ON THE TRACK

On the Track

A Guide to Contemporary Film Scoring

Fred Karlin
Rayburn Wright

Foreword by John Williams

Includes a complete CLICK BOOK by Alexander R. Brinkman

SCHIRMER BOOKS
An Imprint of Simon & Schuster Macmillan
NEW YORK

Prentice Hall International
LONDON MEXICO CITY NEW DELHI SINGAPORE SYDNEY TORONTO

SCHIRMER BOOKS
An Imprint of Simon & Schuster Macmillan
1633 Broadway
New York, N.Y. 10019

Library of Congress Catalog Card Number: 88-39359

Printed in the United States of America

printing number

5 6 7 8 9 10

Library of Congress Cataloging-in-Publication Data

Karlin, Fred.
On the track : a guide to contemporary film scoring / Fred Karlin, Rayburn Wright ; foreword by John Williams ; includes a complete click book by Alexander R. Brinkman.
p. cm.
Filmography: p.
Bibliography: p.
Includes index.
ISBN 0-02-873310-X
1. Motion picture music. 2. Composition (Music) I. Wright, Rayburn. II. Title.
MT737.K37 1989
782.8'5'028—dc19

88-39359
CIP
MN

To Doris, my wife and fellow artist
RW

To my parents, Samuel and Eleanor, who always encouraged and assisted me;
and to my wife, Megan,
who brings so much vision and insight to everything I do
FK

CONTENTS

PART TWO. CONCEPTUALIZING

PART THREE. TIMINGS

PART FOUR. COMPOSING

PART TEN. SPECIALIZED THEMES

FOREWORD

I am often asked by young composers how they might gain entry into the world of film music. The answer, of course, cannot be simple. While there is no magic formula, good training, patience, and a large measure of assistance from lady luck will be indispensable.

To begin with, knowledge of the great films and awareness of current trends in the field are solid prerequisites. After that, experience will be the best teacher. Since practical experience is difficult to come by, the next best thing would be the aid of top-caliber professionals willing to share ideas and techniques that have been gleaned from years of experience. *On the Track* does just that. It sums up the experience of these professionals and offers the reader the opportunity to learn about film composing from their inside point of view.

In the past, most composers approached the world of film music from a variety of backgrounds. They began by studying concert music or playing jazz, rock, or pop music, orchestrating for other composers, writing arrangements for vocalists and big bands, working on theater productions, creating and producing television commercials, and, in general, exploring all styles of music. They also studied the great film scores that led the way for all of us. The broad experience gained from this eclectic background was, and is, probably the best preparation for a film composer. Today, as new composers begin their careers in film, they have access to extremely sophisticated synthesizers and computer technology, but they may find that their background is more limited in scope than their predecessors'. To offset this, these musicians will undoubtedly work in areas other than film in order to gain a wide range of useful experience.

Although the study of music will be ongoing throughout a composer's career, the information contained in this book will help him or her to understand the usage and function of film music as it exists today. Writing, conducting, and playing music while learning about drama through the study of great literature, theater, and films are all essential in preparing for the challenge of scoring films.

Karlin and Wright encourage the reader to apply his or her knowledge by practicing scoring film segments from available videotapes. Because their book is organized by topic, it is easy to use as a reference manual or textbook, yet can be read chapter by chapter if you wish. The many musical examples and references to specific moments in a variety of films make the book a tremendously valuable source of study.

One final note. In the past we've noticed that many of our best musical minds were not interested in film scoring. This was probably the result of the fact that these composers found too many restrictions and technical problems in the film medium, and for some, the practice was simply too "low brow." I do, however, think that in the future we will see more and more "serious" young composers willing to devote some of their energies to film music. If this happens, and I think it will, the resultant music may have an effect, hopefully beneficial, on the development of the art of music itself. Media music is here to stay. It is part of our musical future for better or worse, and this book can help to make it better. For these and other reasons, I celebrate the publication of *On the Track.*

I wish this book had been available when I started in the film industry in the 1950s. It collects and presents so much painfully acquired knowledge that it is a signal advance in the study of our field.

Finally, I wish all students and readers of this book great joy and much success as they enter what is a universe of sight and sound that we are all just beginning to explore.

John Williams

JOHN WILLIAMS

PREFACE

This book has been written to fill a gap on the film-music bookshelf. Rayburn Wright had not been able to find a text for his film-scoring courses at the Eastman School of Music. He wanted a book that discussed traditional film-scoring methods and also the current contemporary practices in the new era of computers, synthesizers, MIDI, and song scores. Coincidentally Fred Karlin had started a book on film scoring in answer to many requests for information explaining how films were scored in contemporary Hollywood. As two longtime friends and colleagues, we decided a collaboration would be ideal.

Our aim has been to create a comprehensive and practical manual detailing the prevailing techniques in the art and craft of contemporary film scoring as practiced by today's leading composers and lyricists. To achieve this goal we have interviewed forty-one composers and lyricists. In addition, because we sought to offer a well-rounded picture of what it is really like to be a professional composer or lyricist in the film world, we have interviewed thrity-six talented professionals from other aspects of the working environment: producers, directors, writers, film editors, music editors, music executives and supervisors, network executives, recording engineers, dubbing mixers, musicians, music contractors, copyists, and composer's agents. Network and music executives' titles are given as they were at the time of their interviews.

To make these candid interviews most useful, quotes have been integrated into our text by topic; for example, quotes about dubbing by composers, directors, and dubbing mixers will be found in Chapter 19, "Dubbing—The Final Mix." We have of necessity edited the tape-recorded comments (with permission) for purposes of clarity and readability. We do not mean to slight in any way those of our colleagues who did not participate in these interviews; any such omissions are due solely to space limitations or, in some cases, scheduling difficulties.

We have limited our discussion and score excerpts to approximately 150 films, most of which are currently available on videocassette. We have not necessarily selected our favorite films and scores (although all the films and scores included have much to recommend them). Rather, we have chosen a well-rounded cross section of works that have yielded invaluable film-music examples. We have placed soaring symphonic scores and funky contemporary scoring solutions side by side, believing that musical style is the language through which the score speaks, and that each film score should find its own appropriate and sometimes even unique musical language.

We have made few distinctions between composing for motion pictures and television. We have pointed out those differences that affect the composer, but the process of scoring a film is basically the same in either medium.

To provide a historical frame of reference, release dates are indicated parenthetically for all motion pictures and television films the first time they are mentioned in each chapter.

This book is addressed to women and men alike. To make this clear we started writing "he/she" and "himself/herself" before we reluctantly recognized that this procedure was both cumbersome and unreadable. Until a nongenderized pronoun comes into usage we are using the generic "he" and "him" to include all people. More and more women are now becoming active in all phases of film production, and we hope the information within this book will encourage women to compete in a field that historically has been heavily dominated by men.

Although our primary goal has been to create a textbook by and for film composers and lyricists, it is our hope that all those involved in or interested in filmmaking and the process of scoring films will find this book helpful in developing a deeper understanding of the art and craft of film scoring and of the men and women who dedicate their lives to this highly demanding profession.

ACKNOWLEDGMENTS

We wish to extend special thanks and gratitude to our seventy-seven colleagues who shared their experiences with us so candidly. Their generous comments during our taped interviews have made it possible for the reader to benefit enormously from their professional experience and know-how.

Many music copyright owners, administrators, and print licensers have generously permitted us to reprint many excerpts from their motion-picture and television-music catalogues. In most cases these musical examples are not available through any other source, and permission to reprint them here has allowed us to integrate these invaluable educational reference materials into our text. Our thanks to ABC-TV, Almo Publications, Brooksfilms Music, Buttermilk Sky Associates, Inc., Chrysalis Music Group, Columbia Pictures, Columbia Pictures Publications, Famous Music Corporation, The Guber-Peters Company, Hal Leonard Publishing Corporation, Hemdale Film Corporation, ITC Films, Inc., Lorimar-Telepictures Music Group, MCA Music, MTM, New Century Entertainment, The Richmond Organization, Screen Gems-EMI, and Warner Bros. Music.

Our thanks to Ruby Armstrong and Harry Lojewski at MGM/UA, Bob Bornstein and Elridge Walker at Paramount Pictures, Julian Brataluvitch at Universal Studios, Harriet Crawford at Columbia Pictures, Danny and Joel Franklin at Warner Bros., and JoAnn Kane at Twentieth-Century Fox for the formidable effort of finding, duplicating, and assembling these manuscripts for inclusion in this text.

Especially helpful were the talented composers who assisted us in researching television-commercial writing and television-theme writing: Keith Foley, Bernard Hoffer, Michael Karp, John LaBarbara, Rod Levitt, Manny Mendelson, and William Waranoff. We wish to thank Douglas Newton, Art Director of Holland & Callaway Advertising Inc., for permission to reproduce the sample Storyboard.

Our thanks to photographer Gay Wallin, who provided us with all the photographs illustrating the equipment and work environment that is so much a part of the scoring process.

Special thanks to Alexander Brinkman, who programmed and printed the click-book pages reproduced herein, and to Marc Gebauer, whose "Click-Calc" chart of digital delay timings we adapted for our Appendix C.

Our thanks also to *Electronic Musician* (Berkeley, CA), *Keyboard Magazine* (Cupertino, CA), *Mix Magazine* (Berkeley, CA), and Elmer Bernstein (*Film Music Notebooks*) for permission to include several excerpts from previously published interviews.

April Rhodes and Ken Warnick were of great help in transcribing some of our lengthy interviews, and Ed Suchow of Captain Video in Montecito, CA, assisted us in making available many of the hundreds of films on videotape that we studied.

Our special thanks to our friends and colleagues who read our completed manuscript. William Russo's and David Wright's many fine suggestions have been incorporated into the final text. Doris Wright and Megan Karlin functioned superbly as overview readers; several readers, including Norman Gimbel, Harry Lojewski, John Richards, and Alan and Marilyn Bergman, read one or more chapters and were most helpful. Especially, in that category, we wish to thank Clark Spangler, whose advice helped shape Chapter 20 ("Electronic Music"). And finally, our deepest gratitude to John Milligan, whose editorial insight and suggestions regarding organization, style, and clarity have been incorporated throughout this book, and contribute greatly to its overall readability.

We wish to extend our appreciation to Schirmer Books; Maribeth Anderson Payne, Editor-in-Chief; Robert J. Axelrod, Associate Editor; Michael Sander, Managing Editor; and Julia Palmore, copy editor, for their editorial contributions and invaluable assistance.

HOW TO USE THIS BOOK

We have tried to make this book as practical, realistic, and up-to-date as possible. Here are some suggestions for using it as a powerful learning tool:

USE VIDEOCASSETTES. In the text when we or those we are interviewing discuss specific film music, we are speaking about the way the music sounds *in conjunction with the film*. The text offers important information about the music and the film, but the reader needs to experience the cinematic effectiveness of the music to understand and feel its dramatic usage and function.

Until recently, the study of film scoring was severely limited by the unavailability of films to study, except for their sporadic reruns on television and in theaters. But now you can rent or buy films on videocassette and replay cues at your own pace, making notes and analyzing the scores. If you are interested enough in film scoring to read this book you will more than likely already be studying film music on videotapes. You can't learn about film music without studying films. Once you have access to a videocassette recorder you can also tape television shows, movies, and miniseries, all of which rarely are available through videocassette distribution.

In the course of a chapter we refer to many different films in order to illustrate scoring solutions to specific dramatic situations. To make research easier we include a "Filmography"—a master list of all films and television series mentioned in the text with their corresponding page numbers for reference. Some chapters include a list of suggested films for further study.

STUDY THE FILMS AND MUSIC EXAMPLES. We recommend that you study the films and music examples along with the text. Screen two or three of the recommended titles at a time. The cues referred to are not recommended as the only possible musical solutions for each scene. They represent the release-print score, and as such they are valuable reference materials. Don't ignore cues and scores (or films) you don't like; there is a great deal to be learned from a cue that you believe doesn't work, and every cue you study is an opportunity to observe your reaction to the specific techniques and dramatic attitudes discussed in the text. With that in mind take notes on the relative effectiveness of each cue, and analyze your value judgments. Then look up the chapter references and reread those passages in the book, studying the specific music cues in the films. Continue taking notes, as this will help you identify and understand your reactions.

We have reduced most of the musical examples from full score to short score or sketch format. All score reductions are in concert pitch, with as much information indicated as is practical. Although in some cases orchestrational touches have been omitted, all musical material is given that a composer would be most likely to include on his sketch. The full scores are all in transposed pitch unless otherwise indicated on the score.

ADD YOUR OWN MUSIC. Some VCRs now have the option of doing an audio-dub recording on one track of the cassette's two available audio tracks. With this feature, if you have made off-the-air copies of films or TV episodes, you will have the capability of composing and recording your own music on the audio-dub track to practice your film-scoring skills. Not all machines have this function; it will be ideal if yours does.

LISTEN TO THE SOUNDTRACK ALBUMS. Soundtrack albums are unrealistic, because a score is never heard in the film with the clarity of a fine stereo recording; nonetheless there is great value in studying such an album *after* studying the score as it plays in its film context, especially to appreciate the musical subtleties that may not be heard on the film soundtrack. Note that music included on the soundtrack album is often not even in the film, is abridged, or is buried under dialogue.

READ OTHER BOOKS ON EACH SUBJECT. The bibliography includes a short list of recommended books and periodicals. READING THE LATEST PERIODICALS AND TRADE PAPERS IS ESSENTIAL IN ORDER TO KEEP CURRENT, ESPECIALLY IN ELECTRONIC AND CONTEMPORARY SCORING.

PRACTICE THE MATH. A guaranteed way to be clear about timing problems and film math is to work through the book's practice problems in Chapters 9 and 10. A guaranteed way to be confused in this area is to skim those chapters without doing the problems. It takes practice to get a real understanding of the math, and handling these numbers can be confusing at first. Computer synchronizing programs also need to be practiced.

LISTEN TO THOSE WHO KNOW. The value of anyone's opinions depends on his credibility. The seventy-seven professionals we have interviewed are among the outstanding experts in Hollywood filmmaking. All work successfully in the field, and all have a self-evident, deep interest in films (see the list of interviewees, with their selected credits, beginning on page 585). Their quotes and the musical examples provided should be an immense help in revealing the techniques and aesthetics of fine film scoring.

ON THE TRACK

PART 1

PRELIMINARIES

INTRODUCTION

You have to be overtrained when the opportunity presents itself. If you're not, then your first time at bat is going to be disastrous. You'll have a short career.
HARRY LOJEWSKI, VICE PRESIDENT OF MOTION PICTURE AND TELEVISION MUSIC, MGM/UA COMMUNICATIONS CO.

What does it take to be a film composer? First and foremost, a film composer should have a natural musical talent and an inherent dramatic sense. A well-rounded technical background is a necessity, but to be successful, a film composer's technical skills must be supported by emotional and psychological discipline. Technique isn't enough. The composer training to work in films must also be prepared for high levels of stress. There are time pressures, commercial pressures, and artistic pressures, and the effectiveness with which the composer deals with these realities will determine to a considerable extent his artistic and professional achievements in the world of motion pictures and television.

Flexibility is essential. There will always be more than one way to score a film. Finding the "right" way will depend in part on the tastes and vision of the director, the producer, and possibly other decision makers involved with the film. If the director believes that a symphonic score will ideally suit his film and the composer cannot demonstrate that there is a better way to score it, the music for that film will probably be a score that uses a symphonic orchestra. This doesn't preclude creativity—it just defines the medium. The film composer must be flexible enough to compose within superimposed (and sometimes arbitrary) guidelines.

Film making is an evolutionary process. The final film results from a series of changes; changes in the script, changes while on location, changes in the editing room, and, of course, changes in the score before, during, and after recording. There will be changes until the film is ready for release, and some of these changes may affect the music in unexpected ways. Preserving the artistic integrity of a :30 cue when the editor has just trimmed :07.4 from the scene requires a flexible approach to the art and craft of film composing. Education and experience are useful only if the composer can accept these changes as part of the filmmaking process.

Rarely will the composer feel he has enough time to compose, and there are many situations that require writing and orchestrating a great amount of music in a very few days. The film for a television series like *Moonlighting* was not always ready for the composer on the Tuesday before a Friday scoring session. On many projects, ongoing film-editing changes add further time pressures to an already-difficult schedule.

The filmmaker's or studio's desire for a chart-busting single or soundtrack album can exert a great influence on film-music decisions, even before a composer is selected to score a film. In these cases the marketplace is an ever-present pressure from the time the composer begins a project, influencing every creative discussion and decision. The pressure to be commercial can sometimes be difficult to accommodate artistically. In general, film composers must work with the constant push and pull between the artistic and commercial elements of the motion picture and television industries—that's how it is.

Not all filmmakers will ask for commercial scores and songs for their projects. There are many times when the film composer will be working with producers and directors who really expect and hope for something else—they will expect (and deserve) a score representing the highest artistic standards.

It is not necessarily safe to rely too much on the filmmaker for artistic validation. Sometimes the filmmaker may not be aware of the potential contribution of a great score, and therefore may settle for much less. "They say, 'It works,'" says composer Ira Newborn. "And it's true, it works—5 percent. As long as it works 5 percent, they think it works. It's like the pass/fail system. They don't have the appreciation, because they're not into it like we are—they don't realize that something can work 95 percent, something can *really* work, almost as perfectly as it possibly can, and squeeze the juice and magnify the scene, or bring something new to the scene that really makes it intense. They don't quite understand that."

Brendon Cahill, Universal Television's former Vice President of Television and Home Video, feels composers should strive for excellence whenever possible, and take the chances sometimes necessary to achieve that excellence. "The composer who comes in today and bases his foundation on the traditional great masters' compositions has to be versatile enough to take a chance. The custom and practice for the composer during the last fifty years has been that if you stay with the tried and true you can't go too far wrong. But it doesn't have to be that way. It all goes back to the director and producer; you hope they'll say to you, 'Look—take a chance. Instead of playing the flute, let's play a clarinet. Instead of putting a string pattern there, let's put a synthesizer there. Or try to look at things differently. Here's the piano, and the mike is normally above the piano; let's turn the mike upside down under the piano and let's see if that creates a different sound. Maybe the knock of the hammer on the string gets a different sound from the string itself. Take the chance.'"

No matter how artistically and technically prepared the composer is, he cannot expect to know everything he'll need to know when he begins his first film-scoring assignment. The fact is that most composers learn most of what they know about film scoring on the job. The successful film composers know what they need to learn when the time comes, and have excellent dramatic instincts that carry them through as they are learning.

It is amazing to hear the stories told by some of the established film composers about their first assignments. **Alan Silvestri's** experience with *Romancing the Stone* (1984), his first major motion picture assignment, is an example. "I got a call one night from the music editor, Tom Carlin, who said they had been looking for a composer and listening to tapes for a long time and were still not happy with anything they had heard. And I mean, they had everybody's tapes on the floor when I got over there. So he said, 'Look, why don't you try something.' So I said, 'Fine.' And he put Bob Zemeckis on the phone and Bob said, 'I've got this one scene with this guy and this girl and they're running through a jungle and they're swinging away with machetes at bamboo and the bad guys are shooting at them. Can you put together three minutes of that and be here for lunch tomorrow?' I said, 'What the hell do I have to lose?' So I did this little demo. It was real makeshift with a LinnDrum and a DX7, and I didn't even have any facilities at my house. I literally had the LinnDrum and I had an 8-track machine, but no board, no echo—nothing. And I put together a three-minute Latin-flavored rhythm track. And I went in the next day to see the guys and that was it. They loved it! They signed me to do the picture the next day."

Silvestri's story illustrates the adaptability and determination that is often necessary to become a successful film composer. He was willing to put something together for the director overnight with inadequate equipment. The filmmakers must have sensed his self-confidence.

Sometimes the most efficient way to prepare to be a pro is to study privately. During **Craig Safan's** early days as a film composer, composer Fred Steiner suggested he study conducting with Hans Beer. "I studied conducting with him for half a year. When I'd conduct I had very bad posture—I used to bend way over when I'd conduct. I was supposed to stand up straight. He would put me against the wall and say, '*Now* conduct in four,' and

I would still bend over. So he went to his file cabinet and took out a ten-inch bayonet—a *real* bayonet—put it up against my chest, and said, 'Now you vill conduct!' He was actually a perfect teacher for me—I can keep the orchestra together and hit all the streamers, and slow down and speed up and get everybody started at the right time."

Safan, who is largely self-taught, was an indefatigable student of motion picture music. "Early in my career I just haunted all the stores. I used to buy every score. I had a huge collection of soundtrack albums, and I'd study everything—every score."

Like most film composers, **Bill Conti** has a very diversified background. He has a bachelor's degree, two master's degrees, and a doctorate in music. But his studies and musical activities cover a wide range of interests and skills. "For my bachelor's degree, I was on scholarship, but it was a bassoon scholarship. And I was a keyboard and composition major. I went to Louisiana State, and then I went to Juilliard. At Juilliard I had to switch to composition. While I was getting all these degrees, I was working playing jazz at night, for about fifteen years. So, the music turned me on in both areas [jazz and classical]. It was a background in all kinds of music."

This background helped prepare Conti for film composition, but it was no guarantee of an entrée into the business. Often, as with Conti, it is the unexpected twist of fate that gets you started. "In Venice, Italy, I was the Italian music supervisor when they were shooting *Blume in Love* [1973]. So, I end up coming back to the States and staying with this still photographer from the film. So I'm sleeping on his couch and he is going off on a one-day shoot for *Harry and Tonto* [1974]. He says, 'Why don't you give me a piece of music to bring to the cutter. I know the cutter; maybe he'll slip it in during the dailies.' I said, 'But I don't even have the script.' 'What do you need to know? It's about an old man and a cat.' 'Well, man, I'm supposed to know more than that. . . .' Anyway, that day, as he was leaving, he forced me to improvise at the piano, just so he could bring a tape. He said, 'You know, make it mellow; there's an old man, there's a cat, there're no chases.' So I did something mellow.

"Now, maybe six months later, I get the job. I actually *get* the job based on that tape. When the director [Paul Mazursky] asked, 'What is this piano stuff, where did it come from?' the editor said, 'This guy. . . .' So, I told the director, 'Well, look, I can really do you a great Main Title. I can really . . .' and he said, 'No, no, I like the piano.' I said, 'But no, no, I understand, this is big time, this is motion pictures. . . .' He said, 'Look, I like the piano.' So I did a take-down of the piano, and I replayed the piano [for the soundtrack], and he said, 'Yea, but I like the way it was.' And I said, 'But that was an old cassette on a funky recorder.' He said, 'Yea, but I cut my main title to it. And it feels so good.' So my first shot, in terms of Hollywood, was this scratchy, thin—I never heard of the movie, never read the script, the guy's leaving for the plane in an hour, and I improvised about three or four minutes, and that's what comes on the screen."

Sometimes a composer has a particularly strong interest and background in one aspect of music, and this can become an important strength in scoring films. **Michael Gore** was involved with pop music and records from an early age. "I started when I was pretty young. My sister, Lesley, was in the business in the early sixties. I basically became involved in music through her. I was ten years old when she started recording. She had some very good people working with her at that time. A lot of people don't know that Quincy Jones was her producer, Phil Ramone was her engineer, and Claus Ogerman was her arranger. I would sit in every weekend she was recording. Occasionally I would do hand claps, occasionally I would play the piano, and this is how I basically got to know a lot about the pop music industry and the recording studio.

"I started writing songs with Lesley when I was about fourteen or fifteen. The first early songs we did were recorded and released as singles for her. We had two songs that were Top-40. I also started writing on staff—after school—at Screen Gems/Columbia, in

New York City, with a variety of lyricists, including Carole Bayer Sager. I spent all those formative years around pop music and the recording studio—that was really my training.

"When I was eighteen I went to Yale. I started taking theory courses, to try to figure out what I was doing instinctively at the piano. I spent the next four years as a music major and became extremely involved in the classical music world. I even started piano lessons again and gave recitals on campus. I also took conducting.

"Then I spent a year abroad in Paris studying with composer Max Deutsch, who was a contemporary of Schoenberg, Webern, and Alban Berg. I continued on with him in the classical area, and spent a year and a half studying conducting and composition.

"After that, I needed to earn some money and I was offered a job at CBS Records in London as a record producer. I produced a great deal of classical recording as well as pop. During that time, I worked with the London Symphony Orchestra and Eric Leinsdorf, guitarist John Williams, opera singer Renata Scotto, pianist Philippe Entremont, and a long list of other artists.

"After two-and-a-half years I wanted a chance to write and work on my own things. I was spending all day in the studio working on somebody else's performances and decided that if I couldn't break away now and try my hand at what I really wanted to do, I would never be able to do it. So I moved to Los Angeles in 1976. The first scoring job that I landed was a Jacques Cousteau special for PBS; I had six instruments and a very, very small budget. I did a few more specials for him, and at the same time I had the good luck to meet producer David Putnam, who became my Hollywood mentor. He thought I had a lot of talent, and he introduced me to [director] Alan Parker. And Alan Parker decided to do a film called *Fame* [1980], and that's how it all began."

You do everything you can to become prepared, and then your break often comes when you least expect it. **John Barry** had two or three instrumental hits with his own group in England in the early sixties. "Noel Rogers, who was the head of United Artists music at that time, called me on a Friday night and said, 'Hey, listen, these two guys, Saltzman and Broccoli, have made this James Bond movie.' And they said that Monty Norman (who I knew essentially as a lyricist) had done the score, but that they weren't all that pleased with it and were in a real bind. 'We need a theme—real quick. Will you come and meet Monty Norman tomorrow morning (Saturday) at the publishing office?' Because they wanted it by Wednesday, believe it or not.

"So I went in and they played me his theme. And I said to Noel, 'Can we go in the other room?' And I said, 'Well what do I do? I cannot work with that material. If you give me a free hand just to go into the studio and do something. . . .' I'd never read a James Bond book. The *Daily Mail* in England used to carry a comic strip of James Bond, and that was the only glimpse I'd ever had of what this guy was. But it was pretty accurate. It didn't take a brain surgeon to figure that one out. So Noel went back in and had a few words with them. He said, 'You know, John doesn't see this thing that you've got.' So Monty Norman's words to Noel were 'I'm not proud. Let him do it. But make sure that he knows that he gets paid but there's no credit.' And that's the way it was. But the only reason I did it was because nobody knew what was going to happen to the Bond movies, believe me—that movie cost $275,000.

"I didn't see any film. I worked on the weekend. I'd written a thing called 'Bees Knees,' which was a twangy guitar-type thing, and it was almost the Bond theme. And Noel said, 'Something like that, that's really interesting.' So, I did it; then, of course, it breaks into a swing tempo and then goes almost be-bop, you know, it was like a Dizzy Gillespie lick, almost. So I did this theme, went into the studio on Wednesday, recorded it and that was it. No strings, just 5 saxes, 9 brass, solo guitar, and rhythm section. And I got paid two-hundred pounds and that was that. Then I don't hear any more from them, except they're pleased with it.

"It was supposed to be just the Main Title. Now then, several weeks later the movie [*Dr. No,* 1964] opens on a Friday in London, and on a Sunday afternoon I went in and saw the movie. Now the goddamn theme is all over the movie.

"I phoned Noel on Monday and I said, 'What is this?' He said, 'Oh-oh, I've been waiting for this phone call. I knew this was going to happen.' He said they went back in and did one more session. They hyped up the main theme several different times. And every time he said, 'I'm Bond—James Bond,' they just laid it in. Very crudely actually. When you look at it now, it sounds like a real glue job, which is exactly what it was.

"And the movie now had gone right through the roof in England. And Monty Norman got all the royalties. And Noel said, 'Well, everybody knows what happened.' So when people say today 'Well, Monty Norman still gets credit at the end of the movie,' I say, 'Well, if he did the first one, then why didn't they keep him on?'"

Even though Barry's start in film scoring would seem to be a singular chance event, there were other fateful factors involved. "Because my father had theaters, I always wanted to write film music. It wasn't a secondhand thing because I wanted to do something else and this came along. I'd always wanted to do it. From a very, very early age. But I always thought, it's America you know, that's where I'm going to have to go ultimately. But then look what happened in the sixties—Carl Foreman was in England, Sam Spiegal was in England. United Artists had all those big successes with the Beatles movies, plus *The Knack* [1965], the Bond movies—the whole United Artists success was coming out of England in the sixties. So I didn't have to go to America. I was right there in the middle of it. So that was another extraordinarily lucky break. I didn't engineer that one either."

Like Michael Gore, **Ira Newborn** had a musical family. "I have a pretty eclectic background. It's hard to say what my roots were. My mother was an opera singer for a while, and my father played trombone and piano in gin mills when he was working his way through college, yet neither of them considered themselves professionals. Early on I was exposed to everything, opera and classical music. My mother likes jazz, my father likes more barrelhouse kind of stuff, stride piano, and stuff. So I listened to that.

"When I first started listening to music I was into the radio, so you figure it was 1954 when I started noticing what music was about. So I heard all of the pop music that was on the radio at that time, and also when it changed into rock-and-roll, away from what it had been before (Patti Page, The Four Freshmen, all that). And then it began to get into regular I, VI, II, V, I rock-and-roll, and I liked that a lot, the girl groups, and the early a cappella groups. When I first started taking guitar lessons, my teacher was a jazz player so I like that a lot. Basically, there's nothing I didn't listen to. And I studied classical guitar too. So everything was coexistent—I'm very eclectic.

"It's all stood me in good stead [in film music]—because I was always fascinated by the different styles. And when I started playing guitar in bands it always fell to me to figure out the chords. So I got myself a nice free music education because they're all deaf and can't hear anything. I had to sit there with the radio or record player in my ear figuring out the chords.

"I went to college, majored in accounting and law, not realizing how ridiculous that was. Transferred into the music department of NYU, which at one time had a very good music department. And they merged with the New York College of Music. It wasn't as rigorous as I would have liked. But since I was already at NYU it was easier to just transfer rather than go to Juilliard or Manhattan which would have given short shrift to my credits. I didn't feel like graduating college when I was twenty-nine.

"I had a couple of unbelievable teachers—I mean inspiring for your whole life. Lenny Frank, Luther Goodheart, and William Kettering, for instance. And all the while I was out doing club dates, bar mitzvahs, the whole routine. Then I started doing jingles and playing guitar in the pits on Broadway. I play very little keyboards. Just composer's piano.

And I don't compose on the guitar. I try to really get most of it in my head. When it gets harmonically complicated I figure it out on the piano.

"So then I started to do jingles and then I became musical director for the Manhattan Transfer. That immediately threw me into big-band writing. I hated big bands because the only kind of thing I'd been exposed to up to that time was that soupy kind of pop big band, like Glenn Miller and "Moonlight Serenade." So when I discovered Count Basie, Duke Ellington, Chick Webb, Jimmy Lunceford, and actually some earlier Glenn Miller charts that he wrote for Ray Noble, then I really got interested in it. And Manhattan Transfer was just a quartet singing four-part harmony and swing music. And they said, 'Do you know how to write for big band?' And I said, 'Of course,' and immediately went out and bought William Russo's book, *Composing for the Jazz Orchestra,* Henry Mancini's *Sounds and Scores,* and a few other books, and immediately wrote my first five big-band charts, which came out great. And to this day when I tell Timmy, the leader of Manhattan Transfer, that those are the first big-band charts I ever wrote in my life he calls me a liar.

"I continued doing jingles and going on the road with them. Then they came out to play in L.A. and do a summer replacement show for the Cher show in 1975, and they decided to move here. That was my gig so I moved with them, and continued to go on the road with them while doing record dates and arranging on records here. Then I quit because I couldn't stand being on the road and stayed in town, still playing a lot of record dates on guitar. And arranging more, then getting into movies. And now I'm in movies."

Now and then a film composer emerges from the ranks of the studio musicians who contribute their talents to film scoring and recording sessions. John Williams was a premier studio pianist, as was Artie Kane. **Michael Melvoin** remains one of the most active studio pianists in Hollywood, even while building his career as a film composer. Here, he explains the progression from instrumentalist to composer.

"In records there's a tradition that goes back to the so-called 'L.A. Rhythm Section' that I took part in. We would actually add equity to the copyrights we were working on. We would improvise an introduction that would become a signature hook that would be called for again in a reintroduction or an interlude, and then repeated once in the fade, or whatever. It would become a part of the tune.

"As a matter of fact, I would find myself playing on original versions of records that would become hits, and then going to other recording sessions to do cover versions of that tune, and discover *my* improvised introduction *in print* in the arrangement that I was about to play for someone else. And I began to notice that at concerts, when the road band would play the introduction to that tune, that before a note of melody had been played, or a word of lyric had been sung, everybody in the stadium knew what the tune was. They had identified it from that now third-generation reading of that improvised piece, and I think that that *drove* me towards composition.

"I realized that was what was happening, and I moved into record arranging almost by default. If I was in charge of the rhythm section in answering all of these questions about how the music should be performed, and providing this particular kind of thematic generation, if you will, I knew that I should at least write the charts. And then, why should somebody else write the sweetening? And then, maybe I should write a tune now and then and maybe I should get into film.

"The very giving of all that thematic material drove me towards composition for film. Because, to me, ultimately, the most satisfaction could be obtained by delineating all of the parts, and what they would sound like together and how they would relate to the film and the story. From the first time I did it I knew that it was graduation time in this town, even from *my* chair, which I think is a blessed chair in the orchestra."

Just how the composer goes about scoring motion picture and television projects will be the focus of this text. When scoring any film, the film composer has a responsibility to himself and to the filmmakers to provide the finest, most creative and artistically satisfying musical solution for the film. This requires a very fine balance between the client's taste, the needs of the film, and the composer's personal vision as a creative artist. Although experience will prove to be the best teacher in learning to achieve this goal, it is our hope that the reader will benefit from the combined experience of many of his colleagues and other members of the film community before he faces his first (or his next) scoring assignment.

CHAPTER 1

THE FILMMAKERS: THE DIRECTOR AND PRODUCER

If I were a composer I would always deal with the director—the man who has the vision.
PAUL WENDKOS, DIRECTOR

How did the director and I get together and solve our differences? We got together in the following way—since I owned the film, that's the way it went.
GERALD ISENBERG, PRODUCER

If you listen to the wrong guy and walk onto the scoring stage, and the guy who really is going to call the shots says, "What's that? I didn't tell you to do that," you're in a lot of trouble.
ALLYN FERGUSON

Any composer who seriously wants to compose for films, and is intent on preparing himself for that work, needs to understand just how film scoring is done, from beginning to end.

By the time he feels "ready" he should not only have studied composition and be able to write in a large variety of styles, but he should have studied the best examples of film scoring and should have a background of practical local/regional studio work: albums, singles, commercials, concerts, personal orchestration projects. He should know as much as possible about how the film industry works. To understand this field and to know what is expected of him, he first needs to look at the actual process that a composer goes through in writing a film, and to understand whom he will be working with in film projects.

In presenting a comprehensive guide to film scoring in this book, we begin with the chronological steps that a composer takes in a typical scoring project:

- Meeting filmmakers, reading script, screening the film
- Spotting the film
- Planning budgets and recording schedules
- Conceptualizing
- Working out timings/synchronization
- Composing
- Orchestrating
- Recording
- Dubbing

Then we go into the special areas of electronic and contemporary scoring, composing in different styles and genres (ethnic, period, comedies, war, mystery, action, TV series), working with songs in films, pre-recording (lip-sync) techniques, and details of the business.

MEETING THE FILMMAKERS

The first step in film composing is usually a meeting with one or more of the filmmakers. Filmmaking is a team effort, and the team includes many experts: actors, cameramen, designers, costumers, writers, recording technicians, dialect coaches, dancing coaches, special-effects persons, sound-effects people, and many more. But the two who have preeminent influence in determining the musical style, tone, and attitude of the film—the crucial factors about which the composer must concern himself—are the director and the producer. Others who may directly influence the score's outcome are the writer, the film editor, the music supervisor or music executive, and the music editor.

The first substantial talks about the film's music needs will probably be with the director, at which time he may give the composer the script, screen early **rough cuts**[1] of the film, or discuss his ideas about the film and its musical needs, or any combination of the above. In the course of developing the score, the composer will encounter varying perceptions of what music is right for the film. These different ideas may come from the different people on the team or, surprisingly, from the same person, as his ideas shift in the course of the composer's work. It is important to know who has the authority. Input is absolutely crucial. You have to know who the leader is. Here are the possibilities:

1. **The producer.**
2. **The director.**
3. **The executive producer.** This person may not play a major role in the day-by-day genesis of the score, but may actually turn out to be the final arbiter when the chips are down.
4. **The editor.** The editor may at some point in post-production be given relatively great authority to supervise dubbing and/or other related tasks. Usually, final approval will come from someone else.
5. **The music supervisor or music executive.** His role depends on his background, abilities, and responsibilities; the specific production company's situation; and whether the supervisor is employed by the production company on a freelance basis or is a salaried executive.

FOLLOW THE LEADER. Don't assume that all executive producers are the final authority. Some may deliberately defer to one or more members of the creative team or another member of the production staff. Other executive producers may not even come to the scoring session, but will exercise final approval of all aspects of **dubbing,**[2] including final music volume levels, placement of a cue (or score) in the film, the relationship between music and sound effects, and so on.

Like every other aspect of the filmmaking process, it is not going to be easy to learn who is in charge because there are no set rules that are absolute—only guidelines. Astonishing as it may seem, the power structure sometimes changes during the course of

---

[1] Rough cut: roughly edited version of the film, often considerably longer than the final cut.

[2] Dubbing: the rerecording of all sound elements onto one piece of sound film (*mag*). This dubbed sound is transferred to the final soundtrack.

the project, and the composer has to rely a great deal on his powers of observation to determine what each person's function really is on a project. First of all, let's meet the director and producer.

THE DIRECTOR

What the director is hearing and feeling is to be respected at all costs.

BILL CONTI

I've learned never to say things like "I hear a music box. I wouldn't dream of telling any distinguished composer exactly how to do his work.

JOHN ERMAN, DIRECTOR

The director is responsible for envisioning and/or approving all creative decisions and overseeing all creative activities on a film. He has specialists in charge of each area (including composing, editing, sound effects, dialogue **looping,**[3] remixing) but they are functioning as his representatives, fulfilling his wishes and realizing his vision. He does not necessarily make all decisions unilaterally, and he often works very closely with the producer, the editor, and the other creative artists. In television (except for specials, made-for-television movies, and miniseries), the producer may be responsible for many of the creative decisions; in those cases, the producer is really functioning as a co-director (as defined above), and the following points relate to the television producer as well.

WHAT THE DIRECTOR EXPECTS FROM THE MUSIC. Directors want the score to reflect and emotionally enhance their idea of what the film is about, and what the scored scenes are about. The director wants the score to reflect the values, texture, and central idea of the film as he sees it. Maurice Jarre defines this as the distinction between concert music and film scoring. "I must say, my philosophy is really the philosophy of the director. And the only thing you have to do, you have to use your imagination and your talent or your technique to satisfy his ideas. When you are doing music for a film, you have to understand it's just a part of the film, and you are not going to write the masterpiece of your life, because if it's a masterpiece you are lucky, because you are part of a masterpiece which has been made basically by the director."

Like many directors, Oliver Stone looks for a dramatic theme (that is, a literary concept). A film's dramatic theme can be defined by describing what the film is really about. Although the theme may be obvious to the composer on first viewing, it is always a good idea to encourage a discussion about this significant issue. As Stone says, "Writing music is much like writing a movie—you wrestle with the theme. You have to convey to the composer what it is you wanted to say. In *Platoon* [1986] I really wanted to hit on the youth theme—the passage of innocence."

THE SCORE'S FUNCTION. Determining the function of music in a film is the single most important decision or group of decisions the composer will make, because these decisions affect the very nature of the score; its style, its musical idiom, its harmonic language, the outer limits of conservatism or reckless abandon. On the surface, determining the score's function may seem easy, but understanding what the director wants and what the film needs can be difficult.

The director's insight is crucial. Paul Wendkos explains his point of view: "The sounds of the score deepen the experience that you are already witnessing on the screen—to deepen

---

[3] Looping: recording a new performance of dialogue to replace original production track.

it, to reinforce it, and not necessarily to comment on it externally. You are trying to get inside the scene. So the music becomes a part of it, not an addition to it. I don't like music to be outside; I don't like doing the score externals. I don't like the score walking or crying or scoring car chases. That's boring. I'd rather get down into the visceral essence of what the chase is about and capture that element, capture the heartbeat of the chase, capture the life and death aspects of the chase. There are all these emotional colors that music can express so well, rather than just the visual excitement of a lot of tires screeching and car crashes, which can become so melodramatic. I like films where the score is very definitely pushed inside, capturing the dark corners, the landscape of the mind. I think that's where the director and composer have a very intimate relationship, in defining that and translating it into musical terms."

THE DIRECTOR/COMPOSER RELATIONSHIP. Some directors are screamers, others are soft-spoken and understated. Still others have more volatile personalities and you never know what their response will be to a particular situation. The ideal atmosphere is one in which communication is open, reflecting mutual respect and thoughtfulness. Alex North, describing his longtime relationship with the late director John Huston, recognizes that if the director inspires the composer's confidence, this can be mutually beneficial. "Huston was a very musical and all-around creative guy, who gave the composer trust in attempting a certain unorthodox approach and concept to a score."

Director John Erman consciously strives to create this comfortable atmosphere, knowing that this is his best chance to get the greatest contribution from his composer. "I'm a believer in what they call in psychological terms 'validation.' And I think the worst thing you can possibly do to a composer is say, 'Well, that's all wrong.' Because it isn't *all* wrong. It's just not what you had in *your* head. But it's what he had in *his* head and maybe you hadn't communicated what you had in your head. So what I try to do is first say all the good things I feel about the cue. And then say, 'In these ways, I don't feel the cue fulfills *my* notion of what this scene is about.' That way, the composer doesn't get his feelings hurt, doesn't feel let down or put down, because the moment you feel put down, it just stifles your creative impulses. And particularly when the poor composer has to redo his cue right there, because generally that's what happens when we do these television movies. There isn't time to say, 'Go away, and two weeks from now we'll get all these musicians back.' Usually I will just say things like 'I feel you're overstating the music; the scene doesn't need that much.' Or, in contrast, I have often said, 'I didn't accomplish everything I wanted in this scene. What can you do to help me give this character a little more heart?' Or whatever. And I'm always thrilled at the way a composer reacts to that, because then you're asking his *help*. And we all respond to that. That's just human nature."

SOMETIMES DIRECTORS DON'T WANT WHAT THEY SAY THEY WANT. David Raksin tells this story: "The new director turned out to be an amiable roughneck, about my own age, bright and shrewd, talented, and still New Yorkish enough to need to let me know that he was not about to have 'any of that Hollywood music' in his picture. What he wanted was 'something different, really powerful—like *Wozzeck*.' To hear the magic name of Alban Berg's operatic masterpiece . . . correctly pronounced was to doubt the evidence of my ears; here was a nonmusician who was not only aware that *Wozzeck* existed but actually thought of his film as one for which so highly expressive a musical style might be appropriate.

"So there we were in my living room, with drinks in hand, the phonograph playing, and the conversation taking its time to get under way. I remember thinking that this was the way things ought to be: I liked his script, I admired him, and I couldn't wait to hear what he had to say and to get working on musical material for the score. Suddenly irritable, he said, 'What's that crap you're playing?' 'That crap,' I replied, 'is *Wozzeck.*'"[4]

INSECURITIES. The director usually suffers from some amount of insecurity during the weeks when the composer is writing the score. Generally speaking, no aspect of the movie-making phase can cause more anxiety for the filmmakers, because ordinarily they can't become very involved in the process of creating the score itself. And so they wait, hoping it will turn out alright. This can be psychologically trying.

The composer must be aware of the director's need for reassurance. Communication is essential, and this will be discussed further as we look at the process of scoring a film. Director-writer David Seltzer's state of mind during the scoring of *Lucas* (1986) is not unusual. "It's a tricky business. Let me only say that having a picture scored was the scariest of all the phases of directing because it comes at the end when there's no money or time to redo it, and also because it's the only thing ever that was out of my control. I could do everything else. I could work with an actor until I got what I wanted, I could work with everyone until I got what I wanted, but I knew that once that music was laid down it was going to be very hard to undo it, and it was going to be someone else's doing. Very scary. I told Dave Grusin he not only had to be my composer but my head shrink at the same time."

Harry Lojewski (Lo-*yef*-ski), former Vice President of Motion Picture and Television Music, MGM/UA, takes this viewpoint: "Directors are very insecure. And also, music is the last element that's added to the film, and it could be disastrous. It is important that the director feel confident that the composer he has selected is someone that is artistic, and is sensitive to the emotional content of his film, and that he is going to be as creative with his score as the director has been in shooting the film."

Allyn Ferguson has found a way to cope with the director's tendency to worry about the score. "I have found that if I verbally prepare the producer and/or director ahead of time to like my score, they're going to come in and like it. And if I have put them off and made them insecure—there have been times when I've been so busy I've had no time to talk to anybody—and you walk in, and they're insecure anyway, and they're *sure* they're not going to like it, I know that if I keep saying, 'It's going to be great, and it's this and it's that,' and you meet them on a level that they can understand—you try to describe the music in terms other than musical—and they feel comfortable about what they think you're doing, they'll love it. The idea is that they should walk in the studio with an extremely positive manner, and a positive feeling about what they're going to hear. And nine times out of ten that's all you need."

COMMUNICATING WITH THE DIRECTOR

> ***Often the directors are really at a disadvantage if they can't verbalize what they want.*** BURT BACHARACH
>
> ***If a director says, "Oh, that temp music sounds perfect," and you have a better idea—well, you'd better blow him out of the saddle if he's already happy with something.*** BILL CONTI

Words used to describe music have different meanings for different people. Sometimes music illustrations can help. How composers and filmmakers communicate through

---

[4] *Film Music Notebook,* Volume I, Fall, 1974, p. 22.

music is the subject of Chapter 4 ("Role Models and Temp Tracks"). In most cases, though, meetings and discussions precede the music.

Sometimes the director can be very specific about his wishes. When you're using music to communicate, you can get very definitive responses from the director. But when the talk turns technical, don't assume the director has mastered the language of music, no matter how basic. Maurice Jarre tells this cautionary tale: "One day a director said, 'You know, Maurice, I would like to have the clarinet playing that.' So I said, 'Fine. I can give the clarinet that melody.' When we went to the recording session he said, 'But I thought you told me you were going to do this theme here with the clarinet.' I said, 'Yes, it's played by the clarinet.' 'No, no, it's not the clarinet, it's not the sound of a clarinet.' I said, 'Look, it's a clarinet player.' And after that he didn't say anything. And so then the oboe played, and he said, 'That's it, that's the clarinet.'"

If such specific words can fail us, how can we possibly hope to discuss the more significant, elusive issues of concept and design? Alexander Courage expresses the frustration of many composers who try to discuss their ideas with the filmmakers. "It's the most difficult thing of all. How do you talk about music? If you're an art director you can show them the model of the set. It's there. They're talking the same vocabulary. It's almost impossible to have a mutual language with the director. Musically, the only thing that's developed over the years is 'Can you play me the theme?'" It can be frustrating, but there are ways to communicate more accurately.

DIRECTORS COMMUNICATE THEIR DRAMATIC VISION. Some of the most effective directors believe their most successful dialogue with the composer is in terms of the drama. What does the film mean to them? What does the scene mean to them? Through describing their vision of the film and the drama, they hope to convey their vision of the score and its role in their film.

Elmer Bernstein's description of his experience with director John Sturges while scoring *The Magnificent Seven* (1960) shows how effective a communication tool dramatic references can be. "I always thought that Sturges was one of the most inspiring directors I ever worked for—not that we talked about music a great deal, but he had a great love for music, a great enthusiasm. He would tell you the story of the film before you ever saw the script, just tell you the story. But the telling had such enthusiasm and such love and such excitement that it was terrifically stimulating. By what he was telling you and the way he told you, he was defining the character of the film, and to a large extent the delineation of the main characters in the film. You would not be in doubt as to what he was looking for, what the dramatic content of the film was."

Individual scenes can be discussed in much the same way. Director Richard Michaels describes his work method: "I communicate with a composer pretty much the same way I do with actors. And that is in the sense of the *feeling* of the scene. Rarely if ever do I give actors instruction on how to read the line. Usually, I find the way to reach them is to tell them what the scene feels like, what it is about. I try to do the same thing with composers. It's a feeling that I want to come out of a scene." If he's ever musically descriptive, "that's my way of saying what the sense of the scene should be and what it should communicate to the audience." He doesn't mean to be taken literally if he says, "It kind of feels like a lonely piano here."

DIRECTORS COMMUNICATE THEIR MUSICAL VISION. Sometimes the director has already decided on a musical approach to scoring his film. The director's musical vision can be expressed subtly, using the power of suggestion, as was the case with director Sidney Lumet and Johnny Mandel on *Deathtrap* (1982). Speaking of his concept for scoring the film with a baroque flavor, played by two harpsichords and orchestra, Mandel remembers, "Actually, I thought we hit on it simultaneously, and later on I happened to remark how it was amazing we both hit on the same thing at the same time, and he didn't say anything—he just smiled. And I knew then I was really being guided by him all the time."

Sometimes the director's musical visions can be confusing. Director William Friedkin often selects music for his films. On *Deal of the Century* (1983), he presented Arthur B. Rubinstein with a complete layout of the score and the type of music it was to include. He demonstrated this to Rubinstein through the use of **temp tracks.**[5] "So I started writing, and halfway into the writing period, I played him stuff. He called me into his office, and he said, 'Listen, I changed my mind. I don't want this. I want *this.*' And the point of reference was now Rossini."

If the director asks you to write two or three different scores, there are only two ways to go: (1) keep giving him what he asks for, and count the days until dubbing is over; (2) tell the producer or music supervisor you can't work this way, and that you won't continue under these circumstances. If you choose the latter course of action, you should discuss this with the director. It would be unprofessional to leave a project without first telling him what you believed the music should be. If he doesn't agree, then the choice is yours. If you think the director's ideas are great but he just can't make up his mind, stay on the job and try to learn from the experience. Compare your ideas to those ultimately used. One final serious word of caution: if an experience like this becomes so intense that you are either driven to drink or start smoking again—walk.

SUPPORT AND GUIDANCE. Sometimes the director's willingness to share the composer's anguish as he thrashes out a creative problem can be the best contribution he can make. David Shire describes a typical moment in the life of a composer: "A couple of times I've been really stuck on pictures. I remember one night on *All the President's Men* [1976]. I'd been working a month trying to find some way to get into that picture. So I called [director] Alan Pakula and said, 'It's so documentary and it's such a wonderful picture, and everything I play I feel is going to make it less good.' And he came over, and I improvised things on the piano, and he said, 'Well, that sounds more in the ballpark than that,' and I can't remember if I found the material that night, but soon after that I had the breakthrough that got me started."

TWO-WAY DIALOGUE BETWEEN DIRECTOR AND COMPOSER

The director and composer communicate on various levels, depending on the circumstances.

1. The Director and Composer Work Together. There can be a real interchange of ideas between the director and the composer. This is always an exciting relationship. It works best when everybody involved is able to sacrifice their ego to the higher benefit of the project, and less successfully when the composer worries about whether an idea originates with him or the director. Craig Safan's experience on the half-hour television sitcom *Cheers* is typical. "When they sent me the first script, my idea was that the music should all sound like it's coming out of a bar—it should sound like a bar band. It should be really unpretentious and sort of sloppy. And [director] Jim Burrows said, 'Yes, well maybe the clarinet or something.' And he just said it in passing, and I immediately went, 'That's it!' Woody Allen, 2:00 AM, playing in a bar somewhere and nobody's hearing him; high clarinet that has a lot of bends in it." And so Safan's bar band met Woody Allen's clarinet, "and it just seemed right."

2. The Director and Composer Disagree. Bill Conti's experience on *The Right Stuff* (1983) is not uncommon. Sometimes the director worries about the score being too big

---

[5]Temp tracks: music tracks temporarily cut into the film's soundtrack prior to the final mix.

or too small, too loud or too soft, too contemporary or too traditional. Director Philip Kaufman wanted his film to project the feeling of the people and their personal stories. But the story was the epic story of the American space race. "It had scope to it," says Conti. "And I saw rockets taking off. So the director and I did not see eye to eye. He felt the personal story would be hurt if the music was big. I agreed with him, but I didn't know how to play rockets going off and circling the moon with just a guitar. So I went for big, and then sometimes he said, 'I think the music is making it too big.' And I kept saying, 'But it's the history of the American space program. Your people are real, you've made a great film, but I don't know how to handle the big moments in a small way. I think it would take away from the film.' So we'd disagree. And he admitted he was intimidated by music. He said that. And brass made him think of the military. So I tried to change the score and tried to make it smaller and smaller. It was a struggle."

It is much more common to have the big/small problem with a film lacking the scope and epic size of *The Right Stuff.* But in any case, the best time to know how the director feels about such things is before scoring, not during or after.

3. The Composer Adapts the Director's Idea. When John Addison scored *Sleuth* (1972), director Joseph Mankiewicz had the idea that the character played by Lawrence Olivier had been intellectually trapped in the thirties. "He was living in the past in his country house in the world of those Agatha Christie detective stories. He therefore thought that the music should have a very strong thirties flavor. And that was something I had to discuss with him a lot, because, in fact, that was going to limit me." The theme for Michael Caine's character, and other music Addison was thinking about for the film was not at all thirties in flavor, and he didn't feel it should be. But he kept the director's idea in mind, and eventually realized that the authentic pop tunes of the thirties would be a perfect accompaniment to the long sequence in the middle of the film that functioned as the equivalent of the act break in the original play. "It worked very, very well there, because it was scored with *source music* coming from his phonograph. And it was completely different from the rest of the score, so it made a wonderful contrast at that point."

4. The Director Edits the Film to Suit the Music. This does occasionally happen if the director chooses to do so, and it illustrates the collaborative process working in both directions. The director can be moved and influenced by the music, and make adjustments to accommodate. When Isaac Hayes was scoring *Shaft* (1971), director Gordon Parks was getting tapes of the cues as he went along. "The more I heard, the more excited I got. I sometimes cut something to fit his music. There were times when I wished I had done something different in the film to go along with the music. And there were times when I said, 'Wow, I wish I had something here to fit this in—how can we use this?'"

Burt Bacharach had a similar experience when he worked with director George Roy Hill on *Butch Cassidy and the Sundance Kid* (1969). Bacharach also mentions the working atmosphere that Hill created: "I think I felt a certain amount of confidence in what I could get away with musically, because he is such a musical director. He almost set up places where he wanted music to be really important—where they would be free of dialogue—when he shot the film. He was great on the scoring stage, too, and I had a wonderful time with the picture. He'd say, 'Hey, you need a few more frames, I'll cut it in. Don't worry about it.' Or, 'I'll stretch that there.'

5. The Composer Asks Questions. The composer should ask as many questions as necessary to understand the director's point of view. It's best if these questions probe into the emotional meaning of the film and of individual sequences. Avoid asking too many specific technical or musical questions. "What attitude do you see the music taking in this scene?" is a question most directors will be comfortable discussing. "Should I write the theme in major or minor?" is not. Music executive Harry Lojewski considers the use of too many questions to be a real danger, especially if the director is insecure about the music to begin with. "The pitfall is that the director cay say, 'What did I hire? I hired him to write the music and now he's asking me to audition the music. He's the composer—doesn't he know this job?'"

On the other hand, with some directors, including John Erman, you can't go too far wrong as long as you talk about the drama. "When Marvin Hamlisch and I did *Streetcar Named Desire* [1984 television movie], he was the most inquisitive composer I've ever worked with. He would literally call me up and say, 'What *exactly* do you intend this scene to mean? What is the entire emotional through line of this scene?' And he would make me talk and talk and talk. And finally he'd say, 'I've got it.' And then he would work on it and then he would call me up almost every day while he was writing the score. And he would always play me themes, and he would say, 'Is this *exactly* what you have in your head?' And if I said, 'No,' then, 'Well, how does it differ from what you want? Or what you hear? Or from what you envision?'"

Many composers are concerned about working that closely with the director. Some believe it to be a time-consuming and fragmented process. Others feel they will end up in the uncomfortable position of depending on the musical insight of someone who may have a very limited musical background and possibly unsophisticated musical instincts. Often, composers are protective of their creative independence, and are leery of becoming solely a mirror image of the director's wishes; they worry they may make serious mistakes in judgment if they rely completely on the director's instructions.

In general, though, each composer must ultimately rely on his own sense of musical creativity to fit the needs of the film and the director.

FIGURE 1-1

James Horner, Harve Bennett, Leonard Nimoy (foreground) during the scoring of *Star Trek III.* Mixer Dan Wallin, far left; music editor Bob Badami, far right. In booth at Record Plant Scoring Stage M.

Photo: Gay Wallin

THE PRODUCER

> ***Producers have an enormous range of ability and taste; some have a sense of aesthetics and some don't. And some of those who don't, think they do.***
> MARC MERSON, PRODUCER

Executive producer; line producer; coproducer; supervising producer; assistant producer. Forget the titles. Function is the key. Function and responsibility. What or whom are they responsible for?

The producer's chief function as a filmmaker is to develop and nurture a project from beginning to end. To do this successfully, he must select the proper writer to work with him on the creation of the ideal script; select the appropriate director; and work with the director in selecting all of the creative and technical talent that is necessary to produce a film. An associate producer often takes care of many of the production details, but the producer may hire someone else as well to follow through on many of the day-to-day tasks that come up in producing a film, including supervision of the shooting of the film. This person may be called the *line producer,* and the producer may consequently become the executive producer.

As a businessman, the producer is responsible for raising the money to produce the film, and/or selling the project to a network, studio, or production company. But there are no absolute definitions that prescribe exactly how much emphasis any individual producer may place on his various creative and financial responsibilities.

CREATIVE PRODUCERS. One way to determine whether a producer is creative is to listen and observe. The creative producers will be the ones presenting and discussing creative issues. They will be interested in the creative process, and eager to hear your solutions. They will be willing to agonize with you a bit if the right musical solution doesn't present itself immediately, because they will understand what you are going through—they are constantly making creative decisions. And most truly creative professionals are wary of quick, slick answers. Some producers, however, may not be looking for the composer's creative input, and may in fact hire the composer to help realize their own creative decisions.

In any case, concept and overall approach will be discussed, and they will probably want to hear the musical theme(s). Producer-writer Marc Merson, who co-creates and develops projects (and sometimes writes them as well), says, "I tend to do a lot of thinking about who's going to be the composer, because I rely on him a lot to suggest things. I have a general idea about music but more often it will be my relying on the composer to come up with, or at least propose, something for me to think about." Once the suggestions are made, expect an open give-and-take dialogue.

EXECUTIVE PRODUCERS. The executive producer may exercise final control over all creative elements, even though he isn't necessarily involved on a daily basis. He is often responsible for the business administration and decisions, and may be chief executive of the production company. He may also be a creative producer—that could be why he is president of the company.

Those producers who are strictly involved with the financial and business side of production will usually (but not always) try to stay clear of the creative discussions, or at the most they will oversee them, checking that they have taken place and so on.

PRODUCERS WITHOUT STRONG MUSIC BACKGROUNDS. Sometimes a producer may want to guide the composer, though he really doesn't have the background for it. His language may reveal his weakness in this area. Agent Alvin Bart often hears the following statement: "I don't know anything about music, but I know what I like." When a composer finds himself working with this kind of producer, he may be able to achieve an open, two-way exchange of ideas by using musical examples (commercial records, other film scores, or the composer's music). If he is comfortable asking the producer, "Do you like this? Do you like that?" they may have a very fruitful dialogue about the score. Musical demonstration is a must in these cases.

Many times Allyn Ferguson gives producers a choice. "On one picture I wasn't really sure what everybody thought. They all had input. And I wrote three themes and played all three of them. They all unanimously picked one—I knew exactly where I was then. I think that's a good idea—I needed their input as to what they wanted, not necessarily what was good, bad, or better. All three themes would have worked beautifully. They picked the most on-the-nose solution. I wouldn't have picked that."

This story suggests that the producer's musical tastes can be important. One producer likes baroque music but hates contemporary jazz. Another loves the alto flute and guitar but never wants to hear timpani. These may seem like curious prejudices to impose on a project, but if the producer really hates alto saxophone solos, it would obviously be a big mistake to feature a David Sanborn–style alto in your score.

THE PRODUCER'S POWER

Everyone agrees that the power is vested differently in television than it is in feature films. In features, the director usually prevails in creative decisions, including those involving the music. There may be an honest, three-way dialogue going between the composer, producer, and director, but in most cases a two-to-one vote against the director won't overrule his wishes. In television, on the other hand, as producer Marc Merson sees it, "The producer is king, and you have more problems dealing with studios and networks than you do with the director. The director is basically armed to do something else, and I find that with television directors things are really negotiable. The composer's basic relationship is going to be with the producer; the basic decisions are going to be made by the producer."

This may be so because the producer sets the deals with the network, develops the project, and then guides it to completion. The directors may have moved on to another project by the time the composer begins a television score. This is especially true in episodic television, but it also pertains to television films. There are times when the composer will never even meet the director of a television film and will work only with the producer.

COMMUNICATING WITH THE PRODUCER

Many times the producer will have an idea of what he feels the score should be. He may describe this in general terms ("contemporary," "romantic and lush," "gritty and hard-hitting"), dramatic terms ("violent," "sentimental" or "nonsentimental," "epic"), or more specifically, in musical terms ("contemporary jazz," "bluesy," "country"). He may offer these ideas as a point of discussion, or he may ask for the score to be written according to his description. In either case he will want to know that you agree with his approach. If you don't agree, suggest one or more alternative approaches.

FOLLOWING THE PRODUCER'S SUGGESTIONS. The producer's suggestions may be very helpful but it can be a major mistake to try to re-create in your score exactly what you think he wants. Duplicating his musical description is not a foolproof method of successfully scoring a film. Some years ago, during the height of popularity of the televison series *Hawaii Five-O,* a producer said to the composer of his new pilot, "I want the theme to be bouncy. I want it bouncy like *Hawaii Five-O*—jazzy." The composer, aiming to please, wrote "bouncy." The opening shots were of a small charter plane taxiing down a dirt runway. The plane was bouncing, the pilot was bouncing, the music was bouncing—everything was bouncing. The producer hated it. He had given the composer an ill-advised directive that he later regretted.

Director John Erman once heard a producer literally destroy a composer by saying, "I don't want any violins, I don't want any piano, and I hear only woodwinds." Erman explains that "this composer (who was very distinguished) was saying. 'Yes. Alright. I can do that for you.' And of course the score was finished and the producer, who was fairly new at the game, said to me, 'I'm so disappointed in the score. It's just not at all what I'd hoped for.' And I said, 'Because you hamstrung him.' "

If the producer *insists* on his musical direction, it's going to be very difficult to convince him that your approach is better unless you have a long history of successful projects together. So the composer in those cases is compelled to give him what he wants and still find a way to make it work for the film and for everybody else, including the composer himself. But remember David Raksin's story—he may not want what he says he wants.

"I suppose producers are a much more varied lot than directors," Merson says. "All directors basically do the same thing, and basically, for better or for worse, have thought fairly carefully about the film. Producers can be lawyers, money men, publicists, and things like that. So producers are a much more difficult lot to deal with, I would think."

THE FILM EDITOR, MUSIC EDITOR, AND MUSIC EXECUTIVE/ SUPERVISOR

I say, "We can always add, we can always trim it. We have a nice, extremely well-put-together piece of film—let's wait for music."

JOHN BURNETT, EDITOR

I've been pleasantly surprised with music so many times. On the other side of the coin, you do a show and you have a main title that really needs the music and a guy doesn't do it and then you go right down the toilet. I mean, you die.

JOHN MARTINELLI, EDITOR

THE FILM EDITOR

THE EDITOR'S RESPONSIBILITIES. The film editor, working with all of the director's **print takes**[1] of each shot, intercuts this footage into a homogenous whole. He works with tens of thousands of feet of film at the outset and collaborates with, and takes his instructions from, the director.

Editors often work on a project from the beginning of shooting. Editor John Martinelli finds that "you're always a tight-knit family, or at least I've always been; the way I work I'm always a part of the picture from day one." Because of this he is often able to make significant creative contributions to the filmmaking process.

THE EDITOR AS INTERMEDIARY. The editor almost always follows a project through scoring and dubbing and usually supervises the lab work on the final **answer print**[2] as well. Because he is one of the few members of the creative team with this kind of continuity on a project, and because he has so much insight into the director's vision of the film, he often has a relatively great amount of authority and responsibility on the dubbing stage. Because of his relationship with the director or producer, he can be an excellent liaison between them and the composer. This can be extremely important if the schedule is very tight and people are difficult to reach, or if there is a misunderstanding that needs clarification.

The editor and his assistant(s) can often help coordinate logistical matters like duplication and delivery of the videocassette to the composer. They are the first to know

[1] Print takes: master takes from recording sessions; master and alternate takes from shooting.

[2] Answer print: a final version of the film with all sound and visual effects combined on one piece of film.

about any changes in schedule. And there are times when a sympathetic editor can be an excellent sounding board, listening to a theme, perhaps, or discussing a difficulty in the production schedule. It helps for the composer to develop a good working relationship with the editor when possible.

The editor is also an excellent liaison between the composer and the sound-effects people and may be the ideal person with whom to discuss the blending of sound effects and music prior to and during scoring and dubbing. These issues should be discussed with the director first, of course, but the editor can help coordinate the execution of any decisions along these lines.

ADDING MUSIC. The editor also is likely to know a great deal about the director's thoughts on the use of music in his film. As a rule he'll have his own ideas as well, sometimes clearly defined by the inclusion of temp tracks prepared by him or the music editor for early screenings or previews. He will often be called upon (or take it upon himself) to add some music here and there to the **work print**[3] for this purpose. He may do this himself, or he may coordinate the music editor's efforts to be sure the director is satisfied with the results.

EDITING TO MUSIC. Editors are sharply divided on the virtues of actually cutting film to music during the early editing process. Those who do, claim that they are able to achieve a better sense of mood and flow by letting an appropriate piece of music guide their editing instincts. They usually choose the music themselves. If the director hears how well it works and likes it enough, this music may find its way onto the temp track. Or, if it is being used strictly as an editing guide track, it may never be heard by anyone other than the editor. The tempo of this guide track rarely has any direct effect on the composer or the final tempo of the cues, unless the film editor specifically cuts to a certain tempo in order to sync a sequence of fast cuts, possibly for a main title or a montage sequence. In cases like that, the editor or music editor will give the composer either the guide track he used, or the tempo, or both, so the composer can exactly duplicate the tempo to which the film was edited.

Those editors who don't like to use music during the editing process believe that the film has its own independent rhythm and flow and that this feeling is best achieved without the external influence of music. Director Paul Wendkos agrees with this school of thought. "I like to be free of the beat of the music. I want to find a visual rhythm and then get music to support that, rather than the other way around." That's how editors John Martinelli and John Burnett work also.

THE MUSIC EDITOR

The job of the music editor (occasionally referred to as the *music cutter* or *cutter*, although music editors dislike the terms) is to provide timing notes for each cue; prepare the film (or videotape) with **punches, streamers,** and any special **click tracks**[4] to assist the conductor at the recording sessions; monitor the recording sessions and operate the digital metronome there as necessary to ensure correct timings; build the **music units**[5] for dubbing; attend the final audio mix on the dubbing stage; assist in any adjustments or changes that may be requested; and keep detailed notes on the whole process.

---

[3] Work print: a copy of the film created by the film editor as he edits. Black-and-white copies of a color work print are called "dupes."

[4] See Chapter 9, "Timings and Clicks."

[5] Music units: 1,000-foot reels of film with music cues edited in sync with the picture.

Ideally music editors come to their jobs with strong musical sensibilities. Their academic background in music varies. Although they may be musically trained, music editor Daniel Allan Carlin says, "I am not convinced that the study of music is necessary to be a well-trained music editor." He believes a strong intuitive sense is probably more valuable than academic training, which can at times lead to the right intellectual ideas utilized in the wrong way. "What's more important for a good music editor is the ability to deal under pressure with people who can get crazy. Almost anybody can cut from a beat to a beat. And anybody can lay in the music. That's not the trick. The trick is that in the back of our minds we know that you've written this score, and we are under an obligation to maintain its integrity as best we can while dealing with film and music changes."

Bruce Broughton recognizes the music editor as an important ally. "My feeling about music editors is that they're the only other people who understand what it is that we do. And you can't talk to the director or producer first on the scoring stage. You have to talk to the music editor and say, 'Did I get close enough to that?' or, 'Does that work for you?' And when I'm worrying, I worry with *them,* rather than with the director or producer."

The music editor is available throughout the composer's assignment to help him in any technical matters that may arise. For example, if the composer wants help in selecting an appropriate **click**[6] for a cue, the music editor will suggest one based on the composer's approximate tempo. If there is on-screen dancing or a marching band moving in tempo, the music editor will determine the most compatible tempo as a specific click.

MUSIC SUPERVISORS AND EXECUTIVES

> ***The music department's expectation of the composer is that he and the director are in direct communication; that they are on the same wavelength; that the musical tastes and desires of the director are implemented by the composer. Those are all goals.***
>
> STEVE BEDELL, VICE PRESIDENT OF MUSIC, PARAMOUNT PICTURES

The major motion picture studios all have executives in charge of music for their television and motion picture divisions. In some cases the same person presides over both divisions; in other cases, there are different people supervising the music used in television and in feature films. Many of the larger independent production companies also have music executives, including Lorimar-Telepictures and Aaron Spelling Productions. There are a number of independent music supervisors, such as Terri Fricon, David Franco, Gaylon Horton, and Becky (Spargo) Mancuso, who assume the same tasks and responsibilities as the studio departments but on a free-lance basis.

THE MUSIC SUPERVISOR'S RESPONSIBILITIES. Generally speaking, the music supervisor (from here on, the term will be used interchangeably with *music executive*) is responsible for everything and anything having to do with music. This covers an enormous range, including some jobs that are strictly business oriented (licensing the rights to use music owned by an outside publishing company, cutting the deal for a major artist to sing on a soundtrack, negotiating the deal with the composer's or lyricist's agent) and some that are much more music oriented. Here is the list of a typical music supervisor's responsibilities:

- Supervise and oversee all music activities (television and/or features)
- Create budget for all projects and sessions; coordinate with contractor
- Conduct preliminary discussions with filmmakers regarding music

---

[6]Click: tempo, traditionally calibrated in eighths of a film frame.

- Research and find composers, lyricists, and songwriters
- Recommend composers and lyricists to producers and directors
- Negotiate their deals
- Seek out recording artists and record producers
- Negotiate soundtrack album deals
- Coordinate studio interests with the outside record company
- Coordinate artists' schedules with film release dates
- Coordinate the in-house music publishing interests
- Attend some screenings of dailies
- Attend advance screening of films prior to spotting
- Attend spotting sessions with producer, director, composer
- Attend scoring sessions; often "produce" the sessions in booth
- Function as liaison between composer and director
- Function as liaison between music production and executives

The specific tasks that a given supervisor will assume usually reflect the experience he brings to the job. Backgrounds can differ widely. For example, Gary LeMel (President, Music, Warner Bros. Inc.), Steve Bedell (Vice President of Music, Paramount Pictures Corporation), Bones Howe (Vice President of Music, Columbia Pictures), and Brendon Cahill (former Vice President, Universal Television Music and Home Video) all have strong record-industry backgrounds. Harry Lojewski (former Vice President of Motion Picture and Television Music, MGM/UA Communications Co.) and Bodie Chandler (former Vice President of Music, Columbia Pictures Television) can play piano, have solid music backgrounds, and have worked as professional musicians. Harry Heitzer (Vice President Business Affairs, Music Operations, CBS Entertainment) has a business affairs—that is, legal—background.

Chandler and Lojewski are both extremely active at all scoring sessions, literally producing the sessions in the booth, checking performances for intonation problems and possible mixing adjustments, calling out cues to the recording mixer, helping to suggest an appropriate change of orchestration if requested by the producer or director. LeMel and Bedell are very involved with the integration of recording artists and songwriters into their studios' films.

All but Heitzer (who is mostly involved in supervising the "operations," not the music) attend scoring sessions and in general act as the studio's diplomatic emissaries to iron out any difficulties that may arise between the composer and the filmmakers. "You referee a few fights," LeMel adds. "It's really tough. There was a film where the director, on every cue, jumped out of the both and ran into the studio and yelled in front of all the players, and after a few of those scenes, the composer just walked out. And I was able to talk with both of them separately and get it back together. But it's difficult because the director really feels 'this is my domain—this is now the moment of truth.'"

RECORD ORIENTATION. There are many film composers who are concerned about the current state of affairs in the motion picture industry, fearing that the venerable art of film scoring may be in danger of extinction due to the increasing use of songs and the emphasis on commercial soundtrack albums. Elmer Bernstein speaks for many when he says, "Today the heads of most of the music departments are basically record-industry people, and their job is basically to sell as many records as they can. That's a legitimate thing for selling records but it does very little for the art of film music. I'm concerned that a generation of film directors could grow up and become so accustomed to this way of scoring films that they really basically don't know what a real score can do for a film. I don't know if it's a realistic concern, but it is a concern."

CHAPTER 3

THE SCRIPT, MEETINGS, AND SCREENINGS

I don't want to know what the script said that I now see is different. All I want to ask from a director is "Show me your final cut."[1]

JERRY FIELDING

THE SCRIPT

In most cases, the composer's first connection with a project will be the script. If it is possible to screen the film soon after being contacted, the composer may wish to see the film without the advance input of the script. (Episodic television moves so fast that if you receive the script at all, you may already be scoring the episode.) Reading the script shortly before a first screening can sometimes soften the emotional impact of that screening, and in some cases may actually mislead you. It has happened to many composers, including Allyn Ferguson. "I don't like to read the script because I have *never* seen a picture with a script that was shot [as written]. If I read a script, I start to get preconceptions about what the picture is, and then I go and see the picture and I think, 'I have to get all that out of my mind—it's not that at all!'"

IF THE FIRST SCREENING IS MORE THAN A FEW DAYS OFF, IT IS PROBABLY A GOOD IDEA TO READ THE SCRIPT ANYWAY. If the film isn't ready to be seen, the script will be the only common ground you and the filmmakers can share in discussing their project. If they are willing to wait until you have seen the film, you may wish to skip the script at this point.

IF YOU HAVE NOT YET RECEIVED AN OFFER TO SCORE THE FILM, YOU MUST READ THE SCRIPT. When a producer decides to inquire about a composer's availability to score his film, he will usually send a script to be sure the composer is really interested in working on the project. This is true whether the composer and producer have worked together before or not. The filmmakers and the composer are testing each other, wanting to be sure that the experience will be a fruitful one.

The filmmakers will be waiting to hear from the composer and will want to know his response to the script. If the composer knows either the producer or the director, he may call them directly to respond. If he has been contacted through his representative (agent, lawyer, manager), he will usually give his representative his reaction to the script; the representative then relays the response to the producer. In either case, the telephone is the medium for the message, not a letter.

There are really only three possible (quotable) responses: (1) "I love it and want to work with you on your project"; (2) "I think it's excellent, but I don't think I can bring the right quality (style/approach) to your film"; or (3) "I'm unavailable, but let's try again next time." Unless you are very well established, the first response will be the best, but rest assured that all three are part of the professional ethic, and nobody really takes offense if you feel the film is not for you. The filmmakers *want* to know this.

[1] *Film Music Notebook,* Volume III, Number 3, 1977, p. 46, interview by Paul Seydor.

WHAT TO LOOK FOR. If you read the script, there will be a lot to learn. There may be specific music indications in it. These should be noted, with any questions that occur to you. Here is what you should look for:

1. *Music may be built into the story line.* When this happens, the scene indicated in the script may already have been shot before the composer is on the project.

As Henry Winkler is starting to make love to his fiancée in *Night Shift* (1982), she complains about the distracting music coming from the adjoining apartment. In exasperation, he gets out of bed, knocks on the neighbor's door, and a six-foot-six redneck opens the door with a ten-gallon hat on and not much else. Although the country western music nearly knocks Winkler over, he doesn't press the issue.

In *10* (1979), Blake Edwards scripted the use of Ravel's *Bolero* into the story line, integrating it carefully into the seduction scene. The scene in part depends on that piece of music. As the scene progresses, he turns it on; she asks him to start it over again; he turns it off as he leaves.

In both of these instances, the scripted music did not need to be recorded prior to shooting the scene, and the composer should take note that these scenes will need to be **post-scored.**[2]

Young Frankenstein (1974) required music before some scenes were even shot. This was because the film's script called for a gypsy theme to be played on camera; it is almost a character in the story. Gene Wilder hears a violin solo and follows the sound of it through the basement of the castle, commenting about it along the way; at the end of the film we see Marty Feldman on the castle turret, playing a French horn obbligato to the solo violin and orchestra, serenading the monster back to the castle. John Morris wrote this theme before the film was shot so that director Mel Brooks could use the rough piano demo of the theme on location[3] (see Figure 4-3). Providing some music or "guide tracks" prior to the start of shooting is not typical, but it can happen. The more musically oriented the project, the more likely that there will be scripted music that calls for preproduction planning and recording.

When the composer subsequently screens the film, he should watch these prerecorded sequences carefully to see whether the scripted music *looks* convincing. If not, it will probably need some more work in postproduction.

2. *The script may indicate visual or nonvisual source music.* Very often a script will call for **source music.**[4] This music can be perceived as coming from an on-screen music source—for example, a radio or juke box (*Ferris Bueller's Day Off,* 1986)—can be played by an on-screen band (*Back to the Future,* 1985; *That's Life!,* 1986), or can be imagined to come from an unseen, possibly imaginary source—perhaps a CD or cassette player (*Sixteen Candles,* 1984) or a television set (such as the opening shoot-out in *48 Hours,* 1982, in which we accept the fact that cartoon music is coming from the television set even when that music continues, actually functioning as score for the subsequent sequence).

Writers often indicate the style of music they imagine coming from the source. They might say "fifties rock and roll" or "the sounds of a Mariachi band drift across the patio." These indications for source music may or may not reflect the tastes and desires of the director and producer, but it is not too soon for the composer to make note of them. They should go on his list of things to consider, and they may give him possible clues as to an appropriate musical direction.

3. *The script may suggest the music's mood or style.* Writer-director Oliver Stone suggested salsa as an appropriate musical style for the ambience music in his script for *Scarface*

[2] Post-scored: recorded after the film is shot.

[3] Final versions of these cues with on-screen solo violin and solo violin and solo French horn with orchestra were post-scored after the film was edited.

[4] Source music: music from a visual or nonvisual source (such as a marching band or juke box.) See Chapter 24, "Ethnic, Period, and Source Music, Documentaries, and Adaptations."

(1983). "My music is described in the script, towards beginnings and ends of scenes, because generally if there's going to be music, the description will be there. Certainly at the end of the scene." In his script for *Midnight Express* (1978) he indicated lyrical, romantic music; "Definitely over very brutal and real images you put very romantic music. I think that heightens the brutality actually; by contrasting it with something very beautiful and fragile it becomes even more horrid. We wanted to evoke a sense of repugnance."

4. The script may include specific songs or instrumental pieces. How seriously should references to pop standards or symphonic classics be taken? It depends on the writer, and on the situation. If the writer is John Hughes (*Sixteen Candles, Pretty in Pink, Ferris Bueller's Day Off*), very seriously, Paramount Vice President of Music Steve Bedell emphasizes. "He's writing to music. John is one of those writer-directors who actually sits down in his room and writes his screenplay listening to very obscure music, so he actually writes songs into the scripts. Some are obvious, like the featured performance of 'Twist and Shout' in *Ferris Bueller.* Others drift by from an unseen source someplace. They're all scripted—specifically, by title. Some are eventually licensed, while others are replaced for practical or monetary reasons."

THE FIRST MEETING BEFORE SCREENING THE FILM

The first meeting will often be very general in character. If you haven't seen the film yet, the director or producer will tell you the story and probably discuss their thoughts about musical style. This meeting is just a chance to get acquainted. Unless there is some immediate music need to take care of, filmmakers rarely expect serious, in-depth discussions at this early stage. If you are "auditioning" for the assignment, however, they will expect your suggestions regarding musical style, instrumentation, and dramatic approach.

THE FIRST SCREENING

The first screening may take place the same day as your first meeting. Someone may or may not sit with you during this screening, but in any event they will be very eager to hear your reactions to their film. Remember that the composer is often the first person outside the production staff to see the edited film, and the producer, director, and editor will be interested in how successful they have been in delivering their emotional message. If it's a comedy, they may want to sit with you just to see if you laugh in the right places. It's an opportunity for them to check the comedic timing and overall pacing of the film. Generally speaking, though, there is really no need for anyone to sit with the composer during this screening, and it can be a much more comfortable experience for the composer if he is alone.

IGNORE THE DETAILS. What should you look for during this first screening? As an overriding principle, IGNORE THE DETAILS AND CONCENTRATE ON THE FILM'S EFFECTIVENESS AND EMOTIONAL IMPACT. MONITOR YOUR EMOTIONAL REACTIONS, AND MAKE MENTAL NOTES ABOUT EMOTIONALLY AFFECTING SCENES AND MOMENTS. Hold on to these first impressions. After you have seen a film a dozen times and studied each scene you are scoring, you can no longer view the entire film with the freshness required to react instinctively. A funny line just isn't as funny the twentieth time you hear it, and you may find yourself reacting with a detached attitude as you watch the heroine die in the tenth reel. This happens, so it is crucial for the composer to notice how he feels the first and second times he sees the film.

At a first screening, watch the film as a member of the audience would, not as a composer. Monitor your reactions to remember them, but with as much objectivity as possible, so you don't lose emotional contact with the film. Look for mood, feeling, texture, the overall nature of the film and its emotional impact. Things to avoid include **spotting**[5] the film, making too many mental notes regarding technical matters, and intellectualizing. Doing these things will tend to interfere with your emotional response to the film.

ROUGH CUT, FINE CUT, AND THE ASSEMBLY

It is important to know how far along the film editing is. What shape is the film in? Editing can cause a major shift in a film's overall impact. More often than not, the natural tightening up of the footage as editing continues adds both power and focus to the final film. It takes experience to sense just exactly what effect this will have on your emotional reaction to the film, but the change may be significant. That's why it is important to ask how much additional editing is planned. The film may be described as an **assembly** (which can be quite a bit longer or shorter than it's ultimate length), as a **rough cut** (usually within five to fifteen minutes of its final length), as an almost fine cut (usually within a few minutes of its final length, but with some polishing still to be done), and as a **fine cut** or **locked** (no intention of further editing).

ASSEMBLY. Is it a first assembly? In that case the film may be quite overlong, with extra footage still in many sequences. Pacing may be much slower than it will ultimately be in action sequences like chases and shootouts, in traveling sequences of any kind, and in key dramatic sports events. Stalking sequences may also be overlong. Montages will usually be overlong, and often in very rough condition.

The first assembly of the feature film *Leadbelly* (1975, Karlin) was over three-and-a-half hours long; the film at that point included one overlong but significant chase, and a lot of musical numbers that were eventually trimmed. The final release print was approximately two hours. The seven-hour television miniseries *Dream West* (1985, Karlin) was two-and-a-half hours longer than the fine cut when the videocassettes were first delivered for scoring. One trek through snow-swept mountains occupied almost an entire ten-minute reel of film. And there was no dialogue at all—just the "slosh, slosh, slosh" of a dozen men slowly walking up a mountain, pushing their way through knee-high snow during a blizzard. Easily an hour and a half of additional music would have been needed just to score this extra footage. EARLY EXPOSURE TO A FILM MAY LEAD YOU TO A FALSE IMPRESSION OF THE BALANCE BETWEEN NARRATIVE AND DRAMATIC ELEMENTS. THIS IN TURN CAN THROW OFF YOUR OVERALL EMOTIONAL REACTION TO THE FILM ITSELF.

ROUGH CUT AND FINE CUT. It can be a shock to watch a work print if you are not used to seeing a film in that condition. First of all, there probably will be no music in it, and music is a convention that composers find as important an element in the viewing experience as anyone else does. It can be an even more startling experience if there is music already. Such music is called temp music or temp tracks. (See Chapter 4.)

There may be lines that can't be understood; the loud sound of an airplane in the master shot of a scene but not in the close-ups; unconvincing gun shots; nonexistent door slams; and lightning without thunder. All of this will be smoothed out by the end of postproduction, but not before the score is composed. If the film happens to rely on dialogue not yet laid in, or sound effects to be added in dubbing, you may miss a great deal. Some rough cuts, on the other hand, will seem comparatively complete.

---

[5] Spotting: determining where music will be.

Fine cuts require no further pictorial editing. The composer and the sound-effects people work from the fine cut whenever possible (there are times when a tight schedule will necessitate working from a film while it is still being edited). Except for any special visual effects (such as dissolves) that may still be missing, the film will be pictorially and dramatically complete, and ready for the final sound elements to be added in dubbing. The missing visual effects will be indicated with a grease-pencil line running the length of the effect. This editorially locked version is timed to the correct length, and can be spotted accurately and scored.

THE FIRST DISCUSSION AFTER SCREENING THE FILM

Composers are not expected to screen a film for the first time and immediately have a detailed discussion of their concept, musical solutions, and recommendations. The filmmakers' first concern will be: Did you like the film? Did it work? What were your impressions? They may also have specific dramatic concerns, and the composer, coming in fresh, has a chance to tell them something about an audience's possible response to their film. If they are worried about a particular story point, they'll want to know if you understood it. If they think a particular performance is weak, they may share that concern with you, or they may hope you'll mention your feelings about it without their asking. Did it feel too long? Was there enough tension or suspense?

Interestingly, they may not ask you these questions, even though these thoughts are on their minds. In fact, they may give you *their* answers to these unspoken questions; if so, you can take that as an invitation. They are probably hoping you will give them feedback on whatever subject they raise. If you say, "We wanted Tom Cruise for the lead, but we got Sidney Katzenbaum," tell them how much you enjoyed the quality Katzenbaum brings to the role. If you did. If you didn't think it worked at all, we can't suggest what to say. Sometimes silence may be appropriate. But if they ask you if you understood something and you didn't, tell them, and tell them why if you can.

Overall, filmmakers appreciate sincerity and candor—if it doesn't hurt too much. But no matter how distinguished the composer, no matter how much respect the filmmakers may have for his abilities as a composer, the composer is rarely one of the filmmakers, unless he has actually written or developed the project himself. *Footloose* (1984) and *Yentl* (1983) are exceptions, in which the lyricists (more than the composers) were deeply involved with the making of the film, due to the total integration of the songs and the script. (See Chapter 26, "Songs.") As a rule, though, you're on safer ground limiting yourself to comments on the musical aspects of the film.

COMPOSING BEFORE THE FILM IS FINISHED

In cases where there is music to prepare for **shooting to playback,**[6] it is mandatory to start composing before the film is finished. Songs are often created early as well. Otherwise, starting to compose the score before the film is finished may be a mistake. This is an area of disagreement between composers, and may depend largely on the project, the people involved, and other unique circumstances.

The late Jerry Fielding explained the potential problems: "Some composers like to be with a film from the beginning, but not me. I don't like to go on location, read scripts, or hang around while they're making movies. I don't want to know what they shot and what they left on the floor. I don't want to know what the intent was; I don't want to

[6] Shooting to playback: filming a sequence to a music track, usually but not necessarily one which has been specifically recorded for the sequence.

know what the script said that I now see is different. If I feel the film isn't working, I'm going to tell the director where I feel that is, and where I think it needs music to help it achieve its proper end. But I don't ever want to see what they took out, what they mixed around, because that's what's confusing the director by this time."[7]

THE OTHER SIDE. David Shire had a distinctly positive experience when he worked on his score for *The Conversation* (1974) with director Francis Coppola and editor Walter Murch. "I wasn't a hired gun who came in at the end after all the work had been done, and tried to fit a score into the picture. The score was being developed as the picture was being edited, and as the picture was being mixed." Working directly with Coppola, who suggested an unusual method for composing, Shire began working on the score before the film was shot, and finished the main theme during the early editing (see Figure 16-16). He even attended a read-through of the script before they started shooting. "One of the great advantages of doing a piano score was that as I wrote cues, I'd go up there and make temp tracks, and we'd lay them in. And Walter was terrific at moving them around, and taking a cue I'd written for one place and moving it some place else." Working this way, Shire was intensely involved throughout production and postproduction, and his experience reflects the power of a successful collaboration of efforts between the director, the composer, and the editor. Shire believes that his theater background helps him in a situation like this. "I'm used to collaborating. And the tendency, more and more, with the Lucas-Coppola-Spielberg school of filmmaking, is to involve the composer earlier." (See Chapter 12, "Composing.")

If the filmmakers and the composer can collaborate in this way, it may be the best of all possible worlds. Still, this kind of work method is not ordinary procedure, and achieves the best results under unique circumstances. Generally speaking, if you are isolated from the ongoing filmmaking, don't compose to the script before seeing footage.

---

[7] *Film Music Notebook,* Volume III, Number 3, 1977, p. 46, interview by Paul Seydor.

ROLE MODELS AND TEMP TRACKS

There is this disease, a demo love. A director will get so used to temp music that it shackles the composer's creativity. It is very difficult to incorporate elements of a working temp score and make it better. But then again, maybe the composer has to be open-minded enough to say, "What is it about this music that works for the scene?"

MICHAEL TRONICK, MUSIC EDITOR

If I am trying to tell a composer specifically what the music has to say through me, then I might as well not have a composer, because I am cutting off his legs at the knees and not stimulating his creative impulses. On the other hand, I want . . . his creative impulses to be in sync with mine.

JAMES GOLDSTONE, DIRECTOR

Even if they say, "I want Stravinsky's* Firebird*" —what part? Play me the part you want.

BRUCE BROUGHTON

When you want to be absolutely specific in describing a musical idea, words are rarely completely reliable. Many times, though, a verbal description of general musical intention can be reasonably clear even to a nonmusician. "Marchlike" means something to everybody. Describing a theme as "a simple, folklike theme, something like 'Home on the Range' or the theme from *High Noon* [1952]," would express a composer's concept of how the music might be approached for a film score. More specific comments would further clarify his ideas in terms a nonmusician could grasp: "I'll use a harmonica and guitar, with soft string chords," for example.

When a director says, "I'd like the theme to sound something like this. . ." and he plays a record for you, he is using a **role model** to demonstrate his wishes. At their best, the use of role models can be an effective way for directors, producers, and composers to communicate accurately with each other. If the filmmakers ask for "a score like *Gone With the Wind* [1939]," ten minutes with the original soundtrack album will remove any uncertainty the composer may have about the filmmakers' intentions. And if the composer suggests scoring a particular cue in the style of Vivaldi, he might be wise to explain his suggestion by playing a recording that sounds stylistically and emotionally close to what he has in mind, especially if he believes the filmmakers may be unclear about the style.

TYPES OF ROLE MODELS. Role models come from the following sources:

1. A specific film score or cue
2. A specific style of film score

3. A specific classical piece or other musical style
4. A specific song

SPECIFIC FILM SCORES OR CUES AS ROLE MODELS

Major landmarks in film scoring are often used as role models, sometimes current, sometimes historical. Scores with enormous impact on the commercial market and those from extraordinarily successful films are often used as references. The following examples of role models from well-known films illustrate both the usefulness and the prevalence of role models in the language of film communication:

- *Lawrence of Arabia* (composed by Maurice Jarre, 1962). Richard Michaels, director of the miniseries *Sadat* (1983), recalls, "I told Charles Bernstein I wanted a *Lawrence of Arabia* type of big full orchestral sounds—as many instruments as we could possibly afford, and that kind of triumph. Basically what we were looking for was a big, big picture." (See Figure 16-5.)
- *Jaws* theme (composed by John Williams, 1975). As the composer Elmer Bernstein began planning his score for *Airplane!* (1980), he remembers, "The Zuckers [directors David and Jerry] helped set the tone, because it was their idea to use the quote from *Jaws* at the beginning and over the main title. You see the fin of the airplane." (See Figure 13-1.)
- *North by Northwest* (composed by Bernard Herrman, 1959). Arthur B. Rubinstein illustrates the necessity of being specific when using role models as points of reference: "I did a television movie starring Audrey Hepburn. And it was a combination of *Charade* [1963], *Two For the Road* [1966], and any number of her films. And the producer said, "The music for this should be, I don't know who it is—it's Cary Grant music.' I said, 'You mean *North by Northwest?*' He said, 'Yes, right.' So I wrote the score, which is very much in that genre. And on the scoring stage, one of the producers said, 'I like that, but that heavy section—you know, it's a comedy.' I said, 'No, it's not a comedy.' And she said, 'Didn't you see *Charade?*' And I said, '*Charade* is not a comedy.' As it turned out, when they dubbed it, everybody called and said, 'You were absolutely right.'"

SPECIFIC FILM-SCORING STYLES USED AS ROLE MODELS

It's not unusual for filmmakers to talk in terms of the style of a particular composer or score, so that the style becomes the role model. A stylistic description like that can go a long way in expressing their vision of the score. Agent Richard Emler notes that "they'll say they want a very 'John Williams-like, *Star Wars* [1977] or *Close Encounters* [1977], symphonic, classical, larger-than-life type of score.' The same applies to Jerry Goldsmith. When they reference a specific Goldsmith score as opposed to referencing a specific John Williams score, you have a good idea of what is meant." In order for this kind of communication to work effectively, everyone involved in the dialogue needs to know the composers and scores being referenced.

SPECIFIC CLASSICAL PIECES OR STYLES USED AS ROLE MODELS

When I say Berlioz, I didn't do Berlioz; I did what Berlioz might have done fifty years later, if he were scoring that film. ALLYN FERGUSON

Very often classical music defines the styles of the score for the composer or filmmakers. But sometimes the use of a role model can communicate without being a specific demand. It becomes a musical illustration of the nature of the music, not the style.

SYMPHONIC MUSIC. Bill Conti's story about the evolution of his score for *Rocky* (1976) is surprising: "John Avildson [the director] said, 'My idea of this is a fairy tale, and it's bigger than life, and it's not just a story about a punchy fighter. Listen to this.' And then he played the 'Eroica' Symphony of Beethoven to slow-motion footage of fighters. And of course the 'Eroica' never needed a picture to help it along. When confronted with the budget, I had to be honest and say, 'I cannot do the "Eroica" Symphony, that symphonic style. What I can hopefully do is go to a baroque feeling.' I suggested maybe a little baroque fanfare, and that we've got to keep in mind it's in the streets of Philadelphia. I didn't think our noses should be held that high. Maybe there's a combination of both there. I did a fugue for the big fight, and it was more 'baroque-y' than the 'Eroica,' which would be overblown for the film. It was kind of baroque rock. I couldn't fight the fact that we were in the streets of Philadelphia, and I don't think John cared if I went straight classical or added something to it, but I knew that he felt classical in the sense that he never spoke of anything else except the 'Eroica.'" (See Figures 4-1, 4-2.)

MIDDLE EUROPEAN LULLABY. John Morris explains his role model for *Young Frankenstein* (1974): "Mel Brooks, in his films, always tries to go for the center of the emotion. *Young Frankenstein* could conceivably have been just another horror movie—it could have been just horror music. However, his instruction to me was to write the most beautiful Middle European lullaby that I could, which would serve as a violin rhapsody, because we needed violin playing during the picture. So that's exactly what I wrote." (See Figure 4-3.)

VIVALDI MANDOLIN CONCERTO. Georges Delerue describes the director's musical role model for *A Little Romance* (1979): "The only thing that was really said was that [director] George [Roy Hill] proposed the sound of the mandolin and guitar to reflect the intimacy of the two kids. He also put in a temp track of Vivaldi, which was fitting very well, and he wanted to keep it for one particular sequence. So I continued that, in order to not have a break in the style of the music. And because it was necessary to have a very clear score, very dynamic and tonal."

USING ROLE MODELS TO COMMUNICATE. There are those times when the filmmaker's suggestions, as expressed by a role model, just don't seem appropriate; the concept just doesn't work for the composer. This is when the composer's powers of persuasion become most important. IN ORDER TO BE CONVINCING, YOU'VE GOT TO STUDY THE PROJECT AS THOROUGHLY AS POSSIBLE, AND FROM EVERY ANGLE. ONLY THEN WILL YOU BE ABLE TO SINCERELY RECOMMEND ANOTHER APPROACH, OR PROPERLY EXPLAIN TO THE FILMMAKER WHY HIS CONCEPT ISN'T GOING TO WORK.

Allyn Ferguson had a challenge like this on the television movie *Camille* (1984). Somebody told producer Norman Rosemount that *Camille* was also the story of *La Traviata*. "So he had said for months, 'I'd like *La Traviata* to be paraphrased as the score.'" says Ferguson. "I had gone through *La Traviata* to find anything that was available. The only thing that could possibly have been used was a part of the overture to the first and third act. There's one little section you could use as score. And I sat Norman down and said, 'Okay, here is this aria and here's that one. This is just vocal music, and can't be done instrumentally. Besides that, even Verdi didn't like it very much—he thought it was trite himself in *those* days. So if it was banal then, what [is] it going to be now?'

FIGURE 4-1

Rocky 13-2 End Scene Bill Conti

FIGURE 4-2

Rocky **13-3 End Title** **Bill Conti**

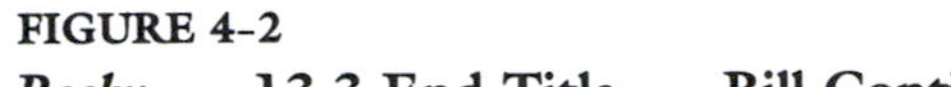

FIGURE 4-3

Young Frankenstein **Transylvania Lullaby** **John Morris**

"Then I played him what I thought it should be, and he said, 'Well, you're breaking my heart. I really think it ought to be *La Traviata.*' And I said, 'Norman, I just won't do that. If you want that, get somebody else to do it. I think it's wrong as hell.'" This is an excellent example of artistic integrity in action. In this case, Ferguson had worked on many of Rosemount's projects, and had developed a very high credibility quotient. And so he was able to compose the score his way, as he felt worked best. But first he did his research, without summarily dismissing Rosemount's idea out of hand.

THE COMPOSER'S USE OF ROLE MODELS

> ***So I will call upon Prokofiev, or I'll call upon Bartok, or will call upon Mahler.*** ARTHUR B. RUBINSTEIN

> ***I would like to thank Beethoven, Brahms, Wagner, Strauss, Rimsky-Korsakov. . . .*** DMITRI TIOMKIN, at the 1955 Academy Awards

CLASSICAL COMPOSERS. Some examples of classical composers used by composers as role models for scores or cues are:

- Bach (Johnny Mandel, for *Deathtrap,* 1982)
- Berlioz (Allyn Ferguson, for the television film *Les Miserables,* 1978)
- Elgar, Mendelssohn (Elmer Bernstein, for *Trading Places,* 1983)
- Rachmaninoff (Randy Edelman, for an episode of the television series *MacGyver*)
- Satie (Johnny Mandel, for *Being There,* 1979)
- Sibelius (Craig Safan, for *The Last Starfighter,* 1984)
- Tchaikovsky (John Morris, for *Young Frankenstein,* 1974)
- Vivaldi (Marvin Hamlisch, for one cue in *Sophie's Choice,* 1982)

FOLK MUSIC AND POP INFLUENCES. Here are examples of folk music and pop sources used by composers as role models for scores or cues:

- Americana/modal harmony (Maurice Jarre, for *Witness,* 1985; see Figure 14-3)
- Bee Gees groove (Marvin Hamlisch, for *The Spy Who Loved Me,* 1977, cue at beginning of film, on ski slopes)
- "A Summer Place" arranged by Percy Faith, late sixties (Patrick Williams, for *Violets Are Blue,* 1986)
- John Barry style (Randy Edelman, for an episode of *MacGyver*)
- Red Army Chorus (Johnny Mandel, for *The Russians Are Coming, The Russians Are Coming,* 1966)

SONGS. The influence of Top-40 songs on today's film scoring is enormous. Agent Richard Emler comments that "more and more in today's film music language, the producers talk in the direction of the type of *song* they have heard on the radio. They like that sound and they want *that* sound for their picture."

ROLE MODELS AND PLAGIARISM

When the role model is a piece of music in the public domain, the composer has the choice of using the music, quoting from it, doing something similar, or something different. When the role model is a copyrighted piece, the situation is more difficult, and the composer may find that anything he composes that is similar to the role model may be challenged as plagiarism. Then come lawyers, musicologists, and other experts to attempt to decide whether an infringement has occurred.

Plagiarism is a slippery business. Cases are not tried in specialized courts as are patent suits (although not very many plagiarism cases actually come to trial because it is expensive and the outcome so unpredictable that each party is afraid a costly decision could go against them). And many of the experts' opinions seem completely farfetched. Ira Newborn tells a story about writing a piece of generic I VI II V music for a dance party. "This guy [a hired musicologist] had me so scared that I wrote it with no melody. I just wrote the chords and a string line, and the guy told me it was 'Rio Rita'!"

The best advice is to try to capture the tone and spirit of a role model without plagiarizing a copyrighted property. If a plagiarism case is lost (through a court suit or through a threat of a suit and a negotiated settlement) the result is that the composer's credits and performance royalties go to the plaintiff. This is a field in which it is nearly impossible to give advice. Legal decisions are unpredictable, and the guidelines are in the hands of lawyers and music departments. You have to follow their advice on particular projects as the questions arise. Legal precedents aren't very helpful. In short, when in doubt—be original.

TEMP TRACKS

If the musical examples being used as role models are actually cut and dubbed into the film prior to scoring, the cues become temp tracks and the score as a whole becomes the *temp score* (or *temp track*). No phrase in the language of film can cause as much anguish and anxiety for the composer as *temp tracks.*

Temp is short for *temporary,* which is something that temp tracks rarely are. Even if they are totally and successfully replaced by original score, there usually is a musical residue left behind. Bruce Broughton finds that the similarity between the temp track and the final score can be too close for comfort. "There are, I think, a lot of obvious cases in films where you see what the temp track was. But there's no disclaimer you can put on the picture saying, 'This is what they wanted. Period.' And yet I know that happens to everybody."

Some film composers are more sanguine than others about temp tracks, and a few actually seem to be at peace with them. But even most producers, directors, and editors recognize the inherent pitfalls in working with them; some, like producer Gerald Isenberg, prefer to do without them if at all possible, finding them "counterproductive."

WHY FILMMAKERS USE TEMP TRACKS

> ***The truth is that temp scores are usually the best scores. Because you get the best of the best. You're up against them all.*** MARVIN HAMLISCH

> ***Sometimes I have been let down eventually when the final music was put in because the temp music was just so good.***
> JAMES GOLDSTONE, DIRECTOR

> ***Often temp tracks are the kiss of death.*** IRA NEWBORN

There are basically four reasons why filmmakers use temp tracks: (1) to help them finish editing their film; (2) to help them screen their film for the producer(s), studio, and/or network executives and preview audiences during various stages of postproduction; (3) to establish a concept for the score; (4) to demonstrate that concept to the composer.

TEMP TRACKS DURING EDITING. At some point during the editing process, the film editor often begins to play around with music, trying available cues from other film scores and various record cuts to see what works. One of the primary reasons for this is to avoid screening the film with no music. There are often sequences in a rough cut that can be improved enormously with the right music.

Editor John Burnett explains a typical situation that calls for a temp track. "You can have a scene that's running very long and *should* be long. If the director is very honest, and he keeps running it, over and over, and over and over, pretty soon he says, 'Do I have to run this turkey again?' He doesn't really mean that, but pretty soon he feels it's just too long, and he starts going, 'Cut it, cut it, cut it.' Until finally it becomes not even an entity within itself that's worth anything. Consequently you start dissipating your movie. But all of a sudden you put in a piece of music, and then do you know what happens? They start saying, 'Wait a minute, that's too short.'"

So that scene now has a temp track. And that temp track stays in the picture for the remainder of the editing phase, right through to the fine cut and the screenings for the networks or the theatrical previews. And it becomes a part of the film during the entire process.

TEMP TRACKS FOR SCREENINGS. Writer-director David Seltzer articulates clearly the reason why everybody uses temp tracks for their screenings. "When you play your film for an audience, and there are audiences all along the way—publicity people and the executives—you find the more theatrical it is the more they respond to it." It's that simple. Almost everyone, including the professionals, finds their response to motion pictures heightened by the appropriate use of music on the soundtrack. Telling your audience that the film isn't finished and that music will be added later doesn't work on an emotional level. When you watch the film, your emotional responses are geared to the film as it is, not as it will be.

TEMP TRACKS TO FIND THE SCORE'S CONCEPT. Even without the pressure of screenings, there are times when the director wants to begin exploring the possibilities of a particular style of music for his film's score. Without the time restrictions and huge expense of the scoring stage, he can search for a musical approach that appeals to him and seems to express his abstract musical impressions of his film. In fact, if he doesn't take the time and effort to do this during the editing stage, it can be a problem later. "For example," music executive Gary LeMel says, "we're doing a film now where the director thought that rap music would work against a particular visual, so we put that music up against it and it didn't work at all. As it turned out, heavy metal music worked."

A carefully designed temp track can leave absolutely no doubt in the composer's mind as to the direction the director wants to take with the score.

HOW COMPOSERS WORK WITH TEMP TRACKS

Even though they know how important these temp tracks can be to the future of their scores, many composers hate to hear them. Some ask that the temp music be completely removed before their first screening of the film to be sure that they are not influenced one way or the other by what they would hear. The big disadvantage of refusing to hear the temp track is that you forfeit the opportunity to discuss this music with the filmmakers. If the music has been carefully considered and represents many of the director's decisions regarding the score, it may be difficult to communicate effectively without referring to the temp track.

Why don't the composers take temp tracks in their stride, listen and discuss them with the filmmakers, and then forget about them? First of all, it can be almost impossible to get the temp track out of your head once you've heard it, especially if it's already been dubbed into the film. If it works, it can be difficult to imagine a better approach. And if it doesn't work, then the chances are it will have spoiled your first emotional reactions to the film. And what's worse, you may still have trouble getting it out of your head.

> *You're stuck an awful lot of the time following the temp score in mood or feeling, or taking a rather extraordinary risk that your score is going to be thrown out.* PATRICK WILLIAMS

> *They always say, "We don't mean this," and I ask, "Then what is it doing there if you don't mean it?" Because they* do *mean it.* ALLYN FERGUSON

> *The director put temp track in there, and he wouldn't have if it felt bad for him, so that's telling you that this feels good to him. If you ignore that as a composer, you're in trouble. You can't do that.* BILL CONTI

FACING THE MUSIC. If Bruce Broughton knows he has been asked to screen a temp-tracked film he will be scoring, he will watch the film with the temp track. And then he talks to the filmmakers right away about the temp track choices, and his reactions to them. "Sometimes the temp track is an appropriate way of going, and I'll note that because I know that they're going to fall in love with it. And whatever they fall in love with, I *know* that I have to pay attention to. If I feel really strongly about a scene, I've said, 'Look, I think your choice of music is really poor in these areas and I would hate to be held to doing something similar to that because I think I know something better for your film.' A common response will be, 'Oh, that's fine.'"

Broughton emphasizes that you must ask if they do in fact really mean for the original music you write to be similar in feel or concept to the temp music. Sometimes the temp track really *is* just there primarily for the practical reasons we've discussed, and not because they are expecting it to be duplicated by the composer.

Broughton continues: "Once or twice the director has said, 'I *love* this piece of music—I love the way it works.' Well, you know you're dead, because you know you've *got to* do that. When I find it particularly a problem is when they really *do* love the temp track, and they mean *that* track. And they know that they can't use it. They know that you have to write something else but they want you to write *that.* And anything that you try to do other than that, including color, melodic contour, and things like that, will not be acceptable. In those cases I really don't know what to do."

When they really do love the temp track, the composer almost invariably ends up duplicating the music. If there is a secret to avoiding that obvious imitation, it may be found in capturing the real essence of the temp music. If you're lucky, that essence may include something that can remain constant, while the rest of the music is not imitative. The original temp music for the montages in *The Sterile Cuckoo* (1969, Karlin) was the song "A Time to Remember," performed by The Sandpipers. The song was definitely very relevant to the film, both musically and lyrically. Ultimately, it wasn't used, but continuity was provided by getting The Sandpipers to perform the new, original song, "Come Saturday Morning" (lyric by Dori Previn, music by Karlin). Director Alan Pakula felt the vocal quality of the group was perfectly suited for the film, and when they sang "Come Saturday Morning" on the final soundtrack, Pakula found it even easier to adjust to the new song.

USING THE COMPOSER'S OWN MUSIC FOR TEMP TRACKS. Many people recommend incorporating into the temp track the composer's own music from previous scores. Whether it makes things any easier for the composer is questionable. However, if the composer actually supervises the selection of appropriate cues, he has the advantage of helping to shape the dramatic thrust of a scene musically. This can prevent everyone from getting used to an inappropriate musical approach.

THE VALUE OF TEMP TRACKS

Temp tracks, like role models, can be made to work for you in the following ways:

- Everyone involved can learn from temp tracks.
- Temp tracks can reveal insights and facilitate communication.
- Temp tracks can be a useful collaborative tool.

EVERYONE CAN LEARN FROM TEMP TRACKS. Charles Fox has never been bothered by temp music. He believes that temp tracks are an excellent opportunity to learn about the film and the potential score. "There have been several times when I've heard things and said, 'That's interesting—that's an interesting approach.' For example, when I did *Oh God, Book II* [1980], there was a lot of Tchaikovsky tracked in and it gave it a quality of largesse, of symphonic proportions, bright and colorful and sparkling, and it almost gave the film a more important feeling because of the symphonic aspect. And although the final score was all my original music, I freely allowed that style to influence me. I might have approached that film more contemporarily, for example. The symphonic temp approach looked good on the screen and it worked."

Fox points out another educational advantage of temp tracks. If you are able to attend previews of theatrical films, you are able to experience the audience's reaction to the film and the temp music.

TEMP TRACKS CAN REVEAL INSIGHTS. Interestingly, temp tracks may contain hidden messages that even the filmmakers cannot or might not necessarily communicate successfully to the composer. If the composer watches for these messages, he can learn a lot about the filmmaker's attitude about his film. Arthur B. Rubinstein illustrates this in describing his first screening of *Blue Thunder* (1983):

"I got to the screening, and the picture was temp-tracked with a couple of Tangerine Dream cues, a couple of the cuts from the electronic tape that I had given him, and—*Raiders of the Lost Ark* [1981]. So I spoke to them afterwards, and the editor said, 'We just put that in there for fun.' Well. I *know* that nobody puts something like that in for fun. Somewhere, somebody had a notion that this picture is more than just Tangerine Dream. It's larger than that." This was doubly surprising to Rubinstein because in his previous discussions with director John Badham, he had been told many times that he wanted an electronic score in the style of Giorgio Moroder. And although the filmmakers were minimizing the importance of the music from *Raiders,* the dramatic impulse inherent in that music was as important to Badham as was the electronic music when it functioned in the film.

When John Barry worked with director Sydney Pollack on the score for *Out of Africa* (1985) they both learned a great deal from their early experimentation with temp music. "Pollack's instincts were initially to listen to various scores of movies that had been done in Africa. And he said none of it worked. Absolutely none of it worked for him at all. In one scene he played *Born Free* [1966] against it, and of course it was so wrong. It was Africa, and all that, but the sentiment was just totally inaccurate. And he said, 'When you look at the picture, there are glimpses, but they are not great shots of elephants and giraffes and lions and landscape.' The focus of the movie was essentially on the characters. And that's exactly the way we went with it. The whole score went that way." (See Figure 13-29.)

TEMP TRACKS AS A COLLABORATIVE TOOL. In a real sense, John Barry and Sydney Pollack were collaborating together in their search for the perfect approach to the score for *Out of Africa*. Barry recounts his experience: "When we first met, there were only one or two little moments of temp track in the film. And then, once I was involved in it, we just got hold of all the stuff that I'd ever done. And he went through it and I went through it to make certain suggestions, so that by the time he was close to a cut for the studio, he had all my stuff in it. It was very helpful. Because it was very on the nose as to what he was looking for in terms of the moods. I temp-tracked the flying scene with the last cue of an obscure movie I did called *The Last Valley* [1970], which was with Michael Caine and Omar Sharif. And it had a choir; it was a story about the Thirty Years War—the religious wars in Europe. . . . But the choir in that cue really worked. I don't think that we would have thought of using a choir until we laid that cue in, and Sydney said, 'Jesus, let's use those voices.' And so that's how that one came about."

For *The Mosquito Coast* (1986) Maurice Jarre and director Peter Weir became collaborators even before shooting began. Jarre created three electronic tracks for Weir to take with him on cassette during the shooting of the film. These pieces were not intended to represent any final solutions to the score, nor were any of them thematically related to the final score. But Jarre says this music gave Weir "moods, to help him set a definite structure for the music in the film. We were constantly in communication. This temporary music helped in a way to find the right musical dimension of the film."

CONTEMPORARY USAGE

Some contemporary filmmakers lock in much of the temp track, and the composer should be prepared for this situation. When Ira Newborn has worked with director John Hughes, he has seen the movie after it is pretty much completely tracked. Hughes conceives many of his teenage-movie scenes with a specific record in mind. He has a gigantic record collection and knows his records well. By the time he finishes a script he has already selected a record for every scene. What's left for the composer to do? "When I would say that something he wanted didn't work, he would keep looking at it, and I'd tell him, 'It's not right, it's not right.' And finally he has this vague gnawing at him that it doesn't work, so he'll let me do it. . . . Then I get to plug the hole." Newborn points out that in *Ferris Bueller's Day Off* (1986) there are more places where the music functions as score, indicating a growing give-and-take collaboration of sorts.

THE TEMP TRACK MAY END UP IN THE FILM. This can be the most difficult blow of all. But many composers have created scores for temp-tracked films only to find out that by the end of dubbing, their score, or a good portion of it, was not in the film. As director James Goldstone says, "Sometimes I have been let down eventually when the final music was put in because the temp music was just so good." And Goldstone is very aware of the dangers of temp music, and consequently very cautious about its use. He knows it's a trap, and consciously works at avoiding the hazards.

Here are some successful films that were released with some of the temp music on the final soundtrack (usually rerecorded specifically for the film):

- *Alien* (1979, composed by Jerry Goldsmith): the film still contains a bit of music from Goldsmith's score for *Freud* (1963), which had been cut into the temp track by one of the editors; a section of Howard Hanson's *Romantic Symphony* is still in the film over the end titles.
- *Breaking Away* (1979, composed by Patrick Williams): the first half of the film uses the Mendelssohn "*Italian*" Symphony, excerpts from Rossini, and other operatic material, all adapted from the temp track and rerecorded for the film.
- *The Exorcist* (1973): the original score composed for the film was not used. Instead, director William Friedkin used his avant-garde concert-music temp track.

- *The Graduate* (1967, songs composed and performed by Simon and Garfunkel): the film's song score, including "The Sound of Silence" and "Mrs. Robinson," was derived from the temp track when director Mike Nichols couldn't find new songs for the film that were as effective for him.
- *Platoon* (1986, composed by Georges Delerue): about half of the temp score was used on the final soundtrack. Thus Samuel Barber's Adagio for Strings became the main theme of the film.
- *The Sting* (1973, adapted by Marvin Hamlisch): most of the score was adapted and rerecorded from director George Roy Hill's self-performed Scott Joplin temp track.
- *2001: A Space Odyssey* (1968): the original score composed for the film by Alex North was not used; instead, director Stanley Kubrick used his own temp track. Hearing the "Blue Danube" as the space ship floated through space was at once startling and effective, and the music from Richard Strauss's *Also sprach Zarathustra* became the "Theme from 2001."

In many of these cases (and countless others like them) the composer actually composed a complete score for the film, not realizing that the temp music might prevail in certain areas. Jerry Goldsmith, commenting about his score for *Alien,* points out that the End Title he wrote for that film is on the soundtrack album, but not in the film. "I must say that I've gotten a lot of condolences for that over the years. They had temp'd the "Romantic" Symphony and I couldn't figure out what the hell that had to do with the picture. And the End Title I did was quite lovely and logical and developed out of the film, and the Hanson piece ended up in the film."

SHOW ME THE WAY TO GO HOME. Many times you know what the score will be right from the start. Allyn Ferguson will never forget the time he screened a film in which they had laid in Carole King's huge hit of the day, "I Feel the Earth Move," as the last cue in the picture—"not the End Title, but the *last cue.* And I heard it go on, and I said, 'Hey, wait a minute! Stop!' And the lights went up in the screening room and the director said, 'What's the matter?' And I said, 'What's *that* doing in there?' And he said, 'Oh, oh, you know, we don't want that, just something *like* that.' And I said, 'Hold it, now. There is *nothing* like that. If you want that, go buy it and use it.' 'No, no, no, we just want something like that.' And I walked away. Because there is nothing like that."

Temp tracks are a risky business. But as we've shown, they *can* work for the composer and the filmmaker. Understand the pitfalls and be ready to explain them to others as necessary. When the filmmakers are aware of their inherent problems the composer and filmmaker can work together to avoid their negative influences, and try to let role models work for them as effective communication devices.

CHAPTER 5

SPOTTING THE FILM

To me the most important aspect of film scoring is the spotting. Everything else is secondary to that. If you make serious mistakes in the spotting, there's no way you can recover. ALLYN FERGUSON

Despite preliminary meetings and screenings, you can't start your serious work until the film editor has locked the picture (that is, until you can see the fine cut). Then the timings are right, the pace and flow are there, the production dialogue is there. (Notes will usually be given regarding the placement of wild lines that may be added later.) It would be great if the sound effects were complete and if the **optical effects**[1] were finished, but they typically aren't and won't be any time before you score. They will be indicated by grease marks scribed on the film. At this point, the film can be spotted. Most composers agree that the sensitive spotting of a film is vital to a successful score.

Decisions about the function of music and its placement in the film are very important, and everyone has an opinion about this. These decisions are made at spotting sessions, during which the film is run and spotted for music. Usually present, at the very least, are the composer, the music editor, and the director, producer, and film editor. Other people associated with the production are often there also. In episodic television, the associate producer may supervise the spotting session.

Spotting is often done in a projection room with a stop-and-go, reversible projector ready to handle the many stops and replays that the process requires. Some directors, like James Goldstone, prefer to spot music on a **KEM** flatbed film editor in a smaller room (see Figure 5-1). "I'm the one who plays it myself, in a small room, with no sense that you're being listened to by twenty-two other people and censoring yourself because of them. It becomes a very intimate collaboration that way and a wonderful asset in spotting music. There should be no rush; you should have the time to explore everything verbally, and go back and forth in the film." Spotting with a KEM is becoming more and more popular among producers and directors.

Some composers make a cassette recording of the spotting session, as well as of other sessions when the director is discussing the musical needs and meaning of the film. For them, taking notes is not fast enough or complete enough. If the director says, "Start music right after that line," a cassette will have the dialogue line and his comments.

PREPARING FOR THE SPOTTING SESSION

When you go in to spot something and you don't know the film, it's all coming from the director. It's ridiculous. I like to go to a spotting session and be able to tell them exactly what's going to happen. Then if they say, "No, I don't need music there," fine—but at least I know

[1] Optical effects: special visual effects shot separately and cut into the film, usually during post production, such as dissolves, fade-ins, fade-outs, supers.

where I'm going. Even on a series, there are videotapes around. Then at least you go in with something, rather than just spotting it not knowing where you're going. RANDY EDELMAN

The filmmakers usually come to spotting with some idea of how music will function and where. As producer Gerald Isenberg says, "If you've seen the picture enough times, unconsciously you've felt music was needed here and not there. And you've made up your mind, so that out of twenty cues there's no doubt on ten, there are five or six that are questionable, and then there are five or six places you don't even know about and never thought of that way, and the fun of spottting is discovery."

Director Robert Wise likes the composer to pre-spot the film before spotting. "When I have a film and I have a cut I want to show a composer, of course I first let the composer see it and find out if he likes it and see if he's right for the film. Then I would like to have him go away and get familiar with the show, then come back to me with his list of cues—where the music should go. Then I might find some places where I hadn't been planning on music; and we talk that out and maybe he'll talk me into it or I might talk him out of it. But I like to get his input initially."

Bodie Chandler, former Vice-President of Music, Columbia Pictures Television, notes that there are times when a composer for television may be asked to spot a film he has never even seen (especially a series episode). That can be difficult, though it is certainly possible, especially if the series has an established style. But whether it's an episode or not, he says, "I'll generally try to get a composer to see a film before he spots it so he doesn't come in cold."

FIGURE 5-1.
KEM flatbed film editor (Michael Palokow, music editor. Lion's Gate Studios).

Photo: Gay Wallin

Henry Mancini likes to pre-spot. In fact, he says, with director Blake Edwards, "I always do it alone, and he's never there—just myself and my music editor. And when he gets the spotting notes, if there's something amiss, or if he was thinking of something else, then I'll do it. I've rarely gotten into any philosophical conversations with Blake. It's a matter of trust.

"Rarely we've had to go back and maybe, after it's completely scored, make adjustments here and there. Because you really don't know what you have in a picture until it's completely scored and dubbed. Then you look at it to find out where you are."

TALKING IT OVER

The spotting session is an ideal time for meaningful communication between the composer and the filmmakers. Ideally at this point, the composer, having studied the videocassette and pre-spotted the film, will know the questions he must ask and may have one or more approaches to present. The director will usually have made final decisions about editing, sound effects, and the tone and attitude of the film—all aspects of the film that influence the music's function.

Good decisions at the spotting stage and a good understanding of the director's conception of what music the film needs can avoid cues being changed or dropped, or even whole scores lost. Nobody wants that to happen—but it *has* happened to almost every film composer.

MAKING DECISIONS

The most obvious decisions to be made at the spotting session are (1) which scenes will have music and (2) where the music will start and stop. While these are important decisions, the underlying question, most significant of all, is What is the right music for the film? There is no single answer to this question because—as with all artistic decisions—the answer is subjective; opinions will differ.

Bodie Chandler finds it very important for the composer to ask as many questions as possible during the spotting. "It may mean bringing a cassette recording of different musical styles or scores that you've gotten off records; if they're asking for something pop, play them cuts from a pop album or soundtrack. Say, 'Is this what you mean by pop?' If somebody says, 'I want a Bruce Springsteen sound,' is that Springsteen when he's singing 'Born in the USA' or when he's singing 'I'm On Fire?' There are twenty different styles of Bruce Springsteen. Or when they say, 'Give me a Dave Grusin score,' you should say, 'Is that Dave Grusin when he's hip or when he's doing *Heaven Can Wait?*'"

Spotting decisions are frequently instinctive for most directors, producers, editors, and composers; although many times all parties agree with those decisions, the authority clearly rests with the director and/or the producer. When differences of opinion arise, as they often do, the composer needs to be sure of the director's intentions. Tact is the byword, but directness is essential, because this is the time for the composer to discuss his own ideas.

The spotting session is the first time the filmmakers will see the composer actually working on their film. Through the proper preparation in advance the composer will be able to make suggestions for the placement and musical approach of cues that will establish the basis for the filmmakers' trust. If there are disagreements, discussion at this point will tell the composer a lot about the filmmakers' attitudes.

WHEN TO USE MUSIC

To justify the placement of music in a scene you must know what contribution music will be able to make. Will it establish a dramatic point of view? Will it get us inside a character's head? Will it emphasize an emotion or provide a rhythmic pulse to drive the action forward?

Allyn Ferguson says, "Sometimes the producer will ask for music, and I'll say, 'Why? Tell me what I'm playing.' Many producers don't know exactly what they mean when they say music. 'Well, you know, just general background.' It doesn't *need* general background.

"I've also argued *for* music when the producer has said, 'No, I don't want any music.' At the bottom line I'll say, 'Let me go ahead and write a cue. You can take it out any time you want if you don't like it. But give me a shot at it.' Most of the time they stay in the movie."

Bruce Broughton says, "On a couple of projects lately I've put much more music into them than I've wanted to and I've said to the director, 'I don't think you'll find that you'll be using this.' And the director has said to me, 'I think you'll find that I will.' And he did.

"If I really don't understand what the music is supposed to do in a particular cue, I have to ask, 'What is it supposed to say?' and if he says he wants it to do this and this, I'll say, 'Okay, I understand that.'"

Curiously, a powerful dramatic scene, especially one with a strong sense of realism or emotion, can be weakened by the addition of music—it can turn earnest drama into maudlin melodrama; it can take the searing edge off gritty, threatening realism and make the scene safely "theatrical" so we no longer see it as reality.

Many times in features the most obvious spotting—putting music under action—is avoided. For the climax of *Breaking Away* (1979), Patrick Williams explains, "it was preplanned that there would not be music for a lot of the bicycle race of the end. [Director] Peter Yates wanted the sound of the bikes and the chains and all that kind of reality, and he didn't want the music to come in until well into the scene."

FINDING THE RIGHT MOMENT. Music sometimes works best in a film by being withheld until it can function in a special way. In *Sophie's Choice* (1984), the story of a Polish girl whose memories of her concentration camp internment still haunt her in New York, Marvin Hamlisch didn't spot music for Meryl Streep's fainting scene. "I've always said that an interesting way of spotting is to decide where you're *not* going to have music. You have to be very careful when you use music with [director] Alan [Pakula] because he wants realism. The reason there was no music when she fainted was that we felt the fainting was still in reality and there was no relationship happening there. Fainting was hers alone. When he brings her to her bed, that's when we started, because that's when you need to have the feeling of there being a combination. There's something to watch regarding the two people." (See Figure 7-7.)

In *Somewhere in Time* (1981) composer John Barry also spotted music to show a relationship between the two people. The film tells the story of a playwright who goes back in time and encounters his old love, lost in a previous incarnation. Barry recalls a scene in which "she's on the stage and virtually starts to talk to him in the audience. I suggested scoring that and the director [Jeannot Szwarc] said, 'I just don't see music there at all.' I said, 'It will totally put these two people together if we put music over them. At that moment she's on the stage and there's an audience; once that music comes in and it's theirs, the two people become totally isolated from the audience. And when the director sees me now he says that was the best cue in the movie—'I would never have thought of that and it just worked like a charm.' The composer has an insight—a fascinating approach to make those things really work. And they are usually the most interesting parts of the score. The obvious things usually take care of themselves."

In the torrid film noir *Body Heat* (1981), Barry recalls, "Larry Kasdan (on his first film as director) and I had talked about the early Bogart movies in terms of style and feel, so we knew the ballpark we were in. His editor was also very aware of the function of music. There were very obvious places where Larry wanted music, but it's always the less obvious places where a composer is more helpful—where you suggest music in a certain area and he says, 'I would never have thought of music there, but let's do it.' Those are the dark areas for directors where they really *don't* see it."

STARTS AND STOPS. Some composers find opportunities to take advantage of the effect of music starting and stopping. In the library sequence in *Ghostbusters* (1984), Elmer Bernstein's music comes in and out several times. "I've always felt that once you have music in a film the music makes a comment; stopping the music also makes a comment, and I've always liked using it in that way. In the case of *Ghostbusters* or in any film comedy the spotting is definitely something I would do with the director. In this rather complex library scene, there was a lot of discussion with Ivan Reitman about those stops and starts."

FIND A POINT OF VIEW. In spotting director Blake Edwards's films, Henry Mancini says that he doesn't pay any attention to the comedy. "If I do it's in an overall sense—it's like dropping a canvas. I think the Main Title for the original *Pink Panther* (1964) sums up the whole approach. That was a cartoon, an animated piece of film. I think that piece of film would have been scored differently at Disney. You know, Inspector Clouseau never had a theme until the fourth or fifth picture because I always felt that Peter [Sellers] was fully capable of having a scene go on his own. So I just stayed out of the way of most of his routines, and Blake never mentioned it because we have a shorthand we use together. And it was a case where I never thought it should be played, he never asked, and that was it."

STARTING A CUE

In general, music starts most effectively at a moment of shifting emphasis. This might be expressed as

1. A new emotional emphasis or subject in the dialogue
2. A new visual emphasis with the camera
3. A camera move, which almost always is conceived for emphasis
4. A new action, such as a car driving off, a person leaving the room, a cop ducking behind a barrier
5. A reaction to something that has been said or has occurred.

Sometimes this new emphasis coincides with an editorial cut to a new shot or angle; keep in mind that the *edit* isn't the focus of the drama, but rather what is happening or what you are seeing. If the best place to start is on a cut, fine, but it is just as effective to start in between cuts. LET THE DRAMA, NOT THE EDITING, BE THE MOTIVATION TO START THE MUSIC.

HOW TO START. Do you start the cue with an aggressive, accented entrance, or with a soft lead-in? The sole criterion for this is the style and nature of the film, and the function of the score at that particular moment. Directorial preference will be important also. Some directors and composers hate **stingers** (heavy music accents on a dramatic shot or moment, like the discovery of a dead body or the reaction to the villain's verbal threat), especially at the start of cue. But in broad comedy or heavy melodrama, these musical accents may be appropriate.

A soft entrance on a dramatic moment or emotional reaction shot can elicit a very emotional response from the audience. It can be chilling, ominous, threatening, poignant. If in doubt, discuss this with the director.

ENDING A CUE

WHEN TO END. Just as you will start for emotional emphasis (whether soft or loud) you will end either for emphasis[2] or de-emphasis, when the dramatic moment or action shifts again (to a different subject, a different level of emotion, a different visual or scene). Sometimes the cut or dissolve to the next scene will feel like the perfect place to end the cue, **tailing out**[3] under the forthcoming dialogue. Sometimes the intrusion of another person or element in an emotional scene or reverie will break the mood, and the music, following this shift in emphasis, will tail out at that time.

And sometimes there just doesn't seem to be a good place to get out of the cue—no convenient sound effect to cover music going out, no timely cut to the next scene. The scene just keeps going, but the music goes out, without apparent motivation. For some reason, this can work better than one would guess. Sometimes when the music goes out, even if it seems arbitrary, it will slightly emphasize the next dialogue or action, and in so doing becomes a part of the dramatic fabric. The reasons for ending a cue in the middle of a scene are (1) the music has gone on as long as it should, and to continue will diminish its effectiveness; (2) the music must enter again shortly, and will be much more effective dramatically if there has been a silence prior to its new entrance; (3) if allowed to continue, the music will actually hurt the dramatic impact of the scene, even though it has been needed up to that point.

HOW TO END. You have the same two choices going out that you have beginning a cue—to end with a fade-out on a held chord or note (to tail out), or to end with a sharp accented note or cut-off (a **hard-out**). Most of the time the flow of the film will suggest tailing out. When you can end a cue with a hard out, it is an effective variation, both in dramas and comedies. When the style of the film allows, it is worth trying to work in some of these cue endings for variety, and for the extra dramatic punch they give the score.

SHORT CUES AND BRIDGES

Very short cues (:05 to :15) are generally avoided in most features, with the exception of genre films that count on short cues as part of the overall effect (horror films and broad comedies, for example). Most directors and composers try to avoid them if possible, preferring to let the music continue once it starts, so that it can make a strong and effective statement. James Horner dislikes short cues. "I like to have cues run for a long period of time because you can then be much more manipulative in a way. Because you are not aware of the music."

The effect of a long cue can be achieved even if there are several stops and starts during the course of an eight-minute section. This can have more dramatic power than

---

[2] See "Highlighting," p. 143.

[3] Tailing out: fading out gradually on a sustained note or chord.

maintaining continuity in the music with rhythm or sustained notes. Horner scored the long hotel shoot-out sequence in *48 Hours* (1982) as though it was one cue, but with starts and stops along the way.

In television, short cues and **bridges**[4] are used more frequently for all types of films, and many times these bridges would not be spotted if the film were a feature.

THE IMPORTANCE OF THE ACTING

If the acting is extraordinary in a scene and relentlessly pulls the audience into the film, the criteria change for spotting music. Where you might have guessed music would be required, none is needed or even wanted; the moment speaks eloquently for itself and the scene will resist any attempt to add music. By the same token, if you find out that what's up there on the screen just doesn't have it, then you may want to jump in to bring out some of the missing qualities.

"I hope the composer would view the film to see what it is the director was trying to do—maybe he didn't accomplish it on the screen," says music executive Harry Lojewski. "But maybe you can help it with the underscoring. You've got to look at it as a whole film. If there's a relationship between the man and woman and there's no emotional involvement, it's difficult for the audience to feel that involvement. Scoring some of those scenes can soften up that coldness."

Lojewski offers *Telefon* (1977) as an example of a film that needed this kind of emotional warm-up in the music. "We scored a scene with Charles Bronson and Lee Remick in which he moved up to her and got closer to her, but then it never went any place. This was a picture about a Russian agent, and they were telling the FBI and the KGB to go to hell and they went off together. Well, you have to have motivation to go off together. They've got to get a little closer than ten feet away."

This gets back to audience expectations. Unless the film establishes another set of guidelines (as does farce, for instance) the audience will always expect credibility. If the film is not credible, at least in its own terms, the audience won't buy it and the film won't work for them.

THE DIRECTORS COMMUNICATE

Elephant Man (1980) is the true story of a grossly deformed man who is rescued from an English freak show and introduced to fashionable society. Describing his experience, John Morris says, "[Director] David Lynch is very sensitive; he is a camera—he has an eye like a camera. He told me what he was going to do with the picture, and he loves sound. And he told me where he would like music, and very little else. He never really said very much about what anything should be, or any feelings about it. And he left me pretty much on my own." (See Figure 7-5.)

Sometimes discussions with the director during spotting can become very involved with style and musical content. Laurence Rosenthal, while working on the miniseries *Peter the Great* (1986), found the spotting sessions with director Marvin Chomsky to be very detailed; they discussed "exactly what the character of the music ought to be. We really got to the point where we were talking about what the absolute function of the music in this scene was. Why is the music there at all? What does it say? Does it really need to be there? And if it does, what is it that the scene can't do without? What is not being seen on the screen that the music can provide? Things like that were discussed in detail."

---

[4] Bridge: a music cue (usually short) that bridges the film from the end of one scene (with its distinctive locale and time) to the beginning of the next scene.

There are times when a few directorial comments can be sufficient. In *Witness* (1985) a young Pennsylvania Amish boy sees a brutal murder in an urban railroad station, and is hidden in an austere rural Amish community to protect him from the killers. Maurice Jarre recalls director Peter Weir's suggestions: "The music should not be sentimental, and it should be a little bit cold. The music should comment in a cold way. And also of course the barn raising should really have the feeling of building something." Besides that, Jarre says, "He left me free. So when I played the theme that I thought was really suitable for the picture, he liked it and said, 'I like it, because it's not sentimental but it is a way to *bring* you somewhere.'" (See Figures 21-4, 21-5, 21-6.)

TRYING IT OUT. In *'night, Mother* (1986) Sissy Spacek plays a girl who feels she must prepare her mother for her planned suicide. David Shire found that "the main opportunity to use music was in the first two reels—the only place where there's no dialogue for a while, where she's setting up the house and before the dialogue actually begins. Again for the end title we just felt there was room to make this positive statement musically. Both [director] Tom Moore (who was doing his first movie) and I adored the original play, which doesn't have a note of music in it, and we were both nervous about using music in the film. . . . What we finally decided was that the music should emphasize whatever positive element there was in the picture, and that was Jessie's courage, her almost Apollonian removal from what you would normally expect as the mood of a girl who's going to kill herself in an hour. She's made peace with herself and with her life, and there is an almost detached courageousness about the way she goes about it.

"We went through twice, spotting it, and it was like a heart-transplant patient rejecting the organ—you'd put music up against it and you'd feel the movie almost physically pushing the music away. I did something with Tom that I'd done before with Herb Ross on *Max Dugan Returns* [1983]—I rented a piano to put in the editing room when we spotted on the KEM. Then as we reached those places where we weren't sure if we should have music I played it on the piano while they ran the film. Tom was used to working on musicals with dance pianists sitting there at the upright improvising stuff. And as we'd get to some scene in the movie he'd say, 'Try playing the theme under this.' I'd play four notes and he's say, 'Stop!' This was really a safe and sane way to work." (See Figure 13-18.)

DIFFERENCES IN TELEVISION AND FILM SPOTTING

Composers are often asked what the difference is between television and film scoring. Usually the answers are about differences in money, schedules, and other practical matters, but another real difference is where and how the music is used—where it is spotted. In the science-fiction film *Brainstorm* (1983), about a futuristic machine that records emotions so faithfully that other people feel them through their own five senses, James Horner didn't spot any music for the dramatic moment when Louise Fletcher gets furious, then walks to the restroom and has a mild heart attack. Horner agrees that this might have been spotted differently for television. "In television you are often asked to **sting**[5] a sequence like that—to put music in. Somehow on film, people are willing to take a few more chances about letting a sequence play in real time without music enhancing it. I always find that when you add music to a scene, unless you are very, very careful, it somehow takes the scene slightly away from being absolutely realistic. There's something very cold and realistic about having a scene play without music; it somehow just seems real. On television, very seldom do you see that. The most effective television shows are when they don't have music on a powerful sequence and it just plays and you have people just looking at each other and then it goes to a commercial.

[5] Sting: accent, or emphasize.

FIGURE 5-2
Moviola editor (Abby Treloggen, music editor).

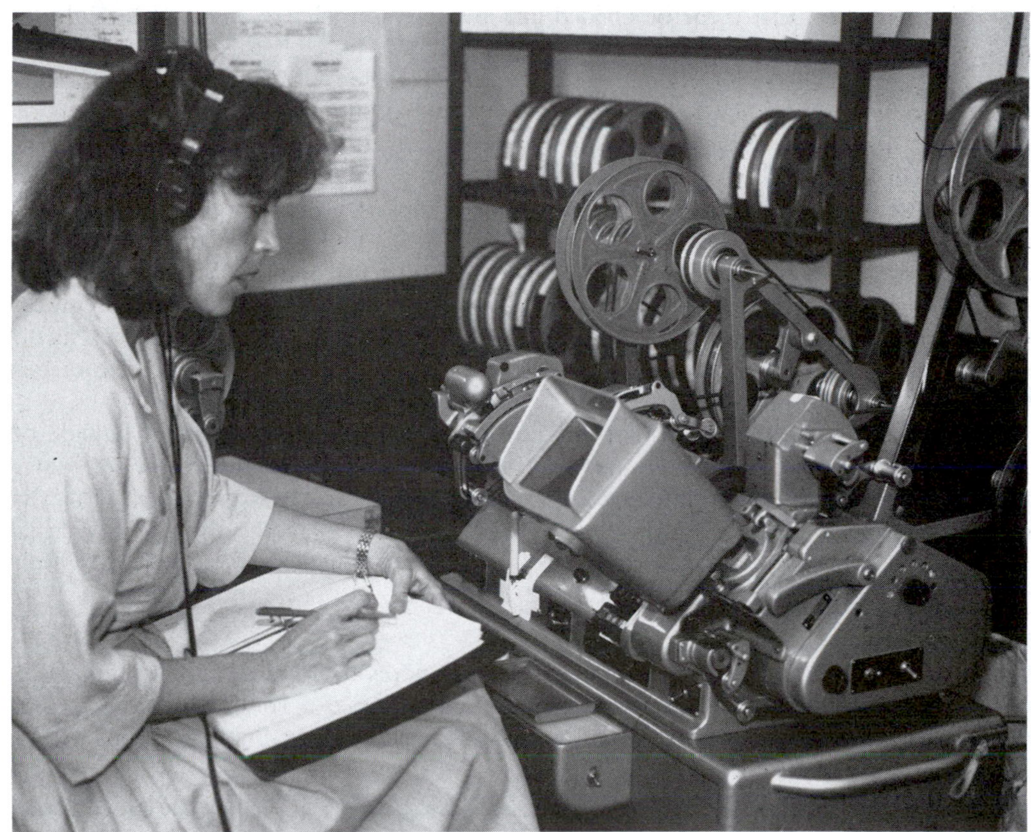

Photo: Gay Wallin

"In a movie like *Testament* [the 1983 film about a small California town affected by a nuclear attack], we had to be very careful because every time you bring in music to underline something there's a very major risk that you'll make the scene maudlin, or sad or something. The places where we put music were in places where the color I used would add a quality to it that was not there.

"In general I also try to avoid scoring dialogue scenes with music; I think the austerity of just the dialogue with no music is great—unless you have a big music section before the dialogue and another one after it, and rather than stop the cue you try to weave it around the dialogue."

SPOTTING NOTES AND TIMING NOTES

After spotting the film, the music editor prepares a music breakdown (**the spotting notes**[6]) listing the music cues and numbering them in a coding system in which the first digit signifies the reel number and the next digits give the cue number within the reel. Thus 1M1 (or M11, or 1/1) means Reel 1, Cue 1. It is always a good idea for the composer to take his own spotting notes as well. This way he has his own record of the

[6] Spotting notes: notes taken by the music editor listing in sequence the beginning and ending points of each music cue in the film, and the overall length of each cue. (See Figure 5-3.)

length of the cues and their function, which can be used until the music editor's notes arrive.

The composer may suggest to the music editor (either at the spotting session or at any time thereafter) that a cue be divided into two or more shorter cues. This might be done to avoid conducting an eight- or nine-minute cue, or possibly to orchestrate the two resultant shorter cues with different-size orchestras. To achieve the sense of a continuous cue, the composer will then be required to overlap the two cues on a compatible note or chord (the first cue coming to a fermata that is overlapped by the second cue).

After preparing the spotting notes, the music editor then prepares the timing notes for each cue, making a detailed list of all dialogue and action within every shot with all timings relative to the cue start. This is done on a Moviola film editor (see Figure 5-2), on a flatbed editor (see Figure 5-1), or on a videotape recorder, using time code. If the music editor is using film rather than videotape, the timings are read from a counter giving the number of feet and frames as counted by sprocketed wheels and gears. If there is no second counter indicating timings in seconds and minutes, he then converts the footages to timings.

Some music editors (particularly in Europe or in smaller film centers outside of Hollywood) will give timings in minutes, seconds, and *frames.* Since there are 24 frames per second, each frame is a time unit of 1/24 second. Any timing expressed in frames is easily converted to seconds by dividing by 24. For example, in the timing 3:16 + 22 fr. (3 minutes, 16 seconds and 22 frames), the 22 fr. is divided by 24 and the result is 92/100 seconds. The total time is now 3:16.92.

TERMINOLOGY. In the course of doing timing notes for a film there are hundreds of shots to be described, and music editors have developed a vocabulary and a set of abbreviations to describe scenes efficiently. These terms are universal and must be learned. Here are the principal ones:

BG	background
CAM	camera
CHOPPER SHOT	high-angle shot from helicopter, typically combined with a zoom shot
CINEMA VERITE [*vare*-ee-tay]	documentary style, usually with hand-held camera
CIRCULAR DOLLY	shot as dolly-mounted camera circles subject
CU	close-up
CUT (BUTT CUT)	direct cut from one shot to another
CUTAWAY or REACTION SHOT	frame shows secondary figure reacting to previous shot
DIAL	dialogue
DISS	dissolve—simultaneous fade-in and fade-out of consecutive shots

DOLLY SHOT	shot from dolly-mounted moving camera
EOL or EL	end of line of dialogue
EXT	exterior
FI	fade-in from black
FF	freeze frame: one frame is multiple-printed to appear as a still picture
FO	fade-out to black
FX	effects: sound effects
INT	interior
LA CAMERA	shot from a low angle
MATTE SHOT	shots in which portions of frame show different images through matte techniques
LS	long shot, full shot
MS	medium shot
MX	music
NARR	narration
O.S.	off-screen (voice, sound)
PAN	panorama shot: camera rotates, revealing sweep of scene
PIX	picture
POP-INS	scene elements that suddenly appear (titles, people)
POV	from the point of view of named actor
SOURCE MUSIC	music that appears to come from the scene; music the actors hear
SUBJECTIVE CAMERA	frame shows what the actor's eyes see, usually by hand-held camera
SUPER	superimposition of two images (a double exposure)
SWISH PAN	a fast blurred pan

TRAVELING MATTE	trick shot with matte techniques
2-SHOT	two subjects in frame (usually people)
3-SHOT	three subjects in frame
SYNC SOUND	sound from people or objects in the frame and in sync with them
UNDERSCORE	supporting music, which the audience hears but the actors don't
V.O.	voice over: a voice that does not lip-sync with subject in frame
XCU or ECU	extreme close-up
XLS or ELS	extreme long shot
ZOOM IN	optical effect of coming closer to subject
ZOOM OUT	optical effect of subject receding

FORMATS. In general, the formats of most spotting notes and timing notes are similar. Figure 5-3 is the spotting notes for *'night, Mother;* Figure 5-4 is a music summary sheet (a short form of the spotting notes) for *Secret of My Success* (1987); Figure 5-5 shows the timing notes for part of cue 8M4 from *Secret of My Success.*

Timing sheets created from (or for) videotape copies can show both the cumulative time code and the individual cue timings. This is very helpful in relating the cue timings to the scene as it appears in the videotape. With these time code timings on videotape the composer and music editor can pinpoint to the frame their communication regarding starts, cuts, and any other necessary information. (See Figures 5-5 and 5-6.)

FIGURE 5-3

***'night, Mother* spotting notes. Prepared by Erma Levin.**

```
'NIGHT, MOTHER   ASP 1885013          19656

M-11   2:49.15  FROM THE TOP OF THE FADE IN.  MELODY TO HIT ON
                THE FIRST CUT TO THE HOUSE ITSELF.  CONTINUE
                THRU UNTIL JESSIE RETURNS TO THE KITCHEN AND
                THE PHONE AND OUT UNDER THE CIRCULATION
                DEPARTMENT OF THE NEWSPAPER TELEPHONE CALL.

M-12    :26.30  AS JESSIE PICKS UP THE CLOCKS (AFTER HEARING
                THE CAR ON GRAVEL) AND PUTS THEM IN THE LIVING
                ROOM .  HEAR THE CAR DOOR CLOSE AND CARRY HER
                TO THE WINDOW.  OUT AS SHE LOOKING THRU THE
                VENETIAN BLINDS.
```

FIGURE 5-3 (*Continued*)

M-13	:28.10	AS CUT TO INTERIOR AND JESSIE TURNING FROM THE WINDOW AND TO THE UTILITY ROOM FOLDING THE LAUNDRY AND OUT AS MAMA SPEAKS TO HER THRU THE WINDOW FROM OUTSIDE.
M-14	1:01.00	AS JESSIE PICKS UP THE LAUNDRY BASKET AND TO THE BATHROOM TO PUT THE LINENS OUT AND OUT AS MAMA CALLS TO HER FROM OUTSIDE.
M-15	:51.75	AS JESSIE FINISHES CROSSING OFF THE LIST AND OUT AS MAMA CALLS HER AGAIN FROM OUTSIDE.
M-21	1:45.30	ON THE INSERT CUT TO THE PHOTO(SOLO HARP OR GUITAR). CHORD TO FALL ON THE INSERT TO THE PHOTO ON THE BEDSIDE TABLE AND TO CONTINUE TO HER PUTTING THE PICTURE DOWN BESIDE THE PICTURE OF MAMA ON THE TABLE BY THE WHITMAN'S SAMPLER BOX. ABOUT :02 BEFORE JESSIE'S "THIS IS WHERE IT'LL STAY."
M-22	:56.25	AFTER MAMA IN THE HALL TALKING ABOUT LETTING THE CRIMINALS HAVE WHAT THEY WANT ON THE CUT TO JESSIE IN THE ATTIC UNDER JESSIE'S LINE "GOOD IDEA, MAMA" AND CONTINUE THRU THE BALANCE OF FINDING OF THE GUN, ETC. UNTIL MAMA'S HAIL "YOU COME DOWN."
		THERE IS NO MUSIC IN REELS THREE THROUGH ELEVEN
M-121	2:45.85	AT JJ2590+06 AS THE CAMERA HAS STARTED ITS MOVEMENT AND TO THE END OF THE CREDITS AS WILL BE INDICATED. AWAITING RECUT AND SPECIFICS ON THIS ENTIRE SEQUENCE.
N.B.	THE M.T.	TEMP WAS MADE TO A 21.7 AND THIS IS THE TEMPO USED TO INITIATE M-12: WITH SIX BARS PRIOR TO THE START OF THE MELODY.
	11:03.70	

FIGURE 5-4
Secret of My Success music summary sheet. Prepared by Daniel Allan Carlin, Segue Music.

Segue Music, Inc. for Film and Video

704 So. Victory Blvd., Suite C • Burbank, California 91502 • Telephone: 818/841-7807

"SUCCESS"

MUSIC SUMMARY SHEET

DECEMBER 22, 1986 (REVISED)

CUE	TITLE	USAGE	TIME
REEL 1			
1M1	MAIN TITLE	SONG SCORE	3:39
1M2	APARTMENT BLDG. SOURCE #1	NEW SOURCE	1:04
1M3	GHETTO-BLASTER SOURCE	PRE-REC. SOURCE	:31
1M4	EXTERIOR BAR SOURCE	NEW SOURCE	1:33
REEL 2			
2M1	KANSAS FLASHBACK	SONG SCORE	1:28
2M2	METROPOLIS #1	UNDERSCORE	:56
3M1	CHRISTY AT WATER FOUNTAIN	SONG SCORE	1:34
2M3	MAILROOM OPERA #1	NEW SOURCE	:29
REEL 3			
4M3	NIGHT WORK MONTAGE	SONG SCORE	2:05
3M3	LIMO TO CONNECTICUT	SONG SCORE	2:41
REEL 4			
4M1	JAWS COMES TO THE POOL	UNDERSCORE	1:03
4M2(1)	BRANTLEY ESCAPES	UNDERSCORE	1:11
4M2(2)	DOG CHASE	UNDERSOCRE	:18
REEL 5			
5M1	BRANTLEY INTO EMPTY OFFICE	SONG SCORE	1:54
5M2	METROPOLIS #2	UNDERSCORE	1:16
5M3	BRANTLEY IN HALL TO CALL	UNDERSCORE	:27
REEL 6			
6M1	EXECUTIVE STRUT	SONG SCORE	2:11
6M2	MAILROOM...'LIKE A RASH'	NEW SOURCE	:24
REEL 7			
7M1	CONDUCTING PROSTITUTION SRC.	NEW SOURCE	1:30
7M2	VERA COMES TO APT. SOURCE	NEW SOURCE	1:26
7M3	HOWARD & CHRISTY AT BAR SRC.	NEW SOURCE	:28
7M4	VERA AT BRANTLEY'S MIRROR SRC.	NEW SOURCE	:20
7M5	HOWARD & CHRISTY SIT & DINE	NEW SOURCE	:50
7M6	CHRISTY STEALS NOTES	UNDERSCORE	:21
REEL 8			
8M1	CHRISTY/BRANTLEY NIGHT-WORK	UNDERSCORE	:13
8M2	MORE C/B NIGHT-WORK	UNDERSCORE	:04
8M3	LOX AROUND THE CLOCK SOURCE	NEW SOURCE	1:23
8M4	SILHOUETTES/SEAPORT MONTAGE	SONG SCORE	2:32
8M5	FERRY/LOVEMAKING MONTAGE	SONG SCORE	2:30

(CONTINUED ON PAGE 2)

FIGURE 5-4 (*Continued*)

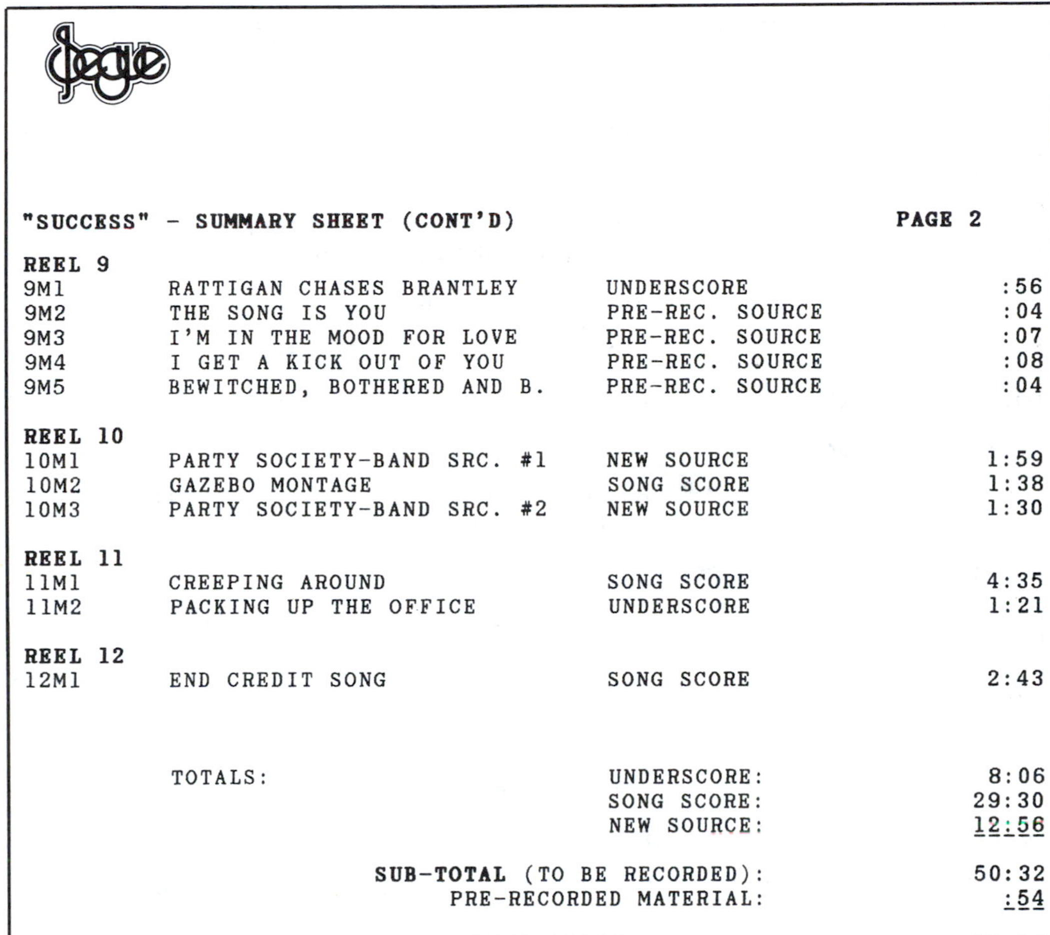

Segue

"SUCCESS" - SUMMARY SHEET (CONT'D) **PAGE 2**

REEL 9			
9M1	RATTIGAN CHASES BRANTLEY	UNDERSCORE	:56
9M2	THE SONG IS YOU	PRE-REC. SOURCE	:04
9M3	I'M IN THE MOOD FOR LOVE	PRE-REC. SOURCE	:07
9M4	I GET A KICK OUT OF YOU	PRE-REC. SOURCE	:08
9M5	BEWITCHED, BOTHERED AND B.	PRE-REC. SOURCE	:04
REEL 10			
10M1	PARTY SOCIETY-BAND SRC. #1	NEW SOURCE	1:59
10M2	GAZEBO MONTAGE	SONG SCORE	1:38
10M3	PARTY SOCIETY-BAND SRC. #2	NEW SOURCE	1:30
REEL 11			
11M1	CREEPING AROUND	SONG SCORE	4:35
11M2	PACKING UP THE OFFICE	UNDERSCORE	1:21
REEL 12			
12M1	END CREDIT SONG	SONG SCORE	2:43
	TOTALS:	UNDERSCORE:	8:06
		SONG SCORE:	29:30
		NEW SOURCE:	12:56
		SUB-TOTAL (TO BE RECORDED):	50:32
		PRE-RECORDED MATERIAL:	:54
		TOTAL MUSIC:	**51:26**

FIGURE 5-5

Secret of My Success cue 8M4 timing notes. Prepared by Jamie Gelb, Segue Music.

TIMING SHEET

TITLE-"SECRET OF MY SUCCESS"

PROD.# DATE: 2-16-88

CUE: 8M4 START: 01:07:31:10

CODE	TIME	
		OUTSIDE RESTAURANT, AS THEY WALK, CHRISTY TELLS BRANTLEY SHE'S BEEN TRYING TO STAY OPEN TO HIS "... BUSINESS IDEAS." HE: "GREAT."
07:31:10	:00.00	MUSIC STARTS A BEAT AFTER THIS LINE OVER TWO SHOT CHRISTY AND BRANTLEY, STARING AT EACH OTHER

FIGURE 5-5 (*Continued*)

TITLE-"SECRET OF MY SUCCESS" CUE: 8M4

CODE	TIME	
07:35:18	:04.27	CHRISTY LOOKS DOWN
07:36:28	:05.61	BEGIN DISSOLVE
07:37:25	:06.51	MID DISSOLVE TO CHRISTY LOOKING AT MANNEQUIN IN WINDOW DISPLAY
07:38:28	:07.61	DISSOLVE FULL IN AS O.S. BRANTLEY: "OK, SO YOU'RE OPEN TO MY BUSINESS IDEAS, NOW HOW ABOUT MY AFTER WORK IDEAS?"
07:44:12	:13.08	E.L. AS CHRISTY: "DON'T PUSH."
07:45:16	:14.21	PAUSE
07:46:10	:15.02	CHRISTY CONTS: "YESTERDAY I THOUGHT YOU WERE OBNOXIOUS."
07:48:16	:17.22	E.L.
07:50:05	:18.85	BRANTLEY ENTERS FRAME AS HE WALKS TOWARD CHRISTY
07:51:08	:19.95	BRANTLEY: "YOU KNOW ALOT OF PEOPLE START OUT THAT WAY..."
07:53:10	:22.02	PAUSE
07:55:15	:24.19	HE CONTS: "THEY USUALLY END UP GETTING MARRIED."
07:56:29	:25.66	E.L.
07:57:11	:26.06	CHRISTY: "DON'T HOLD YOUR BREATH." AS SHE TURNS TOWARD HIM
07:58:20	:27.36	E.L. AS BRANTLEY: "COME ON."
07:59:10	:28.03	PAUSE
08:02:02	:30.76	HE CONTS: "I THINK YOU'RE SECRETLY CRAZY ABOUT ME."
08:04:05	:32.87	PAUSE
08:05:10	:34.03	HE CONTS: "I THINK YOU'LL FEEL ALOT BETTER IF YOU JUST ADMIT IT."
08:07:25	:36.54	PAUSE
08:09:18	:38.30	HE CONTS: "COME ON, YOU LIKE ME."
08:11:01	:39.74	PAUSE AS HE REACHES TOWARD HER
08:11:23	:40.47	HE CONTS: "I'M AN ACQUIRED TASTE."
08:12:13	:41.14	HE BACKS AWAY
08:13:03	:41.81	E.L., BEGIN DISSOLVE

FIGURE 5-5 (*Continued*)

TITLE-"SECRET OF MY SUCCESS" CUE: 8M4

CODE	TIME		
08:13:26	:42.58		MID DISSOLVE TO NIGHT, NEW YORK SKYLINE
08:14:27	:43.61		DISSOLVE FULL IN, CAM HOLDS ON SKYLINE
08:19:00	:47.71		BEGIN DISSOLVE
08:19:29	:48.68		MID DISSOLVE TO EARLY MORNING SKYLINE
08:21:00	:49.72		DISSOLVE FULL IN
08:22:04	:50.85		BEGIN DISSOLVE
08:23:01	:51.75		MID DISSOLVE TO DAY, CLOSER ANGLE SKYLINE
08:24:00	:52.72		DISSOVLE FULL IN
08:25:06	:53.92		BEGIN DISSOLVE
08:26:01	:54.75		MID DISSOLVE TO FULL SHOT BOAT IN HARBOR
08:27:01	:55.76		DISSOLVE FULL IN
08:30:03	:58.83	CUT	MED SHOT BRANTLEY ON BOAT
08:30:15	:59.23		HE LOOKS UP AS HE: "MY DAD INSISTED ON BUYING ME THIS..."
08:32:21	1:01.43		PAUSE
08:34:10	1:03.06		HE HOLDS UP A PLANE TICKET
08:35:10	1:04.06		HE CONTS: "ROUND TRIP TICKET BACK TO KANSAS."
08:37:10	1:06.07	CUT	E.L., TWO SHOT FAVORING CHRISTY
08:37:20	1:06.40		BRANTLEY LOOKS DOWN
08:39:01	1:07.77		HE LOOKS UP AS HE: "I ALMOST TRADED IT IN A COUPLE OF TIMES..."
08:41:07	1:09.97	CUT	MED BRANTLEY, PAUSE
08:42:10	1:11.07		HE BEGINS TO WALK, CAM PANNING WITH HIM AS HE CONTS: "BUT NOW IT'S KIND OF A SYMBOL, YOU KNOW..."
08:44:05	1:12.91		CAM RESTS ON MED SHOT BRANTLEY AS HE CONTS: "THE DAY I USE THIS TICKET...", AS HE HOLDS UP TICKET
08:45:18	1:14.34		PAUSE AS HE LOOKS TOWARD CAM
08:47:06	1:15.94		HE CONTS: "IS THE DAY NEW YORK HAS BEAT

FIGURE 5-6

***Beverly Hills Cop II* cue 9/2 cumulative timing sheets. Prepared by Bob Badami using Streamline Music Scoring System, and printed on a laser printer.**

"BEVERLY HILLS COP"

DATE: 3-1-88

CUE: 9M2 SCORE

I SEE TRUCKS. AS FOLEY, ROSEWOOD AND TAGGERT DRIVE TO THE DENT OIL FIELD, THEY DISCUSS DENT'S MOTIVES AS THE ALPHABET BANDIT. ROSEWOOD MARVELS: "LOOK AT ALL THAT OIL..." AXEL REPLIES: "I DON'T SEE OIL...I SEE TRUCKS..."

02:47:29	:00.00	CUT	MUSIC STARTS ON CUT TO SIDE ANGLE CAR SPEEDING BY AS PASSENGER DOOR STARTS TO OPEN.
02:49:00	:01.03		CAR SCREECHES TO HALT AS...
02:50:05	:02.20		AXEL EMERGES AND...
02:50:10	:02.37		STARTS TO RUN TOWARDS REAR OF CAR AS CAM FOLLOWS.
02:51:12	:03.43		AS AXEL CLEARS BACK OF CAR TAGGERT EMERGES FROM BACK DOOR, CAM CONTS.
02:52:22	:04.77		CAM HOLDS AS AXEL STOPS FRAME LEFT AND LOOKS THRU BINOCULARS, ROSEWOOD AND TAGGERT RUN INTO FRAME.
02:53:15	:05.53		ROSEWOOD AND TAGGERT PULL UP AND GAZE TOWARD OS OIL COMPLEX.
02:53:29	:06.00	CUT	AXEL'S POV ON WAREHOUSE WITH TRUCK PARKED IN FRONT.
02:56:00	:08.03	CUT	FULL 3-SHOT AXEL, ROSEWOOD, TAGGERT.
02:56:29	:09.00		ROSEWOOD STARTS TO REMOVE HIS JACKET, HE TURNS AND...
02:57:21	:09.73		MOVES AWAY BEHIND THE OTHER TWO, AS TAGGERT REACHES FOR AXEL'S BINOCULARS.
02:58:26	:10.90	CUT	FULL SHOT ROSEWOOD REACHES INTO OPEN CAR TRUNK, AXEL AND TAGGERT IN BG.
02:59:01	:11.07		ROSEWOOD PULLS LONG JACKET FROM TRUNK.
03:01:22	:13.70		HE STARTS TO PUT ON JACKET.
03:02:20	:14.63		TAGGERT TURNS FROM AXEL AND DUCKS BACK TOWARD CAR.
03:03:01	:15.00		TAGGERT: "COME ON, BILLY..."
03:03:20	:15.63		PAUSE AS TAGGERT MOVES BEHIND ROSEWOOD.
03:04:09	:16.27		HE NOTICES BILLY'S LONG COAT.

FIGURE 5-6 (*Continued*)

B.H. COP II		CUE: 9M2 PAGE 2
03:04:22	:16.70	CUT MED TAGGERT STARES AT BILLY.
03:06:03	:18.07	TAGGERT: "BILLY, WHAT ARE YOU DOING?"
03:06:23	:18.73	E.L.
03:07:02	:19.03	CUT FULL SHOT ROSEWOOD AND TAGGERT BY OPEN TRUNK.
03:07:03	:19.07	BILLY PULLS A PAIR OF SAWED-OFF SHOTGUNS FROM THE TRUNK.
03:08:13	:20.40	HOISTING THE GUNS OVER HIS SHOULDERS, BILLY: "I'VE BEEN WANTING TO WEAR THIS FOR A WHILE..."
03:09:25	:21.80	CUT CU BACK OF AXEL'S HEAD, HE STARTS TO TURN TOWARDS CAM AS BILLY CONTS: "...SARGE."
03:10:11	:22.33	E.L. AS AXEL LOOKS AT OS BILLY IN DISBELIEF.
03:10:27	:22.87	CUT CLOSE SHOCKED TAGGERT.
03:11:05	:23.13	TAGGERT: "WHAT ARE YOU, NUTS?!..."
03:12:00	:23.97	PAUSE.
03:12:12	:24.37	CUT OTS TAGGERT ON GRINNING BILLY.
03:12:15	:24.47	TAGGERT CONTS: "...JESUS CHRIST, BILLY, WE GOTTA TALK!"
03:14:11	:26.33	CUT (E.L.) FULL SHOT ROSEWOOD WALKS FROM CAR AS TAGGERT STARES INTO TRUNK.
03:15:11	:27.33	GESTURING TOWARDS OPEN TRUNK, TAGGERT: "WHAT THE HELL IS THIS?!!"
03:16:05	:28.13	E.L. AS TAGGERT STARES AT DEPARTING BILLY.
03:16:10	:28.30	CUT CLOSE BEHIND AXEL AND ROSEWOOD, AS ROSEWOOD TURNS AND: "YOU CAN NEVER HAVE TOO MUCH FIREPOWER..."
03:18:05	:30.13	E.L.
03:18:20	:30.63	CUT MED TAGGERT REACHES INTO TRUNK AND...
03:18:23	:30.73	LIFTS OUT A NASTY LOOKING MACHINE GUN AND STARES AT IT.
03:18:29	:30.93	O.S. AXEL: "...HEY, C'MON!!"

The content and style of the music editor's timing notes vary from a minimal description of the frame contents to an interpretive description that almost relates the story line.

DETAILED NOTES. Music editor Erma Levin says, "I usually ask composers, 'How do you like your timings, in tenths or hundredths? Do you like it close? Do you like it loose? Do you like it in lines of action? Do you like it cut for cut?' I try to give a summary of what is going on on the screen so that he can visualize it. Sometimes that's an adverb or an adjective describing the action. One thing I think is essential, though, is never to preempt a point of view."

She differentiates between the ending of a dialogue line and the cut to the next shot and always indicates the timing of important events within the shot. If the needed information is not there, ask the music editor to suppply it.

Like Levin, music editor Gene Marks also likes to be as descriptive as possible. "My timing notes are probably much more detailed than those that many music editors give today," says Marks. "They're almost small novellas in many instances. And one of the most important things I do when I'm timing for a composer is . . . use . . . adjectives and adverbs. I think the more they are used, the easier that makes it for the composer. To say a man comes through the door at :04.7 is meaningless. But if you say he comes through the door with a snarl on his face or he comes through the door happily or he comes through the door dejectedly—that tells the composer, I believe, what mood he should be writing."

VIDEOCASSETTES. Composers now invariably take home a videocassette dub of their film. This has decreased their dependence on detailed timing notes. Gene Marks finds that composers today do much more for themselves. "Many composers now have computers and VCRs—things that were not even dreamed of before. In those days a composer either had his office on the studio lot or, if he worked at home, he had to come in to the studio projection room or run the cue on the Moviola. There are some composers now that don't even want any timings from the editor and I find that to be a handicap from the standpoint of the final product, and very often I will make my own timings anyway so when we're scoring the picture on the stage, I have an idea of what's supposed to be happening where."

THE MUSIC EDITOR'S CREATIVE ROLE

Music editors have to walk a fine line between using their expert knowledge to help the composer or saying too much that might influence him. If music editor Daniel Allan Carlin comes in after discussions have already begun between the composer and the director he realizes he may not be invited to contribute anything to the decisions regarding mood and spotting. "If it's a brand-new discussion and it's a spotting session, I appreciate being asked my opinion. But I won't jump in unless it's appropriate—I wait to be asked. On a television series, though, you build up relationships over the years and everybody speaks freely."

Speaking from the composer's point of view, Bruce Broughton says that he doesn't expect music editors to participate creatively at the spotting session, "but if I need an opinion, I'll ask them, and I'll depend upon it. But, other than that, I'd rather have everything go through me. And I don't like a lot of subjectivity in my timing notes. I have found, particularly with the videotape, that sometimes notes I thought were not subjective were very subjective. Because when I'd look at the scene, I'd read it completely differently from the way the notes read. I'd find an actor's look was misunderstood by the music editor. I have to say in fairness to them that I very often don't understand a show deeply until I start working on it. And even a music editor going through the show and timing it may not understand what the director meant by that look. I like to have notes that are clear without being too subjective."

SCORE LENGTHS

Music score lengths vary widely within each of the main categories of feature films, television movies-of-the-week, television miniseries, and television episodes. The spotting session is the first reliable measure of that length, against which time and money can then be budgeted. The accompanying table offers some samples—but keep in mind that considerably more music may have been spotted and recorded than is now left in the film, especially for the feature-length films.

CATEGORY	COMPOSER	MUSIC	FILM LENGTH
FEATURE FILMS			
Out of Africa	John Barry	35 minutes	120 minutes
Star Trek II	James Horner	68 minutes	114 minutes
Star Trek III	James Horner	76 minutes	105 minutes
Mosquito Coast	Maurice Jarre	25 minutes	117 minutes
Aliens	James Horner	80 minutes	138 minutes
TELEVISION MINISERIES			
The Blue and the Gray	Bruce Broughton	2 1/2 hours	8 hours
Dream West	Fred Karlin	2 1/2 hours	7 hours
North and South	Bill Conti	4 hours	12 hours
Dadah Is Death	Fred Karlin	1 1/2 hours	4 hours
TELEVISION MOVIES			
Autobiography of Miss Jane Pittman	Fred Karlin	50 minutes	96 minutes
Hostage Flight	Fred Karlin	40 minutes	96 minutes
Bitter Harvest	Fred Karlin	25 minutes	96 minutes
Bridge to Silence	Fred Karlin	35 minutes	96 minutes
TELEVISION SERIES (average per episode)			
MacGyver	Randy Edelman	40 minutes	48 minutes
A-Team	Post-Carpenter	15–20 minutes	48 minutes
Magnum, P.I.	Post-Carpenter	7–10 minutes	48 minutes
Murder, She Wrote	David Bell/ Richard Markowitz	7–12 minutes	48 minutes

Sometimes the score will turn out to be shorter than the composer expected. Bruce Broughton says, "On *The Blue and the Gray* [1983], which was 8 hours long, we ended up with 2 ½ hours of music, which I felt was very underspotted, and I worried about that a lot." He checked his instincts against the videotape, and then in discussions with the music editor, Erma Levin. Although he did add another cue or two, he was reassured to find that basically Levin felt the overall spotting was fine. "And I have to say that by the time the picture was done it didn't have much music but it played just fine."

Out of Africa (1985) had only about 35 minutes of music in about 2 hours of movie length. John Barry says, "People think there was a lot of music, a lot more than there was, because when it *was* there [director] Sydney [Pollack] went with the music—like the flying scene, when it was very up-front." *How* the music is used can have significant impact on the audience's overall impression of how much music there is.

Having spotted the film, the composer's first thoughts may have nothing at all to do with music, for even as he is spotting he may be adding up the total number of minutes of music in the score, considering the size of the orchestra and the number of sessions he might need to record the score. There are many inescapable business decisions to be considered now. To deal with them successfully the composer needs to know the facts and figures.

BUDGETS AND SCHEDULES

It is very important for young composers, especially on hourly episodes, to really understand how to break down an orchestra, how to get the most out of it within budgetary limitations.

BODIE CHANDLER, VICE PRESIDENT OF MUSIC, COLUMBIA PICTURES TELEVISION

Suddenly economics have caught up with everybody . . . and it's forced a lot of guys to go in different creative directions that they would not ordinarily have done.

ALVIN BART, AGENT

It may seem completely illogical to be talking about money before the music is written, or even before a clear-cut conception of the music has had a chance to emerge. But every music decision has a price tag that must be considered and agreed upon before the composer can proceed—how many musicians will the budget accommodate, how many minutes of music, how much studio time for overdubbing and postmixing? It is much better if the discussion of budgets comes after the spotting and after the conceptual talks with the director. By then, the amount of required music will be known, and the orchestra sizes will be more clear. In any case the question of costs will come up too soon for comfort, long before the composer has composed anything or is sure of his final orchestral needs. In episodic television the orchestra size and time allotted to record a show are pretty much locked in once the series gets past the **pilot**[1] stage. The composer is told what the orchestra makeup is and the number of hours budgeted for recording. Usually, some extra instruments may be added for special script needs.

On movies made for television, miniseries, and feature films, precise orchestra sizes will not have been set in advance. As a rule, the total music budget for each specific project will have been worked out by the supervising music executive after he has looked at the script and talked to the producer (and director, if one has been engaged at this point). Together they try to forecast the amount of music and the likely orchestra sizes. Usually the amount of money available for musicians, composing, orchestrating, and all other music expenses will be the amount left after licensing any songs.

COST FACTORS

Basic factors that affect the cost are

1. The size and makeup of the orchestra(s), including the number of instrument doubles and overscale players
2. The number of minutes of music
3. The amount of extra studio time needed to do prerecording, song recording and postmixing

[1] Pilot: single television episode, produced for possible production as an ongoing series.

4. The difficulty of the music
5. The usage of electronic instruments with the orchestra (which can be time-consuming and add costly cartage and instrument rentals)

The composer should always ask which elements are part of the music budget, as he will find considerable variation from project to project. Depending on his deal with the producer, the composer may be responsible for all the costs (a **package deal** in which he delivers a mixed-down tape of the score for an agreed amount), or he may be estimating just the composing, copying, and musicians' costs to establish with the music supervisor that they are within the music budget. The music budget may or may not include studio costs, union Pension and Health and Welfare payments, payroll taxes, and the rental and cartage of instruments.

EXPANDING EXPECTATIONS. Sometimes, even after spotting the film, the director may ask for additional music to be sure he is covered on all possible scenes. Music executive Harry Lojewski points out the trap this can become for a young composer who makes a package deal. "The big mistake that can happen on an independent picture is that the producer wants to know, as a rule, how much will it cost for all the music in his film. He will want you to make a budget; he will want to include the recording studio, the copying, the musicians, the whole ball of wax. The composer, in his eagerness to get his feet wet in the business, could very well end up making nothing and possibly even going in the hole. One of the problems is that if you are about to get a picture, you would want to look at it and see what the picture looks like. You might look at this picture and think, There's about 30 minutes of music in it, maybe 30 or 40 minutes. Now you go in to spot the film with the producer or director and then you start getting dialogue like 'I'm not sure that this section shouldn't be scored so you'd better write it and I'll make the decision in dubbing.' You've already made a deal to do the film and you come out of the spotting session discovering that what could have been 30 or 40 minutes is now an hour and ten minutes and it's too late to backtrack. If they're going to get involved in this kind of area, my recommendation to people is to say, 'For up to so many minutes of music the price will be X amount. After that I'll write as much music as you want but it will cost so much a minute beyond that point.'"

An equally disastrous possibility is that the initial assumption of a small orchestra will grow into a big orchestra at the spotting session. Lojewski suggests caution here as well: "You should find out from the director what he's talking about as far as the size of orchestra is concerned so that you can best put together in your mind an A and B orchestra, to try to cut down on that sort of thing."

PLANNING ORCHESTRA SESSIONS. In addition to calculating the total number of minutes of music in the film, a breakdown is needed of how many minutes of music are to be played by each size orchestra. Film scoring sessions are routinely organized to record first all the music cues for the largest orchestra without regard to their sequence in the film. Cues that require smaller instrumentations are recorded either during subsequent sessions or after the larger orchestra is dismissed.

Music executive Bodie Chandler points out, "If you have a budget that allows you only 27 salaries for 4 hours, you may know that's not going to work because your musical needs require more players. You have to learn how to be able to use the orchestra to your best advantage. If you want 30 instruments, or 30 salaries, for 3 hours, do a portion of the score with that orchestra and then break it down and do the rest with a smaller combo. Know how to set up your music; look through the spotting notes so you can say,

'These 5 cues are big cues; I'm going to use the big orchestra. The rest don't require a big orchestra; I can save them for later in the session and cut down to just the violins and a harp.'"

On the miniseries *Sadat* (1983), composer Charles Bernstein worked with Chandler to produce a big score within a tight budget. He used A, B, and C orchestras. "When the budget is this tight," Bernstein says, "and you have to worry about who's doubling what, and about avoiding too many doubles, I make out a chart in which all the cues are listed from top to bottom, and across the graph I put the instrumentation. And then I can see the entire session, and see who's playing what instrument on what cue, and in what orchestral ensemble. In my largest orchestra, which I only had for 3 hours, I had 16 violins, 4 violas, 4 celli, and 2 double basses—I put a lot of my resources into the number of violin players, as you can tell; I had 2 trumpets, 3 French horns, 2 trombones, and 1 bass trombone doubling tuba; I had 3 woodwinds for that 3-hour session; and I had 3 percussion, harp, and piano—in the percussion section I had cimbalom (a mallet player), another playing timps, chimes, and vibes, and another one playing various tom-toms and what have you. That was 42 players. But after 3 hours that orchestra was gone. And then it dropped down to 34 players, and then down to 26 players. The majority of the score was done with 26 players."

Planning this kind of a recording schedule takes many hours, often over several days. Examples indicating the largest orchestra size for specific films and television shows begin on page 328.

FIGURING COSTS

If the budget is tight, you can determine the number of hours needed for each size orchestra by planning to record 4 to 5 minutes of music per hour (during which the American Federation of Musicians agreement calls for the musicians to play for 50 minutes and have 10 minutes off). The minimum-length single session is for 3 hours and overtime is prorated (without overtime premium pay[2]) in 15-minute segments. Main Titles and End Credits (also called the *formats* in episodic television) can take somewhat longer to record, while source music takes less than average because it is usually recorded **wild.**[3] It is not unusual for a television score with 30 minutes of music to be recorded in two 3-hour sessions (called a *double session*).

Every musician can have a different length call. The strings might have a 4-hour call, the trumpets a 3½-hour call, and the trombones a 3-hour call, depending on how much music each musician has to record. In any event, a 3-hour call is the minimum.

If only 5 hours are needed for the session, consideration must be given to the mandated one-hour meal break for musicians, which must be taken sometime between noon and 2 PM or 6 to 8 PM. For a 5-hour morning call this necessitates an 8 AM start to allow for up to an hour of recording time beyond their calls if necessary.

MINIMUM UNION SCALES. There are several different A. F. of M. master agreements; they cover the following categories: Theatrical Motion Picture, Television Film, Television Videotape, Television and Radio Commercial Announcements, and Documentary and Industrial Films. Referring to these agreements one can compute the musicians'

---

[2] With the exception that the 7th hour of recording within an 8-hour period before 8 PM pays 120 percent, and a musician required to remain into the 5th hour of a 3-hour session or the 8th hour of a 6-hour double session is paid 150 percent of the straight-time. Once the 3-hour minimum session is completed some musicians may be dismissed for the day while others are still in session.

[3] Wild: recorded without projection.

costs.[4] These agreements, which are renegotiated every three years by producers and union representatives, include rates for doubling instruments, overtime, premium time, contractor, conductor, orchestration, copying, Pension and Welfare, Health and Welfare, and instrument cartage. Keep in mind that some of the most "in demand" studio players charge either scale-and-one-half or double scale, or a guaranteed instrument double (which guarantees them scale-and-one-half even if they don't play a second instrument). The concertmaster usually gets double scale (sometimes scale-and-one-half for television), first cello scale-and-one-half, first French horn double scale (or for TV, sometimes scale-and-one-half). All overscale fees should be clarified in discussions with the contractor. In Hollywood, the contractor will get double scale as a rule.

The doubling premiums for any musician who plays more than one instrument during a single session include 50 percent extra for the first double and 20 percent extra for each double thereafter.[5]

OVERDUBBING RESTRICTIONS. Union agreements forbid overdubbing (recording additional parts to add to a cue's print take) with the same personnel on the same session without paying those who overdub a duplicate fee for each overdub pass. Stacking the parts (rhythm first, then strings, for instance) is permissible if the entire orchestra remains on the session and is paid accordingly. As an alternative to that, the rhythm section can start earlier than the rest of the orchestra.

COPYING COSTS. The extraction of orchestra parts by copyists is covered by minimum union scales, but it is a budget item that is hard to estimate or control for a specific project because it is based on union-scale page rates for music that at this point has not been written, and therefore is an unknown number of bars. There is a large difference in copying expense between fast and slow music because of the much-greater bar counts in fast music. One known factor is the cost of transposing parts from a concert pitch score, which adds 50 percent to the copying expense for any transposed part. Considering that the transposing instruments (clarinets, English horns, alto flutes, saxophones, French horns, trumpets, and so on) comprise 25 to 30 percent of the parts to be copied in some orchestras, a typical concert score could cost 15 percent more to copy than a transposed score.

The best estimates of the overall copying costs come from previous experience blended with the composer's knowledge of whether his music will be fast or slow, orchestrated in concert or transposed score. Once this estimate is made, be sure to add an additional 25 percent on top of that for the supervising copyist's charge, unless you know there will be enough time for most or all of the score to be copied by one person. Finally, don't forget the amount paid by the hour for photocopying large score pages and various instrumental parts and binding the scores with tape, plus the cost of paper, a messenger service, and other miscellaneous expenses—these charges can add up to hundreds of dollars.

---

[4] According to agreements in force until February 1990, the minimum 3-hour single-session recording scale for theatrical and television films for an orchestra of 35 or more is $166.52 per musician, and each 15-minute overtime segment is $13.88. Premium-time rates from 8 PM to midnight pay 110 percent; 8 PM to midnight after an 8-hour span pays 165 percent; and work beyond 8 hours between midnight and 8 AM pays 200 percent. Players of "electronic musical devices" (synths, etc.) at the producer's option may be paid $200 per hour if one musician is employed at "multi-tracking rates"; $175 per hour if two or more musicians. This special rate includes all electronic and acoustical doubles and all overdubs.

[5] Instruments within the following respective groups are not construed as doubling (and get no additional doubling fees): (a) piano and celeste (when furnished); (b) drummer's standard outfit; (c) timpani; (d) mallet instruments: xylophone, bells, and marimbas; (e) Latin rhythm instruments when used in less than eight bars in connection with other instruments, not used in a rhythm pattern. This means that alto flute, soprano flute, and piccolo are considered to be three separate instruments and must be paid doubling percentages if they are not the primary instrument.

OTHER COSTS. Cartage costs in Hollywood are substantially higher in practice than the union's minimum cartage fees and are billed by instrument-moving companies—the biggest bills being for drums, percussion, guitars, and electronic keyboards, with their associated amplifiers and processors. Rental of instruments can be significant and must also be included.

SINGERS. Singers work through the Screen Actors Guild (SAG) for theatrical films and television films, or the American Federation of Television and Radio Artists (AFTRA) for any nonfilm medium on television, including videotape. The details of any of these union agreements should be obtained through vocal contractors, or through inquiry at those union offices. Note that the orchestra contractor does not contract for the voices.

WORKING WITH THE CONTRACTOR

The music supervisor and contractor work with the composer on estimating the costs, but the starting composer working on a low-budget, independently produced project may find himself on his own in figuring these costs—and it's an area in which he can't afford to be wrong. Recording with orchestras of more than a few musicians always requires a contractor, and the composer should learn as much as possible from him.

BUDGET CONTROL. Some composers simply take the word of the contractor as to the number of musicians available under the budget. However, Universal Studios music contractor Sandy De Crescent thinks composers should know what figures are involved. "You have no idea how many composers don't even want to know about the costs," says De Crescent, "and I think it's serious. I think they should be aware of what it costs so they get the most for their dollars. If they're saying, 'Look—I've got $12,000; why can't I have this, this, and this,' I'll say, 'Here's how much the strings are going to cost you for three hours, and how many doubles do you think you're going to have in the woodwinds?' and I go over it with them, piece by piece. I want them to understand that I will squeeze the last dime out of that $12,000."

BOOKING MUSICIANS, STUDIOS, AND MIXERS EARLY. Even though you may not yet have started to compose your score, this is still the right time to set the recording session dates, book the studio and mixer, and contract any musicians who are vital to the sound of your score. You need to know that the most important musicians for your score and an excellent engineer and studio are engaged. It is always easier to release a player you don't ultimately need than to hire a vital one who isn't available.[6] All of these elements will affect the ultimate success of the score.

In fact, once the scoring sessions have been planned and finalized, it is not too soon to place your call for all or most of the orchestra. The musicians are booked by the contractor after detailed discussions regarding the budget, the number of musicians, the amount of music to be recorded, and the recording schedule approved by the producer or music executive.

Most composers have their favorite musicians whom they ask the contractor to call. Sandy De Crescent advises composers to be open-minded, however, because their favorites may not always be available. "If a composer asks for Attila the Hun, I call him, no matter whether I think he's working or not—that's the fair way to do it," she says. If the composer's choice is not available, she will recommend musicians she knows she can

---

[6] A confirmed call for underscoring may be cancelled upon a 96 or more hours notice. A call for prerecording may be cancelled upon a notice of 48 or more hours.

rely on. But many composers are reluctant to try new people. "A lot of composers are very, very negligent in this. They have this very tight little list, and they can't record without these people. That's serious because many times those people are not available. Working on the kind of schedule that I do, we can't particularly change sessions around to suit players and/or composers."

She feels it is important for composers to keep up-to-date with who's new in town. Once, when a composer with whom she was working couldn't get his first or second choices, he still refused to take her advice about possible musicians. "He got out a list and said, 'I have to go with what's familiar to me,' and began to read me his list, and do you know that about a third of those people were dead!"

Like other conscientious contractors, De Crescent is always interested in new talent. But taking a chance on them is not easy. "Someone can sound absolutely wonderful on a tape, but it really doesn't mean that much. If someone is recommended to me, I prefer it be by someone in his own section—a rhythm player by another rhythm player, for instance. Most of the time, a new person comes to me this way."

COMPOSING FEES

There are A. F. of M. categories for orchestration and conducting but none for composition, hence no minimum scale governs film composition. This results from the union concept that creative work is not measurable with a financial yardstick and should be set individually for each composer and project. (But composers do belong to the A. F. of M. and are governed by the union's minimum scales for orchestration and conducting.) The creative fees cover a wide range from those paid to the top names to those paid beginning composers for whom a film assignment has an important career value regardless of the money. Fees are set in typical marketplace fashion, by negotiating individual strengths against the prevailing norm, except for episodic television shows, where fees are often predetermined and nonnegotiable.

In Hollywood in the 1988–89 season, the following norms for ranges of creative fees were reported by agents and industry executives:

- 30-minute TV shows: $1,000–$3,000; middle range—$1,500.
- One-hour TV episode: $3,000–$5,000; middle range—$3,500.
- Two-hour movie for TV: $12,500–$30,000; middle range—$15,000–$20,000.
- Theatrical feature: starting range—$15,000–$25,000; middle range—$60,000–$75,000; top—$150,000–$200,000.

In episodic television the creative fees usually include orchestration and conducting. If the union scale for those union-regulated tasks exceeds the creative fee, the composer must be paid at least the minimum scale for orchestration and conducting. Typically on feature films (and some miniseries and television movies) the orchestration costs are paid in addition to the creative fee. In cases where there is not enough time for the composer to orchestrate, this should be discussed with the producer at the outset so that payments to an orchestrator due to a schedule bind will be made by the producer, not the composer. Copying fees are universally paid separately.

Fees for lyrics vary a great deal, depending on the songwriter's credits and track record (that is, hits and/or awards). In television, fees range from $1,000 to $5,000; $1,500–$2,500 is the average range. In features, fees start at about $2,500 and can go up to $25,000.

Outside of Hollywood the financial arrangements may vary. If orchestration and conducting fees are paid separately, the composer can take into account the extra monies he will be receiving for these services when he negotiates his creative fee.

PERFORMANCE ROYALTIES. When a composer's music is used on television (or radio), in a film that plays in foreign theaters, or on television in the United States or elsewhere, he will receive performance royalties for each use. Though a motion picture score exhibited theatrically in the United States receives no performance royalties from ASCAP, BMI, or SESAC,[7] every television exhibition earns a performance fee. Since there is no guarantee that a feature film will be successfully distributed in foreign markets or shown on domestic television, the initial creative fee is the only compensation the composer is assured of receiving for a feature. Association with a successful long-running television series can bring in royalties that somewhat mitigate the lower creative fees paid for this television music, but given the number of television pilots and series that do not succeed—and thus bring in no future performance fees—the composer finds himself in the position of gambling on a winner when he accepts the typically lower creative fees for episodic television.

AGENTS. When the composer is successful enough to be represented by an agent, more sophisticated bargaining is likely. But new composers on the scene are naive to expect to break into the business through an agent who finds work for them. In fact, agents are very difficult to find and are typically interested in handling only composers who already have some professional composing credits and some demand for their talents. In addition to finding projects for their established clients, the agent's job is to negotiate contracts and deals and to follow through on the thousand-and-one business details that are so important and time consuming (See Chapter 27, "The Business").

SAMPLE BUDGETS

Working up a budget is a necessary preliminary to serious composing. Budget-estimating methods are not standardized, but the sample work sheets in Figures 6-1a, b, and c are a guide. These samples represent the budget for a hypothetical project entitled *Eagles.*[8] It is a low-budget feature film that is spotted for 52 minutes of music. The composer has planned for three recording sessions, each with different instrumentations. Session 1 will record 18 minutes of music in 4 hours with a 40-piece orchestra; session 2 will record 22 minutes of music in 5 hours with 29 players; and session 3 will record 12 minutes of music in 6 hours with an 8-piece group. The latter uses more studio time because of special electronic effects, and overdubbing.

In estimating the copying costs in the sample budget offered, the assumption was made that it is a moderate, middle-of-the-road example with a fair balance between fast and slow cues, copied from a transposed score.

These work sheets establish for the producer that the creative and performance costs of the music will be roughly within a $65,000 budget, although the composer is not packaging the music and is himself working for his creative fee plus conducting scale. (If the creative fee is to include conducting, as it most often does, that line item should be deleted from the calculations.)

If the producer asks the composer to package the music, a slightly different format should be followed; the package costs for *Eagles* are worked up in Figure 6-2. Though all details of the film's length and its orchestral and song needs may not be available at the time of this negotiation, a guesstimate, with a sufficient margin of error, will have to do since the budget must be set at this time.

---

[7] The performance-rights societies.

[8] Similar blank forms are provided in Appendix B for calculating these costs.

FIGURE 6-1a
Budget work sheet.

FILM SCORING--BUDGET WORK SHEET

TITLE: EAGLES RECORDING SESSION # 1 DATE & TIME:______

A.F.of M. agreement: THEATRICAL MOTION PICTURE (✓); TV FILM ( )
DOCUMENTARY/INDUSTRIAL FILMS ( ); TV/RADIO COMMERCIALS ( ).
No. of musicians 42. Session length 4 hrs. Premium time? ______

APPLICABLE SCALE PER MUSICIAN/UNIT:

Basic session rate for 3 hrs	$166.52	
Overtime: 4 15 min. units @ $13.88	$55.52	
Premium overtime: ___15 min units @ $____	$____.____	
TOTAL SCALE PER MUSICIAN/UNIT		$222.04
Pension: 9%	$19.98	
SUBTOTAL COST PER MUSICIAN/UNIT		$242.02

NUMBER OF UNITS:

Number of players:		40	
Doublers: 1. REED 1	+ 2	.7	
2. PERC	+ 2	.7	
3. KEYBD	+ 1	.5	
4. TRPT 1	+ 1	.5	
Conductor		2	
Contractor		2	
TOTAL NUMBER OF UNITS			46.4
Total cost per unit			x 242.02
SUBTOTAL: MUSICIANS' SCALE + PENSION			$11,229.73

HEALTH AND WELFARE:

$.991 per hour per musician: .991 x 4 X 42 — $166.49
or $______ per original service per musician: ___x______ — $____.____

CARTAGE AND INSTRUMENT RENTAL:______________________
____ total — $500.00

PREMIUM PAY FOR PLAYERS? 3 units @ 222.04 — $666.12

CONTINGENCY ½ hr. o.t. (46.4 units x 13.88 x 2) — $1288.06

ESTIMATED MUSIC COPYING — $2200.00

TOTAL THIS SESSION — $16,050.40

SUMMARY:	SESSION #____	$______.____
	SESSION #____	$______.____
	SESSION #____	&______.____
COMPOSING/ORCHESTRATING FEE		$______.____
	TOTAL	$______.____

FIGURE 6-1b
Budget work sheet.

FILM SCORING--BUDGET WORK SHEET

TITLE: EAGLES RECORDING SESSION # 2 DATE & TIME: ______

A.F.of M. agreement: THEATRICAL MOTION PICTURE (✓); TV FILM ( )
DOCUMENTARY/INDUSTRIAL FILMS ( ); TV/RADIO COMMERCIALS ( ).
No. of musicians 31. Session length ______. Premium time? ______

APPLICABLE SCALE PER MUSICIAN/UNIT:

Basic session rate for 3 hrs	$174.85 (for 30 to 34 players)
Overtime: 4 15 min. units @ $14.57	$58.28
Premium overtime: 4 15 min units @ $21.86 (5th Hour (150%))	$87.42
TOTAL SCALE PER MUSICIAN/UNIT	$320.55
Pension: 9%	$28.85
SUBTOTAL COST PER MUSICIAN/UNIT	$349.40

NUMBER OF UNITS:

Number of players:			29
Doublers:	1. REED 1	+ 3	.9
	2. REED 2	+ 1	.5
	3. REED 3	+ 2	.7
	4. REED 4	+ 1	.5
Conductor			2.0
Contractor			2.0
TOTAL NUMBER OF UNITS			35.6
Total cost per unit			x 349.40
SUBTOTAL: MUSICIANS' SCALE + PENSION			$12,438.64

HEALTH AND WELFARE:

$.991 per hour per musician: .991 x 31 x 5	$153.61
or $______ per original service per musician: ____ x ____	$____.____

CARTAGE AND INSTRUMENT RENTAL: ______ total	$400.00
PREMIUM PAY FOR PLAYERS? 2.5 units @ 320.55	$801.38
CONTINGENCY 15 min. o.t. [14.57 X 35.6 units]	$516.20
ESTIMATED MUSIC COPYING	$2000.00
TOTAL THIS SESSION	$16,309.83

SUMMARY: SESSION #____	$____.____
SESSION #____	$____.____
SESSION #____	&____.____
COMPOSING/ORCHESTRATING FEE	$____.____
TOTAL	$____.____

FIGURE 6-1c
Budget work sheet.

FILM SCORING--BUDGET WORK SHEET

TITLE: EAGLES RECORDING SESSION # 3 DATE & TIME: ______

A.F.of M. agreement: THEATRICAL MOTION PICTURE (✓); TV FILM ( )

DOCUMENTARY/INDUSTRIAL FILMS ( ); TV/RADIO COMMERCIALS ( ).

No. of musicians 9. Session length 6 hrs. Premium time? ______

APPLICABLE SCALE PER MUSICIAN/UNIT:

Basic session rate for 3 hrs	$191.50 (for 23 players or less)	
Overtime: ___ 15 min. units @ $ Second Session	$191.50	
Premium overtime: ___ 15 min units @ $___	$.	
TOTAL SCALE PER MUSICIAN/UNIT		$383.00
Pension: 9%	$34.47	
SUBTOTAL COST PER MUSICIAN/UNIT		$417.47

NUMBER OF UNITS:

Number of players:			8
Doublers:	1. KEYBD	+ 2	.7
	2. PERC	+ 2	.7
	3.	+	
	4.	+	
Conductor			2
Contractor			

TOTAL NUMBER OF UNITS 11.4

Total cost per unit x 417.47

SUBTOTAL: MUSICIANS' SCALE + PENSION $4759.16

HEALTH AND WELFARE:

$.991 per hour per musician: .991 x 6 x 9 $53.51

or $___ per original service per musician: ___ x ___ $.

CARTAGE AND INSTRUMENT RENTAL: ______

______ total $750.00

PREMIUM PAY FOR PLAYERS? 4 units @ 383.00 $1532.00

CONTINGENCY 1 hr. o.t. (4x 15.96 X 11.4 units) $727.78

ESTIMATED MUSIC COPYING $1100.00

TOTAL THIS SESSION $8,922.29

SUMMARY:	SESSION # 1	$16,050.40
	SESSION # 2	$16,309.83
	SESSION # 3	& 8922.29
COMPOSING/ORCHESTRATING FEE		$25,000.00
	TOTAL	$66,282.52

FIGURE 6-2
Package-deal budget.

MUSIC PACKAGE--BUDGET WORK SHEET

PICTURE TITLE EAGLES

TOTAL CREATIVE AND PERFORMANCE COSTS (from Budget Work Sheets) $ 66,282 .52

RECORDING STUDIO:

11 hrs @ $ 450	w/PROJECTION	$ 4950 .00	
7 hrs @ $ 300	wo/PROJECTION	$ 2100 .00	
8 hrs @ $ 180	POST-MIX	$ 1440 .00	
___ hrs @ $___	___	$___ . ___	
4 rolls 2" tape @ $ 120		$ 480.00	
___ rolls 1/2" tape @ $___		$___ . ___	
2 rolls 1/4" tape @ $ 30		$ 60.00	
	Subtotal	$ 9030.	
	TAX 6½%	$ 586 .95	
	SUBTOTAL		$ 9616 .95
OTHER (Lyricists, vocalists): ___		$___ . ___	
___		$___ . ___	
	SUBTOTAL		$___ . ___

PAYROLL/ACCOUNTING:

Total musicians' costs (excluding pension, including premium pay): $ 29,081. 19	
Payroll taxes @ 15.75%	$ 4580 . 29
Total singers' costs: $___ . ___	
Payroll taxes @ 16.95%	$___ . ___
Handling @ 5.5 % of gross $ 70,862.51	$ 3897 . 46
PACKAGE TOTAL	$ 84,377.22

TIME TO COMPOSE

> ***In 1986, for about six months, I was working seven days a week, doing eighteen-hour days. And I always knew if I dropped six hours, I'd miss it.***
> DAVID BELL

Another important part of the planning is to plot the amount of music to be written versus the number of days available to write it. Composers (as well as writers, directors, and actors) universally speak of the relentlessly demanding schedules, especially in television. Each composer eventually learns the average amount of quality music he can write on a daily basis and plans a schedule to allow for that. However, even when decent schedules can be agreed upon, the shooting and editing of films tend to fall behind schedule, and since music is the last element in the production chain, the composer's time gets cut short: he is often not given the fine cut when promised, while the delivery date remains unchanged. Accepting a television assignment will almost inevitably mean accepting their postproduction schedule and doing the best you can with it. Weekly television episodes are sometimes split between two composers who alternate weeks to maintain the grueling production schedules.

Feature films traditionally schedule more time for composing. And the more prestigious composers may sometimes have more clout in setting writing schedules they believe reasonable. But they too feel pressured by circumstances that ultimately shorten those working schedules. Everyone agrees that to be a film composer you must be a fast writer and have the physical stamina to work under extreme pressure and still continue to write music for many days with inadequate sleep.

SAMPLE SCHEDULES. Most composers say that to compose an average of 2 minutes of music per day is reasonable, averaging the slow days and the days with director's conferences and phone calls with the good days when things are going well. Jerry Goldsmith usually figures back from the start of a feature-film recording. "I figure 2 minutes per day and add 10 days to that for that first period of preparation. And those weeks are 7 day weeks—if I stop and lose the momentum I'm lost."

Many composers speak of finding themselves with as much as 10 minutes of score to write per day in extreme cases but generally agree that they can't do their best job if the average goes to more than 3½ to 4. Whether or not they orchestrate their scores will also affect their output.

Although composing schedules for feature films generally are longer than for television, they are for the most part shorter than they were in the pre-1960 era, when 10 weeks was normal. At this writing, 5 or 6 weeks is often planned but 3 or 4 weeks may be the the realistic time after editorial delays. The table shows approximate composing times from spotting sessions to the scoring stage on a variety of feature films.

Time to Compose

COMPOSER	FILM	TIME
Elmer Bernstein	*The Magnificent Seven* (1960)	10 weeks
Jerry Goldsmith	*The Omen* (1976)	6 weeks
John Morris	*Silent Movie* (1976)	5 weeks
Charles Fox	*Foul Play* (1978)	6 weeks
Patrick Williams	*Breaking Away* (1979)	4 weeks
James Horner	*Star Trek II* (1982)	5 weeks
Michael Gore	*Terms of Endearment* (1983)	4 weeks
Arthur B. Rubinstein	*WarGames* (1983)	4 weeks

COMPOSER	FILM	TIME
Craig Safan	*The Last Starfighter* (1984)	6 weeks
James Horner	*Star Trek III* (1984)	5 weeks
Alex North	*Prizzi's Honor* (1985)	6 weeks
Craig Safan	*Remo Williams* (1985)	6 weeks
James Horner	*Aliens* (1986)	3 1/2 weeks
Georges Delerue	*Casanova* (1986)	8 weeks
Jerry Goldsmith	*Lionheart* (1986)	4 weeks

Even in feature films with experienced composers there are more and more reports of last-minute changes that necessitate composing to rough cuts, because editing continues almost to the scoring sessions.

For 2-hour movies-for-TV, music executives report standard schedules for composing to be 2 to 3 weeks, and these can and do sometimes end up as a 1½ week push. Composers (and some producers and executives) consider these schedules unconscionable but they are facts of life the composer must work with.

For the 12-hour television miniseries *North and South* (1985) Bill Conti had only 3 weeks to compose a huge 5½ hours of music. There were 4 hours of underscore and 1½ of source music. Under those circumstances others were brought in to handle the source, but that still left Conti with 4 hours of underscore.

For one-hour television episodes, from 4–5 days to 8–9 days are normal but there are many instances of 3-day schedules for substantial amounts of music (24 to 40 minutes). And there are frequent stories of last-minute director/producer decisions to underscore scenes that had not been spotted.

It seems obvious that in setting up a schedule of composing and recording the composer should ask for as much time as possible, knowing that unforeseen surprise factors beyond his control may leave him without some of that scheduled time.

COPYING TIME

Time must be allotted for orchestrating and extracting the orchestra parts when the sketches are finished. If there is an orchestrator, sketches must be given to him as soon as they are ready so that his work will continue while the composer is sketching. Fortunately, copyists have developed ways to deal with the recurring time binds. Up to six copyists or more will simultaneously copy a last-minute score. Each may be copying a separate instrument's part from photocopies of the score. They copy the strings, percussion, keyboards, and choral parts first, so the necessary extra copies can be duplicated, assembled, and taped while the copyists are finishing the nonduplicated parts.

Planning and maintaining a schedule of composing, orchestrating, and copying is important not only to meet deadlines, but to avoid premium-time copying costs, and mistakes made from rushing and not proofreading. Planning is time-consuming but essential.

The budget and schedule will not go away; these practical matters remain on the composer's desk until the first downbeat of the scoring session, throughout the recording, and sometimes considerably beyond that moment. But if the composer is organized and thoughtful about these details at the beginning of the project, he will have the confidence of knowing that he will be able to follow through smoothly on the practical necessities. With that in mind, he can turn his attention to an infinitely more rewarding step in the process of scoring a film—developing the concept.

PART

CONCEPTUALIZING

CHAPTER 7

DEVELOPING THE CONCEPT

Over the years, I find myself spending more and more time conceptually and less and less time proportionately actually writing the cues.

DAVID SHIRE

I always look at a film and try to find some sort of a hook for it—and the hook might be a melody, or it might be a specific sound or a specific approach.

CRAIG SAFAN

Concept is the heart of the score. It is an *idea,* either small or large, modest or grandiose. It is, in fact, the primary idea that functions as a foundation upon which the score is built. As such, defining and developing this focused, central idea is the first step toward creating a successful film score.

From the time a film composer begins to consider his first thematic material, he is defining his concept for that film. If his choices are consistent, then his score will have a concept—an idea—behind it, and this concept will give his score strength and unity. If he develops the score from a clear concept it will have a consistent attitude and style—a unified approach that helps maintain the film's dramatic integrity.

Concept can often be discussed in terms of musical *style*—a score might be baroque, but with a contemporary rhythm-section feel, for instance. Bill Conti refers to his cues for the last fight and End Credits of *Rocky* (1976; see Figures 4-1 and 4-2) as "baroque-rock." Concept can also be expressed with instrumental *color*—in *Silkwood* (1984), the banjo Georges Delerue introduces during his Main Title (and uses thereafter) represents the quiet, rural nature of the location in which the hard-hitting drama of Karen Silkwood unfolds, contrasting with her struggle to expose corruption and danger at the nuclear plant where she is employed.

Here are some examples of scores with strong concepts:

- Ennio Morricone's *The Good, the Bad and the Ugly* (1967), with its heavily reverbed ocarinas, whistling, wordless voices, and twangy electric guitar, all surprising and fresh. His score is a perfect match for the offbeat, stylized spaghetti Western for which it was designed.
- Johnny Mandel's piano theme for *Being There* (1979), hinting at several influences, including classical composer Erik Satie and the ragtime compositions of Scott Joplin, which seems to express the unusual, slightly off-the-ground, gentle innocence of the gardener played by Peter Sellers.
- The score for *The Godfather* (1971), which Nino Rota composed in the harmonic and melodic language of Italy while at the same time retaining a powerful overview of the universality of the drama.

CHARACTERIZATION

> ***How did we conceptualize the colors for* Rockford Files? *We looked at the character.***
> MIKE POST

In most cases, the concept of the score will be built around the quality and nature of the central character or characters. There are other aspects of the film that the concept can successfully key in to, but more often than not these aspects will relate back to the central character(s).

Mike Post tells us how Pete Carpenter and he looked at the character of Rockford for the hit television series *Rockford Files* (1974): "First of all, [James] Garner is Southwest—Oklahoma. His accent is not real Southern, but he's definitely not East Coast or West Coast. His father was played by Noah Berry, Jr., who's an ex-trucker. Rockford's character is more interested in $200 a day plus expenses than he is in saving the girl or trying to be a hero. So it wasn't heroic music. It was music that had a hand-on-your-hip, tongue-in-cheek, wry attitude to it. And I was real interested in being the first rock-and-roller to score for television. I really wanted to be the first guy to come in there and sound different. I wanted to make some sort of statement."

There's much to be learned from Post's comments. In summary:

1. They analyzed the central character's regional characteristics and accent (Southwest; possibly appropriate regional music).
2. They analyzed his father's personality and background (blue collar, retired working man; implication: string quartets are out—they are not ordinarily associated with blue collar—unless the director wants to create an "against-the-grain" personalized characterization).
3. They analyzed the central character's personality and motivations (he's laid back and has simple motivations; both are qualities that could be represented musically).
4. Through that discovery, they decided what the musical style *wasn't* (Rockford had no heroic impulses; therefore the music shouldn't be heroic).
5. Through all of the above, they decided what the musical style *was,* in terms of attitude (hand-on-hip, tongue-in-cheek, slightly wry; these are also personality characteristics that can be translated into various musical approaches).
6. Post wanted to express all this in a new way for television. (That is, if he could he wanted to characterize all of the above in a way that would sound fresh on television, by making contemporary music compatible with the personality of the chief characters and the show's attitude).

By going through this thought process and verbalizing the concept, Post and Carpenter arrived at an appropriate solution for the main theme and then orchestrated it. "We took a lot of my bluegrass background, used dobro, Minimoog, no trumpets, 2 French horns, 2 trombones, 2 bassoons, oboe, flute, and a small string section with no violins, 2 cellos, and a big rhythm section with 3 guitars (one of them a 5-string guitar finger-picked like a banjo)." And, as a final down-home touch—harmonica. (See Figure 7-1.)

THE CENTRAL CHARACTER

You can't conceptualize the central character unless you understand him. Your musical impression of that character can become the concept. At its simplest, this can be superficial, but if the character has any psychologically interesting reactions or feelings, the music

FIGURE 7-1

Rockford Files Main Title, 1975 Mike Post and Pete Carpenter

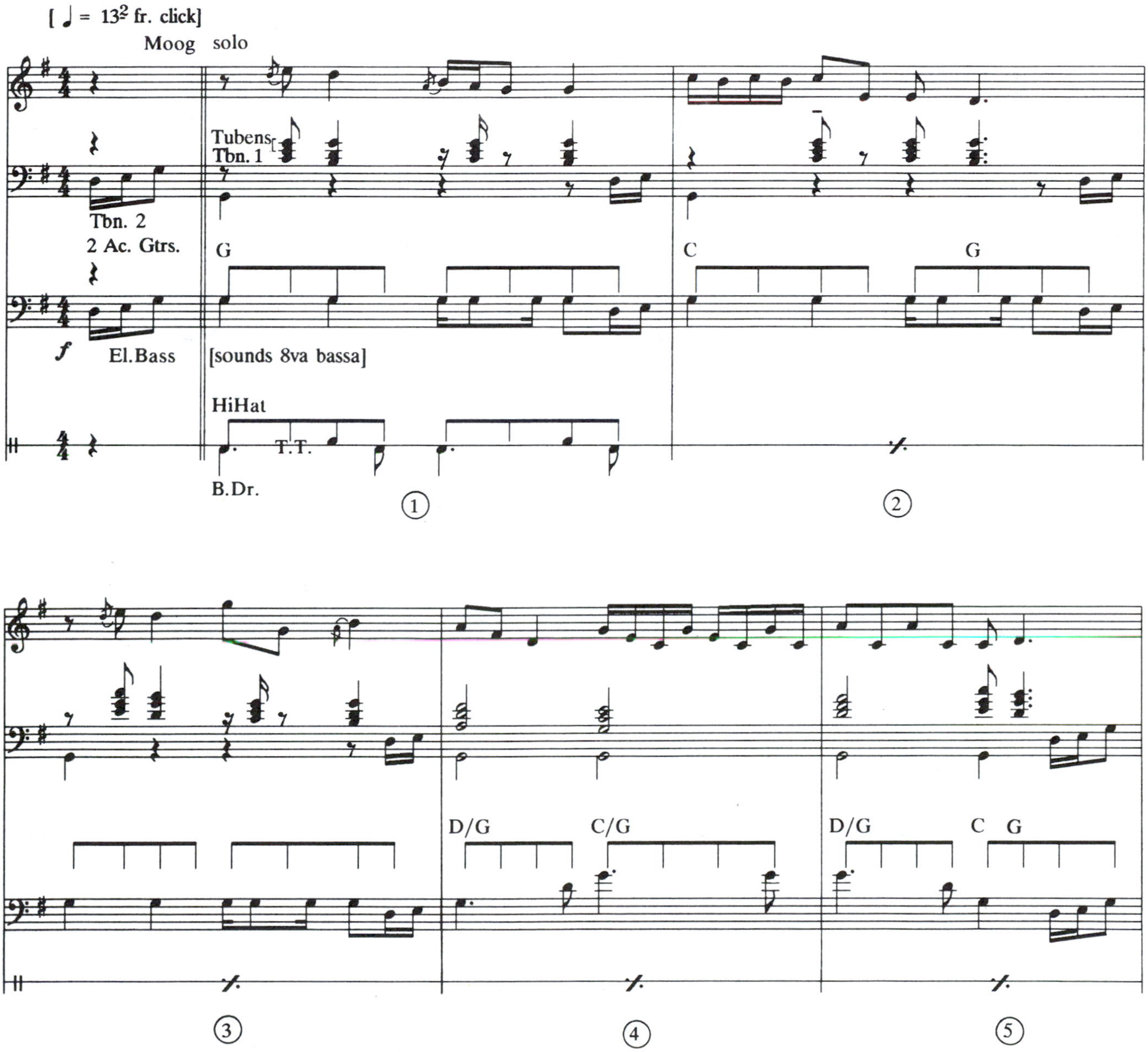

[♩ = 13² fr. click]

Moog solo

Tubens
Tbn. 1

Tbn. 2

2 Ac. Gtrs.

G

C

G

f El.Bass

[sounds 8va bassa]

HiHat

T.T.

B.Dr.

①

②

FIGURE 7-1 (*Continued*)

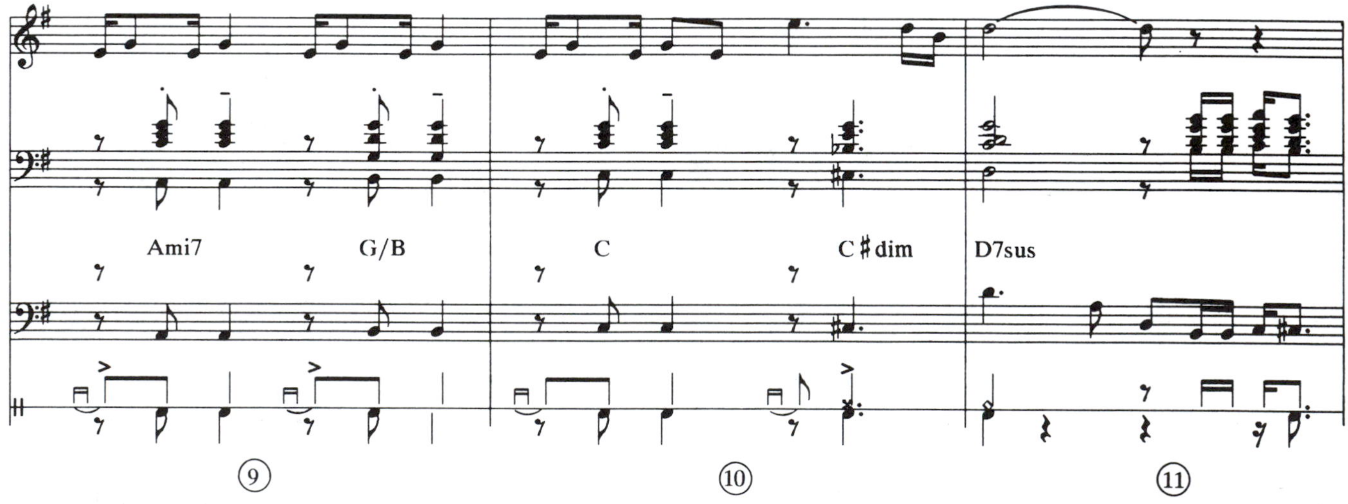

can function most effectively for the film by characterizing these internal attitudes. For example:

The central character in *Superman* (1978)—Clark Kent/Superman—is basically straightforward; he is the prototypical superhero. In the main theme, John Williams took a correspondingly straightforward, heroic, bigger-than-life marchlike approach.

Being There (1979) is more complex. Again, the overall quality of the film is reflected in its central character, an innocent gardener (played by Peter Sellers) cloistered all his life, who is suddenly out on his own on the streets of Washington, D.C., after his employer dies. The gardener's personality is just the opposite of Superman's. Johnny Mandel describes the character: "We're dealing with a guy who is totally divorced from reality. He's a wonderful character, but he relates everything to television. It's a very far-out kind of abstraction—you've got something that's totally unlike life. You've got this guy who's like a child, he's totally naive. He's never been out of the house, he's never been in contact with anyone in the real world, and he doesn't relate to anything or anybody except by way of television. I wanted to get some music that really didn't mean anything [by itself] and probably the closest thing to it was [French composer Erik] Satie. I studied some of his etudes, because he does things that are retrograde a lot of times. He'll go from a C to a G to a D in his harmony. He resolves everything backwards and defies the law of gravity by doing it. His music doesn't follow the normal course and that gives it a kind of spacey, airy quality. And he has the right hand doing stuff that's not too related to the bottom hand rhythmically or harmonically or melodically and that gives a very detached, spaced-out feeling."

In this case, certainly, Mandel was able to find a role model that really related perfectly to the central character. "And also," Mandel adds, "I'd throw in a little Scott Joplin here and there. In other words, just snippets of things he picked up on television. And phrases that start out being very important, just dribble off into absolute gibberish—I did a lot of that." One of the most important qualities that the Sellers character has is the ability to sound profound even while he is talking about something entirely detached from the rest of the world. And Mandel's music captures that essence. (See Figure 7-2.)

In contrast, the film *Patton* (1970) gave Jerry Goldsmith the opportunity to personify musically a legendary military figure (portrayed in an Oscar-winning performance by George C. Scott). "Patton was probably the most intellectual exercise that I ever put forth on a film. On that picture I felt very little demand for music. As a matter of fact, there wasn't very much music in the picture. Only 30 minutes and the picture ran almost

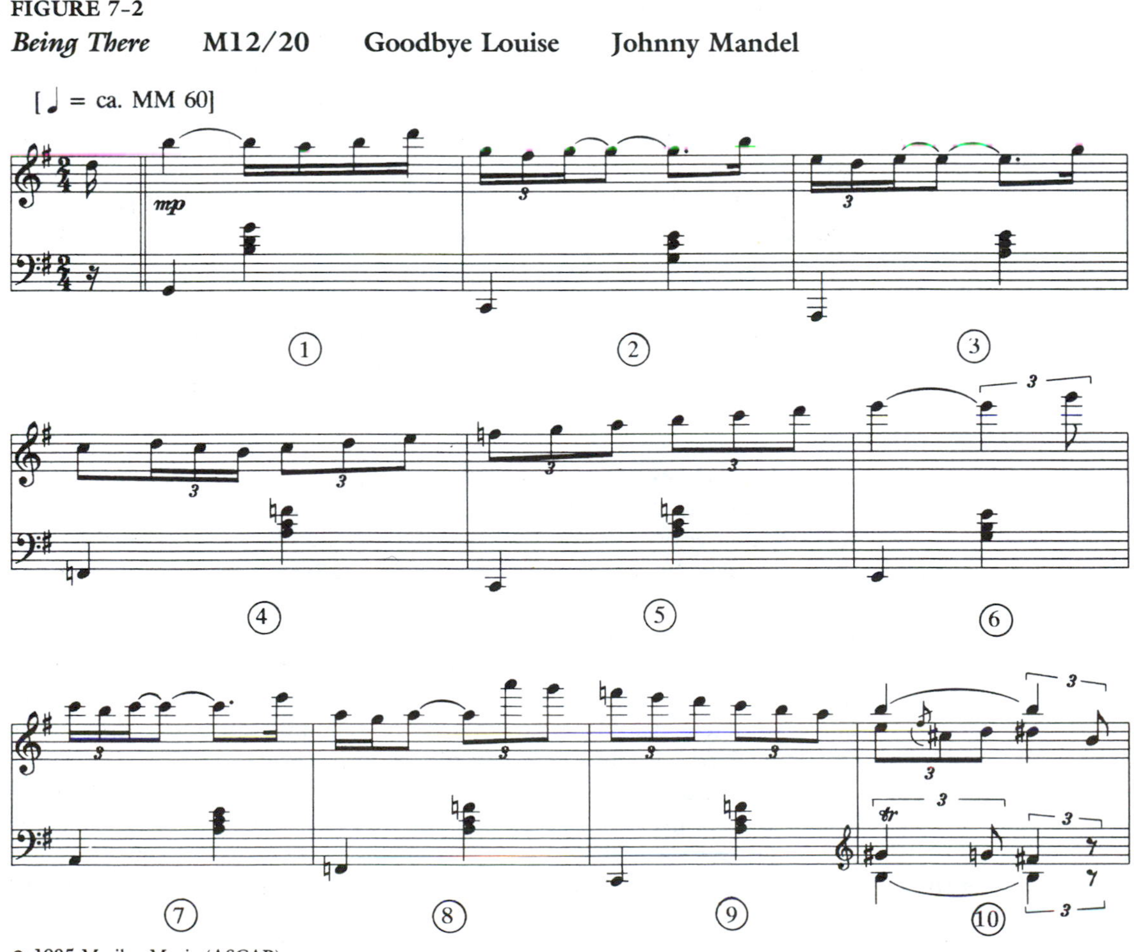

FIGURE 7-2
Being There **M12/20** **Goodbye Louise** **Johnny Mandel**

3 hours. I felt the picture was an antiwar picture. That was my feeling. It wasn't made that way but that was the point of view I took.

"If one looks back in history, there isn't a war that doesn't have some religious implications somewhere, including Vietnam. The man was a religious man and first my idea was to use a doxology, and I told Frank [director Franklin Schaffner] about this and he thought about it and said it might be a good idea. I used that, and said I would write a march as a counterpoint to that and so the actual march I wrote was a counterpoint to the doxology. So now I get a call from him one day (I already anticipated what he was going to say) and he said, 'You can't do it. You are really reaching a little far and insulting the Protestants.' I said, 'You are absolutely right.' So I wrote a reverse counterpoint, but I was still going to make a chorale of religious character, which I did.

"The march was to represent the militaristic character of the man [see Figure 13-16], the chorale the religious part of the man, and the trumpet fanfare [Figure 7-3] was to represent his belief in reincarnation. Doing it electronically added another element. I mean, doing it live still never gets the same effect as doing it electronically. It was one of those things: Oh—how do you get the idea—it just came to me, that's all. I just wanted to somehow subtly be able to remind the audience that this facet of his character was alive.

"This was a three-fold character I was working with. My feeling is that all of these elements musically had to stand by themselves or in various combinations of their parts so that you have the summation of the character when you had all three elements going, or you were seeing one particular facet of the man when he was reliving the battle of Carthaginia. When he was preparing for battle, it was more of a religious rite. I mean it was a ritual. There I took the chorale and expanded it."[1]

The central character in *The Man With the Golden Arm* (1956) is less exalted—he is a professional card dealer with a serious drug habit (played by Frank Sinatra). The setting for the story, Chicago, influenced Elmer Bernstein in devising the concept for his score. "I was helped by some very obvious things. First of all, it was a picture about a man who wanted to be a jazz drummer—that's what he wanted, that's where he lived, that's where his dreams were. He was also involved in the Chicago underworld, and jazz was an easy association to make (unfortunately, because jazz obviously has more worth than just being associated this way). I just liked the particular kind of energy you could generate with jazz."

At that time, in 1957, this was an unusual approach—with the exception of Alex North's score for *Streetcar Named Desire* (1951), Hollywood scores rarely incorporated anything resembling authentic jazz materials (other than for source music).

THE UNSEEN CENTRAL CHARACTER. In *The Stalking Moon* (1968, Karlin), the antagonist is not seen on camera until the last reel. But up until that time he is an unseen presence, stalking loner Gregory Peck as he treks across the West of the 1880s with Eva Marie Saint and her half-Indian son. Peck has saved her from captivity and now the vengeful Indian chief is trying to return them both to his village.

He is no ordinary antagonist, though; director Robert Mulligan intended for him to be bigger than life, a mythic representation of evil, relentlessly stalking his prey. Unseen though he is, the Indian is the central character in this drama. And music had to help provide the sense of imminent danger by this unimaginably powerful, vicious force. The concept of the score involved coloring the entire film with his presence.

Two musical ideas were used to accomplish this. First, a subliminal, sustained string-and-woodwind chord was recorded that could play almost like a sound effect, like a chilly breeze rustling through the trees. Played softly whenever there was the sense that the Indian might be lurking just out of eyesight, just over the next hill, this sound created

[1] *Film Music Notebook,* Volume 111, Number 2, 1977, p. 27, interview by Elmer Bernstein.

FIGURE 7-3
Patton **Trumpet fanfare (with Echoplex)** **Jerry Goldsmith**

Patton R1P2/R2 P1

a quiet, cold tension that never let up for long. It often played simultaneously with cues based on other musical material, giving the impression that nothing was quite calm or safe. The second sound was a single-chord strummed sound, a combination of out-of-tune zithers distorted and manipulated electronically to create an ominous, unreal menace, derived from the more traditional sound of Western folk guitars. As if the menace grew from the Western environment itself, these single chords, written and recorded with a sense of space around them, floated across the skyline in dark contrast with the beautiful scenery and open spaces on the screen. They often worked in conjunction with the ambient chordal sound described above to further increase the tension.

AN INANIMATE OBJECT AS CENTRAL CHARACTER. If a central character can be unseen, it can also be inanimate. John Williams's score for *Close Encounters of the Third Kind* (1977) emphasizes the film's dramatic theme, reflecting the spirituality of Richard Dreyfuss's experiences with the UFOs and the mystical attraction that the spaceship holds for him and Melinda Dillon. In this film, the spaceship, representing the arrival of peaceful space travelers, is really the central character. The score expresses the qualities of this central character (as seen through the eyes of Dreyfuss and Dillon). This cue, illustrated by Figure 7-4, starts as Dreyfuss suddenly brakes to a stop at the roadblock during their search to find out what is happening.

THE SINGLE DRAMATIC THEME

If the musical concept evolves from the dramatic theme of the film, it becomes an *overview* statement; it stands back one step and reflects the overall attitude and thrust of the entire film. To explore the potential of this type of concept, ask the question What is this film really about? Jerry Goldsmith's score for *Hoosiers* (1986), the story of a small Indiana

FIGURE 7-4

Close Encounters of the Third Kind 11/2-12/1 The Mountain

John Williams
Orchestrated by Herb Spencer

high school's basketball team in 1952, has an overview concept, playing the central theme of determination and courage against all odds. A score that plays the dramatic theme as a key statement can also be specifically appropriate for the individuals and the setting. When you see *Hoosiers,* ask yourself if the score would have been exactly the same if the central characters had come from Chicago or Detroit instead of a small country town. If not, what changes would you suggest? (see Figures 22-12 and 22-13.)

FINDING THE OVERVIEW. An overview musical theme is one that musically sums up the emotional thrust of the film. THE OVERVIEW MUSICAL THEME, EXPRESSING THE DRAMATIC THEME OF THE FILM, DESCRIBES MUSICALLY WHAT THE FILM IS ABOUT. Would the type of music you have described as being appropriate for your main character in fact be appropriate as an overview statement?

VERBALIZING THE DRAMATIC THEME. The dramatic theme of a film can often be characterized with a short phrase, like Good vs. evil, or The will to survive. Arthur B. Rubinstein saw *WarGames* (1983) in very dramatic terms. "I decided, as a completely removed, subjective type of theatrical thought, that what this film is about is Faust and the devil. That's the only way I could see it. And that was the whole concept for the score."

Did he discuss his interpretation of the film with the filmmakers? "Well, the wonderful thing was that the person who was Faust, and the one who was the devil—they switched sides; sometimes the machine was the devil, sometimes the machine was Faust, because the kid was manipulating it. So I did this whole literary, theatrical game. Now I know that if I'd gone in at any point and said to any of the producers, 'Well, you see, what this score is about is Faust and the devil,' they would have said, 'Get this bum out of here. This is a picture about kids.'"

Is it a picture about kids? Or about Faust and the devil? The *story* is about two kids who get into a lot of trouble with the government when they tap into a secret computer program that connects with an automated system for missile retaliation. Before long the jeopardy escalates worldwide. The *dramatic theme* is about opposing forces; call them good and evil; call them the military and the citizens; call them scientific values and humanistic values. Or call them Faust and the devil.

SINGLE DRAMATIC THEME SCORES MAKE AN OVERVIEW STATEMENT. THEY SUM UP THE FILM.

TWO DRAMATIC THEMES

Often films have two dramatic themes, and the score can play them both. The development of one and then the other can become the concept of the score. In most cases, one of the two dramatic themes (and therefore musical themes) is personal, while the other is often an ambition of some kind, or a goal. This second dramatic theme becomes an overview of the film's intent and thrust.

Historical dramas are often this way. In the Robert Kennedy television miniseries, Kennedy's personal story was set against the historical backdrop of his times. Even the title of the project clearly articulated this thematic duality: *Robert Kennedy and His Times* (1985, Karlin). And so the film was about Kennedy (and his family) on a personal level, and also about the achievement-oriented, public Robert Kennedy. Here the coexisting dramatic themes are personal and epic. And each of these themes has a dramatic intent or attitude; the personal is close, warm, loving, familial, while the overview is of an intelligent, courageous man—strong, heroic, and American. A score reflecting the dramatic themes of this miniseries would capture those two groups of qualities in at least two main musical themes.

Personal dramas are often approached this way as well. One dramatic theme deals with the personal development of the central character, and possibly his relationship with his family and with others; the second overview theme is about his struggle to achieve a goal, whether it is his determination to save the whales (*Star Trek IV,* 1986), recover from a crippling accident (*The Other Side of the Mountain,* 1975), learn a classic blues tune (*Crossroads,* 1986), become a ballerina (*Flashdance,* 1983), or become an expert at karate and rebuff a bully (*The Karate Kid,* 1984).

Sometimes a group of people are involved in these dual-themed films, but the concept remains the same. The personal story becomes several different personal stories, but all with one unified ambition or goal. *Chariots of Fire* (1981), about the 1924 American Olympics team, and *Fame* (1980), about an entire school's performing arts ambitions, are two good examples of this.

Usually, concept scores turn out to be motivated by the central character(s) or the overall dramatic theme(s), because the other aspects of a film generally relate to these two factors.

MUSICAL STYLES

Established musical styles, whether pop, rock, jazz, or classical, are often the foundation for a concept. If the concept is based upon one distinct musical style, the purest execution of that concept is to be perfectly faithful to that style throughout the score, never changing musical language or composing outside the musical boundaries established by the style. Dave Grusin used the musical styles of twentieth-century French composers Francis Poulenc and Darius Milhaud for his concept for *My Bodyguard* (1980). Regardless of the scene, Grusin is very true to this style throughout the film, always working within that musical language to underscore the drama.

In his score for *Deathtrap* (1982), Johnny Mandel used primarily orchestra plus two harpsichords. Michael Caine plays a has-been playwright preoccupied with antique torture instruments and weapons, all used in his previous murder mysteries. These weapons become very central to the story, as a collective inanimate central character. "I decided to limit the score to Bach or before. I really tried to set that limit of not going past the eighteenth century." Mandel admits to getting "a little Wagnerian" at times, but only out of absolute dramatic necessity. "And there was one scene when Dyan Cannon is tipsy, sitting on the couch, and I start off with a flute duet and then go into a piano thing. And she's giggling and Michael Caine consoles her, telling her she had nothing to do with Christopher Reeve's death. And they're going up the stairs and they're getting pretty spaced out by then. He's leading her up to the bedroom and I got out of the piano and went to a Fender Rhodes at that point, into a deep **chorus**[2]—and broke the style there. And still, it grew out of the style. There's nothing there that Bach hadn't done at one time or another."

COMBINING TWO OR MORE STYLISTIC ELEMENTS

One of the unique features of film music is the combination of several stylistic musical elements to create a composite, sometimes even fresh recipe of musical ingredients. The possible variations are limitless. Ten percent more country-western gives a slightly different slant to the score; leaning more heavily on an element of circus music shifts the sound in that direction. There may not be a single commonly used musical label that accurately describes the composite musical idiom you have created. This is often true of scores

[2] Chorus: an electronically created unison or doubling effect.

with a strong concept, although not always. (*Star Wars* (1977) has a score with a strong and consistent concept, yet the concept is symphonic and orchestral, and not difficult to characterize.)

In his score for *The Elephant Man* (1980), John Morris derived his concept from the central (title) character, a severely deformed young man who had been exhibited in freak shows and carnivals all his life. So the flavor and color of carnival music was an extremely relevant sound (simple waltzes played on mechanical instruments, organ grinders, and steam calliopes). Also, the location of his story, turn-of-the-century London, was also important, because the contemporary reaction of the medical world and public to his deformity was part of the drama. In a different time and place, perhaps he would not have been treated as he was. Morris blended all these elements together to create the main theme, heard first in his Main Title music (see Figure 7-5).

FIGURE 7-5
The Elephant Man **M 11** **Main Title** **John Morris**
Orchestrated by Jack Hayes

FIGURE 7-5 (*Continued*)

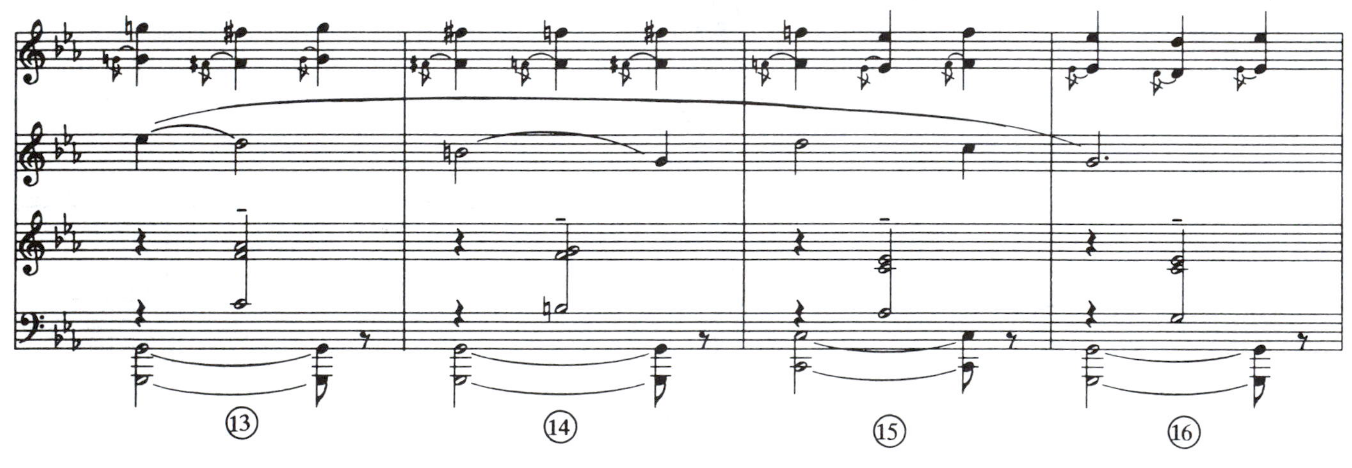

As John Morris describes it, "*Elephant Man* is about a carnival performer. That was the ostinato which was on top of the Main Title, which is like an old-fashioned carnival. The tune itself, though, I thought, should be something that was in his mind from childhood. And that's really it. So it's combining a tune that he would remember from his childhood with a little overtone of the carnival." In retrospect, his explanation makes the solution seem inevitable. This concept still comes from the central character, but deep inside him. To get *inside* the central character, Morris added colors that suggested period, place, and a sense of the musical style of a carnival.

The mixture of musical styles and attitudes can have a great bearing on the ultimate effect of the score. Some of the most memorable and refreshingly ingenious film scores use interesting combinations of several musical ingredients. (See Chapters 23 and 24 for more on the blending of styles—for instance, comedy and adventure, ethnic and period.)

THE PROCESS OF ELIMINATION

For any film, it's like a Chinese menu. I decide what I* don't *want.

JOHN MORRIS

You can start searching for the right music by eliminating certain musical ideas that you *don't* want in your score. For example, when Charles Bernstein was working on his score for the television miniseries *Sadat* (1983), which dramatizes the political and private life of the great Egyptian leader Anwar Sadat, many of his major decisions about style were "avoidance issues." He explains: "If much of the film takes place in the fifties, I'll avoid a harmony that I associate with a later period. In my score for *Sadat,* when I felt myself leaning in directions that, on an intuitive level, violated the time and place, I just nixed it. And took a left turn or a right turn."

These basic decisions can usually be made before you even begin to compose, and they in turn affect the rest of your score. When Laurence Rosenthal was searching for the right quality for the television movie *Who Will Love My Children?* (1983), he reacted emotionally to the film's profoundly moving story. It is the story of a woman who has ten children and a sweet, kind, but alcoholic husband; they live just barely above the poverty line in rural America. Then the woman discovers she has cancer. The film tells how she explains this to her children, and how she tries to find homes for all of them. "And it was so bone simple," says Rosenthal. "I mean there was nothing fancy or sophisticated about the children, and certainly not the woman. I felt that his had to be a melody of great simplicity, as it were, right from the heart—sort of C major simplicity. But at the same time, just with a tiny, tiny little echo of contemporary sound, of a kind of contemporary folk song" (see Figure 7-6).

This process of elimination can lead to both positive and negative choices—you want this, you don't want that—and every time you make another choice like this, you narrow down the possibilities a bit more, bringing you that much closer to your concept. *Sophie's Choice* (1982) is director Alan Pakula's film about a Polish woman (Meryl Streep) who is haunted by her experiences in a Nazi concentration camp, and by the choice she ultimately had to make in order to save one of her young children. Marvin Hamlisch describes this process of negative selection as it worked for him on this film: "The first thing about *Sophie's Choice* that I recall particularly was that I didn't want it to sound like we were doing 'Jewish.' When you write something, and it's supposed to sound Jewish, it's supposed to be in the minor mode, and that's supposed to make it sound sad. Looking at that film, I just knew that the big question mark and the thing that I had to be the most careful of was to capture her spirit, and when I say that, I don't mean her sadness. It's one thing to make that choice she had to make, but that woman throughout that film has a very

FIGURE 7-6
Who Will Love My Children? Theme Laurence Rosenthal

specific spirit about her. And I did not want the music to in any way sound as if this was about a Jewish situation, so for me, 'Marvin's choice' was to try to get a classical melody that was *not* minor."

Hamlisch is describing his deliberate decision to create a theme that would get inside the character and also reflect the dramatic theme of the film. In doing so, he is revealing one way to develop the concept. Sophie's character has a minor strain in her, but the major prevails. The music reflects this paradox. (See Figure 7-7.) Note the minor to major progression in bar 6 (beats 1 to 2); the minor section in bars 7 and 8, which resolves from F♯ minor to F♯ major in bar 8; and the final major cadence in bar 15.

FIGURE 7-7
Sophie's Choice **Theme (transcribed)** **Marvin Hamlisch**

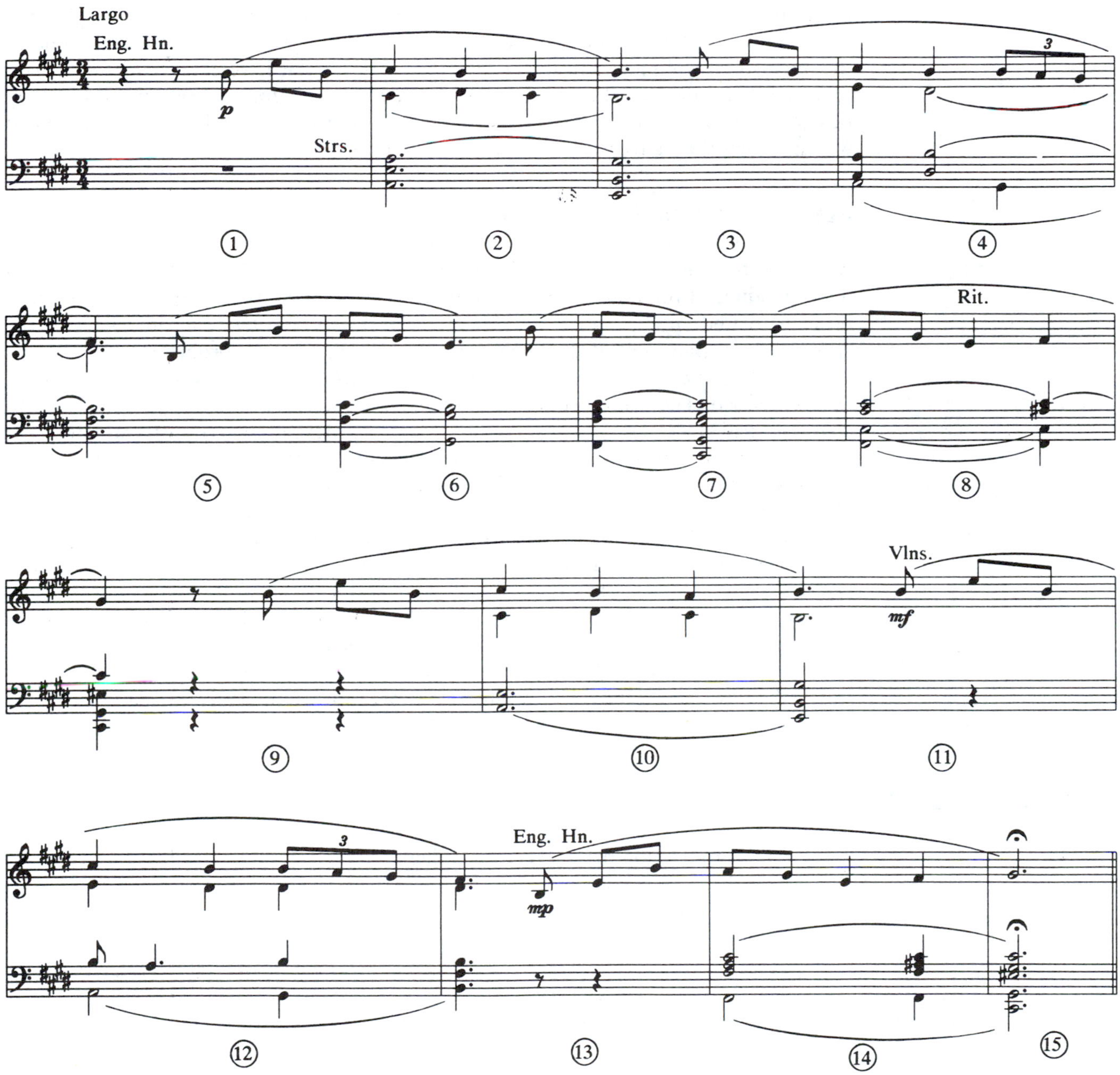
Largo
Eng. Hn.
p
Strs.
Rit.
Vlns.
mf
Eng. Hn.
mp
1
2
3
4
5
6
7
8
9
10
11
12
13
14
15

TONE

The word *tone* is often used in literature and theater to refer to the attitude of a dramatic work. And the dramatic theme of the picture is presented with a certain attitude or tone. When that tone shifts a bit more toward comedy than drama, or is dark and gloomy rather than hopeful and uplifting, this shift in tone in turn redefines the theme. It is undoubtedly the film's tone that has shaped the director's ideas about the score, and the first requisite of a good film score is a sensitivity to this.

A clear and focused tone need not require unidimensional story telling. The comedy/action/adventure genre of film asks the audience to laugh at some points, be thrilled at other times, and even fear for the character's safety in still other scenes. The tone of those films that are successful in this genre is clearly expressed early on, although often there are quick shifts between these emotions. *Raiders of the Lost Ark* (1981) is one of the most successful movies in this genre, and all those that have emulated its style have followed this principle. The audience knows the tone of *Outrageous Fortune* (1987) long before Bette Midler and Shelly Long become involved with the CIA and KGB. And so we can accept their adventures as a lighthearted romp.

READING THE TONE AND ATTITUDE. If the composer misreads this crucial element, the score will misrepresent the director's intentions, seem misplaced, and often be discarded on the cutting-room floor. Sometimes the filmmakers themselves have a blurred understanding of the film's tone, and in those cases the composer may find it extremely difficult to find an appropriate concept. He can do so only by being in sync with the attitude of the film itself. If the film's attitude is fuzzy, it can be problematic.

The dramatic tone of the film *And Justice for All* (1979) seems never to have been clearly defined. Film editor John Burnett remembers the problem. "I think Norman [Jewison] had always said that it was a black comedy. Maybe it was. I wasn't sure that was completely what it was. Norman wasn't sure he had a clear vision. He *wanted* everybody to think he had a clear vision (and I'm not talking out of school—he'd say it himself). He wanted to say such-and-such but every time he explained it people would say, 'I don't know Norman. No, I wouldn't say so.' 'Well what's your idea?' And they were getting everybody's ideas. We just had thirteen or twenty different ideas of what the movie really was. I know that was an extremely difficult scoring assignment."

Most of the time the film's tone will be clear. If it is not, the composer will want to learn as much as possible about the director's attitude toward his film. The best thing to do in such cases is to keep asking questions and demonstrating music in an attempt to define the film's tone (and consequently the music's function).

CONCEPTUALIZING

In order to develop the concept, then, here are the factors to consider:

1. The central character(s)
2. The film's overall dramatic theme
3. The combination of two different aspects of the film (usually a personal aspect, which could be the central character, and an activity or goal, such as Shirley Muldowney's desire in the 1983 film *Heart Like a Wheel* to be the best racing car driver in the country)
4. The period (present, Civil War, the twenties, and so on)
5. The place and ethnic flavor (often combined with the period; Westerns often have the flavor of both period and place, as do historical dramas)
6. An instrumental color or colors (often coming from one or more of the above; for instance, a Civil War banjo, plus a main theme that expresses the love story and aspirations of the protagonists)
7. A musical style that feels appropriate, aside from the above (jazz, rock, classical, or any combination)
8. The combination of several of the film's themes and colors

As a rule, you will find that your basic thematic material evolves from your concept. In some cases, though, the reverse can be true; a piece of music can actually help to clarify and develop your concept. The abstract ideas that you have discussed with the director and producer during spotting will become more specific as soon as you begin working with music, and you will now be able to continue your discussions with your musical choices in mind.

CHAPTER 8

DEMONSTRATING THE SCORE

Most of the scores that I do, I don't play anything ahead of time. If it's a very dramatic thing, I might demonstrate on the piano. But anything with textures or effects, it's impossible to demonstrate. JAMES HORNER

Sometimes I demonstrate. It really depends—it seems to me the more demonstrating you have to do, the more meetings you have to make, the more "advise and consent" there's going to be. MICHAEL MELVOIN

I always like to play the theme for them, because I'd rather they'd be smiling that day when we record it, rather than, "What is this?" BILL CONTI

It seems to me that hearing the main theme is a critically important thing for the composer and the producer or director to share beforehand. MARC MERSON, PRODUCER

At some point the composer may be asked by the director and producer to play some of the score for them, and most especially the main themes. Many composers don't wait for an invitation—they are eager to play themes for the filmmakers as a way of clarifying exactly what they have in mind. Demonstrating the themes, if not the entire score, is a fairly universal practice, and is usually done by the composer on a piano or synthesizer, either at his home (or studio) or at the production facility. It can take place any time during the composing of the score, from before spotting until recording. Scheduling of this demonstration depends primarily upon how much time the composer is given to write the score and how quickly he develops his concept and themes. The earlier it happens the more useful it can be. An early demonstration allows more time for everyone to consider and discuss the score. The time and place is almost always at the discretion of the composer.

By the early seventies composers generally reacted negatively to playing the score for the producer or director. They felt that the filmmakers could never really understand their intentions just from the piano—that if you said, "This high line is flute, the strings are going to do this," the producer and director would not be able to imagine the orchestrated music, and might dismiss cues or whole scores out of hand. Composers felt vulnerable. Their score might be compromised, and since they couldn't accurately demonstrate what it would really sound like they worried about losing a beautiful cue that the producer and director might love if they heard it orchestrated and played with the film.

Some composers still have this concern. "I try not to play the music for them," Allyn Ferguson says. "There isn't anything worse than demonstrations—they don't have any idea what you're saying. I have had more bad luck doing that than good luck."

Composers who are excellent keyboard players are in a position to demonstrate their scores more effectively than others and often are less reluctant to do so. "I've always played the whole score on the piano for people. I'm used to giving a really good description of how the orchestra will sound, singing trumpet lines or banging drums or whatever," says Charles Fox.

Marvin Hamlisch works similarly. "What I normally do is to play themes for any director, and then wait until I get through half the picture, and then I play that half for the director, at my Moviola. I say, 'This is what you're going to hear.' Because I don't like there to be too many surprises." The pro-demonstration composers agree that the demonstration is an important opportunity to communicate with the director. Furthermore, they say, it's better to know earlier rather than later whether you are satisfying the director.

But Bruce Broughton, who is a pianist, explains the potential problem: "Every time we're in the position of having to play a demo for the producer, it is somehow more than a demo to them. They believe that's the score, until they hear the final version. And if we have the misfortune of playing them the sample demo and they like it a lot, then that to them is the sound. Because even the piano, although it's a bland color, is a color. And it has a certain emotional effect."

Regardless of your philosophy about this, demonstrating at least the theme is usually a necessity. Many composers play selected cues that cover the dramatic range of the film. Sometimes, of course, demonstrating even a portion of the score simply isn't practical. The score may be very dependent on color and texture, impossible qualities to suggest on the piano. In television, particularly episodic programs, there isn't time to demonstrate the score, except for themes written for pilots, which are usually very carefully demonstrated regardless of any time restraints, and often changed (sometimes more than once).

WORD POWER

The ability to verbalize a good description of the overall musical effect is an important aspect of the demonstration. Ira Newborn puts it bluntly: "I'm exceedingly voluble and I can speak very well, and I can communicate very well except with the most closed-minded people. For instance, [director] John Hughes and I share certain enthusiasms. We both share a great love of rock-and-roll and he's into a lot of old records too. If he suggests something, I'll say, 'It should be more like Sam and Dave' or some other artist or record we both know, so he believes me. I can paint good word pictures. I've almost never had to rerecord anything."

Bruce Broughton has developed a procedure that might be a model to follow. He demonstrates his music on the piano and will tape it if he has to bring it to the director or producer. "I find it is much better for me to be present when they hear the music demonstrated. I make the tune as simple as I can. I'll play the theme through once, and then I'll play it immediately the second time and start to talk as they're hearing the theme, because they need to hear it a second time before they can make any judgment. And what I talk about is what the theme is doing and what it will do. I make certain promises about the colors and what I'll do with the orchestration. Then I'll play it a third time and preface it with, 'Now let's hear the theme one more time.' By that time they've heard it three times—or at least twice. And they can make some sort of judgment on it."

DEMONSTRATIONS CAN INFLUENCE THE DIRECTOR'S SHOOTING

Director John Erman recalls that for the 1985 television film *Early Frost,* John Kander sent him the theme in the second week of filming: "There was a sequence at the beginning where Gena Rowlands was a piano teacher teaching a child how to play the piano, and I had said, 'I think, rather than play a Chopin Nocturne, it would be wonderful if you could write something that we could then use throughout the movie,' and he said, 'That's difficult without having seen it but let me try.' He wrote this theme after we had talked for a long time about what I and he felt this movie was about. The minute I heard his theme I knew it was absolutely perfect. That was early on and really influenced me a lot about the way I shot the movie."

VIDEORECORDERS AND SYNTHESIZER DEMOS—MUSICAL "POLAROIDS"

Hi-tech developments have changed the basic ways composers work. It has become common practice for them to have a VCR by the piano or synthesizer as a convenient way of trying out music against picture, and directors often go to the composer's studio to hear a demonstration done in this fashion.

Another technical development that has dramatically changed the method of demonstrating a score is the use of synthesizers to compensate for the inadequacy of the piano in these demonstrations. Not only have synthesizers and **sequencers**[1] made possible more effective demonstrations, they have nearly made demonstration a necessity. David Shire comments: "On *The Color Purple* [1985], with Quincy Jones's army of synthesists and keyboard players and arrangers, Spielberg wanted a Synclavier mock-up of every cue so that he could get a feel of exactly what the music was going to do. They call them 'Polaroids' because lighting and cameramen will often take a Polaroid of the set to test the lighting before they shoot. And now we have musical 'Polaroids,' and more and more directors seem to be demanding them. But one can get in trouble with them I think, because the sound of a Synclavier imitating a symphony orchestra is still not an orchestra."

Nevertheless, it is undeniable that synths can give a reasonable approximation of most scores. In the case of *The Color Purple,* Brian Banks and Anthony Marinelli (Sonar Productions) were commissioned to create Polaroids of every cue in the score. To program, perform, and record the enormous amount of music composed for the film in just three weeks' time, they created only rough realizations of each full orchestral score. If a complex woodwind unison was called for in the orchestration, they used just a solo woodwind, or perhaps octaves. Steven Spielberg would then play the synthesized version of the cue against the picture and request changes; these would be incorporated into the orchestration and would then be returned to Sonar Productions for another Polaroid version. This process continued until Spielberg approved every cue.

Since the performance commands are stored on a sequencer, sequencing makes it relatively easy to change the **patches**[2] during a live demonstration if the composer or director wants to hear other options. Of course this adds time-consuming steps to the composition process that can be absolutely impossible on tight schedules, but the payoff is that the composer can avoid making costly changes later, that might be asked for if the director hears the score for the first time on the scoring stage.

---

[1] Sequencers: computer programs or computer-based machines capable of digitally "recording" all the basic musical commands (but not the music, as does a tape recorder) fed into them by a synthesizer or other electronic device.

[2] Patches: synthesizer sounds.

PART 3

TIMINGS

CHAPTER 9

TIMINGS AND CLICKS I

I prefer to work out all the math myself. . . . JAMES HORNER

How much click I use depends on the picture—some pictures I can go through without a click: just the clock and streamers. Others by necessity do have click. HENRY MANCINI

With a clear musical concept and a solid understanding of the film and its dramatic needs you can finally get down to composing. At some point, though, you must deal with the problem of synchronizing the music to the film. This inevitably involves some mathematics, something which has unnecessarily put off many a potential film composer.

The truth is that you rarely need to sync music to film more tightly than within ⅓ of a second, but even when you need to make a **dead hit** (within 2 frames) the process is not unreasonably difficult, and the mathematics involved is straightforward. Experienced composers, working with first-class music editors, aren't hampered by timing and sync problems, although working out the music synchronization does take time. But the neophyte film composer cannot count on having the support of the best music editors and computer timing programs while he serves his apprenticeship scoring the occasional industrial film, documentary, art film, or commercial. You are strongly advised to thoroughly learn the basic mathematics. Even using computer timing programs requires a good grasp of the fundamentals. More important, with a good understanding of film math, you will still be in business when the computer crashes.

With the music editor's timing sheets in hand, you have a list of the film events and the timings where they occur. Your first move is to circle the timings of the events with which you want the music to synchronize. The next step is to select an approximate tempo and to express these timings in music notation on blank music paper. Prepare the sketch with timings above each barline, with scene descriptions and event timings written above the relevant beats on this sketch. You can then see graphically how the music fits the film. Try not to be discouraged if this seems tedious at first. As John Cacavas puts it, "The thing that takes the longest is figuring out the timing. Once I have that done and it's in front of me with the action indicated on the page, things seem to fall into place easier."

FREE TIMING

Click tracks—provided by a digital metronome (calibrated in frames and eighths of frames) or computers (often calibrated in beats per minute)—are now used so often in film recording that one might assume they must always be used. Yet if you had no click available when planning your music synchronization, you could instinctively apply common sense and run a stopwatch as you mentally performed your music (in proper tempo, of course). If you noted the stopwatch timings on your sketch paper as you passed each bar line, you could write into the music the timings and descriptions of the film events above the beats where they occurred. You could then alter the music as needed to make it fit the score. At the recording session it would not be difficult to recreate that tempo and successfully play the music to the scene.

This **free timing** method doesn't provide the sharp **syncing**[1] required in some scenes but it is nonetheless a useful, even preferred method for many cues. Its advantage is the increased musicality and flexibility that results when the conductor and musicians aren't overpowered by the relentless click.

When recording using free timing, the composer watches the film as he conducts to accomplish the synchronization. Even without picture projection, the conductor can use the clock to successfully sync the music to the picture by skillfully varying the tempo as needed to make the timings written in the score conform to the clock's time. This, of course, assumes that the music is basically nonrhythmic and flexible in tempo, usually of a flowing or even rubato nature—and is accompanying film that does not require making dead hits. It can be used when *one* dead hit in the music cue is required, since the music editor can subsequently slide the music forward or backward if necessary. With free timing it is difficult to make more than one dead hit per cue since sliding the music to correct one hit would obviously change the position of the other.

In free timing the music editor can provide two conducting aids: **punches** and **streamers.** Punches (shown in the music as + or ⊕) are multiple holes punched in the film, or electronically added to videotape, that produce a short sequence of fluttering light pulses on the screen. These serve as preparatory signals for the start of a music cue or as barline markers within a cue. If used as conducting aids, they can be prepared to set the tempo of the incoming cue, or can be punched one second apart or one foot of 35mm film (⅔ of a second) apart. A streamer (shown above the score as ━━━━━━━━━┫) is seen as a vertical line which moves across the film frame. This is a guide to help the conductor start a cue or sync a point within the cue.

The conductor may work with 3 foot, 4 foot, or 5 foot streamers on film. Most composer/conductors prefer the 3 foot streamer; be sure to tell the music editor your preference. On videotape, you should specify the streamer length in seconds; however, not all computer programs offer a choice.

Not only do punches and streamers help the conductor make the music fit without the use of clicks, but they can be used in combination with clicks to handle intermixed rubato and *a tempo* sections of the score. As William Goldstein notes, "I just worked on a score where a big chunk was done with streamers only. And there were a number of cues that were combinations of clicks up to a certain point, or we started out just to picture and then brought in the click at a certain point with warning clicks. I also did some cues just following punches on every measure."

ALEATORIC CUES

The coloristic and emotional textures of **aleatoric music**[2] seem just right for some psychological film situations, but this compositional technique may make film sync more difficult. John Corigliano solved this problem when scoring his freely timed, tangled orchestral textures for the hallucinatory scenes in *Altered States* (1980). "The aleatoric sections were no problem to sync. I used a kind of notation that made it possible for the conductor to align it as precisely as he wanted to. I used 'cues' instead of beats. The cues then were simply linked up with the stripes [streamers] and the pops [punches] by conductor Chris Keene. He'd be beating a regular three beat but instead of three equal

---

[1] Syncing: synchronizing.

[2] Aleatoric music: music that contains chance performance elements, usually with the sequence of pitches and timing of notes to be decided by the performers.

beats it would be three cues and each one of them (if it were synced to anything like a stripe) would easily fall into place. For this more abstract kind of music it works well." (See Figure 16-17.)

USING CLICKS AND CLOCK

Free timing is not practical for many music cues because (1) the cues may require a steady tempo that would sound unmusical if varied to make the music fit the timings, or (2) several dead hits must be caught, which is extremely difficult to do in free timing.

When planning to use a steady click you must know the exact time when each beat of a steady tempo occurs so that you can calculate dramatic events in music notation. If the metronome tempo were MM 60, it would be easy to calculate the internal timing, since each ♩ equals one second. Figure 9-1 demonstrates the calculations necessary to make hits at :06.5 and :09.3.

Many film cues have been set in this tempo (or at MM 120, where each ♩ equals ½ second) because of the mathematical simplicity. To be able to use any tempo with assurance and precision the easiest way is to use a **click book.** These books give tables of timings; each page shows timings for one setting of the **digital metronome/variable click generator.** The timing in seconds is given for each numbered click (beat). (See Figure 9-2 for the table for the tempo setting of MM 120). The first click book was assembled by music editor Carroll Knudson in 1965, and the click book is often called the Knudson book. A complete click book by Alexander R. Brinkman, based on new algorithms, may be found on pages 663–841.

THE DIGITAL METRONOME (CLICK GENERATOR)

The digital metronome is an electronic click generator. Before it was developed music editors prepared loops of 35 mm film on which they punched holes in the optical track with a hand punch at regular intervals to produce metronomic clicks. Since film runs at 24 frames per second, 24 frames between clicks produces one click per second (60 beats per minute, or MM 60), 12 frames between clicks produces two clicks per second (120 beats per minute, MM 120), and an 18 frame spacing produces 80 beats per minute (MM 80).

Finer gradations of tempo are possible not only by setting clicks at whole-number intervals (for example, every 7, 8, 9, or 10 frames) but by using fractional spacings like $9\frac{1}{8}$ ($9\underline{1}$), $9\frac{2}{8}$ ($9\underline{2}$), and so on. These finer gradations of tempo are possible by subdividing each frame into eight parts and using the four sprocket holes per frame (of 35 mm-size film) as visual guides to line up the punches (clicks). (See Figure 9-4).

Current electronic digital metronomes and click books still follow this tradition and divide the frame into eighths. Although computer sequencers are often calibrated in beats

FIGURE 9-1
Timing Example.

FIGURE 9-2

Click-book page (12 frame click).

CLICK: 12 0/8 FRAMES; M.M.: 120.00

Click	0	1	2	3	4	5	6	7	8	9
000	0:00.00	0:00.00	0:00.50	0:01.00	0:01.50	0:02.00	0:02.50	0:03.00	0:03.50	0:04.00
010	0:04.50	0:05.00	0:05.50	0:06.00	0:06.50	0:07.00	0:07.50	0:08.00	0:08.50	0:09.00
020	0:09.50	0:10.00	0:10.50	0:11.00	0:11.50	0:12.00	0:12.50	0:13.00	0:13.50	0:14.00
030	0:14.50	0:15.00	0:15.50	0:16.00	0:16.50	0:17.00	0:17.50	0:18.00	0:18.50	0:19.00
040	0:19.50	0:20.00	0:20.50	0:21.00	0:21.50	0:22.00	0:22.50	0:23.00	0:23.50	0:24.00
050	0:24.50	0:25.00	0:25.50	0:26.00	0:26.50	0:27.00	0:27.50	0:28.00	0:28.50	0:29.00
060	0:29.50	0:30.00	0:30.50	0:31.00	0:31.50	0:32.00	0:32.50	0:33.00	0:33.50	0:34.00
070	0:34.50	0:35.00	0:35.50	0:36.00	0:36.50	0:37.00	0:37.50	0:38.00	0:38.50	0:39.00
080	0:39.50	0:40.00	0:40.50	0:41.00	0:41.50	0:42.00	0:42.50	0:43.00	0:43.50	0:44.00
090	0:44.50	0:45.00	0:45.50	0:46.00	0:46.50	0:47.00	0:47.50	0:48.00	0:48.50	0:49.00
100	0:49.50	0:50.00	0:50.50	0:51.00	0:51.50	0:52.00	0:52.50	0:53.00	0:53.50	0:54.00
110	0:54.50	0:55.00	0:55.50	0:56.00	0:56.50	0:57.00	0:57.50	0:58.00	0:58.50	0:59.00
120	0:59.50	1:00.00	1:00.50	1:01.00	1:01.50	1:02.00	1:02.50	1:03.00	1:03.50	1:04.00
130	1:04.50	1:05.00	1:05.50	1:06.00	1:06.50	1:07.00	1:07.50	1:08.00	1:08.50	1:09.00
140	1:09.50	1:10.00	1:10.50	1:11.00	1:11.50	1:12.00	1:12.50	1:13.00	1:13.50	1:14.00
150	1:14.50	1:15.00	1:15.50	1:16.00	1:16.50	1:17.00	1:17.50	1:18.00	1:18.50	1:19.00
160	1:19.50	1:20.00	1:20.50	1:21.00	1:21.50	1:22.00	1:22.50	1:23.00	1:23.50	1:24.00
170	1:24.50	1:25.00	1:25.50	1:26.00	1:26.50	1:27.00	1:27.50	1:28.00	1:28.50	1:29.00
180	1:29.50	1:30.00	1:30.50	1:31.00	1:31.50	1:32.00	1:32.50	1:33.00	1:33.50	1:34.00
190	1:34.50	1:35.00	1:35.50	1:36.00	1:36.50	1:37.00	1:37.50	1:38.00	1:38.50	1:39.00
200	1:39.50	1:40.00	1:40.50	1:41.00	1:41.50	1:42.00	1:42.50	1:43.00	1:43.50	1:44.00
210	1:44.50	1:45.00	1:45.50	1:46.00	1:46.50	1:47.00	1:47.50	1:48.00	1:48.50	1:49.00
220	1:49.50	1:50.00	1:50.50	1:51.00	1:51.50	1:52.00	1:52.50	1:53.00	1:53.50	1:54.00
230	1:54.50	1:55.00	1:55.50	1:56.00	1:56.50	1:57.00	1:57.50	1:58.00	1:58.50	1:59.00
240	1:59.50	2:00.00	2:00.50	2:01.00	2:01.50	2:02.00	2:02.50	2:03.00	2:03.50	2:04.00
250	2:04.50	2:05.00	2:05.50	2:06.00	2:06.50	2:07.00	2:07.50	2:08.00	2:08.50	2:09.00
260	2:09.50	2:10.00	2:10.50	2:11.00	2:11.50	2:12.00	2:12.50	2:13.00	2:13.50	2:14.00
270	2:14.50	2:15.00	2:15.50	2:16.00	2:16.50	2:17.00	2:17.50	2:18.00	2:18.50	2:19.00
280	2:19.50	2:20.00	2:20.50	2:21.00	2:21.50	2:22.00	2:22.50	2:23.00	2:23.50	2:24.00
290	2:24.50	2:25.00	2:25.50	2:26.00	2:26.50	2:27.00	2:27.50	2:28.00	2:28.50	2:29.00
300	2:29.50	2:30.00	2:30.50	2:31.00	2:31.50	2:32.00	2:32.50	2:33.00	2:33.50	2:34.00
310	2:34.50	2:35.00	2:35.50	2:36.00	2:36.50	2:37.00	2:37.50	2:38.00	2:38.50	2:39.00
320	2:39.50	2:40.00	2:40.50	2:41.00	2:41.50	2:42.00	2:42.50	2:43.00	2:43.50	2:44.00
330	2:44.50	2:45.00	2:45.50	2:46.00	2:46.50	2:47.00	2:47.50	2:48.00	2:48.50	2:49.00
340	2:49.50	2:50.00	2:50.50	2:51.00	2:51.50	2:52.00	2:52.50	2:53.00	2:53.50	2:54.00
350	2:54.50	2:55.00	2:55.50	2:56.00	2:56.50	2:57.00	2:57.50	2:58.00	2:58.50	2:59.00
360	2:59.50	3:00.00	3:00.50	3:01.00	3:01.50	3:02.00	3:02.50	3:03.00	3:03.50	3:04.00
370	3:04.50	3:05.00	3:05.50	3:06.00	3:06.50	3:07.00	3:07.50	3:08.00	3:08.50	3:09.00
380	3:09.50	3:10.00	3:10.50	3:11.00	3:11.50	3:12.00	3:12.50	3:13.00	3:13.50	3:14.00
390	3:14.50	3:15.00	3:15.50	3:16.00	3:16.50	3:17.00	3:17.50	3:18.00	3:18.50	3:19.00
400	3:19.50	3:20.00	3:20.50	3:21.00	3:21.50	3:22.00	3:22.50	3:23.00	3:23.50	3:24.00
410	3:24.50	3:25.00	3:25.50	3:26.00	3:26.50	3:27.00	3:27.50	3:28.00	3:28.50	3:29.00
420	3:29.50	3:30.00	3:30.50	3:31.00	3:31.50	3:32.00	3:32.50	3:33.00	3:33.50	3:34.00
430	3:34.50	3:35.00	3:35.50	3:36.00	3:36.50	3:37.00	3:37.50	3:38.00	3:38.50	3:39.00
440	3:39.50	3:40.00	3:40.50	3:41.00	3:41.50	3:42.00	3:42.50	3:43.00	3:43.50	3:44.00
450	3:44.50	3:45.00	3:45.50	3:46.00	3:46.50	3:47.00	3:47.50	3:48.00	3:48.50	3:49.00
460	3:49.50	3:50.00	3:50.50	3:51.00	3:51.50	3:52.00	3:52.50	3:53.00	3:53.50	3:54.00
470	3:54.50	3:55.00	3:55.50	3:56.00	3:56.50	3:57.00	3:57.50	3:58.00	3:58.50	3:59.00
480	3:59.50	4:00.00	4:00.50	4:01.00	4:01.50	4:02.00	4:02.50	4:03.00	4:03.50	4:04.00
490	4:04.50	4:05.00	4:05.50	4:06.00	4:06.50	4:07.00	4:07.50	4:08.00	4:08.50	4:09.00
500	4:09.50	4:10.00	4:10.50	4:11.00	4:11.50	4:12.00	4:12.50	4:13.00	4:13.50	4:14.00
510	4:14.50	4:15.00	4:15.50	4:16.00	4:16.50	4:17.00	4:17.50	4:18.00	4:18.50	4:19.00
520	4:19.50	4:20.00	4:20.50	4:21.00	4:21.50	4:22.00	4:22.50	4:23.00	4:23.50	4:24.00
530	4:24.50	4:25.00	4:25.50	4:26.00	4:26.50	4:27.00	4:27.50	4:28.00	4:28.50	4:29.00
540	4:29.50	4:30.00	4:30.50	4:31.00	4:31.50	4:32.00	4:32.50	4:33.00	4:33.50	4:34.00
550	4:34.50	4:35.00	4:35.50	4:36.00	4:36.50	4:37.00	4:37.50	4:38.00	4:38.50	4:39.00
560	4:39.50	4:40.00	4:40.50	4:41.00	4:41.50	4:42.00	4:42.50	4:43.00	4:43.50	4:44.00
570	4:44.50	4:45.00	4:45.50	4:46.00	4:46.50	4:47.00	4:47.50	4:48.00	4:48.50	4:49.00
580	4:49.50	4:50.00	4:50.50	4:51.00	4:51.50	4:52.00	4:52.50	4:53.00	4:53.50	4:54.00
590	4:54.50	4:55.00	4:55.50	4:56.00	4:56.50	4:57.00	4:57.50	4:58.00	4:58.50	4:59.00

♩. = 0.75; ♩ = 0.50; ♪. = 0.38; (3: ♩ 𝄾) = 0.33; ♪ = 0.25; (3: ♪ 𝄾 𝄾) = 0.17; 𝅘𝅥𝅯 = 0.13 seconds

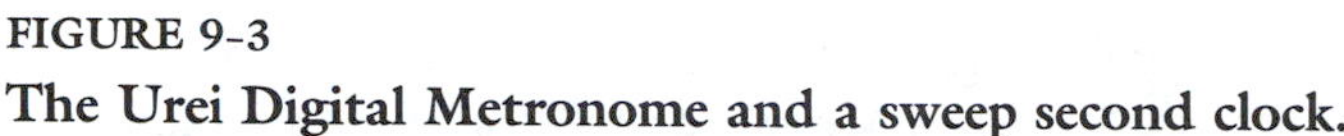

FIGURE 9-3
The Urei Digital Metronome and a sweep second clock.

Photo: Gay Wallin

per minute (to the nearest 10th or 100th), special computer programs are frequently calibrated in eighths of frames. These programs can easily expand the number of usable tempo settings by indicating finer subdivisions expressed in decimal parts of frames (for example, 10.90 frames per click).

DECIMAL EQUIVALENTS. Click tempos are read in the windows of the digital metronome as 091 for 9⅛ and 104 for 10 4/8. Decimal points should not be used in writing these numbers since 9.1 is likely to be read as 9 1/10 rather than 9⅛. However there are many times when using a calculator that you need to express click tempos in true decimals. These eighth-frame equivalents are:

FIGURE 9-4
Film frame divided into eighths.

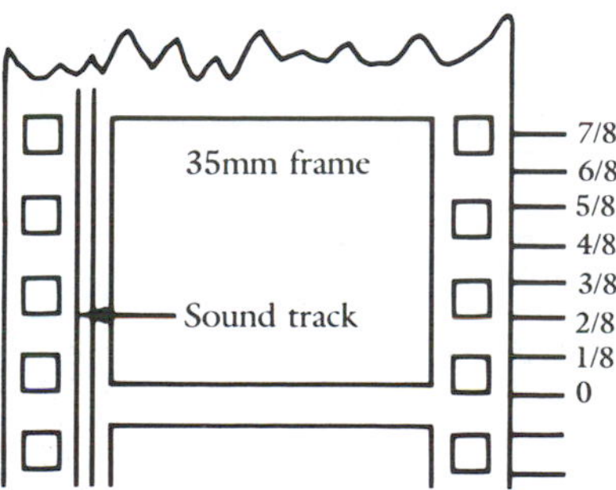

⅛ fr = 0.125 fr
2/8 = .025
⅜ = 0.375
4/8 = 0.5
⅝ = 0.625
6/8 = 0.75
⅞ = 0.875

METRONOME EQUIVALENTS. Digital metronome (click track) numbers, which give frames per click, are inversely proportional to the MM (Maelzel's Metronome) numbers, which give beats per minute (see Figure 9-5). Since there are 1,440 motion-picture frames per minute (24 frames × 60 seconds), you can easily find the metronome equivalent of a click tempo by dividing 1,440 by the number of frames per click. For example: for a 13 3/8 frame click, divide 1,440 by 13.375; the MM equivalent is MM 107.66.

FIGURE 9-5
Table of click track to MM conversions.

CLICK (frames)	MM	CLICK (frames)	MM	CLICK (frames)	MM	CLICK (frames)	MM
6	240	11	130.91	16	90	21	68.57
6 1/8	235.1	11 1/8	129.44	16 1/8	89.3	21 1/8	68.17
6 2/8	230.4	11 2/8	128	16 2/8	88.62	21 2/8	67.76
6 3/8	225.88	11 3/8	126.59	16 3/8	87.94	21 3/8	67.37
6 4/8	221.54	11 4/8	125.22	16 4/8	87.27	21 4/8	66.98
6 5/8	217.36	11 5/8	123.87	16 5/8	86.62	21 5/8	66.69
6 6/8	213.33	11 6/8	122.55	16 6/8	85.97	21 6/8	66.21
6 7/8	209.45	11 7/8	121.26	16 7/8	85.33	21 7/8	65.83
7	205.71	12	120	17	84.71	22	65.45
7 1/8	202.11	12 1/8	118.76	17 1/8	84.09	22 1/8	65.08
7 2/8	198.62	12 2/8	117.55	17 2/8	83.48	22 2/8	64.72
7 3/8	195.25	12 3/8	116.36	17 3/8	82.88	22 3/8	64.36
7 4/8	192	12 4/8	115.2	17 4/8	82.29	22 4/8	64
7 5/8	188.85	12 5/8	114.06	17 5/8	81.70	22 5/8	63.65
7 6/8	185.81	12 6/8	112.94	17 6/8	81.13	22 6/8	63.3
7 7/8	182.86	12 7/8	111.84	17 7/8	80.56	22 7/8	62.95
8	180	13	110.77	18	80	23	62.61
8 1/8	177.23	13 1/8	109.71	18 1/8	79.45	23 1/8	62.27
8 2/8	174.55	13 2/8	108.68	18 2/8	78.90	23 2/8	61.94
8 3/8	171.94	13 3/8	107.65	18 3/8	78.37	23 3/8	61.5
8 4/8	169.41	13 4/8	106.67	18 4/8	77.84	23 4/8	61.25
8 5/8	166.96	13 5/8	105.69	18 5/8	77.32	23 5/8	60.95
8 6/8	164.57	13 6/8	104.73	18 6/8	76.8	23 6/8	60.63
8 7/8	162.25	13 7/8	103.78	18 7/8	76.29	23 7/8	60.31
9	160	14	102.86	19	75.79	24	60
9 1/8	157.81	14 1/8	101.95	19 1/8	75.29	24 1/8	59.69
9 2/8	155.68	14 2/8	101.05	19 2/8	74.81	24 2/8	59.38
9 3/8	153.6	14 3/8	100.17	19 3/8	74.32	24 3/8	59.08
9 4/8	151.58	14 4/8	99.31	19 4/8	73.85	24 4/8	58.78
9 5/8	149.61	14 5/8	98.46	19 5/8	73.38	24 5/8	58.48
9 6/8	147.69	14 6/8	97.63	19 6/8	72.91	24 6/8	58.18
9 7/8	145.82	14 7/8	96.81	19 7/8	72.45	24 7/8	57.89
10	144	15	96	20	72	25	57.6
10 1/8	142.22	15 1/8	95.21	20 1/8	71.55	25 1/8	57.31
10 2/8	140.49	15 2/8	94.43	20 2/8	71.11	25 2/8	57.03
10 3/8	138.8	15 3/8	93.66	20 3/8	70.67	25 3/8	56.75
10 4/8	137.14	15 4/8	92.9	20 4/8	70.24	25 4/8	56.47
10 5/8	135.53	15 5/8	92.16	20 5/8	69.82	25 5/8	56.20
10 6/8	133.95	15 6/8	91.43	20 6/8	69.4	25 6/8	55.92
10 7/8	132.41	15 7/8	90.71	20 7/8	68.98	25 7/8	55.65

SEQUENCER USES. You may need to convert click tempos to MM numbers if you are using a synthesizer sequencer. Most of these programs are still calibrated in MM numbers. In addition, you should check on the accuracy level of the metronome readout of your sequencer, since any error of more than .01 percent will cause a significant error over a 5-minute cue. A direct check would be to time the clicks at ♩ = MM 120 against a reliable digital stopwatch to be sure that the error is no more than an eighth note off after 5 minutes. A call to the manufacturer should get you that information. If the error is more than that, use a digital metronome as the trigger to drive the system.

USING THE CLICK BOOK. The click book has been the universal source used to calculate timings. When using the click-book method, select the page representing your chosen tempo and copy the timings on your sketch's timing line (just above the score's top staff) on successive bars or beats. Then notate the rhythmic position of film events on that line. In tempos faster than ♩ = 15 frames, every other bar may be frequent enough. This method does not require the conductor to actually use the click during the recording; these timings are equally useful whether one uses the click when recording or conducts using the clock (see Figure 9-3).

USING A TABLE OF VARIOUS NOTE VALUES. When you have chosen a tempo and have turned to the appropriate page in the click book, it is helpful to make a small table listing the lengths of several note values, ready to be used in spotting film events. Brinkman's click book already furnishes these tables of note values at the bottom of each page (see sample click pages in Figures 9-2 and 9-6). (It is helpful to copy this table onto the top of the first score page, where it will be instantly available to make the timing adjustments that are often necessary while recording.)

The note-value table for the click-book page in Figure 9-6 was constructed by first taking the value of one click unit (♩ = :00.54), found by reading from the main table the timing at beat number two. (The duration of one click unit is the length of time between beat one and two, since the clock is at zero when the first click sounds.) Dividing :00.54 by 2 gives us the value: ♪ = :00.27. The complete table then is:

♩ = :00.54 sec.
♪ = :00.27 sec.
𝅘𝅥𝅯 = :00.14 sec.
♪. = :00.41 sec.
𝅘𝅥𝅯. = :00.21 sec.
(triplet) ♪ 𝄾 𝄾 = :00.18 sec.
(triplet) ♩ 𝄾 = :00.37 sec.

Figure 9-7 provides a layout of numbered beats (clicks) at this tempo on blank sketch paper, against which there will be hypothetical film hits at

:14.54 Fast pan to boy on hobbyhorse (a "soft" hit)
:21.87 Crash! (a "hard" hit)

The meter is 4/4; the click is a 13-frame click. The click table shows that the first soft hit at :14.54 falls between click numbers 27 and 28. It is :00.46 after click #27's timing of :14.08, and :00.09 before click #28's timing of :14.63. The latter click (#28), less than 1/10 of a second off, will be close enough for this soft hit.

The dead hit at :21.87 comes :00.20 after click #41 (at :21.67). According to the table of assembled note values this is very close to the duration of one triplet (:00.18). The error of :00.02 is less than human ability to detect it. Also this rhythm is easily performed at this tempo, this being one of the essential criteria for any musical solution.

FIGURE 9-6

Click-book page (13 frame click).

CLICK: 13 0/8 FRAMES; M.M.: 110.77

Click	0	1	2	3	4	5	6	7	8	9
000	0:00.00	0:00.00	0:00.54	0:01.08	0:01.62	0:02.17	0:02.71	0:03.25	0:03.79	0:04.33
010	0:04.88	0:05.42	0:05.96	0:06.50	0:07.04	0:07.58	0:08.12	0:08.67	0:09.21	0:09.75
020	0:10.29	0:10.83	0:11.37	0:11.92	0:12.46	0:13.00	0:13.54	0:14.08	0:14.62	0:15.17
030	0:15.71	0:16.25	0:16.79	0:17.33	0:17.88	0:18.42	0:18.96	0:19.50	0:20.04	0:20.58
040	0:21.13	0:21.67	0:22.21	0:22.75	0:23.29	0:23.83	0:24.37	0:24.92	0:25.46	0:26.00
050	0:26.54	0:27.08	0:27.62	0:28.17	0:28.71	0:29.25	0:29.79	0:30.33	0:30.87	0:31.42
060	0:31.96	0:32.50	0:33.04	0:33.58	0:34.12	0:34.67	0:35.21	0:35.75	0:36.29	0:36.83
070	0:37.38	0:37.92	0:38.46	0:39.00	0:39.54	0:40.08	0:40.63	0:41.17	0:41.71	0:42.25
080	0:42.79	0:43.33	0:43.87	0:44.42	0:44.96	0:45.50	0:46.04	0:46.58	0:47.12	0:47.67
090	0:48.21	0:48.75	0:49.29	0:49.83	0:50.37	0:50.92	0:51.46	0:52.00	0:52.54	0:53.08
100	0:53.62	0:54.17	0:54.71	0:55.25	0:55.79	0:56.33	0:56.87	0:57.42	0:57.96	0:58.50
110	0:59.04	0:59.58	1:00.12	1:00.67	1:01.21	1:01.75	1:02.29	1:02.83	1:03.37	1:03.92
120	1:04.46	1:05.00	1:05.54	1:06.08	1:06.62	1:07.17	1:07.71	1:08.25	1:08.79	1:09.33
130	1:09.87	1:10.42	1:10.96	1:11.50	1:12.04	1:12.58	1:13.12	1:13.67	1:14.21	1:14.75
140	1:15.29	1:15.83	1:16.37	1:16.92	1:17.46	1:18.00	1:18.54	1:19.08	1:19.62	1:20.17
150	1:20.71	1:21.25	1:21.79	1:22.33	1:22.87	1:23.42	1:23.96	1:24.50	1:25.04	1:25.58
160	1:26.12	1:26.67	1:27.21	1:27.75	1:28.29	1:28.83	1:29.37	1:29.92	1:30.46	1:31.00
170	1:31.54	1:32.08	1:32.62	1:33.17	1:33.71	1:34.25	1:34.79	1:35.33	1:35.87	1:36.42
180	1:36.96	1:37.50	1:38.04	1:38.58	1:39.12	1:39.67	1:40.21	1:40.75	1:41.29	1:41.83
190	1:42.37	1:42.92	1:43.46	1:44.00	1:44.54	1:45.08	1:45.62	1:46.17	1:46.71	1:47.25
200	1:47.79	1:48.33	1:48.87	1:49.42	1:49.96	1:50.50	1:51.04	1:51.58	1:52.12	1:52.67
210	1:53.21	1:53.75	1:54.29	1:54.83	1:55.37	1:55.92	1:56.46	1:57.00	1:57.54	1:58.08
220	1:58.62	1:59.17	1:59.71	2:00.25	2:00.79	2:01.33	2:01.87	2:02.42	2:02.96	2:03.50
230	2:04.04	2:04.58	2:05.12	2:05.67	2:06.21	2:06.75	2:07.29	2:07.83	2:08.37	2:08.92
240	2:09.46	2:10.00	2:10.54	2:11.08	2:11.62	2:12.17	2:12.71	2:13.25	2:13.79	2:14.33
250	2:14.87	2:15.42	2:15.96	2:16.50	2:17.04	2:17.58	2:18.12	2:18.67	2:19.21	2:19.75
260	2:20.29	2:20.83	2:21.37	2:21.92	2:22.46	2:23.00	2:23.54	2:24.08	2:24.62	2:25.17
270	2:25.71	2:26.25	2:26.79	2:27.33	2:27.87	2:28.42	2:28.96	2:29.50	2:30.04	2:30.58
280	2:31.12	2:31.67	2:32.21	2:32.75	2:33.29	2:33.83	2:34.37	2:34.92	2:35.46	2:36.00
290	2:36.54	2:37.08	2:37.62	2:38.17	2:38.71	2:39.25	2:39.79	2:40.33	2:40.87	2:41.42
300	2:41.96	2:42.50	2:43.04	2:43.58	2:44.12	2:44.67	2:45.21	2:45.75	2:46.29	2:46.83
310	2:47.37	2:47.92	2:48.46	2:49.00	2:49.54	2:50.08	2:50.62	2:51.17	2:51.71	2:52.25
320	2:52.79	2:53.33	2:53.87	2:54.42	2:54.96	2:55.50	2:56.04	2:56.58	2:57.12	2:57.67
330	2:58.21	2:58.75	2:59.29	2:59.83	3:00.37	3:00.92	3:01.46	3:02.00	3:02.54	3:03.08
340	3:03.62	3:04.17	3:04.71	3:05.25	3:05.79	3:06.33	3:06.87	3:07.42	3:07.96	3:08.50
350	3:09.04	3:09.58	3:10.12	3:10.67	3:11.21	3:11.75	3:12.29	3:12.83	3:13.37	3:13.92
360	3:14.46	3:15.00	3:15.54	3:16.08	3:16.62	3:17.17	3:17.71	3:18.25	3:18.79	3:19.33
370	3:19.87	3:20.42	3:20.96	3:21.50	3:22.04	3:22.58	3:23.12	3:23.67	3:24.21	3:24.75
380	3:25.29	3:25.83	3:26.37	3:26.92	3:27.46	3:28.00	3:28.54	3:29.08	3:29.62	3:30.17
390	3:30.71	3:31.25	3:31.79	3:32.33	3:32.87	3:33.42	3:33.96	3:34.50	3:35.04	3:35.58
400	3:36.12	3:36.67	3:37.21	3:37.75	3:38.29	3:38.83	3:39.37	3:39.92	3:40.46	3:41.00
410	3:41.54	3:42.08	3:42.62	3:43.17	3:43.71	3:44.25	3:44.79	3:45.33	3:45.87	3:46.42
420	3:46.96	3:47.50	3:48.04	3:48.58	3:49.12	3:49.67	3:50.21	3:50.75	3:51.29	3:51.83
430	3:52.37	3:52.92	3:53.46	3:54.00	3:54.54	3:55.08	3:55.62	3:56.17	3:56.71	3:57.25
440	3:57.79	3:58.33	3:58.87	3:59.42	3:59.96	4:00.50	4:01.04	4:01.58	4:02.12	4:02.67
450	4:03.21	4:03.75	4:04.29	4:04.83	4:05.37	4:05.92	4:06.46	4:07.00	4:07.54	4:08.08
460	4:08.62	4:09.17	4:09.71	4:10.25	4:10.79	4:11.33	4:11.87	4:12.42	4:12.96	4:13.50
470	4:14.04	4:14.58	4:15.12	4:15.67	4:16.21	4:16.75	4:17.29	4:17.83	4:18.37	4:18.92
480	4:19.46	4:20.00	4:20.54	4:21.08	4:21.62	4:22.17	4:22.71	4:23.25	4:23.79	4:24.33
490	4:24.87	4:25.42	4:25.96	4:26.50	4:27.04	4:27.58	4:28.12	4:28.67	4:29.21	4:29.75
500	4:30.29	4:30.83	4:31.37	4:31.92	4:32.46	4:33.00	4:33.54	4:34.08	4:34.62	4:35.17
510	4:35.71	4:36.25	4:36.79	4:37.33	4:37.87	4:38.42	4:38.96	4:39.50	4:40.04	4:40.58
520	4:41.12	4:41.67	4:42.21	4:42.75	4:43.29	4:43.83	4:44.37	4:44.92	4:45.46	4:46.00
530	4:46.54	4:47.08	4:47.62	4:48.17	4:48.71	4:49.25	4:49.79	4:50.33	4:50.87	4:51.42
540	4:51.96	4:52.50	4:53.04	4:53.58	4:54.12	4:54.67	4:55.21	4:55.75	4:56.29	4:56.83
550	4:57.37	4:57.92	4:58.46	4:59.00	4:59.54	5:00.08	5:00.62	5:01.17	5:01.71	5:02.25
560	5:02.79	5:03.33	5:03.87	5:04.42	5:04.96	5:05.50	5:06.04	5:06.58	5:07.12	5:07.67
570	5:08.21	5:08.75	5:09.29	5:09.83	5:10.37	5:10.92	5:11.46	5:12.00	5:12.54	5:13.08
580	5:13.62	5:14.17	5:14.71	5:15.25	5:15.79	5:16.33	5:16.87	5:17.42	5:17.96	5:18.50
590	5:19.04	5:19.58	5:20.12	5:20.67	5:21.21	5:21.75	5:22.29	5:22.83	5:23.37	5:23.92

♩. = 0.81; ♩ = 0.54; ♪. = 0.41; (3) ♩ 𝄾 = 0.36; ♪ = 0.27; (3) ♪ 𝄾 𝄾 = 0.18; 𝅘𝅥𝅯 = 0.14 seconds

FIGURE 9-7
Timing example.

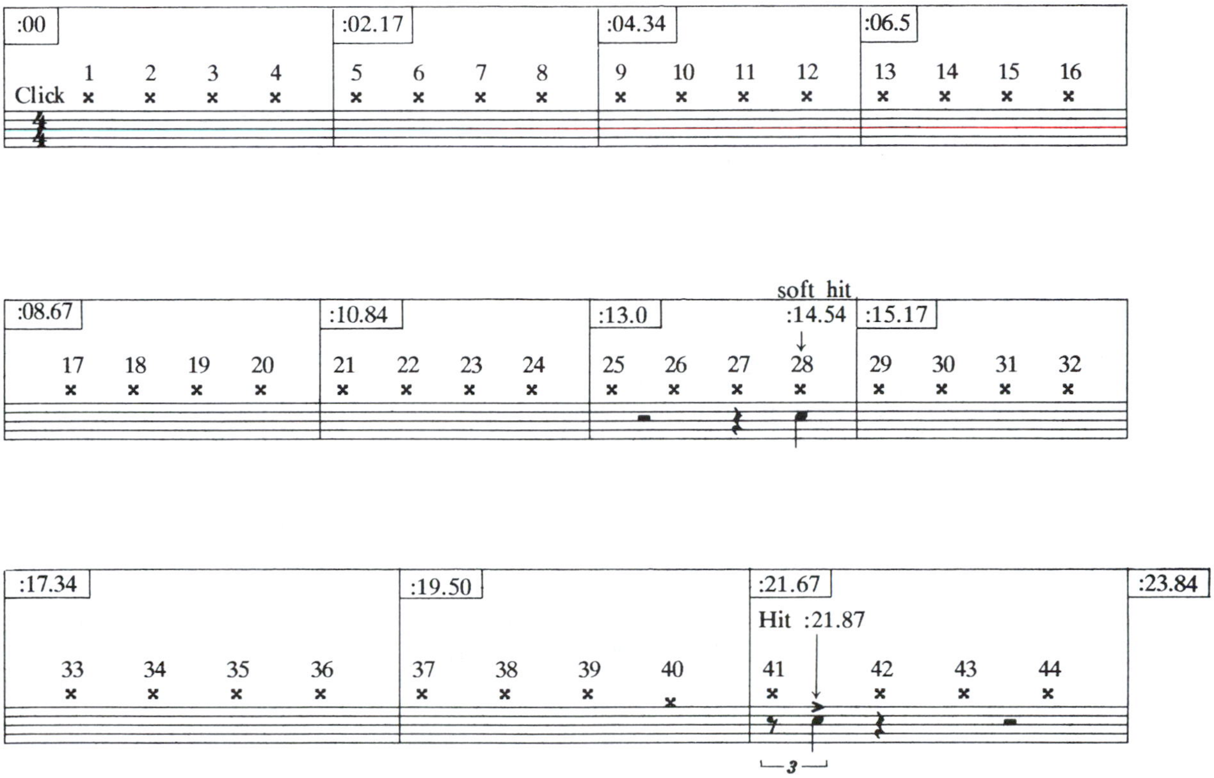

WHEN TIMINGS DON'T SYNC

When several dead hits occur within one music cue, you may not find workable timings in the click table of your chosen tempo.

TEST ADJACENT CLICK TABLES. In that case, examine the click-book pages before and after that page. The *actual* tempo differences of these adjacent pages are undetectable but the *accumulated* timing differences can make the hits correlate better.

TRY OFFSETTING. When the timings in the table are slightly off to a consistent degree faster or slower from the timings of your hits, you don't need to change tempo if you can offset the start of the cue slightly by shifting it a bit earlier or later. For example, if your tempo is a 13-frame click (as in the table in Figure 9-6) and your hits are at :03.71 and :05.86, you will find no click timings that match. When you subtract the hit timings from the nearest clicks you will find that they are, respectively, :00.46 and :00.44 late.

Rather than look for another tempo, you can shift these hits to fall on beats #7 and #11 by starting the whole cue :00.45 later. Remember, you must subtract that offset :00.45 from each timing on the timing sheet to compensate for the later start.

ORIGINAL TIMINGS		OFFSET TIMINGS
:03.71	First hit	:03.26
:05.86	Second hit	:05.41

FIGURE 9-8
Offset cue start.

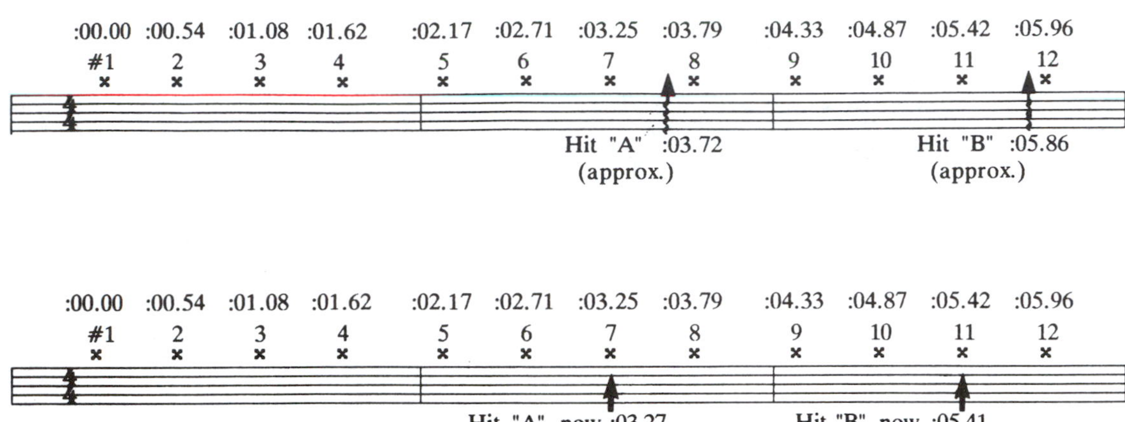

The music notation for the two versions is shown in Figure 9-8.

One of the advantages in using a computerized film-scoring program such as Cue, Streamline, or Auricle (see page 122) is the possibility of using the computer's number-crunching abilities to try out range of tempos to see which one fits the required hits of your film cue. However, the basic process is the same as the manual computation described here, and the latter should be thoroughly understood in order to best utilize the computer method.

AVOIDING THE OBVIOUS. It is not necessary, or even the best choice, to make all film hits fall on the beat. With rhythmic music, this can produce an obvious, even lugubrious effect. It is often more interesting to have hits occur off the beat if they fall naturally into the musical style and flow. For example, if you use the same 13-frame click tempo and a rhythmic theme to write a cue with three hits—(A) :01.88, (B) :04.30, and (C) :06.24—it appears at first that you should change tempos, since only hit B is actually on a beat (#9). However, hits A and C are almost exactly an eighth-note value late (:00.26 and :00.28—at this tempo, at which an eighth note equals :00.27). Actually this makes an interesting rhythmic pattern (see Figure 9-9). The only cost of this sophistication is a little more arithmetic.

ACCURACY REQUIREMENTS ON DEAD HITS

Dead hits require precision. But there is a physiological limit to the human ability to detect sync errors, and it is unnecessary and inefficient to persist in tighter synchronization than can be detected.

Individuals differ in this threshold of perception, but a general rule holds that film experts can easily detect a two-frame sync error ($2/24$ sec., or :00.08) while the general public can detect three-frame errors ($3/24$ sec., or :00.125). One-frame errors are very hard to detect. And slight sync errors can only be perceived when both the music and picture have very sharp changes in their respective sound and look—a sharp musical attack when the picture changes abruptly from light to dark, when a door slams, a bullet hits, and so on.

In addition, a hit that cannot be placed precisely where you want it without error will generally work better if the error makes it sound slightly late rather than early. The

FIGURE 9-9
Offbeat hits.

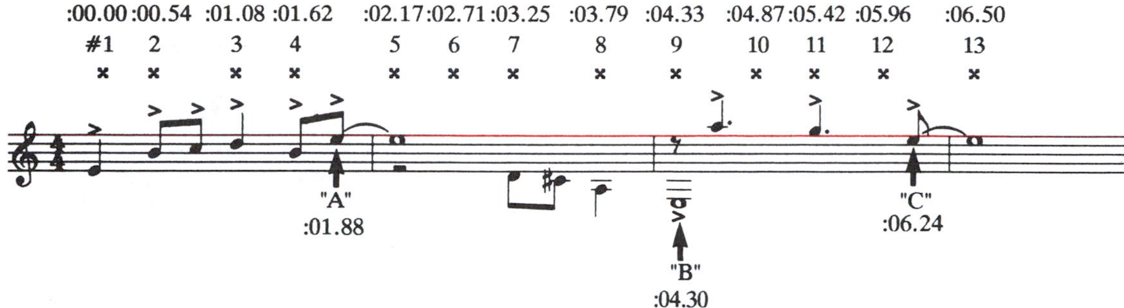

viewer detects an accent that is :00.1 early as being "wrong" because it is ahead of his visual and/or emotional reaction.

Again, with only one dead hit per cue, the music editor can make an adjustment, if necessary, when he lays in the music against picture.

If the sync on hard hits is not well within the two-frame (:00.08) limit you are vulnerable to the additive effects of subsequent technical errors that may creep in. For example, during production, syncing errors are sometimes made in the use of a drop-frame SMPTE time code (discussed in Chapter 10). Other errors may occur in the sound loop after the film is released and are thus beyond the control of the production team. To compensate for these potential errors, the music must be more tightly synchronized than might otherwise be necessary.

THE SOUND LOOP. On the release print of films, it is technically impossible to record the sound on the sound track exactly adjacent to the frame to which it is synced. This is because the sound recording must occur on a steadily moving medium while the picture must stop momentarily for each film frame. During each momentary stop the shutter interrupts the light path two or three times to increase the flicker rate to 50 frames per second or more, a rate at which the human eye does not perceive flicker.

To accommodate these two contradictory technical requirements, the position of the sound recording at any moment is offset from the picture, and leads it by 29 frames. This sound loop is of no concern to you in synchronizing your music since the loop is added automatically at the lab that prepares the release prints. Your only responsibility is to keep the music exactly in sync with the picture.

A common violation of sync often occurs during the showing of old movies on television, when we see the actors' lips move after we hear their voices. The original correct sync can be lost during projection if sprocket hole slippage or operator error changes the size of the sound loop.

It is difficult to conceive of intervals as small as one or two frames (:00.04 to :00.08), but musicians constantly must perform with such accuracy. For example, at the moderately fast tempo of MM 180 (an 8 frame click), each quarter note equals :00.33 and each sixteenth note equals :00.08. If one sets a metronome at 180 and performs the rhythm ♬♩ it is easy to hear the mistake if one player plays it correctly while another plays ♫♩. In the incorrect performance, the second note is :00.08 (2 frames) late.

RITARDS, FERMATAS, ACCELERANDOS

It is important not to let technical considerations force you into rigid, nonmusical results. When the musical concept includes a rhythm section (for jazz/rock/Latin/pop styles), using click works well. Otherwise, playing to a click seems to rob the composer of the chance to use the expressive ritards, accelerandos, and fermatas that make music live. This is no problem in free timing. Yet you often need the higher order of timing accuracy that a click provides. Using clicks also makes it possible to intercut various recording takes (compared to free timing, where comparable beats do not always occur at the same time in various performance takes).

Music editors can build a special click to fit each variable tempo situation. Computer programs will plot such ritards and accelerandos and perform variable click patterns (see page 122). All of these presume the availability of expensive equipment, experts, and the time and budget to use them, as well as a certain dependence on others to do something that you would prefer to keep as personal and as musically instinctive as possible.

You can make tempo variations without such technical dependence. To go into a ritard after an *a tempo* section, first lay out the click-book timings on your music sketch for the *a tempo* segment. Then on the beat when the ritard is to begin, start the stopwatch, and, while mentally singing the ritard, jot down the timings of the passing bar lines. You have to be careful not to rush the ritard or you will ultimately be caught short when recreating it on the scoring stage. With experience there should be no problem in duplicating such ritards during the recording session.

The score must show the cumulative timings from the cue's start. To calculate these timings through the ritard, add the ritard timings to the timing at the moment when you stop the click. In Figures 9-10 and 11, the chosen tempo is a 16-frame click (see Brinkman click book). Say you decide to stay in click tempo until click #53 (:34.67). At that point, start the stopwatch and time the ritard. When you jot down the ritard timings you will arrive at beat #61 at :09.33 (see Figure 9-10). Adding each of the ritard timings to the last click timing of :34.67 at beat #53, you get the cumulative timings from the start of the cue (see Figure 9-11).

When performing this cue you must start the clock on beat #1 and watch the score's cumulative timings. If you conduct without using the click, you can make small tempo variations, adjusting the tempo to the timings written in the score at each bar line, and continuing to adjust tempo as you make the ritard. If you decide to use the click, turn it off as you go into the ritard. You can then start the clock on the first beat of music and rely on the clock as you make the ritard.

When plotting the return to tempo after the ritard, again use the click-book timings but add each of these timings to the cumulative timing of the beat when it returned to tempo (see Figure 9-12.)

When performing this cue, the music editor (or you) must restart the click exactly at the time specified for the *a tempo* to start. One of the excellent features of the digital metronome is its ability to give an instantaneous click as you hit the start button. But keep the clock running to give the cumulative time. Fermatas are handled similarly.

FIGURE 9-10
Ritard timings.

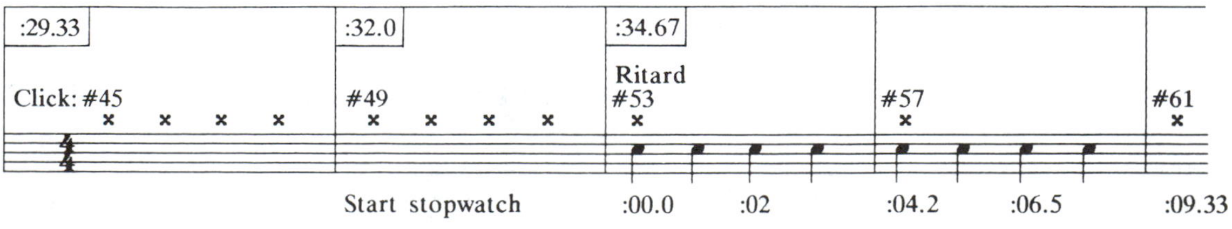

FIGURE 9-11
Ritard timings.

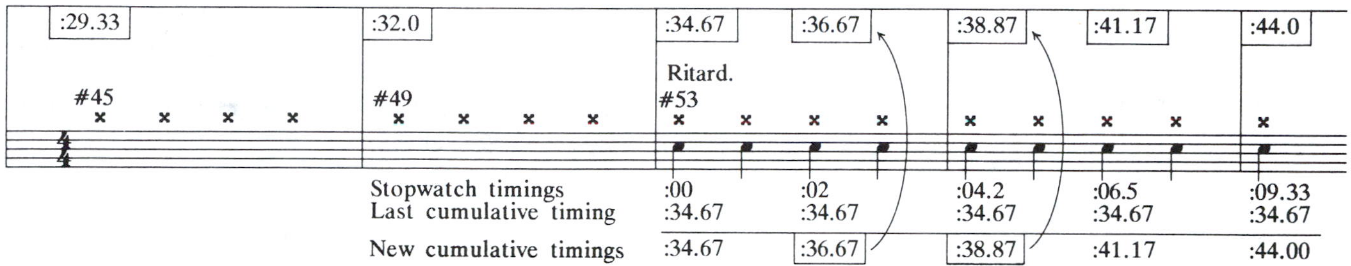

FIGURE 9-12
Ritard timings.

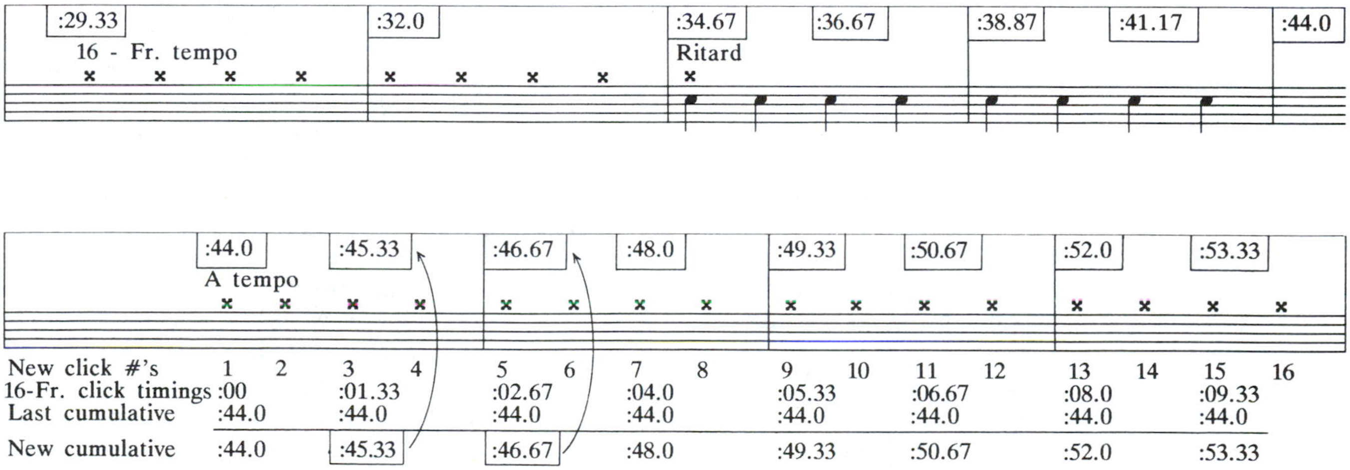

:29.33 — 16 - Fr. tempo
:32.0
:34.67 — Ritard
:36.67
:38.87
:41.17
:44.0

	:44.0 A tempo		:45.33		:46.67		:48.0		:49.33		:50.67		:52.0		:53.33	
New click #'s	1	2	3	4	5	6	7	8	9	10	11	12	13	14	15	16
16-Fr. click timings	:00		:01.33		:02.67		:04.0		:05.33		:06.67		:08.0		:09.33	
Last cumulative	:44.0		:44.0		:44.0		:44.0		:44.0		:44.0		:44.0		:44.0	
New cumulative	:44.0		:45.33		:46.67		:48.0		:49.33		:50.67		:52.0		:53.33	

BACKTRACKING. In planning any of these tempo variations, you will probably need to backtrack from a target time at the end of the desired tempo change. To find the correct time to start a ritard, for example, practice and time the ritard, then subtract that time from the target time. Common sense must prevail. With repeated practice these methods become easy and reliable, and you will be using technology to achieve your musical goals rather than forcing music to be a slave to technology.

TIMINGS AND CLICKS II

I use click a lot, only because of the time factor. JOHN CACAVAS

MUSIC EDITORS

The first step in **hitting cues**[1] is to thoroughly learn the theory and mechanics of timings, clicks, and free timing. The next step is to get to know and trust your music editor. Beyond his role in breaking down the film into music cues and providing the timing notes for each of those segments, the music editor is normally the composer's best ally among the filmmaking team. Everyone is looking after the interests of his own craft, whether it be sound effects, script-writing, acting, or whatever, but the music editor deals with the music and his interests coincide with the composer's.

He can be invaluable in making sure the hits, the composer's calculations, and the click details are correct. Traditionally, the same music editor stays with the picture and the composer all the way through its production. Unfortunately, the bind of tight schedules and economics in television has made that unpredictable. Music editing companies are now often contracted to do this work and the composer may find himself working with not just one editor but with several over the course of the project. This is not as desirable a way to work. Nevertheless, it happens, and the composer would be wise to be largely self-reliant. (This is even more reason for novice film composers to be solid on their math, since television is the medium where they are most likely to work first.)

The best music editors are very helpful, often anticipating and preventing timing problems. Music editor Gene Marks views his relationship with the composer as a collaboration. "I feel it's important to get copies of the scores (or sketches at least) as far in advance of scoring as possible. I feel it's very important to go over them, time allowing. When it's clicks, or even if it's timings that they've indicated on the score, I'll just check it by looking at it and comparing it with the timing notes. If an extra bar is written, or if the clicks numbered across the top, or the bar numbers have a mathematical mistake, I don't want to embarrass the composer, I want to protect him. I want to catch any problem that can be caught before you're on that scoring stage with the tremendous costs involved."

And music editor Michael Tronick adds, "My role is to allow the composer as much freedom as possible, and still understand what is best, almost as a silent partner—being able to handle the workings of the film and video. Awareness pays off—especially in being able to tell the composer how many bars have to be deleted and added when changes have to be made and made quickly because of the time and the pressure in terms of money—the dubbing stage costs something like $600 an hour and the director wants his cue!"

CUT-BACK CUES AND SPLIT CHASES

Everyday sync problems require solutions in postscoring that range from simple to very complex and sophisticated. Many times the composer must change the mood, volume,

[1] Hitting cues: syncing specific moments in the music with specific moments in the film.

and tension levels and other musical elements on each cut back and forth between different scenes. David Shire's score for *The Taking of Pelham One Two Three* (1974) is a fine example of this, as the action frequently cuts back and forth between a subway (on which hostages are being held) and a communications center (where Walter Matthau attempts to save the hostages). In this case, each of these "cut-backs" had to be hit by the composer.

In *Foul Play* (1978), Charles Fox worked out an unusual solution to the typical "split chase" sequence (a specific type of cut-back cue in which the camera cuts back and forth between the actual chase and some other scene). "We see the Pope entering the San Francisco Opera House Hall where Gilbert and Sullivan's *Mikado* is to be performed; with a lot of pomp and circumstance, he walks down the red carpet. Then I started the Overture and we cut inside to the opera in progress. Then there are about seven or eight cutaways—we see the opera in progress; we cut to Chevy Chase and Goldie Hawn in the car; we come back to the opera in progress in another scene and cut back to Chevy and Goldie. Every time we cut back to them they are having an episode with different people: one time with a Japanese couple in the back of a taxi, and at another time with a John Denver–type country-western character. We keep cutting back and forth to the opera in progress, each time moving further along in the first act, so that by the time we get to the opera house at the end of the show they are performing the end of act one of the *Mikado*.

"I saw my job to be to begin with the music of Arthur Sullivan and wherever we cut away to come out of his music into my chase music in a fast, furious tempo that would be contemporary but all the while using themes of *The Mikado,* either the one I just left or the one I was going to. And I would lead from *The Mikado* in whatever key and tempo it was in. While playing the chase I would make a transition to the key and tempo of the next piece we were cutting into, so that finally, when it was put together with all the cuts back and forth between my music and the original Sullivan music, it would almost be a seamless piece of music going from one to the other with all the keys making sense."

Such musical support and integration into the film's fabric can only be realized if the composer is prepared to handle the technical details, both compositional and mathematical, with confidence.

BUILDING CLICK TRACKS

Music editors can help the composer prepare complex sequences for the scoring stage. They can build very sophisticated click patterns, given time to work them out. This would include odd time signatures; changing time signatures; and gradual accelerandos to give the equivalent of a natural increase of a composition's tempo as it moves toward a climax, all of which may need to be tightly tied to timings to make hits. James Horner utilized such technical skills when he organized and composed a long cue in *Star Trek II* (1984), with its many cut-backs from exterior shots of the spaceship in wide open space to interiors that had tension, dialogue, and some forward movement of the script. He first recorded it without click but was ready with a standby built click if the clickless version didn't work in a reasonable amount of time. "That cue was almost 9 minutes long, and that's getting to the limit of what an orchestra can do in perfect performances. What I usually do is free-time the cue and if we get a perfect performance right away so much the better. But if we start to have mistakes I will then use a click, a built click (because not one of those segments is in a firm tempo; they are all sliding, which is why I liked it). I'll have told the editor basically, 'It's a 10-3 that slides 2/10 of a second by the time you get to such and such a timing.' I work it out, and all he has to do is slide it."

USING CLICKS FOR PRACTICAL REASONS

On the first season of the *MacGyver* television series, Randy Edelman used clicks with no projection during his recording sessions, which is quite unique for Hollywood but practical and not uncommon in New York and other film centers. A great advantage of this is the time and money saved during the scoring session. Using projection means extra expenses for renting studios with projection facilities and paying projectionists and technicians to handle the dummies (machines that play back the dialogue and effects tracks). Each time the orchestra stops, for whatever reason, means a short delay while the projector and dummies are rolled back to the start marks. Music playbacks with projection take extra time also.

Ongoing and last-minute picture changes can be a major headache for all composers. Clicks can help. John Cacavas says, "I find that if I hadn't used click track on some of the shows with many changes I'd really have been in trouble on the scoring stage. This happened on *Kojak* all the time. They'd call up a day before the scoring session with changes and I'd say, 'I don't want to know about that—it's too late. When we get to the scoring stage tell me how much time I have to cut or add.' With the click track it's very simple. With some of the independents that don't operate like a major studio, you don't have that luxury, that chain of command. Like on some movies-of-the-week—they'd say, 'We made these cuts—you fix it.'"

TEMPO AND MOOD CHANGES WITHIN CUES

Changing tempo in a musical film sequence can be handled in several different ways, the easiest being to record separately each segment that is in a different tempo and have the music editor assemble them afterward as one apparently continuous cue. That's a safe and efficient way to do it since it is not difficult to get perfect performances on shorter sections in one tempo. But there is a musical continuity that you gain by actually performing a cue that progresses through various tempo changes as one cue, and that was Maurice Jarre's choice in certain of the cues in his electronic score to *Witness* (1985). It doesn't always work well that way—it can get too complicated—but clicks can be very useful. "It depends," Jarre says. "If possible I always prefer to do it in one cue; the feeling is better." The click changes when the tempo changes, and "if we use just a streamer to warn us then we know when to change tempo with the click. . . . After a couple of rehearsals there is no difficulty with the changes of tempo."

CLICKS FOR ODD METERS

Providing clicks for odd meters is a problem. A fast 7/8, for example, is impossible on a conventional digital metronome—if the clicks are fast eighth notes it can be impractical for the musicians to follow. To get a playable click pattern of two quarter notes and three eighth notes, it is usually necessary to have the music editor build a track, or to use a computer-generated tempo map as discussed below.

Jarre uses changing meters now and then. "It could be written in 4/4 with accents, but if you write 5/8 and 3/8 and 6/8 and 4/8 it gives a better flow. That's why Stravinsky at one time tried to reorchestrate *The Rite of Spring*. When you see the first sketch of *Rite of Spring*, visually even, it's more correct. But it's difficult to do these rhythms with electronic instruments because you have to subdivide to the smallest unit. In other words, if you have a 5/8, you have to have your click on the eighth note. The musicians now can really read anything so you can use large clicks to make it easier. Suppose you are in 4/4 or 3/4 and 3/8—depending on the tempo, I might not subdivide for every eighth note."

For episodic television there's rarely time to have the music editor build a special track for those cues, but some computer programs and sequencers (such as Mark of the Unicorn's Performer and Opcode's Cue for the Macintosh) can handle these meters as well as the other complex click tracks described above. Charles Bernstein used a Bulgarian-type sequence of 11/8, 3/4, and 7/8 in one chase scene in the miniseries *Sadat* (1983) (see

FIGURE 10-1

Sadat **M-21 Jeep Chase** **Charles Bernstein**

Figure 10-1) and made up a click chart to use in programming the then newly developed Auricle computer program (described below).

TIMINGS AND CLICKS IN PRACTICE

> ***What I usually do is to have just the drums in the headset.***
>
> JOHN BARRY

> ***The way I work I don't record to picture—I do everything to click, and I compose with the film, so unless I've made a mathematical mistake, it's fine.***
>
> RANDY EDELMAN

Every composer must cope with timings and must continually decide whether to use click or not. Many composers use it, but most wish that technical reasons didn't necessitate click, and that it wasn't frequently so overemphasized. Jerry Goldsmith makes this clear: "One of the things I've noticed about books on film scoring is that they concentrate too much on click tracks. All of that sort of stuff can be taught in two hours. Learn how to write music! Learn how to conduct and get more expression in the music. The technical part is a much overrated thing. Of course, at times you've *got* to use click, there's no question about it."

James Horner works out all of his math by himself. "I indicate my own punches and streamers, and tempo markings [on the top of score pages]. Lately, as I've become more comfortable being controlled less by the mathematics, I'm starting to use it to my advantage. I bend time a tremendous amount in conducting but yet I always know where I am in the score as opposed to the picture. Each performance is tremendously different because I've speeded up in one place and inflected something differently in another place; it is just much more musical to work that way."

"I would love it if I never used click tracks," says Allyn Ferguson, "but unfortunately in this day and age, the time element being what it is, I do use clicks when necessary. I think they're necessary for big chases and things like that where, if you're doing a contemporary score, a click track is almost imperative. When I go to England, if I conduct to a click track I'm the only one who hears the click and they follow me. And that's a joy to me because I can then play with it. And when I know I don't have to be right on it I can lay back or whatever I want to do."

Bruce Broughton uses a click only when he needs to. "I use it for quick tempo things. Anything where I think the orchestra needs to be kept together, either because I can't conduct it accurately enough, or because they can't play it accurately enough. I use it for chases, for fast dramatic scenes, and things that will have possibly a lot of quick metrical changes (if they're not easily conductible). Anything that will get the rehearsal down quicker. I would say I'm at least 50:50 click and free time, with probably a little bit more free time."

John Barry says, "I hate clicks; they screw up performance. But sometimes I'll use them just to ease technical things. Otherwise, I love the give and take of free performance." For the James Bond movies, he doesn't use click on the rhythm cues and his solution for the ever-present problem of getting the rhythm section and the orchestra to hear well enough with the drums in the isolation booth is to have just the drums in the headset, "but I haven't used drums in the Bond things for quite a while. There's percussion but not drums. I write the rhythms orchestrally rather than with a dance set. Like in *Body Heat* [1981] it was mostly just bass guitar, and guitar. I try to keep away from drums, creating the mood with a string **pad**[2] and then the guitar creating the rhythmic movement."

Music editor Gene Marks finds that clicks are used much more now than in the past. Increased emphasis on the contemporary rhythm section has contributed to this change in scoring stage technique. "Coupled with that is the use of more and more electronic instruments." Composer Gerald Fried uses click most of the time now. "Especially with electronic overdubbing now," he says, "it's almost mandatory."

When timing errors occur on the scoring stage, corrections will need to be made. The methods for doing this are discussed beginning on page 355.

TIMINGS WITH A POCKET CALCULATOR

Click books and computer programs are very convenient resources but they are not indispensable. All calculations can be done with a pocket calculator alone. This method is not as easy as using the click book and the newcomer to films is advised to stay with the click book until he is thoroughly confident—then he may find the calculator method given in Appendix E useful. The advantage of this method is that one is never dependent on a click book.

USING VIDEORECORDERS AND SMPTE TIME CODES

It is standard procedure today for the composer to take home a videocassette of the work print as a convenient way to work. Be sure to tell the music editor (or postproduction

---

[2] Pad: sustained harmony.

supervisor or music supervisor) which one of the standard VCR formats you work with at home: ¾" Umatic, ½" VHS, or ½" Betamax.

Whatever the format, the copy should be made with the SMPTE time code burned (inserted) into the picture. SMPTE is the acronym for the Society of Motion Picture and Television Engineers, a standards-setting association. The SMPTE time code is a series of digital audio pulses which can be recorded on audiotape. These pulses encode numbers that give the precise timing address of any point on the tape in terms of hours, minutes, seconds, and parts of seconds (after an arbitrary start mark). They are displayed on the screen as shown in Figure 10-2. The first number on the left is usually assigned the number of the reel rather than the hour, the second window reads minutes, and the third reads seconds. The window on the right reads as one of the following:

1. Tenths of a second (easily identifiable because the counter sequences from 0 to 9)
2. Hundredths of a second (counter sequences 0-99)
3. Videoframes (there are 30 video frames per second so this counter sequences from 0-29)

The difference between television's 30 frames per second and motion-picture film's 24 frames per second should cause no difficulty in determining timings from a videotape. Just convert the frames into their decimal equivalents by dividing the number of extra frames by the total number of video frames per second. In Figure 10-2, divide the 27 by 30, which equals :00.9 seconds. (If that counter is measuring hundredths, the 27 already refers to :00.27.) But whether your timings are calibrated in video frames (at 30 frs./sec.) or motion-picture frames (at 24 frs./sec.), THE CLICK TRACK TEMPOS AS READ ON THE DIGITAL METRONOME ARE ALWAYS CALIBRATED IN MOTION-PICTURE FRAMES. This causes no change in working out your hits so long as the timings are measured in seconds (as opposed to frames or footages).

DROP-FRAME OR NON-DROP-FRAME?

Before your videocassette is made, you may be asked if you want the SMPTE time code in drop-frame or non-drop-frame format. Don't panic. This is just one of a large number of technical considerations in the television and film world that the engineers must deal with. It is safe to order your video copy with time code to run in drop-frame mode; by doing so you will be prepared to interface with integrated video systems. The Auricle Time Processor computer program specifies drop-frame, and other computer timing

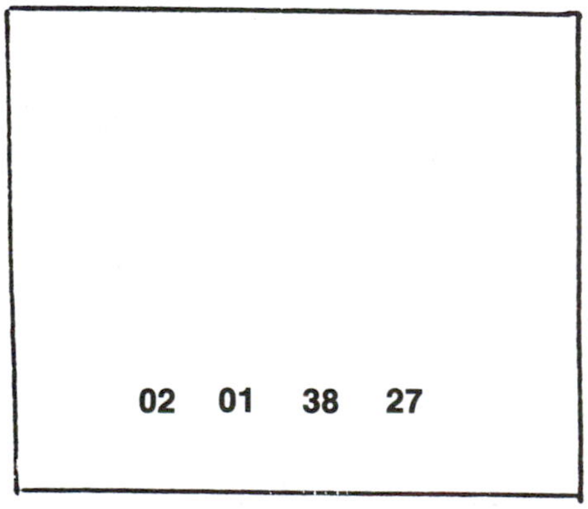

02 01 38 27

FIGURE 10-2
SMPTE time code on videotape.

programs will specify their individual requirements. (For a more complete description, see Appendix F.)

AVOIDING CONFUSION IN MATH PROBLEMS

Working out the timing calculations always consumes valuable time that you would rather spend composing. Sometimes in the middle of an anxious all-nighter while pushing to finish the next day's cues, the math can be burdensome, even confusing at first. In all cases IT IS VITAL THAT YOU KEEP CLEARLY IN MIND WHAT UNITS YOU ARE WORKING WITH. Is it seconds and decimal fractions of seconds? Beats and parts of beats? Video frames, motion-picture frames, 35mm footages, 16mm footages? Normally you can control this by asking your music editor for the format you want to work with.

CUE TIMINGS VS. SMPTE TIMINGS. When you have received the videocassette dub and timing sheets, the SMPTE time code may not read the same as the music editor's individual cue timings, since the code on the cassette is continuous from an arbitrary start mark at the head of a reel. The music editor sets a new zero for the start of each cue. Nonetheless individual timings can be read from the SMPTE code for any scene by subtracting the scene's starting time from each subsequent timing during the scene. It is best to ask for timing notes that provide both the cue timings and the cumulative timings for the reel (as in Figure 5-6). This is a big help in relating the scene to the overall show and helps locate the scene in the videocassette. It also facilitates communication with the music editor if he has the same timings on his cassette. Request that the music editor work with a videocassette. It's a very valuable tool for eventually syncing the score to the film. If you both have cassettes, it is imperative that both tape copies be made with the code starting on exactly the same frame of picture (and in the same drop-frame or non-drop-frame format).

HARDWARE AND SOFTWARE

In an era of rapidly developing computer technology, several computer programs for solving music-timing problems in films and television received attention and praise from Hollywood composers and music editors in 1987/1988. The Auricle Time Processor, developed by composer Ron Grant and his brother, software writer Richard Grant, and released in 1984, is a system set up to deal with the composer's need to quickly find the best tempos and the best options for hitting cues, and to provide a programmed, variable click for the musicians to hear when recording. This click can have programmed ritards and accelerandos as well as subtler, undetectable tempo changes that allow the film hits to come in more natural and acceptable places in the music. It can provide 7/8 and 5/8 meters by combining different building-block units. Corrections can be made quickly on the scoring stage.

Data for the film hits are entered into the computer, where they are displayed on the computer screen against a grid representing the position of the clicks at any chosen tempo (but not limited to the eighth-frame calibrations of the Knudson click system). This "time map" gives a visual display of the way the film hits and music beats relate. Trial runs of different tempos indicate quickly and graphically which tempos provide the best "hit" opportunities. The program runs on the inexpensive Commodore-64 computer, chosen by the inventors for its portability and inexpensive replaceability, as well as for its unpitched click and its color options.[3]

---

[3] The Auricle Time Processor was awarded an Oscar for technical achievement in 1987.

The Streamline Music Scoring System (developed by Bob Badami and Bill and Dick Bernstein) essentially attacks the same problems, but from the slightly different stance of the music editor, who must make any sync system interface with the other equipment and standards of his craft. As described by music editor and coinventor Bob Badami, "At the heart of Streamline is a music calculator that solves the mathematical problems posed by linking rates with timings and beats. Using a spreadsheet-like environment, the user can design or model cues to whatever degree of complexity is required. Rates are referred to either in click rates or metronome settings. It provides a variable click plus warning streamers offered at click starts. It offers streamers and punches in selectable colors that can be quickly changed, deleted, or added at the scoring session. It also includes a play map of the finished cue in a format similar to written music with bar count, cumulative

FIGURE 10-3

Clicks, streamers, and punches chart (*Beverly Hills II,* prepared by Bob Badami on Streamline Music Scoring System).

GRAPHICS MENU — Cue: COPDEMO2

	Bar/Beat	Beats	Time	Type	Color/# Free
--> 1.	1/1	1.00	02:47:29	clix_on	yellow/8
2.	1/1	1.00	02:47:29	streamer	green
3.	4/1	13.00	02:53:28	streamer	white
4.	7/1	23.00	02:58:26	streamer	white
5.	10/1	35.00	03:04:23	clix_off	
6.	10/1	35.00	03:04:23	streamer	blue
7.	11/1	39.00	03:06:23	punch	
8.	13/1	45.00	03:09:24	streamer	white
9.	14/1	49.00	03:11:23	punch	
10.	16/1	57.00	03:15:21	punch	
11.	18/1	63.00	03:18:20	streamer	white
12.	20/1	69.00	03:21:21	streamer	white
13.	20/1	69.00	03:21:21	clix_on	yellow/4
--> 14.	26/1	93.00	03:29:22	streamer	white
15.	30/1	109.00	03:35:02	streamer	white
16.	38/1	139.00	03:45:04	streamer	white
17.	39/1	143.00	03:46:22	punch	
18.	40/1	147.00	03:48:24	punch	
19.	41/1	151.00	03:51:08	punch	
20.	42/1	155.00	03:54:06	clix_off	

Enter Delete Import Clear Quit

beat count, time or footage of each bar start, and rate changes. As each click plays, its corresponding mark lights up, providing a visual guide to the progress of the music." The program runs on IBM PC–compatible computers. Figures 10-3 is a printout of a "graphic menu" created by Streamline indicating the information regarding clicks, punches, and streamers for a hypothetical cue.[4]

Both systems have been used on many films and television episodes. Lorimar-Telepictures, for example, used both the Badami-Bernstein Streamline System and the Auricle Time Processor in 1987. Music editors also speak favorably of Roy Prendergast's VideoScore program, a similar but proprietary system used by music editors at Prendergast's Music Design editorial service. This program also adds streamers and punches very flexibly. Prendergast describes VideoScore as a work tool that has "taken the place of the Moviola as an editorial workbench."

Among Macintosh computer programs that now address film-scoring timing needs are Opcode's Cue and Digidesign's Q-Sheet, while Mark of the Unicorn's Performer and Opcode's Vision sequencing programs respond to SMPTE time code.

In using any computerized timing program, a point to be considered on a cue-to-cue basis is whether the time that is required to enter the timing data for that cue saves a significant amount of time when setting up the right tempo and programming any tempo variations. Some composers do use these programs for preparing all of their music timings. This does not obligate the conductor to use the click on the scoring stage: for a recent television movie Addison only used click on two cues, though the entire score was programmed on Auricle. As he says, this can be very reassuring. "Supposing one had a very tight recording schedule and one got behind, I might decide to simply do certain cues on the click because I know that the fitting will be dead accurate."

---

[4]The Streamline Music Scoring System was awarded as Oscar for technical achievement in 1989.

PART 4

COMPOSING

CHAPTER 11
PLAYING THE DRAMA

There's a certain thing that happens when I've done it right. It's a certain chill I get when I really "get" a scene. There are certain scenes you know are right.
HENRY MANCINI

If the choice is between a great idea or a sincere expression of the film, which do you choose? If possible, try for both. Short of that, tune in to the film, get inside its texture and attitude, and be sincere. More often than not, a sincere (even if unclever) score will serve the film better than a clever idea with no heart.

AUDIENCE EXPECTATIONS

"We're writing for a certain audience," Craig Safan observes, "and that audience has certain expectations. You have to be very careful in any dramatic art, whether you're a playwright or a film composer, to know what these expectations are, because that's your whole tool of manipulation.

"You excite an audience in a certain way, and if you betray them they won't want to go to see your movie. And musically, you can betray your audience. You have to be very careful about that." These expectations are, for the most part, associated with specific genres of films, and are based upon successful films within that genre. The tradition and precedents can go back decades, as they do with Westerns and war dramas, or they can develop more or less contemporaneously, as they have with space/fantasy films like *Star Wars* (1977), *Close Encounters of the Third Kind* (1977), and *E.T.* (1982). These expectations are associated as much with the *function* of the score as the style. The score must do what the audience expects it to do at all the right places—to lift them up, to excite them, to make them curious, and to move them.

DON'T TIP THE STORY

The composer knows how the film is going to end but the audience doesn't. He knows who wins the big race, who walks off into the sunset with whom, who dies before the closing credits. There are times when the director will want music to suggest potential terror before we would otherwise realize it, or help the audience to feel the growing bond between two people even before the characters themselves are fully aware of it. But you don't want to give away the ending before it happens. Marvin Hamlisch faced this challenge while he was working on *Sophie's Choice* (1982): "When you're a composer, you've seen all two or three hours of the film. Now, the thing is, you know that that woman had to make that choice, but the audience doesn't in the first hour and a half. They don't know. So musically, you don't want to tip that off, yet it's part of her. And musically, you have to somehow have that be a part of her theme, and yet not let that dominate.

Sophie wanted to survive, even given that choice. She was still alive." So the essence of the character and/or the circumstances becomes part of the score without revealing the plot in any way. This makes the drama that much stronger.

WHOSE POINT OF VIEW TO PLAY?

Do you play the audience's point of view, or the character's point of view? If you play from the audience's viewpoint, you are scoring their emotional reactions to the film. They may not be reacting as the characters are, or they may know more than the characters do. Watching *Nine to Five* (1980), the audience might laugh when Lily Tomlin steals a corpse on a gurney from the hospital (thinking it is her boss whom she's killed). But within the scene, Tomlin's character is dead serious—she thinks she is in a lot of trouble. The audience knows she's not. This situation might have been played from either the character's terrified point of view, or the audience's. What did Charles Fox do? "I originally played it a little more broadly, from the audience's point of view, allowing them to have a little more of a good time as they watched. The director, Colin Higgins, liked it very much, thought it was amusing, but thought it would be better to play it from the three girls' point of view—they thought they really had actually killed him. So I toned it down, and reapproached it so the music had a little more of their feelings in it."

It will always pay to explore both approaches when this question comes up, and discuss it thoroughly with the director, with demonstration if possible. (See Figures 11-1a and b.)

MAIN TITLES

Main-title music can say to the audience, "The movie you are about to see is . . ." and then establish the overall tone and attitude of the film, or prime the audience's expectation as to what will follow. In cases where the film plays on more than one level—as does *Foul Play* (1978, Charles Fox), which combines romance, comedy, action, and adventure—the composer will likely emphasize just one dramatic element in the score over the main titles. Often the opening scenes dictate which element will be most appropriate. If the film starts with a murder during the main titles, you aren't likely to score it with a romantic pop song—unless you are making an ironic statement. It is appropriate for *Foul Play* to start with a romantic song because Charles Fox's Main-Title music spins off of Goldie Hawn as she leaves a cocktail party, having been told by a friend she should develop more of a social life. Then the mystery/action/adventure quickly follows.

MAIN-TITLE MUSIC CAN SUGGEST THE DRAMA BEFORE IT OCCURS. In *Agnes of God* (1983), Georges Delerue begins with soft string entrances that get progressively more intense. The film's title is religious, and the visuals during the main titles are of the church. But the music tells you immediately that there is more to this film than just the story of a pious nun. It sets up the experience for you, and leads you to expect tension, problems, difficult resolutions. (See Figure 11-2.)

UNDERSCORING THE DIALOGUE

Support the drama without killing the dialogue—that's the challenge. Some classic guidelines for dialogue underscoring are:

1. Voice-overs are more difficult to understand. When the audience can see the lips of the person speaking they can understand the words more easily (because of the chance to lip-read). Conversely, voice-overs, group dialogue, or narration where moving lips are not visible require more caution in underscoring.

FIGURE 11-1a

Nine to Five M-7/1 Violet Steals Body Charles Fox

FIGURE 11-1b
Nine to Five M-7/2 Violet Steals Body Charles Fox

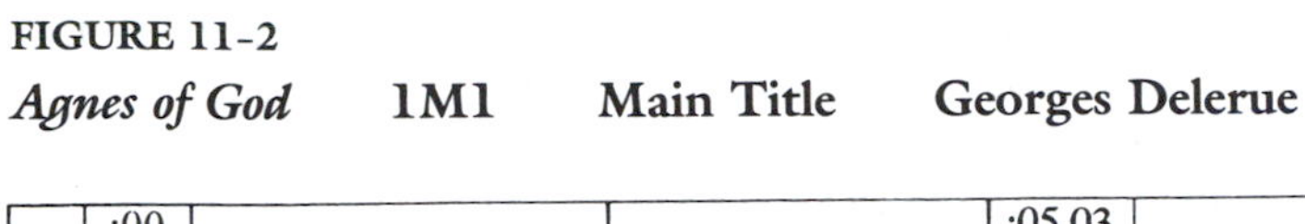

FIGURE 11-2

Agnes of God 1M1 Main Title Georges Delerue

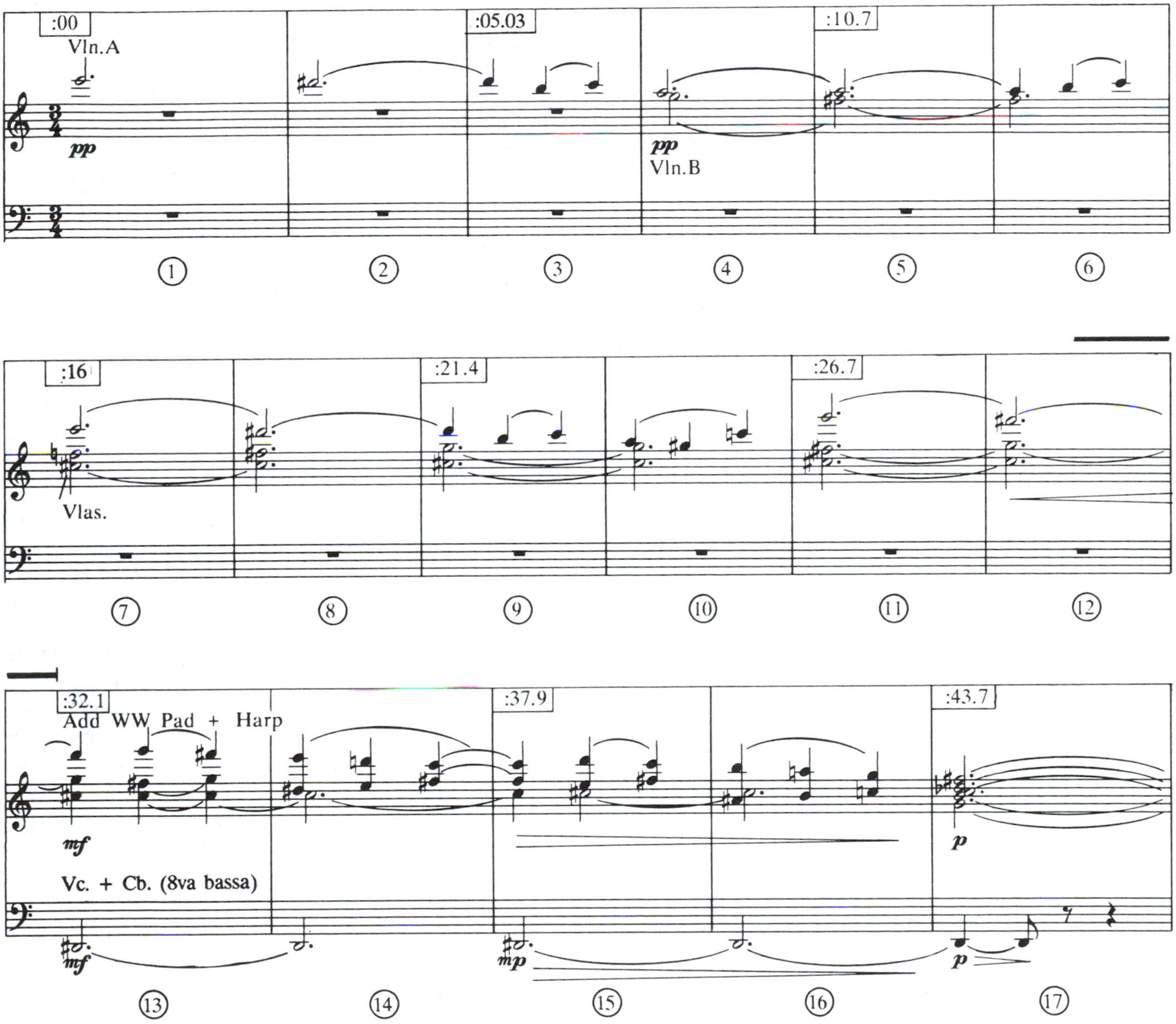

:00
Vln.A
pp
:05.03
pp
Vln.B
:10.7
1
2
3
4
5
6
:16
Vlas.
:21.4
:26.7
7
8
9
10
11
12
:32.1
Add WW Pad + Harp
mf
Vc. + Cb. (8va bassa)
mf
:37.9
mp
:43.7
p
p
13
14
15
16
17

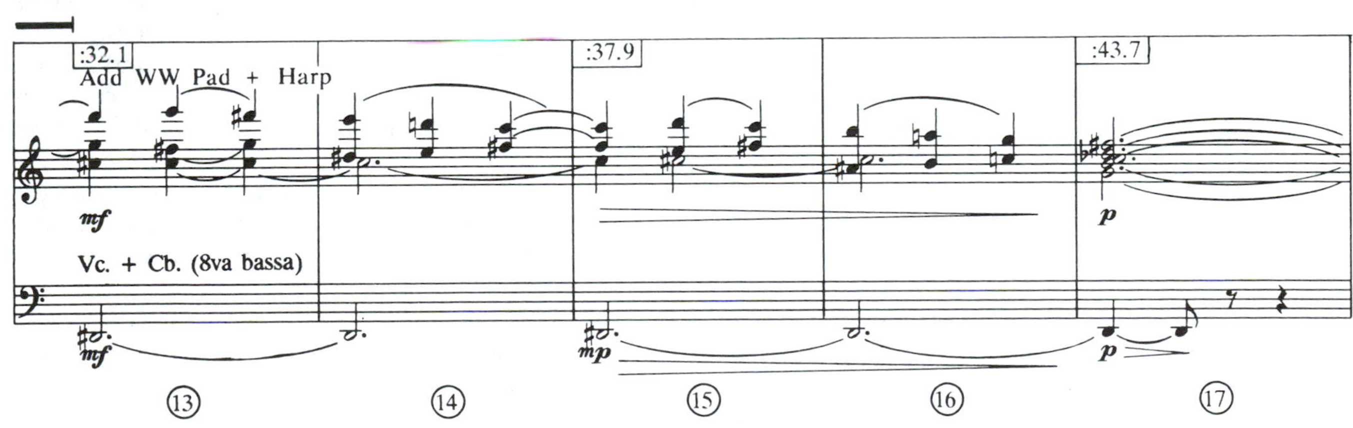

2. Smooth musical textures are less intrusive. Speaking has an articulated textured that stands out better against smooth, legato instrumental textures that do not contain other elements of distraction like large melodic skips, or accents.

3. Keep underscoring out of the voice range. In *Dragonslayer* (1981), Alex North had to underscore action scenes with the dragon and the girl being chased, without hurting the dialogue. "This may be old hat but it's a question of orchestrating it out of the vocal range of the dialogue. With Orson Welles—doing *Sound and the Fury* [1959]—I avoided using bass clarinet and low instruments so they would not conflict with his voice range."

However, the technique of clearing the speaking voice range does not always work. In the television documentary *Ladybird Johnson's Visit to Washington, D.C.* (1964, Wright), the narration was continuous, as Mrs. Johnson talked about Washington's historic buildings and parks. The first lady had been coached to read her lines in a breathy, feminine voice, and the recording was done in documentary style, mostly outdoors with wind and outdoor ambience. Music was clearly needed. The music was scored out of her voice range and was smooth in texture to avoid distracting from her voice. Everybody loved the music at the recording sessions, but when it was played back under her voice she was hard to understand—her voice was so breathy it didn't have any resonance. As it turned out, she actually needed some *support* in her speaking range to give body to her voice, so the rewrite incorporated low G string violins, and French horns and low flutes, all in her voice range, and it immediately worked. Her voice seemed to take on the body of the supporting instruments.

4. Accents and solos can be distracting. North avoids as much as possible any accents in the music, and any solo instruments. He believes that solos "take your mind away from the words, and with solos you're aware of the single instrument." Mellow solos like alto flute and single-note piano can work well under dialogue, but should be mixed softer than they might otherwise be, especially in a mono mix.

5. Avoid extreme highs and lows. Such sounds are intrusive, as are percussive sounds and staccato textures. Experienced sound mixers agree. "No piccolos, or anything really loud under dialogue," suggests recording engineer Dan Wallin. Dubbing mixer Don MacDougall finds that "high woodwinds (piccolo, flute, clarinet) are very difficult with quiet scenes, and brass—things that are percussive. French horns work beautifully. Oboe and English horn are wonderful."

6. Don't overwrite. MacDougall is mostly concerned that "today's composers have a tendency to be a little too busy under dialogue, too fast and hurried. I think maybe the one thing that I find more than anything is this busyness of the background music when it should not be."

Note the effective examples of underscoring in Figures 11-3 and 11-4.

Even solo trumpet *can* work under dialogue, if used with sensitivity. For an example of this, listen to another cue in *Return of the Jedi* (1983) during which Princess Leia and Luke talk about their families.

USING THE APPROPRIATE MUSICAL LANGUAGE

I think the best way to use music is when it's a complement of the film, instead of being an illustration. MAURICE JARRE

I've always said you're putting an emotional hook into the nose of the audience and moving them around this way emotionally while the picture's going on. ALEXANDER COURAGE

Many styles of music already contain visual and emotional associations. Gregorian chant reminds us of monks in a monastery; Dixieland jazz reminds us of New Orleans;

FIGURE 11-3

Star Trek II: The Wrath of Khan M23/30 Khan James Horner

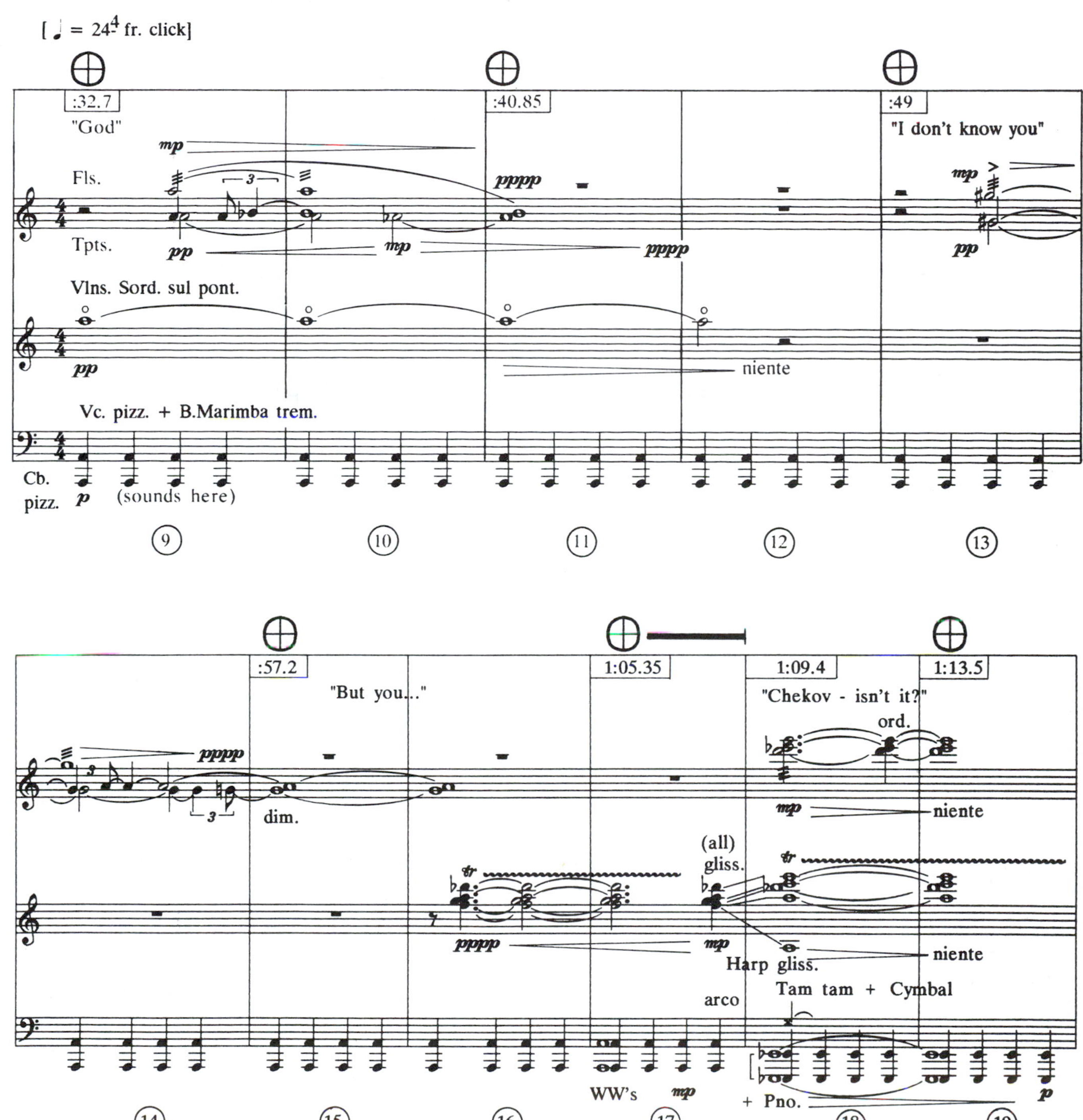

FIGURE 11-4

Return of the Jedi R9 Pt. 2 Brother and Sister John Williams
Orchestrated by Herb Spencer

(a)

FIGURE 11-4 (a) (*Continued*)

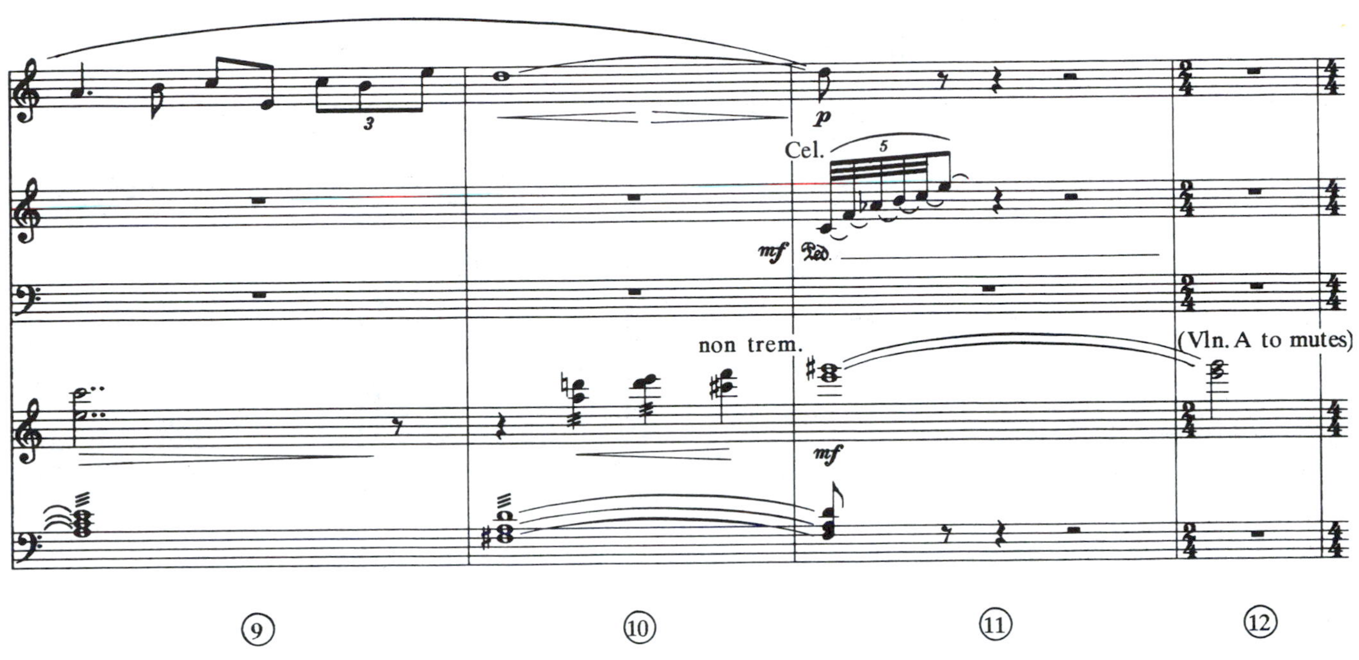

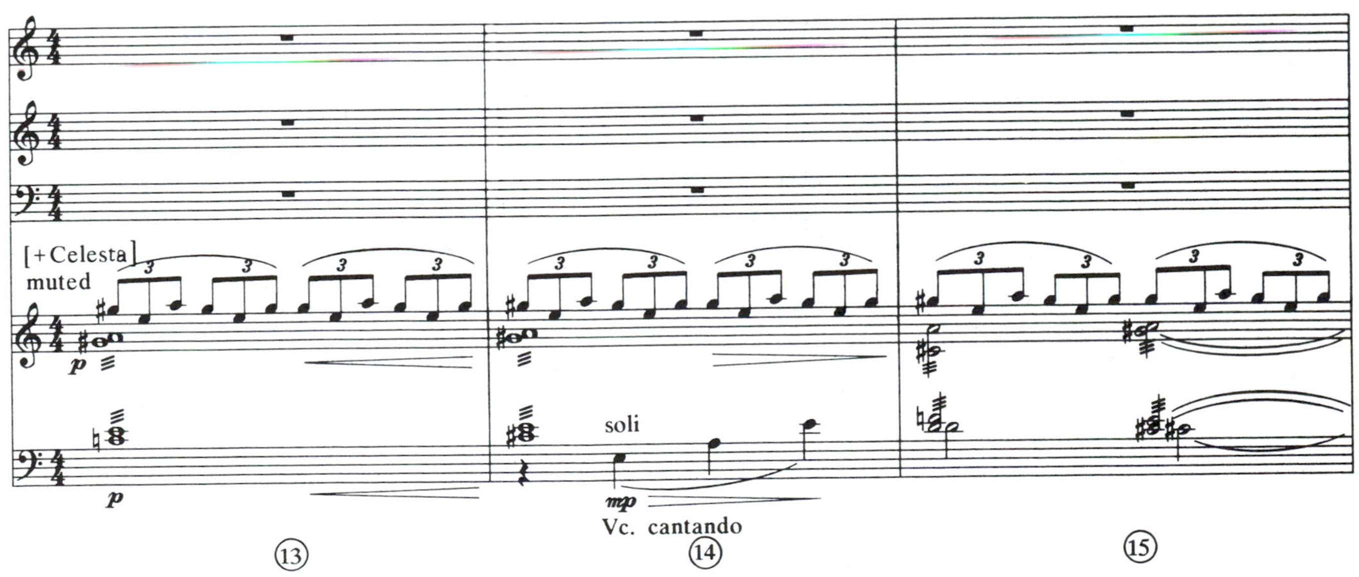

FIGURE 11-4 (a) (*Continued*)

FIGURE 11-4 (*Continued*)

(b)

Woody Guthrie reminds us of the dust bowl in the thirties. Film music can draw upon the power of these musical associations in subtle but potent ways.

Review your notes on your score's concept, and consider the appropriateness of the various musical choices you have made. Does anything seem out of place with the drama? If so, did you intend irony or an "against-the-grain" musical language, or is this accidental?

PLAYING THE OVERVIEW

We have discussed playing the overview and not necessarily the specific emotions of the scene (see Chapter 7). James Horner's score for *Testament* (1983) rarely plays the specific emotions of the moment. And scenes are left unscored to allow the drama itself to create the overview emotion. Often, spotting decisions have a direct effect on the dramatic approach of a composer. Horner wanted to avoid being maudlin.

When Jane Alexander searches for her dead son's lost toy, and later when she hears her husband's last message, there is no score. "It plays so well without music," says Horner. "It's so emotional and I felt that if I added music to that, all I would be doing is making it high anxiety. There is nothing I could say that would transcend that mood, or would enhance that mood. Whereas in the school-play scene, the music can play there. What it does is it pulls you out of the scene. IN A CERTAIN SENSE, IT COMMENTS ON THE WHOLE SCENE. AND IT IS LESS LITERAL, but when she is running around and she is listening to his last message . . . we talked about putting music on the last message and it was too early on in the film to do that. Whereas, running around, where she is looking for the bear, we both felt that we didn't want music there because there was no way that the music could really transform that into anything different. I didn't want to comment on the scene musically."

When music adds another dimension, another personalized color or texture, it can begin to function as overview.

PLAYING WHAT THE SCENE IS *REALLY* ABOUT

When you play *against* the picture, it is possible to play *inside* the picture, by playing the overview or the internal emotions inherent in a scene. Director Richard Michaels tells how he accidentally discovered the value of this approach while working on the television movie *Heart of a Champion* (1985):

"This scene toward the end of the picture was the first fight that 'Boom Boom' Mancini lost when he was fighting for the championship. The score that was written was more or less a traditional boxing score. I never envisioned that the music would not be action music, so the composer wrote action music. It didn't quite work. All of a sudden it seemed like there was too much boxing in the movie. And it wasn't really about boxing anyway—it was about a guy trying to win a championship for his father, and he didn't make it. So the music editor suggested taking a piece of music that was really very slow and sad that was actually part of the Main-Title music—when the fighter was a little boy and was looking at his scrapbook—and trying it behind the fight scene. When he said that, I thought, 'That's crazy, that's not even close to what it should be and what's written for that—but let's try it because we don't like what's happening here.' And it was like magic; it transformed the scene. In fact it was so magical, instead of playing the scene with the sound effects foreground and the music background, we took down the sound effects and brought the music up. And the scene became about this boy's disappointment, instead of about the fight. The fight was almost the background to the disappointment. It was wonderful. None of us intended it that way."

In the scene that Michaels describes, the music scores the subtext of the sequence, the emotion beneath the surface, the *real* story.

In *Revolution* (1985) John Corigliano scored the sadness of the American Revolution by playing directly against the first tragic battle with the British. "They have a 7-minute battle scene which is a massacre, with so much sound and noise and killing that it's ear-splitting. I wrote a 6-minute piece about sorrow, about just how terrible this was, which is very slow while the action is very fast."

In *Blue Thunder* (1983), Arthur B. Rubinstein scores the early dialogue scene between Roy Scheider and Candy Clark with a soft, seemingly simple cue that suggests a disturbed and disturbing relationship between the two, and helps the audience to know what's really going on between them. This cue also gets inside the characters' feelings. (See Figure 11-5.)

GETTING INSIDE THE CHARACTER'S FEELINGS

You often need to "get inside" a character to play what the scene is really about. In novels, the author tells you what the characters are feeling, but in film it is often the score that does this. In *Salvador* (1986), Georges Delerue's music reflects the emotions of James Woods and James Belushi as they first see the dead bodies piled on the hilltop. This cue

FIGURE 11-5

Blue Thunder **M-31** **Arthur B. Rubinstein**
Orchestrated by Bill Brohn

continues under dialogue and goes out as they walk away from the bodies. (See Figure 11-6.)

In *That's Life!* (1986), Julie Andrews sits pensively during the family dinner. Gradually the dialogue diminishes in volume and Henry Mancini's music takes over, playing Andrews's mood and feelings rather than the chatter of the family. Her family is oblivious to her anxiety, but the audience knows she is worried about the possibility of a malignant tumor.

A similar situation occurs in *The Way We Were* (1973), during a classroom scene in which the teacher reads Robert Redford's short story. Marvin Hamlisch's music expresses

FIGURE 11-6
Salvador **4M2 El Playon Georges Delerue**

FIGURE 11-6 (*Continued*)

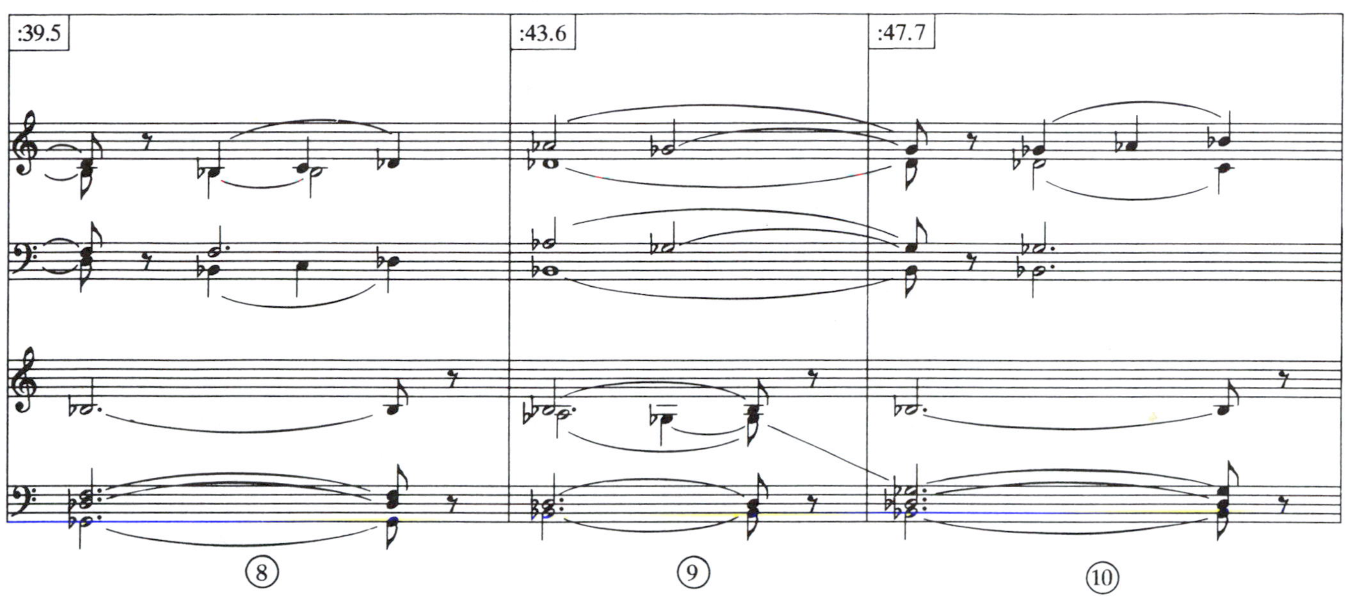

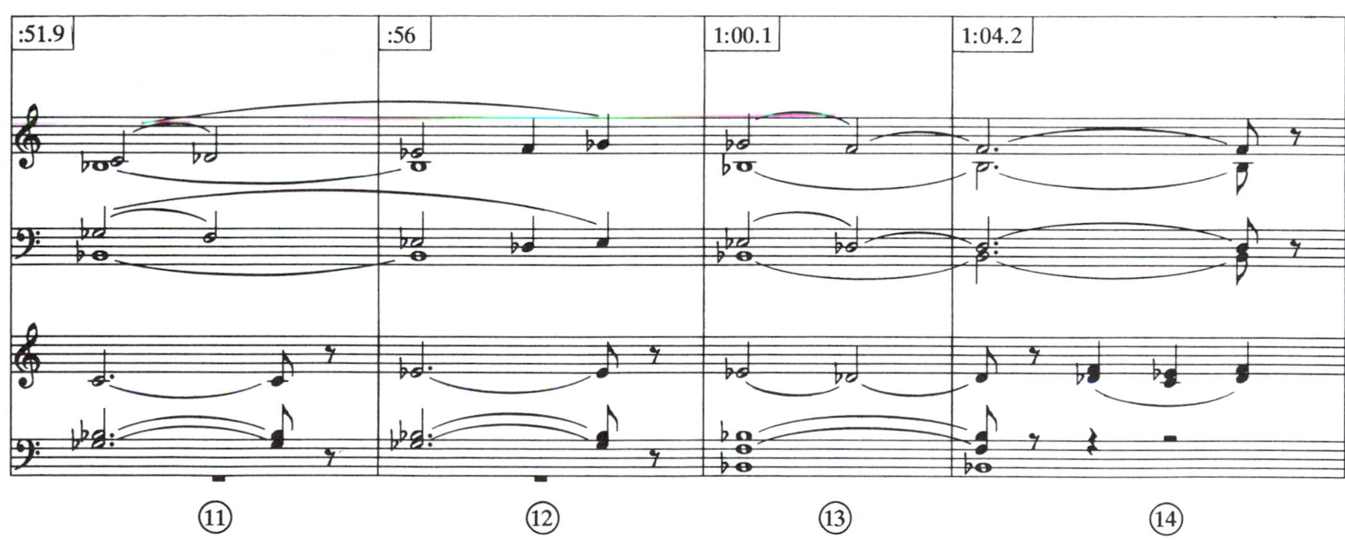

Barbra Streisand's growing admiration for Redford. As the dialogue becomes unimportant, we're learning about Streisand and her emotions.

DE-EMPHASIZING A SCENE

"Most of us are aware of, and do not like, the kind of bad film music that intrudes and italicizes moments that have no need of such emphasis," the late Jerry Fielding observed. "Few realize, however, the ability of music to de-emphasize. Sometimes you look at a scene and think: This is excessively stated, but could I put some music in here that would tone it down? . . . A composer can have a fairly decisive, if subtle, effect on the emphasis in a picture if they'll let him."[1]

LESS IS MORE

If it's a really emotional picture, one of the things I'll be concerned about is that the music doesn't add emotions—because then you start getting close to melodrama. RICHARD MICHAELS, DIRECTOR

That's the subtlety of music, really, it's the subtlety of getting something to start your emotions gurgling, but not going overboard.
MARVIN HAMLISCH

Less is more is an axiom that is difficult to trust. You may look at your score page and wonder how so little could work so well. But in film, you want to aim for just the right amount of music; more than that is always too much. Each film and each score will redefine the limits of the "right amount." Obviously, the right amount for *Close Encounters* (1977) would be too much for an intimate film like *Testament.* In Figure 11-7, notice that Johnny Mandel's score for *The Sandpiper* (1965) is cool and detached from the emotions, lending a dispassionate backdrop to the drama.

For the last scene of *Body Heat* (1981), during which William Hurt confronts Kathleen Turner at the boat house, John Barry used music that was both melodic and melancholy. The score alerts the audience that there *is* a bomb inside and that Hurt might be aware of it. The tension is sustained without being melodramatic. (See Figure 11-8.)

Another example of restrained scoring is shown in Figure 11-9. It accompanies an extremely dramatic moment in *Elephant Man* (1980), when the title character slowly turns around to reveal his face for the first time. Composer John Morris used only strings, playing the sequence with delicacy and touching simplicity.

In *Agnes of God,* Georges Delerue uses simple materials to achieve very dramatic results; the music shown in Figure 11-10 plays during the scene that begins with Anne Bancroft saying, "Let me help you" to Meg Tilly. It works because he is adding music to the texture of a scene that is already very emotional.

Even high levels of dissonance can add drama to a scene without being overstated. At the beginning of the rape sequence in *The Outlaw Josey Wales* (1976), Jerry Fielding begins with a loud piano accent, and then continues with soft strings that almost subliminally play the increasing terror. The harmonic texture is extremely complex, but the soft dynamic level of the divisi strings helps keep the moment understated.

Other understated scores that illustrate this "less is more" philosophy include *Cat People* (1982), *Testament,* and *Sophie's Choice.*

THE SOUND OF SILENCE

You know you can't really listen to two things at once. So if you want something on screen to be heard—don't play. JOHN MORRIS

The art of film scoring involves knowing where to put music, and where *not* to put music. We know this is so in spotting. But even within a cue, silence can be golden. In one of the most touching scenes in *The Elephant Man,* Anne Bancroft is reading *Romeo and Juliet* to the title character. As she slowly leans forward to lightly kiss him, John Morris stops the cue, unresolved—not abruptly, but with a sustained chord as they kiss. After

[1] *Film Music Notebook,* 1977, Volume III, Number 3, pp. 45-46, interview by Paul Seydor.

FIGURE 11-7
The Sandpiper 7/2 **The Seduction** **Johnny Mandel**

some concluding dialogue, the music re-enters with a final resolution of the cue. No music could have been more powerful than that silent moment.

RECURRING SILENCE CAN EMPHASIZE THE DRAMA. Silence can be integrated into the music. We have mentioned the long cues in *48 Hours* (1982) and *Ghostbusters* (1984) that start and stop several times while retaining continuity. In *Brainstorm* (1983) James Horner uses a recurring motif separated by silence (Figure 11-12) to create a feeling of reflection during a scene in which Natalie Wood is alone—just after Christopher Walken has played back her tape (see Figure 14-21 for another excerpt from the same cue).

HIGHLIGHTING

If you build to a specific moment, and then stop the music with an accent, you are highlighting that moment. The effect is always one of *emphasis,* regardless of the film or scene. For example, at the start of *Night Shift* (1982), Burt Bacharach's music goes out as

FIGURE 11-8

Body Heat M12-1 Better Get Him

John Barry
Orchestrated by Al Woodbury

(a)

FIGURE 11-8 (*Continued*)

(b)

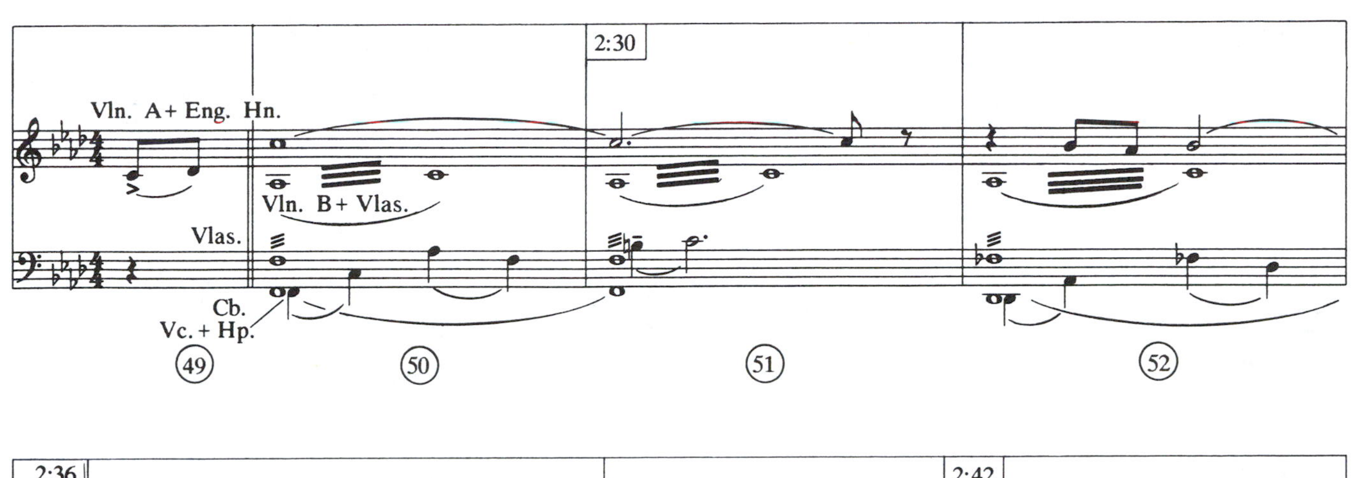

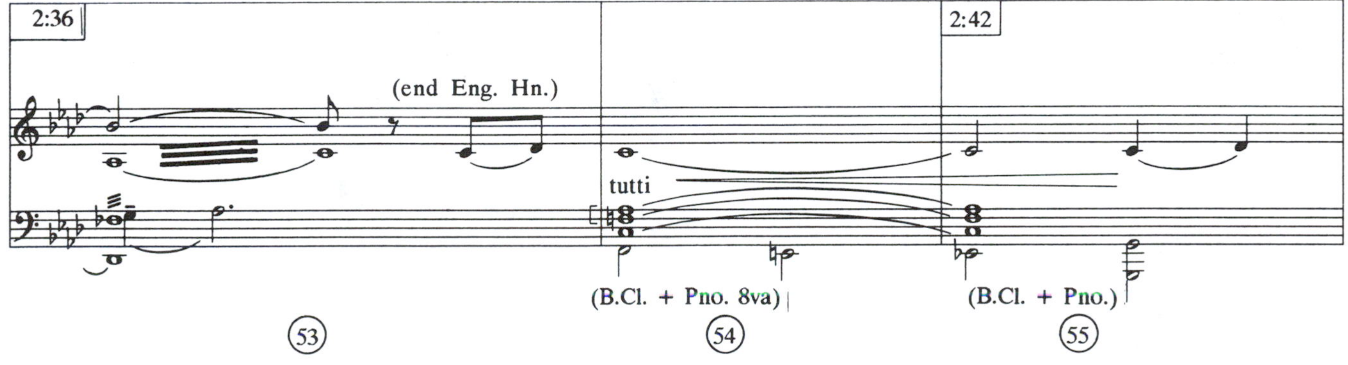

(c)

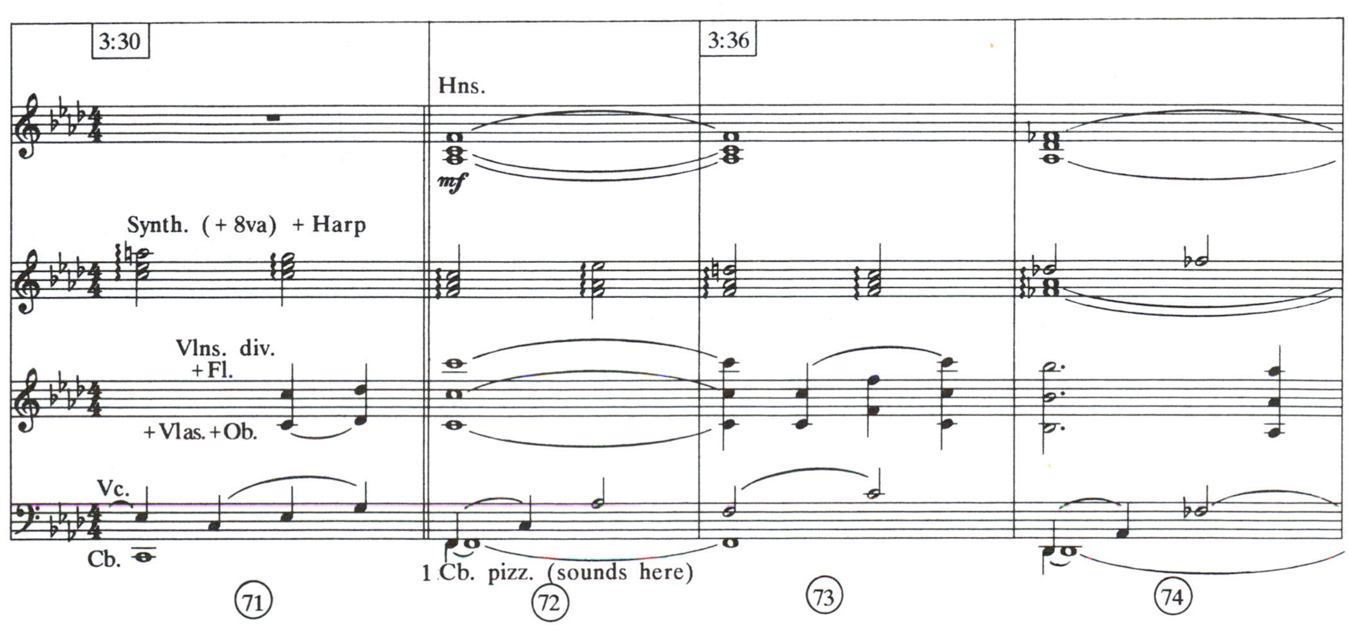

FIGURE 11-8 (*Continued*)

(c)

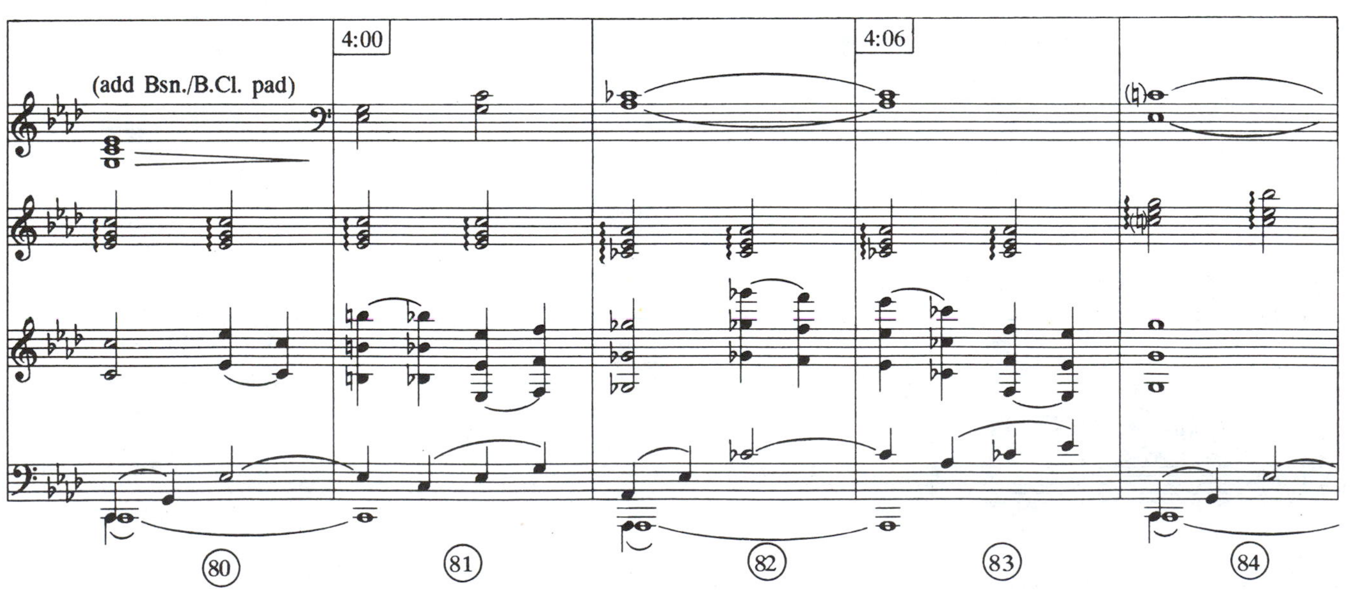

FIGURE 11-9

The Elephant Man M-21 Tear Drop John Morris
Orchestrated by Jack Hayes

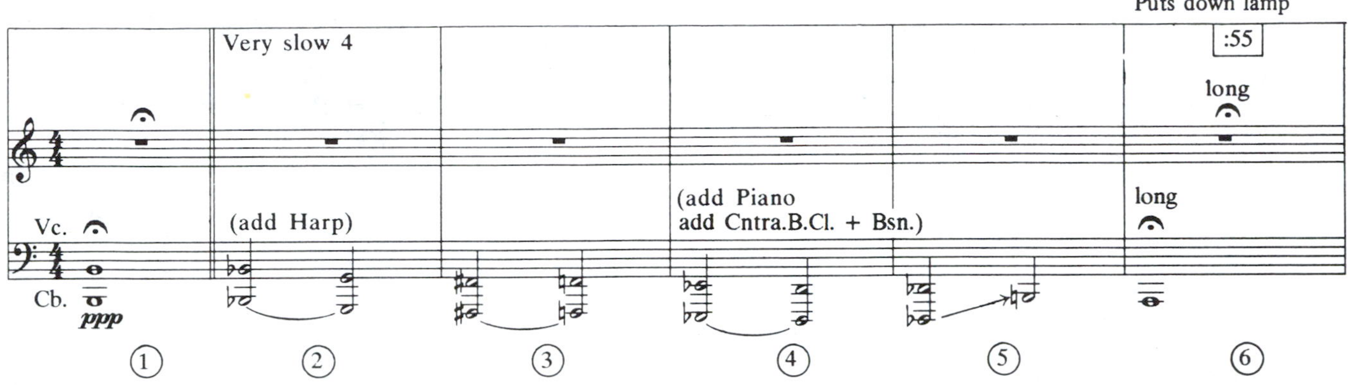

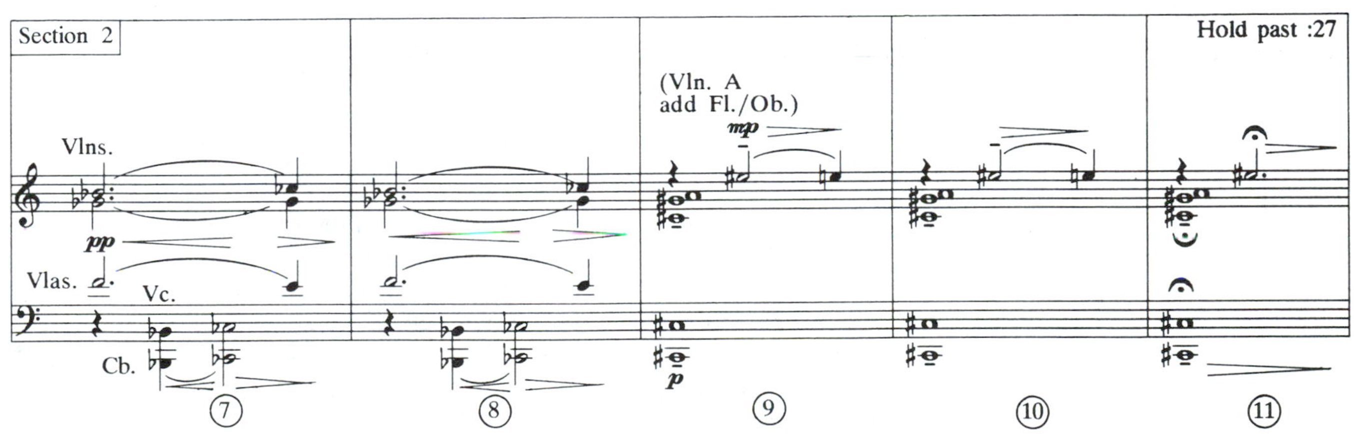

FIGURE 11-10

Agnes of God 7 M1A Let Me Help You Georges Delerue

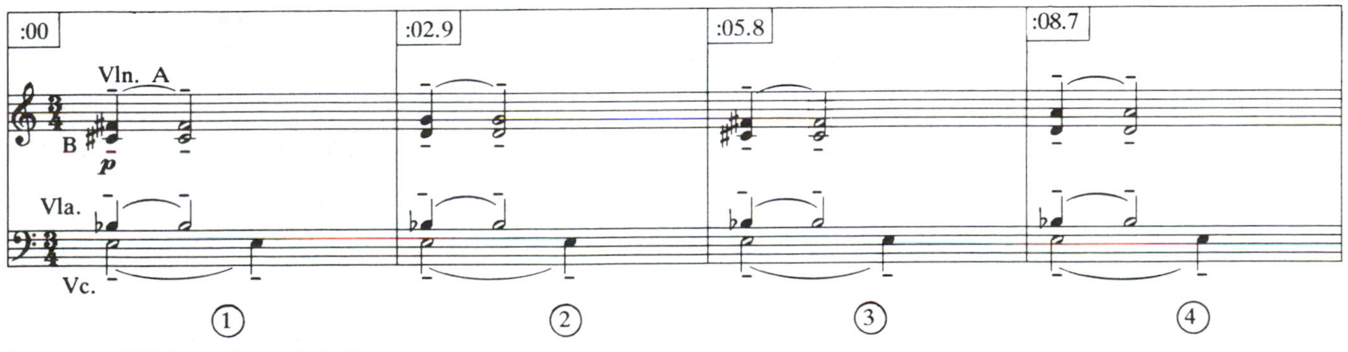

FIGURE 11-10 (*Continued*)

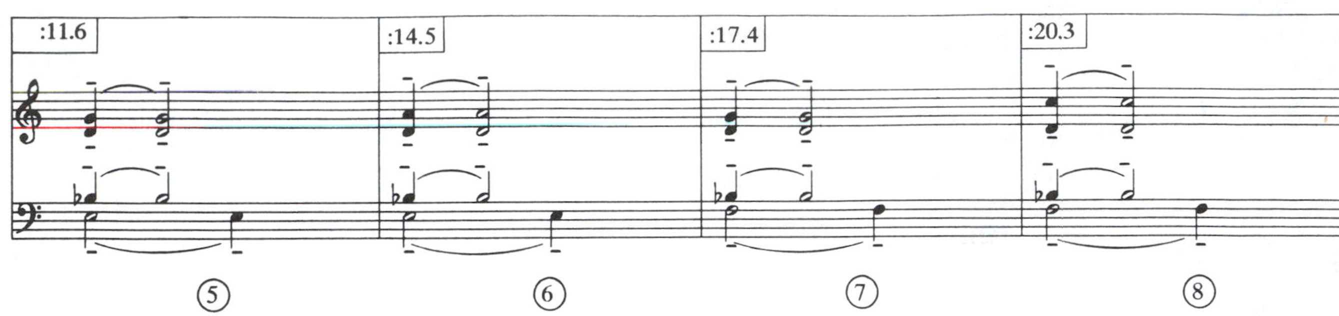

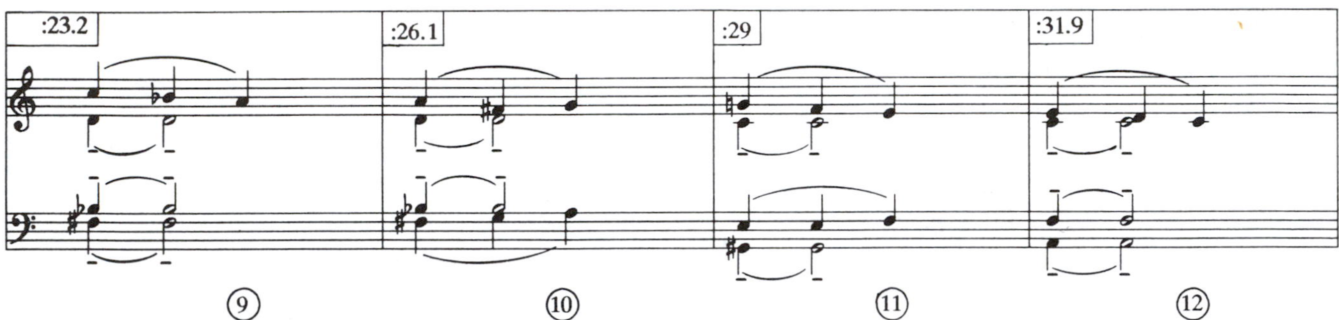

the man falls to the ground. By stopping here, the music highlights the moment, in this case tending to *de*-emphasize the seriousness of the situation.

In *Deathtrap* (1982), Johnny Mandel's music goes out with an accent just before Michael Caine's gun clicks empty, and again just before the arrow strikes Christopher Reeve. And in *White Dawn* (1975) Henry Mancini's music comes to an accented stop just as Warren Oates's knife hits the target, ending a dramatic knife-throwing contest.

In each of these examples, the music stops for emphasis, and the silence becomes a final dramatic accent. This device is often used in comedy, and occurs frequently in John Morris's scores for the Mel Brooks and Gene Wilder films.

RED HERRINGS

Musical **red herrings** are another form of highlighting, in which the music builds to a climax just before something does or doesn't happen. All horror and suspense films use this device. Typically, a red herring ends with a nonthreatening or comical accent—the noise behind the door is just the cat; the strange sounds in the basement become a lonely rat scurrying across the cement floor. In the case of one sequence in *Foul Play,* as Goldie Hawn carefully searches her apartment for something suspicious, the music by Charles Fox builds to an **accent off**[2] to silence as she quickly draws open her curtains. Then, shortly afterwards, she is physically attacked by the menacing "Scarface" as she turns around. The first musical buildup was a red herring; there was no threat behind the curtains—just the open window. Just as we breathe a quick sigh of relief with her, we are jolted into fear and tension as she is attacked (and simultaneously another cue starts). (See Figure 11-13).

[2] Accent off: accented cutoff of the music.

The degree of dramatic musical buildup depends on the overall intention and intensity of the scene. You need to ask, what happens at the climax? Charles Fox describes one scene in *Foul Play* in which a slight buildup was used: "The scene in which the snake moves toward Goldie was clearly not a big buildup because finally Burgess turns around and says softly, 'Oh, there you are' to the snake [the snake is his pet]. So there was no scream involved, no real climax. And she turns and softly says, 'Ooh.' So there was some buildup of anxiety but not much. To be true to the scene, the scene wouldn't have supported doing a lot."

FIGURE 11-11

The Outlaw Josie Wales **9M2 C** **The Violators** **Jerry Fielding**
Orchestrated by Lennie Neihaus

FIGURE 11-11 (*Continued*)

ACCENTING THE DRAMA

Any time the music is highlighting a dramatic moment, the score takes on a more active role. The term *highlighting* has been used here to refer to a buildup to a cutoff for emphasis. If you highlight within a cue, you are *accenting* the drama.

In *Brainstorm,* James Horner accents the stabs of pain Louise Fletcher feels as she succumbs to a heart attack: "There was something about her constantly having these repetitive jabs of pain; as she was trying to make a phone call another jab of pain would hit her, then as she was trying to do something else another jab. It was painful to watch. I didn't know exactly how to score a heart attack; I'd never done that sort of thing before. What I wanted to do was try to enhance this quality of painfulness, and her being alone with it, but not in a way that was underscoring so much as the orchestra being part of the actual heart attack—the experience.

FIGURE 11-12

Brainstorm 6M1 James Horner

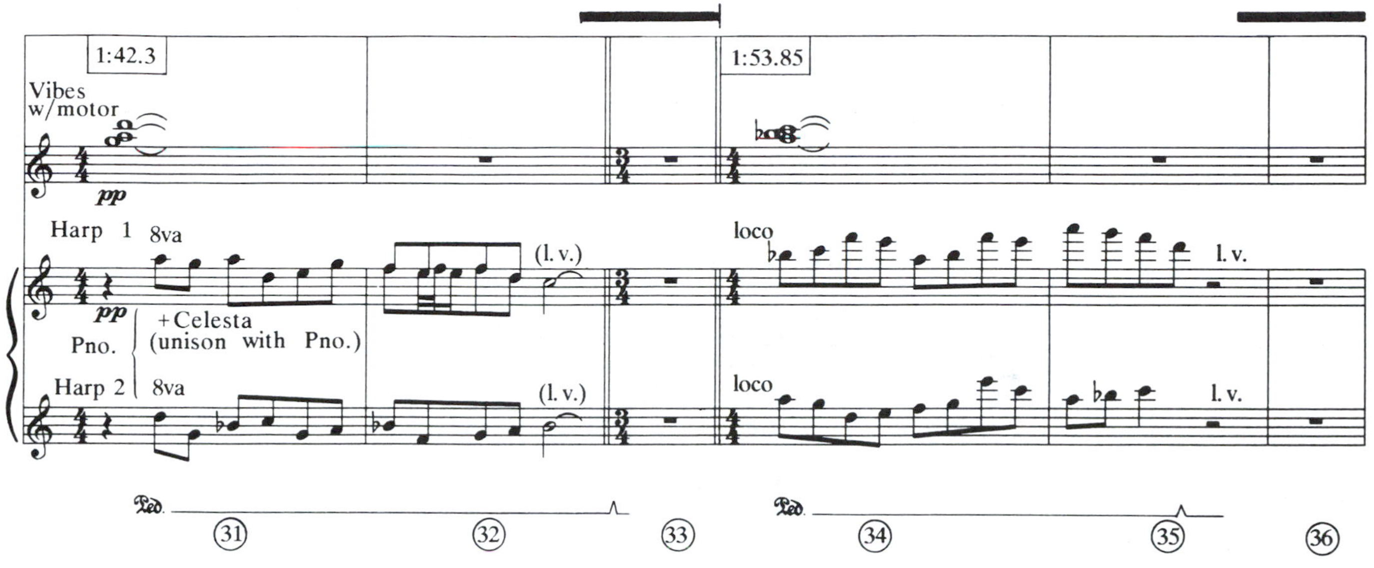

FIGURE 11-12 (*Continued*)

FIGURE 11-13

Foul Play M42 Scarface Charles Fox
Orchestrated by Ruby Raksin

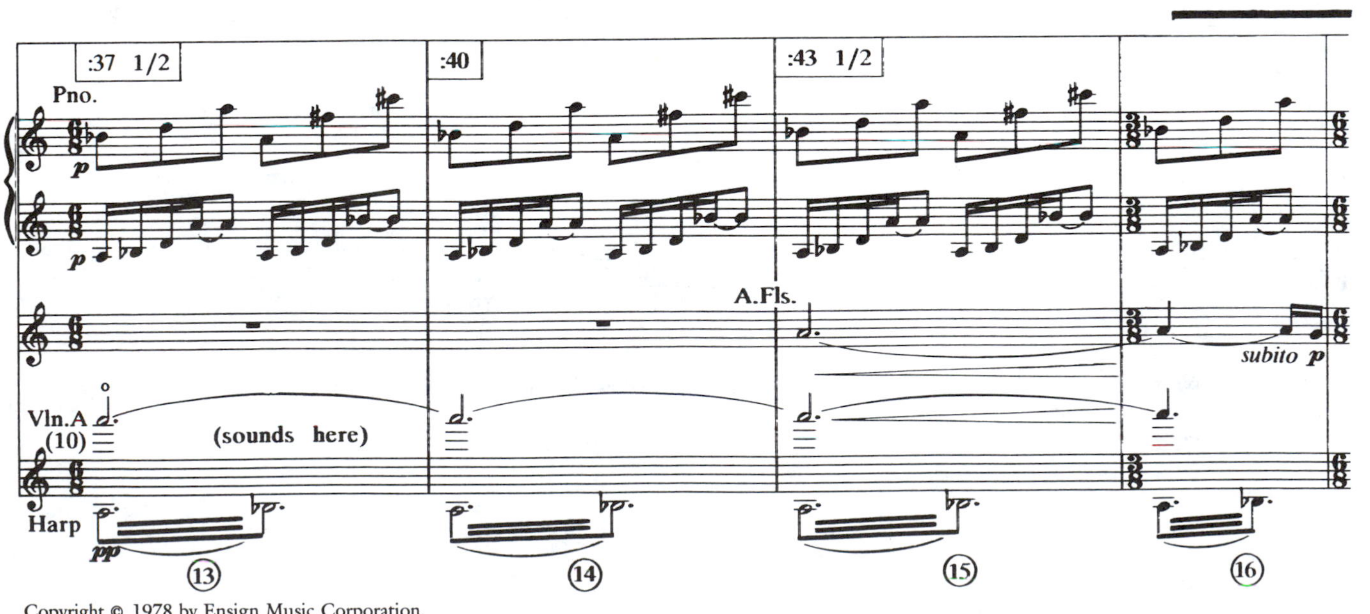

FIGURE 11-13 (*Continued*)

FIGURE 11-13 (*Continued*)

"I had this very Mahlerian figure, with low trumpets—purposely that color. It just keeps repeating; and it emphasized and became like those jabs of pain. I don't very often get into text painting like that, but it was a place where I wanted the heart attack to be as powerful as possible." (See Figure 11-14.)

The film has to be strong enough to accept this kind of approach. Melodramas, suspense films, escape films, and historical dramas are good candidates for this kind of musical support.

SINGLE ACCENTS WITHIN A CUE. If a single musical accent is used to point up a specific cut, person, object, or action within a cue, it may function as a *stinger.* Sometimes the director may feel that an accent in the score is necessary to help emphasize a particular moment. A good example of this occurs in Henry Mancini's score for *Silver Streak* (1976), during the scene in which Gene Wilder is making love to Jill Clayburgh and sees a body suddenly fall into view outside the room. Mancini overlays two sforzando accents into

FIGURE 11-13 (*Continued*)

the texture of an otherwise smooth romantic source cue. These accents help highlight the contrasting action, and heighten the shock value to Wilder and possibly the comedic value to the audience.

SCORING THE FILM LIKE A BALLET

Some directors and composers feel that film is often almost balletic. They equate these moments with a balletic approach to the music. In describing the score he composed for *Shaft's Big Score* (1972), director Gordon Parks says, "Much of it was things like jazz ballets—what we call water ballet—up and down over the bridges and the Hudson River. Helicopters going under the bridges. The helicopters were more or less like ballets. Sort of wild music, disjointed at times."

Referring to his scoring of the television series *Scarecrow and Mrs. King,* Arthur B. Rubinstein says, "I think I treat that show like it's a ballet. You hear things sometimes on some of those episodes I score that are not even film scoring. I will pay no attention to the picture, other than, you start at a certain place, you have a certain locale, you have a certain accent. Other than that, I will not pay attention to what the picture is giving me." In this case, Rubinstein is not musically bringing out the obvious values of the film, but rather adding another dimension perhaps implied by the characters, the locale, and the

FIGURE 11-13 (*Continued*)

situation. And his more balletic approach makes the music almost another character—a narrator, perhaps. In such cases the score often plays the dramatic theme (overview).

John Morris has a solid background in the theater. "I was a dance arranger on Broadway, and I wrote for Bob Fosse, Jerome Robbins, Agnes DeMille, Michael Kidd, Gower Champion—all the wonderful choreographers. Whenever I see anything on the screen in which somebody moves and nobody talks, it's a ballet to me. For instance, in *Elephant Man,* all the drunken people come to torture him in his room at night. And I said, What I'm looking at is a ballet. Pure ballet. The dialogue doesn't mean anything.

FIGURE 11-14

Brainstorm 7M3 James Horner

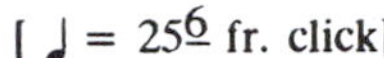

FIGURE 11-14 (*Continued*)

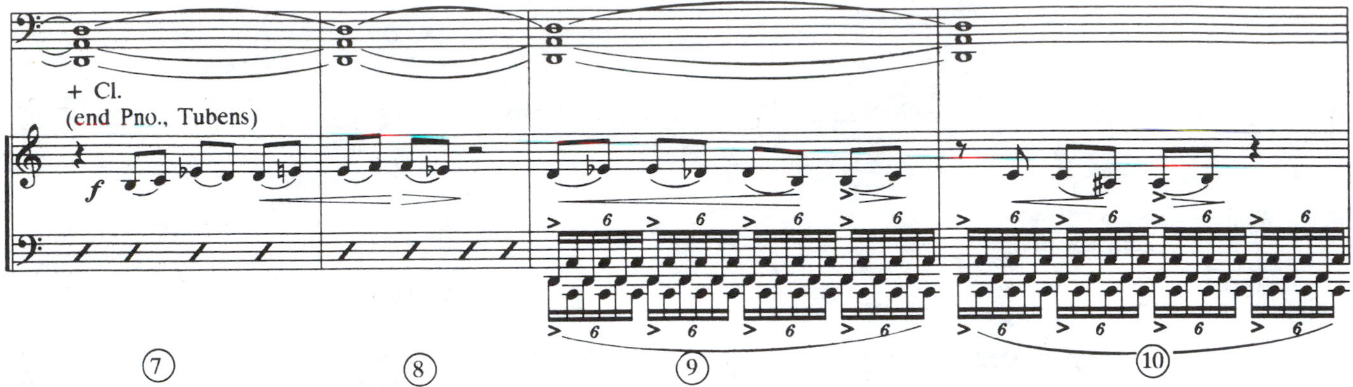

So I scored it like a ballet." He used his theme from the Main Title to do so (see Figure 11-15).

Director Paul Wendkos often thinks of the score as ballet music: "Particularly the way I direct, I try to make a dance out of it, a choreography. You know, the moving cameras, the moving actors, etc. I try to create an event, a behavior, and I find ballet music very effective."

FILMS THAT ILLUSTRATE THIS CHAPTER

ENDING CUES

The Taking of Pelham One Two Three (1974, David Shire). This drama about a hijacked New York subway train allows for a series of accented music outs as the story cuts back and forth between the subway and Walter Matthau at a central command center. (See Figures 14-11, 12, and 13.)

LONG CUES, SHORT CUES

Ghostbusters (1984, Elmer Bernstein). Note the long sectional cue in the library sequence near the beginning of the film, when they first investigate the visiting ghost.

Clue (1985, John Morris) and *Johnny Dangerously* (1984, John Morris). Note the use of short cues in appropriate settings for emphasis and highlighting.

Animal House (1978, Elmer Bernstein). Frequent use of short cues.

PLAYING THE OVERVIEW

Deathtrap (1982). Johnny Mandel's score becomes almost another character, circling around Michael Caine and Christopher Reeve with its baroque filigree.

The White Dawn (1976). Henry Mancini's folk-flavored score colors this drama about Eskimos without dramatizing much of it.

PLAYING WITH THE APPROPRIATE MUSICAL LANGUAGE

'Round Midnight (1986, Herbie Hancock). Watch for use of jazz.

The Way We Were (1973, Marvin Hamlisch). Note the musical language for romance—particularly the first time Robert Redford and Barbra Streisand make love.

American Gigolo (1980, Giorgio Moroder). Again, the musical language for romance—particularly the first time Richard Gere and Lauren Hutton make love—and compare with *The Way We Were.*

The Elephant Man (1980). Notice the quiet string chorale evoking church and religion that John Morris uses to score the scene in which the title character is reading the Bible and building his model church.

Crossroads (1986). Watch for Ry Cooder's use of traditional blues.

PLAYING WHAT THE SCENE IS REALLY ABOUT

Silver Streak (1976). Notice the flying sequence about halfway through the film. Richard Pryor comments on Gene Wilder's preoccupation with Jill Clayburgh, and Henry Mancini's music plays Wilder's thoughts, not the flying or the tension of trying to get back to the train.

Romancing the Stone (1984). Notice Alan Silvestri's score for the cue in the Bronco four-wheeler, when Michael Douglas and Kathleen Turner are being chased and shot at as their host calmly gives them a guided tour of his hometown as though nothing unusual is happening. The music reflects his attitude rather than the jeopardy that we see on screen. (See Figure 23-1.)

Out of Africa (1985). John Barry's score throughout plays the film as a classic romance rather than a period movie set in Africa. His score is playing what the movie is really about. (See Figure 13-29.)

GETTING INSIDE THE CHARACTER'S THOUGHTS AND FEELINGS

Scarface (1983). Giorgio Moroder's electronic score contains several cues that "get inside" Al Pacino's head as he watches his blonde girlfriend/wife and his sister. His tension is mirrored in the score, which plays his feelings of jealousy and protectiveness. Notice that in some cases the sound effects and dialogue gradually fade out, allowing the music full play.

FIGURE 11-15

The Elephant Man 10-1 Terror Night John Morris

Orchestrated by Jack Hayes

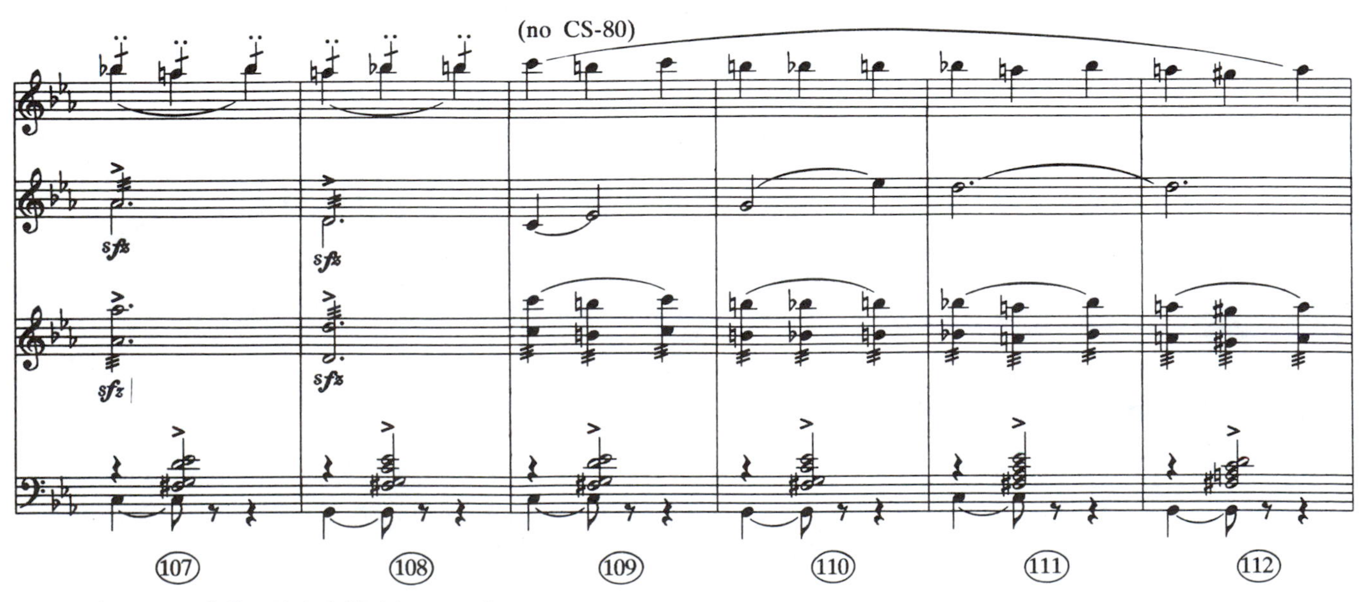

FIGURE 11-15 (*Continued*)

CHAPTER 12

COMPOSING

I know what a great score can do for a picture, and I hunger for a great score. PAUL WENDKOS, DIRECTOR

Even though the young guys coming up say, "Hey, I want to be innovative and different," they still follow the lead of the guys before. BRENDON CAHILL, VICE PRESIDENT OF TELEVISION MUSIC AND HOME VIDEO, UNIVERSAL TELEVISION

Once you stop being daring, you're bankrupt, idea-wise. ALEX NORTH

Of all the primary considerations the composer faces in the process of creating a film score, none should overshadow his search for excellence. If he has only three days instead of three weeks, or three weeks instead of three months, if he has only six strings instead of sixty, if he has only a day to record instead of a week—no matter what the practical restrictions, he can still respond in a creative way.

CREATIVE CONSIDERATIONS

WORK PROCESS

Everyone has a personal way of working. We all bring our own idiosyncrasies to the work process, just as we do to the dining-room table and the family budget discussions. And as in other activities, a certain amount of ritual and routine is helpful. However, too much of the same routine over and over again can turn a fertile imagination into a creative wasteland. Balance is everything.

When David Shire worked with Francis Coppola on his score for *The Conversation* in 1974, Coppola took Shire by the creative lapels and shook him up. "Francis said to me right at the outset, 'I'd like you to work on this film differently than you work on your Hollywood movies. I don't want you to work on it like that at all.'

"After I had read the script and we had talked about it, he gave me seven or eight subjects to write a little piano piece about, because by this time we had decided that we would try to make it a piano score. He said, 'None of these situations are in the movie, but I want you to loosen up and not think about it on the nose.' He was trying to get me to do an end run, so to speak, and think about it tangentially, and not get bogged down in writing for the movie right away. Instead, he wanted me to explore the whole emotional world of the movie and of the particular [dramatic] theme that the score was about.

"He gave me these funny titles, like, 'Harry Picks Up His Laundry'; 'Harry Goes to Thanksgiving Dinner at His Grandmother's'; 'Harry Goes to His High School Reunion.' And he said, 'Take a couple of weeks and write a short piano piece about each of those things.' And I had a great deal of resistance to this. You know, you like to work the way you've worked. He said, 'Don't worry whether they're good or bad, just write them and then we'll talk about them.'

"So I wrote a bunch of pieces, and one of them had a melody in it which I kind of liked, and which Francis was intrigued by, and he said, 'Let's develop that some more.' And that became the theme from *The Conversation* (see Figure 16-16). By not writing directly towards the film right away, I was able to get a theme with a nice ambivalent nature with relation to the film. You can become a victim of your own processes. And that's why Francis was so smart. He forced me to work in a lateral way."

Once you are set in your ways, breaking up your routine may be productive. Write with a new instrument, for instance. Many composers have found the availability of new synthesizers invaluable in suggesting new creative approaches to familiar problems. Creating with a new color other than the piano can change your perception and stimulate different solutions. Another variation is to use no instrument at all. John Cacavas writes at the piano sometimes, but he's found that "if you work at the piano you tend to write music where your hands have been before. But if you look at a score page and say, 'Let's experiment a little.' I'm always amazed at how much more original it is."

This is not by any means a recommendation to compose away from a keyboard, but rather a suggestion to avoid being a slave to your own routine. In the final analysis, whatever works best, works best.

INTUITION AND THE SUBCONSCIOUS

> ***When I watch a film I'm going to score, I'm really like John Q. Public. I just watch it. And I tend to just react to it. And I don't know why. I don't sit there saying, "Rule number forty-seven: Change keys."***
>
> MARVIN HAMLISCH

During the creative process, intuition is your best friend. There is no finer critic, no wiser scholar, no more effective hot line to the gods. The goal during the creative process is to stimulate your intuition and avoid blocking it with your intellect.

Therefore, the creative process generally unfolds in two phases: (1) the verbalizing and intellectualization of the project and the creator's vision; (2) the tapping of intuitive insights and awareness to express this vision. BE VERBAL AND INTELLECTUAL DURING THE PREPARATORY PERIOD; BE INTUITIVE AND EMOTIONAL DURING THE CREATION. LET THE OVERLAP OF THE TWO BE NATURAL AND UNFORCED.

WRITER'S BLOCK

> ***I've found that practically everybody rolls around under the piano, and throws up, and worries that they don't have any talent any more.***
>
> DAVID SHIRE

> ***My recurring nightmare is that I'm walking on the scoring stage and the score isn't finished!***[1]
>
> JERRY GOLDSMITH

> ***You can't wait for the great inspiration.***
>
> LAURENCE ROSENTHAL

An understanding of the creative process can help immeasurably in getting you through the rough times, especially in the early stages. There are those times, of course, when, contrary to all logic, you are just so wired by the project that the music is born fully realized on day one. No labor pains—no prep, no need to sharpen a dozen pencils and then resharpen them ten minutes later without having used them. Enjoy those flashes

[1] *Film Music Notebook,* 1977, Volume III, Number 2, interview by Elmer Bernstein, p. 27.

of inspiration for what they are, but cultivate your work process to take best advantage of your intuitive powers when the going gets tough.

Many creative people find it difficult to get started on a new project. It's the "blank page" syndrome. Georges Delerue speaks for many creative people when he says, "The terrible moment is when I have to start to compose, because I try to avoid doing it. I ask my wife if I have any shopping to do. Is there nothing I can do for her?" He knows that once he starts, he gets completely involved and there is no turning back.

Once you really get plugged into the project, solving the creative problems is no longer an ordeal—it's just a matter of following your instincts from the first cue to the last. The reason for writer's block is not so much because the pages are blank, but because you can't create with instinct alone. The first step in the creative process is to give yourself, and therefore your intuition, as much input as possible to consider. Through the process of verbalizing and developing the musical concept, film composers do just that. All the discussions with the director, producer, and others, all the screenings and spotting, all the listening to role models and temp tracks, and all the music and scores written by the composer in the past—all become input for the project.

LISTEN TO MUSIC YOU ENJOY. When you are ready to start, it can be helpful to "prime the pump" a bit. David Shire sometimes listens to any kind of music that he really enjoys. Not necessarily music that has any real relationship to the film, just music that turns him on. "Just to get me interested in music again. Many times those dark nights come when you're hating music and you hear something you like and even though it isn't something you want to adapt, so to speak, for your own uses, it reminds you again what good music sounds like, and how nice it is to write some."

SLEEP ON IT. If this sounds like a cliché, it is. But it works. Many people believe that if you give yourself a problem to work on before you go to bed at night, you will have the answer when you wake up the next morning. When John Morris was working on *The Elephant Man* (1980), it took him three weeks to get the answer for his Main Title. (Figure 7-5). "Three weeks of going to bed with the problem and getting up with the problem, and I said, 'What—am—I—going—to—do? But then it finally came." One way or another, getting away from the problem can be productive—you stop thinking so much about it, and your relaxation permits your intuition to find the seemingly inevitable solution.

WORK AROUND IT. If, while composing the score, you really jam to a stop, you may have to work around your impasse. Schedules usually prohibit waiting too long for the perfect idea. So at times when you're stuck, work on other cues, work on other themes, do anything productive to stay on schedule. Even preparing the sketch paper with timings or transferring those timings and notes to the orchestration pages can be productive at these times, because these tasks have to be done anyway. By doing something else productive you are also getting away from the problem, which in turn might stimulate a solution.

Laurence Rosenthal describes a common work method: "You start nibbling around the edges. You write an innocuous cue here, a nonthematic cue there. I very often will get up and just dedicate two or three hours to working on themes. And then, whether I've gotten anything good or not, just spend the rest of the day cranking out whatever material I can for what *does* exist."

> ***I do know that if it has to be done by Tuesday, that's a great incentive. There were times when I didn't think that I would get done, and somehow I did.***
> BRUCE BROUGHTON

ACKNOWLEDGE THE DEADLINE. Beginners often fear that deadlines will tighten them up and make the creative process impossible. This is rarely so. It is much more typical for professionals to achieve their greatest motivation during the most severe deadlines. Nothing wires you faster than a tight ten-day schedule. Nothing, that is, except a tight five-day schedule. Sending this message to your subconscious is a very powerful stimulus. At some point in the process, the score often takes on a life of its own, just as fictional characters in a screenplay or novel may seem to "talk" to the writer, leading the story inevitably forward from scene to scene.

USE THE VIDEOCASSETTE OR THE MOVIOLA. One of the best resources for direct input to the subconscious is the film itself. Watch it, either on videocassette or on a Moviola. You can watch a scene or a reel several times; you can skip down three reels to a related scene if you wish; you can stop for a break at any time; and you can be alone, completely absorbed in the film and your emotions.

Does anyone still use a Moviola for this purpose? Marvin Hamlisch does. So does John Barry. They always work with a black-and-white **dupe.**[2] Barry is enthusiastic about working this way: "I love that lever on the Moviola when you're running it through and then you don't quite know where you're going to do something, and you can watch and you can hit that lever and you can freeze the picture so when you're writing you know that's the exact frame you're going to make a switch. I'm sure I'll work on the Moviola till I die. People don't like it because it's noisy or whatever, but I love it. I just love it."

Like many composers, Bruce Broughton uses the videocassette to supplement the timing sheets and to establish an emotional link with the film. "I run the cue before I start composing to remind myself of what the starts were, what the previous scene was, and also to check emotionally those spots that I want to be able to nail dramatically. The timing sheets, though they're very good for the overall cue, can't really determine how great the smile is, or what the wink means, or what the leer means, or what the facial expressions will mean. And I find that I can get a lot closer to the scene just by seeing it again. It also helps to know that this cue follows very closely on the heels of a preceding action. Then you have a better idea of where you're coming from."

ADAPTING TO DIRECTORIAL MUSIC CHANGES

As soon as you play anything for the director, you will get a reaction from him. Does he love it, does he hate it? Is he telling the truth? When Arthur B. Rubinstein played his basic material for *Blue Thunder* (1983) for director John Badham, Badham asked everyone to leave, and then he said, "I hate it." Having worked on the score for two weeks, Rubinstein was at first stunned. "I had been working with a main theme that was very neurotic, a neurotic blues, which is how I perceived Roy Scheider in that picture. And John said, 'Look. When Scheider gets into that helicopter, steals it, and gets up in the air, I want the entire audience to be standing up screaming and cheering.' I said, 'Oh—why didn't you say that to begin with!' So I went home that night, wrote another theme, and started all over."

How was he able to start all over again? "Fear. Fear of not getting it done. Fear of looking foolish—well, that's not entirely true. When a director (especially somebody you know and love) looks at you and says, 'Hey—it's no good. This—is—what—I—want,' then the fear is mingled with a certain amount of challenge, and a certain amount of pride that at least that guy said to you, 'This is what I want,' and didn't call up the producer the next day and say, 'Listen, we're getting another composer.' So he had the faith that the information he was relaying to me would be potent."

---

[2] Dupe: copy of the film (usually black and white).

Under the best of circumstances, most criticism can be helpful. When it comes from a producer or director, *listen to him.* It will not be personal criticism (he is not saying, "I hate you") nor will it necessarily be a musical critique (he is not necessarily saying, "This is rotten music"). This criticism will have to do with the filmmaker's perception of his film. Try to determine why he doesn't like the cue or score. What does he think the film needs that the music may not be providing? Let these questions be your guide in understanding criticism of your film music, and let that criticism work for you.

Under the worst circumstances, the criticism may seem to be irrational, ill-conceived, or even detrimental to the score and the film. When this happens, try logic, try reassuring, and always demonstrate with music. Perhaps a compromise solution—one that works for you and satisfies the filmmaker—can be found.

MUSICAL CONSIDERATIONS

Having developed a concept for the score, move on to develop specific musical solutions. Every decision made about the music—whether it involves writing a theme or considering the orchestration—further defines the score.

TRANSLATE THE CONCEPT INTO MUSICAL TERMS. The four basic musical elements are melody, harmony, rhythm, and instrumental color. When you have decided on the size and composition of your orchestra, you have started defining the sound of the score. Choose a solo color for one of the themes and you are that much further along toward a clear definition of the score. Any familiar stylistic labels clarify the musical language and choices (deciding on a pure country-western style would eliminate the use of flat 9/raised 11th chords). Using an oboe with rock and roll would tend to suggest a hybrid musical idiom. As you continue this process of making these choices, you will begin to find intuitively a consistent approach for your score.

PLANNING THE SCORE

> ***It's very difficult for those of us who have an appreciation for the craft to work with people who don't understand it and don't care about it. What you get now is a scene-by-scene score. Instead of a linear score, you get a collection of cues. Color and motion.***
>
> DANIEL ALLAN CARLIN, MUSIC EDITOR

> ***Of course, there should be a structure, an architecture to any score. It's not a piece here and a piece there. It has to be thought out. You can't approach each cue as a separate piece of music.*** JERRY GOLDSMITH

> ***Sometimes I feel if I joined the end of one cue to another cue, it would make a solid piece.*** ALEX NORTH

> ***I try to look at it as a whole from beginning to end, and not to blow the big moment coming up.*** RANDY EDELMAN

Planning the score takes time and dramatic insight. The first step is to clarify the thematic requirements of the score. Your musical (thematic) materials won't work for the film if they can't provide the necessary dramatic values. These materials become the building blocks upon which the score's structure is designed, so they need to be as strong as possible to bear up to the heavy usage and repetition inherent in a well-constructed score. "I don't wake up the day I'm starting a picture and write Reel 1, Part 1," emphasizes

Jerry Goldsmith. "I wish I could. I've got to get the material to write. Sometimes that can take weeks. Writing the score is the simplest part of it. It's getting the approach."

To "get the approach" you must create the score's concept (which is abstract), thematic materials (which are specific), and structure or form (which is organizational). In Chapter 13 we will explore some ways melody is used by the film composer. But even before you have composed all the basic materials for your score, you must determine what themes the score requires in a general sense—that is, the *nature* of that thematic material. At this stage, you will want to know where and how that material will function. The only way to do this is to get out the spotting notes and begin analyzing what type of music (functionally speaking) goes where. Doing this will tend to clarify the score's requirements and function.

CREATING THE MASTER PLAN. By studying the list of cues, it might be possible to see that there are three cues in which the music supports the central love relationship, so a theme might be needed for those scenes. Although the same theme may not necessarily be used for all three scenes, music that expresses the specific quality of that particular love relationship may be used somehow. Some musical material (thematic, rhythmic, or whatever) may need to be developed for any fights or chase sequences. With the help of the spotting notes you may now be able to organize the cues into thematic categories—a love theme, a piece of material for the sequences when the heroine is alone and suffering, and so on.

The nature of the main theme can now be defined in terms of the concept of the score—will it be an overview theme, or hooked into one or more of the central characters? Will it be the love theme? If not, what?

If special musical effects are needed, this requirement will be obvious now, and should be listed. They can be important thematic colors (like the effect John [Johnny] Green composed for the raintree in the 1958 film *Raintree County,* with its magical shimmering sound)[3] or just a passing moment (like the "beam-up" effect James Horner created for the 1982 *Star Trek II*). Now is a good time to decide on their importance, in case an effect like this might be integrated into the overall design of the score. Here's an organized approach to creating the master plan:

1. List all cues.
2. Add a one or two word description of the overall quality of each cue to the list.
3. Start a second list, sorting all cues by function (chases and shoot-outs might be together; love scenes together; all psychological cues together; and so on.
4. Start a third list, sorting out the cues within each function (separate those love scenes between the two central characters from the family "love scenes" that occur over the Christmas holidays, for instance—even though they eventually may be scored with the same theme).
5. Find those scenes in each of the above lists that seem to relate the most closely to each of the themes already written.
6. Put into words the qualities needed for the remainder of the thematic material for the score.

The above process should help define the function of any themes you still need to create.

[3] See p. 298 for Green's description.

ORGANIZING THE SCORE

Regardless of musical idiom, the best scores include an interaction between the various musical elements and themes. There is often a smooth, sometimes imperceptible flow between one theme and another, a blending of musical materials to serve the drama at any moment. The introduction of new or related material whenever necessary will smooth out the formal structure, making it better developed and more interesting.

Commenting on the thematic organization of a score, Jerry Goldsmith says, "It's not a piece here and a piece there. The idea of film music is to *characterize,* aside from heightening the emotional element for the audience. You're trying to emphasize the character of the people up there. As they evolve, the music must evolve with them. The music has to have a starting point and an ending point. And you've got to develop that music in such a fashion that you have some place to go with it. There has to be a master plan as to where you're going.

"Whether you're doing a picture with one theme like *Chinatown* [1974] or one with five themes, they have to interrelate with each other yet be totally separate and identifiable by themselves."

THE FORM OF THE FILM DETERMINES THE FORM OF THE SCORE. If a film starts off very innocuously, showing a typical American family and giving no hint of any dramatic confrontation, then suddenly turns bizarre and then violent, the music must follow that dramatic sequence one way or the other. The score has three options: (1) to be silent during the neutral, nondramatic scenes, and enter when the tension begins; (2) to play the first part of the film slightly dark and ominously, with a suggestion of the terror that will follow; (3) to play the nondramatic scenes lightly, for warmth and relaxation, as though nothing will ever happen to this pleasant, idyllic family. Quincy Jones and director Richard Brooks decided to play the nondramatic scenes lightly when they scored the 1967 shocker *In Cold Blood,* the story of a brutal mass murder. They wanted the contrast between the daydream and the nightmare.

PACING AND FORM. There are times when the choice of new, possibly unrelated thematic material may be dictated by specific pacing needs of the film. Sometimes a film is basically slow-moving, and any opportunity to add the variety and motion of a change of mood may give the film more impact. In *Sophie's Choice* (1984), Marvin Hamlisch scored one sequence in the style of Vivaldi, with two trumpets, harpsichord, and orchestra, giving the scene a well-placed lift in the midst of slow, downbeat material.

And in *Revolution* (1985), John Corigliano deliberately chose to score a sequence in which Pacino is totally humiliated by the British with a lighter tempo and feeling. "I took the same theme as the 'War Lament' and I made that into a Mendelssohnian aristocratic fox hunt. Completely effervescent. And then in the middle of the scene the theme goes into a kind of tarantella, so you get the idea that this is kind of fun.

"I did this because this is the grimmest film I've ever seen, and I desperately felt that it needed something bright even if it was ironic. I told [director] Hugh Hudson that this film has only one light minute in the whole three-and-a-half hours. You must have something to relieve the dark, sad, oppressive quality."

UNITY AND VARIETY

What I really try to do is to take one simple motif of the material for the picture, and a broad theme, and construct it so they always can work in concert with each other or separately. The repetition of an

> ***identifiable motif does have a cumulative effect upon the audience if they hear it enough times.***
> JERRY GOLDSMITH[4]

> ***I've found if you have a theme that you really love and you can use it, and the choice is: Can I use my theme in a different version or should I write something new?—choose the theme. Because you could play it twenty-five times, but the audience will only really hear it six times.***
> MARVIN HAMLISCH

> ***We've all heard the story where you come onto the scoring stage and you have one great cue, and all of a sudden the whole picture is one cue with a couple of variations, and they've thrown the score out.***
> JOHN MARTINELLI, FILM EDITOR

FORM IS THE RESULT OF REPETITION AND CONTRAST, UNITY AND VARIETY. THE FORM OF A SCORE IS DEVELOPED THROUGH THE REPETITION OF MELODIC, HARMONIC, RHYTHMIC, AND ORCHESTRAL MATERIALS, COMBINED WITH THE VARIATIONS OF THESE AND OTHER MUSICAL MATERIALS. These ideas are exemplified throughout the symphonies of Beethoven, Mozart, and other symphonists.

Strong scores usually have a fine balance between too much and too little repetition. Totally disregard the principle of repetition and the score becomes too abstract, too fragmented. Overuse the principle of repetition and you have a one-note composition that cannot withstand the duration of a full-length film. There have been successful scores that have gone both ways, but these instances can be deceptive in that there may in fact be more variety within a one-theme score than you think, and there may be strong unifying elements in a seemingly unrelated series of cues.

THE POWER OF ASSOCIATION. The reason repetition is so valuable in film scoring is that the music is able to develop tremendous emotional power through the cumulative reactions of an audience to the repetition of a theme developed throughout the course of the film. The music becomes more and more closely associated with the characters and their emotions. When the audience hears that theme later in the film, they remember the way the characters felt and can identify with them more easily—the musical repetition carries with it a powerful accumulation of emotions from earlier scenes. When "Tara's' theme plays at the end of *Gone With the Wind* (1939), it has much more emotional impact for the audience than when it is played at the beginning (even with the same orchestration and volume) because the theme has developed so much associative power by that time.

EXACT REPETITION. When you want to move the audience to emotionally respond with "Oh—here they go again," *exact* repetition can be very effective. It doesn't matter what the emotional quality of the material or the scene is; the principle applies to any emotion. When John Barry's "James Bond theme" begins again, we know immediately what to expect. Henry Mancini's score for *Silver Streak* (1976) has an example of this in a comedic setting. When Gene Wilder falls off the train and lands in the middle of nowhere, Mancini starts a light western-tinged theme played by harmonica as Wilder begins to walk along the railroad tracks. The next time this happens to Wilder, Mancini uses the same theme and setting, which actually heightens the humor of the situation: "Oh, no, there he goes again" (Figure 12-1). The repetition of the short "shark" motif in John Williams's score for *Jaws* (1975) establishes immediate emotional associations with terror; when it begins, the audience quickly begins to feel "not again." (See Figure 13-1.)

[4] *Film Music Notebook,* 1977, Volume III, Number 2, pp. 28–29, interview by Elmer Bernstein.

FIGURE 12-1

Silver Streak 3/3 + 4/1 This Is Terrific

Henry Mancini
Orchestrated by Jack Hayes

SAME THEME, DIFFERENT SETTING. Any one or more of the four basic musical elements (melody, harmony, rhythm, color) can be used to give variety to the repeated use of a theme. If the theme is romantic, as in *The Way We Were* (1973), the melody and harmony are likely to remain much the same throughout, but the rhythmic setting can be quite different. Tempo can change, the rhythm section may be used for a "pop" feel at one time and left out for a more rubato, classical feel at another. The orchestral colors used for the cue may be quite different from previous cues, lending significant variety to thematic repetition. In *The Way We Were,* Marvin Hamlisch integrated the main theme throughout his score, expressing a variety of moods. But the settings change, the "feel" changes, and the theme doesn't necessarily enter at obvious moments. There is also a great deal of variety between the uses of the theme. By the end of the film, when the song introduction begins again, the audience feels the full power of that musical association without feeling that the theme has been overused.

Burt Bacharach learned about the use of thematic unity in film scoring while working on his first score, *What's New, Pussycat?* (1965). "I was totally in the dark. And I didn't understand that you didn't have to have twenty-eight different themes. They took that one theme, the title song, and took one or two cues that I had written, and [producer] Charlie Feldman put them all through the movie because he fell in love with the theme. And I said, 'I never intended it there. I'm going to sue him. I'm going to take my name off this picture.' And then the picture was such a success, and the song was a huge hit."

RESEARCH

Research is often the key to a well-crafted score, and might be used in the following ways:

1. To Define Musical Language and Approach. When Laurence Rosenthal scored his first film, a documentary on the history of Russia, he spent three weeks in the New York Public Library pouring over every collection of Russian folk songs that he could find—and there are thousands of them. He used his recollection of that research when he scored the television miniseries *Peter the Great* (1985; see Figure 24-4). Contemporary music demands the same fidelity to detail. Ry Cooder couldn't have scored *Crossroads* (1986) so authoritatively if he wasn't able to compose with an authentic sense of the blues. Alex North restudied the style of the fourteenth- and fifteenth-century music masters to capture the appropriate period flavor for his score for *The Agony and the Ecstasy* (1965).

2. To Learn About the Authentic Instruments and Locate The Musicians. For *Remo Williams* (1985), Craig Safan specifically wanted to use Korean instruments. "The trick was to find what was Korean and not Chinese or Japanese—that didn't fit our preconception of oriental, which is a bamboo flute and a gong and a koto. So I had to do a lot of research with Korean musicians to find out what sounds uniquely Korean. And there are a number of instruments that *do* sound uniquely Korean, and I only used those instruments." (See Figure 15-5.)

3. To Be Aware of Previous Scores. When Marvin Hamlisch accepted the assignment to score the James Bond movie *The Spy Who Loved Me* (1971), the first thing he did was to screen every James Bond film made up to that point. He brought a cassette recorder with him and taped any scene that really knocked him out. By the end of that research, he had an excellent idea of what had been done already for the Bond movies, what he particularly liked, and what he wanted to do with his score.

Research can be an extremely valuable and often vital tool for the composer, who should look for any promising research projects at the beginning of every new assignment. Used well, musical materials gathered from this research can bring color, personality, and appropriate authenticity to a score.

TEMPO OR PULSE

Just the act of determining what the click will be involves finding some kind of rhythm. And even in order to time the cue out, I think you do have to make that kind of a commitment. I may not actually write a rhythm figure first, but I'm certainly deep into what the basic pulse will be.

MICHAEL MELVOIN

I suppose my first impulse as I compose is movement, not theme.

GERALD FRIED

Developing a feel for the tempo or pulse of any given cue is often the composer's first task when he begins to sketch—even though he may not have developed thematic material at this point. The word *pulse* didn't become standard terminology accidentally—it is the heartbeat and musical life of the scene. Finding an appropriate pulse is an intuitive skill. To sharpen that skill, play the scene several times on videotape or film, and try to imagine the music only as pulse—no notes. Once you feel comfortable with the basic tempo, then you might try adding the thematic material you feel is best suited for the cue. At this point you might ignore every other consideration of scoring the scene, including how the theme synchronizes with the scene, whether it gets in the way of the dialogue, whether or not you feel the harmony is just right for the scene. Your only consideration will be to ascertain whether or not the pulse feels right for the scene. And this is a crucial decision. Here is a check list:

1. Does the tempo feel emotionally compatible with the scene?
2. Does it provide enough basic forward motion?
3. Does it provide too much forward motion?
4. Will it accommodate faster motion (eighth-note patterns, and so on) without feeling too fast or "notey"?
5. Is it a comfortable tempo for the dialogue? (Remember that faster tempos can sound slower by playing half notes instead of quarters or quarter notes instead of eighths. ♩= 24 frame click is not too slow for a legato cue under soft dialogue).
6. If the cue calls for tension, play a repeated low note with the basic pulse. Do you feel a dramatic buildup?
7. Does it sync to the editor's cutting rhythm?

If you are composing a contemporary score, writing to a drum-machine tempo can be helpful. The potential pitfall is that the drum pattern can obscure the basic pulse by providing you with too much ornamental motion. Starting with a very simple bass-drum pattern (possibly including soft quarter notes on the hi hat) is the best way to use the machine. Then, as you become comfortable with a specific tempo for the cue, you can add more motion to the pattern. However, if the score is not contemporary, writing with a drum machine can adversely influence the musical style.

VARIABLE PULSE. The tempo of a cue may not be constant. It might slow down, speed up, slow down, and then return to the original tempo, or remain steady for a while and then speed up to the end of the cue. Bruce Broughton has a classical, rubato background as a classically trained pianist and does not feel tied down to a steady tempo, even on chases and other rhythmic cues:

"Once I had to do an entire show on clicks, and I found it almost impossible because, for me, on the longer pieces the tempo usually gets faster. If I have a chase two or three minutes long, by the end I want to get really fast. To accommodate that on one click is just impossible. I did it, but you start writing triplets or writing across the bar lines, and doing silly rhythmic things which would be really easy to accommodate with free timing or rallentando. If my tempo is a second a beat, by the end of the piece it's usually two-thirds of a second a beat, or a second and a half a beat—it'll really vary. If I go from eighth notes to sixteenth notes, they take a different rate of time, so the music will either slow down or speed up accordingly."

PERSONAL TASTE AND STYLE

All the decisions that a composer makes relate to his overall tastes. Everyone has personal prejudices; if you allow your tastes their natural bent, the concept for your score will be expressed in a stylistically personal way. Director Oliver Stone puts it this way: "Once you choose the actor, you're bound by that style, those parameters. An actor will stretch himself, but he can only go so far. He's not going to become untrue to himself. The same thing with a composer. When you go with a certain type of composer, he will go in a certain direction and get a style and stick to it."

CATCHING THE ACTION

Before you prepare your first sketch of a cue, you'll need to decide how closely synchronized to the action your music will be.

HOW MUCH TO CATCH. How much you actually *catch* or *hit* in any one cue depends upon your style, the style of the film, and your tastes. When a cue catches an action (a vase falling to the floor, a right cross to the jaw, an airplane as it loop-the-loops), it is *Mickey-Mousing* the action. This term is derived from the scoring of the classic animation, which traditionally did catch and illustrate most of the action. When a score seems to catch none of the action or drama, it is *playing through* the scene and not hitting anything. Any variation is possible between these two extremes.

Scores for many contemporary films appear to be playing through the scene. In fact, they are often catching more than you might think, but in a much more subtle way than in the scores of 1930 through 1967. SCORES OFTEN CATCH THE EMOTIONAL SHIFTS AND ACTION ACCENTS BY SUBTLY POINTING UP THE CHANGE OF EMPHASIS IN A SCENE; THE SCORE'S DEVELOPMENT AND ARRANGEMENT RESPONDS TO THE EMOTIONAL AND PICTORIAL FLOW OF THE FILM. This can often be done by phrasing a theme so it begins at a specific moment in the drama, or by changing a color or in some other way adjusting the orchestration at a significant dramatic point.

ANALYZING THE SCENE 1. Note the major shifts of *emotional emphasis* in the drama (such as a turn in the dialogue from a couple's relaxed discussion about the weekend's television schedules to a more intense discussion of why they never go out anymore with their friends). Circle these timings on your notes.

2. Note the major shifts of *emphasis by the camera* in the scene (such as slow move-ins to a close-up on one of the characters as he talks; or a zoom to a close-up of an object outside the window, drawing our attention away from the actors to some inanimate object). Usually, these camera moves will be clues to the director's own emphasis and will have an emotional quality. Music can often highlight, accentuate, or enhance this emphasis. NOTE THAT A SUBTLE MUSICAL STATEMENT CAN BE POTENT IN CONJUNCTION WITH A CAMERA MOVE. Circle the timings for these camera moves also.

3. Note the major shifts of *editorial emphasis* in the scene, and circle those timings on the timing notes. Major emphasis shifts would include cut from one time to another; cuts from one location to another; cuts from one sequence to another (for instance, if a shot of two characters making love cuts to a prisoner escaping). You may not catch these moments, but you should be aware of them, and mark them on your sketch. In montages, for instance, the score often plays through these cuts.

4. Now step back and look at all the timings you have circled by going through the above steps. You should have selected those that you consider to be the most important emotionally for the audience, so you can integrate those moments into your music if you choose.

PHRASING A SEQUENCE

You phrase a sequence by subdividing it into several smaller units. Each of these units will ordinarily have a particular dramatic or emotional quality. For example, if the cue is scoring a dialogue scene between a man and woman, the phrasing might look like this:

:00–:23.4	man tells woman he loves her, and they will be alright
:23.4–:27.1	phone rings—he answers
:27.1–:45.86	he gets message from kidnapper asking for ransom
:45.86–1:22	they decide on course of action and go to car
1:22–1:30	car pulls away

SURFACE OR SUBTEXT EMOTIONS. Each of these dramatic units has its own emotional quality, which the music should enhance. Whether you decide to support these emotions, and to what degree, is your next decision. But this process delineates the phrasing of the *literal* drama of the sequence. If you decide not to phrase the cue this way, it will probably be because you are going to provide another emotional quality to the scene (for example, absolute despair), or emphasize just one of the emotions in the scene (possibly fear or tension in this case). In each instance you are playing a *subtext* to the drama (some quality beneath the surface), and you might play this subtext throughout the entire sequence. This could be a valid approach to the scene; playing the subtext can provide one of music's greatest contributions to a film. (See pp. 13–14 for comments on this subject by director Paul Wendkos.) The style of the film and the score will determine your approach, but in any case you will want to mark the above phrasing on your notes and possibly on your sketch as a reference.

BEGINNING THE SKETCH. Before you phrase a scene, you'll need to commit to a pulse (that is, select a tempo) and rough in the cue on music paper by putting the correct timings (either free or click) at the top of every bar or two bars. Then:

1. Add the significant timings from your analysis list to this layout.
2. Consider adjusting the tempo slightly to accommodate any hits that need to be precise.
3. Compose your thematic material for the scene; or, if you already have the material, play it against the film or video without necessarily trying to fit it exactly to the scene.
4. Place the thematic material on the sketch paper roughly where you would like it to play. This may leave empty bars on one or both sides of the thematic statement(s), which you can fill in later.
5. Now shift the thematic material and try playing it in several different places. When the theme's location seems most compatible to your music in terms of your circled

timings, lock it in by noting its exact placement in the cue. Use the videotape time code or the Moviola footage counter to identify the start. HINT: FIRST ADJUST YOUR THEMATIC MATERIAL TO WORK BEST OVER THE MORE DIFFICULT TRANSITIONS SUCH AS HARD CUTS OR DISSOLVES TO A NEW SCENE, A NEW LOCATION OR A SIGNIFICANT EMOTIONAL THRUST. There will always be a way to work out any other phrasing problems.

6. If everything is still working, make some notes now about compositional or orchestrational changes at your choice timings. Sometimes just adding a new color to the orchestration can be enough acknowledgement of a slight shift in dramatic emphasis on the screen. Adding a soft string pad under the theme in bar 7, as the heroine turns and says, "I love you," can be *very* enhancing to the scene, without disturbing the flow of the theme at all.

Now that the film's dramatic needs are in focus and the musical options have been selected, let's consider the basic musical elements—melody, harmony, rhythm, and color. These elements are completely interactive—none of them function in a vacuum. Nevertheless, it helps to isolate these four elements in order to analyze their roles in the context of effective film scoring.

USING MELODY

Once I wrote that march theme for The Last Starfighter, *that was it. I played it slow, I played it fast, I played it upside down; it worked in three-four, in four-four—it worked everywhere.* CRAIG SAFAN

MOTIFS

That was [director] George Miller's idea, to have a "Mad Max" motif appear every time either he's in trouble or you want to say something with the music which is not too clear visually. MAURICE JARRE

The development of motifs is a powerful compositional device for the film composer, allowing him to bring an overall sense of unity to his score and still leave room for variety. Since motifs are short, they can be used easily for a sequence or shot of any length.

One of the most famous motifs in a contemporary film score is the menacing motif from *Jaws* (1975) composed by John Williams to characterize the shark. Although often referred to as the "Theme From *Jaws*" it is essentially two bass notes that become thematic through repetition (Figure 13-1). As soon as you hear those first two notes, you know it's not safe to go into the water.

The *Jaws* motif uses the interval of a half-step, which brings with it a built-in feeling of tension. In film scoring, the heavy emphasis on one or two intervals establishes those intervals as being characteristic of the sound of the score, and often enables the composer to achieve a consistency of musical texture and harmonic language while at the same time reiterating a central theme. In his score for *WarGames* (1983), Arthur B. Rubinstein uses the interval of a third as a motivic building block (see Figure 13-2).

WarGames is a score without a long-line theme, Rubinstein points out. "Often you're involved in a project where there *is* no big theme. Where the project just can't accept it—you're not given the space for a big theme—so what do you do? You develop 'tinker toys'—motifs. Taking a little motif and developing it, and having the time to use it throughout a picture—it's a game—a wonderful game. I don't know if people respond to it or even sense it subliminally, but that's how I approach that kind of thing." Other melodies in the *WarGames* score sometimes emphasize thirds, which further unifies the musical language and sound (see Figures 13-3a and b).

John Corigliano describes his score for *Revolution* (1985) as relying heavily on the interval of a ninth. "In *Revolution,* the love music at the end was the first thing I developed. I took the love theme, which starts with an upward leap of a ninth, and made the upward leap representative of Al Pacino's struggle through the whole thing, so in the credits you just hear the horns making that leap, and throughout the movie that interval is used to develop the intensity not only of the love relationship but of Pacino himself. So the ninth is used a lot to build things with, and its use throughout the film prepares you for the love theme at the end with full strings."

Longer melodies often rely on the strength of a single interval to establish their identity and personality. In *Star Wars* (1977), John Williams starts his main theme with

FIGURE 13-1

Jaws M-101 Jaws Titles John Williams
Orchestrated by Herb Spencer

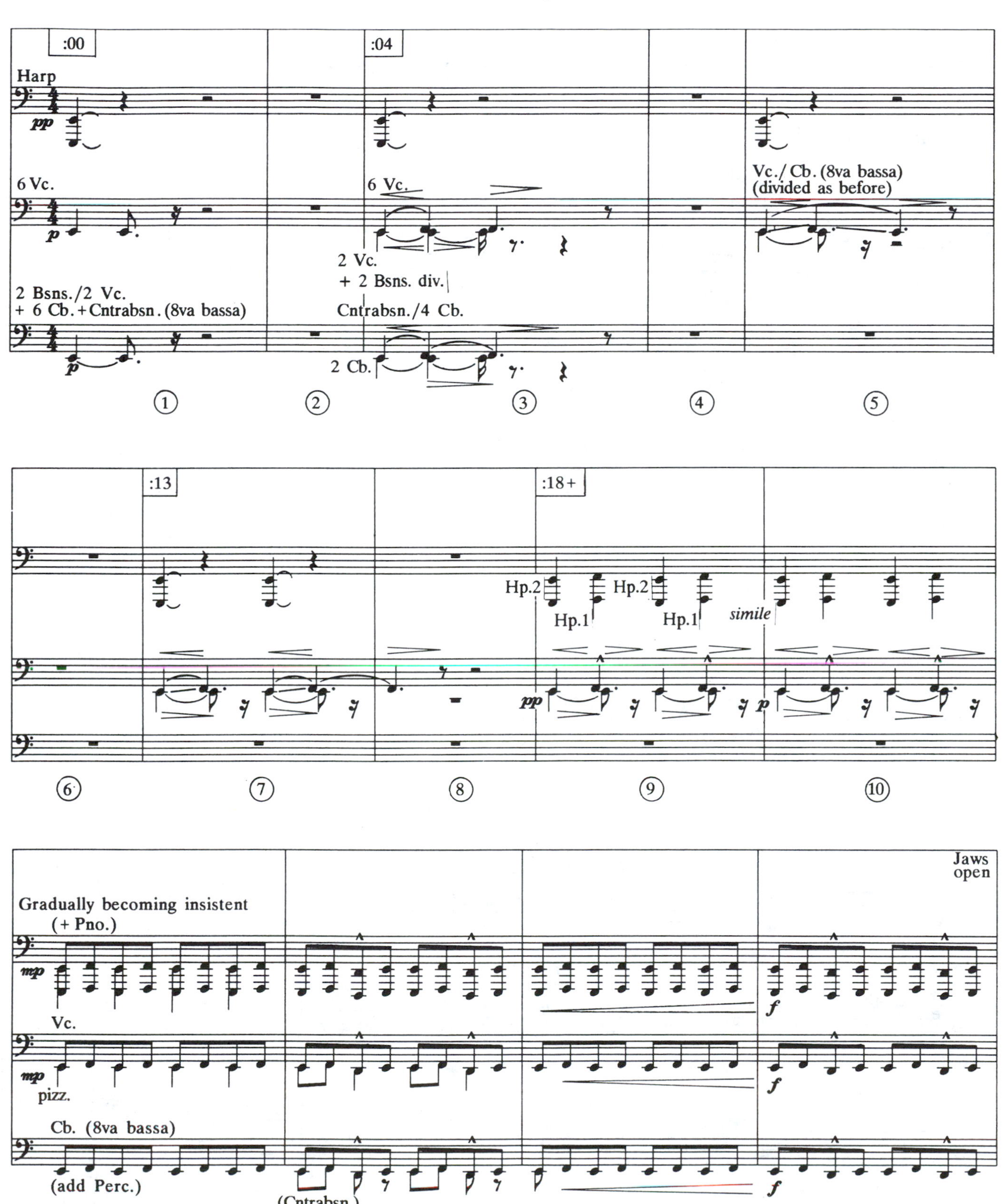

FIGURE 13-2

WarGames M-123A Winner None Arthur B. Rubinstein
Orchestrated by Mark Hoder

FIGURE 13-3a

WarGames M-114 Arthur B. Rubinstein
Orchestrated by Mark Hoder

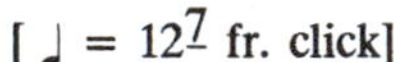

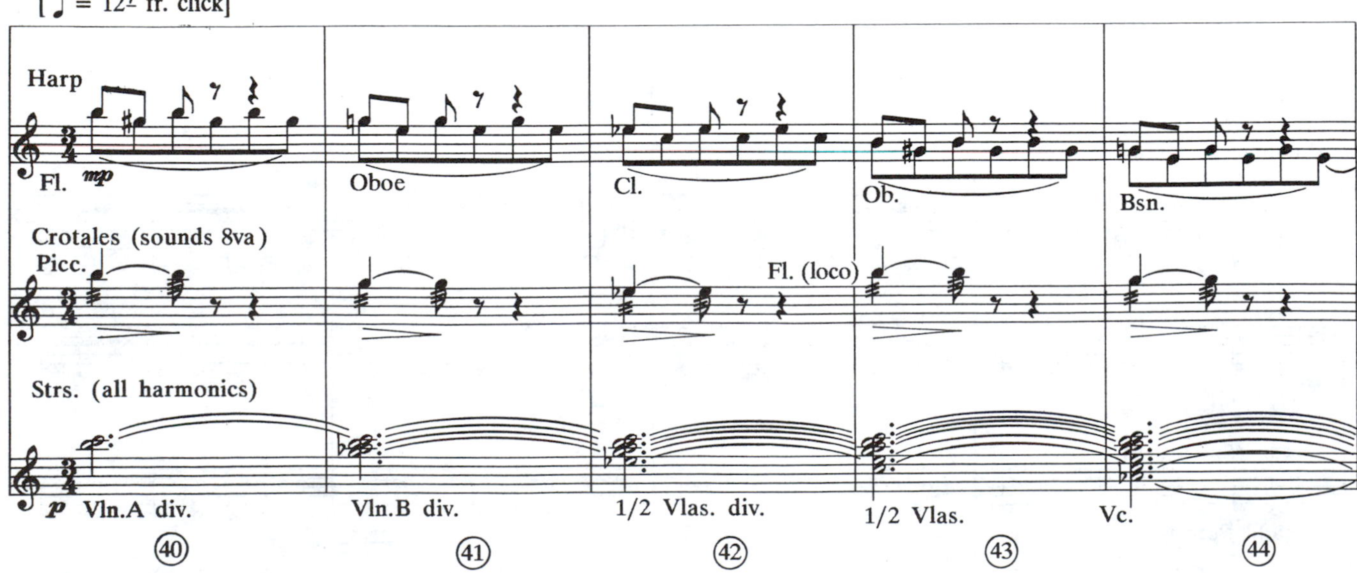

FIGURE 13-3b

WarGames M-62 Arthur B. Rubinstein
Orchestrated by Mark Hoder

an ascending fifth (Figure 13-4). Used this way, the interval itself can become a two-note motif independent of the theme.

In his score for *Brainstorm* (1983), James Horner uses a motif based on a four-note descending minor scale. (See Figure 13-5.) The scale gives the motif unity and strength; the minor scale moving downward gives the piece a driving, "down" feeling in keeping with the film's tone. Elsewhere in the film, the motif is powerfully stated in the brass; here, though it is orchestrated with less impact, it still projects urgency.

Another very well-known theme that is derived from a motif is the "spaceship communication" motif from *Close Encounters of the Third Kind* (1977) by John Williams. In the film, five notes are used by scientists to communicate with the visiting spaceship. Shown here in its simplest form rhythmically, this motif becomes the primary focus of the scene in which the mothership communicates tonally with earth.

FIGURE 13-3b (*Continued*)

FIGURE 13-4

Star Wars **Theme** **John Williams**

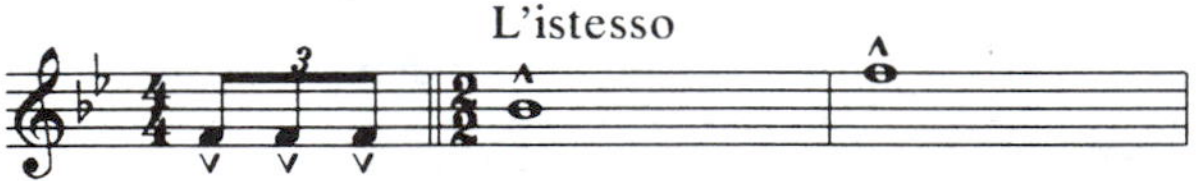

During this scene there is considerable rhythmic variety as the motif is further developed. Williams composed this motif for the demands of the script and then used it several times as part of the score, making this dramatic device into an important musical statement. Since so much associative power attaches itself to this motif through repetition as the scientists and spaceship begin to communicate, his simple melodic motif becomes symbolic of the communication between earth and the space travelers. Note its reappearance as the last cadence of the End Credits, orchestrated for choir and harp.

A second motif, used throughout the score, is shown in Figure 13-6. Note that it has the same contour as the five-note communication motif. See Figure 7-4 for an example of this motif playing in conjunction with the mothership theme.

FIGURE 13-5

Brainstorm 10M3 James Horner

MULTIPLE MOTIFS

When Alex North designed his score for *Dragonslayer* (1981), he developed half-a-dozen motifs. These "cells" were then used as compositional building blocks and functioned as themes (see Figure 13-7a, b, and c). North often used these motifs in conjunction with one another. In Figure 13-8, these three motifs are shown working together simultaneously.

The jazz-oriented James Bond themes are quickly identifiable because of their motivic construction. The first few bars give you an immediate sense of recognition. Most people would know James Bond was nearby if they heard either of the motifs in Figure 13-9, which work together and also function as independent short themes.

UNACCOMPANIED MELODY

Sometimes a single instrument playing the melody is all that the scene requires, and can in fact be a welcome break from more complex orchestration. Scoring this way places all the emphasis on the melodic line, and it is surprising just how emotional an unaccompanied solo melody can be. It is especially effective at the beginning of cues, but works equally well emerging from an orchestral passage. The melody can be orchestrated for a solo instrument, a combined color (like cellos or violins), or a mixed color (like 2 alto flutes, English horn, and subtone clarinet). In *The Verdict* (1982), Johnny Mandel

FIGURE 13-6
Close Encounters of the Third Kind **11/2-12/1** **The Mountain** **John Williams**
Orchestrated by Herb Spencer

FIGURE 13-7
Three cells from *Dragonslayer* Alex North

begins a cue with a single line as the camera slowly moves in on Paul Newman on the telephone with his client. The cue continues through his trip to the hospital (see Figure 13-10).

Although the music is totally exposed, Alex North begins his End Credits for *Under the Volcano* (1984) with a long solo-oboe passage, which enters after the film's very emotional ending. Eventually the orchestra joins in, but not until the solo melodic line has made its statement, playing the tragic aftermath of Albert Finney's murder (see Figure 13-11).

The unaccompanied harp solo in Georges Delerue's score for *The Black Stallion Returns* (1983) is another good example of solo melody, played by a less expressive instrument (see Figure 16-14).

Melodies with solo accompaniment often achieve the same intimate effect. In Goldsmith's Main Title for *Planet of the Apes* (1968), the first 8 bars of the score begin with a solo melody in the violins, accompanied only by log drums (Figure 13-12).

In Nino Rota's Finale for *The Godfather* (1971), he begins with solo oboe on the theme, accompanied only by acoustic guitar (Figure 13-13).

TWO-VOICE TEXTURE

A solo melody line can be enriched through the use of a second part moving in parallel motion with the melody, or a freely moving second part that mirrors the melody's rhythmic motion. In *The Omen* (1976), Jerry Goldsmith uses two freely moving string lines in the first four bars of the scene in which the priest explains that he was there when the baby with Satan's mark was born. Although the rhythms are basically identical, the melodic motion is often contrary, creating interesting intervals with varying degrees of tension (Figure 13-14).

FIGURE 13-8
Dragonslayer Three cells combined Alex North

Free timing

:06 :09.6 :12.5 :15.4

Eng. Hn. solo
mp espr.

Bsn.
mp espr.

Bsn.
mp espr.

Celesta (sounds here)
Harp harmonics

(3) (4) (5) (6)

:18.2 :21.1 :24 :27 :29.6

Vln.A
p espr. Vln.B div.
poco
4
6 *p*

Vlas.
p

Vc.
p dolce
p

Cb. div. *pp*

(7) (8) (9) (10) (11)

FIGURE 13-9

Octopussy **James Bond Suite** **John Barry**

(a)

(b)

FIGURE 13-10

The Verdict **R3 P1** **All Heart** **Johnny Mandel**
Orchestrated by Miles Goodman

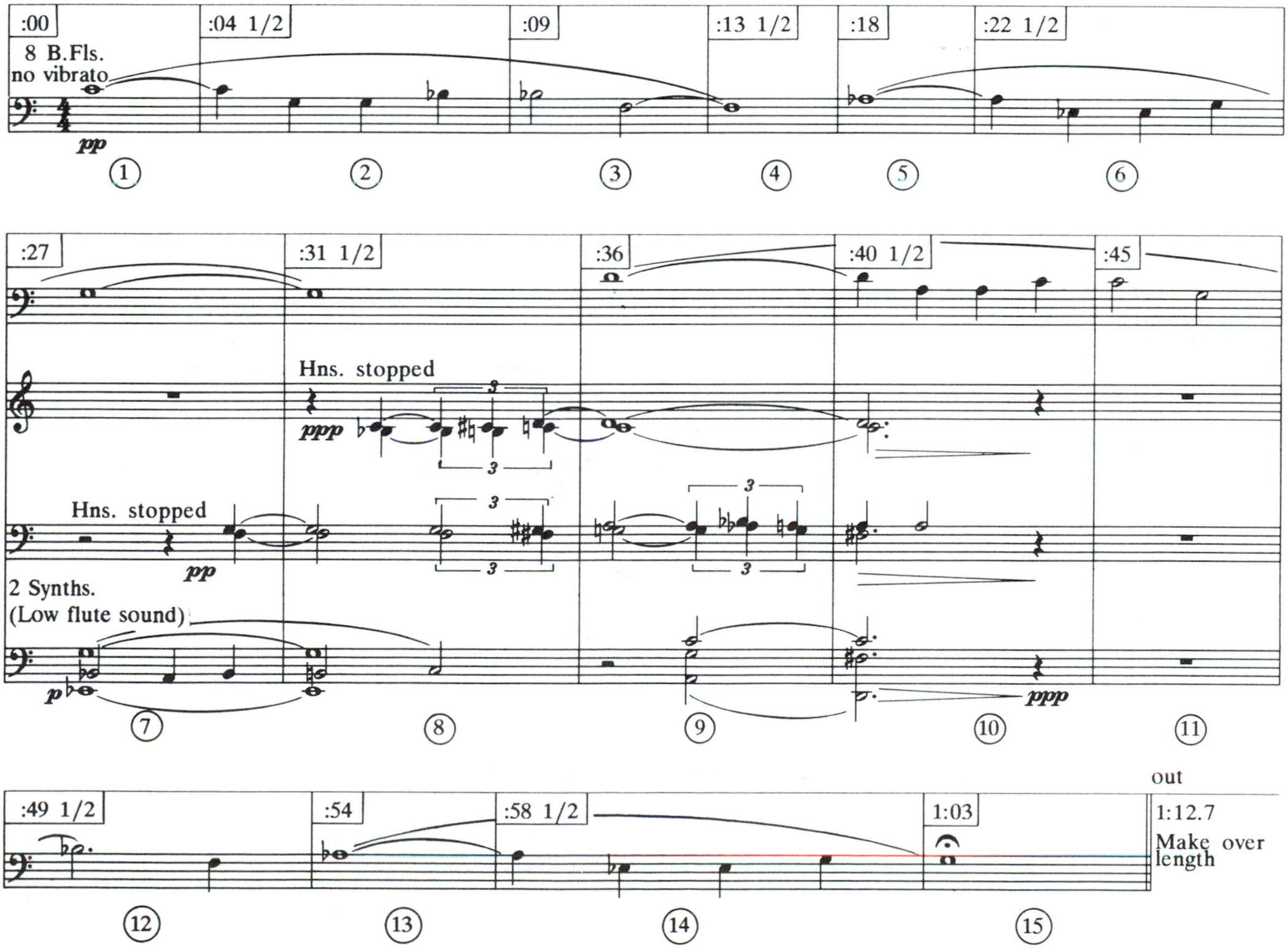

:00 | :04 1/2 | :09 | :13 1/2 | :18 | :22 1/2

8 B.Fls.
no vibrato
pp

① ② ③ ④ ⑤ ⑥

:27 | :31 1/2 | :36 | :40 1/2 | :45

Hns. stopped
ppp

Hns. stopped
pp

2 Synths.
(Low flute sound)
p
ppp

⑦ ⑧ ⑨ ⑩ ⑪

:49 1/2 | :54 | :58 1/2 | 1:03 | out 1:12.7 Make over length

⑫ ⑬ ⑭ ⑮

FIGURE 13-11
Under The Volcano End Title Alex North

FIGURE 13-12
The Planet of the Apes R3 P1 The Search Continues Jerry Goldsmith
Orchestrated by Arthur Morton

FIGURE 13-13

The Godfather 19 M2 Finale Consisting of The Godfather Waltz Nino Rota

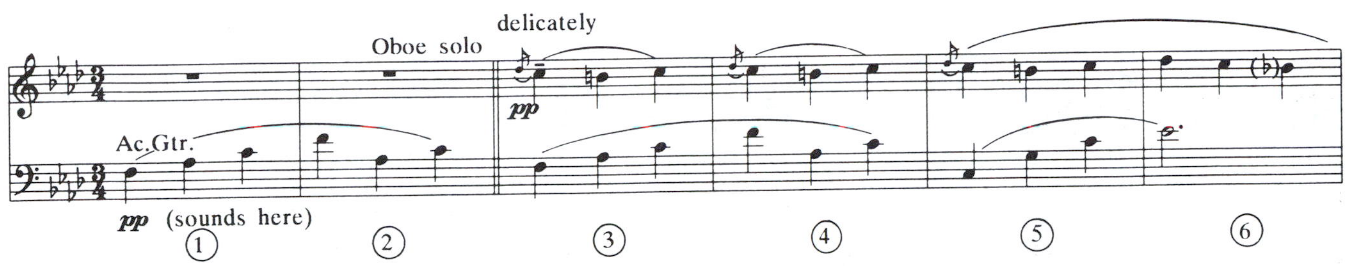

FIGURE 13-14

The Omen R2 P5/R3 P1 I Was There

Jerry Goldsmith
Orchestrated by Arthur Morton

Vlns. sord.

mp *pp*

Vc. sord./Bass Fl.

Vlas.
Vc.

p

14 15 16

Muted Hn. + Cntrabsn.

f

17 18 19 20

Fls. flutter tongue

Eng. Hn. + Vla. pizz.

mf

21 22 23

FIGURE 13-15

Logan's Run **R2 P7/R3 P1** **On the Circuit** **Jerry Goldsmith**
Orchestrated by Arthur Morton

FIGURE 13-15 (*Continued*)

In *Logan's Run* (1976), Goldsmith divides the violins into two parts (Figure 13-15). James Horner uses this technique with the boys choir in *Brainstorm* (1983; see Figure 14-21). Whether accompanied or not, it is a melodic effect that can work with thematic or developmental material.

TWO-PART COUNTERPOINT. The characteristic independence of contrapuntal melodies playing together provides excellent musical resources for the film composer.

For *Patton* (1970), Goldsmith composed a march theme and a counterline to that march theme, each independent of each other, but combining together in counterpoint. In his Main Title, first the organ plays the counterline, and then Goldsmith adds winds on the march theme (heard for the first time) while the organ repeats the counterline. They are combined in Figure 13-16.

FIGURE 13-16

Patton **R1 P2/R2 P1** **Main Title** **Jerry Goldsmith**

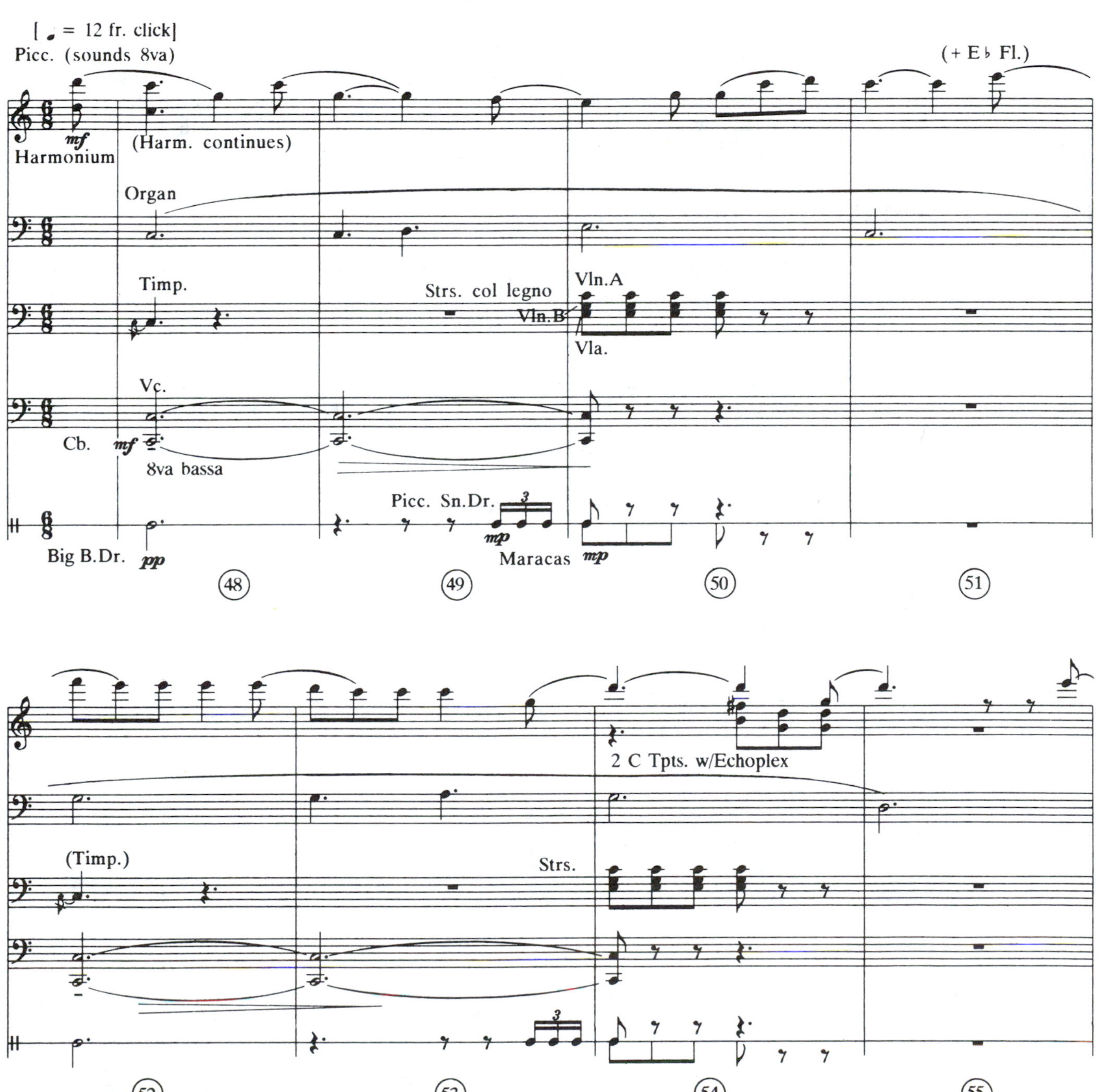

This is a classic usage of two-part counterpoint, harmonized with a simple and traditional chord progression. The same technique can be used within a more sophisticated or intense harmonic structure with chilling results, or may actually be used without a harmonic structure at all, allowing the "harmony" to exist as the combined effect of the two independent lines.

By creating this theme and its independent counterline, Goldsmith had already begun to develop the melodic materials available for his score. This can help achieve the desirable balance of unity and variety, because the counterline actually functions as a separate theme that is also a variation on the original theme.

MELODY AND BASS LINE AS TWO INDEPENDENT THEMES. The score for *Up the Down Staircase* (1967, Karlin) has a theme for solo recorder that can be accompanied by an independent bass line. Sometimes the bass line is played alone as an independent theme. Used in this way, the two melodies can work alone or together, with various orchestral colors. In Figure 13-17 they are shown together.

GIVING THE MELODY CHARACTER

Many melodic themes sum up the essence of a film or its characters, thereby becoming the personification of the film. The following themes project certain emotions or characterize particular people or situations:

COLOR IT CLASSICAL. David Shire wanted to compose a classically oriented melody, based on a Vivaldi role model, for the film *'night, Mother* (1986). (See Figure 13-18).

FIGURE 13-17
Up the Down Staircase **[Theme with bass]** **Fred Karlin**

FIGURE 13–18
'night, Mother **Main Title** **David Shire**

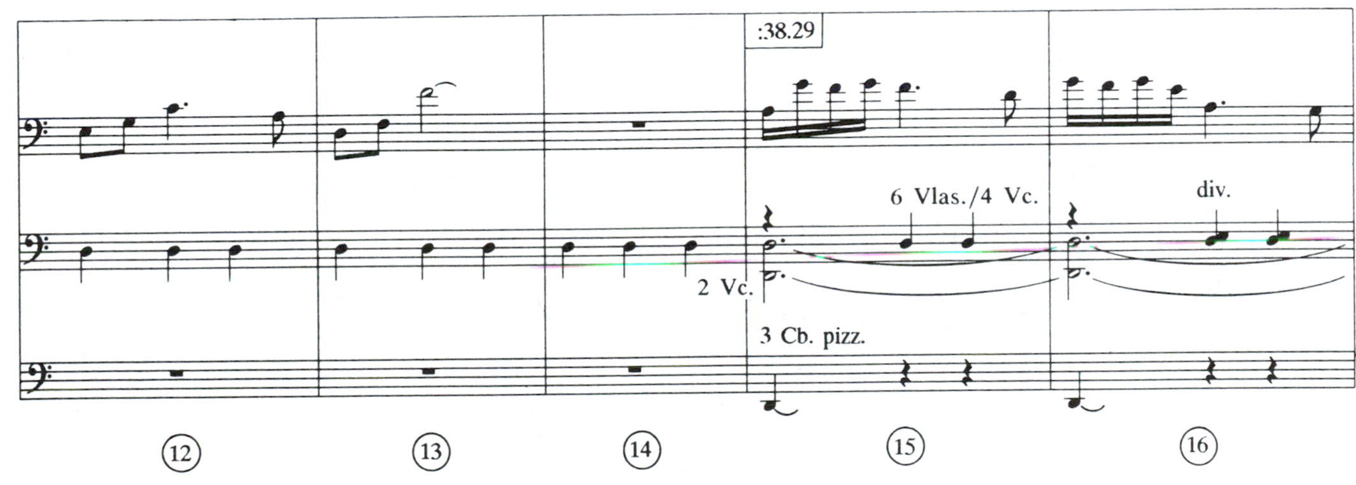

COLOR IT ETHNIC. No film score has been more successful in blending the flavor of Italy within the context of a heavily dramatic story than Nino Rota's score for *The Godfather*. Figures 13-19a and 13-19b contain two of the main themes (see Figure 13-13 for another theme from the score).

COLOR IT PERIOD. By using the solo soprano saxophone and a two-beat feel, Dave Grusin managed to give the contemporary comedy *Heaven Can Wait* (1978) a period flavor. By starting the melody on a major seventh, he gave it a contemporary touch (Figure 13-20).

COLOR IT ETHNIC *AND* PERIOD. The television film *Minstrel Man* (1977, Karlin) is the story of a touring group of black entertainers at the turn of the century who had to rub burnt cork on their faces in order to be acceptable minstrels for the white audiences. The story coincides with the birth of ragtime, a musical idea that is written into the script. The theme suggests the black heritage of the performers as well as the period in time (Figure 13-21).

COLOR IT EVIL. The following two melodic themes both express serious, heavyweight evil. For *The Magnificent Seven* (1960), Elmer Bernstein composed a strong, aggressive melody that nevertheless was clearly villainous, not heroic (Figure 13-22). And John Williams's theme for Darth Vader in *Return of the Jedi* (1983) is a classic essay on big-time evil (Figure 13-23). Notice the minor-mode harmony for the major melody.

COLOR IT HEROIC. Using strong intervals, a marchlike feel, and triadic harmony, the John Williams theme for *Star Wars* (1977) is a bold statement of undisputed heroism (Figure 13-24). It might seem obvious that a fanfare would sound heroic, but give it an interesting offbeat twist and you've got the opening bars of Bill Conti's theme for *Rocky* (1976; see Figure 13-25).

COLOR IT OMINOUS. In *Return of the Jedi,* Williams scores one of the confrontation scenes with only a low, ominous bass line (Figure 13-26). This is another example of a solo melody scoring a sequence.

FIGURE 13-19a

The Godfather **Main Title 1-M1-X** **The Godfather Waltz** **Nino Rota**

FIGURE 13-19b

The Godfather 12M2 Love theme Nino Rota

FIGURE 13-19b (*Continued*)

FIGURE 13-20

Heaven Can Wait **M103/201A** **Heaven Walk** **Dave Grusin**

FIGURE 13-20 (*Continued*)

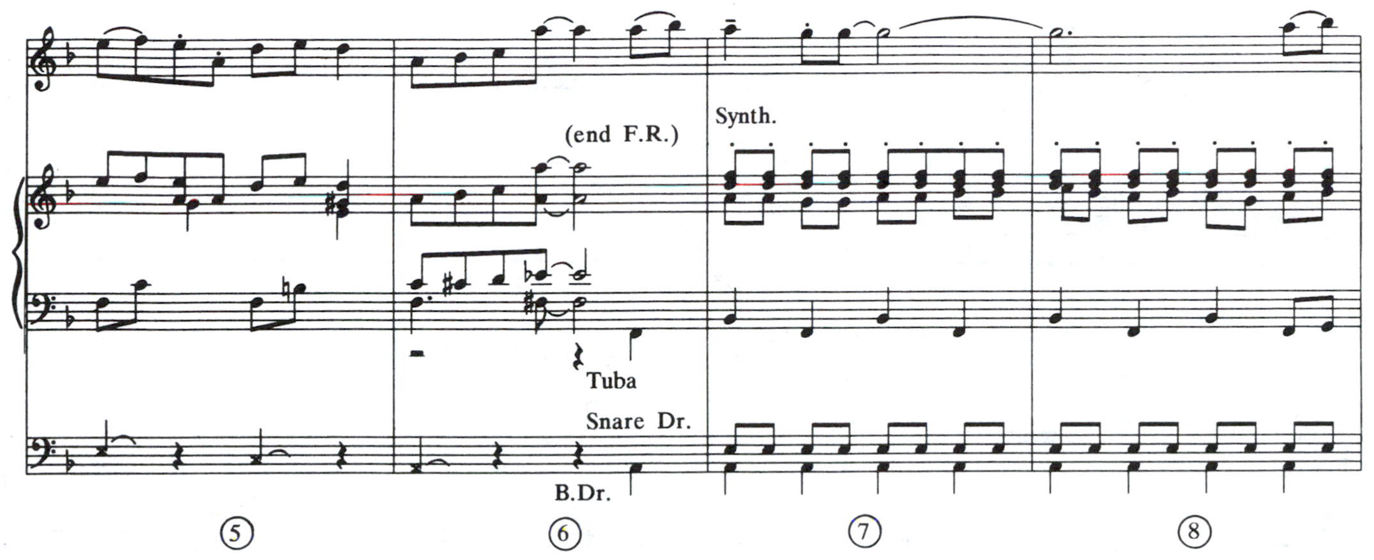

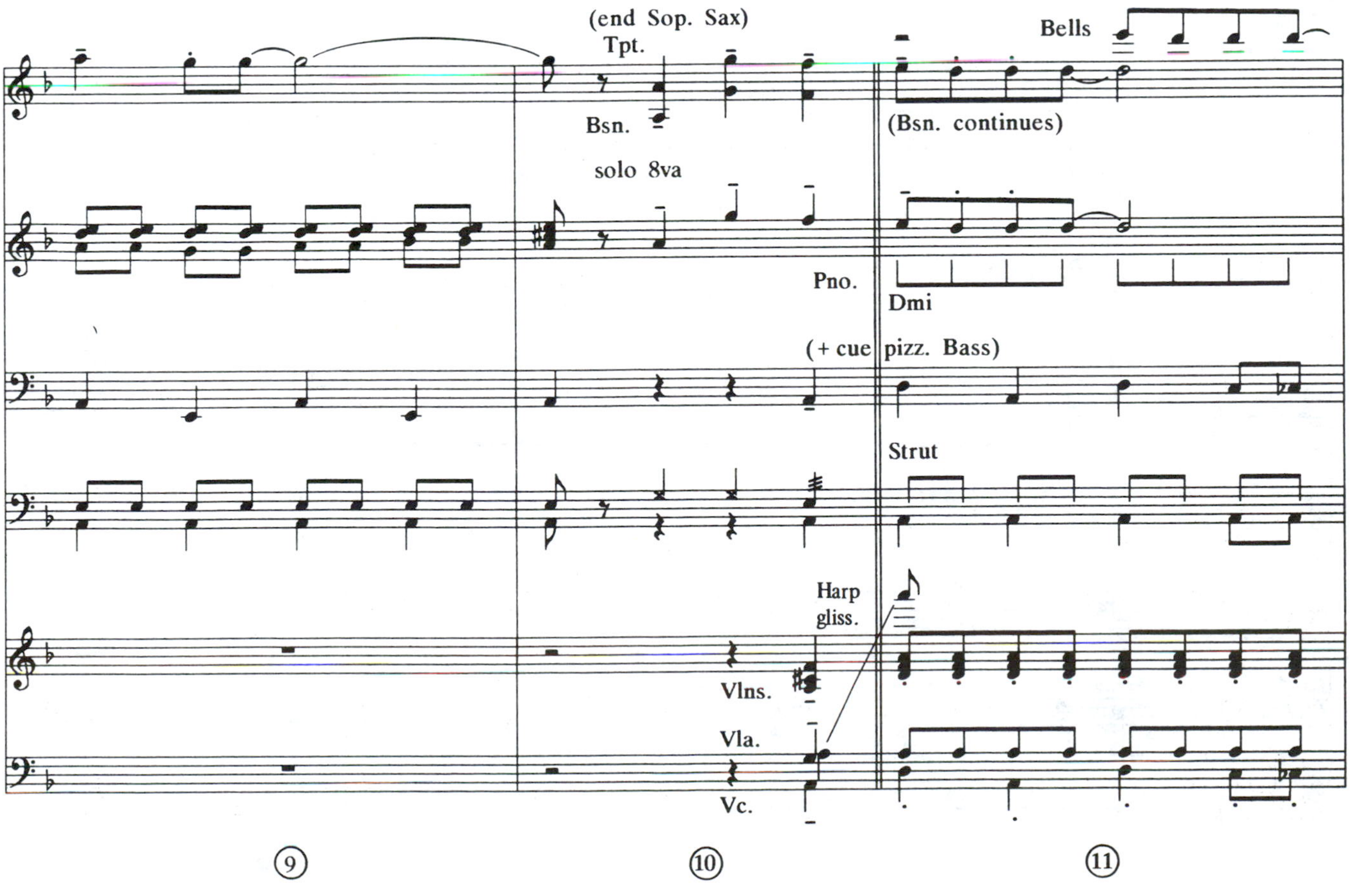

(end F.R.)
Synth.
Tuba
Snare Dr.
B.Dr.
5
6
7
8

(end Sop. Sax)
Tpt.
Bsn.
Bells
(Bsn. continues)
solo 8va
Pno.
Dmi
(+ cue pizz. Bass)
Strut
Harp
gliss.
Vlns.
Vla.
Vc.
9
10
11

FIGURE 13-20 (*Continued*)

FIGURE 13-20 (*Continued*)

FIGURE 13-21
Minstrel Man End Title Fred Karlin

FIGURE 13-21 (*Continued*)

3
10
11
12
13
Slight rit.
pp
Ped.
14
15
16
17

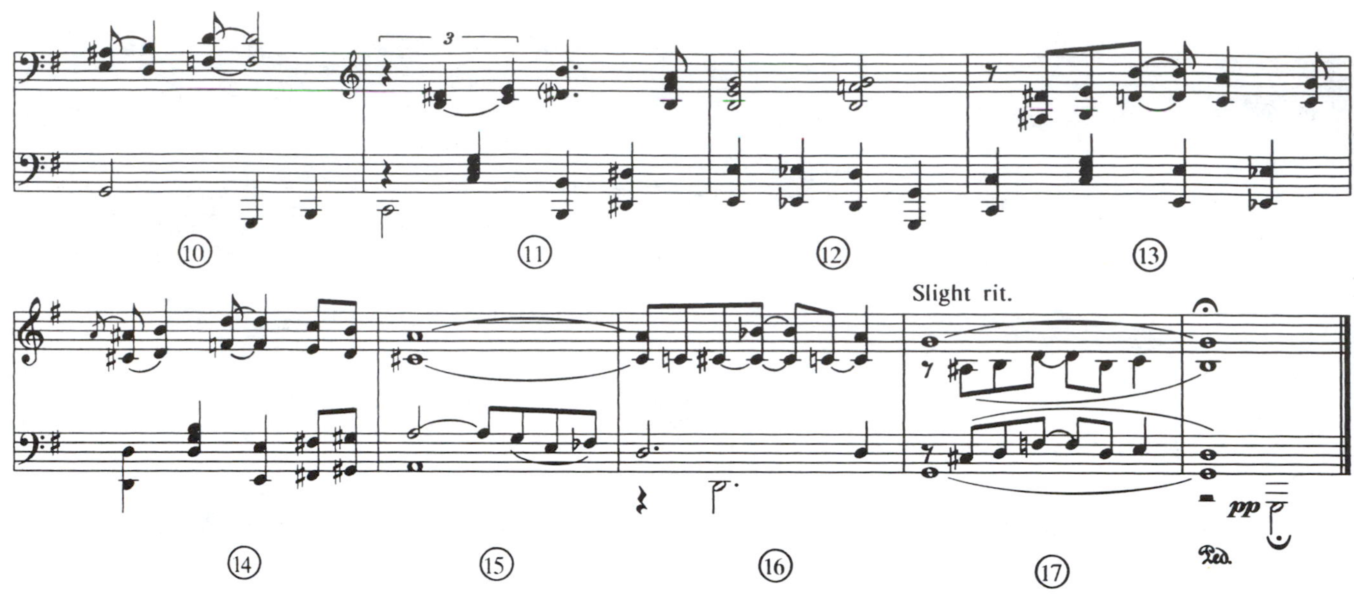

FIGURE 13-22

The Magnificent Seven **Villains' theme** **Elmer Bernstein**

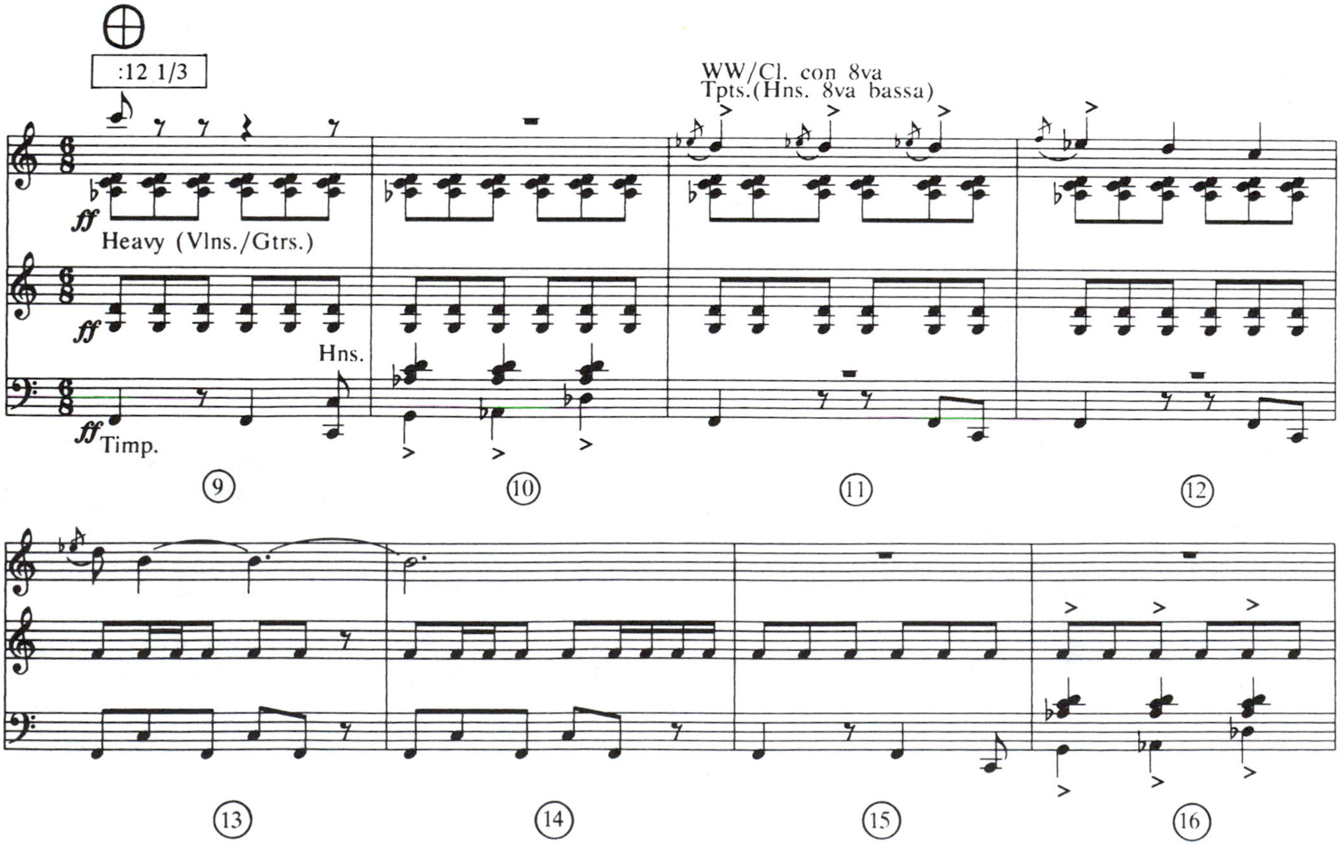

:12 1/3
WW/Cl. con 8va
Tpts.(Hns. 8va bassa)
ff
Heavy (Vlns./Gtrs.)
ff
Hns.
ff Timp.
9
10
11
12
13
14
15
16

FIGURE 13-22 (*Continued*)

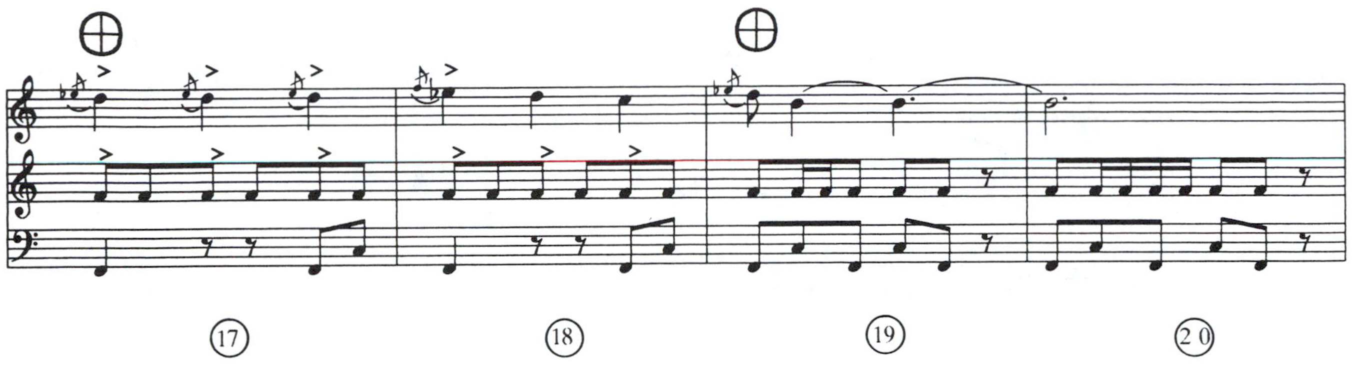

FIGURE 13-23
Return of the Jedi **Darth Vader theme** **John Williams**
Orchestrated by Herb Spencer

FIGURE 13-23 (*Continued*)

FIGURE 13-24
Star Wars Main Title John Williams

FIGURE 13-24 (*Continued*)

FIGURE 13-24 (*Continued*)

FIGURE 13-25

Rocky Fanfare Bill Conti

FIGURE 13-25 *(Continued)*

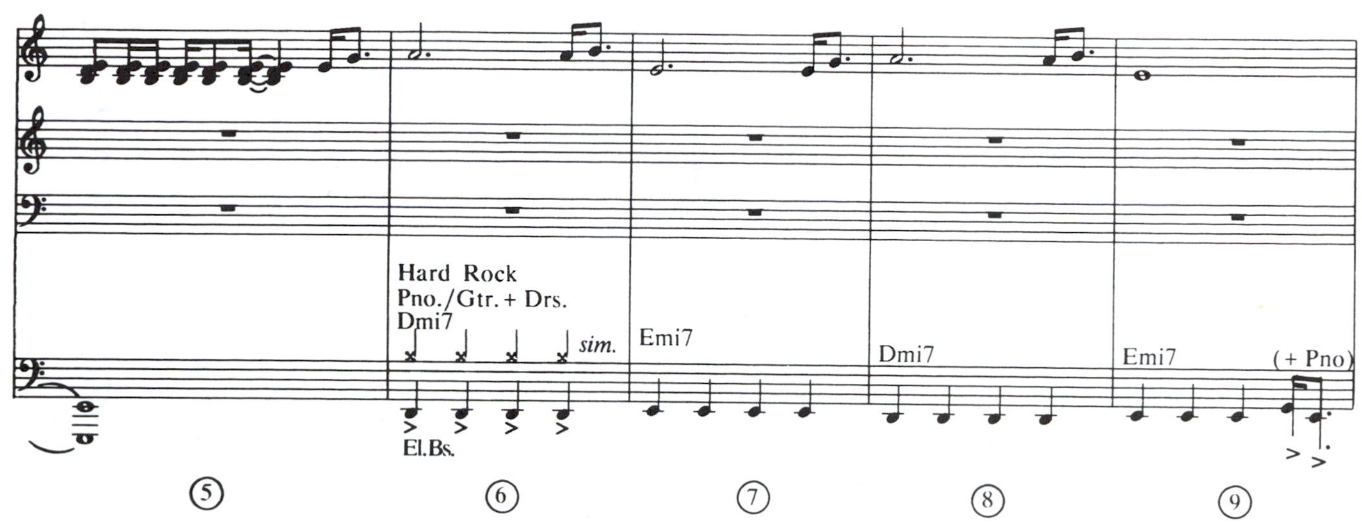

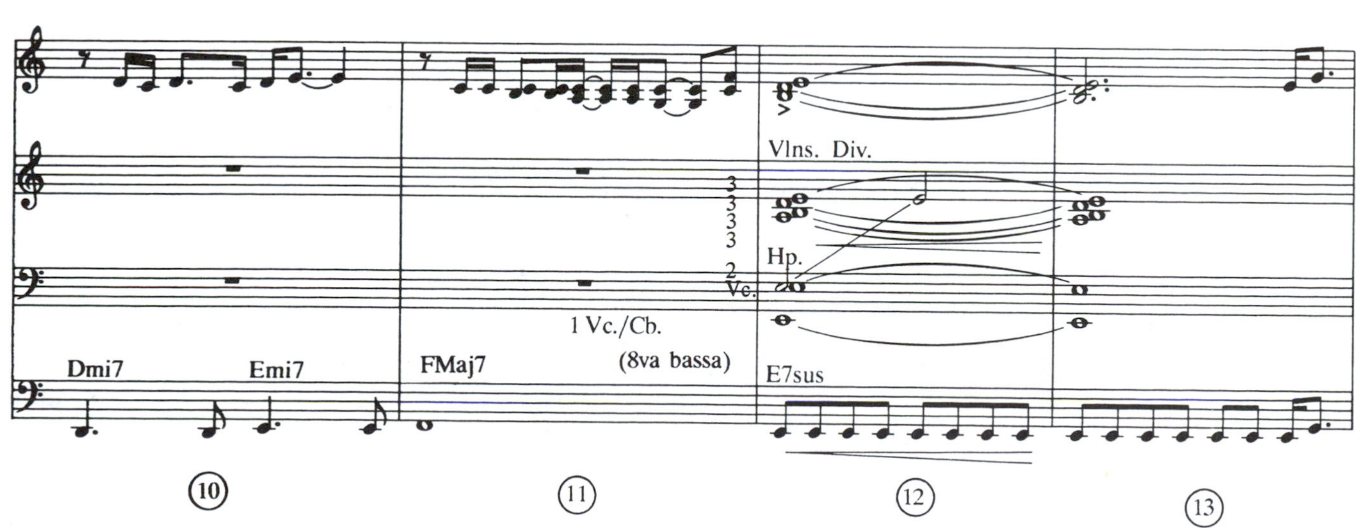

FIGURE 13-26
Return of the Jedi **R12 Pt 3** **More Duel** **John Williams**
Orchestrated by Herb Spencer

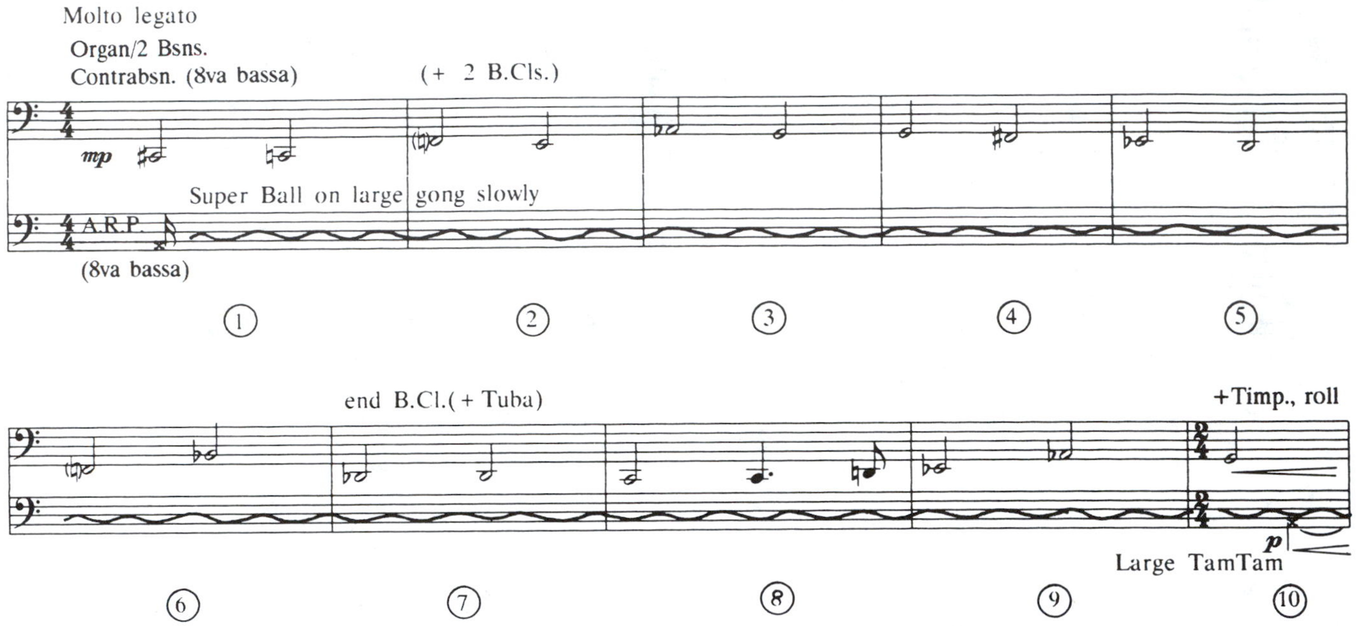

COLOR IT CHARMING. In *Jedi* Williams painted the furry little Ewoks as charming, energetic, lovable rascals (Figure 13-27).

COLOR IT ROMANTIC. The word *romantic* has many different musical implications depending upon the film and the scene. In each of the following examples the director might very well have said to the composer, "Make it romantic."

In *The Yakuza* (1975), Robert Mitchum travels to Tokyo to help a friend, and in so doing finds himself embroiled in dangerous international intrigue with the Japanese underworld. On this, his first trip back to Japan in twenty years, he reunites with his lover. During the course of the film, Mitchum learns that she is married to the man he believed was her brother. See Figure 16-20 for an excerpt of Dave Grusin's score that accompanies the scene in which they say goodbye to each other again, knowing now that their relationship has no future.

When Henry Mancini scored *The Man Who Loved Women* (1983), he captured the overall mood of the film. Burt Reynolds plays the title character, a man who seeks psychiatric help from Julie Andrews in order to understand his loneliness and emotional pain. All the many women in his life fall in love with him, and he is having difficulty dealing with that. Mancini says that he "felt the sadness of the character; it starts out with just a piano." (See Figure 13-28).

John Barry's theme from *Out of Africa* (1985) is a timeless expression of romance, with its classical romantic approach (Figure 13-29).

The tone of *Butch Cassidy and the Sundance Kid* (1969) is light and whimsical even when banks are being robbed and men are being shot. It is appropriate that the film's romantic theme by Burt Bacharach would also have a whimsical flavor. Though the film

FIGURE 13-27

Return of the Jedi R7 Pt 2 Enter the Ewok John Williams
Orchestrated by Herb Spencer

FIGURE 13-28

The Man Who Loved Women **Main Title** **Henry Mancini**

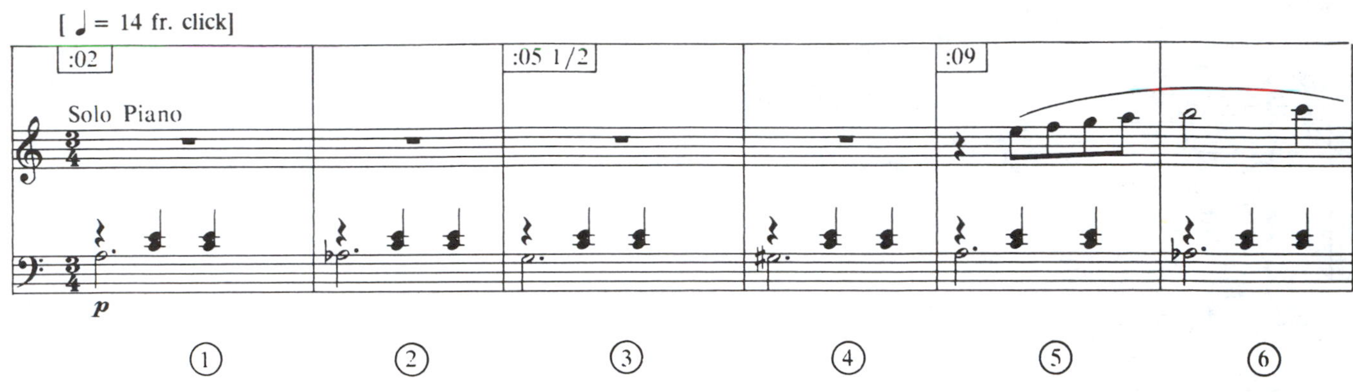

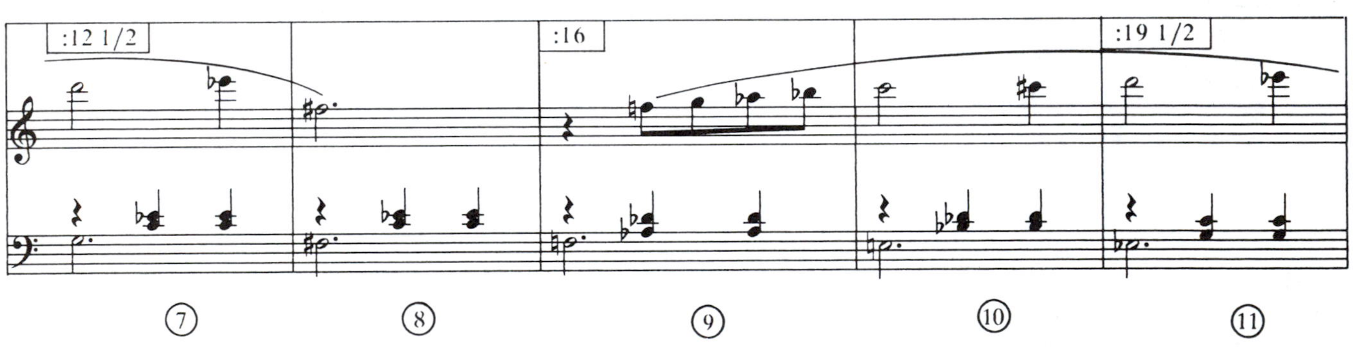

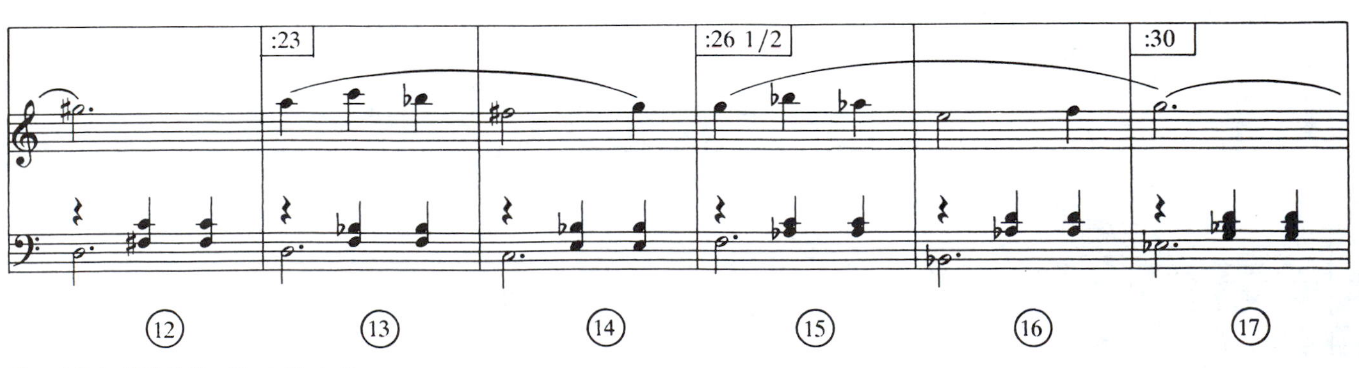

is a period piece, the score incorporates many contemporary elements, including jazz scat singing on some of the chases in Bolivia, and the pop song "Raindrops Keep Falling on Your Head" (lyric: Hal David), a big hit and Oscar winner. Bacharach's theme blends a turn-of-the-century romantic waltz with the hint of a contemporary ballad (emphasized by the Db major seventh chord), orchestrated very simply for clarinet, accordion and piano (Figure 13-30).

In *Body Heat* (1981), John Barry scored another kind of "romantic" mood—sensual and steaming. In the last scene in the film, the melody is orchestrated first for strings (Figure 13-31a) and then solo alto sax (Figure 13-31b).

If Barry's theme plays an intense, passionate romance, Bacharach's theme for *Arthur* (1981) sets off the edgy, quirky personality of the title character (played by Dudley Moore) as he drives to his fiancée's house (Figure 13-32). Originally designed as a pop song for the score, it became a secondary theme when Bacharach co-wrote "Best That You Can Do" with Carole Bayer Sager, Christopher Cross, and Peter Allen.

FIGURE 13-29
Out of Africa **1M2 Main Title** **John Barry**
Orchestrated by Al Woodbury

FIGURE 13-29 (*Continued*)

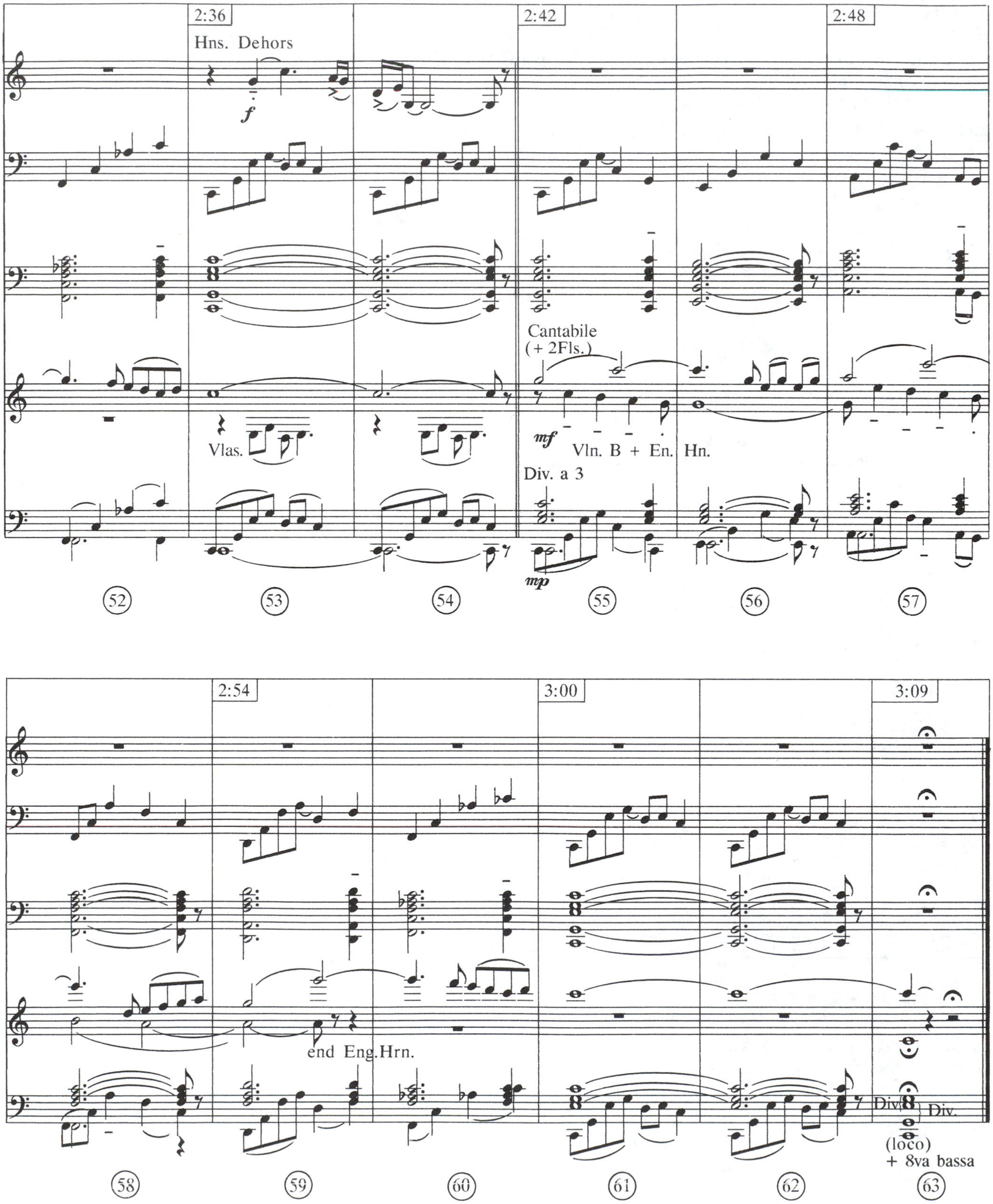

2:36 2:42 2:48

Hns. Dehors

f

Cantabile
(+ 2Fls.)

Vlas.

mf Vln. B + En. Hn.

Div. a 3

mp

(52) (53) (54) (55) (56) (57)

FIGURE 13-30

Butch Cassidy and the Sundance Kid **Waltz theme** **Burt Bacharach**

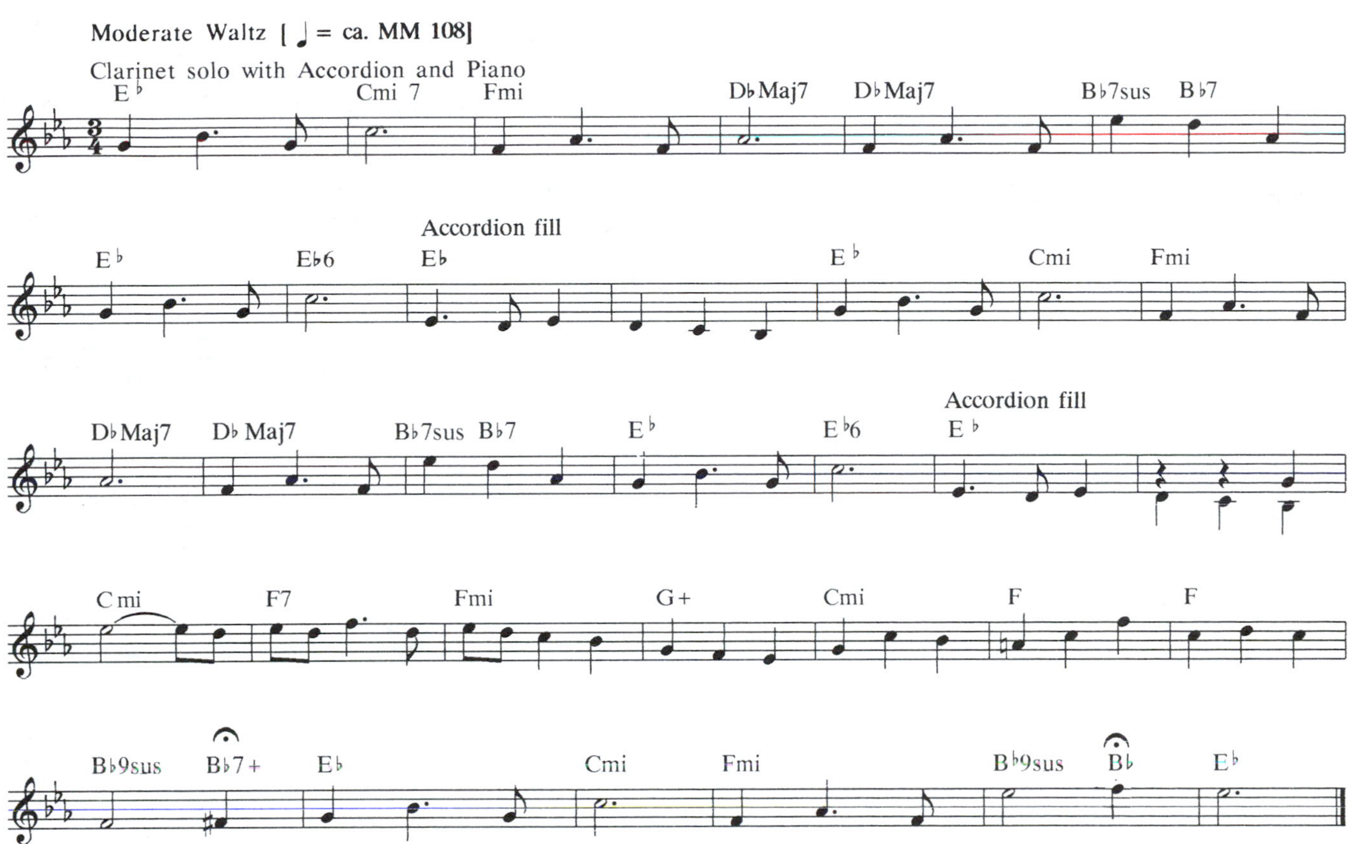

FIGURE 13-31

Body Heat **12/2** **Mattie Was Mary Ann** **John Barry**
Orchestrated by Al Woodbury

(a)

FIGURE 13-31 (a) (*Continued*)

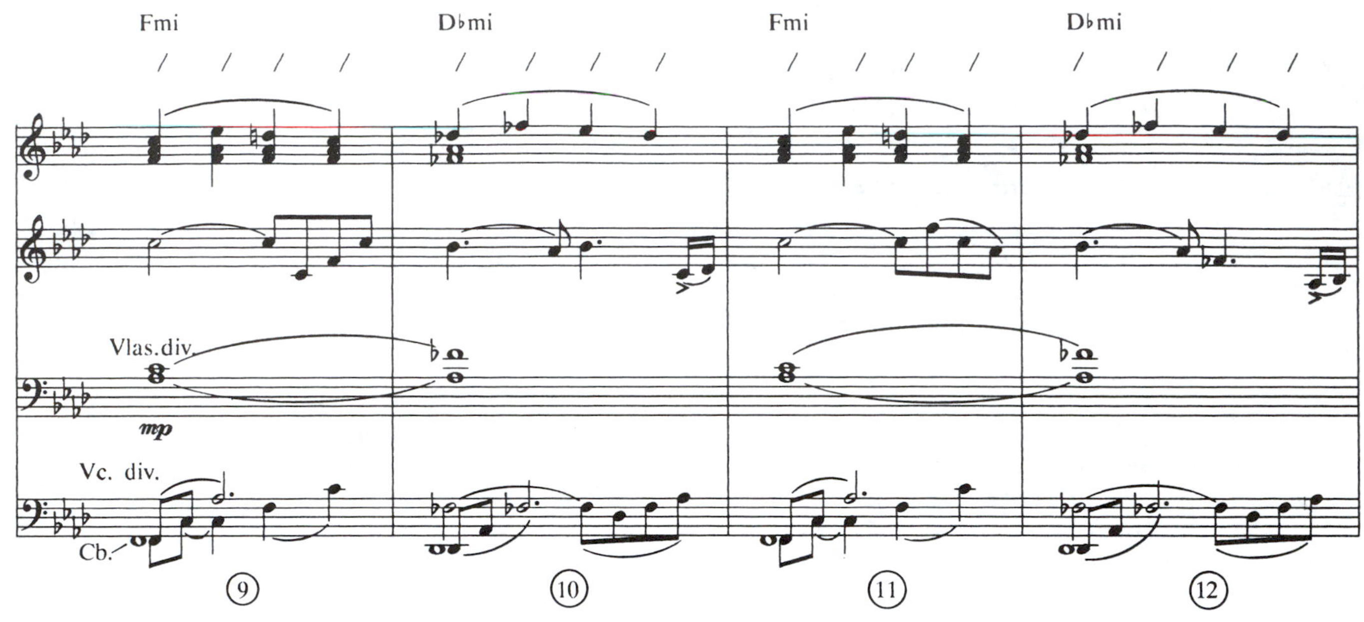

FIGURE 13-31 (a) (*Continued*)

FIGURE 13-31 (a) (*Continued*)

(b)

FIGURE 13-31 (b) (*Continued*)

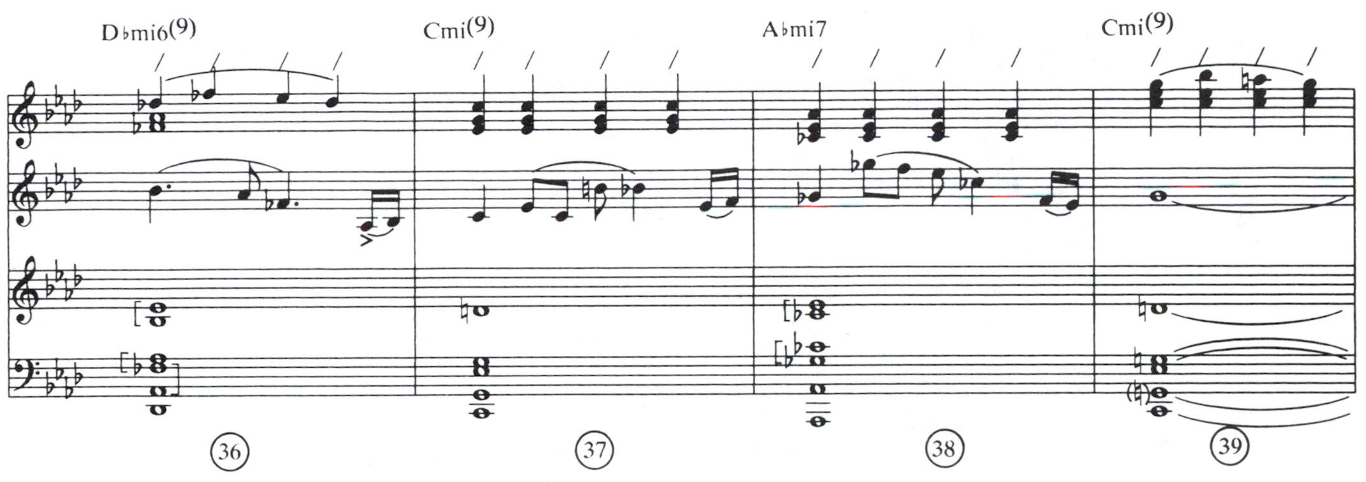

FIGURE 13-32

Arthur Arthur Drives to Fiancee ("Money") Burt Bacharach

FIGURE 13-32 (*Continued*)

HIT RECORDS

One of the great things that can happen to you is to write what we used to call a "standard."
ALEXANDER COURAGE

Every composer would enjoy gold records framed on his wall. Although filmmakers often hope for one or more hit songs for their movies, they aren't averse to a hit instrumental if it happens. And it does, now and then. Most often these hit instrumentals are dependent on contemporary colors and rhythm for their impact (like Vangelis's theme from *Chariots of Fire* (1981) and Harold Faltermeyer's "Axel F" theme from *Beverly Hills Cop* (1984; see Figure 22-11).

If you are asked to write a hit, then that pressure becomes part of the assignment. When possible, though, satisfy the needs of the film also, or you will do everybody a big disservice. John Williams didn't score *Star Wars* with a fusion band. He used a symphonic orchestra and approached his score with an eye toward providing the traditional dramatic values which would best support and enhance the film. The impact of his melodies, well supported by orchestral bravura, has brought his music for that film more recognition and performances than most record-oriented film themes and songs.

CHAPTER 14 USING HARMONY

I relish thinking of the harmony. And there are kinds of stories that would immediately bring that out in me. MICHAEL MELVOIN

You find out that the unison is the strongest sound that you can make. And that the diatonic harmonies used in a sort of four-square way still provide a tremendous amount of strength. ELMER BERNSTEIN

Film composers have available to them all the harmonic resources of the past and present. They have all of the traditional tertian-built harmonies, related to the major and minor scales, of the eighteenth and nineteenth centuries. They have the harmonies resulting from the contrapuntal practices of the sixteenth and seventeenth centuries. And they have the expanded harmonic vocabulary of the twentieth century, during which time composers have extended to the limit the chordal stacking of thirds, have developed every option inherent in the circle of fifths progressions and their substitute-chord possibilities, and have added a number of other harmonic approaches, including bitonality, polytonality, quartal harmony, pandiatonicism, twelve-tone and set-theory technique, and clusters. These harmonic approaches have all been utilized in varying degree by film composers, often within the same score.

HARMONIC LANGUAGES

While the study of compositional techniques is beyond the scope of this book, it will be helpful to review the available harmonic languages and their film applications.

DIATONIC HARMONY AND CHROMATIC HARMONY. The reason diatonic and chromatic harmony, staples for more than two hundred years, are used so often for film music today is that they are still so communicative emotionally. In *Sophie's Choice* (1982), Marvin Hamlisch used a triadic harmonization of the main theme (see Figure 7-7) during the scene after Streep has fainted.

A chromatic approach fits film scores that deal with more sophisticated, sometimes historical, subjects. David Shire's score for *The Hindenburg* (1975), about the German airship that exploded near New York City in 1937, utilizes the style of the postromantic composers. The score for the miniseries *Inside the Third Reich* (1982, Karlin) uses both chromatic sequences and inversions with the third in the bass to evoke this same period of time in Germany (Figure 14-1).

MODAL HARMONY. The term *modal harmony* is essentially a contradiction, since the church modes, which were the foundation of European music through the Middle Ages, were purely melodic devices, predating harmony as a concept. Nonetheless, there is now

FIGURE 14-1

Inside the Third Reich **16/3 The New Building Fred Karlin**

clearly a vocabulary of modal harmony using chords built on these modes, and it is of great use in film scoring.

Music for period films set any time from before recorded history through the Middle Ages has usually been influenced by the modes. Nino Rota's harmonic language (using the Aeolian mode) for Franco Zeffirelli's *Romeo and Juliet* (1968) shows this modal influence (Figure 14-2).

Much of the music brought to America by the settlers from Great Britain was modal, which is why so many of the early American fiddling tunes are modal. Maurice Jarre took this harmonic approach (using major-sounding modes) when he composed his electronic score for *Witness* (1985; see Figure 14-3). He had studied American folk music at the Paris Conservatory in the sixties and says, "I know just how hoedown music and all the hillbilly-style music goes—and basically it's very modal."

Modal harmony also has many contemporary evocations. Techno music uses it. Miles Davis and his fusion band use it, as do Chuck Mangione and Paul Winter. Jazz musicians now have to distinguish between a minor blues and a minor modal blues—just calling

FIGURE 14-2

Romeo and Juliet **M 28** **End Title Love theme** **Nino Rota**

FIGURE 14-3

Witness **8M2** **Building the Barn** **Maurice Jarre**

FIGURE 14-3 (*Continued*)

a blues "minor" isn't precise enough. Contemporary modal harmony has many film applications.

PANDIATONICISM. If all the pitches of a diatonic scale (the white keys of the piano) are used freely without the restrictions of traditional harmony, the resulting dissonances become pandiatonicism, the neoclassical harmonic language used by Stravinsky, Copland, Harris, and Honneger. By keeping these "wrong notes" within the diatonic scales, they sound dissonant but logical, more like errant passing notes and suspensions than harsh dissonances. As an example, pandiatonicism works well when the drama involves a contemporary feeling of strength and Americana; the basic diatonic harmony gives a strong foundation, and the interesting combinations of notes inherent in this approach can add character and personality.

POLYTONALITY. The sound of two different keys playing simultaneously has become very prevalent in film scores. Polytonality is associated with Igor Stravinsky's ballets *The Rite of Spring* and *Petrushka*. In fact, the two chords in Figure 14-4 are sometimes called the "Stravinsky" chords.

Note that Figure 14-4b is a linear version of polytonality. See bar 1 of the cue from *The Omen* (1976) illustrated in Figure 16-15 for another example of this. In this case, Jerry Goldsmith uses the same chord for the string glisses.

Polytonality has been particularly associated with space films and action/adventure films like *Superman* (1978) and *Romancing the Stone* (1984). John Williams uses it in *Star Wars* (1977). In Figure 14-5, the bass pedal point suggests one tonality, playing against the trumpet triads.

Polytonality can help drive things along by enriching the chordal possibilities. In the action-thriller *WarGames* (1983), Arthur B. Rubinstein implies polytonality in the piano chordal passage, giving the music rhythmic propulsion and tension. Although not played simultaneously, the rapidly alternating minor thirds suggest polytonality. (See Figure 14-6). This is also another example of Rubinstein's use of the minor-thirds motif discussed in Chapter 13 (see Figure 13-2).

FIGURE 14-4
"Stravinsky" chords Igor Stravinsky

(a)
Stravinsky: The Rite of Spring

(b)
Stravinsky: Petroushka

FIGURE 14-5

Star Wars **Reel 1 Part 3 The War**

John Williams
Orchestrated by Herb Spencer

(a)

Brightly

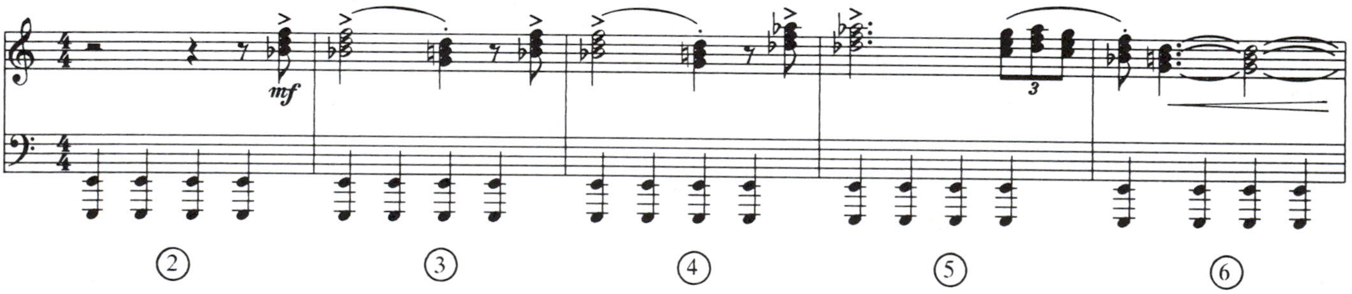

mf

(2) (3) (4) (5)

(6) (7) (8) (9)

(b)

mf

(2) (3) (4) (5) (6)

FIGURE 14-6

WarGames **M-62**

Arthur B. Rubinstein
Orchestrated by Mark Hoder

[♩ = 11⁵ fr. click]

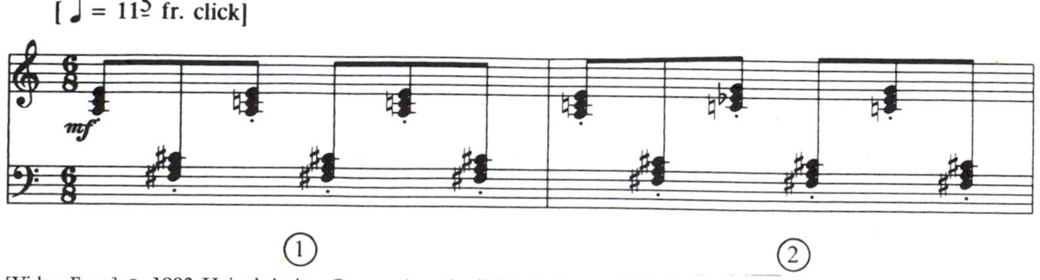

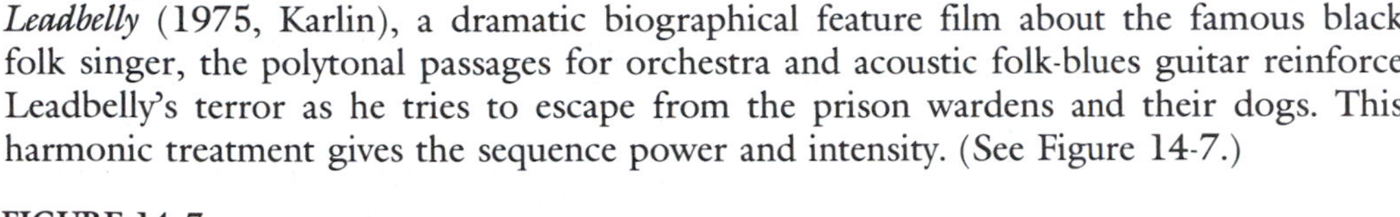

Polytonality can be combined with another musical language for added impact. In *Leadbelly* (1975, Karlin), a dramatic biographical feature film about the famous black folk singer, the polytonal passages for orchestra and acoustic folk-blues guitar reinforce Leadbelly's terror as he tries to escape from the prison wardens and their dogs. This harmonic treatment gives the sequence power and intensity. (See Figure 14-7.)

FIGURE 14-7

Leadbelly **M91 Chase Fred Karlin**

♩ = MM 63

St. mute Tpt./2 A. Fls./2 Eng. Hns.

mp

Hn.

mf

Vlns./Vlas.

p

Vc./Cb.

mp

Gts./El.Bass Ad lib pedal point

139 140 141 142 143

end Hn.

p

144 145 146 147 148

FIGURE 14-7 (*Continued*)

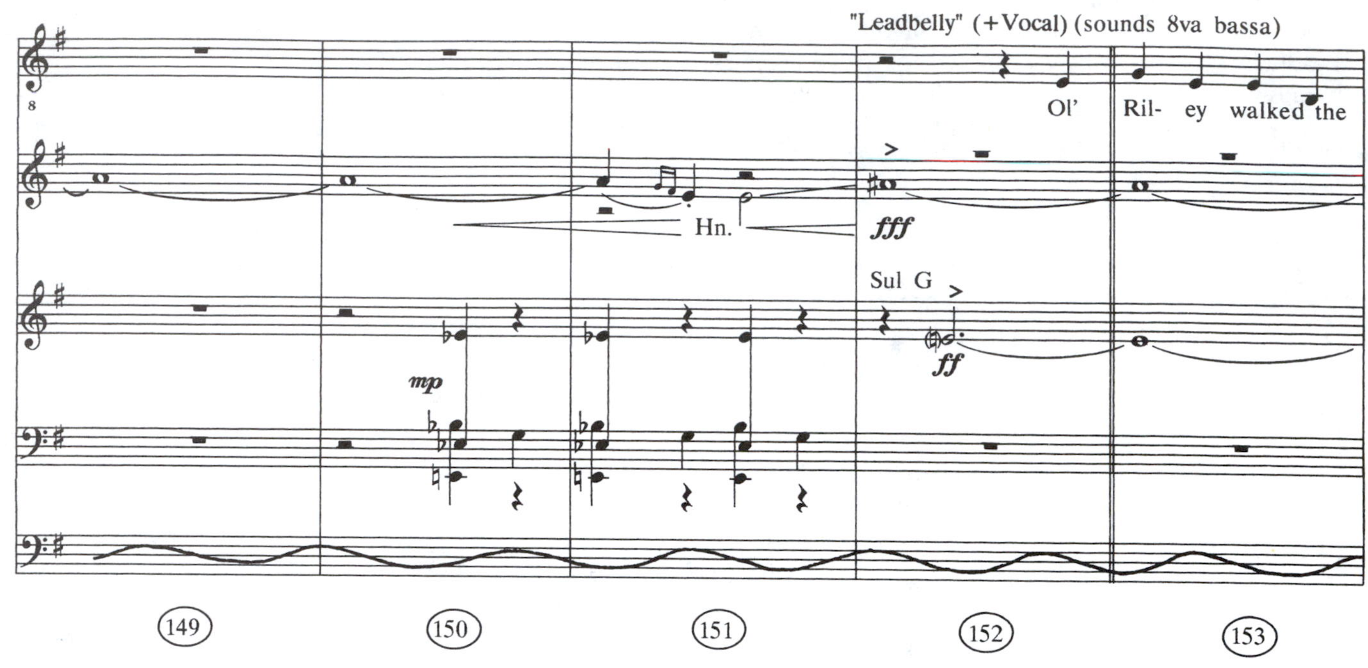

FIGURE 14-7 (*Continued*)

The Lydian mode may also be used in a polytonal way, since the C Lydian mode includes both the C major and D major triads.

This particular mode is often used for expressing a mystical quality, a dreamlike quality, or, in contrast, a grandiose or herioc quality. In a delicate setting it can suggest romance. Figure 14-8 is a four-bar excerpt from the end of John Williams's score for *E.T.* (1982). He used this motif throughout the score.

QUARTAL HARMONY. Chords built on intervals of a fourth or fifth were utilized by Aaron Copland in his well-known symphonic Americana compositions, including *Billy the Kid, Rodeo,* and *Appalachian Spring.* Composers often utilize such chord structures built on fourths and fifths when scoring films with an American theme. It is a harmonic language that often seems appropriate for traditional Westerns, the prototypical Americana.

But, like the other harmonic techniques, quartal writing can be most interesting when applied to dramatic subjects that are not stereotyped. It can be used to sound slightly cool and detached even while being performed with passion—just the flavor Henry Mancini wanted for the moment in *The Man Who Loved Women* (1983) when Burt Reynolds and his psychiatrist, Julie Andrews, make love for the first time (Figure 14-9).

FIGURE 14-8

E.T. M-114/121 The Departure John Williams

Many of the contemporary keyboard-oriented sounds have this harmonic flavor, like the example from Thomas Newman's score for *Desperately Seeking Susan* (1985) quoted in Figure 22-8. The impression is quartal because of the melodic intervals used (including the sixth and ninth), even though the harmony is actually diatonic.

FIGURE 14-9
The Man Who Loved Women **The Analyst Resigns** **Henry Mancini**

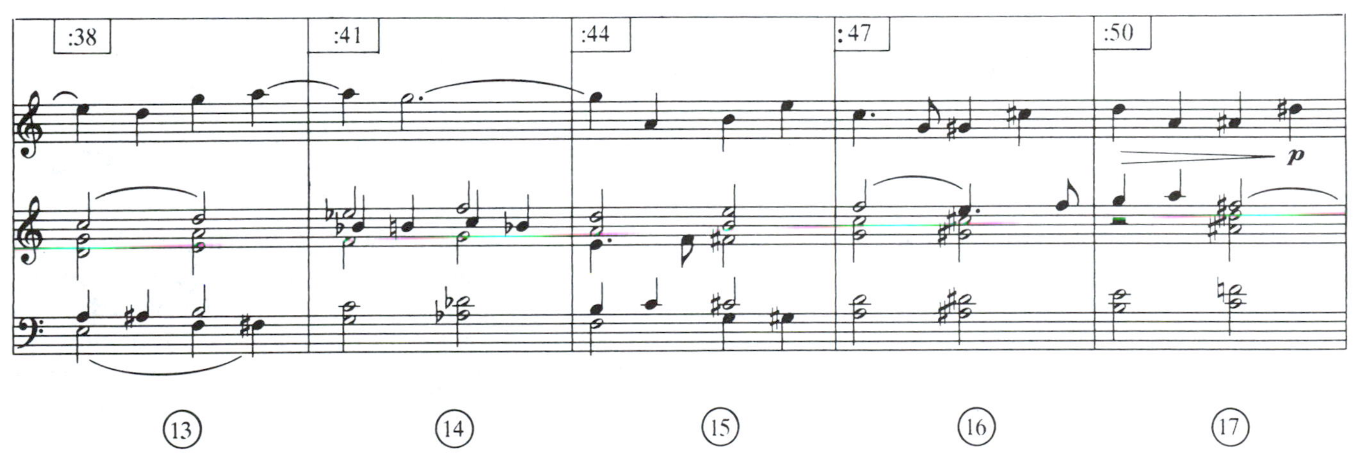

> ***I haven't done a totally serial procedure, but neither have the serial composers. But what difference does it make. No one can tell the difference.***
>
> JERRY GOLDSMITH

TWELVE-TONE TECHNIQUE. Twelve-tone (or *serial*) technique was systematized by Arnold Schoenberg in the early twenties to avoid any implication of a tonality. It is often used by film composers for moments of tangled texture and stress, one of the very effects this post-Wagnerian technique was attempting to achieve (as in Schoenberg's *Transfigured Night,* one of his evolutionary pre-twelve-tone pieces). When desired, it can also give a pointillistic texture with much less overt tension (Berg, Webern, Pierre Boulez).

David Shire found an interesting use of this harmonic language when he began working on *The Taking of Pelham One Two Three* (1974). He had done twelve-tone exercises in college, but composer Paul Glass had pointed out to him that you can use a row for any kind of music you want, depending on how you plan the row. The three diminished chords are a row, the four augmented chords are a row, the two whole-tone scales are a row. Shire describes his usage of the twelve-tone system on *Pelham:*

"*Pelham* was one of the hardest pictures I ever had to crack. I wanted to get that dissonant-sounding jazz, but I didn't want it to sound arbitrary. And I wanted some way of controlling it, because I couldn't write forty minutes of music if I just had to find those dissonances by hunt and peck. At the last possible moment, I stayed up one night practically all night, and at three in the morning it suddenly occurred to me that maybe I could devise a row that sounded jazzy. So I made up a row that was all major thirds, minor seconds, and their inversions [see Figure 14-10], so that it had a lot of major sevenths in it, and whatever you did with it had the flavor that I was looking for, because those were all the main jazz intervals.

"I made, for the first and only time in my life, one of those forty-eight box charts with the twelve transpositions of the row and the retrograde [see Figure 14-11], and propped it up on the piano and started doing this ostinato in the left hand that was a minor third, a minor second away from the basic tonality of the row, so it was related in a way to the row, and just started improvising to my heart's content, just reading down those permutations. And whatever I played came out with that sound that I wanted. It was dissonant, but it had a logic. And I yelled, 'Eureka!' and after that, writing the score was really a lot of fun.

"The theme starts with four groups of three notes each, which comprise the row. And then the four dissonant chords comprise the row, three notes each. The Main Title/End Title [see Figure 14-12] is almost a textbook use of a row. Once I had that material (and it took at least a month to have that breakthrough) it was relatively clear sailing from then on."

Figure 14-13 is an excerpt from Jerry Goldsmith's score for *The Omen,* from the scene near the end of the film in which Mrs. Baylock, the evil nanny, fights Gregory Peck. The music has the sound of twelve-tone procedures without being a strict application of the system. "That's an example where I took the [original] ostinato motif out of it and changed it by transposing the intervals and changing the rhythm and treating it in a quasi-serial way," Goldsmith explains.

Figure 14-14 shows the bass ostinato figure that he refers to. It is from the final "Ave Satani."

The way in which Goldsmith uses the ostinato elements in the fight scene is instructive. The original ostinato (in the bass voice of Figure 14-14) is clearly tonal, starting with

FIGURE 14–10

The Taking of Pelham One Two Three **Twelve-tone row** **David Shire**

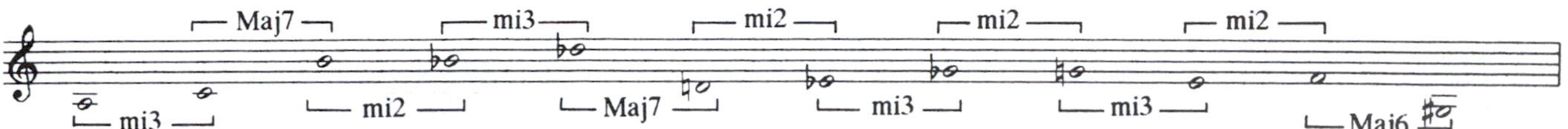

FIGURE 14–11

The Taking of Pelham One Two Three **Twelve-tone Row and Permutations** **David Shire**

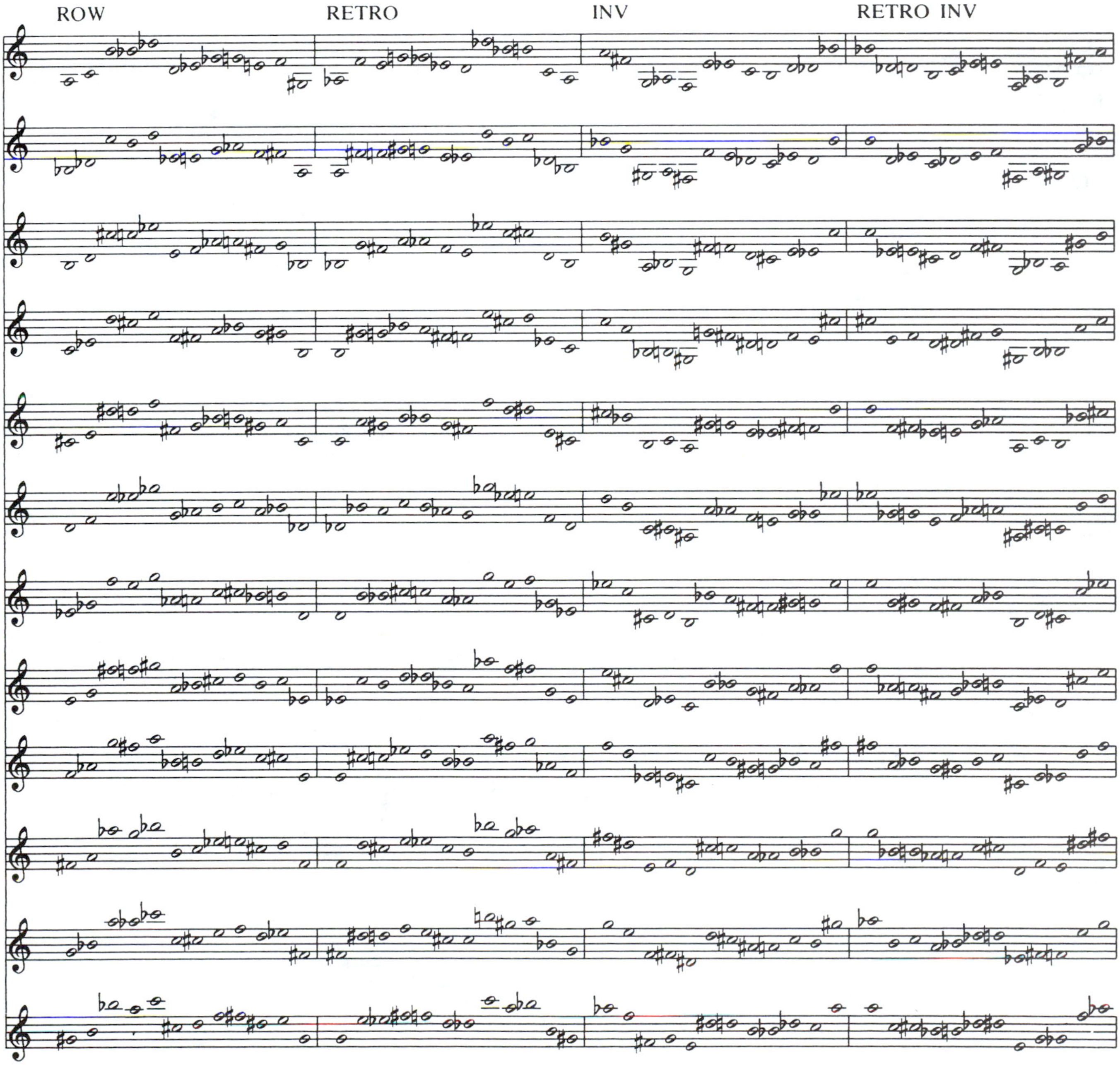

ROW RETRO INV RETRO INV

FIGURE 14-12

The Taking of Pelham One Two Three **End Title** **David Shire**

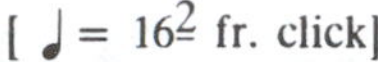

FIGURE 14-12 (*Continued*)

FIGURE 14-13

The Omen R11-P3 The Demise of Mrs. Baylock

Jerry Goldsmith
Orchestrated by Arthur Morton

FIGURE 14-13 *(Continued)*

FIGURE 14-13 (*Continued*)

FIGURE 14-14

The Omen R12-P3 Ave Satani Jerry Goldsmith
Orchestrated by Arthur Morton

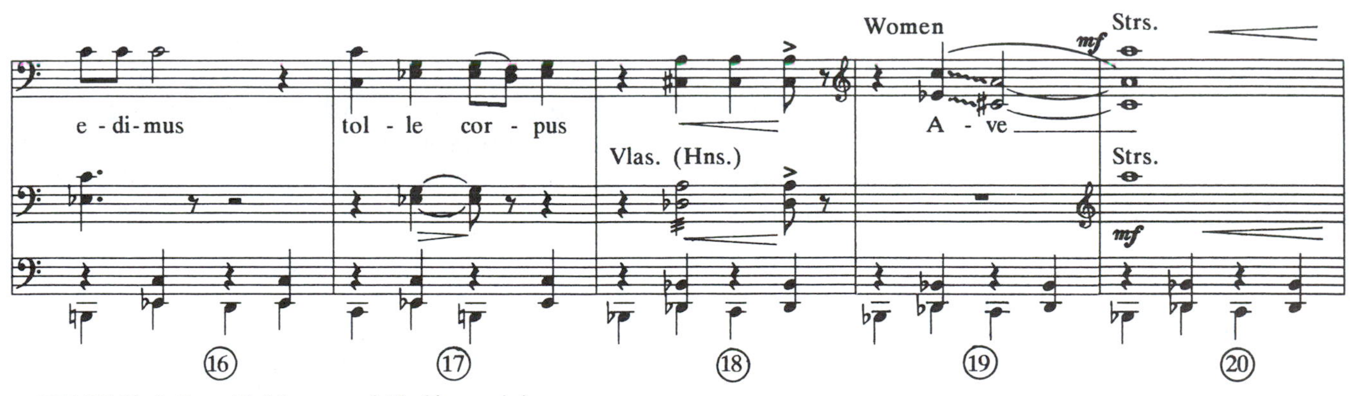

a C minor tonality for the first few bars and then Bb minor before returning to C minor. But within the original ostinato line are several half-step intervals (Eb to D in bar 11, B to the C in the harmony above in bar 12, Db to C in bar 18), all of which he uses as intervallic elements in his music for the fight with Mrs. Baylock in Figure 14-13. These minor 2nd intervals are used in their minor 9th and major 7th inversions and extensions as well as in the original minor 2nd interval (they are found in every bar of Figure 14-13).

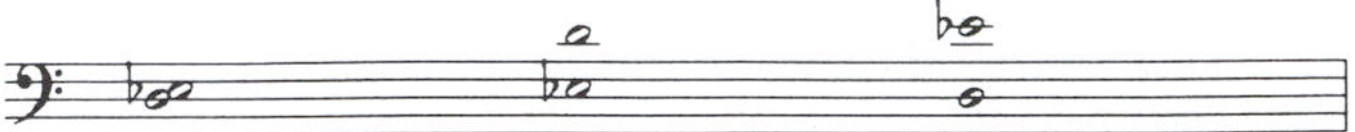

The slow-moving marchlike quarter-note cadence of the ostinato becomes in the fight cue a fast-moving eighth-note pattern (in bar 11). The quasi twelve-tone texture results from the dissonant intervals and the jagged melodic contours, more than from the fact that all 12 tones are actually heard in every bar until bar 11. In that bar only 10 pitches are used, the two omitted pitches significantly being the B and C leading-tone and tonic of the C tonal center inferred by the men's and women's voices who have just been singing prominent Gs and Cs.

The woodwind figure in bar 6 also relates. The upper voice outlines a B7b5 as the lower voice outlines a Bb7b5, again employing the interval of the minor 2nd between the two groups of notes.

Bar 10 is a typical twelve-tone procedure. All 12 tones derived from the intervals of the original bass ostinato are heard without duplications. Much of the rest of the cue is constructed in this way. To get the full impact of these relationships listen to the closing Ave Satani cue to hear the original ostinato and then listen to the fight with Mrs. Baylock ("The Demise of Mrs. Baylock").

Whether used in technical strictness or not, the *sense* of twelve-tone lines and their resulting "harmonies" adds bite and tension to a film score when this quality is desired. It is interesting to note that serial music, along with many twentieth-century techniques, has not been popular with concert-going audiences, yet a huge audience has heard and been moved by such contemporary dissonant music in films where dramatic situations call for tension.

FIGURE 14-15

***Dirty Harry* (1981)** **R 10-P-2** **Francis Drake Boulevard** **Lalo Schifrin**

FIGURE 14-16

The Outlaw Josey Wales (1976) 9M2 C The Violators Jerry Fielding

Orchestrated by Lennie Neihaus

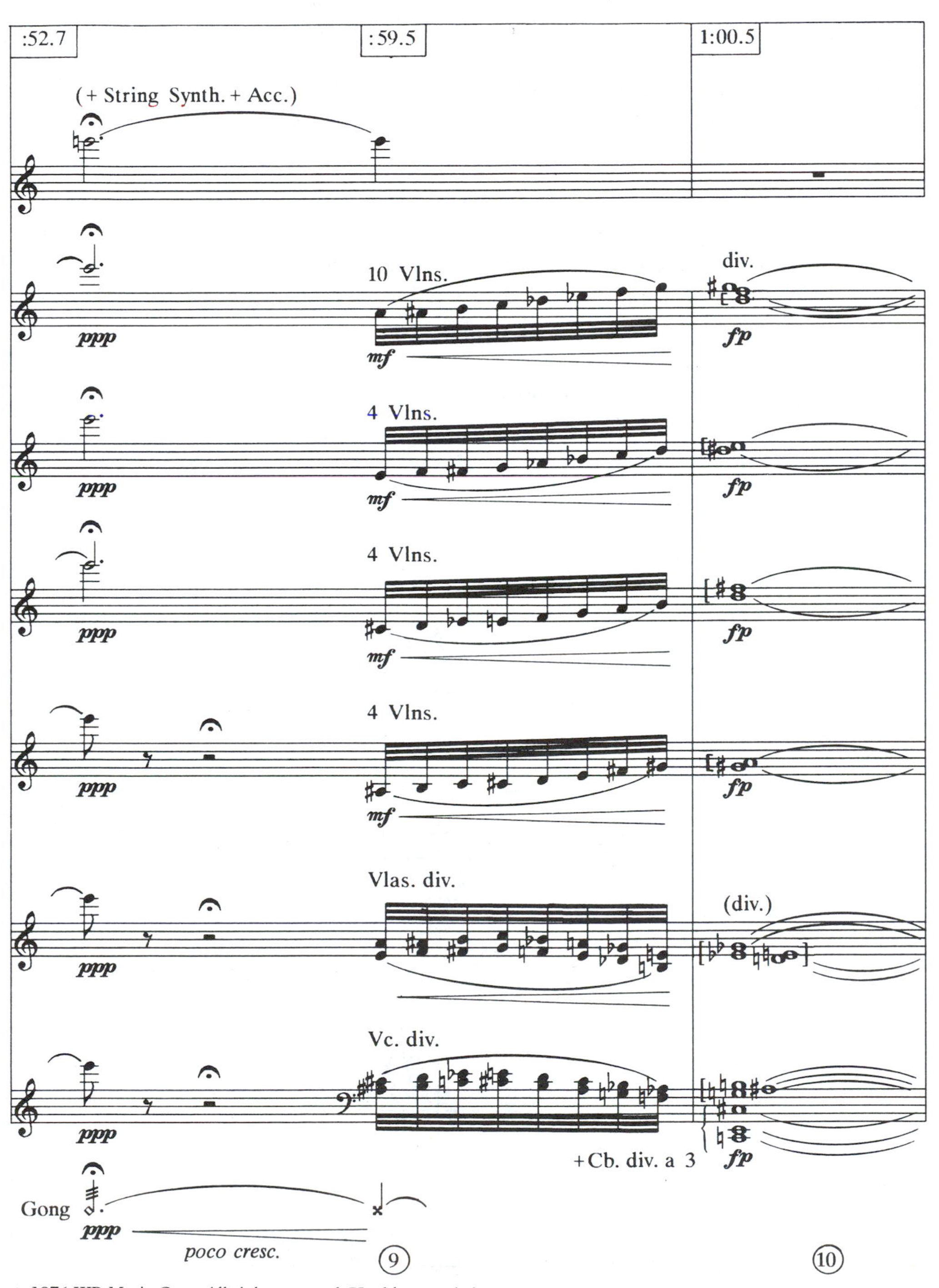

CLUSTERS. These groups of three or more notes, either overlapping or struck simultaneously, are more accurately described as "color accents" than a harmonic language. They fit in any context. They are used for orchestral color and mood, and for varying degrees of tension depending on the intervals used in the cluster. Short, accented clusters can have considerable percussive impact. (See Figure 14-15, 14-16, and 14-17 for examples of use of clusters.)

In his score for *Alien* (1979), Jerry Goldsmith introduces a soft 4-note string cluster in Reel 4, and then expands the cluster during the next few bars (see Figure 14-17).

HARMONY RESULTING FROM LINEAR WRITING

The harmonies of Alex North and Jerry Goldsmith often result from their linear writing. Goldsmith describes the scene in *The Omen* in which Father Brennan first says, "Accept Christ! Accept Christ!": "I think of it strictly linearly. What goes over it is probably

FIGURE 14-17

Alien R4-P2 The Skeleton

Jerry Goldsmith
Orchestrated by Arthur Morton

FIGURE 14-17 (*Continued*)

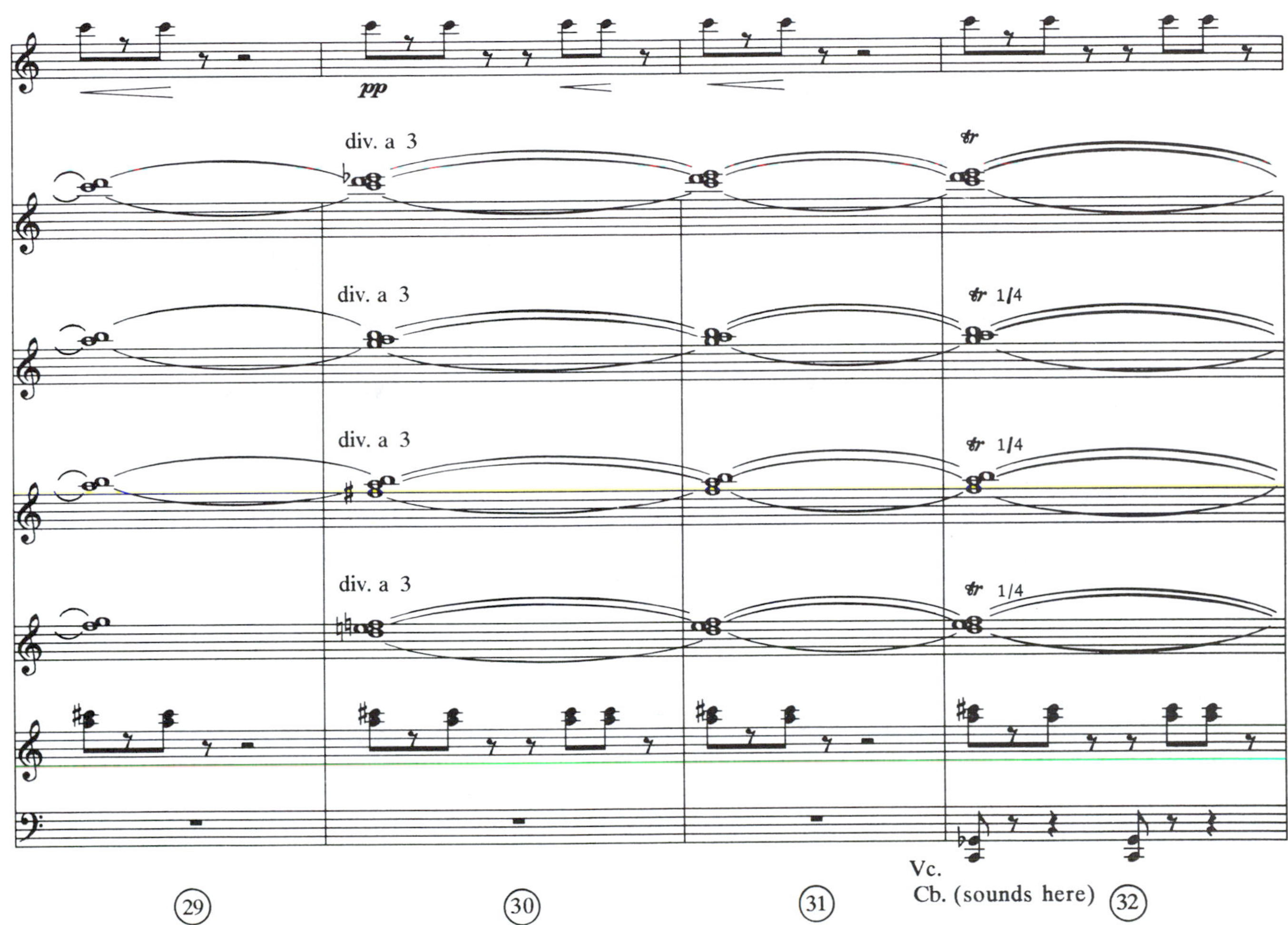

counterpoint, but it's another linear line written over it. As you're going, you develop it rather than staying static in that tonality. You want to move somewhere else with it, whether it's a sequential style or whatever. But it's what you hear; I don't particularly go at it harmonically—it's what you hear in your head."

Alex North explains his concept of a "three-layered construction" of musical lines; "It's more of a linear blocking of one idea that covers the low range of the orchestra, and a middle range, and a high range, and I put these together, and they come out either polytonal or polychordal." It is possible to compose in this way using period lines from the fifteenth and sixteenth centuries, as he did with *The Agony and the Ecstasy* (1965). The melodies have a period flavor, but when two or more of these melodies are played together the resultant harmony is unpredictable. "The lines have their own individuality. They cause dissonances here and there."

In his score for *The Dragonslayer,* North didn't musically represent the Dark Ages, "except in the sense that I used fourths and fifths constantly." These intervals, however, were surrounded and disguised by other intervals. The previously quoted excerpt from *Dragonslayer* shows three of North's short motifs (or "cells") working together (see Figure 13-8).

HARMONIC PEDAL POINT AND OSTINATOS

I consciously try not to use pedal point and ostinatos. But I know that they work. And the repetition does have a tendency to keep the music at a preconscious level in the audience's ear. And to that extent it's useful. But I like more harmonic movement than that. MICHAEL MELVOIN

I use pedal point and ostinatos a lot—one of the three or four great tricks of all time. Talk about mood setting. MIKE POST

PEDAL POINT. The repetition or sustaining of a single pitch (in any octave) while the chords change around it, pedal point is used extensively in film sequences. Rhythmically, the pedal point can be sustained or highly rhythmic and accented. The harmonic language used with pedal point is usually diatonic/chromatic or modal, but any of the above mentioned harmonic styles will work well in the right context. The repeated notes create

FIGURE 14-18

That's Life! M-8 Remember Henry Mancini

a static feeling, but the accompanying moving chords can dissipate that illusion to some extent, especially if there is an increase and decrease of tension as the chords progress.

In *That's Life!* (1986), Henry Mancini composed a pedal-point figure for two synthesizers, set in the middle of the orchestra, to convey a feeling of anxiety while Julie Andrews and the audience wait to find out if her biopsy is negative or positive (see Figure 14-18). "I used two keyboards on the same note, with slightly different sounds, repeating an eighth-note pattern. Used this way, it's like playing a B-natural and a C-flat on the harp at the same time—that kind of concept." Mancini's pedal point plays against shots of the machine that is processing the biopsy.

Michael Small used a repeated bass-note pedal-point figure in *The Star Chamber* (1983) to give an urgency and tension to the statement of the theme (a very useful function of pedal point). Figure 14-19 shows how this works in his Main Title, but the idea recurs throughout the score.

There are several different uses of pedal point in James Horner's score for *Brainstorm* (1983). As Christopher Walken plays back Natalie Wood's recorded emotions for the first time, the pedal point accompanies an important two-part motif played by the French horns and alto flutes (Figure 14-20). A short while later in the film, as he plays back the tape again at home, the harmony over the pedal point establishes a warmer, more reflective feeling as he begins to reminisce and fall in love with her again (Figure 14-21).

In Elmer Bernstein's score for *The Magnificent Seven,* he uses a sixteenth-note pedal-point figure for some of the action sequences. Composed in 1960, the cue shown in Figure 14-22 is an excellent example of rhythmic pedal point for strings.

OSTINATOS. These repeated figures are often (though not necessarily) in the bass register. They may not contain obvious pedal point, but in most cases they function as elaborate pedal points. This is because ostinatos usually reinforce one specific tonality, which to the ear becomes the pedal point. But it would be possible to create an ostinato based on a twelve-tone row, or devised in some other way to diminish the pedal-point effect, making all the notes more or less equal in importance. Since ostinatos are usually rhythmic in nature, they are also mentioned in Chapter 15.

USING HARMONY FOR CHARACTERIZATION

> ***I had the feeling it would be completely wrong if I used something out of character.*** GEORGES DELERUE

Basically, the composer must decide on a harmonic language for the characters, keeping in mind the place and the period. And then he must develop a harmonic language for the dramatic situation. If the people are simple and folksy, for instance, their harmonic language might well be simple, folk-music harmonies and progressions. If the setting and overview are similar, then one harmonic language might do. But if they are in a life-or-death circumstance, the harmonic choices for that aspect of the drama may be much more sophisticated and dissonant. The resultant contrast of harmonic languages would tend to accentuate the bizarre, this-can't-be-happening aspect of the people's lives. The contrast of two harmonic languages in a film score can bring drama to the score.

CAPTURING A CHARACTER'S SPIRIT WITH THE HARMONY. We have mentioned that when Marvin Hamlisch was searching for just the right feeling for his theme for Sophie (played by Meryl Streep) in *Sophie's Choice* (1982) he first decided not to write a theme that was in a minor mode (see page 93). Instead, he chose primarily major chords because he wanted to reflect her inner spirit. This harmonic language worked for him

FIGURE 14-19

Star Chamber M-11 Main Title

Michael Small
Orchestrated by Jack Hayes

FIGURE 14-19 (*Continued*)

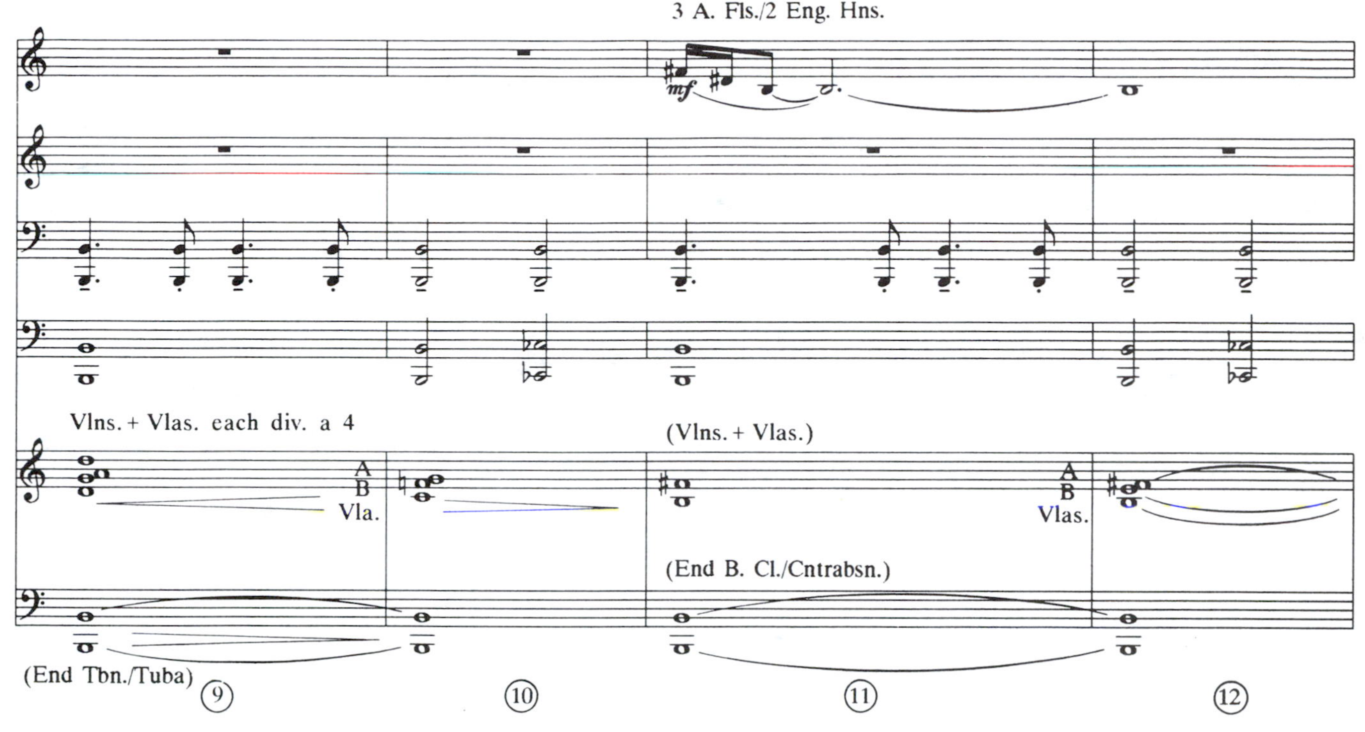

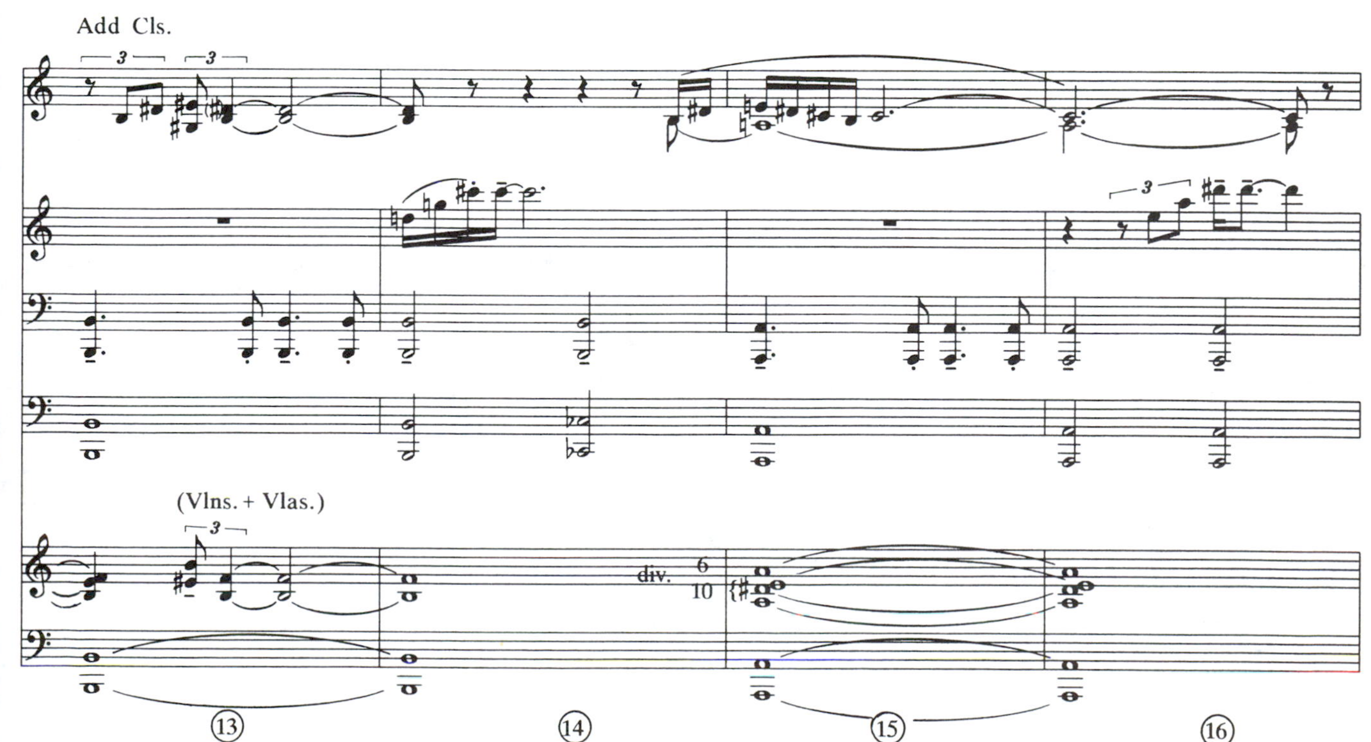

FIGURE 14-20

Brainstorm 5M3 James Horner

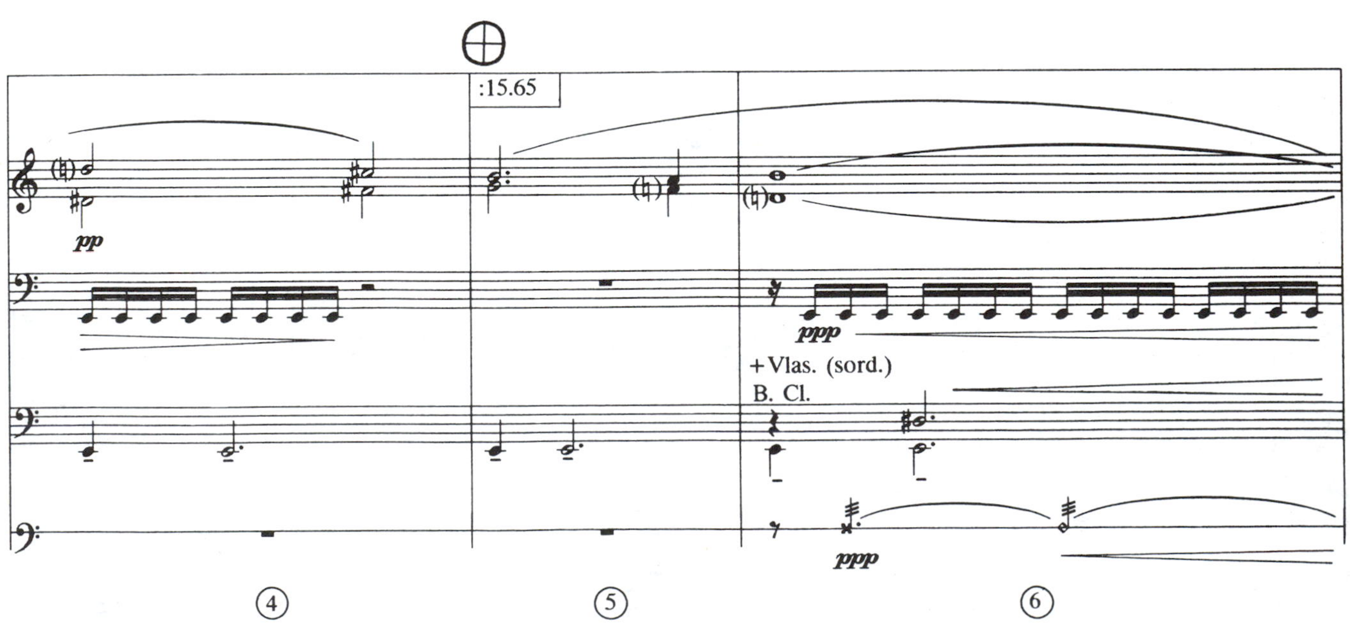

FIGURE 14-20 (*Continued*)

FIGURE 14-21
Brainstorm 6M1 James Horner

because it characterized her will to survive. Hamlisch reflects on his solution: "It's a little bit on the heroic side, but instead of being played big it's taking something that could be played big, but never playing it like that. It would be almost as if you took something like 'La Marseillaise,' for instance, or 'The Star Spangled Banner,' something that's really an imprint on our society, something that's usually very big, a march, and played it as a lullaby. What happens to it is it still retains that marchlike quality and it still maintains that inner dignity to it—it's just all whispered and all held inside her. And in a strange way that's what that theme is. That theme is saying, 'There's a hero here, but we're whispering it.'" (See Figure 7-7.)

Note that the theme and its harmonization are interconnected elements here, as they frequently are. Hamlisch's description of the marchlike, triumphant quality of his prototypes also suggests the harmonic language that is associated with those themes: forthright, diatonic, with triads and strong cadences; simple and marchlike in flavor; and major.

FIGURE 14-22

The Magnificent Seven 1/3 Council Elmer Bernstein

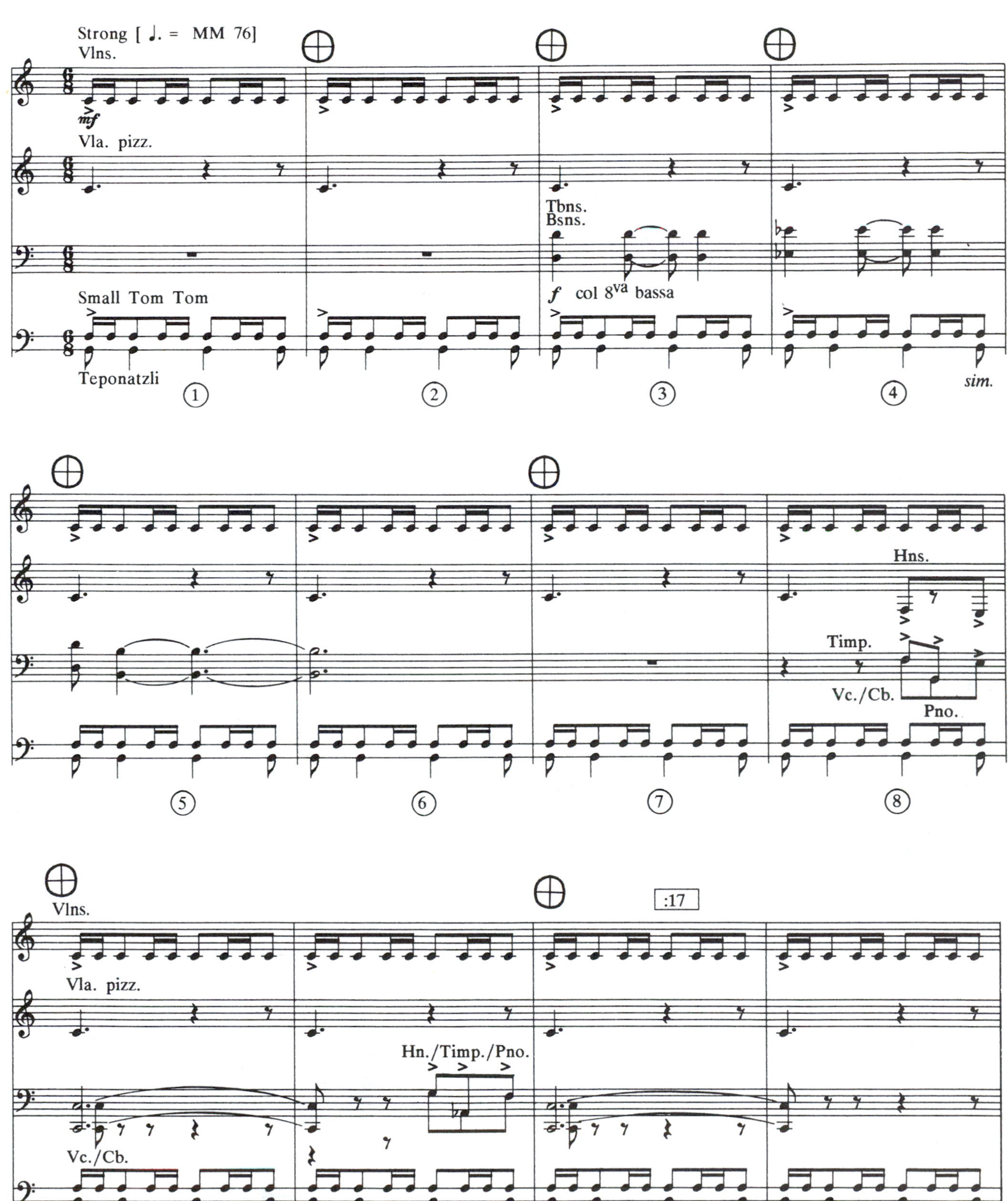

A good test for a theme is to play it without harmony, and A GOOD TEST FOR A HARMONIC LANGUAGE IS TO PLAY IT WITHOUT THE THEME. IF IT WORKS FOR THE FILM WITHOUT MELODY, YOU'LL KNOW IT'S A GOOD PROGRESSION FOR THE SCENE.

SUBTLE HARMONIC VARIATIONS. Harmony faithful to a character's tastes and lifestyle will help relate the score to the film. If you can imagine the character listening to classical music, then a classical approach to harmony could be perfect. If the leading character is a teenager, then the harmonic language heard in the music she likes might be useful. But keep in mind that if these tastes are fairly superficial, then there might be a more important, deeper quality to the character that should be reflected in the music, and therefore in the harmony. And the choice of an appropriate harmonic language is a significant element.

Georges Delerue recalls selecting his harmonic language for the sixteenth-century period film *A Man For All Seasons* (1966): "For me it was absolutely *impossible* to use a nineteenth-century chord progression. For example, I didn't use a dominant seventh or diminished seventh ever. But open fourths and fifths. And used in a similar way as the authentic period music, but with more instruments. Triads, sometimes without the third."

BREAKING THE RULES. Burt Bacharach's score for *Butch Cassidy and the Sundance Kid* (1969) doesn't totally ignore period and place—in fact, the waltz theme has a very period flavor (see Figure 13-30). But Bacharach went for the *spirit* of the film: whimsical; free and loose; contemporary attitudes that contrasted with period, place, and settings; and, ironically, the contrast of the old and the new in the depiction of the death of a lifestyle due to "progress" in the American West. So the score for this nontraditional

FIGURE 14-23

The Postman Always Rings Twice **Main Title** **Michael Small**

FIGURE 14-23 (*Continued*)

Western has a contemporary pop song ("Raindrops Keep Falling On My Head," with Hal David's lyrics), a series of chases in South America scored with up-tempo jazz-oriented scat singing; and the period/contemporary waltz theme mentioned above. The harmony is deliberately not completely related to the time or place. This anachronistic approach depends upon the musical concept being solid and emotionally appropriate for the film. Paul Newman and Robert Redford, wisecracking to the end, were not playing John Wayne and Gary Cooper characters. Bacharach sought to capture their spirit, not their time and place.

FIGURE 14-23 (*Continued*)

TENSION

Generally speaking, an increase in dissonance equates with an increase in tension. Though Laurence Rosenthal's harmonic language for the epic television miniseries *Peter the Great* (1986) uses a great deal of Russian folk music as a role model, he remembers that "the music got really quite twentieth century. In some of the later scenes the story really begins to get frightening with the half-sister, Sophie, trying to poison the mind of Peter's son. And later on, during the scenes of the interrogation and torture of Peter's son, the music is full of bitonality, tone clusters, and all the rest of it. At that point I really felt the only thread that remained [from the period sound] was the echo of the church, which was always there."

As a rule, therefore, composers increase harmonic tension as the dramatic tension increases. In Gerald Fried's score for the docudrama *I Will Fight No More Forever* (1975), about Chief Joseph of the Nez Pierce Indians, much of the thematic material is developed from his thorough research of the various Indian chants and melodies (see Figure 24-1). But, as he points out, "When you get into intense drama, terror, and fright, the music becomes much more atonal, or polytonal, and that's what happens here. The themes were quite modal and monochromatic, and as the drama intensified, I wrote bitonality, polytonality, clusters, etc."

This approach works on an overall level, as a way of harmonically coloring greater tension in the drama with greater tension in the score. Sometimes this results in certain cues being much more harmonically complex and dissonant than others. But you can also have waves of harmonic tension rising and falling within the scene.

TENSION AND RELEASE. Michael Small's score for *The Postman Always Rings Twice* (1981) is set with a relatively dense and dissonant harmonic language, which is introduced in his Main Title (see Figure 14-23). Small calls the thematic passage beginning at bar 20 "thirties romantic." Yet within that framework for his score, Small has sparingly chosen those moments in which to use a greater degree of harmonic tension. When you see the film, listen to the buildup of harmonic tension when Jessica Lange subtly suggests that she and Jack Nicholson might murder her husband.

The film's few lighter moments stand out in bold contrast, since the score's overall attitude is quite dark. Even when Lange and Nicholson first make love in the kitchen, the music begins slowly, with a dark feeling, and progressively gets more and more passionate as their love making gets more intense. The harmony continues to provide the tension that characterizes their relationship (see Figure 14-24). Finally, after they make love, the harmony becomes relatively simple and more consonant.

Later in the film, when Lange has left on the bus, and Nicholson is alone, waiting for her, the harmony is more consonant. When she returns and they dine by candlelight, the harmonic language (which is diatonic) is, again, more "comfortable." As they get married the harmony is also consonant, and in the final cue, as he weeps over her dead body, the harmony is triadic. The emotional impact of these musical moments is heightened because of the harmonic tension that surrounds them.

In *The Verdict* (1982), as Paul Newman tells Charlotte Rampling, "It's over—and it's my fault," Johnny Mandel begins the cue with a single line, which grows to two lines, and then continues to expand, getting progressively more and more harmonically intense. In this cue it is the harmony that makes the emotional statement. (See Figure 14-25.)

FIGURE 14-24

The Postman Always Rings Twice **2/2** **The Kitchen** **Michael Small**

FIGURE 14-24 (*Continued*)

FIGURE 14-25

The Verdict 8M1 Johnny Mandel

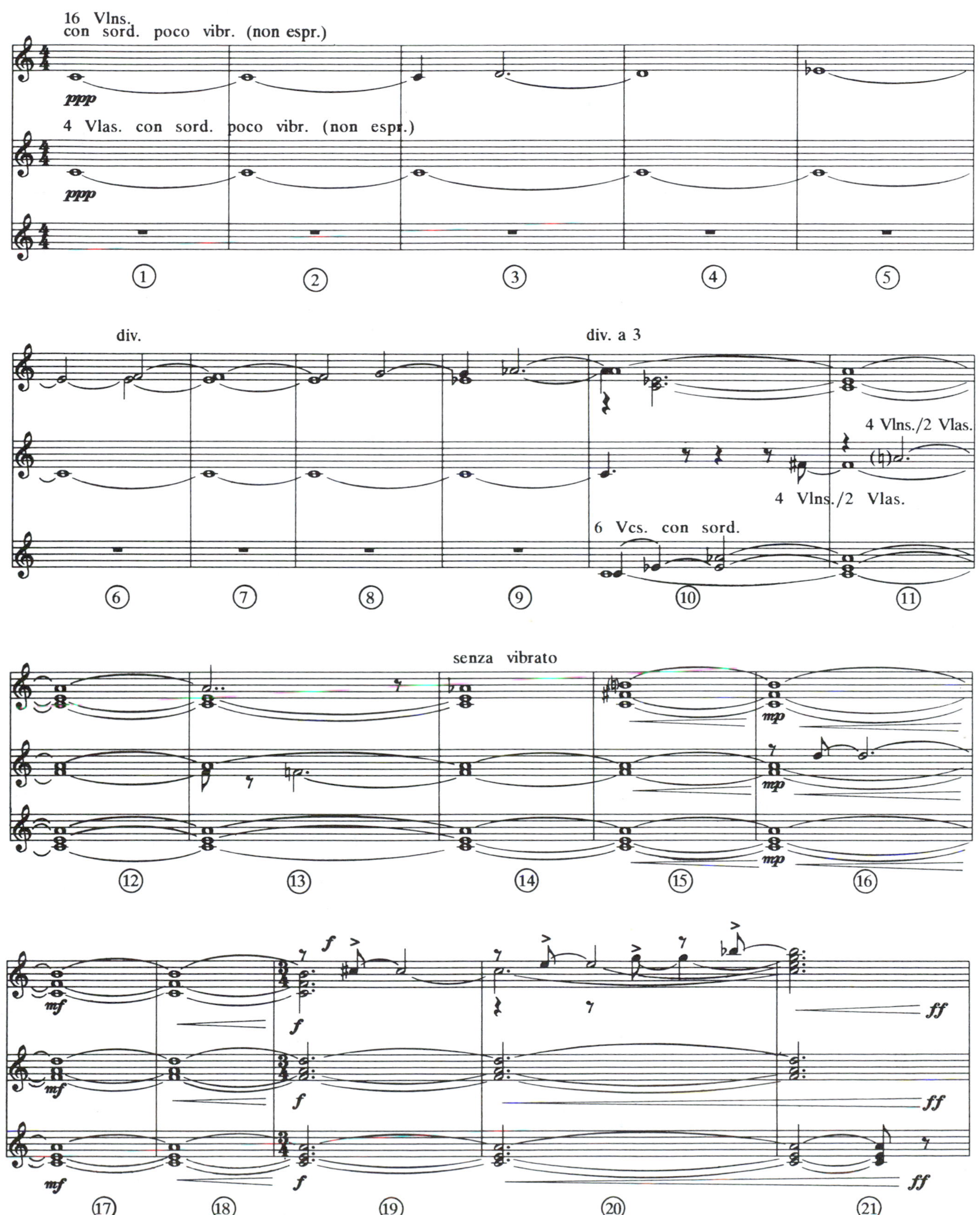

CHAPTER 15

USING RHYTHM

The first thing I do when I lay out an outline is to get my rhythm, my overall motion going. GERALD FRIED

In Airport 1975, *the thing I came up with first was the background rhythm to the main theme, which I used often throughout the picture. Rhythm first, then harmony, then melody.* JOHN CACAVAS

I think the key thing that made The Magnificent Seven *go was a particular sort of rhythmic energy. . .* ELMER BERNSTEIN

TEMPO AND PULSE

Every film has a rhythm—a pace—and either supporting or playing counterpoint to that inherent rhythm is one of a film score's prime functions. That inherent rhythm is the pulse, and we are assuming that the basic decisions regarding tempo and pulse already have been or are now being made (see Chapter 12, "Composing").

SKETCHING THE RHYTHMS

Avoid the quicksand of detail during the early stages of sketching. During this stage, there are many times when you may feel a rhythmic flow without knowing exactly which pitches will be used. If you hear pitches right away, fine. But you can sketch first using slashes without note heads to fill in whatever seems rhythmically appropriate. Later you can fill in any notes or bars that are elusive on the first pass. As an example, Figure 15-1 is a hypothetical pitchless sketch of one of Henry Mancini's cues for *Silver Streak* (1976), which is quoted in Figure 15-2.

In a pinch, some composers will give their sketch to an orchestrator with some slashes notated, usually with an indication to continue a previously sketched passage. In any event, it is much easier to fill in bars after the main body of the cue is finished.

THE PERCUSSION SECTION

The instruments in the percussion family can add both color and rhythm to a composition. The simplest and most abstract expression of rhythm in film writing is scoring with percussion only, and in such cases, the entire thrust of the passage is rhythmic. Alan Silvestri's contemporary score for *Outrageous Fortune* (1987) contains clear examples of this—cues in which the drum machine and percussion carry the musical idea with neither theme nor harmony. More traditionally, in *The Outlaw Josey Wales* (1976)—a Clint Eastwood Western—Jerry Fielding used the percussion section on various drums to score a cue near the end. (See Figure 15-3.)

FIGURE 15-1
Silver Streak **12/1 Runaway Train (nonpitch reduction) Henry Mancini**

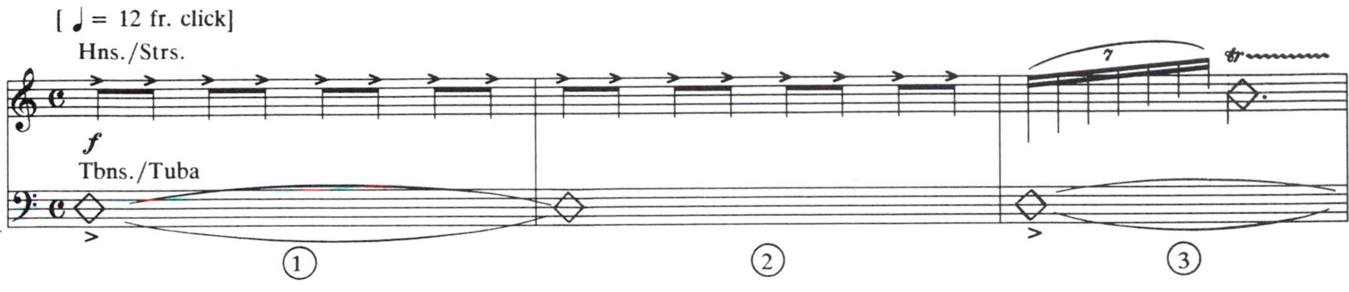

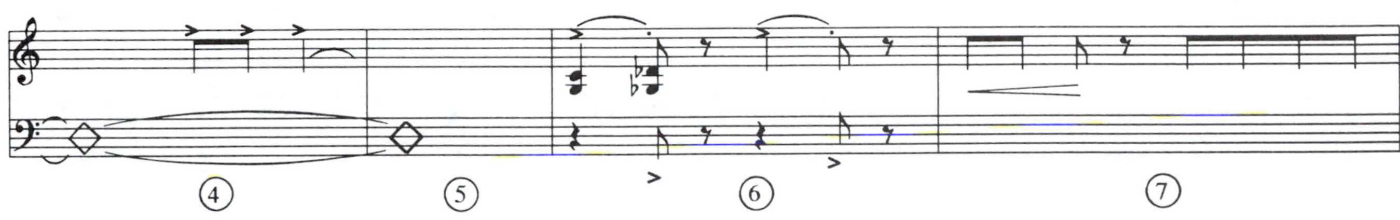

FIGURE 15-2
Silver Streak **12/1 Runaway Train (Part I) Henry Mancini**

FIGURE 15-2 (*Continued*)

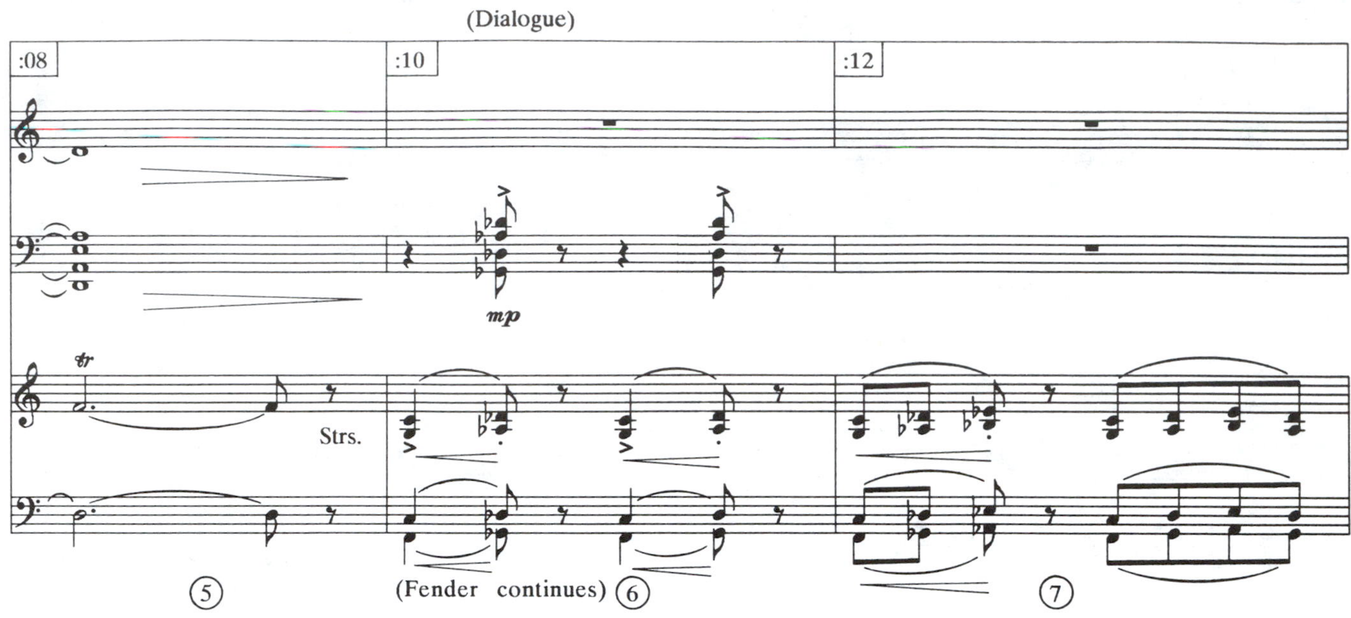

FIGURE 15-3

The Outlaw Josey Wales 14-M3 You're All Alone Now Jerry Fielding

FIGURE 15-3 *(Continued)*

ETHNIC PERCUSSION. A group of ethnic percussion instruments makes an excellent color for an abstract rhythmic statement; combining them with traditional percussion like timpani works very well. Timpani, xylophone, marimba, bells, and vibes all have specific pitches, of course. For *Commando* (1985), in the second cue of his score, James Horner uses seven percussionists and drums plus steel drums, trombones, tuba, two synths, piano, a cello/double bass pedal point, guitar, and solo improvising shakuhachi (the traditional Japanese reed flute). (See Figure 15-4.)

Craig Safan's use of Korean instruments in *Remo Williams* (1985) is another example of how solo ethnic instruments can provide color and rhythm. Figure 15-5 is the first part of his Main Title.

THE ORCHESTRA AS RHYTHM

Frequently, figures are written for the orchestra that are basically rhythmic. Sometimes they are unisons, sometimes harmonized in some way, but the thrust is single-mindedly rhythmic. Propulsion and drive are the objectives. Since film scores are often relied upon to bring these very important qualities to a film, this is a vital film-scoring technique.

In the excerpt from the Main Title of *Remo Williams* shown in Figure 15-5, the brass begin an important rhythmic idea in bar 23, and the Synclavier begins a new rhythmic theme in bar 27.

At one point during the final confrontation in *Romancing the Stone* (1984), Alan Silvestri uses a repeated-note idea harmonized in the strings. Figure 15-6 illustrates the first four bars of this passage; the chords change in the strings as the passage continues to develop, but the rhythmic idea remains the same.

FIGURE 15-4

Commando R1 P2 James Horner

FIGURE 15-5

Remo Williams **Main Title** **Craig Safan**

FIGURE 15-5 (*Continued*)

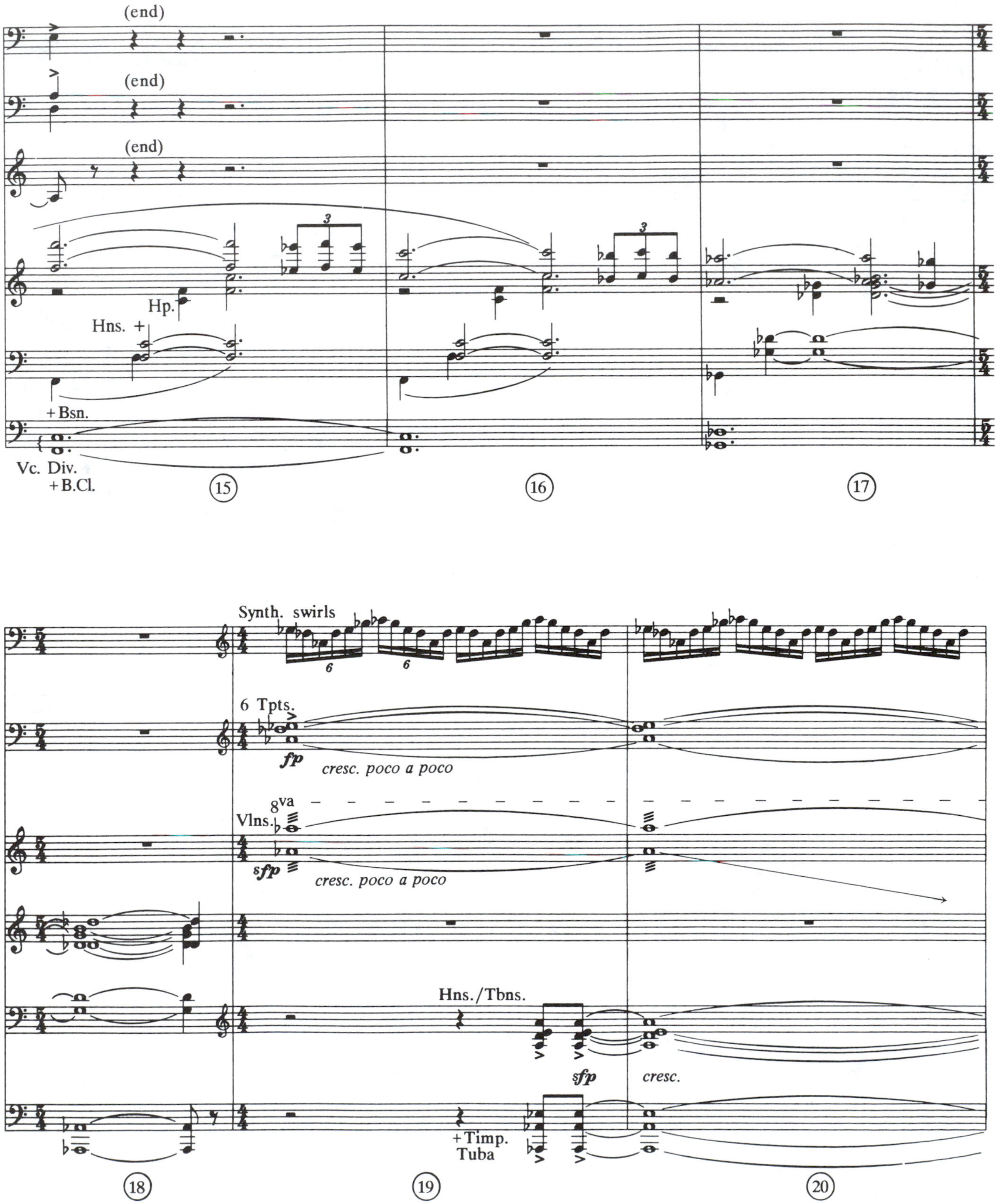

Synth. swirls
6
6
6 Tpts.
fp
cresc. poco a poco
8va
Vlns.
sfp
cresc. poco a poco
Hns./Tbns.
sfp
cresc.
+ Timp.
Tuba
18
19
20

FIGURE 15-5 (*Continued*)

FIGURE 15-5 (*Continued*)

FIGURE 15-6

Romancing the Stone M132 The Big Burn Alan Silvestri

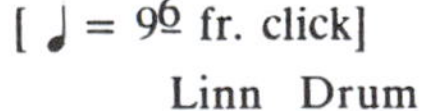

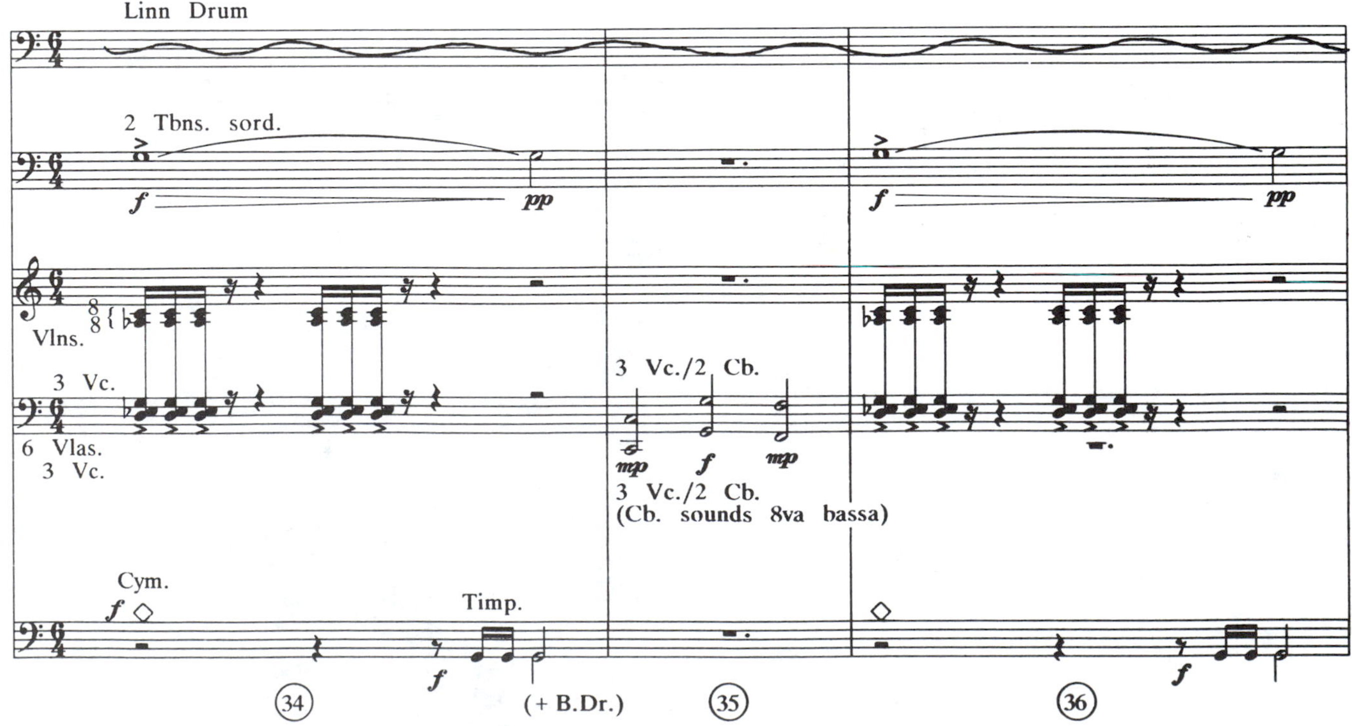

FIGURE 15-6 (*Continued*)

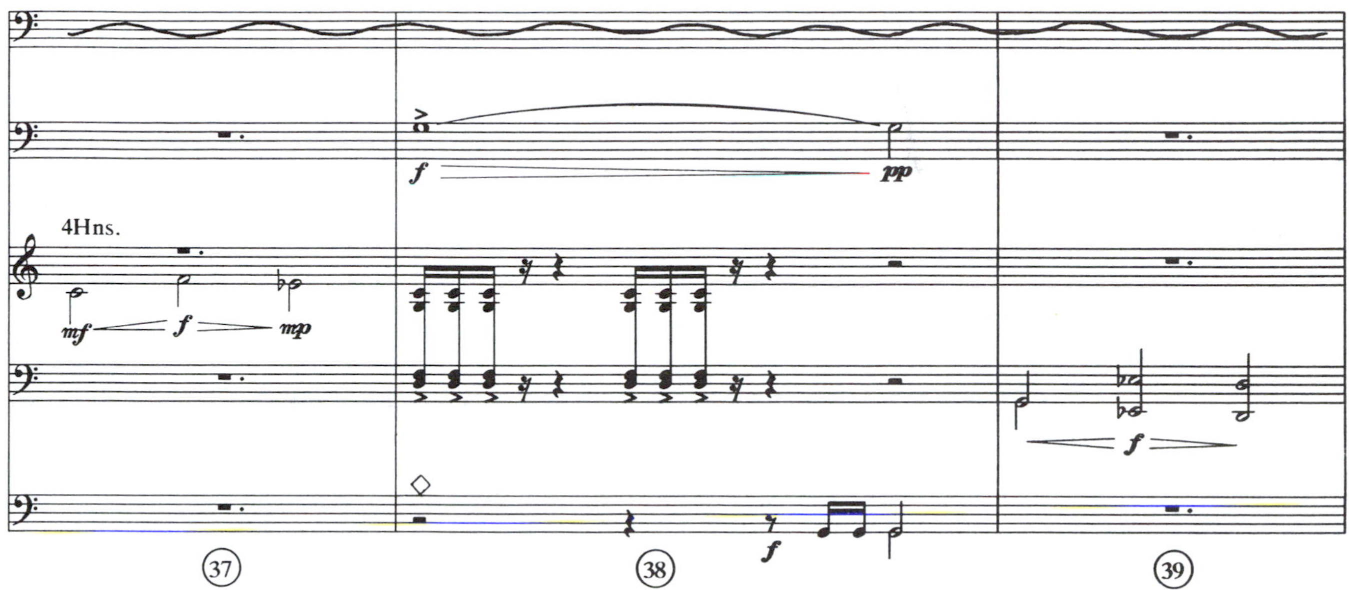

RHYTHM AS A THEMATIC IDEA

> ***I chose a rhythm, or a series of rhythms, and just kept at it, establishing a pulse that was almost irresistible. I wanted just to have the texture thematic.***
> GERALD FRIED

The television movie *Son Rise: A Miracle of Love* (1979) is the story of a young couple who have an autistic child. Everyone told them that there was no hope for the child—that he would always be autistic. But they wouldn't give up. They put aside their careers in advertising and worked with him, getting into the crib and rocking with him in sync with his autistic motions. And little by little the child was cured.

Gerald Fried scored the film. "The first thing I did was to try to establish a rhythm in this seemingly aimless rocking. There was a rhythm inside this boy's head. It may not have looked very organized to an observer, but I chose a series of rhythms that the orchestra played. Partially an electronic cluster, partially woodwinds—it was a light sound, but insistent. A glassy, translucent sound. It had lots of light in it, and it just kept on. There was never a letup of the rocking motion in one way or another till it traveled around the orchestra. No theme. A theme actually would have destroyed what I was trying to do."

RHYTHMIC OSTINATOS

I'll either get some thematic idea and take a fragment of it and develop it into an ostinato, or sometimes I'll take the ostinato and develop it into a theme.

JERRY GOLDSMITH

All ostinatos are rhythmic; some are just more rhythmic than others. Since the sense of tonality is static in a passage with one or more ostinatos, the device is frequently used either as a way of expressing that single harmonic idea with forward motion, or simply as a highly rhythmic device. As such, it is an ideal technique for contemporary music of all sorts, and can often be of dramatic use in scoring. Tangerine Dream's score for *Thief* (1981) is based on ostinatos, often in the mid-low register. The excerpt from *Commando* in Figure 15-4 is another good example of pedal point and ostinato. Ostinatos are used frequently in television scores to provide tension and drive for action sequences.

Jerry Goldsmith uses them throughout his score in *The Omen* (1976). Near the end of the film, the entire orchestra begins a four-bar ostinato that is without a linear theme—only rhythm and the resultant harmony (Figure 15-7a). The voices enter thematically in bar 10 while the ostinato continues. By bar 34, the pitches of the ostinato have changed and the voices have moved up to a different level, but the rhythms remain identical throughout the orchestra (Figure 15-7b).

In a later cue, the "Ave Satani" at the end of the film, the voices begin accompanied by a string drone. In bar 11, organ, strings, and low woodwinds begin another ostinato, which becomes an accompaniment for the voices beginning in bar 13 (Figure 15-8a). This ostinato also develops, changing slightly in bar 29 (Figure 15-8b). There is further orchestral development in bar 37 (Figure 15-8c).

In each of the two cues from *The Omen* cited above, the rhythmic pulse continues throughout but the harmonic and melodic elements develop, adding depth and variety to the repetitive effect of the music.

UNEVEN METERS

You can shift meters without necessarily changing the pulse. This gives variety to the rhythmic effect by slightly changing the emphasis of the basic accents. The composer may have to indicate on a click breakdown chart the click number of any points of dramatic emphasis in the scene and then experiment with various metric patterns to see how they work with the film. Figure 23-5 (from Charles Fox's 1978 score for *Foul Play*) is an example of this.

Sometimes metric shifts can be useful in evoking an ethnic color or derivation, as in the case of Charles Bernstein's score for *Sadat* (1983; see Chapter 24), in which he used Middle Eastern rhythms at times to suggest the locale. Bernstein remembers, "there was one chase scene involving a bungled assassination early on in the film and I was going between 11/8 and 3/4 and 7/8." (See Figure 10-1.)

To perform this fast-moving cue Bernstein used the Auricle Time Processor (see p. 122) and set the click to the lowest common denominator—in this case, very fast eighth notes.

POLYRHYTHMS

> ***I do a lot of polyrhythms electronically. I like to have things completely out of time with each other. But it's not necessarily the kind of thing you would want to do on a live film date unless you have a very luxurious schedule.***
> WILLIAM GOLDSTEIN

There are times when one doesn't want rhythmic precision. Polyrhythms provide a blurred and less synchronous rhythmic feel, which can be an effective approach in some film situations. William Goldstein likes to use the effect electronically. "On the *Oceanscape* album[1] there is a cut called 'Frozen Dream,' and it has at least four or five rhythms going on at the same time. It is very Ravel-like and it works wonderfully. You could certainly do it orchestrally, but it would take a lot of rehearsal time."

ALEATORIC RHYTHMS. One way to get this polyrhythmic effect is to assign certain pitches to one or more musicians and indicate on their parts that they are to improvise freely but rhythmically, using only the indicated pitches. If the musicians are skilled and are directed properly, the resultant aleatoric (improvised) rhythms can become a polyrhythmic web of motion. Any indication of the composer's intentions on each improvising musician's part will help achieve the final effect. Phrases like "not too much motion," "as rapidly as possible," or "short arhythmic figurations" will help. (See the excerpt from John Corigliano's score for *Altered States,* Figure 16-17.)

In *Close Encounters* (1977), John Williams uses a short aleatoric passage beginning in bar 14 of the cue during which the young boy is drawn away from the house to the spaceship. This effect starts during the shot of the spaceship after Melinda Dillon has grabbed her son to bring him inside. In bar 14 the strings are free. The cellos and double basses continue in bar 15, joined by the trombones in bar 16.

Figure 15-9 is reproduced from Herb Spencer's original handwritten orchestration for *Close Encounters.* This score is an example of the way film music looks when delivered to the copyist.

This brief look at some of the musical resources used by film composers should be of help in recognizing these techniques in other scores. In studying these compositional techniques, the question is not only *which* techniques were used, but *why,* and how their usage heightened the drama and enhanced the film.

Having discussed the use of melody, harmony, and rhythm in films, we can now turn our attention to the use of color—the art of orchestration.

---

[1] From Goldstein's 1985 score for the television film *oceanQuest.*

FIGURE 15-7

The Omen R12-P1 The Altar

Jerry Goldsmith
Orchestrated by Arthur Morton

(a)

FIGURE 15-7 (*Continued*)

(b)

FIGURE 15-8
The Omen R12-P3 Ave Satani

Jerry Goldsmith
Orchestrated by Arthur Morton

FIGURE 15-9

Close Encounters of the Third Kind 7/1 **Barry Is Kidnapped**

John Williams
Orchestrated by Herb Spencer

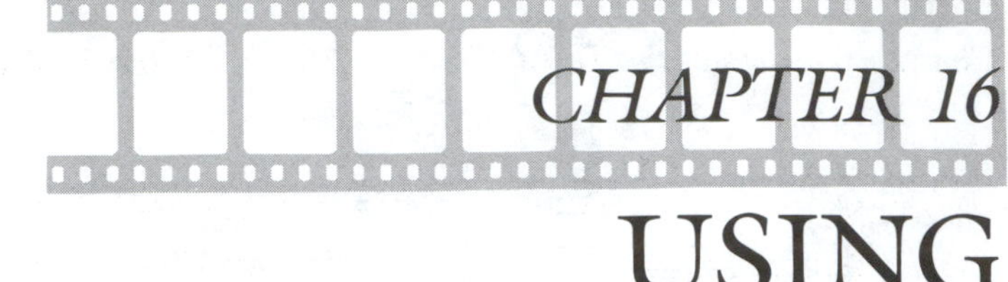

USING ORCHESTRATION

I find the orchestration of the music to be almost as important as the composition. PAUL WENDKOS, DIRECTOR

Is it possible to recall a memorable film score without recalling the very *sound* of the score, particularly if we originally heard it in a theater with a top-quality sound system? Consider the visceral low synthesizer drones of Vangelis's *Chariots of Fire* (1981), the ritualistic and fateful chanting of the chorus in Goldsmith's *Omen* (1976; see Figures 15-7, 15-8). Bernard Herrmann's shrieking strings for the shower-scene murder in *Psycho* (1960), the impact and sweep of James Horner's *Star Trek II* (1984; see Figure 16-6), the echoing, lonely, military trumpet calls in Goldsmith's score for *Patton* (1970; see Figure 7-3).

Orchestral color in film is even more important than in concert music because it must evoke specific emotional responses, thereby becoming powerfully integrated with the character or texture of the film. Instrumental and choral colors are powerful resources for the composer and each composer prides himself on his ability to find the right colors for every dramatic situation. Many film composers who can orchestrate masterfully do not have time to do their own orchestrating, yet almost every composer gives the orchestrator a sketch with detailed instrumental indications as well as the melodic, harmonic, and rhythmic details that one usually thinks of as containing all of the "compositional" elements.

James Horner starts his film assignments by looking for the right colors. "I'll see a film, and looking at the film I'll say, 'What strikes me most about this film is a certain orchestral color,' and I will build my ensemble around that basic pigment of color, whether it's a boys' choir, or some sort of electronic sparkly color, or whatever."

But how can the director know the effectiveness of the colors in the composer's mind? As we keep saying, it's difficult to convey mental musical images and yet you must consistently try to do just that. For Marvin Hamlisch, "the solution for *Sophie's Choice* (1984) was to write the melody and then to score it using the solo cello. And when I showed that melody to [director] Alan [Pakula] I had to explain to him what was going to be playing that melody and how that was going to make it work in terms of the color. To me, orchestration and the way something will sound are as important as what that melody is. I see solo instruments as almost the life of that character. She's a cello, he's some other instrument—with solo instruments you can actually hear the player practically breathe with the character. In *Sophie's Choice* [Figure 16-1] I was keeping things on the small side, trying to keep it very intimate, very contained, because I knew that that would just let the emotions ooze out, that you couldn't get bigger than that. What I mean is, there's *no* way you can get bigger than what that movie is about."

To emphasize this approach, Hamlisch scored the Main Title with unaccompanied solo recorder.

The same considerations must be taken into account for television shows, where music can be an important ingredient in the success of a series. When Mike Post is writing a theme, his first thoughts also include colors. "When I look at a film or read a script I try to think the big thoughts: I answer those three or four big questions: First, what *kind*

FIGURE 16-1
Sophie's Choice **Main Title** **Marvin Hamlisch**

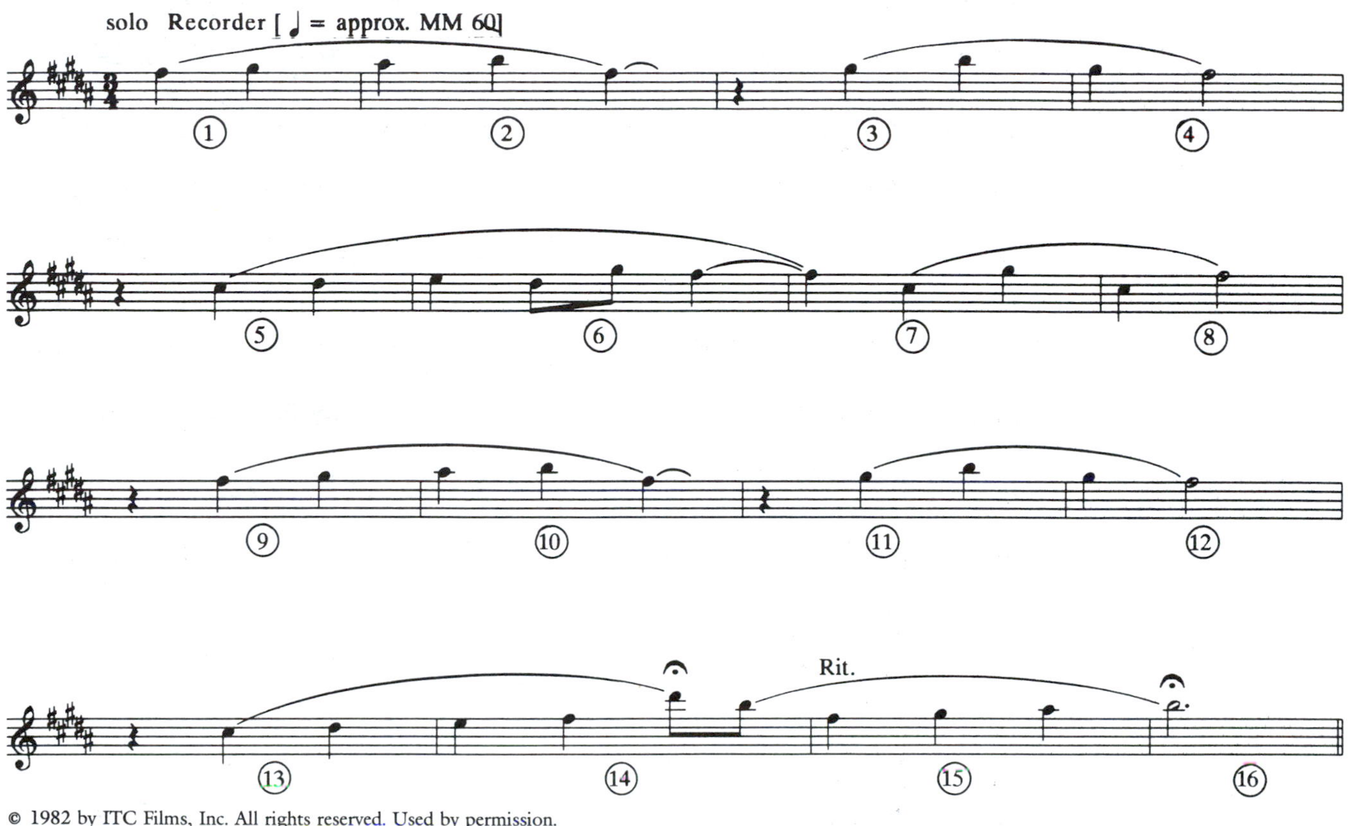

of music is this? Then, what *tempo* is this? And then, before I put my hands down on an instrument I'll ask myself, What kind of orchestra, what kind of *sounds* are in this?"

CHARACTERIZING THE FILM'S THEME

In *Brainstorm* (1983), James Horner was working with a film in which "everything on screen was very hi-tech, from the effects, story, machinery, the whole photo-thrust of the film. But there was a spiritual quality as well that was just beneath the surface. What I was trying to do in the score was play against that hi-tech feeling. The most immediate way to do that for me was to use a boys' choir. When we first discussed *Brainstorm,* [director] Douglas Trumbull wanted an electronic score, a hi-tech sound. I thought about it and came up with the boys' choir, which was sort of horrifying to them at first, because first of all, they didn't know the color very well. Second of all, they didn't know how I would use it. I told them it would be playing *against* what you saw. It has a wonderful quality, and I would write this quasi-sixteenth-century polyphony for the boys to sing. They had to take my word for it, although I played them a record of music from that era. I wanted to combine orchestra and boys' choir [not illustrated here] and also do some avant-garde effects with the orchestra [Figure 16-2]. None of the music I played was a good example of what the choir would sound like against their film. Once they heard the boys' choir they really liked that color, and their whole perception of the music changed. And they allowed me to proceed. We actually had an adult choir, which consisted of about 18 to 24 people and the boys' choir, which consisted of 15 boys, and we had an orchestra all

FIGURE 16-2

Brainstorm 12M3 James Horner

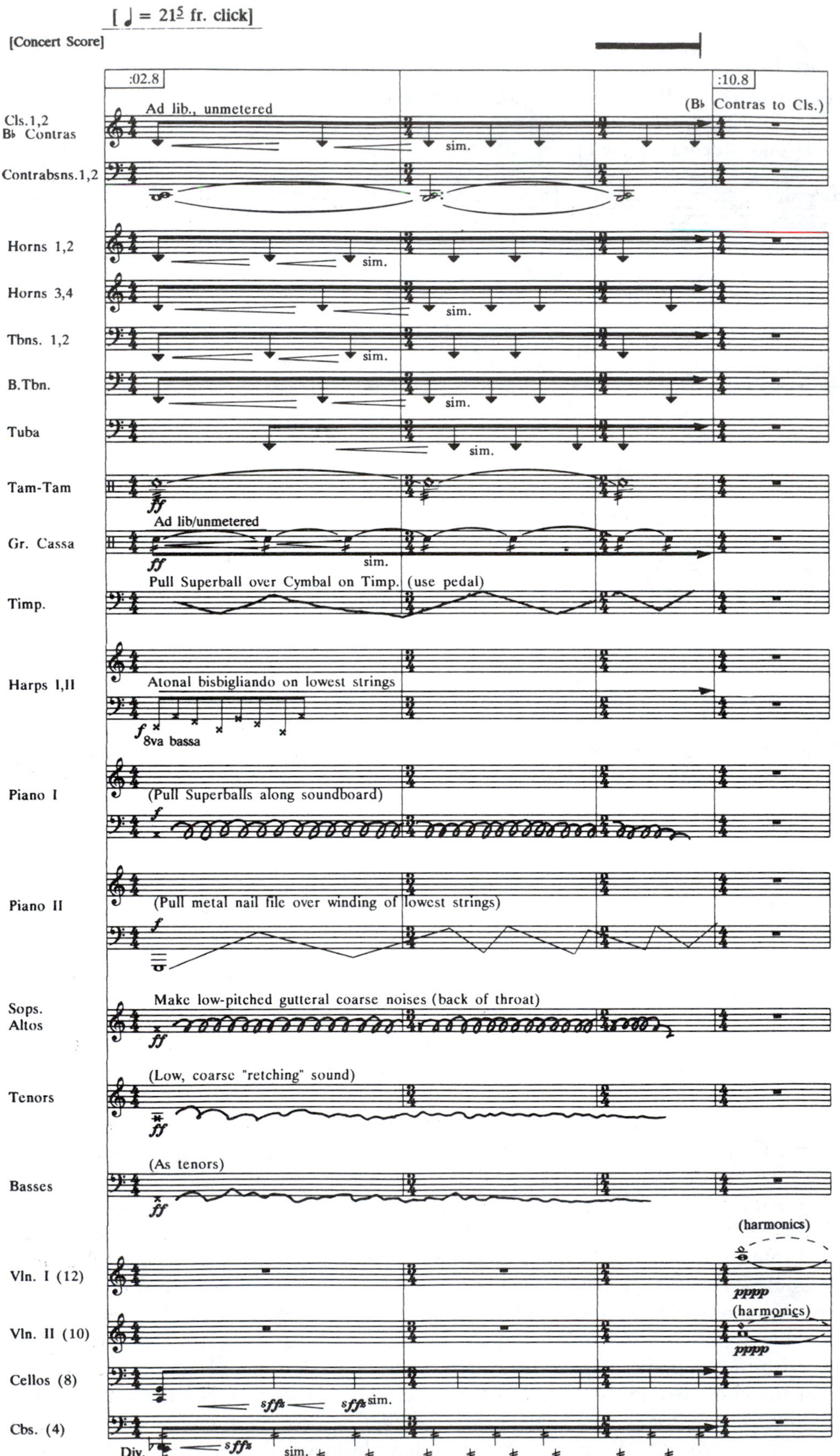

recorded live acoustically in MGM's big barn of a studio. I love to do it all acoustically and not to overdub or isolate the musicians and choir."

SUGGESTING LOCALE WITH COLOR

In *Under the Volcano* (1984), a story of the tragic disintegration of an alcoholic British consul in Mexico, there is an expressive Alex North cue as people are kneeling by the dead body of a Mexican peasant. The plaintive sound of an out-of-tune, primitive flute is set against muted horns, then against strings and bass marimba. The melodic material and instrumental colors combine in making this cue so effective [Figures 16-3 and 16-4, North's sketch and score]. North, who had spent two years in Mexico, recalls, "This was an old religious theme that I used as the basis for this scoring—with muted French horns. That was a strange score in the sense that I tried to establish the locale and the period in the use of the source music and tried to enrich the imagery of what [director John] Huston had done there, in the Mexican landscapes. And also I tried to get in the melancholy of the protagonist, the Consul (Albert Finney), a sort of Latin musical universality, so that the music was not Mexican at all. Just to reflect in a quiet way this man's problems."

Figure 16-3 is reproduced from the composer's original handwritten sketch; Figure 16-4 is reproduced from Henry Brant's orchestration.

North describes the orchestration: "For percussion I used about twelve different instruments. On the Main Title I used: sleigh bells; tambourine; xylophone (struck with

FIGURE 16-3

Under the Volcano 7/2 Death of a Peasant (sketch) Alex North

FIGURE 16-3 *(Continued)*

FIGURE 16-3 ***(Continued)***

large nails); booze bottle (struck with triangle beater); 4 castanets; guiro; Chinese blocks; log drum; cabasa/maraca (one in each hand); marimba; vibes; cowbells; gong/water gong; and a chromatic series of boo-bams (one octave from F below middle C to F above middle C)."

SYMPHONIC ORCHESTRATION

When a film calls for sounds that are bigger than life, full of heroic adventure, you might think of John Williams's *Star Wars* (1977), or, looking back in time, Maurice Jarre's *Lawrence of Arabia* (1962; Figure 16-5), or, looking back even further, Erich Korngold's scores for *The Sea Hawk* (1940) and *Captain Blood* (1935). As familiar as these classics may seem, the orchestration of these grand sounds can no more be taken for granted than that of the special, subtle, unique, recherché sounds. They all must be written *and* orchestrated correctly, and that is a craft and an art.

Today's futuristic space adventures, with their spectacular sci-fi wars, space vistas, supervillains, and superheroes, call for scores in the large orchestra tradition of those heroic films. A huge score like Horner's Main Title for *Star Trek II* is completely filled out (Figure 16-6), but the trick is to maintain clarity and balance within that amount

FIGURE 16-4

Under the Volcano 7/2 Death of a Peasant

Alex North
Orchestrated by Henry Brant

FIGURE 16-4 *(Continued)*

FIGURE 16-4 *(Continued)*

FIGURE 16-4 *(Continued)*

of sound. Figure 16-7 (reproduced from Herb Spencer's handwritten orchestration) illustrates an orchestral setting of the "mothership" theme from John Williams's score for *Close Encounters* (1977; see also Figure 7-4).

The strings are the core of a symphonic approach and can be used for many situations. Figure 16-8 illustrates how important they can be in a romantic score such as *The Way We Were* (1973).

The great composer/orchestrators—Mozart, Rimsky-Korsakov, Tchaikovsky, Wagner, Stravinsky, Respighi, Ravel—have all understood the balances (and imbalances) of the orchestra's sections, and have understood that orchestration is much more than simply assigning the notes from a piano sketch to whatever instruments are available to play them. The scores and recordings of these composers should be studied to see how they have used each orchestral section for its most characteristic and unique sounds. They are always careful not to destroy the effectiveness of the subtle color effects of the strings and woodwinds by using them constantly in combination with the overpowering brass and heavy percussion.

In Figure 16-9, the first bars of John Williams's cue for the bicycle-chase sequence in *E.T.* (1982) illustrate this well-balanced use of the orchestra.

The use of the coloristic instruments (piano, harp, celesta, other keyboards) and percussion instruments can be very effective in film scoring. Williams set his *E.T.* theme for these instruments to suggest the childlike nature of E.T. and his "machine" (Figure 16-10). Each orchestral instrument has its own personality that can bring life to a score when used to best advantage.

FRESH SOUNDS

Not only is the composer looking for colors that will evoke the tone and attitude of the film, but he is looking for the unusual sounds that will make this music and this film unique—"his"—identifiable, different from other film scores of the same genre. Consider Bill Conti's use of panpipes (played on the Electronic Woodwind Instrument) for *Karate Kid II* (1986) instead of the stereotypical Japanese sounds (Figure 16-11); the ominous repetition of a strummed, bizarrely-tuned zither in *Stalking Moon* (1968, Karlin); the airy recorder choir in *Up the Down Staircase* (1967, Karlin; Figure 16-12); Maurice Jarre's anvil-like percussion instruments borrowed from the Balinese gamelan orchestra for *Mad Max Beyond Thunderdome* (1985); and Miklos Rozsa's very early use of the electronic Theremin in *Spellbound* (1945).

In *Wait Until Dark* (1967), Henry Mancini had to sustain an hour-long sequence of tension as a blind woman (Audrey Hepburn) is terrorized in her apartment by murderous crooks in search of a drug-filled doll. One of Mancini's "sounds" was two pianos detuned by a quarter tone. "At the beginning she's waiting for the doll, and the guy's putting heroin in it and setting it up; and she's impatient—it's a pantomime. There's a certain mystery. You certainly don't know what's going on. And the Alan Arkin character is nuts—with a touch of the sadist. Those two things set me off on that piano thing. It's just a recurring A minor triad up in the middle register, played on the regular piano first, and then immediately repeated by the detuned piano (with the pedal down, which gave it the natural reverberation)."

Mancini used another unusual color also. "When I was in Japan some time ago, I brought back several instruments they call the *sho.* And they are reed pipes; it looks like you are holding a cluster of pipes that are pointing towards the air. They're tapered in, and then you put your fingers on the holes in the side, and you play tones. And it sounds like a very reedy out-of-tune instrument in the mouth-organ family. I had three or four of those, and I figured out where the notes were for the woodwind guys to play. When the girl goes looking through the clothes at the beginning of the picture, and she finds the guy in the bag—dead—these instruments are playing."

FIGURE 16-5

Lawrence of Arabia Theme Maurice Jarre

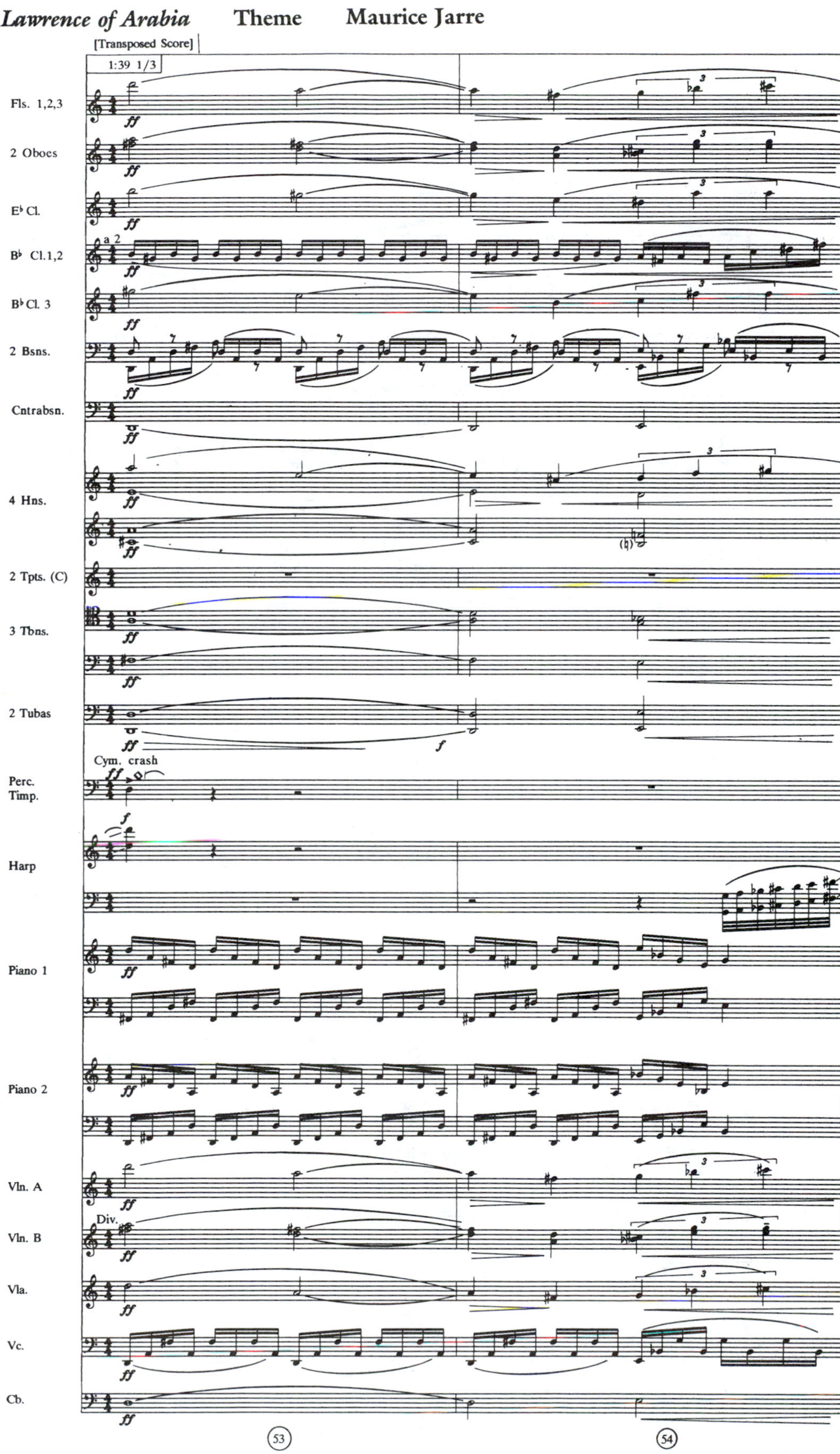

FIGURE 16-5 *(Continued)*

FIGURE 16-6
Star Trek II: The Wrath of Khan **M11 Main Title** **James Horner**

FIGURE 16-6 *(Continued)*

FIGURE 16-6 *(Continued)*

FIGURE 16-6 *(Continued)*

FIGURE 16-7

Close Encounters of the Third Kind **15/3** **John Williams**

The Arrival of the Mother Ship

FIGURE 16-7 *(Continued)*

FIGURE 16-7 *(Continued)*

FIGURE 16-8
The Way We Were M62 You Are Beautiful Marvin Hamlisch
Orchestrated by Herb Spencer

FIGURE 16-8 *(Continued)*

FIGURE 16-8 *(Continued)*

FIGURE 16-8 *(Continued)*

FIGURE 16-9

E.T. M-113 The Bike Chase John Williams

FIGURE 16-9 *(Continued)*

FIGURE 16-9 *(Continued)*

FIGURE 16-9 *(Continued)*

FIGURE 16-10
E.T. M-72/81 E.T.'s Machine John Williams

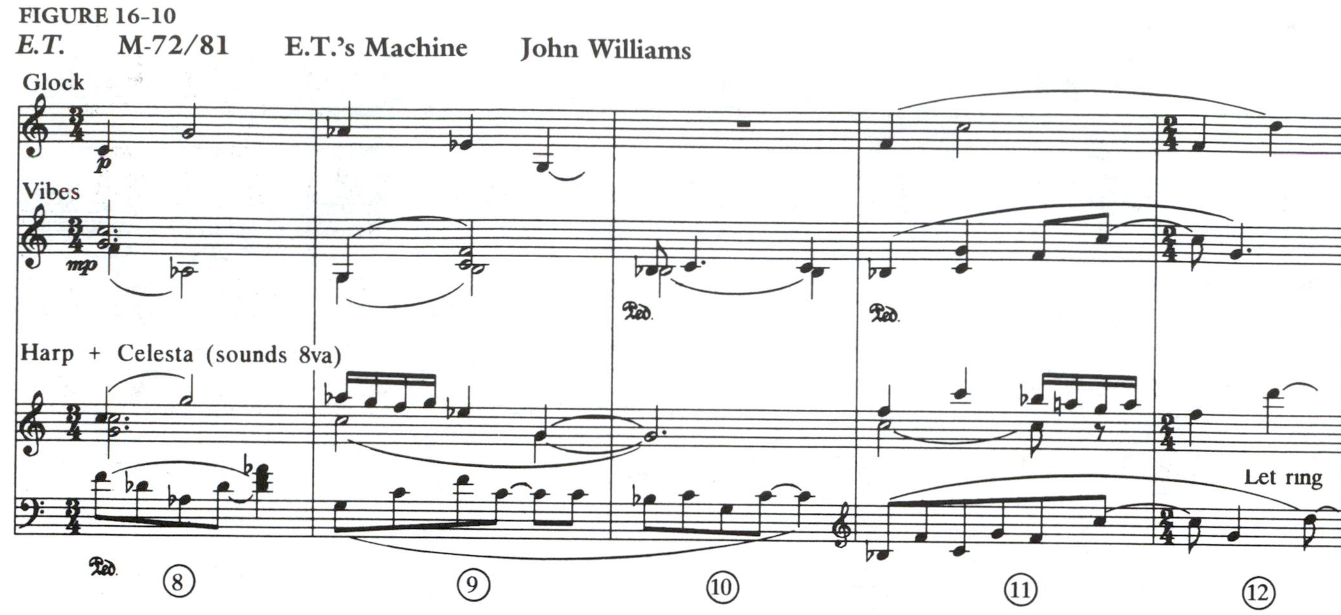

CHANGE THE COLOR, CHANGE THE EMOTION

In his Main Title for the adventure film *The Black Stallion Returns* (1983), Georges Delerue sets the mysterious mood of the film with the bass flute playing over a low string/synthesizer drone (Figure 16-13). "There is something very mysterious and strange about bass flute, which puts you totally outside of your environment. I love the sound—very warm. And sometimes I also used the bass clarinet in octaves with the bass flute—a very interesting color."

Later in the film, when the theme reappears at the reunion of boy and horse, now in a simple harp statement (Figure 16-14), the new color gives a completely different meaning to the same melody.

ORCHESTRAL EFFECTS

Many times the music will sound like an effect—a bit of magic more than a musical idea. In *The Omen* (1976), a clue to the unseen demonic powers is a shaft of light that appears only in photographs of persons marked for tragedy. Goldsmith's ascending dissonant portamentos in muted strings, mixed with vibes, is presented in different versions for a supernatural effect (Figure 16-15).

Raintree County (1958) offered John Green the unusual challenge of inventing a unique, magical color for the tree. His solution was complex. "I used a Chinese bell-tree and four mallets on a vibraphone alternating E major to D major; then I used 2 glockenspiels, each with four hammers, one playing E major, the other playing D major. The celesta played 32nd notes broken—D major, E major. Then the pronouncement of the theme in woodwinds, sometimes interlocked with horns. Each place where that occurred we made two copies each of the Chinese bell-tree and the celesta; one of each we played backwards. And over it all I had 2 sets of tuned finger cymbals, one playing a G♯ and the other playing a D. We combined all of those and I called it a 'jymjyck' (one of Danny Kaye's favorite made-up words). I had a separate score for all of this and just indicated where I wanted it cut into the music. (This was prepared in different keys as needed in

FIGURE 16-11

context.) The strings did different things, sometimes ponticello, sometimes tremolando. The tonal parts of the orchestra were doing the two triads, but we ran the indeterminate sounds with it simultaneously. I didn't know if it was going to work; it was experimental. And it was indicated with a wavy line in the score, because I didn't want to clutter up the score with all those lines."

COLOR AS CONCEPT

The very conception of the music's relation to the film can involve the instrumental colors. David Shire wrote a piano score for *The Conversation* (1974), Francis Coppola's Kafkaesque suspense story about a wiretap expert (Gene Hackman). "Francis said he had always wanted to try that, and he somehow felt it was appropriate on this picture. We first ruled out an electronic score, because the guy was an electronic eavesdropper—that would be much too obvious. We agreed that the score should be about what's going on *inside* Harry Call, not what he does for a living, but the emotional world that he so carefully hides. I was worried that a piano score would get boring, but Francis said, 'Let's see; we can always add an orchestra.' At the mix we put some of the cues through an Arp 2600 [a state of the art synthesizer at the time], and on certain of the later cues we used a little more filtering so that the piano gradually got a little more distorted, a little more off center. Subliminally there were some timbre changes as it went along." (See Figure 16-16.)

Revolution (1985), which tells the story of the American revolution from the point of view of an ordinary colonial soldier (Al Pacino) and his thirteen-year-old drummer-boy son, includes a love relationship between Pacino and Nastassia Kinski, as the daughter of an upper-class pro-British merchant. John Corigliano first of all developed the love music for the story's end. "The children's theme arose later when I realized and felt that the child was in many ways the focus of the film as much as the man. So I decided to pull that into a children's theme as the idea of innocence, first played on a tin whistle for the boy's youth and then on flute when he grew up."

Corigliano's unsettling score for *Altered States* (1980) matched evocative aleatoric textures to William Hurt's hallucinations. Those orchestrational colors were conceptualized when director Ken Russell went to a concert of the Los Angeles Philharmonic to hear Richard Strauss's *Also sprach Zarathustra* and also heard the premiere of Corigliano's *Clarinet Concerto*. He had found the orchestral colors that fitted his film concept and called Corigliano the next day to offer him his first film assignment. The score is notable not only for its power and beauty but for its use of aleatoric procedures and nonmetric notation (Figure 16-17).

In *'night, Mother* (1982), the story of a presuicide dialogue between mother and daughter, David Shire used a small chamber string orchestra with harp and classical guitar, "because I thought the guitar had the rural element. I zeroed in on the sound we would like to have, and then the theme came rather quickly. But it took about a month and a half to know what I was supposed to be looking for." (See Figure 13-18.)

A SPECIFIC COLOR FOR A CHARACTER. In *Tom Jones* (1963), John Addison used small instrumental combinations for a number of his themes. The story takes place in the 1740s, but bawdy sex is timeless. "We decided that all the source music would be as accurate as we could get it. But in the underscore, I was to be free, so that if a saxophone would be

FIGURE 16-12

***Up the Down Staircase* 1B Halls/Classroom Fred Karlin**

FIGURE 16-13

The Black Stallion Returns 1M1 Prologue Georges Delerue

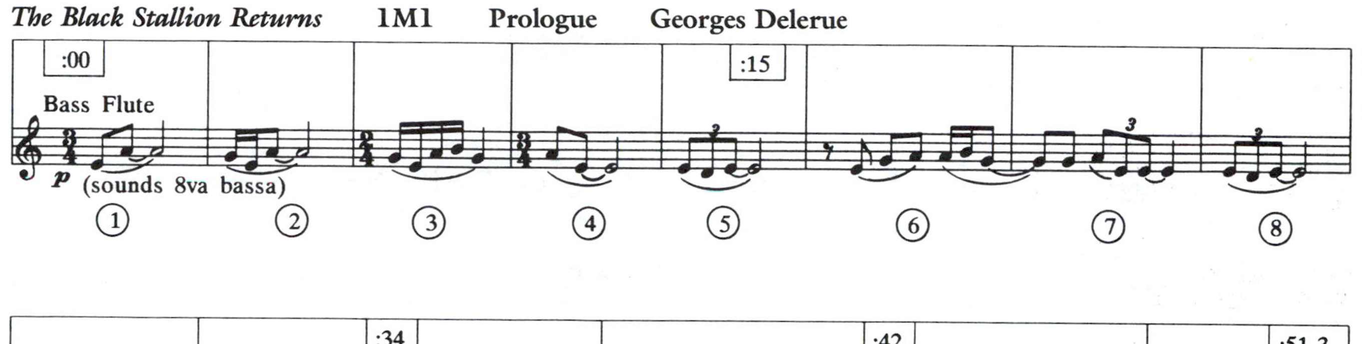

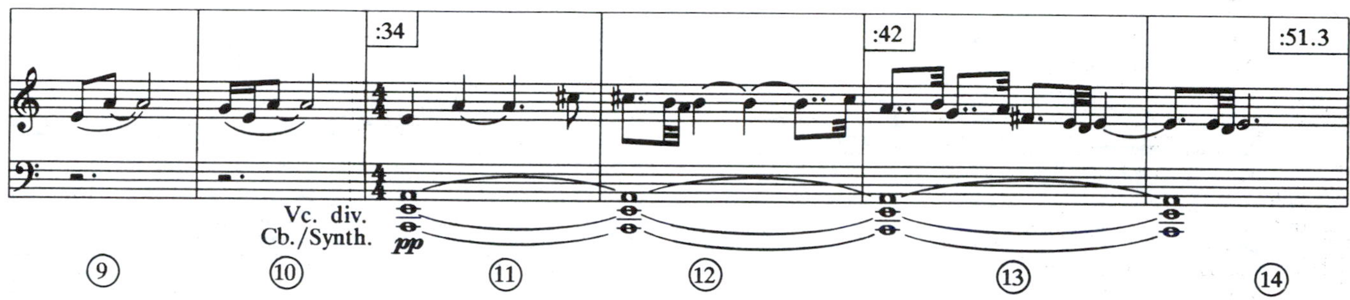

FIGURE 16-14

The Black Stallion Returns 7/4 Reunion Georges Delerue

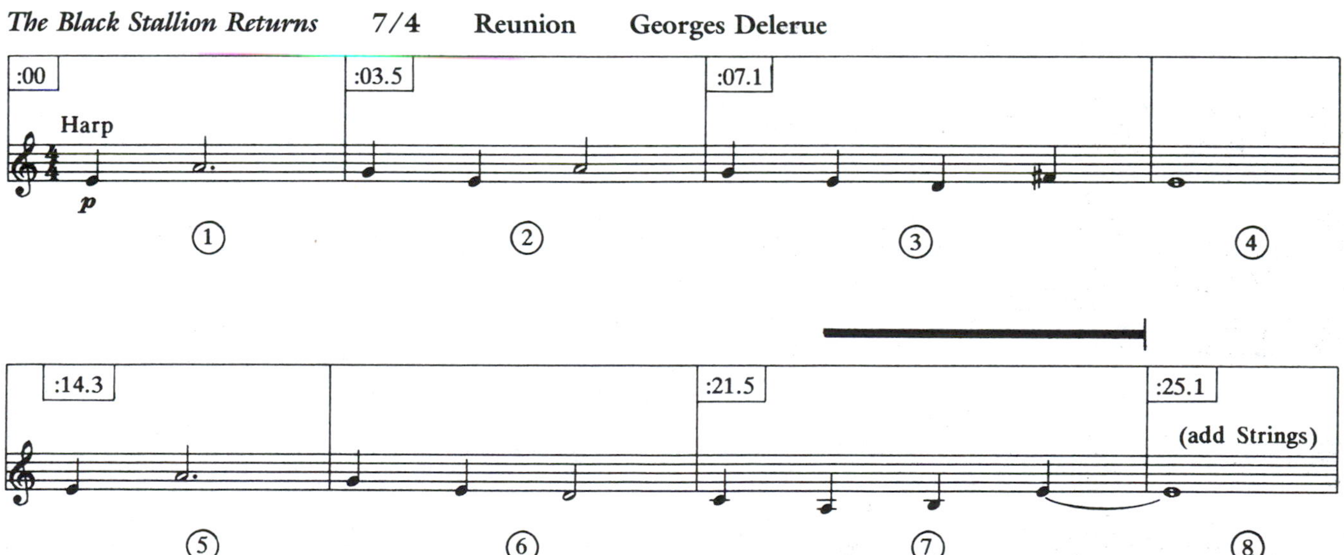

FIGURE 16-15

The Omen R11-P1 The Bed Jerry Goldsmith
Orchestrated by Arthur Morton

FIGURE 16-15 *(Continued)*

FIGURE 16-15 *(Continued)*

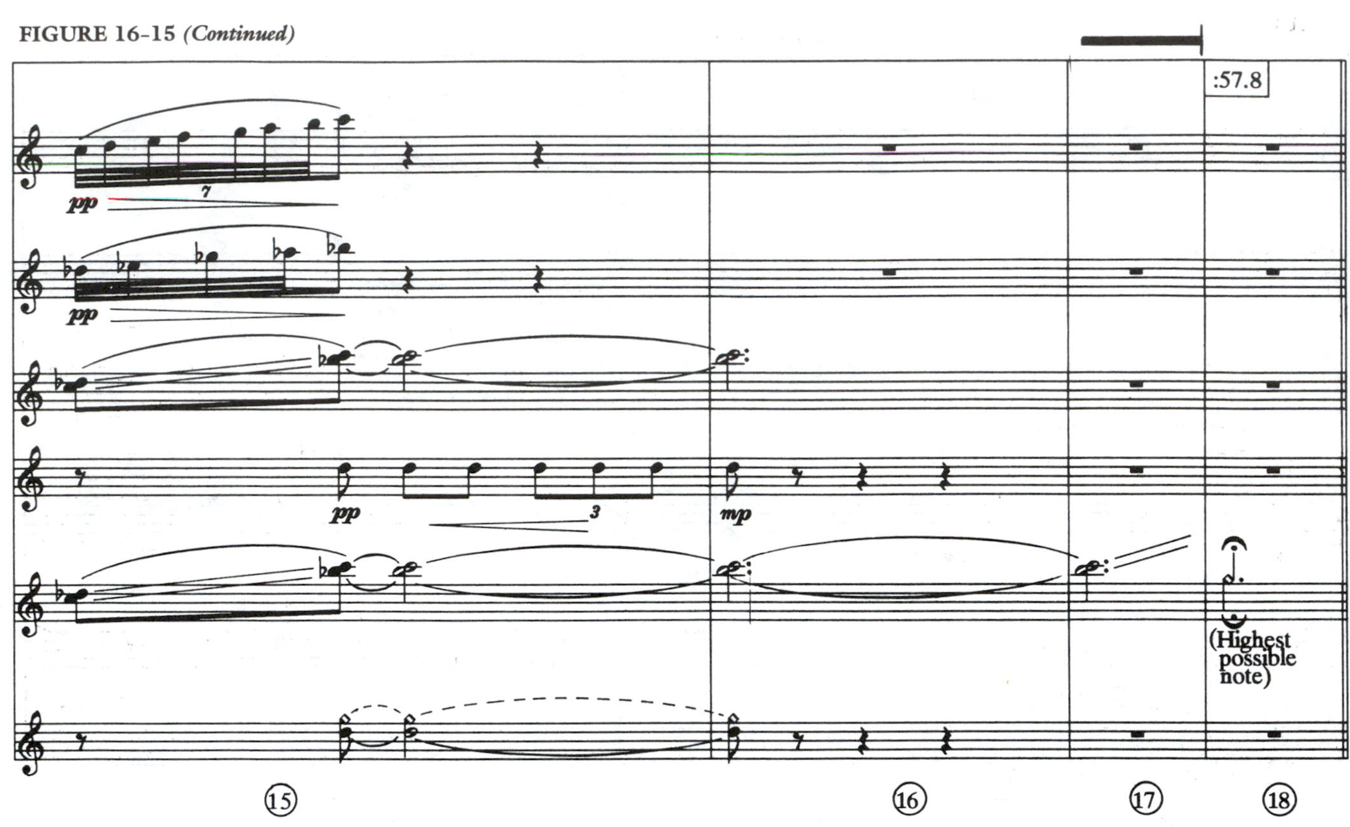

FIGURE 16-16

The Conversation Theme David Shire

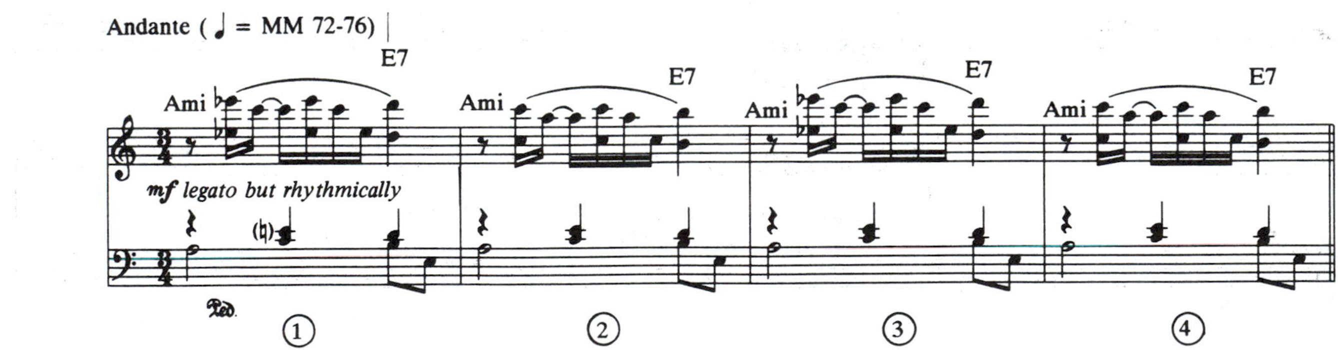

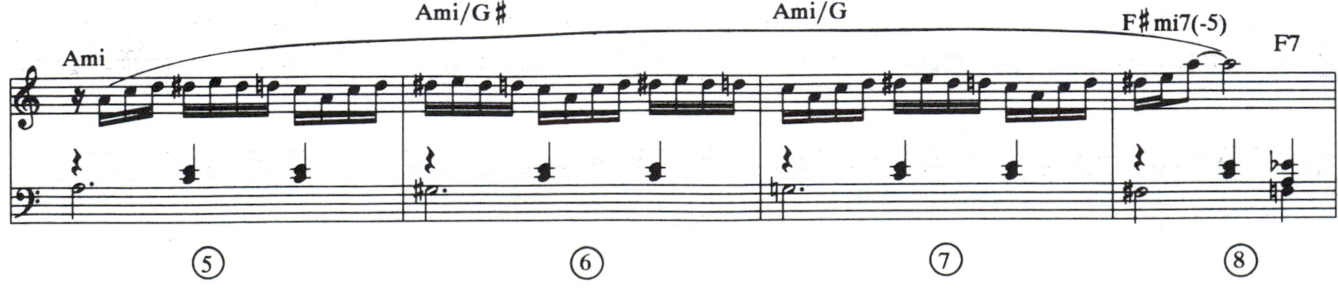

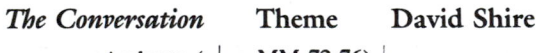

FIGURE 16-16 *(Continued)*

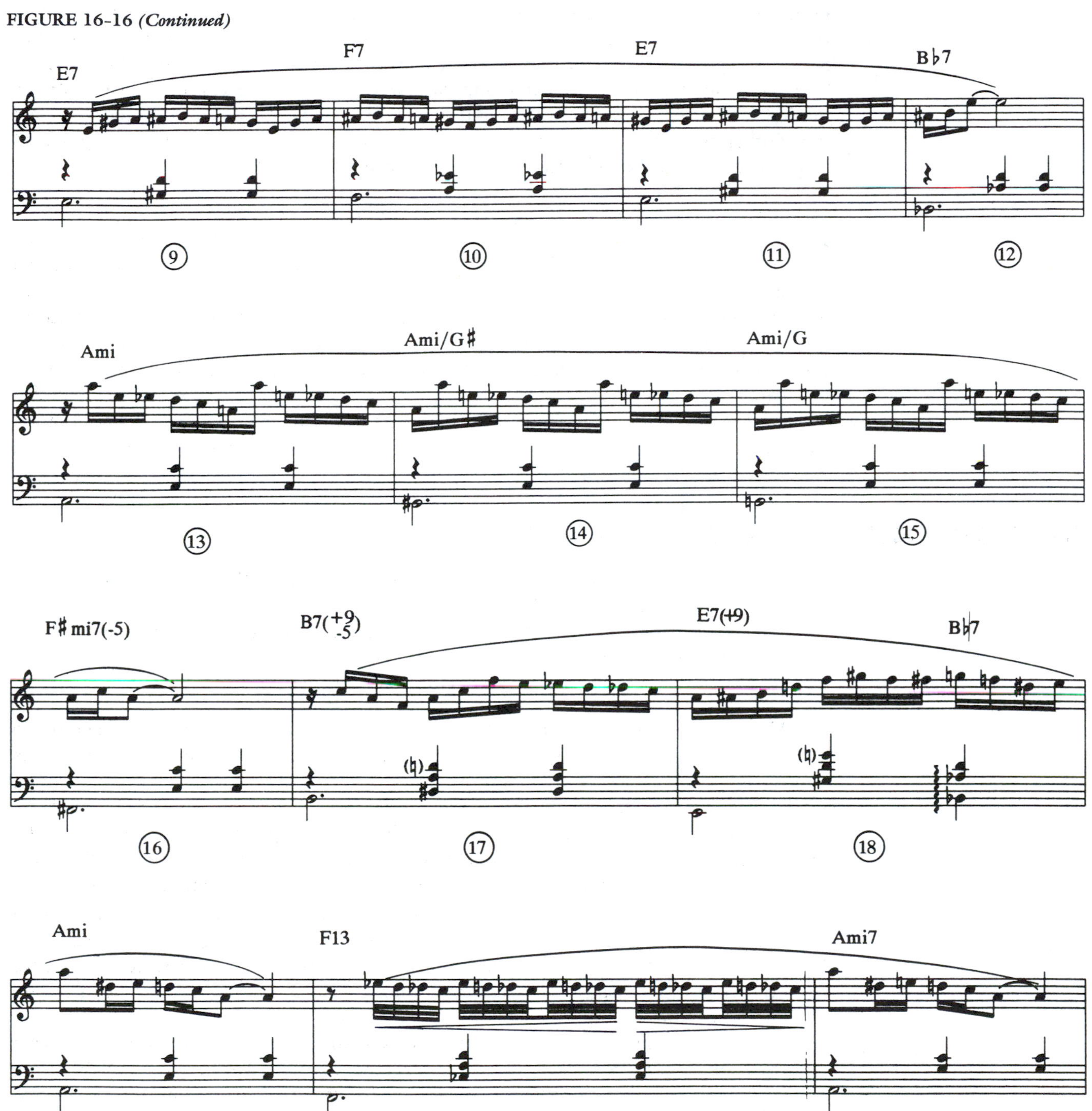

good for a certain character, I would use it even though the instrument didn't exist at that time. In fact, the way it worked out was that there were half a dozen different themes for different characters. And each of those themes featured a few instruments. The pure love theme used solo violin, piano, and harp. We also used the rest of the orchestra as needed. The profane love theme featured alto sax playing with a bassoon. I used the banjo for another character. The opening was done on an out-of-tune piano and a harpsichord [Figure 16-18]. So the full orchestra was seldom playing together."

SMALL BUDGETS. A tight budget can inspire creative decisions on every level. When Randy Edelman was faced with this problem on *Executive Action* (1973), instrumental color became a significant part of his concept. "The film was footage of Kennedy interspersed with a fictional account of the assassination. I wrote something on the piano that was very barbaric and primitive. The drama was very harsh and this music could be translated at the ultimate to 6 cellos playing six different semi-tones—very harsh, barbaric, strident." Edelman knew he wouldn't have 6 cellos if he used any kind of traditional orchestra for his score—there just wasn't enough money for that. "So what I decided to do was go for my 6 cellos. And then I had to figure out a way to do the whole score that way. I didn't want to get a small string section and have the violas play it. I ended up doing the score with 6 cellos, percussion, and piano."

TO ORCHESTRATE OR NOT TO ORCHESTRATE?

> ***And also, I was blessed with magnificent orchestrators. You know, Herb Spencer can write, and we had Jack Hayes.***
>
> ***I never want to put a straight jacket on an orchestrator, because for every time he may do one that you don't love, he may come up with a lot that you do love.*** MARVIN HAMLISCH

Most composers get great satisfaction from orchestrating and would prefer to do their own, but the quantity of music to be written for a film may be so great that it is impossible. Many do as much as they can, up to the point when the deadline approaches. When they can't do their own, they make detailed indications on the sketches so their concept will guide the orchestrator. Yet for television, where the time allowance is the shortest, it also happens that extra money for orchestration is often not provided outside of the composer's fee. Consequently most composers orchestrate their television scores.

John Cacavas's adaptation to this situation is not unusual. "On television there's no money for orchestrators. And by the time I make a neat sketch I might as well do a score. My first sketches are messy, and they must be pretty neat for the orchestrator, so I have to recopy the sketch. Even on the feature *Airport 1975* (1974), where I had just ten days and they allowed me an orchestrator, I didn't use one.

"Another reason I like to do my own orchestrating is that when you do your own orchestration you get a second shot at everything. When you give your sketch to the orchestrator you're through with it. When you orchestrate yourself, you get a chance to improve it as you go."

Georges Delerue prefers to orchestrate after his composition is finished. "I know exactly what kind of orchestration I'll do. I find I prefer to compose everything first, because I play for the director, and if something is not okay with him, it's necessary to reorchestrate it if I don't wait for this. Also, when I begin to compose, it's like a drug—I have to continue."

It often takes a while for a composer to adjust to working with an orchestrator. When John Addison worked on Alfred Hitchcock's *Torn Curtain* in 1966, "it had to be done fast, and I was already exhausted from scoring *A Fine Madness* [1966]. Up until that time I had always scored everything myself. There were not, in England, the equivalent of the

FIGURE 16-17

Altered States M 5/1 Fireworks John Corigliano

FIGURE 16-17 *(Continued)*

* Gliss. to cluster and return. Each div. glisses to a different note in the specified range.

** Tpts. ~~~ = wave pitch, excess vib.

FIGURE 16-17 *(Continued)*

* Ad lib. in this manner: etc. as fast as possible. Stagger breathing.

** Woodwinds vary order of figures and length of fermatas. Should sound sparse and pointillistic. If too full, increase rests (𝄐). Occasionally play 2 figures rapidly.

FIGURE 16-17 *(Continued)*

FIGURE 16-17 *(Continued)*

* Picc., Fls.— Overblow to get harmonics; shape of passage should resemble squiggly line.

** Bsns.—chromatic ♫ notes within specified range. Vary the notes, repeating some occasionally. Ad lib., like a boiling cluster.

FIGURE 16-18

Tom Jones Main Title John Addison

FIGURE 16-18 ***(Continued)***

Hollywood orchestrators. My orchestrator in England put down exactly what was in my sketches.

"Universal assigned Eddie Powell to me, and I was scared stiff. I said that I would like to see the scores before they went in to be copied. In one instance he did get a little bit carried away. I said, 'Well, look, I'm not saying it wouldn't sound good but it isn't what I had intended, so would you mind very much putting it back to the way I had it.' But, conversely, he made certain suggestions which were extremely effective. I had a canonic string passage tremolando, a sort of airy effect, and he suggested just putting in a chord on muted horns, and I said, 'Well, okay, why not?' If I didn't like it, after all, I'd just tell them not to play. But I found it very effective—something I hadn't thought of doing.

"I soon learned that because those orchestrators had worked with all the greats, they knew every single trick of the trade. I would discuss things with them, and they would make suggestions which very often I would take. Since I've been living here, I've learned a lot from orchestrators like Jack Hayes and Gus Levene.

"And I learned from the orchestrators that they were less likely to slip up and miss something if I didn't have situations in which there were arrows going from line to line and all that. So I try to organize my sketches with the woodwinds on 2 staves at the top and the strings on 2 staves at the bottom. Occasionally you'll need a third string staff. Then there's an extra staff at the bottom for percussion plus another line for nonpitch percussion."

SKETCHES

Each composer has his own favorite format for sketching, depending of course on the number of instruments. For full orchestra sounds Delerue favors a 3-line sketch (for his own use since he does his own orchestration), Bill Conti and Patrick Williams like 4-to-6-line sketches, Marvin Hamlisch uses 5, Craig Safan usually 6, Alex North and John Addison use 8. Several of these sketches contain an extra line for nonpitched percussion. Laurence Rosenthal likes 9 lines plus percussion; Ira Newborn 9 to 10; Henry Mancini 10; Alan Silvestri goes up to 14.

The formats vary from composer to composer, and from one size orchestra to another, with clefs inserted as needed. A typical 3-line sketch will have 2 treble-clef staves at the top and a bass clef at the bottom (and probably a percussion single line below). As more staves are added, extra treble clefs are usually added in the upper staves and an extra bass clef in the bottom staff. For full orchestra sketches, with from 8 to 14 staves, one typical layout has double staves for woodwinds and horns at the top, double staves for brass, double staves for mallets and keyboards, double staves for strings, plus percussion lines. But sketches are very personal and there is no standard setup comparable to the standard orchestral score page.

Several composers, including Gerald Fried, like to sketch directly on the score pages, and if they engage an orchestrator they will have him fill in that sketch score. For an example of a handwritten sketch and its subsequent orchestration see David Grusin's cue "Sayonara" for *The Yakuza* (1975; Figures 16-19 and 16-20). (See also Figures 16-3 and 16-4 for Alex North's sketch and the orchestration of a cue for *Under the Volcano.*)

TRANSPOSED OR CONCERT-PITCH SCORES?

"Ninety percent of the scores we see are transposed," says copyist-librarian Rick Vettraino. "The scores in concert pitch usually come from the composers, but in a few cases the orchestrators will give us C scores." There is of course an extra copyist's charge for transposing, but the principal reasons given by orchestrators for scoring in transposed pitch are (1) the ability to see as you orchestrate exactly what the players will see; and (2) to be doubly sure about correctness of the transpositions and to make corrections easier on the scoring stage. The reasons given by the composers who do concert scores are (1) speed; (2) the ability to give the copyist instructions to copy one part from another line without concern for the transpositions of each of the instruments (see Figure 16-23); and (3) to be able to more clearly see complex harmonic relationships.

FIGURE 16-19
The Yakuza **Sayonara (sketch)** **Dave Grusin**

CONTEMPORARY SCORES

Sketches and scores now written for contemporary rock-derived film music look significantly different from those that come out of the orchestral tradition. Scores like Dave Grusin's *Tootsie* (1982; see Figures 22-6 and 22-7) and Giorgio Moroder's *American Gigolo* (1980; see Figure 22-5) are not as completely filled in as traditional scores, especially the staves for the rhythm-section instruments. In the excerpts from the award-winning television series *Hill Street Blues,* Mike Post's handwritten Main Title score (Figure 16-21) indicates quite clearly the sounds and pitches that will be heard, although some of the synthesizer fills that have become identified with that theme are not shown in the score. The episodic cue "Bus" (Figure 16-22) is in a more abbreviated type of notation that nonetheless gives quite definite indications of how it should be played and how it will sound.

Beyond the written notation is the practical understanding that the synthesizer patches may be altered on the spot, reflecting either the synthesist's suggestions, the composer's on-the-spot reactions, the producer's choices, or a combination of all three. This can radically alter the sound without altering the look of the score, as would be the case in a comparable alteration of a traditional orchestral score.

THE ART OF ORCHESTRATION

Beautiful orchestration is greatly respected (although taken for granted) and much can be learned from those who have developed that craft. The late, highly regarded orchestrator Leo Shuken said in a 1975 interview: "I think [a fine orchestrator's] background can vary from formal training to self-training but I think the most important thing is to have communication with the composer, and don't let your ego take over. I like to think I can communicate with the composer and execute what he has in mind and with his feeling."[1]

Sometimes the orchestrator must do the selective editing that the composer would have done if he were orchestrating his own music. "I remember a picture that I orchestrated of Dmitri Tiomkin's, *The Spawn of the North* (1938), and when I looked at the sketch, I felt like I was in a cafeteria—like somebody handing you a tray and telling you to pick something out, because there was no orchestra big enough to play everything that was on the sketch, so I just picked out what I thought were the important points, and fortunately it worked out.

"The melody was harmonized, then he had a sustaining thing from the very bottom to the very top of the orchestra, like a curtain; he had a counterpoint that was harmonized, and he had figures. I did the logical thing—I didn't harmonize the melody and the counterpoint was left in the clear. It was a process of elimination. He seemed to be very pleased, like opening a Christmas package."

Shuken's longtime associate Jack Hayes believes that to be a proficient orchestrator "it helps to be a composer too," and almost all of them are. He feels his task is to orchestrate in the way the composer would orchestrate it himself. "It is a great help to know each composer's style. Henry Mancini, John Morris, and Marvin Hamlisch each have their own style as far as the sketches they make."

Hayes is emphatic in saying that the best way to learn to orchestrate is to pick effective passages from scores and reduce them to condensed sketch scores. "It's very laborious but it's a really good system. When I first learned to write the style of Tchaikovsky, I took those scores and I could see what he did with the horns, the strings. And you have to write it down. You can look at it and say, 'Oh yeah, that's it,' but you've really got to do it. That way you really absorb it. I think that's number one.

[1] *Film Music Notebook,* Spring 1975, p. 16, interview by Elmer Bernstein.

FIGURE 16-20
The Yakuza Sayonara Dave Grusin

FIGURE 16-20 *(Continued)*

FIGURE 16-20 *(Continued)*

FIGURE 16-21

Hill Street Blues **Main Title** **Mike Post**

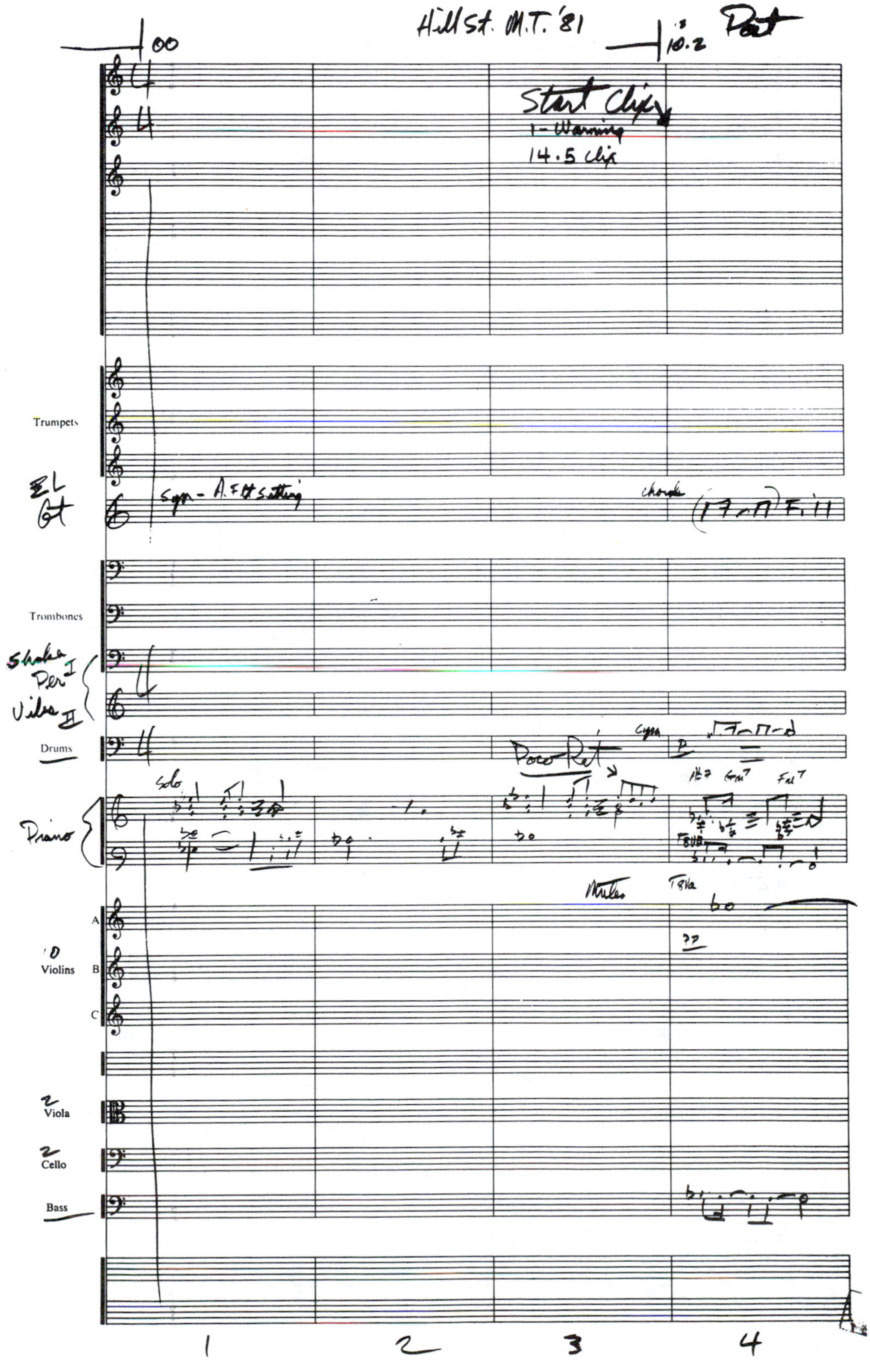
Hill St. M.T. '81
Start Clix
14.5 clix
Trumpets
El Gt
Trombones
Drums
Poco Rit
Solo
Piano
Violins
A
B
C
Viola
Cello
Bass
1
2
3
4

FIGURE 16-21 *(Continued)*

FIGURE 16-21 *(Continued)*

FIGURE 16-21 *(Continued)*

FIGURE 16-21 (*Continued*)

"One composer who is helpful in understanding string writing is the Russian, Miaskovsky. I have an old Columbia record with Ormandy doing his short symphony, a one-movement symphony for strings. If you want to learn beautiful string writing, he did it."

THE COMPOSER/ORCHESTRATOR RELATIONSHIP

In the composer/orchestrator relationship, the orchestrator often must fill in parts of the score, going beyond what the composer sketched. Shuken said, "I think I have

FIGURE 16-22

Hill Street Blues **M41** **The Bus** **Mike Post**

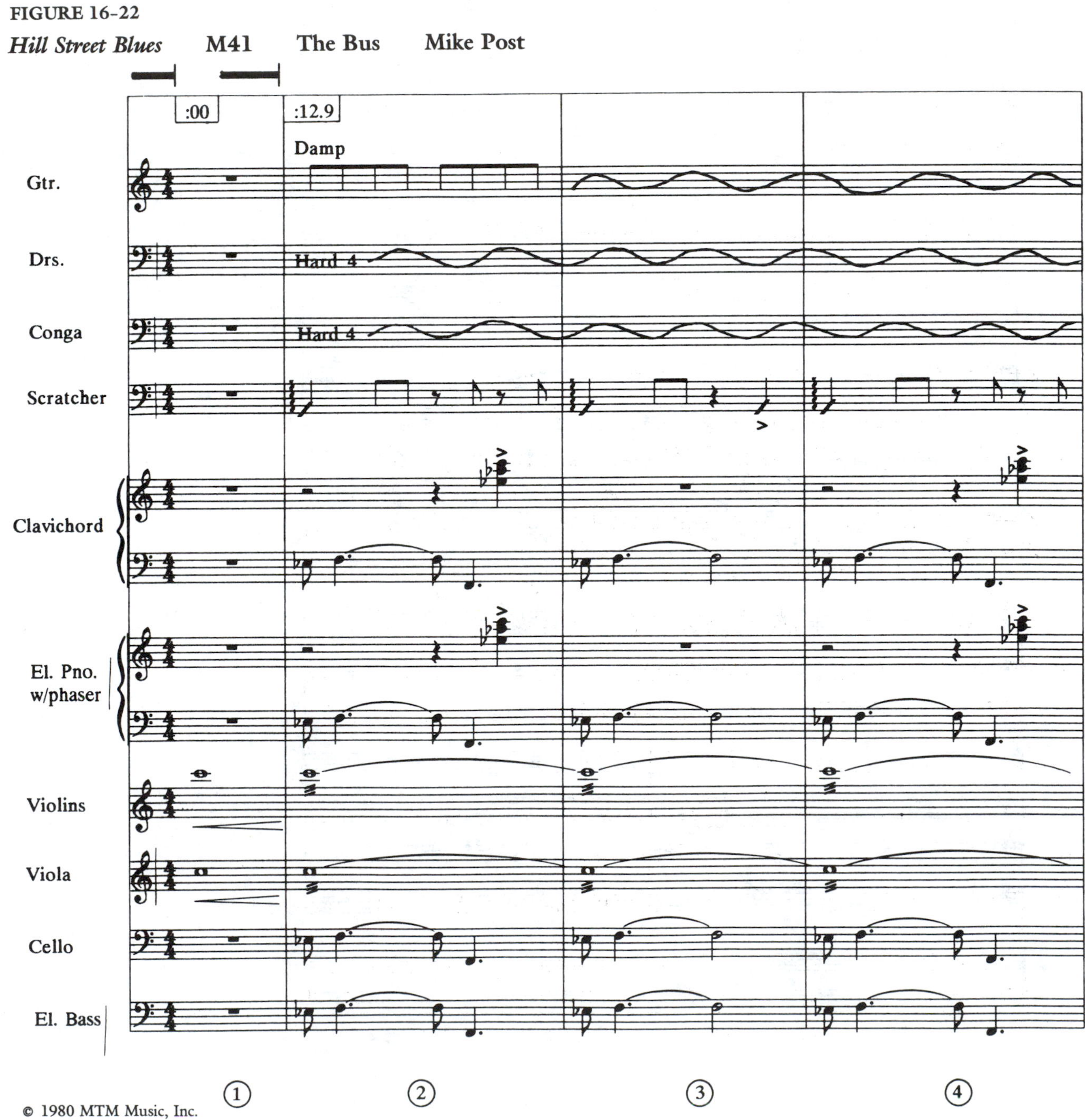

FIGURE 16-22 *(Continued)*

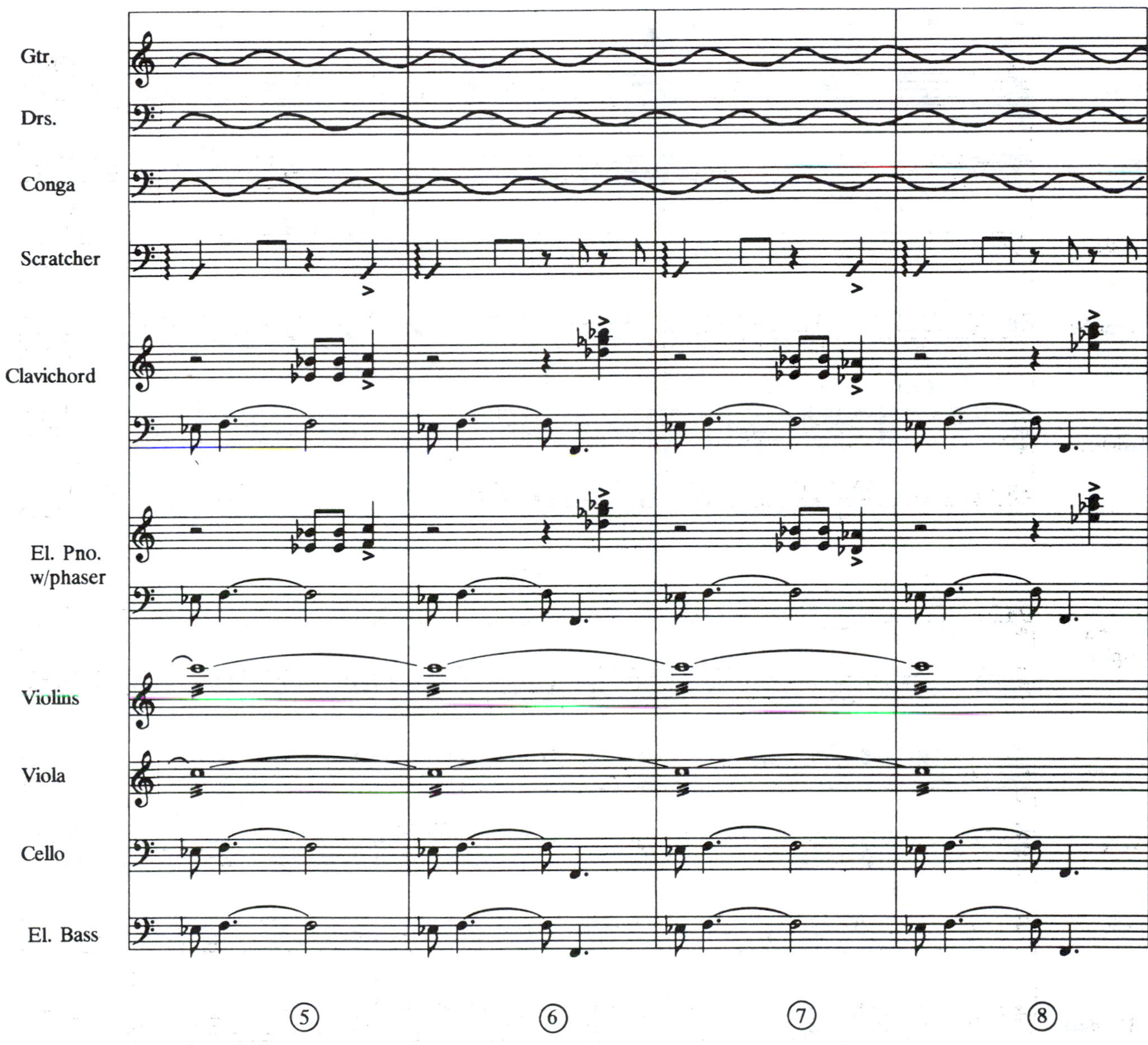

done more composing for other people than I have for myself. But I have enjoyed every minute of it." When answering the question about whether it was a common occurrence to help where a composer was technically incapable of providing him with a full sketch, he said: "Say I'm working with ten composers, two out of the ten don't give you more than a glorified lead sheet—I don't know if you'd call that common or not. I'm thinking of a case where a certain person writes good tunes and has a good dramatic sense but has no orchestral technique. But he makes up for it in other areas. If I were to take a timing sheet and write the music for it, I think it would be immoral if the composer wasn't able to. On the other hand if a good composer gives you a timing sheet because of a deadline problem, I think you should be flattered."

FIGURE 16-22 *(Continued)*

TYPICAL ORCHESTRA SETUPS

In the world of symphony concerts the makeup of the symphony orchestra has conveniently been standardized since the early nineteenth century, but in film work and studio recording of all kinds, only the instrumentalists needed for that day are hired. This has made composers very sensitive to the value of each and every instrument in the orchestra, since budget stringencies usually mean that you can only contract what you absolutely need to get the required sounds. The decisions about the makeup of the orchestra must be faced before composing, based on color needs and the cost of the musicians (including instrument doubles), as detailed in Chapter 6. As mentioned there, you should plan to start the recording sessions with the largest orchestra you will need, then drop down to various smaller size groups in subsequent sessions (or overtime periods of the basic sessions).

There are some favorite orchestra setups to achieve certain orchestral sounds. When the full-bodied, heroic, symphonic scores (like *Star Wars, Star Trek, Airport 1975, The Magnificent Seven*) are orchestrated and recorded, the traditional symphonic orchestra is typically used, with instrumentation of from 65 to 100 players. The string resources may vary, but the winds and percussion will follow a predictable pattern. A typical 85-piece recording orchestra (a full symphony orchestra, often with a basic rhythm section) is: ·

3 flutes (piccolo and 2 flutes)
3 oboes (2 oboes and English horn)
3 clarinets (2 clarinets and bass clarinet)
3 bassoons (2 bassoons and contra-bassoon)
4 French horns
4 trumpets
3 trombones (2 tenor trombones, 1 bass trombone)
1 tuba
4 percussion
1 harp
1 piano (or other keyboards)
1 guitar
1 rhythm bass (upright or electric)
1 drum-set player
33

16 first violins
14 second violins
8 violas
8 cellos
6 basses
52

85 total

STRING-SECTION SIZES. String sections vary in size, depending on the budget and the ability of the mixing engineer to get the "big" string sound on his scoring stage. The preferred minimum string section for orchestrator Jack Hayes is 16 violins, 4 violas, 4 cellos, and 3 basses, but there is common agreement that you can get very good results with 12-4-4-2, a typical section for television movies. For television, though, the budget may not allow even that minimum. For the 1979 television movie *The House on Garibaldi Street,* Charles Bernstein's largest string section was 10-4-4-1, "and it broke down to 8 violins at some point. My philosophy of writing for 8 violins is that they usually sound best not divided if they're going to be in the upper registers. And they don't sound bad divided 4 and 4 if they're in the low register (probably the low part of the staff, depending on the key and context). I'd say the lower two strings on the violin, and particularly the G string, have a rich, warm color, and 4 seem to be quite adequate to hold one voice down there. Whereas up on the E string you can't do wonderful sweeping melodic lines for 8 violins and expect it to sound like much. If I didn't have the resources to do it, I wouldn't assign that to them. Sometimes you can beef it up with a flute, and let harp and/or piano accent the attacks, and that can cover up a multitude of omissions, too. But sometimes (on the E string) you can divide 8 into 3, 3, and 2 and it can sound great if the music is staccato, or if it just happens to fall right in the situation."

Here are the orchestra sizes used for various film projects:

- *American in Paris* (1951, music directors Johnny Green/Saul Chaplin): 94
- *The Sandpiper* (1965, Johnny Mandel): 70: approximately 46 strings (28-8-6-4), 6–8 woodwinds (doublers), 4 horns, 4 trumpets, 4 trombones, tuba, percussion, harp, guitar, drum set
- *The Magnificent Seven* (1960, Elmer Bernstein): 65–70
- *Airport 1975* (1974, John Cacavas): 70
- *The Omen* (1976, Jerry Goldsmith): 50
- *Damien: Omen Two* (1978, Jerry Goldsmith): 80
- *Star Trek II* (1982, James Horner): 86, including 52 strings (26-12-8-6)
- *The Last Starfighter* (1984, Craig Safan): 82
- *Romancing the Stone* (1984, Alan Silvestri): 55, including 6 keyboards, electronic drums
- *Remo Williams* (1985, Craig Safan): 75
- *Back to the Future* (1985, Alan Silvestri): 98, including 2 electronic keyboards and 2 pianos

Some orchestras for television episodes include:

- *Hill Street Blues* (Mike Post): 21, with 10-2-2 strings, 2 percussion, drums, bass, guitar, 2 keyboards
- *A-Team* (Post-Carpenter): 30, with 10 violins, flute, oboe, clarinet, 3 horns, 2 trumpets, 2 trombones, 3 percussion, bass, drums, 2 guitars, 3 keyboards
- *L.A. Law* (Post): 32, with 12-4-4 strings, flute, oboe, clarinet, alto sax, 1 French horn, 2 percussion, 3 keys, bass, and drums
- *Magnum P.I.* (Post-Carpenter): 31, with 10 violins, 4 celli, 2 flutes, oboe, clarinet, 2 horns, 2 trombones, 2 percussion, 3 keyboards, 2 guitars, bass, drums
- *Hunter* (Post-Carpenter): 26, with 10 violins, 4 celli, 2 flutes, oboe, clarinet, 2 percussion, 3 keyboards, bass, drums
- *Murder, She Wrote* (David Bell/Richard Markowitz): 28, with 10-3-4-2 strings, 2 flutes (doubling piccolo, alto flute), 2 clarinets, 2 horns, 1 percussion (usually vibes), harp, piano

Television miniseries:

- *North and South* (Bill Conti): 64, with 20-8-6-4 strings, 8 woodwinds in pairs, 3 horns, 3 trumpets, 3 trombones (including bass trombone), tuba, 6 percussion, harp, and keyboard

CHORAL FORCES. Choral sounds have been important in several of the scores we have discussed. Some typical choral forces have been:

- *The Russians Are Coming* (1966, Johnny Mandel): amateur chorus of 40–50
- *The Omen* (1976, Jerry Goldsmith): mixed choir of 24
- *Damien: Omen II* (1978, Jerry Goldsmith): 32
- *Brainstorm* (1983, James Horner): adult choir of 18–24; boys' choir of 15
- *Testament* (1983, Horner): women's choir of 12
- *Agnes of God* (1985, Georges Delerue): 32, with the full chorus including 8 sopranos, 8 altos, 8 tenors, 8 basses

KNOW THE INSTRUMENTS

A long-standing suggestion for learning to orchestrate has been to learn every instrument. Composer Gerald Fried, who plays oboe in concerts when he can, firmly believes that "every composer should study every single instrument he's going to write for, even if it's for two weeks. You get a feel for the problems. When I was on tour with orchestras I would go out of my way to room with the viola player, room with the bass player, just so I could hear them practice, and they would give me lessons. Just so I knew what it feels like to play a bass part, or a viola part."

SHORT CUTS

> ***Like everybody else I've found ways of getting the music done. I think I'm rather good in the* come sopra *department*** JOHN ADDISON

Come sopras (*coam*-ay *soap*-rah, Italian for "like above") are instructions written in the score telling the copyist to recopy the designated bars. These are indicated in the score by the bar numbers from which they are to be copied (Figure 16-23). Note that the words *come sopra* don't themselves appear in the score, although this is the name used universally to describe the procedure.

Come sopras are much-used time savers that put great responsibility on the copyists who must jump back and forth in the parts to find these "copy-backs." The copyists rarely make mistakes on these instructions but mistakes on such passages are a potential hazard. The toughest and most error-prone, according to copyist Rick Vettraino, "are the *come sopras* from another score because we're not sure what the composer had in mind. We know he's given us numbers, say from cue 1M3, bars 23 to 41, for example. When the *come sopras* look wrong we try to make a phone call and find out if it's right or wrong. The disaster of our lives was a case where the composer asked the copyist for a *come sopra* from another score but also *come sopras* from the same score done in the same cue, plus a *come sopra* where he had to transpose into a new concert key. We were an hour-and-a half on the scoring stage recovering from that because I had nothing on my score except all these *come sopra* indications. I didn't know where we were—I couldn't follow anything. That was really a nightmare. One hundred percent of the time we try to fill in the *come sopras* from the other score and photocopy the pages and paste them in."

Come sopras can be a musically valid as well as a practical compositional technique. "One can use material already used earlier in the score," says John Addison, "but tailor it in such a way that the whole thing sounds as if every note of it was written especially for the cue. Since repetition of themes is quite often a very good thing in film (if it isn't overdone) I found that that was one way of getting more mileage.

"It's usually a question of making little links, cutting them up—different beginnings, different endings—that kind of thing. Once in a while (not often), I might have said to the orchestrator, 'Do that cue, but rescore it as follows.' And sometimes you will use a basic idea and then add in some countermelody or something. In fact, if I'd ever thought of doing it, I might have done it *before* I had a time problem."

Col (*coal*) indications are also time savers. *Col* means "with" in Italian, as in *colla voce* ("with the voice," seen often in opera scores). Instruments playing in unison with each other need not be recopied in the score. The legend "col flute," for example, is sufficient. Indicate the desired octave or correct transposition by also notating the pitch of the first note of the passage in the correct octave.

OTHER PRACTICALITIES

Bar numbers are a necessity on the scoring stage, where references to specific bars are made constantly. Even with bar numbers under every bar it is advisable to additionally insert large rehearsal numbers from time to time (see Figure 16-23) so that players (like percussionists) with many bars of rest will not see "68 bars rest" or something similar.

Phrasings and bowings. Much time can be saved on the scoring stage if all orchestral parts are phrased so session time is not taken up with questions that could have been avoided. Though strings must always be concerned about bowings, violinist/concertmaster Paul Shure recommends that the parts show the musical phrasings rather than bowings. Let the concertmaster select which of many possible bowings will be best for those phrasings. If you have a bowing preference, however, write it as you want it to be played, with the bowings.

FIGURE 16-23

Come sopra/col example

KEYBOARDS

Keyboard parts often have chord symbols, or sketches of orchestral voicings that the players are to double on piano or synthesizer. Michael Melvoin recalls that "the late Jerry Fielding would give me an entire orchestra cut-down sketch on two or three staves. And it would be like 'seventeen fingers.' And he knew perfectly well that I wasn't going to do that. And generally what he meant was (very much like looking at a score in the Basie band), 'Play something where the band isn't doing everything. Put something in a hole.' Whereas some other people usually mean, 'Pick the part that needs reinforcement,' or they'll indicate which parts need reinforcement."

OVERORCHESTRATION

Director Robert Wise recalls an instance where a cue was rejected because the theme that the filmmakers had liked very much was buried in an overorchestration. After the composer brought in a reorchestration that emphasized the theme, they loved it.

In a composer's early scores, the temptation to use available instruments can lead to scores that are too big for the situation. Director James Goldstone remembers Dave Grusin's first big feature score, *Winning* (1969). "I kept saying to Dave, 'What we are essentially scoring, except for the main title and the triumphal moment at the end of the Indianapolis 500 race, is a love story between two people. Keep that in balance between that and this huge background of 350,000 fans at a racetrack of cars.' Yet it was a very big picture and it was the first time that he had had a very large budget, the first time he could use effectively as many instruments as he wanted. He kept coming to me and to the head of the music department at Universal saying, 'Can I have six more strings,' etc., and we always said yes because we had the budget for him. And we scored intentionally in advance in two phases. We scored before previewing, and we laid down enough music that we could track from that music for preview purposes. And we knew we were going to come back and score after the first preview, when I was going to do what in effect became the final cut.

"We had two three-hour sessions and the score was very big for the intimate, small cues. After we finished scoring that day, Dave and I and the head of the music department sat down and while we were listening to the playback of the tape, I said, 'You know Dave, except for the Main Title and the End Title we'll use these for the previews and we'll do everything over again.' Dave was crestfallen, but everything had swelled. Everything that had been intimate—small pieces, small moments—had become big moments because he was carried away by the number of instruments he was allowed to have. And I know that kind of feeling when I've had the chance to have a lot of things on the set, and sometimes I've staged a scene where the *things* became what the scene was about rather than the theme. But he was very, very happy to go back and do exactly the same cues reorchestrated for a smaller group."

TECHNICAL AND PRACTICAL CONSIDERATIONS

You know, it's funny. I don't think about the pressure when I'm doing it—I just think about getting it done. JAMES HORNER

TECHNICAL CONSIDERATIONS

TIMINGS

CALCULATING THE CLICK OF ANY TEMPO, USING A STOPWATCH. To determine the approximate click equivalent of any tempo, start the watch as you start to count from 1 to 25. Stop the watch on the 25th beat. The reading on the watch will be the same numerically as the equivalent click. Remember that clicks are calculated in whole numbers plus eighths, so if the watch reads :10.5, the click equivalent of that tempo is 10 and $4/8$, or simply 10^{4}. If the watch reads :11.25, the click equivalent is 11^{2}. (See Chapter 9, "Timings and Clicks.")

CALCULATING THE CLICK EQUIVALENT OF ANY METRONOME READING. See Figure 9-5 for a chart listing the conversions between digital click and metronome, and page 108 for the method of conversion.

Note that there are only a few *exact* conversions; most of the metronome readings have been rounded off to the nearest hundredth, but metronomes do not usually have fractional subdivisions. So as a rule, the metronomic equivalent of a click will be approximate, and rarely close enough to substitute for the digital click tempo if you are syncing to click and not metronome (a 14-frame click, for example, is equivalent to a metronome reading of ♩ = MM 102.86).

Remember that the click is usually generated by a digital metronome. Although the word "metronome" is part of its name, it is not calibrated in beats per minute (as is a metronome, or MM, reading). It is always calibrated in frames and eighths of a frame. The round number conversions are shown in the table on page 333.

INCLUDE ALL TIMINGS ON SKETCHES. In general, the more information you include on your sketches, the easier it will be to conduct the score. If you will be conducting from the full score and are using an orchestrator, be sure to ask him to transfer all your timing information onto the orchestration. Include the following:

- Timings every bar, unless the tempo is faster than ♩ = 15 or 16 frame click, in which case every other bar is usually sufficient.

DIGITAL METRONOME		METRONOME
8	=	180
9	=	160
10	=	144
$11^{\underline{2}}$	=	128
12	=	120
15	=	96
16	=	90
18	=	80
20	=	72
$22^{\underline{4}}$	=	64
24	=	60

- Entrances and exits of all dialogue lines, plus as much additional dialogue as possible. You can use wavy lines or dots to indicate that dialogue continues.
- Exact placement of every editorial cut. Indicate the dialogue entrances and cuts with rests (see Figure 17-1). This will greatly facilitate conducting. And if you get lost for a moment, or lag behind the clock, all this information will function as landmarks to help you get back in sync during a take with picture.

Some sequencers and drum machines may have fractional metronome readouts for their click generators. If so, they may be used as a reliable substitute for the digital-metronome click equivalents when the final sync will be in terms of digital metronome. But if such sequencers or drum machines are actually being used to lay down a click or a sequenced music track you will need to check the sequencer's accuracy (see p. 109).

If you are using a drum machine or sequencer click to record to, and never need to convert for any reason to digital-metronome film language, it doesn't matter how the click is calibrated—it doesn't need to be in film language unless it is necessary for further sync procedures.

STREAMERS

Streamers and punches (page 104) can be very helpful and often indispensable conducting aids on the scoring stage. Be sure to get all information to the music editor in time for the cues to be properly prepared. The music editor can work from a score copy or from notes given to him over the phone; ask him how much time he needs. If working with film, give him all timing information from a :00 start; if you are both working with videotape, then the cumulative timings (illustrated in Figures 5-5 and 5-6) are best.

FIGURE 17-1

Timings and film information on sketch

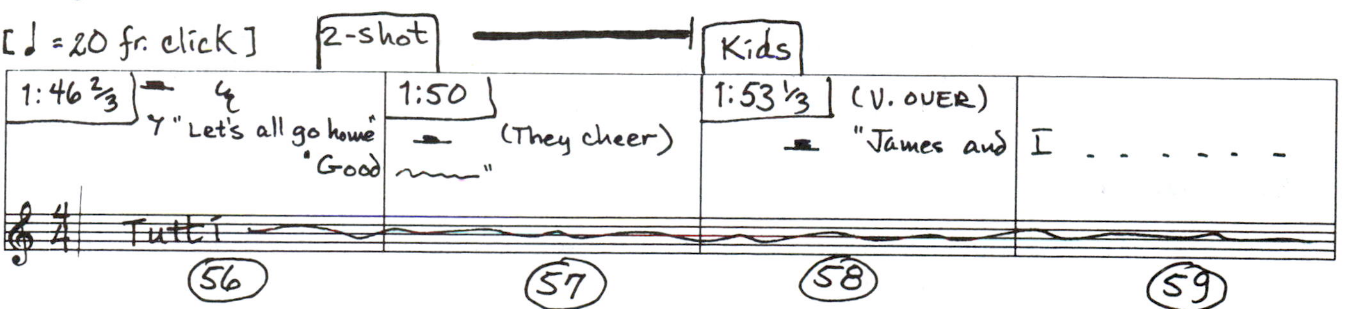

The music editor can use a computer system such as Streamline, Auricle, or Cue to prepare the videotape. These systems are quick and allow for on-the-spot changes on the scoring stage if necessary. Figure 10-3 is a chart created by Streamline for cue 9M2 from *Beverly Hills Cop II*. It shows the beat number and cumulative timing of each streamer, punch, and click change. Even if you are not scoring to videotape, you might still take advantage of these computer programs by asking your music editor to prepare your videocassette ahead of scoring so you can practice conducting any free-timing cues before your record.

SOUND EFFECTS

1. Note the obvious loud effects you may be facing on the dubbing stage (helicopters, jets, battle scenes and chases, thunder, a roaring river, or a stormy ocean).
2. Note those places when sound effects should probably play the scene without music; if not spotted that way, discuss again with the director.
3. Note any moments when stopping the music can heighten the dramatic use of sound effects.

Examples of the use of music with predominant sound effects:

- *Blue Thunder* (1983)—helicopters
- *Uncommon Valor* (1983)—battle scenes
- *Revolution* (1985)—battle scenes
- *Return of the Pink Panther* (1975)—bank alarm
- *Mad Max Beyond Thunderdome* (1985)—very loud vehicles and battle sequences at end of film

Films with sequence(s) with the dramatic use of sound effects without music:

- *Brainstorm* (1983, James Horner)—the first scientific demonstration of the sensory helmet is done with effects only, and remains clinical and real
- *The Elephant Man* (1980, John Morris)—all stylized montages of the elephants are treated only with sound effects
- *Testament* (1983, James Horner)—music gradually takes over during the school recital two thirds of the way through the film, as the clapping of the audience recedes further and further into the background

Example in which music stops for sound effects:

- *Impulse* (1984, Paul Chihara—study the last twenty minutes, in which the music goes out near the end of the film in time for the effective sound of the dogs barking and the pipe with contaminated water in it dripping

RECORDING

1. Don't compose as though you will be recording in layers if you plan to record everything live simultaneously. If you aren't recording the soft bass flute solo as a

separate "pass," you can't expect it to be heard above screaming brass and pounding percussion.

2. Indicate on the score all dynamics and phrasing for the orchestra. This will save time and ensure a sympathetic interpretation of your music.

3. Keep it playable if you want to finish in time and with an excellent performance. You may not have time to properly rehearse extremely complex music.

4. Consider, and make note of, any special effects you may expect the mixer to add on the scoring stage (digital delay, reverb, special stereo placement).

PRACTICAL CONSIDERATIONS

PRIORITIES

Film composing requires the ability to be organized. To bring the most to each project, the film composer should learn to prioritize his responsibilities. Waiting for the last minute may work for sketching a short piece of innocuous roller-derby source music, but you can't book your orchestra the night before the session and be certain of great results. The following suggestions will be helpful:

1. *Work on any songs as soon as possible,* even before delivery of the fine cut if you are able; the whole process of writing a song (including lyrics) takes much more time than underscoring a sequence. Timing the song perfectly with the picture, getting the right artist at the right price, doing one or more demos, getting the filmmaker's approval of the song, considering where else the song might be used in the film—all this will eat into your composing time. Even if you write the music first and have to wait for the lyric to be written, you can continue composing your score in the meantime. Also, if you plan to use the song theme(s) in your score you will need that material early.

2. *Find and book specialists early,* including vocalists, any ethnic instrumentalists, synthesists, rhythm-section musicians, any other instrumentalists with unusual instruments (like the didgeridoo) and special soloists (like the harmonica player or a particular jazz soloist). Remember that vocalists are not booked by the music contractor, but by a vocal contractor.

3. *Review and polish your breakdown chart of all cues.* You need to assign each cue to one of the orchestras before booking the sessions, in order to know how many musicians to book for each session and determine how long each session will be. (If the entire score is budgeted for the same orchestra, this will not be an issue.)

4. *Book the orchestra as soon as possible,* by discussing the budget limitations and all your needs with the music contractor at or around the time of spotting the film. If at all possible, don't wait until you have written half the score. Follow through on each item on the contractor's checklist given later in this chapter.

5. *Book the orchestrator early.* If you are going to use one, you want to be sure he is available when you need him. Good orchestrators are booked in advance and have busy schedules. Keep in close touch with him after spotting, so he knows how much music to expect and exactly what the schedule is. Put him in touch with the copyist, so he can get his orchestrations to him as he finishes.

6. *Give all specific information about cues to the music editor as you go.* This includes either a confirmation or specific change for the start and end of each cue, the digital-click information if the cue is being scored to click, and any information about streamers you are requesting (or copies of the scores if they contain all this information). Give him the copyist's phone number, in case he wants a copy of each cue for study and reference (a must if you expect him to check your timings for errors and know what you are doing).

7. *Get all information you need from the music editor.* Check the spotting notes to see if there are scenes with visual performances, marching, or dancing, which may require

determination of a click. Don't assume the music editor will automatically calculate this click for you. Ask for this information early.

WORK METHODS—THE MECHANICS

Though most composers approach the practical aspects of film scoring in much the same way, there can be many variations and, now and then, eccentricities. Here are some personal choices to consider:

1. *Pen or pencil?* Most composers prefer a pencil to a pen (usually with some kind of soft, number 2 lead)—it's easier to erase a pencil. Why would anybody use pen? Simple—when you're not erasing, it's easier to write. John Cacavas explains: "I write in ink, to save the wrist and go faster. A pencil would ruin you." A pen (either old-fashioned ink or a felt-tipped pen) requires much less pressure, causing less strain on the writing hand. And it's easier to read on the podium from a distance under the glare of the scoring-stage lights.

2. *Which cues first?* Composers seem to be divided on this one. Some, like Bruce Broughton, like to start with the first cue and go straight through to the end of the score in sequence. Others prefer to jump around a bit. One variation is to isolate all of the most significant cues and sketch them first. This would usually include the montages, exposed moments of great triumph or motion (Lawrence of Arabia trekking across the desert), the Main Title, important love scenes, possibly moments of tragedy or perhaps an important action cue or two (those that are more exposed or more organic to the score's concept). Working this way can help to establish the specific use of the most important thematic materials in the score.

PREPARING TO RECORD

1. *Dress comfortably.* It is common to be in a sweater or sport shirt/blouse on the scoring stage, or even a T-shirt if the weather permits. Any clothing is appropriate if it suits you and puts you at ease.

2. *Bring everything you will need.* This might include two batons (keep a second nearby on the podium in case you drop or break one during a cue); water; pencils and/or pens (including several colors in case you want to make easily distinguishable notes on your score; a stopwatch of some sort to keep track of the total elapsed time between breaks (some stages don't have clocks visible from the podium).

3. *If you conduct from the full score, bring along your sketches also.* You may need to refer to them while you are rehearsing to check wrong notes. Organize them in score sequence, or recording sequence if you prefer, so you can find a specific sketch if you need it.

4. *Plan on arriving at the scoring stage early.* There is nothing worse than being stuck in traffic ten minutes before the start of the session.

5. *Say hello to the mixer and crew, and your booth representative.* If you are early enough, this is a good time to go over any last-minute instructions.

CHECKLISTS

The following checklists should be used to ensure that nothing has been overlooked:

MUSIC CONTRACTOR

- Give the music contractor the name of the project.
- Give him the project category (television, feature film, documentary).

- Give him the dates, locations, duration of all sessions.
- Give him the instrumentation for all sessions.
- Give him your first-, second-, and third-choice musicians for each instrument.
- Give him any unusual instruments and instrumentalists needed.
- Give him the duration of call for each musician on all sessions.
- Give him any budget information (for instance, if the budget does not allow for overscale for any musicians, or if rental fees must be under a certain maximum amount).
- Get from him the budget estimate and an itemized breakdown.

MUSIC EDITOR

- Give the music editor your timings preference (to the tenth or hundredth).
- Give him your notes preferences (how subjective, how much detail, all dialogue?).
- Give him your paper preference (8½ × 11 three-holed paper?).
- Give him your final starts and outs for each cue; confirm original start as per notes whenever there is no change.
- Give him all information regarding location of streamers.
- Give him your choice of streamer length (3′, 4′, 5′).
- Give him all information regarding the number of warning clicks you want for each cue (if you are using clicks). You can use these warning clicks to get started, even if you choose not to conduct the cue to click.
- Give him all changes in cue numbers (due to recording one cue as two or more shorter cues).
- Give him all information regarding any new cues added since spotting.
- Give him all information regarding any cues dropped since spotting.
- Give him all information regarding dates, times, and locations of scoring sessions.
- Give him the name, address, and phone number of the copyist.
- Get from him the spotting notes and ask him to send the notes to the copyist, producer, and director.
- Arrange a schedule with the music editor for delivery of all timing notes.
- Get from him the appropriate click for all scenes containing visual performances, marches, dances, and so on, to be postscored.

ORCHESTRATOR(S) AND COPYIST

- Give the names, addresses, and phone numbers of orchestrator(s), supervising copyist, contractor, and scoring stage to orchestrator(s) and copyist.
- Give them all information regarding dates, times, and locations of all scoring sessions.
- Tell them the size of orchestra, and the length and complexity of the score.
- Discuss with the orchestrator whether the scores will be transposed (often the orchestrator's preference) or concert pitch.
- Tell the orchestrator how much timing detail to transfer from your sketches.
- Tell the copyist how many photocopies of the orchestrations to make, and whether to staple the pages or tape them (stapling is cheaper, but more difficult to work with). The conductor's copy should always be taped.

• Prepare a list of the cues to be scored at each session, in the sequence you wish to record them, and give this list to the copyist no later than the day before the session. Keeping similar cues together is usually the most efficient way to organize the cues. If possible, start the session with something relatively easy for the full orchestra, and at least a minute in duration so they can warm up. This also helps the mixer. In general, it is better to avoid starting with an extremely important cue (like the Main Title).

PART 5

RECORDING

RECORDING—THE SCORING STAGE

The scoring stage is the high point—from there on it's all downhill.

JERRY GOLDSMITH

When I walk on that scoring stage and I hear that music, it's probably the single, biggest moment for me—it's absolutely magic time. You spend weeks with a film, in one form, then all of a sudden. . .

JOHN BURNETT, FILM EDITOR

Despite the pressures of time, money, and nervously expectant directors and producers, the recording sessions undoubtedly provide the peak experiences of the whole film-scoring process. It is here that the music first comes alive, and at this time the music is still the principal actor—with the composer calling the shots.

The all-important sessions on the scoring stage are a heady and complex mix of music, recording and film technology, budget control, and psychology. The composer/conductor will be coping with an anxious director and producer(s), musicians, the music editor, contractor, music supervisor, copyist, the technical crew, and the mixing engineer. He must be thoroughly prepared to deal with all of these personalities under high-pressure circumstances.

THE SCORING STAGE

The score is recorded on the **scoring stage,** a term the movie industry uses to loosely differentiate it from a **recording studio,** the scoring stage having full picture-projection facilities (including a machine room with film **dummies**[1] to handle dialogue and effects tracks) and ordinarily a large enough space to record an orchestra of at least thirty musicians. The distinction is not critical—much film music has been recorded in commercial recording studios. The recording studios show picture via closed-circuit monitors or even film projection. And the scoring stages have a full array of multitrack tape recorders, film recorders, digital and analog sound-processing equipment that is roughly comparable to that of the commercial recording studios.

UNDERSCORING, PRERECORDING, AND SET RECORDING

The term **scoring,** or **underscoring,** refers specifically to the process of putting music to film *after* the film is shot (also known as "recording to picture"). When the music is recorded *before* the picture is shot it is termed **prerecording, prescoring,** or **playback recording.** This method is used not only in musicals, where the actors hear the playback recording on set, but for the many situations in nonmusical pictures where an actor has

[1] Dummies: machines that play back sound recorded on sound film ("mag stripe"—1 track; or "full coat"—3 tracks).

FIGURE 18-1

Alex North and Dustin Hoffman in Evergreen Recording Studios booth while scoring *Death of a Salesman*.

Photo: Gay Wallin

FIGURE 18-2

Fred Karlin conducting his score for *Robert Kennedy and His Times*.

Photo: Gay Wallin

occasion to sing or play an instrument. If the music is recorded *simultaneously* as the performance is being shot on the set, it is called **set recording,** or **standard recording.** This gives a very realistic effect. *'Round Midnight* (1986, Herbie Hancock) is an effective example of simultaneous recording and filming. For the film, the shooting set was actually built on a scoring stage.

RECORDING FORMATS

The recording format has to be decided by the producer and the composer. Budget considerations may determine the format, but in any event the scoring stage must always be notified in advance. If the budget can accommodate it, a standard format is to record on 3-stripe mag, plus 24-track tape as a backup. Often, in an alternate procedure, the 3-track mix is recorded on ½-inch 4-track tape (with sync pulse on the fourth track). In either case, the 3-track mix can become the master mix, with no further mix-down necessary, making this an extremely efficient system (it is used almost always for television projects). Otherwise, the cues will have to be mixed down from multitrack tape after the session (see page 360). Stereo feature films are generally postmixed from multitrack.

If one or more cues require a vocal or a special overdubbed instrument, these cues are always recorded on a multitrack machine to facilitate the overdubbing process. Although it was standard practice for years to overdub using mag-stripe, this antiquated technique is a slower and more limited process, lacking the potential for punching in to improve a previously recorded passage.

If a soundtrack album is planned, a multitrack master will give you the control to remix a high-quality stereo recording.

PLANNING

In the United States, a full day of recording is two 3-hour sessions, called a double session (with a possible additional hour overtime). The minimum length for a scoring session is 3 hours. As discussed in Chapter 6, the sessions using the largest orchestra are scheduled first, then the smaller group sessions, and scheduling is planned on the expectation of recording an average of 3 to 5 minutes of music per hour (each "hour" being really 50 minutes after deducting the musicians' 10-minutes-per-hour break). 5 minutes of recorded music per hour is a difficult rate to maintain; feature films are likely to average no more than 2½ to 4 minutes. This averages the slow pace of the first hour (when recording balances are set) with the increased efficiency of the subsequent hours. Any corrections, changes requested by the director or producer, equipment failures, and playbacks are also included in this average. Music for television shows is expected to be recorded at near the 5 minutes per hour maximum allowed by A. F. of M. regulations.[2]

Music executive Harry Lojewski finds that composers and producers of two-hour movies for television, miniseries, and episodes may expect to record 4 minutes per hour but often average 3 to 3½, while features more nearly average 3 minutes per hour. Musical complexity makes a big difference. Bruce Broughton's scoring for the miniseries *The Blue and the Gray* (1983) averaged 4½–5 minutes per hour, while his recordings for the features *The Young Sherlock Holmes* (1985) and *Silverado* (1985) averaged 2½ minutes per hour, due to more difficult music. James Horner found that recording 15 minutes per day in London (or 2½ minutes per hour average) was too much for his difficult score for *Aliens* (1986). He finds that recording goes slower in London and believes that 11 or 12 minutes per day would have been a more realistic expectation. Figure 18-3 is a compilation of recording times for scores (exclusive of songs) in several categories.

---

[2]You can record more than 5 minutes per hour, but the musicians are paid on a prorated basis. For example, if you recorded 30 minutes in 5 hours, the musicians would be paid for 6 hours. Musicians are paid for only those cues (converted to minutes of music) on which they play.

FIGURE 18-3

Scoring session lengths.

TITLE	COMPOSER	MUSIC TIME (MINUTES)	FILM LENGTH (MINUTES)	ORCHESTRA SIZE	RECORDING TIME
FEATURE FILMS					
The Last Starfighter	Craig Safan	60 (w. long cues)	101	82	5 days (30+ hrs)
Romancing the Stone	Alan Silvestri		106	55 (inc. 6 keys, elect. drms)	8 days (48+ hrs)
Body Heat	John Barry	Lots	113		3 days (18+ hrs)
Aliens	James Horner	80	138	85	6 days London
Star Trek II	James Horner	68	114	large	4–5 days
Star Trek III	James Horner	76	105	large	7 days
Cocoon	James Horner	78	117	diff. kinds	6 days (36+)
Just Between Friends	Patrick Williams		110		2 days (12+)
Remo Williams	Craif Safan	60	121		4 days Synclavier 2 days Korean 3 days orch.
War Games	Arthur B. Rubinstein		118	75–80	3 days (18+)
Airport 75	John Cacavas		106		12 hrs
Fame	Michael Gore	10 (underscore portion only)	134		3 hrs (underscore only)
The Spy Who Loved Me	Marvin Hamlisch		125	102	1 day rhythm sect. 4–5 days orchestra
MOVIES FOR TELEVISION					
Return to Oz	David Shire		110	London Symphony	55 hrs
TELEVISION MINI-SERIES					
Mussolini	Laurence Rosenthal	[2 hrs]	[7½ hrs]	Munich Philharmonic	5–6 days (35 hrs)
TELEVISION EPISODES					
A-Team	Mike Post	15–20	48	30	3 hrs
Magnum	Mike Post	7–10	48	31	3 hrs
Hunter	Mike Post	10–12	48	25	3 hrs
Scarecrow	Arthur B. Rubinstein	16–18	48		4 hrs
The Wizard	Arthur B. Rubinstein	28	48		5¼ hrs
Murder, She Wrote	David Bell	7–12	48	28	3 hrs

Factors that slow down the process are difficult music, using large orchestras, adding electronic instruments, overdubbing, multiple playbacks, and changes by the director or producer.

CONDUCTING

The composer/conductor's most important job is to get a fine musical performance from the musicians, taking care that the timings, synchronization, and dramatic approach to the film are correct. Studio musicians are among the finest in the world, with superior sight-reading ability, all-round musicianship, musical flexibility, and experience. Yet with all these skills they won't give the best and most spirited or moving performances without understanding what is expected from them style-wise, and without having some means of performing together in perfect ensemble. A good conductor is the key to both.

The ideal qualities for a scoring stage conductor include flexibility, leadership, communication abilities, and self-confidence. The conductor must realize what a *recording* orchestra needs in order to play together (a good beat and a sensible studio seating setup). He must be able to pinpoint difficulties and stop to correct problems right away, and he must possess enough conducting technique to earn the players' confidence.

Universal Studios orchestra contractor Sandy De Crescent points out how crucial psychological factors can be: "You can take 22 really good violins and put them with one conductor and they are absolutely fantastic—intonation, everything, and you think how lucky we are to have people like this to call. Then, person for person, you can have the same 22 violins a month later on a session and have a disaster, much of which has to do with the conductor—some have no control and the players get very tense."

Many composers have studied conducting formally in music schools or privately, and many others haven't, but all will find that practical experience is a necessity. Music executive Bodie Chandler tells many young composers "to go to conducting classes wherever they can or hire someone to teach them how to conduct. It's really quite difficult—you're so busy following the clock and the streamers that it's tough to focus on the orchestra or vice versa. The art of free timing is very tricky. There are certain ways of getting in and out of free timing that you have to be careful with. If you can't handle this you should write [and conduct] to click until you learn to do otherwise. The one thing you don't want to do is look bad on the stand."

Studio musicians have learned to play to the click and many composers who are not adequate conductors survive in this way. If you are using click, let the click do the time-keeping for you; the musicians won't need you at all for that function. Concentrate instead on distinct downbeats for each bar (which necessitates a slightly larger upbeat), indicating instrumental cues (which can be done with either or both hands—whatever is most comfortable), and adding expression and dynamics to the performance.

However, the ability to evoke musical nuances in free timing requires good conducting, and ASPIRING FILM COMPOSERS NEED TO STUDY CONDUCTING AND PRACTICE IT REGULARLY. Conducting demands the same physical coordination that playing an instrument does, and when you are conducting a cue your attention will be on other details—timing, interpretation, watching the picture. Ideally, your conducting should be so automatic and natural that you can do it well without thinking about it.

TO CONDUCT OR PRODUCE THE MUSIC?

This is the time when the composer would truly like to be in two places at once: to be in the studio conducting the orchestra to get the best performance, and to be in the booth supervising the mix. As a conductor, you want the opportunity to work with the orchestra to interpret the phrasing, to answer musicians' questions, to make the timing work out right, to quickly revise any passages that need a little fine-tuning. But you also want to be in the control room—to work with the mixer to hear the balances as the director and producer are hearing them and to hear and evaluate their comments.

Since you can't perform both functions simultaneously you must choose the one you are best at. Are you a better conductor than an audio producer? Is your first priority direct contact with the orchestra or the mixer? Certainly one of the special bonuses that comes from conducting is the opportunity to respond to the film during a take. If the composer conducts well to picture he can mold the performance skillfully to the dramatic action, adjusting his timings slightly as he conducts in order to bring the most out of the scene.

THE COMPOSER'S BOOTH REPRESENTATIVE. If you decide to conduct (as almost all composers do), you need to have someone in the booth whom you can trust to ensure an excellent recording (one that fits your musical and dramatic intentions), someone who will be honest, responsive, and diplomatic in communicating with you from the booth. Since you will not have the option of postmixing in many film situations (particularly in television), since you can't hear every playback while maintaining the expected output of recorded music, and since you can't always hear mistakes on the scoring stage, you need a representative in the booth who can serve as your alter ego and make these critical observations regarding orchestral performance, intonation, picture sync, instrumental balances, and orchestration. The better the mixer, the less your booth representative (audio producer) has to be concerned about the mixing areas (like balance and sound quality). But there is no chance to go back and rerecord cues after the musicians have gone home; you must be able to trust his judgment when he says a take is okay—and go on to the next cue.

The logical booth representatives are (1) the music supervisor—especially if he is more of a musician than an executive who handles business matters (in any case, if there is a music supervisor, he will be assigned to the project); (2) the orchestrator if there is one; or (3) a hired person of your choice. The contractor might have the requisite skills, although in Hollywood contractors usually prefer to concentrate on their own responsibilities. There is an A.F. of M. price scale for booth supervision.

CUEING THE MIXER. Take time to explain your score and your interpretation of it in advance to your booth representative, whoever he is. There is a good marking system available to identify the principal and secondary instruments in the score: the starts of principal ideas are marked with a red felt-tip pen and secondary ideas with a blue one (Figure 18-4). This can be done very quickly and is easy to follow. Special notes about unusual reverb or other sound processing should be clearly noted on the score, as well as indications about any overdubbing that you intend to do later—the mixer needs this information so that he can be sure to save tracks. The mixer and booth rep should be told about all such details before the session. Keep in mind that the scoring stage is usually set up at the end of the day prior to the next day's session.

SELECTING A CONDUCTOR. If instead of conducting you decide to be in the booth, you will need an excellent conductor, one who will prepare for the session and one who will work well with you. Previous film experience is essential. You must of course go over each cue with him to explain any matters regarding performance and synchronization.

GETTING GOOD PERFORMANCES

No matter how carefully you compose the score, you need to get a performance that really works. The musicians will rely on you to communicate your intentions clearly and

FIGURE 18-4
Afterglow **(marked score) Rayburn Wright**

directly. You know the music and the film and they don't.

Describing the film can be helpful. A few composers do this, but most don't. As a general rule of thumb, the orchestra likes to know the basic story line, but they don't require too much detail. You can supplement a brief outline of the story with a more detailed explanation of an individual scene if you feel it will help them to interpret the cue. Beyond that, although storytelling can increase rapport and generate a relaxed atmosphere, it's expensive to use recording time to talk a great deal.

An occasional touch of humor can contribute to the overall sense of relaxation and well-being on the scoring stage. Use it when it is appropriate. It takes confidence to see the humor in an awkward situation, and the musicians will respond well to the interjection of a humorous comment during a minor crisis. (If a guitarist's top E string snaps just before a take, humor will be more productive than swearing.)

QUESTIONS. Don't misinterpret questions from the musicians as being criticism. They may ask questions such as "Is the A-flat correct?" or "Do you really want that slurred?" The musicians want to get it right and in most cases are simply asking informational questions that should be answered simply and directly.

STRINGS. The strings can be the most difficult section of the orchestra to record. Concertmaster/violinist Paul Shure points out the relationship between string quality and headset use. "No string section plays as well with the clicks on as with them off. When you put the phones [headset] on, you start to listen to yourself more and the tendency is to play louder and more individually, whereas if you don't have anything on your ears (and if you are sensitive at all), you listen to the people around you. Hearing the click in the headset has a tendency to make string players play with less quality and usually more mechanical harshness." If you use clicks on cues with warm string passages, turning down the click volume can help you overcome the musicians' natural reactions to performing with click.

String players also find it very difficult to play when the violins, violas, and celli are either **baffled**[3] or spread out, because they are unable to hear each other as a unified string section. Tuning is difficult under those circumstances. With a symphonic-size string complement, the normal orchestral setup of violins on the left, and violas, cellos, and basses on the right works well (if they are not too spread out). For somewhat smaller complements (12 violins, 6 violas, and 4 cellos or less), seating them together on one side of the stage where they can have acoustical contact works well.

You should be aware of how many strings are necessary to achieve a good sound. If you have less than a realistic minimum number of strings, you may not get the sound you have imagined. Recording mixer John Richards, who worked extensively in England before moving to Hollywood, considers the minimum string section for a full sound to be 22 strings: 12 violins, 4 violas, 4 cellos, 2 double basses. Many television orchestras for two-hour movies-of-the-week have that ratio. But, as mentioned in Chapter 16, orchestrator Jack Hayes's choice for a minimum-size string section is 31 strings (16-6-6-3) and he considers 46 (22-10-8-6) to be best for a full symphonic sound. Another variation of the smaller-sized section is 25 strings: 12-6-4-3.

On *Out of Africa* (1986), mixer Dan Wallin worked with 36 violins with just four mikes for them, Wallin preferring in general to record strings this way. There was no postmix and no remix for the album version.

For *Silkwood* (1983), Georges Delerue used 33 strings (18-6-5-4), a distribution he often writes for, while Elmer Bernstein considers an ideal recording string section to be about 36 (18-8-6-4) "for a really big sound. That puts 10 on a first violin line." Patrick Williams had approximately 40 strings on *Violets Are Blue* (1986).

---

[3]Baffled: isolated with sound-absorbing barriers.

KEYBOARDS. In Hollywood, keyboard players, who are expected to interpret and improvise in different styles, like to be given the option of working out the assignment of parts with the other keyboard players, all of whom know each other's specialties well. However, if you know a specific player's strengths, write for that player and put his name on the part.

If they are to interpret a scene musically or to interact with the story in any way, they need to see the screen and need to be given any conceptual information that could affect their contribution. Improvising to the drama involves many performance decisions that should be directly influenced by the story situation and the composer's input.

CONDUCTING AIDS

Composers who use orchestrators generally prefer to conduct from their own condensed score sketches rather than from the orchestrator's full score—they can have the perspective of seeing more bars of music in one view, turn less pages, and work with their own familiar short scores. Those who conduct from full score do so for the same reason that a symphony conductor does—to know exactly what each instrument is playing. The timings and scene descriptions are of course transferred to the full score in that case.

STREAMERS AND PUNCHES. The music editor can provide these two visual aids that are particularly helpful to the conductor when he is using free timing rather than clicks.

Streamers. A streamer is a line scribed on the film so that it appears as a vertical line that moves across the frame from left to right at a speed that is controlled by the length of the scribed line. If you want something different from the normal three-foot (two-second) streamer you can ask for it in either feet or seconds (one foot equals two-thirds of a second).

Whether you are using free timing or clicks, the music editor will normally prepare for each music cue a warning streamer (usually red) and a start streamer (white). The start will be either the first downbeat (that is, bar 1, beat 1) with any pickup notes coming *ahead* of the streamer, or the first note of music. A reminder to yourself on your score as to which system you are using will be helpful, especially if you use both systems during the course of the session. If you have a preference, inform the music editor before he prepares the film for scoring, and be sure to indicate the placement of :00 on your score.

Punches are short sequences of light pulses produced by punching holes in the film frames. These can be used as preparatory blips to set the start tempo of a free-timing cue, or punched to show the downbeats of each bar in a nonclicked cue. The music editor needs to know your preferences on these matters.

Both streamers and punches can be inserted electronically when the projection medium is videotape. In this case on-the-spot alterations are possible at the recording session, something difficult to do with film streamers and punches.

Warning clicks. If the cue starts with audible clicks, ask the music editor how many warning clicks there are before each cue. Four bars at a fast tempo (♩ = 9-frame click or faster), two bars at a moderate tempo (♩ = 10 to 20), or one bar at a slower tempo (♩ = 20 or slower) will be comfortable for you and the orchestra. Indicate this information on the upper left-hand corner of the first page of your score. It can be very helpful to use only the warning clicks on cues that will be conducted without click. (See page 352 for more.)

THE MIXER

The composer's best efforts will be wasted without a good recording. An expert and experienced mixing engineer is the key. To do his best he needs to know in advance the instrumentation, the composer's point of view (is the score symphonic, keyboard oriented, rhythm-section oriented?), and the type of recording technique (commercial-record oriented, tight sound, or a more open and spacious traditional film sound?). He has many options to choose—whether to use close miking, multimiking, tracking for isolation, tight baffling with everyone wearing headsets, minimum baffling emphasizing acoustic contact between players—and the composer's input can help him set up most effectively. He can make alterations in response to your reactions after hearing the early takes, but time-consuming microphone and seating changes take up precious recording time and quickly raise the total session costs.

FILM SOUND

"There's a difference between an underscore sound and an obvious record sound," says recording engineer Dan Wallin. "I must say that the record things made specifically for films with that idea in mind always sound better. They have to be grander for the big screen than for that tight record mix. . . .You need a much bigger room sound, or more 'space' in the recording."

Recording mixers often blend the sound from an overhead mike into the mix for this reason. "I think it gives that extra dimension to it," Wallin continues. "That kind of overall sound just makes the whole thing sound richer and warmer and more unified as an orchestra."

The lower frequencies of the score become less audible at low listening levels, and recording engineer John Richards considers this an important factor to correct for: "I am always mindful in film and television work that there is enough bass content on the tracks. If you are left with the mids and the highs, it will sound very thin and empty. So just a little more bass needs to be incorporated in the original recording."

Technical knowledge on the part of the composer is not a necessity but in order to get a first-rate recording it is desirable to know as much as possible about the process. Such knowledge will also help the composer to understand what the mixer's concerns and problems are so you can establish a more collaborative relationship during scoring. Dan Wallin feels that a basic technical awareness is important for a film composer. "It would make it a lot easier for them to communicate with me if they knew exactly what they were asking for. They would ask me for a certain amount of delay or flanging on something, or more reverb or a different color." (See the Bibliography for recommended reference materials.)

HEADSET MIXES

Each player will have been given a headset in which he can hear a "cue feed" containing click mixed with music (a variable combination of some or all of the orchestra mixed to best help everyone play together). There are usually at least two cue feeds available (each with different mixes of sounds), since percussionists, keyboard players, singers, and string players may each wish to hear slightly different mixes. Some scoring stages provide headsets for both ears while others provide the option of having single headsets so the players can have one uncovered ear to hear the other instruments acoustically. When single headsets are not provided the players often move one of the two earpieces and place it against their head so that they can hear the orchestra acoustically with one ear.

THE CONDUCTOR'S CUE MIX. The composer/conductor has to decide what he wants to hear in his headset. Although some want only click, and some want to hear what a particular group of musicians are hearing (one of the several cue feeds), many work with the control-room mix, or the "3-stripe mix," as it is called. Without further mix-downs after the scoring sessions, this is the 3-track mix that will go directly to the dubbing stage.

It is possible to hear the dialogue in the headset along with the mix, which gives the conductor a good idea of how these elements will work together. Although most conductors do not want to hear dialogue in their headset, a good headset balance with dialogue is a great help when there isn't enough time to play back everything. Hearing the dialogue allows you to judge on the scoring stage how well your music is working with the dialogue, so that adjustments can be made if necessary. However, hearing dialogue during heavy sound-effects cues (involving, for instance car chases or airplanes) is usually very counterproductive, because these sounds merely obscure your score while recording. If you decide you would like to hear the dialogue, ask for it, because it is not regularly included in the headset mix.

PREVENTING CLICK LEAKAGE. Preventing the sound of the click from being picked up by the mikes is a constant problem. Mixing engineers continually have to ask the players to turn off headsets that are not being used and to turn down the volume of those that are. One problem for the mixer is that very loud passages require a louder click, and when the music becomes softer the click bleeds into the mikes. One sensible solution is to have the click's master volume turned down in the booth by the mixer or booth rep when the softer passages occur. On some scoring stages the music editor will have a click volume control at his desk next to the conductor's podium. Sometimes the composer will be able to control the overall volume level of his own headset from the podium, and sometimes he can change the click volume level also. Whatever the facilities, the conductor and mixer must be alert to this problem, as click leakage can ruin a good take. Some movies and soundtrack albums have even gone out with traces of click audible on them.

CREATIVE RESPONSES

The composer should be constantly open to the creative possibilities that arise on the scoring stage. A player using a different phrasing or playing something unplanned may trigger the realization of some new musical possibility, or hearing a cue may cause you to think of some minor changes that would make it more effective. The goal on the scoring stage is to achieve the most effective results, not simply a perfect rendition of the notes that you have written. Being able to think on your feet is a great advantage and that ability should be developed. It is a good idea to really consider an accidental error in an instrumental part before correcting it without thought.

REHEARSAL PROTOCOL

Each time you start conducting tell the musicians clearly where you are starting and how many free beats you are giving. As simple and logical as these suggestions are, they are often disregarded, causing misunderstandings and wasted time. Make sure every musician can comfortably see you and that the cue mix in the headsets is adjusted for them (with everyone understanding that this may be a "convenience" mix that doesn't represent the final balances).

Also, be sure everyone in the orchestra is ready to play before you give the first downbeat; percussionists may have to set up a different instrument from the previous cue; woodwind doublers need to get out different instruments; synthesists need to set up any patches; the double bassist may now be playing electric bass, requiring a move from one part of the stage to another.

If you are conducting to click, just ask the music editor for the click when you want it; unless otherwise requested, the click will be sent to you and to the entire orchestra. You may have to ask the music editor to turn off the click if it is going during a rehearsal while you are talking to the musicians. If you are not using click to conduct your cue, you may still want to hear a sample of the click that closely approximates the starting tempo of your cue. Ask for a few bars any time you need it.

If you want *only warning clicks* you can ask for this. Just ask for "four warning clicks to zero-zero," or "eight free to the downbeat." This technique will be helpful in getting you started on a free-timing cue and will guarantee that the orchestra and you will start together on the initial downbeat (after which the clicks will be turned off).

The first rehearsal is usually done without picture. If you are recording a cue without click, or are able to rehearse it without click, you may want to conduct this run-through without using the headset. After the first time through, now using **phones**[4] and hearing click if you so wish, you may be ready for the first take. The disadvantage of not using the headset on the first rehearsal is that you don't hear the 3-stripe mix. Regardless of your preference, if time is short, it is usually advantageous to use the headset on the first rehearsal so you can ask the mixer for any balance adjustments you may want before you record.

In general, it is not necessary to get a perfect performance in rehearsal before going for a take. A good studio orchestra will sound even better on a second or third reading of a cue, and a few well-chosen comments by the conductor may correct most mistakes without another complete rehearsal. Notice the performance problems during the first rehearsal; remember wrong notes, misphrasings, faulty dynamics, unwanted sounds. After the rehearsal, quickly go through your notes with the orchestra, making concise corrections to each musician or section as relevant. If there are a few bars that need special attention, rehearse these now.

With experience, a conductor will sense when to take the time to clean up a performance, and when it is not necessary to do so before making a take. In any event, it is a good idea to avoid overrehearsing, which can lead to staleness and even a lack of interest on the part of the musicians.

COMMUNICATING WITH THE BOOTH. Don't assume the people in the booth hear everything you say to them. Your mike is sometimes turned off while they test other circuits or do a quick playback. It's a good idea to encourage your booth representative or mixer to respond when you speak to them so you will know whether they have heard you or not. In a typical interchange the composer might say, "Please put some extra echo on the English horn line at bar 29." A simple "We've got it" from the booth keeps the communication from breaking down.

Any suggestions the composer offers will be productive and appreciated. Otherwise, as John Richards says, "An engineer is left very much to his own devices to create what he hopes is going to be what is required."

PROBLEM SOLVING. When players have ensemble or tuning problems, it is the conductor's job to devise solutions. Musicians don't respond well to being told they are out of tune or are not playing together. Make sure they can hear each other and give them a chance to rehearse those passages together while the rest of the orchestra is quiet so they can have the chance to improve their performance. An impersonal remark like "Let's try bars 7 and 8 to clean it up. Can you hear each other all right?" avoids any accusatory inference. You'll get your best results when you provide a way for them to work it out rather than lecturing them.

The musicians' deportment at sessions depends on the conductor's attitude. If you are

[4]Phones: headsets.

well-organized and know what you want, you will be respected when you insist on good attention and a tight working schedule. If, despite your best efforts, the session runs too loosely—if there is too much talk or people are late coming back from the breaks, deal with this through the orchestra contractor. It is the contractor's responsibility.

PLAYBACKS

There may not be time to hear playbacks after every cue and every take, but it is essential to have one or two playbacks early in the session so the mixer can adjust his levels and overall approach to suit the composer's concept. This also allows the musicians to hear themselves and react. There are many modifications they can make to improve the sound apart from the conductor's requests. On subsequent takes and cues it is no longer as necessary or efficient to hear playbacks; still, time permitting, it is always wise to do so. On television projects, time is always limited. WHEN YOU FEEL A PLAYBACK IS NECESSARY BUT THERE IS NO TIME AVAILABLE DURING THE SESSION, ASK FOR A PLAYBACK OF SELECTED CUES DURING THE TEN-MINUTE BREAKS.

The conductor should ask the mixer any questions he may have regarding the 3-track mix. "The most common question," says John Richards, "is whether we have control of any particular instrument or section. If there is too much of one particular section or instrument, the composer will turn to me and say, 'Do we have control of the trumpets?' Because, as he has obviously picked up, there is either not enough of them or too much, and as soon as he asks me, 'Do we have control?' nothing else has to be said—I know that there is a problem."

If you would like mixing or performance adjustments on a take that cannot be rerecorded because of time constraints, be sure to tell the mixer and musicians anything you feel will help subsequent cues. Overall recording quality can be improved immeasurably by maintaining a continuing dialogue about balance, dynamics, and other performance and recording details.

On feature films, after a cue is recorded, the director will usually ask to have it played back with dialogue. If everyone feels the cue is working, they can play it back again without dialogue to be sure the performance is excellent. For television there is rarely time for many playbacks with dialogue. Listen to them on a break if necessary, but remember, playbacks with dialogue may take a bit longer to prepare because of the extra machine running the dialogue track. It helps to let the music supervisor or mixer know your playback plans in advance of each ten, or the crew may also take a ten and be unavailable during the break.

OVERDUBBING (STACKING OR LAYERING)

Stacking, or overdubbing—the prevailing technique in contemporary commercial recording—is used much less in film scoring, except for songs. When overdubbing is used in underscoring it is usually for control (to provide isolation of sounds), as afterthought **sweeteners,**[5] or for textures that are too complicated or too dense to record simultaneously with the orchestra.

When synthesized sounds are mixed with live sounds, some composers, like Jerry Goldsmith and James Horner, prefer to record them simultaneously, either with the synthesists sitting with the orchestra or playing in the control room. Goldsmith may later electronically process parts of the score, and add sweeteners of live or electronic sounds. Both Goldsmith and Horner also record vocal choruses live (that is, simultaneously) with orchestra.

[5] Sweeteners: added overlays of recorded sound (music usually, but occasionally sound effects).

FIGURE 18-5

Jack Hayes, Dan Wallin (rear), John Morris, and Gene Wilder during the scoring of *Woman in Red*, Evergreen Recording Studios.

Photo: Gay Wallin

When scores have a basic electronic sound blended with live instruments the composer may prerecord the electronic element and bring it to the scoring stage (usually on a 2-inch multitrack master tape) for the orchestra to overdub (see Chapter 21). This process is unrelated to film prerecording, which is done to provide music to bring to the shooting set for shooting to playback (see Chapter 25).

In *Romancing the Stone* (1984), a complex Latin drum track drives a 55-piece orchestra that included 6 keyboard players (all playing electronic instruments). The recording options included either recording it all in layers starting with the electronic drum parts, or recording everything simultaneously. Composer Alan Silvestri first recorded the score and Latin drum tracks (programmed on a LinnDrum, an electronic drum machine) simultaneously, using a digital metronome run through a Doctor Click syncing machine to trigger the LinnDrum. Then, Silvestri overdubbed the percussion. "I spent the whole day with [percussionist] Alex Acuña and picked out the tracks that I wanted him on. The way I like to work with a guy like that is to have everything laid out and have him set up his stuff in the room, and then run the picture with him. And then we talk about the cue and then we build the sections and see what we want and where we want it. The Linn did all the sit-down drums, plus a lot of effects—tom-toms and congas and shakers—then Alex played timbales and all kinds of stuff on top of that.

"It was weird to have the 55 musicians coming in on a tight budget and be depending on Doctor Click to lock up two 24-track machines. The control room was filled with players. Every inch of the place was filled with people. It was pretty intense; fortunately it worked out fine."

It is currently much more common to integrate electronic drum machines into a live orchestra performance. The Hollywood studios are able to provide the composer with the necessary sync hookups. (See Part 6.)

CHANGES ON THE SCORING STAGE

Normally the director or producer will be the authoritative personality in the control room, listening to the orchestrated music for the first time. You must be prepared to react receptively to his opinions and suggestions. While the typical range of opinions varies from throwing out the cue to raving about it, the most common reaction is somewhere in between: an attempt to shape the cue differently—sometimes greatly, sometimes subtly.

Some filmmakers express their dislike of the cues candidly, even in front of the orchestra, but some can't find the ways to express their reaction and the music editor, or music supervisor, or even the mixer, may go out to talk to the composer to try to interpret their objections.

Under ideal circumstances the filmmakers' suggestions will be clear and practical, but under *any* circumstances it is the composer's responsibility to understand the filmmakers' concerns, so he can find the best and most creative solutions. This requires creative flexibility and a keen awareness of what the filmmaker is really saying. His objections will rarely have to do with his reactions to the music abstractly. Usually his concern will be that the music is not doing what he wants for the film.

SURPRISE EDITS. Sometimes the composer will see new changes in the film on the scoring stage. "When I was scoring *The Three Amigos* [1986]," says Elmer Bernstein, "I would get to the scoring stage to find that in the twenty-four hours prior to the recording session a cut had been made or a change had been made which wasn't communicated to anybody. There's an awful lot of that kind of thing. If it's just a question of something being a few seconds shorter that's no great problem. But if the construction of the scene is changed, you have to rethink the whole thing. In some instances, things have to be put off for another day."

QUICK THINKING. When there is a problem, keeping an open and clear mind is a must. In *The White Dawn* (a 1976 film about three men who survive the wreck of a whaling ship), Henry Mancini's first cue after the wreck underscored "the survivors going across the ice, on their last legs. Very stark, very white, very primitive. I wrote a piece which was basically a piccolo solo with strings, orchestra, and flute changing to alto flute. [Director] Phil Kaufman and [producer] Marty Ransohoff didn't feel it was 'primitive' enough. That's the catch phrase here. And I knew the percussionist, Emil Richards, was on the call. And right while we were there listening in the booth I looked at Emil and all of a sudden a light came on in my head. I pushed the talk-back down and said, 'Emil, get the rubber balls out and make that sound of yours on the gong.' I knew it was right before he even played it. But the minute Marty and Phil heard that sound they said, 'That's it.' We put the picture up and did it in one take. I said to Emil, 'Let a lot of space go between sounds, and sometimes play two in a row, and then let it space out.' And it really set it up. It hardly sounds like an instrument.

"Another reason that was effective was because film scoring deals in similars and dissimilars, and here we open the picture with a big, almost Korngoldish kind of music for the old whaler ship, and we're on this boat for thirty days, and then they chase the whale and the boat crashes. All of a sudden you come out of the big orchestra, and there's a period where you hear nothing but the wind. Then you hear this sound. You're in a foreign land both musically and visually. You don't know where you are. That's one of the reasons that worked so well."

Even when the composer and director are in total agreement on the concept and style of the score, changes still may need to be made. During the scoring of *A Man for All Seasons* (1966), Georges Delerue had to rewrite his Main Title music. "When I first played the main theme on the piano fifteen days before the recording session, [director Fred] Zinnemann liked it. It was a piece that used a lot of historical instruments: 2 lutes, 1 crumhorn, 4 recorders, and a quartet of violas da gamba, plus 2 or 3 trumpets and 3 trombones. When I finished recording the entire score Zinnemann liked everything but the Main Title. He wanted something a little more dramatic, which was not then possible after everything else was written for this particular orchestra.

"I panicked; but Zinnemann said, 'Don't worry. Just come back in eight days and we'll do another recording.' But that was not possible for me because I had another film to do. We still had two hours left of the scheduled session, which was booked from 9:00 A.M. until 10:00 P.M. I suggested that we keep the musicians and try to find something very different. And I said, 'If I don't find it in fifteen minutes, forget it.' And Zinnemann said, 'I beg your pardon, Georges—it's terrible trouble for you.' 'No, no don't worry,' I told him. So I sent the musicians out so I could be alone at the piano. The Main Title was long, too—3:40.

"Ten minutes later I found the idea for the main theme. Zinnemann came back in. And once the idea was found it took very little time to orchestrate it. I gave all of the musicians their parts from my piano score. Some of the musicians helped me copy parts for the other players (there was no photocopy machine there). About 9:15 the musicians returned to the stage and I conducted."

CHANGES AND THE BUDGET. Sometimes long discussions and time-consuming changes can jeopardize the recording schedule. "You have to let the producers know that," says music executive Bodie Chandler, "and that's when you say, 'If you get the next two cues exactly to your liking, we'll get no other music for the show and you'll go on the dubbing stage without a score unless you incur significant extra costs.' That seems to impress upon them the fact that we need to move faster. If you go more than an hour overtime, you may lose musicians, and if you don't have an orchestra, you can't record the music." If you see this happening, be sure to talk to the music supervisor to get his advice and assistance.

CREATIVE SCHEDULING. Marvin Hamlisch tries to schedule the most important cues as early as possible during the sessions so that if there's any problem with those cues he will have two or three days to make any adjustments that can't be fixed right on the spot. This procedure points up a big difference between composing for the concert hall and composing for films. In film scoring you are not through with the creative process when you've given your finished score to the copyist. Very often you will find yourself doing revisions right up to the time the film is permanently locked and sent to the lab. Some of the changes may be your own ideas and some may be based on suggestions by the filmmakers. Hamlisch, like others, wisely schedules his sessions with an understanding and acceptance of this filmmaking fact of life.

PRERECORDING

When music is prerecorded, this is done in order to provide a recorded performance to which the actors will lip-sync while filming a scene. Prerecording is done to achieve better sound quality than is possible with ordinary set recording (see Chapter 25). The procedure can be very involved. For example, in *Back to the Future* (1985) Michael J. Fox sits in on guitar with a 1950s band and amazes everyone as he moves through the history of rock-and-roll guitar. To get this effect, composer Alan Silvestri first had guitarist Tim May end his solo with a screaming Van Halen-type guitar solo on "Johnny B. Goode," then a guitar coach transcribed what Tim played, and actor Fox actually learned to play the whole solo in sync with the prerecord.

The filming of live music is often done to prerecorded track. The scene with Hoyt Axton and his country band performing in a club near the beginning of *Heart Like a Wheel* (1983) was prerecorded, and it is a typical usage of the technique.

For vocals, a prerecord with voice, piano, and click is often done as a temp track (or "scratch track"); the piano is well isolated so it can be dropped later when the orchestra is added in a postrecording. John Morris did this with the vocals in *Johnny Dangerously* (1984) and the scenes in which Anne Bancroft sings and plays piano in *To Be Or Not To Be* (1983).

In cases like the "Putting on the Ritz" dance number in *Young Frankenstein* (1974), in which the taps were not prerecorded, you end up with an almost impossible sync job. The music editor has to "chase" the scene by building a track with a click for every beat. The clicks follow the track as it slows down and speeds up. Then the orchestra plays to the clicks they hear, speeding up and slowing down when the clicks do—a nightmarish challenge.

These techniques and others have all been developed extensively for use in musicals and are discussed in more detail in Chapter 25.

TIMING CORRECTIONS WHILE RECORDING

Timing errors of one kind or another often turn up during recording sessions. When that happens it is pointless to spend valuable time trying to discover the reason for the mistake. Just correct the error. A competent music editor can adjust the clicks to help solve the problem or tell you how many beats need to be added or subtracted. However, the composer just getting started may not have this dependable kind of help and should be ready to do his own corrections. It pays to practice in advance some practical solutions to two of the most common situations.

ONE HIT OUT OF SYNC. In a music cue with three dead hits you are told that one is slightly off while two are dead on. Solution: Convert the size of the error (in seconds) into music notation (as on page 109) and have the orchestra move the accent to the new placement in the music. (The music editor may do this for you.) Example: Tempo: 13-frame click. Meter: 4/4. Dead hits at (A) :03.25, (B) :05:70, (C) :09.75. See Figure 18-6 for the music notation of your first version. The music editor tells you that hit B should hit at :06.10 while A and C are dead on. Subtracting :05.70 from :06.10 gives a difference of :00.40 (the amount of time which B is hitting early). At this tempo the musical equivalent of this amount is ♪. The orchestra must delay the accent by that much. See Figure 18-7 for the revised version.

FIGURE 18-6

Timing example.

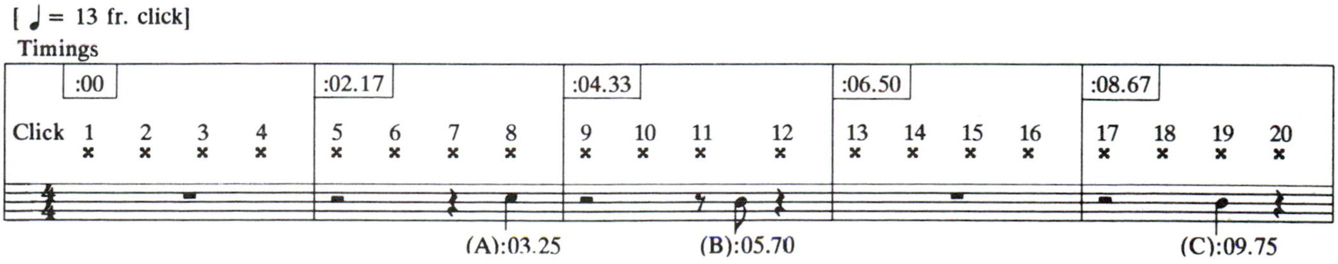

[♩ = 13 fr. click]

Timings

:00	:02.17	:04.33	:06.50	:08.67
Click 1 2 3 4	5 6 7 8	9 10 11 12	13 14 15 16	17 18 19 20
	(A):03.25	(B):05.70		(C):09.75

FIGURE 18-7
Timing example.

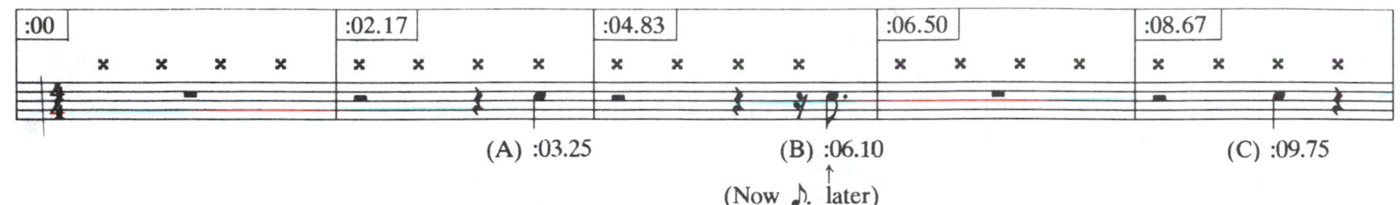

AWKWARD TEMPO. If the original tempo doesn't play well despite rehearsing it and rephrasing it, and you cannot avoid changing tempo, the best solution is to first establish a new tempo that feels better. Then, in the score, circle the crucial timings of any hits, the final resolution, and the out time for the end of the cue. Note the click (beat) number in the old tempo when the circled events happen. In the click track table for the new tempo find the timings of the circled events and note the click numbers at those timings. By comparing the click numbers of the events at the two tempos you can see how many beats to cut or add (by repeating beats) to make the new tempo work. For example: Original tempo = 13-frame click. Meter: 4/4. There are three important timings: a modulation at :08.67, a dead-hit accent at :14.62, and the last fermata at :32.50. Figure 18-8 shows the original tempo. Note which beats (click numbers) the hits fall against.

FIGURE 18-8
Timing example.

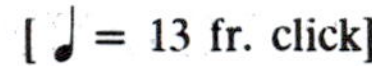

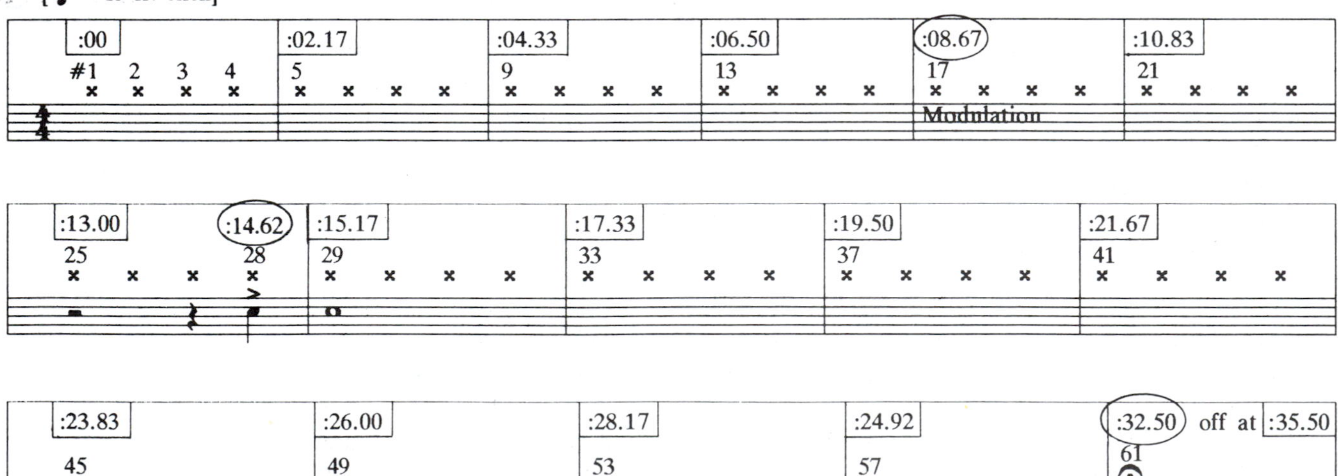

The new chosen tempo is a 14^{3} frame click. The changes required to make the timed hits work in the new tempo can be shown in a quickly prepared chart:

TIMINGS OF HITS	CLICK NUMBERS AT OLD TEMPO	CLICK NUMBERS AT NEW TEMPO	DIFFERENCE	SOLUTION	TOTAL BEATS DELETED
:08.67	#17	#15 1/2	1 1/2	Cut one prior beat and move modulation one ♪ earlier	1
:14.62	#28	#25 1/2	2 1/2	Cut one prior beat and move accent one ♪ earlier.	2
:32.50	#61	#55 1/4	6 1/4	Cut one 4/4 bar and add poco rall. into 𝄐 for 1/4 beat equivalent.	6

Figure 18-9 shows how the hits time out in the new tempo.

FIGURE 18-9
Timing example.

(Old Tempo = 13 fr. click)

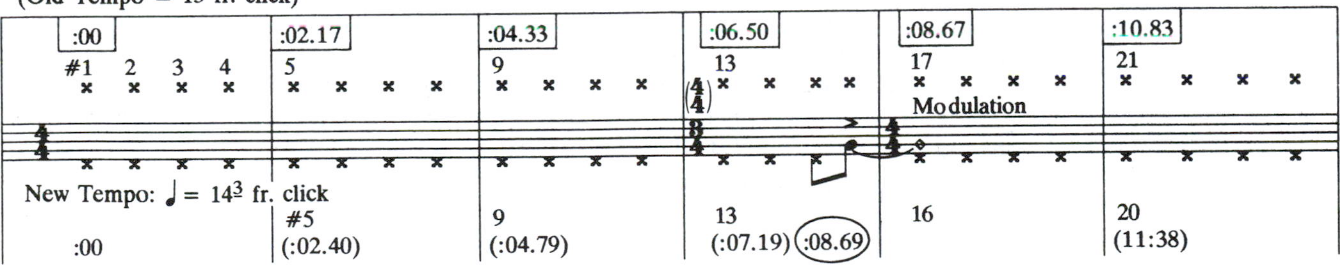

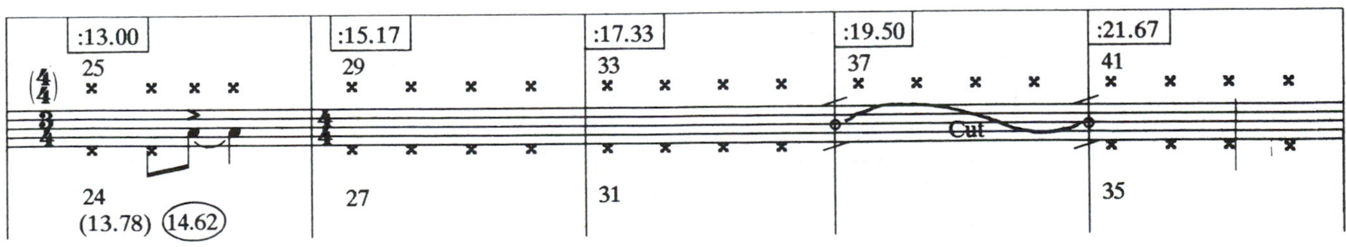

:23.83
45
:26.00
49
:28.17
53
:24.92
57
:32.50
61
39
(:22.76)
43
(:25.16)
47
(:27.55)
51
(:29.95)
55
:32.50

POSTMIXES AND SOUND PROCESSING

Those who have spent time recording contemporary singles and albums may be surprised to hear that most film schedules, especially television schedules, do not allow the days and weeks of elaborate postmixing and processing considered absolutely necessary in commercial recording. In practice, the turn-around time on film and television film production allows you to do only what can be done in a short period of time (and within a budget). Unless the producer wants this kind of detailed recording approach enough to budget the time and money for it, you will have to do without postmixing. With the current popularity of the "song score" for films, special multitrack album-type production has become accepted as part of the scoring process on specific feature films.

In normal film procedure (especially for television) if the session recordings have been recorded on ½-inch tape or 3-track mag, all print takes will be sent to the transfer room for straight one-to-one transfer to 3-stripe 35mm mag film. Any intercuts in the 3-stripe mixes will be **spliced** by the music editor (but the recording mixer will make any tape intercuts). Any music cues that require special processing for exaggerated echo or stylized pop recording processing will be postmixed from the multitrack tapes to 3 or 6 tracks and then transferred to 35mm mag. Any other cues in which the live mix may be found unacceptable can also be postmixed from the multitrack backup tapes, although time allowances usually prevent all of the cues being postmixed, and tight budgets may make even the recording of multitrack backup tapes impossible. Because of these variable methods your chosen procedures must be clearly established with everyone concerned. The music editor and mixing engineer will tell you the possible options and your producer will need to approve the costs.

On feature films where the schedules are less stringent, some composers feel there is a great advantage in postmixing everything. Henry Mancini rarely goes directly to 3-track mag stripe on the scoring stage, preferring to mix everything down to 3-track, "or 6-track, depending. I feel very strongly about the mix-down. But I'll give them a mono track on source music that is not a big stereo thing. As for 3-track recording—3-track is very practical and almost demanded for television where you have to go right from 3-track into the next room within an hour. Then it makes sense to record directly to 3-track. But if I have the time on a movie, I sit down after everybody's gone home and make the mix-downs."

MONO/STEREO

Until the mid-eighties, film music was basically monaural, with the exception of big-buget stereo spectaculars, and television has been monaural until the recent FCC rulings permitting stereo telecasting. Gradually the networks and local stations have changed their policies to broadcast stereo, while more and more feature films and videocassettes are coming out in stereo. At each recording session, the mixer has to provide the format in which the music will be sent to the dubbing stage, where it will then be mixed with the dialogue and sound-effects tracks.

When the desired format is mono the dubbing-stage mixers will want a 3-stripe 35mm mag recording with the strings usually mixed to one track, brass and woodwinds mixed to another, and percussion, keyboards, and rhythm to the third. This leaves some flexibility for changing the dynamic relationship between the three large orchestral groups when they are combined with the dialogue and sound effects at the dubbing. Whatever the origin of the recorded signal, the output is still a 3-stripe mix of all music elements, the object being to record such a good mix that each track is ideally balanced by itself.

The dubbing-stage music mixer then adjusts the relative levels of those 3 tracks. One significant overall concern is that the low end be loud enough to avoid having the music sound thin when the volume is turned down under dialogue. The Fletcher-Munson curves show that at lower volume levels the human ear needs more bass than at louder listening levels. Though mixers like Wallin and Richards add low end on the scoring stage, this still must be adjusted in dubbing. All of the other signal processing—such as echo, digital delay, and compression—is also diminished at softer volumes.

You may, of course, bring in more than 3 tracks; two 3-track units of music would give you up to 6 tracks. But this will always take more time to mix on the dubbing stage, and will rarely prove practical for most television. It should be considered as an option on features whenever time will be available on the dubbing stage to get the proper mix.

STEREO. The current demand for stereo has changed this procedure and actually limits the flexibility of rebalancing at the dubbing. For stereo, the original sound is either mixed on 2 or all 3 of the 3 stripes on the 35mm mag. The music can be delivered to dubbing as a standard 2-track stereo mix, with a phantom center. Or the stereo mix can include a separate track for the "center" channel. In some cases, a discrete third track might be put on the third stripe to give the dubbing stage more control of percussion, rhythm section, and solos or other instruments needing special emphasis. At dubbing, these three music tracks, along with all of the other audio tracks, are remixed to a composite two-track stereo for television and most feature films.

More elaborate feature films have extra tracks to feed the surround speakers in the better equipped theaters. In such cases, 6-track stereo is a very effective format for dubbing with stereo strings, stereo winds and brass, and stereo rhythm, for example. The mixer has to be clear on these variable requirements for each session.

The recording process involves many technical details, but the film composer's main responsibility is to create music that is well performed and recorded, and in sync with the picture both technically and dramatically. His attention should never waver from these goals. If he accomplishes this, his trip to the dubbing stage to mix all the sound elements—dialogue, music, and sound effects—will be accompanied by anticipation, not high anxiety.

CHAPTER 19

DUBBING—THE FINAL MIX

There are many surprises when you get to dubbing, as all composers and all directors know. There are cues that you were sure were going to work, until you put them together with the dialogue and sound effects. When you bring all the elements together in dubbing, things sound different. JAMES GOLDSTONE, DIRECTOR

I can understand why some composers I know don't go to dubbing anymore. On the other hand, if you have the time to go, you learn a lot and also you can affect a lot of things. CRAIG SAFAN

It's like they say, "You've got to go to the dentist twice a year. . ." Yeah, you've got to go to dubbing. MICHAEL MELVOIN

The producers, the director—it's their picture, and we've got to do what they tell us to do. JOHN REITZ, DUBBING DIALOGUE MIXER

We have now reached the final crucial point in fashioning the film, the point at which all of the sound elements are to be combined into a composite sound track. The intricate balancing of dialogue, sound effects, and music must be done. For the first time all of these elements can be heard simultaneously and in sync with the picture; tough decisions must be made.

Director James Goldstone explains the dubbing-stage mystique: "By that time I have seen every shot 300 times and the composer has seen the film many times, and yet it suddenly just becomes a different thing. Sometimes it's wonderful, but sometimes it restructures the storytelling—it's just wrong—and most often those are the times when there is a mutual decision to drop the cue. I remember very few, if any, occasions on the dubbing stage where the composer and I were in real conflict about the overall use of the cue, or the level of the cue, or something of that kind. I very much enjoy having the composer there. I think it is a very delicate balance because part of the composer is saying, 'I want my music to be heard,' and yet the more important part of the composer's function on the dubbing stage is to get the overall balance correct from a musical point of view, but now he is also putting weight on the dramatic effect. Whereas when he was composing the cue and recording it, he was only thinking of his music. We all get to thinking about one element at a time at one time or another."

For composers, it can be a trial. "I don't like to have a cue completely ruined," says Bruce Broughton, "but I don't mind having it altered by editing. What *does* annoy me is to have something dialed in or dialed out. It's like dialing someone out in the middle of a sentence. I try to recommend a more musical way of doing it. Basically I will try and accommodate them; if I think that they're completely wrong, I'll tell them so, but this is a difficult area. I will write a piece of music and [on the scoring stage] they will rave about it—they will love it—accept it entirely. Then we get to the dubbing stage and for whatever reason they decide to make a change in it, or they may want to play a sound effect or they may want to alter the voice, so that the music will be modified somewhat. They will ask me my opinion and I will tell them why I think the cue is working so well, only to find out that's *not* the reason the music is working so well. To them it plays well for a completely different reason.

"I find that my opinion means a little less than the dubbing mixers'. It's frustrating. But whatever happens to the music, I try to have it sound musical. Usually, if you have a good music editor, you don't have to worry about that too much.

"I've found if I try to communicate my frustration and pain I'm just another crying composer. What I really try to do is to figure out just how much of a contribution I'm making and how much abuse I'm taking. Am I taking any more abuse than the writer took when he was asked to rewrite it four times? Or the actor when he thought that he had done the scene as well as he could, and was asked for one more take?

"There are times when I've asked the people to take the music out entirely. I say, 'If that's the way you're going to play it, you obviously don't need it in the scene. Take it out.' They say, 'But we need it, because of such and such.' And I say, 'Play it at a proper level,' or 'Keep it in till the end,' and very often that will do something."

This is the point where music cues can be dropped, where whole scores may be lost. Although most composers feel relatively uninfluential on the dubbing stage, they need to be there if they can to protect their music's contribution to the film. (On episodic television the composer may be unable to come to the dubbing at all because he is already working on the next show.)

It should be stressed here that no composer, no matter how prestigious or how great his track record, is ever contractually granted the right of final decision as to whether his music is used in a film, or in what manner. Film contracts always grant the producer the right to replace a score, interpolate any other composer's work, add lyrics without permission, and in general use or not use the score in any way they see fit.

A positive attitude is a must. As music editor Daniel Allan Carlin says, "Any number of composers could do a show and they'd all do a fine job. They'd just be a little different stylistically. But what they'll remember is if you're a pain in the ass."

Almost all directors, producers, and music executives agree that the composer is valuable at the dubbing, but there are also true stories of cases in which composers were not welcome and were even prevented from coming because the director felt the potential for disagreement would disrupt the process. If the composer can take the larger perspective of the whole film, he should always feel welcome there.

THE SCENE AND THE CAST OF CHARACTERS

The dubbing stage is a projection room adjoined by a machine room with film recorders and dummies (the machines that play back the dialogue, sound effects, and music sound-track "units" so the dubbing mixers can mix them into the final composite audio track). The mixing itself takes place at a long mixing console at the rear of the room, where the music mixer, the effects mixer, and the dialogue mixer are each sitting before their respective sections of the board (see Figure 19-2). Each has charts, often called **dubbing logs,** giving the film footages of the entrances and exits of all of the sounds on their units. On these logs, they make additional notes about fader levels, equalization settings, special signal-processing effects, and any other audio elements with which they should interact (see Figure 19-3). At the front of this small theater, a prominent footage counter is displayed beneath the large movie screen so that each mixer can add the sounds he is responsible for at exact footages while watching the screen.

The central figure in this cast of characters is of course the director or producer.

FIGURE 19-1
Machine room, Dubbing Stage A, Disney Studios.

Photo: Gay Wallin

FIGURE 19-2
Rerecording mixers Gregg Rudloff, John Reitz, and Dave Campbell, Lionsgate Studio Dubbing Stage.

Photo: Gay Wallin

FIGURE 19-3

Dubbing stage log for *Secret of My Success.*

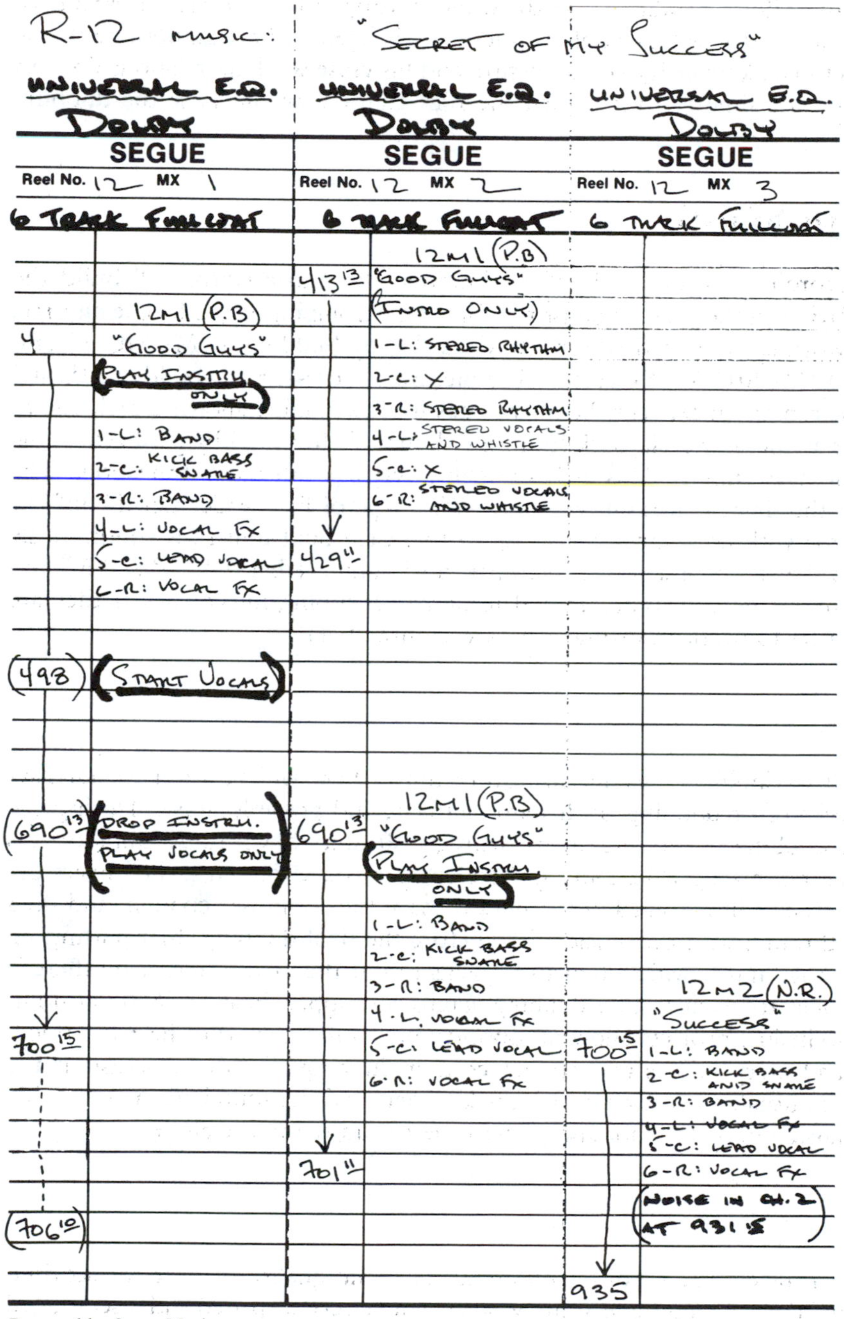

R-12 MUSIC: "SECRET OF MY SUCCESS"

UNIVERSAL E.Q. DOLBY		UNIVERSAL E.Q. DOLBY		UNIVERSAL E.Q. DOLBY	
SEGUE		**SEGUE**		**SEGUE**	
Reel No. 12 MX 1		Reel No. 12 MX 2		Reel No. 12 MX 3	
6 TRACK FULL COAT		6 TRACK FULL COAT		6 TRACK FULL COAT	
			12M1 (P.B)		
		413[13]	"GOOD GUYS"		
	12M1 (P.B)		(INTRO ONLY)		
4	"GOOD GUYS"		1-L: STEREO RHYTHM		
	(PLAY INSTRU. ONLY)		2-C: X		
			3-R: STEREO RHYTHM		
	1-L: BAND		4-L: STEREO VOCALS AND WHISTLE		
	2-C: KICK BASS SNARE		5-C: X		
	3-R: BAND		6-R: STEREO VOCALS AND WHISTLE		
	4-L: VOCAL FX				
	5-C: LEAD VOCAL	429[11]			
	6-R: VOCAL FX				
(498)	(START VOCALS)				
			12M1 (P.B)		
(690[13])	(DROP INSTRU. PLAY VOCALS ONLY)	690[13]	"GOOD GUYS"		
			(PLAY INSTRU. ONLY)		
			1-L: BAND		
			2-C: KICK BASS SNARE		
			3-R: BAND		12M2 (N.R.)
			4-L: VOCAL FX		"SUCCESS"
700[15]			5-C: LEAD VOCAL	700[15]	1-L: BAND
			6-R: VOCAL FX		2-C: KICK BASS AND SNARE
					3-R: BAND
					4-L: VOCAL FX
					5-C: LEAD VOCAL
		701[11]			6-R: VOCAL FX
(706[10])					(NOISE IN CH. 2 AT 931[15])
				935	

Prepared by Segue Music

Others, besides the film editor, the effects editor, and the music editor, are the music supervisor (occasionally), the composer, and perhaps the writer. The music editor and the sound-effects editor will be standing by ready to move, drop, add, or replace elements of their tracks. The film editor will not only be there but is likely to have an important role by virtue of his intimate knowledge of the picture and his close working relationship with the director. There are times, in fact, when the film editor may supervise the dubbing session.

PREPARING THE MUSIC FOR DUBBING

After the recording sessions and before dubbing, the music editor will build the **music units** by laying in the music against the film, synchronizing it cue by cue and reel by reel on the Moviola or flatbed editor. He does this by building a "MUSIC 1" unit (sometimes called "MUSIC A") for each reel of picture. If necessary, he builds a MUSIC 2 unit also, so he can alternately cut the music cues into two units, allowing each cue to overlap the other as the music playback from one dummy is followed by playback of the music unit on the next dummy. This makes possible very smooth music transitions. The music editor fills the silent spaces on each unit with a type of film leader called "fill" (or "slug"), a film base with no magnetic coating, so that each built unit runs continuously from the start to the finish of a reel. Additional music units (labeled "3," "4," "5," and so on) will be built as needed to accommodate new overlapping music cues as they are added, or sweeteners to overlay existing cues (see Figure 19-4).

PREDUBBING

Before the final dubbing sessions on feature films, there will be from several days up to several weeks of predubbing of dialogue, effects, and possibly music. During the predubbing, the dubbing mixers premix as many as 80 units down to 25 units or less to make the final mix manageable. During these rehearsals and predubs, the mixers get to know the material. Editor John Burnett likes to have the composer come in and do a predubbing run-through with the music mixer before the final dubbing, first putting up music alone, and then music with production tracks to test the mix. In television there is rarely time or money to do this, since dubbing stages cost approximately $600 per hour.

Some tight-schedule projects allow no opportunity to pre-dub or to hear the tracks ahead of time, and everyone has to start out cold at dubbing. On those occasions the dialogue mixer will usually first listen to his tracks alone, and the sound effects mixer his tracks, but the music mixer does not always get time to run the music alone.

DUBBING STAGE SOUND

The composer must be aware of the difference in sound quality between the scoring-stage monitors and the dubbing stage. Otherwise he will be very surprised and discouraged the first time he hears his score in dubbing. In general, the music will sound muffled (less high end), less clear in the bass, and be lacking the punch and impact he might expect. The reasons for this are (1) if the film is being dubbed monaurally, the sound will lack the size and spread of stereo or discrete 3-track recording-session playbacks; (2) the monitors on the dubbing stage are behind the screen, which muffles the sound; (3) the dubbing stage may be monitoring the music with an **Academy filter**[1], which rolls off the high

[1] Academy filter: an audio equalization curve, standardized by the Academy of Motion Picture Arts and Sciences, which in the past has limited both high and low frequency content to prevent distortion resulting from oversaturation of the optical soundtracks used in film release prints and compensate for the inadequacy of theater monitors.

FIGURE 19-4
Music editor Abby Treloggen building music units.

Photo: Gay Wallin

end *and* the low end; and (4) the other sound elements can greatly reduce the music's apparent impact. Equalization adjustments are made when recording the music tracks to partially compensate for this reduction in overall sound quality.

Carlin finds that stereo music mixes are increasing the sound quality but decreasing dubbing-stage control. "Now that we are delivering 2-track stereo mixes to the dubbing stage, if one instrumental color or sound goes down, it all goes down. And that's a real drawback. There's no dubbing control, just volume control. A 6-track stereo mix can help compensate."

FIRST ADJUSTMENTS DURING THE MIX

At dubbing, each reel is worked on individually, starting with one or more run-throughs to audition the cumulative effect of all the tracks running simultaneously. These rehearsals will probably be a stop-and-go process, as the dialogue and sound-effects mixers stop the film frequently and back up to correct problems in their tracks. The first adjustments each mixer makes are to set levels, equalization, and reverb to make the blend and balance as smooth as possible. Echo and digital reverb are available as needed, and limiters and compressors are often required to cut down the large differences between the loudest and softest sounds, particularly in dialogue and singing. The music mixer will make additional notes on his log to remind him of any potential problems with dialogue.

Dubbing mixer Don MacDougall (who has mixed both music and dialogue) feels that it is important "that the music mixer have the opportunity to listen to the music isolated without any other kind of extraneous background, dialogue, or effects, so that he can hear the elements of the music. That way he can best judge how the sonorities or complexities of the music work against all the other elements. Presuming that I have predubbed the dialogue, I like to run the dialogue and the music alone, without effects, so the music mixer can hear where people are speaking, to make the scene take hold.

"Then after that run I'll give the music mixer a run all by himself. The effects mixer has an opportunity to do that; the dialogue mixer has the opportunity. Why not the music mixer? If the filmmakers have an opportunity to see the reel with music in a good environment (other than just a playback on the scoring stage), I think they are more likely to understand what the music is doing for the scene."

At this point all conflicts between music and dialogue and between music and effects will have to be resolved. The music editor might be asked to move a cue slightly earlier ("advance" the music) or later ("ritard" the music) to keep from stepping on dialogue lines or sound effects. This can work, but the composer and music editor should be cautious of this, as it may cause the entire cue to be out of sync and miss many of the dramatic elements it originally played.

Although conflicts with dialogue would seem to be the hardest to resolve, since the words must be heard to carry the story line, the more persistent problems involve conflicts between music and effects, each of which require space in which to be heard, with each tending to cancel the other's effectiveness. Very often the most satisfactory solution is to drop one or the other to a secondary role or to drop the music completely, but not without a certain amount of emotional pain for the composer.

On effects-heavy chases and battle scenes, the music doesn't stand a chance. As director James Goldstone has indicated, there is often general agreement in such situations. Alex North speaks for most composers when he says, "I'd rather cut the music entirely than have a jumble of music and sound."

OVERALL MUSIC LEVELS

To contribute anything, music must be dubbed at a certain minimum level, at which all musical elements can be heard distinctly (albeit softly). However, this will only guarantee a ***minimal*** contribution in most cases. Usually, music should be playing louder than this minimum level in order to bring as much value as possible to the film.

This is an area about which filmmakers are frequently unsure, and often err by being unnecessarily conservative. "The dialogue really stands out in the theater more than it does on the dubbing stage," says dubbing dialogue mixer John Reitz. "It's amazing what you can learn in theaters with full houses. The music just goes away." His mixing colleague Dave Campbell agrees. "Even the reverb that you mix in is really at quite a low level. And the music can just disappear with the popcorn noise." "The dialogue," adds Reitz, "never seems to be crowded too much by music. The lines *always* cut through."

CHANGING/LOSING CUES

When the director feels the music is not working—that is, it is stepping on lines, muddying things up, making too busy a texture, or misguiding the audience's emotions—the cue may be dropped or replaced with another cue originally scored for another scene. Although this is a time when the composer would just as soon not be there, directors and producers often want the composer there to offer suggestions. Creativity is still the order of the day. Maybe a sweetener will provide a missing element, maybe a level change, maybe moving the music slightly earlier or later, maybe more echo.

John Cacavas always goes to dubbing for television movies-of-the-week. "Sometimes I'm sorry that I went—you really have to separate your ego there. The first time I did a movie-of-the-week in Hollywood I went to a dubbing session which was run by a sound-effects man. Something came up and he said, 'Take out the music.' I jumped up and the producer put his arm on me and said, 'Take it easy.' And sure enough he was right. The music didn't work there; it shouldn't even have been spotted there."

Interchanging cues has sometimes been a successful initiative. On the 1982 television movie *Executioner's Song,* the true story of murderer Gary Gilmore, Cacavas found that his love theme, though "laid back and not very dramatic at all, still didn't seem to work—Gilmore was just too terrible. On the dubbing stage, it was obvious that it wasn't going to work and I thought I had to do something. The producer said, 'What do you think about that?' and I said, 'I don't know; I don't think it works too well.' And he said, 'I don't either. It's a little too pretty for what the picture's saying.' So we went back to the Moviola and worked out some of those old tried and tested things, and you can't praise a music editor enough for what they can do." This involved using portions of other cues cut together by the music editor to create several new cues for these sequences. In this kind of situation, it is obvious that the composer's presence is important. "I would have been killed otherwise," Cacavas states. And the score and the movie benefited from this interaction between the composer and filmmaker.[2]

When he did the score for *Altered States* (1980), John Corigliano found that "it was a little easier [working] with [director] Ken Russell because he likes and respects composers. . . . But I left the dubbing stage when I entered to hear my stark solo oboes for the first hallucination being overdubbed with gongs right and left and seagull sounds. I got on a plane and went back to New York. The people on the dubbing stages can't understand the possibilities that the composer can envision. We could be of real help to them if they'd let us."

While dubbing a film he had scored, Craig Safan once heard the head mixer say, "If the music wasn't so damned loud you could hear the dialogue." Safan says, "The comment had nothing to do with the music—only the *level* of the music. It was not a critique of the music." Safan's observation is enlightening. DON'T TAKE DUBBING-STAGE COMMENTS PERSONALLY; THEY ARE TALKING ABOUT THE MUSIC'S FUNCTION IN THE FILM, NOT THE PERSONALITY OR CHARACTER OF THE COMPOSER OR THE QUALITY OF THE MUSIC.

AS THE DIRECTOR SEES IT

The experience of running the film with all tracks playing is an all-important one to the director, who must decide what to use and what to change. After months of planning, this is his first chance to see and hear all of the elements of his film together and his last chance to make changes. About the musical choices, director John Erman says, "Sometimes I will love a cue so much that I will tend to sacrifice the other effects. And then I have to

---

[2] Also, see Richard Michael's story about interchanging cues for *Heart of a Champion,* page 138.

say to myself, 'Wait a minute—don't the footsteps mean anything here?' And sometimes the composer won't have left air or space for those footsteps, so when you get on the dubbing stage you may have to bring him down or bring the effects up. The dialogue is more important in certain scenes but sometimes if you just catch part of the dialogue it's enough because the emotional life of the scene may be illustrated better by the music than by the words. Other times there's a plot that has to be gotten across. And as great as the cue may be, if you don't hear that plot you're not going to get through emotionally to the audience.

"We had a cue at the end of *Early Frost* [1985 television movie] that was a beautiful and very dramatic cue. And when I got on the dubbing stage with the producer, who was very creative and who also had a real musical background, we said, 'We don't need any music at all.' Because at the end of that movie the boy was leaving his parents—they knew and he knew he was going to die. They were saying goodbye and the taxi just disappeared in the darkness. We wanted a kind of hopeless, ominous quality that seemed to work better without any music at all. We took the music out and put in some sound effects of a storm brewing—thunder and lightning—and for some reason it had an eloquence that was better. Somehow the elements of nature were the right thing."

DUBBING-STAGE PROTOCOL

In order for the composer to have some practical effect it is necessary to take into account the protocol—the chain of command that governs this complex of artists and technicians. For example, Charles Bernstein describes how he handles the perennial problem of music being masked by a droning sound effect (a helicopter for instance) that continues at a loud level for no obvious purpose. He believes it isn't proper protocol for him to ask the effects mixer to lower the effect. Instead, Bernstein says, "I'll point it out to the director and he'll transmit it. There is a chain of command in the dubbing theater and I try not to violate that. I won't speak to the mixer directly unless I have permission from the director. Sometimes the director will say, 'Charles, feel free to sit with the music mixer and if there is anything you want to discuss with him that will improve the music, by all means do it.'"

Craig Safan agrees with Bernstein's approach. "As a composer at a mix there's only so much you can do. You're really irritating more than anything to most people at a dub. So what you say has to be chosen with care because you're only going to win a few points, and it's very political and you have to do it very gently. What I will do is talk to the producer or director and have them make the change."

The music is there to help the film," as Daniel Allan Carlin reminds us, "and so you cannot lose sight of that when you're on the dubbing stage dealing with the director. Some composers have that problem. Of course, they don't last."

THE FILM EDITOR'S ROLE. Sometimes the film editor will intervene to keep an overreaction by one of the filmmakers from spoiling what could be a good sequence. Editor John Martinelli always sits in on dubbing all the way if he can "because the editor knows all facets—if something is missing I know it and I can say, 'Guys, it's missing.' They never knew it was there so they don't worry about it and it's gone.

"Sometimes they won't give the music a fair shot. The music mixer plays a cue too loud at a rehearsal and immediately a producer or somebody says, 'That's no good, just dump the music.' Many times I'll say, 'Wait a minute, don't just dump it right now; let's go back, give it a fair shot, the way it was scored to work, with the right level, and then, if worst comes to worst, we can take it out. We can come in a couple of bars later, we can go out a couple of bars earlier, we can do whatever we want to do.' And it's amazing—probably 50 percent of the time it will then stay in.

"People overreact and that's wrong. And the composer, when he's there, can say, 'You guys may be right, but may I try this' and they will say, 'Of course. Try it.' And many times it will work. If it isn't going to work, then everybody knows it, including the composer."

COMMUNICATION SKILLS. Don MacDougall likes input from the composer, "probably more than most mixers do—I have a great affinity for those guys. A lot of times composers get bent out of shape for no other reason than that something goes wrong, it doesn't sound right—the producer has a different opinion about something and they're at odds with each other. I think the ability to sit down and communicate with anybody on a dubbing stage is very important. I also believe that the composer should speak to the music mixer on a one-to-one basis—a friendly 'Hello, how are you? Tell me what you have in mind' sort of thing."

He also believes it's important to give the music mixer something to work with. "I think it behooves a composer to realize that a mixer is a human being who as much as the composer wishes for a situation that is happy and productive and enjoyable creatively. I think that composers cheat themselves when they decide that a mono track is far preferable to a multitrack because the mixer can't screw it up; that in itself is very bad thinking. Those composers should really be thinking about being a little more flexible when they come to a dubbing stage, if they have multitrack music."

DUBBING WITH DIALOGUE

Underscoring dialogue is tricky. The fullness and beauty of the music is lost when the music must be turned down to keep it from interfering with the words. And it is not only the composer who feels the loss. Director Richard Michaels finds it very disappointing "to hear a wonderful score on the scoring stage be pushed way down in the background—and I'm remembering what it sounded like when it was full." Remember that some musical textures and colors don't compete with dialogue, while others do. When they don't, a full musical sound can be a satisfying and emotional underpinning to the scene.

Henry Mancini is very conscious of the possibility of the music getting in the way, "and I'm also conscious of overwhelming sound on the track. That bothers me. I'd rather have it too low than too high. I'm always very self-conscious in a scene, especially in dialogue scenes. I'm very conscious of orchestration."[3]

The composer can be most contributive if he *really* listens objectively to the dialogue when there is underscoring, in order to determine if the music is supportive or disruptive.

HEAR IT SOFTLY. Music dubbing mixer David Campbell recommends that the composer "should try listening to his music at a low level and on a small speaker when preparing music with dialogue for television. See what goes away against the noise of the production track." Dialogue dubbing mixer John Reitz agrees. "Judging from what we get, I don't think composers listen to dialogue much anymore. A lot of people don't write around the dialogue anymore."

"When we have to pull music down around dialogue," Campbell continues, "quite often we'll boost low and high end, just to compensate for the volume loss—the Fletcher-Munson curve. And that helps. Keeping a rhythm track going helps—keeping it audible."

Playing back softly or on small speakers prior to dubbing will give the composer a much better sense of how his music will ultimately sound on the dubbing stage. Reitz explains: "On a smaller speaker, the dialogue will punch right out, and the music and everything else seems to drop way back. We try to prove to the filmmakers that, on a smaller speaker, the dialogue is going to be there. Even though it sounds like it's covered up here, in the theater *it really isn't.*"

---

[3] See page 128 for a list of suggestions regarding underscoring dialogue.

SONGS UNDER DIALOGUE. The current vogue of using songs as underscore has even led to attempts to use songs with lyrics behind dialogue. But, as Ira Newborn points out, "They're always struggling to turn down the songs so you can hear the dialogue, and it never really quite works." The composer faced with the task of adding a song to a dialogue scene should try some role-model songs against the scene (preferably dubbed onto videotape for a more realistic appraisal of the effect). If he doesn't think it works, he should play the scene with a song for the director; this will help both the composer and director anticipate and prepare for any dubbing problems.

TECH TALK

Technical mistakes can have a devastating effect on the music, and the composer can feel quite powerless to do anything about them. Surprising sounds may materialize on the dubbing stage, like clicks in the music tracks caused by splices made with magnetized razor blades, or highs missing because of emulsion buildup on the playback heads. Occasionally one music track may not even be coming through the board due to a misconnection in the patch bay. Even when the composer hears flaws like these and can guess what's wrong, it may still be a delicate matter to call them to the engineer's attention without bringing on a defensive reaction from him.

As a musician, the composer's expertise is his ability to hear how things sound, while a recording engineer's domain is to know the technical aspects of why things sound as they do. If you make your comments as a musician, discussing the quality of sound rather than using technical explanations, you're not as likely to challenge the engineer in an unproductive way. For example, subjective comments about the sound seeming dull, or missing lows or highs, or being muddy, or harsh, or thin, are all from the musician's point of view, and are less likely to be irritating than comments about specific equipment, microphones, VU-meter levels or hertz frequencies, comments that should probably be withheld until the engineer has had a chance to satisfy himself that there is a problem and has taken the opportunity to correct it himself. This applies equally well to the scoring stage. In general, once the mixer knows his ability is not being questioned, he will appreciate any appropriate suggestions, technical or otherwise.

LOSING A SCORE

"Losing a score" is a phrase that has an ominous ring for every composer. Nobody can be dispassionate about having a score thrown out, yet "there are very few people in this town—*eminent* people—who haven't had scores thrown out," says John Addison. Losing a score was just as painful for Addison, an eminent composer himself, as it is for every composer. "I'd never had the experience of having a score thrown out until recently. I joined the club. In this case it happened that I was writing very much for the producer, who was the one in control, and everybody was absolutely thrilled at the recording. They did the dubbing, which I wasn't able to go to, and they had a screening for the network person, who hated the score. I'm told that everybody else in the room promptly agreed with network—because they wanted to be employed by that network. And that's an added factor which I'd never realized—you can please the people you are working for, but then somebody at the network says they don't like it." (See Chapter 27, "Business.")

In the case mentioned above, Addison had no opportunity to discuss his score with the network rep, so rapport and understanding were impossible. But when the opportunity is there, a little extra communication may help. Laurence Rosenthal finds it disturbing to hear about scores being thrown out right after recording sessions. He urges taking every precaution to prevent that from happening. "I have strong feelings about having very intense and detailed discussion of the scores with whomever will have any weight later on, whether it's the producer, director, or executive producer. I try to talk about the style, idiom, orchestration, size of orchestra, general approach to any scene which might seem in any way ambiguous, so that we don't get to the recording stage and suddenly he is looking at us and saying, 'Is that what we asked for?' The only time that I have had that kind of objection was when it came from a producer who never said one word to me about the approach of the music, and then suddenly came to dubbing and was full of opinions. That was wrong.

"I really feel that filmmaking is a collaborative effort. It's the very nature of film and no composer can come in and say, 'Look boys, just leave it to me—I know what this picture needs.' Rapport and a genuine exchange between the collaborators on the film is essential if you want to avoid disasters like that."

It might seem logical that, if changes were needed, the original composer would be given the job, but as agent Alvin Bart points out, "Nine-and-a-half times out of ten, if there's to be a rewrite, they'll never go back to the original composer. Instead of saying to him, 'We like these cues and need about 30 percent new material,' they won't go back to him. They'll go hire somebody else."

Losing a score is a point of great sensitivity within the industry and can be traumatic for the composer. The replacing of Jerry Goldsmith's score for *Legend* (1986) by the electronic group Tangerine Dream was more widely publicized than usual. Goldsmith, certainly one of the most highly respected contemporary film composers, and one who doesn't believe in wasting time with negative comments, says, "The only real disaster that I've had in the last ten years is in this thing with *Legend,* where they dropped the entire score and put in Tangerine Dream for distribution in this country. Outside of the United States, they use the original score. It was probably one of the best things I've written. The whole picture was recut, reconceived, and five songs that were actually sung in the picture originally were all cut. That really came as a terrible blow to me. I'd put six months into that picture. But the end result was that there was so damned much publicity on this that I came up smelling like a rose."

But there is always the business angle of trying to predict what the public will pay to hear and see. Music executive Brendon Cahilll recalls the business side of the *Legend* situation. "It was a Fox release outside the U.S. and it was Universal within the U.S., and I had to go along with what the studio wanted to do . . . . The toughest thing was to call Jerry and say, 'Hey Jerry, look, we've got to change the score, because the problem with the movie is that it only appeals to children six years old and under and we're looking to draw a larger audience.' Jerry was pretty upset, but nonetheless the proof of the pudding was that though Tangerine Dream scored the picture in the U.S. and it was a cut-down version from 2 hours and 15 minutes to 98 minutes, the picture still didn't make it. And it went out with Jerry's score around the world.

"You have to forget your ego. Because no matter how great your contribution is, it's the business guys who pull the purse strings. The business side and the financial experts are in $20 million on a picture, and chances are, no matter how great your score is, your portion of the budget is $400,000. Now weigh $20 million against $400,000. How can you have an ego problem?"

That dollar comparison can't be very convincing to the composer's sense of what is dramatically or artistically right for a film, but it can explain why he shouldn't feel personally devastated in such a case, when the decisions are being made on marketing considerations that he may not even be aware of.

It should be understood that when cues or whole scores are thrown out, the composer nonetheless is paid his full fee.

DUBBING SCHEDULES

"The average schedule we see for dubbing a feature these days is anywhere from 5 days or less on a 'B' feature, and probably 15 days or less on an 'A' feature," says dubbing mixer Don MacDougall. "An A feature would be one that is in excess of a $4-million-dollar budget.

"But when we do a stereo optical version like a 4-track stereo mix, then we're given a little more time with things like that. Independent films are a lot different from studio films, too. Time of course is money, and money today is one of the primary concerns of producers all over the world.

"On an A feature I usually spend anywhere from 3 to 5 days predubbing dialogue on a big stereo feature. And usually between 5 to 10 days for the final mix, with everything. On the less highly budgeted feature it's usually 1 day to predub dialogue and 4 days to dub it.

"I just finished a three-hour movie-of-the-week for NBC television called *Mother Courage* [1986, Craig Safan]. That was a film that we did from scratch. Meaning that there was no dialogue predub involved, no effects or music predubbing of any kind. We just put the reels up and did them as we went, and it was very tedious. Television is like that—it taxes you at the outset. It's more difficult than doing features.

"I like to tell a producer, 'I'll go as fast as you want to go.' But everybody wants to make certain that every integral part of a film is perfect. So they want you to do a wonderful job and then they defy you to do it. I've been asked to dub a two-hour movie-of-the-week in two days. We can do it, but obviously there are elements and areas of the mix that suffer because of the lack of time to prepare things properly and do a super job."

On a feature, film editor John Burnett figures 3 to 5 days of dialogue predubbing, with a total predub of dialogue, effects, and music of from 1 week to 3 weeks. For the final mix, "I will turn out anywhere from a reel to 2 reels a day, maybe a reel a day with stereo." By comparison, if the above-mentioned two-hour movie-of-the-week for television is being dubbed in 2 or 3 days, the daily output works out to be between 3 and 4 1,000-foot reels (each 9 to 10 minutes long) per day for a 3-day dub and 5 reels a day for a 2-day dub (rare, but it is done). That's fast, and allows very little time for music rehearsals and polishing.

SOUND ON TELEVISION. Perhaps one of the most astonishing things that can happen to a television score is to learn that the entire show (or television movie) has been slowed down or sped up as much as 3 percent—not just the music but the *master videotape* of the film. Naturally this greatly affects the sound and impact of the score, and can completely ruin its effectiveness. At least one network has done this to compensate for shows that are too short or long.

Even without so drastic a change, there are many other technical steps between the dubbing stage mix and the viewer's television set, all of which influence the final sound. During the final technical stage of transfers and transmission of the shows from Los Angeles to New York and back again to Los Angeles by satellite, the sound is often compressed and/or limited, and may in fact be re-equalized as well to emphasize the dialogue.

David Bell noticed a different on-air sound from the two networks running the two shows he was writing simultaneously, *Blacke's Magic* and *Murder, She Wrote.* "Using the same orchestra, the same scoring stage and recording mixer, and the same dubbing stage and crew, I was not getting the same bass response on one network as on the other. One time I wrote a low solo for contra basses for four beats with nothing else playing, and it came out completely silent. Nothing."

Although the composer (and mixers who also check on-air versions of their work) may not be able to correct such results, they can and do compensate in the way they treat the music for subsequent shows of their continuing television series.

NEXT STEPS

Up to this point we have followed the film-scoring sequence in roughly chronological steps:

1. Meeting the filmmakers
2. The script and screenings
3. Spotting
4. Budget and schedules
5. Developing the concept
6. Timings and clicks
7. Composing
8. Orchestrating
9. Recording
10. Dubbing

The only remaining step in this sequence is to make any alterations that might occur in the case of a feature film that has gone out to preview. Sneak previews are scheduled to test audience reactions before sending multimillion dollar projects out for distribution. Such previews are done in theaters equipped with interlocked projectors and dummies (called "double system" projection) so the picture can be shown without having to make composite prints with picture and sound combined on an optical soundtrack. If that happens, there will usually be revisions, and any picture revisions may affect the music. In such cases the music editor, with suggestions from the composer (if he is available), can usually recut the music to fit the changes. But sometimes previews may prompt major changes, or even a new score.

For purposes of clarity and focus we have not yet discussed variations of the film-composing sequence. However, be aware of the many combinations of factors possible, and as always, be flexible. We now turn our attention to more specialized scores, such as all-electronic scores, contemporary scores (techno/rock/jazz/folk), genre scores, source music, songs and song scores, musicals, and others.

PART

ELECTRONIC AND CONTEMPORARY SCORING

CHAPTER 20

ELECTRONIC MUSIC— THE BASICS

To do an orchestrally provocative synthesizer score takes an orchestral background and familiarization with the technology today.

WILLIAM GOLDSTEIN

Electronic music is everywhere. It is difficult to imagine planning music for film and records without considering all the available electronic techniques. Yet until the mid-seventies, the phrase "electronic music" most often referred to music that could be difficult to create and difficult to integrate into a score. As far back as the early sixties, there were frequent examples of scores utilizing some electronic instruments along with a basically acoustic orchestra. During the seventies, the combination of acoustic and electronic colors became more and more prevalent in television and film scores. Now and then a totally electronic score would surface, taking advantage of the unique potential of electronically created sound (for example, Gil Melle's 1970 score for *The Andromeda Strain*).

With occasional exceptions, most of the all-electronic music used in film and television scores up until the early eighties was rhythm-section-oriented contemporary music, often with sequenced patterns like those used in Tangerine Dream's score for *Thief* (1981). Yet the development of more and more sophisticated equipment and technology has made it possible to score films using a variety of other approaches. Junior Homrich with Brian Gasciogne created an evocative score for *The Emerald Forest* (1985) that suggests sounds indigenous to the film's South American location. Giorgio Moroder's all-electronic scores for *Cat People* (1982) and *Scarface* (1983) are rarely "pop" or record-oriented (the title song for *Cat People* is well integrated instrumentally into the score); rather they utilize traditional scoring techniques and values performed on electronic instruments. Mark Isham's score for *Never Cry Wolf* (1983) uses electronic sounds suggestive of the landscapes of Canada's far north and the story of a man studying the behavior of a pack of wolves.

So the composer has the choice of approaching an electronic score as "classical" music (like chamber music or symphonic music), or "contemporary" music (using a keyboard-oriented rhythm section), or any balance of these two concepts, and then blending his electronic music to any desired degree with acoustic instruments or orchestra. To be able to move freely between these options, the composer will need a solid understanding of electronic techniques in addition to his traditional orchestral background.

THE ELECTRONIC STUDIO

In the seventies, I used to get two phone calls about the Arp 2600: first, "I can't get it to start," followed not too much later by "I can't get it to stop."

CLARK SPANGLER, SYNTHESIST

To remain current all of us have to have not only the understanding of the equipment, but the approaches to the equipment. BILL CONTI

Recording at home is the only way I could dream of finishing everything on time, week in and week out.[1] JAN HAMMER

Whether in a living room, a renovated garage, or a high-tech professional facility, all electronic studios will have the same categories of equipment; synthesizers, samplers, drum machines; sequencers; signal processors; computers and MIDI interfaces; sync boxes and MIDI switchers; mixing consoles; and tape and cassette recorders. For film, add one or more video recorders (¾-inch Umatic or ½-inch format).

Each of these types of equipment requires individual study on a continuing basis. There is an overwhelming flow of new electronic equipment. As synthesist Clark Spangler says, "It seems like there's a new instrument out every Tuesday." Information on current electronic instruments and equipment, as well as computer hardware and software, is readily available in a variety of up-to-date books and periodicals. Owners manuals, though long and complex, are also absolutely essential reading to appreciate the full capability of each instrument.

All this equipment is as relevant to film and television scoring as it has been to records and **MTV.**[2] The following description of electronic studio equipment should help to clarify the basic categories of gear found in any well-equipped film-scoring facility. The ability to work with this technology has become an essential aspect of a film composer's training. With lower-priced instruments with increased **MIDI** (*Mi*-dee) potential now entering the market place, an electronic studio can be set up for a much smaller initial investment than ever before. The composer may therefore choose to finance and create his own personal studiolike environment, possibly at home. Whether or not he makes that choice, however, it is absolutely necessary to understand the basic *possibilities* of electronic music in order to create the most emotionally powerful and dramatically appropriate electronic film music. An understanding of the basics is also recommended for filmmmakers.

SYNTHESIZERS

Contemporary synthesizers represent a potentially enormous repository of sounds that can be used to color a composition. As an example, there are literally thousands of instrumental sounds available for the DX7 and DX7 II. You can organize your own **banks**[3] of these sounds and save them on either a **RAM cartridge,**[4] a computer disc, or a data cassette, whichever is compatible with your available equipment. With these resources, a composer can have at his fingertips a number of different variations of any particular color, some a little brighter or with a bit more buzz on the bottom, others a little more mellow. Once you manipulate these colors through all the variable parameters available on any given instrument, there is no limit. Synthesists sell custom-created patches for most of the more popular synths, and advertise in periodicals such as those listed in the bibliography.

The composer can make use of the available sounds at his disposal as examples of what he has in mind when writing or demonstrating the part for the synthesist who will

[1] © 1987 *Electronic Musician,* interview by Craig Anderton (March 1987, p. 57).

[2] MTV: music television video.

[3] Banks: groups of stored sounds for a synthesizer.

[4] RAM cartridge: random access memory cartridge, designed for the user to store and retrieve sounds.

perform it on the recording session. Top-notch synthesists take pride in their ability to manipulate sound to create exactly what the composer has in mind for any given situation.

Though there are several types of synthesis—including analog, FM, phase distortion, wave-table, and linear arithmetic, as well as sampling (which is not true synthesis)—there are elements common to most instruments, such as envelope generators and low-frequency oscillators (see below). Many instruments produce basically similar effects, such as vibrato, tremolo, and portamento.

CHANGING THE WAVEFORM. Every instrument provides a choice of waveforms. A few standard waveforms include sine wave, saw tooth, triangle wave, square wave, and pulse wave. New synths continue to offer new waveform variations. Some synthesizers give you the option of selecting these various waveforms for each oscillator, thus allowing you to blend a sawtooth wave on one oscillator with a square wave on another, for example. These waveforms are the basic building blocks that can be manipulated and combined to produce a variety of timbres.

NUMBER OF VOICES. The original modular Moog and Minimoog could play only one voice at a time. Although synths have since become polyphonic, there are still limits to the number of notes they can play simultaneously. The Yamaha DX7 is a sixteen-voice instrument (capable of sounding up to sixteen notes simultaneously) and the Kurzweil 250 is twelve-voice. As a practical matter, the more the better.

OCTAVE TRANSPOSITION. Synthesizer pitches are produced by oscillators. You can usually adjust the octave register of any oscillator at least one or two octaves up or down. This change of octaves can make a part more playable by moving it to a more comfortable register of the keyboard, or raising or lowering a particular sound beyond the range of the keyboard.

Not all patches on a synthesizer will be programmed to sound in the expected octave when you strike a key that looks like middle C. Octave transposition is a vital technique for adjusting a part so that it sounds where you want it to sound. An octave discrepancy can occur between two different synths that are playing the same part, due to an inconsistency in the preprogrammed sounds for each instrument. This sometimes makes an octave adjustment necessary when using MIDI (see below) to sync two or more synths together in unison.

PITCH TRANSPOSE. This is a separate adjustment from the octave controller, and the DX7II has this capability, as do many others. If a particular synth doesn't, it's likely that the sequencer you use will. For the film composer, this capability will provide flexibility by allowing two cues sequenced in different keys to be transposed to the same key in order to create a new cue or portion of a cue.

PORTAMENTO. Most synths have some way of moving from one note to another continuously as a portamento (or glide). The rate of portamento can be controlled and can make a big difference in the effect, which can range from very subtle to blatantly obvious.

PITCH BENDER. All synths have a wheel or lever that allows you to bend sustained notes up or down a variable amount, much as guitarists do. This is one of the devices that can make a synth part sound less mechanical. The effective and personal use of pitch bending is something that has to be practiced by the performer, regardless of musical style.

AFTERTOUCH. Most synths provide an aftertouch function. On these, you can often assign a particular performance function to be affected by aftertouch, which allows the performer to manipulate the sound after the attack by pressing harder on a key that is already depressed. Aftertouch can change the vibrato, brilliance, or volume of a sustaining sound. Some synths allow for independent (or "polyphonic") aftertouch (which affects only the specific notes that are pressed after striking).

CHORUSING. Chorusing produces the effect of several voices sounding the same pitch simultaneously when only one key is depressed. This creates the impression of a fuller, doubled sound, much like playing two instruments together.

FLANGING. Flanging combines the original signal with a split-second delay of that signal. This gives a sense of harmonic motion to the sound (something like phasing). Flanging can be very extreme, as the harmonic intrusions created by this effect can be severe.

These effects bring the sound clearly into the electronic, nonacoustic realm and can be deliberately used for this purpose when that is desirable. It is not necessary to know *how* these effects are produced so long as you know the quality of the resultant sound and know how to vary it. (Chorusing and flanging are frequently achieved through external signal processing.)

DIGITAL DELAY. Some synths offer a delay adjustment that manipulates the amount of time between striking the key and the actual sound of the note. This can be used to delay the entrance of the note, or can be combined with the original impact to give multiple attacks.

DETUNING TWO OR MORE OSCILLATORS. Oscillators may be detuned; the detuning can be varied to taste and is an essential ingredient in many electronic sounds and ensemble effects. Gross detuning can be used to create interesting colors, or oscillators may be tuned to different pitches. For example, oscillator number one might be tuned to prime, and oscillator number two to a fifth above prime, so when you strike a middle C, oscillator number one plays middle C and oscillator number two plays the G above middle C. You can tune the second oscillator to *any* note, so it is possible to tune it up a half step or down a major third, thus allowing the performer to play chromatic minor seconds or major thirds by simply playing a chromatic scale on the keyboard.

VOLUME CONTROLS FOR OSCILLATORS. A mixing capability in synths allows you to control the relative volume of the two or more oscillators. In the above-mentioned example of the middle C and G, by greatly reducing the volume of the G, you can *imply* the G without really making the parallel fifths obvious. This technique is often used by synthesists to fatten up chordal sounds.

LFOs. Low-frequency oscillators produce signals at the bottom of or below the range of human hearing. They are typically used to control or modify other oscillators. Common uses of LFOs include modulating the sound to create vibrato or tremolo.

VCFs. Voltage-controlled filters allow you to change the cutoff frequency of a sound. A low-pass filter cuts off all the highs above a certain frequency. A high-pass filter cuts off all the lows below a certain frequency. These filters change the sound of the signal for very useful timbre changes by emphasizing completely different qualities of a particular sound as the lows or highs are removed. In some synths, like the Oberheim Matrix-12, the VCFs also can emphasize the amount of resonance at the frequency cutoff, which further manipulates the original color. If the envelope generator (see below) is moving the resonance point, adding resonance to a sound can give it the "ow" effect sometimes used in conjunction with funky bass or lead sounds. Adding too much resonance creates a feedback effect.

VCAs. Voltage-controlled amplifiers are used to control the volume level of a particular signal.

ENVELOPE GENERATORS. The word *envelope* refers to the dynamic shape of any signal from attack to release. Envelope generators therefore can determine what happens to a note when it is played.

ADSR. This is a type of envelope generator. The four initials stand for "Attack," "Decay," "Sustain," and "Release," the four basic variables of this type of envelope. They are listed in the chronological sequence in which they occur after a note is struck on the keyboard, and they describe the four stages of the consequent sound.

1. *Attack.* Percussive sounds require fast attack. To make a percussive sound more subtle, you would decrease (slow down) the rate of attack somewhat. To cause a stringlike sound to start very gently, you would use a less rapid attack. If a sound lacks punch, you would increase (speed up) the attack.

2. *Decay.* This describes what happens to a note immediately following the attack—how fast the sound diminishes after attack. A xylophone has a very rapid decay, with the sound dropping off drastically immediately after the attack. Plucked sounds would be similar. Piano sounds drop off quite a bit; electric pianos and Fender Rhodes sounds less so. Major changes in the rate of decay of a sound dramatically affect the inherent nature of the sound.

3. *Sustain.* The sustain portion of the envelope determines the duration of the note that sustains after the decay.

4. *Release.* This last portion of the envelope determines what happens to the note at the moment the key is released—how fast the note dies away. If the note stops immediately, the setting is as extreme as possible. To get a note to ring on for several seconds after releasing the keys, increase the release time for that sound (that is, *slow down* its release rate.)

Other types of envelopes exist with more segments. The Kurzweil, for example, has a 256-stage envelope available, as opposed to the 4 stages of an ADSR envelope.

SAMPLING

To "sample" is to convert any sound from any source into digital information for playback with a keyboard (or other **controller**). This sampling is done by recording the sound with a microphone (or using a prerecorded signal from a record, tape recording, or compact disc) and directing the signal into the **sampler.** Samplers either have their own keyboards (like the Synclavier, Kurzweil 250, Emulator) or are modules (designed to be rack mounted) that can be played by another controller. Many are available in either format. Most come with factory-created samples all ready to play, plus the ability for the user to sample whatever he wishes.

It is not easy to record excellent samples. It often takes hours or even days to perfect a difficult sample. But, like synths, you can plug in a sampler, turn on the power, punch up one of the preprogrammed sounds (presets or patches) and instantly play familiar acoustic sounds like classic guitar, voice or flute, various synth sounds or even sound effects on a keyboard.

There is understandable concern about sampling, because as the technology gets better and better, sampled sounds become more and more lifelike. Good samples may sound very much like cellos and harps and oboes. And self-contained studios and composers are now able to "play" and record these acoustic instruments on their keyboards, thereby replacing other musicians. This practice has had a negative effect on some musicians in the recording and film industries. "It doesn't bode too well if you want your son to be an oboe player," says producer Gerald Isenberg.

Burt Bacharach speaks for every composer when he says, "I feel badly for the musicians. And they are friends, and I know they've all got to be hurting. . . . It's rough. I hear what I've got on my Emulator. And I hear what I can just pull out of a box."

There's no easy solution to this problem. Not only is the technology here to stay, but it is improving constantly. And for the film composer, samplers have become a very valuable tool. Maurice Jarre, who *doesn't* use much sampling in his electronic scores, explains one application:

"When you have to deal with very difficult instruments to play, like an instrument from Gambia called the Kora (a kind of harp-lute which is a cross between the European zither and the Argentinian charango) you have maybe one or two guys who are really able to play it, but they can't read music. When you want to introduce an instrument like this into a score, if you have sampling, that is really very interesting. For *The Tin Drum* [1979], I used an instrument from the mountains in Poland, called Fujara. It's another strange instrument. A huge flutelike instrument, but in the shape of a bassoon. And it's a fantastic sound. I didn't need to sample for *Tin Drum* because I found a player who could play this instrument, but in a case like that, sampling would be fine."

Samplers are especially helpful as composers' tools and are effective in sketching and playing back orchestral music quickly and accurately. Whether for a demonstration or the composer's own experimentation, the electronic studio can function as an electronic "sketch pad."

DRUM MACHINES

Contemporary drum machines are dedicated computers that primarily use sampled sounds, and many of them allow user sampling as well. They now offer programmable dynamics, which gives them the potential to be much less machinelike than earlier models. They can be driven in sync with a sequencer or other click source, or they can be the master tempo generator that drives the other instruments and sequencers in the chain.

MIDI

"MIDI" stands for Musical Instrument Digital Interface. It was adapted by all music manufacturers in 1983 as a standardized way of allowing electronic instruments to send controlling messages to each other. Virtually all electronic musical equipment—synths, drum machines, effects boxes, sequencers—manufactured after 1983 are capable of receiving and sending MIDI'd information. There are even retrofits available for pre-MIDI equipment, like the original LinnDrum. MIDI-equipped machines have a MIDI IN receptacle, a MIDI OUT receptacle, and a MIDI THRU receptacle. Cabling is standardized so one type of connector fits everything. If you want to send information from MIDI synth A to MIDI synth B, just plug one end of the cable into synth A's MIDI OUT receptacle, and the other end into synth B's MIDI IN receptacle (Figure 20-1). Now anything you play on synth A (the "master") will be transmitted directly to synth B

FIGURE 20-1
2-synth MIDI hookup.

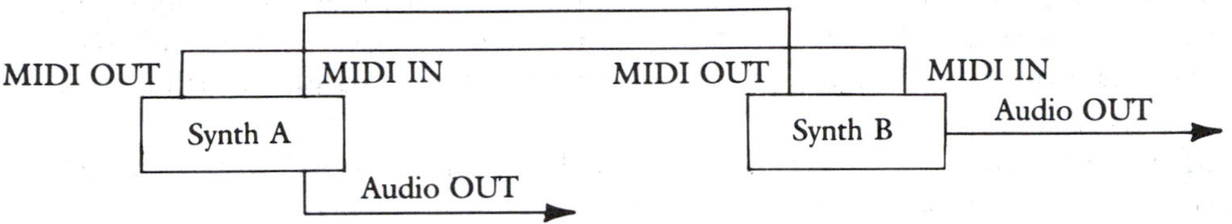

(the "slave"). This includes not only information about pitches (including note on/note off information) but also touch sensitivity, aftertouch, pitch bends, portamento, and so on (assuming both instruments have similar MIDI capabilities). If you change a patch on synth A in bar 13, that information will also be sent to synth B, changing its patch simultaneously.

This describes the most basic MIDI connection. It can get more intricate. To hook up three synths together, you would connect the MIDI OUT of synth A to the MIDI IN of synth B; and then the MIDI THRU of synth B to the MIDI IN of synth C. The THRU terminal sends a direct copy of whatever the synth is receiving, so synth C now gets all the same information as synth B (this is called a "daisy chain"). This means that when you play a chord on synth A, it is now sounding on synth B and synth C simultaneously (Figure 20-2).

There are a total of sixteen MIDI channels available to send and receive information; the user can set synths to receive MIDI information on one specific channel (in poly mode) or on all the channels (omni mode). Thus if synth A were set to receive information on MIDI channel 2 and synth B were set to receive on MIDI channel 3, synth B would not respond to any specific channel information sent to synth A.

FIGURE 20-2
3-synth MIDI hookup.

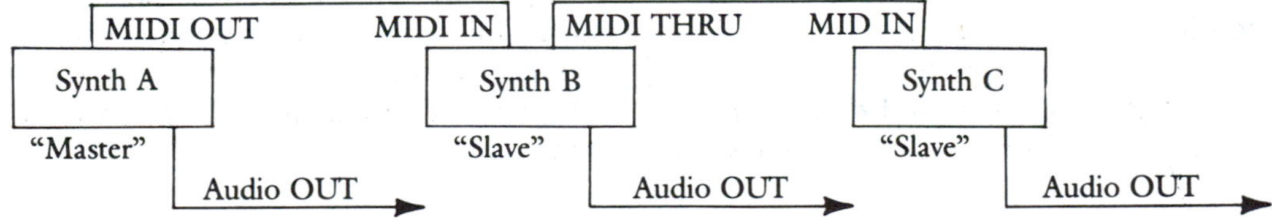

Here are some of the things that MIDI makes possible:

1. You can send any performance information on a real-time basis. That means any number of electronic instruments and effects can be chained together.

2. Sequencers receive and send information via MIDI. So a score can be "recorded" on a sequencer, and then that performance of the score can be sent to as many instruments as you wish.

3. You can send MIDI channel information. With sequenced music, this means that you could assign a particular part to a specific MIDI channel and know that only those instruments set to receive on that channel would play that part.

4. You can control any synth from any keyboard. If you like the feel or size or whatever of your favorite synth, you can play everything on it and send that performance to any other synth or synths you wish. Different synths will have different MIDI capabilities, however.

5. Synths don't need keyboards. You can easily control the sound of synths that are only rack-mounted modules using any MIDI controller.

6. Other instruments can be used as controllers besides keyboards, if they are equipped with MIDI. These are referred to as MIDI controllers. Guitars have been MIDI'd; so have drums, mallet instruments, and wind instruments. Even acoustic pianos have been MIDI'd.

7. Effects units like digital reverb and digital delay units can be MIDI'd so that performance information can be sent to them.

8. MIDI sequencers can be set up to drive an entire electronic ensemble in sync.

9. Drum machines can be incorporated into the MIDI chain, either tied in to a sequencer or playing without a sequencer.

10. Personal computers can be tied into the MIDI chain, so that a sequencer program on a computer can drive everything. You need a special interface for this—a piece of hardware that functions as an adapter between the synth and the computer.

11. Personal computers can be used as patch librarians to allow you to compile a library of sounds.

12. Personal computers also have patch editor programs available, which make the editing of synths more graphic.

HOW MANY SYNTHS?

A typical electronic studio has at least two or three different synths and one sampler. Most composers like the choice of sounds and approaches possible with some variety of instruments. But some composers who work with either the upscale Synclavier or Fairlight find that they are comfortable using one of these instruments almost exclusively. Michael Hoenig's electronic studio centers around his Synclavier, which he supplements with a variety of other synths and effects machines. In 1987 Jan Hammer scored the *Miami Vice* television series episodes on a Fairlight Series III. "It's phenomenal. I'm just totally blown away by it. I was sold on the Fairlight initially with the old Series IIX because of the combination of sampling and different modes of sequencing, which are so well-suited to a musician-like approach. Even though the instrument still looks a bit foreboding—it seems like you can only get to it through the alpha-numeric keyboard—that's not exactly the case. There's so much real time interaction, and it's so well thought-out, that once you get past the first intimidating feelings, you're sold."[5]

SEQUENCERS

> ***I use the sequencer when there should be something perfectly steady, almost like a machine. And that is practically impossible to do with an orchestra.***
>
> MAURICE JARRE

Any machine that converts musical performance commands sent via MIDI into digital information for future playback is called a sequencer. The first sequencers could only play a limited number of notes (which could then be looped) monophonically. Now, anything you play electronically can be digitized by a sequencer. And they will store from 400 to more than 80,000 notes. In some cases, an entire film score can be input on one floppy disc. Some sequencers are housed in dedicated hardware. Yamaha's QX series and Roland's MC-500 are dedicated sequencers. Software programs designed for one of the popular

---

[5] © 1987, *Electronic Musician,* interview by Craig Anderton (March 1987).

personal computers such as the Macintosh, Apple II, Commodore, IBM, and Atari enable them to function as sequencers.

Dedicated or not, they are all basically software programs housed in a computer, and there are many similarities. Here is what the best sequencers can do:

1. Record multiple tracks of electronic musical performance commands via MIDI, including all performance nuances.
2. Play back these tracks simultaneously.
3. Allow the selection of any combination of recorded tracks, muting the others.
4. Offer full editing possibilities, including in many cases the alteration of the dynamic level, rhythmic placement, or even pitch of any individual note on a track. This allows the correction of isolated performance mistakes in an otherwise excellent performance.
5. Transpose any or all tracks. Some programs allow this during playback in real time.
6. Overdub one or more parts onto the same track.
7. Merge two or more separately recorded tracks onto one track.
8. Punch in/punch out recording (accurate to milliseconds) to improve a performance, or change a composition.
9. Move a passage from one track to another. This is especially useful as a compositional tool for film scoring, either because of compositional changes, new timings, or inventive reuse of materials.
10. **Quantize** any portion of a recorded passage, correcting any note played to the nearest whole note, half note, quarter note, eighth note, sixteenth note, or even more minute subdivisions.
11. Copy a track one or more times to shift the entire track rhythmically as a delay effect.
12. Change the rhythmic feel of a passage to make it less mechanical, more swinglike, or whatever.
13. Allow step recording.

You can change the tempo during playback or record. In the playback mode this is extremely useful in finding a more sympathetic performance tempo, or stretching or shortening a cue slightly to fit a re-edited piece of film. In the record mode, passages that would be unplayable at the chosen tempo can be easily played and recorded at a slower tempo, and then played back faster. Phrasing also becomes more controllable at slower tempos.

By quantizing any given passage or individual part, machinelike regularity can be achieved with a sequencer. It is a misconception to think that the use of a sequencer is necessarily related to a mechanical sound; relentless unchanging tempo is just one of the things a sequencer does perfectly. IF YOU RECORD LIVE MUSIC ON THE SEQUENCER, YOU WILL GET LIVE MUSIC BACK (plus whatever else you want to add to it).

What a sequencer *cannot* do is to literally *record* the music. It records only the commands to perform the notes, not the actual sound. This means that if you recorded a track using a plucked sound on the DX7 and you now would like to hear it played back with a quasi-marimba sound, all you need to do is push a button to change the patch on the DX7 to hear it that way. Same performance commands, different color. Or, if you'd rather hear it played back on another synth, that's just as easy. Just MIDI it over to the other synth, select any color you would like, and play it back again. This aspect of sequencers makes them a valuable experimental tool for the composer.

You should always remember to program a two-bar count off on the sequencer at the front of any cue you record. This will be represented by silence on all tracks, allowing the clicks to play alone for those two bars before the cue starts. Some sequencers allow you to insert bars; with those sequencers, these two bars can be added after the cue is finished. Otherwise, you would be wise to make it a practice to start every new cue with two empty bars.

SIGNAL PROCESSORS

Any piece of equipment that is specifically designed to manipulate sound (a "signal") electronically is a signal processor. Digital reverbs, **digital delays,**[6] special equalizers, compressors, and limiters are all considered signal processors. Most of them respond to commands and are programmable. These effects are easy to edit and easy to save. Jerry Goldsmith's trumpet theme from *Patton* (1970; see Figure 7-3) was originally manipulated with an audio tape delay created by an Echoplex. Today, most programmable digital delays would be able to calibrate the amount of delay and the duration of the repeat effect easily, and with much cleaner sound. (See Appendix C for a chart that converts digital metronome click tempos to digital delay settings in milliseconds to achieve specific effects with repeated quarter notes, eighth notes, and so on).

COMPUTERS

With the proper programs, the personal computer is a remarkable piece of equipment able to provide the composer with the following:

1. A sophisticated sequencer, able to generate the master click and sync pulse necessary to drive all the studio equipment in sync.
2. A flexible patch librarian for each synth, with storage space limited only by the space on the disc or hard disc.
3. A notational tool capable of printing out (with limitations) whatever you play or enter into the program.
4. A method of saving user-sampled sounds onto floppy or hard disc.
5. A sophisticated visual analysis of any given sampled sound, and the capability of editing and shaping the contour of that sound to produce the smoothest sample possible.
6. Tone-generators that are built-in basic synthesizers.
7. Any one of hundreds of nonmusical features that everyone is familiar with, including word processing, graphics, accounting, games, tutorials, and an ever-expanding variety of programs (the manuscript for this book was designed and written on two Apple Macintoshes).

Each signal processor, synth, or sequencer is actually a computer that has been dedicated to one specific function. The only difference between this equipment and a personal computer is that the computer can do other things.

---

[6]Digital delay: a signal processor that delays a signal by a variable amount and can repeat that delayed signal for a variable duration, allowing the user to mix the delayed signal with the original signal as desired.

SYNC AND SYNC BOXES

There are a number of different types of sync pulses (signals or codes), all designed for one purpose—to allow two or more pieces of electronic equipment to run simultaneously in perfect sync. Equipment has to be able to run in sync with other equipment, and also with previously recorded material on a tape recorder. We have mentioned that you can tie in a sequencer and a number of synths and a drum machine so that they all play together in sync. This can be done using MIDI itself as a sync controller. Hook up a drum machine with a sequencer, put the drum machine in the proper sync mode, and you can start the drums in sync by starting the sequencer. But a word of caution—things can and do go wrong and take time to straighten out. You won't be the only one that this has happened to.

INTEGRATING WITH TAPE RECORDING. Although sequencers provide multitrack recording capabilities (with the understanding that we have recorded the *commands* to perform our synthesizers, but not the *sounds* of those instruments), electronic music cues are typically recorded on a multitrack tape recorder. This not only allows you to record multiple passes with the same synthesizers, and gives you detailed control of equalization and reverb on mix-down, but most important, gives the option to freely record acoustic instruments and mix them with electronic sounds.

Once you record one or more tracks on tape, you've got to be able to play those tracks back and concurrently drive another synth (or group of synths) so that they can be recorded in sync with the originally recorded tracks. This can be easy or difficult, primarily because not all instruments respond to the same type of sync signal. Some work on the principle of a certain fixed number of pulses per quarter note (referred to as the number of clocks or pulses); common numbers are 24, 48, 96, but others include 12, 64, and 384. To get things in sync, you must know the clock rate of each instrument's sync signal that uses this system. Other equipment uses a sync signal called **FSK** (Frequency Shift Keying). The click from a digital metronome or other source can also be used. SMPTE time code uses digital technology, a big help in syncing sound to video as well. As such, it works well with MIDI information, which is also digital, and is therefore an excellent sync signal. **MIDI time code** (MTC) uses a signal similar to SMPTE but with even finer calibration. MTC in sent through the MIDI chain along with all other MIDI information, and therefore needs no separate interface with the computer (as SMPTE sometimes does).

Each configuration of different sequencers, instruments, and drum machines may require a slightly different sync method. Some of the older equipment may not be compatible, in which case you need a sync box like the Garfield Electronics Doctor Click or Master Beat, or the Roland SBX-80 Sync Box. These are designed to accept any type of sync pulse from any source, and then convert that signal into any other type of sync pulse before sending it on its way.

THE MIXING CONSOLE

The mixing console is usually called the **board.** Every musician and filmmaker has seen plenty of mixing boards, but if you haven't really examined one, you will have missed its real capabilities.

First of all, there is a separate input-output module (controlling pre-amp) for each track that the board can accommodate; a twenty-four track board will start with module number 1 on the extreme left and continue until module number 24. There may be additional modules for sending a group of tracks as a sub-master, or for dedicating to certain effects like reverb or digital delay. THE MODULES REPRESENTING THE TRACKS WILL ALL BE IDENTICAL. This immediately makes the board more logical and understandable.

Learn about one module and you know about many of them. These modules include the following kinds of controls:

1. A way of selecting the source of the sound (from the tape? from an instrument? from a microphone?).

2. A way of adjusting the input level or overall gain of the module itself. This variable adjustment provides the highest possible level without distortion.

3. A way of reducing the overall gain dramatically. This is called a **pad.** It also protects the module from distorting if the source is extremely loud coming into the board.

4. A comprehensive way of adjusting the frequency response of any sound coming into the board through that module. This area of the board is for EQ, or equalizing. There are always a number of knobs on the module that either boost or "roll off" the sound at a particular frequency range. EQ can be very significant in coloring any given sound. Boards usually have three to five EQ controls on each module, but they are calibrated in different ways. On some boards, each control can be switched back and forth from one frequency of operation to another; for example, either 3,000 **hertz**[7] or 5,000, or either 300 or 500. Another type of control allows a complete choice of frequency operation between two given frequencies. These controls are ***parametric.***

5. A way of routing any signal processing so it appears on the module either before the signal is sent to tape (pre) or after (post).

6. A way of controlling the level at which a module's sound is being sent to a signal processor (this is called the ***auxiliary send***). Boards have two or more sends, so the sound passing through that module can be sent to two or more effects. With so many methods of signal processing available, it is very useful to have as many auxiliary sends as possible.

7. A way of controlling the ***monitor level*** of the module, if the board is designed with a separate monitoring function.

8. A way of selecting the proper recording mode for the module: record or mix.

9. A way of controlling the exact left-right placement of the sound in the stereo mix (called a ***pan pot***).

10. A way of turning the module on and off (***muting*** it). This is usually a flat button.

11. A way of monitoring only certain selected modules during a mix without affecting the recording mix-down. This is a "solo" button. If the board has solo "in-place" you will hear the module with reverb, EQ, and so on in its assigned stereo position.

12. A way of controlling the overall level of the signal controlled by that module. This is a sliding lever set into the board, called a **fader.**

13. A way of selecting a specific tape recorder track to which the sound on a module will be sent. An instrument might be coming into the board on module twelve, for instance, but the mixer may wish it to be ***recorded*** on track six. This section of the board is sometimes called the "track assign" section, and also allows you to select the specific placement of each track in the final stereo or 4-track mix.

14. A way of determining the level of the module at any moment. There are two standard techniques for this. The first is the traditional VU meter, in which a needle moves back and forth on a scale that represents a dynamic range from minus 20 db to plus 3 db or more. The newer method uses a vertical LED meter, in which a light appears to be jumping up and down in response to the sound signal. Some mixers prefer one type of meter to another, but most agree that the LEDs are quicker and more responsive to dynamic signals such as those created by contemporary drums and rhythm tracks.

---

[7] Hertz: cycles per second.

Although other modules on the board may be slightly different (often containing less sophisticated EQ, for instance) most of the above-mentioned functions will be the same. Smaller boards specifically designed for small rooms and various home applications may be set up slightly differently in order to double up on some of the individual modules, and to sub-master modules to increase track capability.

The contemporary film composer will find a speaking/working knowledge of signal processing and mixing-board technology to be very helpful in bridging the gap between the *written* score and the *recorded* score—two very different things. Even a totally acoustic score will sound very different when mixed with two different approaches to reverb, for instance.

TAPE RECORDERS

There are several things the composer should know about tape recorders:

1. Recording at a speed of 30 ips is quieter than 15 ips. Without using Dolby noise reduction, 30 ips is definitely the preferred choice. It is also easier to splice intercuts at 30 ips, although that isn't often necessary on the two-inch masters.
2. Although most film recording is still done on analog machines, digital recording is becoming more popular for some films, especially those that may have commercial recording tie-ins. Digital recordings are cleaner and quieter than analog, though some people feel they are not as true and lifelike. Digital is an option sometimes considered when scoring a film to be released in Dolby stereo.
3. For mix-downs going to the typical 3-track format, 4-track ½-inch tape is still the film-scoring medium, with either SMPTE or a 60-cycle sync pulse on the fourth track. Depending on the final requirements of the dubbing stage, there are two possible formats for stereo: (1) three discrete tracks (left, center, and right) with the stereo phantom center actually recorded on the center (second) track; or (2) a true record-type stereo mix with the left on track one and the right on track two, so that the phantom center just *sounds* like it is on a separate center track. A 6-track, with stereo strings, stereo winds, and stereo rhythm is also a possibility and offers more control when the dubbing facility has the necessary 6-track dummies.

SPEAKERS

In general, bigger isn't necessarily better when monitoring electronic music for film. Although Dolby Stereo has vastly increased the frequency response now obtainable on optical film tracks, optical film still is more restricted than the recording-studio spectrum. A good set of smaller near-field speakers that have a nice flat, true sound reproduction will work very well for most film work. Recording mixer John Richards mentions another excellent reason for monitoring with less volume and using smaller near-field speakers: "It is *much* more tiring to work with electronic music for eight hours."

For television, an extra set of smaller speakers makes a good cross-reference, as does sending the mix directly into a television monitor.

MISCELLANEOUS EQUIPMENT

ELECTRONIC CHROMATIC TUNER. Anybody who plans to record electronic instruments should buy two of these (the best money can buy) and put one away for that moment some Sunday evening when the first one isn't working right. Some electronic effects are deliberately a bit out of tune, but they are only effective because everything else is perfectly *in* tune. There is nothing worse than stacking a number of synth tracks on tape, only to realize at three in the morning that somewhere along the line the cue became very out of tune. Tuners run on batteries, so extra batteries are a must.

DIGITAL METRONOME. Since the tempo calibration for films is usually in frames and ⅛ frames, the best and most reliable source of a film-oriented click is the digital metronome. However, without a sync box it can be difficult to integrate a digital metronome into a sequencer/drum machine system, but even if it isn't used to drive the system, the digital metronome is an accurate cross-reference that can be used during the composing process, prior to recording. When sequencers offer frames-per-click calibration of their built-in clicks this won't be necessary anymore. Scores recorded in an electronic studio can use MM tempos if they aren't being combined later on a scoring stage.

MIDI SWITCHER/CONTROLLER. The electronic studio must have the capacity to send each separate synth or module its own dedicated message without changing cables; the MIDI switcher/controller (or MIDI patch bay) does this. The more capacity the better for this piece of equipment. If the composer works with a Yamaha TX816 (as Jerry Goldsmith did while working on *Hoosiers* and other scores in 1987), those eight modules represent the possibility of eight MIDI routings. That's just for one instrument, and without a keyboard at that. The goal is to be able to go to (or program) the switcher box to decide which sequenced track any given instrument will be playing at any given moment.

VIDEOCASSETTE RECORDER (VCR) AND MONITOR. For film work, the recording studio will need either ½-inch or ¾-inch Umatic videocassette format. The film producers will provide videocassettes in either format the composer requests. The ¾-inch is more unwieldy, since a two-hour film will be on two large cassettes of no more than an hour each, and a seven-hour miniseries will take seven cassettes. But the quality is better, and the speed may be more reliable. Although producers don't seem to mention it as a factor, ¾-inch is more expensive. Whatever the format, be sure you have the audio-dub feature, which allows recording new sound on a second channel. It is extremely helpful for any composer, whether he is working electronically or acoustically (and not all machines offer this capability).

INSTRUMENT STANDS. Several companies manufacture synthesizer stands of all sizes, and 19-inch racks for signal processors and synth expander units.

MUSIC STAND. Although anything handy would do in a pinch, there is nothing like the luxury of a music stand when you are working at a synth. Unlike pianos, there is no safe place to write on a synth, so the composer will need something else to write on and something to hold music he has sketched and is performing.

BOOKSHELF FOR INSTRUCTION MANUALS. When the composer isn't using the above-mentioned music stand for music, it will probably be holding one or more instruction manuals. Every electronic studio needs a dedicated space for all the instruction manuals.

The rapid-fire evolution of computer technology has given composers vast new resources of sounds, sound manipulation, and compositional and orchestrational techniques. But the technology is just the means to an artistic end. If the composer reacts to these developments with the same enthusiasm and awareness that Beethoven did when the pianoforte enriched the potential for dynamic keyboard composition, he will discover great opportunities for creating exciting new film music.

CHAPTER 21
ELECTRONIC SCORING

The technique is unimportant compared to what you do with it.
WILLIAM GOLDSTEIN

Electronic music can be conceived in three ways:

1. As an imitation or re-creation of acoustic instruments
2. As a means of creating unique nonacoustic sounds
3. As a blend of electronic and pseudo-acoustic sounds

Each one of these electronic approaches can be used to create an independent ensemble of sounds, or an electronic ensemble of sounds to be incorporated in an acoustic orchestral texture.

ELECTRONIC INSTRUMENTS AS ACOUSTIC RE-CREATIONS

Electronic instruments can and are being used frequently to recreate acoustic ensembles and even large orchestras. In 1986, William Goldstein was asked to compose an electronic score for an NBC-TV film called *Liberty,* about the conception and creation of the Statue of Liberty. In an article by Bob Doerschuk in the July 1986 issue of *Keyboard* magazine (Cupertino, CA), Goldstein says, "I did a period score. Some of the colors do have an electronic tinge, but most of the music has very much of a nineteenth-century character, up to the end of the show, which bridges from the unveiling to contemporary shots of the statue. I wrote a more Coplandesque piece at that point."

The relationship to traditional orchestration is clear-cut, he says. "I think that whatever success I've been having with electronics is absolutely due to my orchestral background, because everything I do here I think of in the same terms I would use if I were writing for an orchestra. It's just that the colors are different colors. It's like you were scoring something for an electronic band."[1]

ELECTRONIC INSTRUMENTS FOR UNIQUE SOUNDS

Synthesizers should do what no other instrument can do.
CLARK SPANGLER, SYNTHESIST

I had to make that shimmer. I wouldn't care if I had the best flutists in the world, no fingers could move that fast. So that was my first use of a synthesizer.
JOHN (JOHNNY) GREEN
(re: They Shoot Horses, Don't They? Main Title, 1969)

[1] © 1986 *Keyboard* magazine, Cupertino, CA. Reprinted by permission.

Synths are machines that are able to do things that are humanly impossible; endless rapid trills on notes that would be difficult to finger on acoustic woodwinds; extremely soft notes in the upper reaches of a "brass" sound; low notes functioning like bass trombones and tubas but not limited by breathing problems; impossible intervals; bowed pianos; smooth woodwind glissandos. With MIDI, add the humanly impossible task of syncing eight "keyboards" together on fast sixteenth notes with machinelike accuracy. Or slightly detuning four keyboard sounds together in ensemble; difficult to achieve on acoustic instruments, this is no problem at all on electronic instruments, since all synths can be detuned easily and exactly.

Many film scores have used an electronic approach. These scores may give the listener the impression that, even if an orchestra could perform the music, the effect would be quite different and might be less satisfying for the dramatic situation. Examples of this include the aforementioned *Emerald Forest* (1985), *Cat People* (1982), and *Scarface* (1983). *Reckless* (1984, composed by Thomas Newman) is hard-edged and contemporary—an orchestra wouldn't produce that sound. *Lucas* (1986, composed by Dave Grusin) takes a somewhat more classical approach to electronic scoring, while still retaining an electronic flavor.

In 1969, when director Robert Wise was in the process of editing *The Andromeda Strain,* a science-fiction film about a group of scientists working against a time limit to neutralize a deadly virus, he knew that the score was going to be very important. Sound effects were light and there was a lot of suspense throughout the film. He decided on an electronic score and worked with composer Gil Mellé. "I told him what I was after," Wise says. "I needed to have a musical score but it needed to sound as mechanical as possible. I said I didn't want any of his electronic stuff to sound like a note, a sustained musical note. And several times, although his cues were very good, there would be some musical notes, something that would sound like a violin or some instrument, and I'd say, 'Gil, that's fine except that part is not right because it sounds identifiably like a piece of music.' And he would take it back that night and fix it."

BLENDING ELECTRONIC AND ACOUSTIC INSTRUMENTS

I've been using electronics for twenty-five years now. But I've never seen it as a substitute for an orchestra. I believe it will someday be an accepted section in a symphony orchestra. JERRY GOLDSMITH

The first uses of electronic scoring were in conjunction with traditional orchestras. And this continues to be an extremely effective medium for utilizing electronic-music techniques in film scores. We have mentioned Craig Safan's score for *Remo Williams* (1985; see Figure 15-5) and Alan Silvestri's *Romancing the Stone* (1984; see Figures 15-6, 22-3, and 23-1). Others include Silvestri's *Back to the Future* (1985) and Jerry Goldsmith's *Hoosiers* (1986; see Figures 22-12 and 22-13). Each establishes its own blend of electronic and acoustic elements, depending on the dramatic needs of the film.

SCORING WITH ELECTRONIC MUSIC

The requisites for a good electronic score of any sort are the same as those for any other good film score. But the process can be quite different.

FINDING SOUNDS. Typically a composer will spend days searching through his library, finding appropriate sounds for a score and possibly editing them to suit his purposes on each specific project as he begins to work. Jerry Goldsmith now adds another week to his schedule on a feature film. "I gather my basic materials. Then I will gather my library of sounds." He doesn't do much editing of the sounds. "I'm not ashamed to use factory patches. There's nothing wrong with a standard sound. An oboe is a standard sound. It's the notes you use." His approach to scheduling the extra time for this part of the process is typical. Ideally, the search for the appropriate sounds to express the musical material a composer has envisioned and possibly already sketched can be a very stimulating and productive phase of the creative process, leading the composer to musical solutions that would not have occurred to him without the availability of those particular colors. Taking the extra time to keep careful notes and create special cartridges or banks of sounds during this phase will pay off in the long run, saving countless hours that would otherwise be spent searching for that special sound that was obvious two weeks ago but can no longer be located.

To get the unique sounds he wants on the scoring stage, the composer can either describe his intentions on the written score, verbalize his intentions to the synthesists on the scoring stage, or bring the specific sounds on RAM cartridges, data cassettes, or computer discs (depending on the equipment), indicating them in the score by number and name.

DESCRIBE THE SOUND ON THE WRITTEN SCORE. Describing the sound in writing demands imagination and the willingness to be redundant or turn a metaphor upside down. In his score for *Brainstorm* (1983), James Horner used the following description above a keyboard part: "Sparkly chord, beautiful, rich Vangelis-like." Synthesist Clark Spangler says that to a synthesist, this means, "Phase shift a CS-80[2] string sound with something that pings, and add a delay device to the sound." The written notes were represented by a mid-range A-major triad. Horner used three different short descriptions to sum up his intentions. This is not unusual, and is really the only effective way to get what you want. Putting a known sound in an unusual situation is also effective. "The sound of an oboe playing under water" will get a good synthesist going.

Spangler remembers the following description on a part: "Brain operation for seven year old. Seven year old survives." Spangler feels that was a very communicative notation. "There's a lot of information within that—my part was just a single line, a piece of string holding it together, and the fact that he survived would have a different implication than if he had not made it. The composer was telling me about the dramatic moment and also the intensity of the picture. What might have been appropriate for a horror film would be quite different from a tender, sad family thing."

Marvin Hamlisch, on an early score of his for a film called *The War Between Men and Women* (1972), asked Spangler for the following: "The sound should be not a flute, not a recorder, not a wind blowing, but in that area." "So we eliminated thousands of things," Spangler says, "and got it to an area, and then we refined that area. It worked very well. It's a concept that works very well for descriptions of the ambiguous sound that doesn't exist in any other form."

VERBALIZE THE SCORE ON THE SCORING STAGE. If the composer decides to describe the sounds on the scoring stage, he should know it will take extra time, since the musicians won't be able to set up any sounds before each cue is rehearsed. The advantage of on-the-spot verbalizing is that the composer can really elaborate his image of what the sound should be like, but THE TIME LOST WHILE SEARCHING FOR THE "RIGHT" SOUND CAN DESTROY THE BUDGET.

---

[2] Yamaha's first 8-voice polyphonic synthesizer.

Maurice Jarre finds that relating his descriptions to orchestral sounds is helpful in some cases. "In electronic music, because there are limitless possibilities, you can't always exactly indicate what you want like you can with an orchestra, especially since you don't even know all the possibilities. But you *can* imagine when you compose what kind of sound you would like to write. If the part is a bass line, you might ask for a kind of classical bass. Or, you can have a woodwind bass like a bassoon or contrabassoon. Or you could also have a brass bass. So already you have three ways to explain to the musician(s) who will play the bass part what you want. So you can say, for instance, 'No, the sound is too stringy,' or, 'It's too brassy.' Unfortunately you have to go by approximation.

"After that, you can also say, 'It is a sunrise sound, it's a kind of combination of beautiful flute and oboe, but it's not really oboe and it's not really flute and it's kind of a combination of basset horn and alto flute,' for instance. And of course, you have to work with people whose imagination you trust. And also their intelligence and their culture." Notice Jarre's allusion to nature, and also to traditional orchestral instruments in unusual combination.

Composers who don't have electronic equipment available to them should make every effort to get together with the synthesists prior to the scoring session, to discuss in detail what sounds they are looking for. Most synthesists, including those who record motion-picture and television scores regularly, will be willing to take a little time to prepare for a session before recording. It takes the pressure off them and is also a big step toward artistically satisfying themselves and the composer on the date. Even a telephone conversation during which you describe the basic types of sounds you will be needing ("punchy bass lines," "silvery floating single notes," "frightening and powerful mid-range clusters") will help enormously.

BRING YOUR OWN. Without question the most fail-safe way to communicate is to bring in the sound on RAM cartridge, computer disc, or whatever. That sound can always be edited by the synthesist; in fact, unless the composer absolutely wants the specific sound he has brought in, he may find it most productive to encourage the synthesist to use the sound only as a demonstration of what he has in mind.

The well-prepared composer will find himself using a combination of all of these techniques, often during the course of a single film session.

DIFFERENT CREATIVE PROCESS. Electronic sounds usually lead a composer down a different creative path. One of the most significant changes in a composer's approach when working on electronic music is that he usually creates on the instruments for which he is composing. Few composers compose their scores on a trumpet or an oboe, but many composers use electronic instruments when composing electronically oriented cues. Burt Bacharach describes how this has affected him: "I write now with a very different process, because one hand plays a synthesizer pad, and the other hand's playing a bass pattern, and there's a drum pattern going. It's framed. That's totally different and *totally* removed from sitting at the piano, playing with both hands."

And again, the electronic colors begin to stimulate new compositional solutions, even for familiar dramatic situations. When Arthur B. Rubinstein looks back on his experience with *Blue Thunder* (1983), he is fascinated by his compositional solutions. "Because it was cast and was orchestrated first for synthesized sounds, it sounds very different than anything else I've ever done. *Very* different. And I listen to it now and I wonder: 'Where the hell did that come from?' I don't know where it came from."

DIFFERENT COMPOSITIONAL PROCESS. The electronic portion of a written score is as likely to be empty bars as a fully fleshed-out sketch. Craig Safan wrote out very little for the Synclavier sections of his score for *Remo Williams* (see Figure 15-5). William Goldstein sometimes sketches out an especially intricate part, but normally he finds it isn't necessary: "Once the basic track is down and I'm doing overdubs, that basic track is my guide." For the composer who performs his own score, that work method is typical (see the following discussion of *Where the River Runs Black*). This is, in fact, one of the stimulating things about creating electronic scores. The composer is much more able to respond to the moment of inspiration; if he does so successfully while sequencing or recording, he has just locked in a bit of his score that might not have evolved in any other environment.

Sometimes composers prepare scores for primarily electronic ensembles in basically sketch format, on three to eight staves. During the 1987 television season, Patrick Williams prepared his scores for the television series *Heart of the City* on a three- or four-line master part, "just as if it were a sketch, but it's all in concert and it just involves four lines and I bracketed things that we played on a particular keyboard." Arthur B. Rubinstein created eight-stave scores for *Blue Thunder* (1983). Depending on each cue's complexity, Maurice Jarre used between three and six staves for his totally notated electronic score for *Witness* (1985; see Figures 14-3, and 21-4, 5, 6). Instruments and colors were determined during the sessions (see the discussion below).

SIMPLICITY. Simplicity is effective in any film, but especially in electronic music. A little synth sound goes a long way, and because of its often unique coloration and potential for doubling, it not only fills a lot of space but also attracts a lot of attention. There are many moments in Alan Silvestri's electronic score for *Clan of the Cave Bear* (1986) when there are only one or two musical elements sounding at one time. Figure 21-1 illustrates how much can be expressed with this kind of simplicity. The sixteenth-note pattern looks much more complicated than it really is; it is performed on a keyboard that controls sampled vocalizing by Silvestri, and has the effect of a primitive percussion sound—an almost nonpitched rhythm.

In order to illustrate the cues from *Clan of the Cave Bear* shown in Figure 21-1, Silvestri utilized his Synclavier's notational capabilities to transcribe his previously unannotated music; this computerized transcription is reproduced in the figure.

William Goldstein's score for *oceanQuest* (1985) strikes a nice balance between the simple and the complex. In the computer-generated notation reproduced in Figure 21-2, the single line in the bass has been joined by a second part above—just two lines going.

TEXTURE. Music created with and for electronic instruments is likely to be more atmospheric than orchestral music created for the same circumstance. In this medium, texture becomes more important musically in and of itself, just because it is a more intrinsic aspect of electronic instruments. As John Cacavas points out, "That's what's happening today with all of these synthesizer scores. It's a texture, but there's no melody. It's strictly sounds, and a lot of directors like that because it doesn't get in the way of what they are doing." Although the music needn't be nonmelodic, electronic music is certainly a textural medium of expression, and texture and atmosphere are two very important cinematic factors.

RECORDING ELECTRONIC MUSIC

Many composers utilize electronic elements in their scores by only using skilled synthesists. One of the rationalizations for going no further toward owning and operating their own home studios (other than the lack of time and good keyboard technique) is that if they hire experts to provide those score elements, they will always have the very latest state-of-the-art equipment and methods, not to mention the refined skills of the synthesists.

FIGURE 21-1

Clan of the Cave Bear The Glacier Trek Alan Silvestri

FIGURE 21-1 *(Continued)*

FIGURE 21-1 *(Continued)*

28

31

FIGURE 21-2
oceanQuest **Whale One** **William Goldstein**

All excerpts from *oceanQuest* performed and printed by M.E.S.A., a software package for the IBM PC/XT/AT and the Roland MPU-401. M.E.S.A. created by composer-synthesist Kentyn Reynolds.

FIGURE 21-2 *(Continued)*

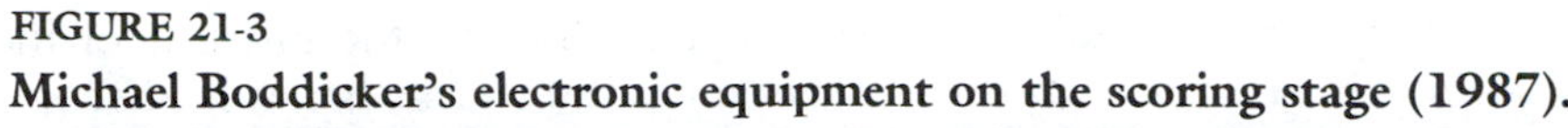

FIGURE 21-3
Michael Boddicker's electronic equipment on the scoring stage (1987).

Photo: Gay Wallin

But at the same time they are missing an opportunity to experiment in a setting that does not cost them by the minute.

Jerry Goldsmith has recorded his electronic music in every possible way over the years. He started out recording the electronic tracks first, because with the early instruments like the Arp 2600 and the Minimoog you couldn't exactly recreate electronic sounds at will, so everything would sound different in the studio. Then he began recording the electronic instruments on the scoring stage with the orchestra: "I tried balancing it acoustically with speakers on the stage along with the orchestra and it was wonderful but it was terribly costly. I tried balancing it in the headset, recording the instruments directly, and I had a mixer who was very good at doing that. But now, when you have three guys playing a MIDI stack together, sometimes I can't remember who's doing what. I find that the only way to do it is to record it and then go mix it down. Then I can go back and sweeten it myself. If I don't like the way somebody played a part I can play it myself during the mix—because the way it's played is a very personal thing. It's very hard to describe to someone how to play an electronic part. I can only tell the degree of modulation I want at the time I'm recording."

RECORDING WITH AN ELECTRONIC ENSEMBLE. Maurice Jarre decided to compose an electronic score for *Witness* (1985) because it was a cold film, and neither he nor the director, Peter Weir, wanted to express any sentimentality. Also, the Amish, main participants in the dramatic action, don't believe in playing musical instruments, and he thought the electronic approach would be sympathetic to that. Additionally, electronic instruments can sustain chords forever, which he felt would be particularly useful for this score.

He composed for six players: four keyboard players (including Michael Boddicker,

Clark Spangler, and Ian Underwood), a pianist, and Nyle Steiner, the inventor of the Electronic Woodwind Instrument (who played his invention). Jarre has since become accustomed to writing for a group like this. "What's best for me is to have an electronic ensemble. About five or six up to maybe ten people, depending on the importance of the music. And then to treat the electronics exactly like chamber music. The only difference is that instead of having a sextette at the end, you have a huge sound."

The same group was on the scoring stage for five straight days recording the score, from about nine in the morning until midnight. Synthesist Clark Spangler describes the sessions: "Maurice would say, 'I need a very large, rich bass sound, something you might associate with cellos and basses in an orchestra, very big and very rich. . . . Maurice would spend anywhere from twenty minutes to a half-hour letting us each try to outdo the other player, and the result was absolutely stunning. There was over $250,000 worth of instruments in the room, so everyone had basically everything available that they owned."

Although they could have MIDI'd themselves together in a gigantic network of keyboards, they didn't. Instead, each of the keyboard players MIDI'd within his own setup as much as he wished to get his own individual sound going for each cue. "Ian had around twenty synthesizers all MIDI'd together," Spangler recalls. He would play a note on one keyboard and this wonderful, rich wall of sound would come out. We all had a number of things we were dealing with individually. Any one of us could have made a perfectly glorious sound, but you take the dedicated focus that we each had toward making a wonderful sound, and then you put them all together and sort them out, which is what Maurice and [mixer] Humberto Gatica were doing in the booth—it was one of the nicest jobs I've ever heard."

Spangler explains that to record each cue, they performed and recorded each part separately. "We laid it down one line at a time. First the 'bass' part. Then the part that would have been played by the cellos. We went back and put parts in that you would have had there been an acoustic orchestra assigned to different parts of the orchestra. That wonderful trumpet sound—Nyle Steiner put that down by himself because there would have been a solo trumpet. So there was a strong consideration given to the difference between solo instruments and ensembles."

Jarre played back the cues every step of the way as they built the tracks. This helped the musicians enormously in shaping the coloration of the next layer of sound. And Spangler didn't feel there was a shortage of anything. "We had a luxurious adequacy of instruments and time. Everything that we wanted was there." They used every instrument but the large computer-based instruments like the Synclavier.

The score was recorded to click. If the tempo changed in the middle of a cue, the click would change also. Jarre notes that "as long as we combined that change with a streamer, then we knew when to change tempo. Either they watched the screen, or after the first rehearsal they knew the basic tempo. With a couple of rehearsals, there was no difficulty with a change of tempo."

Gatica soloed the different sounds so that each player could hear his part during a playback. This helped them to refine and shape their individual colors a little more before making another take.

The score has an atmospheric motif that is a long sustained chord (Figure 21-4), which recurs frequently during the first third of the film. The barn-raising sequence is quite orchestral in concept, and very acoustic in its effect (Figure 21-5). And the materials used for the murder sequence in the men's room, and during the shoot-out sequence at the end of the film, are more "electronic" in approach, with a sequenced moving figure (Figure 21-6).

RECORDING THE COMPOSER-PERFORMER ON THE SCORING STAGE. James Horner never likes to leave anything to chance. But he decided to work in a much more improvisatory way than usual when he scored *Where the River Runs Black* (1986). "The whole

FIGURE 21-4

Witness 1M1 Main Title Maurice Jarre

FIGURE 21-4 (*Continued*)

FIGURE 21-5

Witness **8M2 Building the Barn Maurice Jarre**

FIGURE 21-5 *(Continued)*

FIGURE 21-6

Witness 11M1 The Beginning of the End Maurice Jarre

FIGURE 21-6 *(Continued)*

FIGURE 21-6 *(Continued)*

FIGURE 21-6 *(Continued)*

score was performed by me improvising to the picture. I performed the whole score against picture, so I never prepared. I had a couple of themes, but the whole feeling of the score happened as I looked at the sequence a few times right there in the studio, and I started playing." He layered the score, track by track, in this fashion, recording onto a 32-track digital machine.

"I've never done a score like that before. When you hear it, you'll think those are all ethnic instruments. It all takes place in the Brazilian jungles so I used a lot of ethnic sounds. Panpipes, strings, plucky sounds, percussion, sparkly sounds. The whole score is electronic, including the boy soprano that I used. When I work on electronic music, very seldom do I try to get electronic-type effects, unless I'm asked for them. I try to get effects that sound like instruments. Not so much instruments where I am replacing a violin but instruments where you could say, 'What a marvelous wind instrument of some kind.' I did a lot of preprogramming and working out stuff. I was working with Michael Boddicker and Ian Underwood, who were my programmers, or helped me program."

Horner only used a sequencer for one cue, for some repetitive note patterns. The rest was all performed in real time, pass by pass. "Then I'd say, 'I don't like that performance, let's go back.' We'd do it again or punch in and get it just right." This is exactly the way most solo composer-performers work in their home studios, although they often put much of the music on sequencer, even on a real-time basis, before going to tape.

The cues had from 1 or 2 or 3 tracks to as many as 28 or 30 tracks. It took Horner two weeks in the studio to complete the composing/recording of the 50-minute score. He used the Kurzweil, the DX7, the Oberheim Matrix-12, and a few other instruments, including the Emulator occasionally. And he did use an acoustic French horn. "The French horn is impossible to re-create really beautifully because of the way it's played."

RECORDING THE COMPOSER-PERFORMER IN A HOME STUDIO. William Goldstein works alone at home when he composes and records an electronic score. He sequences on a computer, and has used the M.E.S.A. program by Roland. "The number of tracks is virtually unlimited because you have the ability to merge tracks endlessly, and you also have the ability to go back and separate a merged track. This is all restricted by the 16 MIDI channels. You might use 20 tracks, but they are all on one MIDI channel. So you can have as many tracks times 16 as you want to work with."

On the NBC-TV project *oceanQuest* (1985) Goldstein created a totally electronic score, with no sampling. He records almost everything in 1/4 meter, so that his sync box and sequencer always read out what beat he's at (because the sequencer numbers measures sequentially, and in 1/4 meter every beat is a measure). "I can record in 1/4 and change it into 4/4 later. For editing purposes, if you want to make an insert at a certain beat, it's best to be working in something like 1/4 or 1/8 in that you can start recording very easily at any particular point. And also, of course, with the computer sequencer, you can do a passage that might be great and if there are two or three wrong notes, you don't have to rerecord it. You can just change the two or three wrong notes." Working this way, he uses the click as a reference, not a locked-in tempo guide. "Half of the time I don't even listen to the click. I play free time against the click. It is a reference and editing point, and I don't pay attention to it as far as tempo goes."

He finds signal processing a significant aspect of electronic individuality. "That's a way to get really unique sounds. Everybody is using the same hardware, but there are so many different parameters that can be controlled by signal processing. Like certain phasing or flanging things. Lately, I've been experimenting a lot with delays. Not simple delays, but I've been using the Lexicon PCM-70s. I have a pair of them. They have what they call pan delays, circular delays, and quadra delays, and you hit one tone and the PCM-70 does different things to the sound. Now, JUST LISTENING TO ONE OF THESE EFFECTS IMMEDIATELY GIVES YOU COMPOSITIONAL IDEAS. That is something that is very interesting with electronics. You will come up with things that you would not conceive sitting and writing for an orchestra because you only conceive of it because they occur and you notice them."

Goldstein's days are usually long ones, typically true for a composer/performer. "What I like to do is start working around ten in the morning ideally, and work into the evening, and then just knock off. But most of the time, because of short writing schedules, I'll take a dinner break and come back to work, and work to maybe eleven at night." He doesn't like to schedule more than one to one-and-a-half minutes a day of composing and recording, and often plans on much less.

He mixes down directly without going to multitrack tape. His final medium is a digital master 2-track, either stereo or mono, on videocassette. The notation for an electronic score doesn't show the signal processing, of course, but it does show how linear the music is (Figures 21-7 and 21-8). His score for *oceanQuest* became a record released by CBS Records, retitled "Oceanscape."

PRERECORDING ELECTRONIC TRACKS. The reasons for taking the time and effort to prerecord electronic material prior to a live scoring session are creative control, cost control, technical necessity, and the opportunity for more give and take with the filmmakers than recording *all* of the music electronically in a nonscoring environment that excludes the filmmakers.

By prerecording, the composer really controls the electronic elements of his score. He can fine-tune the colors he wants. He can try things out experimentally without worrying about the thirty (or seventy) musicians sitting idle while he appears to be "wasting" half an hour wrestling with an idea that doesn't work. He can refine the electronic parts so they are as flawless as possible. There are many electronic ideas that simply cannot be recorded well in a commercial studio environment without impractical delays. The parts may be too difficult to play well live in the studio; they may be ideally suited for a sequencer-enhanced performance, where you can slow the sequencer down while sequencing to make an impossible passage playable. Or the use of effects may be a key element in the composition, and the composer will want to control each color's individual rate of delay, time of decay, and so on, and he will need to hear all these instruments on the session with orchestra to know that the orchestral parts are really working properly with the film. The scoring session will be the only opportunity to check everything against film, so these effects must be prerecorded.

Some things to remember when prerecording tracks:

1. If the medium is 24 tracks on two-inch tape, use a standard two-inch tape like Ampex 456, and notify the studio so they can align their machines for that specific tape.

2. Isolate the click track from tracks where it might "bleed" and be audible. To do that, record the click on one of the oustide tracks.

3. Record two bars of solo click before the cue begins. Otherwise you won't have any warning clicks and you won't be able to overdub on the first downbeat.

4. Record the master sync pulse on one of the higher outside tracks (this will be SMPTE or some other sync pulse, and could be generated by the sequencer, the drum machine, or a sync box); record a SMPTE sync pulse (if you need it for video sync, for example) next to the master pulse (if the master is not already SMPTE) or leave a track open for the studio to add SMPTE; record a 60-cycle sync pulse to ensure that the studio's two-inch tape recorder runs at exactly the same speed as the machine on which the pre-record tracks were made. A good distribution of these pulses is: sequencer pulse (if not SMPTE), track 22; SMPTE, track 23; 60-cycle pulse, track 24.

5. If the medium is half-inch 16-track, or a one-inch format, make the necessary arrangements to transfer your prerecorded track to a two-inch copy for the overdubbing session. You may have to bring your own machine into the studio if the studio where you record doesn't have one and you can't rent one.

6. Prepare track sheets for the studio recording mixer indicating what instruments are on which prerecorded tracks.

7. Save enough tracks for the rest of the orchestra, keeping in mind any instruments that will take up two tracks because of stereo or a separate effect track.

8. Record reference tones at the beginning of the tape, so the studio will know what the volume frame of reference was for the prerecord.

9. Bring the tape in to the studio tails out;[3] otherwise, you are starting out unprofessionally, and it may be more difficult to win the professional endorsement of the crew.

10. Check with the studio to be sure there are enough high-quality headsets for the orchestra.

11. Check with the studio also to be sure there is a flexible cue system for feeding information to the headsets. This is especially important when you are overdubbing, because some members of the orchestra may wish to hear only click, while others may want all the prerecorded tracks.

12. Get the master tape to the studio early enough for the crew to prepare for scoring. If you haven't recorded SMPTE, they may have to add it to sync up with video. Or they may have to check out the cue starts to learn exactly how to roll the tape in sync with the picture. This takes time.

13. Give the studio all timing (or sync) information necessary to help them sync up the prerecorded two-inch tape with picture. If the music editor is responsible for this, be sure he has done so.

---

[3] Having been played but not rewound.

FIGURE 21-7
oceanQuest Night Dream William Goldstein

FIGURE 21-8
oceanQuest Oceanscape William Goldstein

PREPROGRAMMING ELECTRONIC TRACKS. Patrick Williams preprogrammed tracks on a sequencer for the 1987 television series *Heart of the City* and then brought three or four synthesists onto the scoring stage to complete his score for each week's episode. By doing this, he was able to engage the producer and director in a dialogue about the scores that would have been impossible had he completed the electronic scores without the chance to play the works in progress for them on the scoring stage. Whether the composer actually prerecords to tape, or simply preprograms a sequencer, the process is very time consuming. In a twelve-hour day he was able to actually record just 8 to 10 minutes of score. Then he had to mix it all down.

RECORDING ELECTRONIC MUSIC LIVE. Here is a checklist for the composer who is going to conduct an electronic-music session with other musicians in a more traditional scoring-stage environment:

1. Be sure the instruments you are writing for are being brought to the session by the keyboard players; if not, make arrangements through your contractor or directly with an instrument rental company to be certain everything is there you need. Don't forget an **effects rack**[4] if needed.
2. Ideally, discuss key sounds with the session synthesists so they can help you create what you need if necessary.
3. Bring the other sounds you are counting on, or be prepared to explain exactly what you want to the musicians.
4. Schedule extra time for the sessions; it takes *much* longer to record a demanding electronic score than an acoustic one.
5. If mixing down after the sessions, try to record any special effects (digital delay, and so on) on separate tracks for complete control later. Otherwise, consider waiting for mix-down to add these effects.
6. To take full advantage of this kind of session, the composer should be open to adventure and accident; it's the nature of the experience, and the best results may include significant contributions from the musicians.
7. Plan the distribution of tracks for each cue before the session so you don't get caught short; if there aren't enough tracks for the material, consider mixing MIDI'd parts onto one track during the session if necessary.
8. Bring emergency telephone numbers for all technical assistance, so you know whom to call and how to reach them if necessary. It's easy to become a victim of malfunctioning electronic equipment if you are not prepared, and that can be a real nightmare.

RECORDING IN A HOME STUDIO

Recording in a home studio can be terrific. In that environment it is possible to enjoy the greatest control and the greatest freedom. Under ideal conditions, working in someone else's home studio is a close second in this department. Many composers who have tried working this way like to work alone as much of the time as possible, often without even a recording mixer to work with them. Jan Hammer can't imagine it any other way: "The way I work is very instinctive and experimental; I try lots of different

[4] Effects rack: rack-mounted group of electronic signal-processing machines, including a digital reverb and digital delay units, and so on.

things. It's like, Throw it up against the wall and see what sticks, and much of it sounds very mundane. I could not do that very freely with someone just sitting here doing a job, like watching the meters. I would feel that I was being judged, with the direct result being that I wouldn't really let go."[5]

HOW TO MAKE IT WORK FOR YOU. All this talk about freedom and relaxation can be misleading in one sense. Working this way requires an enormous amount of focus and discipline. Think about it—how else would the composer-performer know what instrument was on which track; what patch the DX7II played on cue 7M2; what the length of decay was on the digital reverb used on the solo guitar; on which bank he could find the "modified Kalimba"; at which precise SMPTE code number each cue started? And that's not all by any means. Organizational skills and fanatic note taking are absolute musts for success in this type of creative atmosphere. EVERYTHING MUST BE LOGGED. EVERYTHING RECORDED ON COMPUTERS MUST BE SAVED AND BACKED UP WITH A SECOND COPY.

GEARING UP. It is best to invest in equipment bit by bit if possible. It is just too much to assimilate everything that is going on in electronic music without some period of time to become familiar with both the sound and the potential of everything that's out there. Learning about one instrument at a time is advisable, and doing a little analog synthesis before beginning with FM is a good idea.

Learning the specific instruments as you acquire them is a must. The composer should first audition the instruments he will be purchasing, either at a friend's house or a music store. He should know what the instrument can do and what it can sound like. If not, he may find himself in the position of one composer who frantically called the owner of the store that sold him a DX7 manufactured for sale in Japan.[6] Having saved several hundred dollars on the purchase, he had not tried out the instrument before getting it home. He had just plugged it in, turned on the power, and was going through the cartridges of factory preset sounds. He was appalled to find out that almost every sound on the instrument had a decidedly "Japanese" flavor, with a heavy, wide but quick vibrato that sounded like a caricature of a koto. But he figured this was the "Japanese version" of the sounds. When he brought the instrument back to the store for them to look at, he was told the modulation wheel had been accidentally rotated and was actually modulating the sounds, giving them all that crazy vibrato.

It's a good idea to get some one-on-one instruction on every new instrument and piece of equipment in the studio.

PLANNING THE WORK ENVIRONMENT. Although it is well beyond the scope of this book to discuss acoustics, sound insulation, and other engineering refinements, two aspects of the work environment are very important and should be incorporated into the earliest planning stages. They are proper ventilation and comfortable lighting. The more successful you are in creating an airtight and consequently soundproof room, the more important ventilation becomes. Either a sufficient exhaust fan with a separate intake duct, or an air conditioning unit is a crucial part of the studio design. As for lighting, you simply can't work without it.

SETTING IT UP. No matter how simple or elaborate, there are certain constants in setting up an electronic studio. The most basic principle is that the audio and digital

---

[5]© 1987 *Electronic Musician,* interview by Craig Anderton (March, 1987, pp. 52 ff.).

[6]A so-called "gray market" machine, sold by an unauthorized dealer.

information travels through cables to get from one electronic device to another. This may seem simplistic, but everything that goes on in the studio follows from this fact. This creates a lot of cabling, even in an eight-track studio with two synths and a sequencer. If care isn't taken, it may not be possible to walk around in a 24-track room without tripping on the cabling. If you break the chain you are off the air.

Some tips:

1. If at all possible, bring in a separate electrical feed from the main electrical line for the studio equipment. Since you are at home, the studio must at the very least be on different circuits than the air conditioner, refrigerator, and clothes dryer. All computerized equipment has a fairly narrow range of optimum efficiency with regard to voltage requirements. A sudden increase in voltage is a "surge," which can blow fuses and cause loss of computer memory (including any sequencer memory). If the voltage becomes too low the equipment may begin to act very strangely. A synth may begin to detune and change patches with voltage variations. Use surge suppressors as an added precaution.

2. Organize the room for maximum use of the space, and for working comfort. It is very easy to let things pile up. It's natural to bring in a new instrument, attach the cables and get it tied into the system as quickly as possible. Before you know it things begin to stack up, taking up much-needed space. Without precautions, notes (about track information, patches, MIDI, and special effects), manuals, and cartridges will start to get lost and cables will be impossible to trace. Plan things out and save the aggravation.

3. Find one technician to help set up the studio and explain how everything works. Every board has its idiosyncrasies, and recording setups can be very personal. It helps to have a technician who has worked with the room from the outset, who therefore knows the equipment, and who cares. If you don't have someone who will pick up your call at midnight on those occasions when it is really an emergency and the tape recorder won't go into the record mode, you may find your professional reputation in jeopardy.

4. Label *everything*. Period. Every sloppy habit you ever had will haunt you while you are sequencing and recording. The white three-quarter-inch tape used in studios to write on with a magic marker is fine for labeling cables. Just cut a two-inch piece and fold it back on itself around a cable and then write on it for identification. Each end of each cable should have a track number, a MIDI IN, MIDI THRU, or MIDI OUT label, or some other reference like SYNC IN or CLICK OUT.

5. Color code some of the MIDI cables. The permanent cables can be a dark, blending color like brown or black. But the one cable used for the master IN/OUT sequencer cable should be an assertive, one-of-a-kind color. Label one end MIDI OUT, which will go into the MIDI OUT port of whichever instrument you are sequencing at the moment. Label the other end MIDI IN, which will usually be a permanent cable to the MIDI IN port of the sequencer (or computer, if that is functioning as the sequencer). POSSIBLY THE MOST FREQUENT AND ANNOYING SIMPLE MISTAKE IS TO FORGET TO ATTACH THE MIDI OUT TO THE CURRENT INSTRUMENT BEING SEQUENCED. The result—another great performance goes to MIDI heaven. Unless the studio is set up so that one specific keyboard is a dedicated controller for all the keyboards in the studio, this cable will be moved more often than any other, so the chances are great of overlooking this simple necessity. A MIDI patching bay with preset patching routes is a help. (But keep notes.)

MIDI/SMPTE SETUP. Figure 21-9, reproduced from *The MIDI Home Studio,* by Howard Massey, shows a typical MIDI and audio routing to set up a MIDI studio with video-sync capabilities using SMPTE time code. The SMPTE controls the sequencer playback and the audio-tape playback.

In this setup, your videotape dub should have been striped with SMPTE time code on one of the audio channels when the dub was made. The SMPTE generator/converter reads the SMPTE on the videotape and regenerates it onto one track of the multitrack audio tape. (It is regenerated to assure a readable signal.) Then the converter receives the SMPTE from the videotape and controls the sequencer. It also sends SMPTE simultaneously to the transport controller, which locks the multitrack tape recorder with the video. With this system, you can start the videotape anywhere in a cue and the multitrack recorder will seek the appropriate position on the videotape and lock into sync.

USING THE STUDIO. Working in an electronic studio can quickly turn into an intense love/hate relationship. You love it, but if anything malfunctions one more time you are definitely going to chain saw all the cables. There is only one way to survive in this working environment—establish a routine and develop a series of absolutely inviolable work methods. These methods include proper note-taking, the routine procedures for operating each piece of equipment, and those required for the recording process. It sounds easy enough, but it requires a will of iron.

We recommend that the following be made an everyday part of the studio routine:

1. *Never* remove a cable without labeling it and making a note of where it came from and why. Maintain a special area for these notes.

2. Take notes about everything. It will help if you create a special form for recording track sheets and for sequencer-track information. These can then be photocopied and kept available. Keep records about patch numbers for each part, patch edits, sequencer-track information, signal processing, cue numbers and tempos, exact SMPTE code readings for all video cue ins and outs (often difficult to locate a week later), all MIDI information, and any malfunctioning equipment so a tech can fix the problems.

3. Learn how to connect everything in the studio. No one should rely on a mixer or technician to do this. If you do, you're helpless when he's unavailable.

4. Maintain and clean equipment regularly (recorder heads, board faders, and so on) and keep a notebook of maintenance records.

5. Set levels and record reference tones before beginning each new project. This is particularly necessary if you will be taking your master tape to another studio for overdubs. Your technician is the person to help you establish this routine.

6. Use the digital electronic tuner before each new pass with a new patch. Don't assume that just because you tuned an instrument with one patch that another patch will be in tune—they frequently are not.

7. If you start the sequencer or begin to play and nothing happens—check the following:
   (a) Is the master MIDI OUT in the right instrument?
   (b) Are all other MIDI cables inserted in the correct terminals? There is no standardization of where these terminals are located on equipment, so it is easy to make a mistake and plug in to MIDI THRU thinking it is MIDI OUT, or any other permutation. (Keep a small mirror and penlight to read those devilish labels on the backs of instruments in racks.)
   (c) Are all audio cables attached correctly? Did you unplug anything recently?
   (d) Are all power cables still plugged in, and are all power lights on?

If the system is still not functioning, then try some modest troubleshooting. If you don't seem to be recording on the sequencer, change to a different track on the sequencer. If you are sequencing a synth part that doesn't seem to be recording, maybe it *is* recording but it is not playing back properly. To check that out, play back on that same synth any other track that you know has information on it. If it plays back, then the problem is in the recording. If it doesn't play back, then you know

FIGURE 21-9
MIDI/audio-signal routing using SMPTE time code.

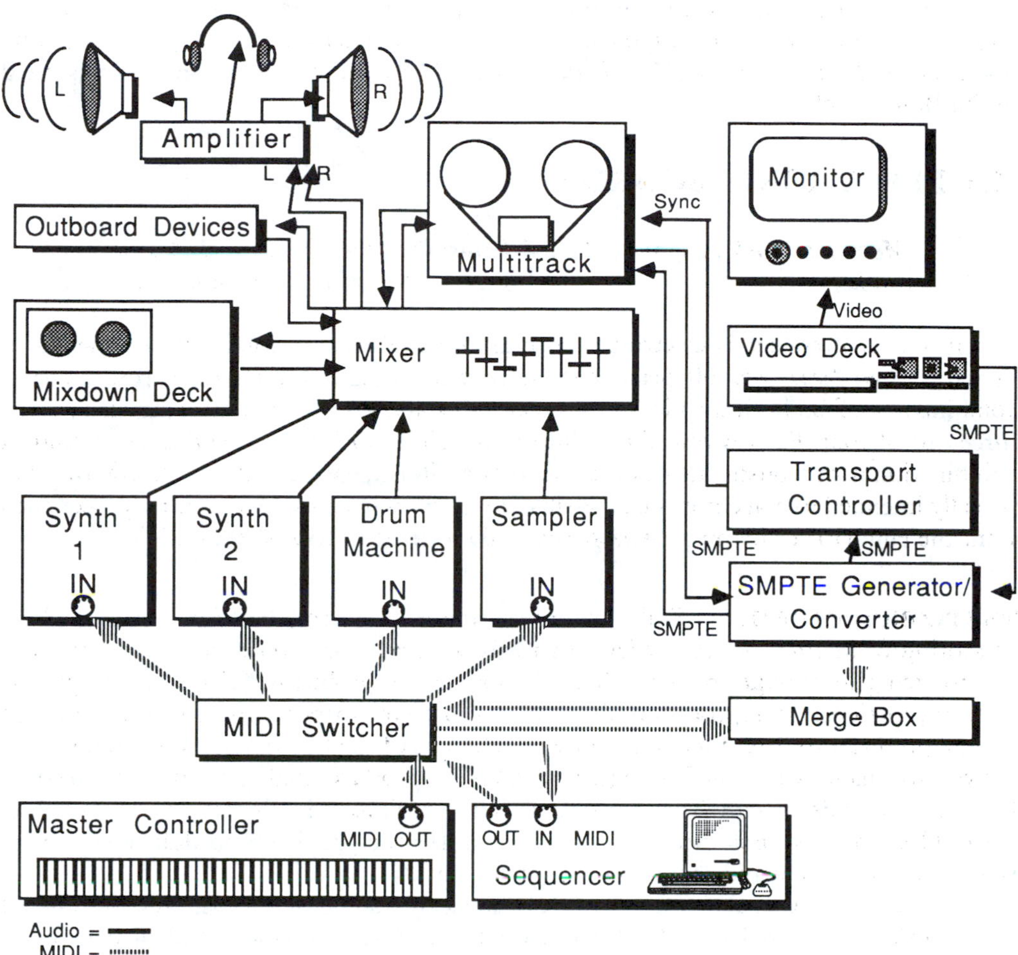

Reprinted with permission from *The MIDI Home Studio.* © 1988 AMSCO Publications.

it might be *recording* correctly, in which case the problem might be in the playback chain. It doesn't take a technician to figure out these things, but it does require developing a way of thinking about the chain of events that takes place in a MIDI studio. This skill definitely improves with experience.

Try calling the manufacturer if there seems to be a malfunction in a specific piece of equipment. All manufacturers have technical help available by phone during business hours. Sometimes their products have individual peculiarities that aren't even mentioned in their manuals. And sometimes the instrument is just going through a revision to remedy this very problem. It may be a software revision, or a new chip or board that the company will retrofit (sometimes without charge). You'll never know if you don't call.

One bit of advice sometimes given by even the most experienced technicians is this: as a last resort, turn off everything, disconnect all cables, and start over again. Sometimes there is simply no explaining why things grind to a halt, but this does happen. The slightest misalignment in connecting two cables can be enough to stop you cold. You may need to try new cables if they are being moved a lot—even cables can fail.

One final caveat: no food, no drinks, no smoking in the studio. They are the natural enemies of electronic studios.

For more detailed information on the components of a MIDI studio and what to look for when investing in equipment, see reference materials such as Howard Massey's book, *The MIDI Home Studio* (New York: Amsco, 1988), and consult the periodicals listed in the Bibliography.

THE PREVALENCE OF ELECTRONIC SCORING

> ***Most of the work I do,*** most ***of it for the last five years, has been electronic music.***
> DON MACDOUGALL, DUBBING MIXER

Just how prevalent is electronic scoring? Agent Richard Emler reports that, as of January 1989, "*way* over 50 percent is electronic, and if not totally electronic, then a combination of both electronic and acoustic. I would say, from our experience, easily three out of four. Even within the realm of television movies. The synthesizer sound or combination with acoustic instruments is way over 50 percent. And the orchestral overdub is really intended to make it more accessible. Even in these cases, however, they frequently want the emphasis to be on a *contemporary,* radio-oriented, Top-40 sound."

THE ECONOMICS OF IT. Emler observes a tremendous growth of interest in this kind of scoring from 1986 on. He believes that this is an economic reflection of the business of producing low-budget pictures. But this does create problems. "There are simply too many inexperienced composers out there willing to do the work inexpensively. It's difficult for the producer to determine in advance the abilities of the less-experienced composer to deliver the quality score his film requires. When the producer makes the wrong selection, he frequently ends up with little or no money left to replace an ineffective score. Therefore, it would seem to be most desirable for everyone for the producers to deal directly with reputable agents, to avoid these costly misjudgments."

Emler isn't happy about the economic squeeze, and sometimes makes low-budget deals work with a "back-end deal" that gives the composer various residual benefits in addition to his up-front package fee. (See Chapter 27, "The Business".)

William Goldstein, who does electronic scores as well as acoustic scores, hopes that the producer's criteria for asking for an electronic score will be aesthetic, not economic. However, he acknowledges the temptation for the producer. "Certainly, economically, in the real world, there are going to be a lot of scores done this way because people don't have the money for an orchestra." And he speculates that these scores will be delivered by new composers eager for such an opportunity.

On the other hand, Maurice Jarre was on the scoring stage for five full days recording his totally electronic score for *Witness*. Recording the score this way cost Paramount as much as recording the score with a conventional 100-piece orchestra for two or three days. In this case, the reasons for using electronic colors were purely artistic.

THE NEW TECHNOLOGY

Today, you can ask for incredible finesse and subtleties with whatever is being played. CLARK SPANGLER, SYNTHESIST

Beyond the machines, you better have a solid song, a solid melody. BURT BACHARACH

To the extent that the lightning-fast technological developments continue to serve the musicians and composers for whom they are marketed, they are a fantasy come true. Philosophical and ethical considerations aside, the higher the tech, the greater the potential for fulfilling artistic aspiration within the strict confines of time and money.

Mozart wrote in his head, and Beethoven couldn't even hear when he wrote his Ninth Symphony. Their talents certainly weren't diminished without the benefit of all of our contemporary technology. But there is no denying the ongoing legacy that the technological revolution has bestowed us with: a vastly expanded range of textures and sounds at our fingertips; the convenience of devices like sequencers and MIDI, **modems**[7] and SMPTE; and the stimulation of it all.

As Bill Conti says, "I was never a resister, but I remember when the things first came out, I was kind of slow to buy. But once you bought, my God, you never came out of the room. Because sound interests us. We deal in that. So it's got to be a turn on. It's great."

Burt Bacharach wonders about the impact of it all: "I don't know, once you switch to machines, how much difference that makes. This great year that Carole and I have had [1986]—two number-one records back to back. Would it all have been possible without the machines?" Having worked with the new technology, many other film composers and songwriters must be asking the same question of their own work—would it all have been possible without the machines?

[7] Modems: telecommunication hookups that allow computer information to be sent and received through the telephone system.

CHAPTER 22

CONTEMPORARY SCORING

The producers don't want it to sound dated. They want it fresh, unique, and to have a today sound. RICHARD EMLER, AGENT

In the film and television world, "contemporary music" never refers to a symphonic or avant-garde style. The term includes the current or "today" sounds and also styles of any given moment in time. The style may be truly current, like disco when it first came to the States from Europe, or folk rock, punk rock and new wave, which were current at the time they became fashionable. Or the style may be a historical resurrection or updating, like the rebirth of pop music from the fifties and sixties. All pop idioms are potentially contemporary—rock, jazz, blues, fusion, punk, disco, heavy metal, folk, country, techno, electronic. It happens that these idioms also have a common element—the rhythm section (keyboards, guitars, basses, drums, and percussion). Without the use of some of these instruments, the score will not likely be regarded as contemporary. Whether the rhythm section plays as a unit or more soloistically is immaterial. Used properly these instruments can make even a symphonic score sound contemporary.

At any given time the current popular success of an artist (for instance, Isaac Hayes—*Shaft,* 1971), group (Tangerine Dream—*Thief,* 1981), or style (disco—*Saturday Night Fever,* 1977) can and does influence the tastes of producers and directors. For filmmakers in the mid-eighties, "contemporary" began to mean synthesizer-oriented pop and/or rock, because that sound was current. But when a producer or director talks about wanting a contemporary score, that is rarely enough information for a composer. He will still need the same sort of clear communication as for any other project; in this case, the names of specific groups and their specific albums and tracks that are most relevant.

USING CONTEMPORARY RHYTHM SECTIONS

There are several basic guidelines for writing for contemporary rhythm sections:

1. Give them bass lines and a well-planned structure.
2. Give them freedom.
3. Tell them the style you are going for.

GIVE THEM BASS LINES AND A STRUCTURE. When Mike Post and Pete Carpenter began their collaboration, Carpenter was an experienced orchestral and film composer. But he didn't have any experience with rock and other contemporary idioms. Post remembers, "Pete would ask if we should give the rhythm section a chord sheet and I'd say, 'No, you've got to be specific with the rhythm section. Don't be afraid of them.'" This is sound advice. The composer must let the rhythm section know what he expects from them, both musically and stylistically. This may be done verbally, with a description of style and content, or may be done with musical notation and rhythms.

Writing the bass line guarantees a certain compatibility between those instrumental parts that may be partially improvised (perhaps with the right hand of a keyboard chording) and those that are more completely written out. It guarantees that any important accents will be picked up in the bass and other low-end instruments. Drums and percussion should also have all these accents. These notations will make the rhythm section sound tight and together quickly (see Figure 22-1).

The film composer is responsible for creating the important compositional material. The rhythm-section musicians, working with the composer to make the best of any given situation, may improve the materials significantly, but at least the composer will have given them an appropriate starting point. The musicians will be more inclined to bring their own suggestions to the project if they know the composer has put his best efforts into planning the score properly. They are used to contributing—composers count on that. As composer/keyboardist Michael Melvoin sees it, "I believe that the habitual creation of thematic material is what makes the top sidemen *premium* players."

GIVE THEM FREEDOM. On the other hand, don't restrict them by overwriting. In any rhythm-oriented style, if you write everything, the performance may sound stiff and nonidiomatic. Even in bands like Chicago, Yellow jackets, or Maynard Ferguson, although the brass and saxes may be totally written, the rhythm parts give the players a lot of freedom. In general, it's best to allow the rhythm players a chance to bring their authority and passion to the project. The goal is to give them all the direction necessary to ensure the proper results, but let them be as free as possible so they can add the style and flavor of the idiom.

FIGURE 22-1

Rhythm section example.

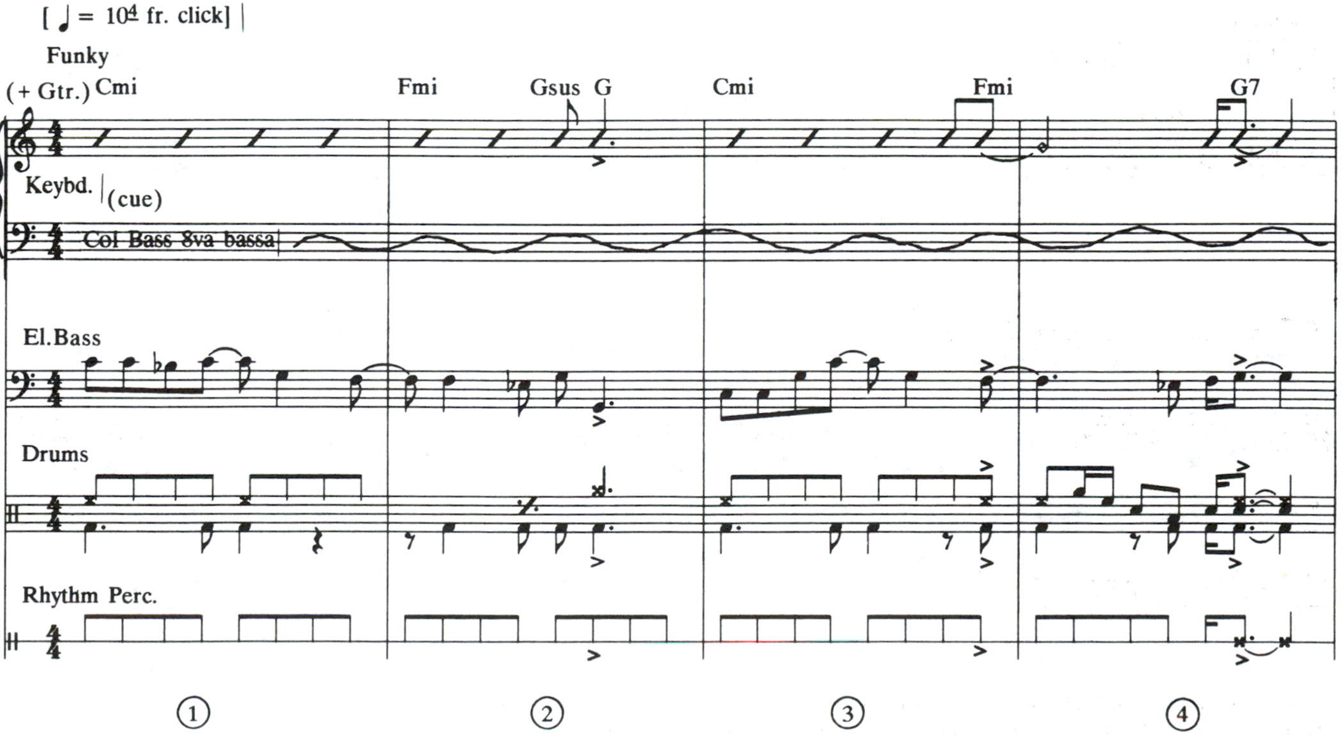

The theme for the television series *Simon and Simon* (by Barry De Vorzon and Michael Towers) begins with rhythm section. The only written parts are the melody (cued in guitars, pedal steel guitar, and piano) and the guitar counterline rhythm (which establishes the overall feel of the piece). The two guitars, pedal steel, piano, and bass all have chord symbols, and that was all they needed (Figure 22-2).

In chases and other extremely rhythm-oriented cues, the entire rhythm section may be playing from nothing more than chord symbols and rhythm slashes. If their functions have been defined, this will probably work out better than anything the composer could write, and will take him much less time. But where their function should be more compositional, their parts will normally be more completely notated. Switching back and forth between written-out parts and chord symbols can be a very effective technique.

TELL THEM THE STYLE. Without question the most effective way for the composer to describe to the rhythm section what he has in mind is through the use of examples; a specific artist, even a specific song, will tell them *exactly* what is expected. The best rhythm-section players are so knowledgeable, in fact, that they can often recognize which

FIGURE 22-2

Simon and Simon **Theme** **Barry DeVorzon and Michael Towers**
Orchestrated by Joseph Conlan

role model the composer is thinking about just from chord symbols. Michael Melvoin speaks as both composer and studio player: "There are a variety of approaches to film writing. And some of them really still just apply a particular style or apply a particular arranging approach or keyboard approach or synthesizer approach from a particular kind of record, or maybe even a specific record, implicit or explicit. Sometimes you can just read a lead sheet and know that the unspoken menu of the day is Prince and 'Keep Us Out of Court.' And then you begin to apply stylistic knowledge that fills that in. But what you're seeing in front of you is a lead sheet." In such a case, indicating "Like 'Keep Us Out of Court,' by Prince" will leave nothing to chance. It is also a good idea to have an audiocassette of the record and a portable cassette player at the session just in case one of the musicians doesn't know the record.

KNOW THE STYLE. The effective composer of contemporary scores is aware of the trademarks that distinguish various styles with which he is working. For example, there are specific idiomatic approaches to heavy-metal guitar that are unique to that style. The composer must be able to lead a rhythm-section musician in the right direction if necessary. He may often find himself suggesting that a certain slide, bend, fall-off, or tone color ***not*** be used for a particular cue because it is not quite the style he had in mind. Stylistic nuances can be very important in film music, and the composer will want to retain control of these elements. And you can't do that unless you have studied the records and know the style.

WRITE FOR THE PLAYER. It helps if you know who is going to be playing a guitar or keyboard part. Individual musicians have their strengths and weaknesses, and when you know their playing you can approach their parts with them in mind. "The great writers write within the capabilities of the player, or write into the strong suit of a player," Melvoin says. If the composer is relying on a friend or contractor to recommend the rhythm-section musicians, he should ask as many questions as possible about their reading, their solos, their stylistic preferences and strengths. Even hearing a tape of their work is a good idea, if one is available.

ELECTRONIC TECHNIQUES

Everything we have discussed about electronic music is relevant to contemporary scoring. Remember that although the use of the rhythm section is necessary to give the score a contemporary feel, that doesn't mean that the composer must have drums and a bass part playing "time" on every cue. It is in fact the judicious mix of rhythm section and nonrhythm section scoring that will add drama and a cinematic flavor to the score. Scores in which the rhythm section plays continuously can get repetitive very quickly, or, even worse, can lose their effectiveness long before the final chase.

SEQUENCING. Several electronic techniques are especially useful in contemporary scoring, but perhaps none more so than sequencing. We have discussed the use of a sequencer to record information played directly on a keyboard in real time. There are two other possibilities, both of which offer the opportunity to perform superhuman passages: slowing down the tempo, so that the sequencer records the live performance slower than the final tempo, and programming the music into the sequencer step by step (that is, note by note).

QUANTIZING. This technique is particularly effective for repeated notes and other repetitive figurations. The word "techno" as in "techno-pop" implies the use of these technically precise figurations played by crisp electronic colors.

We have mentioned that Alan Silvestri recorded the drums and percussion for *Romancing the Stone* (1983) on a preprogrammed LinnDrum live with large orchestra, using Garfield's Doctor Click to keep everything in sync, but this procedure can be technically problematic (Figure 22-3). Hollywood synthesists bring their own sync boxes with them so that the click will activate their equipment in sync with the orchestra (and each other). In general, it takes less time on the scoring stage if you have prerecorded all sequences, as James Horner did for the many sequenced passages in *Commando* (1981; Figure 22-4). Horner's simple bass line ostinato allows for a variety of motifs and textures above it, in any style he chooses; even ethnic elements are used to color the score.

DRUM MACHINES. Many contemporary scores (and records) use electronic drums (like the Simmons drums) and drum machines for rhythm and percussion. The machines are usually preprogrammed by the composer and, like sequencers, are often prerecorded as well. The reader is referred to Silvestri's soundtrack for *Outrageous Fortune* (1987) as an example of a score that uses primarily electronic drums for several cues.

When Stewart Copeland (formerly of the rock group Police) was considering his basic concept for the television series *The Equalizer,* he discussed his ideas with Universal TV Music Executive Brendon Cahill. Cahill recalls: "It was my first introduction to a totally percussion-oriented score which was accented with electronics. I remember Stewart saying to me, 'Wait till you you hear this Main Title—it's going to be like 16 drums, and it's going to pop the tape.' I said, 'Stewart—this is television.' He said, 'I'm going to take chances.' And he did, in spite of the fact that it was so foreign to what normal scoring is."

FIGURE 22-3
Romancing the Stone 5M2 Boo Alan Silvestri

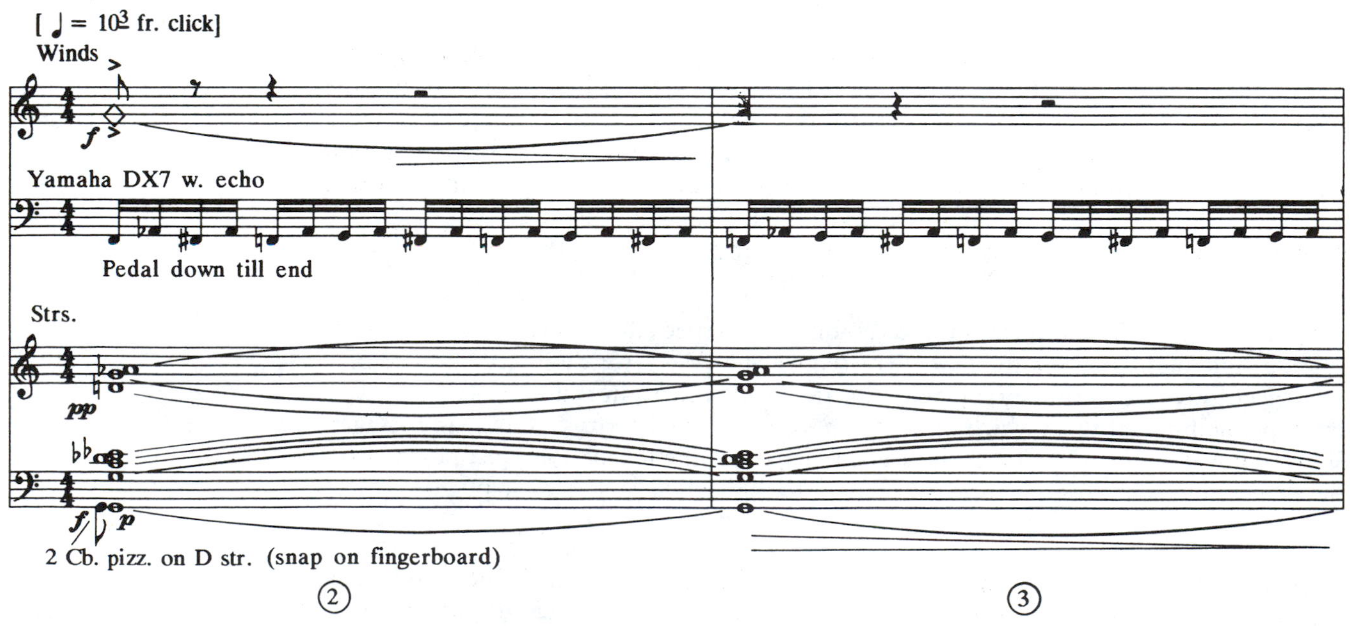

FIGURE 22-3 (*Continued*)

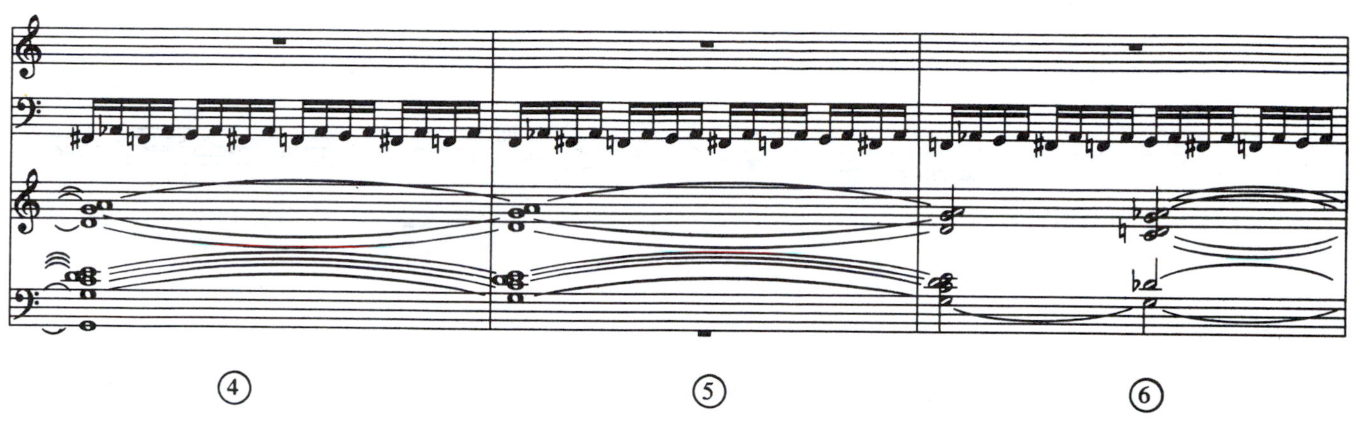

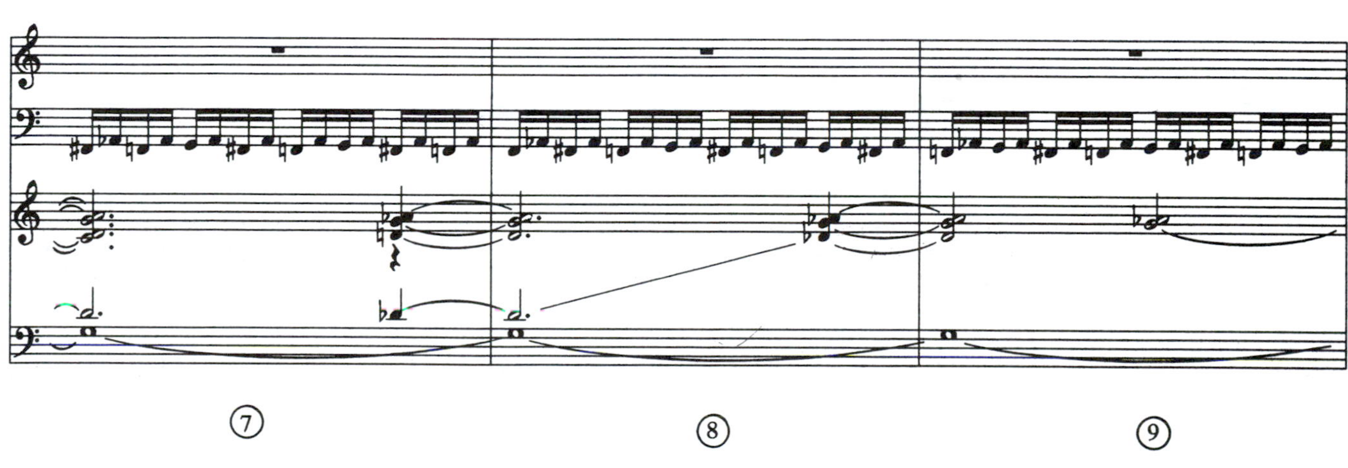

FIGURE 22-4

Commando R1 P4 James Horner

Variable click [♩= 10 3/5]

Synth. I

mf

(Seq.)

① ② ③ ④

Gtr.

Dmi

f

3 Tbns. (Tune dividers)

f

B. Tbn. +Tuba

Chimes

Tam Tam

Hi Hat

Acoustic Drs.

Splash

Sn.

Simmons Drs.

f

Vlns. 8va

ppp *mp*

Synth II

f

(Seq.)

(Seq.)

⑤ ⑥ ⑦ ⑧

CONTEMPORARY SCORES

The written note means less with any kind of contemporary score than with symphonic scoring. Contemporary scores *can* be fully notated, but there is just no way to notate the excitement and the color of idiomatic music, or the performance interpretations so crucial to a contemporary score's final impact. The examples that follow suggest the range of expression possible with a contemporary approach.

AMERICAN GIGOLO. Giorgio Moroder's score for *American Gigolo* (1980), the story of a male prostitute (Richard Gere), is an example of a very straightforward use of synths and rhythm. Moroder's contemporary electronic approach gives the score the raw edge of realism. Blending the score with a song at the beginning ("Call Me") and appropriate source music here and there gives the overall effect further credibility. Bob Badami, music editor on the project, explains Moroder's work methods: "Occasionally Moroder will play bass or something like that. But he has a keyboardist, generally, who plays all the synthesizer parts, who would be the equivalent of an orchestrator. And sometimes they'll bring in a guitarist or any kind of specialty. *American Gigolo* was pre–drum machine so he had a live drummer on that, but ever since he's used the drum machines." The music is by and large very simple, and looks even more so on paper (Figure 22-5).

TOOTSIE. Dave Grusin's score for *Tootsie* (1982) has an opening main theme that underscores a rather complex montage of events in which scenes of New York City are intercut with shots of Dustin Hoffman applying makeup as an actor. Like most main-title cues, its tone sets up the audience for the forthcoming theatrical experience—light, urban hip, yet soulful. Grusin uses a light upper-register synth color for his melody, with rhythm. (See Figures 22-6a,b.) Note that some of the essential elements that define the character of the piece are written out, including the guitar picking and keyboard fills. The bass and keyboard "comping" are free.

FIGURE 22-5

American Gigolo 1M3 Westwood Apartments Giorgio Moroder

FIGURE 22-6
Tootsie M11A Main Title Dave Grusin

(a)

FIGURE 22-6 *(Continued)*

(b)

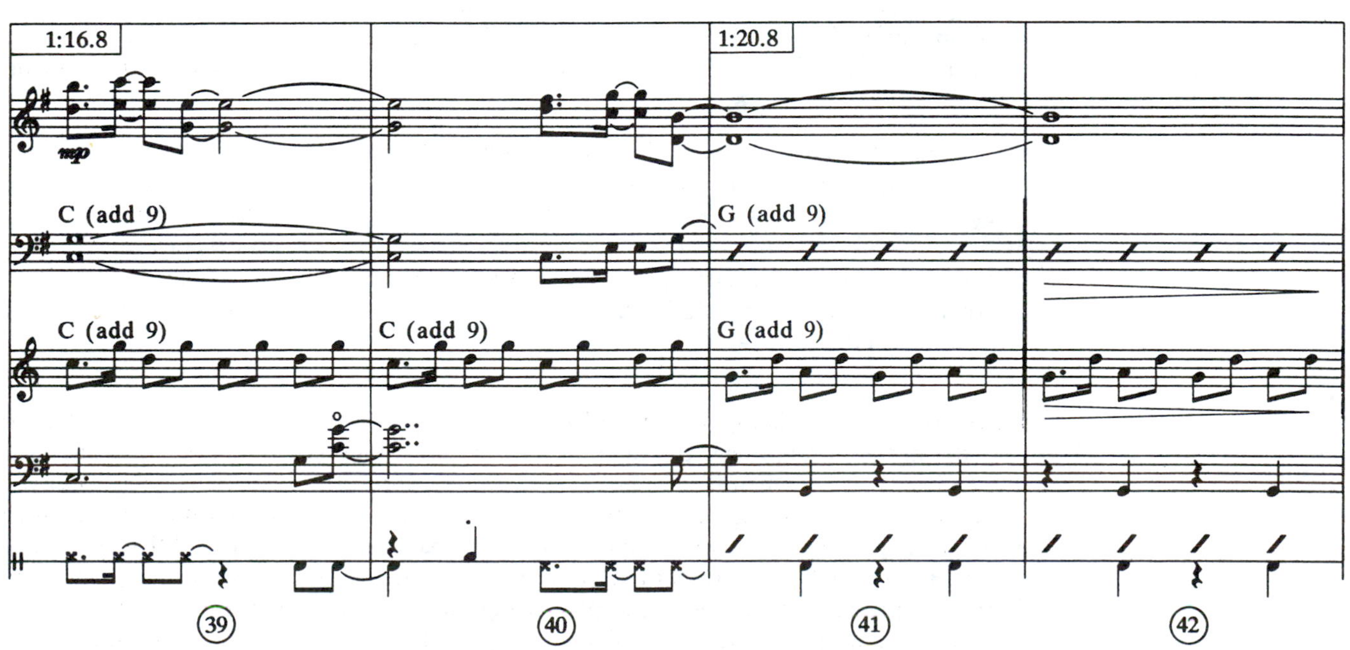

FIGURE 22-6(b) (*Continued*)

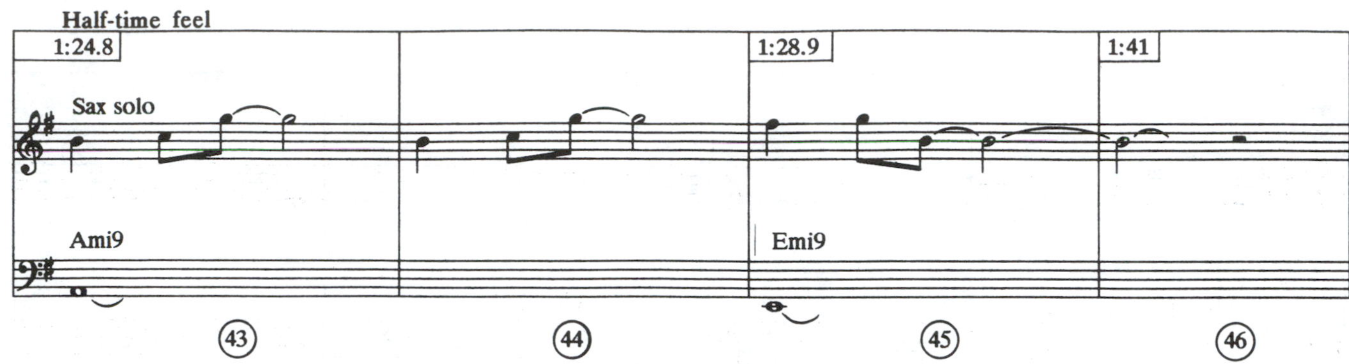

When Hoffman first appears on the streets as a woman, the music also changes style, getting funky and driving, as if to counter the impression that there might be anything feminine about him at that point (Figure 22-7). It also encourages the audience to fully enjoy the visual surprise. Grusin's approach highlights this memorable cinematic moment.

DESPERATELY SEEKING SUSAN. Thomas Newman's score for *Desperately Seeking Susan* (1985) takes another contemporary approach, but also with a light touch. The movie is about a timid housewife (Rosanna Arquette) who becomes fascinated by and involved with a colorful free spirit (Madonna). The score becomes almost a third person, following them around the city on their quirky escapades. The excerpt from Newman's handwritten score in Figure 22-8 plays Madonna's first arrival at the Port Authority at night. Note the digital delay effects.

NINE TO FIVE. Charles Fox provided a multistylistic score for *Nine to Five* (1980) to suit the needs of this freewheeling romp (see Figure 11-1). For the office montage near the end of the film, when Jane Fonda, Dolly Parton, and Lily Tomlin have taken over the office and are issuing executive instructions to change the company's whole approach to office management, Fox used a contemporary big-band sound. (Figure 22-9 shows Fox's handwritten sketch.) The rhythm section gives this cue its contemporary feel, while the brass provide the punch. The brass (plus string pad) also play more compatibly with the action than a more keyboard- or guitar-oriented orchestration would have, by suggesting

FIGURE 22-7
Tootsie **M-33** **Dave Grusin**

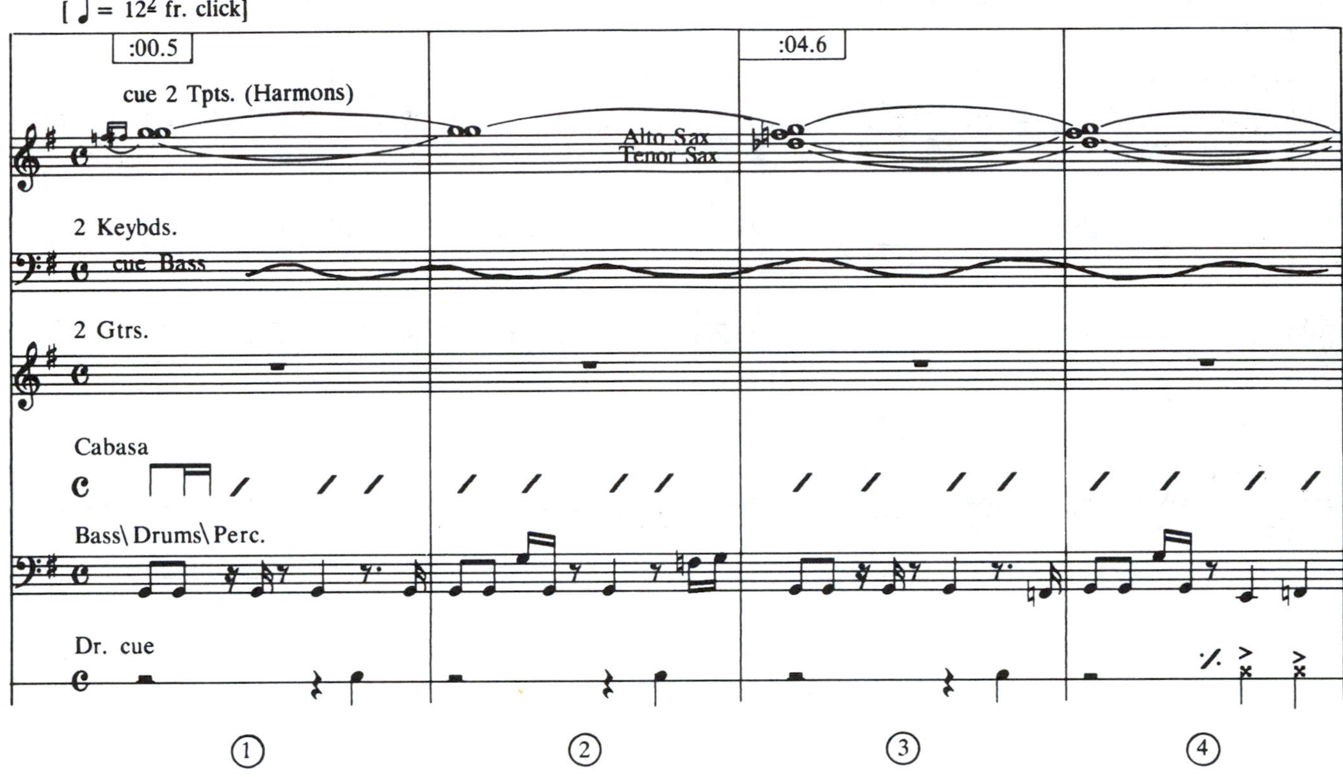

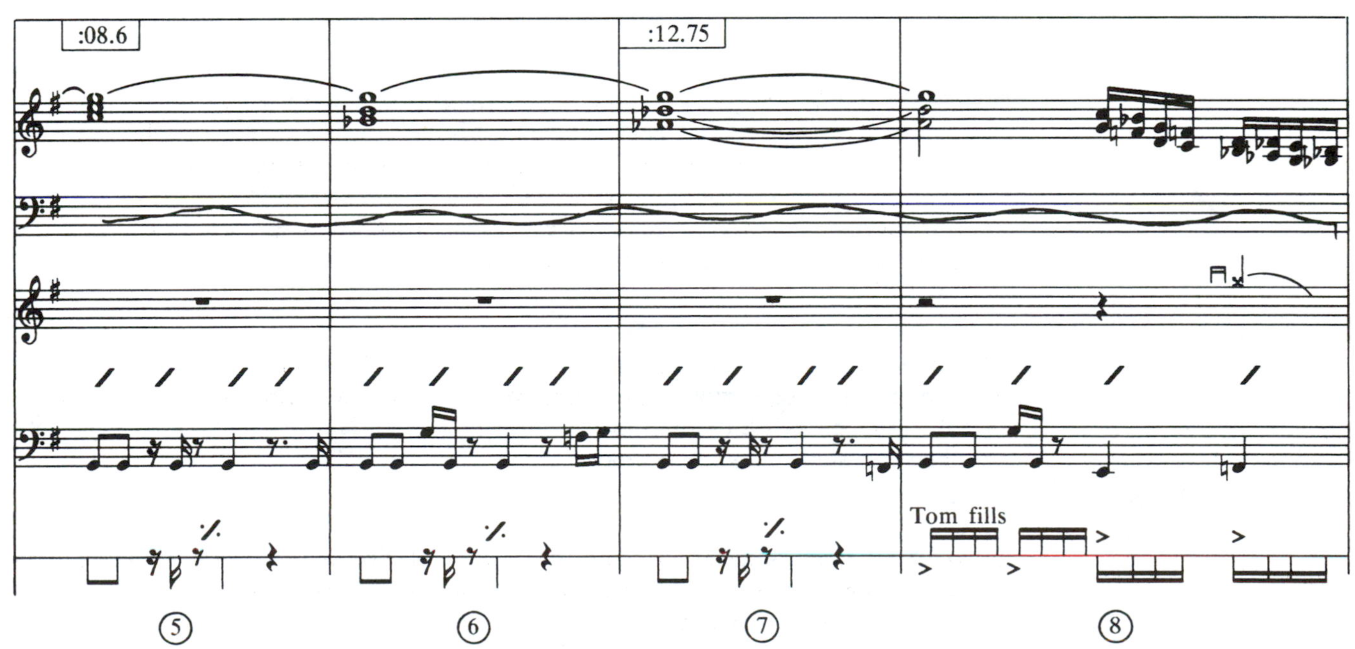

FIGURE 22-7 (*Continued*)

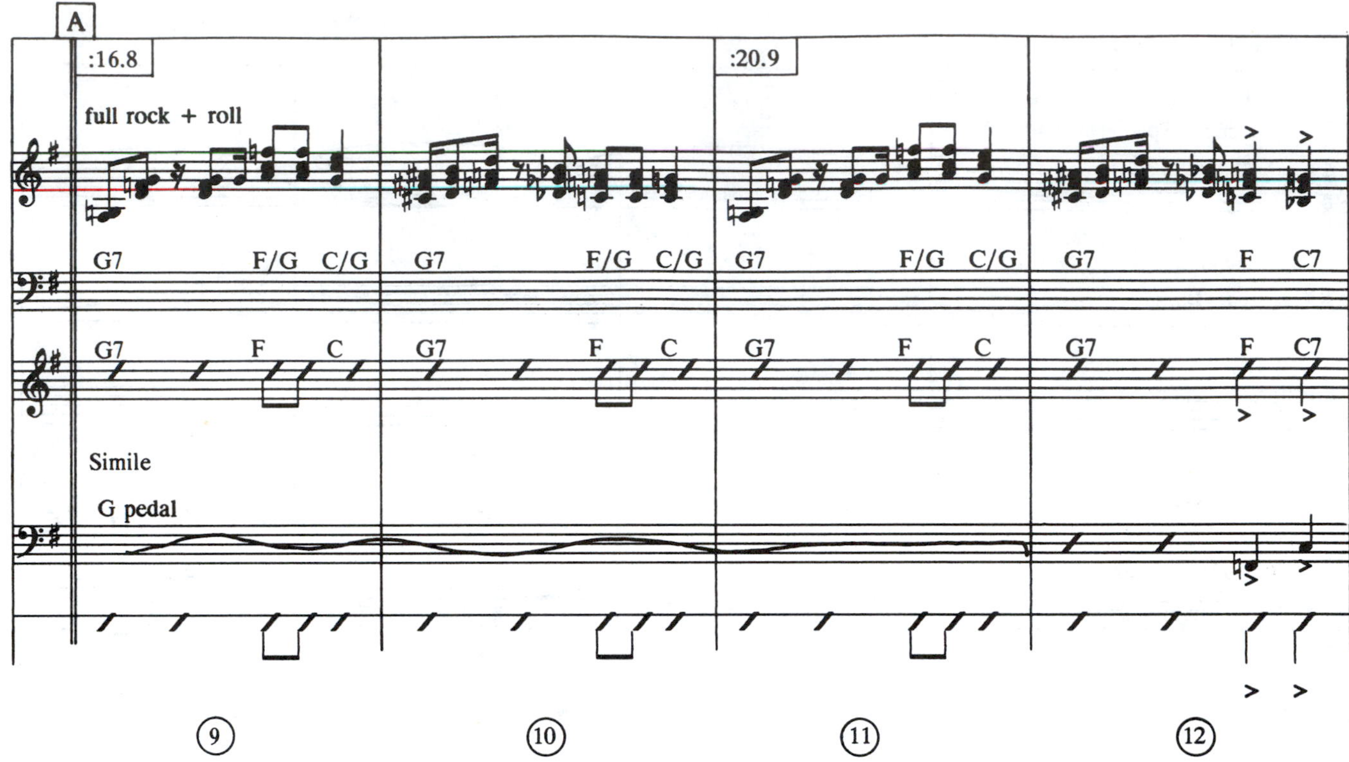

a common denominator sound and impulse that the entire group of workers at the office might relate to. Note that the piano is completely written out, and the first two bars of the bass line are written, giving the player a clear idea of what Fox had in mind for the part.

STIR CRAZY. Tom Scott uses a funky, jazz-oriented score to play dramatic sequences in *Stir Crazy* (1980). In the film, Gene Wilder and Richard Pryor are mistakenly thrown in jail in a redneck western town. The two escape during a climactic prison rodeo contest at the end of the movie, crawling under the stadium and into a friend's van waiting outside. Scott's use of this contemporary idiom gives the sequence both suspense and whimsy—just what is needed under the circumstances (see Figure 22-10).

BEVERLY HILLS COP. Harold Faltermeyer created a lean, hip theme that becomes identified (through repetition) with Eddie Murphy's capers in *Beverly Hills Cop* (1984). "Axel F," Faltermeyer's hit from this film (Figure 22-11), is an example of a theme with a bass line that sometimes works independently (see page 192).

HOOSIERS. Jerry Goldsmith's score for *Hoosiers* (1986) combines electronic and orchestral instruments, and utilizes contemporary electronic drumming. Figures 22-12 and 22-13 are excerpts from his sketches.

FIGURE 22-8

Desperately Seeking Susan Port Authority Thomas Newman

FIGURE 22-9

Nine to Five 10/2 Office Montage Charles Fox

FIGURE 22-9 (*Continued*)

Charles Fox

IN "4" BUT WITH A "2" FEEL

POP/ROCK FEEL • IN "4" BUT WITH A "2" FEEL

W.W.

Brass

Strings

Perc

Drums

Guitar

Bass

Piano

RHYTHM SECTION - NEED NOT PLAY LITERAL PART - CAN USE AS A GUIDE TO THE FEEL

-2-

CF2

FIGURE 22-9 (*Continued*)

FIGURE 22-9 (*Continued*)

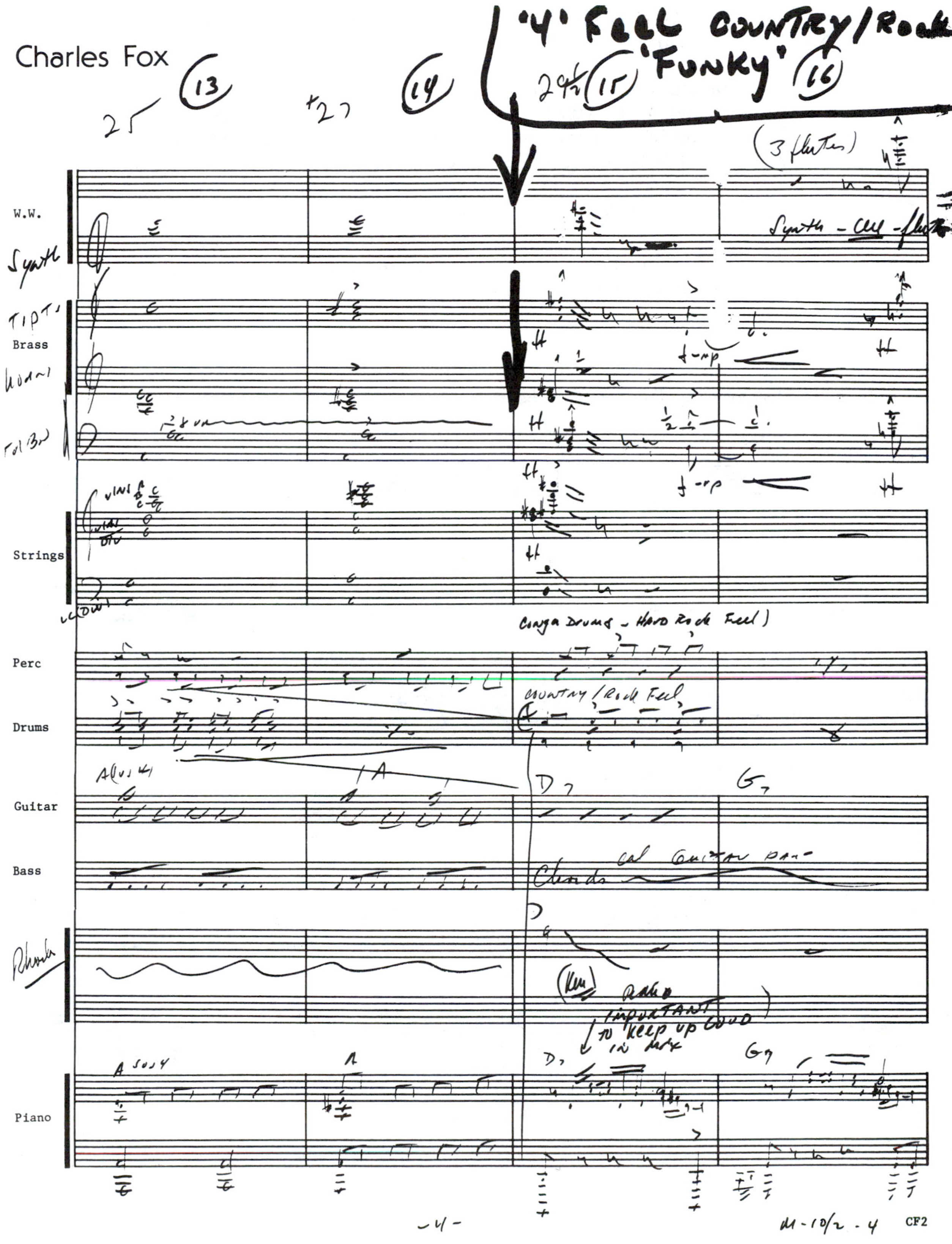

SCORING WITH A SOLO ARTIST

B.B. King was thrilling. He could play the phone book and it would be great.
IRA NEWBORN

Working with a great solo artist can be a real high, it can drive you crazy, or both. If the composer can actually get what he needs on tape, though, it is always worth it. The one overriding criterion is WHAT THE ARTIST DOES MOST NATURALLY MUST BE JUST RIGHT FOR THE FILM. Otherwise you're in trouble. Three other guiding principles:

1. Many solo artists don't read music.
2. The more freedom you give them, the greater their contribution.
3. The most reliable work method is to prerecord the orchestra tracks on multitrack tape and then overdub the artist.

FIGURE 22-10

Stir Crazy **M10-1** **Disappearing Duo** **Tom Scott**

FIGURE 22-10 (*Continued*)

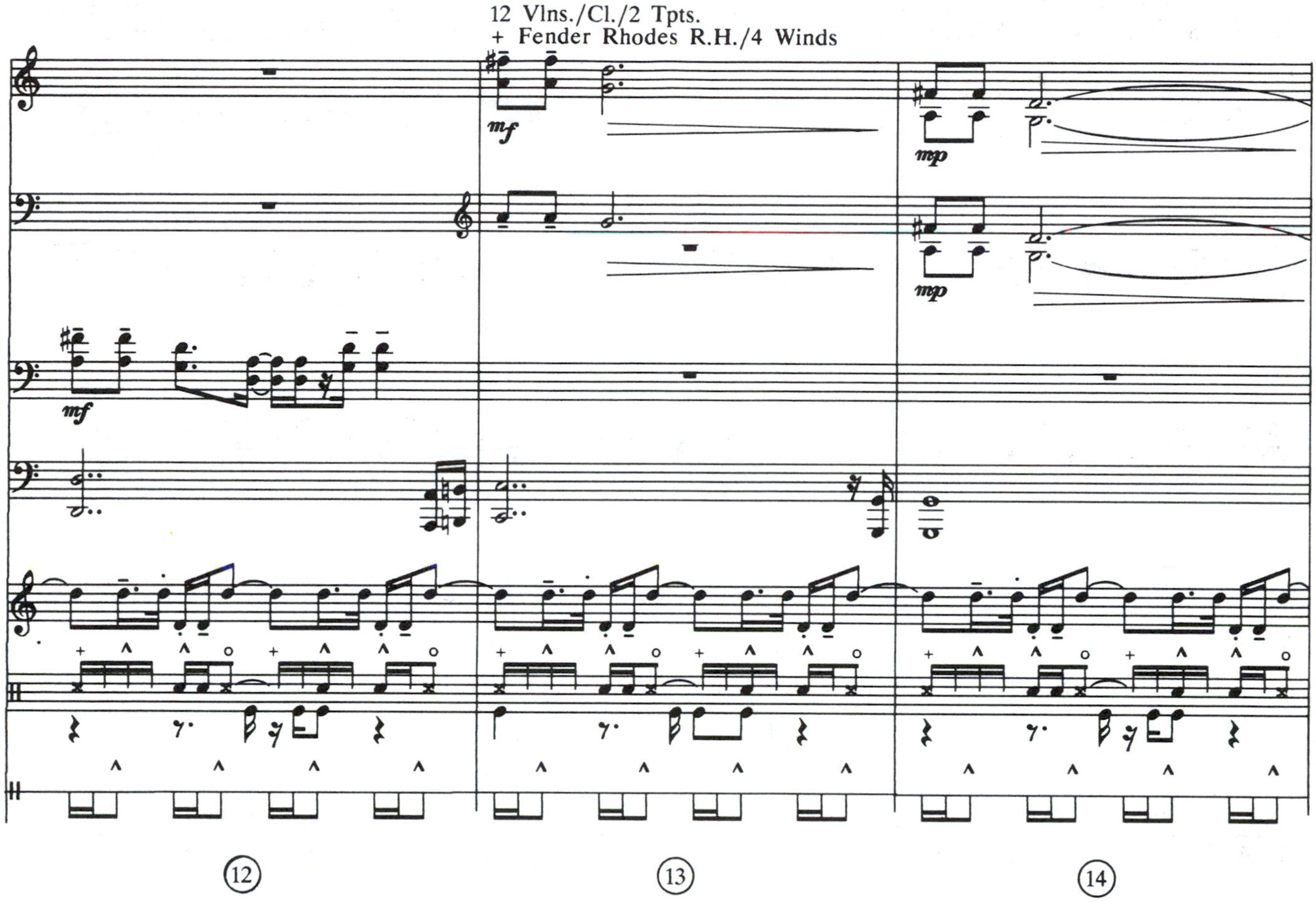

12 Vlns./Cl./2 Tpts.
+ Fender Rhodes R.H./4 Winds
mf
mp
mp
mf
12
13
14

FIGURE 22-11

Beverly Hills Cop **Axel F** **Harold Faltermeyer**

Synth.
solo - no chords

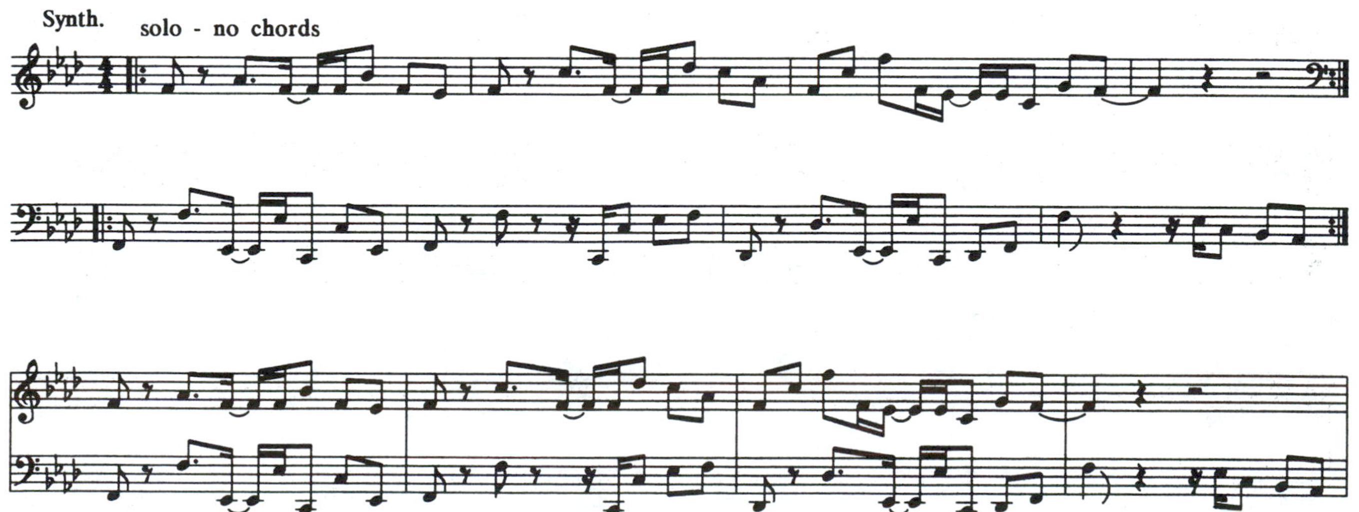

FIGURE 22-11 (*Continued*)

F
E♭
B♭/C
B♭/E♭
B♭/F
F
E♭
B♭/C
F/E♭
F
(Bass fig. cont.)
D♭
E♭
F
E♭
F

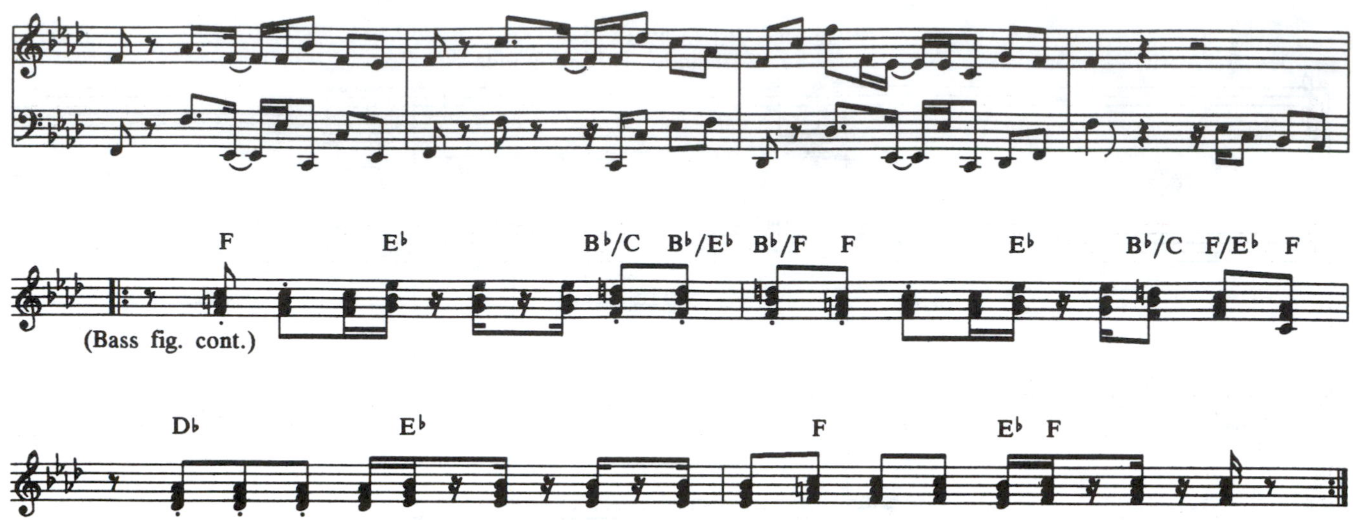

FIGURE 22-12

Hoosiers 1/1 Welcome Jerry Goldsmith

♩ = 18 fr. click

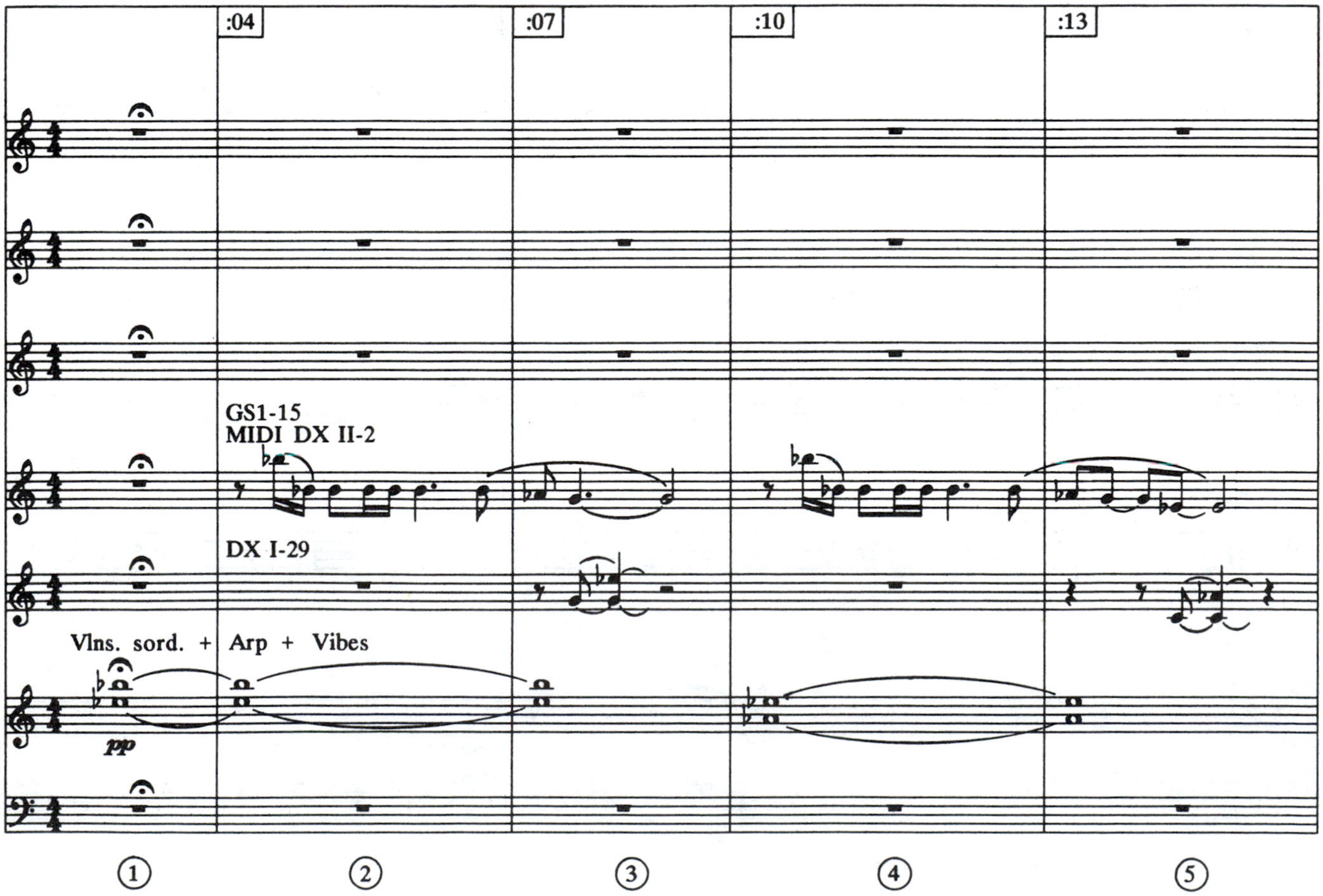

:04
:07
:10
:13
GS1-15
MIDI DX II-2
DX I-29
Vlns. sord. + Arp + Vibes
pp
①
②
③
④
⑤

FIGURE 22-12 (*Continued*)

READING MUSIC. There are artists who do read music. Some, like guitarist Lee Ritenour and jazz-trumpet virtuoso Wynton Marsalis, are schooled musicians who are as at home in the studio as they are on stage. But the composer must ascertain without any doubt the level of the aritst's reading skills before writing a note for him. You can't always rely on the artist to be objective about this; the composer should check with other musicians, contractors, or if necessary a personal manager or recording engineer with whom the artist has worked.

It is always a good idea to get the cues to the artist on cassette before the session, so he can become familiar with the tracks and what he will be playing. If the artist doesn't read, this is mandatory. But even thorough preparation of this sort isn't always foolproof. Before working with legendary guitarist B.B. King on his score for *Into the Night* (1985), Ira Newborn knew King couldn't read. "I gave him no chart because I wrote it so that he could hear it. And he has very, very good ears. He doesn't care what key it's in. I told him what key it's in. He can't read, but he knows keys." On the song Newborn wrote, there was a demo. "I sent a demo to him and he swore to me constantly that he had rehearsed it endlessly. What it really was—I taught it to him in the studio. It was like pulling teeth out of a hippopotamus.

FIGURE 22-12 (*Continued*)

"The guitar performance and the vocal performance on that thing—there are literally millions of pieces. He was sitting out there with a little cassette player playing the demo that I'd made. He'd listen to the phrase and sing it into the microphone. So first I'd get a whole vocal and then I'd start updating each phrase and record each phrase until I got a good one all the way through. Then I'd do the same thing on two or three other tracks. We slaved [interlocked] another 24-track. And we did the same thing with the guitar solos."

GIVE HIM HIS HEAD. When you decide to record a major artist on a soundtrack, you have implicitly decided that the sound and the quality of the music that specific artist plays is perfect for the film. Otherwise, why spend the time and money involved to make it all come together? Having done so, the composer must figure out how to get the most out of the artist and still guide him and control his performance so it becomes totally integrated into the score. If the artist reads, this is somewhat easier because the solo parts can indicate what passages are to be played exactly as written (write "as written" on the part); when the artist should phrase freely (write "phrase freely"); and when the artist is free to improvise on chord changes or a melodic line or both.

FIGURE 22-12 (*Continued*)

When an artist doesn't read music, the process gets more difficult, and sometimes requires great fortitude and patience. Since Newborn realized B. B. King doesn't read, he considered this when he planned and composed his score. "We sat in the studio and I even put the picture up. I would play the music a couple of times and he would sit and listen. I would say, 'Just fool around.' Then I would go out in the studio and watch the movie with him and show him where he should do something. I would just motion to him. But often I didn't have to do anything. He just got into it. I'd say, 'B. B., just look at the picture and play what you think should go there.'"

This technique works beautifully if you really know what to expect from the artist. But the composer should allow ample time for this and be sure to make enough takes on separate tracks for each cue so that he has plenty of material to work with later. Newborn left several empty tracks on the 2-inch master so he could piece together sections of different takes.

STUDIO MUSICIANS. It isn't just a solo recording artist who requires this approach. Many times the composer will write for studio musicians who come to the scoring sessions to play important solo parts. When James Horner began recording his score for *48 Hours*

FIGURE 22-12 (*Continued*)

(1982), he realized he needed to shift his emphasis somewhat from the totally notated score he had written to something that would give the musicians more freedom. "The first cue [saxophonist] Ernie Watts played, I realized after five minutes that this guy was much better off ignoring everything on the page and just getting the feel of what I wrote. And that's what we did. And that's how I told the percussion, drums, and bass, etc., to proceed." Since Horner had written out so much for the musicians, they knew what he was going for and were able to bring their own feel to it.

PRERECORD THE TRACKS; OVERDUB THE ARTIST. Although Horner recorded his score for *48 Hours* live, the safest plan when working on a score with any special solo artist is to record the orchestra (or rhythm) tracks first on multitrack tape and then overdub the artist later, as Ira Newborn did with B. B. King. Even isolating the artist so that he can be recorded live with the orchestra and still be his own tracks is risky business, and doesn't allow for the finessing that can bring out the best in a soloist. It can help if the soloist is present for the recording of the basic tracks, because they become more familiar with the music and can sometimes suggest an adjustment that will help everything go smoother later on. But recording them separately will ordinarily be the best procedure. Maurice Jarre encountered a typical example of this during his score for *Mad Max Beyond Thunderdome* (1985). "At one point we had to mix a hard-rock group—two really hard-rock guitars and drums. Rock musicians never have the opportunity to work with an orchestra, and so I thought it was safer to do that in two parts. We recorded the symphonic part, and then superimposed the rock part so we could spend a little bit more time with them."

SCORING WITH A GROUP

Usually when a group is used in film scoring, they are self-contained and independent. Film composers to date have had little opportunity to work with organized groups. But the guidelines for working with them are the same as for solo artists. With a group, though, it is also a necessity to allow time for as much rehearsal as necessary prior to actually scoring the film, especially since their previous recording experience has been albums, where time schedules are almost unknown.

FIGURE 22-13

Hoosiers **7/1 The Coach Stays Jerry Goldsmith**

FIGURE 22-13 (*Continued*)

SELF-CONTAINED GROUPS; A COLLABORATION. Ever since director Michael Mann engaged the group Tangerine Dream to score *Thief* in 1981, this contemporary electronic group has maintained a high profile in the film world. Originating in Germany, its three members are Johannes Schmoelling, Chris Franke, and Edgar Froese. Froese, who studied art with Salvador Dali, comments on their development: "In the early days we called ourselves surrealists. In our music we tried to turn everything upside down, just to see things differently. We thought that a 4/4 beat should not necessarily be 4/4 anymore; you can break it up and do what you like with it. We found that the mixture between C-major and F-sharp-minor chords and melodies, which normally never fit, suddenly did fit. Once you lose the connection to conventional structures, you find a new structure within your own subjective philosophy. Suddenly you have a new reality, and that's wonderful."[1]

[1] © 1986 *Keyboard* magazine, Cupertino, CA, interview by Bob Doerschuk and Ted Greenwald (January 1987). Reprinted by permission.

FIGURE 22-13 (*Continued*)

CONTEMPORARY SOURCE MUSIC

The source music in contemporary films can be an excellent opportunity to incorporate various styles. Often the choice of these styles is arbitrary and depends on the mutual tastes of the producer, director, and composer. After all, a bar could conceivably have half-a-dozen different kinds of contemporary music coming out of a jukebox, any one of which would be credible and effective for the scene. Sometimes soundtrack-album considerations will dictate a particular style, or, more times than not, a song, either licensed or original for the film. In that case, it is probable that material may already be temp'd onto the track, to be licensed or replaced later.

If the composer is relatively free to decide on the style, anything goes. The one criterion: Make it authoritative. If it doesn't sound authentic, it won't be convincing and can sound as out of place as an English-speaking actor using a Swedish accent to play Shakespeare.

FIGURE 22-13 (*Continued*)

CONTEMPORARY SCORES FOR TELEVISION

> *I thought there ought to be a way, and there was, to make a partnership with Pete Carpenter and learn how contemporary music technically can be put to film. After us the floodgates opened. Also all the rock-and-rollers learned to read and write. Now there are 200 guys doing it.*
>
> MIKE POST

The collaboration of Mike Post and the late Peter Carpenter began in 1971 and has had a tremendous influence on television music. Just as Henry Mancini's use of contemporary music (jazz) in the fifties was irresistible, the themes and scores of Post and Carpenter incorporate and blend many styles of contemporary music and have greatly increased the receptivity of both the filmmakers and the public to their approach to scoring. Their influence was so great that many of their stylistic approaches came to be expected

FIGURE 22-13 (*Continued*)

by producers of televisions series. To do anything less was old-fashioned; anything more—far out.

Post recounts how he and Carpenter got started: "I had a couple of hits and then Andy Williams asked me to be the musical director of his show, which I did for two years. That was my first entrée into TV. Just before that I had met Pete Carpenter, my partner, and we had become close friends and had traded information. He'd been raised in big bands and played primarily jazz. He had no rock-and-roll chops and I had no big-band chops, but we had a love of classical music in common. He had been an assistant to Earle Hagen and had worked on a number of Earle's shows and knew all the techniques for putting music to film.

"I had also in my travels met this young writer, Steven Cannell. When he had heard an album I made for Warner Brothers, he said, 'Jeez, you know your music is just made for film.' When he finally got power as a writer and created a show called *Toma* in '71, he called me up and said, 'Look, you've got to do the music for this show.' I said, 'Fine, but I'm not going to do it alone,'cause I don't even know how to fit the stuff to the picture.' So I called Pete, who was thirty years my senior, and told him my buddy Steve Cannell has this idea and he wants me to do this show, *Toma.* I don't want to do it alone. Pete said, 'I'd love to do it, but I'm getting ready to retire. . . . But I'll give it a shot for one season.'

"We had a little room out in back of his house with a little upright piano. We went out there and started writing and I'd play and he'd write and orchestrate or he'd play and I'd write and orchestrate. I'd write the rhythm section out and he'd do the strings and the woodwinds, etc. We worked that way until we got so busy we had to split some of the stuff up. We never to this day have had an argument—we never even kept track of who wrote what." When Cannell developed *Rockford Files,* Post and Carpenter wrote the music, including the distinctive theme. (See page 82 and Figure 7-1.)

> ***The success of the music in* Miami Vice *is that the major action sequences were in fact cut to the music.***
>
> BRENDON CAHILL, VICE PRESIDENT, UNIVERSAL TELEVISION MUSIC AND HOME VIDEO

Not since Henry Mancini's theme and scores for *Peter Gunn* in 1956 has any television music had the impact of Jan (Yahn) Hammer's music for the television series *Miami Vice.* Bringing his solid experience as a performing musician into his writing, his high-powered electronic contemporary scores almost immediately influenced music supervisors, producers, directors, and composers, both in television and features. His style and approach, the sound and the substance, were suddenly as "in" as anything can be. The fact that he worked as a self-contained composer/performer also has had a tremendous influence on film and television scoring.

In addition to the obvious stylistic characteristics of Hammer's *Miami Vice* scores, there are several other technical factors to note:

1. *He normally created one basic theme and setting of that theme per episode,* and then created variations on that theme throughout the show. For one episode with a central character from Japan, he incorporated some synthesized elements of Japanese music, which worked to make the theme personal and also created significant dramatic tension when needed. Another episode featured the sound of a "Russian" male chorus singing classically in direct counterpoint to high-tension stalking and shoot-outs.

2. *Sometimes the cues seem tailored to the sequences, and sometimes they don't.* Music executive Brendon Cahill explains: "In the beginning, even though they would send a rough cut to Hammer to score, and he would score based on what he saw visually, if he was off a beat he didn't care—he played right through it. At first *they* cared, and then, instead of going back to Jan and saying, 'Hey, rewrite or rerecord that cue,' they said, 'Let's recut the film to fit it.' It's a lot easier. And then also, concurrent with MTV becoming a very prominent force in what's going on in contemporary music today, that all of a sudden gave the show a look of drama; great looking guy, terrific sidekick, exciting area they work in, and God, it's amazing how when you look at the visuals and you hear that music in the action scenes in your own home, you sit on the edge of your chair." Playing *through* a scene, emphasizing the overall emotional content suddenly became the fashion.

3. *The music is dubbed much more prominently than usual.* Cahill explains that producer Michael Mann (who directed *Thief*) is responsible for the execution of that concept. "For the most part, on the dubbing stage, he'll drop effects and play the music. And if you had to say, Well, what is *Miami Vice* all about, other than visual? I would say it's a sound emphasis. And Jan sets the tone of what the effects and the visuals mean to the music."

4. Although totally electronic (synths and samples) except for his own guitar playing, the scores are not effects oriented. By and large, Hammer writes music, not effects, and orchestrates them for an electronic ensemble that he performs and mixes himself.

What was the weekly routine? "Jan would get a first director's cut," Cahill recounts. "Based on the rough cut, he talked with the film editor and the music editor and they told him the progress on cutting down or lengthening whatever scenes were being worked on, and then he got a final version, which could be two or three days before dubbing. At the beginning of the season there might have been 5 to 7 days between the first cut and the final version. At the end of the season, sometimes 3 days."

To compose, perform, record, and mix everything yourself under those circumstances is to work at breakneck speed week after week. Hammer works in his studio at home, and says he just couldn't complete so much work each week without that luxury/necessity. When asked where his ideas come from, he replies: "Compositions happen differently every time. Lots of times I've started from a rhythmic nucleus . . . a typical drum machine approach, using my own drum sounds in the Fairlight, but still the approach where you create an interesting drum beat and go from there. Or it could be a percussion section, samples of real exotic instruments, and creating Cuban, or Haitian, or Asian rhythms. . . . With those patterns, you have a continuum on which you can float."[2]

FIGURE 22-14

Miami Vice **Chase (from pilot)** **Jan Hammer**

Shaker

(sim.)

(sim.)

Dr. Fill

[2] © 1987 *Electronic Musician*, interview by Craig Anderton (March 1987). Reprinted by permission.

FIGURE 22-14 (*Continued*)

Other films that illustrate this chapter:

CONTEMPORARY SCORE

No Mercy (1987). Note Alan Silvestri's sometimes subtle rhythm tracks (percussion tracks don't have to be loud or heavy-impact tracks to be effective), the high synths plus percussion pulse for the first gunfight/car explosion/cattle stampede, and the uses of a contemporary rhythm pulse with an atonal sound above that creates the effect of confusion.

EXAMPLE OF SOLO ARTIST

Sounder (1972), a film about the black experience in the rural South during the Depression, features the music of Taj Mahal, a solo blues artist who scored most of it with blues that he performed on acoustic guitar embellished with blues vocalizing (often wordless) and mouth harp. Only a few chase sequences have orchestra added to his score.

PART

7

STYLES AND GENRES

CHAPTER 23

STYLES AND GENRES

One of the words that I use a lot in evaluating anybody's film score is, "Is it appropriate?" It could be appropriate and bad or it could be appropriate and wonderful, but it can never be inappropriate and wonderful.
ELMER BERNSTEIN

You can't write funny music. . . . I really write it straight. You have to be careful of the vocabulary of the instrumentation, of the harmonies. You just have to be sensitive to the film.
JOHN MORRIS

No, not off-the-wall—we had to be right on the nose.
JOHNNY MANDEL (re: *The Russians Are Coming,* 1966)

Hitting it "right on the nose" is a particular requirement of comedies, adventure romps, horror films, sitcoms, ethnic/geographic stories, science fiction, prime-time soaps, Westerns, cop stories and war films. In every style and genre of film there is an "appropriate" response, an expectation, a vocabulary. The composer who disregards the expectations of these styles and genres will be swimming against the current. In the words of Alexander "Sandy" Courage, "In Hollywood you need to be a master of eclecticism. You have to know how to do whatever your assignment is—just like that. Let's say you're doing one of the nighttime soaps—you should know what's going on musically in the nighttime soap field. There's a certain kind of music that's written for those shows and if you come in and write anything different than that you will not have any legs [that is, staying power] at all and will not be hired back. Come in prepared to write that kind of music instantly."

Every genre will bring with it certain audience expectations regarding both the style of the score, and its function. Because these expectations are based on precedent, a thorough study of classic films in a particular genre is essential to a successful genre score—not to imitate, but to truly understand how these scores have functioned successfully in the past. You must know the language.

COMEDY

The terribly, terribly serious gypsy Romanian violin music was what set the humor off—not to be funny musically, but to let the music be background against which the film could be funny.
CHARLES BERNSTEIN (re: *Love at First Bite,* 1979)

In comedy, playing the music seriously helps the ridiculousness of the character.
ELMER BERNSTEIN

Despite the intuitive nature of comedy, the composer who is scoring a humorous film must probe the director's concept for the proper approach to take. Is it light, obviously broad humor that should be supported with broad musical comments, jokes, quotes of other film music or concert music, or surprises (*Silent Movie,* 1976; *Nine to Five,* 1980; *Ferris Bueller's Day Off,* 1986)? Or is it funny by virtue of absurd contextual relationships where the music must be seriously straight so the absurdity of the context is highlighted (*The Russians Are Coming,* 1966; *Love at First Bite,* 1979)? Is it a story with real danger, jeopardy, even serious problems, against which the humor erupts (*Prizzi's Honor,* 1985; *M*A*S*H,* 1970; *That's Life!,* 1986; *Sleuth,* 1972; *Foul Play,* 1978; *An American Werewolf in London,* 1981)? Is it a breathless romp with thrills and frights and fun that the music keeps whipped up in an endless interplay of suspense and action (*Indiana Jones and the Temple of Doom,* 1984; *Romancing the Stone,* 1984; *Ghostbusters,* 1984)? Or is it a story with such strong comedy projection that the music acts as background without comment (*The Return of the Pink Panther,* 1975; *Blazing Saddles,* 1974)?

IDENTIFYING THE SCORE'S FUNCTION. You must give the music character yet not overwhelm the film with the music, even in a comedy. This requirement necessitates an understanding of the music's function. For the chases in *Romancing the Stone,* Alan Silvestri used percussive sounds on the Yamaha DX7 synthesizer, "plus the LinnDrum going crazy." He used some brassy, big-band pop sounds as his idiom as opposed to a symphony orchestra or string-oriented sounds, which he used elsewhere. Why? "I think it couldn't stand a tremendous orchestra. I didn't want it to be overpowering, yet we wanted it to have a lot of punch and so, generally, it all went more towards a rhythm-section type score."

He didn't always play the jeopardy although the characters were involved in situations of jeopardy. "That was the original concept," says Silvestri. "The whole time the Bronco chase is happening, Douglas and Turner are in the cab of the truck joking around. That's where all the comedy comes from. These crazy soldiers are firing away at them and they're completely scared, and Juan, the driver, is giving them a tour of the city, telling them where he was born, just like it was an everyday deal. So the music played to that." (See Figure 23-1.)

PLAYING IT STRAIGHT. Charles Bernstein describes his music for *Love at First Bite* (1979) as "Romanian romantic/nostalgic. And the juxtaposition of that very serious heart-tugging Romanian music with the absurd, anachronistic count, I think, creates humor just by its juxtaposition. That was our choice—not to be funny musically, but let the film be funny and let the music be the background against which that humor could operate."

Elmer Bernstein's approach for *Ghostbusters* (1984) was similar. "Ivan Reitman and I talked endlessly—we had a great deal of contact on *Ghostbusters.* He is quite knowledgeable about music and he will talk, even sometimes in terms of orchestration and things like that, because he does understand a great deal about it. We had made the decision that the spooky people, the ghosts, would be played straight; *that* fear was awesome. And that the three guys, the Ghostbusters themselves, would be played in a much lighter and airier manner [Figure 23-2]. The music that I wrote doesn't ever make any attempt to make jokes actually."

The difference between Bernstein's approach for comedy and drama is one of emphasis. "If it were a serious drama, I probably would have backed off a bit in terms of the sheer power of some of the things that are in *Ghostbusters.* In general, I would let the music be a little more exaggerated in a comedy than in a serious drama."

FIGURE 23-1

Romancing the Stone M-83 Li'l Mule Alan Silvestri

[♩ = 10^{3} fr. click]

Gtr. fuzz

4 Hns. Brass mutes

3 Tbns. Brass mutes

El.Bass/DX7 "Piano I"

Vc./Cb.

DX7 "Clav.Ens."

(Pedal)

Drums

scrape Cym. + Linn song #11

① ② ③ ④

3 Tpts. + 4 Fls. (Div.)

⑤ ⑥ ⑦ ⑧

FIGURE 23-2

Ghostbusters Theme Elmer Bernstein

MUSICAL QUOTES AND REFERENCES. References to other music and film scores and contextual absurdities are two effective devices. The current use of musical quotes in comedies was influenced by *Airplane!* (1980). "In *Airplane!*" Elmer Bernstein notes, "I definitely made reference by style to very old film scoring. It was meant to be serious, but 'great big' serious. I made a lot of jokes in that film, but the jokes are made through serious scoring. For instance, toward the end of the film there's a love theme with chorus. I keep modulating up, up, up, until the chorus can't do it anymore and they sort of choke, which of course in itself is a joke. I used, for instance, the Notre Dame football fight song at one point, played absolutely seriously, but it's a joke in the context of what is happening in the film."

In the films of writer-director John Hughes there are frequent musical quotes and references to well-known music. These quotes are intended to make a broad comedic comment. When Ferris Bueller comes into the kitchen dressed to kill and says, "Bueller—Ferris Bueller," Ira Newborn's music reminds us of the way John Barry has scored similar moments in James Bond films. He announces his name with hard-hitting brass accents interjected in between "Bueller" and "Ferris Bueller" and then ends with a **button**[1] out. In Hughes's *Weird Science* (1985), the film begins with Newborn's paraphrase of the main theme from *2001: A Space Odyssey* (1968, from Richard Strauss's *Also sprach Zarathustra*).

In *Sixteen Candles* (1984), the nerd walks down the bus aisle to ask the pretty girl for a date accompanied by the *Dragnet* theme. Ira Newborn explains that this had been temp'd in by Hughes by the time they spotted the film. "He just liked that idea. He probably thought of that right from the beginning. The little kid is a nerd, so you play something gigantically overblown and suave which is probably the way the kid sees himself. In that case he temp-dubbed it in. Other times, since I know that style of humor quite well, I will suggest certain things."

Newborn likes the use of quotes now and then, but not as a steady diet. "I find that funny occasionally. I'm not interested in rerecording a million pieces of music that other people wrote. It's an okay gag once in a while. But I prefer to do that thing, when you can do it, without an actual quote. For example, when someone is doing something mundane, you can write tremendous, powerful music that seems totally inappropriate but makes the joke."

REFERRING TO FAMILIAR STYLES. In *Clue* (1985), John Morris had to solve many problems. "I felt *Clue* should have a big orchestra—something that gave it a lot of size [playing on our memories of the old murder-mystery scores]. The introduction of the characters was problematical. When they came to the door one by one, it was a question of whether to play or not to play. And how do you characterize somebody in eight bars? It's like opera—you have to do something with instant clarity. I already knew what the score should be like. It had to have a driving main theme, just to get the film going and support it, and then after that I was just doing legit symphonic solutions to everything I looked at."

In the middle of the film there is a long explanation by the butler of the circumstances of the murder that has taken place that night in the old mansion. "The butler scene was a problem, because what he was doing was a tour de force, and without music it was terrible. You know it's going to be scored when you look at it, but you still have to figure out how to do it—that's the trick." Morris solved this problem by composing a vaudevillian accompaniment to this lengthy sequence, and consequently playing the butler's exposition of the crime as a theatrical performance (Figure 23-3).

---

[1] Button: ending accent.

FIGURE 23-3

Clue **8M6** **Step by Step** **John Morris**

Orchestrated by Jack Hayes

PLAYING IT BROADLY. The musical quote and vaudevillian theatricality are broad approaches to comedy. They work well when the film supports it. Obvious camp also has its place. Regarding *The Russians are Coming* (1966), Johnny Mandel says, "I decided to just go with the very broad comedy of the picture, and in this case there was no such thing as being subtle. The Russians were Russian and you used Russian instruments, and the Americans were 'Yankee Doodle,' and it was that simple. And the only music that departed from that was when you had a little comedy or you had a little love scene. The dramatic scoring was almost silent movie-ish. You overdo it. Some of it is just camp."

SONGS IN COMEDY. Songs can make an excellent contribution to comedy, potentially bringing life, warmth, and a "good time" feeling to a comedic sequence. They are especially useful if the film can take a pop or contemporary musical statement; many soundtracks, like *Ghostbusters* and *Beverly Hills Cop* (1984), have used songs for that purpose.

Songs need some open space on the soundtrack to work most effectively, uninhibited by dialogue and loud effects. Unless they are custom-designed to fit a brief moment, they often sound forced or underdubbed in short cues.

HORROR FILMS

> **Nightmare on Elm Street** ***has become a kind of cult classic. And yet I'd have to say that there's a lightness to it. It does have fun with itself, even being a screamer.*** CHARLES BERNSTEIN

In an era that has seen a record number of bloody, violent films and mad-slasher movies, "there is a genre within the genre," says Charles Bernstein, "which has a lot of imagination. I think that's why *Nightmare on Elm Street* [1984] did as well as it did. It's not a slasher movie, and you're never sure whether you're watching a dream or reality, which is very much the experience you have with James Joyce or Fellini's *8½* [1963]. [Director] Wes Craven is a scholar and a former English professor, who I think has the ability to play with your sense of reality.

"[In the music] I sometimes had to let the audience know they were watching a dream, and sometimes I had to fool them into thinking they were not. My approach is intuitive, but sometimes just the presence of music will indicate that there's something about that reality that's questionable. In the choice of spotting, if you bring in the music at the beginning of a scene, you're letting them know there's something about that scene that's different from the one that preceded it. Whereas holding off and waiting for another moment was one way of fooling the audience into not realizing that there was a major transition when that scene began.

"There were a lot of little tricks in *Nightmare on Elm Street.* I had a theme and also a sub-theme (or a counter theme), and one was evocative of this dream villain that appears in the dreams of these teenagers, and I could bring that sound in. It wasn't as obvious as the shark sound in *Jaws* [see Figure 13-1]. Therefore it wasn't quite 'Oh-oh, here comes Freddie.' But there was a sense of being able to somewhat manipulate the audience into feeling his presence when he wasn't on the screen—to indicate his imminent arrival." (See Figure 23-4.)

KEY TO THE EMOTION. Terror is the objective in a horror film, and music has a powerful ability to communicate emotions, including terror. The scenes of terror are often ones with kinetic action and energy, and it's important to remember that the music is scoring not the action, but the emotion—the throbbing heart, the shrieking voice, the inescapable and overwhelming fear the audience feels.

Throughout film history the ominous low note has been associated with impending, life-threatening danger, and using it implies that depth of jeopardy. But mystery is effectively played with a less ominous feel. Because Charles Fox didn't call upon the obvious low notes in parts of several cues for *Foul Play* (1978; a sometimes comedy, sometimes mystery), he says, he created "almost bone-chilling, mysterious sounds as opposed to the more ominous ones which would lead Goldie Hawn to know what's around the corner—maybe just catching her more off guard and thus becoming more bone chilling to her." (See Figure 23-5.)

FIGURE 23-4
Nightmare on Elm Street Theme Charles Bernstein

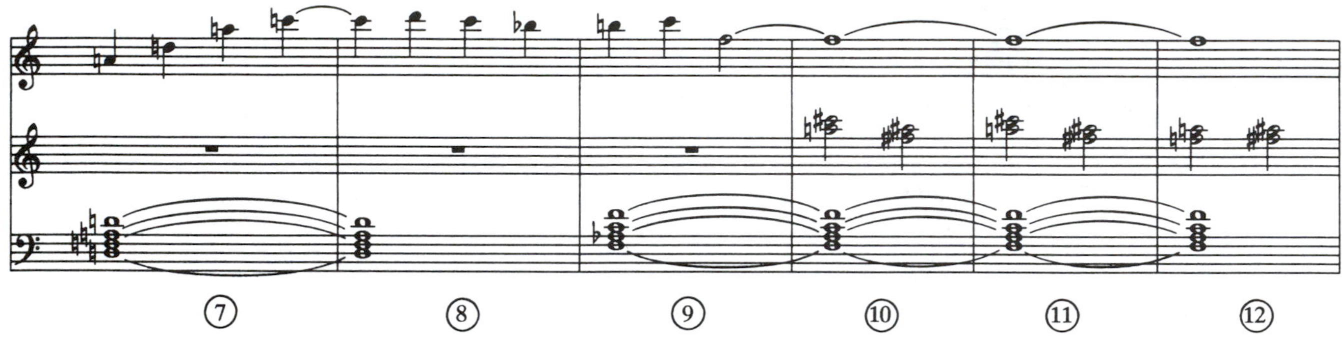

Score by Charles Bernstein from *A Nightmare on Elm Street* appears courtesy of New Line Cinema Corp. © MCMLXXXIV The Elm Street Venture.

MANIPULATING THE AUDIENCE. The composer must take care to use effectively his power to manipulate the audience's reactions. Mysteries make use of "red herring" clues to throw the viewers off and to keep their anxiety alive, and the music must help the illusion (see page 148). But the audience needs to have *some* real clues so they can participate in solving the plot. Music, by its very presence, can give away the new danger that is entering a scene. How many times have we heard the sound from a television mystery show we're not actually watching and suddenly thought, Something's going to happen. At the same time, the music must not "telegraph" coming surprises, thereby ruining their shock value.

WESTERNS

Westerns have been out of favor at times, but historically they have been the most popular of all genres. The basic musical style of the genre has always been orchestral (with harmonica, banjo, and guitar for folk color), depicting the great outdoors and the action of cowboy/Indian chases, cowboy/Mexican battles, bank robberies, train robberies, revenge and love. The classic Western scores the composer should be familiar with include Dmitri Tiomkin's Oscar-winning music for *High Noon* (1952—directed by Fred Zinnemann, with Gary Cooper); André Previn's score for *Bad Day at Black Rock* (1954—John Sturges, director, with Spencer Tracy); Jerome Moross's classic example

FIGURE 23-5
Foul Play M-15 Scotty Followed — Charles Fox, Orchestrated by Ruby Raksin

FIGURE 23-5 (*Continued*)

:23
+:25 1/2
:28 1/2
:30 1/2
div.
subito p
subito p
subito p
10
11
12
13

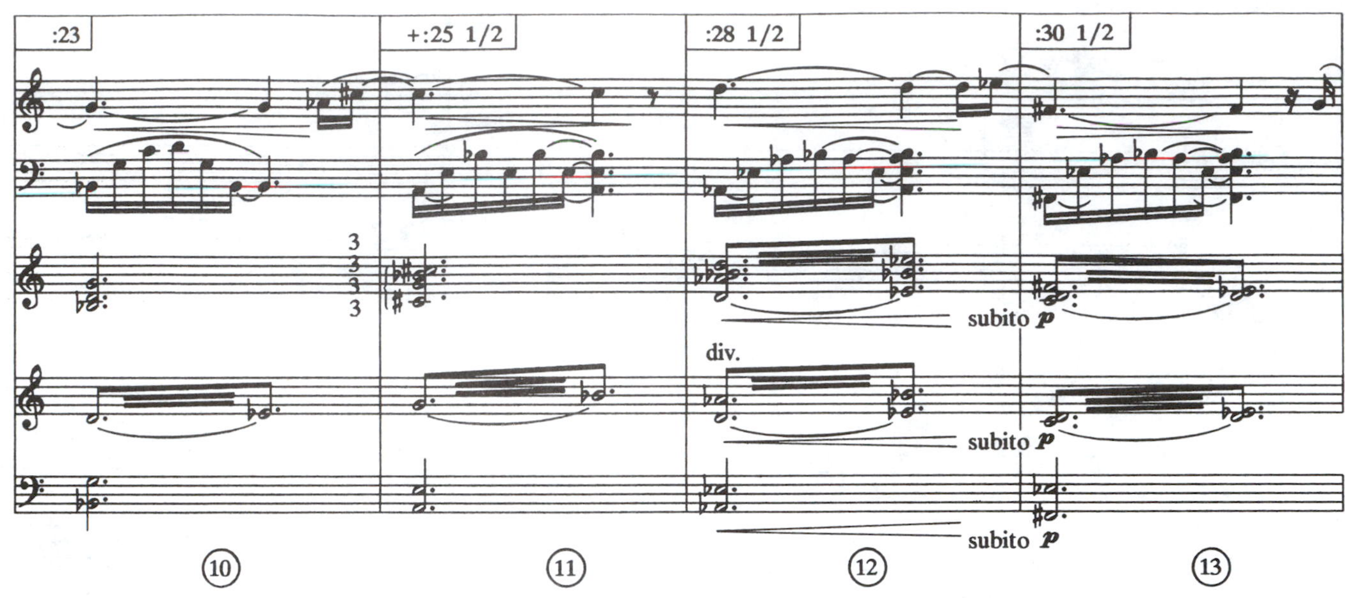

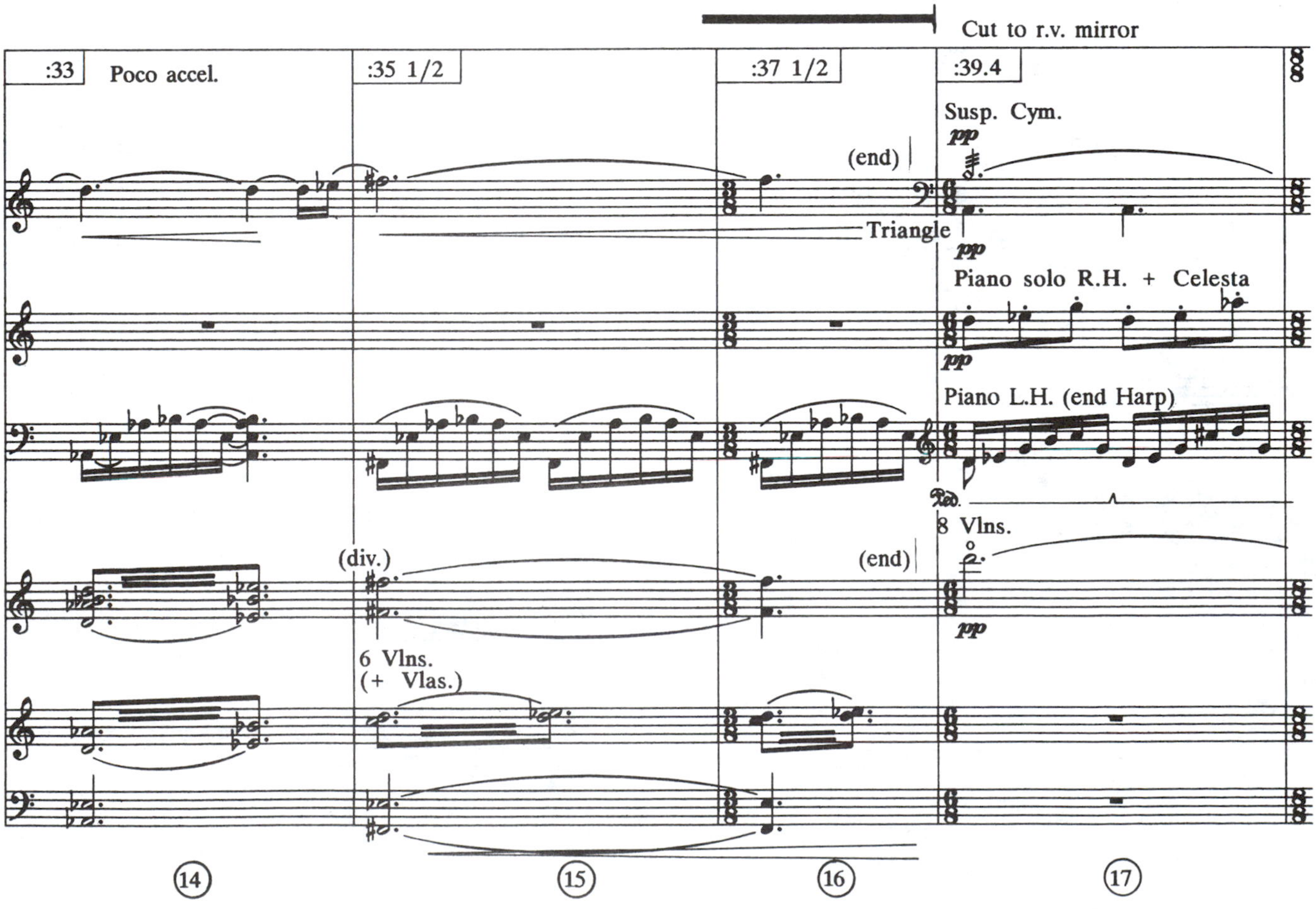

Cut to r.v. mirror
:33
Poco accel.
:35 1/2
:37 1/2
:39.4
Susp. Cym.
pp
(end)
Triangle
pp
Piano solo R.H. + Celesta
pp
Piano L.H. (end Harp)
8 Vlns.
(div.)
(end)
pp
6 Vlns.
(+ Vlas.)
14
15
16
17

FIGURE 23-5 (*Continued*)

of the Western score *The Big Country,* often mentioned as a role model (1958—William Wyler, director, with Gregory Peck and Burl Ives); Elmer Bernstein's famous and definitive score for *The Magnificent Seven* (1960—John Sturges, director, with Yul Brynner and Steve McQueen); Jerry Fielding's scores for *The Wild Bunch* (1969—directed by Sam Peckinpah, with William Holden and Ernest Borgnine, and distinguished by its almost surreal, slow-motion violence) and for the Clint Eastwood film *The Outlaw Josey Wales* (1976); and, more recently, Ry Cooder's folk-flavored music for *The Long Riders* (1983) and Bruce Broughton's provocative orchestral score for *Silverado* (1985).

The distinguished directors, writers, actors, and composers who have worked on Westerns are ample testimony to the classic status of the genre. A composer with an assignment in this field should know exactly what music the filmmakers associate with this genre. Soundtrack albums and videotapes are the textbooks for this study.

Bernstein's score for *The Magnificent Seven* is an absolute classic of its kind—notable for its pulse, propulsion, and lyricism in addition to the use of local color as the story requires. (See Figure 23-6.) As Bernstein reflects, "It was a vehicle which interested me because I'd always been interested in American folk music and, in particular, border folk music. In the thirties interest in American folk music was at a low ebb, compared to countries like England or Ireland. I can remember finding the Lomax books on American folk music, and they were absolutely fascinating, and I was very friendly in those days with Pete Seeger, who was terribly interested in American folk music. So I had some great interest in this and also felt that was a musical element sadly lacking in film scoring and one that should be very useful.

"Just about six months before that, I'd experimented with rhythm in the theme for a television show called *Riverboat,* and I started to really work in the area of underlying rhythms in *The Magnificent Seven.* The harmonic language is very four-square and straightforward. There is a lot of I-IV-V harmonic structure. I didn't look for harmonic sophistication at all in the score, which also clearly roots it in a sort of folk lore.

"The themes had very specific functions. The general theme that people came to know was meant to be a general heroic theme for the Seven. And there was a clear theme for the bad guys [see Figure 13-22]. That was also very clearly delineated. Subsequently there were some other less important themes—there were some guitar themes having to do with some romantic involvement. But they were secondary. Basically the score functioned with two themes.

"Of the scores I've done, I think *The Magnificent Seven* is a score who's style is very consistent and it keeps the picture quite unified stylistically, as well as keeping the picture driving along."

The expansive sweep of the Jerome Moross score for *The Big Country* is often a point of reference for filmmakers working in the genre. Figure 23-7 is a transcription of an excerpt from the Main Title.

WAR FILMS

The many points of view projected in war films cover a huge spectrum; consider the stirring patriotism and nationalism of *The Battle of Britain* (1969), the comedic but patriotic *Mister Roberts* (1955), the comedic but antiwar *M*A*S*H* (1970), and the deeply antiwar *Killing Fields* (1984) and *Platoon* (1986). War films may have terrifyingly noisy battle scenes. They may include scenes of heroism, triumph, defeat, courage, pain, suffering, loss, confusion. Some contain montages representing multiple events during the passage of time. Music can be powerful in expressing the tone and attitude of the film, at times even helping to delineate them. In recent times, war films have mostly abandoned orchestral treatments for the battle scenes, treatments based on role models like Tchaikovsky's *1812* Overture or Shostakovich's Fifth Symphony, and are more likely

FIGURE 23-6

The Magnificent Seven Main Title Elmer Bernstein

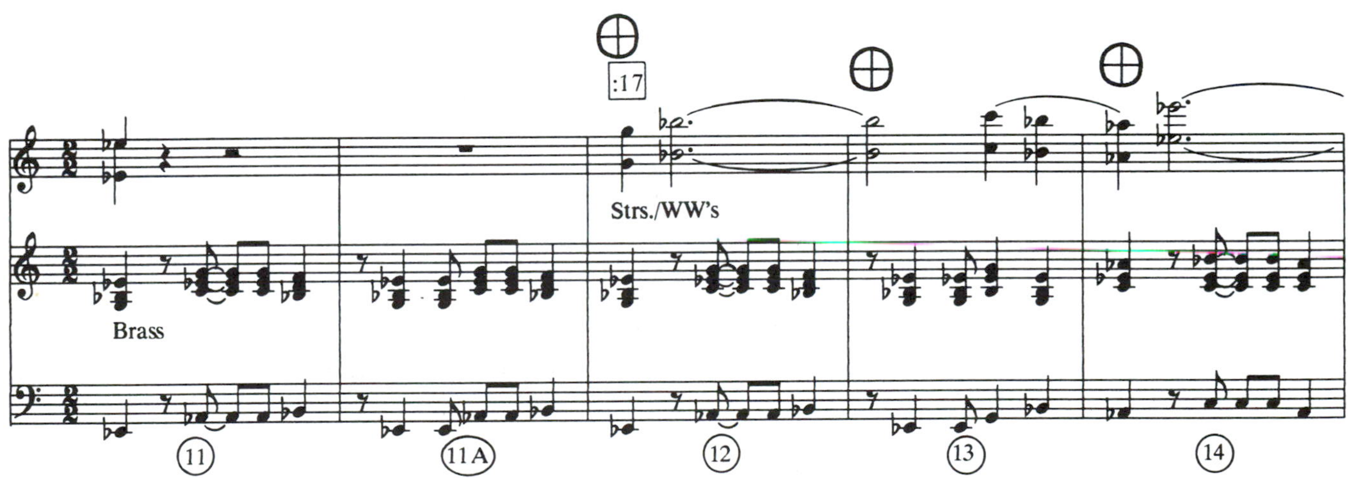

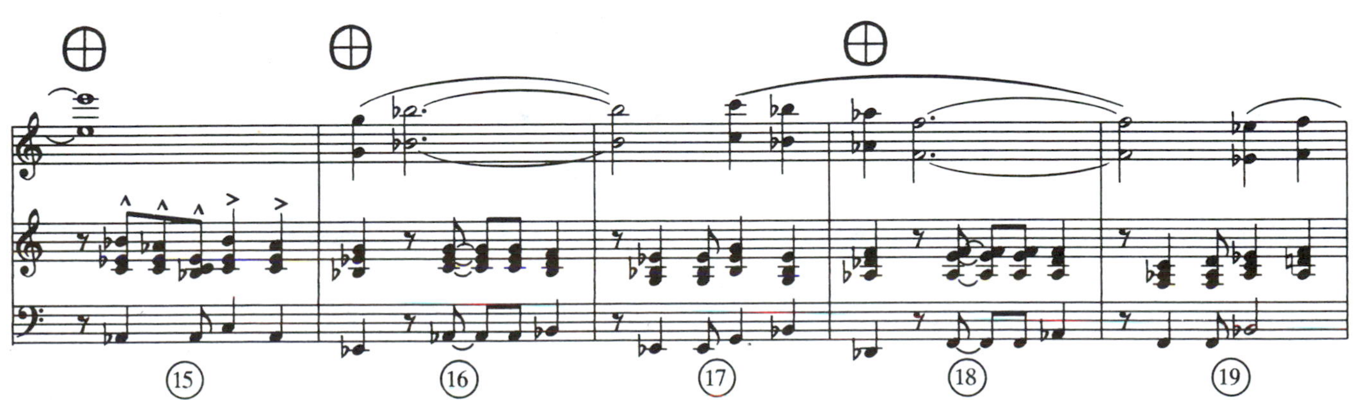

FIGURE 23-6 (*Continued*)

FIGURE 23-7

The Big Country Main Title (transcribed) Jerome Moross

FIGURE 23-7 (*Continued*)

to use only sound effects, or effects plus percussion, or, very typically, a grating rock sound that keeps the nerves frazzled while making the associative connection to the youth of the soldiers and the raw ugliness of the battle (*Apocalypse Now,* 1979; *The Year of Living Dangerously,* 1983).

When events and characters are to be seen as being neither completely good or bad, but complex and variable, the music can greatly help the director and writer in projecting this, although it is a difficult assignment. In *Patton* (1970), the general can be perceived as (and basically is presented as) a domineering, bullying, egocentric, vainglorious, single-minded man of war, but he can also be seen as patriotic, God-fearing, anti-establishment, and a saver of American lives through his efficient and brilliant military moves.

Jerry Goldsmith's music allows us to take either view. The measured march cadences in the background set up an epic perspective to the film, recurring as the foundation for heroic marches to come, propelling and tying together the thrusts and progression of the film. Piccolos remind us of the heroic traditions of the fifes in the *Spirit of '76* (see Figure 13-16). When Patton, in Africa, detours to gaze at the ancient battlefield of Carthage, the distant orchestral murmuring and echoed trumpets tell us that Patton sees himself as being on a sacred mission, in the tradition of the great military campaigns of history. As the story proceeds, Goldsmith's music develops a long, sustained melody with a Mahlerlike epic extension. We can empathize with Patton even as we dislike him. The actual battles are played without music. For the soliloquies, as in most war films, music is used to heighten the character's interior monologue.

In *M*A*S*H,* the emphasis is on the humor that bonds people together in the midst of a war and helps them to survive, just as in the earlier *Bridge on the River Kwai* (1957). The Main Title turned out to be a simple song that played against the helicopters and action of the Korean War setting, much to Johnny Mandel's surprise. "I had just come off a picture with [director] Bob Altman and we were sitting around working on *M*A*S*H.* I had to do the theme for 'Suicide Is Painless' for that last supper scene. He said, 'It's got to be real stupid because of who's going to sing it and play it. We've got a GI who can sing and one who can play a couple of chords on the guitar. I used to write songs. I'll write this.' He came back a couple of days later and said, 'You know something. I can't write anything stupid enough. I've got a 14-year old kid with a guitar who will go through it in five minutes.' And he did. Michael Altman wrote the lyrics, but he dummied the song to a Leonard Cohen song called 'The Gambler.' It took me a couple of weeks to get that song out of my head. In desperation I finally wrote my theme the night before. I just wanted to write something with no chords and that's just what I did. We prerecorded it and everybody loved it. Then they shot the movie and while they were putting it together somebody stuck this song up over the titles, and I said, 'Wait a minute, what is this?' They said, 'We like it.' I said, 'Against those helicopters and the screaming? That's the stupidest thing I ever heard.' And they said, 'We like it.'

"As it turned out I was very happy to be overruled—it's the biggest seller I've ever had. I made a very soft arrangement, using just four men's voices in unison, singing the lyrics with three guys playing three different guitars—a very soft-rock sound. And it worked great."

PRIME-TIME SOAPS

> ***The creators of* Dynasty, *Richard and Esther Shapiro, called and had this project they felt was going to be bigger than life—like a movie—and they wanted scope to it.***
>
> BILL CONTI

> ***Among the most successful of today's television shows are the prime-time soap operas:* Dynasty, Dallas, The Colbys *and* Falcon Crest. *And, in terms of the musical language employed by their composers, how conventional that music is.***
>
> JOHN (JOHNNY) GREEN

> ***I could push even a simple show like* Dallas *as far as I wanted. Or I could have gone back to a triadic system, and that would have worked okay too. So there's never any excuse just to do one or the other.***
>
> BRUCE BROUGHTON

STYLE. John Green observes the scoring for prime-time soaps from a historical perspective. "Some of the music is quite attractive, much of it crashingly boring and dramatically abrasive, but all of it rather well made, brilliantly played, well recorded. But if somebody said to me that it was written in 1955, I wouldn't raise an eyebrow."

Such musicianly reactions to these successful and durable shows should not surprise us. Composers want to use the freshest musical approaches and be up-to-date, but the stylistic parameters of such shows are laid out and their success argues for the correctness of their choices. It might be pointed out that writing in a more traditional style is no tougher or easier an assignment than the other genre assignments, each dictated by dramatic considerations, audience communication, network biases, and precedent. It goes without saying that to come in on a show that's already going (and going successfully), the composer must understand and use the musical language and colors already being heard on the show.

THEMES. Themes for the prime-time soaps are very important to the filmmakers and the networks. Like all other film scoring, they are most successful when they really connect with the show. Bill Conti comments on creating his theme for *Dynasty:* "Esther Shapiro (who, with her husband Richard, created the show) wanted the approach of a feature and wanted scope to it, and she wanted to talk about rich people, etc. The script that she gave me was entitled *Oil.* The script sat around, and I'd go to the piano and nothing would happen. And then one day she called me and said, "The network just changed the name of the show to *Dynasty.* I went, 'Oh, hey—*Dynasty* . . . Dah-guh-dah.' For some reason, one of the rare times, the tune came out—there was the theme."

HARMONY. Even within the requirements of the genre, it is possible to expand the boundaries. In the first season of *Dallas,* Bruce Broughton experimented with how far he could expand the harmonic language, week by week. "Every show was very similar to the one I had just finished. So I asked myself, How can I do this one differently? I tried to see how far I could stretch the harmony before anybody complained. And I found to my own amazement that I could stretch the harmony about as far as I wanted. As long as it worked with the scene I could do the most brittle things, the most convoluted things, and they would still call me back for next week. It was really a wonderful experience.

"It wasn't a simple style at all. Harmonically, I kept trying to do something like late Mahler; he always goes to the wrong note, and creates a chord you couldn't *possibly* expect would be coming up. So I kept thinking, How long can I keep going to the wrong note and keep increasing the harmonic tension, before it completely overburdens the scene? And the answer was that I never found the limit. So there's never any excuse just to do one or the other. (Unless you're doing a rock-and-roll show for fifteen-year-olds—there are times when harmonic sophistication is just not proper.)" Figure 23-8 is a reproduction of Broughton's handwritten sketch for a *Dallas* cue.

FIGURE 23-8

Dallas Assuaging Pam, from the "Winds of War" episode Bruce Broughton

FIGURE 23-8 (*Continued*)

TELEVISION SERIES

> ***Doing episodes is the best schooling possible for a beginning composer, because you get all the variety of styles, the variety of dramatic situations.***
> BRUCE BROUGHTON

> ***In* Dynasty *they wanted it on the nose. On* Cagney & Lacey *they wanted it off the nose. They all have a different little thing, and you'd better deliver that message in the :60 theme.***
> BILL CONTI

> ***To do episodic television, you've got to have a thick skin and no ego.***
> JOHN CACAVAS

Television series—or episodic television, as they are also called—obviously includes more types of shows than prime-time soaps, but there are common elements in them all. Many more pilots are made than reach the screen, and pilot-making represents the television industry at its most hyper. The producers get extremely concerned that the music may not appeal to the one person at the network most responsible for making the decision as to whether the pilot goes or not. The music is replaced much more often on pilots than on other television projects, and the theme is virtually always demonstrated by the composer to the complete satisfaction of the client. But the network reps don't usually hear the demonstration at this point (unless the demo is electronic), and sometimes the networks ask for a replacement of the score after they first receive the pilot (before airing the show). Half-hour and hour pilots rarely have a prescheduled air date, because if they are bought for series production the pilot won't be aired until the series debuts.

THE THEME. Producer-writer Marc Merson finds that in television "there are really two subjects, one of which is the main theme, and the rest of which is scoring the picture. They are related but they are separate, and it seems to me I always talk about the main theme first, because you do that once you have a general sense of the picture and you talk about scoring the picture later. The main theme becomes very important because it tends to carry through the rest of the picture."

"On *Cagney & Lacey,*" Bill Conti says, "Barney Rosenzweig [the producer] said two things to me: 'I don't want anyone to know that this is a cop show. And don't forget, we're following a comedy.' He wants to hold that audience. He doesn't want them to advertise that it's a cop show. So I've got the two alto saxes playing like I'm coming out of a comedy. I go into a little ditty that, at the time, I didn't feel smacked of a cop show. You listen to four or five of them and you say, 'I guess this is how a cop show goes,' and then you don't do that thing." (See Figure 23-9.)

SCORING TELEVISION EPISODES. David Bell's working routine on *Murder, She Wrote* is to get a time-coded videotape of the show each week to study prior to spotting. "Even so the producer [Peter Fischer] thinks of [spotting] things I never would have thought of. I've learned so much from him. There have been shows where I have said, 'I think we're overspotting this—we've got too many little cues'—and I'll be damned if it didn't work. Sometimes I will say, 'Peter, let me try something,' and he usually likes it. There is about 10 minutes of music per show, with many subtle little things that have to be caught, and with this kind of orchestra every note has to be written out." Bell gets 5 to 7 days to write the score and it is recorded in a 3-hour session with an orchestra of 25–28 players. (See the specific instrumentation on page 328.)

ADAPTATION OF THE THEME. Composers who score television series usually work with the Main Title theme(s) for key sequences. These recognizable themes play the action here and there throughout each episode, serving as musical I.D.'s for the show and the characters.

Since another composer has usually written the main theme, the scorer of episodic television is sometimes adapting previously written material. The adaptation of this material is no different than any other adaptation project, except that the musical guidelines are very well established with regard to style, sound, instrumentation, and harmonic language. Figure 23-10 is John Addison's theme for *Murder, She Wrote,* and Figure 23-11 is an excerpt from David Bell's adaptation of this theme. Figure 23-12 is Arthur B. Rubinstein's theme for *Scarecrow and Mrs. King,* and Figure 23-13 is Rubinstein's Christmas adaptation of his own theme for the 1986 *Scarecrow* Christmas episode Main Title.

GETTING HELP. Mike Post manages to score several television shows that are running simultaneously. How did he do it during the 1986–1987 season? "It's really simple. In the case of *Hill Street Blues* [see Figures 16-21 and 16-22], I write and orchestrate every note. That's not hard because there's not much music. They don't want to hear anything, and I have four or five basic generic bags. I never try to pull out old cues and rehang them. I believe that would take more time than just writing. I know what it sounds like when people get killed, I know what it sounds like when people are born, etc. I have my whole little modus operandi for *Hill Street* and it doesn't take long to write one.

"I have a new show called *L. A. Law* that's created by [producer Steven] Bochco that has a bigger orchestra than *Hill Street.* It has a little more music but not much and it takes me a little longer to write and orchestrate, but I have a feeling that this is going to get in line like *Hill Street* has.

FIGURE 23-9

Cagney & Lacey Theme Bill Conti

FIGURE 23-9 (*Continued*)

FIGURE 23-9 (*Continued*)

FIGURE 23-9 (*Continued*)

FIGURE 23-10

Murder, She Wrote Theme John Addison

FIGURE 23-10 (*Continued*)

Picc. (sounds 8va)
Fl.
f
Cls.
f
Triangle
Trpt.solo
(end)
8va Pno.
arco
(+ Bsn.)
+Timp 8va
⑦
⑧
⑨

FIGURE 23-11

Murder, She Wrote Dixon's Diner

David Bell and John Addison
Orchestrated by Fred Paroutaud

FIGURE 23-12

Scarecrow and Mrs. King Theme Arthur B. Rubinstein
Orchestrated by Mark Hoder

"Pete Carpenter [Post's partner] is now retired, but he is keeping *Magnum* on my demand [see Figure 23-14]. We're doing it together at this point. In the case of *Magnum, A-Team,* and *Hunter,* which are the other three shows that we have at this point (aside from *Stingray,* which I just have to write a song for each week), we have six guys that we've trained from the beginning of time to sound like us. What we do is, every week there's a new heavy in *A-Team,* a new little kid, or a new love interest, or a new situation. So I sit down with the producer and we spot the show together and decide where the music is going to start and stop. Then I get the music breakdowns and I write the lick or two licks

FIGURE 23-13

Scarecrow and Mrs. King **Christmas Version** **Show #185912** — **Main Title** — **Arthur B. Rubinstein** **Orchestrated by Mark Hoder**

FIGURE 23-13 (*Continued*)

of the week. We sit there and I say, 'Here's the heavy and here's what it sounds like,' and I write it down on a sheet of sketch paper and photocopy three or four copies and I bring in the guys—Ray Bunch, Jerry Grant, Frank Denson, Ron Jones, Steve Taylor, or Walter Murphy—whoever. They bring in their Walkman tape recorders and we go through the show and I hand them the cues and they put on their tape recorders and I say, 'Okay, it starts at :00 and it starts when the A-Team comes running out of this restaurant. It's about in this tempo (about a 12 frame click, say) and catch that, catch this. Here's the piece of material you use. And here's what you do: do this, do that. Leave the click here and go into free timing here. Now go back into another click here of approximately 13 frames,' and I hand him the cue sheet and he goes away. I show up at the date and I conduct, and I change anything I don't like, and it all sounds like one person wrote it. They see the videotape as I show it to them and they take it home with them. You've got to be real specific about it if you want it to sound like you. It's not enough that they've studied you. You have to tell them specifically what you want.

"And business-wise I'm real proud that there's nothing about this that's considered 'ghosting,' in my opinion. The producers are notified in writing who writes what; the guys split the copyright with us. We pay them a composition fee by the minute plus they get scale for orchestrations. They come to the dates and 'booth' their own cues. They talk to the orchestra and the orchestra knows who wrote what and the producers know who wrote what.

"I conduct all the shows. I'm working for four different companies and we have to juggle times—but everybody's real nice about it.

FIGURE 23-14

Magnum, P.I. Main Title Mike Post and Pete Carpenter

2 Flutes
Oboe

3 Horns

2 Euphoniums
B. Trombone

Guitar
G D
E (no 3rd)

Guitar
E (no 3rd)
G D
E (no 3rd)

Piano/
Rhodes/
Prophet
full chords | G D
E (no 3rd)
octaves
f

Conga/
CowBell
Rock

Drums

10 Violins
f
div.

4 Viola
f
div.

4 Cellos
f

Fender Bass
f

6 7 8 9

FIGURE 23-14 (*Continued*)

FIGURE 23-14 (*Continued*)

FIGURE 23-14 (*Continued*)

"The amount of music goes like this: *A-Team* is the heaviest; it averages 15 to 20 minutes. *Magnum* is much lighter: about 7-10. *Hunter* is maybe 10-12. Last year we had two other shows: '*Riptide*' and *Hardcastle & McCormick,* and those averaged about 11-12 minutes."

THE CLASSICS. Gerald Fried has worked on episodes of some of the most famous television series of all time, including *Star Trek, Man From UNCLE, Mannix,* and *Mission: Impossible.* Fried mentions the differences in each show's point of view: "*Man From UNCLE* was easy—the style was tongue in cheek. You knew they were going to get out of every jam—they didn't try to make any profound points, like *Star Trek* tried and, I think, succeeded. They just were having a nice romp, and it was more sophisticated than anything that came before, and the job of the music was to let the good times roll, like a James Bond movie. This involved using some of the idiomatic sounds of the day, as later shows have done.

"But on *Star Trek* these fellows were saving the world each week by showing us a problem on another world. And it was assumed that we would try to get into the philosophical center of these problems. It's fantasy, like two sides of the coin: you get your wishes and realize that they bring some nasty baggage along with them. . . . You want to involve people on a deeper level. And even though it was a prime-time TV series, I think all of us composers who did it reflected that—we took that show quite seriously. We had 5 days in which to take an hour show seriously, but nevertheless I think we did. And the schedule was as frantic then as on any other TV series."

SAVING TIME. Many composers have thought of reusing cues from other episodes in their series, but it doesn't seem to work. After union rules were changed in 1977 to forbid tracking television episodes from libraries of cues recorded for each series every thirteen weeks, Alexander Courage found he was doing a new show for *The Waltons* every week. "For a while I tried to reuse the old cues, and I had a whole system of labels worked out but it didn't work. It was faster to write than to adapt the old music." Other composers agree.

In certain shows, like *Miami Vice,* the music can ignore the film and simply provide a constant rhythmic motion and tone that supports the general mood of the scene without relating to specific actions or events. In this case, the music editor can take music not timed specifically for a scene and cut it in as needed. But for other shows that can be a disaster. As former Columbia Pictures Television music executive Bodie Chandler points out, "If you take that approach to scoring and put it into a movie that is not filmed with the look or feel of a *Miami Vice,* you can find yourself in trouble. The scene will not breathe the way it should, with music that goes in and out or up and down, catching emotions."

TELEVISION/FILM DIFFERENCES

Writing for episodic television is obviously different from writing for feature films, but writing for two-hour movies-of-the-week or for a television miniseries will be comparable to that of features. But even here there are differences, particularly, as we have noted before, with respect to the time allowed to compose and the budgets, both of which are significantly less in television. Beyond that there are differences in the matter of style, pacing, and organization.

ACT INS AND ACT OUTS. When the stranger suddenly appears out of the darkness and the gun fires and the music comes up to an accented resolution on a minor triad with major seventh, we can be sure we are about to cut to a commercial break. This cadence is called an "act out," something you will not be composing for a feature film. Act ins and act outs are the cues that separate the program content from the advertising messages (the act ins introduce the next act after a commercial break, and the act outs close an act). Another word for act out is "curtain," an apt term since these devices are completely theatrical in function, much like lowering the curtain between acts in the theater.

The decision about whether there will be definitive act outs is a matter of taste, and some television producers love them and some hate them. In the cases when there is not a strong bias one way or the other, the composer can follow what is probably the best compromise procedure: use them at your discretion when they seem most suited to what has preceded.

BUMPERS. Bumpers are short musical signatures used in conjunction with the graphics title card for a show. They are usually based on a short phrase or motif derived from the theme, and are typically either :05 or :07 long, including the reverb "ring off" after the orchestra cuts off their last note. Almost all television shows require them, including movies-of-the-week and miniseries, depending on each network's policy. The editor will tell the music editor or you which length is required. They are recorded once and reprinted as many times as necessary to fulfill the network requirements of the show.

It is a good idea to create a softer and louder version for movies and miniseries to provide a choice in dubbing, in case the producer might like the idea of matching the outgoing mood of a scene with the incoming bumper.

STINGS. A sting is the old radio term for a very short music cue of :05 to :10. They are not used extensively outside of comedies, but will be spotted occasionally by producers who favor them. (See Chapter 11, "Playing the Drama.")

THE PRODUCER. On the matter of creative control in television, producer Marc Merson notes, "You have to distinguish between television and film. In television generally, the director has a great deal less to say. Usually relatively little about music. There are exceptions, but in feature films obviously it's very different—the director has at least as much to say as the producer and usually a lot more."

CREATIVE DIFFERENCES. Music executive Bodie Chandler says, "In television we're going for the more specific scoring, where you're hitting every five or ten seconds and you're carrying the scene along. On movies-of-the-week you have more time to breathe and you can get more of a melody going. Sometimes you really have to go with the film rather than just give it a nice long line and let the visuals carry it, but there are times when you get a longer section of music that can bridge a half-dozen scenes. That's why some composers are better than others—it's what they see on the screen and how they approach it that makes their scoring techniques more desirable than others."

CHAPTER 24

ETHNIC, PERIOD, AND SOURCE MUSIC; DOCUMENTARIES AND ADAPTATIONS

On* Agony and the Ecstasy *I did everything, I got all the fourteenth- and fifteenth-century scores—Gabrielli, Palestrina—and went through and studied them. And when I did* Cheyenne Autumn *I got all the Indian music to study the intervals and what would apply to an original score using so-called indigenous stuff, but tailoring it for my own style.

ALEX NORTH

A great many films have stories with ethnic character (*The Godfather,* 1971, Nino Rota; *Prizzi's Honor,* 1985, Alex North—Italian), geographic settings (*Under the Volcano,* 1984, Alex North—Mexico; *The Black Stallion Returns,* 1983, Georges Delerue—Africa; *The Emerald Forest,* 1985, Junior Homrich with Brian Gasciogne—the Amazon jungle; *The White Dawn,* 1974, Henry Mancini—Eskimo country; *Clue,* 1985, John Morris—England; *Salvador,* Georges Delerue), or period settings (*The Great Gatsby,* 1974, Nelson Riddle—the twenties; *North and South Book I,* 1985, Bill Conti—the Civil War). In each case the composer must decide whether the music should be written totally in an ethnic or period style, just flavored by these musical materials, or not influenced at all by time or place. If the score does utilize these materials, should it be authentic in every detail or simply evocative of the period or locale?

These are recurring questions, and the answers depend on each film's point of view. There are some occasions when musicological accuracy works well, but most composers have found it more satisfactory to use all available musical resources to score these films, including a contemporary harmonic language when called for dramatically, as well as other relevant underscoring techniques to communicate the emotional thrust of the story. The necessary ethnic/geographic and period flavor can be evoked by adding a degree of one or more of the authentic ethnic or period musical elements as desired, whether these be motifs, scales, harmonies, rhythms, or instrumentation.

One way to sort out the options is to rely on your analysis of the function of music in each scene to be scored and in the film as a whole. Two of the principal functions of an ethnic or period score will be (1) to suggest the film's locale and era, and (2) to communicate the emotional flow of the characters in the story and the overall dramatic theme.

ETHNIC/GEOGRAPHIC CONSIDERATIONS

> ***When I wonder sometimes how much the historical, ethnic, national, or racial subject matter of the film should affect the treatment of scoring, I think of Puccini. He may inject a certain color of a Japanese scale, a touch of a Roman canzona here and there, but he is essentially writing his own music. I'm interested in the particular national coloration of the film.***
> LAURENCE ROSENTHAL

Films with foreign settings and characters often require source music for the exterior scenes and bar scenes to solidly establish the locale of the film. In *Salvador,* when James Woods and James Belushi first arrive in the country, soft regional music from their car radio helps set the geographic location, and thereafter it is used wherever possible to provide that local color. Authentic folk songs are used on the soundtrack to heighten the score's connection with the locale. Similarly, in *The Black Stallion Returns,* the street scenes are enriched with source music to establish ethnic/geographic color, yet Georges Delerue basically chose *not* to use these influences in his score. In *Out of Africa* (1985), director Sydney Pollack and John Barry deliberately avoided ethnic/geographic implications in the music.

BLENDING THE ETHNIC ELEMENTS INTO THE SCORE. *The Mission* (1986), which takes place in 1750, tells the story of the Guarani Indians of Brazil and their conversion by the Jesuits. Ennio Morricone was able to blend elements of baroque church music with the native Brazilian music. "It wasn't my intention to reproduce the local folk music," Morricone says. "Rather, I was attempting to unify elements of Indian music with Western music. Towards that end, the score is interwoven with musical patterns common to this particular tribe of Indians, as well as one of their linguistic patterns known as syllabic chant."[1]

The decision to weave ethnic or geographic flavor into the dramatic score and to what degree depends on the film and (sometimes) the filmmakers. In the miniseries *Sadat* (1983), a project set in the Middle East (largely in Egypt), Charles Bernstein considered the options: "I could have scored that movie completely in an Arabic idiom, but I was quite sure that wasn't going to be what they wanted. When I approached the project I realized I could have given it a completely ethnic score with only ethnic instruments and idiomatic music, or I could have gone to the other extreme, which would have been in the tradition of Hollywood film music, where there would be no more ethnicity than let's say Verdi might use in reflecting a similarly exotic locale. When I asked producer Dan Blatt about that he said something very interesting and very helpful. The same question had come up with Lou Gossett, Jr., as to what degree of accent he should use. He was trying to get his character down and wasn't sure whether he should go overboard with some kind of Middle Eastern accent, especially to overcome his own image as a known actor. Dan's attitude was that Lou should do it with just a touch of accent to color it—to give it a sense of the locale without caricaturing it. And that was pretty much the decision about the score; to do it in a neutral idiom and use colorations—accents.

"I used the cimbalom (which is not a Middle Eastern instrument but lent a certain ethnic quality), and the dumbeg and the tambourine, both of which are familiar to Western ears because they are used in Middle Eastern nightclub music (belly dancing, etc.), and lent that little touch of accent. I also used a liberal amount of augmented seconds in the

---

[1] *Los Angeles Times,* April 10, 1987, interview by Kristine McKenna.

scale, being careful not to sound hackneyed or cliché-ridden with them. And I used some very bizarre rhythms.

"When I was dealing with the man himself or his love relationship with his wife, I mostly stayed away from ethnic elements and went with him as a statesman, as neutrally as with any statesman—Winston Churchill, Roosevelt. I just went with the character traits—the nobility and the love and so forth."

Bernstein made a quite different decision for the 1979 television movie *The House on Garibaldi Street.* "The questions here were much more complex. In this film we had Israelis and Germans in Argentina in the late fifties or early sixties. But it didn't have the flavor of the sixties. The environmental aspects were clearly Argentine, and the main characters were the Nazi Adolph Eichmann and the head of Israeli intelligence, who is leading this particular expedition to track him down and bring him back for trial. So there are three rather disparate musical vocabularies: the modern state of Israel, European characters who are Israeli citizens, and Eichmann as a certain aspect of Germany at this time, all set in a South American milieu.

"I was baffled at first, and I had six days to write the score—to plow into *Garibaldi Street* with a very, very tight budget. And yet it turned out to be one of the most satisfying experiences I've had in television.

"I didn't treat it anything like the way I treated *Sadat.* I superseded the issue rather than solved it. There was an overriding issue, which was the pursuit and entrapment of a war criminal. At the beginning of the picture we don't have that element. I asked myself, What kinds of scenes have music in them? There was, for instance, a long monologue in which one of the characters is describing graphically how Eichmann had cruelly murdered a baby. And the music under that had to evoke the Nazi era from the point of view of the victim. That narrowed me down for that particular cue. There was another very dramatic cue where they actually abduct him and I had to create there not only the standard suspense devices, but also, when they abduct him, I wrote into the woodwind parts different rhythms and different pitches of the sound that sirens make in Europe (the kind used in *The Diary of Anne Frank* [1959]) to evoke wartime Europe, to bring us back to that. So he was being abducted to the very sounds which struck fear into the people whom in fact he had abducted—and it created more of an emotional history of that moment. So I found that as I went through the cues, many of the scenes in fact were not rooted in Argentina or Israel, but were memories of where the initial issues and crimes had taken place. Some Argentinian tangos did come into it—in scenes in cafés where you could see somebody playing piano."

RESEARCH. Research will help you to discover the stylistic characteristics that suggest being in Russia, or China, or second-century Greece. Composers dig out this information from recordings, libraries, ethnomusicologists, and foreign musicians when they are available to answer questions.

Research is much easier now than it used to be. Henry Mancini, who uses research materials frequently, says, "When I first started in the fifties, you didn't have all of these catalogues of ethnic music recorded all over the world. And it's such a *great* help now, to have all of this stuff to fall back on. We used to have to go to the public library and pick out music, especially when you get into fourteenth-century music and such, and now there is music [commercially] recorded from that period that is authentic. In the case of *10* [1979], I had a whole library of ethnic music available to me. It gets interesting because you can't trust your ear sometimes. When you start trying to get into the difference between Mexican music and Spanish music, it's a very fine line. And then you start to get into the rest of the Latin American countries—Colombia, for instance, which has its own ethnic style."

QUASI AUTHENTICITY. It is a common experience these days to visit Japan, Hong Kong, and other faraway places, hoping to hear some exotic national music, only to end up hearing no native music at all—only American records of pop hits, or watered-down imitations of them by regional musicians. When the composer sets out to do research on national and regional music, he can often find nothing current that would evoke the deeper associations of that country.

You must know what the authentic sound is for each ethnic or historical project, but you can't necessarily count on that sound to be perceived as authentic by the audience. Gerald Fried, who has scored many National Geographic documentaries with international settings, did one set in Hong Kong. To capture the ethnicity of the film he chose not to use exotic Chinese instruments, other than characteristic gongs, temple blocks, and such. His experience applies to all composers attempting to use authentic ethnic music: "I did research, and it turns out that the genuine music of Hong Kong is such an embarrassing imitation of Western sounds that I had to write my own 'authentic' music. This happens time and time again. And rather than use Chinese instruments, we imitated them. I've had such bad luck in the past. I used to get Hungarians to play cimbaloms, for example. After the first twelve hours on a cue that could have been done by a skilled studio musician in one take, I got smart. I let the studio guitarist adjust his banjo to make it sound like a samisen, and so forth.

"I did a documentary on Tahiti and that was even worse. Tahitian music is like Martin Denny on a drunk night. [As a rule] to be convincing I take out some of the Western influence, and go for what I think is right. I've often done Library of Congress research, and there *are* authentic sounds. I just incorporate those as much as possible into what today's actual music of Tahiti or Hong Kong is."

In his score for the 1975 television movie *I Will Fight No More Forever*—a story about Chief Joseph of the Nez Perce Indians, who spoke the title line when he was finally defeated by the U.S. Army—Fried found that "Once again, the real authentic music of these particular Indians was so primitive, it would have sounded like I was mocking them. The drum just goes bomk, bomk, bomk, on some kind of flabby drum that sounded like a piece of parchment. UCLA has a magnificent library. I've spent lots of time there, and the pentatonic scale of these Indians sounded so Asian that I wouldn't dare use it." Figures 24-1 and 24-2 illustrate solutions by Gerald Fried and Jerry Fielding to this interesting problem.

RECORDING WITH ETHNIC MUSICIANS. It's expensive to record with authentic ethnic musicians who don't have the efficiency and experience of studio musicians, but when time and money are available to work out exotic effects with these musicians, the results can be striking. In *Remo Williams* (1985), composer Craig Safan worked with traditional Korean musicians, but they played their authentic instruments within a contemporary setting (see Figure 15-5).

"Everything was done to click because it was the only way I felt we could sync up all these elements. First I recorded all the Synclavier tracks for all the cues (playing them myself). They were actually all preprogrammed and I just unloaded them in the studio. For cues without Synclavier parts, I just laid down a click track.

"Then I brought in the Korean instruments and players. They had never done overdubbing and it was a tremendous amount of work. If you write a crescendo they can't stay with the click because they speed up. When I said, 'Wait a minute—you're speeding up,' they would say, 'We *always* speed up when we play louder in our music,' I said, 'Well, you can't do that here!' I spent two days conducting sitting on the floor with them trying to hold them in [tempo]."

FIGURE 24–1

I Will Fight No More Forever Main Title Gerald Fried

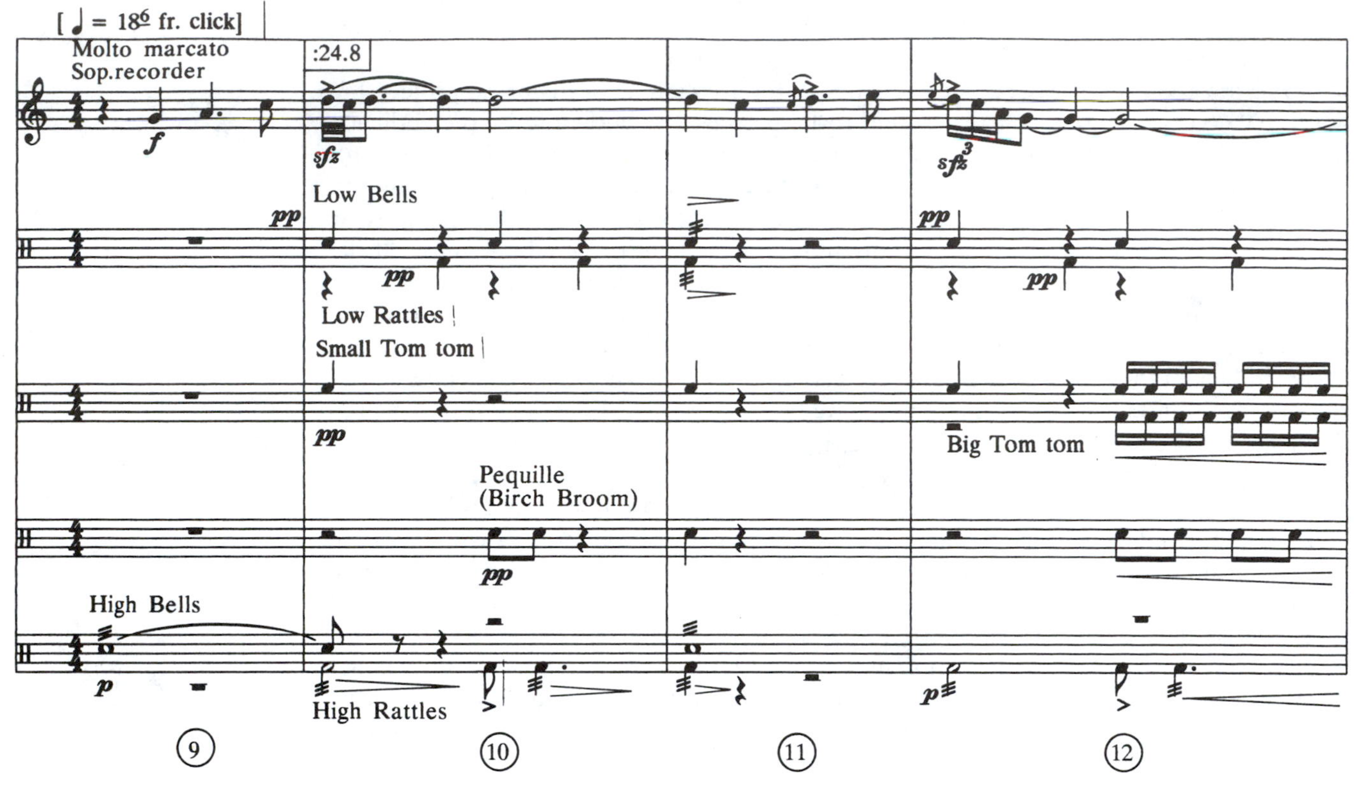

FIGURE 24-1 (*Continued*)

USING AUTHENTIC MUSIC. Laurence Rosenthal felt that there were two authentic Russian musical elements that should be represented in his score for the miniseries *Peter the Great* (1986). "One of them was the whole element of folk music, because one felt very much the presence of the people. And Peter himself, in spite of his Westernization, was a democrat, strangely enough. And then there was the magnificent liturgy of the Russian Orthodox Church. I incorporated both of those elements into the score. Just about all the choral excerpts in the score are directly from the liturgy. I felt that they were inimitable. In the case of the folk songs, it is a mixture. I used about three folk songs which particularly struck me, although one or two I rewrote a bit. There is a very good tradition for that—everybody from Brahms to Stravinsky has rewritten folk material. But there the quality of the melodies was so wonderful that I couldn't resist it. I did actually compose much of the folk-like material throughout the score.

"As far as the effect of these folk-music melodies on the harmonic language of the score, it is a funny thing that when you start dealing with the church music and with the folk music you find that you are drawing on the same sources that Mussorgsky, Glinka, Tchaikovsky, Stravinsky, and many other Russian composers drew on, and inevitably it

FIGURE 24-1 (*Continued*)

seems as though you are starting to sound like them, when actually you are all sounding like the original sources. But in the battle sequences I would be more universal. I invented a kind of Swedish theme which was a rather clean-cut Scandinavian kind of thing." (See Figure 24-3.)

ADDING THE FLAVOR. Bill Conti used the sound of panpipes (played on the Electronic Woodwind Instrument) to add a Japanese flavor to his score for *Karate Kid II* (1986). The panpipes suggest—without directly imitating—a Japanese shakuhachi. Other orchestrational touches that add to the Japanese feeling of the score include occasional pizzicato, synthesizer playing with "lute" and "giant koto" patches, occasional bell trees and wind chimes, and other coloristic synth sounds. Harmonically, Conti often uses the characteristic Japanese minor scale (our natural minor scale, but with different intervals emphasized).

FIGURE 24–2

The Outlaw Josey Wales **11-M-1C Comanche Scouts Jerry Fielding**

FIGURE 24-2 (*Continued*)

Whereas traditional Japanese usage often stresses melodically the E♭ and A in the scale below, Conti has created a more Western approach. The example in Figure 24-4 underscores the end of the cue that begins after Pat Morita's father dies.

Maurice Jarre reminds us that "a director, if he's a good director, may have spent three or four years on a project. He knows what he wants—he gives you his basic idea. When David Lean asked me to do the music for *Lawrence of Arabia* [1962; see Figure 16-5], I started to study Lawrence's life. David said, 'You have to understand *Lawrence;* it's not Arabic. He comes from *his* point of view, not the Arab point of view.' On the contrary, on the film *Mohammed* [1977] I wanted to do almost an Arabic score, not necessarily a composition of Arabic sounds, but the feeling being from the Arab point of view."

AVOIDING ETHNIC REFERENCES. There are other times when the composer gets another directive: *Don't* acknowledge the ethnic background of the characters. When John Cacavas was writing the score for *Kojak,* a detective with great pride in his Greek ancestry, there was one episode with a Spanish or Puerto Rican background. "I borrowed on that kind of music to play it. But many producers today in that same situation are saying, 'I don't want anything to comment on the Puerto Rican-ness of this. I want it to play against it.'"

And when Cacavas was scoring the 1980 television miniseries *The Gangster Chronicles,* the producer did not want anything really ethnic—such as scoring it like *The Godfather* (1972). "They were afraid of backlash from Italian organizations. So we had no mandolins, and so forth. It was treated more symphonically. On the other hand, he wanted that touch of minor—the kind of thing that would be indicative of what people would expect."

FIGURE 24-3

Peter the Great **Theme** **Laurence Rosenthal**

PERIOD MUSIC

> ***I try to make it so it's today's music but has a tinge, a flavor, of the period music as well. And that's not easy—I work hard at it.***
>
> ALEX NORTH

Films that take place in the past are called "period films." *Gone With the Wind* (1939) is a period film. So are *Ragtime* (1981), *How the West Was Won* (1962), and *Out of Africa*

(1985). *Casablanca* is not, because, although it now has become a story about an earlier period in time, at the time it was made in 1942 it was, of course, a contemporary wartime drama.

Swing Shift, a 1984 film about World War II, is a period film. Patrick Williams used a great deal of authentic big-band source music, which blends into his underscoring. Laurence Rosenthal's score for *Heart Like a Wheel* (1983) begins with a 1940s swing-band cue over the main titles, which helps establish the background of champion racing-car driver Shirley Muldowney.

Although period films often use much authentic music from the period as source music, they are not usually *about* that period; that is, the dramatic theme of the film is not about the period itself, it is usually about the people and their particular circumstances.

FIGURE 24-4

Karate Kid II **5-4** **Bill Conti**
Orchestrated by Jack Eskew

FIGURE 24-4 (*Continued*)

Therefore, the chief emotional statement of a period score is not necessarily hooked into the period. The period can definitely flavor the score and can exert a strong influence on the composer's musical choices. There are many times when the musical language of the period becomes the musical language of the score (as in the case of Karlin's 1974 score for the television movie *The Autobiography of Miss Jane Pittman*).

In his score for *Victor/Victoria* (1982), Henry Mancini uses a bluesy twenties/thirties feel for the scene in which James Garner is in bed with Lesley Ann Warren and finds that he is impotent. The style gives an appropriate lightness to the scene and reinforces the period (Figure 24-5). Then, during the long sequence in which Garner sneaks into Julie Andrews's room to see if she is a man or a woman, Mancini elaborates on the same material. In Figure 24-6, the interpolation of a piano solo influenced by Bix Beiderbecke illustrates the effective free use of the period style once it is established.

Period music, then, often supports the era of a film, or a flashback within a film. It can even support the chronological development of musical style to indicate the passage of time, a concept that was developed fully by Gerald Fried in the miniseries *Roots: The Next Generation* (1979). He actually changed his main-title treatment for each episode, matching the styles to the decades as they progressed, starting with the original Afro-American, working up through ragtime, the blues, big-band jazz, up to the present. Each era had appropriate instrumentation. For the post-Civil War music, for example, Fried says, "We

FIGURE 24-4 (*Continued*)

used harmonica, of course, but we used more fiddle, since that was a major instrument in the South at that time."

It is not true that composers always use strong period flavor to match the music to the time and place. In *Dragonslayer* (1981), Alex North didn't overtly acknowledge the Dark Ages. "The score was one of the most dramatic scores I've ever written. The idea of sorcery in the sixth century, and the fantasy and the adventure and the beautifully grotesque monster, all of that gave me an opportunity to go all the way and be free." (See Figure 13-8.)

In the television remake of *The Man in the Iron Mask* (1977), Allyn Ferguson used some Lully played by the Musica Antiqua from London to accompany a dance in Louis XIV's court. But that is source music. What about expressing the terror? As Ferguson describes it, "The score is a sort of takeoff from there, but people in the twentieth century are not going to relate to sixteenth-century music, so I had to do something different there. If you want to convey fear or terror, you need to deal with the kinds of sounds that most people in our society associate with fear or terror. Music can't describe—it's abstract. But all of us come with a set of preconditions. . . . For the dissonant stuff I went almost into a Stravinsky kind of approach. Twentieth-century ears have interpreted

FIGURE 24-5

Victor/Victoria **8M-1 You are Impotent** **Henry Mancini**
Orchestrated by Jack Hayes

Stravinsky to be weird. So you're playing a game all the time, trying to establish an avenue of communication and you're not sure where the listener is."

Georges Delerue's Main Title for *A Man for All Seasons* (1966) is an excellent example of period flavor in an original piece of music. (See page 356.)

Woody Allen has made great use of period music as both source and stylistic underscoring in films like *Radio Days* (1987), *Manhattan* (1979), and *Purple Rose of Cairo* (1985).

DOCUMENTARIES

How should a composer differentiate between the scoring style for a documentary, a docudrama (a dramatized version of a real historical story, like *Sadat*), and a fictional story set in a historical period or an ethnic/geographical context (*Gone With the Wind*, 1939, Max Steiner; *The Pawnbroker*, 1965, Quincy Jones)? The treatment of docudramas may be no different than pure fictional stories set in historical or ethnic/geographic settings, while true documentaries have a noticeably different stylistic treatment. The more a docudrama leans toward a pure documentary approach, the more it will be scored like a documentary, and often with an emphasis on sparseness and cold reality.

Gerald Fried sorts out the differences in this way: "In documentaries you don't try to get inside characters—the drama doesn't happen inside characters. You usually see events that are produced by people, not the events in their own heads. The music seems to be more general—instead of using complex chromatic chords, I would use fourths, for example, which have a drier, more broad effect, almost as if the music lets the audience do the thinking, instead of doing as we do in dramatic music, where we try to do as much thinking for the audience as possible. We have to reach in and grab the audience and make them feel a certain way; in documentaries, I keep it more bland.

"In a feature or a TV series or a thematic show, where a grizzly bear is shown attacking, I would probably think of ways to get as much terror into the music as possible. In a documentary, I would go more for the balance of nature. When we're around a grizzly,

FIGURE 24-6

Victor/Victoria 9M-1 Cat and Mouse Henry Mancini
Orchestrated by Jack Hayes

FIGURE 24-6 (*Continued*)

for example, we are second on the food chain, and I would be more matter of fact about it even though there is some terror. I would keep it more impersonal, larger. The rhythms, the hidden agenda, are based on a larger scale, a larger rhythm. If there's motion on the screen, with something chasing something, I probably would go for the natural turnover of events. It seems to be a more calm, serene, contemplative approach."

In documentaries that deal with countries, cities, or eras, or that pull back to reveal a large perspective, the standard treatment is to use almost constant music behind the omniscient narrator (at least in any place where sound effects are not self-sufficient). Documentary-style dramas that deal with singular events (like *Kent State*) are often more effective using only sync-sound live music, or appropriate source-music-like songs, or no music, rather than using any underscore.

Director James Goldstone describes making the 1981 television movie *Kent State*. "I had grave questions in terms of what music would be scored for this three-hour film. I knew we would use a lot of the popular music of that time, and indeed the picture was written and conceived to use two very famous Crosby, Stills, Nash, and Young songs: 'Teach Your Children,' and 'Four Dead in Ohio.' Because of the tradition of film music, I hired a composer. We tried to unify the score so that what he composed would effectively sound like source music. That is to say, it would not be laid on top of the film or support from underneath the film, but work into the aural texture of the film. As I dubbed the picture I tried playing the scenes without the music (much as I liked it). I dropped about 92 percent of the music he had done, because in each instance where we would put the music in, we lost the 'documentary' flavor of the film. It began to sound like we were trying to tell the audience something rather than immerse them in something that was really happening. Now that is a very special case because there I was trying to duplicate reality."

In documentaries, there may be no script but simply a conceptual story line based on research on that subject. The structure and editing is then opportunistic, taking advantage of beautiful camera shots and propitious and chance action that occurs. Assembling the film can be instinctive and artistic rather than preplanned to be expository. This puts the music in the position of unifying many different sequences of shots, and also delineating and giving form to what sometimes comes across in documentaries as a rather nondramatic, evenly stressed series of scenes. At best, successful scoring turns documentary footage into meaningful and varied sequences. One approach for the composer is to take the point of view that he is creating a kind of ballet music to accompany these "dancing" abstract images, and this can add a dimension to the film beyond the scope of the narration.

SOURCE MUSIC

> ***Source music can really be dull. Source music is always saved until the night before the scoring session, and then tossed off out of hand and out of mind. Source music is always farmed out. Source music is a necessary nuisance. Source music is never taken seriously by the serious film composer.***
>
> FALSE RUMORS

Source music is music that the people on the screen can hear, while underscoring is the music that *they* can't hear but *we* in the audience can. Both are crucial to the effectiveness of a film's score.

The music that seems to be coming from the scene can originate from (1) a known visual source such as a Mariachi band, car radio, or a jukebox, (2) a nonvisual (off screen) source like a marching band or stereo, (3) an imaginary source (something that probably would be believable in a scene, such as a car radio or cassette player. No matter what the originating source, it should always be as authentic as possible.

Since the composer is usually responsible for all source music (other than that recorded as sync sound on the set or on location, or licensed from existing commercial recordings), he must often imitate amateur ensembles and has to get properly amateurish performances from his studio musicians at such times. Georges Delerue composed an on-screen marching-band source piece for *A Little Romance* (1979). "I asked my musicians to play badly. It's hard to do, because sometimes it's too much." Detuning some of the brass and winds helps in cases like this, as does distant miking to facsimile a realistic outdoor recording.

Unless there is a visual or dramatic motivation for starting or stopping source music, it is usually recorded overlong so it can be cut in by the music editor to come in and/or go out in progress. This should be discussed during the spotting session.

When a song or other source music is heard in a film, traditional logic says the scene must show the source of the sound at least for a moment, such as a radio playing or a live band. Yet some contemporary films, especially for the teenage market, are purposely loaded with current recorded music often played loudly, and sometimes no visual explanation accounts for the source of that music. As Ira Newborn points out about his work with John Hughes on *Sixteen Candles* (1984) and other teen films, "As far as your traditional logic about the radio music not sounding loud and present for reality, it should be fudged a little. That's traditional logic, but in films you can do any damn thing you want. [If you can't see the source of the music] it's probably a kid wearing earphones. The point is,

John doesn't feel bound by that anyway. Teenagers aren't bothered by that—momentarily they see something they like, they hear a piece of music they like and—fine!"

Sometimes producers will license the source music they want because they want that exact thing, but that is always the producer's prerogative, and he does not spend that money to save the composer from having to provide source music.

INTERWEAVING SOURCE AND SCORE

Source music is most often used as independent music without any underscoring to accompany or overlap it, but source music (from any point of origin) can also change its function at any time and continue as score, acknowledging the emotions and events of the drama.

SOURCE MUSIC CAN FUNCTION AS SCORE. Sometimes source music can begin to function as powerful dramatic underscoring. Very often, although not always, the source cue is transformed somewhat to achieve this effect, usually through orchestration. Near the end of *Prizzi's Honor* (1985), Kathleen Turner puts an LP on the stereo and we hear pop music, which gets more and more Italian sounding as the strings begin to dominate, building with the intensity of the scene. The music is dubbed louder and louder to increase its effectiveness, continuing right through the slow motion of Jack Nicholson tossing the knife through her throat. At that point the music ends abruptly, highlighting the kill. There is no justification in reality for the LP to stop, but it doesn't matter because the source music has become score.

There is a fine example of source music supporting the emotions and the flow of a scene in *Witness* (1985): when Harrison Ford and the Amish woman flirt and dance with each other in the barn, the song on the soundtrack plays as source music from a visual radio. As they become more involved with each other, the music begins to *function* emotionally more and more like underscore, pulling them closer together and emphasizing their mutual attraction. Here the source music is not changed or adapted in any way as it becomes score—the acting says it all.

SOURCE MUSIC CAN CHANGE INTO SCORE. Source music can turn into score by changing the instrumentation from the reality suggested by a live or "recorded" musical performance into the orchestration of an underscoring ensemble of some sort. In these cases the music will usually change somewhat to function more as underscoring (perhaps being more sensitive to the shifts of emphasis in the dialogue or action, for instance).

In *The Magnificent Seven* (1960), the villains are counting their losses at night, and source guitar is heard under their dialogue. In the middle of this scene, Elmer Bernstein changes the guitar to woodwinds and in the next bar the source music continues as underscoring. The nature of the music doesn't change, but the illusion of reality provided by the solo guitar off in the distance is smoothly replaced by the cinematic convention of an orchestra.

In *Seems Like Old Times* (1980), there is a very clear moment in which a source cue segues to underscore—Marvin Hamlisch changes the live-piano source music during the party into underscoring on a common piano/harp chord, after which the underscoring orchestra takes over, continuing the cue as score.

The transitions from source to underscore are frequently difficult because of pitch problems, since production sound guitars and singing, and actors humming, are rarely tuned to A = 440. In *Animal House* (1978), the on-screen humming of the "Star Spangled Banner" is picked up by the scoring orchestra with a noticeably different pitch.

SOURCE MUSIC CAN CROSSFADE TO SCORE. There are times when source music can be effectively crossfaded into a dramatic cue in dubbing. This technique allows for a more significant change of the music's point of view and function, because the source cue and the underscoring cue can be completely different in sound, orchestration, and character, and the composer can smoothly change from one to the other in dubbing by bringing the level of the source cue down as the level of the underscoring increases. It can work just as well in reverse, by crossfading back to source music from score. The crossover from source to score should be planned prior to scoring, and the composer can then discuss the crossover with the music mixer and the director on the dubbing stage to achieve the most satisfying effect. This must be done with great care and smoothness to avoid sounding like a budget score assembled from a music-library rental service.

Director Paul Wendkos recalls a situation in which he **overscored**[2] source music to support a dramatic scene. "The first time I did an overscore was in *The Death of Richie* [1977 television movie, Karlin], in which we had naturalistic source music [coming from a radio]. There was a particular point in the script when I wanted psychological music in the score. We did a long segue during which we took out the naturalistic sounds and source and went into musical score and it was tremendously effective."

In Giorgio Moroder's electronic score for *Scarface* (1983), there is a highly styled variation of this technique in which the source music gives way to score for a moment, and then continues again. The scene starts with the source cue dance music at a club. Another cue fades up (replacing the source) as Al Pacino sees his sister in the club. This effect only last a few seconds, after which the source music resumes. Then the crossfaded score comes up again on the cut to a 2-shot of Pacino and friend and again fades out back to the source. Finally the score fades up on the move in to Pacino's eyes as his sister leaves; it then cuts off and we hear source again on the cut to Pacino as he follows his sister.

SOURCE MUSIC AND SCORE CAN BE USED SIMULTANEOUSLY. If a sequence is being scored during which a character sits down at the piano and begins to play, usually the score would be spotted to end as the on-screen music begins. However, scoring *through* a scene like this can be very effective if the score is playing an emotional point of view that can continue simultaneously with the on-screen music.

In *Testament* (1985), James Horner scored a scene during which Jane Alexander tries to console her daughter, who is saying, 'Don't come in—I just want to die.' When we see and hear the daughter practicing piano, playing 'Twinkle, Twinkle,' the score continues through this source music so that the source and score actually function together on two different emotional levels. Later in the film, Alexander sings a lullaby to her son as she bathes him, and he sings along. Again the cue continues, playing the drama in counterpoint to the lullaby.

SOURCE MUSIC CAN PLAY THE UNDERSCORING THEME. Sometimes the themes of the source music and the underscoring can be interchanged. This works best when the score is based on idiomatic materials of some type, whether they are contemporary or period.

Along with all the authentic period music in *The Way We Were* (1973), Marvin Hamlisch scored the title-song theme for the 1940s dance band that plays a college dance, thus giving the underscoring theme extra credibility as a melody justifiably identified with that time in the lives of Robert Redford and Barbra Streisand.

---

[2] Overscored: added another layer of music to an existing music track (the term has been coined by Wendkos).

ADAPTATIONS

***Huston is playing* Prizzi *for laughs, and the jokes aren't all in the script. . . . The orchestra acts as an unseen protagonist, commenting on the action and sometimes dictating it. . . . But not a single movie critic that I have read has pointed this out: the joke's on them.*[3]**

MICHAEL WALSH, CRITIC

(re: Alex North's score for *Prizzi's Honor,* 1985)

Many films have used existing music in their scores. In these cases the music must be licensed by the producer if the tunes are not in the public domain. This use of music can include playing actual popular records (Simon and Garfunkel's songs for *The Graduate,* 1967; "Stand By Me" in Rob Reiner's *Stand By Me,* 1986) or rerecording the original versions of existing symphonic compositions (Ravel's *Bolero* in *10,* 1979; Samuel Barber's *Adagio for Strings,* in *Platoon,* 1986; Howard Hanson's *Romantic* Symphony for the ending of *Alien,* 1986; and Alfred Newman's Main Title for *How the West Was Won* in *Romancing the Stone,* 1984).

Many times what sounds like the original may actually be an adaptation to fit the film's timings and needs. *Breaking Away* (1979), the story of an imaginative teenager with a preoccupation with things Italian, contains a climactic bicycle race in which the boy competes against a real Italian cycling team. Composer Patrick Williams found when he entered the picture that the film was already temp'd with Mendelssohn's *Italian* Symphony and some Rossini. "There was no question about the fact that it worked. As it turned out, about half the score is original and half adapted. To make the Mendelssohn and Rossini fit, I had to patch it up and turn corners to get to the right part of the music at the right spot. You have to play a game of taking the most important moments and working backwards, maybe killing time by repeating bars, so you can hit the big moments at the right time."

After Alex North and director, John Huston agreed that opera was the right slant for *Prizzi's Honor,* a film about mafiosi mix-ups, North spent weeks listening to all the Italian operas he could find before coming up with Puccini's *Gianni Schicchi,* an opera whose story parallels that of *Prizzi's Honor,* as well as a string quartet that Puccini wrote when he was eighteen years old, and whose themes he reused in his opera *Manon Lescaut.* North describes the scene in which Maerose (Anjelica Huston) tells her father that Charley Partanna (Jack Nicholson) did it to her "Three times, Papa—right on the floor." "At this point," says North, "I used the famous aria 'O Mio Babbino Caro,' which is sung by Schicchi's daughter Lauretta. This means, 'Oh, dear daddy, I like him—he's so handsome.' And then I used Rossini's overture to *La Gazza Ladra,* which means 'the thieving magpie,' for the corrupt-bank-official kidnapping theme. And I used Donizetti's *L'Elisir d'Amore* for the time when the daughter comes to her father. . . . I was weaving back and forth. It was a combination of adaptation, with changes in musical texture [orchestrational], extending certain thematic material, and digesting some of it."[4]

Some requests for adaptation turn out to be inordinate tasks. "Ricardo Montalban's first picture in this country was called *Fiesta,*" recalls John Green. The story sets up a situation in which the eldest son of a bull-fighting family wants to become a composer. "Jack Cummings, the producer, had the most improbable idea that Ricky Montalban should play at the great big moment, the blow-off of the picture, a piano rhapsody of *El Salon Mexico,* by Aaron Copland. If there ever was an unpianistic work that would be it. I

[3] *Film Comment,* Volume 21, Number 5, September-October 1985.

[4] The original sources of the adapted music were not credited in the film.

told Jack, 'Aaron will laugh you off the telephone.' But Aaron made a monkey out of me. Not at first, but when he heard the fee of $15,000, he said he would license the adaptation on the condition that John Green do the adaptation. Incidentally, it's the only Copland piece published with a split composing credit. It's called *Fantasie Mexicana.* Eighteen-year old André Previn played the original recording."

They Shoot Horses, Don't They? (1969, adapted by John Green and Al Woodbury) is the tragic story of a six-day dance marathon in the early thirties. Full of period dance-band music, it is a very good example of the dramatic use of period source adapted to a demanding dramatic context. (See Chapter 25.)

PART 8

SONGS

CHAPTER 25

MUSICALS AND PRERECORDING

I literally laid out the four-and-a-half minutes of "I Sing the Body Electric" in Fame *for every single vocalist, for the dance break, for what became the a capella section, for what became the orchestral coda. And it was a fairly thick orchestration."*

MICHAEL GORE

Every film composer encounters situations in which singers, dancers, or musicians perform on screen. These pose special problems; the sound is rarely recorded at the same time as the filming because it is almost impossible to get the highest quality picture and best sound recording simultaneously. Even if the obstacles to getting simultaneous great picture and sound could be overcome, it would still be very difficult to get the best musical and dramatic performances when recording during filming. The endless number of retakes needed to shoot different camera angles and to correct technical flaws makes it very unlikely that the musicians/actors would be able to keep giving the spirited peak performances that are so important. It's also excessively expensive, since the whole orchestra would have to be kept there for days of shooting to get the required combination of flawless lighting, camera focus, sound, and high-energy performance.

There are three options available for recording a scene with on screen music: prerecording (playback recording or prescoring), set recording, and postrecording (or postscoring). For the reasons cited above, whenever movies are made that include on-screen performances or dancing, whether it be music videos for MTV, musicians appearing in television commercials, or full-blown film musicals, **prerecording** is almost always the option of choice.

Set recording (simultaneous sound recording and photography) is occasionally used in order to achieve the most lifelike credibility, and for those ad lib musical situations when a singer talks the verse of a song, or when musicians invent new lines in jazz and rock that are difficult to mime convincingly during playback shooting. (Veteran actor Rex Harrison refused to do anything but set recording for most of his numbers in *My Fair Lady,* 1964, which included very "conversational" singing.)

More frequently the choice might be **postrecording** (recording the music after the picture is shot), which offers the ability to upgrade the sound by rerecording the original actor, by replacing the performance of the original actor with that of another (Marni Nixon's voice replaced Audrey Hepburn's in *My Fair Lady* and Natalie Wood's in *West Side Story,* 1961), and Bill Lee replaced Christopher Plummer's vocals in *The Sound of Music,* 1965), or by augmenting the accompaniment. In the Rex Harrison case cited above, there was still postscoring, during which a full orchestra replaced or sweetened the original instrumental track from the live (set) recording. This involves elaborate preparations so that the conductor can "chase" the original piano track with a click track especially built to follow the live performance beat by beat no matter how much its tempo may have varied.

Some isolated scenes—like the one in which the church congregation breaks into song in *The Color Purple* (1985), the scene in which Gene Hackman plays saxophone in *The Conversation* (1974), or the moment when Michael J. Fox plays guitar in *Back to the Future* (1985; see page 357)—require individual solutions to provide the on-screen music.

These same three options are available for television variety shows like Carol Burnett or John Denver, or the annual Oscar presentations, since the same concerns pertain in order to get the best musical performances, the best sound recording and the best picture. A common variation used in these shows is to prerecord the instrumental and vocal backgrounds but record the vocalist live, thus avoiding the dead giveaway of attempting to lip-sync on tight close-ups.

POWER PLANNING. Experienced film editors, music editors, recording engineers, and directors handle the problems of on-screen performances by very disciplined planning of every musical move, dance step, and camera angle, following the precedent of the great musicals listed at the end of this chapter. Careful planning is especially important to the producers, since any overrun can add immeasurably to an already costly project.

PRERECORDING (PRESCORING)

In prerecording a vocal or dance number it is critical that the tempo and interpretation be exactly right so that everything will work perfectly and naturally during the subsequent shooting of the sequence. This includes cinematic technical details like having enough time and space to make the right camera angles.

Director Robert Wise recalls the dance scenes in *West Side Story:* "The music stage was right next to the rehearsal stage over at Goldwyn Studios where Jerry Robbins was rehearsing. When Johnny Green had his orchestra ready to record the 'America' number and he and Jerry had arrived at what they thought was the right tempo, Jerry brought the dancers in and had them rehearse while he made tempo comments. And they would dance to every take. Jerry of course is a stickler for that kind of thing."

INTONATION. As music editor Gene Marks points out, "One of the biggest pitfalls in prerecording is the intonation of the orchestra. If two cues are recorded maybe six months apart, one postscore and one prescore, and they have to segue one right into the other the composer has to make absolutely certain that the pitch is identical between the two." In any case, tracks recorded in Europe can bring a load of grief, since the pitch can be noticeably different there.

DEVELOPMENT OF PRERECORDING METHODS. Composer and music director John Green was around when many of the prerecording methods were developed. He recalls working in New York with orchestrator Conrad Salinger, in the period around 1930, before playback recording was developed. They were using the set recording process to make a short film of an overture that was to be shown in movie theatres before the feature was run. "This overture to *The Vagabond King* was less than a five-minute piece, and the session went on from eight o'clock in the evening until five o'clock in the morning! But before playback recording great compromises were made—principally with the sound and musical aesthetics, rather than the cinematic or photographic aspects. Music was really the stepchild. They were doing close-ups as well as cover shots. Many of these same problems were reincarnated in the days of live television. The advent of the playback made all sorts of choreographic possibilities. You could never have done the Busby Berkeley things without it.

"But it introduced the problem of nuance. What do we do about rallentandi and accelerandi? That's when we got the cue click."

THE CUE CLICK. Prerecording a variable tempo at that time was not too different from what might be done today. For a vocal number the singer and orchestra recorded the song, using a click loop as the metronome. From that recording a cue track was dubbed with audible click for use as playback recording for the shooting stage. When the music ritarded to a fermata, the click of course stopped, but two warning clicks were added just before the note which followed the fermata, returning it to tempo. In Green's words, "By experimentation we found how far apart the clicks should be spread in terms of the human mind and ear. When the singer was in front of the camera and heard these two beats she could come in correctly with the playback recording. On the set, the sound department picked up a guide track [of her actual singing during the shooting]. When you finally got in the cutting room, the music editor had to deal with three tracks (running on his triple-headed Moviola with the picture of that scene) for each camera angle: (1) the original track from the recording stage (with full orchestra); (2) the clicked version of the original track; and (3) the guide track picked up on the shooting stage (including all the sounds from the shooting stage, and lousy sound). From here the music editor reconciled the discrepancies by sliding the music tracks, or if that ultimately failed, by editing picture."

AN AMERICAN IN PARIS. Prerecording can become remarkably complex when a scene includes talking, singing, piano playing, dancing, and orchestral accompaniment, as was the case in "By Strauss," the first trio in *American in Paris* (1951), with Oscar Levant at the piano and Gene Kelly singing. It ultimately evolves into a sextet with everyone dancing. Green was co-music director with Saul Chaplin and conducted all orchestra sessions. He recalls: "That was all prerecorded. We did it on the recording stage as you heard it. What we had to do with that number was to record the piano track with Oscar first; Oscar did not play to click, he played it with me conducting, fermatas and all. We then had to click the piano track for me.

"We had been rehearsing for weeks. The singers were brought in. The clicks were fed to me and to Saul Chaplin while they were recording. Then came the orchestra. The fermati were handled with conventional cue clicks, not tempo clicks. We did sectionalize it, so that the big orchestra section where they all get up and waltz is a separate section. Wherever there was singing, that was cue clicked. Those places where the orchestra played with the piano and they sang, we did it all together. It was a very long recording.

"To try out the takes we went down to the set but we had to do it by the sections (with proper overlaps). So the basic methods applied here. The only problem was that we had a guy singing and playing the piano at the same time.

"When the vocalists were being shot they were hearing the orchestra combined with the prerecorded piano track [and voices] with click. When Oscar spoke, that was recorded on the shooting stage. It was a chore to match the sound but not a problem. When we got into the dubbing room, if there was a problem we fixed it with each cue. We had all the finest equipment.

"All the taps on the songs and dances were postrecorded, whether it was Fred Astaire or Gene Kelly, whoever."

RECENT PRERECORDING

The evolution of commercial recording has greatly raised public expectations. Superior equipment has been a great help, but the basic needs of planning prerecording, set recording, and postrecording still exist. In such cases it is not the composer/music director's task to make all these decisions, but close cooperation with the choreographer, music editor, songwriters, and director is required to solve the many different situations that can arise.

GREASE. Editor John Burnett notes the changes that have occurred: "Years ago everything was very disciplined—whether it was vocals, or dance and instrumental, or vocal and instrumental, everything was done to playback. All of the performers, whether they were actors or dancers or participants in the movie, were rehearsed by choreographers. You coded your music track with a music number and everything that was shot was done from the beginning to bar such and such. Now—you take something like *Grease* [1978]—there is no discipline whatsoever. They don't have everything planned to the beat, the bar, the note, the rest, whatever. They make a playback. But after the first or second take, they panic—start coming up with ideas. By the time they get finished with these dancers they find one very long phrase or section of the number that has a very good beat and they end up playing that same thing over through the whole number. So basically when you get back, you throw the whole thing out and do the music again.

"On *Grease* we would go back and make those adjustments and we'd make the track sound as exciting as we could from the temp track that we had. When we did this, we'd bring the people up to see the sequence. They would sit there and say, 'We don't know how you did it—it's wonderful. Yes, we know we'll have to rerecord. What a great guy.' They were always extremely appreciative. Then the composer would totally rewrite [and rerecord]."

FAME. Composer Michael Gore spent over a year working on *Fame* (1980), a film that was an example of discipline, good planning, and execution. "I was hired about four months before production began. [Director] Alan Parker brought me on as a musical supervisor for the film. At that point he did not really know what he wanted in terms of music, but only knew that the music would be highly eclectic—classical, pop, gospel, rock 'n' roll, etc.

"We planned out the numbers together. The script had not been blueprinted with actual musical sequences. We spent time together trying to figure out where those songs would be (before the shooting). The ones that had to be prerecorded—those that would be sung on screen—had to be done before the shooting.

"Alan Parker did not consider *Fame* a musical. He never really wanted to have people just burst into song. Even if it was a thin excuse, he wanted to have one (like the loudspeaker on top of a taxi during the performance of 'Fame,' for example). . . . When he asked me, 'How can music start, but not really start?' I said, 'The only thing I can think of is a jam, where one person starts, and another begins, and so on.' By the end of that day we had set the 'Hot Lunch Jam' and Alan had laid out all the shots—which instruments and which kids. Then I went into the studio and did a basic track with some session guys in New York to hear what it was going to sound like. I took the track home, and it didn't work. We decided that the playing was too good, too polished. Basically the edges were so rounded and smooth that it lost of a great deal of excitement—it didn't feel like a jam.

"As a result I went in three nights later and worked with the kids in the high school [New York High School of Music and Art, and the Performing Arts High School]. It was a phenomenally talented group—we were extremely lucky. We took them into a session with just a boom mike to get a very rough demo. We laid it out with everybody there and it had a terrific sound. So I took about twenty-five kids into a New York studio and we did the entire thing live (without tracking, with about four or five takes). I then did a pass with all the singers doing their vocals on it, and within that pass we developed a lot of crowd noises—at times they were singing, at times they were talking. Of course in the final film with ADR looping they ended up putting more crowd noises in.

"That track is not locked on a click track. One can feel that the track gets faster, and I think that's wonderful—it adds to the excitement of the piece. That was a deliberate decision, because I felt that on click we would not be able to keep the spontaneity of the jam—people would be following the click.

"Alan was extremely talented. As a director, he truly understood music. He knew exactly what he wanted. The movie that finally emerged was very close to the movie he had in his mind at the beginning of it.

"Where he developed a scene and needed various angle shots, we almost always prerecorded. When he wanted to pick up a shot of somebody playing a cello or a shot of somebody playing the violin, and he wasn't planning on intercutting it with other shots, we occasionally would do it live.

"Putting together the full orchestra plus rock rhythm section for 'I Sing the Body Electric' was technically handled by first laying out the number. We were well into shooting and we still didn't know what the end of the movie was going to be. In fact, Alan originally intended to use a pre-existing song that he was fond of. Lyricist Dean Pitchford and I went away and wrote 'I Sing the Body Electric.' We orchestrated the number—in terms of images and singers—for what we had, including the principals.

"We laid it down with piano, bass, and drums (without click) with studio guys in New York; then I put on all the vocals. Once I knew we had the vocals the way that we wanted them (meaning the principal vocals and also what would become the choir later on), I started to build the track. We then put on the rest of the rhythm section, we put on the strings, we put on the brass. I filled out the orchestra, and we had one section just for the gospel choir. By that time we were on 48 tracks. Alan hadn't shot the scene yet, so he needed the freedom to do a close-up of a flute player and have the flute on its own track. We had to leave every option open. We would give them two or three different mono mixes to use on the shooting stage, one with the vocals a bit above the orchestra, one with the vocals down, so when they were filming the orchestra, that's predominantly what you heard. In playback you really need to use mono so that wherever you are on the set, everybody hears exactly the same thing.

"This piece, even when we did the piano, bass, drums, was charted within an inch of its life. The day of the prerecording, Irene Cara and Paul McCrane were shooting. I took Laura Dean (who is the girl who first sings the opening lines of 'I Sing the Body Electric') and she did the guide vocal from beginning to end. When I knew that we had the right tempo, we came in with each of the singers and had them record their actual part. You should know that we actually did this track about six weeks into shooting on a ten- or eleven-week schedule. We recorded the 'Hot Lunch Jam' on a Friday evening, and the shooting for that sequence began on Monday. We had maybe a week or so on 'Body Electric.'

"As for click, there is something about recording to it which is great for certain kinds of numbers. For example, I think the dance numbers worked incredibly well and click gave them a really solid beat. For something that is more free-form—something that needs air and room to breathe—click just isn't the solution. If you listen to 'Body Electric,' the track starts at one tempo where the vocals enter, and when it moves into the dance break it picks up a little bit. When it moves into the final gospel choir at the end, it picks up yet again. That's part of music—you don't conduct the Brahms Third to a click."

POSTRECORDING (POSTSCORING)

In *That's Life!* (1986), Henry Mancini replaced all the dance-band music at the end of the film with postscoring, and this is typical in such cases. Postscoring also can be an absolute necessity in some situations where musicians play on screen, especially if the on-camera musicians are in some way closely tied in with the drama.

The celebrated film *They Shoot Horses, Don't They?* (1969) was such a case: it might not be regarded as a "musical," but it nonetheless had formidable music sync problems. These occurred because musicians were always visible in the background, and this very tragic drama about marathon dancing in the thirties required a credibility that would be lost if the on-screen musicians were out of sync with the soundtrack.

John Green (functioning as associate producer and music director) spent the better part of a year working out the details of the music recording. "In preshooting rehearsals with the actors and cameras, orchestrator Al Woodbury and I were able throughout the picture to sit with [director] Sydney Pollack [and discuss the actual instruments that should appear in the background to fit the mood of the scene]. And we went into great detail. I remember his saying once, 'I think it would be great, anywhere in these two pages, to see a trombone standing up there with a cup mute.'

"Al and I devised what we called melody/rhythm scores. We picked our tempos on an electronic metronome (in long sessions with Sydney). [For the shooting] everybody had the melody who was capable of playing it. We had to decide whether it was two-beat, four-beat, or waltzes, and how fast. To the degree that we dared prognosticate (in conference with Sydney), we used a red grease pencil on our melody/rhythm scores to indicate that saxes play, brass play, saxes stand up. Sydney had promised that he would stay in meter [when he edited], although he wouldn't promise to complete whole phrases. On the shooting stage we had a piano. The actors, in order to feel the atmosphere, had to have some impression of what they were hearing, but their tracks had to be clean enough to be used [as the final dialogue tracks]. Randy Rayburn, the pianist, was so soft you could hardly hear him. He and the other pianist [who performed this function] were hearing variable click that speeded up since that was part of the essence of these derbies.

"Then the entire picture was postrecorded! Incredible. How in God's name did we do it? I cannot tell you what an impossible job that was. This was a highly sensitive, enormously melodramatic, heart-rending dramatic story. Nine out of ten frames you're looking at a dance band—they're playing all the time. Meanwhile in front of the bandstand a big dramatic scene to tear your heart out is being played by Jane Fonda and Bruce Dern. The pulse of the soundtrack is going on and you can see the bass player (and immediately see if he is playing between the beats you can hear). Normally in such a situation you loop the dialogue. But you couldn't loop *that* dialogue in those soul-searing scenes. And God forbid if the pianist's hands should be up in the air when you hear a piano being played."

THE CLASSIC MUSICALS

Despite the advances in electronics and synchronization and recording techniques, the methods worked out for filming the great song-and-dance musicals of the thirties and forties are mostly still applicable to today's needs. Although we no longer have the steady flow of big Hollywood musicals to train our engineers, cameramen, songwriters, and performers, the following classic musicals are textbook examples of these techniques: *Flying Down to Rio* (1933), *Naughty Marietta* (1935), *Rose Marie* (1936), *The Wizard of Oz* (1939), *Cabin in the Sky* (1943), *Kismet* (1944), *On the Town* (1949), *Show Boat* and *An American in Paris* (1951), *Singing in the Rain* (1952), *Kiss Me Kate* (1953), *Oklahoma* and *Guys and Dolls* (1955), *Carousel* (1956), *Pal Joey* and *The Pajama Game* (1957), *Porgy and Bess* (1959), *West Side Story* (1961), and *The Music Man* (1962). The era is brilliantly summarized with many outstanding highlights in Jack Haley Jr.'s *That's Entertainment* (1974) and Saul Chaplin and Daniel Melnick's *That's Entertainment II* (1976).

Since that time musicals have become less and less frequently produced, but we have still had musicals like *My Fair Lady* (1964), *The Sound of Music* (1965), *Camelot* (1967),

Funny Girl (1968), *Fiddler on the Roof* (1971), *Cabaret* (1972), *Tommy* (1975), *The Wiz* (1978), and *Chorus Line* (1986). All of these have been adapted from Broadway or London musicals and have included important dancing routines as well as singing numbers.

In addition we have seen a number of films in which music played a big role but which were not adaptations of Broadway musicals. The technical considerations, however, are equivalent to those of a Broadway musical adaptation. These films include: *The Entertainer* (1960, with Laurence Olivier), the Beatles' *A Hard Day's Night* (1964) and *Help* (1965), *Alice's Restaurant* (1969), *Gimme Shelter* (with the Rolling Stones, 1970), *Nashville* (1975), *Leadbelly* and *Bound for Glory* (the Woody Guthrie story) (1976), *New York, New York* (1977), *Saturday Night Fever* (1978), *All That Jazz* (1979), *The Coal Miner's Daughter* and *Honeysuckle Rose* (1980), *Tender Mercies* (1982), *Flashdance* and *Staying Alive* (1983), *Cotton Club, Amadeus,* and Prince's *Purple Rain* (1984), and *'Round Midnight* (1986).

CHAPTER 26

SONGS

People don't realize the power—both the contributive power and the detractive power—of songs in films. DEAN PITCHFORD, LYRICIST

Songs can bring a great deal to the film experience. At best, a vocal will humanize the score, and can give the soundtrack either wit ("Ghostbusters," 1984, words and music by Ray Parker Jr.) or warmth ("The Way We Were," 1973, lyric by Alan and Marilyn Bergman, music by Marvin Hamlisch). The lyric can speak for the character ("Ready to Take a Chance Again," in *Foul Play,* 1978, lyric by Norman Gimbel, music by Charles Fox) or reflect an overview of the film, and the right performance can add authenticity to a film's statement (as did the Spanish folk ensemble in *Salvador,* 1986, and Isaac Hayes in *Shaft,* 1971).

The music for the film songs of the sixties and seventies was usually composed first, and then the lyrics were written. Although there was some variation from that work method, especially when the songwriters were not involved in scoring the film, this was the traditional way for film composers to work when they were composing both the score and the songs. The composer was chiefly concerned with creating his main theme for the score, and that theme became the "theme song." Henry Mancini wrote the theme for *Breakfast at Tiffany's* (1961) and then Johnny Mercer wrote the lyric; the song became "Moon River." They wrote "Days of Wine and Roses" (1961) similarly.

When Michel Legrand collaborates with Alan and Marilyn Bergman, he writes the music first for virtually all of their songs (including "The Windmills of Your Mind" and "How Do You Keep the Music Playing?"). Marvin Hamlisch wrote the music first for "The Way We Were" (lyric by the Bergmans) and "Nobody Does It Better" (lyric by Carole Bayer Sager). Karlin wrote the theme for *The Sterile Cuckoo* (1968), and it became "Come Saturday Morning" when director Alan Pakula asked Dori Previn to add a lyric. "For All We Know," written for *Lovers and Other Strangers* (1970), became a song only after Robb Royer and James Griffin (original members of the rock group Bread) added their lyric to Karlin's theme. In each case, although the assignment included writing a song for the film, the music was completed before the lyricists began writing, and few if any changes were made in the music to accommodate the lyrics. Burt Bacharach and Hal David were an exception, comfortably tossing ideas back and forth in much more of a collaboration, probably because they had songwriting backgrounds and therefore approached projects like *Alfie* and *Butch Cassidy* as songwriters, not theme writers.

The advantage to writing the music first is that the music will have been created specifically to satisfy the scoring requirements of the film, and therefore the song can be easily and effectively integrated into the score, sometimes playing under dialogue, and sometimes scoring other dramatically important moments. These songs rarely sound as though they have been arbitrarily added to the soundtrack; their use as score guarantees a more organic effect.

The disadvantage is that these songs are often more suitable as instrumental themes than as songs written to be sung. Although the songs mentioned above have all become vocal standards, there have been many times when the songs that result from this work method are not as idiomatic as they might be. This became more and more significant during the eighties, and filmmakers now expect film songs to be musically and lyrically idiomatic and designed for Top-40 airplay. An instrumental theme with lyrics added will rarely be successful in that context anymore.

With this changing orientation, film songs are now more often than not created by songwriters with commercial recording backgrounds, not by film composers. While this has had a great impact on film songs and soundtracks, the prerequisites for a good film song remain the same. All the artistic criteria for a good song will be relevant to film songs, and the film composer should become aware of the highest standards of excellence in song lyrics so that he can understand the challenges of writing an outstanding lyric and thereby collaborate most effectively with the lyricists with whom he works. When collaborating, he will need to be sure that the resultant song expresses a lyrical and musical tone and attitude consistent with the film, so that the song can be successfully integrated into the score.

The big difference, then, between writing a film song and any other song (other than for theater) is in the creation of the lyric, and our discussion of film songs will therefore concentrate on the art and craft of film song lyrics.

THE FUNCTIONS OF A FILM SONG

> ***Sometimes something's missing from the film, and it needs your help.***
>
> NORMAN GIMBEL, LYRICIST

> ***I will take a job when I feel that something that I write can make a difference.***
>
> DEAN PITCHFORD, LYRICIST

In order to use a song effectively in a score there must be space for that song on the soundtrack, and a reason for its use. Lyricists always want to know whether they will be able to contribute anything to the dramatic whole of the film. "One of the first questions that we ask ourselves when we are shown a film is, Is there a function for us?" says lyricist Marilyn Bergman. If the question is successfully answered—if we can find a real role for the song in the picture—that implies certain things. That implies that we're not going to repeat anything that's happening visually in a kind of show-and-tell way, or repeat anything that's in the screenplay unless we can add some other dimension or fly at another altitude."

Lyricist Dean Pitchford looks at films in the same way. He explains that not all films provide sequences when a song can play a significant role in the drama. "There are more and more cases where I am asked to do songs that are buried under action. I shy away from those because it doesn't challenge me, it doesn't celebrate the song, nor is one song any more or less appropriate than another." When the scene looks right for a song, he says, "I'll look at the sequence in a film and say, 'Ah. I know what to say here. I know how the feeling should go, I know what the rhythm should be, I know what the orchestration should be.' I think of all those things, too. I look at a sequence and I try to figure out, 'Is this a piano and Rhodes ballad or is this a synthesizer, or is this rock and roll (naked guitars and drums); is this a black woman singing or is this a heavy-metal group? What does this moment call for?'

"Sometimes I've been asked to look at a picture and give my opinion. And sometimes I've talked people out of doing a song, because a song would be expensive, it would roll over the final credits, it wouldn't be much of a selling tool, and it wouldn't reinforce the dramatic material."

When a song does feel right for a film sequence, it may be because the film can use the kind of help only a song can provide. As lyricist Norman Gimbel points out, "Sometimes the filmmakers feel that they need words, possibly to help set the film up. If the dramatic setup is a little soft or vague, a song can function over the main titles to create a mood and prepare you for the film."

Occasionally songwriters are required to create a song title that can become the title of the film as well. This is never the only function of a film song, but it can be an important function. Because the filmmakers didn't want the word "death" in their film's title, *Death of a Snow Queen* became *Summer Wishes, Winter Dreams* (1973) after Alan and Marilyn Bergman and Johnny Mandel wrote their title song for the film.

Songwriters should always look for moments when the music, lyric, and performance can make a powerful emotional statement. When Marvin Hamlisch scored the ending of *The Way We Were* (1973), he recorded an instrumental version of the theme, not Streisand singing the Bergmans' lyric. "I thought using the song would be tacky. At the preview, I noticed that people did not cry during the end titles. They were touched, but it wasn't yet what I'd call a handkerchief film.

"And I went to the head of the music department, Jonie Taps, and I said, 'Jonie, you have to let me rerecord the ending, because I know that we've got a mistake here, and in my desire to be perfectly correct, I didn't use my main gun, which would have been Barbra Streisand singing.' And he allowed me to rerecord that wonderful moment when she touches his forehead. And then she sings, 'Memories . . .' And I tell you, the next preview that we had, they all cried."

CONTENT

> ***So often people say, "That song sounds great," and they stick it in the movie and something's happening on screen and something's being sung about on the soundtrack and the two don't mesh.***
>
> DEAN PITCHFORD, LYRICIST
>
> ***On the stage, many of the songs are about what's happening at the moment. On film, you just can't do that."*** ALAN BERGMAN, LYRICIST
>
> ***I synthesize the character, I synthesize the scene.***
>
> NORMAN GIMBEL, LYRICIST

The lyric of a film song can make an enormous contribution. Creating the proper lyric statement is a fine art and a hard-earned craft. Although the content of the lyric and the style of the song must match, the lyricist's challenge is to conceive the content and then create a lyric that perfectly expresses that concept in an appropriate style.

There are four basic approaches to the lyrical content: (1) a direct statement with a conversational, everyday text; (2) a more personal and often more poetic expression of the point of view of the character(s); (3) a more oblique statement, often using interesting images, usually expressing the character's point of view; and (4) an overview statement. The film and the characters dictate the attitude and style of the lyric.

DIRECT LYRIC STATEMENTS. If the characters are involved in situations that require straightforward talk, with no subtleties, then a simple, direct lyrical statement might be perfect. In *Shaft* (1971) Isaac Hayes was as direct as you can be, and even though there is imagery, it too is direct:

Theme From *Shaft*
Words and music: Isaac Hayes

[First line] Who's the Black private dick
That's a sex machine
To all the chicks
Shaft
Spoken by women Damn right
[Third line] Who's the cat that won't
Cop out when there's
Danger all about
Shaft
[Spoken by women] Right on

Shaft is a black private eye who tangles with a powerful racketeer. Even though the lyric tells all, it is an appropriate setup for the film, especially given its strong R & B performance by the songwriter.

The lyric for "Call Me," by Deborah Harry (music by Giorgio Moroder, performed by Deborah Harry), has an equally direct chorus lyric that establishes the theme of *American Gigolo* (the 1980 film about a male hooker and his affair with an older woman). Although obvious and on the surface, the very direct and repetitious statement is effective when combined with Deborah Harry's hard-edged rock performance on the soundtrack.

Call Me
Lyric: Deborah Harry Music: Giorgio Moroder

[Second verse] Cover me with kisses, baby
Cover me with love
Roll me in designer sheets
I'll never get enough
Emotions come, I don't know why
Cover up love's alibi

[Chorus] Call me!
Call me, call me, any, anytime
Call me!
You can call me any day or night
Call me

THE POINT OF VIEW OF THE CHARACTER(S). To write a lyric that gets inside the character requires "getting a sense of the film and what the character means to you," says Norman Gimbel, "and what the character should say in an extended way, or what the vocal should say for the character at that moment."

Gimbel wrote the lyric "Ready to Take a Chance Again" (for which Charles Fox then wrote the music) for *Foul Play* (1978). At the beginning of the film, Goldie Hawn is told by a friend that she should expand her life and start taking some chances. Hawn says she'll think about it, and then gets into her yellow Volkswagon. As she drives along the San Francisco cliffs, the song (performed by Barry Manilow) begins over the main titles. The words are conversational and from Hawn's point of view, but the treatment is full of ironies and surprises.

Ready to Take a Chance Again
Lyric: Norman Gimbel   Music: Charles Fox

You remind me,
I live in a shell,
Safe from the past and doin' okay,
But not very well.
No jolts, no surprises,
No crisis arises
My life goes along as it should,
All very nice,
But not very good.

And I'm ready to take a chance again,
Ready to put my love on the line with you.
Been living with nothing to show for it,
You get what you get when you go for it.
I'm ready to take a chance again,
I'm ready to take a chance again with you.

Arthur (1981) is a romantic comedy about a rich alcoholic (Dudley Moore) who falls in love with a quirky but lovable shoplifter (Liza Minelli). The overall theme of the film is "love" because Moore is forced to choose between Minelli (whom he loves) and an arranged marriage that he must go through with or be disinherited. The song "Best That You Can Do" is by Burt Bacharach, Carole Bayer Sager, Christopher Cross, and Peter Allen (performed by Cross on the soundtrack), and it speaks directly from Arthur's point of view, telling us that when you fall in love time flies, that you cannot shake the feeling, and that falling in love is the "best that you can do." The first lines of the verse sum it up.

Best That You Can Do
Words and music: Burt Bacharach, Carole Bayer Sager, Christopher Cross, and Peter Allen

Once in your life you find her
Someone who turns your heart around and
Next thing you know you're closing down the town

Throughout the verse he continues to ask himself, What is happening to me? The verse ends with the lines:

Wonderin' to yourself
Hey! What have I found?

It is Arthur's joyous speculation and his growing enlightenment that drives the film forward from beginning to end, and the song establishes this over the main titles.

In *An Officer and a Gentleman* (1981), Richard Gere enrolls in Naval Officer Candidate School to improve his life, and Debra Winger seduces Gere in order to improve hers. They are both trying to free themselves of the past, and to raise themselves up and beyond the present. In the chorus, Will Jenning's lyric for "Up Where We Belong" (music by Jack Nitzsche and Buffy Sainte-Marie, performed by Joe Cocker and Jennifer Warnes) captures the ambition of both characters, while at the same time tying them together as a couple.

Up Where We Belong
Lyric: Will Jennings Music: Jack Nitzsche and Buffy Sainte-Marie

Love lift us up where we belong
Where the eagles cry
On a mountain high
Love lift us up where we belong
Far from the world we know
Up where the clear winds blow

Barbra Streisand's voice speaks for both herself and Robert Redford as she sings Alan and Marilyn Bergman's lyric for the title song of *The Way We Were* (1973). By focusing their lyric on the concept of remembrance, the Bergmans are reflecting Streisand's wish in the film that her relationship with Redford could be as she remembers it once was. From the first word, "Mem'ries," the lyric is looking back through the eyes of Streisand at "the way we were." She expresses an uncertainty about her recollections, wondering (in the bridge), "Has time rewritten ev'ry line?" The last stanza reflects a love lost, but treasured.

The Way We Were
Lyric: Alan and Marilyn Bergman Music: Marvin Hamlisch

Mem'ries may be beautiful and yet,
What's too painful to remember
We simply choose to forget.
So it's the laughter we will remember
Whenever we remember the way we were,
The way we were.

AN OBLIQUE STATEMENT. Oblique lyrical statements are frequently from a character's point of view, but with a less obvious connection. Sometimes they rely on well-worked-out imagery for their expression.

For *The Thomas Crown Affair* (a 1968 film starring Steve McQueen as a millionaire bank robber and Faye Dunaway as an insurance investigator determined to catch him), director Norman Jewison knew he wanted a song when he shot the sequence with McQueen in a glider. "He wanted us to write a song that would underline the anxiety that the character was feeling at that moment," says Alan Bergman. "When we first saw that sequence," Marilyn continues, "[the Beatles'] 'Strawberry Fields' was on the temp track.

The only other direction Jewison gave was that he wanted no plot, no character, nothing specific. He just wanted the audience to feel that this was a guy who's skin was too tight for him. So we knew we were dealing with some kind of mind trip." "If we had written a song about flying, who cares—you're seeing it," adds Alan.

As the Bergmans began to work on a concept for their lyric, they realized that "anxiety is a circular emotion. It feeds on itself," explains Marilyn. "And in this case," Alan says, "the style of that movie was fragmented. There were a lot of images going on simultaneously—split screen, different stages of a robbery were going on in four or five different squares on the screen. So we wrote a fragmented lyric." The song became "The Windmills of Your Mind" (music by Michel Legrand).

The Windmills of Your Mind
Lyric: Alan and Marilyn Bergman Music: Michel Legrand

Round, like a circle in a spiral, like a wheel within a wheel,
Never ending or beginning on an ever spinning reel . . .

The imagery of circular motion continues to the end.

Like a clock whose hands are sweeping past the minutes of its face,
And the world is like an apple whirling silently in space,
Like the circles that you find
In the Windmills of Your Mind.

THE OVERVIEW LYRIC. Whether or not the lyric comes from a character's point of view, it may also represent an overview of the dramatic theme of the film, or some other clear overview statement. Marvin Hamlisch and Carole Bayer Sager collaborated on the song for the James Bond movie *The Spy Who Loved Me* (1977). Hamlisch scored the film, and in planning out the score, said to Sager, "I want something that's double entendre, and I want something that's *not* coming out like 'Goldfinger.'" He explains: "I didn't want to come on big. I wanted to come 'Hi, how are ya,' through the back door gently. And I had the first two bars, and said, 'From there is where I want to go. I want to start out with this minuet.' We knew we wanted a woman to sing it. It was all clear what it was going to have to be, but we didn't know what it was until Carole wrote the lyric."

What Sager did was to write a double entendre lyric called "Nobody Does It Better" (performed by Carly Simon) that speaks for one woman or all women and also can refer to Bond's general expertise as a professional spy—the best in the business. The arrangement starts with the chorus.

Nobody Does it Better
Lyric: Carole Bayer Sager Music: Marvin Hamlisch

Nobody does it better
Makes me feel sad for the rest
Nobody does it half as good as you
Baby you're the best.

Although the remainder of the lyric gets even more specifically personal (and sexual), the dual meaning of the above four lines helps carry the overview idea through the song.

In Dean Pitchford's lyric for the title song for *Fame* (1980; music by Michael Gore, performed by Irene Cara), he expresses the viewpoint of every student in the film, and therefore the overview of the drama as well. In the verses, he personalizes the lyric, but it could be any one of the characters speaking.

Fame
Lyric: Dean Pitchford   Music: Michael Gore

Baby, look at me
And tell me what you see
You ain't seen the best of me yet
Give me time, I'll make you forget the rest.

The verses end with the phrase "Remember my name," leading into the chorus, which begins:

FAME
I'm gonna live forever
I'm gonna learn how to fly
HIGH
I feel it comin' together
People will see me and cry

The song ends with the lines:

FAME
I'm gonna live forever
Baby, remember my name.

In *Norma Rae* (1979), Sally Field becomes the voice of her fellow workers in a Southern textile factory, so it is appropriate that Norman Gimbel's lyric for "It Goes Like It Goes" (music by David Shire, performed by Jennifer Warnes) speaks for her and also for the other workers. There is a stoicism in the lyric's philosophy that Field eventually outgrows. But as an overview, it paints the picture of the traditional workers, accepting life as they know it. This idea is clear from the first line of the verse.

It Goes Like it Goes
Lyric: Norman Gimbel   Music: David Shire

Ain't no miracle bein' born,
People doin' it ev'ry day.

The chorus continues this attitude, but allows room for hope as well.

So it goes like it goes,
Like the river flows,

And time it rolls right on.
And maybe what's good
Gets a little bit better,
And maybe what's bad gets gone.

SAME SONG, DIFFERENT MEANING. Some films are structured so that a double use of the song is desirable, once at the beginning or in the first half of the film, and a second time later in the film. Since the characters and the story have developed during the interim between uses, the song often takes on a new and possibly deeper meaning at the end of the film. Writer-director Richard Brooks planned on this kind of emotional transformation of a song when he wrote his script for *The Happy Ending* (1969). "The first time," says Alan Bergman, "you hear it as a proposal of marriage, a real love song. And later on, he wanted to use the song again, not change one word, and hear the irony at that point." Marilyn adds, "Sixteen years later, when this woman's life is falling apart and she walks into a bar and puts a quarter into the jukebox and selects the identical song, it now means something entirely different to the audience."

The song, with music by Michel Legrand, became "What Are You Doing the Rest of Your Life?" and the title itself is an ironic question to ask of a woman whose life is falling apart. The second use is thus particularly poignant. "The Way We Were" is also used in this way, which contributes to its added impact at the end of the film.

SONGWRITING COLLABORATION

When you hear a melody that feels right for a particular place in a film, it somehow evokes the right vocabulary. MARILYN BERGMAN, LYRICIST

A lyric is half of something. And it gets its life from the music. But you put a good lyric with good music and it becomes a great song. DEAN PITCHFORD, LYRICIST

The challenge of lyricist and composer collaborating on a film song is compounded by the intricacies of creating for a specific film sequence. A true collaboration benefits from getting the greatest possible input from all parties.

When Michael Gore and Dean Pitchford collaborated on "Fame," they discussed the song's function in depth, and what it might say. "I came to Michael with a bunch of ideas," says Pitchford, "and we whittled them down, and I began to craft a lyric. And I spent probably three weeks writing a lyric that was punchy and potent and had all kinds of zing to it. And then Michael called me a few days after I had given it to him, and said, 'I've got something. You ought to come hear this.' And when he played me the verse of what eventually became 'Fame,' I said, 'That's wonderful! But I don't see how that fits with the lyric.' And he said, 'Oh, it doesn't.' So I said, 'Okay . . . Well, you still have to write the chorus. Please try to make the chorus work with this chorus lyric.'

"And he called me back the next day, and he said, 'I've got the chorus.' And I went over and sure enough, he did. He had the 'Fame—I'm going to live forever' music, but it didn't fit the original lyric at all."

Pitchford doesn't find this disconcerting anymore. "At first I used to kick and scream and then eventually I calmed down to the point where that is our pattern for working. And I understand that, and it helps me clarify my thinking about a song. It gets me into a second level. The first level lyric is a first-time take. It has energy and it has a rhythmic feel to it. But then when he takes off from that and writes, and then I write to his music, I get real deeply into the songs. Usually my original lines don't fit anymore. I'll use some of the sense of it, but there's something in me that won't let me repeat myself, and so usually I end up scrapping the whole thing and going at his melody with a fresh approach."

HAVING A RHYTHMIC FRAMEWORK. It is very helpful for a lyricist to have a strong rhythmic concept for his lyric, if he writes the words first. Pitchford says he always has a rhythm in mind. "I can always do the drum pattern for my collaborator if I do the lyric first."

USING ROLE MODELS. Sometimes a writer will use a role model just to get started. "I usually walk in with a dummy melody and sing a rhythm or something," says Gimbel. "Not with everybody. Most of the guys won't sit still for it. Sometimes I come to Charles Fox with a whole rhythm, a whole hook with my one continuing melody that he hears for years afterward. He's got to shut that out and just get the bones of the trick. Sometimes I have a little syncopated trick." The Bergmans usually use a prototypical song as a way of getting everybody on the same wavelength. "And even for oneself, to zero in on the flavor," says Marilyn.

Some songwriters have difficulty working with role models, though. "Sometimes I don't let my collaborator know what the role model was," says Pitchford. "Sometimes I just tell him the gene pool that we're trying to draw from."

If the new song isn't written yet, the role-model song may be used during production instead of prerecording for playback for dance numbers. Michael Gore used "Bad Girls" performed by Donna Summer for the playback track for the "Fame" sequence. "I had chosen the number and set it up on a click," says Michael Gore. The decision was very significant, because it determined a great deal about the final song that would eventually become "Fame." "That song has a great deal to do with the way people look in the scene when they're dancing," says Pitchford. "People move in a certain way to one kind of a bass line and not to another. Also, in choosing the Donna Summer record, knowing that we were going to replace it with a song sung by Irene Cara, we were acknowledging that we were going to get a female with a soulful voice, singing an up-tempo dance record with a very strong beat. You start painting yourself into a corner with your role models, and that's why they are very important decisions."

COLLABORATION. When Alan and Marilyn Bergman work with Michel Legrand, they usually have their choice of melodies—sometimes as many as twelve or fifteen. "For 'Windmills,'" says Alan, "he wrote seven or eight melodies." "In that case," Marilyn remembers, "we finally said, 'Let's sleep on it.' The one we ultimately arrived at—all three of us—the next morning, was the one that seemed least likely the night before.

"In discussing the concept, at that time, because of his French and our English, we would speak in terms of abstractions, in terms of colors, or things that had nothing to do with the picture, like the times of day, the seasons. Or we would give him a prose paragraph totally unrelated to what the lyric would eventually say."

When the collaboration is this comfortable, surprising results can occur. Legrand had written many melodies for *The Happy Ending*. "Sometimes complete melodies," says Marilyn, "sometimes just starts, but all of them wonderful. But none of them were really right and he knew it and we knew it. And one of us said to him, 'What happens if the first line of the song is, What are you doing the rest of your life?' And he was sitting at the piano, and he said, 'What are you doing . . . I like that' and he punched, thank God, the cassette player, and said, 'You mean like this?' And he played the whole melody from beginning to end."

The Bergmans and Legrand may be an exception. Norman Gimbel has noticed that very often the traditional film composers are not used to truly collaborating on songs. "Most of the film scorers really satisfy their own needs. They write songs, but they are not songwriters. So you come to the process a little like a stepchild, and it's rare when they can really turn away from film scoring and become a songwriter and sit and generate that kind of heat and comfort and collaborative spirit. They don't know how because they don't have their genesis in songwriting. They have their own problems, they have their own scenes and footage and clicks and things to do and they would probably write better songs if they were able to collaborate with the lyric writer more, but they usually write themes. Piano themes that really basically are not vocal enough to be great songs. They don't write for the throat, they're writing for the keyboard. It is wonderful music, but I feel that they could write better 'songs' if they would give more of a collaboration. Words and music together do not necessarily make a song. A song is a song—a song has to be sung." He points out that Charles Fox prefers to have him write the lyric first and is consequently much more collaborative than most film composers, who don't have a songwriting background.

SYNCING THE LYRIC TO THE VISUALS

One of the cardinal sins is the repetition of what you're seeing, the telling of what you already know.

MARILYN BERGMAN, LYRICIST

More often than not you will want to *avoid* any direct syncing of the lyric with the visual images. "The most powerful things in the film are the images on the screen," says Marilyn Bergman. "Nothing you do should try to repeat those images—you're going to take second place." The circular images in "Windmills" reinforced and supported the symbolic images on the screen (and in McQueen's psyche) but they didn't repeat them (there weren't any windmills on screen).

When the coincidence of verbal and visual imagery occurs, the Bergman's suggest a slight change in the editing to avoid the duplication, or they may rework the line, if possible. "In *The Way We Were,*" Marilyn says, "both Alan and I wince and look away from the screen every time the words 'watercolor memories' hit; at that point there's a cut to a river with people rowing. Nobody else may notice it, but we do. Sydney Pollack moved it a few frames but it is still too close for our comfort."

"Near the end of 'Windmills,'" says Alan, "there's a line, 'When you knew that it was over you are suddenly aware/That the autumn leaves are turning to the color of her hair.' And at that moment, you're watching the glider and the camera moves in on a woman waiting for McQueen, and you see her auburn colored hair." "We didn't know that when we wrote the song," Marilyn says, "because that cut wasn't in the original version." "But that drove us mad," Alan concludes.

It must be added that in broad comedy, anything goes, and in films like *The Revenge of the Nerds* (1984) the obvious or outrageous coincidence of words, music, and film is effective.

REWRITING, OR WRITING ANOTHER SONG

A certain amount of rewriting is part of the songwriting process. Often the songwriters impose a great deal of discipline in their own rewriting prior to anybody else hearing their song. But when the filmmakers hear a song, they may request changes in either the lyric or even the entire song. "You have to be willing to take a few shots," says Gimbel. "If you write something and you love it and they don't feel it's right, you should be prepared to do another one. And if you do another one and *that* isn't right, maybe you would have enough juice to do another one. If you don't, then everybody will agree—you're not getting it. It could be your fault—you're just not grabbing it right or you're not delivering—and the next movie you do could be the next Academy Award song. It's one of those things. Like a baseball hitter can be hitting .300 and then the next season he's down to .210. A smart producer will let you try. He's buying *you,* essentially, your point of view and your skill."

Henry Mancini supports Gimbel's suggestion to try again. One of the songs Mancini and Leslie Bricusse wrote for *Victor/Victoria* (1982)—"You and Me"—was the "second-round choice" for the duet between Robert Preston and Julie Andrews. "We did one," says Mancini, "and they rehearsed it in London, and called Leslie and me and said, 'That didn't seem to work.' And believe me, when someone says that to you, forget it. It's a dead issue. Don't try to put Band-Aids on it. Start something new. Take a hundred-and-eighty degree turn. Because there's nothing worse than trying to salvage something that the people don't like in the first place." Mancini offers advice about your emotional reaction to that kind of professional rejection. "I don't want to be sanguine about it, but I've come to the point now where, when someone says that to me I can completely cut it off and not think about it. I say, 'Alright, I got my kicks doing that.' " And he lets it go, and gets on with the next challenge.

Sometimes everyone loves the song, but you still have to write another one. The Oscar-winning "It Goes Like It Goes," from *Norma Rae,* was the second song David Shire and Norman Gimbel wrote for the film. Shire explains: "Originally, the producers and director [Martin Ritt] had felt that Waylon Jennings, who was hot at the time, was really a good sound for the title song. So they went after him, and Norman and I wrote a Waylon Jennings song. And we made a demo of it. And, with only a week or two to go, it turned out that Waylon Jennings was unavailable. And then we thought, Well, maybe the singing voice should be female and more the sound of Norma herself, rather than a narrative ballad about Norma. So we had about a week to do a whole different concept."

DEMONSTRATING THE SONG

If the film song is based on an important theme in the score and that theme has been written before the lyric, then the composer might have played the theme for the filmmakers before the song is finished. Otherwise, songwriters think of their songs as being incomplete without both melody and lyric. "When I first began writing lyrics," says Dean Pitchford, "I would recite my lyrics for anybody at the drop of a hat. And eventually what I realized is that a lyric is not anything on its own. On a piece of paper a lyric that has no melody to it will read inane ninety-eight percent of the time. Especially if you are working real tightly with the music.

"My lyrics have become shorter, and the lines more compressed, which is why every single syllable has to count. And as a result I've become very protective about the lyric, and I won't even write them into my scripts. Most of the time I just describe the tone of a song in the script. Because I find that lyrics read like Hallmark cards. A good lyric with good music becomes a great song, whereas a good lyric on its own is just—good."

PRESENTING THE SONG TO THE FILMMAKERS. You need a great demo to sell a song for a motion picture. Most songs are selected for inclusion in a film (especially if there will be a soundtrack album) on the basis of a demo. Many times your song will be competing against countless others, and you won't have the opportunity to say to the director, "Wait 'till you hear the artist singing it." The demo is a sales tool, and should be approached from that point of view. Even if you have been specifically hired to write a song for the film, it is wise to record a demo as close to "master quality" as possible. If the song is in the film, this demo will be used to present the song to potential artists, and it may be cut into the work print track as temp track until the final version replaces it.

Pitchford explains the major risk involved with making a demo: "Because the demo aspires to be the record, if not *all* the values are there you can screw yourself. Because in playing it for somebody, they think they're hearing the record and it's either there or not. There's no room for their imaginations to work." Even artists typically respond to what they hear in such cases, not to the song's potential.

THE ARTIST

> ***You can't just think in terms of the lyric. I think of the identity of the people who are singing it and how they reinforce what the picture is all about.***
>
> DEAN PITCHFORD, LYRICIST

Whether the vocalist is going to be a studio singer working for SAG minimum scale or this year's Grammy winner, you still must "cast" the right voice and style for the song in the context of the film. "The worst thing," says Henry Mancini, "is to go to a movie and watch the whole picture and then have the wrong voice come in [singing the song]. And it's such a nice feeling when you have the right sound."

To get the "right" sound for "Through the Looking Glass," which he wrote with Leslie Bricusse for *That's Life!* (1986), Mancini suggested Tony Bennett—"because of the maturity of his voice, and the slight empathy I think that his voice had with the character of Jack Lemmon. It's set off at the beginning when Lemmon sits down and plays the piano. So you know he has some kind of musicality. And in a strange way, at the end of the picture, it kind of pays off. And the voice doesn't shock you." To further match the vocal quality and style of presentation with the central character, they decided not to do any kind of R & B or rhythmic treatment of the song, letting the rhythm be very laid back.

If the lyric has been created from a character's point of view, as in the above instance, you will want the vocalist to come from the feeling of the character. Jennifer Warnes functioned this way for Sally Field in *Norma Rae;* Joe Cocker and Jennifer Warnes functioned this way for Richard Gere and Debra Winger in *An Officer and a Gentleman;* Barbra Streisand functioned this way for herself in *The Way We Were;* and even though the lyric was third person, Isaac Hayes spoke for Richard Roundtree's title characterization in *Shaft.* The question to ask is, Can I hear this artist singing a statement for the character?

In overview songs, the *style* of the vocal becomes the central issue. The title song for *Ghostbusters* is a third person narrative statement about the Ghostbusters; the upbeat attitude of the vocal (and the arrangement) became a key element contributing to its successful integration into the film.

SHOOTING FOR THE STARS. When the producer and the studio invest in a film song, they usually want to attract a commercially successful artist to sing the song. Although the songwriters will often participate in discussions concerning the most appropriate artist for a particular song, the business decisions will not be theirs.

Getting the artist to agree to sing the song is not easy, especially with so much pop music on soundtracks. "For one thing," Warner Bros. President of Music Gary LeMel says, "artists have gotten burned by thinking their song was going to be in an important spot in the film, and then seeing that it's in the background on the radio for ten seconds. They were promised by somebody that the song would be prominent. And they took their word for it. Now a lot of major artists are saying, 'Look, I'm not going to commit to anything until I see the picture,' and this puts everybody in a real time crunch. They can't see the picture until we're close to dubbing, so this is a problem. Just recently we said to a band, 'Look, if the usage of the song in the film changes, then we'll let you out of it.'"

Artists also want to see the film to be sure they want to be associated with it. But there is a much better chance of attracting a major artist if the song *is* prominently featured in the film. "It doesn't flatter an artist," says Pitchford, "to show them some footage and say, 'Listen, we need a song to put on the car radio while they're talking and driving down the street.'"

Their recording and release schedules play an important role in determining their availability. "We're usually talking about projects a year in advance," LeMel explains. "If I want a particular artist, I have to know that he will not have a record in the marketplace when my film is released, or he won't work for me. Because they're not going to put out my record while his record is out there."

LeMel says that record companies and artists usually know about their release schedules twelve months in advance. But no one can predict what will happen to an album when it is released; whether it will have one hit single or three hit singles (with each one on the air for about three months). So schedule projection is almost impossible.

Sometimes the best artist for a film project is one who is up-and-coming. Steve Bedell, Vice President of Music for Paramount Pictures, keeps up to date with all the **A & R**[1] people at the record companies. He has a "constant dialogue [with the A & R people] as to who's happening, what's going on, who are they signing, what's their interest," and he finds himself "listening to music a lot, being involved with all the trade magazines and being intimately involved with all the publishers who are really the developing factors of the new writers and perhaps many of the new artists of tomorrow. And we're always in constant touch. Many of the contemporary agencies—the Traids, the ICMs, the CAAs, the William Morrises—are very actively involved in getting their new artists into motion pictures, so there's a constant flow of information between their agents and us. They are selling based on success, or who's coming up, or who's happening in England or Holland or wherever the music is coming from. If you've got four or five agencies that each push their own, you've covered most of the new happening acts."

THE SONGWRITER'S RESPONSIBILITIES. Film composers are not often involved anymore with the recording production of the songs. If you haven't written the song, you probably will not arrange it or produce it for the soundtrack. Elmer Bernstein scored the film *Ghostbusters,* but Ray Parker Jr. wrote the title song and Bernstein had nothing to do with the arrangement or production of the song for the film (or the record). There were six record producers responsible for recording the songs performed by various artists for *Footloose* (1984) and they were responsible for the arrangers and their arrangements.

If you have written the song, you may very well be able to follow through all the way with it, unless the artist insists on his or her own record producer. Although Charles Fox wrote the music (with Norman Gimbel's lyric) to "Ready to Take a Chance Again" for *Foul Play* and had arranged and produced most of his film songs, Barry Manilow insisted on controlling the production of that song.

When the composer doesn't know who will sing his song, and time is running out before he scores, he has to do the best he can under trying circumstances. "I've actually scored a picture," says Fox, "knowing that we want a singer, with that singer's key in mind, hoping that we were going to get that person." Recording the vocal tracks in several alternate keys is a good option; this may save the expense of recording another track later. And unless you are sure it will be either a man or a woman, it is wise to record at least one version for each, just in case.

---

[1] A & R: Artists and Repertoire. A & R people work with the record-label artists and sometimes advise them with regard to the material they record.

ARTISTS MAY REQUEST REWRITES. When a major artist gets involved in recording a film song, he or she may ask for specific changes. When Norman Jewison, Michel Legrand, and Alan and Marilyn Bergman brought their film song to a best-selling artist with the hope he would sing their song on the soundtrack and record it commercially, the artist said, "I think the melody is fabulous, but I do not understand the lyric. If you rework the lyric, I'll be happy to record this song." Alan Bergman remembers the moment. "Norman said, 'This is exactly what I want for my movie—I wouldn't ask Alan and Marilyn to change a syllable.'" The studio was stunned at Jewison's response because of the commercial possibilities if the artist recorded the song, but fortunately the director believed in "The Windmills of Your Mind" for his film.

HITS AND BIG BUSINESS

> ***Sometimes the studio marketing people look to music to be another marketing tool, especially with videos being as important as they are now. So there are pressures beyond just "Let's have the best music for the film."***
>
> GARY LeMEL,
> PRESIDENT, MUSIC, WARNER BROS.

> ***"On* Top Gun *the record company was trying to get us to put in two more songs. But at Paramount the studio will never compromise the integrity of the film."***
>
> STEVE BEDELL,
> VICE PRESIDENT, MUSIC,
> PARAMOUNT PICTURES CORPORATION

Music editor Bob Badami says that on *Beverly Hills Cop* (1984) and *Top Gun* (1986), "There was a song search, almost a cattle call in a way. They were showing the film to a number of writers and rock and roll people. For example, on *Top Gun* we got well over one hundred cassettes and just started wading through them. The producers, Jerry Bruckheimer and Don Simpson, the director, Tony Scott, composer Harold Faltermeyer and myself, and a representative of the record company. We knew where we needed songs and Harold, because he had a good background in records, had a great deal of input as to whether the song was good."

Culling songs from among stacks of demos has become a commonplace procedure in "scoring" a film with songs. The stakes are high, and everybody involved wants to know what is available. The practice of hiring songwriters in advance to write film songs is less frequent than in the seventies, whereas more and more songwriters are being asked if they wish to submit songs on spec for a particular film.

Most of the time, when a song is called for on a feature film, the filmmakers hope for commercial exploitation of the song, either as a single or as part of a soundtrack album. The pressure is on everybody to produce hits.

When Marvin Hamlisch and Carole Bayer Sager delivered "Nobody Does It Better," performed by Carly Simon, for *The Spy Who Loved Me,* "the producers were very concerned," says Hamlisch, "that it was not going to be a hit. They said it was not at all like anything they had gotten before. When you're used to a big Main Title, and you're used to 'Boom! Pow! Zam!' it's almost shocking that you've spent all that money and all you get out of it is [a whisper]." It was, in fact, a big hit.

"The ultimate is to have a great title song that fits," says Gary LeMel. "It's very difficult because a title song in the main title would be too corny, too on-the-nose and almost never would work. We made it work in *Ghostbusters* by having it come in with the logo, and there had been so much pre-hype that it worked. But it rarely works, and usually the song ends up in the end title. If there's a spot in the body of the film where it really would work, like a montage sequence or something, then that's even better. It's always better if you can marry the music to an emotional piece of film because that's what makes people react. They're not going to react to a song on the end title of a film.

"In *The Big Chill* (1983), they reacted to that music because it was wide open, playing against emotion on the screen, which caused them to go to the record store afterwards. That's the ultimate. And I think that's what a lot of people in films forget."

FOOTLOOSE: AN ORIGINAL COMPILATION SONG SCORE

If the process of putting individual songs into a film is demanding, creating and supervising the production of an original song score can be a full-time job for many months, or even years. *Footloose* (the 1984 film about a big-city boy who movies to a small town in which dancing is banned) was scripted by Dean Pitchford, who also wrote all the lyrics. Although he had a number of different songwriting collaborators, including Kenny Loggins ("Footloose"), Tom Snow ("Let's Hear It for the Boy"), Eric Carmen ("Almost Paradise"), and Bill Wolfer ("Dancing in the Sheets"), Pitchford was the guiding light, giving the project focus and continuity.

THE CREATIVE TEAM. It is vital that the director and editor understand and share the creator's vision of what a musical film can be; otherwise it is bound to fall short of its potential. "It was an enormous give and take," says Pitchford, "and I had to keep track of the whole picture at all times. Serving the song, serving the lyric, serving the artist.

"I was very fortunate to work with [director] Herb Ross, who is so musical. He choreographed on Broadway for years." The editor, Paul Hirsch, was a timpanist, and had previously edited such films as *Star Wars* (1977). "He was very conscious of serving the material. I couldn't have been happier with the collaboration, because he had an innate sense of what works. I've seen pictures where editors cut *off* the beat, and it makes me crazy. They'll arbitrarily snip in the middle of a measure or a beat, and it starts to pull me out of the rhythm. He was impeccable about that. And when the song would build, he would build. Sometimes he'd do funny cut-aways that would punch up a word in the lyric."

USING ROLE MODELS. The only songs written before filming were "Footloose," with Kenny Loggins, and "Somebody's Eyes," with Tom Snow. Pitchford selected role models for all other song sequences. "We went through hundreds of records, trying to find the role models. So when I presented a role model to Herb Ross, I was pointing his head in the direction that the whole scene should go.

"You're not locked into the form of the role model, because of contemporary film editing. If you were doing the older musical style where you would track a dance and film the verse in one long take, then of course you have to acknowledge the form of the role-model song so that you match the film and arrive at the top of the staircase at the same time that Fred Astaire and Ginger Rogers do. But because contemporary choreography and editing is very quick action—cut, cut, cut, cut—almost what has become known as an MTV style, you are not restricted so much to matching the form of the role model when you write your new song."

PREPARING A SCRATCH TRACK FOR SHOOTING. The scratch track (or playback recording) should be prepared to click. That's easy enough if you prerecord the scratch track; if you use preexisting recorded material for your scratch track, you still should have it clicked.

Pitchford decided to use the sixties rock song "Johnny B. Goode" as the scratch track for the sequence that would eventually be scored with the song "Footloose." He needed a track that would keep the dancers going with a high level of energy for eight to ten hours a day. He knew he would never be able to get that amount of excitement from a demo performance of the song, so he asked cowriter Kenny Loggins what tempo he wanted to use. When they found the ideal click they changed the speed of "Johnny B. Goode" to match it. But the record had been cut before pop groups used click, and so the tempo on "Johnny B. Goode" wasn't steady. Since the dancers needed the accuracy that a digital metronome would provide, the music editors transferred the record (now sped up to approximate the chosen clock) to 35mm mag stripe and clicked it out, adjusting the beats as necessary so that every beat fell on the click.

WRITING THE LYRICS. Pitchford's concept of the project and its goals gave the score a continuity that otherwise might be missing. Throughout the lyrics there is a combined sense of celebration and sexual exhilaration, and the image of dancing, so important to the story, is an inherent aspect of the song "Footloose," which is about letting go and dancing, and "Dancing in the Sheets."

Dancing in the Sheets
Lyric: Dean Pitchford Music: Bill Wolfer

[End of first verse] Maybe you don't like the beat
I got a two-track playing in my head
So let me take you somewhere else instead
Dancing in the Sheets

[Chorus] Dancing in the Sheets
Grab your coat and wave goodbye to your friend
I wanna take you where the night never ends
I feel the need to sweep you off-a your feet
You and me we should be
Dancing in the Sheets.

To add further continuity, "Let's Hear It for the Boy" is sung over a montage of Kevin Bacon teaching his inept nondancing friend how to move to the beat, an idea that allows the visual dancing and verbal sexuality images to play together.

Let's Hear It for the Boy
Lyric: Dean Pitchford Music: Tom Snow

[Second verse] Maybe he sings off key
But that's all right by me (yea)
But what he does he does so well
Makes me wanna yell

[Chorus] Let's Hear it for the Boy
Let's give the boy a hand
Let's hear it for my baby
You know you gotta understand

Oh—
Maybe he's no Romeo
But he's my loving one-man show
Oh-wo-wo-wo

Let's Hear it for the Boy.

***FOOTLOOSE* SONG DEMOS.** Because of Ross's background, coproducer Craig Zadan suggested that Pitchford sing each new song for the film to Ross live in his office, rather than making an elaborate demo just to present the song to the director. "He had an upright piano delivered to Herb's office, and we would go in, pass out lyric sheets, and my collaborator would sit at the piano and I would sing just like we were in some hotel room in Boston working on a Broadway musical. And his imagination would fill in the rest. And every time Herb had an objection to something, he was absolutely right. And every time he threw his hands up and said, 'You solved it,' we would go make the record, and it would work."

WORKING WITH THE ARTISTS. "*Footloose* was a musical," Pitchford says. "And because I was giving each one of the artists a chance for a featured performance, they *worked.* They would go back into the studio over and over and over again. If I would call and make comments about a vocal or about a bass line or about a drummer, we'd go back into the studio. We redid Deniece Williams's vocal on 'Let's Hear It for the Boy.' We redid the drum and bass patterns on 'Dancing in the Sheets.' And we redid the vocal that Shalamar had done on 'Dancing.'

"I was there, in every studio, for everything. There was one week where we were cutting four different tunes in four different studios. And I would make a circuit that would take me from early afternoon until maybe four o' clock the next morning—every day. I knew all the [record] producers, and I worked very closely with all of them. I would go in to see what they had done with the tracks, and I was always there for the vocal to be laid down. I flew to San Francisco to work with Sammy Hagar; I flew to Chicago in the middle of a snow storm to pick up the vocals on 'Almost Paradise.'

"I'd occasionally get thrown out of a studio, and I'd come right back the next day. Even though the artist may have seen the footage once or twice, I had the footage playing in my head all the time. Every time I'd go into the studio, I would close my eyes and see the footage and hear the song simultaneously. So when they would get to the point where they thought they had finished a record, yes, they may have finished all that they needed for a record, but it wasn't sufficient for the scoring of that segment of the film. And I'd say, 'No, it needs more uumph, it needs more lift, it needs more vocal, it needs more volume, it needs more punch, it doesn't take off where I want it too, it doesn't lay where I want it to.' And they'd go crazy. Because I was asking them to think about something that they don't normally have to think about. They do ten cuts on album after album, year after year, and suddenly someone comes along and says, 'Yeah, that's a record, but it's not sufficient for films. It's got to be *more* for film.'

TAKING CARE OF BUSINESS. Pitchford not only followed through on every creative aspect of the music production but also was involved with every business detail, working alongside the music supervisor.

"I would never have been able to start if it weren't for Becky Shargo [Mancuso], the music supervisor. She handled all the business and got the deals worked out before we turned them over to the lawyers. We discussed every step of every deal. There were contracts with writers, producers, artists, and the record labels. We had artists on loan-out from some record labels.

"We gave each artist a recording budget, and that budget was to cover studio costs [and all recording costs]. And they were to deliver a finished tape to us, either with their producer or a producer that we would work with or that we would appoint, and what was left over became their fee. She not only played a business role, but a very creative role, so if there was a problem, either one of us could tackle it."

YENTL: AN ORIGINAL SONG SCORE BY ONE TEAM OF WRITERS

Yentl (1983, adapted from Isaac Bashevis Singer's short story) is the story of a young Eastern European woman at the turn of the century who disguises herself as a boy in order to get an education. "We had read the story of 'Yentl' years ago, as Barbra did," says Marilyn Bergman, "and always felt it was a good idea for a musical. But we never mentioned that to her in all of her struggles to get the picture made. Over a period of years she had many scripts written—she never saw it as a musical—and we never discussed it.

"Finally we said, 'Have you ever thought of it as a musical?' At first she said, 'No, it's like a little European picture, that's how I've always seen it.' And then she called back and said, 'How do you see this as a musical? Why is it a musical?' We always saw it as a musical because of the secret life of this character; from the moment she cuts her hair and dons the clothes of a man there is nobody to whom she can talk. So there was a whole inner life that we always thought could be a wonderful interior monologue—that's the score, that's the voice. So we explained that and the work began."

INTEGRATING THE SONG CONCEPT WITH THE SCRIPT. "Every song was spotted in the script and the function of each song was written out," says Marilyn. "Certain ones were very apparent. You knew that there were certain moments where the character had to sing and what she had to sing about. Others we had to dig for, and there was a lot of discarding.

"It was always clear that what this wanted to be was one person's voice. There was a point at which we tried to make a more conventional musical out of it and have some of the other characters sing. It never felt right. We never knew why anybody else was singing. It always then seemed to step into some kind of conventional musical for no organic reason."

DETERMINING THE COMPOSER AND THE MUSICAL STYLE. Streisand and the Bergmans didn't want to approach the score like *Fiddler on the Roof.* "Her voice," says Marilyn, "was a very personal voice. We felt you should never have the feeling that this could not possibly be nineteenth-century European romantic music. And the composer had to be somebody who wrote well for Barbra's voice. We soon realized we were describing Michel Legrand.

"The source music was kind of ethnic, and there were certain modal sounds—little touches here and there, like perfume. Michel came under a lot of fire. A lot of people wanted to know why the music was not more Jewish, more ethnic. They didn't understand. It was a conscious choice."

ESTABLISHING THE CINEMATIC USE OF THE SONGS. "In the very first song we wanted to use every technique for integrating Yentl's vocals that would be used throughout the movie. There is voice-over, on-screen singing, and interspersed dialogue. The music heard in the synagogue is a variation of that first song." "The reason for this," Alan points out, "is so the audience will be subliminally prepared for all the succeeding techniques. To make the first transition from speaking to singing, we have her say a prayer which is halfway between dialogue and song—chantlike. So that when she does begin to sing the audience is prepared for it." "When she goes into her father's room, she sings voice-over," explains Marilyn, "and as soon as she closes the door and turns around, she then is singing on screen because she is again alone. All the ways of using songs are exposed in that first piece."

Where is it Written?
Lyric: Alan and Marilyn Bergman Music: Michel Legrand

[Last refrain] Tell me where,
Where is it written what it is I'm meant to be,
That I can't dare
To find the meanings in the mornings that I see,
Or have my share
Of ev'ry sweet imagined possibility?
Just tell me where,
Where is it written?
Tell me where,
Or if it's written anywhere?

WRITING THE LYRICS AND PRERECORDING THE SONGS. The Bergmans spent their first year on the project doing research on the period and the religious tradition. They worked a great deal with two young rabbis, a man and a woman. "So that when we started writing," says Marilyn, "we felt on solid ground." Because of their complete absorption in the research materials, when they began to write, they worked very quickly, finishing the lyrics in three months. As each song was finished, Streisand would record a piano/vocal demo for reference.

The entire score is very integrated into the drama. In "No Wonder," painstaking planning was necessary to achieve the integration of a voice-over vocal with interjected on-screen spoken lines by Streisand as she dines with her friend Avigdor and his fiancée.

No Wonder
Lyric: Alan and Marilyn Bergman Music: Michel Legrand

[Second half]

No wonder he loves her—no wonder at all.
The moment she sees him her thought is to please him
Before he even knows that he's hungry she's already there with his plate.
Before his glass is even empty she's filling it up, God forbid he should wait!
Before he has the chance to tell her he's chilly she's putting a log on the fire.
No trouble.
No bother.

(spoken) No cabbage?

(spoken) No, thank you.

No wonder she's pretty. What else should she be?
She hasn't a worry—and why should she worry?
When she gets up her biggest decision is figuring out what to wear,
To pick a blouse, a skirt and then there's the problem of what should she do with her hair.
And later as she stands and studies a chicken, the question is to roast or not roast?
Or better yet maybe a pot roast.

(spoken) Tomatoes?

(spoken) No.

(spoken) Potatoes?

No wonder he likes it—it's perfect this way. [etc.]

A week before prerecording began, Alan says, they suddenly realized in reading the script again that there was a moment that needed a song they hadn't originally planned. "It was like a bolt of lightning," says Marilyn. "We said, 'How could we never have seen this before?' It was a moment that always bothered us in the script, and we never knew why. We never realized that it bothered us because it was an important place for a song, when she's finally accepted into the Yeshiva and says, 'I'm a student, I'm a student'; in the script, that was all there was. We always felt there was something unfinished about the moment. We needed a song that talked about her fulfillment—this was why she had done all this. Suddenly she's allowed into this magic kingdom.

"We remembered a story that one of the rabbis had told us two years before about three men on a boat crossing from the old country to America—a silk merchant, a diamond merchant, and a scholar—and they hit a storm at sea and the waves wash over the boat and sweep everything away. And after the storm is over, the three of them are standing there and the silk merchant says, 'Now we are left with nothing. What are we going to do—all my silks are gone'; and the jeweler says, 'All my jewelry's gone'; and the scholar says, 'I have exactly what I came with.' And that story was the genesis of that song ('There are certain things that . . . no wave can wash away, no wind can blow away . . . no fire can burn away . . . ')."

They told Streisand that they *had* to try to write this song. "We wrote a whole page," Marilyn continues, "that we really didn't mean as a lyric, we only meant it as a blueprint for Michel. And he set it. He had never set an English lyric and he set it—every accent was right, every peak was right. It was very exciting."

This Is One of Those Moments
Lyric: Alan and Marilyn Bergman   Music: Michel Legrand

There are moments you remember all your life.
There are moments you wait for and dream of all your life.
This is one of those moments.

She then describes everything about that moment, and declares everything

> Will be written on my mind, will be written in my heart
> As long as I live!

In celebration of learning and of her studies with her father that will always be with her, she sings:

> I can open doors and take from the shelves
> All the books I've longed to hold.
> I can ask all the questions, the whys and the wheres
> As the myst'ries of life unfold.
> Like a link in a chain from the past to the future
> That joins me with the children yet to be,
> I can now be a part of the ongoing stream
> That has always been a part of me!
>
> There are certain things that once you have
> No man can take away,
> No wave can wash away,
> No wind can blow away,
> No tide can turn away,
> No fire can burn away,
> No time can wear away!
> And now they're about to be mine!

PART 9

THE BUSINESS

CHAPTER 27
THE BUSINESS

***There are two words to what we do: the* music business. *You've got to do the* music *and you've got to do the* business.** MIKE POST

GETTING THE JOB

Ultimately, a composer is sold on the basis of his music and his credits. For any given project, one may be a more important credential than the other. In either case, for the composer to be considered, the director or producer must know about him, and this can happen in one of four ways: (1) through an agent or other representative (lawyer, business manager); (2) through direct contact with the producer, director, music executive/supervisor or others (editor, music editor); (3) through third-party recommendation by a mutual acquaintance, family member, or others; (4) through someone who has heard his work and thinks it's right for a particular project (either the producer, director, or someone who then recommends him to them).

Even when a composer has such favorable contacts through previous work with a director, producer, or both, this is not absolute assurance of scoring the picture. More and more these choices must be okayed by others, including the network reps in television and executive producers and music executives in feature films. An impressive demo is a composer's most important marketing device.

DEMOS

You can't even get an agent interested in representing you without a great demo (almost always an audiocassette). These demos are sales tools and should be created with the same attention to overall impact and detail that the composer would devote to any other demanding professional task. Putting together an impressive demo isn't easy, even if the composer has film credits and has ample material to choose from.

HOW TO PREPARE A GOOD DEMO TAPE. Composer's demos should be of high technical quality—you cannot expect the listener to imagine how good it would sound if only you'd had better players and studio, and the length should not be too long. For a new composer in town, agent Alvin Bart suggests: "Not more than fifteen minutes. Make it a kind of combination. If they don't have too much material we'll listen to everything they have and put together something that shows their range—the fact that they can work with a small group, they can work with a large group, there's a romantic thing, a chase thing, an electronic thing. Let's say someone's been doing a lot of commercials, really fine stuff, and some documentaries, whatever. As soon as you log a commercial for Coca-Cola or whatever, you practically get an automatic turndown. If you've composed it, just give it a different title. But it has to be original. Don't use something that's just arranged or orchestrated by you."

Bodie Chandler, former Vice President of Music, Columbia Pictures Television, suggests that "a tape should show me the compositional skill, orchestrational skill, the dramatic skill, and the well-rounded talent of a composer. It should show me that he can do contemporary, a little rock and roll, a little jazz, and of course the standard-type score.

Some composers take ten or fifteen cues and give you ten or twelve seconds of each one of them. That's terrible. I can't really get a feel for the flow of the music, or how the composer gets into and out of a cue or how they build dramatically. I like to hear a full cue from the beginning to the end. There's nothing wrong with a two-and-a-half minute cue if it's representative of some of the composer's best work, but if it's just a two minute holder under dialogue, don't put it on the tape—I'll fall asleep.

"Synthesizer tapes tend to be dull and repetitious. If you've done a score on synthesizer, present the most interesting parts of that score. So many of them sound alike, it's incredible. I find that tapes with an acoustic orchestra can display more of a composer's abilities than can a tape of synthesized music. If somebody hasn't had their first credit yet, even in an episode, I think they should try to facsimilate a cue. Look at a scene in an episode of *Dallas,* or whatever, and take down some overall timing notes and actually write some music for that scene."

Harry Lojewski, former Vice President of Motion Picture and Television Music, MGM/UA, suggests, "If you put a demo together, think of it like a soundtrack LP—put the most exciting piece of music up first, then something very lyrical, completely opposite, and then something interesting. Try to get it together so it all has a lot of interest. You never know at what point the guy's going to stop the cassette. Length doesn't matter if it has enough variety."

Director John Erman listens for something unique. "Basically I look for something that seems original to me because I want somebody to come to a project with an original point of view. If I hear something that is provocative in its originality, I will think, Does this kind of sound mesh with the story that I'm trying to tell?"

PREPARING SPECIAL DEMOS FOR A SPECIFIC PROJECT. Erman's question is very significant in today's marketplace: Does this kind of sound mesh with the story that I'm trying to tell? Agents Richard Emler and Alvin Bart find that more and more requests are being made by producers for custom-made demos for each specific project. Producers and directors want to hear music that they feel is exactly suited to the style and requirements of their film. Consequently, previous credits and experience are becoming less significant in many cases. The question has become: What can the composer play for us that works with our film?

The demand for these custom-made demos is so great that Bart has developed a system to provide samples of a composer's work that fit the description of the music needed for a specific film. "What we've done is hire one of those soundtrack nuts. He has 6,000 soundtracks at home and probably knows every piece of music written by almost every film composer known. We tell him the type of demo we want—this is the picture, here's the rundown, here's the composer. He then goes to our tremendous library of music of every composer we represent and he creates a demo of the composer's work specifically for that project. He'll consult with the composer if necesssary. I would say conservatively that 80 to 85 percent of the assignments we're getting now for the 'new guys' (not the pop people but the guys doing movies-of-the-week and segments and themes and so forth) are strictly due to this system."

This represents a dramatic shift in the way composers are hired in the marketplace and accounts for the much greater percentage of newer composers now scoring motion pictures than ten years ago. Emler points out the recent changes: "Since I started as an agent in 1973, the whole process by which the composer gets an assignment has changed. There's much more auditioning. The creative process from the standpoint of a creative suggestion on the part of the agent, and trust between agent and buyer, is not nearly the same. The buyer very much wants to hear his score in advance of hiring a composer. And this is greatly attributable to the fact that there are so many younger composers in the marketplace who don't have the longevity of writing for feature films and television.

Therefore, many are willing to 'spec' a cue or two on their synthesizers to prove they are capable."

MODELING DEMOS AFTER SPECIFIC ROLE MODELS. Of course there is a verbal dialogue between agents and filmmakers, often using role-model names of composers or specific film scores, or a style of song that they have heard on the radio. Emler says, "They like that sound and they want that sound for their picture. If you're not connected to that particular recording artist or that particular piece of material, the composer or agent must go out and acquaint himself with this material so he can understand the *feel* of the song or score they're wanting in the film."

DEMONSTRATE DIVERSITY ALSO. One additional point: when a filmmaker likes a specific composer for his project, the demo tape is a tool for him to convince others (producers, network reps, music supervisors) of his versatility and quality; when possible, these tapes should be geared to demonstrating those qualities as well as satisfying specific style areas. Sometimes a second tape covering a broader range of music is sent along with the specific one to cover this need.

MAKING COPIES. You'll need a number of duplicate copies of your demo(s). Tape-duplicating companies make multiple cassette copies fast and relatively inexpensively. If you can find a cheaper way to make them without sacrificing quality, do so if you wish. If you make them yourself, be sure to label them clearly with your name, phone number, and address on both the cassette itself and the box legend; the people you will be meeting have stacks of indistinguishable cassettes in their offices (and cars). The labels should look professional without being ostentatious. Every aspect of your presentation should exhibit good taste.

BEING HEARD

There is one overriding generality the aspiring composer should use for guidance: YOU'VE GOT TO BE HEARD TO BE APPRECIATED. The target audience is obvious: agents, studio music executives, production company and independent music supervisors, filmmakers, composers. A standard resource like the Hollywood Reporter Blue Book will give you names. Make calls, write letters, send off demos, and follow up on leads. Revise your demo as often as possible to keep it current and diversified. Send a new demo to an established contact, pointing out in a cover letter what to listen for. If you have a project being performed in public, or your film score is on the air, send out cards letting people know about it; you never know who will watch at an opportune moment. Even those who don't watch will have seen your name connected with some professional activity.

AGENTS

It should be understood from the outset that there are very few agents and it's hard to get representation. It is not generally clear to aspiring new composers that agents don't usually get composers their *first* jobs in any case. That is why the procedure outlined above is so important. But after a composer has acquired several composing credits and can sign with an agent, he still needs help in lining up more work; especially so, since at this point he may feel uncomfortable hustling his own demo tapes to industry people. From here on, the agent can be of help, since agents are among the people contacted by filmmakers to find the right composer for a film project, and they do aggressively submit composers for specific projects.

SIGNING WITH AN AGENT. When you do interest an agent in representing you, the agent will guarantee to use his best efforts to obtain assignments. He will make no promises and may tell you to expect it to "take time." If you sign, he should discuss his efforts with you on a regular basis (not every day, but more than once a month). While he is preparing to submit you for a project, he may discuss the project with you in order to determine whether there is appropriate demo material he may not remember or be aware of. His responsibilities and work methods should be discussed before signing.

THE COMPOSER/AGENT DEAL POINTS. The following are the basic terms the composer should expect to discuss for inclusion in any agency papers presented for signature:

1. *Agent's Responsibilities.* The agent will submit the client for scoring assignments. The agent will collect all money due, deduct his commission (and expenses, if any), and issue an exchange check drawn on his client trust account for the balance within a day or two. In addition to following through on the negotiation of all the deal points (see below) he will remind the production office that money is due, arrange for a messenger paid for by the composer to pick up checks if the composer wishes, and follow through on all details and paperwork related to the project.

2. *Duration.* Usually one year, renewable. Agent and composer may consider negotiating an automatic renewal clause if certain stipulated performance criteria are met by the agent (either in terms of a specific minimum gross[1] for the year, the number of projects, or some other mutually satisfactory formula).

3. *Exclusions.* The composer can negotiate exclusions in areas in which the agent doesn't function (which might include commercials, concert engagements, club dates as a musician, scale orchestrating done for other composers, theater, and so on).

4. *Commissions.* Agents used to receive 10 percent. Now the range is 10 to 15 percent. If the agent has a fixed percentage above 10 percent that he charges all clients, this may be nonnegotiable.

The composer should discuss in detail how the agent calculates commissions on package deals, as this can make a big difference to both parties. It is typical and equitable to commission the *net* package fee after deducting all itemized expenses specific to the project. The agency papers should have a clear definition of "net" in this context.

Film music agents typically commission a percentage of the composer's artist royalties and **mechanical royalties**[2] on soundtrack albums and singles that come from film projects they negotiate. Typically they do not commission performance royalties from ASCAP or BMI.

Overscale orchestration is commissioned. Since orchestration is often an important deal point in an agent's negotiation with the producer (especially in television projects) they feel entitled to commission scale payments to the composer for orchestration performed on his own projects. Television film producers prefer to negotiate a flat fee that may include a certain amount of compensation to the composer for his orchestration. Such agreements set a fixed ceiling for orchestration payments, which producers like; such a ceiling eliminates budgetary surprises if the scale orchestration bill turns out to be $2,000 more than the original budget estimate.

5. *Escape Clause.* All agency papers have escape clauses, which allow the artist to formally withdraw from the agent's representation under certain circumstances. The most

---

[1] Minus packaging expenses.

[2] Mechanical royalties: royalties paid the publisher (who splits 50 percent with the writers) for each cut on a sound recording.

common clause allows the composer to leave the agency if the agent has submitted to him no bona fide offer in a consecutive four-month period. As a matter of policy, agents of Hollywood film composers have traditionally allowed composers and lyricists to cancel representation if they are dissatisfied and the agent feels this dissatisfaction is not just the result of a misunderstanding that could be worked out with some straightforward dialogue.

THE NETWORKS—THE UNSEEN CLIENT

Composers, producers, and agents say that when they have been approached about a television assignment and have reached a tentative agreement, the phrase "subject to network approval" is frequently the final verbal condition. Not uncommonly, word comes back from the producer that the network won't approve that composer for that particular project. In general, the networks deny that they ever disapprove a producer's choice of composer. Harry Heitzer, Vice President for Business Affairs, Music Operations, at CBS, says, "Once in a great while a program executive will call and ask if I'm familiar with the work of composer X because presumably composer X was suggested to the program exec and he or she had not heard of that person and did not know of his or her work himself. If I know the person I know him—if I don't, I don't. If I don't, I might ask around. It's not a formalized thing—it hasn't happened an awful lot."

Regardless of the degree to which the networks participate in these decisions, their influence is felt. Assignments have been lost and so have scores. Composers find it difficult to understand a criticism or rejection of themselves or their scores when it comes from an anonymous network representative with whom they have had no discussion about musical style and attitude. The networks share some of that same frustration, not knowing how much of their creative input ever gets back to the composers. Anthony Masucci, NBC Vice President, Motion Pictures for Television, explains that three-way communication can be unreliable, "because the process is fragmented in terms of the network and the producer and the composer. The worst thing that can happen is that we're surprised. I think if there are no surprises, we can't get into trouble later on.

"There's a lot of dialogue that goes on between meetings in our offices," Masucci continues. "It's very difficult to know what's getting passed on and what's not getting passed on. Recently we at NBC collectively had a meeting with the Writers' Guild to try to figure out ways to make it work better. One of their complaints was that what the producers were telling them and what they ultimately heard from us were two different things. Not all the time, but sometimes. That has to do with direct communications. Our answer to them was, "There are telephones—call us.' "

However, he is not recommending that composers and network reps have direct contact. "It becomes difficult in that one doesn't want to usurp the position of the producer that you've entrusted with the film. It becomes very touchy. Hopefully you have a relationship with the producer where he is conveying things—some do, some don't."

FILM AND TELEVISION DEAL POINTS

Once you get an offer to score a project, you will need to consider what position to take about various negotiable and not so negotiable deal points. There is less flexibility in television movies and miniseries than in feature films, and even less in episodic television. The deal points you will be negotiating are:

1. Fee. This will include conducting (and sometimes orchestration, depending on the medium).[3] When working for small (unknown) independent production companies, the

[3] See page 71 for range of fees.

composer might consider negotiating some method of bonding the entire creative fee (or even the whole music budget), by placing it in a trust fund of some sort, to ensure payment. If the company is legit, this can usually be worked out to everyone's satisfaction.

2. Orchestration. Does the composer receive a separate fee for orchestration, or is it included in his creative fee? Variations include receiving scale for orchestration up to a fixed amount, or scale for any orchestration done by another person (often due to the production company's tight time schedules).

3. Payment Schedule. In episodic television, payment is due upon completion of recording. In television films, composers often receive 50 percent on start (spotting) and 50 percent upon completion of recording. In features, if the composer will be spending more than a month on the project, some other formula of spreading the payments over the length of assignment may be worked out.

4. Credit. The end-title credit in episodic television is standard. Although this is negotiable on television films, usually main-title credit will be given, "equal in size, type, style, and length of time on screen as that accorded the writer, director, and producer."[4] The composer decides how his credit should read: "Music by . . ."; "Music composed and conducted by . . ."; Music composed and performed by . . ." It's good to remember that the less you say about yourself, the more prominent your name will be. Songs will receive separate credit billing, and that must be negotiated as well.

5. Credit in Paid Ads. This is often granted, with standard industry exclusions regarding the minimum-size ad required for credit. Some television producers and production companies do not like to guarantee this.

6. Publishing. Ownership of the publishing rights can be very valuable for the composer, but they are very often nonnegotiable in Hollywood, particularly with the major studios, which have their own gigantic publishing enterprises. Independent production companies are more likely to negotiate the publishing rights and income. Often this deal point is used to help put together a deal on a film with budget problems; a share of the publishing is given as a trade-off for less money in front. The so-called publisher (copyright owner) of the film score or song may or may not actually publish (that is, print) the music, but he receives substantial royalties—equal to those the composer receives—directly from the performing rights societies (ASCAP, BMI) for performances all over the world in any medium (except theatrical film exhibition in the United States). The "publisher" also shares 50/50 all mechanical royalties from the sale of recordings, cassettes, and so on).

6a. Sheet Music. In 1989, composers received from 8 to 12 cents per sheet music copy for television, and 10 to 15 cents per copy for features. This is negotiable, and has been increasing over the years. There is a standard set of terms for other kinds of printed music.

7. Soundtrack Album/Singles. A royalty schedule for the composer as artist (conductor) is negotiated, with the low usually being 5 percent of retail.[5] A formula is devised to prorate the artist royalties, in case there are other performing artists involved. The composer will also receive a separate royalty as record producer if he performs that function. The minimum royalty for that is about 3 percent. It may be prorated if there are other record producers involved on some of the tracks. The composer and lyricists get mechanical royalties on units sold.

8. New-Use Fees. A fee is negotiated for the release of a television film in theaters (50 to 100 percent of the original fee). Deal points for feature films may include new-use fees for a film when released on cable television, network and/or syndicated television, and videocassettes.

9. Exclusivity. The composer is usually considered to be nonexclusive (able to work on other projects also), although production companies may insist that the composer work exclusively for them for the duration of a project with a very tight schedule.

---

[4] Standard wording in Emler's deal memos when this is negotiated.

[5] Recording industry tradition often defines this as "5 percent of 90 percent of retail."

Package deals must clearly articulate up front the exact responsibilities of the composer. The most typical package deals in Hollywood require the composer to pay all expenses involved in delivering a quarter-inch stereo or half-inch 3-track or stereo master tape ready for transfer to film, with the following exceptions: (1) music editor's fee; (2) cost of transferring master tape to 35mm mag strip (including film stock); (3) singers (other than scale studio singers); license fees (see below) for songs or recorded performances the producer and director select to include on the soundtrack. Costs for lyrics must be prenegotiated also, so all parties know who's responsible for what.

BACK-END DEALS. When there isn't enough money up front to pay the composer his established fee and also cover all music-budget expenses for a feature film, creative agents and composers sometimes put together "back-end deals," which strengthen the potential compensation for the composer *after* the film has been released. These deals are gambles for the composer, because if the film isn't successful and isn't released in other ancillary markets, the composer may end up with an impressive back-end percentage of nothing. The operative theory is that if the film does well, the composer will do a bit better than he would have if he had received his normal fee up front.

It takes flexibility on the part of the composer, his agent, and the producer to make back-end deals work. Possible back-end compensations to the composer include (1) a one-time fee when the film is sold to network television, (2) a one-time fee when the film is sold to syndicated television, (3) either a one-time fee or a series of advances against royalties per unit sold when the film is sold for videocassette distribution,[6] (4) a **split publishing** deal, which gives the composer a share (usually 50 percent) of the publishing ownership and revenue, (5) a larger-than-usual artist royalty for any soundtrack records, (6) a deferred payment when and if the film grosses a certain specified amount of revenue, (7) a prenegotiated advance against soundtrack album royalties when and if a soundtrack deal is made with a record company. If the composer already gets some of these deal points, then his participation in any one or more of the points can be increased proportionately.

ASCAP AND BMI

These two organizations license the nonexclusive right (except **grand rights**[7] and **sync rights**[8]) to perform publicly all copyrighted musical works of their members. Both organizations collect license fees from the three major television networks; local and cable television; radio stations; public broadcasters; colleges and universities; taverns and restaurants; Muzak; private clubs; hotels; concert halls; airlines; and so on. They then distribute to their members all income from licensing after deducting operating costs, which are about 15 to 20 percent of gross receipts. Distributions for domestic performances are made quarterly; foreign distributions semiannually. They are based on the number and kind of performances logged in their "surveys."

ASCAP[9] is a nonprofit membership association, with a board of directors made up of twelve writer members and twelve publisher members elected by the entire membership. BMI[10] is a corporation that was established by the broadcasters to provide an alternative to ASCAP. Although its members do not sit on the board of directors, the basic method

---

[6] Royalty participation is becoming more common.

[7] Grand rights: rights to staged versions.

[8] Sync rights: rights to license music synchronized with video or motion picture images.

[9] American Society of Composers, Authors and Publishers (established in 1914).

[10] Broadcast Music, Inc. (established in 1940).

of collecting and distributing performance royalties is similar to that of ASCAP. BMI, however, has more freedom to modify, at its discretion, the amounts distributed to the various categories, such as film music, radio performances, heavily performed works, and so on.

RATES. According to ASCAP's Todd Brabec, members receive the following background music rates:

Prime-time network television:[11]	$180–$200 per minute
Syndicated television:[12]	$50–$60 per minute[13]

When a song becomes the chief focus of attention, it is called a "featured performance." Here are the rates for these:

Prime-time network television (:45 or more in duration):	$1850–$2000[14]
Syndicated television (no minimum duration):[15]	$550–$650[16]

These ASCAP rates are approximate and are given to illustrate the payment structure. BMI representatives say their rates are similar; printed payment schedules are available on request.

MUSIC BUDGETS

The first decision on a new film project is to set a budget. Gary LeMel, the President of Music, Warner Bros. Inc. (including motion pictures and television) describes his activities: "I deal with anything that has to do with music for films and television—which includes meetings with the producer and director to decide what direction we're going. I bring ideas to it and they have ideas. Is there going to be a soundtrack album? If so, what kind of artists are we talking about, what kind of record deal are we going to structure? What labels have the artists that are closest to the feeling of the picture?

"On a green-lighted picture I read the script, then meet with the director—sometimes the director and the producers (or sometimes with producer only, because they haven't hired a director yet). Even before that, we've usually done a budget in order to get the picture green-lighted. For the budget, I try to get as much information as I possibly can. By the nature of the script, if it's a flat-out teenage film and it reads that way and I see all kinds of spots for rock and roll, I know that this is going to be more expensive than a score. Usually there's information floating around on the type of director or the actual director. Knowing that, I can pretty well tell from his track record where his musical tastes lie. So I budget for as many songs as I can see in the picture, plus score, plus licensing if standards are talked about or if titles are talked about."

---

[11] From 7:00 P.M. to 2:00 A.M. based on a 200-plus network hookup.

[12] No time-of-day differences.

[13] Royalties calculated on surveyed shows.

[14] Shared 50-50 by composer(s) and lyricist(s).

[15] No time-of-day differences.

[16] Royalties calculated on surveyed shows; shared 50-50 by composer(s) and lyricist(s).

It is not unusual (especially in television) for the music executive to set a preliminary budget by using the precedent of the last project of the same genre. The range of budgets on a feature film (in 1987), according to Harry Lojewski, including composer, copyist, and musicians (but not pension fund), was from $150,000 to $300,000 for underscoring. On one picture that was song oriented, with artists fees and licenses to pay (not an MGM/UA project), the cost is rumored to have been an astronomical $1,700,000.

By contrast, there are so many young composers who are prepared to do synthesized scores in their own studios, and who want to score a picture as a career move, even if it isn't profitable, that there are music budgets for independent feature films that range as low as $20,000 to $50,000, and sometimes lower, according to Emler. "At $50,000, for a young composer who is just on the rise, to do a synthesized score with limited orchestral overdub, it's financially feasible. But when you get down as low as a $20,000 to $30,000 score and they're asking for orchestral overdubs, then you really start to look for trouble."

A typical music budget for a two-hour television movie in 1988 was from $40,000 (low) to about $65,000. This figure will usually include everything, including lyrics and licenses, if any, and the music supervision fee, if supervised by an independent company.

LICENSING

To use an existing, specific copyrighted piece of music and/or a specific recorded performance of such a piece in a film requires licensing it for this use from the publisher (copyright holder) and record company. This clearance can be complex, depending on a number of factors: Is the usage for the U.S. only or for world rights? For perpetual use or five years only? For network, cable, theater, home video? For background use or main titles? For how many minutes? On screen or off? Are there several separate uses or one continuous use? Do the lyrics refer to the action in some way? Is it a low-budget or major production? Is the recording artist an established star or newcomer? Is the recording an obscure oldie or a new hit? The record company may have to negotiate these "synchronization licenses" with the recording artists since many have the contractual right to approve any use of their material in audiovisual projects. And some artists don't want their music associated with heavy drug culture or organized crime stories, for example.

A struggling recording artist may be less concerned with aesthetics than cash, and the fees can range from $5,000 to as much as $200,000 for a single use in a film. In addition to the record clearance, the publisher must also license the synchronization use of the copyrighted song. Some deals have fallen through because publishers require a unit royalty on videocassettes and studios are reluctant to accept anything other than a one-time "buy-out." It takes time to clear these rights.

This is not the composer's direct concern. It is a director's and producer's decision, one that many come about because the director is sure that this music will support his story best and appeal to his projected audience most effectively. Or it may come about because the newly composed film score cannot ultimately satisfy the director as well as the existing music he temp'd in during the production process. As we have seen in the budgets given above, licensing can be more expensive than scoring, and only directors, producers, and business people can decide whether the increased cost of licensing is worth the value it adds to the film.

LICENSING FEES. The use of the master tape of the licensed recording (for one song) typically will fall in the $30,000 to $100,000 range. For an original song to be written for a film by a middle-ground writer with some track record, a normal fee might be $10,000 to $15,000, while for the artist's performance of the song the low would probably be about $10,000 up to $25,000 or more.

Studios and networks have clearance staffs that do licensing work, and Steve Bedell, Vice President of Music for Paramount Pictures, describes typical procedures: "Ridge Walker clears music, both masters and publishing. If he runs into problems in terms of prices, I get into it, because I have intimate relationships with most of the record publishers and companies. The more the producers and directors have gotten into contemporary music the more extra participation we've had to do. Ridge's department is comprised of him plus two other clearance people, one in television, one in features, each of whom has assistants or secretaries and people that help him."

SPENDING THE BUCKS. LeMel describes the typical chain of events leading to the licensing of popular songs: "Sometimes they are indicated in the script and we budget exactly from that, knowing that they could be replaced. Many scripts call for whatever the big songs of the moment are—most writers have a real penchant for the Rolling Stones and they write in the biggest acts in the world. So that's expensive. Initially, we actually budget for this and then wait and see. Then what really happens is there will be a call saying that the picture can't be made for the 12 million dollars (which is what our budget adds up to with their budget), and it's, 'Can we do the music for $500,000 instead of for $700,000?' And that's when it really takes conversation, primarily with the director, about what he really sees and what we really see. That's up to the studio. In some cases where they really want to make the picture and they're apart by three or four hundred thousand dollars and they absolutely have to get it, we will make an exception and use the advance money from the record company in the music budget. But that's a [judgment] call."

LICENSING CLASSICS. Popular songs are not the only licenses that are acquired. In Oliver Stone's Oscar-winning war story *Platoon* (1986), Samuel Barber's *Adagio for Strings* is used unchanged (in addition to music Georges Delerue wrote for the film). Stone had to consider the advantages and disadvantages of using music that had been used elsewhere. "Nobody has used *Adagio* as the theme for an entire movie. It has been used in pieces—for one scene: one scene in *Elephant Man* (1980), one scene in *El Norte* (1983). So I committed to it fully, and used it as my theme of youth, and nobody has used it like that. Now I don't think anybody will after *Platoon.*"

HIT RECORDS

> ***There's a kind of knee-jerk reaction in the industry right now that whenever you make a movie you get a song, you make a video, you get it on MTV.***
>
> DEAN PITCHFORD, LYRICIST

"There are some pictures that don't merit songs," Pitchford says. "There are some pictures in which the tone would be disturbed. I spend as much time turning down work and talking people out of songs and soundtracks as I do doing them. I've sat through films where I just want the soundtrack to shut up. I want it to please stop playing me one album cut after another so that I can get into the picture. In those cases I become aware of a motion-picture studio on the one hand, and a record label on the other hand, working parallel and never intersecting their interests. Unfortunately, what happens then is you get an album and you get a movie but you don't get the symbiosis of the two."

SOUNDTRACK ALBUMS. Soundtrack albums with songs can be very expensive. As Pitchford sums it up, "It costs a lot to get a composer and a lyricist to write a song, then go into a studio, pay studio costs, engineer costs, tape costs, get an artist and pay him or her something, make the arrangement for the record deal to get a hold-back on his next album; and then you put the single out, press the single, pay promotion costs, you pay for a video—we're talking $400,000 maybe—to put a single in a motion picture and use it properly as a marketing tool."

According to music executive Gary LeMel, "An anthology soundtrack LP, including score and enough songs to almost fill an album, by artists of some note, range from a low of $400,000 to approximately $1,300,000." This doesn't include promotional costs. A confirmation from another source lists a low-end licensing of songs and masters and releasing a soundtrack album at a low-end cost of $250,000 to $280,000—with no original songs composed specifically for the film.

SINGLES. For singles, the quoted costs are $100,000 and as high as $250,000-$300,000 for one song including masters and songwriter and performing fees (including separate versions for the film and for the record, if needed)—with a low of $40,000 per song.

If we compare these figures to the $30,000-$300,000 budgets listed above for full movie scores, the disparity is obvious. But it's often the promotional value of the songs that counts.

THE RECORD PRODUCER. Record producers are objects of both envy (because of the quality and success of their efforts) and disdain (because they are often put into responsible situations in filmmaking even though they may not have the film background to make things work well). The fundamental differences in approach can hardly be more distinct: a record producer may spend six months making an album, polishing, overdubbing, processing the sound, and spending the kind of money quoted above. In film scoring, composers create full-length scores in much less time and for less money.

But when songs are involved, the record producer's skills and experience are in demand. When Burt Bacharach was doing *Night Shift* (1982), songs were conceived as part of it from the beginning. Each song had a different record producer. It is not unusual for the record producers to work on their own on film songs, without much contact with the songwriters. "We got a pretty good tempo and a click for the main title,"[17] says Bacharach, "and John Boylan is very easy to work with, and you give a little input, what you feel, and let him make the record, you know." Record producer Jay Graydon produced the Al Jarreau song. "These people are marvelous record producers."

Sometimes, though, songwriters can be surprised at a record producer's interpretation of their material. Rod Stewart produced his vocal version of "That's What Friends Are For" (Bacharach and Sager), which plays over the end of the film. "Rod cut his song quite different than I'd always heard it in my head. You take an A minor chord—it's a little bit different than an A minor seventh to me. In the song it was really an A minor seventh. Without the seventh it's stark. It doesn't work when you rock-and-roll it or something like that. And I like Rod's record. I thought it was appealing. He can't do too much wrong. He sings a ballad—he's very heartfelt. But was it the record that I visualized there? No. I started producing records originally out of self-defense, just to protect the material. And whenever I can do it now, that's what I prefer."

---

[17]"Night Shift" by Burt Bacharach, Carole Bayer Sager and Marv Ross, produced by John Boylan, performed by Quarterflash.

MUSIC AND BUSINESS

> ***The difference between the music business and music is vast. If you confuse those two things, you're in a lot of trouble. They're simply not the same.***
> ALLYN FERGUSON

Information about the structure and conditions of the film industry should help the reader understand how to handle his business affairs as a film composer. But it's a tricky balance. The fact that many young people are responding solely to the financial side of film composing worries Allyn Ferguson. "There are kids today working in films who don't know anything about music. It doesn't bother anybody. It's appalling to me, some of the nonsense. The medium has truly become the message. I fear for the future of good, fine artists in this business; I don't think there can be any. That's always been the case, but it's extremely different now than it was even five years ago.

"The problem is that the people who have come up *in* the music business have come up as music-business people, and not as serious musicians. I only wanted to be good—I wanted to be the best there was. I didn't know anything about the music business—I just wanted to be good. I have eight kids in my class now; they're all functioning in the business—some of them have weekly credits, and there isn't a kid in there who cares about being good—he cares about being successful. They're products of a society which confuses success with excellence."

The more hopeful view says that the film composer must not only be good musically and dramatically but must be able to understand the business side and handle it well. While some composers are barely functional as business people, others learn to cope very well with the business end. And there are still others who really excel in business and take charge in a fearless, positive way, setting up their own production companies, making package deals, soliciting special accounts.

Mike Post, in recounting his career steps, recalls, "Originally I wanted to become an arranger, but I did a few freelance arranging jobs for some rock-and-roll records and I realized that the producer had control of the arranger—so I started producing records. Then when I got into that position, I thought that it's not enough just to be a hired guy and work for this company and that—you've got to have your own company. And then you've got to press the business thing a little harder so that fewer people have less control over what you do. I don't look at myself as any natural businessman—I just didn't want anybody to have any control."

TAKING CHARGE—THE COMPOSER AS ENTREPRENEUR. Composer Michael Isaacson agrees with Post's outlook, believing that musicians should not just fit into the business pattern but should more positively take charge of their lives, including investing their own money, if necessary, in recording projects, and then marketing the music directly to clients. "I think that the ultimate responsibility for anyone's life is with himself. And if one wants control over their product they have to assume the risk—that's entrepreneurship. We should be developing people who take chances—take chances with their talent, with their money, and with their business acumen—and reap the rewards. A person can invest his own money, write his own music, record his own music, and come back and make a deal and sell that music to whomever wants it, and you are free to do so. It's your property. I'm convinced that once you start to think like an entrepreneur, possibilities open up to you that never existed before. You are not afraid to go to a publisher and suggest a project. You are not afraid to go to a library, a film house, an audiovisual house and suggest a project. You become effectual as opposed to victimized. Victimization always comes when you don't see alternatives or when you don't see yourself empowered to change things."

CHAPTER 28

GETTING STARTED

I would think that the one who would have the best chance in the business would be the one who would have a well-rounded background. Not limited to the classical field, but one who had his feet in every facet of it.

HARRY LOJEWSKI, VICE PRESIDENT, MOTION PICTURE AND TELEVISION MUSIC, MGM/UA COMMUNICATIONS

The film composers currently working in motion pictures and television come to film scoring with a variety of backgrounds. Some have gone to conservatory, some have studied film scoring at schools like the Eastman School of Music, USC, and UCLA, while others are more or less self-trained, yet they all have paid their dues one way or another. But how?

Some have a theatrical background (John Morris, William Goldstein, Arthur B. Rubinstein, David Shire); many have jazz backgrounds, including Johnny Mandel, Jerry Fielding, and Patrick Williams (and many others, like Bill Conti and Shire, were working jazz musicians as well); some, like Jerry Goldsmith, got their early training at the end of the golden age of radio and the beginnings of television; still others came to films directly from commercial work in contemporary music and records (Giorgio Moroder, Harold Faltermeyer, Tangerine Dream, Stewart Copeland, and Vangelis); performing in symphony orchestras provided solid grounding for Gerald Fried and Rubinstein; like many, Elmer Bernstein and Bruce Broughton have developed their abilities as classical pianists.

GETTING STARTED

Still and all, the big hurdle is always getting somebody to give you your first assignment. Bodie Chandler, former Vice President of Music, Columbia Pictures Television, agrees this is a problem. "You can really hurt a scene with the wrong piece of music. The ability of knowing how and what to write for a scene is a very special talent; you're either born with it or you spend years learning it—or both. You will make a lot of mistakes and find out that 'My god, that was too heavy, that was too hard, it's not emotional enough, it's too emotional.' There has to be a training ground if you don't have that great innate film composer inside you. And where do you train? I can't give a composer an opportunity to train himself on a million-dollar episode of one of my shows because I can't go back in and rescore it if the score doesn't work—there's never enough time. They have to hone their talents on student films, on AFI [American Film Institute] films, on industrial films, in a classroom, in their work-study periods, wherever they can get together with a little piece of film and write some music for it and have it performed—like at a music school. It's very important to see how your music plays on the screen."

GHOST WRITING. The new composer may have the opportunity to write a cue or two for an established composer without getting credit or royalties. David Bell is one of many composers who did this early in his career. He attended the scoring sessions for cues he had written, but the composers didn't ask for any help from him regarding interpretation, orchestrational choices, or even possible wrong notes. "It was as though I had just come in for the day as an observer," he says. "I decided early on that that was going to be a one-way street."

Sometimes you may not be aware that you're going to be asked to ghost. "I did one job early on," Bell continues, "in which someone called me up and said, 'I've got some orchestration work for you.' So I went over there and he handed me the timing sheets, and actually said, 'Here, orchestrate these.'"

WHAT IT TAKES

Agent Richard Emler laughs when he says his advice to hopeful film composers is, "Go east, young man, go east." But his suggestion is as candid as it is whimsical. "It's very difficult to move into television and films as a new composer, because there's simply too much competition and not enough opportunity for access that is meaningful. It's not a question of needing more agents in the marketplace—there's simply too much competition between the traditional Hollywood composers and record-oriented composers for the available quality product.

"But the thing I advise them to do depends on their background. If they're not formally trained, I tell them they must be formally trained. They must go to school and learn about composition, theory, harmony, and all the basics that lead them to getting a degree in music composition.

"Once they have that, the next practical step is to try to place themselves where they're going to be able to have hands-on experience in writing music for film. In Los Angeles that is either the UCLA or USC film schools or the American Film Institute. They will likely have to dip into their own pockets to produce the music. Once they have material to be heard, they should contact established composers for work as an orchestrator. This frequently leads to a chance to write an occasional cue.

"I think commercials are important also. Not for filmmakers as much as for attracting the attention of a possible agent. Commercials are not considered to be important as far as film and television writing, but the fact is it is a way for an agent to begin to evaluate the composer. I represent a young composer now (with formal training), whose commercials tape I heard and responded to favorably. He's been able to communicate well with music-department people, and producers, directors and musicians, and he's well on his way to a successful career. It took us a while to get him rolling, but nonetheless he's off and running, with consistent positive response to his work. This last point is important to keep the ball rolling!

"In any event, they should continue to build their repertoire of material through contact on their own with independent film-production companies that are dealing in the area of documentaries, religious programs, or children's programming, and build an audio and ultimately a video reel which they can use as a sales tool. Once they get enough of that material collected, then they're in a position to really attract the attention of an agent—if they're tenacious enough. This approach does work; I've seen it work.

"Once they have enough material, preferably on audio- and videocassette, they can then pursue the independent producers and directors and have a greater degree of access to these people. From time to time these people are more interested in hearing from the younger composers than they are hearing from the agents, because they don't always have enough money to spend to deal with an agent. They feel that their $3,000 or $4,000 or $5,000 music budget isn't going to be worth an agent's time and so they would rather be their own agent and review as many tapes as it takes to find a person who they feel might be able to do the right job.

"It's very difficult to approach the studio music departments, because the music department heads are simply too busy and don't have time to be a screening agent. They are there to do their job in their creative capacity, dealing with all types of music for film and television, working with composers, recording artists, etc. Therefore, they rely on the agents who represent composers and songwriters to keep them aware of available talent. They are able to get from those agents all they need to serve their needs."

When listening to a demo, film composers' agents look for the same qualities as would a producer or director. "For me, it would have to be something very special, very unique. Something that is strong melodically. Different textures, different rhythms, different colors are things that attract me." Would that be enough to sign the composer? "If I heard a piece of material that I really felt was terrific or inventive, I probably would take the time to talk with that individual (again, if he were formally trained), but unless that individual had enough of a foundation of employment established through either independent films, AFI, USC, UCLA films, documentaries, etc., it would be very difficult to represent them.

"And meeting them is *very* important. Because if you meet with somebody and they don't have the type of personality that is conducive to getting other people to like them, then that's a quick turnoff. If they can't communicate well with me, they're not going to be able to communicate very well with the director or producer. And if they can't communicate well with the director and producer they'll have a hard time convincing them they can handle the challenge."

CONSIDER THE POSSIBILITIES

Agent Alvin Bart affirms one proven method of getting started. "The best way, we've found, is to have one of the composers hire the guy, because, especially in features, nine times out of ten the composer [personally] hires the orchestrator. It's either a recommendation from another composer or from us or whatever and there's not too much of a problem—give him a cue or give him a minute or so of music and the composer can tell.

"They start calling the composers and they say, 'Hey, I'm great. I'm an orchestrator,' (or, 'I'm a composer, but I orchestrate') 'and if you get stuck, give me a buzz.' Nine times out of ten you find that they're going to get a call. Guys like Joel Rosenbaum and all these fellows are all orchestrators, working within the circle of composers because you get known. They do a good job and two guys are talking and one says, 'Hey, you ought to use this guy, he's terrific.'

"Then, at some point, the composer they're working for gets busy, goes to the producer, and says 'Mr. Producer, I can't do your next show, but this guy Harry Shradus, who's orchestrated this show for eight, nine segments, he knows it as well or better than I do, give him a shot.' Sure enough, he does the show and there you go. It happened with Dana Kaproff, with Alf Clausen, and with so many of the fellows. A perfect example: Jerry Immel gets to do some *Gunsmoke*s and other shows. He starts to get busy, he hires his old buddy who is sitting next to him at CBS, Bruce Broughton, who then starts to get busy and hires Kenny Harrison. It goes in that kind of a cycle.

"That's the best way, I find, to break into the business—as an orchestrator working for some of the fellows, because you're right there on the firing line and you get the shot immediately. And if they like it, you're on your way. . . ."

Bart sees a real opportunity for new composers interested in film work. "I think there's a great need for new young composers. With all the independents making films, some small, some medium, some big, not having the budget for the so-called top guys, well-known guys, I think there's more and more *place* for new young people. And I think it's very heartening, because if you open up the movie section of the newspaper, you see names that you've never seen before."

PART 10

SPECIALIZED THEMES

CHAPTER 29

TELEVISION COMMERCIALS, SPORTS, NEWS, AND SPECIALIZED TELEVISION THEMES

I think that commercials are also important for the aspiring film composer.
RICHARD EMLER, AGENT

We have suggested that the aspiring film composer get some experience doing television commercials. It's a field that can develop many of the skills needed in film scoring: the techniques of timings and sync, recording, and orchestration; and the psychological skills which come from working in a people-oriented team environment and fitting into a producer/director's conceptual framework. It can also help you test the various ways you can use music to communicate to an audience.

But the advertising music field is more than a training ground for film composers; it is a lucrative, highly competitive, full-time professional field with its own criteria. New York City is the major focus of this activity, with active centers in Chicago, Toronto, Los Angeles, and other cities.

TECHNICAL REQUIREMENTS

In many ways the technical requirements in television commercials exceed those of longer films, since the focus of attention on these 60-second, 30-second, 15- and 10-second spots magnifies details in a way that is unlikely in longer films. Beyond that, the advertising clients demand the finest quality and will go to considerable expense to get it. Advertising agencies hire the best photographers, film editors, *and* composers, musicians, and recording facilities.

The musical needs in commercial spots subdivide into two main categories: (1) the creative development of tunes, themes, and jingles before the spots are filmed; and (2) postscoring (underscoring, usually without singing) after the spot is shot and edited. Most composer/arrangers are more active in one of these fields than the other, depending on their musical strengths. The composer who is working in this field needs to have the same, or even greater, eclectic ability as the film composer—he must be able to write in a variety of old and new styles. He also needs to be able to provide a constant flow of fresh ideas and to keep up with current music trends in Top-40 popular records, television shows, and movies.

THE PRINCIPALS

In this field the persons whom the composer will need to be aware of are:

1. The advertising agency's *creative director*. The creative director is responsible for the current spot or campaign of spots. He would be analogous to a combination director/producer in the film world. Titles for this function vary in different agencies, and titles like Creative Vice-President are sometimes used.

The creative director is typically an experienced agency person who has a background as either a copy writer or art director. That essential distinction of being a "word" person or a "visual" person is usually evident in their creative emphasis. In either case, the creative director will have whatever assistance he needs to handle the copy writing, art design, choreography, special effects, and other creative aspects of the project.

2. The agency *producer*. The creative director usually has a producer, or television producer (or perhaps a member of his creative group[1]), who represents him and is in charge of all production aspects, although some creative directors take a more direct personal role in the spot production. If he does delegate authority to a producer, that person will be the person to whom the composer (and all technical and creative people) will relate. The composer needs to be sure he understands what the producer really wants, without injecting his personal interpretation of what is wanted.

3. The *account executive* is the agency's representative to the client; he personally supervises a particular account in the agency. He is not usually very much in evidence during the production process, but when he's there, his input is carefully considered.

4. *The client*. The advertisers are usually represented by their advertising director, referred to here as the "client." The composer very rarely has direct contact with the client, but must understand that his approval of the spot and its music is mandatory.

5. *The film editor* is the hired expert who creates the spot from the raw footage, analogous to the film editor in Hollywood, and as such, the composer will have contact with him, especially when he is underscoring.

THE MUSIC-PRODUCTION HOUSE

Composer/arrangers may get their work assignments independently from advertising agencies on a project-by-project basis or they may work for a music-production house, which in turn gets its work from the agencies. In the latter case, the music house then handles all the musical details of commercial production, doing the bookkeeping, contracting players and studios, and following through on production details.

The owners of the music-production house are frequently tune writers, sometimes also arrangers. They often possess one or more of the following assets: (1) the ability to work with agency people (some used to work in agencies); (2) a good understanding of film/music relationships; and (3) good music-production skills. They spend a great deal of time finding work, that is, *repping* (representing) their regular composers and arrangers.

[1] Sometimes referred to as "agency persons" or "creatives."

This is one of the reasons that some composers prefer to work for such music houses, despite the somewhat lower shared fees that result from such an arrangement.

THEME DEVELOPMENT (JINGLE WRITING)

THE STORYBOARD. Before the spot is filmed the agency prepares a storyboard to illustrate the sequence of images and copy in the proposed spot (Figure 29-1). It will usually include rough timings of events. The storyboard follows the concept and copy line developed by the agency and approved by the client.

COMPETITIONS. If this is a new campaign that requires a new jingle or tune, the agency will typically invite more than one composer or music house to submit tunes and demos in a competition for the spot. These speculative demos are typically funded in a limited way by the agency to cover some of the basic costs of making the demo. These can be simple tune demonstrations or quite elaborate, with a complete underscore of the storyboard and a polished synthesized score.

The agency (and possibly the client) will then choose one to be put into full production. This practice has, in the eyes of composers, been abused when the agencies have solicited many spec demos for one spot. **SAMPAC**;[2] a trade organization of composers, has worked to try to limit such competitive submissions to three. In general this is being adhered to, but not strictly. The opportunity to do a big national campaign for a major soft-drink or automobile client will stimulate interest from many competing composers. It is not unusual to have an agency call five or six houses, each of whom may have an internal competition among its writers. Each house may then select their nomination for the winning tune and record a full-production treatment in their own demo recording studio, with singers and musicians (especially synthesists) to present to the agency as their "demo."

DEMO SCREENING. The highly competitive nature of the business is exemplified by the fact that quite often the music house must have something on its current demo reel that is very close to what the agency needs before the house is even asked to submit a specific demo. The music house that wins the competition can expect to be given the whole campaign of many spots to do, rather than just the original spot.

By contrast, a competition for a new commercial treatment can be much less elaborate. Several composers may be interviewed and asked to simply give their verbal pictures of how they would handle a certain spot, the decision being based on these responses. But more and more agency people want to hear rather complete demonstrations before making a choice. The fact that many composers now have home synthesizer studios has made it cheap and easy for the agencies to get such elaborate demos.

In any case, it is now true that to succeed in this very competitive field, today's composer (especially a new one without longstanding contacts) must have significant skills in making and recording decent demos on electronic equipment.

Not all jingle development is competitive, and when it is not the process can also be much less formal and less expensive, especially where the creative director and the composer have a good working relationship. A primary demonstration at the piano with the composer singing the tune may be enough for the creative director. The astute composer will probably have two or three tunes to demonstrate. After the creative director has chosen one of these, he may than ask for a more finished demo to make a presentation to the client before proceeding.

---

[2] SAMPAC: Society of Advertising Music Producers, Arrangers, and Composers.

FIGURE 29-1
Agency storyboard.

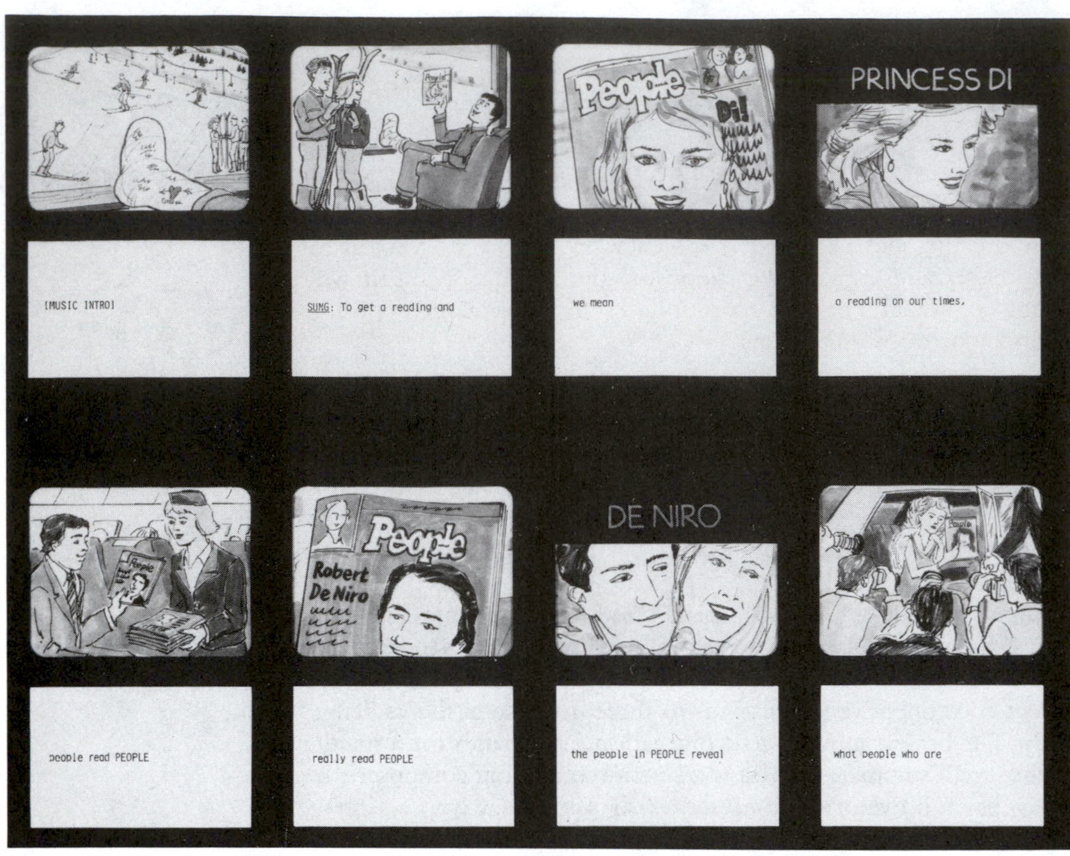

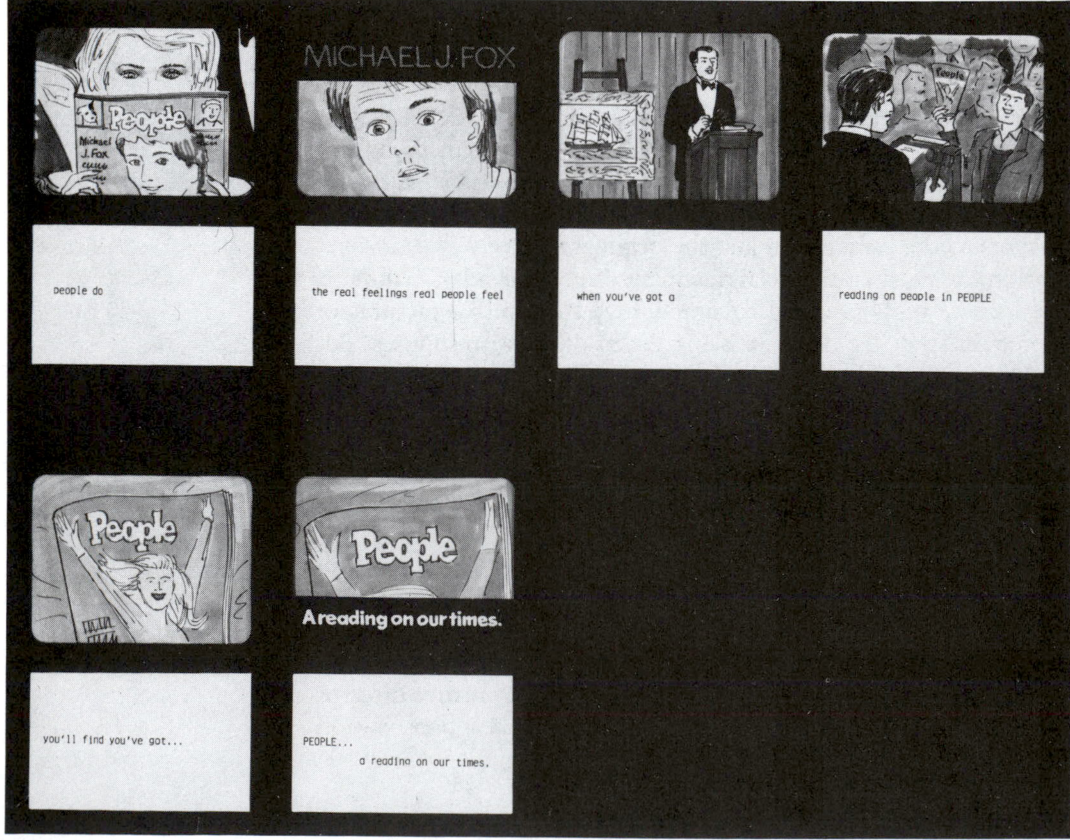

LYRICS. When the situation calls for a jingle (with lyrics) rather than an instrumental tune, the lyrics usually come in final form from the copy writer, especially on large national campaigns. Sometimes the advertising copy does not sing well, and the composer will need to revise the lyrics.

ARRANGING AND RECORDING. The next step in producing the jingle will be to arrange and record the jingle before the agency has the spot filmed and edited (or before animating the spot).

At the recording session, the agency producer (or creative director) and possibly the account executive (but rarely the client) will be in the booth with the mixer. Revisions and rewriting of the music during the session are common and composer/arrangers must always stand ready to find solutions to any problems of style or sound (or timing for that matter) that arise from the creative people or the client.

OVERDUBBING. When the overall musical style of the spot is "orchestral," it is normal that the recording will all be done live, on multitrack tape without overdubbing (except for synth overlays). However, when the spot has a pop-record sound, and strings and wind instruments take on a sweetening role, normal procedure will be to stack (or overdub) the music, mixing it down directly after the recording session. Overdubbing is more common on commercial spots than it is in feature films and television episodes, but not as prevalent as it is in pop-album recording.

When overdubbing is to be employed, the composer may choose to start the session with all forces rehearsing and recording the spot. The reason for this is that the agency people need to hear a complete enough version very early in the session to be able to know if it suits their needs. Corrections can then be made before locking up the idea and starting the overdubbing. If the jingle has already been approved from a full demo, the session can more safely start by laying down the first pass of the overdubbing sequence. However, this is not an inexpensive solution.

Some composer/arrangers take the more assertive point of view that they are hired as the music expert and know best how to produce the best spot for the least cost, so they shouldn't have to use the more expensive method of having all of the musicians there for the complete runthrough before starting the overdubbing process. Typically they will work fast and not risk premature criticism by asking the agency person for comments until the layering is complete.

There are several typical overdubbing sequences. One popular method is to record rhythm section first, then strings, then wind instruments, then vocals, and then additional synthesizers. An excellent variation of this, which helps get a spirited vocal performance, is to first record the rhythm section with a scratch vocal track, and then record the subsequent layers. When using this method, the singer(s) will ultimately be rerecorded for a more perfect result, but the primary vocal pass gives the rhythm section a chance to react to the vocal interpretation rather than having to lay down the **bed**[3] blind to what will follow, and the agency producer is reassured by hearing what he's getting.

Another option is to record the rhythm section and strings, then wind instruments, then vocals, and then additional synthesizer sounds. Or, as a variation, to do the rhythm section first, then the overdubs on which the rhythm section players play, then the vocal, then the brass or strings.

It is also not unusual to use the original demo arrangement—with its recorded rhythm section, voice, and synthesizers—then add strings, then wind instruments, with strings and winds often doubling the synthesizer parts, at which point a decision is made about

[3] Bed: the music recorded first, over which the subsequent passes will be dubbed.

whether to leave the acoustic sounds that double the synthesizers, or to drop some of either the acoustic doubling or the synthesizers. In any cases, additional sweetening or replacing of elements can be continued until the best result is obtained.

Overdubbing infers working to a click, which is recorded on a blank tape track during the first pass. When a good first pass, or bed, is satisfactorily recorded, that take is played back in the earphones with its click on subsequent overdubbing passes, so the musicians can sync to it.

SESSION LENGTHS. The minimum A. F. of M. call for a commercial spot is one hour, with optional overtime in 20-minute segments. A 30-second spot should be recorded (without major changes) in one hour or one hour and twenty minutes.

SYNTHESIZERS AND SEQUENCERS. Synthesizers are frequently used and are often played live on sessions (rather than sequenced) to achieve a more humanized performance. As in film recording, experience shows that using synthesizers in any way takes much more time than using acoustic instruments, and using sequenced synthesizers takes even longer. In cases where sequenced sounds fit the need (as in rock ostinatos and drum machine patterns), you are strongly advised to prerecord all of those sequences directly onto multitrack tape before the musicians do the session, or, as a last resort, have all of the sequenced material loaded into the computer or sequencer, with all the synth patches loaded and ready to go, before the session begins.

SYNTHS, SAMPLERS, AND ACOUSTIC INSTRUMENTS. A much-used method that has evolved with the new technology is to use synths and sampled sounds to form the foundation for the final version, with acoustic instruments being added as solo colors. If a vocal is involved, it is then added (with the understanding that the theme and vocal style was approved as previously recorded on a demo by the songwriter). Typically, the arranger then brings to the recording date his sequenced synths, samples, and drum machines (with twenty or more simultaneous inputs). Different patches and balances are auditioned and balanced for the agency people while the sequencer continuously repeats the spot. When the final choices of color and balance are made, all synths are then committed to tape (with SMPTE sync in case a part needs to be redone later). Next, the all-important human "color" instruments are overdubbed. For pop music, this usually means several tracks of guitar, or other woodwind, brass, or string colors might be added. Finally, any synth touches are added, and in this case, the mix-down is usually quick, since balances and signal processing will have been set throughout the session.

THE MUSIC MIX-DOWN. Usually the music mix-down, which the composer/arranger should obviously attend, is very demanding. All of the balancing, equalization, reverb, digital delay, stereo panning, compressing, and other signal processing will be done there—and with the likelihood of much greater attention to detail than in some film and television situations.

PRODUCTION STUDIO. After the music has been recorded and mixed down, those tracks are usually taken to a different production studio, one that specializes in recording announcers, providing the special sound effects, and syncing up all the audio elements against picture (that is, combining the feature films' jobs of music editor, sound effects editor, and the film editor who lays in the dialogue).

FILM-MIX FACILITY. The spot then goes to yet another facility, a film-mix or television-mix studio, which specializes in doing the final audio mixes (analogous to the Hollywood dubbing stage).

Because of the film's handling by a series of different editors and mixers, it behooves the composer/arranger or someone from the music production house to check on the music sound during every step to ensure the music's quality, correct placement in the film, and correct balance in the final mix. The composer should attend this final film mix-down if possible. He can make sure that, in television stereo production, the final 2-track stereo really works after being mixed down from stereo rhythm section, stereo vocals, and stereo instruments. In the mono version, usually used for radio spots, a separate mix should be made rather than making an automatic composite from the stereo right and left channels. In reality, few composers go to this mix, but music-production-house people sometimes do.

POSTSCORING (UNDERSCORING)

When the spot is already shot and edited before the music is added, the addition of music becomes very much a miniature film assignment. As mentioned, the timings can be more critical than in longer films because of the added attention such a short film gets. Incidentally, almost all major spots for national or regional television still originate on film rather than on videotape. This is essentially true because of the superior color photography with film.

The composer's steps are similar to those in film scoring: the composer may get his timing sheets from the film editor, but more typically he now takes them himself from the visual time code (SMPTE) burned into the video dupe that he takes home with him. He works out the tempo and music timings against the picture and narration, composes, arranges, has music copied, and usually records to click.

OVERALL LENGTH. As the composer lays out his music he is usually told to provide only 59 seconds of music for a 60-second commercial and 29 seconds for a 30-second commercial (including the reverberation of the last note). The music start is delayed for a half second (12 frames) of silence at the beginning and a half second on the ending. This is specified as a safety factor to prevent any swoop of sound as the tape machine, or projector, gets up to speed, and to prevent any unpleasant cut-off of sound at the end. Some editors and composers interpret the 29 seconds to mean that the last note of music should cut off at the end of the 28th second, thus allowing the "ring out" reverb to occupy the last half second thereafter. This works well if the music ends softly. If it ends loudly, a slightly earlier cut-off ensures that the natural reverb will not be chopped off at the end of the final available half second of time. In this debate everyone agrees that the music length should not go beyond 29 seconds. Some less experienced producers may ask for the full 30 seconds, and you should always have an understanding with both the producer and music editor about what length is to be recorded.

THE TRADITIONAL 30-FRAME START-OF-MUSIC DELAY. Not long ago, when commercials were actually run on film projectors at the television stations, rather than being transferred to videotape and then played back via videotape on the air, it was necessary to have a 30-frame delay at the beginning of each spot to take into account the 29-frame sound loop discussed on page 113. This case is unusual now but may be required in some situations, rather than the 12-frame silence discussed above.

CLICK SHEETS. The need for precision and very fast turnover time in commercial spot production has led to some unique techniques. In addition to the normal use of click books and computer timing programs, some composers and music houses have developed special music paper with frame divisions laid out on them in very graphic detail. There are individual variations of these but a good example is one developed by the music house Com/track, Inc., in Chicago. Composer Manny Mendelson's version of this frame sheet is shown in Figure 29-2. In this version, each film frame is shown above the timing line and the bold upper dividing lines with the small numbers above them count footages in 35mm film. Each foot contains 16 frames, and the inclusion of this calibration graphically indicates the extent to which many composers still think in film footages, even when it means converting video time-code timings back into film footages. It's a matter of training and habit.

The bold dividing lines just beneath the timing line represent seconds, since 24 film frames equal one second. At the same time, the small division lines below the timing line symbolize video frames, and these are divided into the corresponding 30 frames per second of videotape. The lower bold dividers, again, equal one second.

The multiple small numbers by the bold footage dividers represent the accumulated footages. Use the first numbers for page one, the second numbers for page two, and the third numbers for page three.

In using this method and this paper, decide the tempo of the click, and mark each click with an X, starting with the first one at 12 frames[4] (to accommodate the 12-frame half-second delay of music). Thereafter, an X is inserted at every 8 frames for an 8 frame click, or every 10 frames for a 10 frame click, and so on.

Scene descriptions and narration are written in just above the timing line exactly where they come. Then the composer selects his music meter (of 4/4, 3/4, 6/8, or whatever the music requires) and draws bar lines on the music stave (Figure 29-3). He now sees in detail where every picture event falls with reference to the frames, seconds, and footages. He can then sketch music on these staves with complete confidence in their accuracy. Since each page contains 24 seconds of time, each 60-second spot requires two-and-one-half pages of this sketch paper. This explains why this system is less likely to be used in film scoring, where cues are longer and where more staves are needed for sketching, but it is very well suited for short commercial spots.

FINDING TEMPO WITH AUDIBLE CLICK. An alternate and quick method of finding the best click (tempo) for a filmed commercial is to test different clicks against the video dupe, listening for the ones with the most natural hits and groove. This is easily managed by freeze framing the video at 15 video frames in (for the half-second delay) and restarting it on a click. When a good tempo match is found you can plot all the hits and musical phrases on a simple hand-fashioned grid of click numbers by simply observing the way the picture hits fall relative to the clicks (Figure 29-4). This nonmathematical method takes advantage of our natural instinctive feelings for what is the best interplay between the film editor's cutting rhythm and the best tempo for the music.

RECORDING SEQUENCE. The sequence of steps for recording, postproduction, and final mixing is exactly the same as given above for recording jingles, except that the music must sync accurately to the picture, usually by using click.

---

[4]Or 11, 13, 14, or 15 frames, at the option of the composer, if any one of those makes the hits work out better.

FIGURE 29-2
Frame-sheet sample.

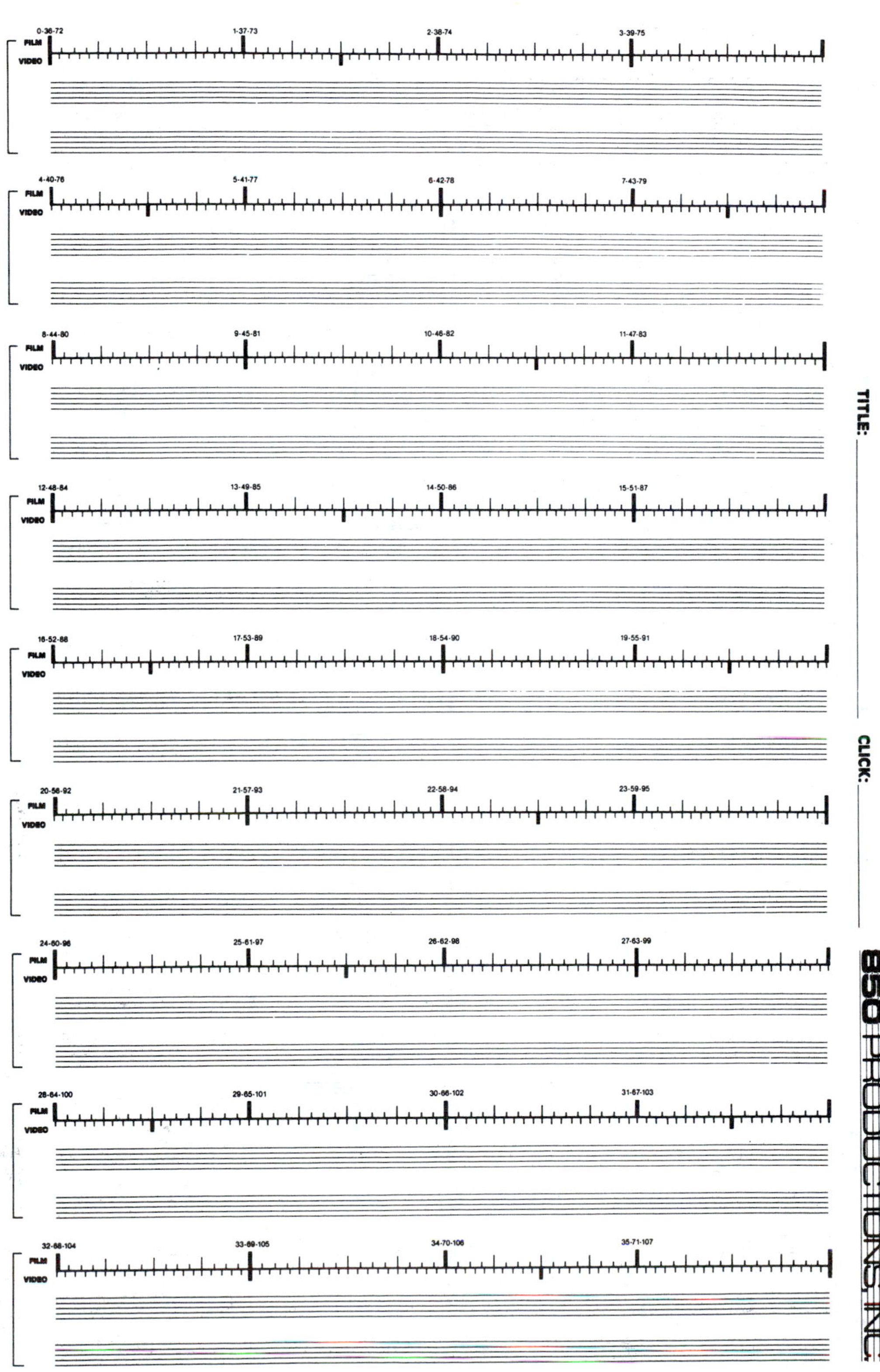

FIGURE 29-3
Filled-out frame sheet.

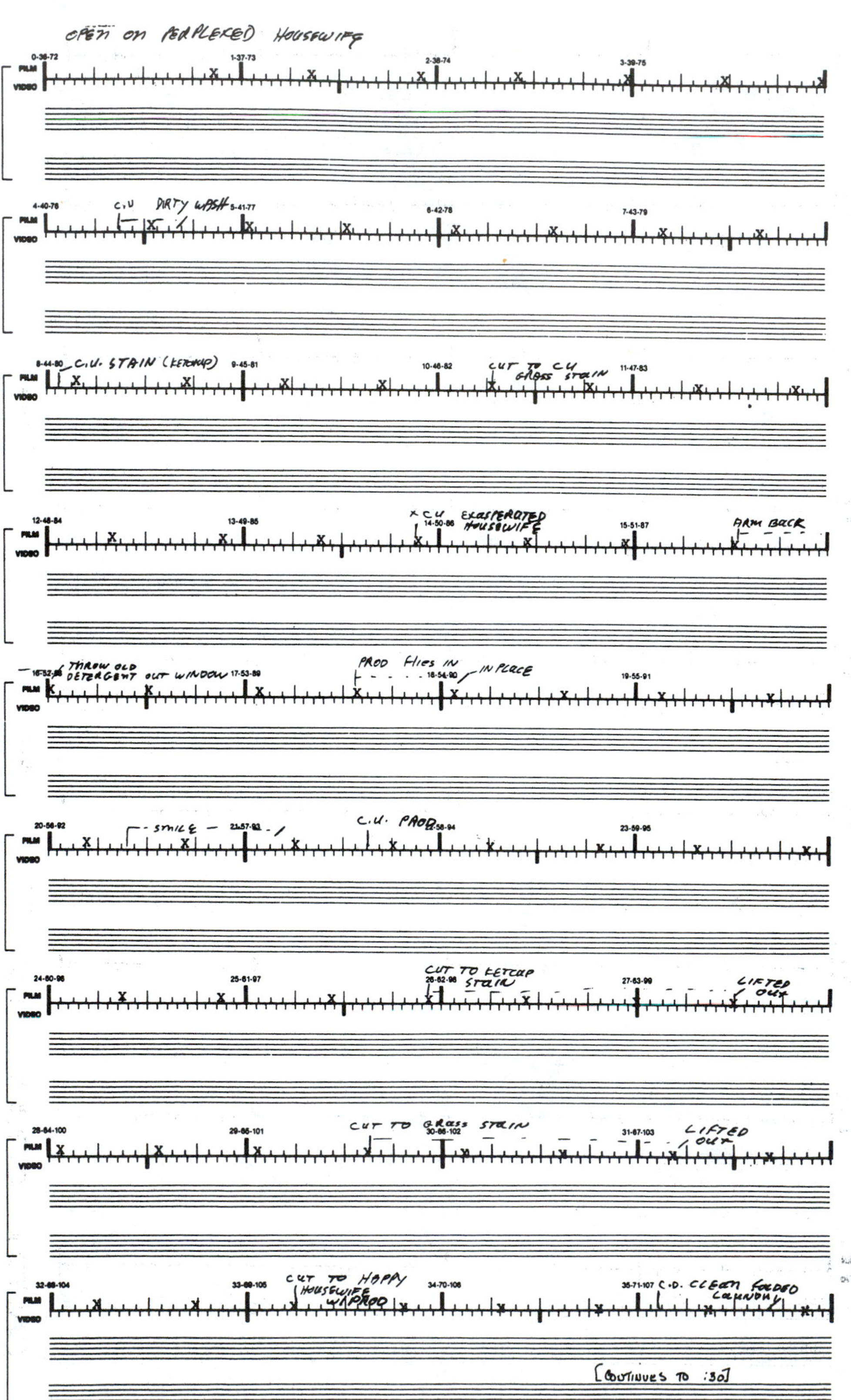

FIGURE 29-4
Click-layout sheet.

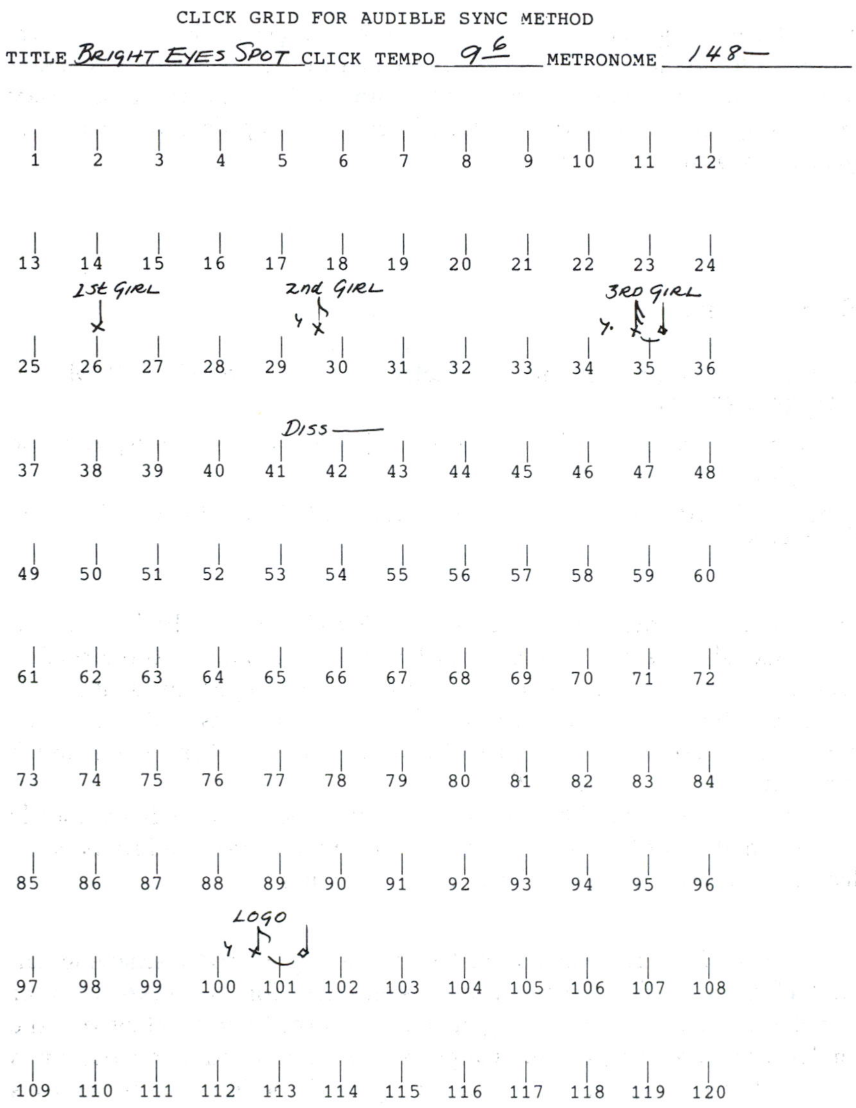

CLICK GRID FOR AUDIBLE SYNC METHOD

TITLE BRIGHT EYES SPOT CLICK TEMPO 9 6/8 METRONOME 148—

1 2 3 4 5 6 7 8 9 10 11 12

13 14 15 16 17 18 19 20 21 22 23 24

1st GIRL 2nd GIRL 3RD GIRL

25 26 27 28 29 30 31 32 33 34 35 36

DISS —

37 38 39 40 41 42 43 44 45 46 47 48

49 50 51 52 53 54 55 56 57 58 59 60

61 62 63 64 65 66 67 68 69 70 71 72

73 74 75 76 77 78 79 80 81 82 83 84

85 86 87 88 89 90 91 92 93 94 95 96

LOGO

97 98 99 100 101 102 103 104 105 106 107 108

109 110 111 112 113 114 115 116 117 118 119 120

TEMP TRACKS, SCRATCH TRACKS. On a postscored project, the composer (or music house) may first do a temp track (or scratch track) for the film editor to cut to. This will typically be a simple keyboard demo (perhaps with drum machine and a simple synth part, plus vocal if a jingle), recorded to click. This is basically a self-protection measure to make sure the final picture will allow for a comfortable and musical performance. Without this, for example, an insufficient time for the final vocal tag can force an awkward tempo change or an alteration of rhythm that destroys the track's mood or groove.

SMPTE SYNCING. Some postscores are more oriented toward the kind of special effects that synthesizers can do. These effects will usually need to be tightly synced to visual events by feeding the audio signal of the SMPTE time code to a sync box (if necessary) or directly to a computer program such as *Performer*. These sync boxes and programs can be set to respond to preset SMPTE time-code numbers, at which points the SMPTE time code triggers "note on" commands to the synths.

COMPETITIONS. Recently agencies have been asking for competing demos for underscore projects as well as for jingles. The two reasons for this are, again, (1) the overabundance of eager young writers with home synthesizer studios, and (2) the desire of agency creative people to hear specific options demonstrated before making decisions. In-house demos at the agencies are also being done.

THE BUSINESS

FEES. Fees for national spots in 1989 were in these ranges:

- Creative fees for songs, tunes, jingles for television: $2,000 to $12,000. Middle range: $2,500—$7,500.
- Creative fees for original underscore (not a jingle theme) can typically be $1,500-$3,000.
- Arranging fees (in addition to any creative fees): $1,200-$6,000. Middle range: $1,500-$2,500.

There can be a somewhat large creative fee for a jingle to be used on both radio and television. Fees for regional spots will be somewhat lower, corresponding to the smaller number of consumers reached. Local commercial spots in the largest cities like New York, Chicago, Los Angeles, Toronto, and Montreal can pay almost as well as regional and national spots, but the normal range of fees for local spots in other cities is much smaller than the national/regional range of fees.

The differences in fees for doing 60 seconds, 30 seconds and 10 seconds are usually small. With the current high costs for television time, there are few 60-second spots being produced; the fees listed above pertain to 30-second commercials.

SESSION FEES. A. F. of M. recording-session fees for arranging and conducting can be considered part of the total fee. There are no residual fees for the composer after payment of the initial creative fees and arranging fees as quoted above. However, the arranger who conducts the recording session will go on the union contract for two units of session pay for conducting, and two units for arranging. In addition, if he does his own copying, he will go on the contract for another unit. This potential total of five units counts toward pension and welfare funds as well as toward residual payments for every subsequent 13-week reuse of the commercial. This can be an important factor in the total amount earned.

VOCALISTS. Singers for commercials belong to both SAG and AFTRA, the same unions as do those singing for feature films and television films. They operate as sister unions, with an unusual overlapping of jurisdiction. Singing done for commercials originating on film is contracted through SAG; that done for radio only is handled through AFTRA. Work done for commercials or films originating on videotape have a split jurisdiction and may be contracted through either union, depending on the producer's affiliations. If he is a signatory to both unions he may choose either, but current practice seems to favor SAG for television commercials.

These fees (particularly the residual payments) are much larger than those paid musicians. When a commercial is used on both television and radio, it increases its potential residual payments substantially. Composer/songwriters who are singers not only have the advantage of being able to demonstrate their tunes to the agencies, but have the opportunity to sing on their jingle dates and be paid significant residuals. Recent economic pressures have tightened up all advertising budgets and large singing groups are no longer being used unless absolutely necessary.

OWNERSHIP OF MUSIC. The agencies maintain control of the music for their spots, and they almost always retain ownership, either through specific contract language or through the copyright law's "made for hire" ruling. Under this ruling the employer of a composer owns the work done for him unless otherwise prenegotiated. Some "in demand" composers do negotiate to retain ASCAP and BMI performance rights in order to be able to use their tunes for other purposes than for commercials, but do not always obtain these rights. Nonetheless, these rights for performing or recording of the music in other forms may be contractually granted to the composer so long as it does not prevent the agency from having full use of the music for advertising purposes. Many composers are reluctant to press for these rights because in doing so they might jeopardize the account. Composers can be more effective in this regard when being represented by a lawyer with copyright expertise. In such a case, a standard contract can be prepared by the lawyer that provides that publishing rights belong to the composer, which, if accepted without change, clarifies the issue at the outset.

IN-HOUSE MUSIC DEPARTMENTS. Some agencies, like J. Walter Thompson, have their own publishing houses. In these cases, composers sometimes earn writers' royalties via ASCAP/BMI, but this is not a certainty and there seems to be no clear-cut procedure. Several of the larger agencies also have their own music directors who take on more of the production details in recording the spots. In these cases, they may avoid using music-production houses, to cut down costs for production work that they do in-house themselves. This is one of the advantages to the composer who works for himself rather than for a music house.

LICENSING. When an agency wishes to use existing copyrighted material in a commercial spot, they must license it. They usually "buy" the tune for one year and the fees can range from $5,000 to $100,000-plus. If there are any lyric changes to be made in the licensed material, the agency will have to clear their use in negotiating the license.

INDEMNIFICATION AGAINST PLAGIARISM. Contracts for commercials, like film-scoring contracts, typically include language that requires that the composer indemnify the agency against any plagiarism charges (typically to a limit of $300,000 for commercials). The agency wants to be absolutely certain that the music is original and free of prior copyright ownership, but no matter how certain a composer is that his music is original, he cannot be sure that someone won't sue him for plagiarism, thereby causing him considerable inconvenience and expense to defend himself. Most composers try to have this clause removed from the contract, or at least limited so that the liability is no greater than the amount of his original fee. The music-production houses handle these details, so their composers don't have to negotiate the issue.

PACKAGING. As in film scoring, the agency may ask the composer to estimate all costs required to deliver a final mixed tape, and to package the whole deal, including recording costs. Under these circumstances, the composer becomes the employer and must handle payroll deductions for withholding tax, must deduct and match social security payments, be liable for unemployment payments, disability insurance, and such. When packaging a project, an add-on payment of 25 percent of the total costs is normal to cover these extra expenses, including the costs of hiring an accountant to handle the financial aspects. Music houses are particularly well set up to do packaging, as are major contractors (who typically charge 10 percent over all costs to handle the payroll as well as the A. F. of M. contract).

TALENT PAYMENT SERVICES. Payroll services have been established to handle all of the talent payments for commercials and are sometimes used by the agencies to take care of all payments on the talent side (including the residual payments that may extend for several years into the future). Music packagers can also hire such talent-payment offices to handle their payroll and taxes.

WORKING FOR A MUSIC-PRODUCTION HOUSE. The two principal ways a composer/arranger is paid when working for or through a music house are:

1. *Freelance basis.* The composer receives individual payments for jingles written or spots arranged. This can be on a fee-basis independent of what the music house receives from the agency; it can be on an approximate 60/40 split of the agency's fee between the composer and the production house (with the 60 percent going to the production house). Or the production house can guarantee a minimum total amount that all the fees for conducting, arranging, and singing on the session will bring.

2. *Staff or exclusive basis.* In these cases the composer/arranger is typically paid a minimum weekly retainer in return for working exclusively for the production house. In addition, he is guaranteed a larger minimum annual salary, to insure that the total of all monies that he receives from his weekly retainer and his scale session fees (A.F. of M., SAG) will not fall below this minimum. He does not participate in additional creative or arranging fees for specific spots.

Music-production houses offer agency creative directors the advantage of having someone else take care of the endless business and production details. The agency benefits from the counsel of experienced trade people, while also gaining the opportunity to hear the creative solutions of several of the composers associated with the music house.

REPS. There are also composer's agents or reps who contact agency people on a continuing basis to find work for the composer/arranger. At fees of 10 to 15 percent, this can be well worth the cost of providing this service. In this field, as in film scoring, it is difficult to find a good rep. Some agency people insist on talking directly to the composer and won't do business with either a rep or a music-production house.

Some composers find that they can more successfully get the work for themselves, but it is not unusual for a self-represented composer to spend as much as 40 percent of his time in this kind of activity.

INFORMATIVE PUBLICATIONS. *Backstage Magazine,* the weekly periodical of the communications and entertainment industry,[5] contains some articles on music in advertising, and publishes an annual directory of music producers, sound-recording studios, music libraries, and sound-effects libraries for New York City, the western zone (essentially Los Angeles), and Chicago. Occasionally a weekly issue will be devoted to articles on music. The weekly publications *Ad Age* and *Ad Week* are widely read and they also include articles on music.

---

[5] 330 W. 42nd St. New York, NY 10036.

SALES TECHNIQUES. Whether the composer does his own roadwork or works through a rep, first-class salesmanship is an indispensable ingredient to success in this field, and the composer who reps himself and makes his own contacts with agency people should do as other people in this field do—read several of the excellent books on sales technique (of the Napoleon Hill/Dale Carnegie genre).

SPECIALIZED TELEVISION THEMES

Another related area of activity for composer/arrangers is that of writing themes for network, syndicated, regional, and local sports shows, news shows, and movie-of-the-week opening titles. The work process differs somewhat from that of advertising music. It is contracted directly by the producers of those shows without going through advertising agencies (unless an agency has been hired to revamp the show's look). The music may be provided through a music-production house or directly by an individual composer.

VERSIONS. The producer usually needs a package of several versions of the theme in a variety of timings to fit various situations. These will include short bumpers, a 15-second and 30-second version, and more—depending on the format of the opening and its video graphics. Sport-show themes are often written as a long version (2 minutes or so) to fit the closing show credits (called the "crawl") and that version is also used for the show opening. In this case it will be faded out at the end of the show opening.

TYPICAL FORMATS. A typical television sports or news visual might start with a computer-generated logo or sequence and continue with divided-screen action panels. In preparing to postscore theme music for such an opening, the composer/arranger may be given rough timings of the computer generated logo, and a storyboard for the subsequent scenes. The final version of the computer-generated logo may be given to him on a video dupe at the last moment (perhaps the day before the session) to do a final trim of the music to fit the timings.

MUSIC FIRST. Often the music is written and recorded first, and the film is then cut to the music and inspired by its musical construction. In such a case, the producer may talk down the music by describing the visual sequences in terms like "We'll start with a five-second computer graphic with NBC sweeping in from the left and expanding to a grid panel of action shots which will hold for about twelve seconds, followed by the four five-second **billboards**[6] announcing the titles of the four events being covered in that show. Then a faster-moving computer graphic like the beginning for about five seconds up to a music button." This verbal description may be accompanied by a storyboard, but not necessarily.

When the longer theme version for the closing credits is used as the opening theme that sequence will typically include the beginning logos and action visuals, with the announcer coming in with the announcements of that day's events. Some opening formats are structured more tightly and call for the music to come up with a synchronized button on an animated or computer-generated graphic after the announcer's lines.

SYNDICATED THEME PACKAGES. Music-production houses also prepare packages of themes in different lengths and versions to license to producers as options for their shows,

[6] Billboard: a short display announcement of one of the show's advertisers or of the title of the sports event being televised.

particularly news shows. The advantage to the producer is that he gets to hear the finished product he is buying; the advantage to the music house is that such packages can be prepared during slack work times.

COMPETITIONS. Producers will sometimes solicit demos for their theme needs, and these competitions are similar to those done for commercial spots. Typically, three to six demos will be solicited, with minimal payments being made to partially defray the costs of doing the demos. Composers are never happy about doing competitions but find them a required aspect of the field. The demos that do not win the competition are not wasted effort for the composer since, if they have high quality, these instrumental themes can be sold to another client.

FEES. Creative and arranging fees for this work are comparable to those expected in commercial spots, with the difference that each network theme will be prepared and recorded in a variety of lengths, as mentioned above, as contrasted with commercial spots, which will usually be produced in one length only. Fees range from $1,500 to $6,000 (or higher) for a set of different-length network themes, with a middle range of $4,000 to $5,000.

ASCAP and BMI performance royalties for such themes are important sources of income for the creative work involved. In contrast with the uncertainty of performance logging by ASCAP/BMI of commercial spots, the regular scheduling of these shows makes it easier to log the themes and to prove that they were aired. Composers need to send in to ASCAP/BMI their own logs of these performances to be sure they receive proper credit. If there is a descrepancy between the performance credits aired and those listed on the royalty statement, if the usage is not determined by a random survey, then notify the performance-rights society to guarantee these credits.

GOALS

To be successful in these fields, the composer/arranger should not forget that his function is a service one, and his goal is to make the music fit the needs of the client and the agency. Composers who are searching for creative outputs for their compositional talents (and all composers should be doing this) must continue composing and performing outside of their commercial assignments to fulfill those goals. A positive side effect of continuing artistic pursuits is that they enhance the composer's status within the advertising field, where the agency people and the music production houses are respectful of the talent and skills necessary for such artistic activities. For this reason, it is important that the composer notify his commercial contacts about any of his extracurricular activities—inviting them to concerts or sending them recordings, for example.

COMMERCIAL WRITING AS TRAINING FOR FILM COMPOSING

Doing jingle work is so competitive, specialized, and demanding that most writers working in that field doubt its usefulness as a way to gain experience for film and television work. However, the composer who is planning to use it as such a training ground must understand the field as it exists and not expect that work will be readily available to him simply because he needs it for his training. The composer should be careful not to assume a patronizing attitude toward the advertising field, which might be as damaging to the composer's chances of getting commercial work as would the opposite hypocritical attitude of treating jingles as supreme works of art.

ON THE TRACK

I know that the impact of some of these pictures that are coming out today would be lessened considerably without the scores that they had. Sometimes they are mediocre pictures. A musical score can transform a picture in an inordinate way. PAUL WENDKOS, DIRECTOR

It's a shame that a lot of scores that are really, really good get lost because the film dies. MARVIN HAMLISCH

With the really great writers, you can take away cues and play them, and they hold up as music. There's musical content as well as dramatic content. DAVID SHIRE

While it is true that composing music for films may require a great deal of technique and craft, the reader should not overlook the fact that there are times when the film composer reaches beyond solid professionalism to create great and sometimes lasting works of art. When this happens, composers are as responsive as their audiences.

"What I find most exciting," says John Addison, "is when someone comes up with a really novel idea for treating a certain scene or a certain character. And I remember being absolutely knocked out years and years ago by *On the Waterfront* [1954], scored by Leonard Bernstein. He appeared to break a lot of rules. For instance, when the characters would kiss, he'd have no music. The music would stop before that.

"As a matter of fact, I was rather impressed with the daring in the film *A Man and a Woman* [composed by Francis Lai in 1966], when they had an actual love-making scene with a song going over it. At *that time* I thought, you can't *do* that. This is where you have your background music doing something if you have it at all. But they had the song over it and it just worked wonderfully.

"I think it's not so much the quality of the music on its own, although that can happen, but it's the way it actually works with the picture. When you say to yourself, My God, I wish I'd thought of that! I think that's what I find most exciting."

Marvin Hamlisch finds that the scores that really stay with him are the ones that intensify the entire film experience. "I love that. My favorite scores are things like *High Noon* [Dmitri Tiomkin, 1952], where, to this day, when I look at one of those Regulator clocks, I hear that theme. I just hear that middle part. And that middle part kills you, and I remember it so well. I remember things like 'Mrs. Robinson'—just seeing that shot and hearing them sing, 'Ho-ho-ho-hey, Mrs. Robinson,'—those things intensify what's up on that screen [*The Graduate,* 1967]. And they intensify them whether it's funny and they make it even funnier, or whether it's romantic and they make it more romantic.

"To me, if you think of a film as a white room and all the walls are white, scoring is not about adding more white. Scoring is about doing something to appreciate that scene, whether you add black or blue or green or whatever. You don't add any more white. You don't need any more white. You add another color, or another shade of white to somehow intensify the thing that's on the screen, and to put it into bas-relief. To bring it out of where it is, and push it out—to '3-D' it, so to speak. That's what music does, I think. And when a picture doesn't need it, then you leave it alone. And when it does need it, that's when you get someone who really knows what they're doing, to make it work."

Filmmakers and composers agree that there are certain scores that have become classics. "There are certain films, if you go back in history, that I remember tremendously," says director Richard Michaels. "The *Gone With the Wind* score [Max Steiner, 1939] was one of my favorites. I think all of it is beautiful. *The Big Country* [1958], by Jerome Moross, was one of the movies from years ago that I thought had a great, great Western film-score sound. That music at the beginning—the way it opened—was just thrilling and exciting! I just love that kind of thing." (see Figure 23-7.)

Jerry Goldsmith and other film composers often single out seminal scores. "I think the landmarks were: Alex North's *Streetcar Named Desire* [1951] with the first jazz-oriented score. It's one of the most successful uses of jazz in a symphonic form. All of the others like *Peter Gunn* and *Man With the Golden Arm* came after that. And *Psycho* [1960], by Bernard Herrmann, is still one of the greatest film scores. *Who's Afraid of Virginia Woolf?* [1966, Alex North] is a picture I wouldn't know how to score. How do you get around that dialogue?"

Alexander Courage mentions "an absolutely marvelous adventure score, [Erich] Korngold's *Adventures of Robin Hood* [1938]. Franz Waxman's *A Place in the Sun* [1951] was a heck of a score. The David Raskin score I've always loved is *The Bad and the Beautiful* [1952], and the way he presented 'Laura' [in *Laura,* 1944] was just gorgeous."

"*East of Eden* [1954], with Leonard Rosenman's music, is a great film on every level," says John Corigliano. "It's like a combination of Berg and Barber and it's beautiful, and it has a simple American melody also of pure innocence. That score is great. It's so powerful, and in addition to that highly chromatic and nervous, wonderful sinewy beauty he also has an innocence like Copland. It should have a symphonic version played by major orchestras."

Director Paul Wendkos was moved by a score from the somewhat more recent *Cutter's Way* (originally released as *Cutter and Bone*), a 1981 film with a score by Jack Nitsche. "I was deeply affected by the movie and the score, which perfectly caught the mood of the piece. It was one of the most fantastic scores I ever heard. He used a series of crystal goblets; it was an unbelievably effective score, it was so psychological, so sophisticated in terms of atonality—psychologically sophisticated."

How do film composers achieve those moments or weeks during which they are working above and beyond the craft of their profession? Elmer Bernstein shares a final thought with us: "I think with film scores, there are moments of inspiration. Strengths and things of imagination that come from sources we can't readily identify, and then there are amazing things that happen. They aren't necessarily once-in-a-lifetime things, but things that happen from time to time. I hear something in a score that I have never heard before—or feel I've never heard before—or such imagination has been brought to bear on a scene, it makes me say, 'I wish I had thought of that'—that kind of feeling. And that makes a score very special. In my career there have been a few moments like that. There are not many, but every once in a while, and you can not describe where you got the idea—but it happens.

"Most often it's something about the film that triggers something in some unconscious part of you, that sets off a whole chain of reactions that leads to something really inspirational. I think it has a lot to do with the film. Now, it could very conceivably be that some incident in the film relates to something that happened in your personal life. It may not just be actually the film. It may trigger some emotion in you.

"It's the old story, though. The music may be able to stand up very nicely outside of the film, but it's the combination that makes a great experience—the combination of music and film."

THE INTERVIEWEES

We have listed representative credits for each of the interviewees who are quoted in this book. These credits have been selected as a sampling of the range and diversity of their work. In no case are they more than a thumbnail sketch of these individuals' many achievements. Network and music executives' titles are given as they were at the time of their interviews.

The following list of abbreviations has been used: AA = Academy Award; AN = Academy Award nomination; E = Emmy; EN = Emmy nomination; DGA = Directors Guild of America Award; G = Grammy; GN = Grammy nomination; scr = score; orch = orchestration; adapt = adaptation; arr = arranger; lyr = lyricist; cond = conductor; m = music; thm = theme; **MP** = motion picture; **TV** = television; ms = miniseries; s = series; ep = episodes; spr = supervisor; c = composer; exec p = executive producer; p = producer; lp = line producer; d = director; w = writer; ed = film editor.

John Addison Composer
MP: *Tom Jones* (AA); *Sleuth* (AN); *A Bridge Too Far* (AN); *Torn Curtain; The Seven Per Cent Solution.* **TV:** *Murder, She Wrote* (E); *Centennial* [ms]; *Ellis Island* [ms]; *Charles and Diana; Strange Voices; Something in Common.*

Burt Bacharach Composer
MP: *Butch Cassidy and the Sundance Kid* (2 AAs/scr and song: "Raindrops Keep Falling on My Head"); *Arthur* (AA/song: "Best That You Can Do"); *Arthur on the Rocks; Night Shift* (including song: "That's What Friends Are For"), *What's New, Pussycat?* (AN/song); *After the Fox.* **TV:** *Burt Bacharach Special* (E).

Bob Badami Music editor
MP: *Broadcast News; Star Trek II* and *III; Beverly Hills Cop I* and *II; Top Gun; American Gigolo; St. Elmo's Fire; Cat People; Pee-Wee's Big Adventure; Thief.*

John Barry Composer
MP: *Out of Africa* (AA); James Bond films [many]; *Body Heat; Born Free* (2 AAs/scr and song); *The Lion in Winter* (AA); *Peggy Sue Got Married; Somewhere in Time.* **TV:** *Eleanor and Franklin* (EN); *Love Among the Ruins.*

Alvin Bart Agent; Bart-Milander Associates
Has represented composers and lyricists since 1960, including Elmer Bernstein, Gerald Fried, and Henry Mancini for more than twenty-five years.

Steve Bedell Music executive
Vice President of Music, Paramount Pictures Corp.; formerly Vice President of Publishing for Casablanca Records. Has worked on many films, including *Footloose; The Untouchables; Beverly Hills Cop II; Fatal Attraction; Terms of Endearment; Witness; Star Trek; Pretty in Pink; Top Gun; Ferris Bueller's Day Off.*

David Bell Composer
TV: *Murder, She Wrote*[ep]; *Simon and Simon*[ep]; *The Return of the Shaggy Dog; Blacke's Magic; Whiz Kids*[ep]; *Killing at Hell's Gate.*

Alan and **Marilyn Bergman** Lyricists
MP: *Yentl*(AA/sng scr); *The Way We Were* (AA/song); *The Thomas Crown Affair*(AA/song: "The Windmills of Your Mind"); *Best Friends*(AN/song: "How Do You Keep the Music Playing?"); *Happy Endings*(AN/song: "What Are You Doing the Rest of Your Life?") **TV:** *Queen of the Stardust Ballroom*(E); *Maude; Good Times; Alice.*

Charles Bernstein Composer
MP: *Dudes; The Entity; Love at First Bite; Nightmare on Elm Street; Cujo; Gator; Outlaw Blues.* **TV:** *Sadat*[ms]; *Little Miss Perfect*(E); *The Long Hot Summer; Scruples; Bogie; House on Garibaldi Street; Winds of Kitty Hawk.*

Elmer Bernstein Composer
MP: *The Magnificent Seven* (AN); *Ghostbusters; Airplane!; Trading Places* (AN); *Thoroughly Modern Millie* (AA); *The Man With the Golden Arm* (AN); *The Ten Commandments; Stripes; Animal House.* **TV:** *The Making of a President—1960* (E); *Captain and Kings* (EN).

Bruce Broughton Composer
MP: *Silverado* (AN); *Harry and the Hendersons; Cross My Heart; Big Shots; Square Dance; Young Sherlock Holmes* (GN); *Boy Who Could Fly.* **TV:** *The First Olympics* [ms] (E); *Dallas* [ep] (2 Es); *Buck Rogers* [ep] (E); *The Blue and the Gray* [ms] (E); *George Washington II* [ms].

John Burnett Film editor
MP: *The Way We Were; Grease; The Wild Rovers; And Justice for All; The Owl and the Pussycat; The Heart Is a Lonely Hunter; Murder by Death.* **TV:** *The Winds of War* [ms]; *War and Remembrance* [ms].

John Cacavas Composer
MP: *Airport 1975; Airport '77; King of Comedy* [source]; *Playing With Fire.* **TV:** *Executioner's Song; Death in California; Dirty Dozen IV; Kojack* [all ep](EN); *Mrs. Columbo* [thm and ep]; *Eischied* [thn & ep] (EN); *Quincy* [ep]; *Bionic Women* [ep]; *The Gangster Chronicles* [ms].

Brendon Cahill Music executive
Vice President, Universal Television Music and Home Video (1980–87). Formerly Music Supervisor, Columbia Pictures TV (1974–79); director of Music/Universal (1979); **MP:** *E.T.; Back to the Future; Somewhere in Time.* **TV:** *Miami Vice; Equalizer; Simon & Simon.*

David Campbell Music rerecording mixer
MP: *Stand by Me; Footloose; Prizzi's Honor; Spinal Tap; Risky Business; Airplane!.* **TV:** *The Ordeal of Dr. Mudd*(E); *An Early Frost*(E); *Peter the Great*[ms]; *Hill Street Blues; The Burning Bed; Call to Glory; Marco Polo*[ms].

Daniel Allan Carlin Music editor; President of Segue Music
MP [by Segue]; *RoboCop; Three Men and a Baby; Lethal Weapon; Ghostbusters; Stand by Me; Witness; Purple Rain; Platoon; Officer and a Gentleman*(cond); *The Secret of My Success; Airplane!; Annie.* **TV:** *Under Siege*(E); [by Segue]: *Hill Street Blues*(EN); *Peter the Great*(EN); *Moonlighting; St. Elsewhere*(EN); *Crime Story.*

Bodie Chandler Music executive
Vice President of Music, Columbia Pictures Television (1983–87). BA from UCLA music school. Formerly Music Director/AIP (1975–1978); Music Director/Lorimar (1978–1983).

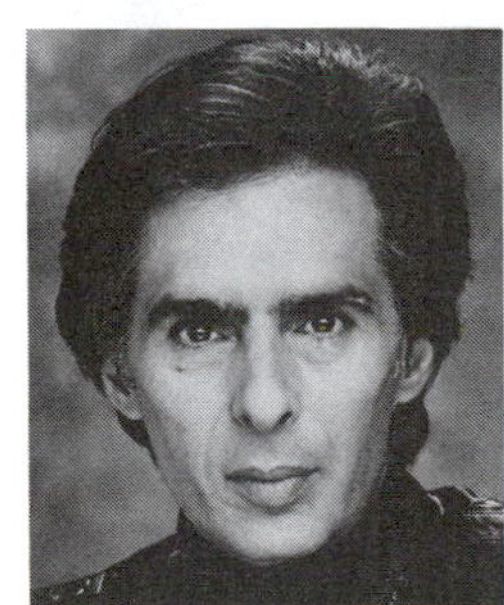

Bill Conti Composer
MP: *The Right Stuff*(AA); *Rocky*(AN/song); *Rocky II* and *III; For Your Eyes Only*(AN/song); *Karate Kid I* and *II; Broadcast News; Private Benjamin.* **TV:** *North and South*[ms] (E); *North and South II*[ms](E); *Dynasty*[thm]; *Cagney & Lacey*[thm]; *Falcon Crest*[thm].

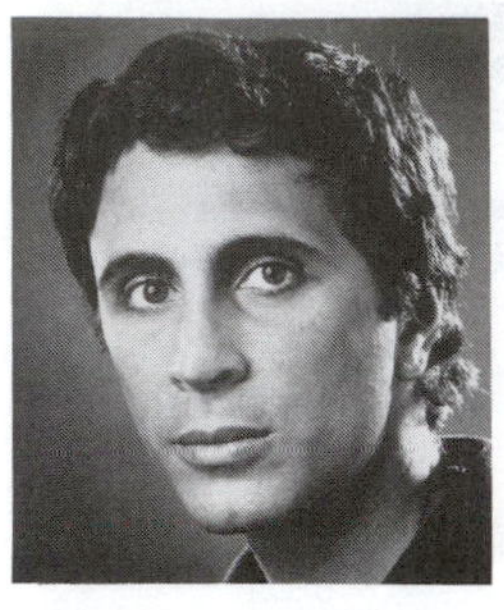

John Corigliano Composer
MP: *Altered States* (AN); *Revolution* (British Film Institute Award). *Concert works:* Clarinet Concerto; Fantasia on an Ostinato; *Pied Piper* Fantasy—Concerto for Flute and Orchestra; Creations for Orchestra and Narrator; Concerto for Oboe and Orchestra.

Alexander Courage Composer-orchestrator
MP: [adapt] *Superman IV;* [orch] *Lionhart; The Poseidon Adventure; The Agony and the Ecstasy;* [orch/arr] *Doctor Dolittle* (AN/with L. Newman); *My Fair Lady; Gigi; Showboat; Guys and Dolls.* **TV:** *Star Trek* [thm]; *The Untouchables* [ep]; *The Waltons* [ep]; *Falcon Crest* [ep].

Sandy De Crescent Music contractor
Universal Studios Music Contractor since 1969; has worked on *Jaws, The Sting, Out of Africa,* and most other Universal films.

Georges Delerue Composer
MP: *Platoon; A Little Romance* (AA); *Biloxi Blues; Salvador; Agnes of God* (AN); *Julie* (AN); *The Day of the Dolphin* (AN); *Anne of the Thousand Days* (AN); *Jules and Jim; Silkwood.* **TV:** *Stone Pillow; A Time to Live; The Execution; Silence of the Heart.*

Randy Edelman Composer-songwriter
MP: *Executive Action; Slow Dancing in the Big City*[lyr], *Feds.* **TV:** *MacGyver* [thm and ep]; *Ryan's Four*[thm and ep]; *Maximum Security*[thm and ep]; *Scandal Street.* **Songs** include: "Weekend in New England."

Richard Emler Agent; Richard Lee Emler Enterprises
Specializes in composers and songwriters for films and TV. Formerly an agent with IFA (1970); began own management company in 1975; own talent agency in 1983.

John Erman Director
TV: *Roots*(DGA and EN); *Who Will Love My Children?*(E); *Streetcar Named Desire*(EN); *An Early Frost*(DGA and EN); *Moviola*[ms](EN); *Roots: The Next Generation*[ms]; *The Two Mrs. Grenvilles; David.*

Allyn Ferguson Composer
MP: *Avalanche Express.* **TV:** *Camille*(E); *Ivanhoe*(EN); *The Woman He Loved; April Morning* (EN); *Les Miserables; Man in the Iron Mask; Master of the Game* [ms](EN); *Charlie's Angels*[thm]; *Barney Miller*[thm].

Charles Fox Composer
MP: *Nine to Five; Foul Play* (AN/song: "Ready to Take a Chance Again"); *The Other Side of the Mountain* (AN/song); *Goodbye Columbus.* **TV:** *Love American Style* (E/song; EN/scr); *Love Boat* [thm]; *The Paper Chase* (EN/song); *Happy Days* [thm]. **Songs** include: "Killing Me Softly With His Song"; "I Got A Name."

Gerald Fried Composer
MP: *Birds Do It, Bees Do It* (AN). **TV:** *Roots* [ms] (E); *Roots: The Next Generation* [ms]; *Mystic Warrior* [ms]; *Moviola* (EN); *Gauguin in Tahiti* (EN); *I Will Fight No More Forever; Dear Mr. Gable; Son-Rise; Star Trek* [ep]; *Mission: Impossible* [ep]; *Police Story* [ep]; *Gunsmoke* [ep].

Norman Gimbel Lyricist
MP: *Norma Rae* (AA/song: "It Goes Like it Goes"); *Foul Play* (AN/song: "Ready to Take a Chance Again"); *The Other Side of the Mountain* (AN/song). **TV:** *The Paper Chase* (EN); *Happy Days; Laverne & Shirely; Love American Style* (E); *Love Boat.* **Songs** include: "Killing Me Softly With His Song"; "I Got a Name"; "Girl From Ipanema."

Jerry Goldsmith Composer
MP: *Hoosiers* (AN); *The Omen* (AA); *Patton* (AN); *Star Trek—the Motion Picture* (AN); *Planet of the Apes* (AN); *Alien; Poltergeist* (AN); *The Wind and the Lion* (AN). **TV:** *Masada* [ms](E); *Babe* (E); *QB-VII* [ms](E); *The Red Pony* (E).

William Goldstein Composer
MP: *Saving Grace; Hello Again; Up the Creek; Eye for an Eye; The Bingo Long Traveling All-Star and Motor Kings.* **TV:** *oceanQuest; Liberty; Six Against the Rock; Fame*[ep](EN); *Happy Endings*[song] (EN); *Omnibus*[thm and ep] (EN); *Twilight Zone*[ep].

James Goldstone Director
MP: *Winning; Roller Coaster; Red Sky at Morning.* **TV:** *Kent State*(E); *Calamity Jane; Studs Lonigan*[ms]; *Clear and Present Danger; Earth* Star Voyager*[ms]; *Star Trek* pilot; *Ironsides* pilot.

Michael Gore Composer-songwriter

MP: *Fame*(2 AAs/scr and song, "Fame"); *Terms of Endearment*(AN); *Pretty in Pink.*

John (Johnny) Green Composer
General Music Director and Executive-in-Charge-of-Music/ MGM (1949–58). **MP:** *Raintree County; American in Paris*(AA/adapt); *West Side Story*(AA/adapt); *Oliver!* (AA/adapt); *Easter Parade*(AA/adapt); *They Shoot Horses, Don't They?*(AN/adapt); *Fiesta; Royal Wedding.* **Songs** include: "Body and Soul"; "I Cover the Waterfront"; "I'm Yours."

Marvin Hamlisch Composer
MP: *The Way We Were* (2 AAs/scr and song); *The Sting* (AA/adapt); *The Spy Who Loved Me* (AN/song: "Nobody Does it Better"); *Little Nikita; Sophie's Choice; Ice Castles; Romantic Comedy; Seems Like Old Times.* **TV:** *A Streetcar Named Desire; The Two Mrs. Grenvilles.* **Musical Theater** includes: *A Chorus Line; They're Playing Our Song; Smile.*

Jack Hayes Orchestrator
MP: *The Way We Were; The Elephant Man; The Natural; Spaceballs; Sophie's Choice; High Anxiety;* [and with Leo Shuken]: *How the West Was Won; The Magnificent Seven; Camelot; The Greatest Story Ever Told; Casino Royale.*

Harry Heitzer Music executive
Vice President, Business Affairs, Music Operations, CBS Entertainment. With CBS since 1956. Formerly director of West Coast Music Operations (1971); director of Business Affairs—Music Operations (1980); Vice President, Music Operations [national] (1981).

James Horner Composer
MP: *Star Trek II and III; Aliens* (AN); *Batteries Not Included; An American Tail* (AN and G/song of the year, 1987: "Somewhere Out There"); *Willow; Project X; 48 Hours; Cocoon; Where the River Runs Black; Testament; Gorky Park.* **TV:** *Angel Dusted; A Piano for Mrs. Cimino.*

Michael Isaacson Composer-orchestrator
MP: *National Lampoon's European Vacation* [orch]; *Billy Jack Goes to Washington* [orch]. **TV:** *Bionic Woman* [ep]; *Hawaii Five-O* [ep]; *Mystic Warrior* [orch]; *Casablanca* [orch]; *Hollywood: The Gift of Laughter* [orch]; *Hart to Hart* [orch].

Gerald Isenberg Producer
MP: *Clan of the Cave Bear; Let the Good Times Roll.* **TV:** [former executive in charge of Production/ABC-TV]; *The Execution of Raymond Graham* [exec p]; *A Time to Triumph; The Defection of Simas Kudirka* [exec pl; *Fame* pilot [exec p].

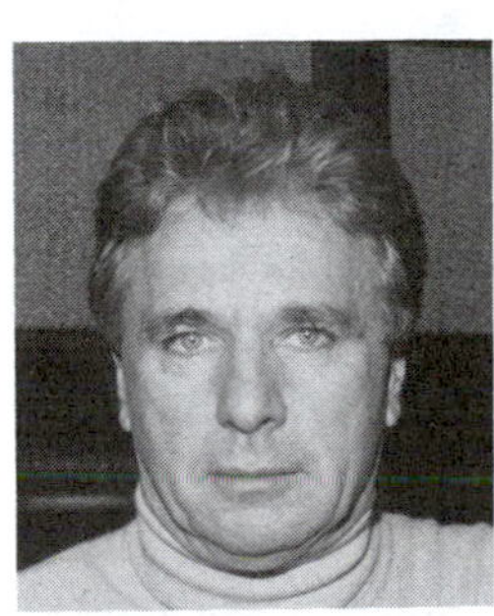

Maurice Jarre Composer
MP: *Lawrence of Arabia* (AA); *Doctor Zhivago* (AA); *Fatal Attraction; Witness; Gorillas in the Mist* (AN); *No Way Out; Mad Max Beyond Thunderdome; A Passage to India* (AA); *The Mosquito Coast; The Tin Drum.* **TV:** *Shogun* [ms].

Gary LeMel Music executive
President, Music, Warner Bros. Inc.; formerly head of Columbia Pictures Music (1983) and senior Vice President and head of A & R of Boardwalk Entertainment. Involved with MP soundtracks like *The Big Chill; St. Elmo's Fire; White Nights; Against All Odds; Arthur on the Rocks; The Lost Boys; Empire of the Sun; Stand and Deliver; Gorillas in the Mist.*

Erma Levin Music editor
MP: *Wait Until Dark; Taking of Pelham 1-2-3; 'night, Mother; Papillon; Who's Afraid of Virginia Woolf?; The Spiral Staircase; I Remember Mama; The Wild One; The Green Berets.* **MP:** *Queen of the Stardust Ballroom; Do You Remember Love?*

Harry Lojewski Music executive
Vice President of Motion Picture and Television Music, MGM/UA Communications (through 1987); with MGM from 1954–87; formerly executive director of music (1973).

Don MacDougall Recording engineer/rerecording mixer
MP: *Star Wars*(AA); *Close Encounters*(AN); *Butch Cassidy*(AN); *Funny Lady*(AN); Patton AN); *The Godfather*(AN) **TV:** *Eleanor and Franklin; Dynasty; Moonlighting.*

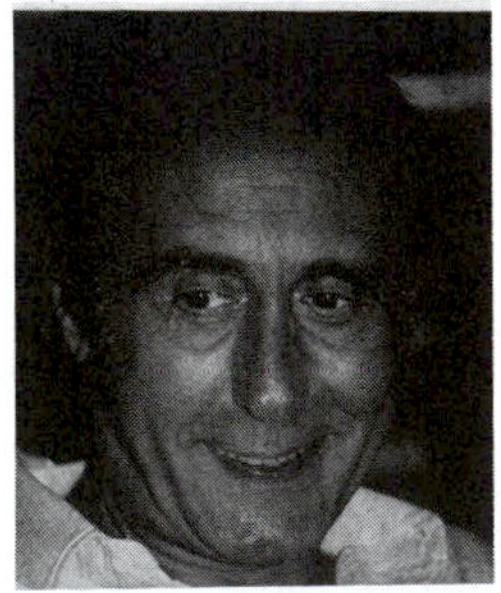

Henry Mancini Composer
MP: *The Pink Panther*(AN); *Days of Wine and Roses*(AA/song); *Breakfast at Tiffany's*(2 AAs/scr and song: "Moon River"); *Victor/Victoria*(AA); *10*(AN); *Wait Until Dark; That's Entertainment; That's Life*(AN/song); *Without a Clue.* **TV:** *The Thorn Birds* [ms](EN); *Remington Steele*[thm]; *Hotel*[thm]; *Newhart*[thm]; *Peter Gunn*[thm].

Johnny Mandel Composer
MP: *M*A*S*H* (including song: "Suicide is Painless"); *Being There; Deathtrap; The Verdict; The Sandpiper* (AA/song: "The Shadow of Your Smile"); *The Russians Are Coming; I Want to Live.* **TV:** *M*A*S*H* [thm and ep]; *LBJ* [ms].

Gene Marks Music editor
With Warner Bros. 1966–85. **MP:** *Spaceballs; Dirty Harry; Blazing Saddles; My Fair Lady; Camelot; Finian's Rainbow.* **TV:** *Roots: The Next Generation* [ms]; *Dream West* [ms].

John Martinelli Film editor
MP: *The Boss's Wife; Hard Country.* **TV:** *Murder in Texas* (E); *The Defection of Simas Kudirka* (E); *The Legend of Lizzie Borden* (E); *A.D. Anno Domini* [ms](EN)[ed/lp].

Anthony Masucci NBC Vice President, Motion Pictures for Television.

Michael Melvoin Composer
MP: *Big Town; King of the Mountain; Main Event; Ashanti.* **TV:** *Aspen; Search For Houdini; Return of the Rebels; The Last Survivors; Fame* [ep]; *MacGyver* [ep]; *Buck Rogers* [ep]; *Lou Grant* [ep]; *Baretta* [ep].

Marc Merson Producer
MP: *The Heart Is a Lonely Hunter; Leadbelly.* **TV:** *Kaz*[s]; *Jessica Novack*[s]; *We'll Get By*[s]; *The Rules of Marriage*[ms].

Richard Michaels Director
MP: *Blue Skies Again.* **TV:** *Sadat*[ms]; *Scared Straight: Another Story; Silence of the Heart; Once an Eagle*[ms]; *Berlin Tunnel 21; Homeward Bound; The Plutonium Incident.*

John Morris Composer
MP: *Dirty Dancing*[scr]; *Ironweed; The Elephant Man*(AN); *Blazing Saddles*(AN/song); *Spaceballs; Young Frankenstein; Silent Movie; The Woman in Red; The Producers; Clue; High Anxiety.* **TV:** *Anne Bancroft Special #2*(E); *S'Lemmon, S'Gershwin, S'Wonderful*(E); *Fresno*[ms]; *Splendor in the Grass.*

Ira Newborn Composer
MP: *Ferris Bueller's Day Off; Dragnet; The Naked Gun; Sixteen Candles; Weird Science; All Night Long; Wise Guys; Into the Night.* **TV:** *Police Squad*[thm and ep]; *SCTV*[thm].

Alex North Composer
MP: AA honorary award (1986); *Under the Volcano*(AN); *Prizzi's Honor; Who's Afraid of Virginia Woolf?*(AN); *A Streetcar Named Desire*(AN); *The Agony and the Ecstasy*(AN); *Spartacus*(AN); *Viva Zapata!*(AN). **TV:** *Rich Man, Poor Man*[ms](E); *Death of a Salesman*(EN).

Gordon Parks Director-composer
MP: *Shaft*[d]; *Leadbelly*[d]; *The Learning Tree*[d/c]; *Shaft's Big Score*[d/c]; *The Odyssey of Solomon Northup*[d/c].

Dean Pitchford Lyricist-writer
MP: *Fame*(AA/song); *Footloose*[lyr/w] (2 ANs/song). *Songs:* "Fame"; "Footloose"; "Let's Hear It for the Boy"; "Almost Paradise"; "Dancing in the Sheets."

Mike Post Composer
TV: *Hill Street Blues*[thm & ep]; *L.A. Law*[thm and ep]; *Rockford Files*[thm and ep]; *Greatest American Hero*[thm and ep]; *Magnum, P.I.*[thm and ep]; *A-Team*[thm and ep].

John Reitz Dialogue rerecording mixer
MP: *Days of Heaven; Footloose; Buckaroo Banzai; Risky Business; Soul Man; Stand by Me; Prizzi's Honor.* **TV:** *An Early Frost*(E); *The Ordeal of Dr. Mudd*(E); *Shogun*[ms]; *Dream West*[ms]; *Peter the Great*[ms]; *Anastasia*[ms]; *Call to Glory.*

John Richards Recording mixer
MP: *The Spy Who Loved Me; White Nights; The Omen; Gandhi; Octopussy; Revenge of the Pink Panther; Victor/Victoria; Murder on the Orient Express.*

Laurence Rosenthal Composer
MP: *Becket*(AN); *Man of La Mancha*(AN/adapt); *Return of a Man Called Horse; Who'll Stop the Rain?; The Miracle Worker.* **TV:** *Anastasia* [ms](E); *Peter the Great* [ms](E); *Michelangelo: The Last Giant*(E); *Who Will Love My Children?*(EN); *Mussolini: The Untold Story*[ms]; *George Washington*[ms]; *Fantasy Island*[thm and ep].

Arthur B. Rubinstein Composer
MP: *WarGames; Stakeout; Blue Thunder; Whose Life is it Anyway?; Lost in America.* **TV:** *Scarecrow & Mrs. King*(E); *The Betty Ford Story; Portrait of a Rebel: Margaret Sanger; The Wizard* [thm and ep]; *Roses Are for the Rich*[ms]; *Bitter Creek; Once Upon a Train.*

Craig Safan Composer
MP: *Stand and Deliver; Remo Williams; The Last Starfighter; Lady Beware; The Legend of Billie Jean; Corvette Summer.* **TV:** *Cheers*[all ep]; *Courage; Timestalkers; Amazing Stories*[ep]; *Twilight Zone*[ep]; *Hitchcock Presents*[ep]; *Call to Glory*[ep].

David Seltzer Director-writer
MP: *The Omen*[w]; *Punchline*[d/w]; *Lucas*[d/w]; *The Other Side of the Mountain*[w]. **TV:** *Green Eyes*[w]; *Larry*[w].

David Shire Composer
MP: *Norma Rae*(AA/song: "It Goes Like It Goes"); *The Promise*(AN); *'night, Mother; Short Circuit; Backfire; Vice Versa; Return to Oz; Saturday Night Fever; 2010; The Taking of Pelham 1-2-3; All the President's Men; The Conversation.* **TV:** *Do You Remember Love?*(EN); *Raid on Entebbe*(EN); **Musical Theater:** *Baby.*

Paul Shure Musician (concertmaster)
Formerly concertmaster at Fox for ten years. Has been concertmaster for many composers, including Bill Conti, Georges Delerue, Charles Fox, Gerald Fried, Jerry Goldsmith, Fred Karlin, and John Williams.

Alan Silvestri Composer
MP: *Who Framed Roger Rabbit; Romancing the Stone; Back to the Future; Outrageous Fortune; No Mercy; Clan of the Cave Bear; Golden Child.* **TV:** *Starsky and Hutch*[ep]; *Amazing Stories*[ep].

Clark Spangler Synthesist
One of the pioneers in studio synthesis; invited by Yamaha to help create the factory preset patches for the original DX7. Has performed and programmed music for numerous motion pictures and television projects.

Oliver Stone Director-writer
MP: *Platoon* (AA); *Wall Street; Midnight Express* (AA/w); *Salvador* (AN/w); *Scarface* [w]; *The Year of the Dragon* [w].

Michael Tronick Music editor-film editor
MP: *Beverly Hills Cop II* [ed]; *Chorus Line; Reds; 48 Hours; Outrageous Fortune; All That Jazz; Streets of Fire; Ruthless People.*

Rick Vettraino Music copyist-librarian
More than twenty years with his own company. **MP:** *Out of Africa; Rocky and Rocky II; In the Heat of the Night; The Thomas Crown Affair; Body Heat; Ghostbusters.* **TV:** *Robert Kennedy and His Times; Inside the Third Reich; Academy Awards Show* [twice].

Dan Wallin Recording mixer-rerecording mixer
Acoustic design of Paramount Stage M; human engineering of Burbank Studios Scoring Stages. **MP:** *The Way We Were; Out of Africa; The Right Stuff; Prizzi's Honor; Body Heat; Star Trek III and IV; The Wild Bunch; Woodstock.*

Paul Wendkos Director
MP: *The Mesphisto Waltz; Guns of the Magnificent Seven.* **TV:** *The Execution; The Ordeal of Dr. Mudd; Hawaii Five-O* pilot; *The Bad Seed; The Legend of Lizzie Borden; Cocaine—One Man's Seduction; The Death of Richie.*

Patrick Williams Composer; founder of Soundwings record label
MP: *All of Me; The Toy; Swing Shift; Breaking Away; Violets Are Blue; Just Between Friends.* **TV:** *Lou Grant*[thm and ep](E); *The Princess and the Cabbie*(E); *Slap Maxwell Story*[thm and ep]; *Days and Nights of Molly Dodd*[thm and ep]; *Bob Newhart Show*[thm and ep]; *Mary Tyler Moore Show*[thm and ep.]. *Records: Threshold*(G); *Suite Memories*(GN); *10th Avenue.*

Robert Wise Director-producer
MP: *West Side Story*(2 AAs/d and p); *The Sound of Music*(2 AAs/d and p); *Star Trek—The Motion Picture; The Hindenburg; Citizen Kane*[ed].

THE AUTHORS

Fred Karlin
Fred Karlin has been scoring motion pictures and television films since *Up the Down Staircase* in 1967. He received an Academy Award for Best Song in 1971 ("For All We Know" with lyrics by Robb Royer and James Griffin) and an Emmy in 1974 for Best Score for the television film *The Autobiography of Miss Jane Pittman.* His score for the television film *Minstrel Man* (with lyrics by his wife Megan) was awarded a special Image Award in 1978 by the NAACP. He has been nominated four times for an Academy Award, and ten times for an Emmy.

He lives in Santa Barbara, California, and divides his film composing between feature films and television projects. A representative sampling of his film music would include his scores for *Westworld; Futureworld; Leadbelly;* and *The Sterile Cuckoo* (including the music for his Grammy-nominated standard, "Come Saturday Morning," with lyrics by Dori Previn). He has scored a number of television miniseries including *Robert Kennedy and His Times; Ike: The War Years; The Awakening Land; Dream West; Dadah Is Death;* and *Inside the Third Reich,* in addition to many other television projects. He plays jazz trumpet, and has written jazz scores featuring his solo performances.

He graduated from Amherst College with honors in music composition, and continued his music studies privately with three masters: William Russo (jazz orchestration), co-author Rayburn Wright (symphonic orchestration), and Tibor Serly (conducting). To develop his conducting coordination, he studied tap dancing with Danny Daniels; to develop his concentration, he practiced meditation with Sri Chinmoy Ghose; to develop endurance and focus, he trained with coach Pat Connolly (1981–1984) for the 800-meter dash and currently races competitively.

Karlin writes at home, and records special projects in his 24-track electronic studio. He is the instructor for the annual ASCAP Film Scoring Workshop. He and Megan have created a historical archive of American music to help preserve America's early popular and folk music.

Rayburn Wright

Rayburn Wright has been a professor at the Eastman School of Music of the University of Rochester in Rochester, New York, since 1970. He teaches film scoring in a laboratory setting including synchronized recording of film and videotape scores. He heads the Jazz Studies and Contemporary Media program, is co-chair of the Conducting and Ensembles Department, and also teaches arranging/orchestration and the business of music.

He was active as a composer/arranger/conductor in New York City from 1950 to 1970, where he composed film scores for ABC/TV. He was twice nominated for Emmys for his work as composer/conductor on the documentary series *The Saga of Western Man.* During this period he was chief arranger and co-director of music at Radio City Music Hall and wrote scores for the Joffrey and Slavenska-Franklin ballet companies. He has been a guest conductor of the Philadelphia Orchestra, the Metropolitan Opera Orchestra, and the Rochester Philharmonic Orchestra.

Wright has produced many recordings and received a citation from the National Academy of Recording Arts and Sciences in 1985 for his producer's role in the Eastman Philharmonia recording of Copland's Lincoln Portrait featuring William Warfield's narration.

He graduated from the Eastman School, where he studied trombone with Emory Remington. He did his graduate work at Juilliard and Columbia University's Teachers' College. He studied orchestration with Bernard Rogers, Burrill Phillips, and Henry Brant, and composition with Henry Brant and Otto Leuning. His conducting teachers were Vladimir Bakaleinakoff, Paul White, Emanuel Balaban, and Fritz Mahler.

He played trombone and arranged for the U.S. Army Band in Washington, D.C., during World War II, and with Tony Pastor and the Tex Beneke/Glenn Miller orchestras after the war.

Wright is the author of *Inside the Score,* an analytical text on jazz arranging published in 1982 by Kendor Music. In 1984 he was awarded the Eisenhart Award for Distinguished Teaching by Eastman School, and in 1986 was named New York State Professor of the Year by the national Council for the Advancement and Support of Education.

Photo credits: Barry, Bart, E. Bernstein, Broughton, Campbell, Courage, De Crescent, Gimbel, Hamlisch, Heitzer, Hayes, Horner, Levin, Lojewski, Mancini, Marks, North, Reitz, Vettraino, Wallin, by Gay Wallin. Badami and Tronick by Peter Londsdale. The Bergmans by Spike Nannarello. Conti by Greg Gorman. Corigliano by Jack Mitchell. Goldstein by Todd Gray. Parks by Stanley Rumbough. Richards by Sherry Rayn Barnett. Seltzer by Suzanne Tenner. Karlin by Jackson R.C. Chao. Wright by Louis Ouzer.

QUESTIONS FOR REVIEW

CHAPTER 1. THE FILMMAKERS: THE DIRECTOR AND PRODUCER

1. Besides the composer, what six people on the filmmaking team may directly influence the outcome of the music score?
2. What are the usual functions and powers of the director on a feature film?
3. Why do some directors say that having a picture scored is the scariest of all the phases of directing a picture?
4. What are several ways the two-way communication between director and composer can be achieved?
5. What are the usual functions and powers of the producer on a feature film?
6. What distinguishes a creative producer from those who are not creatively oriented, and why is this of importance to the composer?
7. The amount and type of music used is often greatly affected by the director's attitude. Study and discuss the basic differences in approach in: (a) Stanley Kubrick's *2001;* (b) Alan Pakula's *All the President's Men;* and (c) Lawrence Kasdan's *Body Heat.*

CHAPTER 2. THE FILM EDITOR, MUSIC EDITOR, AND MUSIC EXECUTIVE SUPERVISOR

1. What are the responsibilities of the film editor?
2. Of the music editor?
3. Of the music supervisor?
4. In what ways can each of these people affect the composer's work? In what ways can each of them help the composer?

CHAPTER 3. THE SCRIPT, MEETINGS, AND SCREENINGS

1. What are the advantages of reading the script before screening the fine cut of the film?
2. What are the disadvantages?
3. What is the difference between a rough cut and the fine cut? Define each.
4. Why do the authors advise the composer to ignore the details at the first screening and watch the film as a member of the audience?

5. What are the potential problems in composing to a rough cut?

6. If, after the first screening, you think a film needs work to make it better, what do you say to the filmmaker when he asks you how you liked the film?

CHAPTER 4. ROLE MODELS AND TEMP TRACKS

1. What is the difference between role models and temp tracks?

2. Why have role models come into use and what are the advantages to the composer and to the director?

3. What are the disadvantages to the composer when a film editor prescores a film with temp tracks?

4. Pick an appropriate musical role model for the the following films: (a) a space epic; (b) an action-packed war story; (c) a bawdy eighteenth-century sex comedy; (d) an epic Western; and (e) a contemporary comedy.

5. It is important to develop a keen sense of what music does for a scene. The following exercise is a practical method using temp tracks to develop this sensitivity: Take a video copy of a film and play it without sound. When you see a scene that is suitable for music, test against it at least five different music selections that you think might work (by playing records or tapes against it). These are your temp tracks. Make careful notes of the different meanings of the scene when different music is used to score it. When you have found something that you like, play the same scene for at least two other people and ask them for their impressions and also for their favorite choices. Compare these with your own choices and solicit their reasons for their choices. Now play the video scene with the original music and compare with your choices.

CHAPTER 5. SPOTTING THE FILM

1. Learn all the terms in the glossary of spotting terms (p. 54).

2. What advantage does the composer have if he has pre-spotted the film before his spotting session with the director?

3. List the most likely motivations for music entrance.

4. Give five examples of moments of shifting dramatic emphasis where music might effectively start.

5. What dramatic situations would justify ending a music cue?

6. What differences are there between television and film spotting?

7. The music editor prepares spotting notes and timing notes. What is the difference between these two lists?

8. What is the advantage of a timing sheet with both cumulative and cue timings?

9. Study thoroughly the sample breakdown sheets and timing notes.

10. If a Moviola or flatbed editor is available, practice operating it, starting with scrap film (since film is very brittle and destructible). Practice threading, starting and stopping, braked stops, uncoupling and coupling the axle which couples the motion of the reels for the sound and picture heads. Practice setting the footage and seconds counters to zero. Take readings from each counter and make timing notes for a scene.

11. Practice making timing notes from a videocassette copy of a scene. List both cumulative and cue timings.

CHAPTER 6. BUDGETS AND SCHEDULES

1. What specific steps can you take in planning the recording sessions to keep the music costs down without sacrificing the overall effectiveness of the score?

2. At what point in the overall film-scoring process should recording dates be set and key players booked for sessions?

3. What is the consensus of opinion about the amount of film music that can be written per day? From your own personal experience, how many minutes of acceptable music do you think you could average per day for two consecutive weeks?

4. How many minutes of music is a composer expected to record for a TV show for each hour of paid orchestra-recording time?

5. Using your answers for the previous two questions, how many days before the final deadline should you start to compose, orchestrate, and record 19 minutes of music for an action-oriented television episode?

6. Using the quoted minimum-union-scales information, compute and estimate only the orchestra costs for a hypothetical feature film that you are scoring. In pre-spotting the film you have timed the music at 35 minutes and estimate the orchestra sizes and playing times to be the following: 15 minutes of music to be played by a 55-piece orchestra with 4 players doubling one extra instrument, 3 players doubling 2 extra instruments (add first-chair premiums for concertmaster, first cello, and first horn, and figure an average of 3 minutes of recorded music per hour of recording time); 20 minutes to be done by a 19-piece orchestra, with 3 players doubling one instrument, and 3 players doubling 3 extra instruments (figure no first-chair premiums, and use the average of 3½ minutes per hour). For this problem ignore the cartage and instrument rental costs, but do include pension payments of 9 percent of the total wages at minimum scale, and Health and Welfare payments of $.991 for each hour worked by each musician. Also include double-scale wages for the nonplaying contractor.

7. See a feature or television film, time the music, estimate the orchestral forces and work up an estimated budget exactly as in question 6.

CHAPTER 7. DEVELOPING THE CONCEPT

1. What are six aspects of a film that can be the basis for a musical concept?

2. See one of the films mentioned in this chapter and describe your interpretation of the score's concept.

3. See a feature film or television movie not mentioned in this chapter and describe the score's concept. Be specific in your description. What aspect of the film do you think the concept was based on (see question 1)?

4. Define the dramatic theme of the following films: (a) *Platoon,* (b) *Body Heat,* (c) *WarGames,* (d) *The Magnificent Seven* and (e) a film of your choice.

CHAPTER 8. DEMONSTRATING THE SCORE

1. Why do many composers not want to demonstrate their scores on the piano or synthesizer before the recording sessions?

2. What's to be gained by demonstrating your score?

3. Would you play your main themes for the director? Why? If so, when?

4. In what way is verbalizing during such a theme demonstration one of the most important communicative techniques?

CHAPTER 9. TIMINGS AND CLICKS I

1. Without using the conversion table in Figure 9-5, calculate the metronomic (beats per minute) equivalent of the click tempo of 15 frames per click. Then check your answer with that table.

2. Do the same for a click tempo of $9^{\underline{5}}$ (9⅝) frame per click. Then check your answer with the table.

3. Calculate the click tempo in frames for the metronome (MM) tempos of 72 and 180. Then check the table.

4. What is the number of motion-picture frames per second for 35mm, 16mm, and 8mm sound film? (They are all the same.)

5. Using Figure 9-7 as a model, express these timings in music notation:
The tempo is a $17^{\underline{3}}$ frame click (refer to the click book) and the meter is 4/4.
Hard hit A at :14.46 = beat # _______.
Hard hit B at :20.29 = beat # _______.

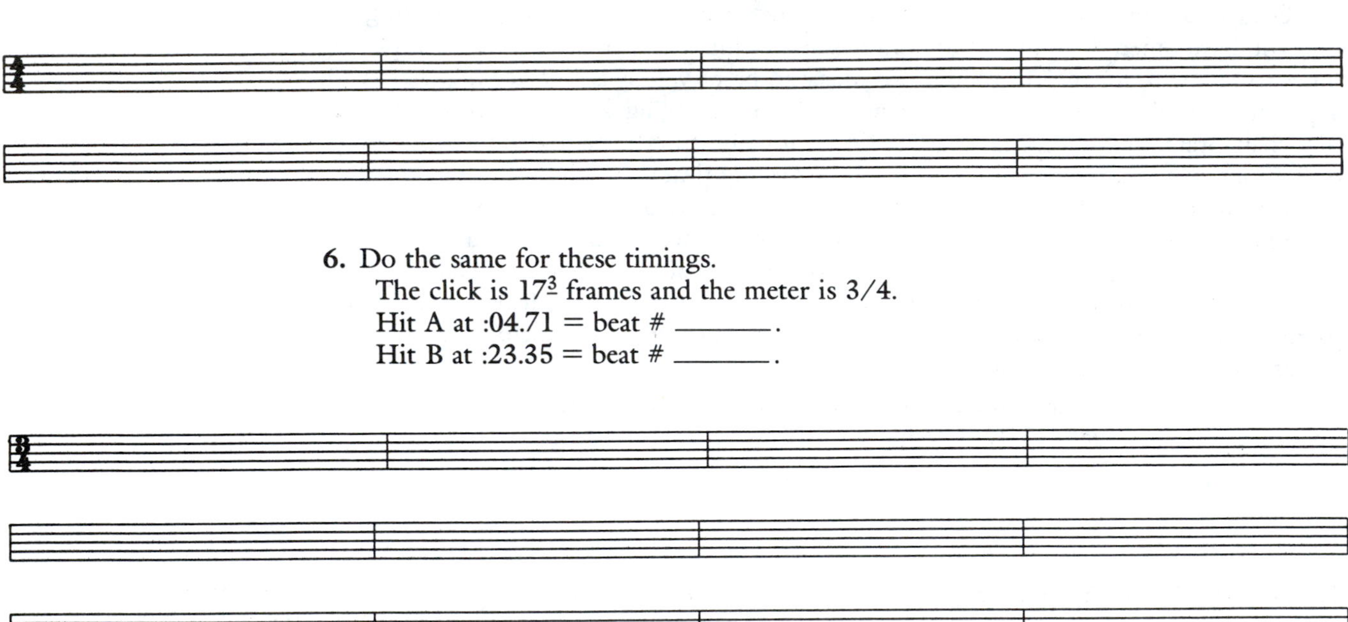

6. Do the same for these timings.
The click is $17^{\underline{3}}$ frames and the meter is 3/4.
Hit A at :04.71 = beat # _______.
Hit B at :23.35 = beat # _______.

7. Do the same for these timings:
The tempo is a 17 frame click and the meter is 4/4.
Hit A at :42.68 = beat # _______.
Hit B at 1:00.45 = beat # _______.

8. Do the same for these timings:
Tempo = $17^{\underline{7}}$ frame click. Meter = 5/4.
Hit A at :30:00 = beat # _______.
Hit B at 1:17.96 = beat # _______.

9. Using the offset method discussed in this chapter and illustrated in Figure 9-8, calculate the offset for these hits and show the amount of the offset (the later start in the cue) and the resulting music notation.
Tempo = 18 frame click. Meter = 4/4.
Hit A at :15.10.
Hit B at :23.34.
Hit C at :33.10.
Amount of offset = _______.
New timings after subtracting offset for later start:
Hit A at _______ = beat # _______.
Hit B at _______ = beat # _______.
Hit C at _______ = beat # _______.

CHAPTER 10. TIMINGS AND CLICKS II

1. Composers agree that recording with click is efficient and helps guarantee syncing dead hits. It is indispensable in recording cues played with a rhythm section. Why then do many composers prefer recording without click whenever possible?

2. How many frames per second are in television?

3. Since the digital metronome (click track) is calibrated in motion picture frames of 24 frames per second and the television frames are different, how can the digital metronome be successfully used when working on television projects?

4. What are "built click tracks" and how are they constructed?

5. Under what circumstances are they needed?

6. What is the SMPTE time code and in what units are its numbers calibrated?

CHAPTER 11. PLAYING THE DRAMA

1. In what way can the music play a scene from the character's point of view or the audience's point of view?

2. In cases where a film plays on more than one level of drama, style, or emotion, how does the composer decide what music to play over the main title?

3. Give five examples of moments of shifting emphasis when music might effectively start.

4. How do you decide whether to start a cue with an aggressive or a soft lead-in?

5. Under what circumstances would a "hard out" music ending be appropriate?

6. Why is underscoring dialogue a continuing challenge?

7. Give six classic guidelines for underscoring dialogue.

8. How does "playing the overview" differ from "playing the scene"?

9. Define "playing against the scene."

10. In what way can music actually de-emphasize a scene?

11. What are the values of silence in a music score?

12. What are musical "red herrings" and how do they contribute to a film?

13. What is "scoring a film like a ballet"?

14. See two of the films listed for suggested viewing under specific categories of playing the drama and discuss how those films handled those dramatic situations.

15. In the above films, what did the Main-Title music say about the pictures? Identify scenes played from the character's or the audience's point of view. Pick five music cues and describe the specific music starts relative to the dramatic situation. Were there any "hard outs" and if so what was the dramatic reason? Was any dialogue underscored? If so how was it handled (starting spot, orchestration, register of instruments, effectiveness)? Pick if you can a sequence in which the music played against the scene. Was there a dramatic use of music silence? Where?

16. Did you find moments when you disagreed with the way the music was spotted or used? Where? What would your choice have been?

CHAPTER 12. COMPOSING

1. What are some approaches to curing writer's block?

2. How can one preplan the score and create a master plan?

3. What is the value of the associative power of music in a film score?

4. Explain the role of musical repetition in a film score?

5. What is the role of research and role models in preparing for composing a film score?

6. How can you define the correct pulse or tempo for a film or for an individual cue?

7. How can one know how much to catch or not catch in a film?

8. What is a good process to use in beginning the sketch?

9. View a film and analyze the reuse of musical materials. What percentage were obvious thematic restatements? What percentage were subtly developed thematic elements? How much of the music was new material?

CHAPTER 13. USING MELODY

1. Composer Oliver Nelson once commented that when the music was turned down under sound effects and dialogue, details of harmony and orchestration were no longer heard and only melody could dependably survive, so you had better have cohesive melodic content. In what other ways does melody function as a vitally important element in most film scores?

2. View a film or television episode and make a list of cues, characterizing each one as having predominantly melody, harmony, or rhythm as the communicative element of the music.

3. Write 6-to-12-bar melodies that communicate an emotion about the following characters or themes. Use no harmony or predominantly rhythmic elements.

a. Fresh young love in a French eighteenth century provincial setting
b. A quiet, positive young contemporary American woman who will ultimately triumph
c. A restless, dynamic, contemporary man with ill-concealed hostility
d. The childish innocence of a mute Indonesian child at play in a dangerous place

4. Imagine two other filmic situations and compose melodic treatments using two linear voices.

CHAPTER 14. USING HARMONY

1. Use your melody from question 3a in Chapter 13 and add a harmonic accompaniment that preserves the dramatic intent of the original.

2. Reharmonize the same melody to support an increasing stress and sadness because of unresolvable conflicts between the romantic characters.

3. Support harmonically the melody you developed in 3b to preserve the stated dramatic situation.

4. Reharmonize the same melody to support a dramatic evolution in which the young women's ambition has changed her from a person with integrity into a person who is ruthless and cold.

5. Harmonize 3c to support a harmless comic set of actions by the character who has previously been seen as vengeful.

6. Harmonize 3d to support the stated dramatic intent.

7. Reharmonize 3d to support the child's nightmarish dream.

8. Take one of your dramatic situations from Chapter 13, question 4 (or one of the setups of question 3) and use only harmonic, nonmelodic elements in composing a musical segment.

9. Add a melodic line to fit the harmonic materials, while still supporting the dramatic situation.

CHAPTER 15. USING RHYTHM

1. View videos of several of the examples given in this chapter. What is the dramatic impact of each one? What about the music is effective?

2. View a theatrical or television action film and analyze the rhythmic development. Are the rhythmic passages repetitious and hypnotic, are they changing and developmental? Is harmony a critical component? Is melody?

3. Set up an extended rhythmic passage for a threatening chase in a primitive jungle. Use no pitches or harmony, only note stems and beams, without heads, but indicate relative registers. Indicate meter, tempo, dynamics, accents. Indicate several subclimaxes (or red herrings) and a real target climax, then one super climax.

4. Add harmonies and pitches to the above sketch.

CHAPTER 16. USING ORCHESTRATION

1. Study each score and sketch in detail, with specific attention to mentally hearing the score. Then listen to the videos and soundtracks of the segments and restudy the scores, taking notes of the orchestrational and textural details of effective passages. Note what dramatic message each passage communicates. Add these observations to your notebook of research results.

2. Reduce each of the full scores to condensed sketch score and analyze the orchestrational details.

3. Set up a plan for keeping a notebook of especially effective film and concert scores, keeping notes about the communicated drama and the orchestral means of achieving those effects. Acquire copies of any of these scores that are available and continue reducing these scores to sketches. Assemble for your use a library of audiocassettes or records of the musical excerpts.

4. Attend orchestra rehearsals and concerts (with scores in hand if possible) to absorb the sounds of the instruments and different orchestrational combinations. When listening to the music, try to visualize how the score looks before studying it. Consider how you would orchestrate it to get that sound.

5. Pick three of the solutions to the following questions and orchestrate them for full orchestra: Chapter 14, questions 1, 2, 3, 4, 5, 6, 7, 8, and 9; Chapter 15, question 4.

6. Pick four of the solutions for the above questions or those of Chapter 13, questions 3a, 3b, 3c, 3d, or 4, and orchestrate them for the smallest group of instruments that can effectively project the drama (under 20 players).

CHAPTER 17. TECHNICAL AND PRACTICAL CONSIDERATIONS

1. Set a steady tempo with a metronome or digital metronome (without looking at its tempo calibration) and practice taking the tempo from a stopwatch from the method on page 332. Check your results directly with the digital-metronome calibration. For the Maelzel's metronome, divide the click tempo into 1,440 to convert it to beats per minute. Compare this with the original MM reading.

2. To get the metronome tempo directly from the stopwatch, start counting the beats as you start the watch. Stop counting as the watch passes 15 seconds. Subtract 1 from this number and multiply the remainder by 4 to get the MM number. Compare results from both systems.

3. View videos of any of the film examples on page 334 and study and note the interrelationship of the sound effects and the music.

4. Study other films and television episodes, similarly noting the interrelationship of the music and the sound effects.

CHAPTER 18. RECORDING—THE SCORING STAGE

1. Define prerecording.

2. Define set recording.

3. Define postscoring.

4. Practice conducting by setting a metronome to about MM 96 and conducting (in front of a mirror) meters of 2/4, 3/4, 4/4, 5/4, 6/4, 7/4, 8/4, and 9/4. After conducting each meter for extended lengths, then conduct one bar of each from 2/4 to 9/4 and continue in reverse order from 9/4 to 2/4. The 5/4 pattern should be practiced as both 2 + 3 and 3 + 2; the 6/4 as both 2 + 2 + 2 and 3 + 3; the 7/4 as 4 + 3 and 3 + 4; the 8/4 as 2 + 2 + 2 + 2; and the 9/4 as both 3 + 3 + 3 and 2 + 2 + 2 + 3. On subsequent practice sessions try faster and slower metronome tempos. (See the Bibliography for texts on conducting.)

5. Attend as many scoring sessions or recording sessions as possible. Observe the mixing boards, control-room equipment, roles of the mixer and other people in the control booth. Note the overdubbing procedures, the way the conductor works with the musicians and engineer. Take every chance to record any music, paying attention to the results obtained with specific setups.

6. In recording a cue with many hits, all are hitting correctly but one. The tempo is a $17^{\underline{4}}$ frame click and the meter is 3/4. it is not clear where the mistake is but one hit seems to be hitting :00.33 early. How many beats should it be moved? Should it be moved earlier or later?

7. After recording the first take of a cue with the orchestra in which you know you have stayed with the click, you are told that one of the three dead hits is incorrect while the other two are exactly on. The tempo is a $17^{\underline{3}}$ frame click; the meter is 4/4. Dead hits are at

:06.49	Hit #I
:15.23	Hit #II
:24.26	Hit #III

Your musical solution has placed the hits here:

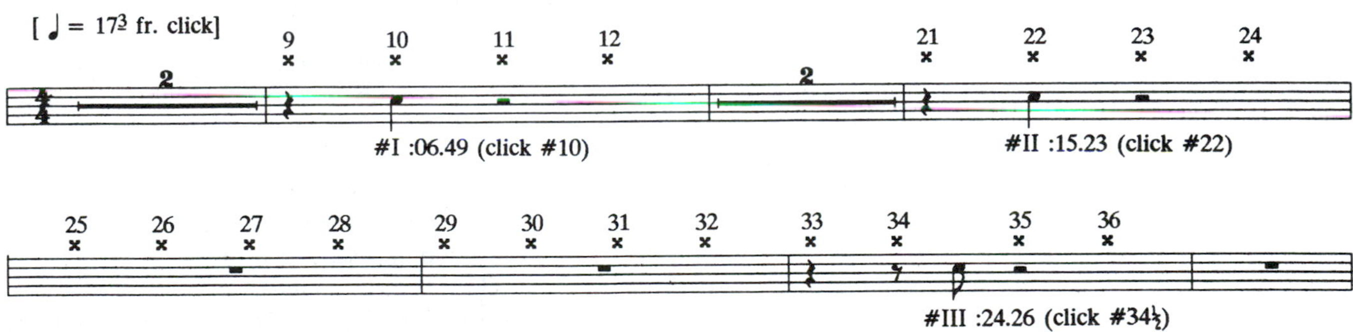

Your music editor tells you that there was a clerical error on Hit #II. It should have been at :14.73 rather than :15.23. To what beat do you tell the orchestra to move the accent?

8. The tempo of a cue seems uncomfortably hurried at the indicated tempo of the $17^{\underline{2}}$ frame click and the only solution seems to be to slow it down to a $17^{\underline{7}}$ frame click. There are no internal hits but the final "accent off" must hit within a quarter-second of 1:04.67. How many beats will you have to cut from the cue to make the timing of the final accent off work out at the slower tempo?

CHAPTER 19. DUBBING—THE FINAL MIX

1. What are the advantages of the composer attending the final mix (the dubbing)?

2. Identify briefly:
   a. dubbing logs
   b. building the music units
   c. predubbing
   d. Academy filter

e. sweetener
f. dubbing-stage protocol
g. dummies
h. machine room
i. interlocked projectors and dummies

3. Why is underscoring dialogue with a song with lyrics ill-advised?

4. Why is it that music which has been enthusiastically approved at the time of the recording sometimes doesn't work at dubbing?

CHAPTER 20. ELECTRONIC MUSIC—THE BASICS

1. Identify briefly:

a. MIDI
b. RAM cartridge
c. ROM memory
d. synthesizer patches
e. waveform
f. oscillator
g. sampling
h. envelope generator
i. ADSR
j. VCA
k. LFO
l. low-pass filter
m. portamento
n. pitch bend
o. aftertouch
p. chorusing
q. detuning
r. sequencer
s. quantize
t. step recording
u. MIDI interface
v. digital delay
w. sync box
x. equalizing
y. pan pot
z. VU meter
aa. LED meter
bb. VCR
cc. FSK
dd. a fader

2. Film composers must learn and experience the operation of synthesizers, sequencers, drum machines, MIDI interfaces, multitrack recording. Analyze where you are in this learning sequence and work on developing experience from there. The normal sequence of learning is:

a. Thoroughly learn to operate one synthesizer at a time until you can produce and modify the sounds and variations of sounds that you hear others using on records and films.
b. Do the same for a drum machine.
c. Learn to operate a sequencer (either a specific dedicated device or a software sequencer program for a general purpose microcomputer) and interconnect it with your synthesizers. Practice until you can sequence musical passages for several synthesizers and a drum machine with assurance.
d. Learn to use signal processing devices such as digital delays, choruses, flangers, digital reverb.
e. Learn to tape-record your synthesizers and live sounds using overdubbing techniques as described in the text.

CHAPTER 21. ELECTRONIC SCORING

1. Study the video of *Witness* and compare with the score excerpts printed in the text (Figures 21-4, 5, 6). Or study the recorded examples of the other excerpts printed in the text. How would you go about composing that kind of music and programming and recording it? What are its distinctive elements?

2. What are five basic options a composer can use in recording a film score that contains electronic sounds?

3. What is the difference between the processes of *prerecording* electronic tracks or *preprogramming* electronic tracks?

4. What are the basic steps to follow in prerecording electronic sounds on a multitrack tape recorder?

5. How can you best prepare for recording electronic music live on a session?

6. What are some advantages and disadvantages to recording electronic music live on a session?

7. What are the advantages and disadvantages to the composer in recording electronic music in a home studio?

8. Identify briefly:
  a. modem
  b. effects rack

9. In what way have composing methods changed because of the availability of electronic-music devices, particularly in the home studio?

10. In what ways have traditional concepts of composing and orchestration been very useful in electronic scoring?

11. Pick two dramatic situations from the following list (or similar ideas) and compose and record 1½-minute cues for them:
  a. Rising tension as police stalk a dangerous suspect
  b. Emerging feelings of young love
  c. Comic, blundering big-game hunters on a safari
  d. Ritual dance of witchcraft
  e. Child lost in scary woods
  f. Supernatural visions
  g. Sci-fi space exploration, at first adventurous fun, which turns threatening

CHAPTER 22. CONTEMPORARY SCORING

1. What is the suggested method for writing for (and in particular, notating) contemporary rhythm sections to get the best results?

2. What is the advantage in recording a special solo artist last after laying down the rhythm tracks and orchestral tracks?

3. View the films listed at the end of the chapter and other films and television episodes that use electronic music. Make notes about the dramatic function of their songs. Does the music play through the scene or underscore the drama? Is the music all produced electronically or are there live elements? If the latter, what instruments and what do they add to the effectiveness of the score? Are there repeated rhythmic patterns that suggest that it was sequenced by cloning bar sequences? Is it "clickless" in feel? Is it effective? If you don't like it, what about it would you avoid in such a cue?

4. Compose and record a one-minute theme for a contemporary television sitcom about inner-city teenagers. Use available resources, with live rhythm section if possible, or all electronic if not.

5. Compose and record a one-minute theme for a television hospital show; the light and caring moments of the program should be reflected in the theme, rather than the dramatic events that occur in the story lines.

6. Invent a hypothetical television story line for a kind of contemporary theme you would like to write. Compose and record it.

CHAPTER 23. STYLES AND GENRES

1. What are several different ways that music plays comedy effectively?

2. What have been some effective approaches to scoring horror films?

3. Westerns?

4. War films?

5. Study and make notes of videos of films and television shows from each category.

6. What differences can be noted in the way feature films and television films are handled musically?

7. Compose cues for selected comedy situations, horror-film excerpts, Western incidents, war films, television police stories, and prime-time soaps. In each case, work from a real work print of a film if available. If not, rent a video and view it with the sound turned off. Invent a story line to fit the action; take timings with a stopwatch. If these materials aren't available, invent an imaginary situation, give it timings, and write a cue to that script and those timings. Record your cues and note the reaction of yourself and others. What does each cue communicate?

CHAPTER 24. ETHNIC, PERIOD, AND SOURCE MUSIC; DOCUMENTARIES AND ADAPTATIONS

1. How can the composer resolve the question of whether a period or ethnic film score should be completely authentic, just be given a flavor of the ethnic/period style, or should be free of those colorations?

2. When emotionally wrenching situations occur in historical films, composers who have been using a period-music flavor often utilize more contemporary harmonic tensions to support the drama. How can those be justified and unified with the rest of the score?

3. How does scoring documentaries differ from scoring similar scenes in films with story lines?

4. How does source music differ from underscore?

5. How can source music believably become underscore under certain circumstances?

6. View several of the films referred to in this chapter. Do you find evidence supporting the points raised in the above questions? How would you have scored scenes differently? Try playing existing records of authentic historical and ethnic music against the film scenes. Do they work? Why? Why not?

CHAPTER 25. MUSICALS AND PRERECORDING

1. When on-screen singing, instrument playing, or dancing occurs, why is the option of choice usually to prerecord and film to playback? Why not simply record the sound as the picture is shot?

2. How does the "cue click" described by John Green deal with the problem of lip-synching out-of-tempo musical passages, ritards, and fermatas?

3. In what ways does contemporary practice in prescoring differ from the traditional methods used in *An American in Paris* and *West Side Story?*

4. View one of the films discussed and try to determine which music was prescored, recorded on set, or postscored.

CHAPTER 26. SONGS

1. What are the functions of songs in films?

2. What are the basic approaches to lyrical content?

3. Why might it be a mistake to repeat the screen images in a song lyric?

4. Write several songs using different approaches:
   a. Write a song based on a role model of a specific song sung by a specific artist.
   b. Write lyrics for the above song and give it a title.
   c. Take existing lyrics (printed in this chapter or from elsewhere) and write new music to accompany them; make the resulting song different in type from the original.

CHAPTER 27. THE BUSINESS

1. What are the guidelines for a first-class demo tape?
2. How may a director or producer know about a composer's talents and availability?
3. What are the responsibilities of a composer's agent?
4. What are typical agent's commissions and what items of the composer's income is typically subject to these commissions?
5. when you get an offer to score a project, what are the negotiable points to consider?
6. Identify briefly:
   a. mechanical royalties
   b. a split publishing deal
   c. back-end deals
   d. ASCAP and BMI royalties
   e. licensing songs
7. What is the range of costs in putting out a soundtrack album that contains songs?
8. Assemble or update your demo tape and test market it with your teachers, fellow composers, industry contacts.

CHAPTER 28. GETTING STARTED

1. Make a list of getting-started options for yourself based on the specific stories related in this chapter. Add to this other options that you can see. Check those that have the best chance for effectiveness for you and outline the steps to follow to exploit them.

CHAPTER 29. TELEVISION COMMERCIALS, SPORTS, NEWS, AND SPECIALIZED TELEVISION THEMES

1. Identify briefly:
   a. the agency's creative director
   b. the agency producer
   c. the account executive
   d. music-production house
   e. storyboard
   f. production studio
   g. film-mix facility
   h. indemnification against plagiarism
   i. talent-payment offices
   j. reps
2. Underscore several different commercials. If film or video copies are not otherwise available from local ad agencies, videotape commercials off the air (that do not contain lip-synched singing or talking), take timing notes by stopwatch, and score and record them.
3. Compose a jingle tune to the storyboard lyrics in this chapter or to lyrics from broadcasted commercials or from a local ad agency.

SELECTED SOLUTIONS

Most answers are found in text. Answers involving computations are given here.

CHAPTER 6. BUDGETS AND SCHEDULES

6. Approximately $33,500. The 55-piece orchestra plays a 5-hour session, the scale of which is $166.52 plus 8 segments of 15 min. @ $13.88 = $111.04 for a total of $277.56. 9% pension payments bring the total to $302.54. The number of musician units is 55 players + 4.1 doubling units, 2 units for a nonplaying contractor = 61.1 units. Total: 61.1 × $302.54 = $18,485.19. Plus 2.5 units of premium pay @$277.56 adds $693.90. Health and Welfare: 56 musicians × 5 hours × $.991 = $277.48. Total for this session: $19,456.

The 19-piece orchestra plays three 3-hour sessions with a total of 25.2 orchestra units. 3 sessions × $166.52 + 9% pension, all times 25.2 musician units = $13,721. Add H & W of $178 for a total of $13,899, the subtotal for the 19-piece sessions. Overall total: $33,355.

CHAPTER 9. TIMINGS AND CLICKS I

4. 24 frames per second.
5. Hit "A" comes on beat #21, Hit "B" falls on beat #29. In music notation:

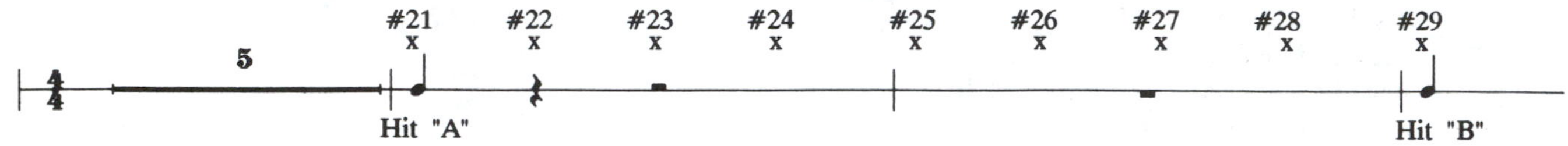

6. Hit "A" = beat #7 ½. Hit "B" = beat #33 ¼.

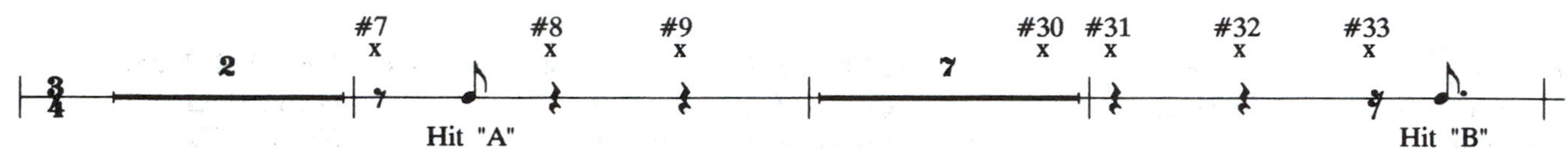

7. Hit "A" = beat #61 ¼. Hit "B" = beat #86 ⅓.

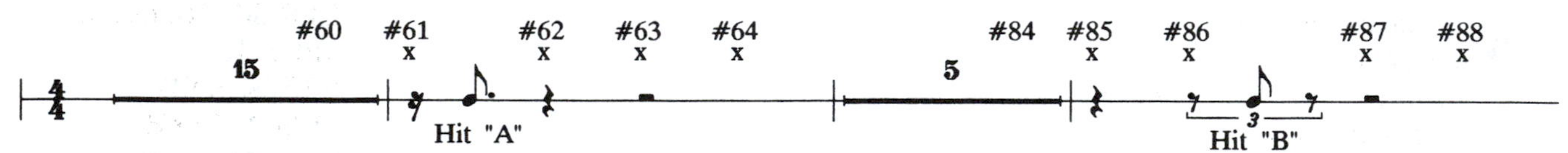

8. Hit "A" = beat #41 ¼. Hit "B" = beat 105 ⅔.

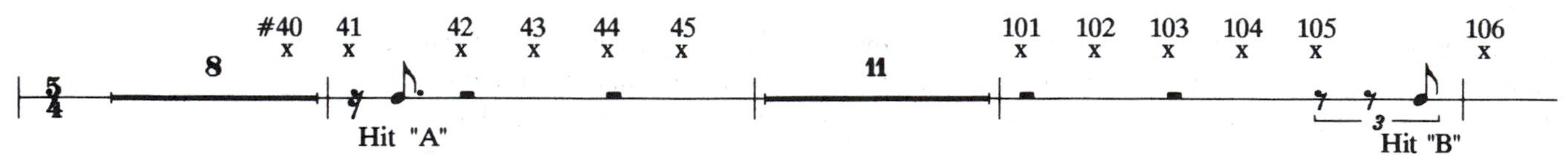

9. Offset = 0.10 sec. Hit "A" at :15.00 = beat #21. Hit "B" at :23.24 = beat #32. Hit "C" at :33.00 = beat #45.

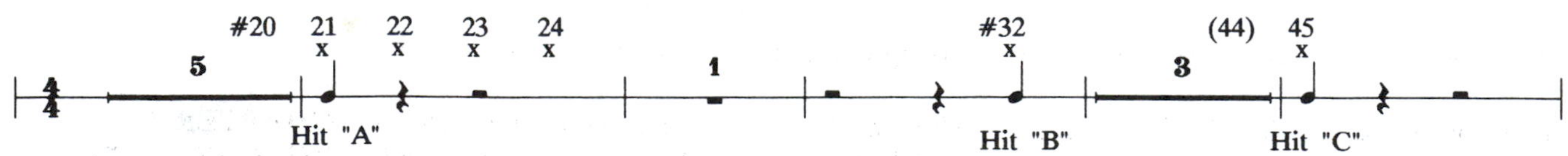

CHAPTER 10. TIMINGS AND CLICKS II

2. 30 frames per second nominally. Actually 29.97 frames per second in color television, although correction allowances are made in the drop-frame mode for this discrepancy. (See appendix F for discussion of drop-frame).

CHAPTER 18. RECORDING

6. The hit should be moved one eighth note later.

7. Hit #II should be moved ⅔ of a beat earlier to the second eighth note triplet of beat one of the same bar.

8. 3 beats. The accent off at 1:04.67 falls on beat #91 at the indicated click of $17\underline{^{2}}$, while the same timing falls on beat #88 at the slower click of $17\underline{^{7}}$.

BUDGET WORK SHEETS

FILM SCORING--BUDGET WORK SHEET

TITLE:________________ RECORDING SESSION #____ DATE & TIME:__________

A.F.of M. agreement: THEATRICAL MOTION PICTURE ( ); TV FILM ( )

DOCUMENTARY/INDUSTRIAL FILMS ( ); TV/RADIO COMMERCIALS ( ).

No. of musicians ____. Session length _______. Premium time? _____

APPLICABLE SCALE PER MUSICIAN/UNIT:

Basic session rate for _____ hrs $_____._____

Overtime: ___ 15 min. units @ $____ $_____._____

Premium overtime: ___15 min units @ $_____ $_____._____

TOTAL SCALE PER MUSICIAN/UNIT $_____._____

Pension: % $_____._____

SUBTOTAL COST PER MUSICIAN/UNIT $_____._____

NUMBER OF UNITS:

Number of players: _____

Doublers: 1.________________ + _________ _____

2.________________ + _________ _____

3.________________ + _________ _____

4.________________ + _________ _____

Conductor _____

Contractor _____

TOTAL NUMBER OF UNITS _______

Total cost per unit x_______._____

SUBTOTAL: MUSICIANS' SCALE + PENSION $__________._____

HEALTH AND WELFARE:

$______per hour per musician: ______x________ $______._____

or $______per original service per musician: ____x_______ $______._____

CARTAGE AND INSTRUMENT RENTAL:_________________________

____total $______._____

PREMIUM PAY FOR PLAYERS?_________units @___________ $______._____

CONTINGENCY____ $______._____

ESTIMATED MUSIC COPYING $________._____

TOTAL THIS SESSION $__________._____

SUMMARY: SESSION #____ $_______._____

SESSION #____ $_______._____

SESSION #____ &_______._____

COMPOSING/ORCHESTRATING FEE $_______._____

TOTAL $_______._____

MUSIC PACKAGE--BUDGET WORK SHEET

PICTURE TITLE______________________

TOTAL CREATIVE AND PERFORMANCE COSTS (from Budget Work Sheets) $__________.______

RECORDING STUDIO:

_____ hrs @ $_______ __________________ $__________.______

_____ hrs @ $_______ __________________ $__________.______

_____ hrs @ $_______ __________________ $__________.______

_____ hrs @ $_______ __________________ $__________.______

_____ rolls 2" tape @ $_________ $__________.______

_____ rolls 1/2" tape @ $_________ $__________.______

_____ rolls 1/4" tape @ $_________ $__________.______

Subtotal $__________.______

TAX $__________.______

SUBTOTAL $__________.______

OTHER (Lyricists, vocalists):__________________ $__________.______

________________________________ $__________.______

SUBTOTAL $__________.______

PAYROLL/ACCOUNTING:

Total musicians' costs (excluding pension, including premium pay): $__________.______

Payroll taxes @ _____% $__________.______

Total singers' costs: ________.____

Payroll taxes @ ____% $__________.______

Handling @ _____% of gross $__________.______ $__________.______

PACKAGE TOTAL $______________

TABLE OF DIGITAL-DELAY TIMINGS

It is very useful to be able to set a digital-delay device so that the repeated notes sound in a prescribed rhythmic relationship to the tempo being played. To use this table, select the desired tempo and set the digital delay to the millesecond delay, which will produce the musical note value of the desired delay. For example: if the tempo is a click of 12 frames and you want the delayed reiteration to sound an eighth note later, set the delay at 250 ms.

TEMPO		**DELAY IN MILLISECONDS FOR**					
FRAMES PER CLICK	MM (BEATS PER MINUTE)	♩	♪	𝅘𝅥𝅯	𝅘𝅥𝅰	3: ♪𝄾𝄾	3: ♩𝄾
8	180	333	167	83	42	111	222
8 1/8	177.23	339	169	85	42	113	226
8 2/8	174.55	344	172	86	43	115	229
8 3/8	171.94	349	174	87	44	116	233
8 4/8	169.41	354	177	89	44	118	236
8 5/8	166.96	359	180	90	45	120	240
8 6/8	162.25	370	185	92	46	123	247
8 7/8	162.25	370	185	92	46	123	247
9	160	375	188	94	47	125	250
9 1/8	157.81	380	190	95	48	127	253
9 2/8	155.68	385	193	96	48	128	257
9 3/8	153.6	391	195	98	49	130	260
9 4/8	151.58	396	198	99	49	132	264
9 5/8	149.61	401	201	100	50	134	267
9 6/8	147.69	406	203	102	51	135	271
9 7/8	145.82	411	206	103	51	137	274

TEMPO		**DELAY IN MILLISECONDS FOR**					
FRAMES PER CLICK	MM (BEATS PER MINUTE)	♩	♪	𝅘𝅥𝅯	𝅘𝅥𝅰	3: ♪𝄾𝄾	3: ♩𝄾
10	144	417	208	104	52	139	278
10 1/8	142.22	422	211	105	53	141	281
10 2/8	140.49	427	214	107	53	142	285
10 3/8	138.8	432	216	108	54	144	288
10 4/8	137.14	438	219	109	55	146	292
10 5/8	135.53	443	221	111	55	148	295
10 6/8	133.95	448	224	112	56	149	299
10 7/8	132.41	453	227	113	57	151	302
11	130.91	458	229	115	57	153	306
11 1/8	129.44	464	232	116	58	155	309
11 2/8	128	469	234	117	59	156	313
11 3/8	126.59	474	237	118	59	158	316
11 4/8	125.22	479	240	120	60	160	319
11 5/8	123.87	484	242	121	61	161	323
11 6/8	122.55	489	245	122	61	163	325
11 7/8	121.26	495	247	124	62	165	330
12	120	500	250	125	63	167	333
12 1/8	118.76	505	253	126	63	168	337
12 2/8	117.55	510	255	128	64	170	340
12 3/8	116.36	516	258	129	64	172	344
12 4/8	115.2	521	260	130	65	174	347
12 5/8	114.06	526	263	132	66	175	351
12 6/8	112.94	531	265	133	66	177	354
12 7/8	111.84	536	268	134	67	179	358
13	110.77	542	271	135	68	181	361
13 1/8	109.71	547	273	137	68	182	365
13 2/8	108.68	552	276	138	69	184	368
13 3/8	107.66	557	279	139	70	186	372
13 4/8	106.67	563	281	141	70	188	375
13 5/8	105.69	568	284	142	71	189	378
13 6/8	104.73	573	286	143	72	191	382
13 7/8	103.78	578	289	145	72	193	385
14	102.86	583	292	146	73	194	389
14 1/8	101.95	589	294	147	74	196	392
14 2/8	101.05	594	297	148	74	198	396
14 3/8	100.17	599	299	150	75	200	399
14 4/8	99.31	604	302	151	76	201	403
14 5/8	98.46	609	305	152	76	203	406
14 6/8	97.63	615	307	154	77	205	410
14 7/8	96.81	620	310	155	77	207	413
15	96	625	313	156	78	208	417
15 1/8	95.21	630	315	158	79	210	420
15 2/8	94.43	635	318	159	79	212	424
15 3/8	93.66	641	320	160	80	214	427
15 4/8	92.9	646	323	161	81	215	431
15 5/8	92.16	651	326	163	81	217	434
15 6/8	91.43	656	328	164	82	219	438
15 7/8	90.71	661	331	165	83	220	441
16	90	667	333	167	83	222	444
16 1/8	89.3	672	336	168	84	224	448
16 2/8	88.62	677	339	169	85	226	451
16 3/8	87.94	682	341	171	85	227	455

TEMPO		DELAY IN MILLISECONDS FOR					
FRAMES PER CLICK	MM (BEATS PER MINUTE)	♩	♪	𝅘𝅥𝅯	𝅘𝅥𝅰	3: ♪ 𝄾 𝄾	3: ♩ 𝄾
16 4/8	87.27	688	344	172	86	229	458
16 5/8	86.62	693	346	173	87	231	462
16 6/8	85.97	698	349	174	87	233	465
16 7/8	85.33	703	352	176	88	234	469
17	84.71	708	354	177	89	236	472
17 1/8	84.09	714	357	178	89	238	476
17 2/8	83.48	719	359	180	90	240	479
17 3/8	82.88	724	362	181	90	241	483
17 4/8	82.29	729	365	182	91	243	486
17 5/8	81.70	734	367	184	92	245	490
17 6/8	81.13	740	370	185	92	247	493
17 7/8	80.56	745	372	186	93	248	497
18	80	750	375	188	94	250	500
18 1/8	79.45	755	378	189	94	252	503
18 2/8	78.90	760	380	190	95	253	507
18 3/8	78.37	766	383	191	96	255	510
18 4/8	77.84	771	385	193	96	257	514
18 5/8	77.32	776	388	194	97	259	517
18 6/8	76.8	781	391	195	98	260	521
18 7/8	76.29	786	393	197	98	262	524
19	75.79	792	396	198	99	264	528
19 1/8	75.29	797	398	199	100	266	531
19 2/8	74.81	802	401	201	100	267	535
19 3/8	74.32	807	404	202	101	269	538
19 4/8	73.85	812	406	203	102	271	542
19 5/8	73.38	818	409	204	102	273	545
19 6/8	72.91	823	411	206	103	274	549
19 7/8	72.45	828	414	207	104	276	552
20	72	833	417	208	104	278	556
20 1/8	71.55	839	419	210	105	280	559
20 2/8	71.11	844	422	211	105	281	563
20 3/8	70.67	849	424	212	106	283	566
20 4/8	70.24	854	427	214	107	285	569
20 5/8	69.82	859	430	215	107	286	573
20 6/8	69.4	865	432	216	108	288	576
20 7/8	68.98	870	435	217	109	290	580
21	68.57	875	438	219	109	292	583
21 1/8	68.17	880	440	220	110	293	587
21 2/8	67.76	885	443	221	111	295	590
21 3/8	67.37	891	445	223	111	297	594
21 4/8	66.98	896	448	224	112	299	597
21 5/8	66.59	901	451	225	113	300	600
21 6/8	66.21	906	453	227	113	302	604
21 7/8	65.83	911	456	228	114	304	608
22	65.45	917	458	229	115	306	611
22 1/8	65.08	922	461	230	115	307	615
22 2/8	64.72	927	464	232	116	309	618
22 3/8	64.36	932	466	233	117	311	622
22 4/8	64	938	469	234	117	313	625
22 5/8	63.65	943	471	236	118	314	628
22 6/8	63.3	948	474	237	118	316	632
22 7/8	62.95	953	477	238	119	318	635

TEMPO		DELAY IN MILLISECONDS FOR					
FRAMES PER CLICK	MM (BEATS PER MINUTE)	♩	♪	𝅘𝅥𝅯	𝅘𝅥𝅰	triplet ♪ 𝄾𝄾	triplet ♩ 𝄾
23	62.61	958	479	240	120	319	639
23 1/8	62.27	964	482	241	120	321	642
23 2/8	61.94	969	484	242	121	323	646
23 3/8	61.6	974	487	243	122	325	649
23 4/8	61.28	979	490	245	122	326	653
23 5/8	60.95	984	492	246	123	328	656
23 6/8	60.63	990	495	247	124	330	660
23 7/8	60.31	995	497	249	124	332	663
24	60	1000	500	250	125	333	667
24 1/8	59.69	1005	503	251	126	335	670
24 2/8	59.38	1010	505	253	126	337	674
24 3/8	59.08	1016	508	254	127	339	677
24 4/8	58.78	1021	510	255	128	340	681
24 5/8	58.48	1026	513	257	128	342	684
24 6/8	58.18	1031	516	258	129	344	688
24 7/8	57.89	1036	518	259	130	345	691
25	57.6	1042	521	260	130	347	694
25 1/8	57.31	1047	523	262	131	349	698
25 2/8	57.03	1052	526	263	132	351	701
25 3/8	56.75	1057	529	264	132	352	705
25 4/8	56.47	1063	531	266	133	354	708
25 5/8	56.20	1068	534	267	133	356	712
25 6/8	55.92	1073	536	268	134	358	715
25 7/8	55.65	1078	539	270	135	359	719
26	55.38	1083	542	271	135	361	722

FOOTAGE/TIMING CONVERSIONS

In dealing with films (as differentiated from videotape), when timings are first expressed as feet and frames, it is necessary to convert these footages to minutes and seconds. Even on Moviolas or flatbed editors that have extra counters calibrated in seconds, music editors often prefer to first take their counts in feet and frames (as this may be the more accurate measurement) before converting them to minutes and seconds. The conversion methods have not been included in the body of the text because the composer is rarely required to convert footages to timings. But there are occasions in smaller productions (including some high-quality art films and experimental projects of the kind beginning composers are likely to encounter) where you will need to be able to do such conversions. Having this ability has other advantages: you are then able to see and correct numerical mistakes by others that could give you false timings and cause costly mistakes at recording sessions.

First of all, here are the relevant mathematical relationships:

FILM FORMAT	PROJECTION SPEED	FRAMES PER FOOT	TIME DURATION PER FOOT	FRAMES PER SECOND
35 mm	90 ft/min	16	2/3 second	24
16 mm	36 ft/min	40	1 2/3 seconds	24
Super 8 mm	20/ft/min	72	3 seconds	24
8 mm	18/ft/min	80	3 1/3 seconds	24

In this array of numbers one important fact is apparent: EACH FILM FORMAT SHOWS THE SAME 24 FRAMES PER SECOND OF PROJECTION SPEED. Stated another way, it shows that each frame in every film format has a time value of 1/24 second. Thus in any film format if we convert all footages to frames and divided by the universal 24 frames per second we will have converted to seconds. With the help of an ordinary pocket calculator with the simplest four mathematical functions and movable decimal point, we can do this very easily. The crucial numbers in each film format then are those that tell you the number of frames per foot.

A 35MM EXAMPLE. Convert a 35mm footage of 9 feet, 12 frames into timings. From the above table, we use 16 frames per foot as the multiplier. $16 \times 9 = 144$ frames. Adding the extra 12 frames gives 156 frames total. Dividing by 24 gives :06.5 seconds.

A 16MM EXAMPLE. Convert a 16mm footage of 28 ft. 22 fr. into timings. The table shows there to be 40 fr. per foot in 16mm format. Hence:

28 ft. × 40 = 1,120 fr.
plus odd frs 22
total 1,142 fr.

$$\frac{1142}{24} = :47.58 \text{ sec.}$$

STUDY ASSIGNMENTS IN FOOTAGE CONVERSIONS

IT IS OBVIOUSLY IMPORTANT ALWAYS TO KNOW WHAT UNITS YOU ARE HANDLING. Film editors have traditionally made these conversions by using the ratio of 3:2 for 35mm feet-to-seconds and the ratio of 3:5 for 16mm feet-to-seconds. The above method is simpler (given a pocket calculator) and still accurate.

1. How many frames per foot in 35mm format?
2. How many frames per foot in 16mm film format?
3. In 35mm format, convert 15 ft. 11 fr. into seconds.
4. In 35mm format, convert 27 ft. 15 fr. into seconds.
5. In 16mm format, convert 21 ft. 28 ft into seconds.
6. In 16mm format, convert 79 ft. 38 fr. into minutes and seconds.
7. Add these 35mm footages: 3 ft. 14 fr.
16 ft. 7 fr.
8. Add these 16mm footages: 3 ft. 14 fr.
16 ft. 7 fr.
9. Add as 35mm footages: 4 ft. 7 fr.
12 ft. 15 fr.
7 ft. 11 fr.
10. Convert your answer from question 9 to minutes and seconds.
11. Add as 16mm footages: 4 ft. 7 fr.
12 ft. 15 fr.
7 ft. 11 fr.
12. Convert your answer from question 11 to minutes and seconds.

ANSWERS

3. :10.46. $\frac{251 \text{ ft.}}{24} = 10.458333$
4. :18.63. $\frac{447 \text{ ft.}}{24} = 18.625$
5. :36.17. $\frac{868 \text{ ft.}}{24} = 36.17$
6. 2:13.25.
7. 20 ft 5 fr.
8. 19 ft 21 fr.
9. 25 ft 1 fr.
10. :16.71 (sec).
11. 23 ft 33 fr.
12. :39.71 (sec).

APPENDIX E CALCULATOR METHOD FOR TIMINGS

A click book is a very convenient tabular listing of timings, but all timings can be computed without one if you have a pocket calculator. This frees you from the dependency of having a click book or computer with you.

The procedure for converting timings into music notation with only a calculator is as follows:

1. Choose your tempo and express it in click-track calibration (that is, frames per click). If it is calibrated in metronome beats per minute, convert it to click-track frames by dividing it into 1,440, and round the answer to the decimal equivalent of the nearest eighth of a frame.

For example, a film has two hits:

:08.00 Stella turns to John

:21.79 Door slams violently

You have chosen a tempo of 116 beats per minute on your quartz metronome.

$$\frac{1440}{116} = 12.413793 \text{ (frames per click)}$$

Rounding to the nearest decimal equivalent of eighths of frames we get 12.375 (decimal equivalent of 12 3/8 fr. click).

2. Convert the timing of the hits from seconds to total frames. This keeps the timings and the click intervals in the same frame units.

In this case the first hit is at :08.00 secs:

:08.00 sec × 24 fr./sec = 192 frames

3. Divide the timing (in frames) by the click (in frames):

$$192 \text{ fr.} \div 12.375 = 15.515151 \text{ beat-units}$$

Round this off to 15.5 beat-units. This is a soft hit, and rounding off to the nearest tenth will provide a sufficient degree of precision.

4. To get the total number of beats, add one to the number of beat-units to account for the first click that occurs while the clock is at zero.

This is sometimes a confusing step, which often causes mistakes, yet it is analogous to similar situations in everyday life. For example, if we measure with a ruler we can see that the first mark has no number. If we were to number the left end of the ruler as mark #1 we can see that the mark numbers are always one greater than the number of units (inches):

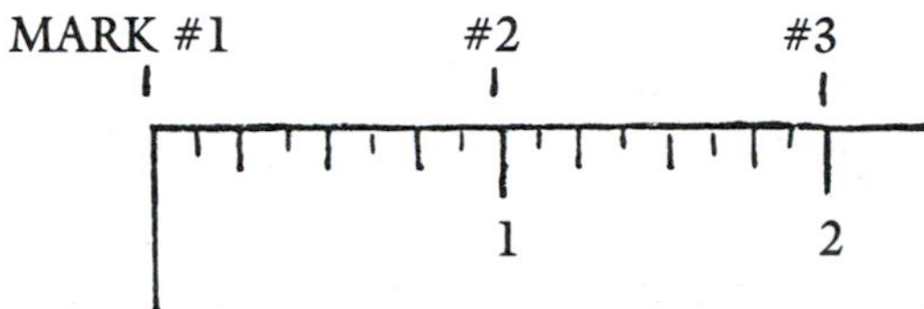

Note that the click book has already taken into account that extra beat number. On every page for every tempo the timing for beat #1 is always :00.00 seconds. And the timing at beat #2 is always the length of one beat-unit.

Continuing with our example: Add 1 to 15.5 beat-units to make 16.5. 16½ is the beat number (or click number) of the hit.

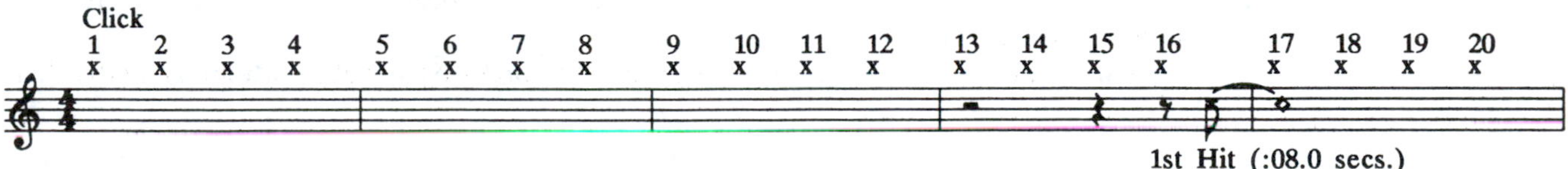

Our second hit must be dead on to match an instantaneous impact in the picture. Following the above procedure of converting timing to total frames and dividing by the click tempo:

$$21.79 \text{ sec} \times 24 = 522.96 \text{ total frames}$$

Round to the nearest frame (523 fr.), since anything smaller than a frame is too small to be observed, and divide by the click tempo:

$$\frac{523 \text{ frs}}{12.375} = 42.262626 \text{ beat-units}$$

Round to 42.25 beat-units and add 1 to make 43.25, the click number where the hit will occur in the music. In music notation, the two hits now show as:

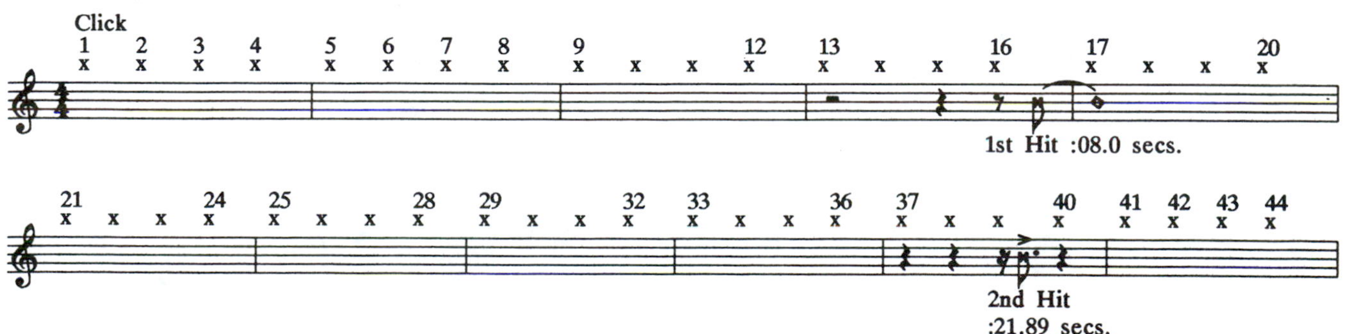

Note: To convert timings to total frames in cases where the timings are expressed as minutes, seconds, and frames, you must remember to add the extra frames after the minutes and seconds are converted to frames. For example: a timing of 1:23 and 9 fr.: 1:23 is first expressed as seconds: 83 sec. 83 × 24 = 1,992 frs. 1992 + the extra 9 frs = 2,001 total frames. From there on the process is identical to the above.

STUDY ASSIGNMENT IN CALCULATOR-DERIVED TIMINGS

Show these hard hits in music notation. Do not use the click book. The click tempo is 13 fr. click. The meter is 4/4.

Hit A at :10.83 sec is click # ____________.

Hit B at :18.69 sec is click # ____________.

In music notation:

ANSWER

Hit A is beat 21, the first beat of bar 6. Hit B is beat 35½, after an eighth rest on the third beat of bar 9.

For further practice, solve problems 5, 6, 7, 8, and 9 on page 608 without using the click book.

APPENDIX F

DROP-FRAME

To understand drop-frame, it is necessary to understand something about the way television signals are controlled and synchronized so that all VCRs are using the same electronic language. Without such agreement, the pictures would be scrambled and unintelligible.

As discussed in Chapter 10, the Society of Motion Picture and Television Engineers (SMPTE) coordinates these standards. The standardization of the SMPTE time code (in 1969) produced a workable system for videotape editing and produced a way to reliably time videotape to the individual frame, as motion-picture film can be timed to the frame. In this system, each individual video frame is encoded with a number representing its hour, minute, second, and frame. In the American NTSC protocol, the time code is normally produced by a generator that counts at 30 frames per second (or in the European PAL/SECAM protocol, at 25 frames per second).

This works for black-and-white television. However, for color television the number of frames per second is actually close to 29.97, an unlikely number that results from other technical requirements.

Because of this, a SMPTE time-code generator that counts video frames at 30 frames per second, when used in color television, produces an error of 3.6 seconds every hour (or 18 frames per ten minutes, almost 2 frames per minute). To compensate for this error build-up, a drop-frame mode has been developed in which 2 frames are dropped each minute, except for every 10th minute (a correction needed, like leap year's February 29, to correct for the fact that the error is slightly less than 2 frames per minute). Each time a new minute number appears, the frame count goes directly from 29 frames to 2 frames of the new minute.

Conventional wisdom says that if you always use SMPTE drop-frame, you will never be more than 2 frames (actually 1.8 frames) off, that being the maximum error. (This is .06 second).

The timing errors that result from using non-drop-frame do not become troublesome until music cues are longer than 3 or 4 minutes and then only when the hits are sharp and obvious.

A complicating situation exists because the SMPTE time code has turned out to be very useful for other purposes than videotape syncing. It is used extensively as a locating device for multitrack recording and for slaving several tape recorders to a master recorder. Digital audiotape editing uses it extensively. It is also being used to drive (time-lock) electronic sequencers. Under these circumstances (that is, when video is not involved) drop-frame is not needed and rarely used (and its maximum recurring error of 2 frames would be intolerable in digital audio editing).

Some SMPTE time-code generators offer the option of producing either drop-frame or non-drop-frame calibration, but many do not offer drop-frame. This is of no consequence in applications other than syncing to videotape, because in either mode the generator is keeping accurate time and will give accurate results if the code-reading device matches the code-generating device. This is a point that remains confusing. In either mode the seconds generated are true seconds and the inaccuracies cited above only occur when a non-drop-frame reader or generator is synced to a VCR or to a drop-frame generator or other device following the drop-frame protocol.

GLOSSARY

The glossary of descriptive terms used in timing sheets can be found on pages 54–56. For definitions of the most-often-used electronic terms, see Chapter 20.

A & R [Artists & Repertoire] person. Someone who works with record-label artists and advises them with regard to the material they record.

Academy filter. An audio-equalization curve, standardized by the Academy of Motion Picture Arts and Sciences, which in the past limited both high- and low-frequency content to prevent distortion resulting from oversaturation of the optical soundtracks used in film release prints. New standards are evolving without these limitations, but existing release prints will still have the Academy curve.

academy leader. The standardized head leader of a film reel, in which numbers from 10 to 2 appear every foot in descending order.

accent off. An accented cut-off to end a music cue.

ADR looping. Automatic dialogue replacement. Recording a new performance of dialogue to replace the original production dialogue track.

AFTRA. The American Federation of Television and Radio Artists.

A. F. of M. The American Federation of Musicians.

aleatoric music. Music that contains chance performance elements within given parameters, usually with the pitch and timing of notes to be decided by the performers.

analog synthesizer. An electronic synthesizer that produces sounds by generating and manipulating electrical voltages whose wave shapes are analogous to their acoustic counterparts. The first generation of synthesizers (Moogs and before) were analog.

answer print. A final version of the film with all sound and visual effects combined on one film base. The answer print is screened for approval and flaws are noted for correction on subsequent answer prints until approved for production of release prints.

ASCAP. The American Society of Composers, Authors, and Publishers. A performing rights society that licenses small rights for performance.

assembly. First version of the film, in which the scenes are assembled in sequence.

audio producer. The person in the recording booth who is responsible for monitoring, producing, and approving the quality of the music recording.

baffle. To isolate instruments in a recording session with sound barriers (called **screens, baffles, flats,** or **gobos**).

bank. Group of stored sounds for a synthesizer or other electronic device.

bed. The music recorded first, prior to overdubbing.

Betamax. The original half-inch videocassette format produced by Sony Corporation.

billboard. A short display announcement of one of a television show's advertisers, or of the title of the sports event being televised on a sports show.

BMI. Broadcast Music Incorporated. A performance rights society that licenses small rights for music performance.

board. Mixing board or console.

booth. Recording booth where the recording engineer works at the mixing console.

booth person. The person in the recording booth who monitors the music quality. (See **audio producer.**)

bridge. A short cue that connects two scenes or sections of a film sequence.

building a click track. Creating a click track (often variable), to follow changing music meters or changing tempos. This can be done on film or on tape, mechanically or electronically.

building music units. To assemble music units (reels of music recorded on film) into synced sequences in which the music cues alternate in placement from one reel to the other for ultimately continuous playback on synchronized dummies.

bumper. A short (:05–:07 sec.) music cue accompanying a visual program logo that is inserted before or after commercials or station breaks to identify the program.

burned in. A time code recorded permanently in the picture of a videocassette.

button. An ending music accent.

cans. Headphones.

cell. A short melodic theme. (Also **motif.**)

chorus. In electronic music, an electronically created unison or doubling effect.

click. A digital metronome tempo calibrated in the number of frames and eighths of frames between beats. Also the sound of an individual beat of the digital metronome.

click book. A collection of tables of timings with one page allotted to each setting of the digital metronome (the click generator).

click track. Any sequence of metronomic clicks for use in synchronizing music to film.

col. Italian for "with"—used as an orchestrational shortcut to tell the orchestrator or copyist to copy a line from another instrument's score line.

come sopra. Italian for "like above"—a term used to describe instructions to copyist or orchestrator written in the score or sketch to copy specific bars.

contractor. The person who engages the musicians or singers for recording sessions, coordinates many of the details (such as instrument rentals), functions as orchestra manager during the sessions, and deposits the contracts with the applicable union. In England, known as the **fixer.**

controller. MIDI-compatible device that can send performance information electronically to another MIDI-compatible device. (Often a keyboard, but can be a guitar, electronic wind controller or other instrument.)

cue. Each individual piece of film music (as in, Cue 21). The term is also used in film scoring to mean an event within a film (as in, hitting the cue precisely).

cue click. A specific series of clicks built to facilitate playback film shooting. These clicks are played back with the prerecorded music and include warning clicks to assist the miming musicians to re-enter properly after a fermata or ritard.

cut-back cue. A cue in which the music changes as the action cuts back and forth between two scenes. (Also **split chase.**)

dead hit. A precisely synced music accent. (Also **hard hit.**)

desk. Mixing console (or board.)

digital delay. A signal processor that delays a signal by a variable amount and may be set to repeat that delayed signal for a variable duration, allowing the user to mix the delayed signal with the original signal as desired.

digital metronome. A click generating device.

digital synthesizer. A synthesizer that generates sound through numerical representation of the sounds.

director. In addition to dramatic and camera directions, the person responsible for making (or approving) all creative decisions and overseeing all creative activities associated with a film project. While shooting the film each day, all personnel are under his direction.

double session. An A. F. of M. stipulated grouping of two three-hour sessions within an eight-hour time period, which allows flexibility in the division of time between the two periods.

double-system projection. Film projection on separate but interlocked projectors and playback dummies when picture and sound are still on separate reels.

doubling. The practice of one musician playing more than one instrument within an engagement. Such a musician is called a doubler.

drop-frame. SMPTE time code with two frames dropped each minute to compensate for the difference between the calibrated 30 frames per second and the actual color video rate of 29.97 frames per second. (See also page 631, Appendix F.)

dub. A duplicate copy of an audio recording. To dub is to record in duplicate. (See also **dubbing.**)

dub down. To mix-down from a multitrack audio recording to a smaller number of tracks, such as a mono version or 2-track or 3-track stereo version.

dubber. An alternate term for "dummy."

dubbing. (1) In film, the rerecording of all sound elements into one composite version (mono or stereo). This is the version that is transferred to the final soundtrack of the release print. (2) In audio recording, any copying of sound from one source to another—tape to tape, film to tape, disk to tape, and so on.

dubbing stage. The rerecording theater where, as the film is projected, the music, dialogue, and sound-effects tracks are mixed down to a final composite audio track.

dummy. A machine that plays back sound recorded on mag film.

dupe. A copy (of film or audiotape).

editor. Film editor, who cuts the picture and dialogue into a homogenous whole.

effects. Sound effects. (Used to denote optical or special effects in another context.)

effects rack. A rack-mounted group of electronic signal processing devices.

effects editor. Sound effects editor, who creates and/or assembles the sound effects and cuts them into the film in sync with the picture.

fader. A volume control, usually seen as a slider on mixing boards.

film noir. A genre of dark mystery films.

fine cut. Final edited version of the film, ready for music and sound effects.

fixer. British term for orchestra contractor.

flats. Theatrical term for vertical stage panels, used in this connection as sound barriers or screens on the scoring stage.

Fletcher-Munson curve. The audio frequency curve developed by Fletcher and Munson that shows how much greater intensity of sound is required on low-frequency and high-frequency pitches when the overall intensity level is low, in order for the average listener to perceive the various frequencies as being of equal volume. This is an important principle to apply in dubbing to prevent music from sounding "thin" when heard at low volume levels, as background music in a film often sounds under dialogue.

FM synthesis. The particular method of synthesizing different tone timbres in digital synthesis, developed by a team of computer scientists headed by Dr. John Chowning at Stanford University in the mid-seventies.

free timing. Composing and/or conducting without the tempo guide provided by a click.

FSK. Frequency shift key. A method of converting electronic signals into audio-frequency signals so they can be recorded or transmitted by audio-frequency devices like tape recorders or telephones. The sounds heard in Touch-Tone telephones are produced by FSK. It is used in audio recording as one of the available synchronizing devices, and an FSK generated by a sequencer will typically be recorded on one track of a multitrack tape recorder to be used as a master sync pulse on subsequent overdubbing passes.

full coat. Synonymous with three-stripe mag, because it is fully coated 35mm mag film that is used to record three tracks of sound.

ghost writing (or **ghosting**). Writing without getting credit (and/or royalties).

gobo. A movable sound barrier used in recording studios.

guide tracks. Music tracks recorded prior to shooting, or prerecorded during rehearsal or camera shoots, to serve as a playback guide for singers, musicians, or dancers. After filming, conductor and musicians postrecord the final version in sync with the people on screen. (Also **scratch tracks.**)

hard hit. A precisely synced music accent. (Also **dead hit.**)

hard out. A sharp or accented cut-off of a music cue.

headset. Earphones, headphones, phones.

hertz. Audio cycles per second.

hitting cues. Syncing specific moments in the music with specific events in the film.

KEM. A brand name of a flatbed film-editing machine.

layer. In recording, to overdub or track (layer by layer). (See also **overdub; stacking.**)

leader. Blank film base used to fill in the silent time between audio segments recorded on mag film. (See also **slug.**)

license music. Obtain the right to use an existing piece of music with a film, video, or stage work.

lock the film. To stop making changes in the fine cut.

log. (1) To list the on-air usage of a music segment. (2) Chart prepared by the various editors for use by the rerecording mixers as a guide to the footage location of the individual sound elements while dubbing.

looping. See ADR looping.

mag. Film coated with magnetic emulsion for audio recording.

mag stripe. Film coated with a single stripe of magnetic emulsion for single-track audio recording. Sometimes used as a generic designation of any film coated with magnetic tape, including three-stripe (full coat).

main title. The music written for the main titles of the picture.

mechanical royalties. Royalties paid by the record manufacturer to the copyright holder (to be shared with the composers and lyricists) for each cut on a sound recording.

MIDI. Musical Instrument Digital Interface; a standard interface allowing electronic instruments and devices to send controlling messages to each other.

MIDI time code (MTC). A SMPTE-like time code in MIDI protocol.

mixer. The mixing engineer in a recording session. Also the electronic mixing board.

mixing console. Mixing board. (Called a **desk** in England.)

mixing engineeer. The engineer who mixes the various musical sounds into the composite recorded version.

modem. A telecommunication device that allows computer information to be transmitted via telephone.

MOS. Filmed without sound.

motif. A short melodic theme. (Also **cell.**)

Moviola. The trade name for the standard vertical movie-editing machine.

MTV. Music TV—a cable television network that presents promotional video presentations of commercial recordings. Also used generically to refer to any music video.

music editor. Person responsible for all physical details regarding the synchronization of the score with the picture.

music supervisor. Representative of the studio, production company, or network, who is responsible for overseeing the business and practical details of the scoring of a film, and often artistic and creative areas as well.

music units. The assembled film reels containing the sequenced and synchronized music cues.

Newman system. A system of film punches devised by Alfred Newman to aid the conductor.

non-drop-frame. SMPTE time code calibrated at 30 frames per second. (See **drop-frame.**)

opticals/optical effects. Special visual effects prepared separately and cut into the film during postproduction, including dissolves, fade ins, fade outs, supers.

ostinato. Repeated musical figure.

overdub. To record additional musical elements on multitrack tape recorders or 35mm mag. (See also **layer; stacking.**)

overview. The overall idea or dramatic tone of the sequence or of the entire film.

package deal. A contract to deliver a master tape of a score for a fixed price that will include all expenses except specified exclusions.

pad. (1) Musically, an accompaniment of sustained harmony. (2) Electronically, a circuit element (usually variable) that attenuates the signal.

patch. A specific setting of synthesizer controls to produce a specific sound color—so-called because the original timbres were obtained by running patch cords between different modular synthesizer elements.

pedal point. A repetition or sustaining of a single pitch, often while the chords change around it.

phantom center channel. The perceived center channel in a 2-track stereo recording when equal levels of the original center sounds are recorded on the right and left tracks, giving the illusion that the sound is coming from the center area between the two speakers.

phones. Headphones, earphones, headsets, "cans."

pilot. Single television episode, produced for possible production as an ongoing series.

playback recording. Music prerecordings prepared to play back on the set for the actors to mime to during camera shooting.

postmix. To mix-down the music from the multitrack tape after the live recording session.

postproduction. All audio processing and manipulation that is done after the recording sessions. Also, all work on the film done after the conclusion of shooting.

postscoring. To score music to a picture after the film is shot and edited.

predub. Premix music, sound effects or dialogue.

prerecord. (1) To record music before the film sequence is shot. To prescore. (2) To record some music elements in advance of the orchestral recording session.

print takes. Master takes from recording sessions or shooting.

producer. Person responsible for developing and obtaining financing for a project, and selecting and overseeing the various people necessary to make the film (often in collaboration with the director).

production dialogue. The dialogue recorded during shooting.

production track. Set recording.

punches. Conducting aids produced by punching holes in the film frames, thus producing short sequences of fluttering light pulses to cue the conductor.

quantize. Adjust the music rhythmically, using a sequencer. Used frequently to correct or perfect rhythmic inaccuracies.

RAM. Random access memory units for computers. Ram cartridges may be used to store and retrieve sound patches.

red herring. A false sense of urgency or terror, often suggested by the music.

release print. The film version that is distributed for public viewing.

role model. A specific piece of music used to exemplify a musical style and/or approach.

ROM. Read-only memory for computers. ROM synthesizer cartridges or internal memories cannot store user-generated patches, but only allow the user to retrieve factory presets.

rough cut. A roughly edited version of the film, sometimes considerably longer than the fine cut will be.

SAG. Screen Actors Guild (union).

sampler. An electronic instrument that records individual sounds digitally, for playback on a keyboard or other electronic controlling device. These sounds can be used as sampled (to approximate acoustic instruments or sound effects, for instance) or can be electronically processed, sometimes radically changing the original sound.

scale. The minimum fees to be paid union members, according to agreements negotiated between business representatives of each field of endeavor (records, films, and so on) and the union.

score. (1) The music for a film. (2) To write the music for a film. (3) To record the music for a film (for instance, "Today I am scoring a television episode from 9 A.M. to 12 noon"). The latter is the most common usage.

scoring stage. A sound stage or recording studio where music is recorded for films. Usually has film projection and/or video monitoring facilities for recording to picture.

scratch tracks. See **guide tracks.**

screens. Sound barriers. (See also **baffles, flats,** or **gobos.**)

seque [seg-way]. Music term meaning to continue directly without pause.

Selsync. A trade name for a system of overdub recording that keeps subsequent passes in sync by using the record head as a playback head during the overdubbing pass, thus aligning that signal with the signal that is recording on the new tracks.

sequencer. Computer programs or computer-based machines capable of digitally "recording" all the basic musical commands (but *not* the *music,* as a tape recorder does), fed them by a synthesizer or other MIDI'd electronic device.

SESAC. A European-based performing rights society.

set recording. (1) Recording sound on the shooting set. (2) Sound recorded on the shooting set.

shooting to playback. Filming a sequence containing music, syncing to a music track.

signal processor. Any piece of equipment specifically designed to manipulate sound (a signal) electronically.

slug. Blank film leader, used as fill in the music units.

small performance royalties. Royalties collected and distributed to writers and publishers by licensing organizations (ASCAP and BMI in the U.S.) for all performances of works in all media except staged versions and versions synced to film and video (also called *petit rights*).

SMPTE. The Society of Motion Picture and Television Engineers—a standards-setting trade association.

SMPTE time code. A standard time code used to sync film and music elements.

sound loop. The 29-frame release print offset of the sound from the picture.

source music. Music from a seen or unseen source in the picture (such as a marching band or jukebox).

split chase. A cue in which the music changes as the action cuts back and forth between two scenes. (Also **cut-back cue.**)

split publishing. Publishing rights shared between two parties according to a negotiated formula.

spotting. Determining where music will be used in a film.

spotting notes. Notes taken by the music editor listing in sequence the beginning and ending points of each music cue in the film.

stacking. In recording, to overdub or track (layer by layer). (See also **layer; overdub.**)

standard recording. Set recording—recording as the picture is shot.

sting. (1) To musically accent or emphasize. (2) A musical accent.

streamer. A scribed vertical line moving across the film frame used as a synchronizing guide for the conductor.

stripes. Striped magnetic coating on films for recording sound.

sweeteners. Added overlays of recorded sound (music usually, but could be sound effects).

syncing. Synchronizing.

tailing out. Fading out the music gradually on a sustained note or chord.

tails out. With the tape having been played but not rewound.

temp tracks. Music tracks temporarily cut into the film's soundtrack prior to the final mix.

three-stripe. One of the conventional formats for 35mm mag sound film—with three audio tracks recorded on it.

Umatic. Three-quarter-inch videotape cassette format, developed by Sony.

underscore. To add music to a film.

Urei. Manufacturer of a much-used digital metronome.

VHS. The predominant half-inch videocassette format.

VSO. Variable speed oscillator, used for correcting off-speed or off-pitch recordings.

wild. Music (or dialogue) that is recorded without timing or syncing it to picture.

work print/work picture. The primary copy of the film assembled by the editor and used during production stages (in color if the film is shot in color). The black-and-white copy used by the music editor is called a dupe. The sound-effects editors also work with a dupe.

FILMOGRAPHY

Year of release is provided for theatrical films and for television miniseries and movies. TV series are indicated by omission of date from year column.

"10" p. 513	1985	Henry Mancini
2001: A SPACE ODYSSEY pp. 44, 263	1968	(various)
48 HOURS pp. 28, 51, 143, 145	1982	James Horner
A-TEAM, THE pp. 65, 328, 344, 486, 492		Mike Post/Pete Carpenter
ADVENTURES OF ROBIN HOOD p. 584	1938	Erich Korngold
AGNES OF GOD pp. 128, 143, 329 Figures 11-2 (p. 131), 11-10 (p. 147)	1983	Georges Delerue
AGONY AND THE ECSTASY, THE pp. 171, 239	1965	Alex North
AIRPLANE! pp. 34, 463	1980	Elmer Bernstein
AIRPORT 1975 pp. 306, 327, 328, 344	1974	John Cacavas
ALIEN pp. 43, 238, 513 Figure 14-17 (p. 238)	1979	Jerry Goldsmith
ALIENS pp. 78, 344	1986	James Horner
ALL THE PRESIDENT'S MEN p. 17	1976	David Shire
ALTERED STATES pp. 104, 269, 300, 369 Figure 16-17 (p. 307)	1980	John Corigliano

AMERICAN GIGOLO pp. 315, 429, 527 Figure 22-5 (p. 429)	1980	Giorgio Moroder (lyric by Deborah Harry)
AMERICAN WEREWOLF IN LONDON, A p. 460	1981	Elmer Bernstein
AN AMERICAN IN PARIS pp. 328, 519, 522	1951	Gershwin; adapted by John Green and Saul Chaplin
AND JUSTICE FOR ALL p. 96	1979	Dave Grusin
ANDROMEDA STRAIN, THE pp. 379, 395	1970	Gil Mellé
ANIMAL HOUSE p. 511	1978	Elmer Bernstein
APOCALYPSE NOW p. 474	1979	Carmine Coppola, Francis Ford Coppola
ARTHUR pp. 209, 528 Figure 13-32 (p. 215)	1982	Burt Bacharach (songs with C. B. Sager, Christopher Cross, Peter Allen)
AUTOBIOGRAPHY OF MISS JANE PITTMAN, THE pp. 65, 505	TV—1974	Fred Karlin
BACK TO THE FUTURE pp. 28, 328, 357, 395, 518	1985	Alan Silvestri
BAD AND THE BEAUTIFUL, THE p. 584	1952	David Raksin
BAD DAY AT BLACK ROCK p. 466	1954	Andre Previn
BATTLE OF BRITAIN p. 470	1969	William Walton, Ron Goodwin
BEING THERE pp. 81, 84 Figure 7-2 (p. 85)	1979	Johnny Mandel
BEVERLY HILLS COP pp. 216, 434, 465, 538 Figure 5-6 (p. 62) 22-11 (p. 441)	1984	Harold Faltermeyer (plus songs)
BEVERLY HILLS COP II pp. 334 Figure 10-3 (p. 123)	1987	Harold Faltermeyer (plus songs)
BIG CHILL, THE p. 539	1983	(anthology)
BIG COUNTRY, THE pp. 470, 584 Figure 23-7 (p. 472)	1958	Jerome Moross
BITTER HARVEST p. 65	TV—1981	Fred Karlin
BLACK STALLION RETURNS, THE pp. 183, 298, 494, 495 Figures 16-13 (p. 301), 16-14 (p. 301)	1983	Georges Delerue
BLACKE'S MAGIC p.374		David Bell
BLAZING SADDLES p. 460	1974	John Morris

BLUE AND THE GRAY, THE pp. 65, 343	TV—1983	Bruce Broughton
BLUE THUNDER pp. 42, 139, 165, 334, 397, 398 Figure 11-5 (p. 139)	1983	Arthur B. Rubinstein
BODY HEAT pp. 49, 130, 143, 209, 344 Figures 11-8a,b,c (p. 144), 13-31a,b (p. 211)	1981	John Barry
BORN FREE p. 42	1965	John Barry
BRAINSTORM pp.52, 143, 150, 179, 190, 241, 271, 329, 334, 396 Figures 11-12 (p. 151), 11-14 (p. 157), 13-5 (p. 181), 14-20 (p. 244), 14-21 (p. 246), 16-2 (p. 272)	1983	James Horner
BREAKFAST AT TIFFANY'S p. 524	1957	Henry Mancini (lyric by Johnny Mercer)
BREAKING AWAY pp. 43, 48, 77, 513	1979	Patrick Williams
BRIDGE ON THE RIVER KWAI p. 474	1957	Malcolm Arnold
BRIDGE TO SILENCE p. 65	TV—1989	Fred Karlin
BUTCH CASSIDY AND THE SUNDANCE KID pp. 18, 206, 248, 524 Figure 13-30 (p. 211)	1969	Burt Bacharach (lyricist: Hal David)
CAGNEY & LACEY p. 478 Figure 23-9 (p. 479)		Bill Conti (theme)
CAMILLE p. 35	TV—1984	Allyn Ferguson
CAPTAIN BLOOD p. 275	1935	Erich Korngold
CASABLANCA p. 504	1942	Max Steiner
CASANOVA p. 78	1986	Georges Delerue
CAT PEOPLE pp. 143, 379, 395	1982	Giorgio Moroder
CHARADE p. 34	1964	Henry Mancini
CHARIOTS OF FIRE pp. 90, 216, 270	1981	Vangelis
CHEERS p. 17		Craig Safan (episodes)
CHEYENNE AUTUMN p. 494	1964	Alex North
CHINATOWN p. 168	1974	Jerry Goldsmith
CLAN OF THE CAVE BEAR p. 398 Figure 21-1 (p. 399)	1986	Alan Silvestri

CLOSE ENCOUNTERS OF THE THIRD KIND pp. 34, 87, 127, 143, 179, 269, 280 Figures 7-4 (p. 88), 13-6 (p. 182), 15-9 (p. 269), 16-7 (p. 287)	1977	John Williams
CLUE pp. 463, 494 Figure 23-3	1985	John Morris
COLBYS, THE p. 475		(various)
COCOON p. 344	1985	James Horner
COLOR PURPLE, THE pp. 100, 518	1985	Quincy Jones
COMMANDO pp. 257, 264, 426 Figures 15-4 (p. 258), 22-4 (p. 428)	1985	James Horner
CONVERSATION, THE pp. 32, 162, 299, 518 Figure 16-16 (p. 304)	1974	David Shire
CROSSROADS pp. 90, 159, 171	1986	Ry Cooder
CUTTER'S WAY (CUTTER AND BONE) p.584	1981	Jack Nitzsche
DADAH IS DEATH p. 65	TV—1988	Fred Karlin
DALLAS pp. 475, 550 Figure 23-8 (p. 476)		(various; Figure by Bruce Broughton)
DAMIEN: OMEN TWO pp. 328, 329	1978	Jerry Goldsmith
DAYS OF WINE AND ROSES p. 524	1962	Henry Mancini (lyricist: Johnny Mercer)
DEAL OF THE CENTURY p. 17	1983	Arthur B. Rubinstein
DEATH OF RICHIE, THE p. 512	TV—1977	Fred Karlin
DEATHTRAP pp. 16, 38, 90, 148, 158	1982	Johnny Mandel
DESPERATELY SEEKING SUSAN pp. 226, 432 Figure 22-8 (p. 435)	1985	Thomas Newman
DIRTY HARRY Figure 14-15 (p. 236)	1971	Lalo Schifrin
DRAGONSLAYER pp. 132, 182, 239, 506 Figures 13-7 (p. 183), 13-8 (p. 184)	1981	Alex North
DREAM WEST pp. 30, 65	TV—1985	Fred Karlin
DYNASTY pp. 475		Bill Conti (theme)
EL NORTE p. 558	1983	(various)

E.T.—THE EXTRA-TERRESTRIAL pp. 225, 280 Figures 14-8 (p. 226), 16-9 (p. 294), 16-10 (p. 298)	1982	John Williams
EARLY FROST, AN pp. 99, 370	TV—1985	John Kander
EAST OF EDEN pp. 584	1944	Leonard Rosenman
ELEPHANT MAN, THE pp. 51, 91, 143, 156, 159, 164, 334, 558 Figures 7-5 (p. 91), 11-9 (p. 147), 11-15 (p. 159)	1980	John Morris
EMERALD FOREST, THE pp. 379, 395, 494	1985	Junior Homrich with Brian Gasciogne
EQUALIZER, THE p. 426		Stewart Copeland
EXECUTIONER'S SONG, THE p. 369	TV—1982	John Cacavas
EXECUTIVE ACTION p. 306	1973	Randy Edelman
EXORCIST, THE p. 43	1973	(anthology)
FALCOLN CREST p. 475		(various)
FAME pp. 6, 90, 344, 520, 531	1980	Michael Gore (lyricist: Dean Pitchford)
FERRIS BUELLER'S DAY OFF pp. 28, 43, 460	1986	Ira Newborn
FIESTA p. 513	1947	John Green
FLASHDANCE p. 90, 523	1983	Giorgio Moroder
FOOTLOOSE pp. 31, 537, 539, 541	1984	Dean Pitchford (various composers)
FOUL PLAY pp. 77, 117, 128, 148, 264, 460, 465, 524, 527 Figures 11-13 (p. 152), 23-5 (p. 467)	1978	Charles Fox (lyric by Norman Gimbel)
FREUD p. 43	1962	Jerry Goldsmith
GANGSTER CHRONICLES, THE p. 503	TV—1980	John Cacavas
GHOSTBUSTERS pp. 49, 143, 158, 460, 465, 536, 537, 538 Figure 23-2 (p. 462)	1984	Elmer Bernstein
GODFATHER, THE pp. 81, 183, 194, 494, 503 Figures 13-13 (p. 187), 13-19a,b (p. 194)	1972	Nino Rota
GONE WITH THE WIND pp. 33, 169, 504, 507, 584	1939	Max Steiner
GOOD, THE BAD, AND THE UGLY, THE p. 81	1966	Ennio Morricone
GRADUATE, THE pp. 44, 513, 583	1967	Simon and Garfunkel

GREASE p. 520	1978	Jacobs and Casey; adapted by Louis St. Louis
GREAT GATSBY, THE p. 494	1974	Nelson Riddle (adaptation)
HAPPY ENDING, THE pp. 532, 533	1969	Michel Legrand (lyricists: A. and M. Bergman)
HARDCASTLE & McCORMICK p. 492		Mike Post/Pete Carpenter
HARRY AND TONTO p. 5	1974	Bill Conti
HEART LIKE A WHEEL pp. 96, 357, 504	1983	Laurence Rosenthal
HEART OF A CHAMPION p. 138	TV—1985	Mike Post
HEART OF THE CITY pp. 398, 415		Patrick Williams
HEAVEN CAN WAIT pp. 47, 194 Figure 13-20 (p. 196)	1978	Dave Grusin
HIGH NOON pp. 33, 466, 583	1952	Dmitri Tiomkin
HILL STREET BLUES pp. 315, 328, 478 Figures 16-21 (p. 319), 16-22 (p. 324)		Mike Post
HINDENBURG, THE p. 217	1975	David Shire
HOOSIERS pp. 87, 392, 395, 434 Figures 22-12 (p. 442), 22-13 (p. 447)	1986	Jerry Goldsmith
HOSTAGE FLIGHT p. 65	TV—1985	Fred Karlin
HOUSE ON GARIBALDI STREET, THE pp. 327, 496	1979	Charles Bernstein
HOW THE WEST WAS WON p. 504	1962	Alfred Newman
HUNTER pp. 328, 344, 486, 492		Mike Post/Pete Carpenter
I WILL FIGHT NO MORE, FOREVER pp. 250, 497 Figure 24-1 (p. 498)	TV—1975	Gerald Fried
IMPULSE p. 334	1984	Paul Chihara
IN COLD BLOOD p. 168	1967	Quincy Jones
INDIANA JONES AND THE TEMPLE OF DOOM p. 460	1984	John Williams
INSIDE THE THIRD REICH p. 217 Figure 14-1 (p. 218)	TV—1982	Fred Karlin
INTO THE NIGHT pp. 443	1985	Ira Newborn

JAWS pp. 169, 176, 465 Figure 13-1 (p. 177)	1975	John Williams
JOHNNY DANGEROUSLY p. 357	1984	John Morris
JUST BETWEEN FRIENDS p. 344	1986	Patrick Williams
KARATE KID, THE p. 90	1984	Bill Conti
KARATE KID II, THE pp. 280, 500 Figures 16-11 (p. 299), 24-4 (p. 504)	1986	Bill Conti
KENT STATE p. 509	TV—1981	Ken Lauber (Songs: Crosby, Stills and Nash)
KILLING FIELDS, THE p. 470	1984	Mike Oldfield
KNACK, THE p. 7	1965	John Barry
KOJAK p. 118, 503		John Cacavas
L.A. LAW pp. 328, 478		Mike Post
LADYBIRD JOHNSON'S VISIT TO WASHINGTON p. 132	TV—1965	Rayburn Wright
LAST STARFIGHTER, THE pp. 38, 78, 328, 344	1984	Craig Safan
LAST VALLEY, THE p. 43	1970	John Barry
LAURA p. 584	1944	David Raksin
LAWRENCE OF ARABIA pp. 34, 275, 502 Figure 16-5 (p. 281)	1962	Maurice Jarre
LEADBELLY pp. 30, 223, 523 Figure 14-7 (p. 223)	1975	Fred Karlin
LEGEND p. 373	1985	Jerry Goldsmith (foreign release); Tangerine Dream (U.S. release)
LES MISERABLES p. 38	TV—1978	Allyn Ferguson
LIBERTY p. 394	TV—1986	William Goldstein
LIONHEART p. 78	1986	Jerry Goldsmith
LITTLE ROMANCE, A pp. 35, 510	1979	Georges Delerue
LOGAN'S RUN p. 190 Figure 13-15	1976	Jerry Goldsmith
LONG RIDERS, THE p. 470	1980	Ry Cooder

Title	Year	Composer
LOVE AT FIRST BITE p. 460	1979	Charles Bernstein
LOVERS AND OTHER STRANGERS p. 524	1969	Fred Karlin (lyricists: Robb Royer and James Griffin)
LUCAS p. 15	1986	Dave Grusin
M*A*S*H pp. 460, 470, 474	1970	Johnny Mandel
MACGYVER pp. 38, 65, 117		(various)
MAD MAX BEYOND THUNDERDOME pp. 280, 334, 447	1985	Maurice Jarre
MAGNIFICENT SEVEN, THE pp. 16, 77, 194, 241, 327, 328, 470, 511 Figures 13-22 (p. 200), 14-22 (p. 247), 23-6 (p. 471)	1960	Elmer Bernstein
MAGNUM, P.I. pp. 65, 328, 344, 486, 492 Figure 23-14 (p. 488)		Mike Post/Pete Carpenter
MAN AND A WOMAN, A p. 583	1966	Francis Lai
MAN FOR ALL SEASONS, A pp. 248, 356, 507	1966	Georges Delerue
MAN FROM UNCLE p. 492		various
MAN IN THE IRON MASK, THE p. 506	TV—1977	Allyn Ferguson
MAN WHO LOVED WOMEN, THE pp. 206, 225 Figures 13-28 (p. 208), 14-9 (p. 227)	TV—1983	Henry Mancini
MAN WITH THE GOLDEN ARM, THE p. 86, 584	1956	Elmer Bernstein
MANHATTAN p. 86, 584	1979	Tom Pierson (music director)
MANNIX p. 492		(various)
MAX DUGAN RETURNS p. 52	1983	David Shire
MIAMI VICE pp. 386, 452, 492 Figure 22-14 (p. 453)		Jan Hammer
MIDNIGHT EXPRESS p. 29	1978	Giorgio Moroder
MINSTREL MAN p. 194 Figure 13-21 (p. 199)	TV—1977	Fred Karlin
MISSION, THE p. 495	1986	Ennio Morricone
MISSION: IMPOSSIBLE p. 492		(various)
MISTER ROBERTS p. 470	1955	Franz Waxman
MOHAMMED, MESSENGER OF GOD p. 503	1977	Maurice Jarre

MOONLIGHTING p. 3		Alf Clausen (episodes)
MOSQUITO COAST pp. 43, 65	1986	Maurice Jarre
MOTHER COURAGE p. 374	TV—1986	Craig Safan
MURDER, SHE WROTE pp. 65, 328, 344, 374, 478 Figures 23-10 (p. 483), 23-11 (p. 484)	1986-87	John Addison (theme); David Bell, Richard Markowitz (episodes)
MUSSOLINI p. 344	TV—1986	Laurence Rosenthal
MY BODYGUARD p. 90	1980	Dave Grusin
MY FAIR LADY p. 517, 522	1964	Lerner and Loewe; adapted by André Previn
NEVER CRY WOLF p. 379	1983	Mark Isham
NIGHT SHIFT pp. 28, 143, 559	1982	Burt Bacharach (lyricist: Carole Bayer Sager)
'NIGHT, MOTHER pp. 52, 56, 192, 300 Figures 5-3 (p. 56), 13-18 (p. 193)	1986	David Shire
NIGHTMARE ON ELM STREET p. 465 Figure 23-4 (p. 466)	1985	Charles Bernstein
NINE TO FIVE pp. 128, 432, 460 Figures 11-1a (p. 129), 11-1b (p. 130), 22-9 (p. 436)	1980	Charles Fox
NO MERCY p. 455	1987	Alan Silvestri
NORMA RAE pp. 531, 535, 536	1979	David Shire (lyricist: Norman Gimbel)
NORTH AND SOUTH pp. 65, 78, 328, 494	TV—1985	Bill Conti
NORTH BY NORTHWEST p. 34	1959	Bernard Herrmann
OCEANQUEST pp. 398, 411 Figures 21-2 (p. 401), 21-7 (p. 413), 21-8 (p. 414)	TV—1985	William Goldstein
OCTOPUSSY Figure 13-9 (p. 185)	1983	John Barry
OFFICER AND A GENTLEMAN, AN pp. 529, 536	1981	Jack Nitzsche (lyricist: Will Jennings, Buffy Sainte-Marie)
OH GOD, BOOK II p. 42	1980	Charles Fox
OMEN, THE pp. 77, 183, 221, 228, 238, 264, 270, 298, 328, 329 Figures 13-14 (p. 188), 14-13 (p. 232), 14-14 (p. 235), 15-7 (p. 266), 15-8 (p. 268), 16-15 (p. 302)	1976	Jerry Goldsmith
ON THE WATERFRONT p. 583	1954	Leonard Bernstein

OTHER SIDE OF THE MOUNTAIN, THE p. 90	1975	Charles Fox (lyricist: Norman Gimbel)
OUT OF AFRICA pp. 42, 65, 159, 206, 348, 495, 504 Figure 13-29 (p. 209)	1986	John Barry
OUTLAW JOSEY WALES, THE pp. 143, 254, 470 Figures 11-11 (p. 149), 14-16 (p. 237), 15-3 (p. 256), 24-2 (p. 501)	1976	Jerry Fielding
OUTRAGEOUS FORTUNE pp. 96, 254, 426	1987	Alan Silvestri
PATTON pp. 85, 191, 270, 388, 474 Figures 7-3 (p. 87), 13-16 (p. 191)	1970	Jerry Goldsmith
PAWNBROKER, THE p. 507	1965	Quincy Jones
PETER GUNN p. 452, 584		Henry Mancini
PETER THE GREAT pp. 51, 171, 250, 499 Figure 24-3 (p. 502)	TV—1986	Laurence Rosenthal
PINK PANTHER, THE p. 49	1963	Henry Mancini
PLACE IN THE SUN, A p. 584	1951	Franz Waxman
PLANET OF THE APES p. 183 Figure 13-12 (p. 186)	1968	Jerry Goldsmith
PLATOON pp. 13, 44, 470, 513, 558	1986	Georges Delerue
POSTMAN ALWAYS RINGS TWICE, THE p. 251 Figures 14-23 (p. 248), 14-24 (p. 251)	1981	Michael Small
PRETTY IN PINK p. 29	1986	Michael Gore
PRIZZI'S HONOR pp. 78, 460, 494, 511, 513	1985	Alex North
PSYCHO pp. 270, 284	1960	Bernard Herrmann
PURPLE ROSE OF CAIRO, THE p. 507	1985	Dick Hyman
RADIO DAYS p. 507	1987	Dick Hyman
RAGTIME p. 504	1981	Randy Newman
RAIDERS OF THE LOST ARK pp. 42, 96	1981	John Williams
RAINTREE COUNTY pp. 167, 298	1958	John Green
RECKLESS p. 395	1984	Thomas Newman
REMO WILLIAMS pp. 78, 171, 257, 328, 344, 395, 398, 497 Figure 15-5 (p. 259)	1985	Craig Safan

RETURN OF THE JEDI pp. 132, 196, 206 Figures 11-4a, b (p. 134), 13-23 (p. 201), 13-26 (p. 206), 13-27 (207)	1983	John Williams
RETURN OF THE PINK PANTHER p. 334, 460	1975	Henry Mancini
RETURN TO OZ p. 344	TV—1985	David Shire
REVENGE OF THE NERDS, THE p. 534	1984	Thomas Newman
REVOLUTION pp. 139, 168, 300, 334	1985	John Corigliano
RIGHT STUFF, THE p. 17	1983	Bill Conti
RIPTIDE p. 492		(various)
RIVERBOAT p. 470		Elmer Bernstein
ROBERT KENNEDY AND HIS TIMES p. 89	TV—1985	Fred Karlin
ROCKFORD FILES pp. 82, 452 Figure 7-1 (p. 83)		Mike Post/Pete Carpenter
ROCKY pp. 35, 81, 194 Figures 4-1 (p. 36), 4-2 (p. 37), 13-25 (p. 204)	1976	Bill Conti
ROMANCING THE STONE pp. 4, 159, 221, 257, 328, 344, 354, 395, 426, 460, 513 Figures 15-6 (p. 262), 22-3 (p. 426), 23-1 (p. 461)	1984	Alan Silvestri
ROMEO AND JULIET p. 143, 218 Figure 14-2 (p. 219)	1968	Nino Rota
ROOTS: THE NEXT GENERATION p. 505	TV—1979	Gerald Fried
'ROUND MIDNIGHT pp. 345, 523	1986	Herbie Hancock
RUSSIANS ARE COMING, THE pp. 38, 329, 460, 464	1966	Johnny Mandel
SADAT pp. 34, 68, 93, 118, 264, 496, 507 Figure 10-1 (p. 119)	TV—1983	Charles Bernstein
SALVADOR pp. 139, 494, 524 Figure 11-6 (p. 140)	1985	Georges Delerue
SANDPIPER, THE pp. 143, 328 Figure 11-7 (p. 142)	1965	Johnny Mandel (lyricist: Paul Francis Webster)
SATURDAY NIGHT FEVER pp. 422, 523	1978	Songs composed and performed by Bee Gees (plus additional music by David Shire)
SCARECROW AND MRS. KING pp. 155, 344, 478 Figures 23-12 (p. 485), 23-13 (p. 486)		Arthur B. Rubinstein

SCARFACE pp. 28, 159, 379, 395, 512	1983	Giorgio Moroder
SEA HAWK, THE p. 275	1940	Erich Korngold
SECRET OF MY SUCCESS p. 56 Figures 5-4 (p. 58, 5-5 (p. 59), 19-3 (p. 365)	1987	David Foster
SEEMS LIKE OLD TIMES p. 511	1980	Marvin Hamlisch
SHAFT pp. 18, 422, 524, 526, 536	1971	Isaac Hayes
SHAFT'S BIG SCORE p. 155	1972	Gordon Parks
SILENT MOVIE pp. 77, 460	1976	John Morris
SILKWOOD pp. 81, 348	1983	Georges Delerue
SILVER STREAK pp. 154, 159, 169, 254 Figures 12-1 (p. 170), 15-1 (p. 255), 15-2 (p. 255)	1976	Henry Mancini
SILVERADO pp. 343, 470	1985	Bruce Broughton
SIMON & SIMON p. 424 Figure 22-2 (p. 424)		Barry DeVorzon/Michael Towers
SIXTEEN CANDLES pp. 28, 463, 510	1984	Ira Newborn
SLEUTH pp. 18, 460	1972	John Addison
SOMEWHERE IN TIME p. 48	1980	John Barry
SON RISE: A MIRACLE OF LOVE p. 263	TV—1979	Gerald Fried
SOPHIE'S CHOICE pp. 38, 48, 93, 127, 143, 168, 217, 241, 270 Figures 7-7 (p. 95), 16-1 (p. 271)	1982	Marvin Hamlisch
SOUND AND THE FURY, THE p. 132	1959	Alex North
SOUND OF MUSIC, THE p. 517, 522	1965	Rodgers and Hammerstein; adapted by Irwin Kostal
SOUNDER p. 455	1972	Taj Mahal
SPAWN OF THE NORTH p. 315	1938	Dmitri Tiomkin
SPELLBOUND p. 280	1945	Miklos Rozsa
SPY WHO LOVED ME, THE pp. 38, 171, 344, 530, 538	1977	Marvin Hamlisch (lyricist: Carole Bayer Sager)
STALKING MOON, THE pp. 86, 280	1968	Fred Karlin
STAND BY ME p. 513	1986	(anthology)

THEY SHOOT HORSES, DON'T THEY? pp. 514, 522	1969	John Green, Albert Woodbury (adaptation)
THIEF pp. 264, 379, 422, 448	1981	Tangerine Dream
THOMAS CROWN AFFAIR, THE pp. 529	1980	Michel Legrand (lyricists: A. and M. Bergman)
THREE AMIGOS, THE p. 355	1986	Elmer Bernstein
TIN DRUM, THE p. 384	1979	Maurice Jarre
TO BE OR NOT TO BE p. 257	1983	John Morris
TOM JONES p. 300 Figure 16-18 (p. 312)	1963	John Addison
TOMA p. 452		Mike Post/Pete Carpenter
TOOTSIE pp. 315, 429 Figures 22-6a,b (p. 430), 22-7 (p. 433)	1982	Dave Grusin
TOP GUN p. 538	1986	Harold Faltermeyer
TORN CURTAIN p. 306	1966	John Addison
TRADING PLACES p. 38	1983	Elmer Bernstein
TWO FOR THE ROAD p. 34	1966	Henry Mancini
UNCOMMON VALOR p. 334	1983	James Horner
UNDER THE VOLCANO pp. 183, 273, 314, 494 Figures 13-11 (p. 186), 16-3 (p. 273), 16-4 (p. 276)	1984	Alex North
UP THE DOWN STAIRCASE pp. 192, 280 Figures 13-17 (p. 192), 16-12 (p. 300)	1967	Fred Karlin
VERDICT, THE pp. 182, 251 Figures 13-10 (p. 185), 14-25 (p. 253)	1982	Johnny Mandel
VICTOR/VICTORIA pp. 505, 535 Figures 24-5 (p. 507), 24-6 (p. 508)	1985	Henry Mancini (lyricist: Leslie Bricusse)
VIOLETS ARE BLUE pp. 38, 348	1986	Patrick Williams
WAIT UNTIL DARK p. 280	1967	Henry Mancini
WALTONS, THE p. 492		(various)
WAR BETWEEN MEN AND WOMEN, THE p. 396	1972	Marvin Hamlisch

WARGAMES pp. 77, 89, 176, 221, 344 Figures 13-2 (p. 178), 13-3a,b (p. 178), 14-6 (p. 222)	1983	Arthur B. Rubinstein
WAY WE WERE, THE pp. 140, 159, 171, 280, 512, 529, 534, 536 Figure 16-8 (p. 290)	1973	Marvin Hamlisch
WEIRD SCIENCE p. 463	1985	Ira Newborn
WEST SIDE STORY p. 517, 518, 522	1961	Leonard Bernstein (lyricist: Stephen Sondheim), conducted by John Green, orchestrations by Sid Ramin and Irwin Kostal
WHAT'S NEW, PUSSYCAT? p. 171	1965	Burt Bacharach (lyricist: Hal David)
WHERE THE RIVER RUNS BLACK pp. 398, 404	1986	James Horner
WHITE DAWN, THE pp. 148, 158, 355, 494	1976	Henry Mancini
WHO WILL LOVE MY CHILDREN? pp. 93 Figure 7-6 (p. 94)	TV—1983	Laurence Rosenthal
WHO'S AFRAID OF VIRGINIA WOOLF? p. 584	1966	Alex North
WILD BUNCH, THE p. 470	1969	Jerry Fielding
WINNING p. 331	1969	Dave Grusin
WITNESS pp. 38, 52, 118, 218, 403, 420, 511 Figures 14-3 (p. 219), 21-4 (p. 405), 21-5 (p. 406), 21-6 (p. 407)	1985	Maurice Jarre
WIZARD, THE p. 344		Arthur Rubinstein
YAKUZA, THE pp. 206, 314 Figures 16-19 (p. 314), 16-20 (p. 316)	1975	Dave Grusin
YEAR OF LIVING DANGEROUSLY, THE p. 474	1982	Maurice Jarre
YENTL pp. 31, 542	1983	Michel Legrand (lyricists: A. and M. Bergman)
YOUNG FRANKENSTEIN pp. 28, 35, 38, 357 Figure 4-3 (p. 37)	1974	John Morris
YOUNG SHERLOCK HOLMES p. 343	1985	Bruce Broughton

BIBLIOGRAPHY

Commercials/ Advertising Music

PERIODICALS

Ad Age. Crain Communications, 740 North Rush, Chicago, IL 60611-2590.

Ad Week. 49 E. 21st St., New York, NY.

Backstage Magazine. 330 W. 42nd St, New York, NY 10036.

Conducting

Hunsberger, Donald, and Roy Ernst. *The Art of Conducting.* New York: Alfred A. Knopf, 1983.

Rudolf, Max. *The Grammar of Conducting.* New York: Schirmer Books, 1950, 1980.

Drop-frame Time Code

Convergence Corporation EECO. *The Time Code Book.* 4th ed. Santa Ana, CA: Convergence Corporation EECO Inc. (1601 E. Chestnut Ave., P.O. Box 659, Santa Ana, CA 92702), 1987.

Electronic Music

Anderton, Craig. *MIDI for Musicians.* New York: Amsco Publications, 1986.

Massey, Howard, and the staff of The Center For Electronic Music. *The Compact Guide to MIDI Software.* New York: Amsco Publications, 1988.

Massey, Howard. *The Complete DX7.* New York: Amsco Publications, 1986.

Massey, Howard. *The Complete DX7II.* New York: Amsco Publications, 1987.

Massey, Howard. *The MIDI Home Studio.* New York: Amsco Publications, 1988.

PERIODICALS

Aftertouch (Yamaha). Box 2338, Northridge, CA 91323.

Electronic Musician. 2608 9th St., Berkeley, CA 94710.

Home Recording. GPI Publications, 20085 Stevens Creek, Cupertino, CA 95014.

Home and Studio Recording. Music Maker Publications, 7361 Topanga Canyon Road, Canoga Park, CA 91303.

Keyboard Magazine. GPI Publications, 20085 Stevens Creek, Cupertino, CA 95014.

Mix Magazine. 2608 9th Street, Berkeley, CA 94710.

Modern Keyboard. Harris Publications, Inc., 1115 Broadway, New York, NY 10010.

Music, Computers and Software. MCS Publications, 190 East Main Street, Huntington, NY 11743

Music and Sound Buyer's Guide. (Published yearly in January by *Music and Sound Output Magazine.*) 220 Westbury Ave., Carle Place, NY 11514.

Music Technology. Music Maker Publications, 2608 Ninth Street, Berkeley, CA 94710.

Musician, Amordian Press. Box 701, 31 Commercial Street, Gloucester, MA 01930.

Roland Users Group. 7200 Dominion Circle, Los Angeles, CA 90040.

Film Directors

Directors Guild of America. *Directors Guild of America Directory* (regularly updated). Los Angeles: Directors Guild of America (7950 W. Sunset Blvd., Los Angeles, CA 90056).

Singer, Michael. *Film Directors: A Complete Guide* (annual). Beverly Hills: Lone Eagle Press (9903 Santa Monica Blvd., #204, Beverly Hills, CA).

Film Editing

Hollyn, Norman. *The Film Editing Room Handbook.* New York: Arlo Publishing, Inc. (215 Park Avenue South, New York, NY 10003), 1984.

Reisz, Karel, and Gavin Millar. *The Technique of Film Editing.* New York: Hastings House, 1968.

Rosenblum, Ralph, and Robert Karen. *When the Shooting Stops . . . The Cutting Begins.* New York: Da Capo Press (233 Spring Street, New York, NY 10013), 1979.

Filmmakers

Chell, David. *Movie Makers at Work.* Redmond, WA: Microsoft Press (16011 N.E. 36th, Box 97017, Redmond, Washington 98073), 1987. Interviews.

Pincus, Edward, and Steven Ascher. *The Film Maker's Handbook.* New York: Plume Books (New American Library, 1633 Broadway, New York, NY 10019), 1984.

Singleton, Ralph. *Film Maker's Dictionary.* Beverly Hills: Lone Eagle Publishing Co. (9903 Santa Monica Blvd, #204, Beverly Hills, CA 90212), 1986.

Film Music

Bazelon, Irwin. *Knowing the Score: Notes on Film Music,* New York: Van Nostrand Reinhold Co., 1975. [Out of print but still available in libraries.]

Eisler, Hanns. *Composing for the Films.* New York: Oxford University Press, 1947. [Out of print but still available in libraries.]

Evans, Mark. *Soundtrack: The Music of the Movies.* New York: Da Capo Press, Inc. (227 West 17th Street, New York, NY 10011), 1979.

Manvell, Roger, and John Huntley. *The Technique of Film Music.* 2d edition. London and New York: Focal Press, 1975.

Prendergast, Roy M. *Film Music: A Neglected Art; A Critical Study of Music in Films.* New York: W.W. Norton & Co., 1977.

Thomas, Tony. *Music for the Movies.* Cranbury, NJ: A.S. Barnes and Co., 1973.

Film Music Thesauruses

Limbacher, James L. *Film Music.* Metuchen, NJ: The Scarecrow Press, Inc. 1974.

———. *Keeping Score; Film Music 1972–1979.* Metuchen, NJ: The Scarecrow Press, Inc., 1981.

Film and Television Producers

Broughton, Irv. *Producers on Producing: The Making of Film and Television.* Jefferson, NC: McFarland & Company, Inc. Publishers (Box 611, Jefferson, NC 28640), 1986.

Film and Television Production

Hollywood Production Manual, The (annual). 1322 N. Cole Ave., Hollywood, CA 90028. Source of union/guild rates and production facilities.

PERIODICALS

Daily Variety, 1400 N. Cahuenga Blvd., Hollywood, CA 90028.

The Hollywood Reporter, 6715 Sunset Blvd., Hollywood CA 90028.

Film Scoring

Hagan, Earle. *Advanced Scoring For Films.* Century City, CA: E.D.J. Music Publishers, Inc., 1989.

Hagen, Earle. *Scoring For Films.* New York: Criterion Music Corp., 1971.

Film Sound

Larry Blake. *Film Sound Today.* Hollywood: Reveille Press (P.O. Box 288, Hollywood, CA 90078), 1984. An anthology of articles from *Recording Engineer/Producer Magazine.*

Weis, Elisabeth, and John Belton, editors. *Theory and Practice of Film Sound.* New York: Columbia University Press, 1985.

Film Thesauruses

Halliwell, Leslie. *Halliwell's Film Guide,* 6th ed. New York: Charles Scribner's Sons, 1987.

Maltin, Leonard. *Leonard Maltin's TV Movies and Video Guide* (annual). New York: Signet Books (New American Library).

Marill, Alvin H. *Movies Made for Televisions (1964–1979).* Westport, CT: Arlington House Publishers, 1980.

Music Business

Baskerville, David. *Music Business Handbook and Career Guide.* Los Angeles and Denver: Sherwood Company, 1985.

Fink, Michael. *Inside the Music Business: Music in Contemporary Life.* New York: Schirmer Books, 1989.

Rachlin, Harvey. *The Encyclopedia of the Music Business.* New York: Harper & Row, 1981.

Shemel, Sidney & M. William Krasilovsky. *More About This Business of Music.* New York: Billboard Publications, Inc. (1515 Broadway, New York, NY 10036), 1985.

———. *This Business of Music.* New York: Billboard Publications, 1979.

Music Composition

Cope, David. *New Directions in Music.* Dubuque, IA: William C. Brown, 1971. Discusses avant-garde procedures and notation.

Dallin, Leon. *Techniques of Twentieth Century Composition.* Dubuque, IA: William C. Brown Company, 1957.

Fink, Robert, and Robert Ricci. *The Language of Twentieth Century Music: A Dictionary of Terms.* New York: Schirmer Books, 1975.

Persichetti, Vincent. *Twentieth-Century Harmony.* New York: W. W. Norton & Co., 1961.

Read, Gardner. *Music Notation: A Manual of Modern Practice.* Boston: Allyn and Bacon, 1964.

Reti, Rudolph. *The Thematic Process in Music.* Westport, CT: Greenwood Press, 1978.

Roemer, Clinton. *The Art of Music Copying,* 2d ed. Sherman Oaks, CA: Roerick Music Co. (4046 Davana Rd, Sherman Oaks, CA 91425), 1985.

Russo, William, with Jeffrey Ainis and David Stevenson. *Composing Music.* Englewood Cliffs, NJ: Prentice Hall, Inc., 1983.

Music Editing

Lustig, Milton. *Music Editing For Motion Pictures.* New York: Hastings House, 1980.

Orchestration/ Arranging

Adler, Samuel. *The Study of Orchestration.* New York: W.W. Norton & Co., 1982.

Mancini, Henry. *Sounds and Scores.* Greenwich, CT: Cherry Lane Music Co., Inc., 1973.

Ostrander, Arthur, and Dana Wilson. *Contemporary Choral Arranging.* Englewood Cliffs, NJ: Prentice-Hall, Inc., 1986.

Read, Owen T., and Joel T. Leach. *Scoring for Percussion.* Melville, NY: Belwyn-Mills, 1978.

Russo, William. *Jazz Composition and Orchestration.* Chicago: University of Chicago Press, 1968.

Wright, Rayburn. *Inside the Score.* Delevan, NY: Kendor Music, 1982.

Recording

Eargle, John. *Sound Recording,* 2d ed. New York: Van Nostrand Reinhold, 1980.

McIan, Peter, and Larry Wichman. *The Musician's Guide to Home Recording.* New York: Linden Press/Fireside, 1988.

Runstein, Robert E., and David Miles Huber. *Modern Recording Techniques,* 2d ed. Indianapolis: Howard W. Sams & Co., 1986.

Tremaine, Howard M. *The Audio Cyclopedia.* Indianapolis: Howard W. Sams and Co., 1982.

Wadhams, Wayne. *Dictionary of Music Production and Engineering Terminology.* New York: Schirmer Books, 1988.

——. *Sound Advice: The Musician's Guide to the Record Industry.* New York: Schirmer Books, 1990.

——. *Sound Advice: The Musician's Guide to the Recording Studio.* New York: Schirmer Books, 1990.

Woram, John M. *The Recording Studio Handbook.* Plainview, NY: Elar Publishing, 1982.

PERIODICAL

Recording Engineer/Producer. 9221 Quivira Rd., P.O. Box 12901, Overland Park, KS 66212-9981.

Songwriting

Davis, Sheila. *The Craft of Lyric Writing.* Cincinnati: Writer's Digest Books, 1985.

Kasha, Al, and Joel Hirschhorn. *If They Ask You, You Can Write a Song.* New York, NY: Simon & Schuster, 1979.

Wilder, Alex. *American Popular Songs: The Great Innovators, 1900–1950.* New York: Oxford University Press, 1972.

Writers

Writers Guild of America Directory (regularly updated). Writers Guide of America, 8955 Beverly Blvd, Los Angeles, CA 90048

CLICK BOOK

Alexander R. Brinkman

CLICK: 6 0/8 FRAMES; M.M.: 240.00

Click	0	1	2	3	4	5	6	7	8	9
000	0:00.00	0:00.00	0:00.25	0:00.50	0:00.75	0:01.00	0:01.25	0:01.50	0:01.75	0:02.00
010	0:02.25	0:02.50	0:02.75	0:03.00	0:03.25	0:03.50	0:03.75	0:04.00	0:04.25	0:04.50
020	0:04.75	0:05.00	0:05.25	0:05.50	0:05.75	0:06.00	0:06.25	0:06.50	0:06.75	0:07.00
030	0:07.25	0:07.50	0:07.75	0:08.00	0:08.25	0:08.50	0:08.75	0:09.00	0:09.25	0:09.50
040	0:09.75	0:10.00	0:10.25	0:10.50	0:10.75	0:11.00	0:11.25	0:11.50	0:11.75	0:12.00
050	0:12.25	0:12.50	0:12.75	0:13.00	0:13.25	0:13.50	0:13.75	0:14.00	0:14.25	0:14.50
060	0:14.75	0:15.00	0:15.25	0:15.50	0:15.75	0:16.00	0:16.25	0:16.50	0:16.75	0:17.00
070	0:17.25	0:17.50	0:17.75	0:18.00	0:18.25	0:18.50	0:18.75	0:19.00	0:19.25	0:19.50
080	0:19.75	0:20.00	0:20.25	0:20.50	0:20.75	0:21.00	0:21.25	0:21.50	0:21.75	0:22.00
090	0:22.25	0:22.50	0:22.75	0:23.00	0:23.25	0:23.50	0:23.75	0:24.00	0:24.25	0:24.50
100	0:24.75	0:25.00	0:25.25	0:25.50	0:25.75	0:26.00	0:26.25	0:26.50	0:26.75	0:27.00
110	0:27.25	0:27.50	0:27.75	0:28.00	0:28.25	0:28.50	0:28.75	0:29.00	0:29.25	0:29.50
120	0:29.75	0:30.00	0:30.25	0:30.50	0:30.75	0:31.00	0:31.25	0:31.50	0:31.75	0:32.00
130	0:32.25	0:32.50	0:32.75	0:33.00	0:33.25	0:33.50	0:33.75	0:34.00	0:34.25	0:34.50
140	0:34.75	0:35.00	0:35.25	0:35.50	0:35.75	0:36.00	0:36.25	0:36.50	0:36.75	0:37.00
150	0:37.25	0:37.50	0:37.75	0:38.00	0:38.25	0:38.50	0:38.75	0:39.00	0:39.25	0:39.50
160	0:39.75	0:40.00	0:40.25	0:40.50	0:40.75	0:41.00	0:41.25	0:41.50	0:41.75	0:42.00
170	0:42.25	0:42.50	0:42.75	0:43.00	0:43.25	0:43.50	0:43.75	0:44.00	0:44.25	0:44.50
180	0:44.75	0:45.00	0:45.25	0:45.50	0:45.75	0:46.00	0:46.25	0:46.50	0:46.75	0:47.00
190	0:47.25	0:47.50	0:47.75	0:48.00	0:48.25	0:48.50	0:48.75	0:49.00	0:49.25	0:49.50
200	0:49.75	0:50.00	0:50.25	0:50.50	0:50.75	0:51.00	0:51.25	0:51.50	0:51.75	0:52.00
210	0:52.25	0:52.50	0:52.75	0:53.00	0:53.25	0:53.50	0:53.75	0:54.00	0:54.25	0:54.50
220	0:54.75	0:55.00	0:55.25	0:55.50	0:55.75	0:56.00	0:56.25	0:56.50	0:56.75	0:57.00
230	0:57.25	0:57.50	0:57.75	0:58.00	0:58.25	0:58.50	0:58.75	0:59.00	0:59.25	0:59.50
240	0:59.75	1:00.00	1:00.25	1:00.50	1:00.75	1:01.00	1:01.25	1:01.50	1:01.75	1:02.00
250	1:02.25	1:02.50	1:02.75	1:03.00	1:03.25	1:03.50	1:03.75	1:04.00	1:04.25	1:04.50
260	1:04.75	1:05.00	1:05.25	1:05.50	1:05.75	1:06.00	1:06.25	1:06.50	1:06.75	1:07.00
270	1:07.25	1:07.50	1:07.75	1:08.00	1:08.25	1:08.50	1:08.75	1:09.00	1:09.25	1:09.50
280	1:09.75	1:10.00	1:10.25	1:10.50	1:10.75	1:11.00	1:11.25	1:11.50	1:11.75	1:12.00
290	1:12.25	1:12.50	1:12.75	1:13.00	1:13.25	1:13.50	1:13.75	1:14.00	1:14.25	1:14.50
300	1:14.75	1:15.00	1:15.25	1:15.50	1:15.75	1:16.00	1:16.25	1:16.50	1:16.75	1:17.00
310	1:17.25	1:17.50	1:17.75	1:18.00	1:18.25	1:18.50	1:18.75	1:19.00	1:19.25	1:19.50
320	1:19.75	1:20.00	1:20.25	1:20.50	1:20.75	1:21.00	1:21.25	1:21.50	1:21.75	1:22.00
330	1:22.25	1:22.50	1:22.75	1:23.00	1:23.25	1:23.50	1:23.75	1:24.00	1:24.25	1:24.50
340	1:24.75	1:25.00	1:25.25	1:25.50	1:25.75	1:26.00	1:26.25	1:26.50	1:26.75	1:27.00
350	1:27.25	1:27.50	1:27.75	1:28.00	1:28.25	1:28.50	1:28.75	1:29.00	1:29.25	1:29.50
360	1:29.75	1:30.00	1:30.25	1:30.50	1:30.75	1:31.00	1:31.25	1:31.50	1:31.75	1:32.00
370	1:32.25	1:32.50	1:32.75	1:33.00	1:33.25	1:33.50	1:33.75	1:34.00	1:34.25	1:34.50
380	1:34.75	1:35.00	1:35.25	1:35.50	1:35.75	1:36.00	1:36.25	1:36.50	1:36.75	1:37.00
390	1:37.25	1:37.50	1:37.75	1:38.00	1:38.25	1:38.50	1:38.75	1:39.00	1:39.25	1:39.50
400	1:39.75	1:40.00	1:40.25	1:40.50	1:40.75	1:41.00	1:41.25	1:41.50	1:41.75	1:42.00
410	1:42.25	1:42.50	1:42.75	1:43.00	1:43.25	1:43.50	1:43.75	1:44.00	1:44.25	1:44.50
420	1:44.75	1:45.00	1:45.25	1:45.50	1:45.75	1:46.00	1:46.25	1:46.50	1:46.75	1:47.00
430	1:47.25	1:47.50	1:47.75	1:48.00	1:48.25	1:48.50	1:48.75	1:49.00	1:49.25	1:49.50
440	1:49.75	1:50.00	1:50.25	1:50.50	1:50.75	1:51.00	1:51.25	1:51.50	1:51.75	1:52.00
450	1:52.25	1:52.50	1:52.75	1:53.00	1:53.25	1:53.50	1:53.75	1:54.00	1:54.25	1:54.50
460	1:54.75	1:55.00	1:55.25	1:55.50	1:55.75	1:56.00	1:56.25	1:56.50	1:56.75	1:57.00
470	1:57.25	1:57.50	1:57.75	1:58.00	1:58.25	1:58.50	1:58.75	1:59.00	1:59.25	1:59.50
480	1:59.75	2:00.00	2:00.25	2:00.50	2:00.75	2:01.00	2:01.25	2:01.50	2:01.75	2:02.00
490	2:02.25	2:02.50	2:02.75	2:03.00	2:03.25	2:03.50	2:03.75	2:04.00	2:04.25	2:04.50
500	2:04.75	2:05.00	2:05.25	2:05.50	2:05.75	2:06.00	2:06.25	2:06.50	2:06.75	2:07.00
510	2:07.25	2:07.50	2:07.75	2:08.00	2:08.25	2:08.50	2:08.75	2:09.00	2:09.25	2:09.50
520	2:09.75	2:10.00	2:10.25	2:10.50	2:10.75	2:11.00	2:11.25	2:11.50	2:11.75	2:12.00
530	2:12.25	2:12.50	2:12.75	2:13.00	2:13.25	2:13.50	2:13.75	2:14.00	2:14.25	2:14.50
540	2:14.75	2:15.00	2:15.25	2:15.50	2:15.75	2:16.00	2:16.25	2:16.50	2:16.75	2:17.00
550	2:17.25	2:17.50	2:17.75	2:18.00	2:18.25	2:18.50	2:18.75	2:19.00	2:19.25	2:19.50
560	2:19.75	2:20.00	2:20.25	2:20.50	2:20.75	2:21.00	2:21.25	2:21.50	2:21.75	2:22.00
570	2:22.25	2:22.50	2:22.75	2:23.00	2:23.25	2:23.50	2:23.75	2:24.00	2:24.25	2:24.50
580	2:24.75	2:25.00	2:25.25	2:25.50	2:25.75	2:26.00	2:26.25	2:26.50	2:26.75	2:27.00
590	2:27.25	2:27.50	2:27.75	2:28.00	2:28.25	2:28.50	2:28.75	2:29.00	2:29.25	2:29.50

(dotted quarter) = 0.38; (quarter) = 0.25; (dotted eighth) = 0.19; (triplet: quarter, eighth rest) = 0.17; (eighth) = 0.13; (triplet: eighth, two eighth rests) = 0.08; (sixteenth) = 0.06 seconds

CLICK: 6⅛ FRAMES; M.M.: 235.10

Click	0	1	2	3	4	5	6	7	8	9
000	0:00.00	0:00.00	0:00.26	0:00.51	0:00.77	0:01.02	0:01.28	0:01.53	0:01.79	0:02.04
010	0:02.30	0:02.55	0:02.81	0:03.06	0:03.32	0:03.57	0:03.83	0:04.08	0:04.34	0:04.59
020	0:04.85	0:05.10	0:05.36	0:05.61	0:05.87	0:06.13	0:06.38	0:06.64	0:06.89	0:07.15
030	0:07.40	0:07.66	0:07.91	0:08.17	0:08.42	0:08.68	0:08.93	0:09.19	0:09.44	0:09.70
040	0:09.95	0:10.21	0:10.46	0:10.72	0:10.97	0:11.23	0:11.48	0:11.74	0:11.99	0:12.25
050	0:12.51	0:12.76	0:13.02	0:13.27	0:13.53	0:13.78	0:14.04	0:14.29	0:14.55	0:14.80
060	0:15.06	0:15.31	0:15.57	0:15.82	0:16.08	0:16.33	0:16.59	0:16.84	0:17.10	0:17.35
070	0:17.61	0:17.86	0:18.12	0:18.38	0:18.63	0:18.89	0:19.14	0:19.40	0:19.65	0:19.91
080	0:20.16	0:20.42	0:20.67	0:20.93	0:21.18	0:21.44	0:21.69	0:21.95	0:22.20	0:22.46
090	0:22.71	0:22.97	0:23.22	0:23.48	0:23.73	0:23.99	0:24.24	0:24.50	0:24.76	0:25.01
100	0:25.27	0:25.52	0:25.78	0:26.03	0:26.29	0:26.54	0:26.80	0:27.05	0:27.31	0:27.56
110	0:27.82	0:28.07	0:28.33	0:28.58	0:28.84	0:29.09	0:29.35	0:29.60	0:29.86	0:30.11
120	0:30.37	0:30.63	0:30.88	0:31.14	0:31.39	0:31.65	0:31.90	0:32.16	0:32.41	0:32.67
130	0:32.92	0:33.18	0:33.43	0:33.69	0:33.94	0:34.20	0:34.45	0:34.71	0:34.96	0:35.22
140	0:35.47	0:35.73	0:35.98	0:36.24	0:36.49	0:36.75	0:37.01	0:37.26	0:37.52	0:37.77
150	0:38.03	0:38.28	0:38.54	0:38.79	0:39.05	0:39.30	0:39.56	0:39.81	0:40.07	0:40.32
160	0:40.58	0:40.83	0:41.09	0:41.34	0:41.60	0:41.85	0:42.11	0:42.36	0:42.62	0:42.88
170	0:43.13	0:43.39	0:43.64	0:43.90	0:44.15	0:44.41	0:44.66	0:44.92	0:45.17	0:45.43
180	0:45.68	0:45.94	0:46.19	0:46.45	0:46.70	0:46.96	0:47.21	0:47.47	0:47.72	0:47.98
190	0:48.23	0:48.49	0:48.74	0:49.00	0:49.26	0:49.51	0:49.77	0:50.02	0:50.28	0:50.53
200	0:50.79	0:51.04	0:51.30	0:51.55	0:51.81	0:52.06	0:52.32	0:52.57	0:52.83	0:53.08
210	0:53.34	0:53.59	0:53.85	0:54.10	0:54.36	0:54.61	0:54.87	0:55.13	0:55.38	0:55.64
220	0:55.89	0:56.15	0:56.40	0:56.66	0:56.91	0:57.17	0:57.42	0:57.68	0:57.93	0:58.19
230	0:58.44	0:58.70	0:58.95	0:59.21	0:59.46	0:59.72	0:59.97	1:00.23	1:00.48	1:00.74
240	1:00.99	1:01.25	1:01.51	1:01.76	1:02.02	1:02.27	1:02.53	1:02.78	1:03.04	1:03.29
250	1:03.55	1:03.80	1:04.06	1:04.31	1:04.57	1:04.82	1:05.08	1:05.33	1:05.59	1:05.84
260	1:06.10	1:06.35	1:06.61	1:06.86	1:07.12	1:07.38	1:07.63	1:07.89	1:08.14	1:08.40
270	1:08.65	1:08.91	1:09.16	1:09.42	1:09.67	1:09.93	1:10.18	1:10.44	1:10.69	1:10.95
280	1:11.20	1:11.46	1:11.71	1:11.97	1:12.22	1:12.48	1:12.73	1:12.99	1:13.24	1:13.50
290	1:13.76	1:14.01	1:14.27	1:14.52	1:14.78	1:15.03	1:15.29	1:15.54	1:15.80	1:16.05
300	1:16.31	1:16.56	1:16.82	1:17.07	1:17.33	1:17.58	1:17.84	1:18.09	1:18.35	1:18.60
310	1:18.86	1:19.11	1:19.37	1:19.63	1:19.88	1:20.14	1:20.39	1:20.65	1:20.90	1:21.16
320	1:21.41	1:21.67	1:21.92	1:22.18	1:22.43	1:22.69	1:22.94	1:23.20	1:23.45	1:23.71
330	1:23.96	1:24.22	1:24.47	1:24.73	1:24.98	1:25.24	1:25.49	1:25.75	1:26.01	1:26.26
340	1:26.52	1:26.77	1:27.03	1:27.28	1:27.54	1:27.79	1:28.05	1:28.30	1:28.56	1:28.81
350	1:29.07	1:29.32	1:29.58	1:29.83	1:30.09	1:30.34	1:30.60	1:30.85	1:31.11	1:31.36
360	1:31.62	1:31.88	1:32.13	1:32.39	1:32.64	1:32.90	1:33.15	1:33.41	1:33.66	1:33.92
370	1:34.17	1:34.43	1:34.68	1:34.94	1:35.19	1:35.45	1:35.70	1:35.96	1:36.21	1:36.47
380	1:36.72	1:36.98	1:37.23	1:37.49	1:37.74	1:38.00	1:38.26	1:38.51	1:38.77	1:39.02
390	1:39.28	1:39.53	1:39.79	1:40.04	1:40.30	1:40.55	1:40.81	1:41.06	1:41.32	1:41.57
400	1:41.83	1:42.08	1:42.34	1:42.59	1:42.85	1:43.10	1:43.36	1:43.61	1:43.87	1:44.13
410	1:44.38	1:44.64	1:44.89	1:45.15	1:45.40	1:45.66	1:45.91	1:46.17	1:46.42	1:46.68
420	1:46.93	1:47.19	1:47.44	1:47.70	1:47.95	1:48.21	1:48.46	1:48.72	1:48.97	1:49.23
430	1:49.48	1:49.74	1:49.99	1:50.25	1:50.51	1:50.76	1:51.02	1:51.27	1:51.53	1:51.78
440	1:52.04	1:52.29	1:52.55	1:52.80	1:53.06	1:53.31	1:53.57	1:53.82	1:54.08	1:54.33
450	1:54.59	1:54.84	1:55.10	1:55.35	1:55.61	1:55.86	1:56.12	1:56.38	1:56.63	1:56.89
460	1:57.14	1:57.40	1:57.65	1:57.91	1:58.16	1:58.42	1:58.67	1:58.93	1:59.18	1:59.44
470	1:59.69	1:59.95	2:00.20	2:00.46	2:00.71	2:00.97	2:01.22	2:01.48	2:01.73	2:01.99
480	2:02.24	2:02.50	2:02.76	2:03.01	2:03.27	2:03.52	2:03.78	2:04.03	2:04.29	2:04.54
490	2:04.80	2:05.05	2:05.31	2:05.56	2:05.82	2:06.07	2:06.33	2:06.58	2:06.84	2:07.09
500	2:07.35	2:07.60	2:07.86	2:08.11	2:08.37	2:08.62	2:08.88	2:09.14	2:09.39	2:09.65
510	2:09.90	2:10.16	2:10.41	2:10.67	2:10.92	2:11.18	2:11.43	2:11.69	2:11.94	2:12.20
520	2:12.45	2:12.71	2:12.96	2:13.22	2:13.47	2:13.73	2:13.98	2:14.24	2:14.49	2:14.75
530	2:15.01	2:15.26	2:15.52	2:15.77	2:16.03	2:16.28	2:16.54	2:16.79	2:17.05	2:17.30
540	2:17.56	2:17.81	2:18.07	2:18.32	2:18.58	2:18.83	2:19.09	2:19.34	2:19.60	2:19.85
550	2:20.11	2:20.36	2:20.62	2:20.87	2:21.13	2:21.39	2:21.64	2:21.90	2:22.15	2:22.41
560	2:22.66	2:22.92	2:23.17	2:23.43	2:23.68	2:23.94	2:24.19	2:24.45	2:24.70	2:24.96
570	2:25.21	2:25.47	2:25.72	2:25.98	2:26.23	2:26.49	2:26.74	2:27.00	2:27.26	2:27.51
580	2:27.77	2:28.02	2:28.28	2:28.53	2:28.79	2:29.04	2:29.30	2:29.55	2:29.81	2:30.06
590	2:30.32	2:30.57	2:30.83	2:31.08	2:31.34	2:31.59	2:31.85	2:32.10	2:32.36	2:32.61

♩. = 0.38; ♩ = 0.26; ♪. = 0.19; (triplet) ♩ 𝄾 = 0.17; ♪ = 0.13; (triplet) ♪ 𝄾 𝄾 = 0.09; 𝅘𝅥𝅯 = 0.06 seconds

CLICK: 6 2/8 FRAMES; M.M.: 230.40

Click	0	1	2	3	4	5	6	7	8	9
000	0:00.00	0:00.00	0:00.26	0:00.52	0:00.78	0:01.04	0:01.30	0:01.56	0:01.82	0:02.08
010	0:02.34	0:02.60	0:02.86	0:03.13	0:03.39	0:03.65	0:03.91	0:04.17	0:04.43	0:04.69
020	0:04.95	0:05.21	0:05.47	0:05.73	0:05.99	0:06.25	0:06.51	0:06.77	0:07.03	0:07.29
030	0:07.55	0:07.81	0:08.07	0:08.33	0:08.59	0:08.85	0:09.11	0:09.38	0:09.64	0:09.90
040	0:10.16	0:10.42	0:10.68	0:10.94	0:11.20	0:11.46	0:11.72	0:11.98	0:12.24	0:12.50
050	0:12.76	0:13.02	0:13.28	0:13.54	0:13.80	0:14.06	0:14.32	0:14.58	0:14.84	0:15.10
060	0:15.36	0:15.63	0:15.89	0:16.15	0:16.41	0:16.67	0:16.93	0:17.19	0:17.45	0:17.71
070	0:17.97	0:18.23	0:18.49	0:18.75	0:19.01	0:19.27	0:19.53	0:19.79	0:20.05	0:20.31
080	0:20.57	0:20.83	0:21.09	0:21.35	0:21.61	0:21.88	0:22.14	0:22.40	0:22.66	0:22.92
090	0:23.18	0:23.44	0:23.70	0:23.96	0:24.22	0:24.48	0:24.74	0:25.00	0:25.26	0:25.52
100	0:25.78	0:26.04	0:26.30	0:26.56	0:26.82	0:27.08	0:27.34	0:27.60	0:27.86	0:28.13
110	0:28.39	0:28.65	0:28.91	0:29.17	0:29.43	0:29.69	0:29.95	0:30.21	0:30.47	0:30.73
120	0:30.99	0:31.25	0:31.51	0:31.77	0:32.03	0:32.29	0:32.55	0:32.81	0:33.07	0:33.33
130	0:33.59	0:33.85	0:34.11	0:34.38	0:34.64	0:34.90	0:35.16	0:35.42	0:35.68	0:35.94
140	0:36.20	0:36.46	0:36.72	0:36.98	0:37.24	0:37.50	0:37.76	0:38.02	0:38.28	0:38.54
150	0:38.80	0:39.06	0:39.32	0:39.58	0:39.84	0:40.10	0:40.36	0:40.63	0:40.89	0:41.15
160	0:41.41	0:41.67	0:41.93	0:42.19	0:42.45	0:42.71	0:42.97	0:43.23	0:43.49	0:43.75
170	0:44.01	0:44.27	0:44.53	0:44.79	0:45.05	0:45.31	0:45.57	0:45.83	0:46.09	0:46.35
180	0:46.61	0:46.88	0:47.14	0:47.40	0:47.66	0:47.92	0:48.18	0:48.44	0:48.70	0:48.96
190	0:49.22	0:49.48	0:49.74	0:50.00	0:50.26	0:50.52	0:50.78	0:51.04	0:51.30	0:51.56
200	0:51.82	0:52.08	0:52.34	0:52.60	0:52.86	0:53.13	0:53.39	0:53.65	0:53.91	0:54.17
210	0:54.43	0:54.69	0:54.95	0:55.21	0:55.47	0:55.73	0:55.99	0:56.25	0:56.51	0:56.77
220	0:57.03	0:57.29	0:57.55	0:57.81	0:58.07	0:58.33	0:58.59	0:58.85	0:59.11	0:59.38
230	0:59.64	0:59.90	1:00.16	1:00.42	1:00.68	1:00.94	1:01.20	1:01.46	1:01.72	1:01.98
240	1:02.24	1:02.50	1:02.76	1:03.02	1:03.28	1:03.54	1:03.80	1:04.06	1:04.32	1:04.58
250	1:04.84	1:05.10	1:05.36	1:05.63	1:05.89	1:06.15	1:06.41	1:06.67	1:06.93	1:07.19
260	1:07.45	1:07.71	1:07.97	1:08.23	1:08.49	1:08.75	1:09.01	1:09.27	1:09.53	1:09.79
270	1:10.05	1:10.31	1:10.57	1:10.83	1:11.09	1:11.35	1:11.61	1:11.88	1:12.14	1:12.40
280	1:12.66	1:12.92	1:13.18	1:13.44	1:13.70	1:13.96	1:14.22	1:14.48	1:14.74	1:15.00
290	1:15.26	1:15.52	1:15.78	1:16.04	1:16.30	1:16.56	1:16.82	1:17.08	1:17.34	1:17.60
300	1:17.86	1:18.13	1:18.39	1:18.65	1:18.91	1:19.17	1:19.43	1:19.69	1:19.95	1:20.21
310	1:20.47	1:20.73	1:20.99	1:21.25	1:21.51	1:21.77	1:22.03	1:22.29	1:22.55	1:22.81
320	1:23.07	1:23.33	1:23.59	1:23.85	1:24.11	1:24.38	1:24.64	1:24.90	1:25.16	1:25.42
330	1:25.68	1:25.94	1:26.20	1:26.46	1:26.72	1:26.98	1:27.24	1:27.50	1:27.76	1:28.02
340	1:28.28	1:28.54	1:28.80	1:29.06	1:29.32	1:29.58	1:29.84	1:30.10	1:30.36	1:30.63
350	1:30.89	1:31.15	1:31.41	1:31.67	1:31.93	1:32.19	1:32.45	1:32.71	1:32.97	1:33.23
360	1:33.49	1:33.75	1:34.01	1:34.27	1:34.53	1:34.79	1:35.05	1:35.31	1:35.57	1:35.83
370	1:36.09	1:36.35	1:36.61	1:36.88	1:37.14	1:37.40	1:37.66	1:37.92	1:38.18	1:38.44
380	1:38.70	1:38.96	1:39.22	1:39.48	1:39.74	1:40.00	1:40.26	1:40.52	1:40.78	1:41.04
390	1:41.30	1:41.56	1:41.82	1:42.08	1:42.34	1:42.60	1:42.86	1:43.13	1:43.39	1:43.65
400	1:43.91	1:44.17	1:44.43	1:44.69	1:44.95	1:45.21	1:45.47	1:45.73	1:45.99	1:46.25
410	1:46.51	1:46.77	1:47.03	1:47.29	1:47.55	1:47.81	1:48.07	1:48.33	1:48.59	1:48.85
420	1:49.11	1:49.38	1:49.64	1:49.90	1:50.16	1:50.42	1:50.68	1:50.94	1:51.20	1:51.46
430	1:51.72	1:51.98	1:52.24	1:52.50	1:52.76	1:53.02	1:53.28	1:53.54	1:53.80	1:54.06
440	1:54.32	1:54.58	1:54.84	1:55.10	1:55.36	1:55.63	1:55.89	1:56.15	1:56.41	1:56.67
450	1:56.93	1:57.19	1:57.45	1:57.71	1:57.97	1:58.23	1:58.49	1:58.75	1:59.01	1:59.27
460	1:59.53	1:59.79	2:00.05	2:00.31	2:00.57	2:00.83	2:01.09	2:01.35	2:01.61	2:01.88
470	2:02.14	2:02.40	2:02.66	2:02.92	2:03.18	2:03.44	2:03.70	2:03.96	2:04.22	2:04.48
480	2:04.74	2:05.00	2:05.26	2:05.52	2:05.78	2:06.04	2:06.30	2:06.56	2:06.82	2:07.08
490	2:07.34	2:07.60	2:07.86	2:08.13	2:08.39	2:08.65	2:08.91	2:09.17	2:09.43	2:09.69
500	2:09.95	2:10.21	2:10.47	2:10.73	2:10.99	2:11.25	2:11.51	2:11.77	2:12.03	2:12.29
510	2:12.55	2:12.81	2:13.07	2:13.33	2:13.59	2:13.85	2:14.11	2:14.38	2:14.64	2:14.90
520	2:15.16	2:15.42	2:15.68	2:15.94	2:16.20	2:16.46	2:16.72	2:16.98	2:17.24	2:17.50
530	2:17.76	2:18.02	2:18.28	2:18.54	2:18.80	2:19.06	2:19.32	2:19.58	2:19.84	2:20.10
540	2:20.36	2:20.63	2:20.89	2:21.15	2:21.41	2:21.67	2:21.93	2:22.19	2:22.45	2:22.71
550	2:22.97	2:23.23	2:23.49	2:23.75	2:24.01	2:24.27	2:24.53	2:24.79	2:25.05	2:25.31
560	2:25.57	2:25.83	2:26.09	2:26.35	2:26.61	2:26.88	2:27.14	2:27.40	2:27.66	2:27.92
570	2:28.18	2:28.44	2:28.70	2:28.96	2:29.22	2:29.48	2:29.74	2:30.00	2:30.26	2:30.52
580	2:30.78	2:31.04	2:31.30	2:31.56	2:31.82	2:32.08	2:32.34	2:32.60	2:32.86	2:33.13
590	2:33.39	2:33.65	2:33.91	2:34.17	2:34.43	2:34.69	2:34.95	2:35.21	2:35.47	2:35.73

♩. = 0.39; ♩ = 0.26; ♪. = 0.20; (triplet) ♩ 𝄾 = 0.17; ♪ = 0.13; (triplet) ♪𝄾𝄾 = 0.09; 𝅘𝅥𝅯 = 0.07 seconds

CLICK: 6⅜ FRAMES; M.M.: 225.88

Click	0	1	2	3	4	5	6	7	8	9
000	0:00.00	0:00.00	0:00.27	0:00.53	0:00.80	0:01.06	0:01.33	0:01.59	0:01.86	0:02.13
010	0:02.39	0:02.66	0:02.92	0:03.19	0:03.45	0:03.72	0:03.98	0:04.25	0:04.52	0:04.78
020	0:05.05	0:05.31	0:05.58	0:05.84	0:06.11	0:06.38	0:06.64	0:06.91	0:07.17	0:07.44
030	0:07.70	0:07.97	0:08.23	0:08.50	0:08.77	0:09.03	0:09.30	0:09.56	0:09.83	0:10.09
040	0:10.36	0:10.63	0:10.89	0:11.16	0:11.42	0:11.69	0:11.95	0:12.22	0:12.48	0:12.75
050	0:13.02	0:13.28	0:13.55	0:13.81	0:14.08	0:14.34	0:14.61	0:14.88	0:15.14	0:15.41
060	0:15.67	0:15.94	0:16.20	0:16.47	0:16.73	0:17.00	0:17.27	0:17.53	0:17.80	0:18.06
070	0:18.33	0:18.59	0:18.86	0:19.13	0:19.39	0:19.66	0:19.92	0:20.19	0:20.45	0:20.72
080	0:20.98	0:21.25	0:21.52	0:21.78	0:22.05	0:22.31	0:22.58	0:22.84	0:23.11	0:23.38
090	0:23.64	0:23.91	0:24.17	0:24.44	0:24.70	0:24.97	0:25.23	0:25.50	0:25.77	0:26.03
100	0:26.30	0:26.56	0:26.83	0:27.09	0:27.36	0:27.63	0:27.89	0:28.16	0:28.42	0:28.69
110	0:28.95	0:29.22	0:29.48	0:29.75	0:30.02	0:30.28	0:30.55	0:30.81	0:31.08	0:31.34
120	0:31.61	0:31.88	0:32.14	0:32.41	0:32.67	0:32.94	0:33.20	0:33.47	0:33.73	0:34.00
130	0:34.27	0:34.53	0:34.80	0:35.06	0:35.33	0:35.59	0:35.86	0:36.13	0:36.39	0:36.66
140	0:36.92	0:37.19	0:37.45	0:37.72	0:37.98	0:38.25	0:38.52	0:38.78	0:39.05	0:39.31
150	0:39.58	0:39.84	0:40.11	0:40.38	0:40.64	0:40.91	0:41.17	0:41.44	0:41.70	0:41.97
160	0:42.23	0:42.50	0:42.77	0:43.03	0:43.30	0:43.56	0:43.83	0:44.09	0:44.36	0:44.63
170	0:44.89	0:45.16	0:45.42	0:45.69	0:45.95	0:46.22	0:46.48	0:46.75	0:47.02	0:47.28
180	0:47.55	0:47.81	0:48.08	0:48.34	0:48.61	0:48.88	0:49.14	0:49.41	0:49.67	0:49.94
190	0:50.20	0:50.47	0:50.73	0:51.00	0:51.27	0:51.53	0:51.80	0:52.06	0:52.33	0:52.59
200	0:52.86	0:53.13	0:53.39	0:53.66	0:53.92	0:54.19	0:54.45	0:54.72	0:54.98	0:55.25
210	0:55.52	0:55.78	0:56.05	0:56.31	0:56.58	0:56.84	0:57.11	0:57.38	0:57.64	0:57.91
220	0:58.17	0:58.44	0:58.70	0:58.97	0:59.23	0:59.50	0:59.77	1:00.03	1:00.30	1:00.56
230	1:00.83	1:01.09	1:01.36	1:01.62	1:01.89	1:02.16	1:02.42	1:02.69	1:02.95	1:03.22
240	1:03.48	1:03.75	1:04.02	1:04.28	1:04.55	1:04.81	1:05.08	1:05.34	1:05.61	1:05.87
250	1:06.14	1:06.41	1:06.67	1:06.94	1:07.20	1:07.47	1:07.73	1:08.00	1:08.27	1:08.53
260	1:08.80	1:09.06	1:09.33	1:09.59	1:09.86	1:10.13	1:10.39	1:10.66	1:10.92	1:11.19
270	1:11.45	1:11.72	1:11.98	1:12.25	1:12.52	1:12.78	1:13.05	1:13.31	1:13.58	1:13.84
280	1:14.11	1:14.38	1:14.64	1:14.91	1:15.17	1:15.44	1:15.70	1:15.97	1:16.23	1:16.50
290	1:16.77	1:17.03	1:17.30	1:17.56	1:17.83	1:18.09	1:18.36	1:18.63	1:18.89	1:19.16
300	1:19.42	1:19.69	1:19.95	1:20.22	1:20.48	1:20.75	1:21.02	1:21.28	1:21.55	1:21.81
310	1:22.08	1:22.34	1:22.61	1:22.88	1:23.14	1:23.41	1:23.67	1:23.94	1:24.20	1:24.47
320	1:24.73	1:25.00	1:25.27	1:25.53	1:25.80	1:26.06	1:26.33	1:26.59	1:26.86	1:27.13
330	1:27.39	1:27.66	1:27.92	1:28.19	1:28.45	1:28.72	1:28.98	1:29.25	1:29.52	1:29.78
340	1:30.05	1:30.31	1:30.58	1:30.84	1:31.11	1:31.38	1:31.64	1:31.91	1:32.17	1:32.44
350	1:32.70	1:32.97	1:33.23	1:33.50	1:33.77	1:34.03	1:34.30	1:34.56	1:34.83	1:35.09
360	1:35.36	1:35.63	1:35.89	1:36.16	1:36.42	1:36.69	1:36.95	1:37.22	1:37.48	1:37.75
370	1:38.02	1:38.28	1:38.55	1:38.81	1:39.08	1:39.34	1:39.61	1:39.88	1:40.14	1:40.41
380	1:40.67	1:40.94	1:41.20	1:41.47	1:41.73	1:42.00	1:42.27	1:42.53	1:42.80	1:43.06
390	1:43.33	1:43.59	1:43.86	1:44.13	1:44.39	1:44.66	1:44.92	1:45.19	1:45.45	1:45.72
400	1:45.98	1:46.25	1:46.52	1:46.78	1:47.05	1:47.31	1:47.58	1:47.84	1:48.11	1:48.38
410	1:48.64	1:48.91	1:49.17	1:49.44	1:49.70	1:49.97	1:50.23	1:50.50	1:50.77	1:51.03
420	1:51.30	1:51.56	1:51.83	1:52.09	1:52.36	1:52.63	1:52.89	1:53.16	1:53.42	1:53.69
430	1:53.95	1:54.22	1:54.48	1:54.75	1:55.02	1:55.28	1:55.55	1:55.81	1:56.08	1:56.34
440	1:56.61	1:56.87	1:57.14	1:57.41	1:57.67	1:57.94	1:58.20	1:58.47	1:58.73	1:59.00
450	1:59.27	1:59.53	1:59.80	2:00.06	2:00.33	2:00.59	2:00.86	2:01.12	2:01.39	2:01.66
460	2:01.92	2:02.19	2:02.45	2:02.72	2:02.98	2:03.25	2:03.52	2:03.78	2:04.05	2:04.31
470	2:04.58	2:04.84	2:05.11	2:05.38	2:05.64	2:05.91	2:06.17	2:06.44	2:06.70	2:06.97
480	2:07.23	2:07.50	2:07.77	2:08.03	2:08.30	2:08.56	2:08.83	2:09.09	2:09.36	2:09.62
490	2:09.89	2:10.16	2:10.42	2:10.69	2:10.95	2:11.22	2:11.48	2:11.75	2:12.02	2:12.28
500	2:12.55	2:12.81	2:13.08	2:13.34	2:13.61	2:13.88	2:14.14	2:14.41	2:14.67	2:14.94
510	2:15.20	2:15.47	2:15.73	2:16.00	2:16.27	2:16.53	2:16.80	2:17.06	2:17.33	2:17.59
520	2:17.86	2:18.12	2:18.39	2:18.66	2:18.92	2:19.19	2:19.45	2:19.72	2:19.98	2:20.25
530	2:20.52	2:20.78	2:21.05	2:21.31	2:21.58	2:21.84	2:22.11	2:22.38	2:22.64	2:22.91
540	2:23.17	2:23.44	2:23.70	2:23.97	2:24.23	2:24.50	2:24.77	2:25.03	2:25.30	2:25.56
550	2:25.83	2:26.09	2:26.36	2:26.62	2:26.89	2:27.16	2:27.42	2:27.69	2:27.95	2:28.22
560	2:28.48	2:28.75	2:29.02	2:29.28	2:29.55	2:29.81	2:30.08	2:30.34	2:30.61	2:30.88
570	2:31.14	2:31.41	2:31.67	2:31.94	2:32.20	2:32.47	2:32.73	2:33.00	2:33.27	2:33.53
580	2:33.80	2:34.06	2:34.33	2:34.59	2:34.86	2:35.12	2:35.39	2:35.66	2:35.92	2:36.19
590	2:36.45	2:36.72	2:36.98	2:37.25	2:37.52	2:37.78	2:38.05	2:38.31	2:38.58	2:38.84

𝅘𝅥. = 0.40; 𝅘𝅥 = 0.27; 𝅘𝅥𝅮. = 0.20; (triplet 𝅘𝅥 𝄾) = 0.18; 𝅘𝅥𝅮 = 0.13; (triplet 𝅘𝅥𝅮 𝄾 𝄾) = 0.09; 𝅘𝅥𝅯 = 0.07 seconds

CLICK: 6 4/8 FRAMES; M.M.: 221.54

Click	0	1	2	3	4	5	6	7	8	9
000	0:00.00	0:00.00	0:00.27	0:00.54	0:00.81	0:01.08	0:01.35	0:01.62	0:01.90	0:02.17
010	0:02.44	0:02.71	0:02.98	0:03.25	0:03.52	0:03.79	0:04.06	0:04.33	0:04.60	0:04.88
020	0:05.15	0:05.42	0:05.69	0:05.96	0:06.23	0:06.50	0:06.77	0:07.04	0:07.31	0:07.58
030	0:07.85	0:08.12	0:08.40	0:08.67	0:08.94	0:09.21	0:09.48	0:09.75	0:10.02	0:10.29
040	0:10.56	0:10.83	0:11.10	0:11.37	0:11.65	0:11.92	0:12.19	0:12.46	0:12.73	0:13.00
050	0:13.27	0:13.54	0:13.81	0:14.08	0:14.35	0:14.62	0:14.90	0:15.17	0:15.44	0:15.71
060	0:15.98	0:16.25	0:16.52	0:16.79	0:17.06	0:17.33	0:17.60	0:17.88	0:18.15	0:18.42
070	0:18.69	0:18.96	0:19.23	0:19.50	0:19.77	0:20.04	0:20.31	0:20.58	0:20.85	0:21.13
080	0:21.40	0:21.67	0:21.94	0:22.21	0:22.48	0:22.75	0:23.02	0:23.29	0:23.56	0:23.83
090	0:24.10	0:24.37	0:24.65	0:24.92	0:25.19	0:25.46	0:25.73	0:26.00	0:26.27	0:26.54
100	0:26.81	0:27.08	0:27.35	0:27.62	0:27.90	0:28.17	0:28.44	0:28.71	0:28.98	0:29.25
110	0:29.52	0:29.79	0:30.06	0:30.33	0:30.60	0:30.87	0:31.15	0:31.42	0:31.69	0:31.96
120	0:32.23	0:32.50	0:32.77	0:33.04	0:33.31	0:33.58	0:33.85	0:34.12	0:34.40	0:34.67
130	0:34.94	0:35.21	0:35.48	0:35.75	0:36.02	0:36.29	0:36.56	0:36.83	0:37.10	0:37.38
140	0:37.65	0:37.92	0:38.19	0:38.46	0:38.73	0:39.00	0:39.27	0:39.54	0:39.81	0:40.08
150	0:40.35	0:40.63	0:40.90	0:41.17	0:41.44	0:41.71	0:41.98	0:42.25	0:42.52	0:42.79
160	0:43.06	0:43.33	0:43.60	0:43.87	0:44.15	0:44.42	0:44.69	0:44.96	0:45.23	0:45.50
170	0:45.77	0:46.04	0:46.31	0:46.58	0:46.85	0:47.12	0:47.40	0:47.67	0:47.94	0:48.21
180	0:48.48	0:48.75	0:49.02	0:49.29	0:49.56	0:49.83	0:50.10	0:50.37	0:50.65	0:50.92
190	0:51.19	0:51.46	0:51.73	0:52.00	0:52.27	0:52.54	0:52.81	0:53.08	0:53.35	0:53.62
200	0:53.90	0:54.17	0:54.44	0:54.71	0:54.98	0:55.25	0:55.52	0:55.79	0:56.06	0:56.33
210	0:56.60	0:56.87	0:57.15	0:57.42	0:57.69	0:57.96	0:58.23	0:58.50	0:58.77	0:59.04
220	0:59.31	0:59.58	0:59.85	1:00.12	1:00.40	1:00.67	1:00.94	1:01.21	1:01.48	1:01.75
230	1:02.02	1:02.29	1:02.56	1:02.83	1:03.10	1:03.37	1:03.65	1:03.92	1:04.19	1:04.46
240	1:04.73	1:05.00	1:05.27	1:05.54	1:05.81	1:06.08	1:06.35	1:06.62	1:06.90	1:07.17
250	1:07.44	1:07.71	1:07.98	1:08.25	1:08.52	1:08.79	1:09.06	1:09.33	1:09.60	1:09.87
260	1:10.15	1:10.42	1:10.69	1:10.96	1:11.23	1:11.50	1:11.77	1:12.04	1:12.31	1:12.58
270	1:12.85	1:13.12	1:13.40	1:13.67	1:13.94	1:14.21	1:14.48	1:14.75	1:15.02	1:15.29
280	1:15.56	1:15.83	1:16.10	1:16.37	1:16.65	1:16.92	1:17.19	1:17.46	1:17.73	1:18.00
290	1:18.27	1:18.54	1:18.81	1:19.08	1:19.35	1:19.62	1:19.90	1:20.17	1:20.44	1:20.71
300	1:20.98	1:21.25	1:21.52	1:21.79	1:22.06	1:22.33	1:22.60	1:22.87	1:23.15	1:23.42
310	1:23.69	1:23.96	1:24.23	1:24.50	1:24.77	1:25.04	1:25.31	1:25.58	1:25.85	1:26.12
320	1:26.40	1:26.67	1:26.94	1:27.21	1:27.48	1:27.75	1:28.02	1:28.29	1:28.56	1:28.83
330	1:29.10	1:29.37	1:29.65	1:29.92	1:30.19	1:30.46	1:30.73	1:31.00	1:31.27	1:31.54
340	1:31.81	1:32.08	1:32.35	1:32.62	1:32.90	1:33.17	1:33.44	1:33.71	1:33.98	1:34.25
350	1:34.52	1:34.79	1:35.06	1:35.33	1:35.60	1:35.87	1:36.15	1:36.42	1:36.69	1:36.96
360	1:37.23	1:37.50	1:37.77	1:38.04	1:38.31	1:38.58	1:38.85	1:39.12	1:39.40	1:39.67
370	1:39.94	1:40.21	1:40.48	1:40.75	1:41.02	1:41.29	1:41.56	1:41.83	1:42.10	1:42.37
380	1:42.65	1:42.92	1:43.19	1:43.46	1:43.73	1:44.00	1:44.27	1:44.54	1:44.81	1:45.08
390	1:45.35	1:45.62	1:45.90	1:46.17	1:46.44	1:46.71	1:46.98	1:47.25	1:47.52	1:47.79
400	1:48.06	1:48.33	1:48.60	1:48.87	1:49.15	1:49.42	1:49.69	1:49.96	1:50.23	1:50.50
410	1:50.77	1:51.04	1:51.31	1:51.58	1:51.85	1:52.12	1:52.40	1:52.67	1:52.94	1:53.21
420	1:53.48	1:53.75	1:54.02	1:54.29	1:54.56	1:54.83	1:55.10	1:55.37	1:55.65	1:55.92
430	1:56.19	1:56.46	1:56.73	1:57.00	1:57.27	1:57.54	1:57.81	1:58.08	1:58.35	1:58.62
440	1:58.90	1:59.17	1:59.44	1:59.71	1:59.98	2:00.25	2:00.52	2:00.79	2:01.06	2:01.33
450	2:01.60	2:01.87	2:02.15	2:02.42	2:02.69	2:02.96	2:03.23	2:03.50	2:03.77	2:04.04
460	2:04.31	2:04.58	2:04.85	2:05.12	2:05.40	2:05.67	2:05.94	2:06.21	2:06.48	2:06.75
470	2:07.02	2:07.29	2:07.56	2:07.83	2:08.10	2:08.37	2:08.65	2:08.92	2:09.19	2:09.46
480	2:09.73	2:10.00	2:10.27	2:10.54	2:10.81	2:11.08	2:11.35	2:11.62	2:11.90	2:12.17
490	2:12.44	2:12.71	2:12.98	2:13.25	2:13.52	2:13.79	2:14.06	2:14.33	2:14.60	2:14.87
500	2:15.15	2:15.42	2:15.69	2:15.96	2:16.23	2:16.50	2:16.77	2:17.04	2:17.31	2:17.58
510	2:17.85	2:18.12	2:18.40	2:18.67	2:18.94	2:19.21	2:19.48	2:19.75	2:20.02	2:20.29
520	2:20.56	2:20.83	2:21.10	2:21.37	2:21.65	2:21.92	2:22.19	2:22.46	2:22.73	2:23.00
530	2:23.27	2:23.54	2:23.81	2:24.08	2:24.35	2:24.62	2:24.90	2:25.17	2:25.44	2:25.71
540	2:25.98	2:26.25	2:26.52	2:26.79	2:27.06	2:27.33	2:27.60	2:27.87	2:28.15	2:28.42
550	2:28.69	2:28.96	2:29.23	2:29.50	2:29.77	2:30.04	2:30.31	2:30.58	2:30.85	2:31.12
560	2:31.40	2:31.67	2:31.94	2:32.21	2:32.48	2:32.75	2:33.02	2:33.29	2:33.56	2:33.83
570	2:34.10	2:34.37	2:34.65	2:34.92	2:35.19	2:35.46	2:35.73	2:36.00	2:36.27	2:36.54
580	2:36.81	2:37.08	2:37.35	2:37.62	2:37.90	2:38.17	2:38.44	2:38.71	2:38.98	2:39.25
590	2:39.52	2:39.79	2:40.06	2:40.33	2:40.60	2:40.87	2:41.15	2:41.42	2:41.69	2:41.96

♩. = 0.41; ♩ = 0.27; ♪. = 0.20; (triplet) ♩ 𝄾 = 0.18; ♪ = 0.14; (triplet) ♪𝄾𝄾 = 0.09; 𝅘𝅥𝅯 = 0.07 seconds

CLICK: 6⅝ FRAMES;   M.M.: 217.36

Click	0	1	2	3	4	5	6	7	8	9
000	0:00.00	0:00.00	0:00.28	0:00.55	0:00.83	0:01.10	0:01.38	0:01.66	0:01.93	0:02.21
010	0:02.48	0:02.76	0:03.04	0:03.31	0:03.59	0:03.86	0:04.14	0:04.42	0:04.69	0:04.97
020	0:05.24	0:05.52	0:05.80	0:06.07	0:06.35	0:06.63	0:06.90	0:07.18	0:07.45	0:07.73
030	0:08.01	0:08.28	0:08.56	0:08.83	0:09.11	0:09.39	0:09.66	0:09.94	0:10.21	0:10.49
040	0:10.77	0:11.04	0:11.32	0:11.59	0:11.87	0:12.15	0:12.42	0:12.70	0:12.97	0:13.25
050	0:13.53	0:13.80	0:14.08	0:14.35	0:14.63	0:14.91	0:15.18	0:15.46	0:15.73	0:16.01
060	0:16.29	0:16.56	0:16.84	0:17.11	0:17.39	0:17.67	0:17.94	0:18.22	0:18.49	0:18.77
070	0:19.05	0:19.32	0:19.60	0:19.88	0:20.15	0:20.43	0:20.70	0:20.98	0:21.26	0:21.53
080	0:21.81	0:22.08	0:22.36	0:22.64	0:22.91	0:23.19	0:23.46	0:23.74	0:24.02	0:24.29
090	0:24.57	0:24.84	0:25.12	0:25.40	0:25.67	0:25.95	0:26.22	0:26.50	0:26.78	0:27.05
100	0:27.33	0:27.60	0:27.88	0:28.16	0:28.43	0:28.71	0:28.98	0:29.26	0:29.54	0:29.81
110	0:30.09	0:30.36	0:30.64	0:30.92	0:31.19	0:31.47	0:31.74	0:32.02	0:32.30	0:32.57
120	0:32.85	0:33.13	0:33.40	0:33.68	0:33.95	0:34.23	0:34.51	0:34.78	0:35.06	0:35.33
130	0:35.61	0:35.89	0:36.16	0:36.44	0:36.71	0:36.99	0:37.27	0:37.54	0:37.82	0:38.09
140	0:38.37	0:38.65	0:38.92	0:39.20	0:39.47	0:39.75	0:40.03	0:40.30	0:40.58	0:40.85
150	0:41.13	0:41.41	0:41.68	0:41.96	0:42.23	0:42.51	0:42.79	0:43.06	0:43.34	0:43.61
160	0:43.89	0:44.17	0:44.44	0:44.72	0:44.99	0:45.27	0:45.55	0:45.82	0:46.10	0:46.38
170	0:46.65	0:46.93	0:47.20	0:47.48	0:47.76	0:48.03	0:48.31	0:48.58	0:48.86	0:49.14
180	0:49.41	0:49.69	0:49.96	0:50.24	0:50.52	0:50.79	0:51.07	0:51.34	0:51.62	0:51.90
190	0:52.17	0:52.45	0:52.72	0:53.00	0:53.28	0:53.55	0:53.83	0:54.10	0:54.38	0:54.66
200	0:54.93	0:55.21	0:55.48	0:55.76	0:56.04	0:56.31	0:56.59	0:56.86	0:57.14	0:57.42
210	0:57.69	0:57.97	0:58.24	0:58.52	0:58.80	0:59.07	0:59.35	0:59.63	0:59.90	1:00.18
220	1:00.45	1:00.73	1:01.01	1:01.28	1:01.56	1:01.83	1:02.11	1:02.39	1:02.66	1:02.94
230	1:03.21	1:03.49	1:03.77	1:04.04	1:04.32	1:04.59	1:04.87	1:05.15	1:05.42	1:05.70
240	1:05.97	1:06.25	1:06.53	1:06.80	1:07.08	1:07.35	1:07.63	1:07.91	1:08.18	1:08.46
250	1:08.73	1:09.01	1:09.29	1:09.56	1:09.84	1:10.11	1:10.39	1:10.67	1:10.94	1:11.22
260	1:11.49	1:11.77	1:12.05	1:12.32	1:12.60	1:12.87	1:13.15	1:13.43	1:13.70	1:13.98
270	1:14.26	1:14.53	1:14.81	1:15.08	1:15.36	1:15.64	1:15.91	1:16.19	1:16.46	1:16.74
280	1:17.02	1:17.29	1:17.57	1:17.84	1:18.12	1:18.40	1:18.67	1:18.95	1:19.22	1:19.50
290	1:19.78	1:20.05	1:20.33	1:20.60	1:20.88	1:21.16	1:21.43	1:21.71	1:21.98	1:22.26
300	1:22.54	1:22.81	1:23.09	1:23.36	1:23.64	1:23.92	1:24.19	1:24.47	1:24.74	1:25.02
310	1:25.30	1:25.57	1:25.85	1:26.13	1:26.40	1:26.68	1:26.95	1:27.23	1:27.51	1:27.78
320	1:28.06	1:28.33	1:28.61	1:28.89	1:29.16	1:29.44	1:29.71	1:29.99	1:30.27	1:30.54
330	1:30.82	1:31.09	1:31.37	1:31.65	1:31.92	1:32.20	1:32.47	1:32.75	1:33.03	1:33.30
340	1:33.58	1:33.85	1:34.13	1:34.41	1:34.68	1:34.96	1:35.23	1:35.51	1:35.79	1:36.06
350	1:36.34	1:36.61	1:36.89	1:37.17	1:37.44	1:37.72	1:37.99	1:38.27	1:38.55	1:38.82
360	1:39.10	1:39.38	1:39.65	1:39.93	1:40.20	1:40.48	1:40.76	1:41.03	1:41.31	1:41.58
370	1:41.86	1:42.14	1:42.41	1:42.69	1:42.96	1:43.24	1:43.52	1:43.79	1:44.07	1:44.34
380	1:44.62	1:44.90	1:45.17	1:45.45	1:45.72	1:46.00	1:46.28	1:46.55	1:46.83	1:47.10
390	1:47.38	1:47.66	1:47.93	1:48.21	1:48.48	1:48.76	1:49.04	1:49.31	1:49.59	1:49.86
400	1:50.14	1:50.42	1:50.69	1:50.97	1:51.24	1:51.52	1:51.80	1:52.07	1:52.35	1:52.63
410	1:52.90	1:53.18	1:53.45	1:53.73	1:54.01	1:54.28	1:54.56	1:54.83	1:55.11	1:55.39
420	1:55.66	1:55.94	1:56.21	1:56.49	1:56.77	1:57.04	1:57.32	1:57.59	1:57.87	1:58.15
430	1:58.42	1:58.70	1:58.97	1:59.25	1:59.53	1:59.80	2:00.08	2:00.35	2:00.63	2:00.91
440	2:01.18	2:01.46	2:01.73	2:02.01	2:02.29	2:02.56	2:02.84	2:03.11	2:03.39	2:03.67
450	2:03.94	2:04.22	2:04.49	2:04.77	2:05.05	2:05.32	2:05.60	2:05.87	2:06.15	2:06.43
460	2:06.70	2:06.98	2:07.26	2:07.53	2:07.81	2:08.08	2:08.36	2:08.64	2:08.91	2:09.19
470	2:09.46	2:09.74	2:10.02	2:10.29	2:10.57	2:10.84	2:11.12	2:11.40	2:11.67	2:11.95
480	2:12.22	2:12.50	2:12.78	2:13.05	2:13.33	2:13.60	2:13.88	2:14.16	2:14.43	2:14.71
490	2:14.98	2:15.26	2:15.54	2:15.81	2:16.09	2:16.36	2:16.64	2:16.92	2:17.19	2:17.47
500	2:17.74	2:18.02	2:18.30	2:18.57	2:18.85	2:19.12	2:19.40	2:19.68	2:19.95	2:20.23
510	2:20.51	2:20.78	2:21.06	2:21.33	2:21.61	2:21.89	2:22.16	2:22.44	2:22.71	2:22.99
520	2:23.27	2:23.54	2:23.82	2:24.09	2:24.37	2:24.65	2:24.92	2:25.20	2:25.47	2:25.75
530	2:26.03	2:26.30	2:26.58	2:26.85	2:27.13	2:27.41	2:27.68	2:27.96	2:28.23	2:28.51
540	2:28.79	2:29.06	2:29.34	2:29.61	2:29.89	2:30.17	2:30.44	2:30.72	2:30.99	2:31.27
550	2:31.55	2:31.82	2:32.10	2:32.37	2:32.65	2:32.93	2:33.20	2:33.48	2:33.76	2:34.03
560	2:34.31	2:34.58	2:34.86	2:35.14	2:35.41	2:35.69	2:35.96	2:36.24	2:36.52	2:36.79
570	2:37.07	2:37.34	2:37.62	2:37.90	2:38.17	2:38.45	2:38.72	2:39.00	2:39.28	2:39.55
580	2:39.83	2:40.10	2:40.38	2:40.66	2:40.93	2:41.21	2:41.48	2:41.76	2:42.04	2:42.31
590	2:42.59	2:42.86	2:43.14	2:43.42	2:43.69	2:43.97	2:44.24	2:44.52	2:44.80	2:45.07

♩. = 0.41; ♩ = 0.28; ♪. = 0.21; (triplet ♩ 𝄾) = 0.18; ♪ = 0.14; (triplet ♪ 𝄾 𝄾) = 0.09; 𝅘𝅥𝅯 = 0.07 seconds

CLICK: 6 6/8 FRAMES; M.M.: 213.33

Click	0	1	2	3	4	5	6	7	8	9
000	0:00.00	0:00.00	0:00.28	0:00.56	0:00.84	0:01.13	0:01.41	0:01.69	0:01.97	0:02.25
010	0:02.53	0:02.81	0:03.09	0:03.38	0:03.66	0:03.94	0:04.22	0:04.50	0:04.78	0:05.06
020	0:05.34	0:05.63	0:05.91	0:06.19	0:06.47	0:06.75	0:07.03	0:07.31	0:07.59	0:07.88
030	0:08.16	0:08.44	0:08.72	0:09.00	0:09.28	0:09.56	0:09.84	0:10.13	0:10.41	0:10.69
040	0:10.97	0:11.25	0:11.53	0:11.81	0:12.09	0:12.38	0:12.66	0:12.94	0:13.22	0:13.50
050	0:13.78	0:14.06	0:14.34	0:14.63	0:14.91	0:15.19	0:15.47	0:15.75	0:16.03	0:16.31
060	0:16.59	0:16.88	0:17.16	0:17.44	0:17.72	0:18.00	0:18.28	0:18.56	0:18.84	0:19.13
070	0:19.41	0:19.69	0:19.97	0:20.25	0:20.53	0:20.81	0:21.09	0:21.38	0:21.66	0:21.94
080	0:22.22	0:22.50	0:22.78	0:23.06	0:23.34	0:23.63	0:23.91	0:24.19	0:24.47	0:24.75
090	0:25.03	0:25.31	0:25.59	0:25.88	0:26.16	0:26.44	0:26.72	0:27.00	0:27.28	0:27.56
100	0:27.84	0:28.13	0:28.41	0:28.69	0:28.97	0:29.25	0:29.53	0:29.81	0:30.09	0:30.38
110	0:30.66	0:30.94	0:31.22	0:31.50	0:31.78	0:32.06	0:32.34	0:32.63	0:32.91	0:33.19
120	0:33.47	0:33.75	0:34.03	0:34.31	0:34.59	0:34.88	0:35.16	0:35.44	0:35.72	0:36.00
130	0:36.28	0:36.56	0:36.84	0:37.13	0:37.41	0:37.69	0:37.97	0:38.25	0:38.53	0:38.81
140	0:39.09	0:39.38	0:39.66	0:39.94	0:40.22	0:40.50	0:40.78	0:41.06	0:41.34	0:41.63
150	0:41.91	0:42.19	0:42.47	0:42.75	0:43.03	0:43.31	0:43.59	0:43.88	0:44.16	0:44.44
160	0:44.72	0:45.00	0:45.28	0:45.56	0:45.84	0:46.13	0:46.41	0:46.69	0:46.97	0:47.25
170	0:47.53	0:47.81	0:48.09	0:48.38	0:48.66	0:48.94	0:49.22	0:49.50	0:49.78	0:50.06
180	0:50.34	0:50.63	0:50.91	0:51.19	0:51.47	0:51.75	0:52.03	0:52.31	0:52.59	0:52.88
190	0:53.16	0:53.44	0:53.72	0:54.00	0:54.28	0:54.56	0:54.84	0:55.13	0:55.41	0:55.69
200	0:55.97	0:56.25	0:56.53	0:56.81	0:57.09	0:57.38	0:57.66	0:57.94	0:58.22	0:58.50
210	0:58.78	0:59.06	0:59.34	0:59.63	0:59.91	1:00.19	1:00.47	1:00.75	1:01.03	1:01.31
220	1:01.59	1:01.88	1:02.16	1:02.44	1:02.72	1:03.00	1:03.28	1:03.56	1:03.84	1:04.13
230	1:04.41	1:04.69	1:04.97	1:05.25	1:05.53	1:05.81	1:06.09	1:06.38	1:06.66	1:06.94
240	1:07.22	1:07.50	1:07.78	1:08.06	1:08.34	1:08.63	1:08.91	1:09.19	1:09.47	1:09.75
250	1:10.03	1:10.31	1:10.59	1:10.88	1:11.16	1:11.44	1:11.72	1:12.00	1:12.28	1:12.56
260	1:12.84	1:13.13	1:13.41	1:13.69	1:13.97	1:14.25	1:14.53	1:14.81	1:15.09	1:15.38
270	1:15.66	1:15.94	1:16.22	1:16.50	1:16.78	1:17.06	1:17.34	1:17.63	1:17.91	1:18.19
280	1:18.47	1:18.75	1:19.03	1:19.31	1:19.59	1:19.88	1:20.16	1:20.44	1:20.72	1:21.00
290	1:21.28	1:21.56	1:21.84	1:22.13	1:22.41	1:22.69	1:22.97	1:23.25	1:23.53	1:23.81
300	1:24.09	1:24.38	1:24.66	1:24.94	1:25.22	1:25.50	1:25.78	1:26.06	1:26.34	1:26.63
310	1:26.91	1:27.19	1:27.47	1:27.75	1:28.03	1:28.31	1:28.59	1:28.88	1:29.16	1:29.44
320	1:29.72	1:30.00	1:30.28	1:30.56	1:30.84	1:31.13	1:31.41	1:31.69	1:31.97	1:32.25
330	1:32.53	1:32.81	1:33.09	1:33.38	1:33.66	1:33.94	1:34.22	1:34.50	1:34.78	1:35.06
340	1:35.34	1:35.63	1:35.91	1:36.19	1:36.47	1:36.75	1:37.03	1:37.31	1:37.59	1:37.88
350	1:38.16	1:38.44	1:38.72	1:39.00	1:39.28	1:39.56	1:39.84	1:40.13	1:40.41	1:40.69
360	1:40.97	1:41.25	1:41.53	1:41.81	1:42.09	1:42.38	1:42.66	1:42.94	1:43.22	1:43.50
370	1:43.78	1:44.06	1:44.34	1:44.63	1:44.91	1:45.19	1:45.47	1:45.75	1:46.03	1:46.31
380	1:46.59	1:46.88	1:47.16	1:47.44	1:47.72	1:48.00	1:48.28	1:48.56	1:48.84	1:49.13
390	1:49.41	1:49.69	1:49.97	1:50.25	1:50.53	1:50.81	1:51.09	1:51.38	1:51.66	1:51.94
400	1:52.22	1:52.50	1:52.78	1:53.06	1:53.34	1:53.63	1:53.91	1:54.19	1:54.47	1:54.75
410	1:55.03	1:55.31	1:55.59	1:55.88	1:56.16	1:56.44	1:56.72	1:57.00	1:57.28	1:57.56
420	1:57.84	1:58.13	1:58.41	1:58.69	1:58.97	1:59.25	1:59.53	1:59.81	2:00.09	2:00.38
430	2:00.66	2:00.94	2:01.22	2:01.50	2:01.78	2:02.06	2:02.34	2:02.63	2:02.91	2:03.19
440	2:03.47	2:03.75	2:04.03	2:04.31	2:04.59	2:04.88	2:05.16	2:05.44	2:05.72	2:06.00
450	2:06.28	2:06.56	2:06.84	2:07.13	2:07.41	2:07.69	2:07.97	2:08.25	2:08.53	2:08.81
460	2:09.09	2:09.38	2:09.66	2:09.94	2:10.22	2:10.50	2:10.78	2:11.06	2:11.34	2:11.63
470	2:11.91	2:12.19	2:12.47	2:12.75	2:13.03	2:13.31	2:13.59	2:13.88	2:14.16	2:14.44
480	2:14.72	2:15.00	2:15.28	2:15.56	2:15.84	2:16.13	2:16.41	2:16.69	2:16.97	2:17.25
490	2:17.53	2:17.81	2:18.09	2:18.38	2:18.66	2:18.94	2:19.22	2:19.50	2:19.78	2:20.06
500	2:20.34	2:20.63	2:20.91	2:21.19	2:21.47	2:21.75	2:22.03	2:22.31	2:22.59	2:22.88
510	2:23.16	2:23.44	2:23.72	2:24.00	2:24.28	2:24.56	2:24.84	2:25.13	2:25.41	2:25.69
520	2:25.97	2:26.25	2:26.53	2:26.81	2:27.09	2:27.38	2:27.66	2:27.94	2:28.22	2:28.50
530	2:28.78	2:29.06	2:29.34	2:29.63	2:29.91	2:30.19	2:30.47	2:30.75	2:31.03	2:31.31
540	2:31.59	2:31.88	2:32.16	2:32.44	2:32.72	2:33.00	2:33.28	2:33.56	2:33.84	2:34.13
550	2:34.41	2:34.69	2:34.97	2:35.25	2:35.53	2:35.81	2:36.09	2:36.38	2:36.66	2:36.94
560	2:37.22	2:37.50	2:37.78	2:38.06	2:38.34	2:38.63	2:38.91	2:39.19	2:39.47	2:39.75
570	2:40.03	2:40.31	2:40.59	2:40.88	2:41.16	2:41.44	2:41.72	2:42.00	2:42.28	2:42.56
580	2:42.84	2:43.13	2:43.41	2:43.69	2:43.97	2:44.25	2:44.53	2:44.81	2:45.09	2:45.38
590	2:45.66	2:45.94	2:46.22	2:46.50	2:46.78	2:47.06	2:47.34	2:47.63	2:47.91	2:48.19

♩. = 0.42; ♩ = 0.28; ♪. = 0.21; (triplet ♩ 𝄾) = 0.19; ♪ = 0.14; (triplet ♪ 𝄾 𝄾) = 0.09; 𝅘𝅥𝅯 = 0.07 seconds

CLICK: 6⅞ FRAMES; M.M.: 209.45

Click	0	1	2	3	4	5	6	7	8	9
000	0:00.00	0:00.00	0:00.29	0:00.57	0:00.86	0:01.15	0:01.43	0:01.72	0:02.01	0:02.29
010	0:02.58	0:02.86	0:03.15	0:03.44	0:03.72	0:04.01	0:04.30	0:04.58	0:04.87	0:05.16
020	0:05.44	0:05.73	0:06.02	0:06.30	0:06.59	0:06.88	0:07.16	0:07.45	0:07.73	0:08.02
030	0:08.31	0:08.59	0:08.88	0:09.17	0:09.45	0:09.74	0:10.03	0:10.31	0:10.60	0:10.89
040	0:11.17	0:11.46	0:11.74	0:12.03	0:12.32	0:12.60	0:12.89	0:13.18	0:13.46	0:13.75
050	0:14.04	0:14.32	0:14.61	0:14.90	0:15.18	0:15.47	0:15.76	0:16.04	0:16.33	0:16.61
060	0:16.90	0:17.19	0:17.47	0:17.76	0:18.05	0:18.33	0:18.62	0:18.91	0:19.19	0:19.48
070	0:19.77	0:20.05	0:20.34	0:20.63	0:20.91	0:21.20	0:21.48	0:21.77	0:22.06	0:22.34
080	0:22.63	0:22.92	0:23.20	0:23.49	0:23.78	0:24.06	0:24.35	0:24.64	0:24.92	0:25.21
090	0:25.49	0:25.78	0:26.07	0:26.35	0:26.64	0:26.93	0:27.21	0:27.50	0:27.79	0:28.07
100	0:28.36	0:28.65	0:28.93	0:29.22	0:29.51	0:29.79	0:30.08	0:30.36	0:30.65	0:30.94
110	0:31.22	0:31.51	0:31.80	0:32.08	0:32.37	0:32.66	0:32.94	0:33.23	0:33.52	0:33.80
120	0:34.09	0:34.38	0:34.66	0:34.95	0:35.23	0:35.52	0:35.81	0:36.09	0:36.38	0:36.67
130	0:36.95	0:37.24	0:37.53	0:37.81	0:38.10	0:38.39	0:38.67	0:38.96	0:39.24	0:39.53
140	0:39.82	0:40.10	0:40.39	0:40.68	0:40.96	0:41.25	0:41.54	0:41.82	0:42.11	0:42.40
150	0:42.68	0:42.97	0:43.26	0:43.54	0:43.83	0:44.11	0:44.40	0:44.69	0:44.97	0:45.26
160	0:45.55	0:45.83	0:46.12	0:46.41	0:46.69	0:46.98	0:47.27	0:47.55	0:47.84	0:48.13
170	0:48.41	0:48.70	0:48.98	0:49.27	0:49.56	0:49.84	0:50.13	0:50.42	0:50.70	0:50.99
180	0:51.28	0:51.56	0:51.85	0:52.14	0:52.42	0:52.71	0:52.99	0:53.28	0:53.57	0:53.85
190	0:54.14	0:54.43	0:54.71	0:55.00	0:55.29	0:55.57	0:55.86	0:56.15	0:56.43	0:56.72
200	0:57.01	0:57.29	0:57.58	0:57.86	0:58.15	0:58.44	0:58.72	0:59.01	0:59.30	0:59.58
210	0:59.87	1:00.16	1:00.44	1:00.73	1:01.02	1:01.30	1:01.59	1:01.88	1:02.16	1:02.45
220	1:02.73	1:03.02	1:03.31	1:03.59	1:03.88	1:04.17	1:04.45	1:04.74	1:05.03	1:05.31
230	1:05.60	1:05.89	1:06.17	1:06.46	1:06.74	1:07.03	1:07.32	1:07.60	1:07.89	1:08.18
240	1:08.46	1:08.75	1:09.04	1:09.32	1:09.61	1:09.90	1:10.18	1:10.47	1:10.76	1:11.04
250	1:11.33	1:11.61	1:11.90	1:12.19	1:12.47	1:12.76	1:13.05	1:13.33	1:13.62	1:13.91
260	1:14.19	1:14.48	1:14.77	1:15.05	1:15.34	1:15.62	1:15.91	1:16.20	1:16.48	1:16.77
270	1:17.06	1:17.34	1:17.63	1:17.92	1:18.20	1:18.49	1:18.78	1:19.06	1:19.35	1:19.64
280	1:19.92	1:20.21	1:20.49	1:20.78	1:21.07	1:21.35	1:21.64	1:21.93	1:22.21	1:22.50
290	1:22.79	1:23.07	1:23.36	1:23.65	1:23.93	1:24.22	1:24.51	1:24.79	1:25.08	1:25.36
300	1:25.65	1:25.94	1:26.22	1:26.51	1:26.80	1:27.08	1:27.37	1:27.66	1:27.94	1:28.23
310	1:28.52	1:28.80	1:29.09	1:29.38	1:29.66	1:29.95	1:30.23	1:30.52	1:30.81	1:31.09
320	1:31.38	1:31.67	1:31.95	1:32.24	1:32.53	1:32.81	1:33.10	1:33.39	1:33.67	1:33.96
330	1:34.24	1:34.53	1:34.82	1:35.10	1:35.39	1:35.68	1:35.96	1:36.25	1:36.54	1:36.82
340	1:37.11	1:37.40	1:37.68	1:37.97	1:38.26	1:38.54	1:38.83	1:39.11	1:39.40	1:39.69
350	1:39.97	1:40.26	1:40.55	1:40.83	1:41.12	1:41.41	1:41.69	1:41.98	1:42.27	1:42.55
360	1:42.84	1:43.13	1:43.41	1:43.70	1:43.98	1:44.27	1:44.56	1:44.84	1:45.13	1:45.42
370	1:45.70	1:45.99	1:46.28	1:46.56	1:46.85	1:47.14	1:47.42	1:47.71	1:47.99	1:48.28
380	1:48.57	1:48.85	1:49.14	1:49.43	1:49.71	1:50.00	1:50.29	1:50.57	1:50.86	1:51.15
390	1:51.43	1:51.72	1:52.01	1:52.29	1:52.58	1:52.86	1:53.15	1:53.44	1:53.72	1:54.01
400	1:54.30	1:54.58	1:54.87	1:55.16	1:55.44	1:55.73	1:56.02	1:56.30	1:56.59	1:56.87
410	1:57.16	1:57.45	1:57.73	1:58.02	1:58.31	1:58.59	1:58.88	1:59.17	1:59.45	1:59.74
420	2:00.03	2:00.31	2:00.60	2:00.89	2:01.17	2:01.46	2:01.74	2:02.03	2:02.32	2:02.60
430	2:02.89	2:03.18	2:03.46	2:03.75	2:04.04	2:04.32	2:04.61	2:04.90	2:05.18	2:05.47
440	2:05.76	2:06.04	2:06.33	2:06.61	2:06.90	2:07.19	2:07.47	2:07.76	2:08.05	2:08.33
450	2:08.62	2:08.91	2:09.19	2:09.48	2:09.77	2:10.05	2:10.34	2:10.62	2:10.91	2:11.20
460	2:11.48	2:11.77	2:12.06	2:12.34	2:12.63	2:12.92	2:13.20	2:13.49	2:13.78	2:14.06
470	2:14.35	2:14.64	2:14.92	2:15.21	2:15.49	2:15.78	2:16.07	2:16.35	2:16.64	2:16.93
480	2:17.21	2:17.50	2:17.79	2:18.07	2:18.36	2:18.65	2:18.93	2:19.22	2:19.51	2:19.79
490	2:20.08	2:20.36	2:20.65	2:20.94	2:21.22	2:21.51	2:21.80	2:22.08	2:22.37	2:22.66
500	2:22.94	2:23.23	2:23.52	2:23.80	2:24.09	2:24.38	2:24.66	2:24.95	2:25.23	2:25.52
510	2:25.81	2:26.09	2:26.38	2:26.67	2:26.95	2:27.24	2:27.53	2:27.81	2:28.10	2:28.39
520	2:28.67	2:28.96	2:29.24	2:29.53	2:29.82	2:30.10	2:30.39	2:30.68	2:30.96	2:31.25
530	2:31.54	2:31.82	2:32.11	2:32.40	2:32.68	2:32.97	2:33.26	2:33.54	2:33.83	2:34.11
540	2:34.40	2:34.69	2:34.97	2:35.26	2:35.55	2:35.83	2:36.12	2:36.41	2:36.69	2:36.98
550	2:37.27	2:37.55	2:37.84	2:38.13	2:38.41	2:38.70	2:38.98	2:39.27	2:39.56	2:39.84
560	2:40.13	2:40.42	2:40.70	2:40.99	2:41.28	2:41.56	2:41.85	2:42.14	2:42.42	2:42.71
570	2:42.99	2:43.28	2:43.57	2:43.85	2:44.14	2:44.43	2:44.71	2:45.00	2:45.29	2:45.57
580	2:45.86	2:46.15	2:46.43	2:46.72	2:47.01	2:47.29	2:47.58	2:47.86	2:48.15	2:48.44
590	2:48.72	2:49.01	2:49.30	2:49.58	2:49.87	2:50.16	2:50.44	2:50.73	2:51.02	2:51.30

♩. = 0.43; ♩ = 0.29; ♪. = 0.21; (3) ♩ 𝄾 = 0.19; ♪ = 0.14; (3) ♪ 𝄾 𝄾 = 0.10; 𝅘𝅥𝅯 = 0.07 seconds

CLICK: 7 0/8 FRAMES; M.M.: 205.71

Click	0	1	2	3	4	5	6	7	8	9
000	0:00.00	0:00.00	0:00.29	0:00.58	0:00.87	0:01.17	0:01.46	0:01.75	0:02.04	0:02.33
010	0:02.63	0:02.92	0:03.21	0:03.50	0:03.79	0:04.08	0:04.38	0:04.67	0:04.96	0:05.25
020	0:05.54	0:05.83	0:06.12	0:06.42	0:06.71	0:07.00	0:07.29	0:07.58	0:07.87	0:08.17
030	0:08.46	0:08.75	0:09.04	0:09.33	0:09.63	0:09.92	0:10.21	0:10.50	0:10.79	0:11.08
040	0:11.37	0:11.67	0:11.96	0:12.25	0:12.54	0:12.83	0:13.12	0:13.42	0:13.71	0:14.00
050	0:14.29	0:14.58	0:14.87	0:15.17	0:15.46	0:15.75	0:16.04	0:16.33	0:16.62	0:16.92
060	0:17.21	0:17.50	0:17.79	0:18.08	0:18.37	0:18.67	0:18.96	0:19.25	0:19.54	0:19.83
070	0:20.12	0:20.42	0:20.71	0:21.00	0:21.29	0:21.58	0:21.87	0:22.17	0:22.46	0:22.75
080	0:23.04	0:23.33	0:23.62	0:23.92	0:24.21	0:24.50	0:24.79	0:25.08	0:25.38	0:25.67
090	0:25.96	0:26.25	0:26.54	0:26.83	0:27.13	0:27.42	0:27.71	0:28.00	0:28.29	0:28.58
100	0:28.87	0:29.17	0:29.46	0:29.75	0:30.04	0:30.33	0:30.62	0:30.92	0:31.21	0:31.50
110	0:31.79	0:32.08	0:32.38	0:32.67	0:32.96	0:33.25	0:33.54	0:33.83	0:34.12	0:34.42
120	0:34.71	0:35.00	0:35.29	0:35.58	0:35.87	0:36.17	0:36.46	0:36.75	0:37.04	0:37.33
130	0:37.63	0:37.92	0:38.21	0:38.50	0:38.79	0:39.08	0:39.37	0:39.67	0:39.96	0:40.25
140	0:40.54	0:40.83	0:41.13	0:41.42	0:41.71	0:42.00	0:42.29	0:42.58	0:42.87	0:43.17
150	0:43.46	0:43.75	0:44.04	0:44.33	0:44.63	0:44.92	0:45.21	0:45.50	0:45.79	0:46.08
160	0:46.37	0:46.67	0:46.96	0:47.25	0:47.54	0:47.83	0:48.13	0:48.42	0:48.71	0:49.00
170	0:49.29	0:49.58	0:49.87	0:50.17	0:50.46	0:50.75	0:51.04	0:51.33	0:51.62	0:51.92
180	0:52.21	0:52.50	0:52.79	0:53.08	0:53.37	0:53.67	0:53.96	0:54.25	0:54.54	0:54.83
190	0:55.12	0:55.42	0:55.71	0:56.00	0:56.29	0:56.58	0:56.87	0:57.17	0:57.46	0:57.75
200	0:58.04	0:58.33	0:58.62	0:58.92	0:59.21	0:59.50	0:59.79	1:00.08	1:00.37	1:00.67
210	1:00.96	1:01.25	1:01.54	1:01.83	1:02.12	1:02.42	1:02.71	1:03.00	1:03.29	1:03.58
220	1:03.87	1:04.17	1:04.46	1:04.75	1:05.04	1:05.33	1:05.62	1:05.92	1:06.21	1:06.50
230	1:06.79	1:07.08	1:07.37	1:07.67	1:07.96	1:08.25	1:08.54	1:08.83	1:09.12	1:09.42
240	1:09.71	1:10.00	1:10.29	1:10.58	1:10.87	1:11.17	1:11.46	1:11.75	1:12.04	1:12.33
250	1:12.62	1:12.92	1:13.21	1:13.50	1:13.79	1:14.08	1:14.37	1:14.67	1:14.96	1:15.25
260	1:15.54	1:15.83	1:16.12	1:16.42	1:16.71	1:17.00	1:17.29	1:17.58	1:17.87	1:18.17
270	1:18.46	1:18.75	1:19.04	1:19.33	1:19.62	1:19.92	1:20.21	1:20.50	1:20.79	1:21.08
280	1:21.37	1:21.67	1:21.96	1:22.25	1:22.54	1:22.83	1:23.12	1:23.42	1:23.71	1:24.00
290	1:24.29	1:24.58	1:24.87	1:25.17	1:25.46	1:25.75	1:26.04	1:26.33	1:26.62	1:26.92
300	1:27.21	1:27.50	1:27.79	1:28.08	1:28.37	1:28.67	1:28.96	1:29.25	1:29.54	1:29.83
310	1:30.12	1:30.42	1:30.71	1:31.00	1:31.29	1:31.58	1:31.87	1:32.17	1:32.46	1:32.75
320	1:33.04	1:33.33	1:33.62	1:33.92	1:34.21	1:34.50	1:34.79	1:35.08	1:35.37	1:35.67
330	1:35.96	1:36.25	1:36.54	1:36.83	1:37.12	1:37.42	1:37.71	1:38.00	1:38.29	1:38.58
340	1:38.87	1:39.17	1:39.46	1:39.75	1:40.04	1:40.33	1:40.62	1:40.92	1:41.21	1:41.50
350	1:41.79	1:42.08	1:42.37	1:42.67	1:42.96	1:43.25	1:43.54	1:43.83	1:44.12	1:44.42
360	1:44.71	1:45.00	1:45.29	1:45.58	1:45.87	1:46.17	1:46.46	1:46.75	1:47.04	1:47.33
370	1:47.62	1:47.92	1:48.21	1:48.50	1:48.79	1:49.08	1:49.37	1:49.67	1:49.96	1:50.25
380	1:50.54	1:50.83	1:51.12	1:51.42	1:51.71	1:52.00	1:52.29	1:52.58	1:52.87	1:53.17
390	1:53.46	1:53.75	1:54.04	1:54.33	1:54.62	1:54.92	1:55.21	1:55.50	1:55.79	1:56.08
400	1:56.37	1:56.67	1:56.96	1:57.25	1:57.54	1:57.83	1:58.12	1:58.42	1:58.71	1:59.00
410	1:59.29	1:59.58	1:59.87	2:00.17	2:00.46	2:00.75	2:01.04	2:01.33	2:01.62	2:01.92
420	2:02.21	2:02.50	2:02.79	2:03.08	2:03.37	2:03.67	2:03.96	2:04.25	2:04.54	2:04.83
430	2:05.12	2:05.42	2:05.71	2:06.00	2:06.29	2:06.58	2:06.87	2:07.17	2:07.46	2:07.75
440	2:08.04	2:08.33	2:08.62	2:08.92	2:09.21	2:09.50	2:09.79	2:10.08	2:10.37	2:10.67
450	2:10.96	2:11.25	2:11.54	2:11.83	2:12.12	2:12.42	2:12.71	2:13.00	2:13.29	2:13.58
460	2:13.87	2:14.17	2:14.46	2:14.75	2:15.04	2:15.33	2:15.62	2:15.92	2:16.21	2:16.50
470	2:16.79	2:17.08	2:17.37	2:17.67	2:17.96	2:18.25	2:18.54	2:18.83	2:19.12	2:19.42
480	2:19.71	2:20.00	2:20.29	2:20.58	2:20.87	2:21.17	2:21.46	2:21.75	2:22.04	2:22.33
490	2:22.62	2:22.92	2:23.21	2:23.50	2:23.79	2:24.08	2:24.37	2:24.67	2:24.96	2:25.25
500	2:25.54	2:25.83	2:26.12	2:26.42	2:26.71	2:27.00	2:27.29	2:27.58	2:27.87	2:28.17
510	2:28.46	2:28.75	2:29.04	2:29.33	2:29.62	2:29.92	2:30.21	2:30.50	2:30.79	2:31.08
520	2:31.37	2:31.67	2:31.96	2:32.25	2:32.54	2:32.83	2:33.12	2:33.42	2:33.71	2:34.00
530	2:34.29	2:34.58	2:34.87	2:35.17	2:35.46	2:35.75	2:36.04	2:36.33	2:36.62	2:36.92
540	2:37.21	2:37.50	2:37.79	2:38.08	2:38.37	2:38.67	2:38.96	2:39.25	2:39.54	2:39.83
550	2:40.12	2:40.42	2:40.71	2:41.00	2:41.29	2:41.58	2:41.87	2:42.17	2:42.46	2:42.75
560	2:43.04	2:43.33	2:43.62	2:43.92	2:44.21	2:44.50	2:44.79	2:45.08	2:45.37	2:45.67
570	2:45.96	2:46.25	2:46.54	2:46.83	2:47.12	2:47.42	2:47.71	2:48.00	2:48.29	2:48.58
580	2:48.87	2:49.17	2:49.46	2:49.75	2:50.04	2:50.33	2:50.62	2:50.92	2:51.21	2:51.50
590	2:51.79	2:52.08	2:52.37	2:52.67	2:52.96	2:53.25	2:53.54	2:53.83	2:54.12	2:54.42

♩. = 0.44; ♩ = 0.29; ♪. = 0.22; (triplet ♩ 𝄾) = 0.19; ♪ = 0.15; (triplet ♪ 𝄾 𝄾) = 0.10; 𝅘𝅥𝅯 = 0.07 seconds

CLICK: 7⅛ FRAMES; M.M.: 202.11

Click	0	1	2	3	4	5	6	7	8	9
000	0:00.00	0:00.00	0:00.30	0:00.59	0:00.89	0:01.19	0:01.48	0:01.78	0:02.08	0:02.38
010	0:02.67	0:02.97	0:03.27	0:03.56	0:03.86	0:04.16	0:04.45	0:04.75	0:05.05	0:05.34
020	0:05.64	0:05.94	0:06.23	0:06.53	0:06.83	0:07.13	0:07.42	0:07.72	0:08.02	0:08.31
030	0:08.61	0:08.91	0:09.20	0:09.50	0:09.80	0:10.09	0:10.39	0:10.69	0:10.98	0:11.28
040	0:11.58	0:11.88	0:12.17	0:12.47	0:12.77	0:13.06	0:13.36	0:13.66	0:13.95	0:14.25
050	0:14.55	0:14.84	0:15.14	0:15.44	0:15.73	0:16.03	0:16.33	0:16.63	0:16.92	0:17.22
060	0:17.52	0:17.81	0:18.11	0:18.41	0:18.70	0:19.00	0:19.30	0:19.59	0:19.89	0:20.19
070	0:20.48	0:20.78	0:21.08	0:21.38	0:21.67	0:21.97	0:22.27	0:22.56	0:22.86	0:23.16
080	0:23.45	0:23.75	0:24.05	0:24.34	0:24.64	0:24.94	0:25.23	0:25.53	0:25.83	0:26.13
090	0:26.42	0:26.72	0:27.02	0:27.31	0:27.61	0:27.91	0:28.20	0:28.50	0:28.80	0:29.09
100	0:29.39	0:29.69	0:29.98	0:30.28	0:30.58	0:30.88	0:31.17	0:31.47	0:31.77	0:32.06
110	0:32.36	0:32.66	0:32.95	0:33.25	0:33.55	0:33.84	0:34.14	0:34.44	0:34.73	0:35.03
120	0:35.33	0:35.63	0:35.92	0:36.22	0:36.52	0:36.81	0:37.11	0:37.41	0:37.70	0:38.00
130	0:38.30	0:38.59	0:38.89	0:39.19	0:39.48	0:39.78	0:40.08	0:40.38	0:40.67	0:40.97
140	0:41.27	0:41.56	0:41.86	0:42.16	0:42.45	0:42.75	0:43.05	0:43.34	0:43.64	0:43.94
150	0:44.23	0:44.53	0:44.83	0:45.13	0:45.42	0:45.72	0:46.02	0:46.31	0:46.61	0:46.91
160	0:47.20	0:47.50	0:47.80	0:48.09	0:48.39	0:48.69	0:48.98	0:49.28	0:49.58	0:49.88
170	0:50.17	0:50.47	0:50.77	0:51.06	0:51.36	0:51.66	0:51.95	0:52.25	0:52.55	0:52.84
180	0:53.14	0:53.44	0:53.73	0:54.03	0:54.33	0:54.63	0:54.92	0:55.22	0:55.52	0:55.81
190	0:56.11	0:56.41	0:56.70	0:57.00	0:57.30	0:57.59	0:57.89	0:58.19	0:58.48	0:58.78
200	0:59.08	0:59.38	0:59.67	0:59.97	1:00.27	1:00.56	1:00.86	1:01.16	1:01.45	1:01.75
210	1:02.05	1:02.34	1:02.64	1:02.94	1:03.23	1:03.53	1:03.83	1:04.13	1:04.42	1:04.72
220	1:05.02	1:05.31	1:05.61	1:05.91	1:06.20	1:06.50	1:06.80	1:07.09	1:07.39	1:07.69
230	1:07.98	1:08.28	1:08.58	1:08.88	1:09.17	1:09.47	1:09.77	1:10.06	1:10.36	1:10.66
240	1:10.95	1:11.25	1:11.55	1:11.84	1:12.14	1:12.44	1:12.73	1:13.03	1:13.33	1:13.63
250	1:13.92	1:14.22	1:14.52	1:14.81	1:15.11	1:15.41	1:15.70	1:16.00	1:16.30	1:16.59
260	1:16.89	1:17.19	1:17.48	1:17.78	1:18.08	1:18.37	1:18.67	1:18.97	1:19.27	1:19.56
270	1:19.86	1:20.16	1:20.45	1:20.75	1:21.05	1:21.34	1:21.64	1:21.94	1:22.23	1:22.53
280	1:22.83	1:23.12	1:23.42	1:23.72	1:24.02	1:24.31	1:24.61	1:24.91	1:25.20	1:25.50
290	1:25.80	1:26.09	1:26.39	1:26.69	1:26.98	1:27.28	1:27.58	1:27.87	1:28.17	1:28.47
300	1:28.77	1:29.06	1:29.36	1:29.66	1:29.95	1:30.25	1:30.55	1:30.84	1:31.14	1:31.44
310	1:31.73	1:32.03	1:32.33	1:32.62	1:32.92	1:33.22	1:33.52	1:33.81	1:34.11	1:34.41
320	1:34.70	1:35.00	1:35.30	1:35.59	1:35.89	1:36.19	1:36.48	1:36.78	1:37.08	1:37.38
330	1:37.67	1:37.97	1:38.27	1:38.56	1:38.86	1:39.16	1:39.45	1:39.75	1:40.05	1:40.34
340	1:40.64	1:40.94	1:41.23	1:41.53	1:41.83	1:42.13	1:42.42	1:42.72	1:43.02	1:43.31
350	1:43.61	1:43.91	1:44.20	1:44.50	1:44.80	1:45.09	1:45.39	1:45.69	1:45.98	1:46.28
360	1:46.58	1:46.88	1:47.17	1:47.47	1:47.77	1:48.06	1:48.36	1:48.66	1:48.95	1:49.25
370	1:49.55	1:49.84	1:50.14	1:50.44	1:50.73	1:51.03	1:51.33	1:51.63	1:51.92	1:52.22
380	1:52.52	1:52.81	1:53.11	1:53.41	1:53.70	1:54.00	1:54.30	1:54.59	1:54.89	1:55.19
390	1:55.48	1:55.78	1:56.08	1:56.38	1:56.67	1:56.97	1:57.27	1:57.56	1:57.86	1:58.16
400	1:58.45	1:58.75	1:59.05	1:59.34	1:59.64	1:59.94	2:00.23	2:00.53	2:00.83	2:01.12
410	2:01.42	2:01.72	2:02.02	2:02.31	2:02.61	2:02.91	2:03.20	2:03.50	2:03.80	2:04.09
420	2:04.39	2:04.69	2:04.98	2:05.28	2:05.58	2:05.87	2:06.17	2:06.47	2:06.77	2:07.06
430	2:07.36	2:07.66	2:07.95	2:08.25	2:08.55	2:08.84	2:09.14	2:09.44	2:09.73	2:10.03
440	2:10.33	2:10.62	2:10.92	2:11.22	2:11.52	2:11.81	2:12.11	2:12.41	2:12.70	2:13.00
450	2:13.30	2:13.59	2:13.89	2:14.19	2:14.48	2:14.78	2:15.08	2:15.37	2:15.67	2:15.97
460	2:16.27	2:16.56	2:16.86	2:17.16	2:17.45	2:17.75	2:18.05	2:18.34	2:18.64	2:18.94
470	2:19.23	2:19.53	2:19.83	2:20.12	2:20.42	2:20.72	2:21.02	2:21.31	2:21.61	2:21.91
480	2:22.20	2:22.50	2:22.80	2:23.09	2:23.39	2:23.69	2:23.98	2:24.28	2:24.58	2:24.87
490	2:25.17	2:25.47	2:25.77	2:26.06	2:26.36	2:26.66	2:26.95	2:27.25	2:27.55	2:27.84
500	2:28.14	2:28.44	2:28.73	2:29.03	2:29.33	2:29.62	2:29.92	2:30.22	2:30.52	2:30.81
510	2:31.11	2:31.41	2:31.70	2:32.00	2:32.30	2:32.59	2:32.89	2:33.19	2:33.48	2:33.78
520	2:34.08	2:34.38	2:34.67	2:34.97	2:35.27	2:35.56	2:35.86	2:36.16	2:36.45	2:36.75
530	2:37.05	2:37.34	2:37.64	2:37.94	2:38.23	2:38.53	2:38.83	2:39.13	2:39.42	2:39.72
540	2:40.02	2:40.31	2:40.61	2:40.91	2:41.20	2:41.50	2:41.80	2:42.09	2:42.39	2:42.69
550	2:42.98	2:43.28	2:43.58	2:43.88	2:44.17	2:44.47	2:44.77	2:45.06	2:45.36	2:45.66
560	2:45.95	2:46.25	2:46.55	2:46.84	2:47.14	2:47.44	2:47.73	2:48.03	2:48.33	2:48.63
570	2:48.92	2:49.22	2:49.52	2:49.81	2:50.11	2:50.41	2:50.70	2:51.00	2:51.30	2:51.59
580	2:51.89	2:52.19	2:52.48	2:52.78	2:53.08	2:53.38	2:53.67	2:53.97	2:54.27	2:54.56
590	2:54.86	2:55.16	2:55.45	2:55.75	2:56.05	2:56.34	2:56.64	2:56.94	2:57.23	2:57.53

♩. = 0.45; ♩ = 0.30; ♪. = 0.22; (3) ♩ 𝄾 = 0.20; ♪ = 0.15; (3) ♪ 𝄾 𝄾 = 0.10; 𝅘𝅥𝅯 = 0.07 seconds

CLICK: 7 2/8 FRAMES; M.M.: 198.62

Click	0	1	2	3	4	5	6	7	8	9
000	0:00.00	0:00.00	0:00.30	0:00.60	0:00.91	0:01.21	0:01.51	0:01.81	0:02.11	0:02.42
010	0:02.72	0:03.02	0:03.32	0:03.63	0:03.93	0:04.23	0:04.53	0:04.83	0:05.14	0:05.44
020	0:05.74	0:06.04	0:06.34	0:06.65	0:06.95	0:07.25	0:07.55	0:07.85	0:08.16	0:08.46
030	0:08.76	0:09.06	0:09.36	0:09.67	0:09.97	0:10.27	0:10.57	0:10.88	0:11.18	0:11.48
040	0:11.78	0:12.08	0:12.39	0:12.69	0:12.99	0:13.29	0:13.59	0:13.90	0:14.20	0:14.50
050	0:14.80	0:15.10	0:15.41	0:15.71	0:16.01	0:16.31	0:16.61	0:16.92	0:17.22	0:17.52
060	0:17.82	0:18.13	0:18.43	0:18.73	0:19.03	0:19.33	0:19.64	0:19.94	0:20.24	0:20.54
070	0:20.84	0:21.15	0:21.45	0:21.75	0:22.05	0:22.35	0:22.66	0:22.96	0:23.26	0:23.56
080	0:23.86	0:24.17	0:24.47	0:24.77	0:25.07	0:25.38	0:25.68	0:25.98	0:26.28	0:26.58
090	0:26.89	0:27.19	0:27.49	0:27.79	0:28.09	0:28.40	0:28.70	0:29.00	0:29.30	0:29.60
100	0:29.91	0:30.21	0:30.51	0:30.81	0:31.11	0:31.42	0:31.72	0:32.02	0:32.32	0:32.63
110	0:32.93	0:33.23	0:33.53	0:33.83	0:34.14	0:34.44	0:34.74	0:35.04	0:35.34	0:35.65
120	0:35.95	0:36.25	0:36.55	0:36.85	0:37.16	0:37.46	0:37.76	0:38.06	0:38.36	0:38.67
130	0:38.97	0:39.27	0:39.57	0:39.88	0:40.18	0:40.48	0:40.78	0:41.08	0:41.39	0:41.69
140	0:41.99	0:42.29	0:42.59	0:42.90	0:43.20	0:43.50	0:43.80	0:44.10	0:44.41	0:44.71
150	0:45.01	0:45.31	0:45.61	0:45.92	0:46.22	0:46.52	0:46.82	0:47.13	0:47.43	0:47.73
160	0:48.03	0:48.33	0:48.64	0:48.94	0:49.24	0:49.54	0:49.84	0:50.15	0:50.45	0:50.75
170	0:51.05	0:51.35	0:51.66	0:51.96	0:52.26	0:52.56	0:52.86	0:53.17	0:53.47	0:53.77
180	0:54.07	0:54.38	0:54.68	0:54.98	0:55.28	0:55.58	0:55.89	0:56.19	0:56.49	0:56.79
190	0:57.09	0:57.40	0:57.70	0:58.00	0:58.30	0:58.60	0:58.91	0:59.21	0:59.51	0:59.81
200	1:00.11	1:00.42	1:00.72	1:01.02	1:01.32	1:01.63	1:01.93	1:02.23	1:02.53	1:02.83
210	1:03.14	1:03.44	1:03.74	1:04.04	1:04.34	1:04.65	1:04.95	1:05.25	1:05.55	1:05.85
220	1:06.16	1:06.46	1:06.76	1:07.06	1:07.36	1:07.67	1:07.97	1:08.27	1:08.57	1:08.88
230	1:09.18	1:09.48	1:09.78	1:10.08	1:10.39	1:10.69	1:10.99	1:11.29	1:11.59	1:11.90
240	1:12.20	1:12.50	1:12.80	1:13.10	1:13.41	1:13.71	1:14.01	1:14.31	1:14.61	1:14.92
250	1:15.22	1:15.52	1:15.82	1:16.13	1:16.43	1:16.73	1:17.03	1:17.33	1:17.64	1:17.94
260	1:18.24	1:18.54	1:18.84	1:19.15	1:19.45	1:19.75	1:20.05	1:20.35	1:20.66	1:20.96
270	1:21.26	1:21.56	1:21.86	1:22.17	1:22.47	1:22.77	1:23.07	1:23.38	1:23.68	1:23.98
280	1:24.28	1:24.58	1:24.89	1:25.19	1:25.49	1:25.79	1:26.09	1:26.40	1:26.70	1:27.00
290	1:27.30	1:27.60	1:27.91	1:28.21	1:28.51	1:28.81	1:29.11	1:29.42	1:29.72	1:30.02
300	1:30.32	1:30.63	1:30.93	1:31.23	1:31.53	1:31.83	1:32.14	1:32.44	1:32.74	1:33.04
310	1:33.34	1:33.65	1:33.95	1:34.25	1:34.55	1:34.85	1:35.16	1:35.46	1:35.76	1:36.06
320	1:36.36	1:36.67	1:36.97	1:37.27	1:37.57	1:37.88	1:38.18	1:38.48	1:38.78	1:39.08
330	1:39.39	1:39.69	1:39.99	1:40.29	1:40.59	1:40.90	1:41.20	1:41.50	1:41.80	1:42.10
340	1:42.41	1:42.71	1:43.01	1:43.31	1:43.61	1:43.92	1:44.22	1:44.52	1:44.82	1:45.13
350	1:45.43	1:45.73	1:46.03	1:46.33	1:46.64	1:46.94	1:47.24	1:47.54	1:47.84	1:48.15
360	1:48.45	1:48.75	1:49.05	1:49.35	1:49.66	1:49.96	1:50.26	1:50.56	1:50.86	1:51.17
370	1:51.47	1:51.77	1:52.07	1:52.38	1:52.68	1:52.98	1:53.28	1:53.58	1:53.89	1:54.19
380	1:54.49	1:54.79	1:55.09	1:55.40	1:55.70	1:56.00	1:56.30	1:56.60	1:56.91	1:57.21
390	1:57.51	1:57.81	1:58.11	1:58.42	1:58.72	1:59.02	1:59.32	1:59.63	1:59.93	2:00.23
400	2:00.53	2:00.83	2:01.14	2:01.44	2:01.74	2:02.04	2:02.34	2:02.65	2:02.95	2:03.25
410	2:03.55	2:03.85	2:04.16	2:04.46	2:04.76	2:05.06	2:05.36	2:05.67	2:05.97	2:06.27
420	2:06.57	2:06.88	2:07.18	2:07.48	2:07.78	2:08.08	2:08.39	2:08.69	2:08.99	2:09.29
430	2:09.59	2:09.90	2:10.20	2:10.50	2:10.80	2:11.10	2:11.41	2:11.71	2:12.01	2:12.31
440	2:12.61	2:12.92	2:13.22	2:13.52	2:13.82	2:14.12	2:14.43	2:14.73	2:15.03	2:15.33
450	2:15.64	2:15.94	2:16.24	2:16.54	2:16.84	2:17.15	2:17.45	2:17.75	2:18.05	2:18.35
460	2:18.66	2:18.96	2:19.26	2:19.56	2:19.86	2:20.17	2:20.47	2:20.77	2:21.07	2:21.38
470	2:21.68	2:21.98	2:22.28	2:22.58	2:22.89	2:23.19	2:23.49	2:23.79	2:24.09	2:24.40
480	2:24.70	2:25.00	2:25.30	2:25.60	2:25.91	2:26.21	2:26.51	2:26.81	2:27.11	2:27.42
490	2:27.72	2:28.02	2:28.32	2:28.63	2:28.93	2:29.23	2:29.53	2:29.83	2:30.14	2:30.44
500	2:30.74	2:31.04	2:31.34	2:31.65	2:31.95	2:32.25	2:32.55	2:32.85	2:33.16	2:33.46
510	2:33.76	2:34.06	2:34.36	2:34.67	2:34.97	2:35.27	2:35.57	2:35.88	2:36.18	2:36.48
520	2:36.78	2:37.08	2:37.39	2:37.69	2:37.99	2:38.29	2:38.59	2:38.90	2:39.20	2:39.50
530	2:39.80	2:40.10	2:40.41	2:40.71	2:41.01	2:41.31	2:41.61	2:41.92	2:42.22	2:42.52
540	2:42.82	2:43.13	2:43.43	2:43.73	2:44.03	2:44.33	2:44.64	2:44.94	2:45.24	2:45.54
550	2:45.84	2:46.15	2:46.45	2:46.75	2:47.05	2:47.35	2:47.66	2:47.96	2:48.26	2:48.56
560	2:48.86	2:49.17	2:49.47	2:49.77	2:50.07	2:50.38	2:50.68	2:50.98	2:51.28	2:51.58
570	2:51.89	2:52.19	2:52.49	2:52.79	2:53.09	2:53.40	2:53.70	2:54.00	2:54.30	2:54.60
580	2:54.91	2:55.21	2:55.51	2:55.81	2:56.11	2:56.42	2:56.72	2:57.02	2:57.32	2:57.63
590	2:57.93	2:58.23	2:58.53	2:58.83	2:59.14	2:59.44	2:59.74	3:00.04	3:00.34	3:00.65

♩. = 0.45; ♩ = 0.30; ♪. = 0.23; (3) ♩ 𝄾 = 0.20; ♪ = 0.15; (3) ♪ 𝄾 𝄾 = 0.10; 𝅘𝅥𝅯 = 0.08 seconds

CLICK: 7⅜ FRAMES; M.M.: 195.25

Click	0	1	2	3	4	5	6	7	8	9
000	0:00.00	0:00.00	0:00.31	0:00.61	0:00.92	0:01.23	0:01.54	0:01.84	0:02.15	0:02.46
010	0:02.77	0:03.07	0:03.38	0:03.69	0:03.99	0:04.30	0:04.61	0:04.92	0:05.22	0:05.53
020	0:05.84	0:06.15	0:06.45	0:06.76	0:07.07	0:07.38	0:07.68	0:07.99	0:08.30	0:08.60
030	0:08.91	0:09.22	0:09.53	0:09.83	0:10.14	0:10.45	0:10.76	0:11.06	0:11.37	0:11.68
040	0:11.98	0:12.29	0:12.60	0:12.91	0:13.21	0:13.52	0:13.83	0:14.14	0:14.44	0:14.75
050	0:15.06	0:15.36	0:15.67	0:15.98	0:16.29	0:16.59	0:16.90	0:17.21	0:17.52	0:17.82
060	0:18.13	0:18.44	0:18.74	0:19.05	0:19.36	0:19.67	0:19.97	0:20.28	0:20.59	0:20.90
070	0:21.20	0:21.51	0:21.82	0:22.13	0:22.43	0:22.74	0:23.05	0:23.35	0:23.66	0:23.97
080	0:24.28	0:24.58	0:24.89	0:25.20	0:25.51	0:25.81	0:26.12	0:26.43	0:26.73	0:27.04
090	0:27.35	0:27.66	0:27.96	0:28.27	0:28.58	0:28.89	0:29.19	0:29.50	0:29.81	0:30.11
100	0:30.42	0:30.73	0:31.04	0:31.34	0:31.65	0:31.96	0:32.27	0:32.57	0:32.88	0:33.19
110	0:33.49	0:33.80	0:34.11	0:34.42	0:34.72	0:35.03	0:35.34	0:35.65	0:35.95	0:36.26
120	0:36.57	0:36.88	0:37.18	0:37.49	0:37.80	0:38.10	0:38.41	0:38.72	0:39.03	0:39.33
130	0:39.64	0:39.95	0:40.26	0:40.56	0:40.87	0:41.18	0:41.48	0:41.79	0:42.10	0:42.41
140	0:42.71	0:43.02	0:43.33	0:43.64	0:43.94	0:44.25	0:44.56	0:44.86	0:45.17	0:45.48
150	0:45.79	0:46.09	0:46.40	0:46.71	0:47.02	0:47.32	0:47.63	0:47.94	0:48.24	0:48.55
160	0:48.86	0:49.17	0:49.47	0:49.78	0:50.09	0:50.40	0:50.70	0:51.01	0:51.32	0:51.63
170	0:51.93	0:52.24	0:52.55	0:52.85	0:53.16	0:53.47	0:53.78	0:54.08	0:54.39	0:54.70
180	0:55.01	0:55.31	0:55.62	0:55.93	0:56.23	0:56.54	0:56.85	0:57.16	0:57.46	0:57.77
190	0:58.08	0:58.39	0:58.69	0:59.00	0:59.31	0:59.61	0:59.92	1:00.23	1:00.54	1:00.84
200	1:01.15	1:01.46	1:01.77	1:02.07	1:02.38	1:02.69	1:02.99	1:03.30	1:03.61	1:03.92
210	1:04.22	1:04.53	1:04.84	1:05.15	1:05.45	1:05.76	1:06.07	1:06.37	1:06.68	1:06.99
220	1:07.30	1:07.60	1:07.91	1:08.22	1:08.53	1:08.83	1:09.14	1:09.45	1:09.76	1:10.06
230	1:10.37	1:10.68	1:10.98	1:11.29	1:11.60	1:11.91	1:12.21	1:12.52	1:12.83	1:13.14
240	1:13.44	1:13.75	1:14.06	1:14.36	1:14.67	1:14.98	1:15.29	1:15.59	1:15.90	1:16.21
250	1:16.52	1:16.82	1:17.13	1:17.44	1:17.74	1:18.05	1:18.36	1:18.67	1:18.97	1:19.28
260	1:19.59	1:19.90	1:20.20	1:20.51	1:20.82	1:21.13	1:21.43	1:21.74	1:22.05	1:22.35
270	1:22.66	1:22.97	1:23.28	1:23.58	1:23.89	1:24.20	1:24.51	1:24.81	1:25.12	1:25.43
280	1:25.73	1:26.04	1:26.35	1:26.66	1:26.96	1:27.27	1:27.58	1:27.89	1:28.19	1:28.50
290	1:28.81	1:29.11	1:29.42	1:29.73	1:30.04	1:30.34	1:30.65	1:30.96	1:31.27	1:31.57
300	1:31.88	1:32.19	1:32.49	1:32.80	1:33.11	1:33.42	1:33.72	1:34.03	1:34.34	1:34.65
310	1:34.95	1:35.26	1:35.57	1:35.87	1:36.18	1:36.49	1:36.80	1:37.10	1:37.41	1:37.72
320	1:38.03	1:38.33	1:38.64	1:38.95	1:39.26	1:39.56	1:39.87	1:40.18	1:40.48	1:40.79
330	1:41.10	1:41.41	1:41.71	1:42.02	1:42.33	1:42.64	1:42.94	1:43.25	1:43.56	1:43.86
340	1:44.17	1:44.48	1:44.79	1:45.09	1:45.40	1:45.71	1:46.02	1:46.32	1:46.63	1:46.94
350	1:47.24	1:47.55	1:47.86	1:48.17	1:48.47	1:48.78	1:49.09	1:49.40	1:49.70	1:50.01
360	1:50.32	1:50.63	1:50.93	1:51.24	1:51.55	1:51.85	1:52.16	1:52.47	1:52.78	1:53.08
370	1:53.39	1:53.70	1:54.01	1:54.31	1:54.62	1:54.93	1:55.23	1:55.54	1:55.85	1:56.16
380	1:56.46	1:56.77	1:57.08	1:57.39	1:57.69	1:58.00	1:58.31	1:58.61	1:58.92	1:59.23
390	1:59.54	1:59.84	2:00.15	2:00.46	2:00.77	2:01.07	2:01.38	2:01.69	2:01.99	2:02.30
400	2:02.61	2:02.92	2:03.22	2:03.53	2:03.84	2:04.15	2:04.45	2:04.76	2:05.07	2:05.38
410	2:05.68	2:05.99	2:06.30	2:06.60	2:06.91	2:07.22	2:07.53	2:07.83	2:08.14	2:08.45
420	2:08.76	2:09.06	2:09.37	2:09.68	2:09.98	2:10.29	2:10.60	2:10.91	2:11.21	2:11.52
430	2:11.83	2:12.14	2:12.44	2:12.75	2:13.06	2:13.36	2:13.67	2:13.98	2:14.29	2:14.59
440	2:14.90	2:15.21	2:15.52	2:15.82	2:16.13	2:16.44	2:16.74	2:17.05	2:17.36	2:17.67
450	2:17.97	2:18.28	2:18.59	2:18.90	2:19.20	2:19.51	2:19.82	2:20.12	2:20.43	2:20.74
460	2:21.05	2:21.35	2:21.66	2:21.97	2:22.28	2:22.58	2:22.89	2:23.20	2:23.51	2:23.81
470	2:24.12	2:24.43	2:24.73	2:25.04	2:25.35	2:25.66	2:25.96	2:26.27	2:26.58	2:26.89
480	2:27.19	2:27.50	2:27.81	2:28.11	2:28.42	2:28.73	2:29.04	2:29.34	2:29.65	2:29.96
490	2:30.27	2:30.57	2:30.88	2:31.19	2:31.49	2:31.80	2:32.11	2:32.42	2:32.72	2:33.03
500	2:33.34	2:33.65	2:33.95	2:34.26	2:34.57	2:34.87	2:35.18	2:35.49	2:35.80	2:36.10
510	2:36.41	2:36.72	2:37.03	2:37.33	2:37.64	2:37.95	2:38.26	2:38.56	2:38.87	2:39.18
520	2:39.48	2:39.79	2:40.10	2:40.41	2:40.71	2:41.02	2:41.33	2:41.64	2:41.94	2:42.25
530	2:42.56	2:42.86	2:43.17	2:43.48	2:43.79	2:44.09	2:44.40	2:44.71	2:45.02	2:45.32
540	2:45.63	2:45.94	2:46.24	2:46.55	2:46.86	2:47.17	2:47.47	2:47.78	2:48.09	2:48.40
550	2:48.70	2:49.01	2:49.32	2:49.63	2:49.93	2:50.24	2:50.55	2:50.85	2:51.16	2:51.47
560	2:51.78	2:52.08	2:52.39	2:52.70	2:53.01	2:53.31	2:53.62	2:53.93	2:54.23	2:54.54
570	2:54.85	2:55.16	2:55.46	2:55.77	2:56.08	2:56.39	2:56.69	2:57.00	2:57.31	2:57.61
580	2:57.92	2:58.23	2:58.54	2:58.84	2:59.15	2:59.46	2:59.77	3:00.07	3:00.38	3:00.69
590	3:00.99	3:01.30	3:01.61	3:01.92	3:02.22	3:02.53	3:02.84	3:03.15	3:03.45	3:03.76

♩. = 0.46; ♩ = 0.31; ♪. = 0.23; (triplet) ♩ 𝄾 = 0.20; ♪ = 0.15; (triplet) ♪𝄾𝄾 = 0.10; 𝅘𝅥𝅯 = 0.08 seconds

CLICK: 7⅛ FRAMES; M.M.: 192.00

Click	0	1	2	3	4	5	6	7	8	9
000	0:00.00	0:00.00	0:00.31	0:00.62	0:00.94	0:01.25	0:01.56	0:01.87	0:02.19	0:02.50
010	0:02.81	0:03.13	0:03.44	0:03.75	0:04.06	0:04.38	0:04.69	0:05.00	0:05.31	0:05.62
020	0:05.94	0:06.25	0:06.56	0:06.87	0:07.19	0:07.50	0:07.81	0:08.12	0:08.44	0:08.75
030	0:09.06	0:09.37	0:09.69	0:10.00	0:10.31	0:10.63	0:10.94	0:11.25	0:11.56	0:11.87
040	0:12.19	0:12.50	0:12.81	0:13.12	0:13.44	0:13.75	0:14.06	0:14.37	0:14.69	0:15.00
050	0:15.31	0:15.62	0:15.94	0:16.25	0:16.56	0:16.87	0:17.19	0:17.50	0:17.81	0:18.12
060	0:18.44	0:18.75	0:19.06	0:19.38	0:19.69	0:20.00	0:20.31	0:20.62	0:20.94	0:21.25
070	0:21.56	0:21.87	0:22.19	0:22.50	0:22.81	0:23.13	0:23.44	0:23.75	0:24.06	0:24.37
080	0:24.69	0:25.00	0:25.31	0:25.62	0:25.94	0:26.25	0:26.56	0:26.87	0:27.19	0:27.50
090	0:27.81	0:28.12	0:28.44	0:28.75	0:29.06	0:29.37	0:29.69	0:30.00	0:30.31	0:30.62
100	0:30.94	0:31.25	0:31.56	0:31.87	0:32.19	0:32.50	0:32.81	0:33.13	0:33.44	0:33.75
110	0:34.06	0:34.37	0:34.69	0:35.00	0:35.31	0:35.62	0:35.94	0:36.25	0:36.56	0:36.88
120	0:37.19	0:37.50	0:37.81	0:38.12	0:38.44	0:38.75	0:39.06	0:39.37	0:39.69	0:40.00
130	0:40.31	0:40.63	0:40.94	0:41.25	0:41.56	0:41.87	0:42.19	0:42.50	0:42.81	0:43.12
140	0:43.44	0:43.75	0:44.06	0:44.38	0:44.69	0:45.00	0:45.31	0:45.62	0:45.94	0:46.25
150	0:46.56	0:46.87	0:47.19	0:47.50	0:47.81	0:48.13	0:48.44	0:48.75	0:49.06	0:49.37
160	0:49.69	0:50.00	0:50.31	0:50.62	0:50.94	0:51.25	0:51.56	0:51.87	0:52.19	0:52.50
170	0:52.81	0:53.12	0:53.44	0:53.75	0:54.06	0:54.37	0:54.69	0:55.00	0:55.31	0:55.62
180	0:55.94	0:56.25	0:56.56	0:56.87	0:57.19	0:57.50	0:57.81	0:58.12	0:58.44	0:58.75
190	0:59.06	0:59.37	0:59.69	0:60.00	1:00.31	1:00.62	1:00.94	1:01.25	1:01.56	1:01.87
200	1:02.19	1:02.50	1:02.81	1:03.12	1:03.44	1:03.75	1:04.06	1:04.37	1:04.69	1:05.00
210	1:05.31	1:05.62	1:05.94	1:06.25	1:06.56	1:06.87	1:07.19	1:07.50	1:07.81	1:08.12
220	1:08.44	1:08.75	1:09.06	1:09.37	1:09.69	1:10.00	1:10.31	1:10.62	1:10.94	1:11.25
230	1:11.56	1:11.87	1:12.19	1:12.50	1:12.81	1:13.12	1:13.44	1:13.75	1:14.06	1:14.37
240	1:14.69	1:15.00	1:15.31	1:15.62	1:15.94	1:16.25	1:16.56	1:16.87	1:17.19	1:17.50
250	1:17.81	1:18.12	1:18.44	1:18.75	1:19.06	1:19.37	1:19.69	1:20.00	1:20.31	1:20.62
260	1:20.94	1:21.25	1:21.56	1:21.87	1:22.19	1:22.50	1:22.81	1:23.12	1:23.44	1:23.75
270	1:24.06	1:24.37	1:24.69	1:25.00	1:25.31	1:25.62	1:25.94	1:26.25	1:26.56	1:26.87
280	1:27.19	1:27.50	1:27.81	1:28.12	1:28.44	1:28.75	1:29.06	1:29.37	1:29.69	1:30.00
290	1:30.31	1:30.62	1:30.94	1:31.25	1:31.56	1:31.87	1:32.19	1:32.50	1:32.81	1:33.12
300	1:33.44	1:33.75	1:34.06	1:34.37	1:34.69	1:35.00	1:35.31	1:35.62	1:35.94	1:36.25
310	1:36.56	1:36.87	1:37.19	1:37.50	1:37.81	1:38.12	1:38.44	1:38.75	1:39.06	1:39.37
320	1:39.69	1:40.00	1:40.31	1:40.62	1:40.94	1:41.25	1:41.56	1:41.87	1:42.19	1:42.50
330	1:42.81	1:43.12	1:43.44	1:43.75	1:44.06	1:44.37	1:44.69	1:45.00	1:45.31	1:45.62
340	1:45.94	1:46.25	1:46.56	1:46.87	1:47.19	1:47.50	1:47.81	1:48.12	1:48.44	1:48.75
350	1:49.06	1:49.37	1:49.69	1:50.00	1:50.31	1:50.62	1:50.94	1:51.25	1:51.56	1:51.87
360	1:52.19	1:52.50	1:52.81	1:53.12	1:53.44	1:53.75	1:54.06	1:54.37	1:54.69	1:55.00
370	1:55.31	1:55.62	1:55.94	1:56.25	1:56.56	1:56.87	1:57.19	1:57.50	1:57.81	1:58.12
380	1:58.44	1:58.75	1:59.06	1:59.37	1:59.69	1:60.00	2:00.31	2:00.62	2:00.94	2:01.25
390	2:01.56	2:01.87	2:02.19	2:02.50	2:02.81	2:03.12	2:03.44	2:03.75	2:04.06	2:04.37
400	2:04.69	2:05.00	2:05.31	2:05.62	2:05.94	2:06.25	2:06.56	2:06.87	2:07.19	2:07.50
410	2:07.81	2:08.12	2:08.44	2:08.75	2:09.06	2:09.37	2:09.69	2:10.00	2:10.31	2:10.62
420	2:10.94	2:11.25	2:11.56	2:11.87	2:12.19	2:12.50	2:12.81	2:13.12	2:13.44	2:13.75
430	2:14.06	2:14.37	2:14.69	2:15.00	2:15.31	2:15.62	2:15.94	2:16.25	2:16.56	2:16.87
440	2:17.19	2:17.50	2:17.81	2:18.12	2:18.44	2:18.75	2:19.06	2:19.37	2:19.69	2:20.00
450	2:20.31	2:20.62	2:20.94	2:21.25	2:21.56	2:21.87	2:22.19	2:22.50	2:22.81	2:23.12
460	2:23.44	2:23.75	2:24.06	2:24.37	2:24.69	2:25.00	2:25.31	2:25.62	2:25.94	2:26.25
470	2:26.56	2:26.87	2:27.19	2:27.50	2:27.81	2:28.12	2:28.44	2:28.75	2:29.06	2:29.37
480	2:29.69	2:30.00	2:30.31	2:30.62	2:30.94	2:31.25	2:31.56	2:31.87	2:32.19	2:32.50
490	2:32.81	2:33.12	2:33.44	2:33.75	2:34.06	2:34.37	2:34.69	2:35.00	2:35.31	2:35.62
500	2:35.94	2:36.25	2:36.56	2:36.87	2:37.19	2:37.50	2:37.81	2:38.12	2:38.44	2:38.75
510	2:39.06	2:39.37	2:39.69	2:40.00	2:40.31	2:40.62	2:40.94	2:41.25	2:41.56	2:41.87
520	2:42.19	2:42.50	2:42.81	2:43.12	2:43.44	2:43.75	2:44.06	2:44.37	2:44.69	2:45.00
530	2:45.31	2:45.62	2:45.94	2:46.25	2:46.56	2:46.87	2:47.19	2:47.50	2:47.81	2:48.12
540	2:48.44	2:48.75	2:49.06	2:49.37	2:49.69	2:50.00	2:50.31	2:50.62	2:50.94	2:51.25
550	2:51.56	2:51.87	2:52.19	2:52.50	2:52.81	2:53.12	2:53.44	2:53.75	2:54.06	2:54.37
560	2:54.69	2:55.00	2:55.31	2:55.62	2:55.94	2:56.25	2:56.56	2:56.87	2:57.19	2:57.50
570	2:57.81	2:58.12	2:58.44	2:58.75	2:59.06	2:59.37	2:59.69	2:60.00	3:00.31	3:00.62
580	3:00.94	3:01.25	3:01.56	3:01.87	3:02.19	3:02.50	3:02.81	3:03.12	3:03.44	3:03.75
590	3:04.06	3:04.37	3:04.69	3:05.00	3:05.31	3:05.62	3:05.94	3:06.25	3:06.56	3:06.87

♩. = 0.47; ♩ = 0.31; ♪. = 0.23; (3: ♩ 𝄾) = 0.21; ♪ = 0.16; (3: ♪ 𝄾 𝄾) = 0.10; 𝅘𝅥𝅯 = 0.08 seconds

CLICK: 7⅝ FRAMES; M.M.: 188.85

Click	0	1	2	3	4	5	6	7	8	9
000	0:00.00	0:00.00	0:00.32	0:00.64	0:00.95	0:01.27	0:01.59	0:01.91	0:02.22	0:02.54
010	0:02.86	0:03.18	0:03.49	0:03.81	0:04.13	0:04.45	0:04.77	0:05.08	0:05.40	0:05.72
020	0:06.04	0:06.35	0:06.67	0:06.99	0:07.31	0:07.63	0:07.94	0:08.26	0:08.58	0:08.90
030	0:09.21	0:09.53	0:09.85	0:10.17	0:10.48	0:10.80	0:11.12	0:11.44	0:11.76	0:12.07
040	0:12.39	0:12.71	0:13.03	0:13.34	0:13.66	0:13.98	0:14.30	0:14.61	0:14.93	0:15.25
050	0:15.57	0:15.89	0:16.20	0:16.52	0:16.84	0:17.16	0:17.47	0:17.79	0:18.11	0:18.43
060	0:18.74	0:19.06	0:19.38	0:19.70	0:20.02	0:20.33	0:20.65	0:20.97	0:21.29	0:21.60
070	0:21.92	0:22.24	0:22.56	0:22.88	0:23.19	0:23.51	0:23.83	0:24.15	0:24.46	0:24.78
080	0:25.10	0:25.42	0:25.73	0:26.05	0:26.37	0:26.69	0:27.01	0:27.32	0:27.64	0:27.96
090	0:28.28	0:28.59	0:28.91	0:29.23	0:29.55	0:29.86	0:30.18	0:30.50	0:30.82	0:31.14
100	0:31.45	0:31.77	0:32.09	0:32.41	0:32.72	0:33.04	0:33.36	0:33.68	0:33.99	0:34.31
110	0:34.63	0:34.95	0:35.27	0:35.58	0:35.90	0:36.22	0:36.54	0:36.85	0:37.17	0:37.49
120	0:37.81	0:38.13	0:38.44	0:38.76	0:39.08	0:39.40	0:39.71	0:40.03	0:40.35	0:40.67
130	0:40.98	0:41.30	0:41.62	0:41.94	0:42.26	0:42.57	0:42.89	0:43.21	0:43.53	0:43.84
140	0:44.16	0:44.48	0:44.80	0:45.11	0:45.43	0:45.75	0:46.07	0:46.39	0:46.70	0:47.02
150	0:47.34	0:47.66	0:47.97	0:48.29	0:48.61	0:48.93	0:49.24	0:49.56	0:49.88	0:50.20
160	0:50.52	0:50.83	0:51.15	0:51.47	0:51.79	0:52.10	0:52.42	0:52.74	0:53.06	0:53.38
170	0:53.69	0:54.01	0:54.33	0:54.65	0:54.96	0:55.28	0:55.60	0:55.92	0:56.23	0:56.55
180	0:56.87	0:57.19	0:57.51	0:57.82	0:58.14	0:58.46	0:58.78	0:59.09	0:59.41	0:59.73
190	1:00.05	1:00.36	1:00.68	1:01.00	1:01.32	1:01.64	1:01.95	1:02.27	1:02.59	1:02.91
200	1:03.22	1:03.54	1:03.86	1:04.18	1:04.49	1:04.81	1:05.13	1:05.45	1:05.77	1:06.08
210	1:06.40	1:06.72	1:07.04	1:07.35	1:07.67	1:07.99	1:08.31	1:08.63	1:08.94	1:09.26
220	1:09.58	1:09.90	1:10.21	1:10.53	1:10.85	1:11.17	1:11.48	1:11.80	1:12.12	1:12.44
230	1:12.76	1:13.07	1:13.39	1:13.71	1:14.03	1:14.34	1:14.66	1:14.98	1:15.30	1:15.61
240	1:15.93	1:16.25	1:16.57	1:16.89	1:17.20	1:17.52	1:17.84	1:18.16	1:18.47	1:18.79
250	1:19.11	1:19.43	1:19.74	1:20.06	1:20.38	1:20.70	1:21.02	1:21.33	1:21.65	1:21.97
260	1:22.29	1:22.60	1:22.92	1:23.24	1:23.56	1:23.88	1:24.19	1:24.51	1:24.83	1:25.15
270	1:25.46	1:25.78	1:26.10	1:26.42	1:26.73	1:27.05	1:27.37	1:27.69	1:28.01	1:28.32
280	1:28.64	1:28.96	1:29.28	1:29.59	1:29.91	1:30.23	1:30.55	1:30.86	1:31.18	1:31.50
290	1:31.82	1:32.14	1:32.45	1:32.77	1:33.09	1:33.41	1:33.72	1:34.04	1:34.36	1:34.68
300	1:34.99	1:35.31	1:35.63	1:35.95	1:36.27	1:36.58	1:36.90	1:37.22	1:37.54	1:37.85
310	1:38.17	1:38.49	1:38.81	1:39.13	1:39.44	1:39.76	1:40.08	1:40.40	1:40.71	1:41.03
320	1:41.35	1:41.67	1:41.98	1:42.30	1:42.62	1:42.94	1:43.26	1:43.57	1:43.89	1:44.21
330	1:44.53	1:44.84	1:45.16	1:45.48	1:45.80	1:46.11	1:46.43	1:46.75	1:47.07	1:47.39
340	1:47.70	1:48.02	1:48.34	1:48.66	1:48.97	1:49.29	1:49.61	1:49.93	1:50.24	1:50.56
350	1:50.88	1:51.20	1:51.52	1:51.83	1:52.15	1:52.47	1:52.79	1:53.10	1:53.42	1:53.74
360	1:54.06	1:54.38	1:54.69	1:55.01	1:55.33	1:55.65	1:55.96	1:56.28	1:56.60	1:56.92
370	1:57.23	1:57.55	1:57.87	1:58.19	1:58.51	1:58.82	1:59.14	1:59.46	1:59.78	2:00.09
380	2:00.41	2:00.73	2:01.05	2:01.36	2:01.68	2:02.00	2:02.32	2:02.64	2:02.95	2:03.27
390	2:03.59	2:03.91	2:04.22	2:04.54	2:04.86	2:05.18	2:05.49	2:05.81	2:06.13	2:06.45
400	2:06.77	2:07.08	2:07.40	2:07.72	2:08.04	2:08.35	2:08.67	2:08.99	2:09.31	2:09.63
410	2:09.94	2:10.26	2:10.58	2:10.90	2:11.21	2:11.53	2:11.85	2:12.17	2:12.48	2:12.80
420	2:13.12	2:13.44	2:13.76	2:14.07	2:14.39	2:14.71	2:15.03	2:15.34	2:15.66	2:15.98
430	2:16.30	2:16.61	2:16.93	2:17.25	2:17.57	2:17.89	2:18.20	2:18.52	2:18.84	2:19.16
440	2:19.47	2:19.79	2:20.11	2:20.43	2:20.74	2:21.06	2:21.38	2:21.70	2:22.02	2:22.33
450	2:22.65	2:22.97	2:23.29	2:23.60	2:23.92	2:24.24	2:24.56	2:24.88	2:25.19	2:25.51
460	2:25.83	2:26.15	2:26.46	2:26.78	2:27.10	2:27.42	2:27.73	2:28.05	2:28.37	2:28.69
470	2:29.01	2:29.32	2:29.64	2:29.96	2:30.28	2:30.59	2:30.91	2:31.23	2:31.55	2:31.86
480	2:32.18	2:32.50	2:32.82	2:33.14	2:33.45	2:33.77	2:34.09	2:34.41	2:34.72	2:35.04
490	2:35.36	2:35.68	2:35.99	2:36.31	2:36.63	2:36.95	2:37.27	2:37.58	2:37.90	2:38.22
500	2:38.54	2:38.85	2:39.17	2:39.49	2:39.81	2:40.13	2:40.44	2:40.76	2:41.08	2:41.40
510	2:41.71	2:42.03	2:42.35	2:42.67	2:42.98	2:43.30	2:43.62	2:43.94	2:44.26	2:44.57
520	2:44.89	2:45.21	2:45.53	2:45.84	2:46.16	2:46.48	2:46.80	2:47.11	2:47.43	2:47.75
530	2:48.07	2:48.39	2:48.70	2:49.02	2:49.34	2:49.66	2:49.97	2:50.29	2:50.61	2:50.93
540	2:51.24	2:51.56	2:51.88	2:52.20	2:52.52	2:52.83	2:53.15	2:53.47	2:53.79	2:54.10
550	2:54.42	2:54.74	2:55.06	2:55.38	2:55.69	2:56.01	2:56.33	2:56.65	2:56.96	2:57.28
560	2:57.60	2:57.92	2:58.23	2:58.55	2:58.87	2:59.19	2:59.51	2:59.82	3:00.14	3:00.46
570	3:00.78	3:01.09	3:01.41	3:01.73	3:02.05	3:02.36	3:02.68	3:03.00	3:03.32	3:03.64
580	3:03.95	3:04.27	3:04.59	3:04.91	3:05.22	3:05.54	3:05.86	3:06.18	3:06.49	3:06.81
590	3:07.13	3:07.45	3:07.77	3:08.08	3:08.40	3:08.72	3:09.04	3:09.35	3:09.67	3:09.99

♩. = 0.48; ♩ = 0.32; ♪. = 0.24; ♩ 𝄾 (triplet) = 0.21; ♪ = 0.16; ♪ 𝄾 𝄾 (triplet) = 0.11; 𝅘𝅥𝅯 = 0.08 seconds

CLICK: 7 6/8 FRAMES; M.M.: 185.81

Click	0	1	2	3	4	5	6	7	8	9
000	0:00.00	0:00.00	0:00.32	0:00.65	0:00.97	0:01.29	0:01.61	0:01.94	0:02.26	0:02.58
010	0:02.91	0:03.23	0:03.55	0:03.88	0:04.20	0:04.52	0:04.84	0:05.17	0:05.49	0:05.81
020	0:06.14	0:06.46	0:06.78	0:07.10	0:07.43	0:07.75	0:08.07	0:08.40	0:08.72	0:09.04
030	0:09.36	0:09.69	0:10.01	0:10.33	0:10.66	0:10.98	0:11.30	0:11.63	0:11.95	0:12.27
040	0:12.59	0:12.92	0:13.24	0:13.56	0:13.89	0:14.21	0:14.53	0:14.85	0:15.18	0:15.50
050	0:15.82	0:16.15	0:16.47	0:16.79	0:17.11	0:17.44	0:17.76	0:18.08	0:18.41	0:18.73
060	0:19.05	0:19.38	0:19.70	0:20.02	0:20.34	0:20.67	0:20.99	0:21.31	0:21.64	0:21.96
070	0:22.28	0:22.60	0:22.93	0:23.25	0:23.57	0:23.90	0:24.22	0:24.54	0:24.86	0:25.19
080	0:25.51	0:25.83	0:26.16	0:26.48	0:26.80	0:27.13	0:27.45	0:27.77	0:28.09	0:28.42
090	0:28.74	0:29.06	0:29.39	0:29.71	0:30.03	0:30.35	0:30.68	0:31.00	0:31.32	0:31.65
100	0:31.97	0:32.29	0:32.61	0:32.94	0:33.26	0:33.58	0:33.91	0:34.23	0:34.55	0:34.88
110	0:35.20	0:35.52	0:35.84	0:36.17	0:36.49	0:36.81	0:37.14	0:37.46	0:37.78	0:38.10
120	0:38.43	0:38.75	0:39.07	0:39.40	0:39.72	0:40.04	0:40.36	0:40.69	0:41.01	0:41.33
130	0:41.66	0:41.98	0:42.30	0:42.63	0:42.95	0:43.27	0:43.59	0:43.92	0:44.24	0:44.56
140	0:44.89	0:45.21	0:45.53	0:45.85	0:46.18	0:46.50	0:46.82	0:47.15	0:47.47	0:47.79
150	0:48.11	0:48.44	0:48.76	0:49.08	0:49.41	0:49.73	0:50.05	0:50.38	0:50.70	0:51.02
160	0:51.34	0:51.67	0:51.99	0:52.31	0:52.64	0:52.96	0:53.28	0:53.60	0:53.93	0:54.25
170	0:54.57	0:54.90	0:55.22	0:55.54	0:55.86	0:56.19	0:56.51	0:56.83	0:57.16	0:57.48
180	0:57.80	0:58.13	0:58.45	0:58.77	0:59.09	0:59.42	0:59.74	1:00.06	1:00.39	1:00.71
190	1:01.03	1:01.35	1:01.68	1:02.00	1:02.32	1:02.65	1:02.97	1:03.29	1:03.61	1:03.94
200	1:04.26	1:04.58	1:04.91	1:05.23	1:05.55	1:05.88	1:06.20	1:06.52	1:06.84	1:07.17
210	1:07.49	1:07.81	1:08.14	1:08.46	1:08.78	1:09.10	1:09.43	1:09.75	1:10.07	1:10.40
220	1:10.72	1:11.04	1:11.36	1:11.69	1:12.01	1:12.33	1:12.66	1:12.98	1:13.30	1:13.63
230	1:13.95	1:14.27	1:14.59	1:14.92	1:15.24	1:15.56	1:15.89	1:16.21	1:16.53	1:16.85
240	1:17.18	1:17.50	1:17.82	1:18.15	1:18.47	1:18.79	1:19.11	1:19.44	1:19.76	1:20.08
250	1:20.41	1:20.73	1:21.05	1:21.38	1:21.70	1:22.02	1:22.34	1:22.67	1:22.99	1:23.31
260	1:23.64	1:23.96	1:24.28	1:24.60	1:24.93	1:25.25	1:25.57	1:25.90	1:26.22	1:26.54
270	1:26.86	1:27.19	1:27.51	1:27.83	1:28.16	1:28.48	1:28.80	1:29.13	1:29.45	1:29.77
280	1:30.09	1:30.42	1:30.74	1:31.06	1:31.39	1:31.71	1:32.03	1:32.35	1:32.68	1:33.00
290	1:33.32	1:33.65	1:33.97	1:34.29	1:34.61	1:34.94	1:35.26	1:35.58	1:35.91	1:36.23
300	1:36.55	1:36.88	1:37.20	1:37.52	1:37.84	1:38.17	1:38.49	1:38.81	1:39.14	1:39.46
310	1:39.78	1:40.10	1:40.43	1:40.75	1:41.07	1:41.40	1:41.72	1:42.04	1:42.36	1:42.69
320	1:43.01	1:43.33	1:43.66	1:43.98	1:44.30	1:44.63	1:44.95	1:45.27	1:45.59	1:45.92
330	1:46.24	1:46.56	1:46.89	1:47.21	1:47.53	1:47.85	1:48.18	1:48.50	1:48.82	1:49.15
340	1:49.47	1:49.79	1:50.11	1:50.44	1:50.76	1:51.08	1:51.41	1:51.73	1:52.05	1:52.38
350	1:52.70	1:53.02	1:53.34	1:53.67	1:53.99	1:54.31	1:54.64	1:54.96	1:55.28	1:55.60
360	1:55.93	1:56.25	1:56.57	1:56.90	1:57.22	1:57.54	1:57.86	1:58.19	1:58.51	1:58.83
370	1:59.16	1:59.48	1:59.80	2:00.12	2:00.45	2:00.77	2:01.09	2:01.42	2:01.74	2:02.06
380	2:02.39	2:02.71	2:03.03	2:03.35	2:03.68	2:04.00	2:04.32	2:04.65	2:04.97	2:05.29
390	2:05.61	2:05.94	2:06.26	2:06.58	2:06.91	2:07.23	2:07.55	2:07.88	2:08.20	2:08.52
400	2:08.84	2:09.17	2:09.49	2:09.81	2:10.14	2:10.46	2:10.78	2:11.10	2:11.43	2:11.75
410	2:12.07	2:12.40	2:12.72	2:13.04	2:13.36	2:13.69	2:14.01	2:14.33	2:14.66	2:14.98
420	2:15.30	2:15.63	2:15.95	2:16.27	2:16.59	2:16.92	2:17.24	2:17.56	2:17.89	2:18.21
430	2:18.53	2:18.85	2:19.18	2:19.50	2:19.82	2:20.15	2:20.47	2:20.79	2:21.11	2:21.44
440	2:21.76	2:22.08	2:22.41	2:22.73	2:23.05	2:23.38	2:23.70	2:24.02	2:24.34	2:24.67
450	2:24.99	2:25.31	2:25.64	2:25.96	2:26.28	2:26.60	2:26.93	2:27.25	2:27.57	2:27.90
460	2:28.22	2:28.54	2:28.86	2:29.19	2:29.51	2:29.83	2:30.16	2:30.48	2:30.80	2:31.12
470	2:31.45	2:31.77	2:32.09	2:32.42	2:32.74	2:33.06	2:33.39	2:33.71	2:34.03	2:34.35
480	2:34.68	2:35.00	2:35.32	2:35.65	2:35.97	2:36.29	2:36.61	2:36.94	2:37.26	2:37.58
490	2:37.91	2:38.23	2:38.55	2:38.88	2:39.20	2:39.52	2:39.84	2:40.17	2:40.49	2:40.81
500	2:41.14	2:41.46	2:41.78	2:42.10	2:42.43	2:42.75	2:43.07	2:43.40	2:43.72	2:44.04
510	2:44.36	2:44.69	2:45.01	2:45.33	2:45.66	2:45.98	2:46.30	2:46.63	2:46.95	2:47.27
520	2:47.59	2:47.92	2:48.24	2:48.56	2:48.89	2:49.21	2:49.53	2:49.85	2:50.18	2:50.50
530	2:50.82	2:51.15	2:51.47	2:51.79	2:52.11	2:52.44	2:52.76	2:53.08	2:53.41	2:53.73
540	2:54.05	2:54.38	2:54.70	2:55.02	2:55.34	2:55.67	2:55.99	2:56.31	2:56.64	2:56.96
550	2:57.28	2:57.60	2:57.93	2:58.25	2:58.57	2:58.90	2:59.22	2:59.54	2:59.86	3:00.19
560	3:00.51	3:00.83	3:01.16	3:01.48	3:01.80	3:02.13	3:02.45	3:02.77	3:03.09	3:03.42
570	3:03.74	3:04.06	3:04.39	3:04.71	3:05.03	3:05.35	3:05.68	3:06.00	3:06.32	3:06.65
580	3:06.97	3:07.29	3:07.61	3:07.94	3:08.26	3:08.58	3:08.91	3:09.23	3:09.55	3:09.88
590	3:10.20	3:10.52	3:10.84	3:11.17	3:11.49	3:11.81	3:12.14	3:12.46	3:12.78	3:13.10

[dotted half note] = 0.48; [quarter note] = 0.32; [dotted eighth note] = 0.24; [triplet: quarter note + eighth rest] = 0.22; [eighth note] = 0.16; [triplet: eighth note + two eighth rests] = 0.11; [sixteenth note] = 0.08 seconds

CLICK: 7⅞ FRAMES; M.M.: 182.86

Click	0	1	2	3	4	5	6	7	8	9
000	0:00.00	0:00.00	0:00.33	0:00.66	0:00.98	0:01.31	0:01.64	0:01.97	0:02.30	0:02.63
010	0:02.95	0:03.28	0:03.61	0:03.94	0:04.27	0:04.59	0:04.92	0:05.25	0:05.58	0:05.91
020	0:06.23	0:06.56	0:06.89	0:07.22	0:07.55	0:07.87	0:08.20	0:08.53	0:08.86	0:09.19
030	0:09.52	0:09.84	0:10.17	0:10.50	0:10.83	0:11.16	0:11.48	0:11.81	0:12.14	0:12.47
040	0:12.80	0:13.13	0:13.45	0:13.78	0:14.11	0:14.44	0:14.77	0:15.09	0:15.42	0:15.75
050	0:16.08	0:16.41	0:16.73	0:17.06	0:17.39	0:17.72	0:18.05	0:18.38	0:18.70	0:19.03
060	0:19.36	0:19.69	0:20.02	0:20.34	0:20.67	0:21.00	0:21.33	0:21.66	0:21.98	0:22.31
070	0:22.64	0:22.97	0:23.30	0:23.62	0:23.95	0:24.28	0:24.61	0:24.94	0:25.27	0:25.59
080	0:25.92	0:26.25	0:26.58	0:26.91	0:27.23	0:27.56	0:27.89	0:28.22	0:28.55	0:28.88
090	0:29.20	0:29.53	0:29.86	0:30.19	0:30.52	0:30.84	0:31.17	0:31.50	0:31.83	0:32.16
100	0:32.48	0:32.81	0:33.14	0:33.47	0:33.80	0:34.12	0:34.45	0:34.78	0:35.11	0:35.44
110	0:35.77	0:36.09	0:36.42	0:36.75	0:37.08	0:37.41	0:37.73	0:38.06	0:38.39	0:38.72
120	0:39.05	0:39.38	0:39.70	0:40.03	0:40.36	0:40.69	0:41.02	0:41.34	0:41.67	0:42.00
130	0:42.33	0:42.66	0:42.98	0:43.31	0:43.64	0:43.97	0:44.30	0:44.63	0:44.95	0:45.28
140	0:45.61	0:45.94	0:46.27	0:46.59	0:46.92	0:47.25	0:47.58	0:47.91	0:48.23	0:48.56
150	0:48.89	0:49.22	0:49.55	0:49.88	0:50.20	0:50.53	0:50.86	0:51.19	0:51.52	0:51.84
160	0:52.17	0:52.50	0:52.83	0:53.16	0:53.48	0:53.81	0:54.14	0:54.47	0:54.80	0:55.13
170	0:55.45	0:55.78	0:56.11	0:56.44	0:56.77	0:57.09	0:57.42	0:57.75	0:58.08	0:58.41
180	0:58.73	0:59.06	0:59.39	0:59.72	1:00.05	1:00.38	1:00.70	1:01.03	1:01.36	1:01.69
190	1:02.02	1:02.34	1:02.67	1:03.00	1:03.33	1:03.66	1:03.98	1:04.31	1:04.64	1:04.97
200	1:05.30	1:05.63	1:05.95	1:06.28	1:06.61	1:06.94	1:07.27	1:07.59	1:07.92	1:08.25
210	1:08.58	1:08.91	1:09.23	1:09.56	1:09.89	1:10.22	1:10.55	1:10.87	1:11.20	1:11.53
220	1:11.86	1:12.19	1:12.52	1:12.84	1:13.17	1:13.50	1:13.83	1:14.16	1:14.48	1:14.81
230	1:15.14	1:15.47	1:15.80	1:16.12	1:16.45	1:16.78	1:17.11	1:17.44	1:17.77	1:18.09
240	1:18.42	1:18.75	1:19.08	1:19.41	1:19.73	1:20.06	1:20.39	1:20.72	1:21.05	1:21.37
250	1:21.70	1:22.03	1:22.36	1:22.69	1:23.02	1:23.34	1:23.67	1:24.00	1:24.33	1:24.66
260	1:24.98	1:25.31	1:25.64	1:25.97	1:26.30	1:26.63	1:26.95	1:27.28	1:27.61	1:27.94
270	1:28.27	1:28.59	1:28.92	1:29.25	1:29.58	1:29.91	1:30.23	1:30.56	1:30.89	1:31.22
280	1:31.55	1:31.88	1:32.20	1:32.53	1:32.86	1:33.19	1:33.52	1:33.84	1:34.17	1:34.50
290	1:34.83	1:35.16	1:35.48	1:35.81	1:36.14	1:36.47	1:36.80	1:37.13	1:37.45	1:37.78
300	1:38.11	1:38.44	1:38.77	1:39.09	1:39.42	1:39.75	1:40.08	1:40.41	1:40.73	1:41.06
310	1:41.39	1:41.72	1:42.05	1:42.37	1:42.70	1:43.03	1:43.36	1:43.69	1:44.02	1:44.34
320	1:44.67	1:45.00	1:45.33	1:45.66	1:45.98	1:46.31	1:46.64	1:46.97	1:47.30	1:47.62
330	1:47.95	1:48.28	1:48.61	1:48.94	1:49.27	1:49.59	1:49.92	1:50.25	1:50.58	1:50.91
340	1:51.23	1:51.56	1:51.89	1:52.22	1:52.55	1:52.88	1:53.20	1:53.53	1:53.86	1:54.19
350	1:54.52	1:54.84	1:55.17	1:55.50	1:55.83	1:56.16	1:56.48	1:56.81	1:57.14	1:57.47
360	1:57.80	1:58.13	1:58.45	1:58.78	1:59.11	1:59.44	1:59.77	2:00.09	2:00.42	2:00.75
370	2:01.08	2:01.41	2:01.73	2:02.06	2:02.39	2:02.72	2:03.05	2:03.37	2:03.70	2:04.03
380	2:04.36	2:04.69	2:05.02	2:05.34	2:05.67	2:06.00	2:06.33	2:06.66	2:06.98	2:07.31
390	2:07.64	2:07.97	2:08.30	2:08.62	2:08.95	2:09.28	2:09.61	2:09.94	2:10.27	2:10.59
400	2:10.92	2:11.25	2:11.58	2:11.91	2:12.23	2:12.56	2:12.89	2:13.22	2:13.55	2:13.88
410	2:14.20	2:14.53	2:14.86	2:15.19	2:15.52	2:15.84	2:16.17	2:16.50	2:16.83	2:17.16
420	2:17.48	2:17.81	2:18.14	2:18.47	2:18.80	2:19.12	2:19.45	2:19.78	2:20.11	2:20.44
430	2:20.77	2:21.09	2:21.42	2:21.75	2:22.08	2:22.41	2:22.73	2:23.06	2:23.39	2:23.72
440	2:24.05	2:24.38	2:24.70	2:25.03	2:25.36	2:25.69	2:26.02	2:26.34	2:26.67	2:27.00
450	2:27.33	2:27.66	2:27.98	2:28.31	2:28.64	2:28.97	2:29.30	2:29.62	2:29.95	2:30.28
460	2:30.61	2:30.94	2:31.27	2:31.59	2:31.92	2:32.25	2:32.58	2:32.91	2:33.23	2:33.56
470	2:33.89	2:34.22	2:34.55	2:34.87	2:35.20	2:35.53	2:35.86	2:36.19	2:36.52	2:36.84
480	2:37.17	2:37.50	2:37.83	2:38.16	2:38.48	2:38.81	2:39.14	2:39.47	2:39.80	2:40.13
490	2:40.45	2:40.78	2:41.11	2:41.44	2:41.77	2:42.09	2:42.42	2:42.75	2:43.08	2:43.41
500	2:43.73	2:44.06	2:44.39	2:44.72	2:45.05	2:45.37	2:45.70	2:46.03	2:46.36	2:46.69
510	2:47.02	2:47.34	2:47.67	2:48.00	2:48.33	2:48.66	2:48.98	2:49.31	2:49.64	2:49.97
520	2:50.30	2:50.63	2:50.95	2:51.28	2:51.61	2:51.94	2:52.27	2:52.59	2:52.92	2:53.25
530	2:53.58	2:53.91	2:54.23	2:54.56	2:54.89	2:55.22	2:55.55	2:55.87	2:56.20	2:56.53
540	2:56.86	2:57.19	2:57.52	2:57.84	2:58.17	2:58.50	2:58.83	2:59.16	2:59.48	2:59.81
550	3:00.14	3:00.47	3:00.80	3:01.12	3:01.45	3:01.78	3:02.11	3:02.44	3:02.77	3:03.09
560	3:03.42	3:03.75	3:04.08	3:04.41	3:04.73	3:05.06	3:05.39	3:05.72	3:06.05	3:06.38
570	3:06.70	3:07.03	3:07.36	3:07.69	3:08.02	3:08.34	3:08.67	3:09.00	3:09.33	3:09.66
580	3:09.98	3:10.31	3:10.64	3:10.97	3:11.30	3:11.62	3:11.95	3:12.28	3:12.61	3:12.94
590	3:13.27	3:13.59	3:13.92	3:14.25	3:14.58	3:14.91	3:15.23	3:15.56	3:15.89	3:16.22

♩. = 0.49; ♩ = 0.33; ♪. = 0.25; (triplet ♩ 𝄾) = 0.22; ♪ = 0.16; (triplet ♪ 𝄾 𝄾) = 0.11; 𝅘𝅥𝅯 = 0.08 seconds

CLICK: 8 0/8 FRAMES; M.M.: 180.00

Click	0	1	2	3	4	5	6	7	8	9
000	0:00.00	0:00.00	0:00.33	0:00.67	0:01.00	0:01.33	0:01.67	0:02.00	0:02.33	0:02.67
010	0:03.00	0:03.33	0:03.67	0:04.00	0:04.33	0:04.67	0:05.00	0:05.33	0:05.67	0:06.00
020	0:06.33	0:06.67	0:07.00	0:07.33	0:07.67	0:08.00	0:08.33	0:08.67	0:09.00	0:09.33
030	0:09.67	0:10.00	0:10.33	0:10.67	0:11.00	0:11.33	0:11.67	0:12.00	0:12.33	0:12.67
040	0:13.00	0:13.33	0:13.67	0:14.00	0:14.33	0:14.67	0:15.00	0:15.33	0:15.67	0:16.00
050	0:16.33	0:16.67	0:17.00	0:17.33	0:17.67	0:18.00	0:18.33	0:18.67	0:19.00	0:19.33
060	0:19.67	0:20.00	0:20.33	0:20.67	0:21.00	0:21.33	0:21.67	0:22.00	0:22.33	0:22.67
070	0:23.00	0:23.33	0:23.67	0:24.00	0:24.33	0:24.67	0:25.00	0:25.33	0:25.67	0:26.00
080	0:26.33	0:26.67	0:27.00	0:27.33	0:27.67	0:28.00	0:28.33	0:28.67	0:29.00	0:29.33
090	0:29.67	0:30.00	0:30.33	0:30.67	0:31.00	0:31.33	0:31.67	0:32.00	0:32.33	0:32.67
100	0:33.00	0:33.33	0:33.67	0:34.00	0:34.33	0:34.67	0:35.00	0:35.33	0:35.67	0:36.00
110	0:36.33	0:36.67	0:37.00	0:37.33	0:37.67	0:38.00	0:38.33	0:38.67	0:39.00	0:39.33
120	0:39.67	0:40.00	0:40.33	0:40.67	0:41.00	0:41.33	0:41.67	0:42.00	0:42.33	0:42.67
130	0:43.00	0:43.33	0:43.67	0:44.00	0:44.33	0:44.67	0:45.00	0:45.33	0:45.67	0:46.00
140	0:46.33	0:46.67	0:47.00	0:47.33	0:47.67	0:48.00	0:48.33	0:48.67	0:49.00	0:49.33
150	0:49.67	0:50.00	0:50.33	0:50.67	0:51.00	0:51.33	0:51.67	0:52.00	0:52.33	0:52.67
160	0:53.00	0:53.33	0:53.67	0:54.00	0:54.33	0:54.67	0:55.00	0:55.33	0:55.67	0:56.00
170	0:56.33	0:56.67	0:57.00	0:57.33	0:57.67	0:58.00	0:58.33	0:58.67	0:59.00	0:59.33
180	0:59.67	1:00.00	1:00.33	1:00.67	1:01.00	1:01.33	1:01.67	1:02.00	1:02.33	1:02.67
190	1:03.00	1:03.33	1:03.67	1:04.00	1:04.33	1:04.67	1:05.00	1:05.33	1:05.67	1:06.00
200	1:06.33	1:06.67	1:07.00	1:07.33	1:07.67	1:08.00	1:08.33	1:08.67	1:09.00	1:09.33
210	1:09.67	1:10.00	1:10.33	1:10.67	1:11.00	1:11.33	1:11.67	1:12.00	1:12.33	1:12.67
220	1:13.00	1:13.33	1:13.67	1:14.00	1:14.33	1:14.67	1:15.00	1:15.33	1:15.67	1:16.00
230	1:16.33	1:16.67	1:17.00	1:17.33	1:17.67	1:18.00	1:18.33	1:18.67	1:19.00	1:19.33
240	1:19.67	1:20.00	1:20.33	1:20.67	1:21.00	1:21.33	1:21.67	1:22.00	1:22.33	1:22.67
250	1:23.00	1:23.33	1:23.67	1:24.00	1:24.33	1:24.67	1:25.00	1:25.33	1:25.67	1:26.00
260	1:26.33	1:26.67	1:27.00	1:27.33	1:27.67	1:28.00	1:28.33	1:28.67	1:29.00	1:29.33
270	1:29.67	1:30.00	1:30.33	1:30.67	1:31.00	1:31.33	1:31.67	1:32.00	1:32.33	1:32.67
280	1:33.00	1:33.33	1:33.67	1:34.00	1:34.33	1:34.67	1:35.00	1:35.33	1:35.67	1:36.00
290	1:36.33	1:36.67	1:37.00	1:37.33	1:37.67	1:38.00	1:38.33	1:38.67	1:39.00	1:39.33
300	1:39.67	1:40.00	1:40.33	1:40.67	1:41.00	1:41.33	1:41.67	1:42.00	1:42.33	1:42.67
310	1:43.00	1:43.33	1:43.67	1:44.00	1:44.33	1:44.67	1:45.00	1:45.33	1:45.67	1:46.00
320	1:46.33	1:46.67	1:47.00	1:47.33	1:47.67	1:48.00	1:48.33	1:48.67	1:49.00	1:49.33
330	1:49.67	1:50.00	1:50.33	1:50.67	1:51.00	1:51.33	1:51.67	1:52.00	1:52.33	1:52.67
340	1:53.00	1:53.33	1:53.67	1:54.00	1:54.33	1:54.67	1:55.00	1:55.33	1:55.67	1:56.00
350	1:56.33	1:56.67	1:57.00	1:57.33	1:57.67	1:58.00	1:58.33	1:58.67	1:59.00	1:59.33
360	1:59.67	2:00.00	2:00.33	2:00.67	2:01.00	2:01.33	2:01.67	2:02.00	2:02.33	2:02.67
370	2:03.00	2:03.33	2:03.67	2:04.00	2:04.33	2:04.67	2:05.00	2:05.33	2:05.67	2:06.00
380	2:06.33	2:06.67	2:07.00	2:07.33	2:07.67	2:08.00	2:08.33	2:08.67	2:09.00	2:09.33
390	2:09.67	2:10.00	2:10.33	2:10.67	2:11.00	2:11.33	2:11.67	2:12.00	2:12.33	2:12.67
400	2:13.00	2:13.33	2:13.67	2:14.00	2:14.33	2:14.67	2:15.00	2:15.33	2:15.67	2:16.00
410	2:16.33	2:16.67	2:17.00	2:17.33	2:17.67	2:18.00	2:18.33	2:18.67	2:19.00	2:19.33
420	2:19.67	2:20.00	2:20.33	2:20.67	2:21.00	2:21.33	2:21.67	2:22.00	2:22.33	2:22.67
430	2:23.00	2:23.33	2:23.67	2:24.00	2:24.33	2:24.67	2:25.00	2:25.33	2:25.67	2:26.00
440	2:26.33	2:26.67	2:27.00	2:27.33	2:27.67	2:28.00	2:28.33	2:28.67	2:29.00	2:29.33
450	2:29.67	2:30.00	2:30.33	2:30.67	2:31.00	2:31.33	2:31.67	2:32.00	2:32.33	2:32.67
460	2:33.00	2:33.33	2:33.67	2:34.00	2:34.33	2:34.67	2:35.00	2:35.33	2:35.67	2:36.00
470	2:36.33	2:36.67	2:37.00	2:37.33	2:37.67	2:38.00	2:38.33	2:38.67	2:39.00	2:39.33
480	2:39.67	2:40.00	2:40.33	2:40.67	2:41.00	2:41.33	2:41.67	2:42.00	2:42.33	2:42.67
490	2:43.00	2:43.33	2:43.67	2:44.00	2:44.33	2:44.67	2:45.00	2:45.33	2:45.67	2:46.00
500	2:46.33	2:46.67	2:47.00	2:47.33	2:47.67	2:48.00	2:48.33	2:48.67	2:49.00	2:49.33
510	2:49.67	2:50.00	2:50.33	2:50.67	2:51.00	2:51.33	2:51.67	2:52.00	2:52.33	2:52.67
520	2:53.00	2:53.33	2:53.67	2:54.00	2:54.33	2:54.67	2:55.00	2:55.33	2:55.67	2:56.00
530	2:56.33	2:56.67	2:57.00	2:57.33	2:57.67	2:58.00	2:58.33	2:58.67	2:59.00	2:59.33
540	2:59.67	3:00.00	3:00.33	3:00.67	3:01.00	3:01.33	3:01.67	3:02.00	3:02.33	3:02.67
550	3:03.00	3:03.33	3:03.67	3:04.00	3:04.33	3:04.67	3:05.00	3:05.33	3:05.67	3:06.00
560	3:06.33	3:06.67	3:07.00	3:07.33	3:07.67	3:08.00	3:08.33	3:08.67	3:09.00	3:09.33
570	3:09.67	3:10.00	3:10.33	3:10.67	3:11.00	3:11.33	3:11.67	3:12.00	3:12.33	3:12.67
580	3:13.00	3:13.33	3:13.67	3:14.00	3:14.33	3:14.67	3:15.00	3:15.33	3:15.67	3:16.00
590	3:16.33	3:16.67	3:17.00	3:17.33	3:17.67	3:18.00	3:18.33	3:18.67	3:19.00	3:19.33

♩. = 0.50; ♩ = 0.33; ♪. = 0.25; (3: ♩ 𝄾) = 0.22; ♪ = 0.17; (3: ♪ 𝄾 𝄾) = 0.11; 𝅘𝅥𝅯 = 0.08 seconds

CLICK: 8⅛ FRAMES; M.M.: 177.23

Click	0	1	2	3	4	5	6	7	8	9
000	0:00.00	0:00.00	0:00.34	0:00.68	0:01.02	0:01.35	0:01.69	0:02.03	0:02.37	0:02.71
010	0:03.05	0:03.39	0:03.72	0:04.06	0:04.40	0:04.74	0:05.08	0:05.42	0:05.76	0:06.09
020	0:06.43	0:06.77	0:07.11	0:07.45	0:07.79	0:08.13	0:08.46	0:08.80	0:09.14	0:09.48
030	0:09.82	0:10.16	0:10.49	0:10.83	0:11.17	0:11.51	0:11.85	0:12.19	0:12.53	0:12.86
040	0:13.20	0:13.54	0:13.88	0:14.22	0:14.56	0:14.90	0:15.23	0:15.57	0:15.91	0:16.25
050	0:16.59	0:16.93	0:17.27	0:17.60	0:17.94	0:18.28	0:18.62	0:18.96	0:19.30	0:19.64
060	0:19.97	0:20.31	0:20.65	0:20.99	0:21.33	0:21.67	0:22.01	0:22.34	0:22.68	0:23.02
070	0:23.36	0:23.70	0:24.04	0:24.38	0:24.71	0:25.05	0:25.39	0:25.73	0:26.07	0:26.41
080	0:26.74	0:27.08	0:27.42	0:27.76	0:28.10	0:28.44	0:28.78	0:29.11	0:29.45	0:29.79
090	0:30.13	0:30.47	0:30.81	0:31.15	0:31.48	0:31.82	0:32.16	0:32.50	0:32.84	0:33.18
100	0:33.52	0:33.85	0:34.19	0:34.53	0:34.87	0:35.21	0:35.55	0:35.89	0:36.22	0:36.56
110	0:36.90	0:37.24	0:37.58	0:37.92	0:38.26	0:38.59	0:38.93	0:39.27	0:39.61	0:39.95
120	0:40.29	0:40.63	0:40.96	0:41.30	0:41.64	0:41.98	0:42.32	0:42.66	0:42.99	0:43.33
130	0:43.67	0:44.01	0:44.35	0:44.69	0:45.03	0:45.36	0:45.70	0:46.04	0:46.38	0:46.72
140	0:47.06	0:47.40	0:47.73	0:48.07	0:48.41	0:48.75	0:49.09	0:49.43	0:49.77	0:50.10
150	0:50.44	0:50.78	0:51.12	0:51.46	0:51.80	0:52.14	0:52.47	0:52.81	0:53.15	0:53.49
160	0:53.83	0:54.17	0:54.51	0:54.84	0:55.18	0:55.52	0:55.86	0:56.20	0:56.54	0:56.87
170	0:57.21	0:57.55	0:57.89	0:58.23	0:58.57	0:58.91	0:59.24	0:59.58	0:59.92	1:00.26
180	1:00.60	1:00.94	1:01.28	1:01.61	1:01.95	1:02.29	1:02.63	1:02.97	1:03.31	1:03.65
190	1:03.98	1:04.32	1:04.66	1:05.00	1:05.34	1:05.68	1:06.02	1:06.35	1:06.69	1:07.03
200	1:07.37	1:07.71	1:08.05	1:08.39	1:08.72	1:09.06	1:09.40	1:09.74	1:10.08	1:10.42
210	1:10.76	1:11.09	1:11.43	1:11.77	1:12.11	1:12.45	1:12.79	1:13.13	1:13.46	1:13.80
220	1:14.14	1:14.48	1:14.82	1:15.16	1:15.49	1:15.83	1:16.17	1:16.51	1:16.85	1:17.19
230	1:17.53	1:17.86	1:18.20	1:18.54	1:18.88	1:19.22	1:19.56	1:19.90	1:20.23	1:20.57
240	1:20.91	1:21.25	1:21.59	1:21.93	1:22.27	1:22.60	1:22.94	1:23.28	1:23.62	1:23.96
250	1:24.30	1:24.64	1:24.97	1:25.31	1:25.65	1:25.99	1:26.33	1:26.67	1:27.01	1:27.34
260	1:27.68	1:28.02	1:28.36	1:28.70	1:29.04	1:29.37	1:29.71	1:30.05	1:30.39	1:30.73
270	1:31.07	1:31.41	1:31.74	1:32.08	1:32.42	1:32.76	1:33.10	1:33.44	1:33.78	1:34.11
280	1:34.45	1:34.79	1:35.13	1:35.47	1:35.81	1:36.15	1:36.48	1:36.82	1:37.16	1:37.50
290	1:37.84	1:38.18	1:38.52	1:38.85	1:39.19	1:39.53	1:39.87	1:40.21	1:40.55	1:40.89
300	1:41.22	1:41.56	1:41.90	1:42.24	1:42.58	1:42.92	1:43.26	1:43.59	1:43.93	1:44.27
310	1:44.61	1:44.95	1:45.29	1:45.62	1:45.96	1:46.30	1:46.64	1:46.98	1:47.32	1:47.66
320	1:47.99	1:48.33	1:48.67	1:49.01	1:49.35	1:49.69	1:50.03	1:50.36	1:50.70	1:51.04
330	1:51.38	1:51.72	1:52.06	1:52.40	1:52.73	1:53.07	1:53.41	1:53.75	1:54.09	1:54.43
340	1:54.77	1:55.10	1:55.44	1:55.78	1:56.12	1:56.46	1:56.80	1:57.14	1:57.47	1:57.81
350	1:58.15	1:58.49	1:58.83	1:59.17	1:59.51	1:59.84	2:00.18	2:00.52	2:00.86	2:01.20
360	2:01.54	2:01.88	2:02.21	2:02.55	2:02.89	2:03.23	2:03.57	2:03.91	2:04.24	2:04.58
370	2:04.92	2:05.26	2:05.60	2:05.94	2:06.28	2:06.61	2:06.95	2:07.29	2:07.63	2:07.97
380	2:08.31	2:08.65	2:08.98	2:09.32	2:09.66	2:10.00	2:10.34	2:10.68	2:11.02	2:11.35
390	2:11.69	2:12.03	2:12.37	2:12.71	2:13.05	2:13.39	2:13.72	2:14.06	2:14.40	2:14.74
400	2:15.08	2:15.42	2:15.76	2:16.09	2:16.43	2:16.77	2:17.11	2:17.45	2:17.79	2:18.12
410	2:18.46	2:18.80	2:19.14	2:19.48	2:19.82	2:20.16	2:20.49	2:20.83	2:21.17	2:21.51
420	2:21.85	2:22.19	2:22.53	2:22.86	2:23.20	2:23.54	2:23.88	2:24.22	2:24.56	2:24.90
430	2:25.23	2:25.57	2:25.91	2:26.25	2:26.59	2:26.93	2:27.27	2:27.60	2:27.94	2:28.28
440	2:28.62	2:28.96	2:29.30	2:29.64	2:29.97	2:30.31	2:30.65	2:30.99	2:31.33	2:31.67
450	2:32.01	2:32.34	2:32.68	2:33.02	2:33.36	2:33.70	2:34.04	2:34.37	2:34.71	2:35.05
460	2:35.39	2:35.73	2:36.07	2:36.41	2:36.74	2:37.08	2:37.42	2:37.76	2:38.10	2:38.44
470	2:38.78	2:39.11	2:39.45	2:39.79	2:40.13	2:40.47	2:40.81	2:41.15	2:41.48	2:41.82
480	2:42.16	2:42.50	2:42.84	2:43.18	2:43.52	2:43.85	2:44.19	2:44.53	2:44.87	2:45.21
490	2:45.55	2:45.89	2:46.22	2:46.56	2:46.90	2:47.24	2:47.58	2:47.92	2:48.26	2:48.59
500	2:48.93	2:49.27	2:49.61	2:49.95	2:50.29	2:50.63	2:50.96	2:51.30	2:51.64	2:51.98
510	2:52.32	2:52.66	2:52.99	2:53.33	2:53.67	2:54.01	2:54.35	2:54.69	2:55.03	2:55.36
520	2:55.70	2:56.04	2:56.38	2:56.72	2:57.06	2:57.40	2:57.73	2:58.07	2:58.41	2:58.75
530	2:59.09	2:59.43	2:59.77	3:00.10	3:00.44	3:00.78	3:01.12	3:01.46	3:01.80	3:02.14
540	3:02.47	3:02.81	3:03.15	3:03.49	3:03.83	3:04.17	3:04.51	3:04.84	3:05.18	3:05.52
550	3:05.86	3:06.20	3:06.54	3:06.87	3:07.21	3:07.55	3:07.89	3:08.23	3:08.57	3:08.91
560	3:09.24	3:09.58	3:09.92	3:10.26	3:10.60	3:10.94	3:11.28	3:11.61	3:11.95	3:12.29
570	3:12.63	3:12.97	3:13.31	3:13.65	3:13.98	3:14.32	3:14.66	3:15.00	3:15.34	3:15.68
580	3:16.02	3:16.35	3:16.69	3:17.03	3:17.37	3:17.71	3:18.05	3:18.39	3:18.72	3:19.06
590	3:19.40	3:19.74	3:20.08	3:20.42	3:20.76	3:21.09	3:21.43	3:21.77	3:22.11	3:22.45

♩. = 0.51; ♩ = 0.34; ♪. = 0.25; [triplet: ♩ 𝄾] = 0.23; ♪ = 0.17; [triplet: ♪ 𝄾 𝄾] = 0.11; 𝅘𝅥𝅯 = 0.08 seconds

CLICK: 8 2/8 FRAMES; M.M.: 174.55

Click	0	1	2	3	4	5	6	7	8	9
000	0:00.00	0:00.00	0:00.34	0:00.69	0:01.03	0:01.38	0:01.72	0:02.06	0:02.41	0:02.75
010	0:03.09	0:03.44	0:03.78	0:04.13	0:04.47	0:04.81	0:05.16	0:05.50	0:05.84	0:06.19
020	0:06.53	0:06.88	0:07.22	0:07.56	0:07.91	0:08.25	0:08.59	0:08.94	0:09.28	0:09.63
030	0:09.97	0:10.31	0:10.66	0:11.00	0:11.34	0:11.69	0:12.03	0:12.38	0:12.72	0:13.06
040	0:13.41	0:13.75	0:14.09	0:14.44	0:14.78	0:15.13	0:15.47	0:15.81	0:16.16	0:16.50
050	0:16.84	0:17.19	0:17.53	0:17.88	0:18.22	0:18.56	0:18.91	0:19.25	0:19.59	0:19.94
060	0:20.28	0:20.63	0:20.97	0:21.31	0:21.66	0:22.00	0:22.34	0:22.69	0:23.03	0:23.38
070	0:23.72	0:24.06	0:24.41	0:24.75	0:25.09	0:25.44	0:25.78	0:26.13	0:26.47	0:26.81
080	0:27.16	0:27.50	0:27.84	0:28.19	0:28.53	0:28.88	0:29.22	0:29.56	0:29.91	0:30.25
090	0:30.59	0:30.94	0:31.28	0:31.63	0:31.97	0:32.31	0:32.66	0:33.00	0:33.34	0:33.69
100	0:34.03	0:34.38	0:34.72	0:35.06	0:35.41	0:35.75	0:36.09	0:36.44	0:36.78	0:37.13
110	0:37.47	0:37.81	0:38.16	0:38.50	0:38.84	0:39.19	0:39.53	0:39.88	0:40.22	0:40.56
120	0:40.91	0:41.25	0:41.59	0:41.94	0:42.28	0:42.63	0:42.97	0:43.31	0:43.66	0:44.00
130	0:44.34	0:44.69	0:45.03	0:45.38	0:45.72	0:46.06	0:46.41	0:46.75	0:47.09	0:47.44
140	0:47.78	0:48.13	0:48.47	0:48.81	0:49.16	0:49.50	0:49.84	0:50.19	0:50.53	0:50.88
150	0:51.22	0:51.56	0:51.91	0:52.25	0:52.59	0:52.94	0:53.28	0:53.63	0:53.97	0:54.31
160	0:54.66	0:55.00	0:55.34	0:55.69	0:56.03	0:56.38	0:56.72	0:57.06	0:57.41	0:57.75
170	0:58.09	0:58.44	0:58.78	0:59.13	0:59.47	0:59.81	1:00.16	1:00.50	1:00.84	1:01.19
180	1:01.53	1:01.88	1:02.22	1:02.56	1:02.91	1:03.25	1:03.59	1:03.94	1:04.28	1:04.63
190	1:04.97	1:05.31	1:05.66	1:06.00	1:06.34	1:06.69	1:07.03	1:07.38	1:07.72	1:08.06
200	1:08.41	1:08.75	1:09.09	1:09.44	1:09.78	1:10.13	1:10.47	1:10.81	1:11.16	1:11.50
210	1:11.84	1:12.19	1:12.53	1:12.88	1:13.22	1:13.56	1:13.91	1:14.25	1:14.59	1:14.94
220	1:15.28	1:15.63	1:15.97	1:16.31	1:16.66	1:17.00	1:17.34	1:17.69	1:18.03	1:18.37
230	1:18.72	1:19.06	1:19.41	1:19.75	1:20.09	1:20.44	1:20.78	1:21.13	1:21.47	1:21.81
240	1:22.16	1:22.50	1:22.84	1:23.19	1:23.53	1:23.88	1:24.22	1:24.56	1:24.91	1:25.25
250	1:25.59	1:25.94	1:26.28	1:26.63	1:26.97	1:27.31	1:27.66	1:28.00	1:28.34	1:28.69
260	1:29.03	1:29.38	1:29.72	1:30.06	1:30.41	1:30.75	1:31.09	1:31.44	1:31.78	1:32.13
270	1:32.47	1:32.81	1:33.16	1:33.50	1:33.84	1:34.19	1:34.53	1:34.88	1:35.22	1:35.56
280	1:35.91	1:36.25	1:36.59	1:36.94	1:37.28	1:37.63	1:37.97	1:38.31	1:38.66	1:39.00
290	1:39.34	1:39.69	1:40.03	1:40.38	1:40.72	1:41.06	1:41.41	1:41.75	1:42.09	1:42.44
300	1:42.78	1:43.13	1:43.47	1:43.81	1:44.16	1:44.50	1:44.84	1:45.19	1:45.53	1:45.88
310	1:46.22	1:46.56	1:46.91	1:47.25	1:47.59	1:47.94	1:48.28	1:48.63	1:48.97	1:49.31
320	1:49.66	1:50.00	1:50.34	1:50.69	1:51.03	1:51.38	1:51.72	1:52.06	1:52.41	1:52.75
330	1:53.09	1:53.44	1:53.78	1:54.13	1:54.47	1:54.81	1:55.16	1:55.50	1:55.84	1:56.19
340	1:56.53	1:56.88	1:57.22	1:57.56	1:57.91	1:58.25	1:58.59	1:58.94	1:59.28	1:59.63
350	1:59.97	2:00.31	2:00.66	2:01.00	2:01.34	2:01.69	2:02.03	2:02.38	2:02.72	2:03.06
360	2:03.41	2:03.75	2:04.09	2:04.44	2:04.78	2:05.13	2:05.47	2:05.81	2:06.16	2:06.50
370	2:06.84	2:07.19	2:07.53	2:07.88	2:08.22	2:08.56	2:08.91	2:09.25	2:09.59	2:09.94
380	2:10.28	2:10.63	2:10.97	2:11.31	2:11.66	2:12.00	2:12.34	2:12.69	2:13.03	2:13.37
390	2:13.72	2:14.06	2:14.41	2:14.75	2:15.09	2:15.44	2:15.78	2:16.12	2:16.47	2:16.81
400	2:17.16	2:17.50	2:17.84	2:18.19	2:18.53	2:18.87	2:19.22	2:19.56	2:19.91	2:20.25
410	2:20.59	2:20.94	2:21.28	2:21.63	2:21.97	2:22.31	2:22.66	2:23.00	2:23.34	2:23.69
420	2:24.03	2:24.38	2:24.72	2:25.06	2:25.41	2:25.75	2:26.09	2:26.44	2:26.78	2:27.13
430	2:27.47	2:27.81	2:28.16	2:28.50	2:28.84	2:29.19	2:29.53	2:29.88	2:30.22	2:30.56
440	2:30.91	2:31.25	2:31.59	2:31.94	2:32.28	2:32.63	2:32.97	2:33.31	2:33.66	2:34.00
450	2:34.34	2:34.69	2:35.03	2:35.38	2:35.72	2:36.06	2:36.41	2:36.75	2:37.09	2:37.44
460	2:37.78	2:38.13	2:38.47	2:38.81	2:39.16	2:39.50	2:39.84	2:40.19	2:40.53	2:40.88
470	2:41.22	2:41.56	2:41.91	2:42.25	2:42.59	2:42.94	2:43.28	2:43.63	2:43.97	2:44.31
480	2:44.66	2:45.00	2:45.34	2:45.69	2:46.03	2:46.38	2:46.72	2:47.06	2:47.41	2:47.75
490	2:48.09	2:48.44	2:48.78	2:49.13	2:49.47	2:49.81	2:50.16	2:50.50	2:50.84	2:51.19
500	2:51.53	2:51.88	2:52.22	2:52.56	2:52.91	2:53.25	2:53.59	2:53.94	2:54.28	2:54.63
510	2:54.97	2:55.31	2:55.66	2:56.00	2:56.34	2:56.69	2:57.03	2:57.37	2:57.72	2:58.06
520	2:58.41	2:58.75	2:59.09	2:59.44	2:59.78	3:00.12	3:00.47	3:00.81	3:01.16	3:01.50
530	3:01.84	3:02.19	3:02.53	3:02.87	3:03.22	3:03.56	3:03.91	3:04.25	3:04.59	3:04.94
540	3:05.28	3:05.63	3:05.97	3:06.31	3:06.66	3:07.00	3:07.34	3:07.69	3:08.03	3:08.38
550	3:08.72	3:09.06	3:09.41	3:09.75	3:10.09	3:10.44	3:10.78	3:11.13	3:11.47	3:11.81
560	3:12.16	3:12.50	3:12.84	3:13.19	3:13.53	3:13.88	3:14.22	3:14.56	3:14.91	3:15.25
570	3:15.59	3:15.94	3:16.28	3:16.63	3:16.97	3:17.31	3:17.66	3:18.00	3:18.34	3:18.69
580	3:19.03	3:19.38	3:19.72	3:20.06	3:20.41	3:20.75	3:21.09	3:21.44	3:21.78	3:22.13
590	3:22.47	3:22.81	3:23.16	3:23.50	3:23.84	3:24.19	3:24.53	3:24.88	3:25.22	3:25.56

𝅗𝅥. = 0.52; ♩ = 0.34; ♪. = 0.26; (triplet) ♩ 𝄾 = 0.23; ♪ = 0.17; (triplet) ♪𝄾𝄾 = 0.11; 𝅘𝅥𝅯 = 0.09 seconds

CLICK: 8 3/8 FRAMES; M.M.: 171.94

Click	0	1	2	3	4	5	6	7	8	9
000	0:00.00	0:00.00	0:00.35	0:00.70	0:01.05	0:01.40	0:01.74	0:02.09	0:02.44	0:02.79
010	0:03.14	0:03.49	0:03.84	0:04.19	0:04.54	0:04.89	0:05.23	0:05.58	0:05.93	0:06.28
020	0:06.63	0:06.98	0:07.33	0:07.68	0:08.03	0:08.38	0:08.72	0:09.07	0:09.42	0:09.77
030	0:10.12	0:10.47	0:10.82	0:11.17	0:11.52	0:11.86	0:12.21	0:12.56	0:12.91	0:13.26
040	0:13.61	0:13.96	0:14.31	0:14.66	0:15.01	0:15.35	0:15.70	0:16.05	0:16.40	0:16.75
050	0:17.10	0:17.45	0:17.80	0:18.15	0:18.49	0:18.84	0:19.19	0:19.54	0:19.89	0:20.24
060	0:20.59	0:20.94	0:21.29	0:21.64	0:21.98	0:22.33	0:22.68	0:23.03	0:23.38	0:23.73
070	0:24.08	0:24.43	0:24.78	0:25.13	0:25.47	0:25.82	0:26.17	0:26.52	0:26.87	0:27.22
080	0:27.57	0:27.92	0:28.27	0:28.61	0:28.96	0:29.31	0:29.66	0:30.01	0:30.36	0:30.71
090	0:31.06	0:31.41	0:31.76	0:32.10	0:32.45	0:32.80	0:33.15	0:33.50	0:33.85	0:34.20
100	0:34.55	0:34.90	0:35.24	0:35.59	0:35.94	0:36.29	0:36.64	0:36.99	0:37.34	0:37.69
110	0:38.04	0:38.39	0:38.73	0:39.08	0:39.43	0:39.78	0:40.13	0:40.48	0:40.83	0:41.18
120	0:41.53	0:41.88	0:42.22	0:42.57	0:42.92	0:43.27	0:43.62	0:43.97	0:44.32	0:44.67
130	0:45.02	0:45.36	0:45.71	0:46.06	0:46.41	0:46.76	0:47.11	0:47.46	0:47.81	0:48.16
140	0:48.51	0:48.85	0:49.20	0:49.55	0:49.90	0:50.25	0:50.60	0:50.95	0:51.30	0:51.65
150	0:51.99	0:52.34	0:52.69	0:53.04	0:53.39	0:53.74	0:54.09	0:54.44	0:54.79	0:55.14
160	0:55.48	0:55.83	0:56.18	0:56.53	0:56.88	0:57.23	0:57.58	0:57.93	0:58.28	0:58.63
170	0:58.97	0:59.32	0:59.67	1:00.02	1:00.37	1:00.72	1:01.07	1:01.42	1:01.77	1:02.11
180	1:02.46	1:02.81	1:03.16	1:03.51	1:03.86	1:04.21	1:04.56	1:04.91	1:05.26	1:05.60
190	1:05.95	1:06.30	1:06.65	1:07.00	1:07.35	1:07.70	1:08.05	1:08.40	1:08.74	1:09.09
200	1:09.44	1:09.79	1:10.14	1:10.49	1:10.84	1:11.19	1:11.54	1:11.89	1:12.23	1:12.58
210	1:12.93	1:13.28	1:13.63	1:13.98	1:14.33	1:14.68	1:15.03	1:15.38	1:15.72	1:16.07
220	1:16.42	1:16.77	1:17.12	1:17.47	1:17.82	1:18.17	1:18.52	1:18.86	1:19.21	1:19.56
230	1:19.91	1:20.26	1:20.61	1:20.96	1:21.31	1:21.66	1:22.01	1:22.35	1:22.70	1:23.05
240	1:23.40	1:23.75	1:24.10	1:24.45	1:24.80	1:25.15	1:25.49	1:25.84	1:26.19	1:26.54
250	1:26.89	1:27.24	1:27.59	1:27.94	1:28.29	1:28.64	1:28.98	1:29.33	1:29.68	1:30.03
260	1:30.38	1:30.73	1:31.08	1:31.43	1:31.78	1:32.13	1:32.47	1:32.82	1:33.17	1:33.52
270	1:33.87	1:34.22	1:34.57	1:34.92	1:35.27	1:35.61	1:35.96	1:36.31	1:36.66	1:37.01
280	1:37.36	1:37.71	1:38.06	1:38.41	1:38.76	1:39.10	1:39.45	1:39.80	1:40.15	1:40.50
290	1:40.85	1:41.20	1:41.55	1:41.90	1:42.24	1:42.59	1:42.94	1:43.29	1:43.64	1:43.99
300	1:44.34	1:44.69	1:45.04	1:45.39	1:45.73	1:46.08	1:46.43	1:46.78	1:47.13	1:47.48
310	1:47.83	1:48.18	1:48.53	1:48.88	1:49.22	1:49.57	1:49.92	1:50.27	1:50.62	1:50.97
320	1:51.32	1:51.67	1:52.02	1:52.36	1:52.71	1:53.06	1:53.41	1:53.76	1:54.11	1:54.46
330	1:54.81	1:55.16	1:55.51	1:55.85	1:56.20	1:56.55	1:56.90	1:57.25	1:57.60	1:57.95
340	1:58.30	1:58.65	1:58.99	1:59.34	1:59.69	2:00.04	2:00.39	2:00.74	2:01.09	2:01.44
350	2:01.79	2:02.14	2:02.48	2:02.83	2:03.18	2:03.53	2:03.88	2:04.23	2:04.58	2:04.93
360	2:05.28	2:05.63	2:05.97	2:06.32	2:06.67	2:07.02	2:07.37	2:07.72	2:08.07	2:08.42
370	2:08.77	2:09.11	2:09.46	2:09.81	2:10.16	2:10.51	2:10.86	2:11.21	2:11.56	2:11.91
380	2:12.26	2:12.60	2:12.95	2:13.30	2:13.65	2:14.00	2:14.35	2:14.70	2:15.05	2:15.40
390	2:15.74	2:16.09	2:16.44	2:16.79	2:17.14	2:17.49	2:17.84	2:18.19	2:18.54	2:18.89
400	2:19.23	2:19.58	2:19.93	2:20.28	2:20.63	2:20.98	2:21.33	2:21.68	2:22.03	2:22.38
410	2:22.72	2:23.07	2:23.42	2:23.77	2:24.12	2:24.47	2:24.82	2:25.17	2:25.52	2:25.86
420	2:26.21	2:26.56	2:26.91	2:27.26	2:27.61	2:27.96	2:28.31	2:28.66	2:29.01	2:29.35
430	2:29.70	2:30.05	2:30.40	2:30.75	2:31.10	2:31.45	2:31.80	2:32.15	2:32.49	2:32.84
440	2:33.19	2:33.54	2:33.89	2:34.24	2:34.59	2:34.94	2:35.29	2:35.64	2:35.98	2:36.33
450	2:36.68	2:37.03	2:37.38	2:37.73	2:38.08	2:38.43	2:38.78	2:39.13	2:39.47	2:39.82
460	2:40.17	2:40.52	2:40.87	2:41.22	2:41.57	2:41.92	2:42.27	2:42.61	2:42.96	2:43.31
470	2:43.66	2:44.01	2:44.36	2:44.71	2:45.06	2:45.41	2:45.76	2:46.10	2:46.45	2:46.80
480	2:47.15	2:47.50	2:47.85	2:48.20	2:48.55	2:48.90	2:49.24	2:49.59	2:49.94	2:50.29
490	2:50.64	2:50.99	2:51.34	2:51.69	2:52.04	2:52.39	2:52.73	2:53.08	2:53.43	2:53.78
500	2:54.13	2:54.48	2:54.83	2:55.18	2:55.53	2:55.88	2:56.22	2:56.57	2:56.92	2:57.27
510	2:57.62	2:57.97	2:58.32	2:58.67	2:59.02	2:59.36	2:59.71	3:00.06	3:00.41	3:00.76
520	3:01.11	3:01.46	3:01.81	3:02.16	3:02.51	3:02.85	3:03.20	3:03.55	3:03.90	3:04.25
530	3:04.60	3:04.95	3:05.30	3:05.65	3:05.99	3:06.34	3:06.69	3:07.04	3:07.39	3:07.74
540	3:08.09	3:08.44	3:08.79	3:09.14	3:09.48	3:09.83	3:10.18	3:10.53	3:10.88	3:11.23
550	3:11.58	3:11.93	3:12.28	3:12.63	3:12.97	3:13.32	3:13.67	3:14.02	3:14.37	3:14.72
560	3:15.07	3:15.42	3:15.77	3:16.11	3:16.46	3:16.81	3:17.16	3:17.51	3:17.86	3:18.21
570	3:18.56	3:18.91	3:19.26	3:19.60	3:19.95	3:20.30	3:20.65	3:21.00	3:21.35	3:21.70
580	3:22.05	3:22.40	3:22.74	3:23.09	3:23.44	3:23.79	3:24.14	3:24.49	3:24.84	3:25.19
590	3:25.54	3:25.89	3:26.23	3:26.58	3:26.93	3:27.28	3:27.63	3:27.98	3:28.33	3:28.68

𝅘𝅥. = 0.52; 𝅘𝅥 = 0.35; 𝅘𝅥𝅮. = 0.26; (triplet 3: 𝅘𝅥 𝄾) = 0.23; 𝅘𝅥𝅮 = 0.17; (triplet 3: 𝅘𝅥𝅮 𝄾 𝄾) = 0.12; 𝅘𝅥𝅯 = 0.09 seconds

CLICK: 8 4/8 FRAMES; M.M.: 169.41

Click	0	1	2	3	4	5	6	7	8	9
000	0:00.00	0:00.00	0:00.35	0:00.71	0:01.06	0:01.42	0:01.77	0:02.13	0:02.48	0:02.83
010	0:03.19	0:03.54	0:03.90	0:04.25	0:04.60	0:04.96	0:05.31	0:05.67	0:06.02	0:06.38
020	0:06.73	0:07.08	0:07.44	0:07.79	0:08.15	0:08.50	0:08.85	0:09.21	0:09.56	0:09.92
030	0:10.27	0:10.63	0:10.98	0:11.33	0:11.69	0:12.04	0:12.40	0:12.75	0:13.10	0:13.46
040	0:13.81	0:14.17	0:14.52	0:14.88	0:15.23	0:15.58	0:15.94	0:16.29	0:16.65	0:17.00
050	0:17.35	0:17.71	0:18.06	0:18.42	0:18.77	0:19.13	0:19.48	0:19.83	0:20.19	0:20.54
060	0:20.90	0:21.25	0:21.60	0:21.96	0:22.31	0:22.67	0:23.02	0:23.38	0:23.73	0:24.08
070	0:24.44	0:24.79	0:25.15	0:25.50	0:25.85	0:26.21	0:26.56	0:26.92	0:27.27	0:27.63
080	0:27.98	0:28.33	0:28.69	0:29.04	0:29.40	0:29.75	0:30.10	0:30.46	0:30.81	0:31.17
090	0:31.52	0:31.88	0:32.23	0:32.58	0:32.94	0:33.29	0:33.65	0:34.00	0:34.35	0:34.71
100	0:35.06	0:35.42	0:35.77	0:36.13	0:36.48	0:36.83	0:37.19	0:37.54	0:37.90	0:38.25
110	0:38.60	0:38.96	0:39.31	0:39.67	0:40.02	0:40.38	0:40.73	0:41.08	0:41.44	0:41.79
120	0:42.15	0:42.50	0:42.85	0:43.21	0:43.56	0:43.92	0:44.27	0:44.63	0:44.98	0:45.33
130	0:45.69	0:46.04	0:46.40	0:46.75	0:47.10	0:47.46	0:47.81	0:48.17	0:48.52	0:48.88
140	0:49.23	0:49.58	0:49.94	0:50.29	0:50.65	0:51.00	0:51.35	0:51.71	0:52.06	0:52.42
150	0:52.77	0:53.13	0:53.48	0:53.83	0:54.19	0:54.54	0:54.90	0:55.25	0:55.60	0:55.96
160	0:56.31	0:56.67	0:57.02	0:57.38	0:57.73	0:58.08	0:58.44	0:58.79	0:59.15	0:59.50
170	0:59.85	1:00.21	1:00.56	1:00.92	1:01.27	1:01.63	1:01.98	1:02.33	1:02.69	1:03.04
180	1:03.40	1:03.75	1:04.10	1:04.46	1:04.81	1:05.17	1:05.52	1:05.88	1:06.23	1:06.58
190	1:06.94	1:07.29	1:07.65	1:08.00	1:08.35	1:08.71	1:09.06	1:09.42	1:09.77	1:10.13
200	1:10.48	1:10.83	1:11.19	1:11.54	1:11.90	1:12.25	1:12.60	1:12.96	1:13.31	1:13.67
210	1:14.02	1:14.38	1:14.73	1:15.08	1:15.44	1:15.79	1:16.15	1:16.50	1:16.85	1:17.21
220	1:17.56	1:17.92	1:18.27	1:18.63	1:18.98	1:19.33	1:19.69	1:20.04	1:20.40	1:20.75
230	1:21.10	1:21.46	1:21.81	1:22.17	1:22.52	1:22.88	1:23.23	1:23.58	1:23.94	1:24.29
240	1:24.65	1:25.00	1:25.35	1:25.71	1:26.06	1:26.42	1:26.77	1:27.13	1:27.48	1:27.83
250	1:28.19	1:28.54	1:28.90	1:29.25	1:29.60	1:29.96	1:30.31	1:30.67	1:31.02	1:31.38
260	1:31.73	1:32.08	1:32.44	1:32.79	1:33.15	1:33.50	1:33.85	1:34.21	1:34.56	1:34.92
270	1:35.27	1:35.63	1:35.98	1:36.33	1:36.69	1:37.04	1:37.40	1:37.75	1:38.10	1:38.46
280	1:38.81	1:39.17	1:39.52	1:39.88	1:40.23	1:40.58	1:40.94	1:41.29	1:41.65	1:42.00
290	1:42.35	1:42.71	1:43.06	1:43.42	1:43.77	1:44.13	1:44.48	1:44.83	1:45.19	1:45.54
300	1:45.90	1:46.25	1:46.60	1:46.96	1:47.31	1:47.67	1:48.02	1:48.38	1:48.73	1:49.08
310	1:49.44	1:49.79	1:50.15	1:50.50	1:50.85	1:51.21	1:51.56	1:51.92	1:52.27	1:52.63
320	1:52.98	1:53.33	1:53.69	1:54.04	1:54.40	1:54.75	1:55.10	1:55.46	1:55.81	1:56.17
330	1:56.52	1:56.88	1:57.23	1:57.58	1:57.94	1:58.29	1:58.65	1:59.00	1:59.35	1:59.71
340	2:00.06	2:00.42	2:00.77	2:01.12	2:01.48	2:01.83	2:02.19	2:02.54	2:02.90	2:03.25
350	2:03.60	2:03.96	2:04.31	2:04.67	2:05.02	2:05.38	2:05.73	2:06.08	2:06.44	2:06.79
360	2:07.15	2:07.50	2:07.85	2:08.21	2:08.56	2:08.92	2:09.27	2:09.62	2:09.98	2:10.33
370	2:10.69	2:11.04	2:11.40	2:11.75	2:12.10	2:12.46	2:12.81	2:13.17	2:13.52	2:13.88
380	2:14.23	2:14.58	2:14.94	2:15.29	2:15.65	2:16.00	2:16.35	2:16.71	2:17.06	2:17.42
390	2:17.77	2:18.13	2:18.48	2:18.83	2:19.19	2:19.54	2:19.90	2:20.25	2:20.60	2:20.96
400	2:21.31	2:21.67	2:22.02	2:22.38	2:22.73	2:23.08	2:23.44	2:23.79	2:24.15	2:24.50
410	2:24.85	2:25.21	2:25.56	2:25.92	2:26.27	2:26.63	2:26.98	2:27.33	2:27.69	2:28.04
420	2:28.40	2:28.75	2:29.10	2:29.46	2:29.81	2:30.17	2:30.52	2:30.88	2:31.23	2:31.58
430	2:31.94	2:32.29	2:32.65	2:33.00	2:33.35	2:33.71	2:34.06	2:34.42	2:34.77	2:35.13
440	2:35.48	2:35.83	2:36.19	2:36.54	2:36.90	2:37.25	2:37.60	2:37.96	2:38.31	2:38.67
450	2:39.02	2:39.38	2:39.73	2:40.08	2:40.44	2:40.79	2:41.15	2:41.50	2:41.85	2:42.21
460	2:42.56	2:42.92	2:43.27	2:43.63	2:43.98	2:44.33	2:44.69	2:45.04	2:45.40	2:45.75
470	2:46.10	2:46.46	2:46.81	2:47.17	2:47.52	2:47.88	2:48.23	2:48.58	2:48.94	2:49.29
480	2:49.65	2:50.00	2:50.35	2:50.71	2:51.06	2:51.42	2:51.77	2:52.13	2:52.48	2:52.83
490	2:53.19	2:53.54	2:53.90	2:54.25	2:54.60	2:54.96	2:55.31	2:55.67	2:56.02	2:56.38
500	2:56.73	2:57.08	2:57.44	2:57.79	2:58.15	2:58.50	2:58.85	2:59.21	2:59.56	2:59.92
510	3:00.27	3:00.63	3:00.98	3:01.33	3:01.69	3:02.04	3:02.40	3:02.75	3:03.10	3:03.46
520	3:03.81	3:04.17	3:04.52	3:04.87	3:05.23	3:05.58	3:05.94	3:06.29	3:06.65	3:07.00
530	3:07.35	3:07.71	3:08.06	3:08.42	3:08.77	3:09.13	3:09.48	3:09.83	3:10.19	3:10.54
540	3:10.90	3:11.25	3:11.60	3:11.96	3:12.31	3:12.67	3:13.02	3:13.38	3:13.73	3:14.08
550	3:14.44	3:14.79	3:15.15	3:15.50	3:15.85	3:16.21	3:16.56	3:16.92	3:17.27	3:17.63
560	3:17.98	3:18.33	3:18.69	3:19.04	3:19.40	3:19.75	3:20.10	3:20.46	3:20.81	3:21.17
570	3:21.52	3:21.88	3:22.23	3:22.58	3:22.94	3:23.29	3:23.65	3:24.00	3:24.35	3:24.71
580	3:25.06	3:25.42	3:25.77	3:26.13	3:26.48	3:26.83	3:27.19	3:27.54	3:27.90	3:28.25
590	3:28.60	3:28.96	3:29.31	3:29.67	3:30.02	3:30.38	3:30.73	3:31.08	3:31.44	3:31.79

♩. = 0.53; ♩ = 0.35; ♪. = 0.27; (triplet ♩ 𝄾) = 0.24; ♪ = 0.18; (triplet ♪ 𝄾 𝄾) = 0.12; 𝅘𝅥𝅯 = 0.09 seconds

CLICK: 8⅝ FRAMES; M.M.: 166.96

Click	0	1	2	3	4	5	6	7	8	9
000	0:00.00	0:00.00	0:00.36	0:00.72	0:01.08	0:01.44	0:01.80	0:02.16	0:02.52	0:02.88
010	0:03.23	0:03.59	0:03.95	0:04.31	0:04.67	0:05.03	0:05.39	0:05.75	0:06.11	0:06.47
020	0:06.83	0:07.19	0:07.55	0:07.91	0:08.27	0:08.63	0:08.98	0:09.34	0:09.70	0:10.06
030	0:10.42	0:10.78	0:11.14	0:11.50	0:11.86	0:12.22	0:12.58	0:12.94	0:13.30	0:13.66
040	0:14.02	0:14.38	0:14.73	0:15.09	0:15.45	0:15.81	0:16.17	0:16.53	0:16.89	0:17.25
050	0:17.61	0:17.97	0:18.33	0:18.69	0:19.05	0:19.41	0:19.77	0:20.13	0:20.48	0:20.84
060	0:21.20	0:21.56	0:21.92	0:22.28	0:22.64	0:23.00	0:23.36	0:23.72	0:24.08	0:24.44
070	0:24.80	0:25.16	0:25.52	0:25.88	0:26.23	0:26.59	0:26.95	0:27.31	0:27.67	0:28.03
080	0:28.39	0:28.75	0:29.11	0:29.47	0:29.83	0:30.19	0:30.55	0:30.91	0:31.27	0:31.63
090	0:31.98	0:32.34	0:32.70	0:33.06	0:33.42	0:33.78	0:34.14	0:34.50	0:34.86	0:35.22
100	0:35.58	0:35.94	0:36.30	0:36.66	0:37.02	0:37.38	0:37.73	0:38.09	0:38.45	0:38.81
110	0:39.17	0:39.53	0:39.89	0:40.25	0:40.61	0:40.97	0:41.33	0:41.69	0:42.05	0:42.41
120	0:42.77	0:43.13	0:43.48	0:43.84	0:44.20	0:44.56	0:44.92	0:45.28	0:45.64	0:46.00
130	0:46.36	0:46.72	0:47.08	0:47.44	0:47.80	0:48.16	0:48.52	0:48.88	0:49.23	0:49.59
140	0:49.95	0:50.31	0:50.67	0:51.03	0:51.39	0:51.75	0:52.11	0:52.47	0:52.83	0:53.19
150	0:53.55	0:53.91	0:54.27	0:54.63	0:54.98	0:55.34	0:55.70	0:56.06	0:56.42	0:56.78
160	0:57.14	0:57.50	0:57.86	0:58.22	0:58.58	0:58.94	0:59.30	0:59.66	1:00.02	1:00.38
170	1:00.73	1:01.09	1:01.45	1:01.81	1:02.17	1:02.53	1:02.89	1:03.25	1:03.61	1:03.97
180	1:04.33	1:04.69	1:05.05	1:05.41	1:05.77	1:06.12	1:06.48	1:06.84	1:07.20	1:07.56
190	1:07.92	1:08.28	1:08.64	1:09.00	1:09.36	1:09.72	1:10.08	1:10.44	1:10.80	1:11.16
200	1:11.52	1:11.87	1:12.23	1:12.59	1:12.95	1:13.31	1:13.67	1:14.03	1:14.39	1:14.75
210	1:15.11	1:15.47	1:15.83	1:16.19	1:16.55	1:16.91	1:17.27	1:17.62	1:17.98	1:18.34
220	1:18.70	1:19.06	1:19.42	1:19.78	1:20.14	1:20.50	1:20.86	1:21.22	1:21.58	1:21.94
230	1:22.30	1:22.66	1:23.02	1:23.38	1:23.73	1:24.09	1:24.45	1:24.81	1:25.17	1:25.53
240	1:25.89	1:26.25	1:26.61	1:26.97	1:27.33	1:27.69	1:28.05	1:28.41	1:28.77	1:29.13
250	1:29.48	1:29.84	1:30.20	1:30.56	1:30.92	1:31.28	1:31.64	1:32.00	1:32.36	1:32.72
260	1:33.08	1:33.44	1:33.80	1:34.16	1:34.52	1:34.87	1:35.23	1:35.59	1:35.95	1:36.31
270	1:36.67	1:37.03	1:37.39	1:37.75	1:38.11	1:38.47	1:38.83	1:39.19	1:39.55	1:39.91
280	1:40.27	1:40.62	1:40.98	1:41.34	1:41.70	1:42.06	1:42.42	1:42.78	1:43.14	1:43.50
290	1:43.86	1:44.22	1:44.58	1:44.94	1:45.30	1:45.66	1:46.02	1:46.38	1:46.73	1:47.09
300	1:47.45	1:47.81	1:48.17	1:48.53	1:48.89	1:49.25	1:49.61	1:49.97	1:50.33	1:50.69
310	1:51.05	1:51.41	1:51.77	1:52.13	1:52.48	1:52.84	1:53.20	1:53.56	1:53.92	1:54.28
320	1:54.64	1:55.00	1:55.36	1:55.72	1:56.08	1:56.44	1:56.80	1:57.16	1:57.52	1:57.87
330	1:58.23	1:58.59	1:58.95	1:59.31	1:59.67	2:00.03	2:00.39	2:00.75	2:01.11	2:01.47
340	2:01.83	2:02.19	2:02.55	2:02.91	2:03.27	2:03.63	2:03.98	2:04.34	2:04.70	2:05.06
350	2:05.42	2:05.78	2:06.14	2:06.50	2:06.86	2:07.22	2:07.58	2:07.94	2:08.30	2:08.66
360	2:09.02	2:09.38	2:09.73	2:10.09	2:10.45	2:10.81	2:11.17	2:11.53	2:11.89	2:12.25
370	2:12.61	2:12.97	2:13.33	2:13.69	2:14.05	2:14.41	2:14.77	2:15.12	2:15.48	2:15.84
380	2:16.20	2:16.56	2:16.92	2:17.28	2:17.64	2:18.00	2:18.36	2:18.72	2:19.08	2:19.44
390	2:19.80	2:20.16	2:20.52	2:20.87	2:21.23	2:21.59	2:21.95	2:22.31	2:22.67	2:23.03
400	2:23.39	2:23.75	2:24.11	2:24.47	2:24.83	2:25.19	2:25.55	2:25.91	2:26.27	2:26.62
410	2:26.98	2:27.34	2:27.70	2:28.06	2:28.42	2:28.78	2:29.14	2:29.50	2:29.86	2:30.22
420	2:30.58	2:30.94	2:31.30	2:31.66	2:32.02	2:32.37	2:32.73	2:33.09	2:33.45	2:33.81
430	2:34.17	2:34.53	2:34.89	2:35.25	2:35.61	2:35.97	2:36.33	2:36.69	2:37.05	2:37.41
440	2:37.77	2:38.12	2:38.48	2:38.84	2:39.20	2:39.56	2:39.92	2:40.28	2:40.64	2:41.00
450	2:41.36	2:41.72	2:42.08	2:42.44	2:42.80	2:43.16	2:43.52	2:43.88	2:44.23	2:44.59
460	2:44.95	2:45.31	2:45.67	2:46.03	2:46.39	2:46.75	2:47.11	2:47.47	2:47.83	2:48.19
470	2:48.55	2:48.91	2:49.27	2:49.63	2:49.98	2:50.34	2:50.70	2:51.06	2:51.42	2:51.78
480	2:52.14	2:52.50	2:52.86	2:53.22	2:53.58	2:53.94	2:54.30	2:54.66	2:55.02	2:55.38
490	2:55.73	2:56.09	2:56.45	2:56.81	2:57.17	2:57.53	2:57.89	2:58.25	2:58.61	2:58.97
500	2:59.33	2:59.69	3:00.05	3:00.41	3:00.77	3:01.12	3:01.48	3:01.84	3:02.20	3:02.56
510	3:02.92	3:03.28	3:03.64	3:04.00	3:04.36	3:04.72	3:05.08	3:05.44	3:05.80	3:06.16
520	3:06.52	3:06.87	3:07.23	3:07.59	3:07.95	3:08.31	3:08.67	3:09.03	3:09.39	3:09.75
530	3:10.11	3:10.47	3:10.83	3:11.19	3:11.55	3:11.91	3:12.27	3:12.62	3:12.98	3:13.34
540	3:13.70	3:14.06	3:14.42	3:14.78	3:15.14	3:15.50	3:15.86	3:16.22	3:16.58	3:16.94
550	3:17.30	3:17.66	3:18.02	3:18.37	3:18.73	3:19.09	3:19.45	3:19.81	3:20.17	3:20.53
560	3:20.89	3:21.25	3:21.61	3:21.97	3:22.33	3:22.69	3:23.05	3:23.41	3:23.77	3:24.12
570	3:24.48	3:24.84	3:25.20	3:25.56	3:25.92	3:26.28	3:26.64	3:27.00	3:27.36	3:27.72
580	3:28.08	3:28.44	3:28.80	3:29.16	3:29.52	3:29.88	3:30.23	3:30.59	3:30.95	3:31.31
590	3:31.67	3:32.03	3:32.39	3:32.75	3:33.11	3:33.47	3:33.83	3:34.19	3:34.55	3:34.91

♩. = 0.54; ♩ = 0.36; ♪. = 0.27; (triplet ♩ 𝄾) = 0.24; ♪ = 0.18; (triplet ♪ 𝄾 𝄾) = 0.12; 𝅘𝅥𝅯 = 0.09 seconds

CLICK: 8 6/8 FRAMES; M.M.: 164.57

Click	0	1	2	3	4	5	6	7	8	9
000	0:00.00	0:00.00	0:00.36	0:00.73	0:01.09	0:01.46	0:01.82	0:02.19	0:02.55	0:02.92
010	0:03.28	0:03.65	0:04.01	0:04.38	0:04.74	0:05.10	0:05.47	0:05.83	0:06.20	0:06.56
020	0:06.93	0:07.29	0:07.66	0:08.02	0:08.39	0:08.75	0:09.11	0:09.48	0:09.84	0:10.21
030	0:10.57	0:10.94	0:11.30	0:11.67	0:12.03	0:12.40	0:12.76	0:13.13	0:13.49	0:13.85
040	0:14.22	0:14.58	0:14.95	0:15.31	0:15.68	0:16.04	0:16.41	0:16.77	0:17.14	0:17.50
050	0:17.86	0:18.23	0:18.59	0:18.96	0:19.32	0:19.69	0:20.05	0:20.42	0:20.78	0:21.15
060	0:21.51	0:21.88	0:22.24	0:22.60	0:22.97	0:23.33	0:23.70	0:24.06	0:24.43	0:24.79
070	0:25.16	0:25.52	0:25.89	0:26.25	0:26.61	0:26.98	0:27.34	0:27.71	0:28.07	0:28.44
080	0:28.80	0:29.17	0:29.53	0:29.90	0:30.26	0:30.63	0:30.99	0:31.35	0:31.72	0:32.08
090	0:32.45	0:32.81	0:33.18	0:33.54	0:33.91	0:34.27	0:34.64	0:35.00	0:35.36	0:35.73
100	0:36.09	0:36.46	0:36.82	0:37.19	0:37.55	0:37.92	0:38.28	0:38.65	0:39.01	0:39.38
110	0:39.74	0:40.10	0:40.47	0:40.83	0:41.20	0:41.56	0:41.93	0:42.29	0:42.66	0:43.02
120	0:43.39	0:43.75	0:44.11	0:44.48	0:44.84	0:45.21	0:45.57	0:45.94	0:46.30	0:46.67
130	0:47.03	0:47.40	0:47.76	0:48.13	0:48.49	0:48.85	0:49.22	0:49.58	0:49.95	0:50.31
140	0:50.68	0:51.04	0:51.41	0:51.77	0:52.14	0:52.50	0:52.86	0:53.23	0:53.59	0:53.96
150	0:54.32	0:54.69	0:55.05	0:55.42	0:55.78	0:56.15	0:56.51	0:56.88	0:57.24	0:57.60
160	0:57.97	0:58.33	0:58.70	0:59.06	0:59.43	0:59.79	1:00.16	1:00.52	1:00.89	1:01.25
170	1:01.61	1:01.98	1:02.34	1:02.71	1:03.07	1:03.44	1:03.80	1:04.17	1:04.53	1:04.90
180	1:05.26	1:05.63	1:05.99	1:06.35	1:06.72	1:07.08	1:07.45	1:07.81	1:08.18	1:08.54
190	1:08.91	1:09.27	1:09.64	1:10.00	1:10.36	1:10.73	1:11.09	1:11.46	1:11.82	1:12.19
200	1:12.55	1:12.92	1:13.28	1:13.65	1:14.01	1:14.38	1:14.74	1:15.10	1:15.47	1:15.83
210	1:16.20	1:16.56	1:16.93	1:17.29	1:17.66	1:18.02	1:18.39	1:18.75	1:19.11	1:19.48
220	1:19.84	1:20.21	1:20.57	1:20.94	1:21.30	1:21.67	1:22.03	1:22.40	1:22.76	1:23.13
230	1:23.49	1:23.85	1:24.22	1:24.58	1:24.95	1:25.31	1:25.68	1:26.04	1:26.41	1:26.77
240	1:27.14	1:27.50	1:27.86	1:28.23	1:28.59	1:28.96	1:29.32	1:29.69	1:30.05	1:30.42
250	1:30.78	1:31.15	1:31.51	1:31.88	1:32.24	1:32.60	1:32.97	1:33.33	1:33.70	1:34.06
260	1:34.43	1:34.79	1:35.16	1:35.52	1:35.89	1:36.25	1:36.61	1:36.98	1:37.34	1:37.71
270	1:38.07	1:38.44	1:38.80	1:39.17	1:39.53	1:39.90	1:40.26	1:40.63	1:40.99	1:41.35
280	1:41.72	1:42.08	1:42.45	1:42.81	1:43.18	1:43.54	1:43.91	1:44.27	1:44.64	1:45.00
290	1:45.36	1:45.73	1:46.09	1:46.46	1:46.82	1:47.19	1:47.55	1:47.92	1:48.28	1:48.65
300	1:49.01	1:49.38	1:49.74	1:50.10	1:50.47	1:50.83	1:51.20	1:51.56	1:51.93	1:52.29
310	1:52.66	1:53.02	1:53.39	1:53.75	1:54.11	1:54.48	1:54.84	1:55.21	1:55.57	1:55.94
320	1:56.30	1:56.67	1:57.03	1:57.40	1:57.76	1:58.13	1:58.49	1:58.85	1:59.22	1:59.58
330	1:59.95	2:00.31	2:00.68	2:01.04	2:01.41	2:01.77	2:02.14	2:02.50	2:02.86	2:03.23
340	2:03.59	2:03.96	2:04.32	2:04.69	2:05.05	2:05.42	2:05.78	2:06.15	2:06.51	2:06.87
350	2:07.24	2:07.60	2:07.97	2:08.33	2:08.70	2:09.06	2:09.43	2:09.79	2:10.16	2:10.52
360	2:10.89	2:11.25	2:11.61	2:11.98	2:12.34	2:12.71	2:13.07	2:13.44	2:13.80	2:14.17
370	2:14.53	2:14.90	2:15.26	2:15.63	2:15.99	2:16.35	2:16.72	2:17.08	2:17.45	2:17.81
380	2:18.18	2:18.54	2:18.91	2:19.27	2:19.64	2:20.00	2:20.36	2:20.73	2:21.09	2:21.46
390	2:21.82	2:22.19	2:22.55	2:22.92	2:23.28	2:23.65	2:24.01	2:24.38	2:24.74	2:25.10
400	2:25.47	2:25.83	2:26.20	2:26.56	2:26.93	2:27.29	2:27.66	2:28.02	2:28.39	2:28.75
410	2:29.11	2:29.48	2:29.84	2:30.21	2:30.57	2:30.94	2:31.30	2:31.67	2:32.03	2:32.40
420	2:32.76	2:33.13	2:33.49	2:33.85	2:34.22	2:34.58	2:34.95	2:35.31	2:35.68	2:36.04
430	2:36.41	2:36.77	2:37.14	2:37.50	2:37.86	2:38.23	2:38.59	2:38.96	2:39.32	2:39.69
440	2:40.05	2:40.42	2:40.78	2:41.15	2:41.51	2:41.88	2:42.24	2:42.60	2:42.97	2:43.33
450	2:43.70	2:44.06	2:44.43	2:44.79	2:45.16	2:45.52	2:45.89	2:46.25	2:46.61	2:46.98
460	2:47.34	2:47.71	2:48.07	2:48.44	2:48.80	2:49.17	2:49.53	2:49.90	2:50.26	2:50.63
470	2:50.99	2:51.35	2:51.72	2:52.08	2:52.45	2:52.81	2:53.18	2:53.54	2:53.91	2:54.27
480	2:54.64	2:55.00	2:55.36	2:55.73	2:56.09	2:56.46	2:56.82	2:57.19	2:57.55	2:57.92
490	2:58.28	2:58.65	2:59.01	2:59.38	2:59.74	3:00.10	3:00.47	3:00.83	3:01.20	3:01.56
500	3:01.93	3:02.29	3:02.66	3:03.02	3:03.39	3:03.75	3:04.11	3:04.48	3:04.84	3:05.21
510	3:05.57	3:05.94	3:06.30	3:06.67	3:07.03	3:07.40	3:07.76	3:08.13	3:08.49	3:08.85
520	3:09.22	3:09.58	3:09.95	3:10.31	3:10.68	3:11.04	3:11.41	3:11.77	3:12.14	3:12.50
530	3:12.86	3:13.23	3:13.59	3:13.96	3:14.32	3:14.69	3:15.05	3:15.42	3:15.78	3:16.15
540	3:16.51	3:16.88	3:17.24	3:17.60	3:17.97	3:18.33	3:18.70	3:19.06	3:19.43	3:19.79
550	3:20.16	3:20.52	3:20.89	3:21.25	3:21.61	3:21.98	3:22.34	3:22.71	3:23.07	3:23.44
560	3:23.80	3:24.17	3:24.53	3:24.90	3:25.26	3:25.63	3:25.99	3:26.35	3:26.72	3:27.08
570	3:27.45	3:27.81	3:28.18	3:28.54	3:28.91	3:29.27	3:29.64	3:30.00	3:30.36	3:30.73
580	3:31.09	3:31.46	3:31.82	3:32.19	3:32.55	3:32.92	3:33.28	3:33.65	3:34.01	3:34.38
590	3:34.74	3:35.10	3:35.47	3:35.83	3:36.20	3:36.56	3:36.93	3:37.29	3:37.66	3:38.02

♩. = 0.55; ♩ = 0.36; ♪. = 0.27; (triplet ♩ 𝄾) = 0.24; ♪ = 0.18; (triplet ♪ 𝄾 𝄾) = 0.12; 𝅘𝅥𝅯 = 0.09 seconds

CLICK: 8⅞ FRAMES; M.M.: 162.25

Click	0	1	2	3	4	5	6	7	8	9
000	0:00.00	0:00.00	0:00.37	0:00.74	0:01.11	0:01.48	0:01.85	0:02.22	0:02.59	0:02.96
010	0:03.33	0:03.70	0:04.07	0:04.44	0:04.81	0:05.18	0:05.55	0:05.92	0:06.29	0:06.66
020	0:07.03	0:07.40	0:07.77	0:08.14	0:08.51	0:08.88	0:09.24	0:09.61	0:09.98	0:10.35
030	0:10.72	0:11.09	0:11.46	0:11.83	0:12.20	0:12.57	0:12.94	0:13.31	0:13.68	0:14.05
040	0:14.42	0:14.79	0:15.16	0:15.53	0:15.90	0:16.27	0:16.64	0:17.01	0:17.38	0:17.75
050	0:18.12	0:18.49	0:18.86	0:19.23	0:19.60	0:19.97	0:20.34	0:20.71	0:21.08	0:21.45
060	0:21.82	0:22.19	0:22.56	0:22.93	0:23.30	0:23.67	0:24.04	0:24.41	0:24.78	0:25.15
070	0:25.52	0:25.89	0:26.26	0:26.63	0:26.99	0:27.36	0:27.73	0:28.10	0:28.47	0:28.84
080	0:29.21	0:29.58	0:29.95	0:30.32	0:30.69	0:31.06	0:31.43	0:31.80	0:32.17	0:32.54
090	0:32.91	0:33.28	0:33.65	0:34.02	0:34.39	0:34.76	0:35.13	0:35.50	0:35.87	0:36.24
100	0:36.61	0:36.98	0:37.35	0:37.72	0:38.09	0:38.46	0:38.83	0:39.20	0:39.57	0:39.94
110	0:40.31	0:40.68	0:41.05	0:41.42	0:41.79	0:42.16	0:42.53	0:42.90	0:43.27	0:43.64
120	0:44.01	0:44.38	0:44.74	0:45.11	0:45.48	0:45.85	0:46.22	0:46.59	0:46.96	0:47.33
130	0:47.70	0:48.07	0:48.44	0:48.81	0:49.18	0:49.55	0:49.92	0:50.29	0:50.66	0:51.03
140	0:51.40	0:51.77	0:52.14	0:52.51	0:52.88	0:53.25	0:53.62	0:53.99	0:54.36	0:54.73
150	0:55.10	0:55.47	0:55.84	0:56.21	0:56.58	0:56.95	0:57.32	0:57.69	0:58.06	0:58.43
160	0:58.80	0:59.17	0:59.54	0:59.91	1:00.28	1:00.65	1:01.02	1:01.39	1:01.76	1:02.12
170	1:02.49	1:02.86	1:03.23	1:03.60	1:03.97	1:04.34	1:04.71	1:05.08	1:05.45	1:05.82
180	1:06.19	1:06.56	1:06.93	1:07.30	1:07.67	1:08.04	1:08.41	1:08.78	1:09.15	1:09.52
190	1:09.89	1:10.26	1:10.63	1:11.00	1:11.37	1:11.74	1:12.11	1:12.48	1:12.85	1:13.22
200	1:13.59	1:13.96	1:14.33	1:14.70	1:15.07	1:15.44	1:15.81	1:16.18	1:16.55	1:16.92
210	1:17.29	1:17.66	1:18.03	1:18.40	1:18.77	1:19.14	1:19.51	1:19.87	1:20.24	1:20.61
220	1:20.98	1:21.35	1:21.72	1:22.09	1:22.46	1:22.83	1:23.20	1:23.57	1:23.94	1:24.31
230	1:24.68	1:25.05	1:25.42	1:25.79	1:26.16	1:26.53	1:26.90	1:27.27	1:27.64	1:28.01
240	1:28.38	1:28.75	1:29.12	1:29.49	1:29.86	1:30.23	1:30.60	1:30.97	1:31.34	1:31.71
250	1:32.08	1:32.45	1:32.82	1:33.19	1:33.56	1:33.93	1:34.30	1:34.67	1:35.04	1:35.41
260	1:35.78	1:36.15	1:36.52	1:36.89	1:37.26	1:37.63	1:37.99	1:38.36	1:38.73	1:39.10
270	1:39.47	1:39.84	1:40.21	1:40.58	1:40.95	1:41.32	1:41.69	1:42.06	1:42.43	1:42.80
280	1:43.17	1:43.54	1:43.91	1:44.28	1:44.65	1:45.02	1:45.39	1:45.76	1:46.13	1:46.50
290	1:46.87	1:47.24	1:47.61	1:47.98	1:48.35	1:48.72	1:49.09	1:49.46	1:49.83	1:50.20
300	1:50.57	1:50.94	1:51.31	1:51.68	1:52.05	1:52.42	1:52.79	1:53.16	1:53.53	1:53.90
310	1:54.27	1:54.64	1:55.01	1:55.38	1:55.74	1:56.11	1:56.48	1:56.85	1:57.22	1:57.59
320	1:57.96	1:58.33	1:58.70	1:59.07	1:59.44	1:59.81	2:00.18	2:00.55	2:00.92	2:01.29
330	2:01.66	2:02.03	2:02.40	2:02.77	2:03.14	2:03.51	2:03.88	2:04.25	2:04.62	2:04.99
340	2:05.36	2:05.73	2:06.10	2:06.47	2:06.84	2:07.21	2:07.58	2:07.95	2:08.32	2:08.69
350	2:09.06	2:09.43	2:09.80	2:10.17	2:10.54	2:10.91	2:11.28	2:11.65	2:12.02	2:12.39
360	2:12.76	2:13.13	2:13.49	2:13.86	2:14.23	2:14.60	2:14.97	2:15.34	2:15.71	2:16.08
370	2:16.45	2:16.82	2:17.19	2:17.56	2:17.93	2:18.30	2:18.67	2:19.04	2:19.41	2:19.78
380	2:20.15	2:20.52	2:20.89	2:21.26	2:21.63	2:22.00	2:22.37	2:22.74	2:23.11	2:23.48
390	2:23.85	2:24.22	2:24.59	2:24.96	2:25.33	2:25.70	2:26.07	2:26.44	2:26.81	2:27.18
400	2:27.55	2:27.92	2:28.29	2:28.66	2:29.03	2:29.40	2:29.77	2:30.14	2:30.51	2:30.88
410	2:31.24	2:31.61	2:31.98	2:32.35	2:32.72	2:33.09	2:33.46	2:33.83	2:34.20	2:34.57
420	2:34.94	2:35.31	2:35.68	2:36.05	2:36.42	2:36.79	2:37.16	2:37.53	2:37.90	2:38.27
430	2:38.64	2:39.01	2:39.38	2:39.75	2:40.12	2:40.49	2:40.86	2:41.23	2:41.60	2:41.97
440	2:42.34	2:42.71	2:43.08	2:43.45	2:43.82	2:44.19	2:44.56	2:44.93	2:45.30	2:45.67
450	2:46.04	2:46.41	2:46.78	2:47.15	2:47.52	2:47.89	2:48.26	2:48.63	2:48.99	2:49.36
460	2:49.73	2:50.10	2:50.47	2:50.84	2:51.21	2:51.58	2:51.95	2:52.32	2:52.69	2:53.06
470	2:53.43	2:53.80	2:54.17	2:54.54	2:54.91	2:55.28	2:55.65	2:56.02	2:56.39	2:56.76
480	2:57.13	2:57.50	2:57.87	2:58.24	2:58.61	2:58.98	2:59.35	2:59.72	3:00.09	3:00.46
490	3:00.83	3:01.20	3:01.57	3:01.94	3:02.31	3:02.68	3:03.05	3:03.42	3:03.79	3:04.16
500	3:04.53	3:04.90	3:05.27	3:05.64	3:06.01	3:06.38	3:06.74	3:07.11	3:07.48	3:07.85
510	3:08.22	3:08.59	3:08.96	3:09.33	3:09.70	3:10.07	3:10.44	3:10.81	3:11.18	3:11.55
520	3:11.92	3:12.29	3:12.66	3:13.03	3:13.40	3:13.77	3:14.14	3:14.51	3:14.88	3:15.25
530	3:15.62	3:15.99	3:16.36	3:16.73	3:17.10	3:17.47	3:17.84	3:18.21	3:18.58	3:18.95
540	3:19.32	3:19.69	3:20.06	3:20.43	3:20.80	3:21.17	3:21.54	3:21.91	3:22.28	3:22.65
550	3:23.02	3:23.39	3:23.76	3:24.12	3:24.49	3:24.86	3:25.23	3:25.60	3:25.97	3:26.34
560	3:26.71	3:27.08	3:27.45	3:27.82	3:28.19	3:28.56	3:28.93	3:29.30	3:29.67	3:30.04
570	3:30.41	3:30.78	3:31.15	3:31.52	3:31.89	3:32.26	3:32.63	3:33.00	3:33.37	3:33.74
580	3:34.11	3:34.48	3:34.85	3:35.22	3:35.59	3:35.96	3:36.33	3:36.70	3:37.07	3:37.44
590	3:37.81	3:38.18	3:38.55	3:38.92	3:39.29	3:39.66	3:40.03	3:40.40	3:40.77	3:41.14

♩. = 0.55; ♩ = 0.37; ♪. = 0.28; (triplet ♩ 𝄾) = 0.25; ♪ = 0.18; (triplet ♪ 𝄾 𝄾) = 0.12; 𝅘𝅥𝅯 = 0.09 seconds

CLICK: 9⅜ FRAMES; M.M.: 160.00

Click	0	1	2	3	4	5	6	7	8	9
000	0:00.00	0:00.00	0:00.38	0:00.75	0:01.13	0:01.50	0:01.88	0:02.25	0:02.63	0:03.00
010	0:03.38	0:03.75	0:04.13	0:04.50	0:04.88	0:05.25	0:05.63	0:06.00	0:06.38	0:06.75
020	0:07.13	0:07.50	0:07.88	0:08.25	0:08.63	0:09.00	0:09.38	0:09.75	0:10.13	0:10.50
030	0:10.88	0:11.25	0:11.63	0:12.00	0:12.38	0:12.75	0:13.13	0:13.50	0:13.88	0:14.25
040	0:14.63	0:15.00	0:15.38	0:15.75	0:16.13	0:16.50	0:16.88	0:17.25	0:17.63	0:18.00
050	0:18.38	0:18.75	0:19.13	0:19.50	0:19.88	0:20.25	0:20.63	0:21.00	0:21.38	0:21.75
060	0:22.13	0:22.50	0:22.88	0:23.25	0:23.63	0:24.00	0:24.38	0:24.75	0:25.13	0:25.50
070	0:25.88	0:26.25	0:26.63	0:27.00	0:27.38	0:27.75	0:28.13	0:28.50	0:28.88	0:29.25
080	0:29.63	0:30.00	0:30.38	0:30.75	0:31.13	0:31.50	0:31.88	0:32.25	0:32.63	0:33.00
090	0:33.38	0:33.75	0:34.13	0:34.50	0:34.88	0:35.25	0:35.63	0:36.00	0:36.38	0:36.75
100	0:37.13	0:37.50	0:37.88	0:38.25	0:38.63	0:39.00	0:39.38	0:39.75	0:40.13	0:40.50
110	0:40.88	0:41.25	0:41.63	0:42.00	0:42.38	0:42.75	0:43.13	0:43.50	0:43.88	0:44.25
120	0:44.63	0:45.00	0:45.38	0:45.75	0:46.13	0:46.50	0:46.88	0:47.25	0:47.63	0:48.00
130	0:48.38	0:48.75	0:49.13	0:49.50	0:49.88	0:50.25	0:50.63	0:51.00	0:51.38	0:51.75
140	0:52.13	0:52.50	0:52.88	0:53.25	0:53.63	0:54.00	0:54.38	0:54.75	0:55.13	0:55.50
150	0:55.88	0:56.25	0:56.63	0:57.00	0:57.38	0:57.75	0:58.13	0:58.50	0:58.88	0:59.25
160	0:59.63	1:00.00	1:00.38	1:00.75	1:01.13	1:01.50	1:01.88	1:02.25	1:02.63	1:03.00
170	1:03.37	1:03.75	1:04.13	1:04.50	1:04.88	1:05.25	1:05.63	1:06.00	1:06.38	1:06.75
180	1:07.12	1:07.50	1:07.88	1:08.25	1:08.63	1:09.00	1:09.38	1:09.75	1:10.13	1:10.50
190	1:10.87	1:11.25	1:11.63	1:12.00	1:12.38	1:12.75	1:13.13	1:13.50	1:13.88	1:14.25
200	1:14.62	1:15.00	1:15.38	1:15.75	1:16.13	1:16.50	1:16.88	1:17.25	1:17.63	1:18.00
210	1:18.37	1:18.75	1:19.13	1:19.50	1:19.88	1:20.25	1:20.63	1:21.00	1:21.38	1:21.75
220	1:22.12	1:22.50	1:22.88	1:23.25	1:23.63	1:24.00	1:24.38	1:24.75	1:25.13	1:25.50
230	1:25.87	1:26.25	1:26.63	1:27.00	1:27.38	1:27.75	1:28.13	1:28.50	1:28.88	1:29.25
240	1:29.62	1:30.00	1:30.38	1:30.75	1:31.13	1:31.50	1:31.88	1:32.25	1:32.63	1:33.00
250	1:33.38	1:33.75	1:34.13	1:34.50	1:34.88	1:35.25	1:35.63	1:36.00	1:36.38	1:36.75
260	1:37.13	1:37.50	1:37.88	1:38.25	1:38.63	1:39.00	1:39.38	1:39.75	1:40.13	1:40.50
270	1:40.88	1:41.25	1:41.63	1:42.00	1:42.38	1:42.75	1:43.13	1:43.50	1:43.88	1:44.25
280	1:44.63	1:45.00	1:45.38	1:45.75	1:46.13	1:46.50	1:46.88	1:47.25	1:47.63	1:48.00
290	1:48.38	1:48.75	1:49.13	1:49.50	1:49.88	1:50.25	1:50.63	1:51.00	1:51.38	1:51.75
300	1:52.13	1:52.50	1:52.88	1:53.25	1:53.63	1:54.00	1:54.38	1:54.75	1:55.13	1:55.50
310	1:55.88	1:56.25	1:56.63	1:57.00	1:57.38	1:57.75	1:58.13	1:58.50	1:58.88	1:59.25
320	1:59.63	2:00.00	2:00.38	2:00.75	2:01.12	2:01.50	2:01.88	2:02.25	2:02.63	2:03.00
330	2:03.38	2:03.75	2:04.13	2:04.50	2:04.87	2:05.25	2:05.63	2:06.00	2:06.38	2:06.75
340	2:07.13	2:07.50	2:07.88	2:08.25	2:08.62	2:09.00	2:09.38	2:09.75	2:10.13	2:10.50
350	2:10.88	2:11.25	2:11.63	2:12.00	2:12.37	2:12.75	2:13.13	2:13.50	2:13.88	2:14.25
360	2:14.63	2:15.00	2:15.38	2:15.75	2:16.12	2:16.50	2:16.88	2:17.25	2:17.63	2:18.00
370	2:18.38	2:18.75	2:19.13	2:19.50	2:19.87	2:20.25	2:20.63	2:21.00	2:21.38	2:21.75
380	2:22.13	2:22.50	2:22.88	2:23.25	2:23.62	2:24.00	2:24.38	2:24.75	2:25.13	2:25.50
390	2:25.88	2:26.25	2:26.63	2:27.00	2:27.37	2:27.75	2:28.13	2:28.50	2:28.88	2:29.25
400	2:29.63	2:30.00	2:30.38	2:30.75	2:31.12	2:31.50	2:31.88	2:32.25	2:32.63	2:33.00
410	2:33.38	2:33.75	2:34.13	2:34.50	2:34.87	2:35.25	2:35.63	2:36.00	2:36.38	2:36.75
420	2:37.13	2:37.50	2:37.88	2:38.25	2:38.62	2:39.00	2:39.38	2:39.75	2:40.13	2:40.50
430	2:40.88	2:41.25	2:41.63	2:42.00	2:42.37	2:42.75	2:43.13	2:43.50	2:43.88	2:44.25
440	2:44.63	2:45.00	2:45.38	2:45.75	2:46.12	2:46.50	2:46.88	2:47.25	2:47.63	2:48.00
450	2:48.38	2:48.75	2:49.13	2:49.50	2:49.87	2:50.25	2:50.63	2:51.00	2:51.38	2:51.75
460	2:52.13	2:52.50	2:52.88	2:53.25	2:53.62	2:54.00	2:54.38	2:54.75	2:55.13	2:55.50
470	2:55.88	2:56.25	2:56.63	2:57.00	2:57.37	2:57.75	2:58.13	2:58.50	2:58.88	2:59.25
480	2:59.63	3:00.00	3:00.38	3:00.75	3:01.12	3:01.50	3:01.88	3:02.25	3:02.63	3:03.00
490	3:03.38	3:03.75	3:04.13	3:04.50	3:04.87	3:05.25	3:05.63	3:06.00	3:06.38	3:06.75
500	3:07.13	3:07.50	3:07.88	3:08.25	3:08.62	3:09.00	3:09.38	3:09.75	3:10.13	3:10.50
510	3:10.88	3:11.25	3:11.63	3:12.00	3:12.37	3:12.75	3:13.13	3:13.50	3:13.88	3:14.25
520	3:14.63	3:15.00	3:15.38	3:15.75	3:16.12	3:16.50	3:16.88	3:17.25	3:17.63	3:18.00
530	3:18.38	3:18.75	3:19.13	3:19.50	3:19.87	3:20.25	3:20.63	3:21.00	3:21.38	3:21.75
540	3:22.13	3:22.50	3:22.88	3:23.25	3:23.62	3:24.00	3:24.38	3:24.75	3:25.13	3:25.50
550	3:25.88	3:26.25	3:26.63	3:27.00	3:27.37	3:27.75	3:28.13	3:28.50	3:28.88	3:29.25
560	3:29.63	3:30.00	3:30.38	3:30.75	3:31.12	3:31.50	3:31.88	3:32.25	3:32.63	3:33.00
570	3:33.38	3:33.75	3:34.13	3:34.50	3:34.87	3:35.25	3:35.63	3:36.00	3:36.38	3:36.75
580	3:37.13	3:37.50	3:37.88	3:38.25	3:38.62	3:39.00	3:39.38	3:39.75	3:40.13	3:40.50
590	3:40.88	3:41.25	3:41.63	3:42.00	3:42.37	3:42.75	3:43.13	3:43.50	3:43.88	3:44.25

♩. = 0.56; ♩ = 0.38; ♪. = 0.28; (triplet ♩ 𝄾) = 0.25; ♪ = 0.19; (triplet ♪ 𝄾 𝄾) = 0.13; 𝅘𝅥𝅯 = 0.09 seconds

CLICK: 9⅛ FRAMES; M.M.: 157.81

Click	0	1	2	3	4	5	6	7	8	9
000	0:00.00	0:00.00	0:00.38	0:00.76	0:01.14	0:01.52	0:01.90	0:02.28	0:02.66	0:03.04
010	0:03.42	0:03.80	0:04.18	0:04.56	0:04.94	0:05.32	0:05.70	0:06.08	0:06.46	0:06.84
020	0:07.22	0:07.60	0:07.98	0:08.36	0:08.74	0:09.13	0:09.51	0:09.89	0:10.27	0:10.65
030	0:11.03	0:11.41	0:11.79	0:12.17	0:12.55	0:12.93	0:13.31	0:13.69	0:14.07	0:14.45
040	0:14.83	0:15.21	0:15.59	0:15.97	0:16.35	0:16.73	0:17.11	0:17.49	0:17.87	0:18.25
050	0:18.63	0:19.01	0:19.39	0:19.77	0:20.15	0:20.53	0:20.91	0:21.29	0:21.67	0:22.05
060	0:22.43	0:22.81	0:23.19	0:23.57	0:23.95	0:24.33	0:24.71	0:25.09	0:25.47	0:25.85
070	0:26.23	0:26.61	0:26.99	0:27.38	0:27.76	0:28.14	0:28.52	0:28.90	0:29.28	0:29.66
080	0:30.04	0:30.42	0:30.80	0:31.18	0:31.56	0:31.94	0:32.32	0:32.70	0:33.08	0:33.46
090	0:33.84	0:34.22	0:34.60	0:34.98	0:35.36	0:35.74	0:36.12	0:36.50	0:36.88	0:37.26
100	0:37.64	0:38.02	0:38.40	0:38.78	0:39.16	0:39.54	0:39.92	0:40.30	0:40.68	0:41.06
110	0:41.44	0:41.82	0:42.20	0:42.58	0:42.96	0:43.34	0:43.72	0:44.10	0:44.48	0:44.86
120	0:45.24	0:45.63	0:46.01	0:46.39	0:46.77	0:47.15	0:47.53	0:47.91	0:48.29	0:48.67
130	0:49.05	0:49.43	0:49.81	0:50.19	0:50.57	0:50.95	0:51.33	0:51.71	0:52.09	0:52.47
140	0:52.85	0:53.23	0:53.61	0:53.99	0:54.37	0:54.75	0:55.13	0:55.51	0:55.89	0:56.27
150	0:56.65	0:57.03	0:57.41	0:57.79	0:58.17	0:58.55	0:58.93	0:59.31	0:59.69	1:00.07
160	1:00.45	1:00.83	1:01.21	1:01.59	1:01.97	1:02.35	1:02.73	1:03.11	1:03.49	1:03.88
170	1:04.26	1:04.64	1:05.02	1:05.40	1:05.78	1:06.16	1:06.54	1:06.92	1:07.30	1:07.68
180	1:08.06	1:08.44	1:08.82	1:09.20	1:09.58	1:09.96	1:10.34	1:10.72	1:11.10	1:11.48
190	1:11.86	1:12.24	1:12.62	1:13.00	1:13.38	1:13.76	1:14.14	1:14.52	1:14.90	1:15.28
200	1:15.66	1:16.04	1:16.42	1:16.80	1:17.18	1:17.56	1:17.94	1:18.32	1:18.70	1:19.08
210	1:19.46	1:19.84	1:20.22	1:20.60	1:20.98	1:21.36	1:21.74	1:22.13	1:22.51	1:22.89
220	1:23.27	1:23.65	1:24.03	1:24.41	1:24.79	1:25.17	1:25.55	1:25.93	1:26.31	1:26.69
230	1:27.07	1:27.45	1:27.83	1:28.21	1:28.59	1:28.97	1:29.35	1:29.73	1:30.11	1:30.49
240	1:30.87	1:31.25	1:31.63	1:32.01	1:32.39	1:32.77	1:33.15	1:33.53	1:33.91	1:34.29
250	1:34.67	1:35.05	1:35.43	1:35.81	1:36.19	1:36.57	1:36.95	1:37.33	1:37.71	1:38.09
260	1:38.47	1:38.85	1:39.23	1:39.61	1:39.99	1:40.38	1:40.76	1:41.14	1:41.52	1:41.90
270	1:42.28	1:42.66	1:43.04	1:43.42	1:43.80	1:44.18	1:44.56	1:44.94	1:45.32	1:45.70
280	1:46.08	1:46.46	1:46.84	1:47.22	1:47.60	1:47.98	1:48.36	1:48.74	1:49.12	1:49.50
290	1:49.88	1:50.26	1:50.64	1:51.02	1:51.40	1:51.78	1:52.16	1:52.54	1:52.92	1:53.30
300	1:53.68	1:54.06	1:54.44	1:54.82	1:55.20	1:55.58	1:55.96	1:56.34	1:56.72	1:57.10
310	1:57.48	1:57.86	1:58.24	1:58.63	1:59.01	1:59.39	1:59.77	2:00.15	2:00.53	2:00.91
320	2:01.29	2:01.67	2:02.05	2:02.43	2:02.81	2:03.19	2:03.57	2:03.95	2:04.33	2:04.71
330	2:05.09	2:05.47	2:05.85	2:06.23	2:06.61	2:06.99	2:07.37	2:07.75	2:08.13	2:08.51
340	2:08.89	2:09.27	2:09.65	2:10.03	2:10.41	2:10.79	2:11.17	2:11.55	2:11.93	2:12.31
350	2:12.69	2:13.07	2:13.45	2:13.83	2:14.21	2:14.59	2:14.97	2:15.35	2:15.73	2:16.11
360	2:16.49	2:16.88	2:17.26	2:17.64	2:18.02	2:18.40	2:18.78	2:19.16	2:19.54	2:19.92
370	2:20.30	2:20.68	2:21.06	2:21.44	2:21.82	2:22.20	2:22.58	2:22.96	2:23.34	2:23.72
380	2:24.10	2:24.48	2:24.86	2:25.24	2:25.62	2:26.00	2:26.38	2:26.76	2:27.14	2:27.52
390	2:27.90	2:28.28	2:28.66	2:29.04	2:29.42	2:29.80	2:30.18	2:30.56	2:30.94	2:31.32
400	2:31.70	2:32.08	2:32.46	2:32.84	2:33.22	2:33.60	2:33.98	2:34.36	2:34.74	2:35.13
410	2:35.51	2:35.89	2:36.27	2:36.65	2:37.03	2:37.41	2:37.79	2:38.17	2:38.55	2:38.93
420	2:39.31	2:39.69	2:40.07	2:40.45	2:40.83	2:41.21	2:41.59	2:41.97	2:42.35	2:42.73
430	2:43.11	2:43.49	2:43.87	2:44.25	2:44.63	2:45.01	2:45.39	2:45.77	2:46.15	2:46.53
440	2:46.91	2:47.29	2:47.67	2:48.05	2:48.43	2:48.81	2:49.19	2:49.57	2:49.95	2:50.33
450	2:50.71	2:51.09	2:51.47	2:51.85	2:52.23	2:52.61	2:52.99	2:53.38	2:53.76	2:54.14
460	2:54.52	2:54.90	2:55.28	2:55.66	2:56.04	2:56.42	2:56.80	2:57.18	2:57.56	2:57.94
470	2:58.32	2:58.70	2:59.08	2:59.46	2:59.84	3:00.22	3:00.60	3:00.98	3:01.36	3:01.74
480	3:02.12	3:02.50	3:02.88	3:03.26	3:03.64	3:04.02	3:04.40	3:04.78	3:05.16	3:05.54
490	3:05.92	3:06.30	3:06.68	3:07.06	3:07.44	3:07.82	3:08.20	3:08.58	3:08.96	3:09.34
500	3:09.72	3:10.10	3:10.48	3:10.86	3:11.24	3:11.63	3:12.01	3:12.39	3:12.77	3:13.15
510	3:13.53	3:13.91	3:14.29	3:14.67	3:15.05	3:15.43	3:15.81	3:16.19	3:16.57	3:16.95
520	3:17.33	3:17.71	3:18.09	3:18.47	3:18.85	3:19.23	3:19.61	3:19.99	3:20.37	3:20.75
530	3:21.13	3:21.51	3:21.89	3:22.27	3:22.65	3:23.03	3:23.41	3:23.79	3:24.17	3:24.55
540	3:24.93	3:25.31	3:25.69	3:26.07	3:26.45	3:26.83	3:27.21	3:27.59	3:27.97	3:28.35
550	3:28.73	3:29.11	3:29.49	3:29.88	3:30.26	3:30.64	3:31.02	3:31.40	3:31.78	3:32.16
560	3:32.54	3:32.92	3:33.30	3:33.68	3:34.06	3:34.44	3:34.82	3:35.20	3:35.58	3:35.96
570	3:36.34	3:36.72	3:37.10	3:37.48	3:37.86	3:38.24	3:38.62	3:39.00	3:39.38	3:39.76
580	3:40.14	3:40.52	3:40.90	3:41.28	3:41.66	3:42.04	3:42.42	3:42.80	3:43.18	3:43.56
590	3:43.94	3:44.32	3:44.70	3:45.08	3:45.46	3:45.84	3:46.22	3:46.60	3:46.98	3:47.36

♩. = 0.57; ♩ = 0.38; ♪. = 0.29; (3) ♩ 𝄿 = 0.25; ♪ = 0.19; (3) ♪𝄿𝄿 = 0.13; 𝅘𝅥𝅯 = 0.10 seconds

CLICK: 9 2/8 FRAMES; M.M.: 155.68

Click	0	1	2	3	4	5	6	7	8	9
000	0:00.00	0:00.00	0:00.39	0:00.77	0:01.16	0:01.54	0:01.93	0:02.31	0:02.70	0:03.08
010	0:03.47	0:03.85	0:04.24	0:04.63	0:05.01	0:05.40	0:05.78	0:06.17	0:06.55	0:06.94
020	0:07.32	0:07.71	0:08.09	0:08.48	0:08.86	0:09.25	0:09.64	0:10.02	0:10.41	0:10.79
030	0:11.18	0:11.56	0:11.95	0:12.33	0:12.72	0:13.10	0:13.49	0:13.88	0:14.26	0:14.65
040	0:15.03	0:15.42	0:15.80	0:16.19	0:16.57	0:16.96	0:17.34	0:17.73	0:18.11	0:18.50
050	0:18.89	0:19.27	0:19.66	0:20.04	0:20.43	0:20.81	0:21.20	0:21.58	0:21.97	0:22.35
060	0:22.74	0:23.13	0:23.51	0:23.90	0:24.28	0:24.67	0:25.05	0:25.44	0:25.82	0:26.21
070	0:26.59	0:26.98	0:27.36	0:27.75	0:28.14	0:28.52	0:28.91	0:29.29	0:29.68	0:30.06
080	0:30.45	0:30.83	0:31.22	0:31.60	0:31.99	0:32.38	0:32.76	0:33.15	0:33.53	0:33.92
090	0:34.30	0:34.69	0:35.07	0:35.46	0:35.84	0:36.23	0:36.61	0:37.00	0:37.39	0:37.77
100	0:38.16	0:38.54	0:38.93	0:39.31	0:39.70	0:40.08	0:40.47	0:40.85	0:41.24	0:41.63
110	0:42.01	0:42.40	0:42.78	0:43.17	0:43.55	0:43.94	0:44.32	0:44.71	0:45.09	0:45.48
120	0:45.86	0:46.25	0:46.64	0:47.02	0:47.41	0:47.79	0:48.18	0:48.56	0:48.95	0:49.33
130	0:49.72	0:50.10	0:50.49	0:50.88	0:51.26	0:51.65	0:52.03	0:52.42	0:52.80	0:53.19
140	0:53.57	0:53.96	0:54.34	0:54.73	0:55.11	0:55.50	0:55.89	0:56.27	0:56.66	0:57.04
150	0:57.43	0:57.81	0:58.20	0:58.58	0:58.97	0:59.35	0:59.74	1:00.12	1:00.51	1:00.90
160	1:01.28	1:01.67	1:02.05	1:02.44	1:02.82	1:03.21	1:03.59	1:03.98	1:04.36	1:04.75
170	1:05.14	1:05.52	1:05.91	1:06.29	1:06.68	1:07.06	1:07.45	1:07.83	1:08.22	1:08.60
180	1:08.99	1:09.38	1:09.76	1:10.15	1:10.53	1:10.92	1:11.30	1:11.69	1:12.07	1:12.46
190	1:12.84	1:13.23	1:13.61	1:14.00	1:14.39	1:14.77	1:15.16	1:15.54	1:15.93	1:16.31
200	1:16.70	1:17.08	1:17.47	1:17.85	1:18.24	1:18.63	1:19.01	1:19.40	1:19.78	1:20.17
210	1:20.55	1:20.94	1:21.32	1:21.71	1:22.09	1:22.48	1:22.86	1:23.25	1:23.64	1:24.02
220	1:24.41	1:24.79	1:25.18	1:25.56	1:25.95	1:26.33	1:26.72	1:27.10	1:27.49	1:27.88
230	1:28.26	1:28.65	1:29.03	1:29.42	1:29.80	1:30.19	1:30.57	1:30.96	1:31.34	1:31.73
240	1:32.11	1:32.50	1:32.89	1:33.27	1:33.66	1:34.04	1:34.43	1:34.81	1:35.20	1:35.58
250	1:35.97	1:36.35	1:36.74	1:37.13	1:37.51	1:37.90	1:38.28	1:38.67	1:39.05	1:39.44
260	1:39.82	1:40.21	1:40.59	1:40.98	1:41.36	1:41.75	1:42.14	1:42.52	1:42.91	1:43.29
270	1:43.68	1:44.06	1:44.45	1:44.83	1:45.22	1:45.60	1:45.99	1:46.38	1:46.76	1:47.15
280	1:47.53	1:47.92	1:48.30	1:48.69	1:49.07	1:49.46	1:49.84	1:50.23	1:50.61	1:51.00
290	1:51.39	1:51.77	1:52.16	1:52.54	1:52.93	1:53.31	1:53.70	1:54.08	1:54.47	1:54.85
300	1:55.24	1:55.63	1:56.01	1:56.40	1:56.78	1:57.17	1:57.55	1:57.94	1:58.32	1:58.71
310	1:59.09	1:59.48	1:59.86	2:00.25	2:00.64	2:01.02	2:01.41	2:01.79	2:02.18	2:02.56
320	2:02.95	2:03.33	2:03.72	2:04.10	2:04.49	2:04.87	2:05.26	2:05.65	2:06.03	2:06.42
330	2:06.80	2:07.19	2:07.57	2:07.96	2:08.34	2:08.73	2:09.11	2:09.50	2:09.89	2:10.27
340	2:10.66	2:11.04	2:11.43	2:11.81	2:12.20	2:12.58	2:12.97	2:13.35	2:13.74	2:14.12
350	2:14.51	2:14.90	2:15.28	2:15.67	2:16.05	2:16.44	2:16.82	2:17.21	2:17.59	2:17.98
360	2:18.36	2:18.75	2:19.14	2:19.52	2:19.91	2:20.29	2:20.68	2:21.06	2:21.45	2:21.83
370	2:22.22	2:22.60	2:22.99	2:23.38	2:23.76	2:24.15	2:24.53	2:24.92	2:25.30	2:25.69
380	2:26.07	2:26.46	2:26.84	2:27.23	2:27.61	2:28.00	2:28.39	2:28.77	2:29.16	2:29.54
390	2:29.93	2:30.31	2:30.70	2:31.08	2:31.47	2:31.85	2:32.24	2:32.63	2:33.01	2:33.40
400	2:33.78	2:34.17	2:34.55	2:34.94	2:35.32	2:35.71	2:36.09	2:36.48	2:36.86	2:37.25
410	2:37.64	2:38.02	2:38.41	2:38.79	2:39.18	2:39.56	2:39.95	2:40.33	2:40.72	2:41.10
420	2:41.49	2:41.88	2:42.26	2:42.65	2:43.03	2:43.42	2:43.80	2:44.19	2:44.57	2:44.96
430	2:45.34	2:45.73	2:46.11	2:46.50	2:46.89	2:47.27	2:47.66	2:48.04	2:48.43	2:48.81
440	2:49.20	2:49.58	2:49.97	2:50.35	2:50.74	2:51.13	2:51.51	2:51.90	2:52.28	2:52.67
450	2:53.05	2:53.44	2:53.82	2:54.21	2:54.59	2:54.98	2:55.36	2:55.75	2:56.14	2:56.52
460	2:56.91	2:57.29	2:57.68	2:58.06	2:58.45	2:58.83	2:59.22	2:59.60	2:59.99	3:00.38
470	3:00.76	3:01.15	3:01.53	3:01.92	3:02.30	3:02.69	3:03.07	3:03.46	3:03.84	3:04.23
480	3:04.61	3:05.00	3:05.39	3:05.77	3:06.16	3:06.54	3:06.93	3:07.31	3:07.70	3:08.08
490	3:08.47	3:08.85	3:09.24	3:09.62	3:10.01	3:10.40	3:10.78	3:11.17	3:11.55	3:11.94
500	3:12.32	3:12.71	3:13.09	3:13.48	3:13.86	3:14.25	3:14.64	3:15.02	3:15.41	3:15.79
510	3:16.18	3:16.56	3:16.95	3:17.33	3:17.72	3:18.10	3:18.49	3:18.87	3:19.26	3:19.65
520	3:20.03	3:20.42	3:20.80	3:21.19	3:21.57	3:21.96	3:22.34	3:22.73	3:23.11	3:23.50
530	3:23.89	3:24.27	3:24.66	3:25.04	3:25.43	3:25.81	3:26.20	3:26.58	3:26.97	3:27.35
540	3:27.74	3:28.13	3:28.51	3:28.90	3:29.28	3:29.67	3:30.05	3:30.44	3:30.82	3:31.21
550	3:31.59	3:31.98	3:32.36	3:32.75	3:33.14	3:33.52	3:33.91	3:34.29	3:34.68	3:35.06
560	3:35.45	3:35.83	3:36.22	3:36.60	3:36.99	3:37.38	3:37.76	3:38.15	3:38.53	3:38.92
570	3:39.30	3:39.69	3:40.07	3:40.46	3:40.84	3:41.23	3:41.61	3:42.00	3:42.39	3:42.77
580	3:43.16	3:43.54	3:43.93	3:44.31	3:44.70	3:45.08	3:45.47	3:45.85	3:46.24	3:46.63
590	3:47.01	3:47.40	3:47.78	3:48.17	3:48.55	3:48.94	3:49.32	3:49.71	3:50.09	3:50.48

𝅗𝅥. = 0.58; ♩ = 0.39; ♪. = 0.29; (triplet ♩ 𝄾) = 0.26; ♪ = 0.19; (triplet ♪ 𝄾 𝄾) = 0.13; ♬ = 0.10 seconds

CLICK: 9⅜ FRAMES; M.M.: 153.60

Click	0	1	2	3	4	5	6	7	8	9
000	0:00.00	0:00.00	0:00.39	0:00.78	0:01.17	0:01.56	0:01.95	0:02.34	0:02.73	0:03.13
010	0:03.52	0:03.91	0:04.30	0:04.69	0:05.08	0:05.47	0:05.86	0:06.25	0:06.64	0:07.03
020	0:07.42	0:07.81	0:08.20	0:08.59	0:08.98	0:09.38	0:09.77	0:10.16	0:10.55	0:10.94
030	0:11.33	0:11.72	0:12.11	0:12.50	0:12.89	0:13.28	0:13.67	0:14.06	0:14.45	0:14.84
040	0:15.23	0:15.62	0:16.02	0:16.41	0:16.80	0:17.19	0:17.58	0:17.97	0:18.36	0:18.75
050	0:19.14	0:19.53	0:19.92	0:20.31	0:20.70	0:21.09	0:21.48	0:21.87	0:22.27	0:22.66
060	0:23.05	0:23.44	0:23.83	0:24.22	0:24.61	0:25.00	0:25.39	0:25.78	0:26.17	0:26.56
070	0:26.95	0:27.34	0:27.73	0:28.13	0:28.52	0:28.91	0:29.30	0:29.69	0:30.08	0:30.47
080	0:30.86	0:31.25	0:31.64	0:32.03	0:32.42	0:32.81	0:33.20	0:33.59	0:33.98	0:34.37
090	0:34.77	0:35.16	0:35.55	0:35.94	0:36.33	0:36.72	0:37.11	0:37.50	0:37.89	0:38.28
100	0:38.67	0:39.06	0:39.45	0:39.84	0:40.23	0:40.63	0:41.02	0:41.41	0:41.80	0:42.19
110	0:42.58	0:42.97	0:43.36	0:43.75	0:44.14	0:44.53	0:44.92	0:45.31	0:45.70	0:46.09
120	0:46.48	0:46.88	0:47.27	0:47.66	0:48.05	0:48.44	0:48.83	0:49.22	0:49.61	0:50.00
130	0:50.39	0:50.78	0:51.17	0:51.56	0:51.95	0:52.34	0:52.73	0:53.12	0:53.52	0:53.91
140	0:54.30	0:54.69	0:55.08	0:55.47	0:55.86	0:56.25	0:56.64	0:57.03	0:57.42	0:57.81
150	0:58.20	0:58.59	0:58.98	0:59.38	0:59.77	1:00.16	1:00.55	1:00.94	1:01.33	1:01.72
160	1:02.11	1:02.50	1:02.89	1:03.28	1:03.67	1:04.06	1:04.45	1:04.84	1:05.23	1:05.63
170	1:06.02	1:06.41	1:06.80	1:07:19	1:07.58	1:07.97	1:08.36	1:08.75	1:09.14	1:09.53
180	1:09.92	1:10.31	1:10.70	1:11.09	1:11.48	1:11.87	1:12.27	1:12.66	1:13.05	1:13.44
190	1:13.83	1:14.22	1:14.61	1:15.00	1:15.39	1:15.78	1:16.17	1:16.56	1:16.95	1:17.34
200	1:17.73	1:18.12	1:18.52	1:18.91	1:19.30	1:19.69	1:20.08	1:20.47	1:20.86	1:21.25
210	1:21.64	1:22.03	1:22.42	1:22.81	1:23.20	1:23.59	1:23.98	1:24.38	1:24.77	1:25.16
220	1:25.55	1:25.94	1:26.33	1:26.72	1:27.11	1:27.50	1:27.89	1:28.28	1:28.67	1:29.06
230	1:29.45	1:29.84	1:30.23	1:30.62	1:31.02	1:31.41	1:31.80	1:32.19	1:32.58	1:32.97
240	1:33.36	1:33.75	1:34.14	1:34.53	1:34.92	1:35.31	1:35.70	1:36.09	1:36.48	1:36.87
250	1:37.27	1:37.66	1:38.05	1:38.44	1:38.83	1:39.22	1:39.61	1:40.00	1:40.39	1:40.78
260	1:41.17	1:41.56	1:41.95	1:42.34	1:42.73	1:43.13	1:43.52	1:43.91	1:44.30	1:44.69
270	1:45.08	1:45.47	1:45.86	1:46.25	1:46.64	1:47.03	1:47.42	1:47.81	1:48.20	1:48.59
280	1:48.98	1:49.37	1:49.77	1:50.16	1:50.55	1:50.94	1:51.33	1:51.72	1:52.11	1:52.50
290	1:52.89	1:53.28	1:53.67	1:54.06	1:54.45	1:54.84	1:55.23	1:55.62	1:56.02	1:56.41
300	1:56.80	1:57.19	1:57.58	1:57.97	1:58.36	1:58.75	1:59.14	1:59.53	1:59.92	2:00.31
310	2:00.70	2:01.09	2:01.48	2:01.88	2:02.27	2:02.66	2:03.05	2:03.44	2:03.83	2:04.22
320	2:04.61	2:05.00	2:05.39	2:05.78	2:06.17	2:06.56	2:06.95	2:07.34	2:07.73	2:08.12
330	2:08.52	2:08.91	2:09.30	2:09.69	2:10.08	2:10.47	2:10.86	2:11.25	2:11.64	2:12.03
340	2:12.42	2:12.81	2:13.20	2:13.59	2:13.98	2:14.37	2:14.77	2:15.16	2:15.55	2:15.94
350	2:16.33	2:16.72	2:17.11	2:17.50	2:17.89	2:18.28	2:18.67	2:19.06	2:19.45	2:19.84
360	2:20.23	2:20.63	2:21.02	2:21.41	2:21.80	2:22.19	2:22.58	2:22.97	2:23.36	2:23.75
370	2:24.14	2:24.53	2:24.92	2:25.31	2:25.70	2:26.09	2:26.48	2:26.87	2:27.27	2:27.66
380	2:28.05	2:28.44	2:28.83	2:29.22	2:29.61	2:30.00	2:30.39	2:30.78	2:31.17	2:31.56
390	2:31.95	2:32.34	2:32.73	2:33.12	2:33.52	2:33.91	2:34.30	2:34.69	2:35.08	2:35.47
400	2:35.86	2:36.25	2:36.64	2:37.03	2:37.42	2:37.81	2:38.20	2:38.59	2:38.98	2:39.38
410	2:39.77	2:40.16	2:40.55	2:40.94	2:41.33	2:41.72	2:42.11	2:42.50	2:42.89	2:43.28
420	2:43.67	2:44.06	2:44.45	2:44.84	2:45.23	2:45.62	2:46.02	2:46.41	2:46.80	2:47.19
430	2:47.58	2:47.97	2:48.36	2:48.75	2:49.14	2:49.53	2:49.92	2:50.31	2:50.70	2:51.09
440	2:51.48	2:51.87	2:52.27	2:52.66	2:53.05	2:53.44	2:53.83	2:54.22	2:54.61	2:55.00
450	2:55.39	2:55.78	2:56.17	2:56.56	2:56.95	2:57.34	2:57.73	2:58.13	2:58.52	2:58.91
460	2:59.30	2:59.69	3:00.08	3:00.47	3:00.86	3:01.25	3:01.64	3:02.03	3:02.42	3:02.81
470	3:03.20	3:03.59	3:03.98	3:04.37	3:04.77	3:05.16	3:05.55	3:05.94	3:06.33	3:06.72
480	3:07.11	3:07.50	3:07.89	3:08.28	3:08.67	3:09.06	3:09.45	3:09.84	3:10.23	3:10.62
490	3:11.02	3:11.41	3:11.80	3:12.19	3:12.58	3:12.97	3:13.36	3:13.75	3:14.14	3:14.53
500	3:14.92	3:15.31	3:15.70	3:16.09	3:16.48	3:16.88	3:17.27	3:17.66	3:18.05	3:18.44
510	3:18.83	3:19.22	3:19.61	3:20.00	3:20.39	3:20.78	3:21.17	3:21.56	3:21.95	3:22.34
520	3:22.73	3:23.12	3:23.52	3:23.91	3:24.30	3:24.69	3:25.08	3:25.47	3:25.86	3:26.25
530	3:26.64	3:27.03	3:27.42	3:27.81	3:28.20	3:28.59	3:28.98	3:29.37	3:29.77	3:30.16
540	3:30.55	3:30.94	3:31.33	3:31.72	3:32.11	3:32.50	3:32.89	3:33.28	3:33.67	3:34.06
550	3:34.45	3:34.84	3:35.23	3:35.63	3:36.02	3:36.41	3:36.80	3:37.19	3:37.58	3:37.97
560	3:38.36	3:38.75	3:39.14	3:39.53	3:39.92	3:40.31	3:40.70	3:41.09	3:41.48	3:41.87
570	3:42.27	3:42.66	3:43.05	3:43.44	3:43.83	3:44.22	3:44.61	3:45.00	3:45.39	3:45.78
580	3:46.17	3:46.56	3:46.95	3:47.34	3:47.73	3:48.12	3:48.52	3:48.91	3:49.30	3:49.69
590	3:50.08	3:50.47	3:50.86	3:51.25	3:51.64	3:52.03	3:52.42	3:52.81	3:53.20	3:53.59

♩. = 0.59; ♩ = 0.39; ♪. = 0.29; (3: ♩ 𝄾) = 0.26; ♪ = 0.20; (3: ♪ 𝄾 𝄾) = 0.13; 𝅘𝅥𝅯 = 0.10 seconds

CLICK: 9 4/8 FRAMES; M.M.: 151.58

Click	0	1	2	3	4	5	6	7	8	9
000	0:00.00	0:00.00	0:00.40	0:00.79	0:01.19	0:01.58	0:01.98	0:02.38	0:02.77	0:03.17
010	0:03.56	0:03.96	0:04.35	0:04.75	0:05.15	0:05.54	0:05.94	0:06.33	0:06.73	0:07.13
020	0:07.52	0:07.92	0:08.31	0:08.71	0:09.10	0:09.50	0:09.90	0:10.29	0:10.69	0:11.08
030	0:11.48	0:11.88	0:12.27	0:12.67	0:13.06	0:13.46	0:13.85	0:14.25	0:14.65	0:15.04
040	0:15.44	0:15.83	0:16.23	0:16.63	0:17.02	0:17.42	0:17.81	0:18.21	0:18.60	0:19.00
050	0:19.40	0:19.79	0:20.19	0:20.58	0:20.98	0:21.38	0:21.77	0:22.17	0:22.56	0:22.96
060	0:23.35	0:23.75	0:24.15	0:24.54	0:24.94	0:25.33	0:25.73	0:26.13	0:26.52	0:26.92
070	0:27.31	0:27.71	0:28.10	0:28.50	0:28.90	0:29.29	0:29.69	0:30.08	0:30.48	0:30.88
080	0:31.27	0:31.67	0:32.06	0:32.46	0:32.85	0:33.25	0:33.65	0:34.04	0:34.44	0:34.83
090	0:35.23	0:35.63	0:36.02	0:36.42	0:36.81	0:37.21	0:37.60	0:38.00	0:38.40	0:38.79
100	0:39.19	0:39.58	0:39.98	0:40.38	0:40.77	0:41.17	0:41.56	0:41.96	0:42.35	0:42.75
110	0:43.15	0:43.54	0:43.94	0:44.33	0:44.73	0:45.13	0:45.52	0:45.92	0:46.31	0:46.71
120	0:47.10	0:47.50	0:47.90	0:48.29	0:48.69	0:49.08	0:49.48	0:49.88	0:50.27	0:50.67
130	0:51.06	0:51.46	0:51.85	0:52.25	0:52.65	0:53.04	0:53.44	0:53.83	0:54.23	0:54.63
140	0:55.02	0:55.42	0:55.81	0:56.21	0:56.60	0:57.00	0:57.40	0:57.79	0:58.19	0:58.58
150	0:58.98	0:59.38	0:59.77	1:00.17	1:00.56	1:00.96	1:01.35	1:01.75	1:02.15	1:02.54
160	1:02.94	1:03.33	1:03.73	1:04.13	1:04.52	1:04.92	1:05.31	1:05.71	1:06.10	1:06.50
170	1:06.90	1:07.29	1:07.69	1:08.08	1:08.48	1:08.88	1:09.27	1:09.67	1:10.06	1:10.46
180	1:10.85	1:11.25	1:11.65	1:12.04	1:12.44	1:12.83	1:13.23	1:13.63	1:14.02	1:14.42
190	1:14.81	1:15.21	1:15.60	1:16.00	1:16.40	1:16.79	1:17.19	1:17.58	1:17.98	1:18.37
200	1:18.77	1:19.17	1:19.56	1:19.96	1:20.35	1:20.75	1:21.15	1:21.54	1:21.94	1:22.33
210	1:22.73	1:23.12	1:23.52	1:23.92	1:24.31	1:24.71	1:25.10	1:25.50	1:25.90	1:26.29
220	1:26.69	1:27.08	1:27.48	1:27.88	1:28.27	1:28.67	1:29.06	1:29.46	1:29.85	1:30.25
230	1:30.65	1:31.04	1:31.44	1:31.83	1:32.23	1:32.63	1:33.02	1:33.42	1:33.81	1:34.21
240	1:34.60	1:35.00	1:35.40	1:35.79	1:36.19	1:36.58	1:36.98	1:37.38	1:37.77	1:38.17
250	1:38.56	1:38.96	1:39.35	1:39.75	1:40.15	1:40.54	1:40.94	1:41.33	1:41.73	1:42.13
260	1:42.52	1:42.92	1:43.31	1:43.71	1:44.10	1:44.50	1:44.90	1:45.29	1:45.69	1:46.08
270	1:46.48	1:46.88	1:47.27	1:47.67	1:48.06	1:48.46	1:48.85	1:49.25	1:49.65	1:50.04
280	1:50.44	1:50.83	1:51.23	1:51.63	1:52.02	1:52.42	1:52.81	1:53.21	1:53.60	1:54.00
290	1:54.40	1:54.79	1:55.19	1:55.58	1:55.98	1:56.38	1:56.77	1:57.17	1:57.56	1:57.96
300	1:58.35	1:58.75	1:59.15	1:59.54	1:59.94	2:00.33	2:00.73	2:01.12	2:01.52	2:01.92
310	2:02.31	2:02.71	2:03.10	2:03.50	2:03.90	2:04.29	2:04.69	2:05.08	2:05.48	2:05.87
320	2:06.27	2:06.67	2:07.06	2:07.46	2:07.85	2:08.25	2:08.65	2:09.04	2:09.44	2:09.83
330	2:10.23	2:10.62	2:11.02	2:11.42	2:11.81	2:12.21	2:12.60	2:13.00	2:13.40	2:13.79
340	2:14.19	2:14.58	2:14.98	2:15.38	2:15.77	2:16.17	2:16.56	2:16.96	2:17.35	2:17.75
350	2:18.15	2:18.54	2:18.94	2:19.33	2:19.73	2:20.13	2:20.52	2:20.92	2:21.31	2:21.71
360	2:22.10	2:22.50	2:22.90	2:23.29	2:23.69	2:24.08	2:24.48	2:24.88	2:25.27	2:25.67
370	2:26.06	2:26.46	2:26.85	2:27.25	2:27.65	2:28.04	2:28.44	2:28.83	2:29.23	2:29.63
380	2:30.02	2:30.42	2:30.81	2:31.21	2:31.60	2:32.00	2:32.40	2:32.79	2:33.19	2:33.58
390	2:33.98	2:34.38	2:34.77	2:35.17	2:35.56	2:35.96	2:36.35	2:36.75	2:37.15	2:37.54
400	2:37.94	2:38.33	2:38.73	2:39.13	2:39.52	2:39.92	2:40.31	2:40.71	2:41.10	2:41.50
410	2:41.90	2:42.29	2:42.69	2:43.08	2:43.48	2:43.88	2:44.27	2:44.67	2:45.06	2:45.46
420	2:45.85	2:46.25	2:46.65	2:47.04	2:47.44	2:47.83	2:48.23	2:48.63	2:49.02	2:49.42
430	2:49.81	2:50.21	2:50.60	2:51.00	2:51.40	2:51.79	2:52.19	2:52.58	2:52.98	2:53.38
440	2:53.77	2:54.17	2:54.56	2:54.96	2:55.35	2:55.75	2:56.15	2:56.54	2:56.94	2:57.33
450	2:57.73	2:58.13	2:58.52	2:58.92	2:59.31	2:59.71	3:00.10	3:00.50	3:00.90	3:01.29
460	3:01.69	3:02.08	3:02.48	3:02.87	3:03.27	3:03.67	3:04.06	3:04.46	3:04.85	3:05.25
470	3:05.65	3:06.04	3:06.44	3:06.83	3:07.23	3:07.62	3:08.02	3:08.42	3:08.81	3:09.21
480	3:09.60	3:10.00	3:10.40	3:10.79	3:11.19	3:11.58	3:11.98	3:12.37	3:12.77	3:13.17
490	3:13.56	3:13.96	3:14.35	3:14.75	3:15.15	3:15.54	3:15.94	3:16.33	3:16.73	3:17.12
500	3:17.52	3:17.92	3:18.31	3:18.71	3:19.10	3:19.50	3:19.90	3:20.29	3:20.69	3:21.08
510	3:21.48	3:21.87	3:22.27	3:22.67	3:23.06	3:23.46	3:23.85	3:24.25	3:24.65	3:25.04
520	3:25.44	3:25.83	3:26.23	3:26.63	3:27.02	3:27.42	3:27.81	3:28.21	3:28.60	3:29.00
530	3:29.40	3:29.79	3:30.19	3:30.58	3:30.98	3:31.38	3:31.77	3:32.17	3:32.56	3:32.96
540	3:33.35	3:33.75	3:34.15	3:34.54	3:34.94	3:35.33	3:35.73	3:36.13	3:36.52	3:36.92
550	3:37.31	3:37.71	3:38.10	3:38.50	3:38.90	3:39.29	3:39.69	3:40.08	3:40.48	3:40.88
560	3:41.27	3:41.67	3:42.06	3:42.46	3:42.85	3:43.25	3:43.65	3:44.04	3:44.44	3:44.83
570	3:45.23	3:45.63	3:46.02	3:46.42	3:46.81	3:47.21	3:47.60	3:48.00	3:48.40	3:48.79
580	3:49.19	3:49.58	3:49.98	3:50.38	3:50.77	3:51.17	3:51.56	3:51.96	3:52.35	3:52.75
590	3:53.15	3:53.54	3:53.94	3:54.33	3:54.73	3:55.13	3:55.52	3:55.92	3:56.31	3:56.71

♩. = 0.59; ♩ = 0.40; ♪. = 0.30; (3: ♩ 𝄾) = 0.26; ♪ = 0.20; (3: ♪ 𝄾 𝄾) = 0.13; 𝅘𝅥𝅯 = 0.10 seconds

CLICK: 9⅝ FRAMES; M.M.: 149.61

Click	0	1	2	3	4	5	6	7	8	9
000	0:00.00	0:00.00	0:00.40	0:00.80	0:01.20	0:01.60	0:02.01	0:02.41	0:02.81	0:03.21
010	0:03.61	0:04.01	0:04.41	0:04.81	0:05.21	0:05.61	0:06.02	0:06.42	0:06.82	0:07.22
020	0:07.62	0:08.02	0:08.42	0:08.82	0:09.22	0:09.63	0:10.03	0:10.43	0:10.83	0:11.23
030	0:11.63	0:12.03	0:12.43	0:12.83	0:13.23	0:13.64	0:14.04	0:14.44	0:14.84	0:15.24
040	0:15.64	0:16.04	0:16.44	0:16.84	0:17.24	0:17.65	0:18.05	0:18.45	0:18.85	0:19.25
050	0:19.65	0:20.05	0:20.45	0:20.85	0:21.26	0:21.66	0:22.06	0:22.46	0:22.86	0:23.26
060	0:23.66	0:24.06	0:24.46	0:24.86	0:25.27	0:25.67	0:26.07	0:26.47	0:26.87	0:27.27
070	0:27.67	0:28.07	0:28.47	0:28.88	0:29.28	0:29.68	0:30.08	0:30.48	0:30.88	0:31.28
080	0:31.68	0:32.08	0:32.48	0:32.89	0:33.29	0:33.69	0:34.09	0:34.49	0:34.89	0:35.29
090	0:35.69	0:36.09	0:36.49	0:36.90	0:37.30	0:37.70	0:38.10	0:38.50	0:38.90	0:39.30
100	0:39.70	0:40.10	0:40.51	0:40.91	0:41.31	0:41.71	0:42.11	0:42.51	0:42.91	0:43.31
110	0:43.71	0:44.11	0:44.52	0:44.92	0:45.32	0:45.72	0:46.12	0:46.52	0:46.92	0:47.32
120	0:47.72	0:48.13	0:48.53	0:48.93	0:49.33	0:49.73	0:50.13	0:50.53	0:50.93	0:51.33
130	0:51.73	0:52.14	0:52.54	0:52.94	0:53.34	0:53.74	0:54.14	0:54.54	0:54.94	0:55.34
140	0:55.74	0:56.15	0:56.55	0:56.95	0:57.35	0:57.75	0:58.15	0:58.55	0:58.95	0:59.35
150	0:59.76	1:00.16	1:00.56	1:00.96	1:01.36	1:01.76	1:02.16	1:02.56	1:02.96	1:03.36
160	1:03.77	1:04.17	1:04.57	1:04.97	1:05.37	1:05.77	1:06.17	1:06.57	1:06.97	1:07.38
170	1:07.78	1:08.18	1:08.58	1:08.98	1:09.38	1:09.78	1:10.18	1:10.58	1:10.98	1:11.39
180	1:11.79	1:12.19	1:12.59	1:12.99	1:13.39	1:13.79	1:14.19	1:14.59	1:14.99	1:15.40
190	1:15.80	1:16.20	1:16.60	1:17.00	1:17.40	1:17.80	1:18.20	1:18.60	1:19.01	1:19.41
200	1:19.81	1:20.21	1:20.61	1:21.01	1:21.41	1:21.81	1:22.21	1:22.61	1:23.02	1:23.42
210	1:23.82	1:24.22	1:24.62	1:25.02	1:25.42	1:25.82	1:26.22	1:26.63	1:27.03	1:27.43
220	1:27.83	1:28.23	1:28.63	1:29.03	1:29.43	1:29.83	1:30.23	1:30.64	1:31.04	1:31.44
230	1:31.84	1:32.24	1:32.64	1:33.04	1:33.44	1:33.84	1:34.24	1:34.65	1:35.05	1:35.45
240	1:35.85	1:36.25	1:36.65	1:37.05	1:37.45	1:37.85	1:38.26	1:38.66	1:39.06	1:39.46
250	1:39.86	1:40.26	1:40.66	1:41.06	1:41.46	1:41.86	1:42.27	1:42.67	1:43.07	1:43.47
260	1:43.87	1:44.27	1:44.67	1:45.07	1:45.47	1:45.88	1:46.28	1:46.68	1:47.08	1:47.48
270	1:47.88	1:48.28	1:48.68	1:49.08	1:49.48	1:49.89	1:50.29	1:50.69	1:51.09	1:51.49
280	1:51.89	1:52.29	1:52.69	1:53.09	1:53.49	1:53.90	1:54.30	1:54.70	1:55.10	1:55.50
290	1:55.90	1:56.30	1:56.70	1:57.10	1:57.51	1:57.91	1:58.31	1:58.71	1:59.11	1:59.51
300	1:59.91	2:00.31	2:00.71	2:01.11	2:01.52	2:01.92	2:02.32	2:02.72	2:03.12	2:03.52
310	2:03.92	2:04.32	2:04.72	2:05.13	2:05.53	2:05.93	2:06.33	2:06.73	2:07.13	2:07.53
320	2:07.93	2:08.33	2:08.73	2:09.14	2:09.54	2:09.94	2:10.34	2:10.74	2:11.14	2:11.54
330	2:11.94	2:12.34	2:12.74	2:13.15	2:13.55	2:13.95	2:14.35	2:14.75	2:15.15	2:15.55
340	2:15.95	2:16.35	2:16.76	2:17.16	2:17.56	2:17.96	2:18.36	2:18.76	2:19.16	2:19.56
350	2:19.96	2:20.36	2:20.77	2:21.17	2:21.57	2:21.97	2:22.37	2:22.77	2:23.17	2:23.57
360	2:23.97	2:24.38	2:24.78	2:25.18	2:25.58	2:25.98	2:26.38	2:26.78	2:27.18	2:27.58
370	2:27.98	2:28.39	2:28.79	2:29.19	2:29.59	2:29.99	2:30.39	2:30.79	2:31.19	2:31.59
380	2:31.99	2:32.40	2:32.80	2:33.20	2:33.60	2:34.00	2:34.40	2:34.80	2:35.20	2:35.60
390	2:36.01	2:36.41	2:36.81	2:37.21	2:37.61	2:38.01	2:38.41	2:38.81	2:39.21	2:39.61
400	2:40.02	2:40.42	2:40.82	2:41.22	2:41.62	2:42.02	2:42.42	2:42.82	2:43.22	2:43.63
410	2:44.03	2:44.43	2:44.83	2:45.23	2:45.63	2:46.03	2:46.43	2:46.83	2:47.23	2:47.64
420	2:48.04	2:48.44	2:48.84	2:49.24	2:49.64	2:50.04	2:50.44	2:50.84	2:51.24	2:51.65
430	2:52.05	2:52.45	2:52.85	2:53.25	2:53.65	2:54.05	2:54.45	2:54.85	2:55.26	2:55.66
440	2:56.06	2:56.46	2:56.86	2:57.26	2:57.66	2:58.06	2:58.46	2:58.86	2:59.27	2:59.67
450	3:00.07	3:00.47	3:00.87	3:01.27	3:01.67	3:02.07	3:02.47	3:02.88	3:03.28	3:03.68
460	3:04.08	3:04.48	3:04.88	3:05.28	3:05.68	3:06.08	3:06.48	3:06.89	3:07.29	3:07.69
470	3:08.09	3:08.49	3:08.89	3:09.29	3:09.69	3:10.09	3:10.49	3:10.90	3:11.30	3:11.70
480	3:12.10	3:12.50	3:12.90	3:13.30	3:13.70	3:14.10	3:14.51	3:14.91	3:15.31	3:15.71
490	3:16.11	3:16.51	3:16.91	3:17.31	3:17.71	3:18.11	3:18.52	3:18.92	3:19.32	3:19.72
500	3:20.12	3:20.52	3:20.92	3:21.32	3:21.72	3:22.13	3:22.53	3:22.93	3:23.33	3:23.73
510	3:24.13	3:24.53	3:24.93	3:25.33	3:25.73	3:26.14	3:26.54	3:26.94	3:27.34	3:27.74
520	3:28.14	3:28.54	3:28.94	3:29.34	3:29.74	3:30.15	3:30.55	3:30.95	3:31.35	3:31.75
530	3:32.15	3:32.55	3:32.95	3:33.35	3:33.76	3:34.16	3:34.56	3:34.96	3:35.36	3:35.76
540	3:36.16	3:36.56	3:36.96	3:37.36	3:37.77	3:38.17	3:38.57	3:38.97	3:39.37	3:39.77
550	3:40.17	3:40.57	3:40.97	3:41.38	3:41.78	3:42.18	3:42.58	3:42.98	3:43.38	3:43.78
560	3:44.18	3:44.58	3:44.98	3:45.39	3:45.79	3:46.19	3:46.59	3:46.99	3:47.39	3:47.79
570	3:48.19	3:48.59	3:48.99	3:49.40	3:49.80	3:50.20	3:50.60	3:51.00	3:51.40	3:51.80
580	3:52.20	3:52.60	3:53.01	3:53.41	3:53.81	3:54.21	3:54.61	3:55.01	3:55.41	3:55.81
590	3:56.21	3:56.61	3:57.02	3:57.42	3:57.82	3:58.22	3:58.62	3:59.02	3:59.42	3:59.82

♩. = 0.60; ♩ = 0.40; ♪. = 0.30; ⌐3¬ ♩𝄾 = 0.27; ♪ = 0.20; ⌐3¬ ♪𝄾𝄾 = 0.13; 𝅘𝅥𝅯 = 0.10 seconds

CLICK: 9 6/8 FRAMES; M.M.: 147.69

Click	0	1	2	3	4	5	6	7	8	9
000	0:00.00	0:00.00	0:00.41	0:00.81	0:01.22	0:01.63	0:02.03	0:02.44	0:02.84	0:03.25
010	0:03.66	0:04.06	0:04.47	0:04.88	0:05.28	0:05.69	0:06.09	0:06.50	0:06.91	0:07.31
020	0:07.72	0:08.13	0:08.53	0:08.94	0:09.34	0:09.75	0:10.16	0:10.56	0:10.97	0:11.38
030	0:11.78	0:12.19	0:12.59	0:13.00	0:13.41	0:13.81	0:14.22	0:14.63	0:15.03	0:15.44
040	0:15.84	0:16.25	0:16.66	0:17.06	0:17.47	0:17.88	0:18.28	0:18.69	0:19.09	0:19.50
050	0:19.91	0:20.31	0:20.72	0:21.13	0:21.53	0:21.94	0:22.34	0:22.75	0:23.16	0:23.56
060	0:23.97	0:24.38	0:24.78	0:25.19	0:25.59	0:26.00	0:26.41	0:26.81	0:27.22	0:27.63
070	0:28.03	0:28.44	0:28.84	0:29.25	0:29.66	0:30.06	0:30.47	0:30.88	0:31.28	0:31.69
080	0:32.09	0:32.50	0:32.91	0:33.31	0:33.72	0:34.13	0:34.53	0:34.94	0:35.34	0:35.75
090	0:36.16	0:36.56	0:36.97	0:37.38	0:37.78	0:38.19	0:38.59	0:39.00	0:39.41	0:39.81
100	0:40.22	0:40.63	0:41.03	0:41.44	0:41.84	0:42.25	0:42.66	0:43.06	0:43.47	0:43.88
110	0:44.28	0:44.69	0:45.09	0:45.50	0:45.91	0:46.31	0:46.72	0:47.13	0:47.53	0:47.94
120	0:48.34	0:48.75	0:49.16	0:49.56	0:49.97	0:50.38	0:50.78	0:51.19	0:51.59	0:52.00
130	0:52.41	0:52.81	0:53.22	0:53.63	0:54.03	0:54.44	0:54.84	0:55.25	0:55.66	0:56.06
140	0:56.47	0:56.88	0:57.28	0:57.69	0:58.09	0:58.50	0:58.91	0:59.31	0:59.72	1:00.12
150	1:00.53	1:00.94	1:01.34	1:01.75	1:02.16	1:02.56	1:02.97	1:03.37	1:03.78	1:04.19
160	1:04.59	1:05.00	1:05.41	1:05.81	1:06.22	1:06.62	1:07.03	1:07.44	1:07.84	1:08.25
170	1:08.66	1:09.06	1:09.47	1:09.88	1:10.28	1:10.69	1:11.09	1:11.50	1:11.91	1:12.31
180	1:12.72	1:13.13	1:13.53	1:13.94	1:14.34	1:14.75	1:15.16	1:15.56	1:15.97	1:16.38
190	1:16.78	1:17.19	1:17.59	1:18.00	1:18.41	1:18.81	1:19.22	1:19.63	1:20.03	1:20.44
200	1:20.84	1:21.25	1:21.66	1:22.06	1:22.47	1:22.88	1:23.28	1:23.69	1:24.09	1:24.50
210	1:24.91	1:25.31	1:25.72	1:26.13	1:26.53	1:26.94	1:27.34	1:27.75	1:28.16	1:28.56
220	1:28.97	1:29.38	1:29.78	1:30.19	1:30.59	1:31.00	1:31.41	1:31.81	1:32.22	1:32.63
230	1:33.03	1:33.44	1:33.84	1:34.25	1:34.66	1:35.06	1:35.47	1:35.88	1:36.28	1:36.69
240	1:37.09	1:37.50	1:37.91	1:38.31	1:38.72	1:39.13	1:39.53	1:39.94	1:40.34	1:40.75
250	1:41.16	1:41.56	1:41.97	1:42.38	1:42.78	1:43.19	1:43.59	1:44.00	1:44.41	1:44.81
260	1:45.22	1:45.62	1:46.03	1:46.44	1:46.84	1:47.25	1:47.66	1:48.06	1:48.47	1:48.88
270	1:49.28	1:49.69	1:50.09	1:50.50	1:50.91	1:51.31	1:51.72	1:52.13	1:52.53	1:52.94
280	1:53.34	1:53.75	1:54.16	1:54.56	1:54.97	1:55.38	1:55.78	1:56.19	1:56.59	1:57.00
290	1:57.41	1:57.81	1:58.22	1:58.63	1:59.03	1:59.44	1:59.84	2:00.25	2:00.66	2:01.06
300	2:01.47	2:01.88	2:02.28	2:02.69	2:03.09	2:03.50	2:03.91	2:04.31	2:04.72	2:05.13
310	2:05.53	2:05.94	2:06.34	2:06.75	2:07.16	2:07.56	2:07.97	2:08.38	2:08.78	2:09.19
320	2:09.59	2:10.00	2:10.41	2:10.81	2:11.22	2:11.62	2:12.03	2:12.44	2:12.84	2:13.25
330	2:13.66	2:14.06	2:14.47	2:14.88	2:15.28	2:15.69	2:16.09	2:16.50	2:16.91	2:17.31
340	2:17.72	2:18.12	2:18.53	2:18.94	2:19.34	2:19.75	2:20.16	2:20.56	2:20.97	2:21.38
350	2:21.78	2:22.19	2:22.59	2:23.00	2:23.41	2:23.81	2:24.22	2:24.62	2:25.03	2:25.44
360	2:25.84	2:26.25	2:26.66	2:27.06	2:27.47	2:27.88	2:28.28	2:28.69	2:29.09	2:29.50
370	2:29.91	2:30.31	2:30.72	2:31.12	2:31.53	2:31.94	2:32.34	2:32.75	2:33.16	2:33.56
380	2:33.97	2:34.38	2:34.78	2:35.19	2:35.59	2:36.00	2:36.41	2:36.81	2:37.22	2:37.63
390	2:38.03	2:38.44	2:38.84	2:39.25	2:39.66	2:40.06	2:40.47	2:40.88	2:41.28	2:41.69
400	2:42.09	2:42.50	2:42.91	2:43.31	2:43.72	2:44.13	2:44.53	2:44.94	2:45.34	2:45.75
410	2:46.16	2:46.56	2:46.97	2:47.38	2:47.78	2:48.19	2:48.59	2:49.00	2:49.41	2:49.81
420	2:50.22	2:50.63	2:51.03	2:51.44	2:51.84	2:52.25	2:52.66	2:53.06	2:53.47	2:53.88
430	2:54.28	2:54.69	2:55.09	2:55.50	2:55.91	2:56.31	2:56.72	2:57.13	2:57.53	2:57.94
440	2:58.34	2:58.75	2:59.16	2:59.56	2:59.97	3:00.38	3:00.78	3:01.19	3:01.59	3:02.00
450	3:02.41	3:02.81	3:03.22	3:03.63	3:04.03	3:04.44	3:04.84	3:05.25	3:05.66	3:06.06
460	3:06.47	3:06.87	3:07.28	3:07.69	3:08.09	3:08.50	3:08.91	3:09.31	3:09.72	3:10.13
470	3:10.53	3:10.94	3:11.34	3:11.75	3:12.16	3:12.56	3:12.97	3:13.37	3:13.78	3:14.19
480	3:14.59	3:15.00	3:15.41	3:15.81	3:16.22	3:16.63	3:17.03	3:17.44	3:17.84	3:18.25
490	3:18.66	3:19.06	3:19.47	3:19.87	3:20.28	3:20.69	3:21.09	3:21.50	3:21.91	3:22.31
500	3:22.72	3:23.13	3:23.53	3:23.94	3:24.34	3:24.75	3:25.16	3:25.56	3:25.97	3:26.37
510	3:26.78	3:27.19	3:27.59	3:28.00	3:28.41	3:28.81	3:29.22	3:29.63	3:30.03	3:30.44
520	3:30.84	3:31.25	3:31.66	3:32.06	3:32.47	3:32.88	3:33.28	3:33.69	3:34.09	3:34.50
530	3:34.91	3:35.31	3:35.72	3:36.13	3:36.53	3:36.94	3:37.34	3:37.75	3:38.16	3:38.56
540	3:38.97	3:39.38	3:39.78	3:40.19	3:40.59	3:41.00	3:41.41	3:41.81	3:42.22	3:42.63
550	3:43.03	3:43.44	3:43.84	3:44.25	3:44.66	3:45.06	3:45.47	3:45.88	3:46.28	3:46.69
560	3:47.09	3:47.50	3:47.91	3:48.31	3:48.72	3:49.13	3:49.53	3:49.94	3:50.34	3:50.75
570	3:51.16	3:51.56	3:51.97	3:52.38	3:52.78	3:53.19	3:53.59	3:54.00	3:54.41	3:54.81
580	3:55.22	3:55.62	3:56.03	3:56.44	3:56.84	3:57.25	3:57.66	3:58.06	3:58.47	3:58.88
590	3:59.28	3:59.69	4:00.09	4:00.50	4:00.91	4:01.31	4:01.72	4:02.12	4:02.53	4:02.94

♩. = 0.61; ♩ = 0.41; ♪. = 0.30; (triplet) ♩ 𝄾 = 0.27; ♪ = 0.20; (triplet) ♪ 𝄾 𝄾 = 0.14; 𝅘𝅥𝅯 = 0.10 seconds

CLICK: 9⅞ FRAMES; M.M.: 145.82

Click	0	1	2	3	4	5	6	7	8	9
000	0:00.00	0:00.00	0:00.41	0:00.82	0:01.23	0:01.65	0:02.06	0:02.47	0:02.88	0:03.29
010	0:03.70	0:04.11	0:04.53	0:04.94	0:05.35	0:05.76	0:06.17	0:06.58	0:06.99	0:07.41
020	0:07.82	0:08.23	0:08.64	0:09.05	0:09.46	0:09.88	0:10.29	0:10.70	0:11.11	0:11.52
030	0:11.93	0:12.34	0:12.76	0:13.17	0:13.58	0:13.99	0:14.40	0:14.81	0:15.22	0:15.64
040	0:16.05	0:16.46	0:16.87	0:17.28	0:17.69	0:18.10	0:18.52	0:18.93	0:19.34	0:19.75
050	0:20.16	0:20.57	0:20.98	0:21.40	0:21.81	0:22.22	0:22.63	0:23.04	0:23.45	0:23.86
060	0:24.28	0:24.69	0:25.10	0:25.51	0:25.92	0:26.33	0:26.74	0:27.16	0:27.57	0:27.98
070	0:28.39	0:28.80	0:29.21	0:29.62	0:30.04	0:30.45	0:30.86	0:31.27	0:31.68	0:32.09
080	0:32.51	0:32.92	0:33.33	0:33.74	0:34.15	0:34.56	0:34.97	0:35.39	0:35.80	0:36.21
090	0:36.62	0:37.03	0:37.44	0:37.85	0:38.27	0:38.68	0:39.09	0:39.50	0:39.91	0:40.32
100	0:40.73	0:41.15	0:41.56	0:41.97	0:42.38	0:42.79	0:43.20	0:43.61	0:44.03	0:44.44
110	0:44.85	0:45.26	0:45.67	0:46.08	0:46.49	0:46.91	0:47.32	0:47.73	0:48.14	0:48.55
120	0:48.96	0:49.37	0:49.79	0:50.20	0:50.61	0:51.02	0:51.43	0:51.84	0:52.26	0:52.67
130	0:53.08	0:53.49	0:53.90	0:54.31	0:54.72	0:55.14	0:55.55	0:55.96	0:56.37	0:56.78
140	0:57.19	0:57.60	0:58.02	0:58.43	0:58.84	0:59.25	0:59.66	1:00.07	1:00.48	1:00.90
150	1:01.31	1:01.72	1:02.13	1:02.54	1:02.95	1:03.36	1:03.78	1:04.19	1:04.60	1:05.01
160	1:05.42	1:05.83	1:06.24	1:06.66	1:07.07	1:07.48	1:07.89	1:08.30	1:08.71	1:09.12
170	1:09.54	1:09.95	1:10.36	1:10.77	1:11.18	1:11.59	1:12.01	1:12.42	1:12.83	1:13.24
180	1:13.65	1:14.06	1:14.47	1:14.89	1:15.30	1:15.71	1:16.12	1:16.53	1:16.94	1:17.35
190	1:17.77	1:18.18	1:18.59	1:19.00	1:19.41	1:19.82	1:20.23	1:20.65	1:21.06	1:21.47
200	1:21.88	1:22.29	1:22.70	1:23.11	1:23.53	1:23.94	1:24.35	1:24.76	1:25.17	1:25.58
210	1:25.99	1:26.41	1:26.82	1:27.23	1:27.64	1:28.05	1:28.46	1:28.87	1:29.29	1:29.70
220	1:30.11	1:30.52	1:30.93	1:31.34	1:31.76	1:32.17	1:32.58	1:32.99	1:33.40	1:33.81
230	1:34.22	1:34.64	1:35.05	1:35.46	1:35.87	1:36.28	1:36.69	1:37.10	1:37.52	1:37.93
240	1:38.34	1:38.75	1:39.16	1:39.57	1:39.98	1:40.40	1:40.81	1:41.22	1:41.63	1:42.04
250	1:42.45	1:42.86	1:43.28	1:43.69	1:44.10	1:44.51	1:44.92	1:45.33	1:45.74	1:46.16
260	1:46.57	1:46.98	1:47.39	1:47.80	1:48.21	1:48.62	1:49.04	1:49.45	1:49.86	1:50.27
270	1:50.68	1:51.09	1:51.51	1:51.92	1:52.33	1:52.74	1:53.15	1:53.56	1:53.97	1:54.39
280	1:54.80	1:55.21	1:55.62	1:56.03	1:56.44	1:56.85	1:57.27	1:57.68	1:58.09	1:58.50
290	1:58.91	1:59.32	1:59.73	2:00.15	2:00.56	2:00.97	2:01.38	2:01.79	2:02.20	2:02.61
300	2:03.03	2:03.44	2:03.85	2:04.26	2:04.67	2:05.08	2:05.49	2:05.91	2:06.32	2:06.73
310	2:07.14	2:07.55	2:07.96	2:08.38	2:08.79	2:09.20	2:09.61	2:10.02	2:10.43	2:10.84
320	2:11.26	2:11.67	2:12.08	2:12.49	2:12.90	2:13.31	2:13.72	2:14.14	2:14.55	2:14.96
330	2:15.37	2:15.78	2:16.19	2:16.60	2:17.02	2:17.43	2:17.84	2:18.25	2:18.66	2:19.07
340	2:19.48	2:19.90	2:20.31	2:20.72	2:21.13	2:21.54	2:21.95	2:22.36	2:22.78	2:23.19
350	2:23.60	2:24.01	2:24.42	2:24.83	2:25.24	2:25.66	2:26.07	2:26.48	2:26.89	2:27.30
360	2:27.71	2:28.13	2:28.54	2:28.95	2:29.36	2:29.77	2:30.18	2:30.59	2:31.01	2:31.42
370	2:31.83	2:32.24	2:32.65	2:33.06	2:33.47	2:33.89	2:34.30	2:34.71	2:35.12	2:35.53
380	2:35.94	2:36.35	2:36.77	2:37.18	2:37.59	2:38.00	2:38.41	2:38.82	2:39.23	2:39.65
390	2:40.06	2:40.47	2:40.88	2:41.29	2:41.70	2:42.11	2:42.53	2:42.94	2:43.35	2:43.76
400	2:44.17	2:44.58	2:44.99	2:45.41	2:45.82	2:46.23	2:46.64	2:47.05	2:47.46	2:47.88
410	2:48.29	2:48.70	2:49.11	2:49.52	2:49.93	2:50.34	2:50.76	2:51.17	2:51.58	2:51.99
420	2:52.40	2:52.81	2:53.22	2:53.64	2:54.05	2:54.46	2:54.87	2:55.28	2:55.69	2:56.10
430	2:56.52	2:56.93	2:57.34	2:57.75	2:58.16	2:58.57	2:58.98	2:59.40	2:59.81	3:00.22
440	3:00.63	3:01.04	3:01.45	3:01.86	3:02.28	3:02.69	3:03.10	3:03.51	3:03.92	3:04.33
450	3:04.74	3:05.16	3:05.57	3:05.98	3:06.39	3:06.80	3:07.21	3:07.62	3:08.04	3:08.45
460	3:08.86	3:09.27	3:09.68	3:10.09	3:10.51	3:10.92	3:11.33	3:11.74	3:12.15	3:12.56
470	3:12.97	3:13.39	3:13.80	3:14.21	3:14.62	3:15.03	3:15.44	3:15.85	3:16.27	3:16.68
480	3:17.09	3:17.50	3:17.91	3:18.32	3:18.73	3:19.15	3:19.56	3:19.97	3:20.38	3:20.79
490	3:21.20	3:21.61	3:22.03	3:22.44	3:22.85	3:23.26	3:23.67	3:24.08	3:24.49	3:24.91
500	3:25.32	3:25.73	3:26.14	3:26.55	3:26.96	3:27.37	3:27.79	3:28.20	3:28.61	3:29.02
510	3:29.43	3:29.84	3:30.26	3:30.67	3:31.08	3:31.49	3:31.90	3:32.31	3:32.72	3:33.14
520	3:33.55	3:33.96	3:34.37	3:34.78	3:35.19	3:35.60	3:36.02	3:36.43	3:36.84	3:37.25
530	3:37.66	3:38.07	3:38.48	3:38.90	3:39.31	3:39.72	3:40.13	3:40.54	3:40.95	3:41.36
540	3:41.78	3:42.19	3:42.60	3:43.01	3:43.42	3:43.83	3:44.24	3:44.66	3:45.07	3:45.48
550	3:45.89	3:46.30	3:46.71	3:47.12	3:47.54	3:47.95	3:48.36	3:48.77	3:49.18	3:49.59
560	3:50.01	3:50.42	3:50.83	3:51.24	3:51.65	3:52.06	3:52.47	3:52.89	3:53.30	3:53.71
570	3:54.12	3:54.53	3:54.94	3:55.35	3:55.77	3:56.18	3:56.59	3:57.00	3:57.41	3:57.82
580	3:58.23	3:58.65	3:59.06	3:59.47	3:59.88	4:00.29	4:00.70	4:01.11	4:01.53	4:01.94
590	4:02.35	4:02.76	4:03.17	4:03.58	4:03.99	4:04.41	4:04.82	4:05.23	4:05.64	4:06.05

♩. = 0.62; ♩ = 0.41; ♪. = 0.31; (triplet) ♩ 𝄾 = 0.27; ♪ = 0.21; (triplet) ♪ 𝄾 𝄾 = 0.14; 𝅘𝅥𝅯 = 0.10 seconds

CLICK: 10 0/8 FRAMES; M.M.: 144.00

Click	0	1	2	3	4	5	6	7	8	9
000	0:00.00	0:00.00	0:00.42	0:00.83	0:01.25	0:01.67	0:02.08	0:02.50	0:02.92	0:03.33
010	0:03.75	0:04.17	0:04.58	0:05.00	0:05.42	0:05.83	0:06.25	0:06.67	0:07.08	0:07.50
020	0:07.92	0:08.33	0:08.75	0:09.17	0:09.58	0:10.00	0:10.42	0:10.83	0:11.25	0:11.67
030	0:12.08	0:12.50	0:12.92	0:13.33	0:13.75	0:14.17	0:14.58	0:15.00	0:15.42	0:15.83
040	0:16.25	0:16.67	0:17.08	0:17.50	0:17.92	0:18.33	0:18.75	0:19.17	0:19.58	0:20.00
050	0:20.42	0:20.83	0:21.25	0:21.67	0:22.08	0:22.50	0:22.92	0:23.33	0:23.75	0:24.17
060	0:24.58	0:25.00	0:25.42	0:25.83	0:26.25	0:26.67	0:27.08	0:27.50	0:27.92	0:28.33
070	0:28.75	0:29.17	0:29.58	0:30.00	0:30.42	0:30.83	0:31.25	0:31.67	0:32.08	0:32.50
080	0:32.92	0:33.33	0:33.75	0:34.17	0:34.58	0:35.00	0:35.42	0:35.83	0:36.25	0:36.67
090	0:37.08	0:37.50	0:37.92	0:38.33	0:38.75	0:39.17	0:39.58	0:40.00	0:40.42	0:40.83
100	0:41.25	0:41.67	0:42.08	0:42.50	0:42.92	0:43.33	0:43.75	0:44.17	0:44.58	0:45.00
110	0:45.42	0:45.83	0:46.25	0:46.67	0:47.08	0:47.50	0:47.92	0:48.33	0:48.75	0:49.17
120	0:49.58	0:50.00	0:50.42	0:50.83	0:51.25	0:51.67	0:52.08	0:52.50	0:52.92	0:53.33
130	0:53.75	0:54.17	0:54.58	0:55.00	0:55.42	0:55.83	0:56.25	0:56.67	0:57.08	0:57.50
140	0:57.92	0:58.33	0:58.75	0:59.17	0:59.58	1:00.00	1:00.42	1:00.83	1:01.25	1:01.67
150	1:02.08	1:02.50	1:02.92	1:03.33	1:03.75	1:04.17	1:04.58	1:05.00	1:05.42	1:05.83
160	1:06.25	1:06.67	1:07.08	1:07.50	1:07.92	1:08.33	1:08.75	1:09.17	1:09.58	1:10.00
170	1:10.42	1:10.83	1:11.25	1:11.67	1:12.08	1:12.50	1:12.92	1:13.33	1:13.75	1:14.17
180	1:14.58	1:15.00	1:15.42	1:15.83	1:16.25	1:16.67	1:17.08	1:17.50	1:17.92	1:18.33
190	1:18.75	1:19.17	1:19.58	1:20.00	1:20.42	1:20.83	1:21.25	1:21.67	1:22.08	1:22.50
200	1:22.92	1:23.33	1:23.75	1:24.17	1:24.58	1:25.00	1:25.42	1:25.83	1:26.25	1:26.67
210	1:27.08	1:27.50	1:27.92	1:28.33	1:28.75	1:29.17	1:29.58	1:30.00	1:30.42	1:30.83
220	1:31.25	1:31.67	1:32.08	1:32.50	1:32.92	1:33.33	1:33.75	1:34.17	1:34.58	1:35.00
230	1:35.42	1:35.83	1:36.25	1:36.67	1:37.08	1:37.50	1:37.92	1:38.33	1:38.75	1:39.17
240	1:39.58	1:40.00	1:40.42	1:40.83	1:41.25	1:41.67	1:42.08	1:42.50	1:42.92	1:43.33
250	1:43.75	1:44.17	1:44.58	1:45.00	1:45.42	1:45.83	1:46.25	1:46.67	1:47.08	1:47.50
260	1:47.92	1:48.33	1:48.75	1:49.17	1:49.58	1:50.00	1:50.42	1:50.83	1:51.25	1:51.67
270	1:52.08	1:52.50	1:52.92	1:53.33	1:53.75	1:54.17	1:54.58	1:55.00	1:55.42	1:55.83
280	1:56.25	1:56.67	1:57.08	1:57.50	1:57.92	1:58.33	1:58.75	1:59.17	1:59.58	2:00.00
290	2:00.42	2:00.83	2:01.25	2:01.67	2:02.08	2:02.50	2:02.92	2:03.33	2:03.75	2:04.17
300	2:04.58	2:05.00	2:05.42	2:05.83	2:06.25	2:06.67	2:07.08	2:07.50	2:07.92	2:08.33
310	2:08.75	2:09.17	2:09.58	2:10.00	2:10.42	2:10.83	2:11.25	2:11.67	2:12.08	2:12.50
320	2:12.92	2:13.33	2:13.75	2:14.17	2:14.58	2:15.00	2:15.42	2:15.83	2:16.25	2:16.67
330	2:17.08	2:17.50	2:17.92	2:18.33	2:18.75	2:19.17	2:19.58	2:20.00	2:20.42	2:20.83
340	2:21.25	2:21.67	2:22.08	2:22.50	2:22.92	2:23.33	2:23.75	2:24.17	2:24.58	2:25.00
350	2:25.42	2:25.83	2:26.25	2:26.67	2:27.08	2:27.50	2:27.92	2:28.33	2:28.75	2:29.17
360	2:29.58	2:30.00	2:30.42	2:30.83	2:31.25	2:31.67	2:32.08	2:32.50	2:32.92	2:33.33
370	2:33.75	2:34.17	2:34.58	2:35.00	2:35.42	2:35.83	2:36.25	2:36.67	2:37.08	2:37.50
380	2:37.92	2:38.33	2:38.75	2:39.17	2:39.58	2:40.00	2:40.42	2:40.83	2:41.25	2:41.67
390	2:42.08	2:42.50	2:42.92	2:43.33	2:43.75	2:44.17	2:44.58	2:45.00	2:45.42	2:45.83
400	2:46.25	2:46.67	2:47.08	2:47.50	2:47.92	2:48.33	2:48.75	2:49.17	2:49.58	2:50.00
410	2:50.42	2:50.83	2:51.25	2:51.67	2:52.08	2:52.50	2:52.92	2:53.33	2:53.75	2:54.17
420	2:54.58	2:55.00	2:55.42	2:55.83	2:56.25	2:56.67	2:57.08	2:57.50	2:57.92	2:58.33
430	2:58.75	2:59.17	2:59.58	3:00.00	3:00.42	3:00.83	3:01.25	3:01.67	3:02.08	3:02.50
440	3:02.92	3:03.33	3:03.75	3:04.17	3:04.58	3:05.00	3:05.42	3:05.83	3:06.25	3:06.67
450	3:07.08	3:07.50	3:07.92	3:08.33	3:08.75	3:09.17	3:09.58	3:10.00	3:10.42	3:10.83
460	3:11.25	3:11.67	3:12.08	3:12.50	3:12.92	3:13.33	3:13.75	3:14.17	3:14.58	3:15.00
470	3:15.42	3:15.83	3:16.25	3:16.67	3:17.08	3:17.50	3:17.92	3:18.33	3:18.75	3:19.17
480	3:19.58	3:20.00	3:20.42	3:20.83	3:21.25	3:21.67	3:22.08	3:22.50	3:22.92	3:23.33
490	3:23.75	3:24.17	3:24.58	3:25.00	3:25.42	3:25.83	3:26.25	3:26.67	3:27.08	3:27.50
500	3:27.92	3:28.33	3:28.75	3:29.17	3:29.58	3:30.00	3:30.42	3:30.83	3:31.25	3:31.67
510	3:32.08	3:32.50	3:32.92	3:33.33	3:33.75	3:34.17	3:34.58	3:35.00	3:35.42	3:35.83
520	3:36.25	3:36.67	3:37.08	3:37.50	3:37.92	3:38.33	3:38.75	3:39.17	3:39.58	3:40.00
530	3:40.42	3:40.83	3:41.25	3:41.67	3:42.08	3:42.50	3:42.92	3:43.33	3:43.75	3:44.17
540	3:44.58	3:45.00	3:45.42	3:45.83	3:46.25	3:46.67	3:47.08	3:47.50	3:47.92	3:48.33
550	3:48.75	3:49.17	3:49.58	3:50.00	3:50.42	3:50.83	3:51.25	3:51.67	3:52.08	3:52.50
560	3:52.92	3:53.33	3:53.75	3:54.17	3:54.58	3:55.00	3:55.42	3:55.83	3:56.25	3:56.67
570	3:57.08	3:57.50	3:57.92	3:58.33	3:58.75	3:59.17	3:59.58	4:00.00	4:00.42	4:00.83
580	4:01.25	4:01.67	4:02.08	4:02.50	4:02.92	4:03.33	4:03.75	4:04.17	4:04.58	4:05.00
590	4:05.42	4:05.83	4:06.25	4:06.67	4:07.08	4:07.50	4:07.92	4:08.33	4:08.75	4:09.17

♩. = 0.63; ♩ = 0.42; ♪. = 0.31; (triplet ♩ 𝄾) = 0.28; ♪ = 0.21; (triplet ♪ 𝄾 𝄾) = 0.14; 𝅘𝅥𝅯 = 0.10 seconds

CLICK: 10⅛ FRAMES; M.M.: 142.22

Click	0	1	2	3	4	5	6	7	8	9
000	0:00.00	0:00.00	0:00.42	0:00.84	0:01.27	0:01.69	0:02.11	0:02.53	0:02.95	0:03.38
010	0:03.80	0:04.22	0:04.64	0:05.06	0:05.48	0:05.91	0:06.33	0:06.75	0:07.17	0:07.59
020	0:08.02	0:08.44	0:08.86	0:09.28	0:09.70	0:10.13	0:10.55	0:10.97	0:11.39	0:11.81
030	0:12.23	0:12.66	0:13.08	0:13.50	0:13.92	0:14.34	0:14.77	0:15.19	0:15.61	0:16.03
040	0:16.45	0:16.88	0:17.30	0:17.72	0:18.14	0:18.56	0:18.98	0:19.41	0:19.83	0:20.25
050	0:20.67	0:21.09	0:21.52	0:21.94	0:22.36	0:22.78	0:23.20	0:23.62	0:24.05	0:24.47
060	0:24.89	0:25.31	0:25.73	0:26.16	0:26.58	0:27.00	0:27.42	0:27.84	0:28.27	0:28.69
070	0:29.11	0:29.53	0:29.95	0:30.37	0:30.80	0:31.22	0:31.64	0:32.06	0:32.48	0:32.91
080	0:33.33	0:33.75	0:34.17	0:34.59	0:35.02	0:35.44	0:35.86	0:36.28	0:36.70	0:37.13
090	0:37.55	0:37.97	0:38.39	0:38.81	0:39.23	0:39.66	0:40.08	0:40.50	0:40.92	0:41.34
100	0:41.77	0:42.19	0:42.61	0:43.03	0:43.45	0:43.88	0:44.30	0:44.72	0:45.14	0:45.56
110	0:45.98	0:46.41	0:46.83	0:47.25	0:47.67	0:48.09	0:48.52	0:48.94	0:49.36	0:49.78
120	0:50.20	0:50.63	0:51.05	0:51.47	0:51.89	0:52.31	0:52.73	0:53.16	0:53.58	0:54.00
130	0:54.42	0:54.84	0:55.27	0:55.69	0:56.11	0:56.53	0:56.95	0:57.37	0:57.80	0:58.22
140	0:58.64	0:59.06	0:59.48	0:59.91	1:00.33	1:00.75	1:01.17	1:01.59	1:02.02	1:02.44
150	1:02.86	1:03.28	1:03.70	1:04.13	1:04.55	1:04.97	1:05.39	1:05.81	1:06.23	1:06.66
160	1:07.08	1:07.50	1:07.92	1:08.34	1:08.77	1:09.19	1:09.61	1:10.03	1:10.45	1:10.87
170	1:11.30	1:11.72	1:12.14	1:12.56	1:12.98	1:13.41	1:13.83	1:14.25	1:14.67	1:15.09
180	1:15.52	1:15.94	1:16.36	1:16.78	1:17.20	1:17.62	1:18.05	1:18.47	1:18.89	1:19.31
190	1:19.73	1:20.16	1:20.58	1:21.00	1:21.42	1:21.84	1:22.27	1:22.69	1:23.11	1:23.53
200	1:23.95	1:24.38	1:24.80	1:25.22	1:25.64	1:26.06	1:26.48	1:26.91	1:27.33	1:27.75
210	1:28.17	1:28.59	1:29.02	1:29.44	1:29.86	1:30.28	1:30.70	1:31.12	1:31.55	1:31.97
220	1:32.39	1:32.81	1:33.23	1:33.66	1:34.08	1:34.50	1:34.92	1:35.34	1:35.77	1:36.19
230	1:36.61	1:37.03	1:37.45	1:37.87	1:38.30	1:38.72	1:39.14	1:39.56	1:39.98	1:40.41
240	1:40.83	1:41.25	1:41.67	1:42.09	1:42.52	1:42.94	1:43.36	1:43.78	1:44.20	1:44.63
250	1:45.05	1:45.47	1:45.89	1:46.31	1:46.73	1:47.16	1:47.58	1:48.00	1:48.42	1:48.84
260	1:49.27	1:49.69	1:50.11	1:50.53	1:50.95	1:51.37	1:51.80	1:52.22	1:52.64	1:53.06
270	1:53.48	1:53.91	1:54.33	1:54.75	1:55.17	1:55.59	1:56.02	1:56.44	1:56.86	1:57.28
280	1:57.70	1:58.13	1:58.55	1:58.97	1:59.39	1:59.81	2:00.23	2:00.66	2:01.08	2:01.50
290	2:01.92	2:02.34	2:02.77	2:03.19	2:03.61	2:04.03	2:04.45	2:04.87	2:05.30	2:05.72
300	2:06.14	2:06.56	2:06.98	2:07.41	2:07.83	2:08.25	2:08.67	2:09.09	2:09.52	2:09.94
310	2:10.36	2:10.78	2:11.20	2:11.62	2:12.05	2:12.47	2:12.89	2:13.31	2:13.73	2:14.16
320	2:14.58	2:15.00	2:15.42	2:15.84	2:16.27	2:16.69	2:17.11	2:17.53	2:17.95	2:18.37
330	2:18.80	2:19.22	2:19.64	2:20.06	2:20.48	2:20.91	2:21.33	2:21.75	2:22.17	2:22.59
340	2:23.02	2:23.44	2:23.86	2:24.28	2:24.70	2:25.13	2:25.55	2:25.97	2:26.39	2:26.81
350	2:27.23	2:27.66	2:28.08	2:28.50	2:28.92	2:29.34	2:29.77	2:30.19	2:30.61	2:31.03
360	2:31.45	2:31.88	2:32.30	2:32.72	2:33.14	2:33.56	2:33.98	2:34.41	2:34.83	2:35.25
370	2:35.67	2:36.09	2:36.52	2:36.94	2:37.36	2:37.78	2:38.20	2:38.62	2:39.05	2:39.47
380	2:39.89	2:40.31	2:40.73	2:41.16	2:41.58	2:42.00	2:42.42	2:42.84	2:43.27	2:43.69
390	2:44.11	2:44.53	2:44.95	2:45.37	2:45.80	2:46.22	2:46.64	2:47.06	2:47.48	2:47.91
400	2:48.33	2:48.75	2:49.17	2:49.59	2:50.02	2:50.44	2:50.86	2:51.28	2:51.70	2:52.12
410	2:52.55	2:52.97	2:53.39	2:53.81	2:54.23	2:54.66	2:55.08	2:55.50	2:55.92	2:56.34
420	2:56.77	2:57.19	2:57.61	2:58.03	2:58.45	2:58.87	2:59.30	2:59.72	3:00.14	3:00.56
430	3:00.98	3:01.41	3:01.83	3:02.25	3:02.67	3:03.09	3:03.52	3:03.94	3:04.36	3:04.78
440	3:05.20	3:05.63	3:06.05	3:06.47	3:06.89	3:07.31	3:07.73	3:08.16	3:08.58	3:09.00
450	3:09.42	3:09.84	3:10.27	3:10.69	3:11.11	3:11.53	3:11.95	3:12.37	3:12.80	3:13.22
460	3:13.64	3:14.06	3:14.48	3:14.91	3:15.33	3:15.75	3:16.17	3:16.59	3:17.02	3:17.44
470	3:17.86	3:18.28	3:18.70	3:19.12	3:19.55	3:19.97	3:20.39	3:20.81	3:21.23	3:21.66
480	3:22.08	3:22.50	3:22.92	3:23.34	3:23.77	3:24.19	3:24.61	3:25.03	3:25.45	3:25.87
490	3:26.30	3:26.72	3:27.14	3:27.56	3:27.98	3:28.41	3:28.83	3:29.25	3:29.67	3:30.09
500	3:30.52	3:30.94	3:31.36	3:31.78	3:32.20	3:32.62	3:33.05	3:33.47	3:33.89	3:34.31
510	3:34.73	3:35.16	3:35.58	3:36.00	3:36.42	3:36.84	3:37.27	3:37.69	3:38.11	3:38.53
520	3:38.95	3:39.38	3:39.80	3:40.22	3:40.64	3:41.06	3:41.48	3:41.91	3:42.33	3:42.75
530	3:43.17	3:43.59	3:44.02	3:44.44	3:44.86	3:45.28	3:45.70	3:46.12	3:46.55	3:46.97
540	3:47.39	3:47.81	3:48.23	3:48.66	3:49.08	3:49.50	3:49.92	3:50.34	3:50.77	3:51.19
550	3:51.61	3:52.03	3:52.45	3:52.87	3:53.30	3:53.72	3:54.14	3:54.56	3:54.98	3:55.41
560	3:55.83	3:56.25	3:56.67	3:57.09	3:57.52	3:57.94	3:58.36	3:58.78	3:59.20	3:59.62
570	4:00.05	4:00.47	4:00.89	4:01.31	4:01.73	4:02.16	4:02.58	4:03.00	4:03.42	4:03.84
580	4:04.27	4:04.69	4:05.11	4:05.53	4:05.95	4:06.37	4:06.80	4:07.22	4:07.64	4:08.06
590	4:08.48	4:08.91	4:09.33	4:09.75	4:10.17	4:10.59	4:11.02	4:11.44	4:11.86	4:12.28

♩. = 0.63; ♩ = 0.42; ♪. = 0.32; (triplet ♩ 𝄾) = 0.28; ♪ = 0.21; (triplet ♪ 𝄾 𝄾) = 0.14; 𝅘𝅥𝅯 = 0.11 seconds

CLICK: 10 2/8 FRAMES; M.M.: 140.49

Click	0	1	2	3	4	5	6	7	8	9
000	0:00.00	0:00.00	0:00.43	0:00.85	0:01.28	0:01.71	0:02.14	0:02.56	0:02.99	0:03.42
010	0:03.84	0:04.27	0:04.70	0:05.13	0:05.55	0:05.98	0:06.41	0:06.83	0:07.26	0:07.69
020	0:08.11	0:08.54	0:08.97	0:09.40	0:09.82	0:10.25	0:10.68	0:11.10	0:11.53	0:11.96
030	0:12.39	0:12.81	0:13.24	0:13.67	0:14.09	0:14.52	0:14.95	0:15.38	0:15.80	0:16.23
040	0:16.66	0:17.08	0:17.51	0:17.94	0:18.36	0:18.79	0:19.22	0:19.65	0:20.07	0:20.50
050	0:20.93	0:21.35	0:21.78	0:22.21	0:22.64	0:23.06	0:23.49	0:23.92	0:24.34	0:24.77
060	0:25.20	0:25.63	0:26.05	0:26.48	0:26.91	0:27.33	0:27.76	0:28.19	0:28.61	0:29.04
070	0:29.47	0:29.90	0:30.32	0:30.75	0:31.18	0:31.60	0:32.03	0:32.46	0:32.89	0:33.31
080	0:33.74	0:34.17	0:34.59	0:35.02	0:35.45	0:35.88	0:36.30	0:36.73	0:37.16	0:37.58
090	0:38.01	0:38.44	0:38.86	0:39.29	0:39.72	0:40.15	0:40.57	0:41.00	0:41.43	0:41.85
100	0:42.28	0:42.71	0:43.14	0:43.56	0:43.99	0:44.42	0:44.84	0:45.27	0:45.70	0:46.13
110	0:46.55	0:46.98	0:47.41	0:47.83	0:48.26	0:48.69	0:49.11	0:49.54	0:49.97	0:50.40
120	0:50.82	0:51.25	0:51.68	0:52.10	0:52.53	0:52.96	0:53.39	0:53.81	0:54.24	0:54.67
130	0:55.09	0:55.52	0:55.95	0:56.38	0:56.80	0:57.23	0:57.66	0:58.08	0:58.51	0:58.94
140	0:59.36	0:59.79	1:00.22	1:00.65	1:01.07	1:01.50	1:01.93	1:02.35	1:02.78	1:03.21
150	1:03.64	1:04.06	1:04.49	1:04.92	1:05.34	1:05.77	1:06.20	1:06.63	1:07.05	1:07.48
160	1:07.91	1:08.33	1:08.76	1:09.19	1:09.61	1:10.04	1:10.47	1:10.90	1:11.32	1:11.75
170	1:12.18	1:12.60	1:13.03	1:13.46	1:13.89	1:14.31	1:14.74	1:15.17	1:15.59	1:16.02
180	1:16.45	1:16.88	1:17.30	1:17.73	1:18.16	1:18.58	1:19.01	1:19.44	1:19.86	1:20.29
190	1:20.72	1:21.15	1:21.57	1:22.00	1:22.43	1:22.85	1:23.28	1:23.71	1:24.14	1:24.56
200	1:24.99	1:25.42	1:25.84	1:26.27	1:26.70	1:27.13	1:27.55	1:27.98	1:28.41	1:28.83
210	1:29.26	1:29.69	1:30.11	1:30.54	1:30.97	1:31.40	1:31.82	1:32.25	1:32.68	1:33.10
220	1:33.53	1:33.96	1:34.39	1:34.81	1:35.24	1:35.67	1:36.09	1:36.52	1:36.95	1:37.38
230	1:37.80	1:38.23	1:38.66	1:39.08	1:39.51	1:39.94	1:40.36	1:40.79	1:41.22	1:41.65
240	1:42.07	1:42.50	1:42.93	1:43.35	1:43.78	1:44.21	1:44.64	1:45.06	1:45.49	1:45.92
250	1:46.34	1:46.77	1:47.20	1:47.63	1:48.05	1:48.48	1:48.91	1:49.33	1:49.76	1:50.19
260	1:50.61	1:51.04	1:51.47	1:51.90	1:52.32	1:52.75	1:53.18	1:53.60	1:54.03	1:54.46
270	1:54.89	1:55.31	1:55.74	1:56.17	1:56.59	1:57.02	1:57.45	1:57.88	1:58.30	1:58.73
280	1:59.16	1:59.58	2:00.01	2:00.44	2:00.86	2:01.29	2:01.72	2:02.15	2:02.57	2:03.00
290	2:03.43	2:03.85	2:04.28	2:04.71	2:05.14	2:05.56	2:05.99	2:06.42	2:06.84	2:07.27
300	2:07.70	2:08.13	2:08.55	2:08.98	2:09.41	2:09.83	2:10.26	2:10.69	2:11.11	2:11.54
310	2:11.97	2:12.40	2:12.82	2:13.25	2:13.68	2:14.10	2:14.53	2:14.96	2:15.39	2:15.81
320	2:16.24	2:16.67	2:17.09	2:17.52	2:17.95	2:18.38	2:18.80	2:19.23	2:19.66	2:20.08
330	2:20.51	2:20.94	2:21.36	2:21.79	2:22.22	2:22.65	2:23.07	2:23.50	2:23.93	2:24.35
340	2:24.78	2:25.21	2:25.64	2:26.06	2:26.49	2:26.92	2:27.34	2:27.77	2:28.20	2:28.63
350	2:29.05	2:29.48	2:29.91	2:30.33	2:30.76	2:31.19	2:31.61	2:32.04	2:32.47	2:32.90
360	2:33.32	2:33.75	2:34.18	2:34.60	2:35.03	2:35.46	2:35.89	2:36.31	2:36.74	2:37.17
370	2:37.59	2:38.02	2:38.45	2:38.88	2:39.30	2:39.73	2:40.16	2:40.58	2:41.01	2:41.44
380	2:41.86	2:42.29	2:42.72	2:43.15	2:43.57	2:44.00	2:44.43	2:44.85	2:45.28	2:45.71
390	2:46.14	2:46.56	2:46.99	2:47.42	2:47.84	2:48.27	2:48.70	2:49.13	2:49.55	2:49.98
400	2:50.41	2:50.83	2:51.26	2:51.69	2:52.11	2:52.54	2:52.97	2:53.40	2:53.82	2:54.25
410	2:54.68	2:55.10	2:55.53	2:55.96	2:56.39	2:56.81	2:57.24	2:57.67	2:58.09	2:58.52
420	2:58.95	2:59.38	2:59.80	3:00.23	3:00.66	3:01.08	3:01.51	3:01.94	3:02.36	3:02.79
430	3:03.22	3:03.65	3:04.07	3:04.50	3:04.93	3:05.35	3:05.78	3:06.21	3:06.64	3:07.06
440	3:07.49	3:07.92	3:08.34	3:08.77	3:09.20	3:09.63	3:10.05	3:10.48	3:10.91	3:11.33
450	3:11.76	3:12.19	3:12.61	3:13.04	3:13.47	3:13.90	3:14.32	3:14.75	3:15.18	3:15.60
460	3:16.03	3:16.46	3:16.89	3:17.31	3:17.74	3:18.17	3:18.59	3:19.02	3:19.45	3:19.88
470	3:20.30	3:20.73	3:21.16	3:21.58	3:22.01	3:22.44	3:22.86	3:23.29	3:23.72	3:24.15
480	3:24.57	3:25.00	3:25.43	3:25.85	3:26.28	3:26.71	3:27.14	3:27.56	3:27.99	3:28.42
490	3:28.84	3:29.27	3:29.70	3:30.13	3:30.55	3:30.98	3:31.41	3:31.83	3:32.26	3:32.69
500	3:33.11	3:33.54	3:33.97	3:34.40	3:34.82	3:35.25	3:35.68	3:36.10	3:36.53	3:36.96
510	3:37.39	3:37.81	3:38.24	3:38.67	3:39.09	3:39.52	3:39.95	3:40.38	3:40.80	3:41.23
520	3:41.66	3:42.08	3:42.51	3:42.94	3:43.36	3:43.79	3:44.22	3:44.65	3:45.07	3:45.50
530	3:45.93	3:46.35	3:46.78	3:47.21	3:47.64	3:48.06	3:48.49	3:48.92	3:49.34	3:49.77
540	3:50.20	3:50.63	3:51.05	3:51.48	3:51.91	3:52.33	3:52.76	3:53.19	3:53.61	3:54.04
550	3:54.47	3:54.90	3:55.32	3:55.75	3:56.18	3:56.60	3:57.03	3:57.46	3:57.89	3:58.31
560	3:58.74	3:59.17	3:59.59	4:00.02	4:00.45	4:00.88	4:01.30	4:01.73	4:02.16	4:02.58
570	4:03.01	4:03.44	4:03.86	4:04.29	4:04.72	4:05.15	4:05.57	4:06.00	4:06.43	4:06.85
580	4:07.28	4:07.71	4:08.14	4:08.56	4:08.99	4:09.42	4:09.84	4:10.27	4:10.70	4:11.13
590	4:11.55	4:11.98	4:12.41	4:12.83	4:13.26	4:13.69	4:14.11	4:14.54	4:14.97	4:15.40

♩. = 0.64; ♩ = 0.43; ♪. = 0.32; (triplet ♩ 𝄾) = 0.28; ♪ = 0.21; (triplet ♪ 𝄾 𝄾) = 0.14; 𝅘𝅥𝅯 = 0.11 seconds

CLICK: 10⅜ FRAMES; M.M.: 138.80

Click	0	1	2	3	4	5	6	7	8	9
000	0:00.00	0:00.00	0:00.43	0:00.86	0:01.30	0:01.73	0:02.16	0:02.59	0:03.03	0:03.46
010	0:03.89	0:04.32	0:04.76	0:05.19	0:05.62	0:06.05	0:06.48	0:06.92	0:07.35	0:07.78
020	0:08.21	0:08.65	0:09.08	0:09.51	0:09.94	0:10.38	0:10.81	0:11.24	0:11.67	0:12.10
030	0:12.54	0:12.97	0:13.40	0:13.83	0:14.27	0:14.70	0:15.13	0:15.56	0:15.99	0:16.43
040	0:16.86	0:17.29	0:17.72	0:18.16	0:18.59	0:19.02	0:19.45	0:19.89	0:20.32	0:20.75
050	0:21.18	0:21.61	0:22.05	0:22.48	0:22.91	0:23.34	0:23.78	0:24.21	0:24.64	0:25.07
060	0:25.51	0:25.94	0:26.37	0:26.80	0:27.23	0:27.67	0:28.10	0:28.53	0:28.96	0:29.40
070	0:29.83	0:30.26	0:30.69	0:31.13	0:31.56	0:31.99	0:32.42	0:32.85	0:33.29	0:33.72
080	0:34.15	0:34.58	0:35.02	0:35.45	0:35.88	0:36.31	0:36.74	0:37.18	0:37.61	0:38.04
090	0:38.47	0:38.91	0:39.34	0:39.77	0:40.20	0:40.64	0:41.07	0:41.50	0:41.93	0:42.36
100	0:42.80	0:43.23	0:43.66	0:44.09	0:44.53	0:44.96	0:45.39	0:45.82	0:46.26	0:46.69
110	0:47.12	0:47.55	0:47.98	0:48.42	0:48.85	0:49.28	0:49.71	0:50.15	0:50.58	0:51.01
120	0:51.44	0:51.88	0:52.31	0:52.74	0:53.17	0:53.60	0:54.04	0:54.47	0:54.90	0:55.33
130	0:55.77	0:56.20	0:56.63	0:57.06	0:57.49	0:57.93	0:58.36	0:58.79	0:59.22	0:59.66
140	1:00.09	1:00.52	1:00.95	1:01.39	1:01.82	1:02.25	1:02.68	1:03.11	1:03.55	1:03.98
150	1:04.41	1:04.84	1:05.28	1:05.71	1:06.14	1:06.57	1:07.01	1:07.44	1:07.87	1:08.30
160	1:08.73	1:09.17	1:09.60	1:10.03	1:10.46	1:10.90	1:11.33	1:11.76	1:12.19	1:12.63
170	1:13.06	1:13.49	1:13.92	1:14.35	1:14.79	1:15.22	1:15.65	1:16.08	1:16.52	1:16.95
180	1:17.38	1:17.81	1:18.24	1:18.68	1:19.11	1:19.54	1:19.97	1:20.41	1:20.84	1:21.27
190	1:21.70	1:22.14	1:22.57	1:23.00	1:23.43	1:23.86	1:24.30	1:24.73	1:25.16	1:25.59
200	1:26.03	1:26.46	1:26.89	1:27.32	1:27.76	1:28.19	1:28.62	1:29.05	1:29.48	1:29.92
210	1:30.35	1:30.78	1:31.21	1:31.65	1:32.08	1:32.51	1:32.94	1:33.38	1:33.81	1:34.24
220	1:34.67	1:35.10	1:35.54	1:35.97	1:36.40	1:36.83	1:37.27	1:37.70	1:38.13	1:38.56
230	1:38.99	1:39.43	1:39.86	1:40.29	1:40.72	1:41.16	1:41.59	1:42.02	1:42.45	1:42.89
240	1:43.32	1:43.75	1:44.18	1:44.61	1:45.05	1:45.48	1:45.91	1:46.34	1:46.78	1:47.21
250	1:47.64	1:48.07	1:48.51	1:48.94	1:49.37	1:49.80	1:50.23	1:50.67	1:51.10	1:51.53
260	1:51.96	1:52.40	1:52.83	1:53.26	1:53.69	1:54.12	1:54.56	1:54.99	1:55.42	1:55.85
270	1:56.29	1:56.72	1:57.15	1:57.58	1:58.02	1:58.45	1:58.88	1:59.31	1:59.74	2:00.18
280	2:00.61	2:01.04	2:01.47	2:01.91	2:02.34	2:02.77	2:03.20	2:03.64	2:04.07	2:04.50
290	2:04.93	2:05.36	2:05.80	2:06.23	2:06.66	2:07.09	2:07.53	2:07.96	2:08.39	2:08.82
300	2:09.26	2:09.69	2:10.12	2:10.55	2:10.98	2:11.42	2:11.85	2:12.28	2:12.71	2:13.15
310	2:13.58	2:14.01	2:14.44	2:14.88	2:15.31	2:15.74	2:16.17	2:16.60	2:17.04	2:17.47
320	2:17.90	2:18.33	2:18.77	2:19.20	2:19.63	2:20.06	2:20.49	2:20.93	2:21.36	2:21.79
330	2:22.22	2:22.66	2:23.09	2:23.52	2:23.95	2:24.39	2:24.82	2:25.25	2:25.68	2:26.11
340	2:26.55	2:26.98	2:27.41	2:27.84	2:28.28	2:28.71	2:29.14	2:29.57	2:30.01	2:30.44
350	2:30.87	2:31.30	2:31.73	2:32.17	2:32.60	2:33.03	2:33.46	2:33.90	2:34.33	2:34.76
360	2:35.19	2:35.63	2:36.06	2:36.49	2:36.92	2:37.35	2:37.79	2:38.22	2:38.65	2:39.08
370	2:39.52	2:39.95	2:40.38	2:40.81	2:41.24	2:41.68	2:42.11	2:42.54	2:42.97	2:43.41
380	2:43.84	2:44.27	2:44.70	2:45.14	2:45.57	2:46.00	2:46.43	2:46.86	2:47.30	2:47.73
390	2:48.16	2:48.59	2:49.03	2:49.46	2:49.89	2:50.32	2:50.76	2:51.19	2:51.62	2:52.05
400	2:52.48	2:52.92	2:53.35	2:53.78	2:54.21	2:54.65	2:55.08	2:55.51	2:55.94	2:56.38
410	2:56.81	2:57.24	2:57.67	2:58.10	2:58.54	2:58.97	2:59.40	2:59.83	3:00.27	3:00.70
420	3:01.13	3:01.56	3:01.99	3:02.43	3:02.86	3:03.29	3:03.72	3:04.16	3:04.59	3:05.02
430	3:05.45	3:05.89	3:06.32	3:06.75	3:07.18	3:07.61	3:08.05	3:08.48	3:08.91	3:09.34
440	3:09.78	3:10.21	3:10.64	3:11.07	3:11.51	3:11.94	3:12.37	3:12.80	3:13.23	3:13.67
450	3:14.10	3:14.53	3:14.96	3:15.40	3:15.83	3:16.26	3:16.69	3:17.12	3:17.56	3:17.99
460	3:18.42	3:18.85	3:19.29	3:19.72	3:20.15	3:20.58	3:21.02	3:21.45	3:21.88	3:22.31
470	3:22.74	3:23.18	3:23.61	3:24.04	3:24.47	3:24.91	3:25.34	3:25.77	3:26.20	3:26.64
480	3:27.07	3:27.50	3:27.93	3:28.36	3:28.80	3:29.23	3:29.66	3:30.09	3:30.53	3:30.96
490	3:31.39	3:31.82	3:32.26	3:32.69	3:33.12	3:33.55	3:33.98	3:34.42	3:34.85	3:35.28
500	3:35.71	3:36.15	3:36.58	3:37.01	3:37.44	3:37.87	3:38.31	3:38.74	3:39.17	3:39.60
510	3:40.04	3:40.47	3:40.90	3:41.33	3:41.77	3:42.20	3:42.63	3:43.06	3:43.49	3:43.93
520	3:44.36	3:44.79	3:45.22	3:45.66	3:46.09	3:46.52	3:46.95	3:47.39	3:47.82	3:48.25
530	3:48.68	3:49.11	3:49.55	3:49.98	3:50.41	3:50.84	3:51.28	3:51.71	3:52.14	3:52.57
540	3:53.01	3:53.44	3:53.87	3:54.30	3:54.73	3:55.17	3:55.60	3:56.03	3:56.46	3:56.90
550	3:57.33	3:57.76	3:58.19	3:58.62	3:59.06	3:59.49	3:59.92	4:00.35	4:00.79	4:01.22
560	4:01.65	4:02.08	4:02.52	4:02.95	4:03.38	4:03.81	4:04.24	4:04.68	4:05.11	4:05.54
570	4:05.97	4:06.41	4:06.84	4:07.27	4:07.70	4:08.14	4:08.57	4:09.00	4:09.43	4:09.86
580	4:10.30	4:10.73	4:11.16	4:11.59	4:12.03	4:12.46	4:12.89	4:13.32	4:13.76	4:14.19
590	4:14.62	4:15.05	4:15.48	4:15.92	4:16.35	4:16.78	4:17.21	4:17.65	4:18.08	4:18.51

♩. = 0.65; ♩ = 0.43; ♪. = 0.32; ♩𝄾 (triplet 3) = 0.29; ♪ = 0.22; ♪𝄾𝄾 (triplet 3) = 0.14; 𝅘𝅥𝅯 = 0.11 seconds

CLICK: 10 4/8 FRAMES; M.M.: 137.14

Click	0	1	2	3	4	5	6	7	8	9
000	0:00.00	0:00.00	0:00.44	0:00.88	0:01.31	0:01.75	0:02.19	0:02.63	0:03.06	0:03.50
010	0:03.94	0:04.38	0:04.81	0:05.25	0:05.69	0:06.13	0:06.56	0:07.00	0:07.44	0:07.87
020	0:08.31	0:08.75	0:09.19	0:09.63	0:10.06	0:10.50	0:10.94	0:11.38	0:11.81	0:12.25
030	0:12.69	0:13.13	0:13.56	0:14.00	0:14.44	0:14.88	0:15.31	0:15.75	0:16.19	0:16.63
040	0:17.06	0:17.50	0:17.94	0:18.38	0:18.81	0:19.25	0:19.69	0:20.13	0:20.56	0:21.00
050	0:21.44	0:21.88	0:22.31	0:22.75	0:23.19	0:23.63	0:24.06	0:24.50	0:24.94	0:25.38
060	0:25.81	0:26.25	0:26.69	0:27.13	0:27.56	0:28.00	0:28.44	0:28.88	0:29.31	0:29.75
070	0:30.19	0:30.63	0:31.06	0:31.50	0:31.94	0:32.38	0:32.81	0:33.25	0:33.69	0:34.13
080	0:34.56	0:35.00	0:35.44	0:35.88	0:36.31	0:36.75	0:37.19	0:37.63	0:38.06	0:38.50
090	0:38.94	0:39.38	0:39.81	0:40.25	0:40.69	0:41.13	0:41.56	0:42.00	0:42.44	0:42.88
100	0:43.31	0:43.75	0:44.19	0:44.63	0:45.06	0:45.50	0:45.94	0:46.38	0:46.81	0:47.25
110	0:47.69	0:48.13	0:48.56	0:49.00	0:49.44	0:49.88	0:50.31	0:50.75	0:51.19	0:51.63
120	0:52.06	0:52.50	0:52.94	0:53.38	0:53.81	0:54.25	0:54.69	0:55.13	0:55.56	0:56.00
130	0:56.44	0:56.88	0:57.31	0:57.75	0:58.19	0:58.63	0:59.06	0:59.50	0:59.94	1:00.38
140	1:00.81	1:01.25	1:01.69	1:02.13	1:02.56	1:03.00	1:03.44	1:03.87	1:04.31	1:04.75
150	1:05.19	1:05.63	1:06.06	1:06.50	1:06.94	1:07.38	1:07.81	1:08.25	1:08.69	1:09.13
160	1:09.56	1:10.00	1:10.44	1:10.87	1:11.31	1:11.75	1:12.19	1:12.63	1:13.06	1:13.50
170	1:13.94	1:14.38	1:14.81	1:15.25	1:15.69	1:16.12	1:16.56	1:17.00	1:17.44	1:17.88
180	1:18.31	1:18.75	1:19.19	1:19.63	1:20.06	1:20.50	1:20.94	1:21.38	1:21.81	1:22.25
190	1:22.69	1:23.12	1:23.56	1:24.00	1:24.44	1:24.88	1:25.31	1:25.75	1:26.19	1:26.63
200	1:27.06	1:27.50	1:27.94	1:28.38	1:28.81	1:29.25	1:29.69	1:30.12	1:30.56	1:31.00
210	1:31.44	1:31.88	1:32.31	1:32.75	1:33.19	1:33.63	1:34.06	1:34.50	1:34.94	1:35.38
220	1:35.81	1:36.25	1:36.69	1:37.13	1:37.56	1:38.00	1:38.44	1:38.88	1:39.31	1:39.75
230	1:40.19	1:40.63	1:41.06	1:41.50	1:41.94	1:42.37	1:42.81	1:43.25	1:43.69	1:44.13
240	1:44.56	1:45.00	1:45.44	1:45.88	1:46.31	1:46.75	1:47.19	1:47.63	1:48.06	1:48.50
250	1:48.94	1:49.37	1:49.81	1:50.25	1:50.69	1:51.13	1:51.56	1:52.00	1:52.44	1:52.88
260	1:53.31	1:53.75	1:54.19	1:54.63	1:55.06	1:55.50	1:55.94	1:56.38	1:56.81	1:57.25
270	1:57.69	1:58.13	1:58.56	1:59.00	1:59.44	1:59.88	2:00.31	2:00.75	2:01.19	2:01.63
280	2:02.06	2:02.50	2:02.94	2:03.38	2:03.81	2:04.25	2:04.69	2:05.13	2:05.56	2:06.00
290	2:06.44	2:06.87	2:07.31	2:07.75	2:08.19	2:08.62	2:09.06	2:09.50	2:09.94	2:10.37
300	2:10.81	2:11.25	2:11.69	2:12.13	2:12.56	2:13.00	2:13.44	2:13.88	2:14.31	2:14.75
310	2:15.19	2:15.63	2:16.06	2:16.50	2:16.94	2:17.38	2:17.81	2:18.25	2:18.69	2:19.12
320	2:19.56	2:20.00	2:20.44	2:20.87	2:21.31	2:21.75	2:22.19	2:22.62	2:23.06	2:23.50
330	2:23.94	2:24.38	2:24.81	2:25.25	2:25.69	2:26.13	2:26.56	2:27.00	2:27.44	2:27.88
340	2:28.31	2:28.75	2:29.19	2:29.63	2:30.06	2:30.50	2:30.94	2:31.38	2:31.81	2:32.25
350	2:32.69	2:33.12	2:33.56	2:34.00	2:34.44	2:34.87	2:35.31	2:35.75	2:36.19	2:36.63
360	2:37.06	2:37.50	2:37.94	2:38.38	2:38.81	2:39.25	2:39.69	2:40.13	2:40.56	2:41.00
370	2:41.44	2:41.88	2:42.31	2:42.75	2:43.19	2:43.63	2:44.06	2:44.50	2:44.94	2:45.37
380	2:45.81	2:46.25	2:46.69	2:47.12	2:47.56	2:48.00	2:48.44	2:48.88	2:49.31	2:49.75
390	2:50.19	2:50.63	2:51.06	2:51.50	2:51.94	2:52.38	2:52.81	2:53.25	2:53.69	2:54.13
400	2:54.56	2:55.00	2:55.44	2:55.88	2:56.31	2:56.75	2:57.19	2:57.63	2:58.06	2:58.50
410	2:58.94	2:59.37	2:59.81	3:00.25	3:00.69	3:01.12	3:01.56	3:02.00	3:02.44	3:02.87
420	3:03.31	3:03.75	3:04.19	3:04.63	3:05.06	3:05.50	3:05.94	3:06.38	3:06.81	3:07.25
430	3:07.69	3:08.13	3:08.56	3:09.00	3:09.44	3:09.88	3:10.31	3:10.75	3:11.19	3:11.62
440	3:12.06	3:12.50	3:12.94	3:13.37	3:13.81	3:14.25	3:14.69	3:15.12	3:15.56	3:16.00
450	3:16.44	3:16.88	3:17.31	3:17.75	3:18.19	3:18.63	3:19.06	3:19.50	3:19.94	3:20.38
460	3:20.81	3:21.25	3:21.69	3:22.13	3:22.56	3:23.00	3:23.44	3:23.88	3:24.31	3:24.75
470	3:25.19	3:25.62	3:26.06	3:26.50	3:26.94	3:27.37	3:27.81	3:28.25	3:28.69	3:29.13
480	3:29.56	3:30.00	3:30.44	3:30.88	3:31.31	3:31.75	3:32.19	3:32.63	3:33.06	3:33.50
490	3:33.94	3:34.38	3:34.81	3:35.25	3:35.69	3:36.13	3:36.56	3:37.00	3:37.44	3:37.87
500	3:38.31	3:38.75	3:39.19	3:39.62	3:40.06	3:40.50	3:40.94	3:41.38	3:41.81	3:42.25
510	3:42.69	3:43.13	3:43.56	3:44.00	3:44.44	3:44.88	3:45.31	3:45.75	3:46.19	3:46.63
520	3:47.06	3:47.50	3:47.94	3:48.38	3:48.81	3:49.25	3:49.69	3:50.13	3:50.56	3:51.00
530	3:51.44	3:51.87	3:52.31	3:52.75	3:53.19	3:53.62	3:54.06	3:54.50	3:54.94	3:55.38
540	3:55.81	3:56.25	3:56.69	3:57.13	3:57.56	3:58.00	3:58.44	3:58.88	3:59.31	3:59.75
550	4:00.19	4:00.62	4:01.06	4:01.50	4:01.94	4:02.37	4:02.81	4:03.25	4:03.69	4:04.12
560	4:04.56	4:05.00	4:05.44	4:05.87	4:06.31	4:06.75	4:07.19	4:07.62	4:08.06	4:08.50
570	4:08.94	4:09.38	4:09.81	4:10.25	4:10.69	4:11.13	4:11.56	4:12.00	4:12.44	4:12.88
580	4:13.31	4:13.75	4:14.19	4:14.63	4:15.06	4:15.50	4:15.94	4:16.38	4:16.81	4:17.25
590	4:17.69	4:18.13	4:18.56	4:19.00	4:19.44	4:19.88	4:20.31	4:20.75	4:21.19	4:21.63

♩. = 0.66; ♩ = 0.44; ♪. = 0.33; (triplet ♩ 𝄾) = 0.29; ♪ = 0.22; (triplet ♪ 𝄾 𝄾) = 0.15; 𝅘𝅥𝅯 = 0.11 seconds

CLICK: 10⅝ FRAMES; M.M.: 135.53

Click	0	1	2	3	4	5	6	7	8	9
000	0:00.00	0:00.00	0:00.44	0:00.89	0:01.33	0:01.77	0:02.21	0:02.66	0:03.10	0:03.54
010	0:03.98	0:04.43	0:04.87	0:05.31	0:05.76	0:06.20	0:06.64	0:07.08	0:07.53	0:07.97
020	0:08.41	0:08.85	0:09.30	0:09.74	0:10.18	0:10.63	0:11.07	0:11.51	0:11.95	0:12.40
030	0:12.84	0:13.28	0:13.72	0:14.17	0:14.61	0:15.05	0:15.49	0:15.94	0:16.38	0:16.82
040	0:17.27	0:17.71	0:18.15	0:18.59	0:19.04	0:19.48	0:19.92	0:20.36	0:20.81	0:21.25
050	0:21.69	0:22.14	0:22.58	0:23.02	0:23.46	0:23.91	0:24.35	0:24.79	0:25.23	0:25.68
060	0:26.12	0:26.56	0:27.01	0:27.45	0:27.89	0:28.33	0:28.78	0:29.22	0:29.66	0:30.10
070	0:30.55	0:30.99	0:31.43	0:31.88	0:32.32	0:32.76	0:33.20	0:33.65	0:34.09	0:34.53
080	0:34.97	0:35.42	0:35.86	0:36.30	0:36.74	0:37.19	0:37.63	0:38.07	0:38.52	0:38.96
090	0:39.40	0:39.84	0:40.29	0:40.73	0:41.17	0:41.61	0:42.06	0:42.50	0:42.94	0:43.39
100	0:43.83	0:44.27	0:44.71	0:45.16	0:45.60	0:46.04	0:46.48	0:46.93	0:47.37	0:47.81
110	0:48.26	0:48.70	0:49.14	0:49.58	0:50.03	0:50.47	0:50.91	0:51.35	0:51.80	0:52.24
120	0:52.68	0:53.12	0:53.57	0:54.01	0:54.45	0:54.90	0:55.34	0:55.78	0:56.22	0:56.67
130	0:57.11	0:57.55	0:57.99	0:58.44	0:58.88	0:59.32	0:59.77	1:00.21	1:00.65	1:01.09
140	1:01.54	1:01.98	1:02.42	1:02.86	1:03.31	1:03.75	1:04.19	1:04.64	1:05.08	1:05.52
150	1:05.96	1:06.41	1:06.85	1:07.29	1:07.73	1:08.18	1:08.62	1:09.06	1:09.51	1:09.95
160	1:10.39	1:10.83	1:11.28	1:11.72	1:12.16	1:12.60	1:13.05	1:13.49	1:13.93	1:14.37
170	1:14.82	1:15.26	1:15.70	1:16.15	1:16.59	1:17.03	1:17.47	1:17.92	1:18.36	1:18.80
180	1:19.24	1:19.69	1:20.13	1:20.57	1:21.02	1:21.46	1:21.90	1:22.34	1:22.79	1:23.23
190	1:23.67	1:24.11	1:24.56	1:25.00	1:25.44	1:25.89	1:26.33	1:26.77	1:27.21	1:27.66
200	1:28.10	1:28.54	1:28.98	1:29.43	1:29.87	1:30.31	1:30.76	1:31.20	1:31.64	1:32.08
210	1:32.53	1:32.97	1:33.41	1:33.85	1:34.30	1:34.74	1:35.18	1:35.63	1:36.07	1:36.51
220	1:36.95	1:37.40	1:37.84	1:38.28	1:38.72	1:39.17	1:39.61	1:40.05	1:40.49	1:40.94
230	1:41.38	1:41.82	1:42.27	1:42.71	1:43.15	1:43.59	1:44.04	1:44.48	1:44.92	1:45.36
240	1:45.81	1:46.25	1:46.69	1:47.14	1:47.58	1:48.02	1:48.46	1:48.91	1:49.35	1:49.79
250	1:50.23	1:50.68	1:51.12	1:51.56	1:52.01	1:52.45	1:52.89	1:53.33	1:53.78	1:54.22
260	1:54.66	1:55.10	1:55.55	1:55.99	1:56.43	1:56.87	1:57.32	1:57.76	1:58.20	1:58.65
270	1:59.09	1:59.53	1:59.97	2:00.42	2:00.86	2:01.30	2:01.74	2:02.19	2:02.63	2:03.07
280	2:03.52	2:03.96	2:04.40	2:04.84	2:05.29	2:05.73	2:06.17	2:06.61	2:07.06	2:07.50
290	2:07.94	2:08.39	2:08.83	2:09.27	2:09.71	2:10.16	2:10.60	2:11.04	2:11.48	2:11.93
300	2:12.37	2:12.81	2:13.26	2:13.70	2:14.14	2:14.58	2:15.03	2:15.47	2:15.91	2:16.35
310	2:16.80	2:17.24	2:17.68	2:18.12	2:18.57	2:19.01	2:19.45	2:19.90	2:20.34	2:20.78
320	2:21.22	2:21.67	2:22.11	2:22.55	2:22.99	2:23.44	2:23.88	2:24.32	2:24.77	2:25.21
330	2:25.65	2:26.09	2:26.54	2:26.98	2:27.42	2:27.86	2:28.31	2:28.75	2:29.19	2:29.64
340	2:30.08	2:30.52	2:30.96	2:31.41	2:31.85	2:32.29	2:32.73	2:33.18	2:33.62	2:34.06
350	2:34.51	2:34.95	2:35.39	2:35.83	2:36.28	2:36.72	2:37.16	2:37.60	2:38.05	2:38.49
360	2:38.93	2:39.38	2:39.82	2:40.26	2:40.70	2:41.15	2:41.59	2:42.03	2:42.47	2:42.92
370	2:43.36	2:43.80	2:44.24	2:44.69	2:45.13	2:45.57	2:46.02	2:46.46	2:46.90	2:47.34
380	2:47.79	2:48.23	2:48.67	2:49.11	2:49.56	2:50.00	2:50.44	2:50.89	2:51.33	2:51.77
390	2:52.21	2:52.66	2:53.10	2:53.54	2:53.98	2:54.43	2:54.87	2:55.31	2:55.76	2:56.20
400	2:56.64	2:57.08	2:57.53	2:57.97	2:58.41	2:58.85	2:59.30	2:59.74	3:00.18	3:00.62
410	3:01.07	3:01.51	3:01.95	3:02.40	3:02.84	3:03.28	3:03.72	3:04.17	3:04.61	3:05.05
420	3:05.49	3:05.94	3:06.38	3:06.82	3:07.27	3:07.71	3:08.15	3:08.59	3:09.04	3:09.48
430	3:09.92	3:10.36	3:10.81	3:11.25	3:11.69	3:12.14	3:12.58	3:13.02	3:13.46	3:13.91
440	3:14.35	3:14.79	3:15.23	3:15.68	3:16.12	3:16.56	3:17.01	3:17.45	3:17.89	3:18.33
450	3:18.78	3:19.22	3:19.66	3:20.10	3:20.55	3:20.99	3:21.43	3:21.87	3:22.32	3:22.76
460	3:23.20	3:23.65	3:24.09	3:24.53	3:24.97	3:25.42	3:25.86	3:26.30	3:26.74	3:27.19
470	3:27.63	3:28.07	3:28.52	3:28.96	3:29.40	3:29.84	3:30.29	3:30.73	3:31.17	3:31.61
480	3:32.06	3:32.50	3:32.94	3:33.39	3:33.83	3:34.27	3:34.71	3:35.16	3:35.60	3:36.04
490	3:36.48	3:36.93	3:37.37	3:37.81	3:38.26	3:38.70	3:39.14	3:39.58	3:40.03	3:40.47
500	3:40.91	3:41.35	3:41.80	3:42.24	3:42.68	3:43.13	3:43.57	3:44.01	3:44.45	3:44.90
510	3:45.34	3:45.78	3:46.22	3:46.67	3:47.11	3:47.55	3:47.99	3:48.44	3:48.88	3:49.32
520	3:49.77	3:50.21	3:50.65	3:51.09	3:51.54	3:51.98	3:52.42	3:52.86	3:53.31	3:53.75
530	3:54.19	3:54.64	3:55.08	3:55.52	3:55.96	3:56.41	3:56.85	3:57.29	3:57.73	3:58.18
540	3:58.62	3:59.06	3:59.51	3:59.95	4:00.39	4:00.83	4:01.28	4:01.72	4:02.16	4:02.60
550	4:03.05	4:03.49	4:03.93	4:04.37	4:04.82	4:05.26	4:05.70	4:06.15	4:06.59	4:07.03
560	4:07.47	4:07.92	4:08.36	4:08.80	4:09.24	4:09.69	4:10.13	4:10.57	4:11.02	4:11.46
570	4:11.90	4:12.34	4:12.79	4:13.23	4:13.67	4:14.11	4:14.56	4:15.00	4:15.44	4:15.89
580	4:16.33	4:16.77	4:17.21	4:17.66	4:18.10	4:18.54	4:18.98	4:19.43	4:19.87	4:20.31
590	4:20.76	4:21.20	4:21.64	4:22.08	4:22.53	4:22.97	4:23.41	4:23.85	4:24.30	4:24.74

♩. = 0.66; ♩ = 0.44; ♪. = 0.33; (3) ♩ 𝄾 = 0.30; ♪ = 0.22; (3) ♪𝄾𝄾 = 0.15; 𝅘𝅥𝅯 = 0.11 seconds

CLICK: 10 6/8 FRAMES; M.M.: 133.95

Click	0	1	2	3	4	5	6	7	8	9
000	0:00.00	0:00.00	0:00.45	0:00.90	0:01.34	0:01.79	0:02.24	0:02.69	0:03.14	0:03.58
010	0:04.03	0:04.48	0:04.93	0:05.38	0:05.82	0:06.27	0:06.72	0:07.17	0:07.61	0:08.06
020	0:08.51	0:08.96	0:09.41	0:09.85	0:10.30	0:10.75	0:11.20	0:11.65	0:12.09	0:12.54
030	0:12.99	0:13.44	0:13.89	0:14.33	0:14.78	0:15.23	0:15.68	0:16.13	0:16.57	0:17.02
040	0:17.47	0:17.92	0:18.36	0:18.81	0:19.26	0:19.71	0:20.16	0:20.60	0:21.05	0:21.50
050	0:21.95	0:22.40	0:22.84	0:23.29	0:23.74	0:24.19	0:24.64	0:25.08	0:25.53	0:25.98
060	0:26.43	0:26.88	0:27.32	0:27.77	0:28.22	0:28.67	0:29.11	0:29.56	0:30.01	0:30.46
070	0:30.91	0:31.35	0:31.80	0:32.25	0:32.70	0:33.15	0:33.59	0:34.04	0:34.49	0:34.94
080	0:35.39	0:35.83	0:36.28	0:36.73	0:37.18	0:37.63	0:38.07	0:38.52	0:38.97	0:39.42
090	0:39.86	0:40.31	0:40.76	0:41.21	0:41.66	0:42.10	0:42.55	0:43.00	0:43.45	0:43.90
100	0:44.34	0:44.79	0:45.24	0:45.69	0:46.14	0:46.58	0:47.03	0:47.48	0:47.93	0:48.38
110	0:48.82	0:49.27	0:49.72	0:50.17	0:50.61	0:51.06	0:51.51	0:51.96	0:52.41	0:52.85
120	0:53.30	0:53.75	0:54.20	0:54.65	0:55.09	0:55.54	0:55.99	0:56.44	0:56.89	0:57.33
130	0:57.78	0:58.23	0:58.68	0:59.13	0:59.57	1:00.02	1:00.47	1:00.92	1:01.36	1:01.81
140	1:02.26	1:02.71	1:03.16	1:03.60	1:04.05	1:04.50	1:04.95	1:05.40	1:05.84	1:06.29
150	1:06.74	1:07.19	1:07.64	1:08.08	1:08.53	1:08.98	1:09.43	1:09.88	1:10.32	1:10.77
160	1:11.22	1:11.67	1:12.11	1:12.56	1:13.01	1:13.46	1:13.91	1:14.35	1:14.80	1:15.25
170	1:15.70	1:16.15	1:16.59	1:17.04	1:17.49	1:17.94	1:18.39	1:18.83	1:19.28	1:19.73
180	1:20.18	1:20.63	1:21.07	1:21.52	1:21.97	1:22.42	1:22.86	1:23.31	1:23.76	1:24.21
190	1:24.66	1:25.10	1:25.55	1:26.00	1:26.45	1:26.90	1:27.34	1:27.79	1:28.24	1:28.69
200	1:29.14	1:29.58	1:30.03	1:30.48	1:30.93	1:31.38	1:31.82	1:32.27	1:32.72	1:33.17
210	1:33.61	1:34.06	1:34.51	1:34.96	1:35.41	1:35.85	1:36.30	1:36.75	1:37.20	1:37.65
220	1:38.09	1:38.54	1:38.99	1:39.44	1:39.89	1:40.33	1:40.78	1:41.23	1:41.68	1:42.13
230	1:42.57	1:43.02	1:43.47	1:43.92	1:44.36	1:44.81	1:45.26	1:45.71	1:46.16	1:46.60
240	1:47.05	1:47.50	1:47.95	1:48.40	1:48.84	1:49.29	1:49.74	1:50.19	1:50.64	1:51.08
250	1:51.53	1:51.98	1:52.43	1:52.88	1:53.32	1:53.77	1:54.22	1:54.67	1:55.11	1:55.56
260	1:56.01	1:56.46	1:56.91	1:57.35	1:57.80	1:58.25	1:58.70	1:59.15	1:59.59	2:00.04
270	2:00.49	2:00.94	2:01.39	2:01.83	2:02.28	2:02.73	2:03.18	2:03.63	2:04.07	2:04.52
280	2:04.97	2:05.42	2:05.86	2:06.31	2:06.76	2:07.21	2:07.66	2:08.10	2:08.55	2:09.00
290	2:09.45	2:09.90	2:10.34	2:10.79	2:11.24	2:11.69	2:12.14	2:12.58	2:13.03	2:13.48
300	2:13.93	2:14.37	2:14.82	2:15.27	2:15.72	2:16.17	2:16.61	2:17.06	2:17.51	2:17.96
310	2:18.41	2:18.85	2:19.30	2:19.75	2:20.20	2:20.65	2:21.09	2:21.54	2:21.99	2:22.44
320	2:22.89	2:23.33	2:23.78	2:24.23	2:24.68	2:25.13	2:25.57	2:26.02	2:26.47	2:26.92
330	2:27.36	2:27.81	2:28.26	2:28.71	2:29.16	2:29.60	2:30.05	2:30.50	2:30.95	2:31.40
340	2:31.84	2:32.29	2:32.74	2:33.19	2:33.64	2:34.08	2:34.53	2:34.98	2:35.43	2:35.87
350	2:36.32	2:36.77	2:37.22	2:37.67	2:38.11	2:38.56	2:39.01	2:39.46	2:39.91	2:40.35
360	2:40.80	2:41.25	2:41.70	2:42.15	2:42.59	2:43.04	2:43.49	2:43.94	2:44.39	2:44.83
370	2:45.28	2:45.73	2:46.18	2:46.63	2:47.07	2:47.52	2:47.97	2:48.42	2:48.86	2:49.31
380	2:49.76	2:50.21	2:50.66	2:51.10	2:51.55	2:52.00	2:52.45	2:52.90	2:53.34	2:53.79
390	2:54.24	2:54.69	2:55.14	2:55.58	2:56.03	2:56.48	2:56.93	2:57.37	2:57.82	2:58.27
400	2:58.72	2:59.17	2:59.61	3:00.06	3:00.51	3:00.96	3:01.41	3:01.85	3:02.30	3:02.75
410	3:03.20	3:03.65	3:04.09	3:04.54	3:04.99	3:05.44	3:05.89	3:06.33	3:06.78	3:07.23
420	3:07.68	3:08.13	3:08.57	3:09.02	3:09.47	3:09.92	3:10.36	3:10.81	3:11.26	3:11.71
430	3:12.16	3:12.60	3:13.05	3:13.50	3:13.95	3:14.40	3:14.84	3:15.29	3:15.74	3:16.19
440	3:16.64	3:17.08	3:17.53	3:17.98	3:18.43	3:18.87	3:19.32	3:19.77	3:20.22	3:20.67
450	3:21.11	3:21.56	3:22.01	3:22.46	3:22.91	3:23.35	3:23.80	3:24.25	3:24.70	3:25.15
460	3:25.59	3:26.04	3:26.49	3:26.94	3:27.39	3:27.83	3:28.28	3:28.73	3:29.18	3:29.63
470	3:30.07	3:30.52	3:30.97	3:31.42	3:31.86	3:32.31	3:32.76	3:33.21	3:33.66	3:34.10
480	3:34.55	3:35.00	3:35.45	3:35.90	3:36.34	3:36.79	3:37.24	3:37.69	3:38.14	3:38.58
490	3:39.03	3:39.48	3:39.93	3:40.38	3:40.82	3:41.27	3:41.72	3:42.17	3:42.61	3:43.06
500	3:43.51	3:43.96	3:44.41	3:44.85	3:45.30	3:45.75	3:46.20	3:46.65	3:47.09	3:47.54
510	3:47.99	3:48.44	3:48.89	3:49.33	3:49.78	3:50.23	3:50.68	3:51.13	3:51.57	3:52.02
520	3:52.47	3:52.92	3:53.36	3:53.81	3:54.26	3:54.71	3:55.16	3:55.60	3:56.05	3:56.50
530	3:56.95	3:57.40	3:57.84	3:58.29	3:58.74	3:59.19	3:59.64	4:00.08	4:00.53	4:00.98
540	4:01.43	4:01.88	4:02.32	4:02.77	4:03.22	4:03.67	4:04.11	4:04.56	4:05.01	4:05.46
550	4:05.91	4:06.35	4:06.80	4:07.25	4:07.70	4:08.15	4:08.59	4:09.04	4:09.49	4:09.94
560	4:10.39	4:10.83	4:11.28	4:11.73	4:12.18	4:12.63	4:13.07	4:13.52	4:13.97	4:14.42
570	4:14.86	4:15.31	4:15.76	4:16.21	4:16.66	4:17.10	4:17.55	4:18.00	4:18.45	4:18.90
580	4:19.34	4:19.79	4:20.24	4:20.69	4:21.14	4:21.58	4:22.03	4:22.48	4:22.93	4:23.37
590	4:23.82	4:24.27	4:24.72	4:25.17	4:25.61	4:26.06	4:26.51	4:26.96	4:27.41	4:27.85

♩. = 0.67; ♩ = 0.45; ♪. = 0.34; (triplet ♩ 𝄾) = 0.30; ♪ = 0.22; (triplet ♪ 𝄾 𝄾) = 0.15; 𝅘𝅥𝅯 = 0.11 seconds

CLICK: 10⅞ FRAMES; M.M.: 132.41

Click	0	1	2	3	4	5	6	7	8	9
000	0:00.00	0:00.00	0:00.45	0:00.91	0:01.36	0:01.81	0:02.27	0:02.72	0:03.17	0:03.63
010	0:04.08	0:04.53	0:04.98	0:05.44	0:05.89	0:06.34	0:06.80	0:07.25	0:07.70	0:08.16
020	0:08.61	0:09.06	0:09.52	0:09.97	0:10.42	0:10.88	0:11.33	0:11.78	0:12.23	0:12.69
030	0:13.14	0:13.59	0:14.05	0:14.50	0:14.95	0:15.41	0:15.86	0:16.31	0:16.77	0:17.22
040	0:17.67	0:18.13	0:18.58	0:19.03	0:19.48	0:19.94	0:20.39	0:20.84	0:21.30	0:21.75
050	0:22.20	0:22.66	0:23.11	0:23.56	0:24.02	0:24.47	0:24.92	0:25.38	0:25.83	0:26.28
060	0:26.73	0:27.19	0:27.64	0:28.09	0:28.55	0:29.00	0:29.45	0:29.91	0:30.36	0:30.81
070	0:31.27	0:31.72	0:32.17	0:32.63	0:33.08	0:33.53	0:33.98	0:34.44	0:34.89	0:35.34
080	0:35.80	0:36.25	0:36.70	0:37.16	0:37.61	0:38.06	0:38.52	0:38.97	0:39.42	0:39.88
090	0:40.33	0:40.78	0:41.23	0:41.69	0:42.14	0:42.59	0:43.05	0:43.50	0:43.95	0:44.41
100	0:44.86	0:45.31	0:45.77	0:46.22	0:46.67	0:47.13	0:47.58	0:48.03	0:48.48	0:48.94
110	0:49.39	0:49.84	0:50.30	0:50.75	0:51.20	0:51.66	0:52.11	0:52.56	0:53.02	0:53.47
120	0:53.92	0:54.38	0:54.83	0:55.28	0:55.73	0:56.19	0:56.64	0:57.09	0:57.55	0:58.00
130	0:58.45	0:58.91	0:59.36	0:59.81	1:00.27	1:00.72	1:01.17	1:01.63	1:02.08	1:02.53
140	1:02.98	1:03.44	1:03.89	1:04.34	1:04.80	1:05.25	1:05.70	1:06.16	1:06.61	1:07.06
150	1:07.52	1:07.97	1:08.42	1:08.88	1:09.33	1:09.78	1:10.23	1:10.69	1:11.14	1:11.59
160	1:12.05	1:12.50	1:12.95	1:13.41	1:13.86	1:14.31	1:14.77	1:15.22	1:15.67	1:16.13
170	1:16.58	1:17.03	1:17.48	1:17.94	1:18.39	1:18.84	1:19.30	1:19.75	1:20.20	1:20.66
180	1:21.11	1:21.56	1:22.02	1:22.47	1:22.92	1:23.38	1:23.83	1:24.28	1:24.73	1:25.19
190	1:25.64	1:26.09	1:26.55	1:27.00	1:27.45	1:27.91	1:28.36	1:28.81	1:29.27	1:29.72
200	1:30.17	1:30.63	1:31.08	1:31.53	1:31.98	1:32.44	1:32.89	1:33.34	1:33.80	1:34.25
210	1:34.70	1:35.16	1:35.61	1:36.06	1:36.52	1:36.97	1:37.42	1:37.88	1:38.33	1:38.78
220	1:39.23	1:39.69	1:40.14	1:40.59	1:41.05	1:41.50	1:41.95	1:42.41	1:42.86	1:43.31
230	1:43.77	1:44.22	1:44.67	1:45.13	1:45.58	1:46.03	1:46.48	1:46.94	1:47.39	1:47.84
240	1:48.30	1:48.75	1:49.20	1:49.66	1:50.11	1:50.56	1:51.02	1:51.47	1:51.92	1:52.38
250	1:52.83	1:53.28	1:53.73	1:54.19	1:54.64	1:55.09	1:55.55	1:56.00	1:56.45	1:56.91
260	1:57.36	1:57.81	1:58.27	1:58.72	1:59.17	1:59.63	2:00.08	2:00.53	2:00.98	2:01.44
270	2:01.89	2:02.34	2:02.80	2:03.25	2:03.70	2:04.16	2:04.61	2:05.06	2:05.52	2:05.97
280	2:06.42	2:06.88	2:07.33	2:07.78	2:08.23	2:08.69	2:09.14	2:09.59	2:10.05	2:10.50
290	2:10.95	2:11.41	2:11.86	2:12.31	2:12.77	2:13.22	2:13.67	2:14.12	2:14.58	2:15.03
300	2:15.48	2:15.94	2:16.39	2:16.84	2:17.30	2:17.75	2:18.20	2:18.66	2:19.11	2:19.56
310	2:20.02	2:20.47	2:20.92	2:21.38	2:21.83	2:22.28	2:22.73	2:23.19	2:23.64	2:24.09
320	2:24.55	2:25.00	2:25.45	2:25.91	2:26.36	2:26.81	2:27.27	2:27.72	2:28.17	2:28.63
330	2:29.08	2:29.53	2:29.98	2:30.44	2:30.89	2:31.34	2:31.80	2:32.25	2:32.70	2:33.16
340	2:33.61	2:34.06	2:34.52	2:34.97	2:35.42	2:35.88	2:36.33	2:36.78	2:37.23	2:37.69
350	2:38.14	2:38.59	2:39.05	2:39.50	2:39.95	2:40.41	2:40.86	2:41.31	2:41.77	2:42.22
360	2:42.67	2:43.13	2:43.58	2:44.03	2:44.48	2:44.94	2:45.39	2:45.84	2:46.30	2:46.75
370	2:47.20	2:47.66	2:48.11	2:48.56	2:49.02	2:49.47	2:49.92	2:50.38	2:50.83	2:51.28
380	2:51.73	2:52.19	2:52.64	2:53.09	2:53.55	2:54.00	2:54.45	2:54.91	2:55.36	2:55.81
390	2:56.27	2:56.72	2:57.17	2:57.63	2:58.08	2:58.53	2:58.98	2:59.44	2:59.89	3:00.34
400	3:00.80	3:01.25	3:01.70	3:02.16	3:02.61	3:03.06	3:03.52	3:03.97	3:04.42	3:04.88
410	3:05.33	3:05.78	3:06.23	3:06.69	3:07.14	3:07.59	3:08.05	3:08.50	3:08.95	3:09.41
420	3:09.86	3:10.31	3:10.77	3:11.22	3:11.67	3:12.13	3:12.58	3:13.03	3:13.48	3:13.94
430	3:14.39	3:14.84	3:15.30	3:15.75	3:16.20	3:16.66	3:17.11	3:17.56	3:18.02	3:18.47
440	3:18.92	3:19.38	3:19.83	3:20.28	3:20.73	3:21.19	3:21.64	3:22.09	3:22.55	3:23.00
450	3:23.45	3:23.91	3:24.36	3:24.81	3:25.27	3:25.72	3:26.17	3:26.63	3:27.08	3:27.53
460	3:27.98	3:28.44	3:28.89	3:29.34	3:29.80	3:30.25	3:30.70	3:31.16	3:31.61	3:32.06
470	3:32.52	3:32.97	3:33.42	3:33.88	3:34.33	3:34.78	3:35.23	3:35.69	3:36.14	3:36.59
480	3:37.05	3:37.50	3:37.95	3:38.41	3:38.86	3:39.31	3:39.77	3:40.22	3:40.67	3:41.13
490	3:41.58	3:42.03	3:42.48	3:42.94	3:43.39	3:43.84	3:44.30	3:44.75	3:45.20	3:45.66
500	3:46.11	3:46.56	3:47.02	3:47.47	3:47.92	3:48.38	3:48.83	3:49.28	3:49.73	3:50.19
510	3:50.64	3:51.09	3:51.55	3:52.00	3:52.45	3:52.91	3:53.36	3:53.81	3:54.27	3:54.72
520	3:55.17	3:55.63	3:56.08	3:56.53	3:56.98	3:57.44	3:57.89	3:58.34	3:58.80	3:59.25
530	3:59.70	4:00.16	4:00.61	4:01.06	4:01.52	4:01.97	4:02.42	4:02.88	4:03.33	4:03.78
540	4:04.23	4:04.69	4:05.14	4:05.59	4:06.05	4:06.50	4:06.95	4:07.41	4:07.86	4:08.31
550	4:08.77	4:09.22	4:09.67	4:10.13	4:10.58	4:11.03	4:11.48	4:11.94	4:12.39	4:12.84
560	4:13.30	4:13.75	4:14.20	4:14.66	4:15.11	4:15.56	4:16.02	4:16.47	4:16.92	4:17.38
570	4:17.83	4:18.28	4:18.73	4:19.19	4:19.64	4:20.09	4:20.55	4:21.00	4:21.45	4:21.91
580	4:22.36	4:22.81	4:23.27	4:23.72	4:24.17	4:24.62	4:25.08	4:25.53	4:25.98	4:26.44
590	4:26.89	4:27.34	4:27.80	4:28.25	4:28.70	4:29.16	4:29.61	4:30.06	4:30.52	4:30.97

♩. = 0.68; ♩ = 0.45; ♪. = 0.34; (3) ♩ 𝄾 = 0.30; ♪ = 0.23; (3) ♪𝄾𝄾 = 0.15; 𝅘𝅥𝅯 = 0.11 seconds

CLICK: 11 0/8 FRAMES; M.M.: 130.91

Click	0	1	2	3	4	5	6	7	8	9
000	0:00.00	0:00.00	0:00.46	0:00.92	0:01.38	0:01.83	0:02.29	0:02.75	0:03.21	0:03.67
010	0:04.13	0:04.58	0:05.04	0:05.50	0:05.96	0:06.42	0:06.88	0:07.33	0:07.79	0:08.25
020	0:08.71	0:09.17	0:09.63	0:10.08	0:10.54	0:11.00	0:11.46	0:11.92	0:12.38	0:12.83
030	0:13.29	0:13.75	0:14.21	0:14.67	0:15.13	0:15.58	0:16.04	0:16.50	0:16.96	0:17.42
040	0:17.88	0:18.33	0:18.79	0:19.25	0:19.71	0:20.17	0:20.63	0:21.08	0:21.54	0:22.00
050	0:22.46	0:22.92	0:23.38	0:23.83	0:24.29	0:24.75	0:25.21	0:25.67	0:26.13	0:26.58
060	0:27.04	0:27.50	0:27.96	0:28.42	0:28.88	0:29.33	0:29.79	0:30.25	0:30.71	0:31.17
070	0:31.63	0:32.08	0:32.54	0:33.00	0:33.46	0:33.92	0:34.38	0:34.83	0:35.29	0:35.75
080	0:36.21	0:36.67	0:37.13	0:37.58	0:38.04	0:38.50	0:38.96	0:39.42	0:39.88	0:40.33
090	0:40.79	0:41.25	0:41.71	0:42.17	0:42.63	0:43.08	0:43.54	0:44.00	0:44.46	0:44.92
100	0:45.38	0:45.83	0:46.29	0:46.75	0:47.21	0:47.67	0:48.13	0:48.58	0:49.04	0:49.50
110	0:49.96	0:50.42	0:50.88	0:51.33	0:51.79	0:52.25	0:52.71	0:53.17	0:53.63	0:54.08
120	0:54.54	0:55.00	0:55.46	0:55.92	0:56.38	0:56.83	0:57.29	0:57.75	0:58.21	0:58.67
130	0:59.13	0:59.58	1:00.04	1:00.50	1:00.96	1:01.42	1:01.88	1:02.33	1:02.79	1:03.25
140	1:03.71	1:04.17	1:04.63	1:05.08	1:05.54	1:06.00	1:06.46	1:06.92	1:07.38	1:07.83
150	1:08.29	1:08.75	1:09.21	1:09.67	1:10.13	1:10.58	1:11.04	1:11.50	1:11.96	1:12.42
160	1:12.87	1:13.33	1:13.79	1:14.25	1:14.71	1:15.17	1:15.62	1:16.08	1:16.54	1:17.00
170	1:17.46	1:17.92	1:18.37	1:18.83	1:19.29	1:19.75	1:20.21	1:20.67	1:21.13	1:21.58
180	1:22.04	1:22.50	1:22.96	1:23.42	1:23.88	1:24.33	1:24.79	1:25.25	1:25.71	1:26.17
190	1:26.63	1:27.08	1:27.54	1:28.00	1:28.46	1:28.92	1:29.38	1:29.83	1:30.29	1:30.75
200	1:31.21	1:31.67	1:32.13	1:32.58	1:33.04	1:33.50	1:33.96	1:34.42	1:34.87	1:35.33
210	1:35.79	1:36.25	1:36.71	1:37.17	1:37.63	1:38.08	1:38.54	1:39.00	1:39.46	1:39.92
220	1:40.38	1:40.83	1:41.29	1:41.75	1:42.21	1:42.67	1:43.13	1:43.58	1:44.04	1:44.50
230	1:44.96	1:45.42	1:45.88	1:46.33	1:46.79	1:47.25	1:47.71	1:48.17	1:48.63	1:49.08
240	1:49.54	1:50.00	1:50.46	1:50.92	1:51.38	1:51.83	1:52.29	1:52.75	1:53.21	1:53.67
250	1:54.12	1:54.58	1:55.04	1:55.50	1:55.96	1:56.42	1:56.87	1:57.33	1:57.79	1:58.25
260	1:58.71	1:59.17	1:59.63	2:00.08	2:00.54	2:01.00	2:01.46	2:01.92	2:02.38	2:02.83
270	2:03.29	2:03.75	2:04.21	2:04.67	2:05.12	2:05.58	2:06.04	2:06.50	2:06.96	2:07.42
280	2:07.87	2:08.33	2:08.79	2:09.25	2:09.71	2:10.17	2:10.62	2:11.08	2:11.54	2:12.00
290	2:12.46	2:12.92	2:13.37	2:13.83	2:14.29	2:14.75	2:15.21	2:15.67	2:16.12	2:16.58
300	2:17.04	2:17.50	2:17.96	2:18.42	2:18.87	2:19.33	2:19.79	2:20.25	2:20.71	2:21.17
310	2:21.63	2:22.08	2:22.54	2:23.00	2:23.46	2:23.92	2:24.38	2:24.83	2:25.29	2:25.75
320	2:26.21	2:26.67	2:27.13	2:27.58	2:28.04	2:28.50	2:28.96	2:29.42	2:29.88	2:30.33
330	2:30.79	2:31.25	2:31.71	2:32.17	2:32.63	2:33.08	2:33.54	2:34.00	2:34.46	2:34.92
340	2:35.38	2:35.83	2:36.29	2:36.75	2:37.21	2:37.67	2:38.13	2:38.58	2:39.04	2:39.50
350	2:39.96	2:40.42	2:40.88	2:41.33	2:41.79	2:42.25	2:42.71	2:43.17	2:43.63	2:44.08
360	2:44.54	2:45.00	2:45.46	2:45.92	2:46.37	2:46.83	2:47.29	2:47.75	2:48.21	2:48.67
370	2:49.12	2:49.58	2:50.04	2:50.50	2:50.96	2:51.42	2:51.87	2:52.33	2:52.79	2:53.25
380	2:53.71	2:54.17	2:54.62	2:55.08	2:55.54	2:56.00	2:56.46	2:56.92	2:57.37	2:57.83
390	2:58.29	2:58.75	2:59.21	2:59.67	3:00.12	3:00.58	3:01.04	3:01.50	3:01.96	3:02.42
400	3:02.87	3:03.33	3:03.79	3:04.25	3:04.71	3:05.17	3:05.63	3:06.08	3:06.54	3:07.00
410	3:07.46	3:07.92	3:08.38	3:08.83	3:09.29	3:09.75	3:10.21	3:10.67	3:11.13	3:11.58
420	3:12.04	3:12.50	3:12.96	3:13.42	3:13.88	3:14.33	3:14.79	3:15.25	3:15.71	3:16.17
430	3:16.63	3:17.08	3:17.54	3:18.00	3:18.46	3:18.92	3:19.38	3:19.83	3:20.29	3:20.75
440	3:21.21	3:21.67	3:22.13	3:22.58	3:23.04	3:23.50	3:23.96	3:24.42	3:24.88	3:25.33
450	3:25.79	3:26.25	3:26.71	3:27.17	3:27.62	3:28.08	3:28.54	3:29.00	3:29.46	3:29.92
460	3:30.37	3:30.83	3:31.29	3:31.75	3:32.21	3:32.67	3:33.12	3:33.58	3:34.04	3:34.50
470	3:34.96	3:35.42	3:35.87	3:36.33	3:36.79	3:37.25	3:37.71	3:38.17	3:38.62	3:39.08
480	3:39.54	3:40.00	3:40.46	3:40.92	3:41.38	3:41.83	3:42.29	3:42.75	3:43.21	3:43.67
490	3:44.13	3:44.58	3:45.04	3:45.50	3:45.96	3:46.42	3:46.88	3:47.33	3:47.79	3:48.25
500	3:48.71	3:49.17	3:49.63	3:50.08	3:50.54	3:51.00	3:51.46	3:51.92	3:52.38	3:52.83
510	3:53.29	3:53.75	3:54.21	3:54.67	3:55.13	3:55.58	3:56.04	3:56.50	3:56.96	3:57.42
520	3:57.88	3:58.33	3:58.79	3:59.25	3:59.71	4:00.17	4:00.62	4:01.08	4:01.54	4:02.00
530	4:02.46	4:02.92	4:03.38	4:03.83	4:04.29	4:04.75	4:05.21	4:05.67	4:06.12	4:06.58
540	4:07.04	4:07.50	4:07.96	4:08.42	4:08.88	4:09.33	4:09.79	4:10.25	4:10.71	4:11.17
550	4:11.62	4:12.08	4:12.54	4:13.00	4:13.46	4:13.92	4:14.38	4:14.83	4:15.29	4:15.75
560	4:16.21	4:16.67	4:17.12	4:17.58	4:18.04	4:18.50	4:18.96	4:19.42	4:19.88	4:20.33
570	4:20.79	4:21.25	4:21.71	4:22.17	4:22.62	4:23.08	4:23.54	4:24.00	4:24.46	4:24.92
580	4:25.38	4:25.83	4:26.29	4:26.75	4:27.21	4:27.67	4:28.13	4:28.58	4:29.04	4:29.50
590	4:29.96	4:30.42	4:30.87	4:31.33	4:31.79	4:32.25	4:32.71	4:33.17	4:33.63	4:34.08

♩. = 0.69; ♩ = 0.46; ♪. = 0.34; (triplet ♩ 𝄾) = 0.31; ♪ = 0.23; (triplet ♪ 𝄾 𝄾) = 0.15; 𝅘𝅥𝅯 = 0.11 seconds

CLICK: 11⅛ FRAMES; M.M.: 129.44

Click	0	1	2	3	4	5	6	7	8	9
000	0:00.00	0:00.00	0:00.46	0:00.93	0:01.39	0:01.85	0:02.32	0:02.78	0:03.24	0:03.71
010	0:04.17	0:04.64	0:05.10	0:05.56	0:06.03	0:06.49	0:06.95	0:07.42	0:07.88	0:08.34
020	0:08.81	0:09.27	0:09.73	0:10.20	0:10.66	0:11.13	0:11.59	0:12.05	0:12.52	0:12.98
030	0:13.44	0:13.91	0:14.37	0:14.83	0:15.30	0:15.76	0:16.22	0:16.69	0:17.15	0:17.61
040	0:18.08	0:18.54	0:19.01	0:19.47	0:19.93	0:20.40	0:20.86	0:21.32	0:21.79	0:22.25
050	0:22.71	0:23.18	0:23.64	0:24.10	0:24.57	0:25.03	0:25.49	0:25.96	0:26.42	0:26.89
060	0:27.35	0:27.81	0:28.28	0:28.74	0:29.20	0:29.67	0:30.13	0:30.59	0:31.06	0:31.52
070	0:31.98	0:32.45	0:32.91	0:33.38	0:33.84	0:34.30	0:34.77	0:35.23	0:35.69	0:36.16
080	0:36.62	0:37.08	0:37.55	0:38.01	0:38.47	0:38.94	0:39.40	0:39.86	0:40.33	0:40.79
090	0:41.26	0:41.72	0:42.18	0:42.65	0:43.11	0:43.57	0:44.04	0:44.50	0:44.96	0:45.43
100	0:45.89	0:46.35	0:46.82	0:47.28	0:47.74	0:48.21	0:48.67	0:49.14	0:49.60	0:50.06
110	0:50.53	0:50.99	0:51.45	0:51.92	0:52.38	0:52.84	0:53.31	0:53.77	0:54.23	0:54.70
120	0:55.16	0:55.63	0:56.09	0:56.55	0:57.02	0:57.48	0:57.94	0:58.41	0:58.87	0:59.33
130	0:59.80	1:00.26	1:00.72	1:01.19	1:01.65	1:02.11	1:02.58	1:03.04	1:03.51	1:03.97
140	1:04.43	1:04.90	1:05.36	1:05.82	1:06.29	1:06.75	1:07.21	1:07.68	1:08.14	1:08.60
150	1:09.07	1:09.53	1:09.99	1:10.46	1:10.92	1:11.39	1:11.85	1:12.31	1:12.78	1:13.24
160	1:13.70	1:14.17	1:14.63	1:15.09	1:15.56	1:16.02	1:16.48	1:16.95	1:17.41	1:17.88
170	1:18.34	1:18.80	1:19.27	1:19.73	1:20.19	1:20.66	1:21.12	1:21.58	1:22.05	1:22.51
180	1:22.97	1:23.44	1:23.90	1:24.36	1:24.83	1:25.29	1:25.76	1:26.22	1:26.68	1:27.15
190	1:27.61	1:28.07	1:28.54	1:29.00	1:29.46	1:29.93	1:30.39	1:30.85	1:31.32	1:31.78
200	1:32.24	1:32.71	1:33.17	1:33.64	1:34.10	1:34.56	1:35.03	1:35.49	1:35.95	1:36.42
210	1:36.88	1:37.34	1:37.81	1:38.27	1:38.73	1:39.20	1:39.66	1:40.13	1:40.59	1:41.05
220	1:41.52	1:41.98	1:42.44	1:42.91	1:43.37	1:43.83	1:44.30	1:44.76	1:45.22	1:45.69
230	1:46.15	1:46.61	1:47.08	1:47.54	1:48.01	1:48.47	1:48.93	1:49.40	1:49.86	1:50.32
240	1:50.79	1:51.25	1:51.71	1:52.18	1:52.64	1:53.10	1:53.57	1:54.03	1:54.49	1:54.96
250	1:55.42	1:55.89	1:56.35	1:56.81	1:57.28	1:57.74	1:58.20	1:58.67	1:59.13	1:59.59
260	2:00.06	2:00.52	2:00.98	2:01.45	2:01.91	2:02.38	2:02.84	2:03.30	2:03.77	2:04.23
270	2:04.69	2:05.16	2:05.62	2:06.08	2:06.55	2:07.01	2:07.47	2:07.94	2:08.40	2:08.86
280	2:09.33	2:09.79	2:10.26	2:10.72	2:11.18	2:11.65	2:12.11	2:12.57	2:13.04	2:13.50
290	2:13.96	2:14.43	2:14.89	2:15.35	2:15.82	2:16.28	2:16.74	2:17.21	2:17.67	2:18.14
300	2:18.60	2:19.06	2:19.53	2:19.99	2:20.45	2:20.92	2:21.38	2:21.84	2:22.31	2:22.77
310	2:23.23	2:23.70	2:24.16	2:24.63	2:25.09	2:25.55	2:26.02	2:26.48	2:26.94	2:27.41
320	2:27.87	2:28.33	2:28.80	2:29.26	2:29.72	2:30.19	2:30.65	2:31.11	2:31.58	2:32.04
330	2:32.51	2:32.97	2:33.43	2:33.90	2:34.36	2:34.82	2:35.29	2:35.75	2:36.21	2:36.68
340	2:37.14	2:37.60	2:38.07	2:38.53	2:38.99	2:39.46	2:39.92	2:40.39	2:40.85	2:41.31
350	2:41.78	2:42.24	2:42.70	2:43.17	2:43.63	2:44.09	2:44.56	2:45.02	2:45.48	2:45.95
360	2:46.41	2:46.88	2:47.34	2:47.80	2:48.27	2:48.73	2:49.19	2:49.66	2:50.12	2:50.58
370	2:51.05	2:51.51	2:51.97	2:52.44	2:52.90	2:53.36	2:53.83	2:54.29	2:54.76	2:55.22
380	2:55.68	2:56.15	2:56.61	2:57.07	2:57.54	2:58.00	2:58.46	2:58.93	2:59.39	2:59.85
390	3:00.32	3:00.78	3:01.24	3:01.71	3:02.17	3:02.64	3:03.10	3:03.56	3:04.03	3:04.49
400	3:04.95	3:05.42	3:05.88	3:06.34	3:06.81	3:07.27	3:07.73	3:08.20	3:08.66	3:09.13
410	3:09.59	3:10.05	3:10.52	3:10.98	3:11.44	3:11.91	3:12.37	3:12.83	3:13.30	3:13.76
420	3:14.22	3:14.69	3:15.15	3:15.61	3:16.08	3:16.54	3:17.01	3:17.47	3:17.93	3:18.40
430	3:18.86	3:19.32	3:19.79	3:20.25	3:20.71	3:21.18	3:21.64	3:22.10	3:22.57	3:23.03
440	3:23.49	3:23.96	3:24.42	3:24.89	3:25.35	3:25.81	3:26.28	3:26.74	3:27.20	3:27.67
450	3:28.13	3:28.59	3:29.06	3:29.52	3:29.98	3:30.45	3:30.91	3:31.38	3:31.84	3:32.30
460	3:32.77	3:33.23	3:33.69	3:34.16	3:34.62	3:35.08	3:35.55	3:36.01	3:36.47	3:36.94
470	3:37.40	3:37.86	3:38.33	3:38.79	3:39.26	3:39.72	3:40.18	3:40.65	3:41.11	3:41.57
480	3:42.04	3:42.50	3:42.96	3:43.43	3:43.89	3:44.35	3:44.82	3:45.28	3:45.74	3:46.21
490	3:46.67	3:47.14	3:47.60	3:48.06	3:48.53	3:48.99	3:49.45	3:49.92	3:50.38	3:50.84
500	3:51.31	3:51.77	3:52.23	3:52.70	3:53.16	3:53.63	3:54.09	3:54.55	3:55.02	3:55.48
510	3:55.94	3:56.41	3:56.87	3:57.33	3:57.80	3:58.26	3:58.72	3:59.19	3:59.65	4:00.11
520	4:00.58	4:01.04	4:01.51	4:01.97	4:02.43	4:02.90	4:03.36	4:03.82	4:04.29	4:04.75
530	4:05.21	4:05.68	4:06.14	4:06.60	4:07.07	4:07.53	4:07.99	4:08.46	4:08.92	4:09.39
540	4:09.85	4:10.31	4:10.78	4:11.24	4:11.70	4:12.17	4:12.63	4:13.09	4:13.56	4:14.02
550	4:14.48	4:14.95	4:15.41	4:15.88	4:16.34	4:16.80	4:17.27	4:17.73	4:18.19	4:18.66
560	4:19.12	4:19.58	4:20.05	4:20.51	4:20.97	4:21.44	4:21.90	4:22.36	4:22.83	4:23.29
570	4:23.76	4:24.22	4:24.68	4:25.15	4:25.61	4:26.07	4:26.54	4:27.00	4:27.46	4:27.93
580	4:28.39	4:28.85	4:29.32	4:29.78	4:30.24	4:30.71	4:31.17	4:31.64	4:32.10	4:32.56
590	4:33.03	4:33.49	4:33.95	4:34.42	4:34.88	4:35.34	4:35.81	4:36.27	4:36.73	4:37.20

♩. = 0.70; ♩ = 0.46; ♪. = 0.35; (3) ♩ 𝄾 = 0.31; ♪ = 0.23; (3) ♪𝄾𝄾 = 0.15; 𝅘𝅥𝅯 = 0.12 seconds

CLICK: 11 2/8 FRAMES; M.M.: 128.00

Click	0	1	2	3	4	5	6	7	8	9
000	0:00.00	0:00.00	0:00.47	0:00.94	0:01.41	0:01.88	0:02.34	0:02.81	0:03.28	0:03.75
010	0:04.22	0:04.69	0:05.16	0:05.63	0:06.09	0:06.56	0:07.03	0:07.50	0:07.97	0:08.44
020	0:08.91	0:09.38	0:09.84	0:10.31	0:10.78	0:11.25	0:11.72	0:12.19	0:12.66	0:13.13
030	0:13.59	0:14.06	0:14.53	0:15.00	0:15.47	0:15.94	0:16.41	0:16.88	0:17.34	0:17.81
040	0:18.28	0:18.75	0:19.22	0:19.69	0:20.16	0:20.63	0:21.09	0:21.56	0:22.03	0:22.50
050	0:22.97	0:23.44	0:23.91	0:24.38	0:24.84	0:25.31	0:25.78	0:26.25	0:26.72	0:27.19
060	0:27.66	0:28.13	0:28.59	0:29.06	0:29.53	0:30.00	0:30.47	0:30.94	0:31.41	0:31.88
070	0:32.34	0:32.81	0:33.28	0:33.75	0:34.22	0:34.69	0:35.16	0:35.63	0:36.09	0:36.56
080	0:37.03	0:37.50	0:37.97	0:38.44	0:38.91	0:39.38	0:39.84	0:40.31	0:40.78	0:41.25
090	0:41.72	0:42.19	0:42.66	0:43.13	0:43.59	0:44.06	0:44.53	0:45.00	0:45.47	0:45.94
100	0:46.41	0:46.88	0:47.34	0:47.81	0:48.28	0:48.75	0:49.22	0:49.69	0:50.16	0:50.63
110	0:51.09	0:51.56	0:52.03	0:52.50	0:52.97	0:53.44	0:53.91	0:54.38	0:54.84	0:55.31
120	0:55.78	0:56.25	0:56.72	0:57.19	0:57.66	0:58.13	0:58.59	0:59.06	0:59.53	1:00.00
130	1:00.47	1:00.94	1:01.41	1:01.88	1:02.34	1:02.81	1:03.28	1:03.75	1:04.22	1:04.69
140	1:05.16	1:05.63	1:06.09	1:06.56	1:07.03	1:07.50	1:07.97	1:08.44	1:08.91	1:09.38
150	1:09.84	1:10.31	1:10.78	1:11.25	1:11.72	1:12.19	1:12.66	1:13.13	1:13.59	1:14.06
160	1:14.53	1:15.00	1:15.47	1:15.94	1:16.41	1:16.88	1:17.34	1:17.81	1:18.28	1:18.75
170	1:19.22	1:19.69	1:20.16	1:20.63	1:21.09	1:21.56	1:22.03	1:22.50	1:22.97	1:23.44
180	1:23.91	1:24.38	1:24.84	1:25.31	1:25.78	1:26.25	1:26.72	1:27.19	1:27.66	1:28.13
190	1:28.59	1:29.06	1:29.53	1:30.00	1:30.47	1:30.94	1:31.41	1:31.88	1:32.34	1:32.81
200	1:33.28	1:33.75	1:34.22	1:34.69	1:35.16	1:35.63	1:36.09	1:36.56	1:37.03	1:37.50
210	1:37.97	1:38.44	1:38.91	1:39.38	1:39.84	1:40.31	1:40.78	1:41.25	1:41.72	1:42.19
220	1:42.66	1:43.13	1:43.59	1:44.06	1:44.53	1:45.00	1:45.47	1:45.94	1:46.41	1:46.88
230	1:47.34	1:47.81	1:48.28	1:48.75	1:49.22	1:49.69	1:50.16	1:50.63	1:51.09	1:51.56
240	1:52.03	1:52.50	1:52.97	1:53.44	1:53.91	1:54.38	1:54.84	1:55.31	1:55.78	1:56.25
250	1:56.72	1:57.19	1:57.66	1:58.13	1:58.59	1:59.06	1:59.53	2:00.00	2:00.47	2:00.94
260	2:01.41	2:01.88	2:02.34	2:02.81	2:03.28	2:03.75	2:04.22	2:04.69	2:05.16	2:05.63
270	2:06.09	2:06.56	2:07.03	2:07.50	2:07.97	2:08.44	2:08.91	2:09.38	2:09.84	2:10.31
280	2:10.78	2:11.25	2:11.72	2:12.19	2:12.66	2:13.13	2:13.59	2:14.06	2:14.53	2:15.00
290	2:15.47	2:15.94	2:16.41	2:16.88	2:17.34	2:17.81	2:18.28	2:18.75	2:19.22	2:19.69
300	2:20.16	2:20.63	2:21.09	2:21.56	2:22.03	2:22.50	2:22.97	2:23.44	2:23.91	2:24.38
310	2:24.84	2:25.31	2:25.78	2:26.25	2:26.72	2:27.19	2:27.66	2:28.13	2:28.59	2:29.06
320	2:29.53	2:30.00	2:30.47	2:30.94	2:31.41	2:31.88	2:32.34	2:32.81	2:33.28	2:33.75
330	2:34.22	2:34.69	2:35.16	2:35.63	2:36.09	2:36.56	2:37.03	2:37.50	2:37.97	2:38.44
340	2:38.91	2:39.38	2:39.84	2:40.31	2:40.78	2:41.25	2:41.72	2:42.19	2:42.66	2:43.13
350	2:43.59	2:44.06	2:44.53	2:45.00	2:45.47	2:45.94	2:46.41	2:46.88	2:47.34	2:47.81
360	2:48.28	2:48.75	2:49.22	2:49.69	2:50.16	2:50.63	2:51.09	2:51.56	2:52.03	2:52.50
370	2:52.97	2:53.44	2:53.91	2:54.38	2:54.84	2:55.31	2:55.78	2:56.25	2:56.72	2:57.19
380	2:57.66	2:58.13	2:58.59	2:59.06	2:59.53	3:00.00	3:00.47	3:00.94	3:01.41	3:01.88
390	3:02.34	3:02.81	3:03.28	3:03.75	3:04.22	3:04.69	3:05.16	3:05.63	3:06.09	3:06.56
400	3:07.03	3:07.50	3:07.97	3:08.44	3:08.91	3:09.38	3:09.84	3:10.31	3:10.78	3:11.25
410	3:11.72	3:12.19	3:12.66	3:13.13	3:13.59	3:14.06	3:14.53	3:15.00	3:15.47	3:15.94
420	3:16.41	3:16.88	3:17.34	3:17.81	3:18.28	3:18.75	3:19.22	3:19.69	3:20.16	3:20.63
430	3:21.09	3:21.56	3:22.03	3:22.50	3:22.97	3:23.44	3:23.91	3:24.38	3:24.84	3:25.31
440	3:25.78	3:26.25	3:26.72	3:27.19	3:27.66	3:28.13	3:28.59	3:29.06	3:29.53	3:30.00
450	3:30.47	3:30.94	3:31.41	3:31.88	3:32.34	3:32.81	3:33.28	3:33.75	3:34.22	3:34.69
460	3:35.16	3:35.63	3:36.09	3:36.56	3:37.03	3:37.50	3:37.97	3:38.44	3:38.91	3:39.38
470	3:39.84	3:40.31	3:40.78	3:41.25	3:41.72	3:42.19	3:42.66	3:43.13	3:43.59	3:44.06
480	3:44.53	3:45.00	3:45.47	3:45.94	3:46.41	3:46.88	3:47.34	3:47.81	3:48.28	3:48.75
490	3:49.22	3:49.69	3:50.16	3:50.63	3:51.09	3:51.56	3:52.03	3:52.50	3:52.97	3:53.44
500	3:53.91	3:54.38	3:54.84	3:55.31	3:55.78	3:56.25	3:56.72	3:57.19	3:57.66	3:58.13
510	3:58.59	3:59.06	3:59.53	4:00.00	4:00.47	4:00.94	4:01.41	4:01.88	4:02.34	4:02.81
520	4:03.28	4:03.75	4:04.22	4:04.69	4:05.16	4:05.63	4:06.09	4:06.56	4:07.03	4:07.50
530	4:07.97	4:08.44	4:08.91	4:09.38	4:09.84	4:10.31	4:10.78	4:11.25	4:11.72	4:12.19
540	4:12.66	4:13.13	4:13.59	4:14.06	4:14.53	4:15.00	4:15.47	4:15.94	4:16.41	4:16.88
550	4:17.34	4:17.81	4:18.28	4:18.75	4:19.22	4:19.69	4:20.16	4:20.63	4:21.09	4:21.56
560	4:22.03	4:22.50	4:22.97	4:23.44	4:23.91	4:24.38	4:24.84	4:25.31	4:25.78	4:26.25
570	4:26.72	4:27.19	4:27.66	4:28.13	4:28.59	4:29.06	4:29.53	4:30.00	4:30.47	4:30.94
580	4:31.41	4:31.88	4:32.34	4:32.81	4:33.28	4:33.75	4:34.22	4:34.69	4:35.16	4:35.63
590	4:36.09	4:36.56	4:37.03	4:37.50	4:37.97	4:38.44	4:38.91	4:39.38	4:39.84	4:40.31

♩. = 0.70; ♩ = 0.47; ♪. = 0.35; (triplet ♩ 𝄾) = 0.31; ♪ = 0.23; (triplet ♪ 𝄾 𝄾) = 0.16; 𝅘𝅥𝅯 = 0.12 seconds

CLICK: 11⅜ FRAMES; M.M.: 126.59

Click	0	1	2	3	4	5	6	7	8	9
000	0:00.00	0:00.00	0:00.47	0:00.95	0:01.42	0:01.90	0:02.37	0:02.84	0:03.32	0:03.79
010	0:04.27	0:04.74	0:05.21	0:05.69	0:06.16	0:06.64	0:07.11	0:07.58	0:08.06	0:08.53
020	0:09.01	0:09.48	0:09.95	0:10.43	0:10.90	0:11.38	0:11.85	0:12.32	0:12.80	0:13.27
030	0:13.74	0:14.22	0:14.69	0:15.17	0:15.64	0:16.11	0:16.59	0:17.06	0:17.54	0:18.01
040	0:18.48	0:18.96	0:19.43	0:19.91	0:20.38	0:20.85	0:21.33	0:21.80	0:22.28	0:22.75
050	0:23.22	0:23.70	0:24.17	0:24.65	0:25.12	0:25.59	0:26.07	0:26.54	0:27.02	0:27.49
060	0:27.96	0:28.44	0:28.91	0:29.39	0:29.86	0:30.33	0:30.81	0:31.28	0:31.76	0:32.23
070	0:32.70	0:33.18	0:33.65	0:34.13	0:34.60	0:35.07	0:35.55	0:36.02	0:36.49	0:36.97
080	0:37.44	0:37.92	0:38.39	0:38.86	0:39.34	0:39.81	0:40.29	0:40.76	0:41.23	0:41.71
090	0:42.18	0:42.66	0:43.13	0:43.60	0:44.08	0:44.55	0:45.03	0:45.50	0:45.97	0:46.45
100	0:46.92	0:47.40	0:47.87	0:48.34	0:48.82	0:49.29	0:49.77	0:50.24	0:50.71	0:51.19
110	0:51.66	0:52.14	0:52.61	0:53.08	0:53.56	0:54.03	0:54.51	0:54.98	0:55.45	0:55.93
120	0:56.40	0:56.88	0:57.35	0:57.82	0:58.30	0:58.77	0:59.24	0:59.72	1:00.19	1:00.67
130	1:01.14	1:01.61	1:02.09	1:02.56	1:03.04	1:03.51	1:03.98	1:04.46	1:04.93	1:05.41
140	1:05.88	1:06.35	1:06.83	1:07.30	1:07.78	1:08.25	1:08.72	1:09.20	1:09.67	1:10.15
150	1:10.62	1:11.09	1:11.57	1:12.04	1:12.52	1:12.99	1:13.46	1:13.94	1:14.41	1:14.89
160	1:15.36	1:15.83	1:16.31	1:16.78	1:17.26	1:17.73	1:18.20	1:18.68	1:19.15	1:19.63
170	1:20.10	1:20.57	1:21.05	1:21.52	1:21.99	1:22.47	1:22.94	1:23.42	1:23.89	1:24.36
180	1:24.84	1:25.31	1:25.79	1:26.26	1:26.73	1:27.21	1:27.68	1:28.16	1:28.63	1:29.10
190	1:29.58	1:30.05	1:30.53	1:31.00	1:31.47	1:31.95	1:32.42	1:32.90	1:33.37	1:33.84
200	1:34.32	1:34.79	1:35.27	1:35.74	1:36.21	1:36.69	1:37.16	1:37.64	1:38.11	1:38.58
210	1:39.06	1:39.53	1:40.01	1:40.48	1:40.95	1:41.43	1:41.90	1:42.38	1:42.85	1:43.32
220	1:43.80	1:44.27	1:44.74	1:45.22	1:45.69	1:46.17	1:46.64	1:47.11	1:47.59	1:48.06
230	1:48.54	1:49.01	1:49.48	1:49.96	1:50.43	1:50.91	1:51.38	1:51.85	1:52.33	1:52.80
240	1:53.28	1:53.75	1:54.22	1:54.70	1:55.17	1:55.65	1:56.12	1:56.59	1:57.07	1:57.54
250	1:58.02	1:58.49	1:58.96	1:59.44	1:59.91	2:00.39	2:00.86	2:01.33	2:01.81	2:02.28
260	2:02.76	2:03.23	2:03.70	2:04.18	2:04.65	2:05.13	2:05.60	2:06.07	2:06.55	2:07.02
270	2:07.49	2:07.97	2:08.44	2:08.92	2:09.39	2:09.86	2:10.34	2:10.81	2:11.29	2:11.76
280	2:12.23	2:12.71	2:13.18	2:13.66	2:14.13	2:14.60	2:15.08	2:15.55	2:16.03	2:16.50
290	2:16.97	2:17.45	2:17.92	2:18.40	2:18.87	2:19.34	2:19.82	2:20.29	2:20.77	2:21.24
300	2:21.71	2:22.19	2:22.66	2:23.14	2:23.61	2:24.08	2:24.56	2:25.03	2:25.51	2:25.98
310	2:26.45	2:26.93	2:27.40	2:27.88	2:28.35	2:28.82	2:29.30	2:29.77	2:30.24	2:30.72
320	2:31.19	2:31.67	2:32.14	2:32.61	2:33.09	2:33.56	2:34.04	2:34.51	2:34.98	2:35.46
330	2:35.93	2:36.41	2:36.88	2:37.35	2:37.83	2:38.30	2:38.78	2:39.25	2:39.72	2:40.20
340	2:40.67	2:41.15	2:41.62	2:42.09	2:42.57	2:43.04	2:43.52	2:43.99	2:44.46	2:44.94
350	2:45.41	2:45.89	2:46.36	2:46.83	2:47.31	2:47.78	2:48.26	2:48.73	2:49.20	2:49.68
360	2:50.15	2:50.63	2:51.10	2:51.57	2:52.05	2:52.52	2:52.99	2:53.47	2:53.94	2:54.42
370	2:54.89	2:55.36	2:55.84	2:56.31	2:56.79	2:57.26	2:57.73	2:58.21	2:58.68	2:59.16
380	2:59.63	3:00.10	3:00.58	3:01.05	3:01.53	3:02.00	3:02.47	3:02.95	3:03.42	3:03.90
390	3:04.37	3:04.84	3:05.32	3:05.79	3:06.27	3:06.74	3:07.21	3:07.69	3:08.16	3:08.64
400	3:09.11	3:09.58	3:10.06	3:10.53	3:11.01	3:11.48	3:11.95	3:12.43	3:12.90	3:13.38
410	3:13.85	3:14.32	3:14.80	3:15.27	3:15.74	3:16.22	3:16.69	3:17.17	3:17.64	3:18.11
420	3:18.59	3:19.06	3:19.54	3:20.01	3:20.48	3:20.96	3:21.43	3:21.91	3:22.38	3:22.85
430	3:23.33	3:23.80	3:24.28	3:24.75	3:25.22	3:25.70	3:26.17	3:26.65	3:27.12	3:27.59
440	3:28.07	3:28.54	3:29.02	3:29.49	3:29.96	3:30.44	3:30.91	3:31.39	3:31.86	3:32.33
450	3:32.81	3:33.28	3:33.76	3:34.23	3:34.70	3:35.18	3:35.65	3:36.13	3:36.60	3:37.07
460	3:37.55	3:38.02	3:38.49	3:38.97	3:39.44	3:39.92	3:40.39	3:40.86	3:41.34	3:41.81
470	3:42.29	3:42.76	3:43.23	3:43.71	3:44.18	3:44.66	3:45.13	3:45.60	3:46.08	3:46.55
480	3:47.03	3:47.50	3:47.97	3:48.45	3:48.92	3:49.40	3:49.87	3:50.34	3:50.82	3:51.29
490	3:51.77	3:52.24	3:52.71	3:53.19	3:53.66	3:54.14	3:54.61	3:55.08	3:55.56	3:56.03
500	3:56.51	3:56.98	3:57.45	3:57.93	3:58.40	3:58.88	3:59.35	3:59.82	4:00.30	4:00.77
510	4:01.24	4:01.72	4:02.19	4:02.67	4:03.14	4:03.61	4:04.09	4:04.56	4:05.04	4:05.51
520	4:05.98	4:06.46	4:06.93	4:07.41	4:07.88	4:08.35	4:08.83	4:09.30	4:09.78	4:10.25
530	4:10.72	4:11.20	4:11.67	4:12.15	4:12.62	4:13.09	4:13.57	4:14.04	4:14.52	4:14.99
540	4:15.46	4:15.94	4:16.41	4:16.89	4:17.36	4:17.83	4:18.31	4:18.78	4:19.26	4:19.73
550	4:20.20	4:20.68	4:21.15	4:21.63	4:22.10	4:22.57	4:23.05	4:23.52	4:23.99	4:24.47
560	4:24.94	4:25.42	4:25.89	4:26.36	4:26.84	4:27.31	4:27.79	4:28.26	4:28.73	4:29.21
570	4:29.68	4:30.16	4:30.63	4:31.10	4:31.58	4:32.05	4:32.53	4:33.00	4:33.47	4:33.95
580	4:34.42	4:34.90	4:35.37	4:35.84	4:36.32	4:36.79	4:37.27	4:37.74	4:38.21	4:38.69
590	4:39.16	4:39.64	4:40.11	4:40.58	4:41.06	4:41.53	4:42.01	4:42.48	4:42.95	4:43.43

𝅗𝅥. = 0.71; ♩ = 0.47; ♪. = 0.36; ♩ 𝄾 (triplet 3) = 0.32; ♪ = 0.24; ♪ 𝄾 𝄾 (triplet 3) = 0.16; 𝅘𝅥𝅯 = 0.12 seconds

CLICK: 11 4/8 FRAMES; M.M.: 125.22

Click	0	1	2	3	4	5	6	7	8	9
000	0:00.00	0:00.00	0:00.48	0:00.96	0:01.44	0:01.92	0:02.40	0:02.88	0:03.35	0:03.83
010	0:04.31	0:04.79	0:05.27	0:05.75	0:06.23	0:06.71	0:07.19	0:07.67	0:08.15	0:08.63
020	0:09.10	0:09.58	0:10.06	0:10.54	0:11.02	0:11.50	0:11.98	0:12.46	0:12.94	0:13.42
030	0:13.90	0:14.37	0:14.85	0:15.33	0:15.81	0:16.29	0:16.77	0:17.25	0:17.73	0:18.21
040	0:18.69	0:19.17	0:19.65	0:20.12	0:20.60	0:21.08	0:21.56	0:22.04	0:22.52	0:23.00
050	0:23.48	0:23.96	0:24.44	0:24.92	0:25.40	0:25.87	0:26.35	0:26.83	0:27.31	0:27.79
060	0:28.27	0:28.75	0:29.23	0:29.71	0:30.19	0:30.67	0:31.15	0:31.62	0:32.10	0:32.58
070	0:33.06	0:33.54	0:34.02	0:34.50	0:34.98	0:35.46	0:35.94	0:36.42	0:36.90	0:37.38
080	0:37.85	0:38.33	0:38.81	0:39.29	0:39.77	0:40.25	0:40.73	0:41.21	0:41.69	0:42.17
090	0:42.65	0:43.12	0:43.60	0:44.08	0:44.56	0:45.04	0:45.52	0:46.00	0:46.48	0:46.96
100	0:47.44	0:47.92	0:48.40	0:48.88	0:49.35	0:49.83	0:50.31	0:50.79	0:51.27	0:51.75
110	0:52.23	0:52.71	0:53.19	0:53.67	0:54.15	0:54.62	0:55.10	0:55.58	0:56.06	0:56.54
120	0:57.02	0:57.50	0:57.98	0:58.46	0:58.94	0:59.42	0:59.90	1:00.37	1:00.85	1:01.33
130	1:01.81	1:02.29	1:02.77	1:03.25	1:03.73	1:04.21	1:04.69	1:05.17	1:05.65	1:06.12
140	1:06.60	1:07.08	1:07.56	1:08.04	1:08.52	1:09.00	1:09.48	1:09.96	1:10.44	1:10.92
150	1:11.40	1:11.87	1:12.35	1:12.83	1:13.31	1:13.79	1:14.27	1:14.75	1:15.23	1:15.71
160	1:16.19	1:16.67	1:17.15	1:17.62	1:18.10	1:18.58	1:19.06	1:19.54	1:20.02	1:20.50
170	1:20.98	1:21.46	1:21.94	1:22.42	1:22.90	1:23.37	1:23.85	1:24.33	1:24.81	1:25.29
180	1:25.77	1:26.25	1:26.73	1:27.21	1:27.69	1:28.17	1:28.65	1:29.12	1:29.60	1:30.08
190	1:30.56	1:31.04	1:31.52	1:32.00	1:32.48	1:32.96	1:33.44	1:33.92	1:34.40	1:34.87
200	1:35.35	1:35.83	1:36.31	1:36.79	1:37.27	1:37.75	1:38.23	1:38.71	1:39.19	1:39.67
210	1:40.15	1:40.62	1:41.10	1:41.58	1:42.06	1:42.54	1:43.02	1:43.50	1:43.98	1:44.46
220	1:44.94	1:45.42	1:45.90	1:46.37	1:46.85	1:47.33	1:47.81	1:48.29	1:48.77	1:49.25
230	1:49.73	1:50.21	1:50.69	1:51.17	1:51.65	1:52.12	1:52.60	1:53.08	1:53.56	1:54.04
240	1:54.52	1:55.00	1:55.48	1:55.96	1:56.44	1:56.92	1:57.40	1:57.87	1:58.35	1:58.83
250	1:59.31	1:59.79	2:00.27	2:00.75	2:01.23	2:01.71	2:02.19	2:02.67	2:03.15	2:03.62
260	2:04.10	2:04.58	2:05.06	2:05.54	2:06.02	2:06.50	2:06.98	2:07.46	2:07.94	2:08.42
270	2:08.90	2:09.37	2:09.85	2:10.33	2:10.81	2:11.29	2:11.77	2:12.25	2:12.73	2:13.21
280	2:13.69	2:14.17	2:14.65	2:15.12	2:15.60	2:16.08	2:16.56	2:17.04	2:17.52	2:18.00
290	2:18.48	2:18.96	2:19.44	2:19.92	2:20.40	2:20.87	2:21.35	2:21.83	2:22.31	2:22.79
300	2:23.27	2:23.75	2:24.23	2:24.71	2:25.19	2:25.67	2:26.15	2:26.62	2:27.10	2:27.58
310	2:28.06	2:28.54	2:29.02	2:29.50	2:29.98	2:30.46	2:30.94	2:31.42	2:31.90	2:32.37
320	2:32.85	2:33.33	2:33.81	2:34.29	2:34.77	2:35.25	2:35.73	2:36.21	2:36.69	2:37.17
330	2:37.65	2:38.12	2:38.60	2:39.08	2:39.56	2:40.04	2:40.52	2:41.00	2:41.48	2:41.96
340	2:42.44	2:42.92	2:43.40	2:43.87	2:44.35	2:44.83	2:45.31	2:45.79	2:46.27	2:46.75
350	2:47.23	2:47.71	2:48.19	2:48.67	2:49.15	2:49.62	2:50.10	2:50.58	2:51.06	2:51.54
360	2:52.02	2:52.50	2:52.98	2:53.46	2:53.94	2:54.42	2:54.90	2:55.37	2:55.85	2:56.33
370	2:56.81	2:57.29	2:57.77	2:58.25	2:58.73	2:59.21	2:59.69	3:00.17	3:00.65	3:01.12
380	3:01.60	3:02.08	3:02.56	3:03.04	3:03.52	3:04.00	3:04.48	3:04.96	3:05.44	3:05.92
390	3:06.40	3:06.87	3:07.35	3:07.83	3:08.31	3:08.79	3:09.27	3:09.75	3:10.23	3:10.71
400	3:11.19	3:11.67	3:12.15	3:12.62	3:13.10	3:13.58	3:14.06	3:14.54	3:15.02	3:15.50
410	3:15.98	3:16.46	3:16.94	3:17.42	3:17.90	3:18.37	3:18.85	3:19.33	3:19.81	3:20.29
420	3:20.77	3:21.25	3:21.73	3:22.21	3:22.69	3:23.17	3:23.65	3:24.12	3:24.60	3:25.08
430	3:25.56	3:26.04	3:26.52	3:27.00	3:27.48	3:27.96	3:28.44	3:28.92	3:29.40	3:29.87
440	3:30.35	3:30.83	3:31.31	3:31.79	3:32.27	3:32.75	3:33.23	3:33.71	3:34.19	3:34.67
450	3:35.15	3:35.62	3:36.10	3:36.58	3:37.06	3:37.54	3:38.02	3:38.50	3:38.98	3:39.46
460	3:39.94	3:40.42	3:40.90	3:41.37	3:41.85	3:42.33	3:42.81	3:43.29	3:43.77	3:44.25
470	3:44.73	3:45.21	3:45.69	3:46.17	3:46.65	3:47.12	3:47.60	3:48.08	3:48.56	3:49.04
480	3:49.52	3:50.00	3:50.48	3:50.96	3:51.44	3:51.92	3:52.40	3:52.87	3:53.35	3:53.83
490	3:54.31	3:54.79	3:55.27	3:55.75	3:56.23	3:56.71	3:57.19	3:57.67	3:58.15	3:58.62
500	3:59.10	3:59.58	4:00.06	4:00.54	4:01.02	4:01.50	4:01.98	4:02.46	4:02.94	4:03.42
510	4:03.90	4:04.37	4:04.85	4:05.33	4:05.81	4:06.29	4:06.77	4:07.25	4:07.73	4:08.21
520	4:08.69	4:09.17	4:09.65	4:10.12	4:10.60	4:11.08	4:11.56	4:12.04	4:12.52	4:13.00
530	4:13.48	4:13.96	4:14.44	4:14.92	4:15.40	4:15.87	4:16.35	4:16.83	4:17.31	4:17.79
540	4:18.27	4:18.75	4:19.23	4:19.71	4:20.19	4:20.67	4:21.15	4:21.62	4:22.10	4:22.58
550	4:23.06	4:23.54	4:24.02	4:24.50	4:24.98	4:25.46	4:25.94	4:26.42	4:26.90	4:27.37
560	4:27.85	4:28.33	4:28.81	4:29.29	4:29.77	4:30.25	4:30.73	4:31.21	4:31.69	4:32.17
570	4:32.65	4:33.12	4:33.60	4:34.08	4:34.56	4:35.04	4:35.52	4:36.00	4:36.48	4:36.96
580	4:37.44	4:37.92	4:38.40	4:38.87	4:39.35	4:39.83	4:40.31	4:40.79	4:41.27	4:41.75
590	4:42.23	4:42.71	4:43.19	4:43.67	4:44.15	4:44.62	4:45.10	4:45.58	4:46.06	4:46.54

♩. = 0.72; ♩ = 0.48; ♪. = 0.36; (triplet ♩ 𝄾) = 0.32; ♪ = 0.24; (triplet ♪ 𝄾 𝄾) = 0.16; 𝅘𝅥𝅯 = 0.12 seconds

CLICK: 11⅝ FRAMES; M.M.: 123.87

Click	0	1	2	3	4	5	6	7	8	9
000	0:00.00	0:00.00	0:00.48	0:00.97	0:01.45	0:01.94	0:02.42	0:02.91	0:03.39	0:03.88
010	0:04.36	0:04.84	0:05.33	0:05.81	0:06.30	0:06.78	0:07.27	0:07.75	0:08.23	0:08.72
020	0:09.20	0:09.69	0:10.17	0:10.66	0:11.14	0:11.63	0:12.11	0:12.59	0:13.08	0:13.56
030	0:14.05	0:14.53	0:15.02	0:15.50	0:15.98	0:16.47	0:16.95	0:17.44	0:17.92	0:18.41
040	0:18.89	0:19.38	0:19.86	0:20.34	0:20.83	0:21.31	0:21.80	0:22.28	0:22.77	0:23.25
050	0:23.73	0:24.22	0:24.70	0:25.19	0:25.67	0:26.16	0:26.64	0:27.13	0:27.61	0:28.09
060	0:28.58	0:29.06	0:29.55	0:30.03	0:30.52	0:31.00	0:31.48	0:31.97	0:32.45	0:32.94
070	0:33.42	0:33.91	0:34.39	0:34.88	0:35.36	0:35.84	0:36.33	0:36.81	0:37.30	0:37.78
080	0:38.27	0:38.75	0:39.23	0:39.72	0:40.20	0:40.69	0:41.17	0:41.66	0:42.14	0:42.63
090	0:43.11	0:43.59	0:44.08	0:44.56	0:45.05	0:45.53	0:46.02	0:46.50	0:46.98	0:47.47
100	0:47.95	0:48.44	0:48.92	0:49.41	0:49.89	0:50.38	0:50.86	0:51.34	0:51.83	0:52.31
110	0:52.80	0:53.28	0:53.77	0:54.25	0:54.73	0:55.22	0:55.70	0:56.19	0:56.67	0:57.16
120	0:57.64	0:58.13	0:58.61	0:59.09	0:59.58	1:00.06	1:00.55	1:01.03	1:01.52	1:02.00
130	1:02.48	1:02.97	1:03.45	1:03.94	1:04.42	1:04.91	1:05.39	1:05.88	1:06.36	1:06.84
140	1:07.33	1:07.81	1:08.30	1:08.78	1:09.27	1:09.75	1:10.23	1:10.72	1:11.20	1:11.69
150	1:12.17	1:12.66	1:13.14	1:13.63	1:14.11	1:14.59	1:15.08	1:15.56	1:16.05	1:16.53
160	1:17.02	1:17.50	1:17.98	1:18.47	1:18.95	1:19.44	1:19.92	1:20.41	1:20.89	1:21.38
170	1:21.86	1:22.34	1:22.83	1:23.31	1:23.80	1:24.28	1:24.77	1:25.25	1:25.73	1:26.22
180	1:26.70	1:27.19	1:27.67	1:28.16	1:28.64	1:29.13	1:29.61	1:30.09	1:30.58	1:31.06
190	1:31.55	1:32.03	1:32.52	1:33.00	1:33.48	1:33.97	1:34.45	1:34.94	1:35.42	1:35.91
200	1:36.39	1:36.88	1:37.36	1:37.84	1:38.33	1:38.81	1:39.30	1:39.78	1:40.27	1:40.75
210	1:41.23	1:41.72	1:42.20	1:42.69	1:43.17	1:43.66	1:44.14	1:44.63	1:45.11	1:45.59
220	1:46.08	1:46.56	1:47.05	1:47.53	1:48.02	1:48.50	1:48.98	1:49.47	1:49.95	1:50.44
230	1:50.92	1:51.41	1:51.89	1:52.38	1:52.86	1:53.34	1:53.83	1:54.31	1:54.80	1:55.28
240	1:55.77	1:56.25	1:56.73	1:57.22	1:57.70	1:58.19	1:58.67	1:59.16	1:59.64	2:00.13
250	2:00.61	2:01.09	2:01.58	2:02.06	2:02.55	2:03.03	2:03.52	2:04.00	2:04.48	2:04.97
260	2:05.45	2:05.94	2:06.42	2:06.91	2:07.39	2:07.88	2:08.36	2:08.84	2:09.33	2:09.81
270	2:10.30	2:10.78	2:11.27	2:11.75	2:12.23	2:12.72	2:13.20	2:13.69	2:14.17	2:14.66
280	2:15.14	2:15.63	2:16.11	2:16.59	2:17.08	2:17.56	2:18.05	2:18.53	2:19.02	2:19.50
290	2:19.98	2:20.47	2:20.95	2:21.44	2:21.92	2:22.41	2:22.89	2:23.38	2:23.86	2:24.34
300	2:24.83	2:25.31	2:25.80	2:26.28	2:26.77	2:27.25	2:27.73	2:28.22	2:28.70	2:29.19
310	2:29.67	2:30.16	2:30.64	2:31.13	2:31.61	2:32.09	2:32.58	2:33.06	2:33.55	2:34.03
320	2:34.52	2:35.00	2:35.48	2:35.97	2:36.45	2:36.94	2:37.42	2:37.91	2:38.39	2:38.88
330	2:39.36	2:39.84	2:40.33	2:40.81	2:41.30	2:41.78	2:42.27	2:42.75	2:43.23	2:43.72
340	2:44.20	2:44.69	2:45.17	2:45.66	2:46.14	2:46.63	2:47.11	2:47.59	2:48.08	2:48.56
350	2:49.05	2:49.53	2:50.02	2:50.50	2:50.98	2:51.47	2:51.95	2:52.44	2:52.92	2:53.41
360	2:53.89	2:54.38	2:54.86	2:55.34	2:55.83	2:56.31	2:56.80	2:57.28	2:57.77	2:58.25
370	2:58.73	2:59.22	2:59.70	3:00.19	3:00.67	3:01.16	3:01.64	3:02.13	3:02.61	3:03.09
380	3:03.58	3:04.06	3:04.55	3:05.03	3:05.52	3:06.00	3:06.48	3:06.97	3:07.45	3:07.94
390	3:08.42	3:08.91	3:09.39	3:09.88	3:10.36	3:10.84	3:11.33	3:11.81	3:12.30	3:12.78
400	3:13.27	3:13.75	3:14.23	3:14.72	3:15.20	3:15.69	3:16.17	3:16.66	3:17.14	3:17.63
410	3:18.11	3:18.59	3:19.08	3:19.56	3:20.05	3:20.53	3:21.02	3:21.50	3:21.98	3:22.47
420	3:22.95	3:23.44	3:23.92	3:24.41	3:24.89	3:25.38	3:25.86	3:26.34	3:26.83	3:27.31
430	3:27.80	3:28.28	3:28.77	3:29.25	3:29.73	3:30.22	3:30.70	3:31.19	3:31.67	3:32.16
440	3:32.64	3:33.13	3:33.61	3:34.09	3:34.58	3:35.06	3:35.55	3:36.03	3:36.52	3:37.00
450	3:37.48	3:37.97	3:38.45	3:38.94	3:39.42	3:39.91	3:40.39	3:40.88	3:41.36	3:41.84
460	3:42.33	3:42.81	3:43.30	3:43.78	3:44.27	3:44.75	3:45.23	3:45.72	3:46.20	3:46.69
470	3:47.17	3:47.66	3:48.14	3:48.63	3:49.11	3:49.59	3:50.08	3:50.56	3:51.05	3:51.53
480	3:52.02	3:52.50	3:52.98	3:53.47	3:53.95	3:54.44	3:54.92	3:55.41	3:55.89	3:56.38
490	3:56.86	3:57.34	3:57.83	3:58.31	3:58.80	3:59.28	3:59.77	4:00.25	4:00.73	4:01.22
500	4:01.70	4:02.19	4:02.67	4:03.16	4:03.64	4:04.13	4:04.61	4:05.09	4:05.58	4:06.06
510	4:06.55	4:07.03	4:07.52	4:08.00	4:08.48	4:08.97	4:09.45	4:09.94	4:10.42	4:10.91
520	4:11.39	4:11.88	4:12.36	4:12.84	4:13.33	4:13.81	4:14.30	4:14.78	4:15.27	4:15.75
530	4:16.23	4:16.72	4:17.20	4:17.69	4:18.17	4:18.66	4:19.14	4:19.63	4:20.11	4:20.59
540	4:21.08	4:21.56	4:22.05	4:22.53	4:23.02	4:23.50	4:23.98	4:24.47	4:24.95	4:25.44
550	4:25.92	4:26.41	4:26.89	4:27.38	4:27.86	4:28.34	4:28.83	4:29.31	4:29.80	4:30.28
560	4:30.77	4:31.25	4:31.73	4:32.22	4:32.70	4:33.19	4:33.67	4:34.16	4:34.64	4:35.13
570	4:35.61	4:36.09	4:36.58	4:37.06	4:37.55	4:38.03	4:38.52	4:39.00	4:39.48	4:39.97
580	4:40.45	4:40.94	4:41.42	4:41.91	4:42.39	4:42.88	4:43.36	4:43.84	4:44.33	4:44.81
590	4:45.30	4:45.78	4:46.27	4:46.75	4:47.23	4:47.72	4:48.20	4:48.69	4:49.17	4:49.66

♩. = 0.73; ♩ = 0.48; ♪. = 0.36; (triplet ♩ 𝄾) = 0.32; ♪ = 0.24; (triplet ♪ 𝄾 𝄾) = 0.16; 𝅘𝅥𝅯 = 0.12 seconds

CLICK: 11 6/8 FRAMES; M.M.: 122.55

Click	0	1	2	3	4	5	6	7	8	9
000	0:00.00	0:00.00	0:00.49	0:00.98	0:01.47	0:01.96	0:02.45	0:02.94	0:03.43	0:03.92
010	0:04.41	0:04.90	0:05.39	0:05.88	0:06.36	0:06.85	0:07.34	0:07.83	0:08.32	0:08.81
020	0:09.30	0:09.79	0:10.28	0:10.77	0:11.26	0:11.75	0:12.24	0:12.73	0:13.22	0:13.71
030	0:14.20	0:14.69	0:15.18	0:15.67	0:16.16	0:16.65	0:17.14	0:17.63	0:18.11	0:18.60
040	0:19.09	0:19.58	0:20.07	0:20.56	0:21.05	0:21.54	0:22.03	0:22.52	0:23.01	0:23.50
050	0:23.99	0:24.48	0:24.97	0:25.46	0:25.95	0:26.44	0:26.93	0:27.42	0:27.91	0:28.40
060	0:28.89	0:29.38	0:29.86	0:30.35	0:30.84	0:31.33	0:31.82	0:32.31	0:32.80	0:33.29
070	0:33.78	0:34.27	0:34.76	0:35.25	0:35.74	0:36.23	0:36.72	0:37.21	0:37.70	0:38.19
080	0:38.68	0:39.17	0:39.66	0:40.15	0:40.64	0:41.13	0:41.61	0:42.10	0:42.59	0:43.08
090	0:43.57	0:44.06	0:44.55	0:45.04	0:45.53	0:46.02	0:46.51	0:47.00	0:47.49	0:47.98
100	0:48.47	0:48.96	0:49.45	0:49.94	0:50.43	0:50.92	0:51.41	0:51.90	0:52.39	0:52.88
110	0:53.36	0:53.85	0:54.34	0:54.83	0:55.32	0:55.81	0:56.30	0:56.79	0:57.28	0:57.77
120	0:58.26	0:58.75	0:59.24	0:59.73	1:00.22	1:00.71	1:01.20	1:01.69	1:02.18	1:02.67
130	1:03.16	1:03.65	1:04.14	1:04.63	1:05.11	1:05.60	1:06.09	1:06.58	1:07.07	1:07.56
140	1:08.05	1:08.54	1:09.03	1:09.52	1:10.01	1:10.50	1:10.99	1:11.48	1:11.97	1:12.46
150	1:12.95	1:13.44	1:13.93	1:14.42	1:14.91	1:15.40	1:15.89	1:16.38	1:16.86	1:17.35
160	1:17.84	1:18.33	1:18.82	1:19.31	1:19.80	1:20.29	1:20.78	1:21.27	1:21.76	1:22.25
170	1:22.74	1:23.23	1:23.72	1:24.21	1:24.70	1:25.19	1:25.68	1:26.17	1:26.66	1:27.15
180	1:27.64	1:28.13	1:28.61	1:29.10	1:29.59	1:30.08	1:30.57	1:31.06	1:31.55	1:32.04
190	1:32.53	1:33.02	1:33.51	1:34.00	1:34.49	1:34.98	1:35.47	1:35.96	1:36.45	1:36.94
200	1:37.43	1:37.92	1:38.41	1:38.90	1:39.39	1:39.88	1:40.36	1:40.85	1:41.34	1:41.83
210	1:42.32	1:42.81	1:43.30	1:43.79	1:44.28	1:44.77	1:45.26	1:45.75	1:46.24	1:46.73
220	1:47.22	1:47.71	1:48.20	1:48.69	1:49.18	1:49.67	1:50.16	1:50.65	1:51.14	1:51.63
230	1:52.11	1:52.60	1:53.09	1:53.58	1:54.07	1:54.56	1:55.05	1:55.54	1:56.03	1:56.52
240	1:57.01	1:57.50	1:57.99	1:58.48	1:58.97	1:59.46	1:59.95	2:00.44	2:00.93	2:01.42
250	2:01.91	2:02.40	2:02.89	2:03.38	2:03.86	2:04.35	2:04.84	2:05.33	2:05.82	2:06.31
260	2:06.80	2:07.29	2:07.78	2:08.27	2:08.76	2:09.25	2:09.74	2:10.23	2:10.72	2:11.21
270	2:11.70	2:12.19	2:12.68	2:13.17	2:13.66	2:14.15	2:14.64	2:15.13	2:15.61	2:16.10
280	2:16.59	2:17.08	2:17.57	2:18.06	2:18.55	2:19.04	2:19.53	2:20.02	2:20.51	2:21.00
290	2:21.49	2:21.98	2:22.47	2:22.96	2:23.45	2:23.94	2:24.43	2:24.92	2:25.41	2:25.90
300	2:26.39	2:26.88	2:27.36	2:27.85	2:28.34	2:28.83	2:29.32	2:29.81	2:30.30	2:30.79
310	2:31.28	2:31.77	2:32.26	2:32.75	2:33.24	2:33.73	2:34.22	2:34.71	2:35.20	2:35.69
320	2:36.18	2:36.67	2:37.16	2:37.65	2:38.14	2:38.63	2:39.11	2:39.60	2:40.09	2:40.58
330	2:41.07	2:41.56	2:42.05	2:42.54	2:43.03	2:43.52	2:44.01	2:44.50	2:44.99	2:45.48
340	2:45.97	2:46.46	2:46.95	2:47.44	2:47.93	2:48.42	2:48.91	2:49.40	2:49.89	2:50.38
350	2:50.86	2:51.35	2:51.84	2:52.33	2:52.82	2:53.31	2:53.80	2:54.29	2:54.78	2:55.27
360	2:55.76	2:56.25	2:56.74	2:57.23	2:57.72	2:58.21	2:58.70	2:59.19	2:59.68	3:00.17
370	3:00.66	3:01.15	3:01.64	3:02.13	3:02.61	3:03.10	3:03.59	3:04.08	3:04.57	3:05.06
380	3:05.55	3:06.04	3:06.53	3:07.02	3:07.51	3:08.00	3:08.49	3:08.98	3:09.47	3:09.96
390	3:10.45	3:10.94	3:11.43	3:11.92	3:12.41	3:12.90	3:13.39	3:13.88	3:14.36	3:14.85
400	3:15.34	3:15.83	3:16.32	3:16.81	3:17.30	3:17.79	3:18.28	3:18.77	3:19.26	3:19.75
410	3:20.24	3:20.73	3:21.22	3:21.71	3:22.20	3:22.69	3:23.18	3:23.67	3:24.16	3:24.65
420	3:25.14	3:25.63	3:26.11	3:26.60	3:27.09	3:27.58	3:28.07	3:28.56	3:29.05	3:29.54
430	3:30.03	3:30.52	3:31.01	3:31.50	3:31.99	3:32.48	3:32.97	3:33.46	3:33.95	3:34.44
440	3:34.93	3:35.42	3:35.91	3:36.40	3:36.89	3:37.38	3:37.86	3:38.35	3:38.84	3:39.33
450	3:39.82	3:40.31	3:40.80	3:41.29	3:41.78	3:42.27	3:42.76	3:43.25	3:43.74	3:44.23
460	3:44.72	3:45.21	3:45.70	3:46.19	3:46.68	3:47.17	3:47.66	3:48.15	3:48.64	3:49.13
470	3:49.61	3:50.10	3:50.59	3:51.08	3:51.57	3:52.06	3:52.55	3:53.04	3:53.53	3:54.02
480	3:54.51	3:55.00	3:55.49	3:55.98	3:56.47	3:56.96	3:57.45	3:57.94	3:58.43	3:58.92
490	3:59.41	3:59.90	4:00.39	4:00.88	4:01.36	4:01.85	4:02.34	4:02.83	4:03.32	4:03.81
500	4:04.30	4:04.79	4:05.28	4:05.77	4:06.26	4:06.75	4:07.24	4:07.73	4:08.22	4:08.71
510	4:09.20	4:09.69	4:10.18	4:10.67	4:11.16	4:11.65	4:12.14	4:12.63	4:13.11	4:13.60
520	4:14.09	4:14.58	4:15.07	4:15.56	4:16.05	4:16.54	4:17.03	4:17.52	4:18.01	4:18.50
530	4:18.99	4:19.48	4:19.97	4:20.46	4:20.95	4:21.44	4:21.93	4:22.42	4:22.91	4:23.40
540	4:23.89	4:24.38	4:24.86	4:25.35	4:25.84	4:26.33	4:26.82	4:27.31	4:27.80	4:28.29
550	4:28.78	4:29.27	4:29.76	4:30.25	4:30.74	4:31.23	4:31.72	4:32.21	4:32.70	4:33.19
560	4:33.68	4:34.17	4:34.66	4:35.15	4:35.64	4:36.13	4:36.61	4:37.10	4:37.59	4:38.08
570	4:38.57	4:39.06	4:39.55	4:40.04	4:40.53	4:41.02	4:41.51	4:42.00	4:42.49	4:42.98
580	4:43.47	4:43.96	4:44.45	4:44.94	4:45.43	4:45.92	4:46.41	4:46.90	4:47.39	4:47.88
590	4:48.36	4:48.85	4:49.34	4:49.83	4:50.32	4:50.81	4:51.30	4:51.79	4:52.28	4:52.77

♩. = 0.73; ♩ = 0.49; ♪. = 0.37; (triplet ♩ 𝄾) = 0.33; ♪ = 0.24; (triplet ♪ 𝄾 𝄾) = 0.16; 𝅘𝅥𝅯 = 0.12 seconds

CLICK: 11⅞ FRAMES; M.M.: 121.26

Click	0	1	2	3	4	5	6	7	8	9
000	0:00.00	0:00.00	0:00.49	0:00.99	0:01.48	0:01.98	0:02.47	0:02.97	0:03.46	0:03.96
010	0:04.45	0:04.95	0:05.44	0:05.94	0:06.43	0:06.93	0:07.42	0:07.92	0:08.41	0:08.91
020	0:09.40	0:09.90	0:10.39	0:10.89	0:11.38	0:11.88	0:12.37	0:12.86	0:13.36	0:13.85
030	0:14.35	0:14.84	0:15.34	0:15.83	0:16.33	0:16.82	0:17.32	0:17.81	0:18.31	0:18.80
040	0:19.30	0:19.79	0:20.29	0:20.78	0:21.28	0:21.77	0:22.27	0:22.76	0:23.26	0:23.75
050	0:24.24	0:24.74	0:25.23	0:25.73	0:26.22	0:26.72	0:27.21	0:27.71	0:28.20	0:28.70
060	0:29.19	0:29.69	0:30.18	0:30.68	0:31.17	0:31.67	0:32.16	0:32.66	0:33.15	0:33.65
070	0:34.14	0:34.64	0:35.13	0:35.63	0:36.12	0:36.61	0:37.11	0:37.60	0:38.10	0:38.59
080	0:39.09	0:39.58	0:40.08	0:40.57	0:41.07	0:41.56	0:42.06	0:42.55	0:43.05	0:43.54
090	0:44.04	0:44.53	0:45.03	0:45.52	0:46.02	0:46.51	0:47.01	0:47.50	0:47.99	0:48.49
100	0:48.98	0:49.48	0:49.97	0:50.47	0:50.96	0:51.46	0:51.95	0:52.45	0:52.94	0:53.44
110	0:53.93	0:54.43	0:54.92	0:55.42	0:55.91	0:56.41	0:56.90	0:57.40	0:57.89	0:58.39
120	0:58.88	0:59.38	0:59.87	1:00.36	1:00.86	1:01.35	1:01.85	1:02.34	1:02.84	1:03.33
130	1:03.83	1:04.32	1:04.82	1:05.31	1:05.81	1:06.30	1:06.80	1:07.29	1:07.79	1:08.28
140	1:08.78	1:09.27	1:09.77	1:10.26	1:10.76	1:11.25	1:11.74	1:12.24	1:12.73	1:13.23
150	1:13.72	1:14.22	1:14.71	1:15.21	1:15.70	1:16.20	1:16.69	1:17.19	1:17.68	1:18.18
160	1:18.67	1:19.17	1:19.66	1:20.16	1:20.65	1:21.15	1:21.64	1:22.14	1:22.63	1:23.13
170	1:23.62	1:24.11	1:24.61	1:25.10	1:25.60	1:26.09	1:26.59	1:27.08	1:27.58	1:28.07
180	1:28.57	1:29.06	1:29.56	1:30.05	1:30.55	1:31.04	1:31.54	1:32.03	1:32.53	1:33.02
190	1:33.52	1:34.01	1:34.51	1:35.00	1:35.49	1:35.99	1:36.48	1:36.98	1:37.47	1:37.97
200	1:38.46	1:38.96	1:39.45	1:39.95	1:40.44	1:40.94	1:41.43	1:41.93	1:42.42	1:42.92
210	1:43.41	1:43.91	1:44.40	1:44.90	1:45.39	1:45.89	1:46.38	1:46.88	1:47.37	1:47.86
220	1:48.36	1:48.85	1:49.35	1:49.84	1:50.34	1:50.83	1:51.33	1:51.82	1:52.32	1:52.81
230	1:53.31	1:53.80	1:54.30	1:54.79	1:55.29	1:55.78	1:56.28	1:56.77	1:57.27	1:57.76
240	1:58.26	1:58.75	1:59.24	1:59.74	2:00.23	2:00.73	2:01.22	2:01.72	2:02.21	2:02.71
250	2:03.20	2:03.70	2:04.19	2:04.69	2:05.18	2:05.68	2:06.17	2:06.67	2:07.16	2:07.66
260	2:08.15	2:08.65	2:09.14	2:09.64	2:10.13	2:10.63	2:11.12	2:11.61	2:12.11	2:12.60
270	2:13.10	2:13.59	2:14.09	2:14.58	2:15.08	2:15.57	2:16.07	2:16.56	2:17.06	2:17.55
280	2:18.05	2:18.54	2:19.04	2:19.53	2:20.03	2:20.52	2:21.02	2:21.51	2:22.01	2:22.50
290	2:22.99	2:23.49	2:23.98	2:24.48	2:24.97	2:25.47	2:25.96	2:26.46	2:26.95	2:27.45
300	2:27.94	2:28.44	2:28.93	2:29.43	2:29.92	2:30.42	2:30.91	2:31.41	2:31.90	2:32.40
310	2:32.89	2:33.39	2:33.88	2:34.38	2:34.87	2:35.36	2:35.86	2:36.35	2:36.85	2:37.34
320	2:37.84	2:38.33	2:38.83	2:39.32	2:39.82	2:40.31	2:40.81	2:41.30	2:41.80	2:42.29
330	2:42.79	2:43.28	2:43.78	2:44.27	2:44.77	2:45.26	2:45.76	2:46.25	2:46.74	2:47.24
340	2:47.73	2:48.23	2:48.72	2:49.22	2:49.71	2:50.21	2:50.70	2:51.20	2:51.69	2:52.19
350	2:52.68	2:53.18	2:53.67	2:54.17	2:54.66	2:55.16	2:55.65	2:56.15	2:56.64	2:57.14
360	2:57.63	2:58.13	2:58.62	2:59.11	2:59.61	3:00.10	3:00.60	3:01.09	3:01.59	3:02.08
370	3:02.58	3:03.07	3:03.57	3:04.06	3:04.56	3:05.05	3:05.55	3:06.04	3:06.54	3:07.03
380	3:07.53	3:08.02	3:08.52	3:09.01	3:09.51	3:10.00	3:10.49	3:10.99	3:11.48	3:11.98
390	3:12.47	3:12.97	3:13.46	3:13.96	3:14.45	3:14.95	3:15.44	3:15.94	3:16.43	3:16.93
400	3:17.42	3:17.92	3:18.41	3:18.91	3:19.40	3:19.90	3:20.39	3:20.89	3:21.38	3:21.88
410	3:22.37	3:22.86	3:23.36	3:23.85	3:24.35	3:24.84	3:25.34	3:25.83	3:26.33	3:26.82
420	3:27.32	3:27.81	3:28.31	3:28.80	3:29.30	3:29.79	3:30.29	3:30.78	3:31.28	3:31.77
430	3:32.27	3:32.76	3:33.26	3:33.75	3:34.24	3:34.74	3:35.23	3:35.73	3:36.22	3:36.72
440	3:37.21	3:37.71	3:38.20	3:38.70	3:39.19	3:39.69	3:40.18	3:40.68	3:41.17	3:41.67
450	3:42.16	3:42.66	3:43.15	3:43.65	3:44.14	3:44.64	3:45.13	3:45.63	3:46.12	3:46.61
460	3:47.11	3:47.60	3:48.10	3:48.59	3:49.09	3:49.58	3:50.08	3:50.57	3:51.07	3:51.56
470	3:52.06	3:52.55	3:53.05	3:53.54	3:54.04	3:54.53	3:55.03	3:55.52	3:56.02	3:56.51
480	3:57.01	3:57.50	3:57.99	3:58.49	3:58.98	3:59.48	3:59.97	4:00.47	4:00.96	4:01.46
490	4:01.95	4:02.45	4:02.94	4:03.44	4:03.93	4:04.43	4:04.92	4:05.42	4:05.91	4:06.41
500	4:06.90	4:07.40	4:07.89	4:08.39	4:08.88	4:09.38	4:09.87	4:10.36	4:10.86	4:11.35
510	4:11.85	4:12.34	4:12.84	4:13.33	4:13.83	4:14.32	4:14.82	4:15.31	4:15.81	4:16.30
520	4:16.80	4:17.29	4:17.79	4:18.28	4:18.78	4:19.27	4:19.77	4:20.26	4:20.76	4:21.25
530	4:21.74	4:22.24	4:22.73	4:23.23	4:23.72	4:24.22	4:24.71	4:25.21	4:25.70	4:26.20
540	4:26.69	4:27.19	4:27.68	4:28.18	4:28.67	4:29.17	4:29.66	4:30.16	4:30.65	4:31.15
550	4:31.64	4:32.14	4:32.63	4:33.13	4:33.62	4:34.11	4:34.61	4:35.10	4:35.60	4:36.09
560	4:36.59	4:37.08	4:37.58	4:38.07	4:38.57	4:39.06	4:39.56	4:40.05	4:40.55	4:41.04
570	4:41.54	4:42.03	4:42.53	4:43.02	4:43.52	4:44.01	4:44.51	4:45.00	4:45.49	4:45.99
580	4:46.48	4:46.98	4:47.47	4:47.97	4:48.46	4:48.96	4:49.45	4:49.95	4:50.44	4:50.94
590	4:51.43	4:51.93	4:52.42	4:52.92	4:53.41	4:53.91	4:54.40	4:54.90	4:55.39	4:55.89

𝅗𝅥. = 0.74; ♩ = 0.49; ♪. = 0.37; (triplet ♩ 𝄾) = 0.33; ♪ = 0.25; (triplet ♪ 𝄾 𝄾) = 0.16; 𝅘𝅥𝅯 = 0.12 seconds

CLICK: 12 0/8 FRAMES; M.M.: 120.00

Click	0	1	2	3	4	5	6	7	8	9
000	0:00.00	0:00.00	0:00.50	0:01.00	0:01.50	0:02.00	0:02.50	0:03.00	0:03.50	0:04.00
010	0:04.50	0:05.00	0:05.50	0:06.00	0:06.50	0:07.00	0:07.50	0:08.00	0:08.50	0:09.00
020	0:09.50	0:10.00	0:10.50	0:11.00	0:11.50	0:12.00	0:12.50	0:13.00	0:13.50	0:14.00
030	0:14.50	0:15.00	0:15.50	0:16.00	0:16.50	0:17.00	0:17.50	0:18.00	0:18.50	0:19.00
040	0:19.50	0:20.00	0:20.50	0:21.00	0:21.50	0:22.00	0:22.50	0:23.00	0:23.50	0:24.00
050	0:24.50	0:25.00	0:25.50	0:26.00	0:26.50	0:27.00	0:27.50	0:28.00	0:28.50	0:29.00
060	0:29.50	0:30.00	0:30.50	0:31.00	0:31.50	0:32.00	0:32.50	0:33.00	0:33.50	0:34.00
070	0:34.50	0:35.00	0:35.50	0:36.00	0:36.50	0:37.00	0:37.50	0:38.00	0:38.50	0:39.00
080	0:39.50	0:40.00	0:40.50	0:41.00	0:41.50	0:42.00	0:42.50	0:43.00	0:43.50	0:44.00
090	0:44.50	0:45.00	0:45.50	0:46.00	0:46.50	0:47.00	0:47.50	0:48.00	0:48.50	0:49.00
100	0:49.50	0:50.00	0:50.50	0:51.00	0:51.50	0:52.00	0:52.50	0:53.00	0:53.50	0:54.00
110	0:54.50	0:55.00	0:55.50	0:56.00	0:56.50	0:57.00	0:57.50	0:58.00	0:58.50	0:59.00
120	0:59.50	1:00.00	1:00.50	1:01.00	1:01.50	1:02.00	1:02.50	1:03.00	1:03.50	1:04.00
130	1:04.50	1:05.00	1:05.50	1:06.00	1:06.50	1:07.00	1:07.50	1:08.00	1:08.50	1:09.00
140	1:09.50	1:10.00	1:10.50	1:11.00	1:11.50	1:12.00	1:12.50	1:13.00	1:13.50	1:14.00
150	1:14.50	1:15.00	1:15.50	1:16.00	1:16.50	1:17.00	1:17.50	1:18.00	1:18.50	1:19.00
160	1:19.50	1:20.00	1:20.50	1:21.00	1:21.50	1:22.00	1:22.50	1:23.00	1:23.50	1:24.00
170	1:24.50	1:25.00	1:25.50	1:26.00	1:26.50	1:27.00	1:27.50	1:28.00	1:28.50	1:29.00
180	1:29.50	1:30.00	1:30.50	1:31.00	1:31.50	1:32.00	1:32.50	1:33.00	1:33.50	1:34.00
190	1:34.50	1:35.00	1:35.50	1:36.00	1:36.50	1:37.00	1:37.50	1:38.00	1:38.50	1:39.00
200	1:39.50	1:40.00	1:40.50	1:41.00	1:41.50	1:42.00	1:42.50	1:43.00	1:43.50	1:44.00
210	1:44.50	1:45.00	1:45.50	1:46.00	1:46.50	1:47.00	1:47.50	1:48.00	1:48.50	1:49.00
220	1:49.50	1:50.00	1:50.50	1:51.00	1:51.50	1:52.00	1:52.50	1:53.00	1:53.50	1:54.00
230	1:54.50	1:55.00	1:55.50	1:56.00	1:56.50	1:57.00	1:57.50	1:58.00	1:58.50	1:59.00
240	1:59.50	2:00.00	2:00.50	2:01.00	2:01.50	2:02.00	2:02.50	2:03.00	2:03.50	2:04.00
250	2:04.50	2:05.00	2:05.50	2:06.00	2:06.50	2:07.00	2:07.50	2:08.00	2:08.50	2:09.00
260	2:09.50	2:10.00	2:10.50	2:11.00	2:11.50	2:12.00	2:12.50	2:13.00	2:13.50	2:14.00
270	2:14.50	2:15.00	2:15.50	2:16.00	2:16.50	2:17.00	2:17.50	2:18.00	2:18.50	2:19.00
280	2:19.50	2:20.00	2:20.50	2:21.00	2:21.50	2:22.00	2:22.50	2:23.00	2:23.50	2:24.00
290	2:24.50	2:25.00	2:25.50	2:26.00	2:26.50	2:27.00	2:27.50	2:28.00	2:28.50	2:29.00
300	2:29.50	2:30.00	2:30.50	2:31.00	2:31.50	2:32.00	2:32.50	2:33.00	2:33.50	2:34.00
310	2:34.50	2:35.00	2:35.50	2:36.00	2:36.50	2:37.00	2:37.50	2:38.00	2:38.50	2:39.00
320	2:39.50	2:40.00	2:40.50	2:41.00	2:41.50	2:42.00	2:42.50	2:43.00	2:43.50	2:44.00
330	2:44.50	2:45.00	2:45.50	2:46.00	2:46.50	2:47.00	2:47.50	2:48.00	2:48.50	2:49.00
340	2:49.50	2:50.00	2:50.50	2:51.00	2:51.50	2:52.00	2:52.50	2:53.00	2:53.50	2:54.00
350	2:54.50	2:55.00	2:55.50	2:56.00	2:56.50	2:57.00	2:57.50	2:58.00	2:58.50	2:59.00
360	2:59.50	3:00.00	3:00.50	3:01.00	3:01.50	3:02.00	3:02.50	3:03.00	3:03.50	3:04.00
370	3:04.50	3:05.00	3:05.50	3:06.00	3:06.50	3:07.00	3:07.50	3:08.00	3:08.50	3:09.00
380	3:09.50	3:10.00	3:10.50	3:11.00	3:11.50	3:12.00	3:12.50	3:13.00	3:13.50	3:14.00
390	3:14.50	3:15.00	3:15.50	3:16.00	3:16.50	3:17.00	3:17.50	3:18.00	3:18.50	3:19.00
400	3:19.50	3:20.00	3:20.50	3:21.00	3:21.50	3:22.00	3:22.50	3:23.00	3:23.50	3:24.00
410	3:24.50	3:25.00	3:25.50	3:26.00	3:26.50	3:27.00	3:27.50	3:28.00	3:28.50	3:29.00
420	3:29.50	3:30.00	3:30.50	3:31.00	3:31.50	3:32.00	3:32.50	3:33.00	3:33.50	3:34.00
430	3:34.50	3:35.00	3:35.50	3:36.00	3:36.50	3:37.00	3:37.50	3:38.00	3:38.50	3:39.00
440	3:39.50	3:40.00	3:40.50	3:41.00	3:41.50	3:42.00	3:42.50	3:43.00	3:43.50	3:44.00
450	3:44.50	3:45.00	3:45.50	3:46.00	3:46.50	3:47.00	3:47.50	3:48.00	3:48.50	3:49.00
460	3:49.50	3:50.00	3:50.50	3:51.00	3:51.50	3:52.00	3:52.50	3:53.00	3:53.50	3:54.00
470	3:54.50	3:55.00	3:55.50	3:56.00	3:56.50	3:57.00	3:57.50	3:58.00	3:58.50	3:59.00
480	3:59.50	4:00.00	4:00.50	4:01.00	4:01.50	4:02.00	4:02.50	4:03.00	4:03.50	4:04.00
490	4:04.50	4:05.00	4:05.50	4:06.00	4:06.50	4:07.00	4:07.50	4:08.00	4:08.50	4:09.00
500	4:09.50	4:10.00	4:10.50	4:11.00	4:11.50	4:12.00	4:12.50	4:13.00	4:13.50	4:14.00
510	4:14.50	4:15.00	4:15.50	4:16.00	4:16.50	4:17.00	4:17.50	4:18.00	4:18.50	4:19.00
520	4:19.50	4:20.00	4:20.50	4:21.00	4:21.50	4:22.00	4:22.50	4:23.00	4:23.50	4:24.00
530	4:24.50	4:25.00	4:25.50	4:26.00	4:26.50	4:27.00	4:27.50	4:28.00	4:28.50	4:29.00
540	4:29.50	4:30.00	4:30.50	4:31.00	4:31.50	4:32.00	4:32.50	4:33.00	4:33.50	4:34.00
550	4:34.50	4:35.00	4:35.50	4:36.00	4:36.50	4:37.00	4:37.50	4:38.00	4:38.50	4:39.00
560	4:39.50	4:40.00	4:40.50	4:41.00	4:41.50	4:42.00	4:42.50	4:43.00	4:43.50	4:44.00
570	4:44.50	4:45.00	4:45.50	4:46.00	4:46.50	4:47.00	4:47.50	4:48.00	4:48.50	4:49.00
580	4:49.50	4:50.00	4:50.50	4:51.00	4:51.50	4:52.00	4:52.50	4:53.00	4:53.50	4:54.00
590	4:54.50	4:55.00	4:55.50	4:56.00	4:56.50	4:57.00	4:57.50	4:58.00	4:58.50	4:59.00

♩. = 0.75; ♩ = 0.50; ♪. = 0.38; (triplet ♩ 𝄾) = 0.33; ♪ = 0.25; (triplet ♪ 𝄾 𝄾) = 0.17; 𝅘𝅥𝅯 = 0.13 seconds

CLICK: 12⅛ FRAMES; M.M.: 118.76

Click	0	1	2	3	4	5	6	7	8	9
000	0:00.00	0:00.00	0:00.51	0:01.01	0:01.52	0:02.02	0:02.53	0:03.03	0:03.54	0:04.04
010	0:04.55	0:05.05	0:05.56	0:06.06	0:06.57	0:07.07	0:07.58	0:08.08	0:08.59	0:09.09
020	0:09.60	0:10.10	0:10.61	0:11.11	0:11.62	0:12.13	0:12.63	0:13.14	0:13.64	0:14.15
030	0:14.65	0:15.16	0:15.66	0:16.17	0:16.67	0:17.18	0:17.68	0:18.19	0:18.69	0:19.20
040	0:19.70	0:20.21	0:20.71	0:21.22	0:21.72	0:22.23	0:22.73	0:23.24	0:23.74	0:24.25
050	0:24.76	0:25.26	0:25.77	0:26.27	0:26.78	0:27.28	0:27.79	0:28.29	0:28.80	0:29.30
060	0:29.81	0:30.31	0:30.82	0:31.32	0:31.83	0:32.33	0:32.84	0:33.34	0:33.85	0:34.35
070	0:34.86	0:35.36	0:35.87	0:36.38	0:36.88	0:37.39	0:37.89	0:38.40	0:38.90	0:39.41
080	0:39.91	0:40.42	0:40.92	0:41.43	0:41.93	0:42.44	0:42.94	0:43.45	0:43.95	0:44.46
090	0:44.96	0:45.47	0:45.97	0:46.48	0:46.98	0:47.49	0:47.99	0:48.50	0:49.01	0:49.51
100	0:50.02	0:50.52	0:51.03	0:51.53	0:52.04	0:52.54	0:53.05	0:53.55	0:54.06	0:54.56
110	0:55.07	0:55.57	0:56.08	0:56.58	0:57.09	0:57.59	0:58.10	0:58.60	0:59.11	0:59.61
120	1:00.12	1:00.62	1:01.13	1:01.64	1:02.14	1:02.65	1:03.15	1:03.66	1:04.16	1:04.67
130	1:05.17	1:05.68	1:06.18	1:06.69	1:07.19	1:07.70	1:08.20	1:08.71	1:09.21	1:09.72
140	1:10.22	1:10.73	1:11.23	1:11.74	1:12.24	1:12.75	1:13.26	1:13.76	1:14.27	1:14.77
150	1:15.28	1:15.78	1:16.29	1:16.79	1:17.30	1:17.80	1:18.31	1:18.81	1:19.32	1:19.82
160	1:20.33	1:20.83	1:21.34	1:21.84	1:22.35	1:22.85	1:23.36	1:23.86	1:24.37	1:24.88
170	1:25.38	1:25.89	1:26.39	1:26.90	1:27.40	1:27.91	1:28.41	1:28.92	1:29.42	1:29.93
180	1:30.43	1:30.94	1:31.44	1:31.95	1:32.45	1:32.96	1:33.46	1:33.97	1:34.47	1:34.98
190	1:35.48	1:35.99	1:36.49	1:37.00	1:37.51	1:38.01	1:38.52	1:39.02	1:39.53	1:40.03
200	1:40.54	1:41.04	1:41.55	1:42.05	1:42.56	1:43.06	1:43.57	1:44.07	1:44.58	1:45.08
210	1:45.59	1:46.09	1:46.60	1:47.10	1:47.61	1:48.11	1:48.62	1:49.12	1:49.63	1:50.14
220	1:50.64	1:51.15	1:51.65	1:52.16	1:52.66	1:53.17	1:53.67	1:54.18	1:54.68	1:55.19
230	1:55.69	1:56.20	1:56.70	1:57.21	1:57.71	1:58.22	1:58.72	1:59.23	1:59.73	2:00.24
240	2:00.74	2:01.25	2:01.76	2:02.26	2:02.77	2:03.27	2:03.78	2:04.28	2:04.79	2:05.29
250	2:05.80	2:06.30	2:06.81	2:07.31	2:07.82	2:08.32	2:08.83	2:09.33	2:09.84	2:10.34
260	2:10.85	2:11.35	2:11.86	2:12.36	2:12.87	2:13.37	2:13.88	2:14.39	2:14.89	2:15.40
270	2:15.90	2:16.41	2:16.91	2:17.42	2:17.92	2:18.43	2:18.93	2:19.44	2:19.94	2:20.45
280	2:20.95	2:21.46	2:21.96	2:22.47	2:22.97	2:23.48	2:23.98	2:24.49	2:24.99	2:25.50
290	2:26.01	2:26.51	2:27.02	2:27.52	2:28.03	2:28.53	2:29.04	2:29.54	2:30.05	2:30.55
300	2:31.06	2:31.56	2:32.07	2:32.57	2:33.08	2:33.58	2:34.09	2:34.59	2:35.10	2:35.60
310	2:36.11	2:36.61	2:37.12	2:37.63	2:38.13	2:38.64	2:39.14	2:39.65	2:40.15	2:40.66
320	2:41.16	2:41.67	2:42.17	2:42.68	2:43.18	2:43.69	2:44.19	2:44.70	2:45.20	2:45.71
330	2:46.21	2:46.72	2:47.22	2:47.73	2:48.23	2:48.74	2:49.24	2:49.75	2:50.26	2:50.76
340	2:51.27	2:51.77	2:52.28	2:52.78	2:53.29	2:53.79	2:54.30	2:54.80	2:55.31	2:55.81
350	2:56.32	2:56.82	2:57.33	2:57.83	2:58.34	2:58.84	2:59.35	2:59.85	3:00.36	3:00.86
360	3:01.37	3:01.88	3:02.38	3:02.89	3:03.39	3:03.90	3:04.40	3:04.91	3:05.41	3:05.92
370	3:06.42	3:06.93	3:07.43	3:07.94	3:08.44	3:08.95	3:09.45	3:09.96	3:10.46	3:10.97
380	3:11.47	3:11.98	3:12.48	3:12.99	3:13.49	3:14.00	3:14.51	3:15.01	3:15.52	3:16.02
390	3:16.53	3:17.03	3:17.54	3:18.04	3:18.55	3:19.05	3:19.56	3:20.06	3:20.57	3:21.07
400	3:21.58	3:22.08	3:22.59	3:23.09	3:23.60	3:24.10	3:24.61	3:25.11	3:25.62	3:26.12
410	3:26.63	3:27.14	3:27.64	3:28.15	3:28.65	3:29.16	3:29.66	3:30.17	3:30.67	3:31.18
420	3:31.68	3:32.19	3:32.69	3:33.20	3:33.70	3:34.21	3:34.71	3:35.22	3:35.72	3:36.23
430	3:36.73	3:37.24	3:37.74	3:38.25	3:38.76	3:39.26	3:39.77	3:40.27	3:40.78	3:41.28
440	3:41.79	3:42.29	3:42.80	3:43.30	3:43.81	3:44.31	3:44.82	3:45.32	3:45.83	3:46.33
450	3:46.84	3:47.34	3:47.85	3:48.35	3:48.86	3:49.36	3:49.87	3:50.37	3:50.88	3:51.39
460	3:51.89	3:52.40	3:52.90	3:53.41	3:53.91	3:54.42	3:54.92	3:55.43	3:55.93	3:56.44
470	3:56.94	3:57.45	3:57.95	3:58.46	3:58.96	3:59.47	3:59.97	4:00.48	4:00.98	4:01.49
480	4:01.99	4:02.50	4:03.01	4:03.51	4:04.02	4:04.52	4:05.03	4:05.53	4:06.04	4:06.54
490	4:07.05	4:07.55	4:08.06	4:08.56	4:09.07	4:09.57	4:10.08	4:10.58	4:11.09	4:11.59
500	4:12.10	4:12.60	4:13.11	4:13.61	4:14.12	4:14.63	4:15.13	4:15.64	4:16.14	4:16.65
510	4:17.15	4:17.66	4:18.16	4:18.67	4:19.17	4:19.68	4:20.18	4:20.69	4:21.19	4:21.70
520	4:22.20	4:22.71	4:23.21	4:23.72	4:24.22	4:24.73	4:25.23	4:25.74	4:26.24	4:26.75
530	4:27.26	4:27.76	4:28.27	4:28.77	4:29.28	4:29.78	4:30.29	4:30.79	4:31.30	4:31.80
540	4:32.31	4:32.81	4:33.32	4:33.82	4:34.33	4:34.83	4:35.34	4:35.84	4:36.35	4:36.85
550	4:37.36	4:37.86	4:38.37	4:38.87	4:39.38	4:39.89	4:40.39	4:40.90	4:41.40	4:41.91
560	4:42.41	4:42.92	4:43.42	4:43.93	4:44.43	4:44.94	4:45.44	4:45.95	4:46.45	4:46.96
570	4:47.46	4:47.97	4:48.47	4:48.98	4:49.48	4:49.99	4:50.49	4:51.00	4:51.51	4:52.01
580	4:52.52	4:53.02	4:53.53	4:54.03	4:54.54	4:55.04	4:55.55	4:56.05	4:56.56	4:57.06
590	4:57.57	4:58.07	4:58.58	4:59.08	4:59.59	5:00.09	5:00.60	5:01.10	5:01.61	5:02.11

♩. = 0.76; ♩ = 0.51; ♪. = 0.38; (3: ♩ 𝄾) = 0.34; ♪ = 0.25; (3: ♪ 𝄾 𝄾) = 0.17; 𝅘𝅥𝅯 = 0.13 seconds

CLICK: 12 2/8 FRAMES; M.M.: 117.55

Click	0	1	2	3	4	5	6	7	8	9
000	0:00.00	0:00.00	0:00.51	0:01.02	0:01.53	0:02.04	0:02.55	0:03.06	0:03.57	0:04.08
010	0:04.59	0:05.10	0:05.61	0:06.13	0:06.64	0:07.15	0:07.66	0:08.17	0:08.68	0:09.19
020	0:09.70	0:10.21	0:10.72	0:11.23	0:11.74	0:12.25	0:12.76	0:13.27	0:13.78	0:14.29
030	0:14.80	0:15.31	0:15.82	0:16.33	0:16.84	0:17.35	0:17.86	0:18.38	0:18.89	0:19.40
040	0:19.91	0:20.42	0:20.93	0:21.44	0:21.95	0:22.46	0:22.97	0:23.48	0:23.99	0:24.50
050	0:25.01	0:25.52	0:26.03	0:26.54	0:27.05	0:27.56	0:28.07	0:28.58	0:29.09	0:29.60
060	0:30.11	0:30.63	0:31.14	0:31.65	0:32.16	0:32.67	0:33.18	0:33.69	0:34.20	0:34.71
070	0:35.22	0:35.73	0:36.24	0:36.75	0:37.26	0:37.77	0:38.28	0:38.79	0:39.30	0:39.81
080	0:40.32	0:40.83	0:41.34	0:41.85	0:42.36	0:42.88	0:43.39	0:43.90	0:44.41	0:44.92
090	0:45.43	0:45.94	0:46.45	0:46.96	0:47.47	0:47.98	0:48.49	0:49.00	0:49.51	0:50.02
100	0:50.53	0:51.04	0:51.55	0:52.06	0:52.57	0:53.08	0:53.59	0:54.10	0:54.61	0:55.13
110	0:55.64	0:56.15	0:56.66	0:57.17	0:57.68	0:58.19	0:58.70	0:59.21	0:59.72	1:00.23
120	1:00.74	1:01.25	1:01.76	1:02.27	1:02.78	1:03.29	1:03.80	1:04.31	1:04.82	1:05.33
130	1:05.84	1:06.35	1:06.86	1:07.38	1:07.89	1:08.40	1:08.91	1:09.42	1:09.93	1:10.44
140	1:10.95	1:11.46	1:11.97	1:12.48	1:12.99	1:13.50	1:14.01	1:14.52	1:15.03	1:15.54
150	1:16.05	1:16.56	1:17.07	1:17.58	1:18.09	1:18.60	1:19.11	1:19.63	1:20.14	1:20.65
160	1:21.16	1:21.67	1:22.18	1:22.69	1:23.20	1:23.71	1:24.22	1:24.73	1:25.24	1:25.75
170	1:26.26	1:26.77	1:27.28	1:27.79	1:28.30	1:28.81	1:29.32	1:29.83	1:30.34	1:30.85
180	1:31.36	1:31.88	1:32.39	1:32.90	1:33.41	1:33.92	1:34.43	1:34.94	1:35.45	1:35.96
190	1:36.47	1:36.98	1:37.49	1:38.00	1:38.51	1:39.02	1:39.53	1:40.04	1:40.55	1:41.06
200	1:41.57	1:42.08	1:42.59	1:43.10	1:43.61	1:44.13	1:44.64	1:45.15	1:45.66	1:46.17
210	1:46.68	1:47.19	1:47.70	1:48.21	1:48.72	1:49.23	1:49.74	1:50.25	1:50.76	1:51.27
220	1:51.78	1:52.29	1:52.80	1:53.31	1:53.82	1:54.33	1:54.84	1:55.35	1:55.86	1:56.38
230	1:56.89	1:57.40	1:57.91	1:58.42	1:58.93	1:59.44	1:59.95	2:00.46	2:00.97	2:01.48
240	2:01.99	2:02.50	2:03.01	2:03.52	2:04.03	2:04.54	2:05.05	2:05.56	2:06.07	2:06.58
250	2:07.09	2:07.60	2:08.11	2:08.62	2:09.14	2:09.65	2:10.16	2:10.67	2:11.18	2:11.69
260	2:12.20	2:12.71	2:13.22	2:13.73	2:14.24	2:14.75	2:15.26	2:15.77	2:16.28	2:16.79
270	2:17.30	2:17.81	2:18.32	2:18.83	2:19.34	2:19.85	2:20.36	2:20.87	2:21.39	2:21.90
280	2:22.41	2:22.92	2:23.43	2:23.94	2:24.45	2:24.96	2:25.47	2:25.98	2:26.49	2:27.00
290	2:27.51	2:28.02	2:28.53	2:29.04	2:29.55	2:30.06	2:30.57	2:31.08	2:31.59	2:32.10
300	2:32.61	2:33.12	2:33.64	2:34.15	2:34.66	2:35.17	2:35.68	2:36.19	2:36.70	2:37.21
310	2:37.72	2:38.23	2:38.74	2:39.25	2:39.76	2:40.27	2:40.78	2:41.29	2:41.80	2:42.31
320	2:42.82	2:43.33	2:43.84	2:44.35	2:44.86	2:45.37	2:45.89	2:46.40	2:46.91	2:47.42
330	2:47.93	2:48.44	2:48.95	2:49.46	2:49.97	2:50.48	2:50.99	2:51.50	2:52.01	2:52.52
340	2:53.03	2:53.54	2:54.05	2:54.56	2:55.07	2:55.58	2:56.09	2:56.60	2:57.11	2:57.62
350	2:58.14	2:58.65	2:59.16	2:59.67	3:00.18	3:00.69	3:01.20	3:01.71	3:02.22	3:02.73
360	3:03.24	3:03.75	3:04.26	3:04.77	3:05.28	3:05.79	3:06.30	3:06.81	3:07.32	3:07.83
370	3:08.34	3:08.85	3:09.36	3:09.87	3:10.39	3:10.90	3:11.41	3:11.92	3:12.43	3:12.94
380	3:13.45	3:13.96	3:14.47	3:14.98	3:15.49	3:16.00	3:16.51	3:17.02	3:17.53	3:18.04
390	3:18.55	3:19.06	3:19.57	3:20.08	3:20.59	3:21.10	3:21.61	3:22.13	3:22.64	3:23.15
400	3:23.66	3:24.17	3:24.68	3:25.19	3:25.70	3:26.21	3:26.72	3:27.23	3:27.74	3:28.25
410	3:28.76	3:29.27	3:29.78	3:30.29	3:30.80	3:31.31	3:31.82	3:32.33	3:32.84	3:33.35
420	3:33.86	3:34.38	3:34.89	3:35.40	3:35.91	3:36.42	3:36.93	3:37.44	3:37.95	3:38.46
430	3:38.97	3:39.48	3:39.99	3:40.50	3:41.01	3:41.52	3:42.03	3:42.54	3:43.05	3:43.56
440	3:44.07	3:44.58	3:45.09	3:45.60	3:46.11	3:46.63	3:47.14	3:47.65	3:48.16	3:48.67
450	3:49.18	3:49.69	3:50.20	3:50.71	3:51.22	3:51.73	3:52.24	3:52.75	3:53.26	3:53.77
460	3:54.28	3:54.79	3:55.30	3:55.81	3:56.32	3:56.83	3:57.34	3:57.85	3:58.36	3:58.88
470	3:59.39	3:59.90	4:00.41	4:00.92	4:01.43	4:01.94	4:02.45	4:02.96	4:03.47	4:03.98
480	4:04.49	4:05.00	4:05.51	4:06.02	4:06.53	4:07.04	4:07.55	4:08.06	4:08.57	4:09.08
490	4:09.59	4:10.10	4:10.61	4:11.13	4:11.64	4:12.15	4:12.66	4:13.17	4:13.68	4:14.19
500	4:14.70	4:15.21	4:15.72	4:16.23	4:16.74	4:17.25	4:17.76	4:18.27	4:18.78	4:19.29
510	4:19.80	4:20.31	4:20.82	4:21.33	4:21.84	4:22.35	4:22.86	4:23.37	4:23.89	4:24.40
520	4:24.91	4:25.42	4:25.93	4:26.44	4:26.95	4:27.46	4:27.97	4:28.48	4:28.99	4:29.50
530	4:30.01	4:30.52	4:31.03	4:31.54	4:32.05	4:32.56	4:33.07	4:33.58	4:34.09	4:34.60
540	4:35.11	4:35.63	4:36.14	4:36.65	4:37.16	4:37.67	4:38.18	4:38.69	4:39.20	4:39.71
550	4:40.22	4:40.73	4:41.24	4:41.75	4:42.26	4:42.77	4:43.28	4:43.79	4:44.30	4:44.81
560	4:45.32	4:45.83	4:46.34	4:46.85	4:47.36	4:47.87	4:48.39	4:48.90	4:49.41	4:49.92
570	4:50.43	4:50.94	4:51.45	4:51.96	4:52.47	4:52.98	4:53.49	4:54.00	4:54.51	4:55.02
580	4:55.53	4:56.04	4:56.55	4:57.06	4:57.57	4:58.08	4:58.59	4:59.10	4:59.61	5:00.12
590	5:00.64	5:01.15	5:01.66	5:02.17	5:02.68	5:03.19	5:03.70	5:04.21	5:04.72	5:05.23

♩. = 0.77; ♩ = 0.51; ♪. = 0.38; ♩ 𝄾 (3) = 0.34; ♪ = 0.26; ♪ 𝄾 𝄾 (3) = 0.17; 𝅘𝅥𝅯 = 0.13 seconds

CLICK: 12⅜ FRAMES; M.M.: 116.36

Click	0	1	2	3	4	5	6	7	8	9
000	0:00.00	0:00.00	0:00.52	0:01.03	0:01.55	0:02.06	0:02.58	0:03.09	0:03.61	0:04.13
010	0:04.64	0:05.16	0:05.67	0:06.19	0:06.70	0:07.22	0:07.73	0:08.25	0:08.77	0:09.28
020	0:09.80	0:10.31	0:10.83	0:11.34	0:11.86	0:12.38	0:12.89	0:13.41	0:13.92	0:14.44
030	0:14.95	0:15.47	0:15.98	0:16.50	0:17.02	0:17.53	0:18.05	0:18.56	0:19.08	0:19.59
040	0:20.11	0:20.63	0:21.14	0:21.66	0:22.17	0:22.69	0:23.20	0:23.72	0:24.23	0:24.75
050	0:25.27	0:25.78	0:26.30	0:26.81	0:27.33	0:27.84	0:28.36	0:28.88	0:29.39	0:29.91
060	0:30.42	0:30.94	0:31.45	0:31.97	0:32.48	0:33.00	0:33.52	0:34.03	0:34.55	0:35.06
070	0:35.58	0:36.09	0:36.61	0:37.13	0:37.64	0:38.16	0:38.67	0:39.19	0:39.70	0:40.22
080	0:40.73	0:41.25	0:41.77	0:42.28	0:42.80	0:43.31	0:43.83	0:44.34	0:44.86	0:45.38
090	0:45.89	0:46.41	0:46.92	0:47.44	0:47.95	0:48.47	0:48.98	0:49.50	0:50.02	0:50.53
100	0:51.05	0:51.56	0:52.08	0:52.59	0:53.11	0:53.63	0:54.14	0:54.66	0:55.17	0:55.69
110	0:56.20	0:56.72	0:57.23	0:57.75	0:58.27	0:58.78	0:59.30	0:59.81	1:00.33	1:00.84
120	1:01.36	1:01.88	1:02.39	1:02.91	1:03.42	1:03.94	1:04.45	1:04.97	1:05.48	1:06.00
130	1:06.52	1:07.03	1:07.55	1:08.06	1:08.58	1:09.09	1:09.61	1:10.13	1:10.64	1:11.16
140	1:11.67	1:12.19	1:12.70	1:13.22	1:13.73	1:14.25	1:14.77	1:15.28	1:15.80	1:16.31
150	1:16.83	1:17.34	1:17.86	1:18.37	1:18.89	1:19.41	1:19.92	1:20.44	1:20.95	1:21.47
160	1:21.98	1:22.50	1:23.02	1:23.53	1:24.05	1:24.56	1:25.08	1:25.59	1:26.11	1:26.63
170	1:27.14	1:27.66	1:28.17	1:28.69	1:29.20	1:29.72	1:30.23	1:30.75	1:31.27	1:31.78
180	1:32.30	1:32.81	1:33.33	1:33.84	1:34.36	1:34.88	1:35.39	1:35.91	1:36.42	1:36.94
190	1:37.45	1:37.97	1:38.48	1:39.00	1:39.52	1:40.03	1:40.55	1:41.06	1:41.58	1:42.09
200	1:42.61	1:43.13	1:43.64	1:44.16	1:44.67	1:45.19	1:45.70	1:46.22	1:46.73	1:47.25
210	1:47.77	1:48.28	1:48.80	1:49.31	1:49.83	1:50.34	1:50.86	1:51.38	1:51.89	1:52.41
220	1:52.92	1:53.44	1:53.95	1:54.47	1:54.98	1:55.50	1:56.02	1:56.53	1:57.05	1:57.56
230	1:58.08	1:58.59	1:59.11	1:59.63	2:00.14	2:00.66	2:01.17	2:01.69	2:02.20	2:02.72
240	2:03.23	2:03.75	2:04.27	2:04.78	2:05.30	2:05.81	2:06.33	2:06.84	2:07.36	2:07.88
250	2:08.39	2:08.91	2:09.42	2:09.94	2:10.45	2:10.97	2:11.48	2:12.00	2:12.52	2:13.03
260	2:13.55	2:14.06	2:14.58	2:15.09	2:15.61	2:16.12	2:16.64	2:17.16	2:17.67	2:18.19
270	2:18.70	2:19.22	2:19.73	2:20.25	2:20.77	2:21.28	2:21.80	2:22.31	2:22.83	2:23.34
280	2:23.86	2:24.38	2:24.89	2:25.41	2:25.92	2:26.44	2:26.95	2:27.47	2:27.98	2:28.50
290	2:29.02	2:29.53	2:30.05	2:30.56	2:31.08	2:31.59	2:32.11	2:32.63	2:33.14	2:33.66
300	2:34.17	2:34.69	2:35.20	2:35.72	2:36.23	2:36.75	2:37.27	2:37.78	2:38.30	2:38.81
310	2:39.33	2:39.84	2:40.36	2:40.88	2:41.39	2:41.91	2:42.42	2:42.94	2:43.45	2:43.97
320	2:44.48	2:45.00	2:45.52	2:46.03	2:46.55	2:47.06	2:47.58	2:48.09	2:48.61	2:49.13
330	2:49.64	2:50.16	2:50.67	2:51.19	2:51.70	2:52.22	2:52.73	2:53.25	2:53.77	2:54.28
340	2:54.80	2:55.31	2:55.83	2:56.34	2:56.86	2:57.37	2:57.89	2:58.41	2:58.92	2:59.44
350	2:59.95	3:00.47	3:00.98	3:01.50	3:02.02	3:02.53	3:03.05	3:03.56	3:04.08	3:04.59
360	3:05.11	3:05.63	3:06.14	3:06.66	3:07.17	3:07.69	3:08.20	3:08.72	3:09.23	3:09.75
370	3:10.27	3:10.78	3:11.30	3:11.81	3:12.33	3:12.84	3:13.36	3:13.88	3:14.39	3:14.91
380	3:15.42	3:15.94	3:16.45	3:16.97	3:17.48	3:18.00	3:18.52	3:19.03	3:19.55	3:20.06
390	3:20.58	3:21.09	3:21.61	3:22.13	3:22.64	3:23.16	3:23.67	3:24.19	3:24.70	3:25.22
400	3:25.73	3:26.25	3:26.77	3:27.28	3:27.80	3:28.31	3:28.83	3:29.34	3:29.86	3:30.38
410	3:30.89	3:31.41	3:31.92	3:32.44	3:32.95	3:33.47	3:33.98	3:34.50	3:35.02	3:35.53
420	3:36.05	3:36.56	3:37.08	3:37.59	3:38.11	3:38.63	3:39.14	3:39.66	3:40.17	3:40.69
430	3:41.20	3:41.72	3:42.23	3:42.75	3:43.27	3:43.78	3:44.30	3:44.81	3:45.33	3:45.84
440	3:46.36	3:46.88	3:47.39	3:47.91	3:48.42	3:48.94	3:49.45	3:49.97	3:50.48	3:51.00
450	3:51.52	3:52.03	3:52.55	3:53.06	3:53.58	3:54.09	3:54.61	3:55.13	3:55.64	3:56.16
460	3:56.67	3:57.19	3:57.70	3:58.22	3:58.73	3:59.25	3:59.77	4:00.28	4:00.80	4:01.31
470	4:01.83	4:02.34	4:02.86	4:03.38	4:03.89	4:04.41	4:04.92	4:05.44	4:05.95	4:06.47
480	4:06.98	4:07.50	4:08.02	4:08.53	4:09.05	4:09.56	4:10.08	4:10.59	4:11.11	4:11.62
490	4:12.14	4:12.66	4:13.17	4:13.69	4:14.20	4:14.72	4:15.23	4:15.75	4:16.27	4:16.78
500	4:17.30	4:17.81	4:18.33	4:18.84	4:19.36	4:19.88	4:20.39	4:20.91	4:21.42	4:21.94
510	4:22.45	4:22.97	4:23.48	4:24.00	4:24.52	4:25.03	4:25.55	4:26.06	4:26.58	4:27.09
520	4:27.61	4:28.13	4:28.64	4:29.16	4:29.67	4:30.19	4:30.70	4:31.22	4:31.73	4:32.25
530	4:32.77	4:33.28	4:33.80	4:34.31	4:34.83	4:35.34	4:35.86	4:36.38	4:36.89	4:37.41
540	4:37.92	4:38.44	4:38.95	4:39.47	4:39.98	4:40.50	4:41.02	4:41.53	4:42.05	4:42.56
550	4:43.08	4:43.59	4:44.11	4:44.63	4:45.14	4:45.66	4:46.17	4:46.69	4:47.20	4:47.72
560	4:48.23	4:48.75	4:49.27	4:49.78	4:50.30	4:50.81	4:51.33	4:51.84	4:52.36	4:52.87
570	4:53.39	4:53.91	4:54.42	4:54.94	4:55.45	4:55.97	4:56.48	4:57.00	4:57.52	4:58.03
580	4:58.55	4:59.06	4:59.58	5:00.09	5:00.61	5:01.13	5:01.64	5:02.16	5:02.67	5:03.19
590	5:03.70	5:04.22	5:04.73	5:05.25	5:05.77	5:06.28	5:06.80	5:07.31	5:07.83	5:08.34

♩. = 0.77; ♩ = 0.52; ♪. = 0.39; (triplet ♩ 𝄾) = 0.34; ♪ = 0.26; (triplet ♪ 𝄾 𝄾) = 0.17; 𝅘𝅥𝅯 = 0.13 seconds

CLICK: 12 4/8 FRAMES; M.M.: 115.20

Click	0	1	2	3	4	5	6	7	8	9
000	0:00.00	0:00.00	0:00.52	0:01.04	0:01.56	0:02.08	0:02.60	0:03.13	0:03.65	0:04.17
010	0:04.69	0:05.21	0:05.73	0:06.25	0:06.77	0:07.29	0:07.81	0:08.33	0:08.85	0:09.38
020	0:09.90	0:10.42	0:10.94	0:11.46	0:11.98	0:12.50	0:13.02	0:13.54	0:14.06	0:14.58
030	0:15.10	0:15.63	0:16.15	0:16.67	0:17.19	0:17.71	0:18.23	0:18.75	0:19.27	0:19.79
040	0:20.31	0:20.83	0:21.35	0:21.88	0:22.40	0:22.92	0:23.44	0:23.96	0:24.48	0:25.00
050	0:25.52	0:26.04	0:26.56	0:27.08	0:27.60	0:28.13	0:28.65	0:29.17	0:29.69	0:30.21
060	0:30.73	0:31.25	0:31.77	0:32.29	0:32.81	0:33.33	0:33.85	0:34.38	0:34.90	0:35.42
070	0:35.94	0:36.46	0:36.98	0:37.50	0:38.02	0:38.54	0:39.06	0:39.58	0:40.10	0:40.63
080	0:41.15	0:41.67	0:42.19	0:42.71	0:43.23	0:43.75	0:44.27	0:44.79	0:45.31	0:45.83
090	0:46.35	0:46.88	0:47.40	0:47.92	0:48.44	0:48.96	0:49.48	0:50.00	0:50.52	0:51.04
100	0:51.56	0:52.08	0:52.60	0:53.13	0:53.65	0:54.17	0:54.69	0:55.21	0:55.73	0:56.25
110	0:56.77	0:57.29	0:57.81	0:58.33	0:58.85	0:59.38	0:59.90	1:00.42	1:00.94	1:01.46
120	1:01.98	1:02.50	1:03.02	1:03.54	1:04.06	1:04.58	1:05.10	1:05.63	1:06.15	1:06.67
130	1:07.19	1:07.71	1:08.23	1:08.75	1:09.27	1:09.79	1:10.31	1:10.83	1:11.35	1:11.88
140	1:12.40	1:12.92	1:13.44	1:13.96	1:14.48	1:15.00	1:15.52	1:16.04	1:16.56	1:17.08
150	1:17.60	1:18.13	1:18.65	1:19.17	1:19.69	1:20.21	1:20.73	1:21.25	1:21.77	1:22.29
160	1:22.81	1:23.33	1:23.85	1:24.38	1:24.90	1:25.42	1:25.94	1:26.46	1:26.98	1:27.50
170	1:28.02	1:28.54	1:29.06	1:29.58	1:30.10	1:30.63	1:31.15	1:31.67	1:32.19	1:32.71
180	1:33.23	1:33.75	1:34.27	1:34.79	1:35.31	1:35.83	1:36.35	1:36.88	1:37.40	1:37.92
190	1:38.44	1:38.96	1:39.48	1:40.00	1:40.52	1:41.04	1:41.56	1:42.08	1:42.60	1:43.13
200	1:43.65	1:44.17	1:44.69	1:45.21	1:45.73	1:46.25	1:46.77	1:47.29	1:47.81	1:48.33
210	1:48.85	1:49.38	1:49.90	1:50.42	1:50.94	1:51.46	1:51.98	1:52.50	1:53.02	1:53.54
220	1:54.06	1:54.58	1:55.10	1:55.63	1:56.15	1:56.67	1:57.19	1:57.71	1:58.23	1:58.75
230	1:59.27	1:59.79	2:00.31	2:00.83	2:01.35	2:01.88	2:02.40	2:02.92	2:03.44	2:03.96
240	2:04.48	2:05.00	2:05.52	2:06.04	2:06.56	2:07.08	2:07.60	2:08.13	2:08.65	2:09.17
250	2:09.69	2:10.21	2:10.73	2:11.25	2:11.77	2:12.29	2:12.81	2:13.33	2:13.85	2:14.38
260	2:14.90	2:15.42	2:15.94	2:16.46	2:16.98	2:17.50	2:18.02	2:18.54	2:19.06	2:19.58
270	2:20.10	2:20.63	2:21.15	2:21.67	2:22.19	2:22.71	2:23.23	2:23.75	2:24.27	2:24.79
280	2:25.31	2:25.83	2:26.35	2:26.88	2:27.40	2:27.92	2:28.44	2:28.96	2:29.48	2:30.00
290	2:30.52	2:31.04	2:31.56	2:32.08	2:32.60	2:33.13	2:33.65	2:34.17	2:34.69	2:35.21
300	2:35.73	2:36.25	2:36.77	2:37.29	2:37.81	2:38.33	2:38.85	2:39.38	2:39.90	2:40.42
310	2:40.94	2:41.46	2:41.98	2:42.50	2:43.02	2:43.54	2:44.06	2:44.58	2:45.10	2:45.63
320	2:46.15	2:46.67	2:47.19	2:47.71	2:48.23	2:48.75	2:49.27	2:49.79	2:50.31	2:50.83
330	2:51.35	2:51.88	2:52.40	2:52.92	2:53.44	2:53.96	2:54.48	2:55.00	2:55.52	2:56.04
340	2:56.56	2:57.08	2:57.60	2:58.13	2:58.65	2:59.17	2:59.69	3:00.21	3:00.73	3:01.25
350	3:01.77	3:02.29	3:02.81	3:03.33	3:03.85	3:04.38	3:04.90	3:05.42	3:05.94	3:06.46
360	3:06.98	3:07.50	3:08.02	3:08.54	3:09.06	3:09.58	3:10.10	3:10.63	3:11.15	3:11.67
370	3:12.19	3:12.71	3:13.23	3:13.75	3:14.27	3:14.79	3:15.31	3:15.83	3:16.35	3:16.88
380	3:17.40	3:17.92	3:18.44	3:18.96	3:19.48	3:20.00	3:20.52	3:21.04	3:21.56	3:22.08
390	3:22.60	3:23.13	3:23.65	3:24.17	3:24.69	3:25.21	3:25.73	3:26.25	3:26.77	3:27.29
400	3:27.81	3:28.33	3:28.85	3:29.38	3:29.90	3:30.42	3:30.94	3:31.46	3:31.98	3:32.50
410	3:33.02	3:33.54	3:34.06	3:34.58	3:35.10	3:35.63	3:36.15	3:36.67	3:37.19	3:37.71
420	3:38.23	3:38.75	3:39.27	3:39.79	3:40.31	3:40.83	3:41.35	3:41.88	3:42.40	3:42.92
430	3:43.44	3:43.96	3:44.48	3:45.00	3:45.52	3:46.04	3:46.56	3:47.08	3:47.60	3:48.13
440	3:48.65	3:49.17	3:49.69	3:50.21	3:50.73	3:51.25	3:51.77	3:52.29	3:52.81	3:53.33
450	3:53.85	3:54.38	3:54.90	3:55.42	3:55.94	3:56.46	3:56.98	3:57.50	3:58.02	3:58.54
460	3:59.06	3:59.58	4:00.10	4:00.63	4:01.15	4:01.67	4:02.19	4:02.71	4:03.23	4:03.75
470	4:04.27	4:04.79	4:05.31	4:05.83	4:06.35	4:06.88	4:07.40	4:07.92	4:08.44	4:08.96
480	4:09.48	4:10.00	4:10.52	4:11.04	4:11.56	4:12.08	4:12.60	4:13.13	4:13.65	4:14.17
490	4:14.69	4:15.21	4:15.73	4:16.25	4:16.77	4:17.29	4:17.81	4:18.33	4:18.85	4:19.38
500	4:19.90	4:20.42	4:20.94	4:21.46	4:21.98	4:22.50	4:23.02	4:23.54	4:24.06	4:24.58
510	4:25.10	4:25.63	4:26.15	4:26.67	4:27.19	4:27.71	4:28.23	4:28.75	4:29.27	4:29.79
520	4:30.31	4:30.83	4:31.35	4:31.88	4:32.40	4:32.92	4:33.44	4:33.96	4:34.48	4:35.00
530	4:35.52	4:36.04	4:36.56	4:37.08	4:37.60	4:38.13	4:38.65	4:39.17	4:39.69	4:40.21
540	4:40.73	4:41.25	4:41.77	4:42.29	4:42.81	4:43.33	4:43.85	4:44.38	4:44.90	4:45.42
550	4:45.94	4:46.46	4:46.98	4:47.50	4:48.02	4:48.54	4:49.06	4:49.58	4:50.10	4:50.63
560	4:51.15	4:51.67	4:52.19	4:52.71	4:53.23	4:53.75	4:54.27	4:54.79	4:55.31	4:55.83
570	4:56.35	4:56.88	4:57.40	4:57.92	4:58.44	4:58.96	4:59.48	5:00.00	5:00.52	5:01.04
580	5:01.56	5:02.08	5:02.60	5:03.13	5:03.65	5:04.17	5:04.69	5:05.21	5:05.73	5:06.25
590	5:06.77	5:07.29	5:07.81	5:08.33	5:08.85	5:09.38	5:09.90	5:10.42	5:10.94	5:11.46

♩. = 0.78; ♩ = 0.52; ♪. = 0.39; (triplet ♩ 𝄾) = 0.35; ♪ = 0.26; (triplet ♪ 𝄾 𝄾) = 0.17; 𝅘𝅥𝅯 = 0.13 seconds

CLICK: 12⅝ FRAMES; M.M.: 114.06

Click	0	1	2	3	4	5	6	7	8	9
000	0:00.00	0:00.00	0:00.53	0:01.05	0:01.58	0:02.10	0:02.63	0:03.16	0:03.68	0:04.21
010	0:04.73	0:05.26	0:05.79	0:06.31	0:06.84	0:07.36	0:07.89	0:08.42	0:08.94	0:09.47
020	0:09.99	0:10.52	0:11.05	0:11.57	0:12.10	0:12.63	0:13.15	0:13.68	0:14.20	0:14.73
030	0:15.26	0:15.78	0:16.31	0:16.83	0:17.36	0:17.89	0:18.41	0:18.94	0:19.46	0:19.99
040	0:20.52	0:21.04	0:21.57	0:22.09	0:22.62	0:23.15	0:23.67	0:24.20	0:24.72	0:25.25
050	0:25.78	0:26.30	0:26.83	0:27.35	0:27.88	0:28.41	0:28.93	0:29.46	0:29.98	0:30.51
060	0:31.04	0:31.56	0:32.09	0:32.61	0:33.14	0:33.67	0:34.19	0:34.72	0:35.24	0:35.77
070	0:36.30	0:36.82	0:37.35	0:37.88	0:38.40	0:38.93	0:39.45	0:39.98	0:40.51	0:41.03
080	0:41.56	0:42.08	0:42.61	0:43.14	0:43.66	0:44.19	0:44.71	0:45.24	0:45.77	0:46.29
090	0:46.82	0:47.34	0:47.87	0:48.40	0:48.92	0:49.45	0:49.97	0:50.50	0:51.03	0:51.55
100	0:52.08	0:52.60	0:53.13	0:53.66	0:54.18	0:54.71	0:55.23	0:55.76	0:56.29	0:56.81
110	0:57.34	0:57.86	0:58.39	0:58.92	0:59.44	0:59.97	1:00.49	1:01.02	1:01.55	1:02.07
120	1:02.60	1:03.13	1:03.65	1:04.18	1:04.70	1:05.23	1:05.76	1:06.28	1:06.81	1:07.33
130	1:07.86	1:08.39	1:08.91	1:09.44	1:09.96	1:10.49	1:11.02	1:11.54	1:12.07	1:12.59
140	1:13.12	1:13.65	1:14.17	1:14.70	1:15.22	1:15.75	1:16.28	1:16.80	1:17.33	1:17.85
150	1:18.38	1:18.91	1:19.43	1:19.96	1:20.48	1:21.01	1:21.54	1:22.06	1:22.59	1:23.11
160	1:23.64	1:24.17	1:24.69	1:25.22	1:25.74	1:26.27	1:26.80	1:27.32	1:27.85	1:28.38
170	1:28.90	1:29.43	1:29.95	1:30.48	1:31.01	1:31.53	1:32.06	1:32.58	1:33.11	1:33.64
180	1:34.16	1:34.69	1:35.21	1:35.74	1:36.27	1:36.79	1:37.32	1:37.84	1:38.37	1:38.90
190	1:39.42	1:39.95	1:40.47	1:41.00	1:41.53	1:42.05	1:42.58	1:43.10	1:43.63	1:44.16
200	1:44.68	1:45.21	1:45.73	1:46.26	1:46.79	1:47.31	1:47.84	1:48.36	1:48.89	1:49.42
210	1:49.94	1:50.47	1:50.99	1:51.52	1:52.05	1:52.57	1:53.10	1:53.63	1:54.15	1:54.68
220	1:55.20	1:55.73	1:56.26	1:56.78	1:57.31	1:57.83	1:58.36	1:58.89	1:59.41	1:59.94
230	2:00.46	2:00.99	2:01.52	2:02.04	2:02.57	2:03.09	2:03.62	2:04.15	2:04.67	2:05.20
240	2:05.72	2:06.25	2:06.78	2:07.30	2:07.83	2:08.35	2:08.88	2:09.41	2:09.93	2:10.46
250	2:10.98	2:11.51	2:12.04	2:12.56	2:13.09	2:13.61	2:14.14	2:14.67	2:15.19	2:15.72
260	2:16.24	2:16.77	2:17.30	2:17.82	2:18.35	2:18.88	2:19.40	2:19.93	2:20.45	2:20.98
270	2:21.51	2:22.03	2:22.56	2:23.08	2:23.61	2:24.14	2:24.66	2:25.19	2:25.71	2:26.24
280	2:26.77	2:27.29	2:27.82	2:28.34	2:28.87	2:29.40	2:29.92	2:30.45	2:30.97	2:31.50
290	2:32.03	2:32.55	2:33.08	2:33.60	2:34.13	2:34.66	2:35.18	2:35.71	2:36.23	2:36.76
300	2:37.29	2:37.81	2:38.34	2:38.86	2:39.39	2:39.92	2:40.44	2:40.97	2:41.49	2:42.02
310	2:42.55	2:43.07	2:43.60	2:44.13	2:44.65	2:45.18	2:45.70	2:46.23	2:46.76	2:47.28
320	2:47.81	2:48.33	2:48.86	2:49.39	2:49.91	2:50.44	2:50.96	2:51.49	2:52.02	2:52.54
330	2:53.07	2:53.59	2:54.12	2:54.65	2:55.17	2:55.70	2:56.22	2:56.75	2:57.28	2:57.80
340	2:58.33	2:58.85	2:59.38	2:59.91	3:00.43	3:00.96	3:01.48	3:02.01	3:02.54	3:03.06
350	3:03.59	3:04.11	3:04.64	3:05.17	3:05.69	3:06.22	3:06.74	3:07.27	3:07.80	3:08.32
360	3:08.85	3:09.38	3:09.90	3:10.43	3:10.95	3:11.48	3:12.01	3:12.53	3:13.06	3:13.58
370	3:14.11	3:14.64	3:15.16	3:15.69	3:16.21	3:16.74	3:17.27	3:17.79	3:18.32	3:18.84
380	3:19.37	3:19.90	3:20.42	3:20.95	3:21.47	3:22.00	3:22.53	3:23.05	3:23.58	3:24.10
390	3:24.63	3:25.16	3:25.68	3:26.21	3:26.73	3:27.26	3:27.79	3:28.31	3:28.84	3:29.36
400	3:29.89	3:30.42	3:30.94	3:31.47	3:31.99	3:32.52	3:33.05	3:33.57	3:34.10	3:34.63
410	3:35.15	3:35.68	3:36.20	3:36.73	3:37.26	3:37.78	3:38.31	3:38.83	3:39.36	3:39.89
420	3:40.41	3:40.94	3:41.46	3:41.99	3:42.52	3:43.04	3:43.57	3:44.09	3:44.62	3:45.15
430	3:45.67	3:46.20	3:46.72	3:47.25	3:47.78	3:48.30	3:48.83	3:49.35	3:49.88	3:50.41
440	3:50.93	3:51.46	3:51.98	3:52.51	3:53.04	3:53.56	3:54.09	3:54.61	3:55.14	3:55.67
450	3:56.19	3:56.72	3:57.24	3:57.77	3:58.30	3:58.82	3:59.35	3:59.88	4:00.40	4:00.93
460	4:01.45	4:01.98	4:02.51	4:03.03	4:03.56	4:04.08	4:04.61	4:05.14	4:05.66	4:06.19
470	4:06.71	4:07.24	4:07.77	4:08.29	4:08.82	4:09.34	4:09.87	4:10.40	4:10.92	4:11.45
480	4:11.97	4:12.50	4:13.03	4:13.55	4:14.08	4:14.60	4:15.13	4:15.66	4:16.18	4:16.71
490	4:17.23	4:17.76	4:18.29	4:18.81	4:19.34	4:19.86	4:20.39	4:20.92	4:21.44	4:21.97
500	4:22.49	4:23.02	4:23.55	4:24.07	4:24.60	4:25.13	4:25.65	4:26.18	4:26.70	4:27.23
510	4:27.76	4:28.28	4:28.81	4:29.33	4:29.86	4:30.39	4:30.91	4:31.44	4:31.96	4:32.49
520	4:33.02	4:33.54	4:34.07	4:34.59	4:35.12	4:35.65	4:36.17	4:36.70	4:37.22	4:37.75
530	4:38.28	4:38.80	4:39.33	4:39.85	4:40.38	4:40.91	4:41.43	4:41.96	4:42.48	4:43.01
540	4:43.54	4:44.06	4:44.59	4:45.11	4:45.64	4:46.17	4:46.69	4:47.22	4:47.74	4:48.27
550	4:48.80	4:49.32	4:49.85	4:50.38	4:50.90	4:51.43	4:51.95	4:52.48	4:53.01	4:53.53
560	4:54.06	4:54.58	4:55.11	4:55.64	4:56.16	4:56.69	4:57.21	4:57.74	4:58.27	4:58.79
570	4:59.32	4:59.84	5:00.37	5:00.90	5:01.42	5:01.95	5:02.47	5:03.00	5:03.53	5:04.05
580	5:04.58	5:05.10	5:05.63	5:06.16	5:06.68	5:07.21	5:07.73	5:08.26	5:08.79	5:09.31
590	5:09.84	5:10.36	5:10.89	5:11.42	5:11.94	5:12.47	5:12.99	5:13.52	5:14.05	5:14.57

♩. = 0.79; ♩ = 0.53; ♪. = 0.39; (triplet) ♩ 𝄾 = 0.35; ♪ = 0.26; (triplet) ♪ 𝄾 𝄾 = 0.18; 𝅘𝅥𝅯 = 0.13 seconds

CLICK: 12 6/8 FRAMES; M.M.: 112.94

Click	0	1	2	3	4	5	6	7	8	9
000	0:00.00	0:00.00	0:00.53	0:01.06	0:01.59	0:02.13	0:02.66	0:03.19	0:03.72	0:04.25
010	0:04.78	0:05.31	0:05.84	0:06.38	0:06.91	0:07.44	0:07.97	0:08.50	0:09.03	0:09.56
020	0:10.09	0:10.63	0:11.16	0:11.69	0:12.22	0:12.75	0:13.28	0:13.81	0:14.34	0:14.88
030	0:15.41	0:15.94	0:16.47	0:17.00	0:17.53	0:18.06	0:18.59	0:19.13	0:19.66	0:20.19
040	0:20.72	0:21.25	0:21.78	0:22.31	0:22.84	0:23.38	0:23.91	0:24.44	0:24.97	0:25.50
050	0:26.03	0:26.56	0:27.09	0:27.63	0:28.16	0:28.69	0:29.22	0:29.75	0:30.28	0:30.81
060	0:31.34	0:31.88	0:32.41	0:32.94	0:33.47	0:34.00	0:34.53	0:35.06	0:35.59	0:36.13
070	0:36.66	0:37.19	0:37.72	0:38.25	0:38.78	0:39.31	0:39.84	0:40.38	0:40.91	0:41.44
080	0:41.97	0:42.50	0:43.03	0:43.56	0:44.09	0:44.63	0:45.16	0:45.69	0:46.22	0:46.75
090	0:47.28	0:47.81	0:48.34	0:48.88	0:49.41	0:49.94	0:50.47	0:51.00	0:51.53	0:52.06
100	0:52.59	0:53.13	0:53.66	0:54.19	0:54.72	0:55.25	0:55.78	0:56.31	0:56.84	0:57.38
110	0:57.91	0:58.44	0:58.97	0:59.50	1:00.03	1:00.56	1:01.09	1:01.62	1:02.16	1:02.69
120	1:03.22	1:03.75	1:04.28	1:04.81	1:05.34	1:05.87	1:06.41	1:06.94	1:07.47	1:08.00
130	1:08.53	1:09.06	1:09.59	1:10.13	1:10.66	1:11.19	1:11.72	1:12.25	1:12.78	1:13.31
140	1:13.84	1:14.38	1:14.91	1:15.44	1:15.97	1:16.50	1:17.03	1:17.56	1:18.09	1:18.63
150	1:19.16	1:19.69	1:20.22	1:20.75	1:21.28	1:21.81	1:22.34	1:22.88	1:23.41	1:23.94
160	1:24.47	1:25.00	1:25.53	1:26.06	1:26.59	1:27.13	1:27.66	1:28.19	1:28.72	1:29.25
170	1:29.78	1:30.31	1:30.84	1:31.38	1:31.91	1:32.44	1:32.97	1:33.50	1:34.03	1:34.56
180	1:35.09	1:35.63	1:36.16	1:36.69	1:37.22	1:37.75	1:38.28	1:38.81	1:39.34	1:39.88
190	1:40.41	1:40.94	1:41.47	1:42.00	1:42.53	1:43.06	1:43.59	1:44.13	1:44.66	1:45.19
200	1:45.72	1:46.25	1:46.78	1:47.31	1:47.84	1:48.38	1:48.91	1:49.44	1:49.97	1:50.50
210	1:51.03	1:51.56	1:52.09	1:52.63	1:53.16	1:53.69	1:54.22	1:54.75	1:55.28	1:55.81
220	1:56.34	1:56.87	1:57.41	1:57.94	1:58.47	1:59.00	1:59.53	2:00.06	2:00.59	2:01.12
230	2:01.66	2:02.19	2:02.72	2:03.25	2:03.78	2:04.31	2:04.84	2:05.38	2:05.91	2:06.44
240	2:06.97	2:07.50	2:08.03	2:08.56	2:09.09	2:09.62	2:10.16	2:10.69	2:11.22	2:11.75
250	2:12.28	2:12.81	2:13.34	2:13.88	2:14.41	2:14.94	2:15.47	2:16.00	2:16.53	2:17.06
260	2:17.59	2:18.12	2:18.66	2:19.19	2:19.72	2:20.25	2:20.78	2:21.31	2:21.84	2:22.38
270	2:22.91	2:23.44	2:23.97	2:24.50	2:25.03	2:25.56	2:26.09	2:26.62	2:27.16	2:27.69
280	2:28.22	2:28.75	2:29.28	2:29.81	2:30.34	2:30.88	2:31.41	2:31.94	2:32.47	2:33.00
290	2:33.53	2:34.06	2:34.59	2:35.12	2:35.66	2:36.19	2:36.72	2:37.25	2:37.78	2:38.31
300	2:38.84	2:39.38	2:39.91	2:40.44	2:40.97	2:41.50	2:42.03	2:42.56	2:43.09	2:43.62
310	2:44.16	2:44.69	2:45.22	2:45.75	2:46.28	2:46.81	2:47.34	2:47.88	2:48.41	2:48.94
320	2:49.47	2:50.00	2:50.53	2:51.06	2:51.59	2:52.13	2:52.66	2:53.19	2:53.72	2:54.25
330	2:54.78	2:55.31	2:55.84	2:56.38	2:56.91	2:57.44	2:57.97	2:58.50	2:59.03	2:59.56
340	3:00.09	3:00.63	3:01.16	3:01.69	3:02.22	3:02.75	3:03.28	3:03.81	3:04.34	3:04.87
350	3:05.41	3:05.94	3:06.47	3:07.00	3:07.53	3:08.06	3:08.59	3:09.13	3:09.66	3:10.19
360	3:10.72	3:11.25	3:11.78	3:12.31	3:12.84	3:13.37	3:13.91	3:14.44	3:14.97	3:15.50
370	3:16.03	3:16.56	3:17.09	3:17.63	3:18.16	3:18.69	3:19.22	3:19.75	3:20.28	3:20.81
380	3:21.34	3:21.87	3:22.41	3:22.94	3:23.47	3:24.00	3:24.53	3:25.06	3:25.59	3:26.13
390	3:26.66	3:27.19	3:27.72	3:28.25	3:28.78	3:29.31	3:29.84	3:30.37	3:30.91	3:31.44
400	3:31.97	3:32.50	3:33.03	3:33.56	3:34.09	3:34.63	3:35.16	3:35.69	3:36.22	3:36.75
410	3:37.28	3:37.81	3:38.34	3:38.87	3:39.41	3:39.94	3:40.47	3:41.00	3:41.53	3:42.06
420	3:42.59	3:43.13	3:43.66	3:44.19	3:44.72	3:45.25	3:45.78	3:46.31	3:46.84	3:47.37
430	3:47.91	3:48.44	3:48.97	3:49.50	3:50.03	3:50.56	3:51.09	3:51.63	3:52.16	3:52.69
440	3:53.22	3:53.75	3:54.28	3:54.81	3:55.34	3:55.87	3:56.41	3:56.94	3:57.47	3:58.00
450	3:58.53	3:59.06	3:59.59	4:00.12	4:00.66	4:01.19	4:01.72	4:02.25	4:02.78	4:03.31
460	4:03.84	4:04.37	4:04.91	4:05.44	4:05.97	4:06.50	4:07.03	4:07.56	4:08.09	4:08.63
470	4:09.16	4:09.69	4:10.22	4:10.75	4:11.28	4:11.81	4:12.34	4:12.88	4:13.41	4:13.94
480	4:14.47	4:15.00	4:15.53	4:16.06	4:16.59	4:17.12	4:17.66	4:18.19	4:18.72	4:19.25
490	4:19.78	4:20.31	4:20.84	4:21.37	4:21.91	4:22.44	4:22.97	4:23.50	4:24.03	4:24.56
500	4:25.09	4:25.63	4:26.16	4:26.69	4:27.22	4:27.75	4:28.28	4:28.81	4:29.34	4:29.88
510	4:30.41	4:30.94	4:31.47	4:32.00	4:32.53	4:33.06	4:33.59	4:34.12	4:34.66	4:35.19
520	4:35.72	4:36.25	4:36.78	4:37.31	4:37.84	4:38.37	4:38.91	4:39.44	4:39.97	4:40.50
530	4:41.03	4:41.56	4:42.09	4:42.63	4:43.16	4:43.69	4:44.22	4:44.75	4:45.28	4:45.81
540	4:46.34	4:46.88	4:47.41	4:47.94	4:48.47	4:49.00	4:49.53	4:50.06	4:50.59	4:51.12
550	4:51.66	4:52.19	4:52.72	4:53.25	4:53.78	4:54.31	4:54.84	4:55.37	4:55.91	4:56.44
560	4:56.97	4:57.50	4:58.03	4:58.56	4:59.09	4:59.63	5:00.16	5:00.69	5:01.22	5:01.75
570	5:02.28	5:02.81	5:03.34	5:03.87	5:04.41	5:04.94	5:05.47	5:06.00	5:06.53	5:07.06
580	5:07.59	5:08.12	5:08.66	5:09.19	5:09.72	5:10.25	5:10.78	5:11.31	5:11.84	5:12.38
590	5:12.91	5:13.44	5:13.97	5:14.50	5:15.03	5:15.56	5:16.09	5:16.63	5:17.16	5:17.69

♩. = 0.80; ♩ = 0.53; ♪. = 0.40; (3: ♩ 𝄾) = 0.35; ♪ = 0.27; (3: ♪ 𝄾 𝄾) = 0.18; 𝅘𝅥𝅯 = 0.13 seconds

CLICK: 12⅞ FRAMES; M.M.: 111.84

Click	0	1	2	3	4	5	6	7	8	9
000	0:00.00	0:00.00	0:00.54	0:01.07	0:01.61	0:02.15	0:02.68	0:03.22	0:03.76	0:04.29
010	0:04.83	0:05.36	0:05.90	0:06.44	0:06.97	0:07.51	0:08.05	0:08.58	0:09.12	0:09.66
020	0:10.19	0:10.73	0:11.27	0:11.80	0:12.34	0:12.88	0:13.41	0:13.95	0:14.48	0:15.02
030	0:15.56	0:16.09	0:16.63	0:17.17	0:17.70	0:18.24	0:18.78	0:19.31	0:19.85	0:20.39
040	0:20.92	0:21.46	0:21.99	0:22.53	0:23.07	0:23.60	0:24.14	0:24.68	0:25.21	0:25.75
050	0:26.29	0:26.82	0:27.36	0:27.90	0:28.43	0:28.97	0:29.51	0:30.04	0:30.58	0:31.11
060	0:31.65	0:32.19	0:32.72	0:33.26	0:33.80	0:34.33	0:34.87	0:35.41	0:35.94	0:36.48
070	0:37.02	0:37.55	0:38.09	0:38.63	0:39.16	0:39.70	0:40.23	0:40.77	0:41.31	0:41.84
080	0:42.38	0:42.92	0:43.45	0:43.99	0:44.53	0:45.06	0:45.60	0:46.14	0:46.67	0:47.21
090	0:47.74	0:48.28	0:48.82	0:49.35	0:49.89	0:50.43	0:50.96	0:51.50	0:52.04	0:52.57
100	0:53.11	0:53.65	0:54.18	0:54.72	0:55.26	0:55.79	0:56.33	0:56.86	0:57.40	0:57.94
110	0:58.47	0:59.01	0:59.55	1:00.08	1:00.62	1:01.16	1:01.69	1:02.23	1:02.77	1:03.30
120	1:03.84	1:04.38	1:04.91	1:05.45	1:05.98	1:06.52	1:07.06	1:07.59	1:08.13	1:08.67
130	1:09.20	1:09.74	1:10.28	1:10.81	1:11.35	1:11.89	1:12.42	1:12.96	1:13.49	1:14.03
140	1:14.57	1:15.10	1:15.64	1:16.18	1:16.71	1:17.25	1:17.79	1:18.32	1:18.86	1:19.40
150	1:19.93	1:20.47	1:21.01	1:21.54	1:22.08	1:22.61	1:23.15	1:23.69	1:24.22	1:24.76
160	1:25.30	1:25.83	1:26.37	1:26.91	1:27.44	1:27.98	1:28.52	1:29.05	1:29.59	1:30.13
170	1:30.66	1:31.20	1:31.73	1:32.27	1:32.81	1:33.34	1:33.88	1:34.42	1:34.95	1:35.49
180	1:36.03	1:36.56	1:37.10	1:37.64	1:38.17	1:38.71	1:39.24	1:39.78	1:40.32	1:40.85
190	1:41.39	1:41.93	1:42.46	1:43.00	1:43.54	1:44.07	1:44.61	1:45.15	1:45.68	1:46.22
200	1:46.76	1:47.29	1:47.83	1:48.36	1:48.90	1:49.44	1:49.97	1:50.51	1:51.05	1:51.58
210	1:52.12	1:52.66	1:53.19	1:53.73	1:54.27	1:54.80	1:55.34	1:55.88	1:56.41	1:56.95
220	1:57.48	1:58.02	1:58.56	1:59.09	1:59.63	2:00.17	2:00.70	2:01.24	2:01.78	2:02.31
230	2:02.85	2:03.39	2:03.92	2:04.46	2:04.99	2:05.53	2:06.07	2:06.60	2:07.14	2:07.68
240	2:08.21	2:08.75	2:09.29	2:09.82	2:10.36	2:10.90	2:11.43	2:11.97	2:12.51	2:13.04
250	2:13.58	2:14.11	2:14.65	2:15.19	2:15.72	2:16.26	2:16.80	2:17.33	2:17.87	2:18.41
260	2:18.94	2:19.48	2:20.02	2:20.55	2:21.09	2:21.63	2:22.16	2:22.70	2:23.23	2:23.77
270	2:24.31	2:24.84	2:25.38	2:25.92	2:26.45	2:26.99	2:27.53	2:28.06	2:28.60	2:29.14
280	2:29.67	2:30.21	2:30.74	2:31.28	2:31.82	2:32.35	2:32.89	2:33.43	2:33.96	2:34.50
290	2:35.04	2:35.57	2:36.11	2:36.65	2:37.18	2:37.72	2:38.26	2:38.79	2:39.33	2:39.86
300	2:40.40	2:40.94	2:41.47	2:42.01	2:42.55	2:43.08	2:43.62	2:44.16	2:44.69	2:45.23
310	2:45.77	2:46.30	2:46.84	2:47.38	2:47.91	2:48.45	2:48.98	2:49.52	2:50.06	2:50.59
320	2:51.13	2:51.67	2:52.20	2:52.74	2:53.28	2:53.81	2:54.35	2:54.89	2:55.42	2:55.96
330	2:56.49	2:57.03	2:57.57	2:58.10	2:58.64	2:59.18	2:59.71	3:00.25	3:00.79	3:01.32
340	3:01.86	3:02.40	3:02.93	3:03.47	3:04.01	3:04.54	3:05.08	3:05.61	3:06.15	3:06.69
350	3:07.22	3:07.76	3:08.30	3:08.83	3:09.37	3:09.91	3:10.44	3:10.98	3:11.52	3:12.05
360	3:12.59	3:13.13	3:13.66	3:14.20	3:14.73	3:15.27	3:15.81	3:16.34	3:16.88	3:17.42
370	3:17.95	3:18.49	3:19.03	3:19.56	3:20.10	3:20.64	3:21.17	3:21.71	3:22.24	3:22.78
380	3:23.32	3:23.85	3:24.39	3:24.93	3:25.46	3:26.00	3:26.54	3:27.07	3:27.61	3:28.15
390	3:28.68	3:29.22	3:29.76	3:30.29	3:30.83	3:31.36	3:31.90	3:32.44	3:32.97	3:33.51
400	3:34.05	3:34.58	3:35.12	3:35.66	3:36.19	3:36.73	3:37.27	3:37.80	3:38.34	3:38.88
410	3:39.41	3:39.95	3:40.48	3:41.02	3:41.56	3:42.09	3:42.63	3:43.17	3:43.70	3:44.24
420	3:44.78	3:45.31	3:45.85	3:46.39	3:46.92	3:47.46	3:47.99	3:48.53	3:49.07	3:49.60
430	3:50.14	3:50.68	3:51.21	3:51.75	3:52.29	3:52.82	3:53.36	3:53.90	3:54.43	3:54.97
440	3:55.51	3:56.04	3:56.58	3:57.11	3:57.65	3:58.19	3:58.72	3:59.26	3:59.80	4:00.33
450	4:00.87	4:01.41	4:01.94	4:02.48	4:03.02	4:03.55	4:04.09	4:04.63	4:05.16	4:05.70
460	4:06.23	4:06.77	4:07.31	4:07.84	4:08.38	4:08.92	4:09.45	4:09.99	4:10.53	4:11.06
470	4:11.60	4:12.14	4:12.67	4:13.21	4:13.74	4:14.28	4:14.82	4:15.35	4:15.89	4:16.43
480	4:16.96	4:17.50	4:18.04	4:18.57	4:19.11	4:19.65	4:20.18	4:20.72	4:21.26	4:21.79
490	4:22.33	4:22.86	4:23.40	4:23.94	4:24.47	4:25.01	4:25.55	4:26.08	4:26.62	4:27.16
500	4:27.69	4:28.23	4:28.77	4:29.30	4:29.84	4:30.37	4:30.91	4:31.45	4:31.98	4:32.52
510	4:33.06	4:33.59	4:34.13	4:34.67	4:35.20	4:35.74	4:36.28	4:36.81	4:37.35	4:37.89
520	4:38.42	4:38.96	4:39.49	4:40.03	4:40.57	4:41.10	4:41.64	4:42.18	4:42.71	4:43.25
530	4:43.79	4:44.32	4:44.86	4:45.40	4:45.93	4:46.47	4:47.01	4:47.54	4:48.08	4:48.61
540	4:49.15	4:49.69	4:50.22	4:50.76	4:51.30	4:51.83	4:52.37	4:52.91	4:53.44	4:53.98
550	4:54.52	4:55.05	4:55.59	4:56.13	4:56.66	4:57.20	4:57.73	4:58.27	4:58.81	4:59.34
560	4:59.88	5:00.42	5:00.95	5:01.49	5:02.03	5:02.56	5:03.10	5:03.64	5:04.17	5:04.71
570	5:05.24	5:05.78	5:06.32	5:06.85	5:07.39	5:07.93	5:08.46	5:09.00	5:09.54	5:10.07
580	5:10.61	5:11.15	5:11.68	5:12.22	5:12.76	5:13.29	5:13.83	5:14.36	5:14.90	5:15.44
590	5:15.97	5:16.51	5:17.05	5:17.58	5:18.12	5:18.66	5:19.19	5:19.73	5:20.27	5:20.80

♩. = 0.80; ♩ = 0.54; ♪. = 0.40; (triplet ♩ 𝄾) = 0.36; ♪ = 0.27; (triplet ♪ 𝄾 𝄾) = 0.18; 𝅘𝅥𝅯 = 0.13 seconds

CLICK: 13 0/8 FRAMES; M.M.: 110.77

Click	0	1	2	3	4	5	6	7	8	9
000	0:00.00	0:00.00	0:00.54	0:01.08	0:01.62	0:02.17	0:02.71	0:03.25	0:03.79	0:04.33
010	0:04.88	0:05.42	0:05.96	0:06.50	0:07.04	0:07.58	0:08.12	0:08.67	0:09.21	0:09.75
020	0:10.29	0:10.83	0:11.37	0:11.92	0:12.46	0:13.00	0:13.54	0:14.08	0:14.62	0:15.17
030	0:15.71	0:16.25	0:16.79	0:17.33	0:17.88	0:18.42	0:18.96	0:19.50	0:20.04	0:20.58
040	0:21.13	0:21.67	0:22.21	0:22.75	0:23.29	0:23.83	0:24.37	0:24.92	0:25.46	0:26.00
050	0:26.54	0:27.08	0:27.62	0:28.17	0:28.71	0:29.25	0:29.79	0:30.33	0:30.87	0:31.42
060	0:31.96	0:32.50	0:33.04	0:33.58	0:34.12	0:34.67	0:35.21	0:35.75	0:36.29	0:36.83
070	0:37.38	0:37.92	0:38.46	0:39.00	0:39.54	0:40.08	0:40.63	0:41.17	0:41.71	0:42.25
080	0:42.79	0:43.33	0:43.87	0:44.42	0:44.96	0:45.50	0:46.04	0:46.58	0:47.12	0:47.67
090	0:48.21	0:48.75	0:49.29	0:49.83	0:50.37	0:50.92	0:51.46	0:52.00	0:52.54	0:53.08
100	0:53.62	0:54.17	0:54.71	0:55.25	0:55.79	0:56.33	0:56.87	0:57.42	0:57.96	0:58.50
110	0:59.04	0:59.58	1:00.12	1:00.67	1:01.21	1:01.75	1:02.29	1:02.83	1:03.37	1:03.92
120	1:04.46	1:05.00	1:05.54	1:06.08	1:06.62	1:07.17	1:07.71	1:08.25	1:08.79	1:09.33
130	1:09.87	1:10.42	1:10.96	1:11.50	1:12.04	1:12.58	1:13.12	1:13.67	1:14.21	1:14.75
140	1:15.29	1:15.83	1:16.37	1:16.92	1:17.46	1:18.00	1:18.54	1:19.08	1:19.62	1:20.17
150	1:20.71	1:21.25	1:21.79	1:22.33	1:22.87	1:23.42	1:23.96	1:24.50	1:25.04	1:25.58
160	1:26.12	1:26.67	1:27.21	1:27.75	1:28.29	1:28.83	1:29.37	1:29.92	1:30.46	1:31.00
170	1:31.54	1:32.08	1:32.62	1:33.17	1:33.71	1:34.25	1:34.79	1:35.33	1:35.87	1:36.42
180	1:36.96	1:37.50	1:38.04	1:38.58	1:39.12	1:39.67	1:40.21	1:40.75	1:41.29	1:41.83
190	1:42.37	1:42.92	1:43.46	1:44.00	1:44.54	1:45.08	1:45.62	1:46.17	1:46.71	1:47.25
200	1:47.79	1:48.33	1:48.87	1:49.42	1:49.96	1:50.50	1:51.04	1:51.58	1:52.12	1:52.67
210	1:53.21	1:53.75	1:54.29	1:54.83	1:55.37	1:55.92	1:56.46	1:57.00	1:57.54	1:58.08
220	1:58.62	1:59.17	1:59.71	2:00.25	2:00.79	2:01.33	2:01.87	2:02.42	2:02.96	2:03.50
230	2:04.04	2:04.58	2:05.12	2:05.67	2:06.21	2:06.75	2:07.29	2:07.83	2:08.37	2:08.92
240	2:09.46	2:10.00	2:10.54	2:11.08	2:11.62	2:12.17	2:12.71	2:13.25	2:13.79	2:14.33
250	2:14.87	2:15.42	2:15.96	2:16.50	2:17.04	2:17.58	2:18.12	2:18.67	2:19.21	2:19.75
260	2:20.29	2:20.83	2:21.37	2:21.92	2:22.46	2:23.00	2:23.54	2:24.08	2:24.62	2:25.17
270	2:25.71	2:26.25	2:26.79	2:27.33	2:27.87	2:28.42	2:28.96	2:29.50	2:30.04	2:30.58
280	2:31.12	2:31.67	2:32.21	2:32.75	2:33.29	2:33.83	2:34.37	2:34.92	2:35.46	2:36.00
290	2:36.54	2:37.08	2:37.62	2:38.17	2:38.71	2:39.25	2:39.79	2:40.33	2:40.87	2:41.42
300	2:41.96	2:42.50	2:43.04	2:43.58	2:44.12	2:44.67	2:45.21	2:45.75	2:46.29	2:46.83
310	2:47.37	2:47.92	2:48.46	2:49.00	2:49.54	2:50.08	2:50.62	2:51.17	2:51.71	2:52.25
320	2:52.79	2:53.33	2:53.87	2:54.42	2:54.96	2:55.50	2:56.04	2:56.58	2:57.12	2:57.67
330	2:58.21	2:58.75	2:59.29	2:59.83	3:00.37	3:00.92	3:01.46	3:02.00	3:02.54	3:03.08
340	3:03.62	3:04.17	3:04.71	3:05.25	3:05.79	3:06.33	3:06.87	3:07.42	3:07.96	3:08.50
350	3:09.04	3:09.58	3:10.12	3:10.67	3:11.21	3:11.75	3:12.29	3:12.83	3:13.37	3:13.92
360	3:14.46	3:15.00	3:15.54	3:16.08	3:16.62	3:17.17	3:17.71	3:18.25	3:18.79	3:19.33
370	3:19.87	3:20.42	3:20.96	3:21.50	3:22.04	3:22.58	3:23.12	3:23.67	3:24.21	3:24.75
380	3:25.29	3:25.83	3:26.37	3:26.92	3:27.46	3:28.00	3:28.54	3:29.08	3:29.62	3:30.17
390	3:30.71	3:31.25	3:31.79	3:32.33	3:32.87	3:33.42	3:33.96	3:34.50	3:35.04	3:35.58
400	3:36.12	3:36.67	3:37.21	3:37.75	3:38.29	3:38.83	3:39.37	3:39.92	3:40.46	3:41.00
410	3:41.54	3:42.08	3:42.62	3:43.17	3:43.71	3:44.25	3:44.79	3:45.33	3:45.87	3:46.42
420	3:46.96	3:47.50	3:48.04	3:48.58	3:49.12	3:49.67	3:50.21	3:50.75	3:51.29	3:51.83
430	3:52.37	3:52.92	3:53.46	3:54.00	3:54.54	3:55.08	3:55.62	3:56.17	3:56.71	3:57.25
440	3:57.79	3:58.33	3:58.87	3:59.42	3:59.96	4:00.50	4:01.04	4:01.58	4:02.12	4:02.67
450	4:03.21	4:03.75	4:04.29	4:04.83	4:05.37	4:05.92	4:06.46	4:07.00	4:07.54	4:08.08
460	4:08.62	4:09.17	4:09.71	4:10.25	4:10.79	4:11.33	4:11.87	4:12.42	4:12.96	4:13.50
470	4:14.04	4:14.58	4:15.12	4:15.67	4:16.21	4:16.75	4:17.29	4:17.83	4:18.37	4:18.92
480	4:19.46	4:20.00	4:20.54	4:21.08	4:21.62	4:22.17	4:22.71	4:23.25	4:23.79	4:24.33
490	4:24.87	4:25.42	4:25.96	4:26.50	4:27.04	4:27.58	4:28.12	4:28.67	4:29.21	4:29.75
500	4:30.29	4:30.83	4:31.37	4:31.92	4:32.46	4:33.00	4:33.54	4:34.08	4:34.62	4:35.17
510	4:35.71	4:36.25	4:36.79	4:37.33	4:37.87	4:38.42	4:38.96	4:39.50	4:40.04	4:40.58
520	4:41.12	4:41.67	4:42.21	4:42.75	4:43.29	4:43.83	4:44.37	4:44.92	4:45.46	4:46.00
530	4:46.54	4:47.08	4:47.62	4:48.17	4:48.71	4:49.25	4:49.79	4:50.33	4:50.87	4:51.42
540	4:51.96	4:52.50	4:53.04	4:53.58	4:54.12	4:54.67	4:55.21	4:55.75	4:56.29	4:56.83
550	4:57.37	4:57.92	4:58.46	4:59.00	4:59.54	5:00.08	5:00.62	5:01.17	5:01.71	5:02.25
560	5:02.79	5:03.33	5:03.87	5:04.42	5:04.96	5:05.50	5:06.04	5:06.58	5:07.12	5:07.67
570	5:08.21	5:08.75	5:09.29	5:09.83	5:10.37	5:10.92	5:11.46	5:12.00	5:12.54	5:13.08
580	5:13.62	5:14.17	5:14.71	5:15.25	5:15.79	5:16.33	5:16.87	5:17.42	5:17.96	5:18.50
590	5:19.04	5:19.58	5:20.12	5:20.67	5:21.21	5:21.75	5:22.29	5:22.83	5:23.37	5:23.92

𝅗𝅥. = 0.81; ♩ = 0.54; ♪. = 0.41; (triplet ♩ 𝄾) = 0.36; ♪ = 0.27; (triplet ♪ 𝄾 𝄾) = 0.18; 𝅘𝅥𝅯 = 0.14 seconds

CLICK: 13⅛ FRAMES; M.M.: 109.71

Click	0	1	2	3	4	5	6	7	8	9
000	0:00.00	0:00.00	0:00.55	0:01.09	0:01.64	0:02.19	0:02.73	0:03.28	0:03.83	0:04.38
010	0:04.92	0:05.47	0:06.02	0:06.56	0:07.11	0:07.66	0:08.20	0:08.75	0:09.30	0:09.84
020	0:10.39	0:10.94	0:11.48	0:12.03	0:12.58	0:13.13	0:13.67	0:14.22	0:14.77	0:15.31
030	0:15.86	0:16.41	0:16.95	0:17.50	0:18.05	0:18.59	0:19.14	0:19.69	0:20.23	0:20.78
040	0:21.33	0:21.87	0:22.42	0:22.97	0:23.52	0:24.06	0:24.61	0:25.16	0:25.70	0:26.25
050	0:26.80	0:27.34	0:27.89	0:28.44	0:28.98	0:29.53	0:30.08	0:30.62	0:31.17	0:31.72
060	0:32.27	0:32.81	0:33.36	0:33.91	0:34.45	0:35.00	0:35.55	0:36.09	0:36.64	0:37.19
070	0:37.73	0:38.28	0:38.83	0:39.38	0:39.92	0:40.47	0:41.02	0:41.56	0:42.11	0:42.66
080	0:43.20	0:43.75	0:44.30	0:44.84	0:45.39	0:45.94	0:46.48	0:47.03	0:47.58	0:48.13
090	0:48.67	0:49.22	0:49.77	0:50.31	0:50.86	0:51.41	0:51.95	0:52.50	0:53.05	0:53.59
100	0:54.14	0:54.69	0:55.23	0:55.78	0:56.33	0:56.87	0:57.42	0:57.97	0:58.52	0:59.06
110	0:59.61	1:00.16	1:00.70	1:01.25	1:01.80	1:02.34	1:02.89	1:03.44	1:03.98	1:04.53
120	1:05.08	1:05.63	1:06.17	1:06.72	1:07.27	1:07.81	1:08.36	1:08.91	1:09.45	1:10.00
130	1:10.55	1:11.09	1:11.64	1:12.19	1:12.73	1:13.28	1:13.83	1:14.37	1:14.92	1:15.47
140	1:16.02	1:16.56	1:17.11	1:17.66	1:18.20	1:18.75	1:19.30	1:19.84	1:20.39	1:20.94
150	1:21.48	1:22.03	1:22.58	1:23.12	1:23.67	1:24.22	1:24.77	1:25.31	1:25.86	1:26.41
160	1:26.95	1:27.50	1:28.05	1:28.59	1:29.14	1:29.69	1:30.23	1:30.78	1:31.33	1:31.88
170	1:32.42	1:32.97	1:33.52	1:34.06	1:34.61	1:35.16	1:35.70	1:36.25	1:36.80	1:37.34
180	1:37.89	1:38.44	1:38.98	1:39.53	1:40.08	1:40.62	1:41.17	1:41.72	1:42.27	1:42.81
190	1:43.36	1:43.91	1:44.45	1:45.00	1:45.55	1:46.09	1:46.64	1:47.19	1:47.73	1:48.28
200	1:48.83	1:49.37	1:49.92	1:50.47	1:51.02	1:51.56	1:52.11	1:52.66	1:53.20	1:53.75
210	1:54.30	1:54.84	1:55.39	1:55.94	1:56.48	1:57.03	1:57.58	1:58.12	1:58.67	1:59.22
220	1:59.77	2:00.31	2:00.86	2:01.41	2:01.95	2:02.50	2:03.05	2:03.59	2:04.14	2:04.69
230	2:05.23	2:05.78	2:06.33	2:06.87	2:07.42	2:07.97	2:08.52	2:09.06	2:09.61	2:10.16
240	2:10.70	2:11.25	2:11.80	2:12.34	2:12.89	2:13.44	2:13.98	2:14.53	2:15.08	2:15.62
250	2:16.17	2:16.72	2:17.27	2:17.81	2:18.36	2:18.91	2:19.45	2:20.00	2:20.55	2:21.09
260	2:21.64	2:22.19	2:22.73	2:23.28	2:23.83	2:24.38	2:24.92	2:25.47	2:26.02	2:26.56
270	2:27.11	2:27.66	2:28.20	2:28.75	2:29.30	2:29.84	2:30.39	2:30.94	2:31.48	2:32.03
280	2:32.58	2:33.12	2:33.67	2:34.22	2:34.77	2:35.31	2:35.86	2:36.41	2:36.95	2:37.50
290	2:38.05	2:38.59	2:39.14	2:39.69	2:40.23	2:40.78	2:41.33	2:41.87	2:42.42	2:42.97
300	2:43.52	2:44.06	2:44.61	2:45.16	2:45.70	2:46.25	2:46.80	2:47.34	2:47.89	2:48.44
310	2:48.98	2:49.53	2:50.08	2:50.63	2:51.17	2:51.72	2:52.27	2:52.81	2:53.36	2:53.91
320	2:54.45	2:55.00	2:55.55	2:56.09	2:56.64	2:57.19	2:57.73	2:58.28	2:58.83	2:59.37
330	2:59.92	3:00.47	3:01.02	3:01.56	3:02.11	3:02.66	3:03.20	3:03.75	3:04.30	3:04.84
340	3:05.39	3:05.94	3:06.48	3:07.03	3:07.58	3:08.12	3:08.67	3:09.22	3:09.77	3:10.31
350	3:10.86	3:11.41	3:11.95	3:12.50	3:13.05	3:13.59	3:14.14	3:14.69	3:15.23	3:15.78
360	3:16.33	3:16.88	3:17.42	3:17.97	3:18.52	3:19.06	3:19.61	3:20.16	3:20.70	3:21.25
370	3:21.80	3:22.34	3:22.89	3:23.44	3:23.98	3:24.53	3:25.08	3:25.62	3:26.17	3:26.72
380	3:27.27	3:27.81	3:28.36	3:28.91	3:29.45	3:30.00	3:30.55	3:31.09	3:31.64	3:32.19
390	3:32.73	3:33.28	3:33.83	3:34.37	3:34.92	3:35.47	3:36.02	3:36.56	3:37.11	3:37.66
400	3:38.20	3:38.75	3:39.30	3:39.84	3:40.39	3:40.94	3:41.48	3:42.03	3:42.58	3:43.12
410	3:43.67	3:44.22	3:44.77	3:45.31	3:45.86	3:46.41	3:46.95	3:47.50	3:48.05	3:48.59
420	3:49.14	3:49.69	3:50.23	3:50.78	3:51.33	3:51.87	3:52.42	3:52.97	3:53.52	3:54.06
430	3:54.61	3:55.16	3:55.70	3:56.25	3:56.80	3:57.34	3:57.89	3:58.44	3:58.98	3:59.53
440	4:00.08	4:00.62	4:01.17	4:01.72	4:02.27	4:02.81	4:03.36	4:03.91	4:04.45	4:05.00
450	4:05.55	4:06.09	4:06.64	4:07.19	4:07.73	4:08.28	4:08.83	4:09.38	4:09.92	4:10.47
460	4:11.02	4:11.56	4:12.11	4:12.66	4:13.20	4:13.75	4:14.30	4:14.84	4:15.39	4:15.94
470	4:16.48	4:17.03	4:17.58	4:18.12	4:18.67	4:19.22	4:19.77	4:20.31	4:20.86	4:21.41
480	4:21.95	4:22.50	4:23.05	4:23.59	4:24.14	4:24.69	4:25.23	4:25.78	4:26.33	4:26.87
490	4:27.42	4:27.97	4:28.52	4:29.06	4:29.61	4:30.16	4:30.70	4:31.25	4:31.80	4:32.34
500	4:32.89	4:33.44	4:33.98	4:34.53	4:35.08	4:35.63	4:36.17	4:36.72	4:37.27	4:37.81
510	4:38.36	4:38.91	4:39.45	4:40.00	4:40.55	4:41.09	4:41.64	4:42.19	4:42.73	4:43.28
520	4:43.83	4:44.37	4:44.92	4:45.47	4:46.02	4:46.56	4:47.11	4:47.66	4:48.20	4:48.75
530	4:49.30	4:49.84	4:50.39	4:50.94	4:51.48	4:52.03	4:52.58	4:53.12	4:53.67	4:54.22
540	4:54.77	4:55.31	4:55.86	4:56.41	4:56.95	4:57.50	4:58.05	4:58.59	4:59.14	4:59.69
550	5:00.23	5:00.78	5:01.33	5:01.88	5:02.42	5:02.97	5:03.52	5:04.06	5:04.61	5:05.16
560	5:05.70	5:06.25	5:06.80	5:07.34	5:07.89	5:08.44	5:08.98	5:09.53	5:10.08	5:10.62
570	5:11.17	5:11.72	5:12.27	5:12.81	5:13.36	5:13.91	5:14.45	5:15.00	5:15.55	5:16.09
580	5:16.64	5:17.19	5:17.73	5:18.28	5:18.83	5:19.37	5:19.92	5:20.47	5:21.02	5:21.56
590	5:22.11	5:22.66	5:23.20	5:23.75	5:24.30	5:24.84	5:25.39	5:25.94	5:26.48	5:27.03

♩. = 0.82; ♩ = 0.55; ♪. = 0.41; (triplet) ♩ 𝄾 = 0.36; ♪ = 0.27; (triplet) ♪ 𝄾 𝄾 = 0.18; 𝅘𝅥𝅯 = 0.14 seconds

CLICK: 13⅞ FRAMES; M.M.: 108.68

Click	0	1	2	3	4	5	6	7	8	9
000	0:00.00	0:00.00	0:00.55	0:01.10	0:01.66	0:02.21	0:02.76	0:03.31	0:03.86	0:04.42
010	0:04.97	0:05.52	0:06.07	0:06.63	0:07.18	0:07.73	0:08.28	0:08.83	0:09.39	0:09.94
020	0:10.49	0:11.04	0:11.59	0:12.15	0:12.70	0:13.25	0:13.80	0:14.35	0:14.91	0:15.46
030	0:16.01	0:16.56	0:17.11	0:17.67	0:18.22	0:18.77	0:19.32	0:19.88	0:20.43	0:20.98
040	0:21.53	0:22.08	0:22.64	0:23.19	0:23.74	0:24.29	0:24.84	0:25.40	0:25.95	0:26.50
050	0:27.05	0:27.60	0:28.16	0:28.71	0:29.26	0:29.81	0:30.36	0:30.92	0:31.47	0:32.02
060	0:32.57	0:33.13	0:33.68	0:34.23	0:34.78	0:35.33	0:35.89	0:36.44	0:36.99	0:37.54
070	0:38.09	0:38.65	0:39.20	0:39.75	0:40.30	0:40.85	0:41.41	0:41.96	0:42.51	0:43.06
080	0:43.61	0:44.17	0:44.72	0:45.27	0:45.82	0:46.38	0:46.93	0:47.48	0:48.03	0:48.58
090	0:49.14	0:49.69	0:50.24	0:50.79	0:51.34	0:51.90	0:52.45	0:53.00	0:53.55	0:54.10
100	0:54.66	0:55.21	0:55.76	0:56.31	0:56.86	0:57.42	0:57.97	0:58.52	0:59.07	0:59.63
110	1:00.18	1:00.73	1:01.28	1:01.83	1:02.39	1:02.94	1:03.49	1:04.04	1:04.59	1:05.15
120	1:05.70	1:06.25	1:06.80	1:07.35	1:07.91	1:08.46	1:09.01	1:09.56	1:10.11	1:10.67
130	1:11.22	1:11.77	1:12.32	1:12.87	1:13.43	1:13.98	1:14.53	1:15.08	1:15.64	1:16.19
140	1:16.74	1:17.29	1:17.84	1:18.40	1:18.95	1:19.50	1:20.05	1:20.60	1:21.16	1:21.71
150	1:22.26	1:22.81	1:23.36	1:23.92	1:24.47	1:25.02	1:25.57	1:26.13	1:26.68	1:27.23
160	1:27.78	1:28.33	1:28.89	1:29.44	1:29.99	1:30.54	1:31.09	1:31.65	1:32.20	1:32.75
170	1:33.30	1:33.85	1:34.41	1:34.96	1:35.51	1:36.06	1:36.61	1:37.17	1:37.72	1:38.27
180	1:38.82	1:39.38	1:39.93	1:40.48	1:41.03	1:41.58	1:42.14	1:42.69	1:43.24	1:43.79
190	1:44.34	1:44.90	1:45.45	1:46.00	1:46.55	1:47.10	1:47.66	1:48.21	1:48.76	1:49.31
200	1:49.86	1:50.42	1:50.97	1:51.52	1:52.07	1:52.63	1:53.18	1:53.73	1:54.28	1:54.83
210	1:55.39	1:55.94	1:56.49	1:57.04	1:57.59	1:58.15	1:58.70	1:59.25	1:59.80	2:00.35
220	2:00.91	2:01.46	2:02.01	2:02.56	2:03.11	2:03.67	2:04.22	2:04.77	2:05.32	2:05.87
230	2:06.43	2:06.98	2:07.53	2:08.08	2:08.64	2:09.19	2:09.74	2:10.29	2:10.84	2:11.40
240	2:11.95	2:12.50	2:13.05	2:13.60	2:14.16	2:14.71	2:15.26	2:15.81	2:16.36	2:16.92
250	2:17.47	2:18.02	2:18.57	2:19.12	2:19.68	2:20.23	2:20.78	2:21.33	2:21.89	2:22.44
260	2:22.99	2:23.54	2:24.09	2:24.65	2:25.20	2:25.75	2:26.30	2:26.85	2:27.41	2:27.96
270	2:28.51	2:29.06	2:29.61	2:30.17	2:30.72	2:31.27	2:31.82	2:32.37	2:32.93	2:33.48
280	2:34.03	2:34.58	2:35.14	2:35.69	2:36.24	2:36.79	2:37.34	2:37.90	2:38.45	2:39.00
290	2:39.55	2:40.10	2:40.66	2:41.21	2:41.76	2:42.31	2:42.86	2:43.42	2:43.97	2:44.52
300	2:45.07	2:45.63	2:46.18	2:46.73	2:47.28	2:47.83	2:48.39	2:48.94	2:49.49	2:50.04
310	2:50.59	2:51.15	2:51.70	2:52.25	2:52.80	2:53.35	2:53.91	2:54.46	2:55.01	2:55.56
320	2:56.11	2:56.67	2:57.22	2:57.77	2:58.32	2:58.88	2:59.43	2:59.98	3:00.53	3:01.08
330	3:01.64	3:02.19	3:02.74	3:03.29	3:03.84	3:04.40	3:04.95	3:05.50	3:06.05	3:06.60
340	3:07.16	3:07.71	3:08.26	3:08.81	3:09.36	3:09.92	3:10.47	3:11.02	3:11.57	3:12.13
350	3:12.68	3:13.23	3:13.78	3:14.33	3:14.89	3:15.44	3:15.99	3:16.54	3:17.09	3:17.65
360	3:18.20	3:18.75	3:19.30	3:19.85	3:20.41	3:20.96	3:21.51	3:22.06	3:22.61	3:23.17
370	3:23.72	3:24.27	3:24.82	3:25.38	3:25.93	3:26.48	3:27.03	3:27.58	3:28.14	3:28.69
380	3:29.24	3:29.79	3:30.34	3:30.90	3:31.45	3:32.00	3:32.55	3:33.10	3:33.66	3:34.21
390	3:34.76	3:35.31	3:35.86	3:36.42	3:36.97	3:37.52	3:38.07	3:38.62	3:39.18	3:39.73
400	3:40.28	3:40.83	3:41.39	3:41.94	3:42.49	3:43.04	3:43.59	3:44.15	3:44.70	3:45.25
410	3:45.80	3:46.35	3:46.91	3:47.46	3:48.01	3:48.56	3:49.11	3:49.67	3:50.22	3:50.77
420	3:51.32	3:51.87	3:52.43	3:52.98	3:53.53	3:54.08	3:54.64	3:55.19	3:55.74	3:56.29
430	3:56.84	3:57.40	3:57.95	3:58.50	3:59.05	3:59.60	4:00.16	4:00.71	4:01.26	4:01.81
440	4:02.36	4:02.92	4:03.47	4:04.02	4:04.57	4:05.13	4:05.68	4:06.23	4:06.78	4:07.33
450	4:07.89	4:08.44	4:08.99	4:09.54	4:10.09	4:10.65	4:11.20	4:11.75	4:12.30	4:12.85
460	4:13.41	4:13.96	4:14.51	4:15.06	4:15.61	4:16.17	4:16.72	4:17.27	4:17.82	4:18.38
470	4:18.93	4:19.48	4:20.03	4:20.58	4:21.14	4:21.69	4:22.24	4:22.79	4:23.34	4:23.90
480	4:24.45	4:25.00	4:25.55	4:26.10	4:26.66	4:27.21	4:27.76	4:28.31	4:28.86	4:29.42
490	4:29.97	4:30.52	4:31.07	4:31.63	4:32.18	4:32.73	4:33.28	4:33.83	4:34.39	4:34.94
500	4:35.49	4:36.04	4:36.59	4:37.15	4:37.70	4:38.25	4:38.80	4:39.35	4:39.91	4:40.46
510	4:41.01	4:41.56	4:42.11	4:42.67	4:43.22	4:43.77	4:44.32	4:44.88	4:45.43	4:45.98
520	4:46.53	4:47.08	4:47.64	4:48.19	4:48.74	4:49.29	4:49.84	4:50.40	4:50.95	4:51.50
530	4:52.05	4:52.60	4:53.16	4:53.71	4:54.26	4:54.81	4:55.36	4:55.92	4:56.47	4:57.02
540	4:57.57	4:58.13	4:58.68	4:59.23	4:59.78	5:00.33	5:00.89	5:01.44	5:01.99	5:02.54
550	5:03.09	5:03.65	5:04.20	5:04.75	5:05.30	5:05.85	5:06.41	5:06.96	5:07.51	5:08.06
560	5:08.61	5:09.17	5:09.72	5:10.27	5:10.82	5:11.37	5:11.93	5:12.48	5:13.03	5:13.58
570	5:14.14	5:14.69	5:15.24	5:15.79	5:16.34	5:16.90	5:17.45	5:18.00	5:18.55	5:19.10
580	5:19.66	5:20.21	5:20.76	5:21.31	5:21.86	5:22.42	5:22.97	5:23.52	5:24.07	5:24.62
590	5:25.18	5:25.73	5:26.28	5:26.83	5:27.39	5:27.94	5:28.49	5:29.04	5:29.59	5:30.15

♩. = 0.83; ♩ = 0.55; ♪. = 0.41; (triplet) ♩ 𝄾 = 0.37; ♪ = 0.28; (triplet) ♪𝄾𝄾 = 0.18; 𝅘𝅥𝅯 = 0.14 seconds

CLICK: 13⅜ FRAMES; M.M.: 107.66

Click	0	1	2	3	4	5	6	7	8	9
000	0:00.00	0:00.00	0:00.56	0:01.11	0:01.67	0:02.23	0:02.79	0:03.34	0:03.90	0:04.46
010	0:05.02	0:05.57	0:06.13	0:06.69	0:07.24	0:07.80	0:08.36	0:08.92	0:09.47	0:10.03
020	0:10.59	0:11.15	0:11.70	0:12.26	0:12.82	0:13.38	0:13.93	0:14.49	0:15.05	0:15.60
030	0:16.16	0:16.72	0:17.28	0:17.83	0:18.39	0:18.95	0:19.51	0:20.06	0:20.62	0:21.18
040	0:21.73	0:22.29	0:22.85	0:23.41	0:23.96	0:24.52	0:25.08	0:25.64	0:26.19	0:26.75
050	0:27.31	0:27.86	0:28.42	0:28.98	0:29.54	0:30.09	0:30.65	0:31.21	0:31.77	0:32.32
060	0:32.88	0:33.44	0:33.99	0:34.55	0:35.11	0:35.67	0:36.22	0:36.78	0:37.34	0:37.90
070	0:38.45	0:39.01	0:39.57	0:40.13	0:40.68	0:41.24	0:41.80	0:42.35	0:42.91	0:43.47
080	0:44.03	0:44.58	0:45.14	0:45.70	0:46.26	0:46.81	0:47.37	0:47.93	0:48.48	0:49.04
090	0:49.60	0:50.16	0:50.71	0:51.27	0:51.83	0:52.39	0:52.94	0:53.50	0:54.06	0:54.61
100	0:55.17	0:55.73	0:56.29	0:56.84	0:57.40	0:57.96	0:58.52	0:59.07	0:59.63	1:00.19
110	1:00.74	1:01.30	1:01.86	1:02.42	1:02.97	1:03.53	1:04.09	1:04.65	1:05.20	1:05.76
120	1:06.32	1:06.88	1:07.43	1:07.99	1:08.55	1:09.10	1:09.66	1:10.22	1:10.78	1:11.33
130	1:11.89	1:12.45	1:13.01	1:13.56	1:14.12	1:14.68	1:15.23	1:15.79	1:16.35	1:16.91
140	1:17.46	1:18.02	1:18.58	1:19.14	1:19.69	1:20.25	1:20.81	1:21.36	1:21.92	1:22.48
150	1:23.04	1:23.59	1:24.15	1:24.71	1:25.27	1:25.82	1:26.38	1:26.94	1:27.49	1:28.05
160	1:28.61	1:29.17	1:29.72	1:30.28	1:30.84	1:31.40	1:31.95	1:32.51	1:33.07	1:33.63
170	1:34.18	1:34.74	1:35.30	1:35.85	1:36.41	1:36.97	1:37.53	1:38.08	1:38.64	1:39.20
180	1:39.76	1:40.31	1:40.87	1:41.43	1:41.98	1:42.54	1:43.10	1:43.66	1:44.21	1:44.77
190	1:45.33	1:45.89	1:46.44	1:47.00	1:47.56	1:48.11	1:48.67	1:49.23	1:49.79	1:50.34
200	1:50.90	1:51.46	1:52.02	1:52.57	1:53.13	1:53.69	1:54.24	1:54.80	1:55.36	1:55.92
210	1:56.47	1:57.03	1:57.59	1:58.15	1:58.70	1:59.26	1:59.82	2:00.38	2:00.93	2:01.49
220	2:02.05	2:02.60	2:03.16	2:03.72	2:04.28	2:04.83	2:05.39	2:05.95	2:06.51	2:07.06
230	2:07.62	2:08.18	2:08.73	2:09.29	2:09.85	2:10.41	2:10.96	2:11.52	2:12.08	2:12.64
240	2:13.19	2:13.75	2:14.31	2:14.86	2:15.42	2:15.98	2:16.54	2:17.09	2:17.65	2:18.21
250	2:18.77	2:19.32	2:19.88	2:20.44	2:20.99	2:21.55	2:22.11	2:22.67	2:23.22	2:23.78
260	2:24.34	2:24.90	2:25.45	2:26.01	2:26.57	2:27.13	2:27.68	2:28.24	2:28.80	2:29.35
270	2:29.91	2:30.47	2:31.03	2:31.58	2:32.14	2:32.70	2:33.26	2:33.81	2:34.37	2:34.93
280	2:35.48	2:36.04	2:36.60	2:37.16	2:37.71	2:38.27	2:38.83	2:39.39	2:39.94	2:40.50
290	2:41.06	2:41.61	2:42.17	2:42.73	2:43.29	2:43.84	2:44.40	2:44.96	2:45.52	2:46.07
300	2:46.63	2:47.19	2:47.74	2:48.30	2:48.86	2:49.42	2:49.97	2:50.53	2:51.09	2:51.65
310	2:52.20	2:52.76	2:53.32	2:53.88	2:54.43	2:54.99	2:55.55	2:56.10	2:56.66	2:57.22
320	2:57.78	2:58.33	2:58.89	2:59.45	3:00.01	3:00.56	3:01.12	3:01.68	3:02.23	3:02.79
330	3:03.35	3:03.91	3:04.46	3:05.02	3:05.58	3:06.14	3:06.69	3:07.25	3:07.81	3:08.36
340	3:08.92	3:09.48	3:10.04	3:10.59	3:11.15	3:11.71	3:12.27	3:12.82	3:13.38	3:13.94
350	3:14.49	3:15.05	3:15.61	3:16.17	3:16.72	3:17.28	3:17.84	3:18.40	3:18.95	3:19.51
360	3:20.07	3:20.63	3:21.18	3:21.74	3:22.30	3:22.85	3:23.41	3:23.97	3:24.53	3:25.08
370	3:25.64	3:26.20	3:26.76	3:27.31	3:27.87	3:28.43	3:28.98	3:29.54	3:30.10	3:30.66
380	3:31.21	3:31.77	3:32.33	3:32.89	3:33.44	3:34.00	3:34.56	3:35.11	3:35.67	3:36.23
390	3:36.79	3:37.34	3:37.90	3:38.46	3:39.02	3:39.57	3:40.13	3:40.69	3:41.24	3:41.80
400	3:42.36	3:42.92	3:43.47	3:44.03	3:44.59	3:45.15	3:45.70	3:46.26	3:46.82	3:47.38
410	3:47.93	3:48.49	3:49.05	3:49.60	3:50.16	3:50.72	3:51.28	3:51.83	3:52.39	3:52.95
420	3:53.51	3:54.06	3:54.62	3:55.18	3:55.73	3:56.29	3:56.85	3:57.41	3:57.96	3:58.52
430	3:59.08	3:59.64	4:00.19	4:00.75	4:01.31	4:01.86	4:02.42	4:02.98	4:03.54	4:04.09
440	4:04.65	4:05.21	4:05.77	4:06.32	4:06.88	4:07.44	4:07.99	4:08.55	4:09.11	4:09.67
450	4:10.22	4:10.78	4:11.34	4:11.90	4:12.45	4:13.01	4:13.57	4:14.13	4:14.68	4:15.24
460	4:15.80	4:16.35	4:16.91	4:17.47	4:18.03	4:18.58	4:19.14	4:19.70	4:20.26	4:20.81
470	4:21.37	4:21.93	4:22.48	4:23.04	4:23.60	4:24.16	4:24.71	4:25.27	4:25.83	4:26.39
480	4:26.94	4:27.50	4:28.06	4:28.61	4:29.17	4:29.73	4:30.29	4:30.84	4:31.40	4:31.96
490	4:32.52	4:33.07	4:33.63	4:34.19	4:34.74	4:35.30	4:35.86	4:36.42	4:36.97	4:37.53
500	4:38.09	4:38.65	4:39.20	4:39.76	4:40.32	4:40.88	4:41.43	4:41.99	4:42.55	4:43.10
510	4:43.66	4:44.22	4:44.78	4:45.33	4:45.89	4:46.45	4:47.01	4:47.56	4:48.12	4:48.68
520	4:49.23	4:49.79	4:50.35	4:50.91	4:51.46	4:52.02	4:52.58	4:53.14	4:53.69	4:54.25
530	4:54.81	4:55.36	4:55.92	4:56.48	4:57.04	4:57.59	4:58.15	4:58.71	4:59.27	4:59.82
540	5:00.38	5:00.94	5:01.49	5:02.05	5:02.61	5:03.17	5:03.72	5:04.28	5:04.84	5:05.40
550	5:05.95	5:06.51	5:07.07	5:07.62	5:08.18	5:08.74	5:09.30	5:09.85	5:10.41	5:10.97
560	5:11.53	5:12.08	5:12.64	5:13.20	5:13.76	5:14.31	5:14.87	5:15.43	5:15.98	5:16.54
570	5:17.10	5:17.66	5:18.21	5:18.77	5:19.33	5:19.89	5:20.44	5:21.00	5:21.56	5:22.11
580	5:22.67	5:23.23	5:23.79	5:24.34	5:24.90	5:25.46	5:26.02	5:26.57	5:27.13	5:27.69
590	5:28.24	5:28.80	5:29.36	5:29.92	5:30.47	5:31.03	5:31.59	5:32.15	5:32.70	5:33.26

♩. = 0.84; ♩ = 0.56; ♪. = 0.42; (triplet: ♩ 𝄾) = 0.37; ♪ = 0.28; (triplet: ♪ 𝄾 𝄾) = 0.19; 𝅘𝅥𝅯 = 0.14 seconds

CLICK: 13 4/8 FRAMES; M.M.: 106.67

Click	0	1	2	3	4	5	6	7	8	9
000	0:00.00	0:00.00	0:00.56	0:01.13	0:01.69	0:02.25	0:02.81	0:03.38	0:03.94	0:04.50
010	0:05.06	0:05.63	0:06.19	0:06.75	0:07.31	0:07.88	0:08.44	0:09.00	0:09.56	0:10.13
020	0:10.69	0:11.25	0:11.81	0:12.38	0:12.94	0:13.50	0:14.06	0:14.63	0:15.19	0:15.75
030	0:16.31	0:16.88	0:17.44	0:18.00	0:18.56	0:19.13	0:19.69	0:20.25	0:20.81	0:21.38
040	0:21.94	0:22.50	0:23.06	0:23.63	0:24.19	0:24.75	0:25.31	0:25.88	0:26.44	0:27.00
050	0:27.56	0:28.13	0:28.69	0:29.25	0:29.81	0:30.38	0:30.94	0:31.50	0:32.06	0:32.63
060	0:33.19	0:33.75	0:34.31	0:34.88	0:35.44	0:36.00	0:36.56	0:37.13	0:37.69	0:38.25
070	0:38.81	0:39.38	0:39.94	0:40.50	0:41.06	0:41.63	0:42.19	0:42.75	0:43.31	0:43.88
080	0:44.44	0:45.00	0:45.56	0:46.13	0:46.69	0:47.25	0:47.81	0:48.38	0:48.94	0:49.50
090	0:50.06	0:50.63	0:51.19	0:51.75	0:52.31	0:52.88	0:53.44	0:54.00	0:54.56	0:55.13
100	0:55.69	0:56.25	0:56.81	0:57.38	0:57.94	0:58.50	0:59.06	0:59.63	1:00.19	1:00.75
110	1:01.31	1:01.88	1:02.44	1:03.00	1:03.56	1:04.13	1:04.69	1:05.25	1:05.81	1:06.38
120	1:06.94	1:07.50	1:08.06	1:08.63	1:09.19	1:09.75	1:10.31	1:10.88	1:11.44	1:12.00
130	1:12.56	1:13.13	1:13.69	1:14.25	1:14.81	1:15.38	1:15.94	1:16.50	1:17.06	1:17.63
140	1:18.19	1:18.75	1:19.31	1:19.88	1:20.44	1:21.00	1:21.56	1:22.13	1:22.69	1:23.25
150	1:23.81	1:24.38	1:24.94	1:25.50	1:26.06	1:26.63	1:27.19	1:27.75	1:28.31	1:28.88
160	1:29.44	1:30.00	1:30.56	1:31.13	1:31.69	1:32.25	1:32.81	1:33.38	1:33.94	1:34.50
170	1:35.06	1:35.63	1:36.19	1:36.75	1:37.31	1:37.88	1:38.44	1:39.00	1:39.56	1:40.13
180	1:40.69	1:41.25	1:41.81	1:42.38	1:42.94	1:43.50	1:44.06	1:44.63	1:45.19	1:45.75
190	1:46.31	1:46.88	1:47.44	1:48.00	1:48.56	1:49.13	1:49.69	1:50.25	1:50.81	1:51.38
200	1:51.94	1:52.50	1:53.06	1:53.63	1:54.19	1:54.75	1:55.31	1:55.88	1:56.44	1:57.00
210	1:57.56	1:58.13	1:58.69	1:59.25	1:59.81	2:00.38	2:00.94	2:01.50	2:02.06	2:02.63
220	2:03.19	2:03.75	2:04.31	2:04.88	2:05.44	2:06.00	2:06.56	2:07.13	2:07.69	2:08.25
230	2:08.81	2:09.38	2:09.94	2:10.50	2:11.06	2:11.63	2:12.19	2:12.75	2:13.31	2:13.88
240	2:14.44	2:15.00	2:15.56	2:16.13	2:16.69	2:17.25	2:17.81	2:18.38	2:18.94	2:19.50
250	2:20.06	2:20.63	2:21.19	2:21.75	2:22.31	2:22.88	2:23.44	2:24.00	2:24.56	2:25.13
260	2:25.69	2:26.25	2:26.81	2:27.38	2:27.94	2:28.50	2:29.06	2:29.63	2:30.19	2:30.75
270	2:31.31	2:31.88	2:32.44	2:33.00	2:33.56	2:34.13	2:34.69	2:35.25	2:35.81	2:36.38
280	2:36.94	2:37.50	2:38.06	2:38.63	2:39.19	2:39.75	2:40.31	2:40.88	2:41.44	2:42.00
290	2:42.56	2:43.13	2:43.69	2:44.25	2:44.81	2:45.38	2:45.94	2:46.50	2:47.06	2:47.63
300	2:48.19	2:48.75	2:49.31	2:49.88	2:50.44	2:51.00	2:51.56	2:52.13	2:52.69	2:53.25
310	2:53.81	2:54.38	2:54.94	2:55.50	2:56.06	2:56.63	2:57.19	2:57.75	2:58.31	2:58.88
320	2:59.44	3:00.00	3:00.56	3:01.13	3:01.69	3:02.25	3:02.81	3:03.38	3:03.94	3:04.50
330	3:05.06	3:05.63	3:06.19	3:06.75	3:07.31	3:07.88	3:08.44	3:09.00	3:09.56	3:10.13
340	3:10.69	3:11.25	3:11.81	3:12.38	3:12.94	3:13.50	3:14.06	3:14.63	3:15.19	3:15.75
350	3:16.31	3:16.88	3:17.44	3:18.00	3:18.56	3:19.13	3:19.69	3:20.25	3:20.81	3:21.38
360	3:21.94	3:22.50	3:23.06	3:23.63	3:24.19	3:24.75	3:25.31	3:25.88	3:26.44	3:27.00
370	3:27.56	3:28.13	3:28.69	3:29.25	3:29.81	3:30.38	3:30.94	3:31.50	3:32.06	3:32.63
380	3:33.19	3:33.75	3:34.31	3:34.88	3:35.44	3:36.00	3:36.56	3:37.13	3:37.69	3:38.25
390	3:38.81	3:39.38	3:39.94	3:40.50	3:41.06	3:41.63	3:42.19	3:42.75	3:43.31	3:43.88
400	3:44.44	3:45.00	3:45.56	3:46.13	3:46.69	3:47.25	3:47.81	3:48.38	3:48.94	3:49.50
410	3:50.06	3:50.63	3:51.19	3:51.75	3:52.31	3:52.88	3:53.44	3:54.00	3:54.56	3:55.13
420	3:55.69	3:56.25	3:56.81	3:57.38	3:57.94	3:58.50	3:59.06	3:59.63	4:00.19	4:00.75
430	4:01.31	4:01.88	4:02.44	4:03.00	4:03.56	4:04.13	4:04.69	4:05.25	4:05.81	4:06.38
440	4:06.94	4:07.50	4:08.06	4:08.63	4:09.19	4:09.75	4:10.31	4:10.88	4:11.44	4:12.00
450	4:12.56	4:13.13	4:13.69	4:14.25	4:14.81	4:15.38	4:15.94	4:16.50	4:17.06	4:17.63
460	4:18.19	4:18.75	4:19.31	4:19.88	4:20.44	4:21.00	4:21.56	4:22.13	4:22.69	4:23.25
470	4:23.81	4:24.38	4:24.94	4:25.50	4:26.06	4:26.63	4:27.19	4:27.75	4:28.31	4:28.88
480	4:29.44	4:30.00	4:30.56	4:31.13	4:31.69	4:32.25	4:32.81	4:33.38	4:33.94	4:34.50
490	4:35.06	4:35.63	4:36.19	4:36.75	4:37.31	4:37.88	4:38.44	4:39.00	4:39.56	4:40.13
500	4:40.69	4:41.25	4:41.81	4:42.38	4:42.94	4:43.50	4:44.06	4:44.63	4:45.19	4:45.75
510	4:46.31	4:46.88	4:47.44	4:48.00	4:48.56	4:49.13	4:49.69	4:50.25	4:50.81	4:51.38
520	4:51.94	4:52.50	4:53.06	4:53.63	4:54.19	4:54.75	4:55.31	4:55.88	4:56.44	4:57.00
530	4:57.56	4:58.13	4:58.69	4:59.25	4:59.81	5:00.38	5:00.94	5:01.50	5:02.06	5:02.63
540	5:03.19	5:03.75	5:04.31	5:04.88	5:05.44	5:06.00	5:06.56	5:07.13	5:07.69	5:08.25
550	5:08.81	5:09.38	5:09.94	5:10.50	5:11.06	5:11.63	5:12.19	5:12.75	5:13.31	5:13.88
560	5:14.44	5:15.00	5:15.56	5:16.13	5:16.69	5:17.25	5:17.81	5:18.38	5:18.94	5:19.50
570	5:20.06	5:20.63	5:21.19	5:21.75	5:22.31	5:22.88	5:23.44	5:24.00	5:24.56	5:25.13
580	5:25.69	5:26.25	5:26.81	5:27.38	5:27.94	5:28.50	5:29.06	5:29.63	5:30.19	5:30.75
590	5:31.31	5:31.88	5:32.44	5:33.00	5:33.56	5:34.13	5:34.69	5:35.25	5:35.81	5:36.38

♩. = 0.84; ♩ = 0.56; ♪. = 0.42; (3: ♩ 𝄾) = 0.38; ♪ = 0.28; (3: ♪ 𝄾 𝄾) = 0.19; 𝅘𝅥𝅯 = 0.14 seconds

CLICK: 13⅝ FRAMES; M.M.: 105.69

Click	0	1	2	3	4	5	6	7	8	9
000	0:00.00	0:00.00	0:00.57	0:01.14	0:01.70	0:02.27	0:02.84	0:03.41	0:03.97	0:04.54
010	0:05.11	0:05.68	0:06.24	0:06.81	0:07.38	0:07.95	0:08.52	0:09.08	0:09.65	0:10.22
020	0:10.79	0:11.35	0:11.92	0:12.49	0:13.06	0:13.63	0:14.19	0:14.76	0:15.33	0:15.90
030	0:16.46	0:17.03	0:17.60	0:18.17	0:18.73	0:19.30	0:19.87	0:20.44	0:21.01	0:21.57
040	0:22.14	0:22.71	0:23.28	0:23.84	0:24.41	0:24.98	0:25.55	0:26.11	0:26.68	0:27.25
050	0:27.82	0:28.39	0:28.95	0:29.52	0:30.09	0:30.66	0:31.22	0:31.79	0:32.36	0:32.93
060	0:33.49	0:34.06	0:34.63	0:35.20	0:35.77	0:36.33	0:36.90	0:37.47	0:38.04	0:38.60
070	0:39.17	0:39.74	0:40.31	0:40.88	0:41.44	0:42.01	0:42.58	0:43.15	0:43.71	0:44.28
080	0:44.85	0:45.42	0:45.98	0:46.55	0:47.12	0:47.69	0:48.26	0:48.82	0:49.39	0:49.96
090	0:50.53	0:51.09	0:51.66	0:52.23	0:52.80	0:53.36	0:53.93	0:54.50	0:55.07	0:55.64
100	0:56.20	0:56.77	0:57.34	0:57.91	0:58.47	0:59.04	0:59.61	1:00.18	1:00.74	1:01.31
110	1:01.88	1:02.45	1:03.02	1:03.58	1:04.15	1:04.72	1:05.29	1:05.85	1:06.42	1:06.99
120	1:07.56	1:08.12	1:08.69	1:09.26	1:09.83	1:10.40	1:10.96	1:11.53	1:12.10	1:12.67
130	1:13.23	1:13.80	1:14.37	1:14.94	1:15.51	1:16.07	1:16.64	1:17.21	1:17.78	1:18.34
140	1:18.91	1:19.48	1:20.05	1:20.61	1:21.18	1:21.75	1:22.32	1:22.89	1:23.45	1:24.02
150	1:24.59	1:25.16	1:25.72	1:26.29	1:26.86	1:27.43	1:27.99	1:28.56	1:29.13	1:29.70
160	1:30.27	1:30.83	1:31.40	1:31.97	1:32.54	1:33.10	1:33.67	1:34.24	1:34.81	1:35.37
170	1:35.94	1:36.51	1:37.08	1:37.65	1:38.21	1:38.78	1:39.35	1:39.92	1:40.48	1:41.05
180	1:41.62	1:42.19	1:42.76	1:43.32	1:43.89	1:44.46	1:45.03	1:45.59	1:46.16	1:46.73
190	1:47.30	1:47.86	1:48.43	1:49.00	1:49.57	1:50.14	1:50.70	1:51.27	1:51.84	1:52.41
200	1:52.97	1:53.54	1:54.11	1:54.68	1:55.24	1:55.81	1:56.38	1:56.95	1:57.52	1:58.08
210	1:58.65	1:59.22	1:59.79	2:00.35	2:00.92	2:01.49	2:02.06	2:02.63	2:03.19	2:03.76
220	2:04.33	2:04.90	2:05.46	2:06.03	2:06.60	2:07.17	2:07.73	2:08.30	2:08.87	2:09.44
230	2:10.01	2:10.57	2:11.14	2:11.71	2:12.28	2:12.84	2:13.41	2:13.98	2:14.55	2:15.11
240	2:15.68	2:16.25	2:16.82	2:17.39	2:17.95	2:18.52	2:19.09	2:19.66	2:20.22	2:20.79
250	2:21.36	2:21.93	2:22.49	2:23.06	2:23.63	2:24.20	2:24.77	2:25.33	2:25.90	2:26.47
260	2:27.04	2:27.60	2:28.17	2:28.74	2:29.31	2:29.88	2:30.44	2:31.01	2:31.58	2:32.15
270	2:32.71	2:33.28	2:33.85	2:34.42	2:34.98	2:35.55	2:36.12	2:36.69	2:37.26	2:37.82
280	2:38.39	2:38.96	2:39.53	2:40.09	2:40.66	2:41.23	2:41.80	2:42.36	2:42.93	2:43.50
290	2:44.07	2:44.64	2:45.20	2:45.77	2:46.34	2:46.91	2:47.47	2:48.04	2:48.61	2:49.18
300	2:49.74	2:50.31	2:50.88	2:51.45	2:52.02	2:52.58	2:53.15	2:53.72	2:54.29	2:54.85
310	2:55.42	2:55.99	2:56.56	2:57.13	2:57.69	2:58.26	2:58.83	2:59.40	2:59.96	3:00.53
320	3:01.10	3:01.67	3:02.23	3:02.80	3:03.37	3:03.94	3:04.51	3:05.07	3:05.64	3:06.21
330	3:06.78	3:07.34	3:07.91	3:08.48	3:09.05	3:09.61	3:10.18	3:10.75	3:11.32	3:11.89
340	3:12.45	3:13.02	3:13.59	3:14.16	3:14.72	3:15.29	3:15.86	3:16.43	3:16.99	3:17.56
350	3:18.13	3:18.70	3:19.27	3:19.83	3:20.40	3:20.97	3:21.54	3:22.10	3:22.67	3:23.24
360	3:23.81	3:24.38	3:24.94	3:25.51	3:26.08	3:26.65	3:27.21	3:27.78	3:28.35	3:28.92
370	3:29.48	3:30.05	3:30.62	3:31.19	3:31.76	3:32.32	3:32.89	3:33.46	3:34.03	3:34.59
380	3:35.16	3:35.73	3:36.30	3:36.86	3:37.43	3:38.00	3:38.57	3:39.14	3:39.70	3:40.27
390	3:40.84	3:41.41	3:41.97	3:42.54	3:43.11	3:43.68	3:44.24	3:44.81	3:45.38	3:45.95
400	3:46.52	3:47.08	3:47.65	3:48.22	3:48.79	3:49.35	3:49.92	3:50.49	3:51.06	3:51.63
410	3:52.19	3:52.76	3:53.33	3:53.90	3:54.46	3:55.03	3:55.60	3:56.17	3:56.73	3:57.30
420	3:57.87	3:58.44	3:59.01	3:59.57	4:00.14	4:00.71	4:01.28	4:01.84	4:02.41	4:02.98
430	4:03.55	4:04.11	4:04.68	4:05.25	4:05.82	4:06.39	4:06.95	4:07.52	4:08.09	4:08.66
440	4:09.22	4:09.79	4:10.36	4:10.93	4:11.49	4:12.06	4:12.63	4:13.20	4:13.77	4:14.33
450	4:14.90	4:15.47	4:16.04	4:16.60	4:17.17	4:17.74	4:18.31	4:18.87	4:19.44	4:20.01
460	4:20.58	4:21.15	4:21.71	4:22.28	4:22.85	4:23.42	4:23.98	4:24.55	4:25.12	4:25.69
470	4:26.26	4:26.82	4:27.39	4:27.96	4:28.53	4:29.09	4:29.66	4:30.23	4:30.80	4:31.36
480	4:31.93	4:32.50	4:33.07	4:33.64	4:34.20	4:34.77	4:35.34	4:35.91	4:36.47	4:37.04
490	4:37.61	4:38.18	4:38.74	4:39.31	4:39.88	4:40.45	4:41.02	4:41.58	4:42.15	4:42.72
500	4:43.29	4:43.85	4:44.42	4:44.99	4:45.56	4:46.12	4:46.69	4:47.26	4:47.83	4:48.40
510	4:48.96	4:49.53	4:50.10	4:50.67	4:51.23	4:51.80	4:52.37	4:52.94	4:53.51	4:54.07
520	4:54.64	4:55.21	4:55.78	4:56.34	4:56.91	4:57.48	4:58.05	4:58.61	4:59.18	4:59.75
530	5:00.32	5:00.89	5:01.45	5:02.02	5:02.59	5:03.16	5:03.72	5:04.29	5:04.86	5:05.43
540	5:05.99	5:06.56	5:07.13	5:07.70	5:08.27	5:08.83	5:09.40	5:09.97	5:10.54	5:11.10
550	5:11.67	5:12.24	5:12.81	5:13.37	5:13.94	5:14.51	5:15.08	5:15.65	5:16.21	5:16.78
560	5:17.35	5:17.92	5:18.48	5:19.05	5:19.62	5:20.19	5:20.76	5:21.32	5:21.89	5:22.46
570	5:23.03	5:23.59	5:24.16	5:24.73	5:25.30	5:25.86	5:26.43	5:27.00	5:27.57	5:28.14
580	5:28.70	5:29.27	5:29.84	5:30.41	5:30.97	5:31.54	5:32.11	5:32.68	5:33.24	5:33.81
590	5:34.38	5:34.95	5:35.52	5:36.08	5:36.65	5:37.22	5:37.79	5:38.35	5:38.92	5:39.49

♩. = 0.85; ♩ = 0.57; ♪. = 0.43; (triplet 3) ♩ 𝄾 = 0.38; ♪ = 0.28; (triplet 3) ♪𝄾𝄾 = 0.19; 𝅘𝅥𝅯 = 0.14 seconds

CLICK: 13 6/8 FRAMES; M.M.: 104.73

Click	0	1	2	3	4	5	6	7	8	9
000	0:00.00	0:00.00	0:00.57	0:01.15	0:01.72	0:02.29	0:02.86	0:03.44	0:04.01	0:04.58
010	0:05.16	0:05.73	0:06.30	0:06.88	0:07.45	0:08.02	0:08.59	0:09.17	0:09.74	0:10.31
020	0:10.89	0:11.46	0:12.03	0:12.60	0:13.18	0:13.75	0:14.32	0:14.90	0:15.47	0:16.04
030	0:16.61	0:17.19	0:17.76	0:18.33	0:18.91	0:19.48	0:20.05	0:20.63	0:21.20	0:21.77
040	0:22.34	0:22.92	0:23.49	0:24.06	0:24.64	0:25.21	0:25.78	0:26.35	0:26.93	0:27.50
050	0:28.07	0:28.65	0:29.22	0:29.79	0:30.36	0:30.94	0:31.51	0:32.08	0:32.66	0:33.23
060	0:33.80	0:34.38	0:34.95	0:35.52	0:36.09	0:36.67	0:37.24	0:37.81	0:38.39	0:38.96
070	0:39.53	0:40.10	0:40.68	0:41.25	0:41.82	0:42.40	0:42.97	0:43.54	0:44.11	0:44.69
080	0:45.26	0:45.83	0:46.41	0:46.98	0:47.55	0:48.13	0:48.70	0:49.27	0:49.84	0:50.42
090	0:50.99	0:51.56	0:52.14	0:52.71	0:53.28	0:53.85	0:54.43	0:55.00	0:55.57	0:56.15
100	0:56.72	0:57.29	0:57.86	0:58.44	0:59.01	0:59.58	1:00.16	1:00.73	1:01.30	1:01.88
110	1:02.45	1:03.02	1:03.59	1:04.17	1:04.74	1:05.31	1:05.89	1:06.46	1:07.03	1:07.60
120	1:08.18	1:08.75	1:09.32	1:09.90	1:10.47	1:11.04	1:11.61	1:12.19	1:12.76	1:13.33
130	1:13.91	1:14.48	1:15.05	1:15.62	1:16.20	1:16.77	1:17.34	1:17.92	1:18.49	1:19.06
140	1:19.64	1:20.21	1:20.78	1:21.35	1:21.93	1:22.50	1:23.07	1:23.65	1:24.22	1:24.79
150	1:25.36	1:25.94	1:26.51	1:27.08	1:27.66	1:28.23	1:28.80	1:29.38	1:29.95	1:30.52
160	1:31.09	1:31.67	1:32.24	1:32.81	1:33.39	1:33.96	1:34.53	1:35.10	1:35.68	1:36.25
170	1:36.82	1:37.40	1:37.97	1:38.54	1:39.11	1:39.69	1:40.26	1:40.83	1:41.41	1:41.98
180	1:42.55	1:43.13	1:43.70	1:44.27	1:44.84	1:45.42	1:45.99	1:46.56	1:47.14	1:47.71
190	1:48.28	1:48.85	1:49.43	1:50.00	1:50.57	1:51.15	1:51.72	1:52.29	1:52.86	1:53.44
200	1:54.01	1:54.58	1:55.16	1:55.73	1:56.30	1:56.87	1:57.45	1:58.02	1:58.59	1:59.17
210	1:59.74	2:00.31	2:00.89	2:01.46	2:02.03	2:02.60	2:03.18	2:03.75	2:04.32	2:04.90
220	2:05.47	2:06.04	2:06.61	2:07.19	2:07.76	2:08.33	2:08.91	2:09.48	2:10.05	2:10.62
230	2:11.20	2:11.77	2:12.34	2:12.92	2:13.49	2:14.06	2:14.64	2:15.21	2:15.78	2:16.35
240	2:16.93	2:17.50	2:18.07	2:18.65	2:19.22	2:19.79	2:20.36	2:20.94	2:21.51	2:22.08
250	2:22.66	2:23.23	2:23.80	2:24.38	2:24.95	2:25.52	2:26.09	2:26.67	2:27.24	2:27.81
260	2:28.39	2:28.96	2:29.53	2:30.10	2:30.68	2:31.25	2:31.82	2:32.40	2:32.97	2:33.54
270	2:34.11	2:34.69	2:35.26	2:35.83	2:36.41	2:36.98	2:37.55	2:38.13	2:38.70	2:39.27
280	2:39.84	2:40.42	2:40.99	2:41.56	2:42.14	2:42.71	2:43.28	2:43.85	2:44.43	2:45.00
290	2:45.57	2:46.15	2:46.72	2:47.29	2:47.86	2:48.44	2:49.01	2:49.58	2:50.16	2:50.73
300	2:51.30	2:51.87	2:52.45	2:53.02	2:53.59	2:54.17	2:54.74	2:55.31	2:55.89	2:56.46
310	2:57.03	2:57.60	2:58.18	2:58.75	2:59.32	2:59.90	3:00.47	3:01.04	3:01.61	3:02.19
320	3:02.76	3:03.33	3:03.91	3:04.48	3:05.05	3:05.63	3:06.20	3:06.77	3:07.34	3:07.92
330	3:08.49	3:09.06	3:09.64	3:10.21	3:10.78	3:11.35	3:11.93	3:12.50	3:13.07	3:13.65
340	3:14.22	3:14.79	3:15.36	3:15.94	3:16.51	3:17.08	3:17.66	3:18.23	3:18.80	3:19.38
350	3:19.95	3:20.52	3:21.09	3:21.67	3:22.24	3:22.81	3:23.39	3:23.96	3:24.53	3:25.10
360	3:25.68	3:26.25	3:26.82	3:27.40	3:27.97	3:28.54	3:29.11	3:29.69	3:30.26	3:30.83
370	3:31.41	3:31.98	3:32.55	3:33.12	3:33.70	3:34.27	3:34.84	3:35.42	3:35.99	3:36.56
380	3:37.14	3:37.71	3:38.28	3:38.85	3:39.43	3:40.00	3:40.57	3:41.15	3:41.72	3:42.29
390	3:42.86	3:43.44	3:44.01	3:44.58	3:45.16	3:45.73	3:46.30	3:46.88	3:47.45	3:48.02
400	3:48.59	3:49.17	3:49.74	3:50.31	3:50.89	3:51.46	3:52.03	3:52.60	3:53.18	3:53.75
410	3:54.32	3:54.90	3:55.47	3:56.04	3:56.61	3:57.19	3:57.76	3:58.33	3:58.91	3:59.48
420	4:00.05	4:00.62	4:01.20	4:01.77	4:02.34	4:02.92	4:03.49	4:04.06	4:04.64	4:05.21
430	4:05.78	4:06.35	4:06.93	4:07.50	4:08.07	4:08.65	4:09.22	4:09.79	4:10.36	4:10.94
440	4:11.51	4:12.08	4:12.66	4:13.23	4:13.80	4:14.38	4:14.95	4:15.52	4:16.09	4:16.67
450	4:17.24	4:17.81	4:18.39	4:18.96	4:19.53	4:20.10	4:20.68	4:21.25	4:21.82	4:22.40
460	4:22.97	4:23.54	4:24.11	4:24.69	4:25.26	4:25.83	4:26.41	4:26.98	4:27.55	4:28.13
470	4:28.70	4:29.27	4:29.84	4:30.42	4:30.99	4:31.56	4:32.14	4:32.71	4:33.28	4:33.85
480	4:34.43	4:35.00	4:35.57	4:36.15	4:36.72	4:37.29	4:37.86	4:38.44	4:39.01	4:39.58
490	4:40.16	4:40.73	4:41.30	4:41.87	4:42.45	4:43.02	4:43.59	4:44.17	4:44.74	4:45.31
500	4:45.89	4:46.46	4:47.03	4:47.60	4:48.18	4:48.75	4:49.32	4:49.90	4:50.47	4:51.04
510	4:51.61	4:52.19	4:52.76	4:53.33	4:53.91	4:54.48	4:55.05	4:55.63	4:56.20	4:56.77
520	4:57.34	4:57.92	4:58.49	4:59.06	4:59.64	5:00.21	5:00.78	5:01.35	5:01.93	5:02.50
530	5:03.07	5:03.65	5:04.22	5:04.79	5:05.36	5:05.94	5:06.51	5:07.08	5:07.66	5:08.23
540	5:08.80	5:09.38	5:09.95	5:10.52	5:11.09	5:11.67	5:12.24	5:12.81	5:13.39	5:13.96
550	5:14.53	5:15.10	5:15.68	5:16.25	5:16.82	5:17.40	5:17.97	5:18.54	5:19.11	5:19.69
560	5:20.26	5:20.83	5:21.41	5:21.98	5:22.55	5:23.12	5:23.70	5:24.27	5:24.84	5:25.42
570	5:25.99	5:26.56	5:27.14	5:27.71	5:28.28	5:28.85	5:29.43	5:30.00	5:30.57	5:31.15
580	5:31.72	5:32.29	5:32.86	5:33.44	5:34.01	5:34.58	5:35.16	5:35.73	5:36.30	5:36.88
590	5:37.45	5:38.02	5:38.59	5:39.17	5:39.74	5:40.31	5:40.89	5:41.46	5:42.03	5:42.60

♩. = 0.86; ♩ = 0.57; ♪. = 0.43; (triplet ♩ 𝄾) = 0.38; ♪ = 0.29; (triplet ♪ 𝄾 𝄾) = 0.19; ♬ = 0.14 seconds

CLICK: 13⅞ FRAMES; M.M.: 103.78

Click	0	1	2	3	4	5	6	7	8	9
000	0:00.00	0:00.00	0:00.58	0:01.16	0:01.73	0:02.31	0:02.89	0:03.47	0:04.05	0:04.63
010	0:05.20	0:05.78	0:06.36	0:06.94	0:07.52	0:08.09	0:08.67	0:09.25	0:09.83	0:10.41
020	0:10.98	0:11.56	0:12.14	0:12.72	0:13.30	0:13.88	0:14.45	0:15.03	0:15.61	0:16.19
030	0:16.77	0:17.34	0:17.92	0:18.50	0:19.08	0:19.66	0:20.23	0:20.81	0:21.39	0:21.97
040	0:22.55	0:23.13	0:23.70	0:24.28	0:24.86	0:25.44	0:26.02	0:26.59	0:27.17	0:27.75
050	0:28.33	0:28.91	0:29.48	0:30.06	0:30.64	0:31.22	0:31.80	0:32.38	0:32.95	0:33.53
060	0:34.11	0:34.69	0:35.27	0:35.84	0:36.42	0:37.00	0:37.58	0:38.16	0:38.73	0:39.31
070	0:39.89	0:40.47	0:41.05	0:41.63	0:42.20	0:42.78	0:43.36	0:43.94	0:44.52	0:45.09
080	0:45.67	0:46.25	0:46.83	0:47.41	0:47.98	0:48.56	0:49.14	0:49.72	0:50.30	0:50.88
090	0:51.45	0:52.03	0:52.61	0:53.19	0:53.77	0:54.34	0:54.92	0:55.50	0:56.08	0:56.66
100	0:57.23	0:57.81	0:58.39	0:58.97	0:59.55	1:00.12	1:00.70	1:01.28	1:01.86	1:02.44
110	1:03.02	1:03.59	1:04.17	1:04.75	1:05.33	1:05.91	1:06.48	1:07.06	1:07.64	1:08.22
120	1:08.80	1:09.38	1:09.95	1:10.53	1:11.11	1:11.69	1:12.27	1:12.84	1:13.42	1:14.00
130	1:14.58	1:15.16	1:15.73	1:16.31	1:16.89	1:17.47	1:18.05	1:18.63	1:19.20	1:19.78
140	1:20.36	1:20.94	1:21.52	1:22.09	1:22.67	1:23.25	1:23.83	1:24.41	1:24.98	1:25.56
150	1:26.14	1:26.72	1:27.30	1:27.88	1:28.45	1:29.03	1:29.61	1:30.19	1:30.77	1:31.34
160	1:31.92	1:32.50	1:33.08	1:33.66	1:34.23	1:34.81	1:35.39	1:35.97	1:36.55	1:37.13
170	1:37.70	1:38.28	1:38.86	1:39.44	1:40.02	1:40.59	1:41.17	1:41.75	1:42.33	1:42.91
180	1:43.48	1:44.06	1:44.64	1:45.22	1:45.80	1:46.38	1:46.95	1:47.53	1:48.11	1:48.69
190	1:49.27	1:49.84	1:50.42	1:51.00	1:51.58	1:52.16	1:52.73	1:53.31	1:53.89	1:54.47
200	1:55.05	1:55.63	1:56.20	1:56.78	1:57.36	1:57.94	1:58.52	1:59.09	1:59.67	2:00.25
210	2:00.83	2:01.41	2:01.98	2:02.56	2:03.14	2:03.72	2:04.30	2:04.87	2:05.45	2:06.03
220	2:06.61	2:07.19	2:07.77	2:08.34	2:08.92	2:09.50	2:10.08	2:10.66	2:11.23	2:11.81
230	2:12.39	2:12.97	2:13.55	2:14.12	2:14.70	2:15.28	2:15.86	2:16.44	2:17.02	2:17.59
240	2:18.17	2:18.75	2:19.33	2:19.91	2:20.48	2:21.06	2:21.64	2:22.22	2:22.80	2:23.38
250	2:23.95	2:24.53	2:25.11	2:25.69	2:26.27	2:26.84	2:27.42	2:28.00	2:28.58	2:29.16
260	2:29.73	2:30.31	2:30.89	2:31.47	2:32.05	2:32.63	2:33.20	2:33.78	2:34.36	2:34.94
270	2:35.52	2:36.09	2:36.67	2:37.25	2:37.83	2:38.41	2:38.98	2:39.56	2:40.14	2:40.72
280	2:41.30	2:41.88	2:42.45	2:43.03	2:43.61	2:44.19	2:44.77	2:45.34	2:45.92	2:46.50
290	2:47.08	2:47.66	2:48.23	2:48.81	2:49.39	2:49.97	2:50.55	2:51.13	2:51.70	2:52.28
300	2:52.86	2:53.44	2:54.02	2:54.59	2:55.17	2:55.75	2:56.33	2:56.91	2:57.48	2:58.06
310	2:58.64	2:59.22	2:59.80	3:00.38	3:00.95	3:01.53	3:02.11	3:02.69	3:03.27	3:03.84
320	3:04.42	3:05.00	3:05.58	3:06.16	3:06.73	3:07.31	3:07.89	3:08.47	3:09.05	3:09.62
330	3:10.20	3:10.78	3:11.36	3:11.94	3:12.52	3:13.09	3:13.67	3:14.25	3:14.83	3:15.41
340	3:15.98	3:16.56	3:17.14	3:17.72	3:18.30	3:18.87	3:19.45	3:20.03	3:20.61	3:21.19
350	3:21.77	3:22.34	3:22.92	3:23.50	3:24.08	3:24.66	3:25.23	3:25.81	3:26.39	3:26.97
360	3:27.55	3:28.13	3:28.70	3:29.28	3:29.86	3:30.44	3:31.02	3:31.59	3:32.17	3:32.75
370	3:33.33	3:33.91	3:34.48	3:35.06	3:35.64	3:36.22	3:36.80	3:37.38	3:37.95	3:38.53
380	3:39.11	3:39.69	3:40.27	3:40.84	3:41.42	3:42.00	3:42.58	3:43.16	3:43.73	3:44.31
390	3:44.89	3:45.47	3:46.05	3:46.63	3:47.20	3:47.78	3:48.36	3:48.94	3:49.52	3:50.09
400	3:50.67	3:51.25	3:51.83	3:52.41	3:52.98	3:53.56	3:54.14	3:54.72	3:55.30	3:55.88
410	3:56.45	3:57.03	3:57.61	3:58.19	3:58.77	3:59.34	3:59.92	4:00.50	4:01.08	4:01.66
420	4:02.23	4:02.81	4:03.39	4:03.97	4:04.55	4:05.13	4:05.70	4:06.28	4:06.86	4:07.44
430	4:08.02	4:08.59	4:09.17	4:09.75	4:10.33	4:10.91	4:11.48	4:12.06	4:12.64	4:13.22
440	4:13.80	4:14.38	4:14.95	4:15.53	4:16.11	4:16.69	4:17.27	4:17.84	4:18.42	4:19.00
450	4:19.58	4:20.16	4:20.73	4:21.31	4:21.89	4:22.47	4:23.05	4:23.63	4:24.20	4:24.78
460	4:25.36	4:25.94	4:26.52	4:27.09	4:27.67	4:28.25	4:28.83	4:29.41	4:29.98	4:30.56
470	4:31.14	4:31.72	4:32.30	4:32.88	4:33.45	4:34.03	4:34.61	4:35.19	4:35.77	4:36.34
480	4:36.92	4:37.50	4:38.08	4:38.66	4:39.23	4:39.81	4:40.39	4:40.97	4:41.55	4:42.13
490	4:42.70	4:43.28	4:43.86	4:44.44	4:45.02	4:45.59	4:46.17	4:46.75	4:47.33	4:47.91
500	4:48.48	4:49.06	4:49.64	4:50.22	4:50.80	4:51.38	4:51.95	4:52.53	4:53.11	4:53.69
510	4:54.27	4:54.84	4:55.42	4:56.00	4:56.58	4:57.16	4:57.73	4:58.31	4:58.89	4:59.47
520	5:00.05	5:00.62	5:01.20	5:01.78	5:02.36	5:02.94	5:03.52	5:04.09	5:04.67	5:05.25
530	5:05.83	5:06.41	5:06.98	5:07.56	5:08.14	5:08.72	5:09.30	5:09.87	5:10.45	5:11.03
540	5:11.61	5:12.19	5:12.77	5:13.34	5:13.92	5:14.50	5:15.08	5:15.66	5:16.23	5:16.81
550	5:17.39	5:17.97	5:18.55	5:19.12	5:19.70	5:20.28	5:20.86	5:21.44	5:22.02	5:22.59
560	5:23.17	5:23.75	5:24.33	5:24.91	5:25.48	5:26.06	5:26.64	5:27.22	5:27.80	5:28.37
570	5:28.95	5:29.53	5:30.11	5:30.69	5:31.27	5:31.84	5:32.42	5:33.00	5:33.58	5:34.16
580	5:34.73	5:35.31	5:35.89	5:36.47	5:37.05	5:37.63	5:38.20	5:38.78	5:39.36	5:39.94
590	5:40.52	5:41.09	5:41.67	5:42.25	5:42.83	5:43.41	5:43.98	5:44.56	5:45.14	5:45.72

♩. = 0.87; ♩ = 0.58; ♪. = 0.43; (triplet) ♩ 𝄾 = 0.39; ♪ = 0.29; (triplet) ♪𝄾𝄾 = 0.19; 𝅘𝅥𝅯 = 0.14 seconds

CLICK: 14 0/8 FRAMES; M.M.: 102.86

Click	0	1	2	3	4	5	6	7	8	9
000	0:00.00	0:00.00	0:00.58	0:01.17	0:01.75	0:02.33	0:02.92	0:03.50	0:04.08	0:04.67
010	0:05.25	0:05.83	0:06.42	0:07.00	0:07.58	0:08.17	0:08.75	0:09.33	0:09.92	0:10.50
020	0:11.08	0:11.67	0:12.25	0:12.83	0:13.42	0:14.00	0:14.58	0:15.17	0:15.75	0:16.33
030	0:16.92	0:17.50	0:18.08	0:18.67	0:19.25	0:19.83	0:20.42	0:21.00	0:21.58	0:22.17
040	0:22.75	0:23.33	0:23.92	0:24.50	0:25.08	0:25.67	0:26.25	0:26.83	0:27.42	0:28.00
050	0:28.58	0:29.17	0:29.75	0:30.33	0:30.92	0:31.50	0:32.08	0:32.67	0:33.25	0:33.83
060	0:34.42	0:35.00	0:35.58	0:36.17	0:36.75	0:37.33	0:37.92	0:38.50	0:39.08	0:39.67
070	0:40.25	0:40.83	0:41.42	0:42.00	0:42.58	0:43.17	0:43.75	0:44.33	0:44.92	0:45.50
080	0:46.08	0:46.67	0:47.25	0:47.83	0:48.42	0:49.00	0:49.58	0:50.17	0:50.75	0:51.33
090	0:51.92	0:52.50	0:53.08	0:53.67	0:54.25	0:54.83	0:55.42	0:56.00	0:56.58	0:57.17
100	0:57.75	0:58.33	0:58.92	0:59.50	1:00.08	1:00.67	1:01.25	1:01.83	1:02.42	1:03.00
110	1:03.58	1:04.17	1:04.75	1:05.33	1:05.92	1:06.50	1:07.08	1:07.67	1:08.25	1:08.83
120	1:09.42	1:10.00	1:10.58	1:11.17	1:11.75	1:12.33	1:12.92	1:13.50	1:14.08	1:14.67
130	1:15.25	1:15.83	1:16.42	1:17.00	1:17.58	1:18.17	1:18.75	1:19.33	1:19.92	1:20.50
140	1:21.08	1:21.67	1:22.25	1:22.83	1:23.42	1:24.00	1:24.58	1:25.17	1:25.75	1:26.33
150	1:26.92	1:27.50	1:28.08	1:28.67	1:29.25	1:29.83	1:30.42	1:31.00	1:31.58	1:32.17
160	1:32.75	1:33.33	1:33.92	1:34.50	1:35.08	1:35.67	1:36.25	1:36.83	1:37.42	1:38.00
170	1:38.58	1:39.17	1:39.75	1:40.33	1:40.92	1:41.50	1:42.08	1:42.67	1:43.25	1:43.83
180	1:44.42	1:45.00	1:45.58	1:46.17	1:46.75	1:47.33	1:47.92	1:48.50	1:49.08	1:49.67
190	1:50.25	1:50.83	1:51.42	1:52.00	1:52.58	1:53.17	1:53.75	1:54.33	1:54.92	1:55.50
200	1:56.08	1:56.67	1:57.25	1:57.83	1:58.42	1:59.00	1:59.58	2:00.17	2:00.75	2:01.33
210	2:01.92	2:02.50	2:03.08	2:03.67	2:04.25	2:04.83	2:05.42	2:06.00	2:06.58	2:07.17
220	2:07.75	2:08.33	2:08.92	2:09.50	2:10.08	2:10.67	2:11.25	2:11.83	2:12.42	2:13.00
230	2:13.58	2:14.17	2:14.75	2:15.33	2:15.92	2:16.50	2:17.08	2:17.67	2:18.25	2:18.83
240	2:19.42	2:20.00	2:20.58	2:21.17	2:21.75	2:22.33	2:22.92	2:23.50	2:24.08	2:24.67
250	2:25.25	2:25.83	2:26.42	2:27.00	2:27.58	2:28.17	2:28.75	2:29.33	2:29.92	2:30.50
260	2:31.08	2:31.67	2:32.25	2:32.83	2:33.42	2:34.00	2:34.58	2:35.17	2:35.75	2:36.33
270	2:36.92	2:37.50	2:38.08	2:38.67	2:39.25	2:39.83	2:40.42	2:41.00	2:41.58	2:42.17
280	2:42.75	2:43.33	2:43.92	2:44.50	2:45.08	2:45.67	2:46.25	2:46.83	2:47.42	2:48.00
290	2:48.58	2:49.17	2:49.75	2:50.33	2:50.92	2:51.50	2:52.08	2:52.67	2:53.25	2:53.83
300	2:54.42	2:55.00	2:55.58	2:56.17	2:56.75	2:57.33	2:57.92	2:58.50	2:59.08	2:59.67
310	3:00.25	3:00.83	3:01.42	3:02.00	3:02.58	3:03.17	3:03.75	3:04.33	3:04.92	3:05.50
320	3:06.08	3:06.67	3:07.25	3:07.83	3:08.42	3:09.00	3:09.58	3:10.17	3:10.75	3:11.33
330	3:11.92	3:12.50	3:13.08	3:13.67	3:14.25	3:14.83	3:15.42	3:16.00	3:16.58	3:17.17
340	3:17.75	3:18.33	3:18.92	3:19.50	3:20.08	3:20.67	3:21.25	3:21.83	3:22.42	3:23.00
350	3:23.58	3:24.17	3:24.75	3:25.33	3:25.92	3:26.50	3:27.08	3:27.67	3:28.25	3:28.83
360	3:29.42	3:30.00	3:30.58	3:31.17	3:31.75	3:32.33	3:32.92	3:33.50	3:34.08	3:34.67
370	3:35.25	3:35.83	3:36.42	3:37.00	3:37.58	3:38.17	3:38.75	3:39.33	3:39.92	3:40.50
380	3:41.08	3:41.67	3:42.25	3:42.83	3:43.42	3:44.00	3:44.58	3:45.17	3:45.75	3:46.33
390	3:46.92	3:47.50	3:48.08	3:48.67	3:49.25	3:49.83	3:50.42	3:51.00	3:51.58	3:52.17
400	3:52.75	3:53.33	3:53.92	3:54.50	3:55.08	3:55.67	3:56.25	3:56.83	3:57.42	3:58.00
410	3:58.58	3:59.17	3:59.75	4:00.33	4:00.92	4:01.50	4:02.08	4:02.67	4:03.25	4:03.83
420	4:04.42	4:05.00	4:05.58	4:06.17	4:06.75	4:07.33	4:07.92	4:08.50	4:09.08	4:09.67
430	4:10.25	4:10.83	4:11.42	4:12.00	4:12.58	4:13.17	4:13.75	4:14.33	4:14.92	4:15.50
440	4:16.08	4:16.67	4:17.25	4:17.83	4:18.42	4:19.00	4:19.58	4:20.17	4:20.75	4:21.33
450	4:21.92	4:22.50	4:23.08	4:23.67	4:24.25	4:24.83	4:25.42	4:26.00	4:26.58	4:27.17
460	4:27.75	4:28.33	4:28.92	4:29.50	4:30.08	4:30.67	4:31.25	4:31.83	4:32.42	4:33.00
470	4:33.58	4:34.17	4:34.75	4:35.33	4:35.92	4:36.50	4:37.08	4:37.67	4:38.25	4:38.83
480	4:39.42	4:40.00	4:40.58	4:41.17	4:41.75	4:42.33	4:42.92	4:43.50	4:44.08	4:44.67
490	4:45.25	4:45.83	4:46.42	4:47.00	4:47.58	4:48.17	4:48.75	4:49.33	4:49.92	4:50.50
500	4:51.08	4:51.67	4:52.25	4:52.83	4:53.42	4:54.00	4:54.58	4:55.17	4:55.75	4:56.33
510	4:56.92	4:57.50	4:58.08	4:58.67	4:59.25	4:59.83	5:00.42	5:01.00	5:01.58	5:02.17
520	5:02.75	5:03.33	5:03.92	5:04.50	5:05.08	5:05.67	5:06.25	5:06.83	5:07.42	5:08.00
530	5:08.58	5:09.17	5:09.75	5:10.33	5:10.92	5:11.50	5:12.08	5:12.67	5:13.25	5:13.83
540	5:14.42	5:15.00	5:15.58	5:16.17	5:16.75	5:17.33	5:17.92	5:18.50	5:19.08	5:19.67
550	5:20.25	5:20.83	5:21.42	5:22.00	5:22.58	5:23.17	5:23.75	5:24.33	5:24.92	5:25.50
560	5:26.08	5:26.67	5:27.25	5:27.83	5:28.42	5:29.00	5:29.58	5:30.17	5:30.75	5:31.33
570	5:31.92	5:32.50	5:33.08	5:33.67	5:34.25	5:34.83	5:35.42	5:36.00	5:36.58	5:37.17
580	5:37.75	5:38.33	5:38.92	5:39.50	5:40.08	5:40.67	5:41.25	5:41.83	5:42.42	5:43.00
590	5:43.58	5:44.17	5:44.75	5:45.33	5:45.92	5:46.50	5:47.08	5:47.67	5:48.25	5:48.83

♩. = 0.88; ♩ = 0.58; ♪. = 0.44; triplet (♩ 𝄾) = 0.39; ♪ = 0.29; triplet (♪ 𝄾 𝄾) = 0.19; 𝅘𝅥𝅯 = 0.15 seconds

CLICK: 14⅛ FRAMES; M.M.: 101.95

Click	0	1	2	3	4	5	6	7	8	9
000	0:00.00	0:00.00	0:00.59	0:01.18	0:01.77	0:02.35	0:02.94	0:03.53	0:04.12	0:04.71
010	0:05.30	0:05.89	0:06.47	0:07.06	0:07.65	0:08.24	0:08.83	0:09.42	0:10.01	0:10.59
020	0:11.18	0:11.77	0:12.36	0:12.95	0:13.54	0:14.13	0:14.71	0:15.30	0:15.89	0:16.48
030	0:17.07	0:17.66	0:18.24	0:18.83	0:19.42	0:20.01	0:20.60	0:21.19	0:21.78	0:22.36
040	0:22.95	0:23.54	0:24.13	0:24.72	0:25.31	0:25.90	0:26.48	0:27.07	0:27.66	0:28.25
050	0:28.84	0:29.43	0:30.02	0:30.60	0:31.19	0:31.78	0:32.37	0:32.96	0:33.55	0:34.14
060	0:34.72	0:35.31	0:35.90	0:36.49	0:37.08	0:37.67	0:38.26	0:38.84	0:39.43	0:40.02
070	0:40.61	0:41.20	0:41.79	0:42.38	0:42.96	0:43.55	0:44.14	0:44.73	0:45.32	0:45.91
080	0:46.49	0:47.08	0:47.67	0:48.26	0:48.85	0:49.44	0:50.03	0:50.61	0:51.20	0:51.79
090	0:52.38	0:52.97	0:53.56	0:54.15	0:54.73	0:55.32	0:55.91	0:56.50	0:57.09	0:57.68
100	0:58.27	0:58.85	0:59.44	1:00.03	1:00.62	1:01.21	1:01.80	1:02.39	1:02.97	1:03.56
110	1:04.15	1:04.74	1:05.33	1:05.92	1:06.51	1:07.09	1:07.68	1:08.27	1:08.86	1:09.45
120	1:10.04	1:10.63	1:11.21	1:11.80	1:12.39	1:12.98	1:13.57	1:14.16	1:14.74	1:15.33
130	1:15.92	1:16.51	1:17.10	1:17.69	1:18.28	1:18.86	1:19.45	1:20.04	1:20.63	1:21.22
140	1:21.81	1:22.40	1:22.98	1:23.57	1:24.16	1:24.75	1:25.34	1:25.93	1:26.52	1:27.10
150	1:27.69	1:28.28	1:28.87	1:29.46	1:30.05	1:30.64	1:31.22	1:31.81	1:32.40	1:32.99
160	1:33.58	1:34.17	1:34.76	1:35.34	1:35.93	1:36.52	1:37.11	1:37.70	1:38.29	1:38.88
170	1:39.46	1:40.05	1:40.64	1:41.23	1:41.82	1:42.41	1:42.99	1:43.58	1:44.17	1:44.76
180	1:45.35	1:45.94	1:46.53	1:47.11	1:47.70	1:48.29	1:48.88	1:49.47	1:50.06	1:50.65
190	1:51.23	1:51.82	1:52.41	1:53.00	1:53.59	1:54.18	1:54.77	1:55.35	1:55.94	1:56.53
200	1:57.12	1:57.71	1:58.30	1:58.89	1:59.47	2:00.06	2:00.65	2:01.24	2:01.83	2:02.42
210	2:03.01	2:03.59	2:04.18	2:04.77	2:05.36	2:05.95	2:06.54	2:07.13	2:07.71	2:08.30
220	2:08.89	2:09.48	2:10.07	2:10.66	2:11.24	2:11.83	2:12.42	2:13.01	2:13.60	2:14.19
230	2:14.78	2:15.36	2:15.95	2:16.54	2:17.13	2:17.72	2:18.31	2:18.90	2:19.48	2:20.07
240	2:20.66	2:21.25	2:21.84	2:22.43	2:23.02	2:23.60	2:24.19	2:24.78	2:25.37	2:25.96
250	2:26.55	2:27.14	2:27.72	2:28.31	2:28.90	2:29.49	2:30.08	2:30.67	2:31.26	2:31.84
260	2:32.43	2:33.02	2:33.61	2:34.20	2:34.79	2:35.38	2:35.96	2:36.55	2:37.14	2:37.73
270	2:38.32	2:38.91	2:39.49	2:40.08	2:40.67	2:41.26	2:41.85	2:42.44	2:43.03	2:43.61
280	2:44.20	2:44.79	2:45.38	2:45.97	2:46.56	2:47.15	2:47.73	2:48.32	2:48.91	2:49.50
290	2:50.09	2:50.68	2:51.27	2:51.85	2:52.44	2:53.03	2:53.62	2:54.21	2:54.80	2:55.39
300	2:55.97	2:56.56	2:57.15	2:57.74	2:58.33	2:58.92	2:59.51	3:00.09	3:00.68	3:01.27
310	3:01.86	3:02.45	3:03.04	3:03.63	3:04.21	3:04.80	3:05.39	3:05.98	3:06.57	3:07.16
320	3:07.74	3:08.33	3:08.92	3:09.51	3:10.10	3:10.69	3:11.28	3:11.86	3:12.45	3:13.04
330	3:13.63	3:14.22	3:14.81	3:15.40	3:15.98	3:16.57	3:17.16	3:17.75	3:18.34	3:18.93
340	3:19.52	3:20.10	3:20.69	3:21.28	3:21.87	3:22.46	3:23.05	3:23.64	3:24.22	3:24.81
350	3:25.40	3:25.99	3:26.58	3:27.17	3:27.76	3:28.34	3:28.93	3:29.52	3:30.11	3:30.70
360	3:31.29	3:31.88	3:32.46	3:33.05	3:33.64	3:34.23	3:34.82	3:35.41	3:35.99	3:36.58
370	3:37.17	3:37.76	3:38.35	3:38.94	3:39.53	3:40.11	3:40.70	3:41.29	3:41.88	3:42.47
380	3:43.06	3:43.65	3:44.23	3:44.82	3:45.41	3:46.00	3:46.59	3:47.18	3:47.77	3:48.35
390	3:48.94	3:49.53	3:50.12	3:50.71	3:51.30	3:51.89	3:52.47	3:53.06	3:53.65	3:54.24
400	3:54.83	3:55.42	3:56.01	3:56.59	3:57.18	3:57.77	3:58.36	3:58.95	3:59.54	4:00.13
410	4:00.71	4:01.30	4:01.89	4:02.48	4:03.07	4:03.66	4:04.24	4:04.83	4:05.42	4:06.01
420	4:06.60	4:07.19	4:07.78	4:08.36	4:08.95	4:09.54	4:10.13	4:10.72	4:11.31	4:11.90
430	4:12.48	4:13.07	4:13.66	4:14.25	4:14.84	4:15.43	4:16.02	4:16.60	4:17.19	4:17.78
440	4:18.37	4:18.96	4:19.55	4:20.14	4:20.72	4:21.31	4:21.90	4:22.49	4:23.08	4:23.67
450	4:24.26	4:24.84	4:25.43	4:26.02	4:26.61	4:27.20	4:27.79	4:28.38	4:28.96	4:29.55
460	4:30.14	4:30.73	4:31.32	4:31.91	4:32.49	4:33.08	4:33.67	4:34.26	4:34.85	4:35.44
470	4:36.03	4:36.61	4:37.20	4:37.79	4:38.38	4:38.97	4:39.56	4:40.15	4:40.73	4:41.32
480	4:41.91	4:42.50	4:43.09	4:43.68	4:44.27	4:44.85	4:45.44	4:46.03	4:46.62	4:47.21
490	4:47.80	4:48.39	4:48.97	4:49.56	4:50.15	4:50.74	4:51.33	4:51.92	4:52.51	4:53.09
500	4:53.68	4:54.27	4:54.86	4:55.45	4:56.04	4:56.63	4:57.21	4:57.80	4:58.39	4:58.98
510	4:59.57	5:00.16	5:00.74	5:01.33	5:01.92	5:02.51	5:03.10	5:03.69	5:04.28	5:04.86
520	5:05.45	5:06.04	5:06.63	5:07.22	5:07.81	5:08.40	5:08.98	5:09.57	5:10.16	5:10.75
530	5:11.34	5:11.93	5:12.52	5:13.10	5:13.69	5:14.28	5:14.87	5:15.46	5:16.05	5:16.64
540	5:17.22	5:17.81	5:18.40	5:18.99	5:19.58	5:20.17	5:20.76	5:21.34	5:21.93	5:22.52
550	5:23.11	5:23.70	5:24.29	5:24.88	5:25.46	5:26.05	5:26.64	5:27.23	5:27.82	5:28.41
560	5:28.99	5:29.58	5:30.17	5:30.76	5:31.35	5:31.94	5:32.53	5:33.11	5:33.70	5:34.29
570	5:34.88	5:35.47	5:36.06	5:36.65	5:37.23	5:37.82	5:38.41	5:39.00	5:39.59	5:40.18
580	5:40.77	5:41.35	5:41.94	5:42.53	5:43.12	5:43.71	5:44.30	5:44.89	5:45.47	5:46.06
590	5:46.65	5:47.24	5:47.83	5:48.42	5:49.01	5:49.59	5:50.18	5:50.77	5:51.36	5:51.95

♩. = 0.88; ♩ = 0.59; ♪. = 0.44; (triplet) ♩ 𝄾 = 0.39; ♪ = 0.29; (triplet) ♪ 𝄾 𝄾 = 0.20; 𝅘𝅥𝅯 = 0.15 seconds

CLICK: 14 2/8 FRAMES; M.M.: 101.05

Click	0	1	2	3	4	5	6	7	8	9
000	0:00.00	0:00.00	0:00.59	0:01.19	0:01.78	0:02.38	0:02.97	0:03.56	0:04.16	0:04.75
010	0:05.34	0:05.94	0:06.53	0:07.13	0:07.72	0:08.31	0:08.91	0:09.50	0:10.09	0:10.69
020	0:11.28	0:11.88	0:12.47	0:13.06	0:13.66	0:14.25	0:14.84	0:15.44	0:16.03	0:16.63
030	0:17.22	0:17.81	0:18.41	0:19.00	0:19.59	0:20.19	0:20.78	0:21.38	0:21.97	0:22.56
040	0:23.16	0:23.75	0:24.34	0:24.94	0:25.53	0:26.13	0:26.72	0:27.31	0:27.91	0:28.50
050	0:29.09	0:29.69	0:30.28	0:30.88	0:31.47	0:32.06	0:32.66	0:33.25	0:33.84	0:34.44
060	0:35.03	0:35.63	0:36.22	0:36.81	0:37.41	0:38.00	0:38.59	0:39.19	0:39.78	0:40.38
070	0:40.97	0:41.56	0:42.16	0:42.75	0:43.34	0:43.94	0:44.53	0:45.13	0:45.72	0:46.31
080	0:46.91	0:47.50	0:48.09	0:48.69	0:49.28	0:49.88	0:50.47	0:51.06	0:51.66	0:52.25
090	0:52.84	0:53.44	0:54.03	0:54.63	0:55.22	0:55.81	0:56.41	0:57.00	0:57.59	0:58.19
100	0:58.78	0:59.38	0:59.97	1:00.56	1:01.16	1:01.75	1:02.34	1:02.94	1:03.53	1:04.13
110	1:04.72	1:05.31	1:05.91	1:06.50	1:07.09	1:07.69	1:08.28	1:08.88	1:09.47	1:10.06
120	1:10.66	1:11.25	1:11.84	1:12.44	1:13.03	1:13.63	1:14.22	1:14.81	1:15.41	1:16.00
130	1:16.59	1:17.19	1:17.78	1:18.37	1:18.97	1:19.56	1:20.16	1:20.75	1:21.34	1:21.94
140	1:22.53	1:23.12	1:23.72	1:24.31	1:24.91	1:25.50	1:26.09	1:26.69	1:27.28	1:27.87
150	1:28.47	1:29.06	1:29.66	1:30.25	1:30.84	1:31.44	1:32.03	1:32.62	1:33.22	1:33.81
160	1:34.41	1:35.00	1:35.59	1:36.19	1:36.78	1:37.38	1:37.97	1:38.56	1:39.16	1:39.75
170	1:40.34	1:40.94	1:41.53	1:42.13	1:42.72	1:43.31	1:43.91	1:44.50	1:45.09	1:45.69
180	1:46.28	1:46.88	1:47.47	1:48.06	1:48.66	1:49.25	1:49.84	1:50.44	1:51.03	1:51.63
190	1:52.22	1:52.81	1:53.41	1:54.00	1:54.59	1:55.19	1:55.78	1:56.38	1:56.97	1:57.56
200	1:58.16	1:58.75	1:59.34	1:59.94	2:00.53	2:01.12	2:01.72	2:02.31	2:02.91	2:03.50
210	2:04.09	2:04.69	2:05.28	2:05.87	2:06.47	2:07.06	2:07.66	2:08.25	2:08.84	2:09.44
220	2:10.03	2:10.62	2:11.22	2:11.81	2:12.41	2:13.00	2:13.59	2:14.19	2:14.78	2:15.37
230	2:15.97	2:16.56	2:17.16	2:17.75	2:18.34	2:18.94	2:19.53	2:20.12	2:20.72	2:21.31
240	2:21.91	2:22.50	2:23.09	2:23.69	2:24.28	2:24.87	2:25.47	2:26.06	2:26.66	2:27.25
250	2:27.84	2:28.44	2:29.03	2:29.62	2:30.22	2:30.81	2:31.41	2:32.00	2:32.59	2:33.19
260	2:33.78	2:34.38	2:34.97	2:35.56	2:36.16	2:36.75	2:37.34	2:37.94	2:38.53	2:39.13
270	2:39.72	2:40.31	2:40.91	2:41.50	2:42.09	2:42.69	2:43.28	2:43.88	2:44.47	2:45.06
280	2:45.66	2:46.25	2:46.84	2:47.44	2:48.03	2:48.63	2:49.22	2:49.81	2:50.41	2:51.00
290	2:51.59	2:52.19	2:52.78	2:53.38	2:53.97	2:54.56	2:55.16	2:55.75	2:56.34	2:56.94
300	2:57.53	2:58.13	2:58.72	2:59.31	2:59.91	3:00.50	3:01.09	3:01.69	3:02.28	3:02.87
310	3:03.47	3:04.06	3:04.66	3:05.25	3:05.84	3:06.44	3:07.03	3:07.62	3:08.22	3:08.81
320	3:09.41	3:10.00	3:10.59	3:11.19	3:11.78	3:12.37	3:12.97	3:13.56	3:14.16	3:14.75
330	3:15.34	3:15.94	3:16.53	3:17.12	3:17.72	3:18.31	3:18.91	3:19.50	3:20.09	3:20.69
340	3:21.28	3:21.87	3:22.47	3:23.06	3:23.66	3:24.25	3:24.84	3:25.44	3:26.03	3:26.62
350	3:27.22	3:27.81	3:28.41	3:29.00	3:29.59	3:30.19	3:30.78	3:31.37	3:31.97	3:32.56
360	3:33.16	3:33.75	3:34.34	3:34.94	3:35.53	3:36.12	3:36.72	3:37.31	3:37.91	3:38.50
370	3:39.09	3:39.69	3:40.28	3:40.87	3:41.47	3:42.06	3:42.66	3:43.25	3:43.84	3:44.44
380	3:45.03	3:45.62	3:46.22	3:46.81	3:47.41	3:48.00	3:48.59	3:49.19	3:49.78	3:50.38
390	3:50.97	3:51.56	3:52.16	3:52.75	3:53.34	3:53.94	3:54.53	3:55.13	3:55.72	3:56.31
400	3:56.91	3:57.50	3:58.09	3:58.69	3:59.28	3:59.88	4:00.47	4:01.06	4:01.66	4:02.25
410	4:02.84	4:03.44	4:04.03	4:04.62	4:05.22	4:05.81	4:06.41	4:07.00	4:07.59	4:08.19
420	4:08.78	4:09.38	4:09.97	4:10.56	4:11.16	4:11.75	4:12.34	4:12.94	4:13.53	4:14.12
430	4:14.72	4:15.31	4:15.91	4:16.50	4:17.09	4:17.69	4:18.28	4:18.87	4:19.47	4:20.06
440	4:20.66	4:21.25	4:21.84	4:22.44	4:23.03	4:23.62	4:24.22	4:24.81	4:25.41	4:26.00
450	4:26.59	4:27.19	4:27.78	4:28.37	4:28.97	4:29.56	4:30.16	4:30.75	4:31.34	4:31.94
460	4:32.53	4:33.13	4:33.72	4:34.31	4:34.91	4:35.50	4:36.09	4:36.69	4:37.28	4:37.87
470	4:38.47	4:39.06	4:39.66	4:40.25	4:40.84	4:41.44	4:42.03	4:42.63	4:43.22	4:43.81
480	4:44.41	4:45.00	4:45.59	4:46.19	4:46.78	4:47.37	4:47.97	4:48.56	4:49.16	4:49.75
490	4:50.34	4:50.94	4:51.53	4:52.13	4:52.72	4:53.31	4:53.91	4:54.50	4:55.09	4:55.69
500	4:56.28	4:56.87	4:57.47	4:58.06	4:58.66	4:59.25	4:59.84	5:00.44	5:01.03	5:01.63
510	5:02.22	5:02.81	5:03.41	5:04.00	5:04.59	5:05.19	5:05.78	5:06.37	5:06.97	5:07.56
520	5:08.16	5:08.75	5:09.34	5:09.94	5:10.53	5:11.13	5:11.72	5:12.31	5:12.91	5:13.50
530	5:14.09	5:14.69	5:15.28	5:15.87	5:16.47	5:17.06	5:17.66	5:18.25	5:18.84	5:19.44
540	5:20.03	5:20.63	5:21.22	5:21.81	5:22.41	5:23.00	5:23.59	5:24.19	5:24.78	5:25.37
550	5:25.97	5:26.56	5:27.16	5:27.75	5:28.34	5:28.94	5:29.53	5:30.12	5:30.72	5:31.31
560	5:31.91	5:32.50	5:33.09	5:33.69	5:34.28	5:34.87	5:35.47	5:36.06	5:36.66	5:37.25
570	5:37.84	5:38.44	5:39.03	5:39.62	5:40.22	5:40.81	5:41.41	5:42.00	5:42.59	5:43.19
580	5:43.78	5:44.38	5:44.97	5:45.56	5:46.16	5:46.75	5:47.34	5:47.94	5:48.53	5:49.12
590	5:49.72	5:50.31	5:50.91	5:51.50	5:52.09	5:52.69	5:53.28	5:53.88	5:54.47	5:55.06

♩. = 0.89; ♩ = 0.59; ♪. = 0.45; (triplet) ♩ 𝄾 = 0.40; ♪ = 0.30; (triplet) ♪ 𝄾 𝄾 = 0.20; 𝅘𝅥𝅯 = 0.15 seconds

CLICK: 14⅜ FRAMES; M.M.: 100.17

Click	0	1	2	3	4	5	6	7	8	9
000	0:00.00	0:00.00	0:00.60	0:01.20	0:01.80	0:02.40	0:02.99	0:03.59	0:04.19	0:04.79
010	0:05.39	0:05.99	0:06.59	0:07.19	0:07.79	0:08.39	0:08.98	0:09.58	0:10.18	0:10.78
020	0:11.38	0:11.98	0:12.58	0:13.18	0:13.78	0:14.38	0:14.97	0:15.57	0:16.17	0:16.77
030	0:17.37	0:17.97	0:18.57	0:19.17	0:19.77	0:20.36	0:20.96	0:21.56	0:22.16	0:22.76
040	0:23.36	0:23.96	0:24.56	0:25.16	0:25.76	0:26.35	0:26.95	0:27.55	0:28.15	0:28.75
050	0:29.35	0:29.95	0:30.55	0:31.15	0:31.74	0:32.34	0:32.94	0:33.54	0:34.14	0:34.74
060	0:35.34	0:35.94	0:36.54	0:37.14	0:37.73	0:38.33	0:38.93	0:39.53	0:40.13	0:40.73
070	0:41.33	0:41.93	0:42.53	0:43.13	0:43.72	0:44.32	0:44.92	0:45.52	0:46.12	0:46.72
080	0:47.32	0:47.92	0:48.52	0:49.11	0:49.71	0:50.31	0:50.91	0:51.51	0:52.11	0:52.71
090	0:53.31	0:53.91	0:54.51	0:55.10	0:55.70	0:56.30	0:56.90	0:57.50	0:58.10	0:58.70
100	0:59.30	0:59.90	1:00.49	1:01.09	1:01.69	1:02.29	1:02.89	1:03.49	1:04.09	1:04.69
110	1:05.29	1:05.89	1:06.48	1:07.08	1:07.68	1:08.28	1:08.88	1:09.48	1:10.08	1:10.68
120	1:11.28	1:11.87	1:12.47	1:13.07	1:13.67	1:14.27	1:14.87	1:15.47	1:16.07	1:16.67
130	1:17.27	1:17.86	1:18.46	1:19.06	1:19.66	1:20.26	1:20.86	1:21.46	1:22.06	1:22.66
140	1:23.26	1:23.85	1:24.45	1:25.05	1:25.65	1:26.25	1:26.85	1:27.45	1:28.05	1:28.65
150	1:29.24	1:29.84	1:30.44	1:31.04	1:31.64	1:32.24	1:32.84	1:33.44	1:34.04	1:34.64
160	1:35.23	1:35.83	1:36.43	1:37.03	1:37.63	1:38.23	1:38.83	1:39.43	1:40.03	1:40.63
170	1:41.22	1:41.82	1:42.42	1:43.02	1:43.62	1:44.22	1:44.82	1:45.42	1:46.02	1:46.61
180	1:47.21	1:47.81	1:48.41	1:49.01	1:49.61	1:50.21	1:50.81	1:51.41	1:52.01	1:52.60
190	1:53.20	1:53.80	1:54.40	1:55.00	1:55.60	1:56.20	1:56.80	1:57.40	1:57.99	1:58.59
200	1:59.19	1:59.79	2:00.39	2:00.99	2:01.59	2:02.19	2:02.79	2:03.39	2:03.98	2:04.58
210	2:05.18	2:05.78	2:06.38	2:06.98	2:07.58	2:08.18	2:08.78	2:09.38	2:09.97	2:10.57
220	2:11.17	2:11.77	2:12.37	2:12.97	2:13.57	2:14.17	2:14.77	2:15.36	2:15.96	2:16.56
230	2:17.16	2:17.76	2:18.36	2:18.96	2:19.56	2:20.16	2:20.76	2:21.35	2:21.95	2:22.55
240	2:23.15	2:23.75	2:24.35	2:24.95	2:25.55	2:26.15	2:26.74	2:27.34	2:27.94	2:28.54
250	2:29.14	2:29.74	2:30.34	2:30.94	2:31.54	2:32.14	2:32.73	2:33.33	2:33.93	2:34.53
260	2:35.13	2:35.73	2:36.33	2:36.93	2:37.53	2:38.13	2:38.72	2:39.32	2:39.92	2:40.52
270	2:41.12	2:41.72	2:42.32	2:42.92	2:43.52	2:44.11	2:44.71	2:45.31	2:45.91	2:46.51
280	2:47.11	2:47.71	2:48.31	2:48.91	2:49.51	2:50.10	2:50.70	2:51.30	2:51.90	2:52.50
290	2:53.10	2:53.70	2:54.30	2:54.90	2:55.49	2:56.09	2:56.69	2:57.29	2:57.89	2:58.49
300	2:59.09	2:59.69	3:00.29	3:00.89	3:01.48	3:02.08	3:02.68	3:03.28	3:03.88	3:04.48
310	3:05.08	3:05.68	3:06.28	3:06.87	3:07.47	3:08.07	3:08.67	3:09.27	3:09.87	3:10.47
320	3:11.07	3:11.67	3:12.27	3:12.86	3:13.46	3:14.06	3:14.66	3:15.26	3:15.86	3:16.46
330	3:17.06	3:17.66	3:18.26	3:18.85	3:19.45	3:20.05	3:20.65	3:21.25	3:21.85	3:22.45
340	3:23.05	3:23.65	3:24.24	3:24.84	3:25.44	3:26.04	3:26.64	3:27.24	3:27.84	3:28.44
350	3:29.04	3:29.64	3:30.23	3:30.83	3:31.43	3:32.03	3:32.63	3:33.23	3:33.83	3:34.43
360	3:35.03	3:35.63	3:36.22	3:36.82	3:37.42	3:38.02	3:38.62	3:39.22	3:39.82	3:40.42
370	3:41.02	3:41.61	3:42.21	3:42.81	3:43.41	3:44.01	3:44.61	3:45.21	3:45.81	3:46.41
380	3:47.01	3:47.60	3:48.20	3:48.80	3:49.40	3:50.00	3:50.60	3:51.20	3:51.80	3:52.40
390	3:52.99	3:53.59	3:54.19	3:54.79	3:55.39	3:55.99	3:56.59	3:57.19	3:57.79	3:58.39
400	3:58.98	3:59.58	4:00.18	4:00.78	4:01.38	4:01.98	4:02.58	4:03.18	4:03.78	4:04.37
410	4:04.97	4:05.57	4:06.17	4:06.77	4:07.37	4:07.97	4:08.57	4:09.17	4:09.77	4:10.36
420	4:10.96	4:11.56	4:12.16	4:12.76	4:13.36	4:13.96	4:14.56	4:15.16	4:15.76	4:16.35
430	4:16.95	4:17.55	4:18.15	4:18.75	4:19.35	4:19.95	4:20.55	4:21.15	4:21.74	4:22.34
440	4:22.94	4:23.54	4:24.14	4:24.74	4:25.34	4:25.94	4:26.54	4:27.14	4:27.73	4:28.33
450	4:28.93	4:29.53	4:30.13	4:30.73	4:31.33	4:31.93	4:32.53	4:33.13	4:33.72	4:34.32
460	4:34.92	4:35.52	4:36.12	4:36.72	4:37.32	4:37.92	4:38.52	4:39.11	4:39.71	4:40.31
470	4:40.91	4:41.51	4:42.11	4:42.71	4:43.31	4:43.91	4:44.51	4:45.10	4:45.70	4:46.30
480	4:46.90	4:47.50	4:48.10	4:48.70	4:49.30	4:49.90	4:50.49	4:51.09	4:51.69	4:52.29
490	4:52.89	4:53.49	4:54.09	4:54.69	4:55.29	4:55.89	4:56.48	4:57.08	4:57.68	4:58.28
500	4:58.88	4:59.48	5:00.08	5:00.68	5:01.28	5:01.88	5:02.47	5:03.07	5:03.67	5:04.27
510	5:04.87	5:05.47	5:06.07	5:06.67	5:07.27	5:07.86	5:08.46	5:09.06	5:09.66	5:10.26
520	5:10.86	5:11.46	5:12.06	5:12.66	5:13.26	5:13.85	5:14.45	5:15.05	5:15.65	5:16.25
530	5:16.85	5:17.45	5:18.05	5:18.65	5:19.24	5:19.84	5:20.44	5:21.04	5:21.64	5:22.24
540	5:22.84	5:23.44	5:24.04	5:24.64	5:25.23	5:25.83	5:26.43	5:27.03	5:27.63	5:28.23
550	5:28.83	5:29.43	5:30.03	5:30.62	5:31.22	5:31.82	5:32.42	5:33.02	5:33.62	5:34.22
560	5:34.82	5:35.42	5:36.02	5:36.61	5:37.21	5:37.81	5:38.41	5:39.01	5:39.61	5:40.21
570	5:40.81	5:41.41	5:42.01	5:42.60	5:43.20	5:43.80	5:44.40	5:45.00	5:45.60	5:46.20
580	5:46.80	5:47.40	5:47.99	5:48.59	5:49.19	5:49.79	5:50.39	5:50.99	5:51.59	5:52.19
590	5:52.79	5:53.39	5:53.98	5:54.58	5:55.18	5:55.78	5:56.38	5:56.98	5:57.58	5:58.18

♩. = 0.90; ♩ = 0.60; ♪. = 0.45; (triplet 3: ♩ 𝄾) = 0.40; ♪ = 0.30; (triplet 3: ♪ 𝄾 𝄾) = 0.20; 𝅘𝅥𝅯 = 0.15 seconds

CLICK: 14 4/8 FRAMES; M.M.: 99.31

Click	0	1	2	3	4	5	6	7	8	9
000	0:00.00	0:00.00	0:00.60	0:01.21	0:01.81	0:02.42	0:03.02	0:03.63	0:04.23	0:04.83
010	0:05.44	0:06.04	0:06.65	0:07.25	0:07.85	0:08.46	0:09.06	0:09.67	0:10.27	0:10.88
020	0:11.48	0:12.08	0:12.69	0:13.29	0:13.90	0:14.50	0:15.10	0:15.71	0:16.31	0:16.92
030	0:17.52	0:18.13	0:18.73	0:19.33	0:19.94	0:20.54	0:21.15	0:21.75	0:22.35	0:22.96
040	0:23.56	0:24.17	0:24.77	0:25.38	0:25.98	0:26.58	0:27.19	0:27.79	0:28.40	0:29.00
050	0:29.60	0:30.21	0:30.81	0:31.42	0:32.02	0:32.63	0:33.23	0:33.83	0:34.44	0:35.04
060	0:35.65	0:36.25	0:36.85	0:37.46	0:38.06	0:38.67	0:39.27	0:39.88	0:40.48	0:41.08
070	0:41.69	0:42.29	0:42.90	0:43.50	0:44.10	0:44.71	0:45.31	0:45.92	0:46.52	0:47.13
080	0:47.73	0:48.33	0:48.94	0:49.54	0:50.15	0:50.75	0:51.35	0:51.96	0:52.56	0:53.17
090	0:53.77	0:54.38	0:54.98	0:55.58	0:56.19	0:56.79	0:57.40	0:58.00	0:58.60	0:59.21
100	0:59.81	1:00.42	1:01.02	1:01.63	1:02.23	1:02.83	1:03.44	1:04.04	1:04.65	1:05.25
110	1:05.85	1:06.46	1:07.06	1:07.67	1:08.27	1:08.88	1:09.48	1:10.08	1:10.69	1:11.29
120	1:11.90	1:12.50	1:13.10	1:13.71	1:14.31	1:14.92	1:15.52	1:16.13	1:16.73	1:17.33
130	1:17.94	1:18.54	1:19.15	1:19.75	1:20.35	1:20.96	1:21.56	1:22.17	1:22.77	1:23.38
140	1:23.98	1:24.58	1:25.19	1:25.79	1:26.40	1:27.00	1:27.60	1:28.21	1:28.81	1:29.42
150	1:30.02	1:30.63	1:31.23	1:31.83	1:32.44	1:33.04	1:33.65	1:34.25	1:34.85	1:35.46
160	1:36.06	1:36.67	1:37.27	1:37.88	1:38.48	1:39.08	1:39.69	1:40.29	1:40.90	1:41.50
170	1:42.10	1:42.71	1:43.31	1:43.92	1:44.52	1:45.13	1:45.73	1:46.33	1:46.94	1:47.54
180	1:48.15	1:48.75	1:49.35	1:49.96	1:50.56	1:51.17	1:51.77	1:52.38	1:52.98	1:53.58
190	1:54.19	1:54.79	1:55.40	1:56.00	1:56.60	1:57.21	1:57.81	1:58.42	1:59.02	1:59.63
200	2:00.23	2:00.83	2:01.44	2:02.04	2:02.65	2:03.25	2:03.85	2:04.46	2:05.06	2:05.67
210	2:06.27	2:06.88	2:07.48	2:08.08	2:08.69	2:09.29	2:09.90	2:10.50	2:11.10	2:11.71
220	2:12.31	2:12.92	2:13.52	2:14.12	2:14.73	2:15.33	2:15.94	2:16.54	2:17.15	2:17.75
230	2:18.35	2:18.96	2:19.56	2:20.17	2:20.77	2:21.38	2:21.98	2:22.58	2:23.19	2:23.79
240	2:24.40	2:25.00	2:25.60	2:26.21	2:26.81	2:27.42	2:28.02	2:28.63	2:29.23	2:29.83
250	2:30.44	2:31.04	2:31.65	2:32.25	2:32.85	2:33.46	2:34.06	2:34.67	2:35.27	2:35.88
260	2:36.48	2:37.08	2:37.69	2:38.29	2:38.90	2:39.50	2:40.10	2:40.71	2:41.31	2:41.92
270	2:42.52	2:43.13	2:43.73	2:44.33	2:44.94	2:45.54	2:46.15	2:46.75	2:47.35	2:47.96
280	2:48.56	2:49.17	2:49.77	2:50.38	2:50.98	2:51.58	2:52.19	2:52.79	2:53.40	2:54.00
290	2:54.60	2:55.21	2:55.81	2:56.42	2:57.02	2:57.63	2:58.23	2:58.83	2:59.44	3:00.04
300	3:00.65	3:01.25	3:01.85	3:02.46	3:03.06	3:03.67	3:04.27	3:04.88	3:05.48	3:06.08
310	3:06.69	3:07.29	3:07.90	3:08.50	3:09.10	3:09.71	3:10.31	3:10.92	3:11.52	3:12.13
320	3:12.73	3:13.33	3:13.94	3:14.54	3:15.15	3:15.75	3:16.35	3:16.96	3:17.56	3:18.17
330	3:18.77	3:19.38	3:19.98	3:20.58	3:21.19	3:21.79	3:22.40	3:23.00	3:23.60	3:24.21
340	3:24.81	3:25.42	3:26.02	3:26.63	3:27.23	3:27.83	3:28.44	3:29.04	3:29.65	3:30.25
350	3:30.85	3:31.46	3:32.06	3:32.67	3:33.27	3:33.88	3:34.48	3:35.08	3:35.69	3:36.29
360	3:36.90	3:37.50	3:38.10	3:38.71	3:39.31	3:39.92	3:40.52	3:41.13	3:41.73	3:42.33
370	3:42.94	3:43.54	3:44.15	3:44.75	3:45.35	3:45.96	3:46.56	3:47.17	3:47.77	3:48.38
380	3:48.98	3:49.58	3:50.19	3:50.79	3:51.40	3:52.00	3:52.60	3:53.21	3:53.81	3:54.42
390	3:55.02	3:55.63	3:56.23	3:56.83	3:57.44	3:58.04	3:58.65	3:59.25	3:59.85	4:00.46
400	4:01.06	4:01.67	4:02.27	4:02.88	4:03.48	4:04.08	4:04.69	4:05.29	4:05.90	4:06.50
410	4:07.10	4:07.71	4:08.31	4:08.92	4:09.52	4:10.13	4:10.73	4:11.33	4:11.94	4:12.54
420	4:13.15	4:13.75	4:14.35	4:14.96	4:15.56	4:16.17	4:16.77	4:17.38	4:17.98	4:18.58
430	4:19.19	4:19.79	4:20.40	4:21.00	4:21.60	4:22.21	4:22.81	4:23.42	4:24.02	4:24.62
440	4:25.23	4:25.83	4:26.44	4:27.04	4:27.65	4:28.25	4:28.85	4:29.46	4:30.06	4:30.67
450	4:31.27	4:31.88	4:32.48	4:33.08	4:33.69	4:34.29	4:34.90	4:35.50	4:36.10	4:36.71
460	4:37.31	4:37.92	4:38.52	4:39.13	4:39.73	4:40.33	4:40.94	4:41.54	4:42.15	4:42.75
470	4:43.35	4:43.96	4:44.56	4:45.17	4:45.77	4:46.38	4:46.98	4:47.58	4:48.19	4:48.79
480	4:49.40	4:50.00	4:50.60	4:51.21	4:51.81	4:52.42	4:53.02	4:53.63	4:54.23	4:54.83
490	4:55.44	4:56.04	4:56.65	4:57.25	4:57.85	4:58.46	4:59.06	4:59.67	5:00.27	5:00.88
500	5:01.48	5:02.08	5:02.69	5:03.29	5:03.90	5:04.50	5:05.10	5:05.71	5:06.31	5:06.92
510	5:07.52	5:08.13	5:08.73	5:09.33	5:09.94	5:10.54	5:11.15	5:11.75	5:12.35	5:12.96
520	5:13.56	5:14.17	5:14.77	5:15.38	5:15.98	5:16.58	5:17.19	5:17.79	5:18.40	5:19.00
530	5:19.60	5:20.21	5:20.81	5:21.42	5:22.02	5:22.62	5:23.23	5:23.83	5:24.44	5:25.04
540	5:25.65	5:26.25	5:26.85	5:27.46	5:28.06	5:28.67	5:29.27	5:29.88	5:30.48	5:31.08
550	5:31.69	5:32.29	5:32.90	5:33.50	5:34.10	5:34.71	5:35.31	5:35.92	5:36.52	5:37.13
560	5:37.73	5:38.33	5:38.94	5:39.54	5:40.15	5:40.75	5:41.35	5:41.96	5:42.56	5:43.17
570	5:43.77	5:44.38	5:44.98	5:45.58	5:46.19	5:46.79	5:47.40	5:48.00	5:48.60	5:49.21
580	5:49.81	5:50.42	5:51.02	5:51.63	5:52.23	5:52.83	5:53.44	5:54.04	5:54.65	5:55.25
590	5:55.85	5:56.46	5:57.06	5:57.67	5:58.27	5:58.88	5:59.48	6:00.08	6:00.69	6:01.29

♩. = 0.91; ♩ = 0.60; ♪. = 0.45; (triplet ♩ 𝄾) = 0.40; ♪ = 0.30; (triplet ♪ 𝄾 𝄾) = 0.20; 𝅘𝅥𝅯 = 0.15 seconds

CLICK: 14⅝ FRAMES; M.M.: 98.46

Click	0	1	2	3	4	5	6	7	8	9
000	0:00.00	0:00.00	0:00.61	0:01.22	0:01.83	0:02.44	0:03.05	0:03.66	0:04.27	0:04.88
010	0:05.48	0:06.09	0:06.70	0:07.31	0:07.92	0:08.53	0:09.14	0:09.75	0:10.36	0:10.97
020	0:11.58	0:12.19	0:12.80	0:13.41	0:14.02	0:14.62	0:15.23	0:15.84	0:16.45	0:17.06
030	0:17.67	0:18.28	0:18.89	0:19.50	0:20.11	0:20.72	0:21.33	0:21.94	0:22.55	0:23.16
040	0:23.77	0:24.38	0:24.98	0:25.59	0:26.20	0:26.81	0:27.42	0:28.03	0:28.64	0:29.25
050	0:29.86	0:30.47	0:31.08	0:31.69	0:32.30	0:32.91	0:33.52	0:34.12	0:34.73	0:35.34
060	0:35.95	0:36.56	0:37.17	0:37.78	0:38.39	0:39.00	0:39.61	0:40.22	0:40.83	0:41.44
070	0:42.05	0:42.66	0:43.27	0:43.88	0:44.48	0:45.09	0:45.70	0:46.31	0:46.92	0:47.53
080	0:48.14	0:48.75	0:49.36	0:49.97	0:50.58	0:51.19	0:51.80	0:52.41	0:53.02	0:53.62
090	0:54.23	0:54.84	0:55.45	0:56.06	0:56.67	0:57.28	0:57.89	0:58.50	0:59.11	0:59.72
100	1:00.33	1:00.94	1:01.55	1:02.16	1:02.77	1:03.37	1:03.98	1:04.59	1:05.20	1:05.81
110	1:06.42	1:07.03	1:07.64	1:08.25	1:08.86	1:09.47	1:10.08	1:10.69	1:11.30	1:11.91
120	1:12.52	1:13.13	1:13.73	1:14.34	1:14.95	1:15.56	1:16.17	1:16.78	1:17.39	1:18.00
130	1:18.61	1:19.22	1:19.83	1:20.44	1:21.05	1:21.66	1:22.27	1:22.87	1:23.48	1:24.09
140	1:24.70	1:25.31	1:25.92	1:26.53	1:27.14	1:27.75	1:28.36	1:28.97	1:29.58	1:30.19
150	1:30.80	1:31.41	1:32.02	1:32.62	1:33.23	1:33.84	1:34.45	1:35.06	1:35.67	1:36.28
160	1:36.89	1:37.50	1:38.11	1:38.72	1:39.33	1:39.94	1:40.55	1:41.16	1:41.77	1:42.37
170	1:42.98	1:43.59	1:44.20	1:44.81	1:45.42	1:46.03	1:46.64	1:47.25	1:47.86	1:48.47
180	1:49.08	1:49.69	1:50.30	1:50.91	1:51.52	1:52.13	1:52.73	1:53.34	1:53.95	1:54.56
190	1:55.17	1:55.78	1:56.39	1:57.00	1:57.61	1:58.22	1:58.83	1:59.44	2:00.05	2:00.66
200	2:01.27	2:01.88	2:02.48	2:03.09	2:03.70	2:04.31	2:04.92	2:05.53	2:06.14	2:06.75
210	2:07.36	2:07.97	2:08.58	2:09.19	2:09.80	2:10.41	2:11.02	2:11.62	2:12.23	2:12.84
220	2:13.45	2:14.06	2:14.67	2:15.28	2:15.89	2:16.50	2:17.11	2:17.72	2:18.33	2:18.94
230	2:19.55	2:20.16	2:20.77	2:21.37	2:21.98	2:22.59	2:23.20	2:23.81	2:24.42	2:25.03
240	2:25.64	2:26.25	2:26.86	2:27.47	2:28.08	2:28.69	2:29.30	2:29.91	2:30.52	2:31.12
250	2:31.73	2:32.34	2:32.95	2:33.56	2:34.17	2:34.78	2:35.39	2:36.00	2:36.61	2:37.22
260	2:37.83	2:38.44	2:39.05	2:39.66	2:40.27	2:40.87	2:41.48	2:42.09	2:42.70	2:43.31
270	2:43.92	2:44.53	2:45.14	2:45.75	2:46.36	2:46.97	2:47.58	2:48.19	2:48.80	2:49.41
280	2:50.02	2:50.63	2:51.23	2:51.84	2:52.45	2:53.06	2:53.67	2:54.28	2:54.89	2:55.50
290	2:56.11	2:56.72	2:57.33	2:57.94	2:58.55	2:59.16	2:59.77	3:00.37	3:00.98	3:01.59
300	3:02.20	3:02.81	3:03.42	3:04.03	3:04.64	3:05.25	3:05.86	3:06.47	3:07.08	3:07.69
310	3:08.30	3:08.91	3:09.52	3:10.12	3:10.73	3:11.34	3:11.95	3:12.56	3:13.17	3:13.78
320	3:14.39	3:15.00	3:15.61	3:16.22	3:16.83	3:17.44	3:18.05	3:18.66	3:19.27	3:19.87
330	3:20.48	3:21.09	3:21.70	3:22.31	3:22.92	3:23.53	3:24.14	3:24.75	3:25.36	3:25.97
340	3:26.58	3:27.19	3:27.80	3:28.41	3:29.02	3:29.62	3:30.23	3:30.84	3:31.45	3:32.06
350	3:32.67	3:33.28	3:33.89	3:34.50	3:35.11	3:35.72	3:36.33	3:36.94	3:37.55	3:38.16
360	3:38.77	3:39.37	3:39.98	3:40.59	3:41.20	3:41.81	3:42.42	3:43.03	3:43.64	3:44.25
370	3:44.86	3:45.47	3:46.08	3:46.69	3:47.30	3:47.91	3:48.52	3:49.12	3:49.73	3:50.34
380	3:50.95	3:51.56	3:52.17	3:52.78	3:53.39	3:54.00	3:54.61	3:55.22	3:55.83	3:56.44
390	3:57.05	3:57.66	3:58.27	3:58.87	3:59.48	4:00.09	4:00.70	4:01.31	4:01.92	4:02.53
400	4:03.14	4:03.75	4:04.36	4:04.97	4:05.58	4:06.19	4:06.80	4:07.41	4:08.02	4:08.62
410	4:09.23	4:09.84	4:10.45	4:11.06	4:11.67	4:12.28	4:12.89	4:13.50	4:14.11	4:14.72
420	4:15.33	4:15.94	4:16.55	4:17.16	4:17.77	4:18.37	4:18.98	4:19.59	4:20.20	4:20.81
430	4:21.42	4:22.03	4:22.64	4:23.25	4:23.86	4:24.47	4:25.08	4:25.69	4:26.30	4:26.91
440	4:27.52	4:28.13	4:28.73	4:29.34	4:29.95	4:30.56	4:31.17	4:31.78	4:32.39	4:33.00
450	4:33.61	4:34.22	4:34.83	4:35.44	4:36.05	4:36.66	4:37.27	4:37.87	4:38.48	4:39.09
460	4:39.70	4:40.31	4:40.92	4:41.53	4:42.14	4:42.75	4:43.36	4:43.97	4:44.58	4:45.19
470	4:45.80	4:46.41	4:47.02	4:47.62	4:48.23	4:48.84	4:49.45	4:50.06	4:50.67	4:51.28
480	4:51.89	4:52.50	4:53.11	4:53.72	4:54.33	4:54.94	4:55.55	4:56.16	4:56.77	4:57.37
490	4:57.98	4:58.59	4:59.20	4:59.81	5:00.42	5:01.03	5:01.64	5:02.25	5:02.86	5:03.47
500	5:04.08	5:04.69	5:05.30	5:05.91	5:06.52	5:07.12	5:07.73	5:08.34	5:08.95	5:09.56
510	5:10.17	5:10.78	5:11.39	5:12.00	5:12.61	5:13.22	5:13.83	5:14.44	5:15.05	5:15.66
520	5:16.27	5:16.88	5:17.48	5:18.09	5:18.70	5:19.31	5:19.92	5:20.53	5:21.14	5:21.75
530	5:22.36	5:22.97	5:23.58	5:24.19	5:24.80	5:25.41	5:26.02	5:26.62	5:27.23	5:27.84
540	5:28.45	5:29.06	5:29.67	5:30.28	5:30.89	5:31.50	5:32.11	5:32.72	5:33.33	5:33.94
550	5:34.55	5:35.16	5:35.77	5:36.37	5:36.98	5:37.59	5:38.20	5:38.81	5:39.42	5:40.03
560	5:40.64	5:41.25	5:41.86	5:42.47	5:43.08	5:43.69	5:44.30	5:44.91	5:45.52	5:46.12
570	5:46.73	5:47.34	5:47.95	5:48.56	5:49.17	5:49.78	5:50.39	5:51.00	5:51.61	5:52.22
580	5:52.83	5:53.44	5:54.05	5:54.66	5:55.27	5:55.87	5:56.48	5:57.09	5:57.70	5:58.31
590	5:58.92	5:59.53	6:00.14	6:00.75	6:01.36	6:01.97	6:02.58	6:03.19	6:03.80	6:04.41

♩. = 0.91; ♩ = 0.61; ♪. = 0.46; (3: ♩ 𝄾) = 0.41; ♪ = 0.30; (3: ♪ 𝄾 𝄾) = 0.20; 𝅘𝅥𝅯 = 0.15 seconds

CLICK: $14\frac{6}{8}$ FRAMES; M.M.: 97.63

Click	0	1	2	3	4	5	6	7	8	9
000	0:00.00	0:00.00	0:00.61	0:01.23	0:01.84	0:02.46	0:03.07	0:03.69	0:04.30	0:04.92
010	0:05.53	0:06.15	0:06.76	0:07.38	0:07.99	0:08.60	0:09.22	0:09.83	0:10.45	0:11.06
020	0:11.68	0:12.29	0:12.91	0:13.52	0:14.14	0:14.75	0:15.36	0:15.98	0:16.59	0:17.21
030	0:17.82	0:18.44	0:19.05	0:19.67	0:20.28	0:20.90	0:21.51	0:22.13	0:22.74	0:23.35
040	0:23.97	0:24.58	0:25.20	0:25.81	0:26.43	0:27.04	0:27.66	0:28.27	0:28.89	0:29.50
050	0:30.11	0:30.73	0:31.34	0:31.96	0:32.57	0:33.19	0:33.80	0:34.42	0:35.03	0:35.65
060	0:36.26	0:36.88	0:37.49	0:38.10	0:38.72	0:39.33	0:39.95	0:40.56	0:41.18	0:41.79
070	0:42.41	0:43.02	0:43.64	0:44.25	0:44.86	0:45.48	0:46.09	0:46.71	0:47.32	0:47.94
080	0:48.55	0:49.17	0:49.78	0:50.40	0:51.01	0:51.63	0:52.24	0:52.85	0:53.47	0:54.08
090	0:54.70	0:55.31	0:55.93	0:56.54	0:57.16	0:57.77	0:58.39	0:59.00	0:59.61	1:00.23
100	1:00.84	1:01.46	1:02.07	1:02.69	1:03.30	1:03.92	1:04.53	1:05.15	1:05.76	1:06.37
110	1:06.99	1:07.60	1:08.22	1:08.83	1:09.45	1:10.06	1:10.68	1:11.29	1:11.91	1:12.52
120	1:13.14	1:13.75	1:14.36	1:14.98	1:15.59	1:16.21	1:16.82	1:17.44	1:18.05	1:18.67
130	1:19.28	1:19.90	1:20.51	1:21.13	1:21.74	1:22.35	1:22.97	1:23.58	1:24.20	1:24.81
140	1:25.43	1:26.04	1:26.66	1:27.27	1:27.89	1:28.50	1:29.11	1:29.73	1:30.34	1:30.96
150	1:31.57	1:32.19	1:32.80	1:33.42	1:34.03	1:34.65	1:35.26	1:35.87	1:36.49	1:37.10
160	1:37.72	1:38.33	1:38.95	1:39.56	1:40.18	1:40.79	1:41.41	1:42.02	1:42.64	1:43.25
170	1:43.86	1:44.48	1:45.09	1:45.71	1:46.32	1:46.94	1:47.55	1:48.17	1:48.78	1:49.40
180	1:50.01	1:50.63	1:51.24	1:51.85	1:52.47	1:53.08	1:53.70	1:54.31	1:54.93	1:55.54
190	1:56.16	1:56.77	1:57.39	1:58.00	1:58.61	1:59.23	1:59.84	2:00.46	2:01.07	2:01.69
200	2:02.30	2:02.92	2:03.53	2:04.15	2:04.76	2:05.38	2:05.99	2:06.60	2:07.22	2:07.83
210	2:08.45	2:09.06	2:09.68	2:10.29	2:10.91	2:11.52	2:12.14	2:12.75	2:13.36	2:13.98
220	2:14.59	2:15.21	2:15.82	2:16.44	2:17.05	2:17.67	2:18.28	2:18.90	2:19.51	2:20.12
230	2:20.74	2:21.35	2:21.97	2:22.58	2:23.20	2:23.81	2:24.43	2:25.04	2:25.66	2:26.27
240	2:26.89	2:27.50	2:28.11	2:28.73	2:29.34	2:29.96	2:30.57	2:31.19	2:31.80	2:32.42
250	2:33.03	2:33.65	2:34.26	2:34.87	2:35.49	2:36.10	2:36.72	2:37.33	2:37.95	2:38.56
260	2:39.18	2:39.79	2:40.41	2:41.02	2:41.64	2:42.25	2:42.86	2:43.48	2:44.09	2:44.71
270	2:45.32	2:45.94	2:46.55	2:47.17	2:47.78	2:48.40	2:49.01	2:49.63	2:50.24	2:50.85
280	2:51.47	2:52.08	2:52.70	2:53.31	2:53.93	2:54.54	2:55.16	2:55.77	2:56.39	2:57.00
290	2:57.61	2:58.23	2:58.84	2:59.46	3:00.07	3:00.69	3:01.30	3:01.92	3:02.53	3:03.15
300	3:03.76	3:04.37	3:04.99	3:05.60	3:06.22	3:06.83	3:07.45	3:08.06	3:08.68	3:09.29
310	3:09.91	3:10.52	3:11.14	3:11.75	3:12.36	3:12.98	3:13.59	3:14.21	3:14.82	3:15.44
320	3:16.05	3:16.67	3:17.28	3:17.90	3:18.51	3:19.12	3:19.74	3:20.35	3:20.97	3:21.58
330	3:22.20	3:22.81	3:23.43	3:24.04	3:24.66	3:25.27	3:25.89	3:26.50	3:27.11	3:27.73
340	3:28.34	3:28.96	3:29.57	3:30.19	3:30.80	3:31.42	3:32.03	3:32.65	3:33.26	3:33.88
350	3:34.49	3:35.10	3:35.72	3:36.33	3:36.95	3:37.56	3:38.18	3:38.79	3:39.41	3:40.02
360	3:40.64	3:41.25	3:41.86	3:42.48	3:43.09	3:43.71	3:44.32	3:44.94	3:45.55	3:46.17
370	3:46.78	3:47.40	3:48.01	3:48.63	3:49.24	3:49.85	3:50.47	3:51.08	3:51.70	3:52.31
380	3:52.93	3:53.54	3:54.16	3:54.77	3:55.39	3:56.00	3:56.61	3:57.23	3:57.84	3:58.46
390	3:59.07	3:59.69	4:00.30	4:00.92	4:01.53	4:02.15	4:02.76	4:03.38	4:03.99	4:04.60
400	4:05.22	4:05.83	4:06.45	4:07.06	4:07.68	4:08.29	4:08.91	4:09.52	4:10.14	4:10.75
410	4:11.36	4:11.98	4:12.59	4:13.21	4:13.82	4:14.44	4:15.05	4:15.67	4:16.28	4:16.90
420	4:17.51	4:18.13	4:18.74	4:19.35	4:19.97	4:20.58	4:21.20	4:21.81	4:22.43	4:23.04
430	4:23.66	4:24.27	4:24.89	4:25.50	4:26.11	4:26.73	4:27.34	4:27.96	4:28.57	4:29.19
440	4:29.80	4:30.42	4:31.03	4:31.65	4:32.26	4:32.87	4:33.49	4:34.10	4:34.72	4:35.33
450	4:35.95	4:36.56	4:37.18	4:37.79	4:38.41	4:39.02	4:39.64	4:40.25	4:40.86	4:41.48
460	4:42.09	4:42.71	4:43.32	4:43.94	4:44.55	4:45.17	4:45.78	4:46.40	4:47.01	4:47.62
470	4:48.24	4:48.85	4:49.47	4:50.08	4:50.70	4:51.31	4:51.93	4:52.54	4:53.16	4:53.77
480	4:54.39	4:55.00	4:55.61	4:56.23	4:56.84	4:57.46	4:58.07	4:58.69	4:59.30	4:59.92
490	5:00.53	5:01.15	5:01.76	5:02.37	5:02.99	5:03.60	5:04.22	5:04.83	5:05.45	5:06.06
500	5:06.68	5:07.29	5:07.91	5:08.52	5:09.14	5:09.75	5:10.36	5:10.98	5:11.59	5:12.21
510	5:12.82	5:13.44	5:14.05	5:14.67	5:15.28	5:15.90	5:16.51	5:17.12	5:17.74	5:18.35
520	5:18.97	5:19.58	5:20.20	5:20.81	5:21.43	5:22.04	5:22.66	5:23.27	5:23.89	5:24.50
530	5:25.11	5:25.73	5:26.34	5:26.96	5:27.57	5:28.19	5:28.80	5:29.42	5:30.03	5:30.65
540	5:31.26	5:31.88	5:32.49	5:33.10	5:33.72	5:34.33	5:34.95	5:35.56	5:36.18	5:36.79
550	5:37.41	5:38.02	5:38.64	5:39.25	5:39.86	5:40.48	5:41.09	5:41.71	5:42.32	5:42.94
560	5:43.55	5:44.17	5:44.78	5:45.40	5:46.01	5:46.63	5:47.24	5:47.85	5:48.47	5:49.08
570	5:49.70	5:50.31	5:50.93	5:51.54	5:52.16	5:52.77	5:53.39	5:54.00	5:54.61	5:55.23
580	5:55.84	5:56.46	5:57.07	5:57.69	5:58.30	5:58.92	5:59.53	6:00.15	6:00.76	6:01.38
590	6:01.99	6:02.60	6:03.22	6:03.83	6:04.45	6:05.06	6:05.68	6:06.29	6:06.91	6:07.52

♩. = 0.92; ♩ = 0.61; ♪. = 0.46; (triplet ♩ 𝄾) = 0.41; ♪ = 0.31; (triplet ♪ 𝄾 𝄾) = 0.20; 𝅘𝅥𝅯 = 0.15 seconds

CLICK: 14⅞ FRAMES; M.M.: 96.81

Click	0	1	2	3	4	5	6	7	8	9
000	0:00.00	0:00.00	0:00.62	0:01.24	0:01.86	0:02.48	0:03.10	0:03.72	0:04.34	0:04.96
010	0:05.58	0:06.20	0:06.82	0:07.44	0:08.06	0:08.68	0:09.30	0:09.92	0:10.54	0:11.16
020	0:11.78	0:12.40	0:13.02	0:13.64	0:14.26	0:14.88	0:15.49	0:16.11	0:16.73	0:17.35
030	0:17.97	0:18.59	0:19.21	0:19.83	0:20.45	0:21.07	0:21.69	0:22.31	0:22.93	0:23.55
040	0:24.17	0:24.79	0:25.41	0:26.03	0:26.65	0:27.27	0:27.89	0:28.51	0:29.13	0:29.75
050	0:30.37	0:30.99	0:31.61	0:32.23	0:32.85	0:33.47	0:34.09	0:34.71	0:35.33	0:35.95
060	0:36.57	0:37.19	0:37.81	0:38.43	0:39.05	0:39.67	0:40.29	0:40.91	0:41.53	0:42.15
070	0:42.77	0:43.39	0:44.01	0:44.63	0:45.24	0:45.86	0:46.48	0:47.10	0:47.72	0:48.34
080	0:48.96	0:49.58	0:50.20	0:50.82	0:51.44	0:52.06	0:52.68	0:53.30	0:53.92	0:54.54
090	0:55.16	0:55.78	0:56.40	0:57.02	0:57.64	0:58.26	0:58.88	0:59.50	1:00.12	1:00.74
100	1:01.36	1:01.98	1:02.60	1:03.22	1:03.84	1:04.46	1:05.08	1:05.70	1:06.32	1:06.94
110	1:07.56	1:08.18	1:08.80	1:09.42	1:10.04	1:10.66	1:11.28	1:11.90	1:12.52	1:13.14
120	1:13.76	1:14.38	1:14.99	1:15.61	1:16.23	1:16.85	1:17.47	1:18.09	1:18.71	1:19.33
130	1:19.95	1:20.57	1:21.19	1:21.81	1:22.43	1:23.05	1:23.67	1:24.29	1:24.91	1:25.53
140	1:26.15	1:26.77	1:27.39	1:28.01	1:28.63	1:29.25	1:29.87	1:30.49	1:31.11	1:31.73
150	1:32.35	1:32.97	1:33.59	1:34.21	1:34.83	1:35.45	1:36.07	1:36.69	1:37.31	1:37.93
160	1:38.55	1:39.17	1:39.79	1:40.41	1:41.03	1:41.65	1:42.27	1:42.89	1:43.51	1:44.13
170	1:44.74	1:45.36	1:45.98	1:46.60	1:47.22	1:47.84	1:48.46	1:49.08	1:49.70	1:50.32
180	1:50.94	1:51.56	1:52.18	1:52.80	1:53.42	1:54.04	1:54.66	1:55.28	1:55.90	1:56.52
190	1:57.14	1:57.76	1:58.38	1:59.00	1:59.62	2:00.24	2:00.86	2:01.48	2:02.10	2:02.72
200	2:03.34	2:03.96	2:04.58	2:05.20	2:05.82	2:06.44	2:07.06	2:07.68	2:08.30	2:08.92
210	2:09.54	2:10.16	2:10.78	2:11.40	2:12.02	2:12.64	2:13.26	2:13.88	2:14.49	2:15.11
220	2:15.73	2:16.35	2:16.97	2:17.59	2:18.21	2:18.83	2:19.45	2:20.07	2:20.69	2:21.31
230	2:21.93	2:22.55	2:23.17	2:23.79	2:24.41	2:25.03	2:25.65	2:26.27	2:26.89	2:27.51
240	2:28.13	2:28.75	2:29.37	2:29.99	2:30.61	2:31.23	2:31.85	2:32.47	2:33.09	2:33.71
250	2:34.33	2:34.95	2:35.57	2:36.19	2:36.81	2:37.43	2:38.05	2:38.67	2:39.29	2:39.91
260	2:40.53	2:41.15	2:41.77	2:42.39	2:43.01	2:43.63	2:44.24	2:44.86	2:45.48	2:46.10
270	2:46.72	2:47.34	2:47.96	2:48.58	2:49.20	2:49.82	2:50.44	2:51.06	2:51.68	2:52.30
280	2:52.92	2:53.54	2:54.16	2:54.78	2:55.40	2:56.02	2:56.64	2:57.26	2:57.88	2:58.50
290	2:59.12	2:59.74	3:00.36	3:00.98	3:01.60	3:02.22	3:02.84	3:03.46	3:04.08	3:04.70
300	3:05.32	3:05.94	3:06.56	3:07.18	3:07.80	3:08.42	3:09.04	3:09.66	3:10.28	3:10.90
310	3:11.52	3:12.14	3:12.76	3:13.37	3:13.99	3:14.61	3:15.23	3:15.85	3:16.47	3:17.09
320	3:17.71	3:18.33	3:18.95	3:19.57	3:20.19	3:20.81	3:21.43	3:22.05	3:22.67	3:23.29
330	3:23.91	3:24.53	3:25.15	3:25.77	3:26.39	3:27.01	3:27.63	3:28.25	3:28.87	3:29.49
340	3:30.11	3:30.73	3:31.35	3:31.97	3:32.59	3:33.21	3:33.83	3:34.45	3:35.07	3:35.69
350	3:36.31	3:36.93	3:37.55	3:38.17	3:38.79	3:39.41	3:40.03	3:40.65	3:41.27	3:41.89
360	3:42.51	3:43.13	3:43.74	3:44.36	3:44.98	3:45.60	3:46.22	3:46.84	3:47.46	3:48.08
370	3:48.70	3:49.32	3:49.94	3:50.56	3:51.18	3:51.80	3:52.42	3:53.04	3:53.66	3:54.28
380	3:54.90	3:55.52	3:56.14	3:56.76	3:57.38	3:58.00	3:58.62	3:59.24	3:59.86	4:00.48
390	4:01.10	4:01.72	4:02.34	4:02.96	4:03.58	4:04.20	4:04.82	4:05.44	4:06.06	4:06.68
400	4:07.30	4:07.92	4:08.54	4:09.16	4:09.78	4:10.40	4:11.02	4:11.64	4:12.26	4:12.88
410	4:13.49	4:14.11	4:14.73	4:15.35	4:15.97	4:16.59	4:17.21	4:17.83	4:18.45	4:19.07
420	4:19.69	4:20.31	4:20.93	4:21.55	4:22.17	4:22.79	4:23.41	4:24.03	4:24.65	4:25.27
430	4:25.89	4:26.51	4:27.13	4:27.75	4:28.37	4:28.99	4:29.61	4:30.23	4:30.85	4:31.47
440	4:32.09	4:32.71	4:33.33	4:33.95	4:34.57	4:35.19	4:35.81	4:36.43	4:37.05	4:37.67
450	4:38.29	4:38.91	4:39.53	4:40.15	4:40.77	4:41.39	4:42.01	4:42.63	4:43.24	4:43.86
460	4:44.48	4:45.10	4:45.72	4:46.34	4:46.96	4:47.58	4:48.20	4:48.82	4:49.44	4:50.06
470	4:50.68	4:51.30	4:51.92	4:52.54	4:53.16	4:53.78	4:54.40	4:55.02	4:55.64	4:56.26
480	4:56.88	4:57.50	4:58.12	4:58.74	4:59.36	4:59.98	5:00.60	5:01.22	5:01.84	5:02.46
490	5:03.08	5:03.70	5:04.32	5:04.94	5:05.56	5:06.18	5:06.80	5:07.42	5:08.04	5:08.66
500	5:09.28	5:09.90	5:10.52	5:11.14	5:11.76	5:12.38	5:12.99	5:13.61	5:14.23	5:14.85
510	5:15.47	5:16.09	5:16.71	5:17.33	5:17.95	5:18.57	5:19.19	5:19.81	5:20.43	5:21.05
520	5:21.67	5:22.29	5:22.91	5:23.53	5:24.15	5:24.77	5:25.39	5:26.01	5:26.63	5:27.25
530	5:27.87	5:28.49	5:29.11	5:29.73	5:30.35	5:30.97	5:31.59	5:32.21	5:32.83	5:33.45
540	5:34.07	5:34.69	5:35.31	5:35.93	5:36.55	5:37.17	5:37.79	5:38.41	5:39.03	5:39.65
550	5:40.27	5:40.89	5:41.51	5:42.13	5:42.74	5:43.36	5:43.98	5:44.60	5:45.22	5:45.84
560	5:46.46	5:47.08	5:47.70	5:48.32	5:48.94	5:49.56	5:50.18	5:50.80	5:51.42	5:52.04
570	5:52.66	5:53.28	5:53.90	5:54.52	5:55.14	5:55.76	5:56.38	5:57.00	5:57.62	5:58.24
580	5:58.86	5:59.48	6:00.10	6:00.72	6:01.34	6:01.96	6:02.58	6:03.20	6:03.82	6:04.44
590	6:05.06	6:05.68	6:06.30	6:06.92	6:07.54	6:08.16	6:08.78	6:09.40	6:10.02	6:10.64

♩. = 0.93; ♩ = 0.62; ♪. = 0.46; (triplet) ♩ 𝄾 = 0.41; ♪ = 0.31; (triplet) ♪ 𝄾 𝄾 = 0.21; 𝅘𝅥𝅯 = 0.15 seconds

CLICK: 15 0/8 FRAMES; M.M.: 96.00

Click	0	1	2	3	4	5	6	7	8	9
000	0:00.00	0:00.00	0:00.62	0:01.25	0:01.87	0:02.50	0:03.13	0:03.75	0:04.38	0:05.00
010	0:05.62	0:06.25	0:06.87	0:07.50	0:08.12	0:08.75	0:09.37	0:10.00	0:10.63	0:11.25
020	0:11.87	0:12.50	0:13.12	0:13.75	0:14.37	0:15.00	0:15.62	0:16.25	0:16.87	0:17.50
030	0:18.12	0:18.75	0:19.38	0:20.00	0:20.62	0:21.25	0:21.87	0:22.50	0:23.13	0:23.75
040	0:24.37	0:25.00	0:25.62	0:26.25	0:26.87	0:27.50	0:28.12	0:28.75	0:29.37	0:30.00
050	0:30.62	0:31.25	0:31.87	0:32.50	0:33.13	0:33.75	0:34.37	0:35.00	0:35.62	0:36.25
060	0:36.88	0:37.50	0:38.12	0:38.75	0:39.37	0:40.00	0:40.63	0:41.25	0:41.87	0:42.50
070	0:43.12	0:43.75	0:44.38	0:45.00	0:45.62	0:46.25	0:46.87	0:47.50	0:48.13	0:48.75
080	0:49.37	0:50.00	0:50.62	0:51.25	0:51.87	0:52.50	0:53.12	0:53.75	0:54.37	0:55.00
090	0:55.62	0:56.25	0:56.87	0:57.50	0:58.12	0:58.75	0:59.37	0:60.00	1:00.62	1:01.25
100	1:01.87	1:02.50	1:03.12	1:03.75	1:04.37	1:05.00	1:05.62	1:06.25	1:06.87	1:07.50
110	1:08.12	1:08.75	1:09.37	1:10.00	1:10.62	1:11.25	1:11.87	1:12.50	1:13.12	1:13.75
120	1:14.37	1:15.00	1:15.62	1:16.25	1:16.87	1:17.50	1:18.12	1:18.75	1:19.37	1:20.00
130	1:20.62	1:21.25	1:21.87	1:22.50	1:23.12	1:23.75	1:24.37	1:25.00	1:25.62	1:26.25
140	1:26.87	1:27.50	1:28.12	1:28.75	1:29.37	1:30.00	1:30.62	1:31.25	1:31.87	1:32.50
150	1:33.12	1:33.75	1:34.37	1:35.00	1:35.62	1:36.25	1:36.87	1:37.50	1:38.12	1:38.75
160	1:39.37	1:40.00	1:40.62	1:41.25	1:41.87	1:42.50	1:43.12	1:43.75	1:44.37	1:45.00
170	1:45.62	1:46.25	1:46.87	1:47.50	1:48.12	1:48.75	1:49.37	1:50.00	1:50.62	1:51.25
180	1:51.87	1:52.50	1:53.12	1:53.75	1:54.37	1:55.00	1:55.62	1:56.25	1:56.87	1:57.50
190	1:58.12	1:58.75	1:59.37	1:60.00	2:00.62	2:01.25	2:01.87	2:02.50	2:03.12	2:03.75
200	2:04.37	2:05.00	2:05.62	2:06.25	2:06.87	2:07.50	2:08.12	2:08.75	2:09.37	2:10.00
210	2:10.62	2:11.25	2:11.87	2:12.50	2:13.12	2:13.75	2:14.37	2:15.00	2:15.62	2:16.25
220	2:16.87	2:17.50	2:18.12	2:18.75	2:19.37	2:20.00	2:20.62	2:21.25	2:21.87	2:22.50
230	2:23.12	2:23.75	2:24.37	2:25.00	2:25.62	2:26.25	2:26.87	2:27.50	2:28.12	2:28.75
240	2:29.37	2:30.00	2:30.62	2:31.25	2:31.87	2:32.50	2:33.12	2:33.75	2:34.37	2:35.00
250	2:35.62	2:36.25	2:36.87	2:37.50	2:38.12	2:38.75	2:39.37	2:40.00	2:40.62	2:41.25
260	2:41.87	2:42.50	2:43.12	2:43.75	2:44.37	2:45.00	2:45.62	2:46.25	2:46.87	2:47.50
270	2:48.12	2:48.75	2:49.37	2:50.00	2:50.62	2:51.25	2:51.87	2:52.50	2:53.12	2:53.75
280	2:54.37	2:55.00	2:55.62	2:56.25	2:56.87	2:57.50	2:58.12	2:58.75	2:59.37	2:60.00
290	3:00.62	3:01.25	3:01.87	3:02.50	3:03.12	3:03.75	3:04.37	3:05.00	3:05.62	3:06.25
300	3:06.87	3:07.50	3:08.12	3:08.75	3:09.37	3:10.00	3:10.62	3:11.25	3:11.87	3:12.50
310	3:13.12	3:13.75	3:14.37	3:15.00	3:15.62	3:16.25	3:16.87	3:17.50	3:18.12	3:18.75
320	3:19.37	3:20.00	3:20.62	3:21.25	3:21.87	3:22.50	3:23.12	3:23.75	3:24.37	3:25.00
330	3:25.62	3:26.25	3:26.87	3:27.50	3:28.12	3:28.75	3:29.37	3:30.00	3:30.62	3:31.25
340	3:31.87	3:32.50	3:33.12	3:33.75	3:34.37	3:35.00	3:35.62	3:36.25	3:36.87	3:37.50
350	3:38.12	3:38.75	3:39.37	3:40.00	3:40.62	3:41.25	3:41.87	3:42.50	3:43.12	3:43.75
360	3:44.37	3:45.00	3:45.62	3:46.25	3:46.87	3:47.50	3:48.12	3:48.75	3:49.37	3:50.00
370	3:50.62	3:51.25	3:51.87	3:52.50	3:53.12	3:53.75	3:54.37	3:55.00	3:55.62	3:56.25
380	3:56.87	3:57.50	3:58.12	3:58.75	3:59.37	3:60.00	4:00.62	4:01.25	4:01.87	4:02.50
390	4:03.12	4:03.75	4:04.37	4:05.00	4:05.62	4:06.25	4:06.87	4:07.50	4:08.12	4:08.75
400	4:09.37	4:10.00	4:10.62	4:11.25	4:11.87	4:12.50	4:13.12	4:13.75	4:14.37	4:15.00
410	4:15.62	4:16.25	4:16.87	4:17.50	4:18.12	4:18.75	4:19.37	4:20.00	4:20.62	4:21.25
420	4:21.87	4:22.50	4:23.12	4:23.75	4:24.37	4:25.00	4:25.62	4:26.25	4:26.87	4:27.50
430	4:28.12	4:28.75	4:29.37	4:30.00	4:30.62	4:31.25	4:31.87	4:32.50	4:33.12	4:33.75
440	4:34.37	4:35.00	4:35.62	4:36.25	4:36.87	4:37.50	4:38.12	4:38.75	4:39.37	4:40.00
450	4:40.62	4:41.25	4:41.87	4:42.50	4:43.12	4:43.75	4:44.37	4:45.00	4:45.62	4:46.25
460	4:46.87	4:47.50	4:48.12	4:48.75	4:49.37	4:50.00	4:50.62	4:51.25	4:51.87	4:52.50
470	4:53.12	4:53.75	4:54.37	4:55.00	4:55.62	4:56.25	4:56.87	4:57.50	4:58.12	4:58.75
480	4:59.37	4:60.00	5:00.62	5:01.25	5:01.87	5:02.50	5:03.12	5:03.75	5:04.37	5:05.00
490	5:05.62	5:06.25	5:06.87	5:07.50	5:08.12	5:08.75	5:09.37	5:10.00	5:10.62	5:11.25
500	5:11.87	5:12.50	5:13.12	5:13.75	5:14.37	5:15.00	5:15.62	5:16.25	5:16.87	5:17.50
510	5:18.12	5:18.75	5:19.37	5:20.00	5:20.62	5:21.25	5:21.87	5:22.50	5:23.12	5:23.75
520	5:24.37	5:25.00	5:25.62	5:26.25	5:26.87	5:27.50	5:28.12	5:28.75	5:29.37	5:30.00
530	5:30.62	5:31.25	5:31.87	5:32.50	5:33.12	5:33.75	5:34.37	5:35.00	5:35.62	5:36.25
540	5:36.87	5:37.50	5:38.12	5:38.75	5:39.37	5:40.00	5:40.62	5:41.25	5:41.87	5:42.50
550	5:43.12	5:43.75	5:44.37	5:45.00	5:45.62	5:46.25	5:46.87	5:47.50	5:48.12	5:48.75
560	5:49.37	5:50.00	5:50.62	5:51.25	5:51.87	5:52.50	5:53.12	5:53.75	5:54.37	5:55.00
570	5:55.62	5:56.25	5:56.87	5:57.50	5:58.12	5:58.75	5:59.37	5:60.00	6:00.62	6:01.25
580	6:01.87	6:02.50	6:03.12	6:03.75	6:04.37	6:05.00	6:05.62	6:06.25	6:06.87	6:07.50
590	6:08.12	6:08.75	6:09.37	6:10.00	6:10.62	6:11.25	6:11.87	6:12.50	6:13.12	6:13.75

♩. = 0.94; ♩ = 0.62; ♪. = 0.47; (3) ♩ 𝄾 = 0.42; ♪ = 0.31; (3) ♪ 𝄾 𝄾 = 0.21; 𝅘𝅥𝅯 = 0.16 seconds

CLICK: 15⅛ FRAMES; M.M.: 95.21

Click	0	1	2	3	4	5	6	7	8	9
000	0:00.00	0:00.00	0:00.63	0:01.26	0:01.89	0:02.52	0:03.15	0:03.78	0:04.41	0:05.04
010	0:05.67	0:06.30	0:06.93	0:07.56	0:08.19	0:08.82	0:09.45	0:10.08	0:10.71	0:11.34
020	0:11.97	0:12.60	0:13.23	0:13.86	0:14.49	0:15.13	0:15.76	0:16.39	0:17.02	0:17.65
030	0:18.28	0:18.91	0:19.54	0:20.17	0:20.80	0:21.43	0:22.06	0:22.69	0:23.32	0:23.95
040	0:24.58	0:25.21	0:25.84	0:26.47	0:27.10	0:27.73	0:28.36	0:28.99	0:29.62	0:30.25
050	0:30.88	0:31.51	0:32.14	0:32.77	0:33.40	0:34.03	0:34.66	0:35.29	0:35.92	0:36.55
060	0:37.18	0:37.81	0:38.44	0:39.07	0:39.70	0:40.33	0:40.96	0:41.59	0:42.22	0:42.85
070	0:43.48	0:44.11	0:44.74	0:45.38	0:46.01	0:46.64	0:47.27	0:47.90	0:48.53	0:49.16
080	0:49.79	0:50.42	0:51.05	0:51.68	0:52.31	0:52.94	0:53.57	0:54.20	0:54.83	0:55.46
090	0:56.09	0:56.72	0:57.35	0:57.98	0:58.61	0:59.24	0:59.87	1:00.50	1:01.13	1:01.76
100	1:02.39	1:03.02	1:03.65	1:04.28	1:04.91	1:05.54	1:06.17	1:06.80	1:07.43	1:08.06
110	1:08.69	1:09.32	1:09.95	1:10.58	1:11.21	1:11.84	1:12.47	1:13.10	1:13.73	1:14.36
120	1:14.99	1:15.63	1:16.26	1:16.89	1:17.52	1:18.15	1:18.78	1:19.41	1:20.04	1:20.67
130	1:21.30	1:21.93	1:22.56	1:23.19	1:23.82	1:24.45	1:25.08	1:25.71	1:26.34	1:26.97
140	1:27.60	1:28.23	1:28.86	1:29.49	1:30.12	1:30.75	1:31.38	1:32.01	1:32.64	1:33.27
150	1:33.90	1:34.53	1:35.16	1:35.79	1:36.42	1:37.05	1:37.68	1:38.31	1:38.94	1:39.57
160	1:40.20	1:40.83	1:41.46	1:42.09	1:42.72	1:43.35	1:43.98	1:44.61	1:45.24	1:45.88
170	1:46.51	1:47.14	1:47.77	1:48.40	1:49.03	1:49.66	1:50.29	1:50.92	1:51.55	1:52.18
180	1:52.81	1:53.44	1:54.07	1:54.70	1:55.33	1:55.96	1:56.59	1:57.22	1:57.85	1:58.48
190	1:59.11	1:59.74	2:00.37	2:01.00	2:01.63	2:02.26	2:02.89	2:03.52	2:04.15	2:04.78
200	2:05.41	2:06.04	2:06.67	2:07.30	2:07.93	2:08.56	2:09.19	2:09.82	2:10.45	2:11.08
210	2:11.71	2:12.34	2:12.97	2:13.60	2:14.23	2:14.86	2:15.49	2:16.13	2:16.76	2:17.39
220	2:18.02	2:18.65	2:19.28	2:19.91	2:20.54	2:21.17	2:21.80	2:22.43	2:23.06	2:23.69
230	2:24.32	2:24.95	2:25.58	2:26.21	2:26.84	2:27.47	2:28.10	2:28.73	2:29.36	2:29.99
240	2:30.62	2:31.25	2:31.88	2:32.51	2:33.14	2:33.77	2:34.40	2:35.03	2:35.66	2:36.29
250	2:36.92	2:37.55	2:38.18	2:38.81	2:39.44	2:40.07	2:40.70	2:41.33	2:41.96	2:42.59
260	2:43.22	2:43.85	2:44.48	2:45.11	2:45.74	2:46.38	2:47.01	2:47.64	2:48.27	2:48.90
270	2:49.53	2:50.16	2:50.79	2:51.42	2:52.05	2:52.68	2:53.31	2:53.94	2:54.57	2:55.20
280	2:55.83	2:56.46	2:57.09	2:57.72	2:58.35	2:58.98	2:59.61	3:00.24	3:00.87	3:01.50
290	3:02.13	3:02.76	3:03.39	3:04.02	3:04.65	3:05.28	3:05.91	3:06.54	3:07.17	3:07.80
300	3:08.43	3:09.06	3:09.69	3:10.32	3:10.95	3:11.58	3:12.21	3:12.84	3:13.47	3:14.10
310	3:14.73	3:15.36	3:15.99	3:16.63	3:17.26	3:17.89	3:18.52	3:19.15	3:19.78	3:20.41
320	3:21.04	3:21.67	3:22.30	3:22.93	3:23.56	3:24.19	3:24.82	3:25.45	3:26.08	3:26.71
330	3:27.34	3:27.97	3:28.60	3:29.23	3:29.86	3:30.49	3:31.12	3:31.75	3:32.38	3:33.01
340	3:33.64	3:34.27	3:34.90	3:35.53	3:36.16	3:36.79	3:37.42	3:38.05	3:38.68	3:39.31
350	3:39.94	3:40.57	3:41.20	3:41.83	3:42.46	3:43.09	3:43.72	3:44.35	3:44.98	3:45.61
360	3:46.24	3:46.88	3:47.51	3:48.14	3:48.77	3:49.40	3:50.03	3:50.66	3:51.29	3:51.92
370	3:52.55	3:53.18	3:53.81	3:54.44	3:55.07	3:55.70	3:56.33	3:56.96	3:57.59	3:58.22
380	3:58.85	3:59.48	4:00.11	4:00.74	4:01.37	4:02.00	4:02.63	4:03.26	4:03.89	4:04.52
390	4:05.15	4:05.78	4:06.41	4:07.04	4:07.67	4:08.30	4:08.93	4:09.56	4:10.19	4:10.82
400	4:11.45	4:12.08	4:12.71	4:13.34	4:13.97	4:14.60	4:15.23	4:15.86	4:16.49	4:17.13
410	4:17.76	4:18.39	4:19.02	4:19.65	4:20.28	4:20.91	4:21.54	4:22.17	4:22.80	4:23.43
420	4:24.06	4:24.69	4:25.32	4:25.95	4:26.58	4:27.21	4:27.84	4:28.47	4:29.10	4:29.73
430	4:30.36	4:30.99	4:31.62	4:32.25	4:32.88	4:33.51	4:34.14	4:34.77	4:35.40	4:36.03
440	4:36.66	4:37.29	4:37.92	4:38.55	4:39.18	4:39.81	4:40.44	4:41.07	4:41.70	4:42.33
450	4:42.96	4:43.59	4:44.22	4:44.85	4:45.48	4:46.11	4:46.74	4:47.38	4:48.01	4:48.64
460	4:49.27	4:49.90	4:50.53	4:51.16	4:51.79	4:52.42	4:53.05	4:53.68	4:54.31	4:54.94
470	4:55.57	4:56.20	4:56.83	4:57.46	4:58.09	4:58.72	4:59.35	4:59.98	5:00.61	5:01.24
480	5:01.87	5:02.50	5:03.13	5:03.76	5:04.39	5:05.02	5:05.65	5:06.28	5:06.91	5:07.54
490	5:08.17	5:08.80	5:09.43	5:10.06	5:10.69	5:11.32	5:11.95	5:12.58	5:13.21	5:13.84
500	5:14.47	5:15.10	5:15.73	5:16.36	5:16.99	5:17.63	5:18.26	5:18.89	5:19.52	5:20.15
510	5:20.78	5:21.41	5:22.04	5:22.67	5:23.30	5:23.93	5:24.56	5:25.19	5:25.82	5:26.45
520	5:27.08	5:27.71	5:28.34	5:28.97	5:29.60	5:30.23	5:30.86	5:31.49	5:32.12	5:32.75
530	5:33.38	5:34.01	5:34.64	5:35.27	5:35.90	5:36.53	5:37.16	5:37.79	5:38.42	5:39.05
540	5:39.68	5:40.31	5:40.94	5:41.57	5:42.20	5:42.83	5:43.46	5:44.09	5:44.72	5:45.35
550	5:45.98	5:46.61	5:47.24	5:47.88	5:48.51	5:49.14	5:49.77	5:50.40	5:51.03	5:51.66
560	5:52.29	5:52.92	5:53.55	5:54.18	5:54.81	5:55.44	5:56.07	5:56.70	5:57.33	5:57.96
570	5:58.59	5:59.22	5:59.85	6:00.48	6:01.11	6:01.74	6:02.37	6:03.00	6:03.63	6:04.26
580	6:04.89	6:05.52	6:06.15	6:06.78	6:07.41	6:08.04	6:08.67	6:09.30	6:09.93	6:10.56
590	6:11.19	6:11.82	6:12.45	6:13.08	6:13.71	6:14.34	6:14.97	6:15.60	6:16.23	6:16.86

♩. = 0.95; ♩ = 0.63; ♪. = 0.47; (triplet ♩ 𝄾) = 0.42; ♪ = 0.32; (triplet ♪ 𝄾 𝄾) = 0.21; 𝅘𝅥𝅯 = 0.16 seconds

CLICK: 15⅝ FRAMES; M.M.: 94.43

Click	0	1	2	3	4	5	6	7	8	9
000	0:00.00	0:00.00	0:00.64	0:01.27	0:01.91	0:02.54	0:03.18	0:03.81	0:04.45	0:05.08
010	0:05.72	0:06.35	0:06.99	0:07.63	0:08.26	0:08.90	0:09.53	0:10.17	0:10.80	0:11.44
020	0:12.07	0:12.71	0:13.34	0:13.98	0:14.61	0:15.25	0:15.89	0:16.52	0:17.16	0:17.79
030	0:18.43	0:19.06	0:19.70	0:20.33	0:20.97	0:21.60	0:22.24	0:22.88	0:23.51	0:24.15
040	0:24.78	0:25.42	0:26.05	0:26.69	0:27.32	0:27.96	0:28.59	0:29.23	0:29.86	0:30.50
050	0:31.14	0:31.77	0:32.41	0:33.04	0:33.68	0:34.31	0:34.95	0:35.58	0:36.22	0:36.85
060	0:37.49	0:38.13	0:38.76	0:39.40	0:40.03	0:40.67	0:41.30	0:41.94	0:42.57	0:43.21
070	0:43.84	0:44.48	0:45.11	0:45.75	0:46.39	0:47.02	0:47.66	0:48.29	0:48.93	0:49.56
080	0:50.20	0:50.83	0:51.47	0:52.10	0:52.74	0:53.38	0:54.01	0:54.65	0:55.28	0:55.92
090	0:56.55	0:57.19	0:57.82	0:58.46	0:59.09	0:59.73	1:00.36	1:01.00	1:01.64	1:02.27
100	1:02.91	1:03.54	1:04.18	1:04.81	1:05.45	1:06.08	1:06.72	1:07.35	1:07.99	1:08.63
110	1:09.26	1:09.90	1:10.53	1:11.17	1:11.80	1:12.44	1:13.07	1:13.71	1:14.34	1:14.98
120	1:15.61	1:16.25	1:16.89	1:17.52	1:18.16	1:18.79	1:19.43	1:20.06	1:20.70	1:21.33
130	1:21.97	1:22.60	1:23.24	1:23.88	1:24.51	1:25.15	1:25.78	1:26.42	1:27.05	1:27.69
140	1:28.32	1:28.96	1:29.59	1:30.23	1:30.86	1:31.50	1:32.14	1:32.77	1:33.41	1:34.04
150	1:34.68	1:35.31	1:35.95	1:36.58	1:37.22	1:37.85	1:38.49	1:39.13	1:39.76	1:40.40
160	1:41.03	1:41.67	1:42.30	1:42.94	1:43.57	1:44.21	1:44.84	1:45.48	1:46.11	1:46.75
170	1:47.39	1:48.02	1:48.66	1:49.29	1:49.93	1:50.56	1:51.20	1:51.83	1:52.47	1:53.10
180	1:53.74	1:54.38	1:55.01	1:55.65	1:56.28	1:56.92	1:57.55	1:58.19	1:58.82	1:59.46
190	2:00.09	2:00.73	2:01.36	2:02.00	2:02.64	2:03.27	2:03.91	2:04.54	2:05.18	2:05.81
200	2:06.45	2:07.08	2:07.72	2:08.35	2:08.99	2:09.63	2:10.26	2:10.90	2:11.53	2:12.17
210	2:12.80	2:13.44	2:14.07	2:14.71	2:15.34	2:15.98	2:16.61	2:17.25	2:17.89	2:18.52
220	2:19.16	2:19.79	2:20.43	2:21.06	2:21.70	2:22.33	2:22.97	2:23.60	2:24.24	2:24.88
230	2:25.51	2:26.15	2:26.78	2:27.42	2:28.05	2:28.69	2:29.32	2:29.96	2:30.59	2:31.23
240	2:31.86	2:32.50	2:33.14	2:33.77	2:34.41	2:35.04	2:35.68	2:36.31	2:36.95	2:37.58
250	2:38.22	2:38.85	2:39.49	2:40.13	2:40.76	2:41.40	2:42.03	2:42.67	2:43.30	2:43.94
260	2:44.57	2:45.21	2:45.84	2:46.48	2:47.11	2:47.75	2:48.39	2:49.02	2:49.66	2:50.29
270	2:50.93	2:51.56	2:52.20	2:52.83	2:53.47	2:54.10	2:54.74	2:55.38	2:56.01	2:56.65
280	2:57.28	2:57.92	2:58.55	2:59.19	2:59.82	3:00.46	3:01.09	3:01.73	3:02.36	3:03.00
290	3:03.64	3:04.27	3:04.91	3:05.54	3:06.18	3:06.81	3:07.45	3:08.08	3:08.72	3:09.35
300	3:09.99	3:10.63	3:11.26	3:11.90	3:12.53	3:13.17	3:13.80	3:14.44	3:15.07	3:15.71
310	3:16.34	3:16.98	3:17.61	3:18.25	3:18.89	3:19.52	3:20.16	3:20.79	3:21.43	3:22.06
320	3:22.70	3:23.33	3:23.97	3:24.60	3:25.24	3:25.88	3:26.51	3:27.15	3:27.78	3:28.42
330	3:29.05	3:29.69	3:30.32	3:30.96	3:31.59	3:32.23	3:32.86	3:33.50	3:34.14	3:34.77
340	3:35.41	3:36.04	3:36.68	3:37.31	3:37.95	3:38.58	3:39.22	3:39.85	3:40.49	3:41.13
350	3:41.76	3:42.40	3:43.03	3:43.67	3:44.30	3:44.94	3:45.57	3:46.21	3:46.84	3:47.48
360	3:48.11	3:48.75	3:49.39	3:50.02	3:50.66	3:51.29	3:51.93	3:52.56	3:53.20	3:53.83
370	3:54.47	3:55.10	3:55.74	3:56.38	3:57.01	3:57.65	3:58.28	3:58.92	3:59.55	4:00.19
380	4:00.82	4:01.46	4:02.09	4:02.73	4:03.36	4:04.00	4:04.64	4:05.27	4:05.91	4:06.54
390	4:07.18	4:07.81	4:08.45	4:09.08	4:09.72	4:10.35	4:10.99	4:11.63	4:12.26	4:12.90
400	4:13.53	4:14.17	4:14.80	4:15.44	4:16.07	4:16.71	4:17.34	4:17.98	4:18.61	4:19.25
410	4:19.89	4:20.52	4:21.16	4:21.79	4:22.43	4:23.06	4:23.70	4:24.33	4:24.97	4:25.60
420	4:26.24	4:26.88	4:27.51	4:28.15	4:28.78	4:29.42	4:30.05	4:30.69	4:31.32	4:31.96
430	4:32.59	4:33.23	4:33.86	4:34.50	4:35.14	4:35.77	4:36.41	4:37.04	4:37.68	4:38.31
440	4:38.95	4:39.58	4:40.22	4:40.85	4:41.49	4:42.13	4:42.76	4:43.40	4:44.03	4:44.67
450	4:45.30	4:45.94	4:46.57	4:47.21	4:47.84	4:48.48	4:49.11	4:49.75	4:50.39	4:51.02
460	4:51.66	4:52.29	4:52.93	4:53.56	4:54.20	4:54.83	4:55.47	4:56.10	4:56.74	4:57.38
470	4:58.01	4:58.65	4:59.28	4:59.92	5:00.55	5:01.19	5:01.82	5:02.46	5:03.09	5:03.73
480	5:04.36	5:05.00	5:05.64	5:06.27	5:06.91	5:07.54	5:08.18	5:08.81	5:09.45	5:10.08
490	5:10.72	5:11.35	5:11.99	5:12.63	5:13.26	5:13.90	5:14.53	5:15.17	5:15.80	5:16.44
500	5:17.07	5:17.71	5:18.34	5:18.98	5:19.61	5:20.25	5:20.89	5:21.52	5:22.16	5:22.79
510	5:23.43	5:24.06	5:24.70	5:25.33	5:25.97	5:26.60	5:27.24	5:27.88	5:28.51	5:29.15
520	5:29.78	5:30.42	5:31.05	5:31.69	5:32.32	5:32.96	5:33.59	5:34.23	5:34.86	5:35.50
530	5:36.14	5:36.77	5:37.41	5:38.04	5:38.68	5:39.31	5:39.95	5:40.58	5:41.22	5:41.85
540	5:42.49	5:43.13	5:43.76	5:44.40	5:45.03	5:45.67	5:46.30	5:46.94	5:47.57	5:48.21
550	5:48.84	5:49.48	5:50.11	5:50.75	5:51.39	5:52.02	5:52.66	5:53.29	5:53.93	5:54.56
560	5:55.20	5:55.83	5:56.47	5:57.10	5:57.74	5:58.38	5:59.01	5:59.65	6:00.28	6:00.92
570	6:01.55	6:02.19	6:02.82	6:03.46	6:04.09	6:04.73	6:05.36	6:06.00	6:06.64	6:07.27
580	6:07.91	6:08.54	6:09.18	6:09.81	6:10.45	6:11.08	6:11.72	6:12.35	6:12.99	6:13.63
590	6:14.26	6:14.90	6:15.53	6:16.17	6:16.80	6:17.44	6:18.07	6:18.71	6:19.34	6:19.98

♩. = 0.95; ♩ = 0.64; ♪. = 0.48; (3: ♩ 𝄾) = 0.42; ♪ = 0.32; (3: ♪ 𝄾 𝄾) = 0.21; 𝅘𝅥𝅯 = 0.16 seconds

CLICK: 15⅜ FRAMES; M.M.: 93.66

Click	0	1	2	3	4	5	6	7	8	9
000	0:00.00	0:00.00	0:00.64	0:01.28	0:01.92	0:02.56	0:03.20	0:03.84	0:04.48	0:05.13
010	0:05.77	0:06.41	0:07.05	0:07.69	0:08.33	0:08.97	0:09.61	0:10.25	0:10.89	0:11.53
020	0:12.17	0:12.81	0:13.45	0:14.09	0:14.73	0:15.38	0:16.02	0:16.66	0:17.30	0:17.94
030	0:18.58	0:19.22	0:19.86	0:20.50	0:21.14	0:21.78	0:22.42	0:23.06	0:23.70	0:24.34
040	0:24.98	0:25.63	0:26.27	0:26.91	0:27.55	0:28.19	0:28.83	0:29.47	0:30.11	0:30.75
050	0:31.39	0:32.03	0:32.67	0:33.31	0:33.95	0:34.59	0:35.23	0:35.88	0:36.52	0:37.16
060	0:37.80	0:38.44	0:39.08	0:39.72	0:40.36	0:41.00	0:41.64	0:42.28	0:42.92	0:43.56
070	0:44.20	0:44.84	0:45.48	0:46.13	0:46.77	0:47.41	0:48.05	0:48.69	0:49.33	0:49.97
080	0:50.61	0:51.25	0:51.89	0:52.53	0:53.17	0:53.81	0:54.45	0:55.09	0:55.73	0:56.38
090	0:57.02	0:57.66	0:58.30	0:58.94	0:59.58	1:00.22	1:00.86	1:01.50	1:02.14	1:02.78
100	1:03.42	1:04.06	1:04.70	1:05.34	1:05.98	1:06.63	1:07.27	1:07.91	1:08.55	1:09.19
110	1:09.83	1:10.47	1:11.11	1:11.75	1:12.39	1:13.03	1:13.67	1:14.31	1:14.95	1:15.59
120	1:16.23	1:16.88	1:17.52	1:18.16	1:18.80	1:19.44	1:20.08	1:20.72	1:21.36	1:22.00
130	1:22.64	1:23.28	1:23.92	1:24.56	1:25.20	1:25.84	1:26.48	1:27.13	1:27.77	1:28.41
140	1:29.05	1:29.69	1:30.33	1:30.97	1:31.61	1:32.25	1:32.89	1:33.53	1:34.17	1:34.81
150	1:35.45	1:36.09	1:36.73	1:37.38	1:38.02	1:38.66	1:39.30	1:39.94	1:40.58	1:41.22
160	1:41.86	1:42.50	1:43.14	1:43.78	1:44.42	1:45.06	1:45.70	1:46.34	1:46.98	1:47.63
170	1:48.27	1:48.91	1:49.55	1:50.19	1:50.83	1:51.47	1:52.11	1:52.75	1:53.39	1:54.03
180	1:54.67	1:55.31	1:55.95	1:56.59	1:57.23	1:57.88	1:58.52	1:59.16	1:59.80	2:00.44
190	2:01.08	2:01.72	2:02.36	2:03.00	2:03.64	2:04.28	2:04.92	2:05.56	2:06.20	2:06.84
200	2:07.48	2:08.13	2:08.77	2:09.41	2:10.05	2:10.69	2:11.33	2:11.97	2:12.61	2:13.25
210	2:13.89	2:14.53	2:15.17	2:15.81	2:16.45	2:17.09	2:17.73	2:18.38	2:19.02	2:19.66
220	2:20.30	2:20.94	2:21.58	2:22.22	2:22.86	2:23.50	2:24.14	2:24.78	2:25.42	2:26.06
230	2:26.70	2:27.34	2:27.98	2:28.63	2:29.27	2:29.91	2:30.55	2:31.19	2:31.83	2:32.47
240	2:33.11	2:33.75	2:34.39	2:35.03	2:35.67	2:36.31	2:36.95	2:37.59	2:38.23	2:38.88
250	2:39.52	2:40.16	2:40.80	2:41.44	2:42.08	2:42.72	2:43.36	2:44.00	2:44.64	2:45.28
260	2:45.92	2:46.56	2:47.20	2:47.84	2:48.48	2:49.13	2:49.77	2:50.41	2:51.05	2:51.69
270	2:52.33	2:52.97	2:53.61	2:54.25	2:54.89	2:55.53	2:56.17	2:56.81	2:57.45	2:58.09
280	2:58.73	2:59.38	3:00.02	3:00.66	3:01.30	3:01.94	3:02.58	3:03.22	3:03.86	3:04.50
290	3:05.14	3:05.78	3:06.42	3:07.06	3:07.70	3:08.34	3:08.98	3:09.63	3:10.27	3:10.91
300	3:11.55	3:12.19	3:12.83	3:13.47	3:14.11	3:14.75	3:15.39	3:16.03	3:16.67	3:17.31
310	3:17.95	3:18.59	3:19.23	3:19.88	3:20.52	3:21.16	3:21.80	3:22.44	3:23.08	3:23.72
320	3:24.36	3:25.00	3:25.64	3:26.28	3:26.92	3:27.56	3:28.20	3:28.84	3:29.48	3:30.13
330	3:30.77	3:31.41	3:32.05	3:32.69	3:33.33	3:33.97	3:34.61	3:35.25	3:35.89	3:36.53
340	3:37.17	3:37.81	3:38.45	3:39.09	3:39.73	3:40.38	3:41.02	3:41.66	3:42.30	3:42.94
350	3:43.58	3:44.22	3:44.86	3:45.50	3:46.14	3:46.78	3:47.42	3:48.06	3:48.70	3:49.34
360	3:49.98	3:50.63	3:51.27	3:51.91	3:52.55	3:53.19	3:53.83	3:54.47	3:55.11	3:55.75
370	3:56.39	3:57.03	3:57.67	3:58.31	3:58.95	3:59.59	4:00.23	4:00.88	4:01.52	4:02.16
380	4:02.80	4:03.44	4:04.08	4:04.72	4:05.36	4:06.00	4:06.64	4:07.28	4:07.92	4:08.56
390	4:09.20	4:09.84	4:10.48	4:11.13	4:11.77	4:12.41	4:13.05	4:13.69	4:14.33	4:14.97
400	4:15.61	4:16.25	4:16.89	4:17.53	4:18.17	4:18.81	4:19.45	4:20.09	4:20.73	4:21.38
410	4:22.02	4:22.66	4:23.30	4:23.94	4:24.58	4:25.22	4:25.86	4:26.50	4:27.14	4:27.78
420	4:28.42	4:29.06	4:29.70	4:30.34	4:30.98	4:31.63	4:32.27	4:32.91	4:33.55	4:34.19
430	4:34.83	4:35.47	4:36.11	4:36.75	4:37.39	4:38.03	4:38.67	4:39.31	4:39.95	4:40.59
440	4:41.23	4:41.88	4:42.52	4:43.16	4:43.80	4:44.44	4:45.08	4:45.72	4:46.36	4:47.00
450	4:47.64	4:48.28	4:48.92	4:49.56	4:50.20	4:50.84	4:51.48	4:52.13	4:52.77	4:53.41
460	4:54.05	4:54.69	4:55.33	4:55.97	4:56.61	4:57.25	4:57.89	4:58.53	4:59.17	4:59.81
470	5:00.45	5:01.09	5:01.73	5:02.38	5:03.02	5:03.66	5:04.30	5:04.94	5:05.58	5:06.22
480	5:06.86	5:07.50	5:08.14	5:08.78	5:09.42	5:10.06	5:10.70	5:11.34	5:11.98	5:12.63
490	5:13.27	5:13.91	5:14.55	5:15.19	5:15.83	5:16.47	5:17.11	5:17.75	5:18.39	5:19.03
500	5:19.67	5:20.31	5:20.95	5:21.59	5:22.23	5:22.88	5:23.52	5:24.16	5:24.80	5:25.44
510	5:26.08	5:26.72	5:27.36	5:28.00	5:28.64	5:29.28	5:29.92	5:30.56	5:31.20	5:31.84
520	5:32.48	5:33.13	5:33.77	5:34.41	5:35.05	5:35.69	5:36.33	5:36.97	5:37.61	5:38.25
530	5:38.89	5:39.53	5:40.17	5:40.81	5:41.45	5:42.09	5:42.73	5:43.38	5:44.02	5:44.66
540	5:45.30	5:45.94	5:46.58	5:47.22	5:47.86	5:48.50	5:49.14	5:49.78	5:50.42	5:51.06
550	5:51.70	5:52.34	5:52.98	5:53.63	5:54.27	5:54.91	5:55.55	5:56.19	5:56.83	5:57.47
560	5:58.11	5:58.75	5:59.39	6:00.03	6:00.67	6:01.31	6:01.95	6:02.59	6:03.23	6:03.88
570	6:04.52	6:05.16	6:05.80	6:06.44	6:07.08	6:07.72	6:08.36	6:09.00	6:09.64	6:10.28
580	6:10.92	6:11.56	6:12.20	6:12.84	6:13.48	6:14.13	6:14.77	6:15.41	6:16.05	6:16.69
590	6:17.33	6:17.97	6:18.61	6:19.25	6:19.89	6:20.53	6:21.17	6:21.81	6:22.45	6:23.09

♩. = 0.96; ♩ = 0.64; ♪. = 0.48; (triplet ♩ 𝄾) = 0.43; ♪ = 0.32; (triplet ♪ 𝄾 𝄾) = 0.21; 𝅘𝅥𝅯 = 0.16 seconds

CLICK: 15 4/8 FRAMES; M.M.: 92.90

Click	0	1	2	3	4	5	6	7	8	9
000	0:00.00	0:00.00	0:00.65	0:01.29	0:01.94	0:02.58	0:03.23	0:03.88	0:04.52	0:05.17
010	0:05.81	0:06.46	0:07.10	0:07.75	0:08.40	0:09.04	0:09.69	0:10.33	0:10.98	0:11.63
020	0:12.27	0:12.92	0:13.56	0:14.21	0:14.85	0:15.50	0:16.15	0:16.79	0:17.44	0:18.08
030	0:18.73	0:19.38	0:20.02	0:20.67	0:21.31	0:21.96	0:22.60	0:23.25	0:23.90	0:24.54
040	0:25.19	0:25.83	0:26.48	0:27.13	0:27.77	0:28.42	0:29.06	0:29.71	0:30.35	0:31.00
050	0:31.65	0:32.29	0:32.94	0:33.58	0:34.23	0:34.88	0:35.52	0:36.17	0:36.81	0:37.46
060	0:38.10	0:38.75	0:39.40	0:40.04	0:40.69	0:41.33	0:41.98	0:42.63	0:43.27	0:43.92
070	0:44.56	0:45.21	0:45.85	0:46.50	0:47.15	0:47.79	0:48.44	0:49.08	0:49.73	0:50.38
080	0:51.02	0:51.67	0:52.31	0:52.96	0:53.60	0:54.25	0:54.90	0:55.54	0:56.19	0:56.83
090	0:57.48	0:58.13	0:58.77	0:59.42	1:00.06	1:00.71	1:01.35	1:02.00	1:02.65	1:03.29
100	1:03.94	1:04.58	1:05.23	1:05.88	1:06.52	1:07.17	1:07.81	1:08.46	1:09.10	1:09.75
110	1:10.40	1:11.04	1:11.69	1:12.33	1:12.98	1:13.63	1:14.27	1:14.92	1:15.56	1:16.21
120	1:16.85	1:17.50	1:18.15	1:18.79	1:19.44	1:20.08	1:20.73	1:21.38	1:22.02	1:22.67
130	1:23.31	1:23.96	1:24.60	1:25.25	1:25.90	1:26.54	1:27.19	1:27.83	1:28.48	1:29.13
140	1:29.77	1:30.42	1:31.06	1:31.71	1:32.35	1:33.00	1:33.65	1:34.29	1:34.94	1:35.58
150	1:36.23	1:36.88	1:37.52	1:38.17	1:38.81	1:39.46	1:40.10	1:40.75	1:41.40	1:42.04
160	1:42.69	1:43.33	1:43.98	1:44.63	1:45.27	1:45.92	1:46.56	1:47.21	1:47.85	1:48.50
170	1:49.15	1:49.79	1:50.44	1:51.08	1:51.73	1:52.38	1:53.02	1:53.67	1:54.31	1:54.96
180	1:55.60	1:56.25	1:56.90	1:57.54	1:58.19	1:58.83	1:59.48	2:00.12	2:00.77	2:01.42
190	2:02.06	2:02.71	2:03.35	2:04.00	2:04.65	2:05.29	2:05.94	2:06.58	2:07.23	2:07.88
200	2:08.52	2:09.17	2:09.81	2:10.46	2:11.10	2:11.75	2:12.40	2:13.04	2:13.69	2:14.33
210	2:14.98	2:15.63	2:16.27	2:16.92	2:17.56	2:18.21	2:18.85	2:19.50	2:20.15	2:20.79
220	2:21.44	2:22.08	2:22.73	2:23.38	2:24.02	2:24.67	2:25.31	2:25.96	2:26.60	2:27.25
230	2:27.90	2:28.54	2:29.19	2:29.83	2:30.48	2:31.12	2:31.77	2:32.42	2:33.06	2:33.71
240	2:34.35	2:35.00	2:35.65	2:36.29	2:36.94	2:37.58	2:38.23	2:38.88	2:39.52	2:40.17
250	2:40.81	2:41.46	2:42.10	2:42.75	2:43.40	2:44.04	2:44.69	2:45.33	2:45.98	2:46.63
260	2:47.27	2:47.92	2:48.56	2:49.21	2:49.85	2:50.50	2:51.15	2:51.79	2:52.44	2:53.08
270	2:53.73	2:54.38	2:55.02	2:55.67	2:56.31	2:56.96	2:57.60	2:58.25	2:58.90	2:59.54
280	3:00.19	3:00.83	3:01.48	3:02.13	3:02.77	3:03.42	3:04.06	3:04.71	3:05.35	3:06.00
290	3:06.65	3:07.29	3:07.94	3:08.58	3:09.23	3:09.88	3:10.52	3:11.17	3:11.81	3:12.46
300	3:13.10	3:13.75	3:14.40	3:15.04	3:15.69	3:16.33	3:16.98	3:17.63	3:18.27	3:18.92
310	3:19.56	3:20.21	3:20.85	3:21.50	3:22.15	3:22.79	3:23.44	3:24.08	3:24.73	3:25.38
320	3:26.02	3:26.67	3:27.31	3:27.96	3:28.60	3:29.25	3:29.90	3:30.54	3:31.19	3:31.83
330	3:32.48	3:33.13	3:33.77	3:34.42	3:35.06	3:35.71	3:36.35	3:37.00	3:37.65	3:38.29
340	3:38.94	3:39.58	3:40.23	3:40.88	3:41.52	3:42.17	3:42.81	3:43.46	3:44.10	3:44.75
350	3:45.40	3:46.04	3:46.69	3:47.33	3:47.98	3:48.63	3:49.27	3:49.92	3:50.56	3:51.21
360	3:51.85	3:52.50	3:53.15	3:53.79	3:54.44	3:55.08	3:55.73	3:56.38	3:57.02	3:57.67
370	3:58.31	3:58.96	3:59.60	4:00.25	4:00.90	4:01.54	4:02.19	4:02.83	4:03.48	4:04.12
380	4:04.77	4:05.42	4:06.06	4:06.71	4:07.35	4:08.00	4:08.65	4:09.29	4:09.94	4:10.58
390	4:11.23	4:11.88	4:12.52	4:13.17	4:13.81	4:14.46	4:15.10	4:15.75	4:16.40	4:17.04
400	4:17.69	4:18.33	4:18.98	4:19.63	4:20.27	4:20.92	4:21.56	4:22.21	4:22.85	4:23.50
410	4:24.15	4:24.79	4:25.44	4:26.08	4:26.73	4:27.38	4:28.02	4:28.67	4:29.31	4:29.96
420	4:30.60	4:31.25	4:31.90	4:32.54	4:33.19	4:33.83	4:34.48	4:35.13	4:35.77	4:36.42
430	4:37.06	4:37.71	4:38.35	4:39.00	4:39.65	4:40.29	4:40.94	4:41.58	4:42.23	4:42.88
440	4:43.52	4:44.17	4:44.81	4:45.46	4:46.10	4:46.75	4:47.40	4:48.04	4:48.69	4:49.33
450	4:49.98	4:50.63	4:51.27	4:51.92	4:52.56	4:53.21	4:53.85	4:54.50	4:55.15	4:55.79
460	4:56.44	4:57.08	4:57.73	4:58.37	4:59.02	4:59.67	5:00.31	5:00.96	5:01.60	5:02.25
470	5:02.90	5:03.54	5:04.19	5:04.83	5:05.48	5:06.13	5:06.77	5:07.42	5:08.06	5:08.71
480	5:09.35	5:10.00	5:10.65	5:11.29	5:11.94	5:12.58	5:13.23	5:13.88	5:14.52	5:15.17
490	5:15.81	5:16.46	5:17.10	5:17.75	5:18.40	5:19.04	5:19.69	5:20.33	5:20.98	5:21.63
500	5:22.27	5:22.92	5:23.56	5:24.21	5:24.85	5:25.50	5:26.15	5:26.79	5:27.44	5:28.08
510	5:28.73	5:29.38	5:30.02	5:30.67	5:31.31	5:31.96	5:32.60	5:33.25	5:33.90	5:34.54
520	5:35.19	5:35.83	5:36.48	5:37.13	5:37.77	5:38.42	5:39.06	5:39.71	5:40.35	5:41.00
530	5:41.65	5:42.29	5:42.94	5:43.58	5:44.23	5:44.88	5:45.52	5:46.17	5:46.81	5:47.46
540	5:48.10	5:48.75	5:49.40	5:50.04	5:50.69	5:51.33	5:51.98	5:52.63	5:53.27	5:53.92
550	5:54.56	5:55.21	5:55.85	5:56.50	5:57.15	5:57.79	5:58.44	5:59.08	5:59.73	6:00.38
560	6:01.02	6:01.67	6:02.31	6:02.96	6:03.60	6:04.25	6:04.90	6:05.54	6:06.19	6:06.83
570	6:07.48	6:08.13	6:08.77	6:09.42	6:10.06	6:10.71	6:11.35	6:12.00	6:12.65	6:13.29
580	6:13.94	6:14.58	6:15.23	6:15.88	6:16.52	6:17.17	6:17.81	6:18.46	6:19.10	6:19.75
590	6:20.40	6:21.04	6:21.69	6:22.33	6:22.98	6:23.63	6:24.27	6:24.92	6:25.56	6:26.21

♩. = 0.97; ♩ = 0.65; ♪. = 0.48; (triplet ♩ 𝄾) = 0.43; ♪ = 0.32; (triplet ♪ 𝄾 𝄾) = 0.22; 𝅘𝅥𝅯 = 0.16 seconds

CLICK: 15⅝ FRAMES; M.M.: 92.16

Click	0	1	2	3	4	5	6	7	8	9
000	0:00.00	0:00.00	0:00.65	0:01.30	0:01.95	0:02.60	0:03.26	0:03.91	0:04.56	0:05.21
010	0:05.86	0:06.51	0:07.16	0:07.81	0:08.46	0:09.11	0:09.77	0:10.42	0:11.07	0:11.72
020	0:12.37	0:13.02	0:13.67	0:14.32	0:14.97	0:15.62	0:16.28	0:16.93	0:17.58	0:18.23
030	0:18.88	0:19.53	0:20.18	0:20.83	0:21.48	0:22.14	0:22.79	0:23.44	0:24.09	0:24.74
040	0:25.39	0:26.04	0:26.69	0:27.34	0:27.99	0:28.65	0:29.30	0:29.95	0:30.60	0:31.25
050	0:31.90	0:32.55	0:33.20	0:33.85	0:34.51	0:35.16	0:35.81	0:36.46	0:37.11	0:37.76
060	0:38.41	0:39.06	0:39.71	0:40.36	0:41.02	0:41.67	0:42.32	0:42.97	0:43.62	0:44.27
070	0:44.92	0:45.57	0:46.22	0:46.88	0:47.53	0:48.18	0:48.83	0:49.48	0:50.13	0:50.78
080	0:51.43	0:52.08	0:52.73	0:53.39	0:54.04	0:54.69	0:55.34	0:55.99	0:56.64	0:57.29
090	0:57.94	0:58.59	0:59.24	0:59.90	1:00.55	1:01.20	1:01.85	1:02.50	1:03.15	1:03.80
100	1:04.45	1:05.10	1:05.76	1:06.41	1:07.06	1:07.71	1:08.36	1:09.01	1:09.66	1:10.31
110	1:10.96	1:11.61	1:12.27	1:12.92	1:13.57	1:14.22	1:14.87	1:15.52	1:16.17	1:16.82
120	1:17.47	1:18.12	1:18.78	1:19.43	1:20.08	1:20.73	1:21.38	1:22.03	1:22.68	1:23.33
130	1:23.98	1:24.64	1:25.29	1:25.94	1:26.59	1:27.24	1:27.89	1:28.54	1:29.19	1:29.84
140	1:30.49	1:31.15	1:31.80	1:32.45	1:33.10	1:33.75	1:34.40	1:35.05	1:35.70	1:36.35
150	1:37.01	1:37.66	1:38.31	1:38.96	1:39.61	1:40.26	1:40.91	1:41.56	1:42.21	1:42.86
160	1:43.52	1:44.17	1:44.82	1:45.47	1:46.12	1:46.77	1:47.42	1:48.07	1:48.72	1:49.37
170	1:50.03	1:50.68	1:51.33	1:51.98	1:52.63	1:53.28	1:53.93	1:54.58	1:55.23	1:55.89
180	1:56.54	1:57.19	1:57.84	1:58.49	1:59.14	1:59.79	2:00.44	2:01.09	2:01.74	2:02.40
190	2:03.05	2:03.70	2:04.35	2:05.00	2:05.65	2:06.30	2:06.95	2:07.60	2:08.26	2:08.91
200	2:09.56	2:10.21	2:10.86	2:11.51	2:12.16	2:12.81	2:13.46	2:14.11	2:14.77	2:15.42
210	2:16.07	2:16.72	2:17.37	2:18.02	2:18.67	2:19.32	2:19.97	2:20.63	2:21.28	2:21.93
220	2:22.58	2:23.23	2:23.88	2:24.53	2:25.18	2:25.83	2:26.48	2:27.14	2:27.79	2:28.44
230	2:29.09	2:29.74	2:30.39	2:31.04	2:31.69	2:32.34	2:32.99	2:33.65	2:34.30	2:34.95
240	2:35.60	2:36.25	2:36.90	2:37.55	2:38.20	2:38.85	2:39.51	2:40.16	2:40.81	2:41.46
250	2:42.11	2:42.76	2:43.41	2:44.06	2:44.71	2:45.36	2:46.02	2:46.67	2:47.32	2:47.97
260	2:48.62	2:49.27	2:49.92	2:50.57	2:51.22	2:51.87	2:52.53	2:53.18	2:53.83	2:54.48
270	2:55.13	2:55.78	2:56.43	2:57.08	2:57.73	2:58.39	2:59.04	2:59.69	3:00.34	3:00.99
280	3:01.64	3:02.29	3:02.94	3:03.59	3:04.24	3:04.90	3:05.55	3:06.20	3:06.85	3:07.50
290	3:08.15	3:08.80	3:09.45	3:10.10	3:10.76	3:11.41	3:12.06	3:12.71	3:13.36	3:14.01
300	3:14.66	3:15.31	3:15.96	3:16.61	3:17.27	3:17.92	3:18.57	3:19.22	3:19.87	3:20.52
310	3:21.17	3:21.82	3:22.47	3:23.12	3:23.78	3:24.43	3:25.08	3:25.73	3:26.38	3:27.03
320	3:27.68	3:28.33	3:28.98	3:29.64	3:30.29	3:30.94	3:31.59	3:32.24	3:32.89	3:33.54
330	3:34.19	3:34.84	3:35.49	3:36.15	3:36.80	3:37.45	3:38.10	3:38.75	3:39.40	3:40.05
340	3:40.70	3:41.35	3:42.01	3:42.66	3:43.31	3:43.96	3:44.61	3:45.26	3:45.91	3:46.56
350	3:47.21	3:47.86	3:48.52	3:49.17	3:49.82	3:50.47	3:51.12	3:51.77	3:52.42	3:53.07
360	3:53.72	3:54.37	3:55.03	3:55.68	3:56.33	3:56.98	3:57.63	3:58.28	3:58.93	3:59.58
370	4:00.23	4:00.89	4:01.54	4:02.19	4:02.84	4:03.49	4:04.14	4:04.79	4:05.44	4:06.09
380	4:06.74	4:07.40	4:08.05	4:08.70	4:09.35	4:10.00	4:10.65	4:11.30	4:11.95	4:12.60
390	4:13.26	4:13.91	4:14.56	4:15.21	4:15.86	4:16.51	4:17.16	4:17.81	4:18.46	4:19.11
400	4:19.77	4:20.42	4:21.07	4:21.72	4:22.37	4:23.02	4:23.67	4:24.32	4:24.97	4:25.62
410	4:26.28	4:26.93	4:27.58	4:28.23	4:28.88	4:29.53	4:30.18	4:30.83	4:31.48	4:32.14
420	4:32.79	4:33.44	4:34.09	4:34.74	4:35.39	4:36.04	4:36.69	4:37.34	4:37.99	4:38.65
430	4:39.30	4:39.95	4:40.60	4:41.25	4:41.90	4:42.55	4:43.20	4:43.85	4:44.51	4:45.16
440	4:45.81	4:46.46	4:47.11	4:47.76	4:48.41	4:49.06	4:49.71	4:50.36	4:51.02	4:51.67
450	4:52.32	4:52.97	4:53.62	4:54.27	4:54.92	4:55.57	4:56.22	4:56.87	4:57.53	4:58.18
460	4:58.83	4:59.48	5:00.13	5:00.78	5:01.43	5:02.08	5:02.73	5:03.39	5:04.04	5:04.69
470	5:05.34	5:05.99	5:06.64	5:07.29	5:07.94	5:08.59	5:09.24	5:09.90	5:10.55	5:11.20
480	5:11.85	5:12.50	5:13.15	5:13.80	5:14.45	5:15.10	5:15.76	5:16.41	5:17.06	5:17.71
490	5:18.36	5:19.01	5:19.66	5:20.31	5:20.96	5:21.61	5:22.27	5:22.92	5:23.57	5:24.22
500	5:24.87	5:25.52	5:26.17	5:26.82	5:27.47	5:28.13	5:28.78	5:29.43	5:30.08	5:30.73
510	5:31.38	5:32.03	5:32.68	5:33.33	5:33.98	5:34.64	5:35.29	5:35.94	5:36.59	5:37.24
520	5:37.89	5:38.54	5:39.19	5:39.84	5:40.49	5:41.15	5:41.80	5:42.45	5:43.10	5:43.75
530	5:44.40	5:45.05	5:45.70	5:46.35	5:47.01	5:47.66	5:48.31	5:48.96	5:49.61	5:50.26
540	5:50.91	5:51.56	5:52.21	5:52.86	5:53.52	5:54.17	5:54.82	5:55.47	5:56.12	5:56.77
550	5:57.42	5:58.07	5:58.72	5:59.37	6:00.03	6:00.68	6:01.33	6:01.98	6:02.63	6:03.28
560	6:03.93	6:04.58	6:05.23	6:05.89	6:06.54	6:07.19	6:07.84	6:08.49	6:09.14	6:09.79
570	6:10.44	6:11.09	6:11.74	6:12.40	6:13.05	6:13.70	6:14.35	6:15.00	6:15.65	6:16.30
580	6:16.95	6:17.60	6:18.26	6:18.91	6:19.56	6:20.21	6:20.86	6:21.51	6:22.16	6:22.81
590	6:23.46	6:24.11	6:24.77	6:25.42	6:26.07	6:26.72	6:27.37	6:28.02	6:28.67	6:29.32

♩. = 0.98; ♩ = 0.65; ♪. = 0.49; ♩ 𝄾 (triplet, 3) = 0.43; ♪ = 0.33; ♪ 𝄾 𝄾 (triplet, 3) = 0.22; 𝅘𝅥𝅯 = 0.16 seconds

CLICK: 15 6/8 FRAMES; M.M.: 91.43

Click	0	1	2	3	4	5	6	7	8	9
000	0:00.00	0:00.00	0:00.66	0:01.31	0:01.97	0:02.63	0:03.28	0:03.94	0:04.59	0:05.25
010	0:05.91	0:06.56	0:07.22	0:07.87	0:08.53	0:09.19	0:09.84	0:10.50	0:11.16	0:11.81
020	0:12.47	0:13.13	0:13.78	0:14.44	0:15.09	0:15.75	0:16.41	0:17.06	0:17.72	0:18.38
030	0:19.03	0:19.69	0:20.34	0:21.00	0:21.66	0:22.31	0:22.97	0:23.62	0:24.28	0:24.94
040	0:25.59	0:26.25	0:26.91	0:27.56	0:28.22	0:28.88	0:29.53	0:30.19	0:30.84	0:31.50
050	0:32.16	0:32.81	0:33.47	0:34.12	0:34.78	0:35.44	0:36.09	0:36.75	0:37.41	0:38.06
060	0:38.72	0:39.38	0:40.03	0:40.69	0:41.34	0:42.00	0:42.66	0:43.31	0:43.97	0:44.63
070	0:45.28	0:45.94	0:46.59	0:47.25	0:47.91	0:48.56	0:49.22	0:49.88	0:50.53	0:51.19
080	0:51.84	0:52.50	0:53.16	0:53.81	0:54.47	0:55.13	0:55.78	0:56.44	0:57.09	0:57.75
090	0:58.41	0:59.06	0:59.72	1:00.38	1:01.03	1:01.69	1:02.34	1:03.00	1:03.66	1:04.31
100	1:04.97	1:05.63	1:06.28	1:06.94	1:07.59	1:08.25	1:08.91	1:09.56	1:10.22	1:10.87
110	1:11.53	1:12.19	1:12.84	1:13.50	1:14.16	1:14.81	1:15.47	1:16.12	1:16.78	1:17.44
120	1:18.09	1:18.75	1:19.41	1:20.06	1:20.72	1:21.37	1:22.03	1:22.69	1:23.34	1:24.00
130	1:24.66	1:25.31	1:25.97	1:26.63	1:27.28	1:27.94	1:28.59	1:29.25	1:29.91	1:30.56
140	1:31.22	1:31.88	1:32.53	1:33.19	1:33.84	1:34.50	1:35.16	1:35.81	1:36.47	1:37.13
150	1:37.78	1:38.44	1:39.09	1:39.75	1:40.41	1:41.06	1:41.72	1:42.37	1:43.03	1:43.69
160	1:44.34	1:45.00	1:45.66	1:46.31	1:46.97	1:47.62	1:48.28	1:48.94	1:49.59	1:50.25
170	1:50.91	1:51.56	1:52.22	1:52.88	1:53.53	1:54.19	1:54.84	1:55.50	1:56.16	1:56.81
180	1:57.47	1:58.13	1:58.78	1:59.44	2:00.09	2:00.75	2:01.41	2:02.06	2:02.72	2:03.37
190	2:04.03	2:04.69	2:05.34	2:06.00	2:06.66	2:07.31	2:07.97	2:08.62	2:09.28	2:09.94
200	2:10.59	2:11.25	2:11.91	2:12.56	2:13.22	2:13.88	2:14.53	2:15.19	2:15.84	2:16.50
210	2:17.16	2:17.81	2:18.47	2:19.12	2:19.78	2:20.44	2:21.09	2:21.75	2:22.41	2:23.06
220	2:23.72	2:24.38	2:25.03	2:25.69	2:26.34	2:27.00	2:27.66	2:28.31	2:28.97	2:29.62
230	2:30.28	2:30.94	2:31.59	2:32.25	2:32.91	2:33.56	2:34.22	2:34.87	2:35.53	2:36.19
240	2:36.84	2:37.50	2:38.16	2:38.81	2:39.47	2:40.13	2:40.78	2:41.44	2:42.09	2:42.75
250	2:43.41	2:44.06	2:44.72	2:45.37	2:46.03	2:46.69	2:47.34	2:48.00	2:48.66	2:49.31
260	2:49.97	2:50.63	2:51.28	2:51.94	2:52.59	2:53.25	2:53.91	2:54.56	2:55.22	2:55.87
270	2:56.53	2:57.19	2:57.84	2:58.50	2:59.16	2:59.81	3:00.47	3:01.12	3:01.78	3:02.44
280	3:03.09	3:03.75	3:04.41	3:05.06	3:05.72	3:06.38	3:07.03	3:07.69	3:08.34	3:09.00
290	3:09.66	3:10.31	3:10.97	3:11.62	3:12.28	3:12.94	3:13.59	3:14.25	3:14.91	3:15.56
300	3:16.22	3:16.88	3:17.53	3:18.19	3:18.84	3:19.50	3:20.16	3:20.81	3:21.47	3:22.12
310	3:22.78	3:23.44	3:24.09	3:24.75	3:25.41	3:26.06	3:26.72	3:27.37	3:28.03	3:28.69
320	3:29.34	3:30.00	3:30.66	3:31.31	3:31.97	3:32.63	3:33.28	3:33.94	3:34.59	3:35.25
330	3:35.91	3:36.56	3:37.22	3:37.87	3:38.53	3:39.19	3:39.84	3:40.50	3:41.16	3:41.81
340	3:42.47	3:43.13	3:43.78	3:44.44	3:45.09	3:45.75	3:46.41	3:47.06	3:47.72	3:48.37
350	3:49.03	3:49.69	3:50.34	3:51.00	3:51.66	3:52.31	3:52.97	3:53.62	3:54.28	3:54.94
360	3:55.59	3:56.25	3:56.91	3:57.56	3:58.22	3:58.88	3:59.53	4:00.19	4:00.84	4:01.50
370	4:02.16	4:02.81	4:03.47	4:04.12	4:04.78	4:05.44	4:06.09	4:06.75	4:07.41	4:08.06
380	4:08.72	4:09.38	4:10.03	4:10.69	4:11.34	4:12.00	4:12.66	4:13.31	4:13.97	4:14.63
390	4:15.28	4:15.94	4:16.59	4:17.25	4:17.91	4:18.56	4:19.22	4:19.87	4:20.53	4:21.19
400	4:21.84	4:22.50	4:23.16	4:23.81	4:24.47	4:25.12	4:25.78	4:26.44	4:27.09	4:27.75
410	4:28.41	4:29.06	4:29.72	4:30.37	4:31.03	4:31.69	4:32.34	4:33.00	4:33.66	4:34.31
420	4:34.97	4:35.63	4:36.28	4:36.94	4:37.59	4:38.25	4:38.91	4:39.56	4:40.22	4:40.88
430	4:41.53	4:42.19	4:42.84	4:43.50	4:44.16	4:44.81	4:45.47	4:46.12	4:46.78	4:47.44
440	4:48.09	4:48.75	4:49.41	4:50.06	4:50.72	4:51.37	4:52.03	4:52.69	4:53.34	4:54.00
450	4:54.66	4:55.31	4:55.97	4:56.62	4:57.28	4:57.94	4:58.59	4:59.25	4:59.91	5:00.56
460	5:01.22	5:01.88	5:02.53	5:03.19	5:03.84	5:04.50	5:05.16	5:05.81	5:06.47	5:07.13
470	5:07.78	5:08.44	5:09.09	5:09.75	5:10.41	5:11.06	5:11.72	5:12.37	5:13.03	5:13.69
480	5:14.34	5:15.00	5:15.66	5:16.31	5:16.97	5:17.62	5:18.28	5:18.94	5:19.59	5:20.25
490	5:20.91	5:21.56	5:22.22	5:22.87	5:23.53	5:24.19	5:24.84	5:25.50	5:26.16	5:26.81
500	5:27.47	5:28.13	5:28.78	5:29.44	5:30.09	5:30.75	5:31.41	5:32.06	5:32.72	5:33.38
510	5:34.03	5:34.69	5:35.34	5:36.00	5:36.66	5:37.31	5:37.97	5:38.62	5:39.28	5:39.94
520	5:40.59	5:41.25	5:41.91	5:42.56	5:43.22	5:43.87	5:44.53	5:45.19	5:45.84	5:46.50
530	5:47.16	5:47.81	5:48.47	5:49.12	5:49.78	5:50.44	5:51.09	5:51.75	5:52.41	5:53.06
540	5:53.72	5:54.38	5:55.03	5:55.69	5:56.34	5:57.00	5:57.66	5:58.31	5:58.97	5:59.63
550	6:00.28	6:00.94	6:01.59	6:02.25	6:02.91	6:03.56	6:04.22	6:04.87	6:05.53	6:06.19
560	6:06.84	6:07.50	6:08.16	6:08.81	6:09.47	6:10.12	6:10.78	6:11.44	6:12.09	6:12.75
570	6:13.41	6:14.06	6:14.72	6:15.37	6:16.03	6:16.69	6:17.34	6:18.00	6:18.66	6:19.31
580	6:19.97	6:20.63	6:21.28	6:21.94	6:22.59	6:23.25	6:23.91	6:24.56	6:25.22	6:25.88
590	6:26.53	6:27.19	6:27.84	6:28.50	6:29.16	6:29.81	6:30.47	6:31.12	6:31.78	6:32.44

♩. = 0.98; ♩ = 0.66; ♪. = 0.49; (triplet ♩ 𝄾) = 0.44; ♪ = 0.33; (triplet ♪ 𝄾 𝄾) = 0.22; 𝅘𝅥𝅯 = 0.16 seconds

CLICK: 15⅞ FRAMES; M.M.: 90.71

Click	0	1	2	3	4	5	6	7	8	9
000	0:00.00	0:00.00	0:00.66	0:01.32	0:01.98	0:02.65	0:03.31	0:03.97	0:04.63	0:05.29
010	0:05.95	0:06.61	0:07.28	0:07.94	0:08.60	0:09.26	0:09.92	0:10.58	0:11.24	0:11.91
020	0:12.57	0:13.23	0:13.89	0:14.55	0:15.21	0:15.88	0:16.54	0:17.20	0:17.86	0:18.52
030	0:19.18	0:19.84	0:20.51	0:21.17	0:21.83	0:22.49	0:23.15	0:23.81	0:24.47	0:25.14
040	0:25.80	0:26.46	0:27.12	0:27.78	0:28.44	0:29.10	0:29.77	0:30.43	0:31.09	0:31.75
050	0:32.41	0:33.07	0:33.73	0:34.40	0:35.06	0:35.72	0:36.38	0:37.04	0:37.70	0:38.36
060	0:39.03	0:39.69	0:40.35	0:41.01	0:41.67	0:42.33	0:42.99	0:43.66	0:44.32	0:44.98
070	0:45.64	0:46.30	0:46.96	0:47.63	0:48.29	0:48.95	0:49.61	0:50.27	0:50.93	0:51.59
080	0:52.26	0:52.92	0:53.58	0:54.24	0:54.90	0:55.56	0:56.22	0:56.89	0:57.55	0:58.21
090	0:58.87	0:59.53	1:00.19	1:00.85	1:01.52	1:02.18	1:02.84	1:03.50	1:04.16	1:04.82
100	1:05.48	1:06.15	1:06.81	1:07.47	1:08.13	1:08.79	1:09.45	1:10.11	1:10.78	1:11.44
110	1:12.10	1:12.76	1:13.42	1:14.08	1:14.74	1:15.41	1:16.07	1:16.73	1:17.39	1:18.05
120	1:18.71	1:19.37	1:20.04	1:20.70	1:21.36	1:22.02	1:22.68	1:23.34	1:24.01	1:24.67
130	1:25.33	1:25.99	1:26.65	1:27.31	1:27.97	1:28.64	1:29.30	1:29.96	1:30.62	1:31.28
140	1:31.94	1:32.60	1:33.27	1:33.93	1:34.59	1:35.25	1:35.91	1:36.57	1:37.23	1:37.90
150	1:38.56	1:39.22	1:39.88	1:40.54	1:41.20	1:41.86	1:42.53	1:43.19	1:43.85	1:44.51
160	1:45.17	1:45.83	1:46.49	1:47.16	1:47.82	1:48.48	1:49.14	1:49.80	1:50.46	1:51.13
170	1:51.79	1:52.45	1:53.11	1:53.77	1:54.43	1:55.09	1:55.76	1:56.42	1:57.08	1:57.74
180	1:58.40	1:59.06	1:59.72	2:00.39	2:01.05	2:01.71	2:02.37	2:03.03	2:03.69	2:04.35
190	2:05.02	2:05.68	2:06.34	2:07.00	2:07.66	2:08.32	2:08.98	2:09.65	2:10.31	2:10.97
200	2:11.63	2:12.29	2:12.95	2:13.61	2:14.28	2:14.94	2:15.60	2:16.26	2:16.92	2:17.58
210	2:18.24	2:18.91	2:19.57	2:20.23	2:20.89	2:21.55	2:22.21	2:22.87	2:23.54	2:24.20
220	2:24.86	2:25.52	2:26.18	2:26.84	2:27.51	2:28.17	2:28.83	2:29.49	2:30.15	2:30.81
230	2:31.47	2:32.14	2:32.80	2:33.46	2:34.12	2:34.78	2:35.44	2:36.10	2:36.77	2:37.43
240	2:38.09	2:38.75	2:39.41	2:40.07	2:40.73	2:41.40	2:42.06	2:42.72	2:43.38	2:44.04
250	2:44.70	2:45.36	2:46.03	2:46.69	2:47.35	2:48.01	2:48.67	2:49.33	2:49.99	2:50.66
260	2:51.32	2:51.98	2:52.64	2:53.30	2:53.96	2:54.62	2:55.29	2:55.95	2:56.61	2:57.27
270	2:57.93	2:58.59	2:59.26	2:59.92	3:00.58	3:01.24	3:01.90	3:02.56	3:03.22	3:03.89
280	3:04.55	3:05.21	3:05.87	3:06.53	3:07.19	3:07.85	3:08.52	3:09.18	3:09.84	3:10.50
290	3:11.16	3:11.82	3:12.48	3:13.15	3:13.81	3:14.47	3:15.13	3:15.79	3:16.45	3:17.11
300	3:17.78	3:18.44	3:19.10	3:19.76	3:20.42	3:21.08	3:21.74	3:22.41	3:23.07	3:23.73
310	3:24.39	3:25.05	3:25.71	3:26.37	3:27.04	3:27.70	3:28.36	3:29.02	3:29.68	3:30.34
320	3:31.01	3:31.67	3:32.33	3:32.99	3:33.65	3:34.31	3:34.97	3:35.64	3:36.30	3:36.96
330	3:37.62	3:38.28	3:38.94	3:39.60	3:40.27	3:40.93	3:41.59	3:42.25	3:42.91	3:43.57
340	3:44.23	3:44.90	3:45.56	3:46.22	3:46.88	3:47.54	3:48.20	3:48.86	3:49.53	3:50.19
350	3:50.85	3:51.51	3:52.17	3:52.83	3:53.49	3:54.16	3:54.82	3:55.48	3:56.14	3:56.80
360	3:57.46	3:58.13	3:58.79	3:59.45	4:00.11	4:00.77	4:01.43	4:02.09	4:02.76	4:03.42
370	4:04.08	4:04.74	4:05.40	4:06.06	4:06.72	4:07.39	4:08.05	4:08.71	4:09.37	4:10.03
380	4:10.69	4:11.35	4:12.02	4:12.68	4:13.34	4:14.00	4:14.66	4:15.32	4:15.98	4:16.65
390	4:17.31	4:17.97	4:18.63	4:19.29	4:19.95	4:20.61	4:21.28	4:21.94	4:22.60	4:23.26
400	4:23.92	4:24.58	4:25.24	4:25.91	4:26.57	4:27.23	4:27.89	4:28.55	4:29.21	4:29.88
410	4:30.54	4:31.20	4:31.86	4:32.52	4:33.18	4:33.84	4:34.51	4:35.17	4:35.83	4:36.49
420	4:37.15	4:37.81	4:38.47	4:39.14	4:39.80	4:40.46	4:41.12	4:41.78	4:42.44	4:43.10
430	4:43.77	4:44.43	4:45.09	4:45.75	4:46.41	4:47.07	4:47.73	4:48.40	4:49.06	4:49.72
440	4:50.38	4:51.04	4:51.70	4:52.36	4:53.03	4:53.69	4:54.35	4:55.01	4:55.67	4:56.33
450	4:56.99	4:57.66	4:58.32	4:58.98	4:59.64	5:00.30	5:00.96	5:01.63	5:02.29	5:02.95
460	5:03.61	5:04.27	5:04.93	5:05.59	5:06.26	5:06.92	5:07.58	5:08.24	5:08.90	5:09.56
470	5:10.22	5:10.89	5:11.55	5:12.21	5:12.87	5:13.53	5:14.19	5:14.85	5:15.52	5:16.18
480	5:16.84	5:17.50	5:18.16	5:18.82	5:19.48	5:20.15	5:20.81	5:21.47	5:22.13	5:22.79
490	5:23.45	5:24.11	5:24.78	5:25.44	5:26.10	5:26.76	5:27.42	5:28.08	5:28.74	5:29.41
500	5:30.07	5:30.73	5:31.39	5:32.05	5:32.71	5:33.38	5:34.04	5:34.70	5:35.36	5:36.02
510	5:36.68	5:37.34	5:38.01	5:38.67	5:39.33	5:39.99	5:40.65	5:41.31	5:41.97	5:42.64
520	5:43.30	5:43.96	5:44.62	5:45.28	5:45.94	5:46.60	5:47.27	5:47.93	5:48.59	5:49.25
530	5:49.91	5:50.57	5:51.23	5:51.90	5:52.56	5:53.22	5:53.88	5:54.54	5:55.20	5:55.86
540	5:56.53	5:57.19	5:57.85	5:58.51	5:59.17	5:59.83	6:00.49	6:01.16	6:01.82	6:02.48
550	6:03.14	6:03.80	6:04.46	6:05.13	6:05.79	6:06.45	6:07.11	6:07.77	6:08.43	6:09.09
560	6:09.76	6:10.42	6:11.08	6:11.74	6:12.40	6:13.06	6:13.72	6:14.39	6:15.05	6:15.71
570	6:16.37	6:17.03	6:17.69	6:18.35	6:19.02	6:19.68	6:20.34	6:21.00	6:21.66	6:22.32
580	6:22.98	6:23.65	6:24.31	6:24.97	6:25.63	6:26.29	6:26.95	6:27.61	6:28.28	6:28.94
590	6:29.60	6:30.26	6:30.92	6:31.58	6:32.24	6:32.91	6:33.57	6:34.23	6:34.89	6:35.55

♩. = 0.99; ♩ = 0.66; ♪. = 0.50; (triplet ♩ 𝄾) = 0.44; ♪ = 0.33; (triplet ♪ 𝄾 𝄾) = 0.22; 𝅘𝅥𝅯 = 0.17 seconds

CLICK: 16⅔ FRAMES; M.M.: 90.00

Click	0	1	2	3	4	5	6	7	8	9
000	0:00.00	0:00.00	0:00.67	0:01.33	0:02.00	0:02.67	0:03.33	0:04.00	0:04.67	0:05.33
010	0:06.00	0:06.67	0:07.33	0:08.00	0:08.67	0:09.33	0:10.00	0:10.67	0:11.33	0:12.00
020	0:12.67	0:13.33	0:14.00	0:14.67	0:15.33	0:16.00	0:16.67	0:17.33	0:18.00	0:18.67
030	0:19.33	0:20.00	0:20.67	0:21.33	0:22.00	0:22.67	0:23.33	0:24.00	0:24.67	0:25.33
040	0:26.00	0:26.67	0:27.33	0:28.00	0:28.67	0:29.33	0:30.00	0:30.67	0:31.33	0:32.00
050	0:32.67	0:33.33	0:34.00	0:34.67	0:35.33	0:36.00	0:36.67	0:37.33	0:38.00	0:38.67
060	0:39.33	0:40.00	0:40.67	0:41.33	0:42.00	0:42.67	0:43.33	0:44.00	0:44.67	0:45.33
070	0:46.00	0:46.67	0:47.33	0:48.00	0:48.67	0:49.33	0:50.00	0:50.67	0:51.33	0:52.00
080	0:52.67	0:53.33	0:54.00	0:54.67	0:55.33	0:56.00	0:56.67	0:57.33	0:58.00	0:58.67
090	0:59.33	1:00.00	1:00.67	1:01.33	1:02.00	1:02.67	1:03.33	1:04.00	1:04.67	1:05.33
100	1:06.00	1:06.67	1:07.33	1:08.00	1:08.67	1:09.33	1:10.00	1:10.67	1:11.33	1:12.00
110	1:12.67	1:13.33	1:14.00	1:14.67	1:15.33	1:16.00	1:16.67	1:17.33	1:18.00	1:18.67
120	1:19.33	1:20.00	1:20.67	1:21.33	1:22.00	1:22.67	1:23.33	1:24.00	1:24.67	1:25.33
130	1:26.00	1:26.67	1:27.33	1:28.00	1:28.67	1:29.33	1:30.00	1:30.67	1:31.33	1:32.00
140	1:32.67	1:33.33	1:34.00	1:34.67	1:35.33	1:36.00	1:36.67	1:37.33	1:38.00	1:38.67
150	1:39.33	1:40.00	1:40.67	1:41.33	1:42.00	1:42.67	1:43.33	1:44.00	1:44.67	1:45.33
160	1:46.00	1:46.67	1:47.33	1:48.00	1:48.67	1:49.33	1:50.00	1:50.67	1:51.33	1:52.00
170	1:52.67	1:53.33	1:54.00	1:54.67	1:55.33	1:56.00	1:56.67	1:57.33	1:58.00	1:58.67
180	1:59.33	2:00.00	2:00.67	2:01.33	2:02.00	2:02.67	2:03.33	2:04.00	2:04.67	2:05.33
190	2:06.00	2:06.67	2:07.33	2:08.00	2:08.67	2:09.33	2:10.00	2:10.67	2:11.33	2:12.00
200	2:12.67	2:13.33	2:14.00	2:14.67	2:15.33	2:16.00	2:16.67	2:17.33	2:18.00	2:18.67
210	2:19.33	2:20.00	2:20.67	2:21.33	2:22.00	2:22.67	2:23.33	2:24.00	2:24.67	2:25.33
220	2:26.00	2:26.67	2:27.33	2:28.00	2:28.67	2:29.33	2:30.00	2:30.67	2:31.33	2:32.00
230	2:32.67	2:33.33	2:34.00	2:34.67	2:35.33	2:36.00	2:36.67	2:37.33	2:38.00	2:38.67
240	2:39.33	2:40.00	2:40.67	2:41.33	2:42.00	2:42.67	2:43.33	2:44.00	2:44.67	2:45.33
250	2:46.00	2:46.67	2:47.33	2:48.00	2:48.67	2:49.33	2:50.00	2:50.67	2:51.33	2:52.00
260	2:52.67	2:53.33	2:54.00	2:54.67	2:55.33	2:56.00	2:56.67	2:57.33	2:58.00	2:58.67
270	2:59.33	3:00.00	3:00.67	3:01.33	3:02.00	3:02.67	3:03.33	3:04.00	3:04.67	3:05.33
280	3:06.00	3:06.67	3:07.33	3:08.00	3:08.67	3:09.33	3:10.00	3:10.67	3:11.33	3:12.00
290	3:12.67	3:13.33	3:14.00	3:14.67	3:15.33	3:16.00	3:16.67	3:17.33	3:18.00	3:18.67
300	3:19.33	3:20.00	3:20.67	3:21.33	3:22.00	3:22.67	3:23.33	3:24.00	3:24.67	3:25.33
310	3:26.00	3:26.67	3:27.33	3:28.00	3:28.67	3:29.33	3:30.00	3:30.67	3:31.33	3:32.00
320	3:32.67	3:33.33	3:34.00	3:34.67	3:35.33	3:36.00	3:36.67	3:37.33	3:38.00	3:38.67
330	3:39.33	3:40.00	3:40.67	3:41.33	3:42.00	3:42.67	3:43.33	3:44.00	3:44.67	3:45.33
340	3:46.00	3:46.67	3:47.33	3:48.00	3:48.67	3:49.33	3:50.00	3:50.67	3:51.33	3:52.00
350	3:52.67	3:53.33	3:54.00	3:54.67	3:55.33	3:56.00	3:56.67	3:57.33	3:58.00	3:58.67
360	3:59.33	4:00.00	4:00.67	4:01.33	4:02.00	4:02.67	4:03.33	4:04.00	4:04.67	4:05.33
370	4:06.00	4:06.67	4:07.33	4:08.00	4:08.67	4:09.33	4:10.00	4:10.67	4:11.33	4:12.00
380	4:12.67	4:13.33	4:14.00	4:14.67	4:15.33	4:16.00	4:16.67	4:17.33	4:18.00	4:18.67
390	4:19.33	4:20.00	4:20.67	4:21.33	4:22.00	4:22.67	4:23.33	4:24.00	4:24.67	4:25.33
400	4:26.00	4:26.67	4:27.33	4:28.00	4:28.67	4:29.33	4:30.00	4:30.67	4:31.33	4:32.00
410	4:32.67	4:33.33	4:34.00	4:34.67	4:35.33	4:36.00	4:36.67	4:37.33	4:38.00	4:38.67
420	4:39.33	4:40.00	4:40.67	4:41.33	4:42.00	4:42.67	4:43.33	4:44.00	4:44.67	4:45.33
430	4:46.00	4:46.67	4:47.33	4:48.00	4:48.67	4:49.33	4:50.00	4:50.67	4:51.33	4:52.00
440	4:52.67	4:53.33	4:54.00	4:54.67	4:55.33	4:56.00	4:56.67	4:57.33	4:58.00	4:58.67
450	4:59.33	5:00.00	5:00.67	5:01.33	5:02.00	5:02.67	5:03.33	5:04.00	5:04.67	5:05.33
460	5:06.00	5:06.67	5:07.33	5:08.00	5:08.67	5:09.33	5:10.00	5:10.67	5:11.33	5:12.00
470	5:12.67	5:13.33	5:14.00	5:14.67	5:15.33	5:16.00	5:16.67	5:17.33	5:18.00	5:18.67
480	5:19.33	5:20.00	5:20.67	5:21.33	5:22.00	5:22.67	5:23.33	5:24.00	5:24.67	5:25.33
490	5:26.00	5:26.67	5:27.33	5:28.00	5:28.67	5:29.33	5:30.00	5:30.67	5:31.33	5:32.00
500	5:32.67	5:33.33	5:34.00	5:34.67	5:35.33	5:36.00	5:36.67	5:37.33	5:38.00	5:38.67
510	5:39.33	5:40.00	5:40.67	5:41.33	5:42.00	5:42.67	5:43.33	5:44.00	5:44.67	5:45.33
520	5:46.00	5:46.67	5:47.33	5:48.00	5:48.67	5:49.33	5:50.00	5:50.67	5:51.33	5:52.00
530	5:52.67	5:53.33	5:54.00	5:54.67	5:55.33	5:56.00	5:56.67	5:57.33	5:58.00	5:58.67
540	5:59.33	6:00.00	6:00.67	6:01.33	6:02.00	6:02.67	6:03.33	6:04.00	6:04.67	6:05.33
550	6:06.00	6:06.67	6:07.33	6:08.00	6:08.67	6:09.33	6:10.00	6:10.67	6:11.33	6:12.00
560	6:12.67	6:13.33	6:14.00	6:14.67	6:15.33	6:16.00	6:16.67	6:17.33	6:18.00	6:18.67
570	6:19.33	6:20.00	6:20.67	6:21.33	6:22.00	6:22.67	6:23.33	6:24.00	6:24.67	6:25.33
580	6:26.00	6:26.67	6:27.33	6:28.00	6:28.67	6:29.33	6:30.00	6:30.67	6:31.33	6:32.00
590	6:32.67	6:33.33	6:34.00	6:34.67	6:35.33	6:36.00	6:36.67	6:37.33	6:38.00	6:38.67

♩. = 1.00; ♩ = 0.67; ♪. = 0.50; (3) ♩ 𝄾 = 0.44; ♪ = 0.33; (3) ♪𝄾𝄾 = 0.22; 𝅘𝅥𝅯 = 0.17 seconds

CLICK: 16⅛ FRAMES; M.M.: 89.30

Click	0	1	2	3	4	5	6	7	8	9
000	0:00.00	0:00.00	0:00.67	0:01.34	0:02.02	0:02.69	0:03.36	0:04.03	0:04.70	0:05.38
010	0:06.05	0:06.72	0:07.39	0:08.06	0:08.73	0:09.41	0:10.08	0:10.75	0:11.42	0:12.09
020	0:12.77	0:13.44	0:14.11	0:14.78	0:15.45	0:16.13	0:16.80	0:17.47	0:18.14	0:18.81
030	0:19.48	0:20.16	0:20.83	0:21.50	0:22.17	0:22.84	0:23.52	0:24.19	0:24.86	0:25.53
040	0:26.20	0:26.88	0:27.55	0:28.22	0:28.89	0:29.56	0:30.23	0:30.91	0:31.58	0:32.25
050	0:32.92	0:33.59	0:34.27	0:34.94	0:35.61	0:36.28	0:36.95	0:37.63	0:38.30	0:38.97
060	0:39.64	0:40.31	0:40.98	0:41.66	0:42.33	0:43.00	0:43.67	0:44.34	0:45.02	0:45.69
070	0:46.36	0:47.03	0:47.70	0:48.38	0:49.05	0:49.72	0:50.39	0:51.06	0:51.73	0:52.41
080	0:53.08	0:53.75	0:54.42	0:55.09	0:55.77	0:56.44	0:57.11	0:57.78	0:58.45	0:59.13
090	0:59.80	1:00.47	1:01.14	1:01.81	1:02.48	1:03.16	1:03.83	1:04.50	1:05.17	1:05.84
100	1:06.52	1:07.19	1:07.86	1:08.53	1:09.20	1:09.88	1:10.55	1:11.22	1:11.89	1:12.56
110	1:13.23	1:13.91	1:14.58	1:15.25	1:15.92	1:16.59	1:17.27	1:17.94	1:18.61	1:19.28
120	1:19.95	1:20.63	1:21.30	1:21.97	1:22.64	1:23.31	1:23.98	1:24.66	1:25.33	1:26.00
130	1:26.67	1:27.34	1:28.02	1:28.69	1:29.36	1:30.03	1:30.70	1:31.38	1:32.05	1:32.72
140	1:33.39	1:34.06	1:34.73	1:35.41	1:36.08	1:36.75	1:37.42	1:38.09	1:38.77	1:39.44
150	1:40.11	1:40.78	1:41.45	1:42.13	1:42.80	1:43.47	1:44.14	1:44.81	1:45.48	1:46.16
160	1:46.83	1:47.50	1:48.17	1:48.84	1:49.52	1:50.19	1:50.86	1:51.53	1:52.20	1:52.88
170	1:53.55	1:54.22	1:54.89	1:55.56	1:56.23	1:56.91	1:57.58	1:58.25	1:58.92	1:59.59
180	2:00.27	2:00.94	2:01.61	2:02.28	2:02.95	2:03.63	2:04.30	2:04.97	2:05.64	2:06.31
190	2:06.98	2:07.66	2:08.33	2:09.00	2:09.67	2:10.34	2:11.02	2:11.69	2:12.36	2:13.03
200	2:13.70	2:14.38	2:15.05	2:15.72	2:16.39	2:17.06	2:17.73	2:18.41	2:19.08	2:19.75
210	2:20.42	2:21.09	2:21.77	2:22.44	2:23.11	2:23.78	2:24.45	2:25.13	2:25.80	2:26.47
220	2:27.14	2:27.81	2:28.48	2:29.16	2:29.83	2:30.50	2:31.17	2:31.84	2:32.52	2:33.19
230	2:33.86	2:34.53	2:35.20	2:35.88	2:36.55	2:37.22	2:37.89	2:38.56	2:39.23	2:39.91
240	2:40.58	2:41.25	2:41.92	2:42.59	2:43.27	2:43.94	2:44.61	2:45.28	2:45.95	2:46.63
250	2:47.30	2:47.97	2:48.64	2:49.31	2:49.98	2:50.66	2:51.33	2:52.00	2:52.67	2:53.34
260	2:54.02	2:54.69	2:55.36	2:56.03	2:56.70	2:57.38	2:58.05	2:58.72	2:59.39	3:00.06
270	3:00.73	3:01.41	3:02.08	3:02.75	3:03.42	3:04.09	3:04.77	3:05.44	3:06.11	3:06.78
280	3:07.45	3:08.13	3:08.80	3:09.47	3:10.14	3:10.81	3:11.48	3:12.16	3:12.83	3:13.50
290	3:14.17	3:14.84	3:15.52	3:16.19	3:16.86	3:17.53	3:18.20	3:18.88	3:19.55	3:20.22
300	3:20.89	3:21.56	3:22.23	3:22.91	3:23.58	3:24.25	3:24.92	3:25.59	3:26.27	3:26.94
310	3:27.61	3:28.28	3:28.95	3:29.63	3:30.30	3:30.97	3:31.64	3:32.31	3:32.98	3:33.66
320	3:34.33	3:35.00	3:35.67	3:36.34	3:37.02	3:37.69	3:38.36	3:39.03	3:39.70	3:40.38
330	3:41.05	3:41.72	3:42.39	3:43.06	3:43.73	3:44.41	3:45.08	3:45.75	3:46.42	3:47.09
340	3:47.77	3:48.44	3:49.11	3:49.78	3:50.45	3:51.13	3:51.80	3:52.47	3:53.14	3:53.81
350	3:54.48	3:55.16	3:55.83	3:56.50	3:57.17	3:57.84	3:58.52	3:59.19	3:59.86	4:00.53
360	4:01.20	4:01.88	4:02.55	4:03.22	4:03.89	4:04.56	4:05.23	4:05.91	4:06.58	4:07.25
370	4:07.92	4:08.59	4:09.27	4:09.94	4:10.61	4:11.28	4:11.95	4:12.63	4:13.30	4:13.97
380	4:14.64	4:15.31	4:15.98	4:16.66	4:17.33	4:18.00	4:18.67	4:19.34	4:20.02	4:20.69
390	4:21.36	4:22.03	4:22.70	4:23.38	4:24.05	4:24.72	4:25.39	4:26.06	4:26.73	4:27.41
400	4:28.08	4:28.75	4:29.42	4:30.09	4:30.77	4:31.44	4:32.11	4:32.78	4:33.45	4:34.13
410	4:34.80	4:35.47	4:36.14	4:36.81	4:37.48	4:38.16	4:38.83	4:39.50	4:40.17	4:40.84
420	4:41.52	4:42.19	4:42.86	4:43.53	4:44.20	4:44.88	4:45.55	4:46.22	4:46.89	4:47.56
430	4:48.23	4:48.91	4:49.58	4:50.25	4:50.92	4:51.59	4:52.27	4:52.94	4:53.61	4:54.28
440	4:54.95	4:55.63	4:56.30	4:56.97	4:57.64	4:58.31	4:58.98	4:59.66	5:00.33	5:01.00
450	5:01.67	5:02.34	5:03.02	5:03.69	5:04.36	5:05.03	5:05.70	5:06.38	5:07.05	5:07.72
460	5:08.39	5:09.06	5:09.73	5:10.41	5:11.08	5:11.75	5:12.42	5:13.09	5:13.77	5:14.44
470	5:15.11	5:15.78	5:16.45	5:17.13	5:17.80	5:18.47	5:19.14	5:19.81	5:20.48	5:21.16
480	5:21.83	5:22.50	5:23.17	5:23.84	5:24.52	5:25.19	5:25.86	5:26.53	5:27.20	5:27.88
490	5:28.55	5:29.22	5:29.89	5:30.56	5:31.23	5:31.91	5:32.58	5:33.25	5:33.92	5:34.59
500	5:35.27	5:35.94	5:36.61	5:37.28	5:37.95	5:38.63	5:39.30	5:39.97	5:40.64	5:41.31
510	5:41.98	5:42.66	5:43.33	5:44.00	5:44.67	5:45.34	5:46.02	5:46.69	5:47.36	5:48.03
520	5:48.70	5:49.38	5:50.05	5:50.72	5:51.39	5:52.06	5:52.73	5:53.41	5:54.08	5:54.75
530	5:55.42	5:56.09	5:56.77	5:57.44	5:58.11	5:58.78	5:59.45	6:00.13	6:00.80	6:01.47
540	6:02.14	6:02.81	6:03.48	6:04.16	6:04.83	6:05.50	6:06.17	6:06.84	6:07.52	6:08.19
550	6:08.86	6:09.53	6:10.20	6:10.88	6:11.55	6:12.22	6:12.89	6:13.56	6:14.23	6:14.91
560	6:15.58	6:16.25	6:16.92	6:17.59	6:18.27	6:18.94	6:19.61	6:20.28	6:20.95	6:21.63
570	6:22.30	6:22.97	6:23.64	6:24.31	6:24.98	6:25.66	6:26.33	6:27.00	6:27.67	6:28.34
580	6:29.02	6:29.69	6:30.36	6:31.03	6:31.70	6:32.38	6:33.05	6:33.72	6:34.39	6:35.06
590	6:35.73	6:36.41	6:37.08	6:37.75	6:38.42	6:39.09	6:39.77	6:40.44	6:41.11	6:41.78

♩. = 1.01; ♩ = 0.67; ♪. = 0.50; (triplet ♩ 𝄾) = 0.45; ♪ = 0.34; (triplet ♪ 𝄾 𝄾) = 0.22; 𝅘𝅥𝅯 = 0.17 seconds

CLICK: 16 2/8 FRAMES; M.M.: 88.62

Click	0	1	2	3	4	5	6	7	8	9
000	0:00.00	0:00.00	0:00.68	0:01.35	0:02.03	0:02.71	0:03.39	0:04.06	0:04.74	0:05.42
010	0:06.09	0:06.77	0:07.45	0:08.13	0:08.80	0:09.48	0:10.16	0:10.83	0:11.51	0:12.19
020	0:12.86	0:13.54	0:14.22	0:14.90	0:15.57	0:16.25	0:16.93	0:17.60	0:18.28	0:18.96
030	0:19.64	0:20.31	0:20.99	0:21.67	0:22.34	0:23.02	0:23.70	0:24.38	0:25.05	0:25.73
040	0:26.41	0:27.08	0:27.76	0:28.44	0:29.11	0:29.79	0:30.47	0:31.15	0:31.82	0:32.50
050	0:33.18	0:33.85	0:34.53	0:35.21	0:35.89	0:36.56	0:37.24	0:37.92	0:38.59	0:39.27
060	0:39.95	0:40.63	0:41.30	0:41.98	0:42.66	0:43.33	0:44.01	0:44.69	0:45.36	0:46.04
070	0:46.72	0:47.40	0:48.07	0:48.75	0:49.43	0:50.10	0:50.78	0:51.46	0:52.14	0:52.81
080	0:53.49	0:54.17	0:54.84	0:55.52	0:56.20	0:56.87	0:57.55	0:58.23	0:58.91	0:59.58
090	1:00.26	1:00.94	1:01.61	1:02.29	1:02.97	1:03.65	1:04.32	1:05.00	1:05.68	1:06.35
100	1:07.03	1:07.71	1:08.39	1:09.06	1:09.74	1:10.42	1:11.09	1:11.77	1:12.45	1:13.13
110	1:13.80	1:14.48	1:15.16	1:15.83	1:16.51	1:17.19	1:17.86	1:18.54	1:19.22	1:19.90
120	1:20.57	1:21.25	1:21.93	1:22.60	1:23.28	1:23.96	1:24.64	1:25.31	1:25.99	1:26.67
130	1:27.34	1:28.02	1:28.70	1:29.37	1:30.05	1:30.73	1:31.41	1:32.08	1:32.76	1:33.44
140	1:34.11	1:34.79	1:35.47	1:36.15	1:36.82	1:37.50	1:38.18	1:38.85	1:39.53	1:40.21
150	1:40.89	1:41.56	1:42.24	1:42.92	1:43.59	1:44.27	1:44.95	1:45.62	1:46.30	1:46.98
160	1:47.66	1:48.33	1:49.01	1:49.69	1:50.36	1:51.04	1:51.72	1:52.40	1:53.07	1:53.75
170	1:54.43	1:55.10	1:55.78	1:56.46	1:57.14	1:57.81	1:58.49	1:59.17	1:59.84	2:00.52
180	2:01.20	2:01.88	2:02.55	2:03.23	2:03.91	2:04.58	2:05.26	2:05.94	2:06.61	2:07.29
190	2:07.97	2:08.65	2:09.32	2:10.00	2:10.68	2:11.35	2:12.03	2:12.71	2:13.39	2:14.06
200	2:14.74	2:15.42	2:16.09	2:16.77	2:17.45	2:18.12	2:18.80	2:19.48	2:20.16	2:20.83
210	2:21.51	2:22.19	2:22.86	2:23.54	2:24.22	2:24.90	2:25.57	2:26.25	2:26.93	2:27.60
220	2:28.28	2:28.96	2:29.64	2:30.31	2:30.99	2:31.67	2:32.34	2:33.02	2:33.70	2:34.37
230	2:35.05	2:35.73	2:36.41	2:37.08	2:37.76	2:38.44	2:39.11	2:39.79	2:40.47	2:41.15
240	2:41.82	2:42.50	2:43.18	2:43.85	2:44.53	2:45.21	2:45.89	2:46.56	2:47.24	2:47.92
250	2:48.59	2:49.27	2:49.95	2:50.63	2:51.30	2:51.98	2:52.66	2:53.33	2:54.01	2:54.69
260	2:55.36	2:56.04	2:56.72	2:57.40	2:58.07	2:58.75	2:59.43	3:00.10	3:00.78	3:01.46
270	3:02.14	3:02.81	3:03.49	3:04.17	3:04.84	3:05.52	3:06.20	3:06.87	3:07.55	3:08.23
280	3:08.91	3:09.58	3:10.26	3:10.94	3:11.61	3:12.29	3:12.97	3:13.65	3:14.32	3:15.00
290	3:15.68	3:16.35	3:17.03	3:17.71	3:18.39	3:19.06	3:19.74	3:20.42	3:21.09	3:21.77
300	3:22.45	3:23.12	3:23.80	3:24.48	3:25.16	3:25.83	3:26.51	3:27.19	3:27.86	3:28.54
310	3:29.22	3:29.90	3:30.57	3:31.25	3:31.93	3:32.60	3:33.28	3:33.96	3:34.64	3:35.31
320	3:35.99	3:36.67	3:37.34	3:38.02	3:38.70	3:39.38	3:40.05	3:40.73	3:41.41	3:42.08
330	3:42.76	3:43.44	3:44.11	3:44.79	3:45.47	3:46.15	3:46.82	3:47.50	3:48.18	3:48.85
340	3:49.53	3:50.21	3:50.89	3:51.56	3:52.24	3:52.92	3:53.59	3:54.27	3:54.95	3:55.62
350	3:56.30	3:56.98	3:57.66	3:58.33	3:59.01	3:59.69	4:00.36	4:01.04	4:01.72	4:02.40
360	4:03.07	4:03.75	4:04.43	4:05.10	4:05.78	4:06.46	4:07.14	4:07.81	4:08.49	4:09.17
370	4:09.84	4:10.52	4:11.20	4:11.87	4:12.55	4:13.23	4:13.91	4:14.58	4:15.26	4:15.94
380	4:16.61	4:17.29	4:17.97	4:18.65	4:19.32	4:20.00	4:20.68	4:21.35	4:22.03	4:22.71
390	4:23.39	4:24.06	4:24.74	4:25.42	4:26.09	4:26.77	4:27.45	4:28.13	4:28.80	4:29.48
400	4:30.16	4:30.83	4:31.51	4:32.19	4:32.86	4:33.54	4:34.22	4:34.90	4:35.57	4:36.25
410	4:36.93	4:37.60	4:38.28	4:38.96	4:39.64	4:40.31	4:40.99	4:41.67	4:42.34	4:43.02
420	4:43.70	4:44.37	4:45.05	4:45.73	4:46.41	4:47.08	4:47.76	4:48.44	4:49.11	4:49.79
430	4:50.47	4:51.15	4:51.82	4:52.50	4:53.18	4:53.85	4:54.53	4:55.21	4:55.89	4:56.56
440	4:57.24	4:57.92	4:58.59	4:59.27	4:59.95	5:00.62	5:01.30	5:01.98	5:02.66	5:03.33
450	5:04.01	5:04.69	5:05.36	5:06.04	5:06.72	5:07.40	5:08.07	5:08.75	5:09.43	5:10.10
460	5:10.78	5:11.46	5:12.14	5:12.81	5:13.49	5:14.17	5:14.84	5:15.52	5:16.20	5:16.88
470	5:17.55	5:18.23	5:18.91	5:19.58	5:20.26	5:20.94	5:21.61	5:22.29	5:22.97	5:23.65
480	5:24.32	5:25.00	5:25.68	5:26.35	5:27.03	5:27.71	5:28.39	5:29.06	5:29.74	5:30.42
490	5:31.09	5:31.77	5:32.45	5:33.12	5:33.80	5:34.48	5:35.16	5:35.83	5:36.51	5:37.19
500	5:37.86	5:38.54	5:39.22	5:39.90	5:40.57	5:41.25	5:41.93	5:42.60	5:43.28	5:43.96
510	5:44.64	5:45.31	5:45.99	5:46.67	5:47.34	5:48.02	5:48.70	5:49.37	5:50.05	5:50.73
520	5:51.41	5:52.08	5:52.76	5:53.44	5:54.11	5:54.79	5:55.47	5:56.15	5:56.82	5:57.50
530	5:58.18	5:58.85	5:59.53	6:00.21	6:00.89	6:01.56	6:02.24	6:02.92	6:03.59	6:04.27
540	6:04.95	6:05.63	6:06.30	6:06.98	6:07.66	6:08.33	6:09.01	6:09.69	6:10.36	6:11.04
550	6:11.72	6:12.40	6:13.07	6:13.75	6:14.43	6:15.10	6:15.78	6:16.46	6:17.14	6:17.81
560	6:18.49	6:19.17	6:19.84	6:20.52	6:21.20	6:21.87	6:22.55	6:23.23	6:23.91	6:24.58
570	6:25.26	6:25.94	6:26.61	6:27.29	6:27.97	6:28.65	6:29.32	6:30.00	6:30.68	6:31.35
580	6:32.03	6:32.71	6:33.39	6:34.06	6:34.74	6:35.42	6:36.09	6:36.77	6:37.45	6:38.12
590	6:38.80	6:39.48	6:40.16	6:40.83	6:41.51	6:42.19	6:42.86	6:43.54	6:44.22	6:44.90

𝅗𝅥. = 1.02; ♩ = 0.68; ♪. = 0.51; (triplet ♩ 𝄾) = 0.45; ♪ = 0.34; (triplet ♪ 𝄾 𝄾) = 0.23; 𝅘𝅥𝅯 = 0.17 seconds

CLICK: 16⅜ FRAMES; M.M.: 87.94

Click	0	1	2	3	4	5	6	7	8	9
000	0:00.00	0:00.00	0:00.68	0:01.36	0:02.05	0:02.73	0:03.41	0:04.09	0:04.78	0:05.46
010	0:06.14	0:06.82	0:07.51	0:08.19	0:08.87	0:09.55	0:10.23	0:10.92	0:11.60	0:12.28
020	0:12.96	0:13.65	0:14.33	0:15.01	0:15.69	0:16.38	0:17.06	0:17.74	0:18.42	0:19.10
030	0:19.79	0:20.47	0:21.15	0:21.83	0:22.52	0:23.20	0:23.88	0:24.56	0:25.24	0:25.93
040	0:26.61	0:27.29	0:27.97	0:28.66	0:29.34	0:30.02	0:30.70	0:31.39	0:32.07	0:32.75
050	0:33.43	0:34.11	0:34.80	0:35.48	0:36.16	0:36.84	0:37.53	0:38.21	0:38.89	0:39.57
060	0:40.26	0:40.94	0:41.62	0:42.30	0:42.98	0:43.67	0:44.35	0:45.03	0:45.71	0:46.40
070	0:47.08	0:47.76	0:48.44	0:49.13	0:49.81	0:50.49	0:51.17	0:51.85	0:52.54	0:53.22
080	0:53.90	0:54.58	0:55.27	0:55.95	0:56.63	0:57.31	0:57.99	0:58.68	0:59.36	1:00.04
090	1:00.72	1:01.41	1:02.09	1:02.77	1:03.45	1:04.14	1:04.82	1:05.50	1:06.18	1:06.86
100	1:07.55	1:08.23	1:08.91	1:09.59	1:10.28	1:10.96	1:11.64	1:12.32	1:13.01	1:13.69
110	1:14.37	1:15.05	1:15.73	1:16.42	1:17.10	1:17.78	1:18.46	1:19.15	1:19.83	1:20.51
120	1:21.19	1:21.88	1:22.56	1:23.24	1:23.92	1:24.60	1:25.29	1:25.97	1:26.65	1:27.33
130	1:28.02	1:28.70	1:29.38	1:30.06	1:30.74	1:31.43	1:32.11	1:32.79	1:33.47	1:34.16
140	1:34.84	1:35.52	1:36.20	1:36.89	1:37.57	1:38.25	1:38.93	1:39.61	1:40.30	1:40.98
150	1:41.66	1:42.34	1:43.03	1:43.71	1:44.39	1:45.07	1:45.76	1:46.44	1:47.12	1:47.80
160	1:48.48	1:49.17	1:49.85	1:50.53	1:51.21	1:51.90	1:52.58	1:53.26	1:53.94	1:54.63
170	1:55.31	1:55.99	1:56.67	1:57.35	1:58.04	1:58.72	1:59.40	2:00.08	2:00.77	2:01.45
180	2:02.13	2:02.81	2:03.49	2:04.18	2:04.86	2:05.54	2:06.22	2:06.91	2:07.59	2:08.27
190	2:08.95	2:09.64	2:10.32	2:11.00	2:11.68	2:12.36	2:13.05	2:13.73	2:14.41	2:15.09
200	2:15.78	2:16.46	2:17.14	2:17.82	2:18.51	2:19.19	2:19.87	2:20.55	2:21.23	2:21.92
210	2:22.60	2:23.28	2:23.96	2:24.65	2:25.33	2:26.01	2:26.69	2:27.37	2:28.06	2:28.74
220	2:29.42	2:30.10	2:30.79	2:31.47	2:32.15	2:32.83	2:33.52	2:34.20	2:34.88	2:35.56
230	2:36.24	2:36.93	2:37.61	2:38.29	2:38.97	2:39.66	2:40.34	2:41.02	2:41.70	2:42.39
240	2:43.07	2:43.75	2:44.43	2:45.11	2:45.80	2:46.48	2:47.16	2:47.84	2:48.53	2:49.21
250	2:49.89	2:50.57	2:51.26	2:51.94	2:52.62	2:53.30	2:53.98	2:54.67	2:55.35	2:56.03
260	2:56.71	2:57.40	2:58.08	2:58.76	2:59.44	3:00.12	3:00.81	3:01.49	3:02.17	3:02.85
270	3:03.54	3:04.22	3:04.90	3:05.58	3:06.27	3:06.95	3:07.63	3:08.31	3:08.99	3:09.68
280	3:10.36	3:11.04	3:11.72	3:12.41	3:13.09	3:13.77	3:14.45	3:15.14	3:15.82	3:16.50
290	3:17.18	3:17.86	3:18.55	3:19.23	3:19.91	3:20.59	3:21.28	3:21.96	3:22.64	3:23.32
300	3:24.01	3:24.69	3:25.37	3:26.05	3:26.73	3:27.42	3:28.10	3:28.78	3:29.46	3:30.15
310	3:30.83	3:31.51	3:32.19	3:32.88	3:33.56	3:34.24	3:34.92	3:35.60	3:36.29	3:36.97
320	3:37.65	3:38.33	3:39.02	3:39.70	3:40.38	3:41.06	3:41.74	3:42.43	3:43.11	3:43.79
330	3:44.47	3:45.16	3:45.84	3:46.52	3:47.20	3:47.89	3:48.57	3:49.25	3:49.93	3:50.61
340	3:51.30	3:51.98	3:52.66	3:53.34	3:54.03	3:54.71	3:55.39	3:56.07	3:56.76	3:57.44
350	3:58.12	3:58.80	3:59.48	4:00.17	4:00.85	4:01.53	4:02.21	4:02.90	4:03.58	4:04.26
360	4:04.94	4:05.63	4:06.31	4:06.99	4:07.67	4:08.35	4:09.04	4:09.72	4:10.40	4:11.08
370	4:11.77	4:12.45	4:13.13	4:13.81	4:14.49	4:15.18	4:15.86	4:16.54	4:17.22	4:17.91
380	4:18.59	4:19.27	4:19.95	4:20.64	4:21.32	4:22.00	4:22.68	4:23.36	4:24.05	4:24.73
390	4:25.41	4:26.09	4:26.78	4:27.46	4:28.14	4:28.82	4:29.51	4:30.19	4:30.87	4:31.55
400	4:32.23	4:32.92	4:33.60	4:34.28	4:34.96	4:35.65	4:36.33	4:37.01	4:37.69	4:38.37
410	4:39.06	4:39.74	4:40.42	4:41.10	4:41.79	4:42.47	4:43.15	4:43.83	4:44.52	4:45.20
420	4:45.88	4:46.56	4:47.24	4:47.93	4:48.61	4:49.29	4:49.97	4:50.66	4:51.34	4:52.02
430	4:52.70	4:53.39	4:54.07	4:54.75	4:55.43	4:56.11	4:56.80	4:57.48	4:58.16	4:58.84
440	4:59.53	5:00.21	5:00.89	5:01.57	5:02.26	5:02.94	5:03.62	5:04.30	5:04.98	5:05.67
450	5:06.35	5:07.03	5:07.71	5:08.40	5:09.08	5:09.76	5:10.44	5:11.13	5:11.81	5:12.49
460	5:13.17	5:13.85	5:14.54	5:15.22	5:15.90	5:16.58	5:17.27	5:17.95	5:18.63	5:19.31
470	5:19.99	5:20.68	5:21.36	5:22.04	5:22.72	5:23.41	5:24.09	5:24.77	5:25.45	5:26.14
480	5:26.82	5:27.50	5:28.18	5:28.86	5:29.55	5:30.23	5:30.91	5:31.59	5:32.28	5:32.96
490	5:33.64	5:34.32	5:35.01	5:35.69	5:36.37	5:37.05	5:37.73	5:38.42	5:39.10	5:39.78
500	5:40.46	5:41.15	5:41.83	5:42.51	5:43.19	5:43.87	5:44.56	5:45.24	5:45.92	5:46.60
510	5:47.29	5:47.97	5:48.65	5:49.33	5:50.02	5:50.70	5:51.38	5:52.06	5:52.74	5:53.43
520	5:54.11	5:54.79	5:55.47	5:56.16	5:56.84	5:57.52	5:58.20	5:58.89	5:59.57	6:00.25
530	6:00.93	6:01.61	6:02.30	6:02.98	6:03.66	6:04.34	6:05.03	6:05.71	6:06.39	6:07.07
540	6:07.76	6:08.44	6:09.12	6:09.80	6:10.48	6:11.17	6:11.85	6:12.53	6:13.21	6:13.90
550	6:14.58	6:15.26	6:15.94	6:16.63	6:17.31	6:17.99	6:18.67	6:19.35	6:20.04	6:20.72
560	6:21.40	6:22.08	6:22.77	6:23.45	6:24.13	6:24.81	6:25.49	6:26.18	6:26.86	6:27.54
570	6:28.22	6:28.91	6:29.59	6:30.27	6:30.95	6:31.64	6:32.32	6:33.00	6:33.68	6:34.36
580	6:35.05	6:35.73	6:36.41	6:37.09	6:37.78	6:38.46	6:39.14	6:39.82	6:40.51	6:41.19
590	6:41.87	6:42.55	6:43.23	6:43.92	6:44.60	6:45.28	6:45.96	6:46.65	6:47.33	6:48.01

♩. = 1.02; ♩ = 0.68; ♪. = 0.51; (triplet) ♩ 𝄾 = 0.45; ♪ = 0.34; (triplet) ♪ 𝄾 𝄾 = 0.23; 𝅘𝅥𝅯 = 0.17 seconds

CLICK: 16 4/8 FRAMES; M.M.: 87.27

Click	0	1	2	3	4	5	6	7	8	9
000	0:00.00	0:00.00	0:00.69	0:01.38	0:02.06	0:02.75	0:03.44	0:04.13	0:04.81	0:05.50
010	0:06.19	0:06.88	0:07.56	0:08.25	0:08.94	0:09.63	0:10.31	0:11.00	0:11.69	0:12.38
020	0:13.06	0:13.75	0:14.44	0:15.13	0:15.81	0:16.50	0:17.19	0:17.88	0:18.56	0:19.25
030	0:19.94	0:20.63	0:21.31	0:22.00	0:22.69	0:23.38	0:24.06	0:24.75	0:25.44	0:26.13
040	0:26.81	0:27.50	0:28.19	0:28.88	0:29.56	0:30.25	0:30.94	0:31.63	0:32.31	0:33.00
050	0:33.69	0:34.38	0:35.06	0:35.75	0:36.44	0:37.13	0:37.81	0:38.50	0:39.19	0:39.88
060	0:40.56	0:41.25	0:41.94	0:42.63	0:43.31	0:44.00	0:44.69	0:45.38	0:46.06	0:46.75
070	0:47.44	0:48.13	0:48.81	0:49.50	0:50.19	0:50.88	0:51.56	0:52.25	0:52.94	0:53.63
080	0:54.31	0:55.00	0:55.69	0:56.38	0:57.06	0:57.75	0:58.44	0:59.13	0:59.81	1:00.50
090	1:01.19	1:01.88	1:02.56	1:03.25	1:03.94	1:04.63	1:05.31	1:06.00	1:06.69	1:07.38
100	1:08.06	1:08.75	1:09.44	1:10.13	1:10.81	1:11.50	1:12.19	1:12.88	1:13.56	1:14.25
110	1:14.94	1:15.63	1:16.31	1:17.00	1:17.69	1:18.37	1:19.06	1:19.75	1:20.44	1:21.13
120	1:21.81	1:22.50	1:23.19	1:23.88	1:24.56	1:25.25	1:25.94	1:26.63	1:27.31	1:28.00
130	1:28.69	1:29.38	1:30.06	1:30.75	1:31.44	1:32.13	1:32.81	1:33.50	1:34.19	1:34.88
140	1:35.56	1:36.25	1:36.94	1:37.63	1:38.31	1:39.00	1:39.69	1:40.38	1:41.06	1:41.75
150	1:42.44	1:43.13	1:43.81	1:44.50	1:45.19	1:45.88	1:46.56	1:47.25	1:47.94	1:48.63
160	1:49.31	1:50.00	1:50.69	1:51.38	1:52.06	1:52.75	1:53.44	1:54.13	1:54.81	1:55.50
170	1:56.19	1:56.88	1:57.56	1:58.25	1:58.94	1:59.63	2:00.31	2:01.00	2:01.69	2:02.38
180	2:03.06	2:03.75	2:04.44	2:05.13	2:05.81	2:06.50	2:07.19	2:07.88	2:08.56	2:09.25
190	2:09.94	2:10.63	2:11.31	2:12.00	2:12.69	2:13.37	2:14.06	2:14.75	2:15.44	2:16.12
200	2:16.81	2:17.50	2:18.19	2:18.87	2:19.56	2:20.25	2:20.94	2:21.63	2:22.31	2:23.00
210	2:23.69	2:24.38	2:25.06	2:25.75	2:26.44	2:27.13	2:27.81	2:28.50	2:29.19	2:29.88
220	2:30.56	2:31.25	2:31.94	2:32.63	2:33.31	2:34.00	2:34.69	2:35.38	2:36.06	2:36.75
230	2:37.44	2:38.13	2:38.81	2:39.50	2:40.19	2:40.88	2:41.56	2:42.25	2:42.94	2:43.63
240	2:44.31	2:45.00	2:45.69	2:46.38	2:47.06	2:47.75	2:48.44	2:49.13	2:49.81	2:50.50
250	2:51.19	2:51.88	2:52.56	2:53.25	2:53.94	2:54.63	2:55.31	2:56.00	2:56.69	2:57.37
260	2:58.06	2:58.75	2:59.44	3:00.12	3:00.81	3:01.50	3:02.19	3:02.87	3:03.56	3:04.25
270	3:04.94	3:05.63	3:06.31	3:07.00	3:07.69	3:08.38	3:09.06	3:09.75	3:10.44	3:11.13
280	3:11.81	3:12.50	3:13.19	3:13.88	3:14.56	3:15.25	3:15.94	3:16.63	3:17.31	3:18.00
290	3:18.69	3:19.38	3:20.06	3:20.75	3:21.44	3:22.13	3:22.81	3:23.50	3:24.19	3:24.88
300	3:25.56	3:26.25	3:26.94	3:27.63	3:28.31	3:29.00	3:29.69	3:30.38	3:31.06	3:31.75
310	3:32.44	3:33.13	3:33.81	3:34.50	3:35.19	3:35.88	3:36.56	3:37.25	3:37.94	3:38.63
320	3:39.31	3:40.00	3:40.69	3:41.38	3:42.06	3:42.75	3:43.44	3:44.13	3:44.81	3:45.50
330	3:46.19	3:46.88	3:47.56	3:48.25	3:48.94	3:49.63	3:50.31	3:51.00	3:51.69	3:52.38
340	3:53.06	3:53.75	3:54.44	3:55.13	3:55.81	3:56.50	3:57.19	3:57.88	3:58.56	3:59.25
350	3:59.94	4:00.63	4:01.31	4:02.00	4:02.69	4:03.38	4:04.06	4:04.75	4:05.44	4:06.12
360	4:06.81	4:07.50	4:08.19	4:08.88	4:09.56	4:10.25	4:10.94	4:11.62	4:12.31	4:13.00
370	4:13.69	4:14.38	4:15.06	4:15.75	4:16.44	4:17.12	4:17.81	4:18.50	4:19.19	4:19.88
380	4:20.56	4:21.25	4:21.94	4:22.62	4:23.31	4:24.00	4:24.69	4:25.38	4:26.06	4:26.75
390	4:27.44	4:28.13	4:28.81	4:29.50	4:30.19	4:30.88	4:31.56	4:32.25	4:32.94	4:33.63
400	4:34.31	4:35.00	4:35.69	4:36.38	4:37.06	4:37.75	4:38.44	4:39.13	4:39.81	4:40.50
410	4:41.19	4:41.88	4:42.56	4:43.25	4:43.94	4:44.63	4:45.31	4:46.00	4:46.69	4:47.37
420	4:48.06	4:48.75	4:49.44	4:50.13	4:50.81	4:51.50	4:52.19	4:52.87	4:53.56	4:54.25
430	4:54.94	4:55.63	4:56.31	4:57.00	4:57.69	4:58.37	4:59.06	4:59.75	5:00.44	5:01.13
440	5:01.81	5:02.50	5:03.19	5:03.87	5:04.56	5:05.25	5:05.94	5:06.63	5:07.31	5:08.00
450	5:08.69	5:09.38	5:10.06	5:10.75	5:11.44	5:12.13	5:12.81	5:13.50	5:14.19	5:14.88
460	5:15.56	5:16.25	5:16.94	5:17.63	5:18.31	5:19.00	5:19.69	5:20.38	5:21.06	5:21.75
470	5:22.44	5:23.13	5:23.81	5:24.50	5:25.19	5:25.88	5:26.56	5:27.25	5:27.94	5:28.63
480	5:29.31	5:30.00	5:30.69	5:31.38	5:32.06	5:32.75	5:33.44	5:34.12	5:34.81	5:35.50
490	5:36.19	5:36.88	5:37.56	5:38.25	5:38.94	5:39.62	5:40.31	5:41.00	5:41.69	5:42.38
500	5:43.06	5:43.75	5:44.44	5:45.13	5:45.81	5:46.50	5:47.19	5:47.88	5:48.56	5:49.25
510	5:49.94	5:50.63	5:51.31	5:52.00	5:52.69	5:53.38	5:54.06	5:54.75	5:55.44	5:56.13
520	5:56.81	5:57.50	5:58.19	5:58.88	5:59.56	6:00.25	6:00.94	6:01.63	6:02.31	6:03.00
530	6:03.69	6:04.38	6:05.06	6:05.75	6:06.44	6:07.13	6:07.81	6:08.50	6:09.19	6:09.88
540	6:10.56	6:11.25	6:11.94	6:12.63	6:13.31	6:14.00	6:14.69	6:15.37	6:16.06	6:16.75
550	6:17.44	6:18.13	6:18.81	6:19.50	6:20.19	6:20.87	6:21.56	6:22.25	6:22.94	6:23.63
560	6:24.31	6:25.00	6:25.69	6:26.37	6:27.06	6:27.75	6:28.44	6:29.13	6:29.81	6:30.50
570	6:31.19	6:31.88	6:32.56	6:33.25	6:33.94	6:34.63	6:35.31	6:36.00	6:36.69	6:37.38
580	6:38.06	6:38.75	6:39.44	6:40.13	6:40.81	6:41.50	6:42.19	6:42.88	6:43.56	6:44.25
590	6:44.94	6:45.63	6:46.31	6:47.00	6:47.69	6:48.38	6:49.06	6:49.75	6:50.44	6:51.13

♩. = 1.03; ♩ = 0.69; ♪. = 0.52; (triplet 3) ♩ 𝄾 = 0.46; ♪ = 0.34; (triplet 3) ♪𝄾𝄾 = 0.23; 𝅘𝅥𝅯 = 0.17 seconds

CLICK: 16⅝ FRAMES; M.M.: 86.62

Click	0	1	2	3	4	5	6	7	8	9
000	0:00.00	0:00.00	0:00.69	0:01.39	0:02.08	0:02.77	0:03.46	0:04.16	0:04.85	0:05.54
010	0:06.23	0:06.93	0:07.62	0:08.31	0:09.01	0:09.70	0:10.39	0:11.08	0:11.78	0:12.47
020	0:13.16	0:13.85	0:14.55	0:15.24	0:15.93	0:16.63	0:17.32	0:18.01	0:18.70	0:19.40
030	0:20.09	0:20.78	0:21.47	0:22.17	0:22.86	0:23.55	0:24.24	0:24.94	0:25.63	0:26.32
040	0:27.02	0:27.71	0:28.40	0:29.09	0:29.79	0:30.48	0:31.17	0:31.86	0:32.56	0:33.25
050	0:33.94	0:34.64	0:35.33	0:36.02	0:36.71	0:37.41	0:38.10	0:38.79	0:39.48	0:40.18
060	0:40.87	0:41.56	0:42.26	0:42.95	0:43.64	0:44.33	0:45.03	0:45.72	0:46.41	0:47.10
070	0:47.80	0:48.49	0:49.18	0:49.87	0:50.57	0:51.26	0:51.95	0:52.65	0:53.34	0:54.03
080	0:54.72	0:55.42	0:56.11	0:56.80	0:57.49	0:58.19	0:58.88	0:59.57	1:00.27	1:00.96
090	1:01.65	1:02.34	1:03.04	1:03.73	1:04.42	1:05.11	1:05.81	1:06.50	1:07.19	1:07.89
100	1:08.58	1:09.27	1:09.96	1:10.66	1:11.35	1:12.04	1:12.73	1:13.43	1:14.12	1:14.81
110	1:15.51	1:16.20	1:16.89	1:17.58	1:18.28	1:18.97	1:19.66	1:20.35	1:21.05	1:21.74
120	1:22.43	1:23.12	1:23.82	1:24.51	1:25.20	1:25.90	1:26.59	1:27.28	1:27.97	1:28.67
130	1:29.36	1:30.05	1:30.74	1:31.44	1:32.13	1:32.82	1:33.52	1:34.21	1:34.90	1:35.59
140	1:36.29	1:36.98	1:37.67	1:38.36	1:39.06	1:39.75	1:40.44	1:41.14	1:41.83	1:42.52
150	1:43.21	1:43.91	1:44.60	1:45.29	1:45.98	1:46.68	1:47.37	1:48.06	1:48.76	1:49.45
160	1:50.14	1:50.83	1:51.53	1:52.22	1:52.91	1:53.60	1:54.30	1:54.99	1:55.68	1:56.38
170	1:57.07	1:57.76	1:58.45	1:59.15	1:59.84	2:00.53	2:01.22	2:01.92	2:02.61	2:03.30
180	2:03.99	2:04.69	2:05.38	2:06.07	2:06.77	2:07.46	2:08.15	2:08.84	2:09.54	2:10.23
190	2:10.92	2:11.61	2:12.31	2:13.00	2:13.69	2:14.39	2:15.08	2:15.77	2:16.46	2:17.16
200	2:17.85	2:18.54	2:19.23	2:19.93	2:20.62	2:21.31	2:22.01	2:22.70	2:23.39	2:24.08
210	2:24.78	2:25.47	2:26.16	2:26.85	2:27.55	2:28.24	2:28.93	2:29.62	2:30.32	2:31.01
220	2:31.70	2:32.40	2:33.09	2:33.78	2:34.47	2:35.17	2:35.86	2:36.55	2:37.24	2:37.94
230	2:38.63	2:39.32	2:40.02	2:40.71	2:41.40	2:42.09	2:42.79	2:43.48	2:44.17	2:44.86
240	2:45.56	2:46.25	2:46.94	2:47.64	2:48.33	2:49.02	2:49.71	2:50.41	2:51.10	2:51.79
250	2:52.48	2:53.18	2:53.87	2:54.56	2:55.26	2:55.95	2:56.64	2:57.33	2:58.03	2:58.72
260	2:59.41	3:00.10	3:00.80	3:01.49	3:02.18	3:02.87	3:03.57	3:04.26	3:04.95	3:05.65
270	3:06.34	3:07.03	3:07.72	3:08.42	3:09.11	3:09.80	3:10.49	3:11.19	3:11.88	3:12.57
280	3:13.27	3:13.96	3:14.65	3:15.34	3:16.04	3:16.73	3:17.42	3:18.11	3:18.81	3:19.50
290	3:20.19	3:20.89	3:21.58	3:22.27	3:22.96	3:23.66	3:24.35	3:25.04	3:25.73	3:26.43
300	3:27.12	3:27.81	3:28.51	3:29.20	3:29.89	3:30.58	3:31.28	3:31.97	3:32.66	3:33.35
310	3:34.05	3:34.74	3:35.43	3:36.12	3:36.82	3:37.51	3:38.20	3:38.90	3:39.59	3:40.28
320	3:40.97	3:41.67	3:42.36	3:43.05	3:43.74	3:44.44	3:45.13	3:45.82	3:46.52	3:47.21
330	3:47.90	3:48.59	3:49.29	3:49.98	3:50.67	3:51.36	3:52.06	3:52.75	3:53.44	3:54.14
340	3:54.83	3:55.52	3:56.21	3:56.91	3:57.60	3:58.29	3:58.98	3:59.68	4:00.37	4:01.06
350	4:01.76	4:02.45	4:03.14	4:03.83	4:04.53	4:05.22	4:05.91	4:06.60	4:07.30	4:07.99
360	4:08.68	4:09.38	4:10.07	4:10.76	4:11.45	4:12.15	4:12.84	4:13.53	4:14.22	4:14.92
370	4:15.61	4:16.30	4:16.99	4:17.69	4:18.38	4:19.07	4:19.77	4:20.46	4:21.15	4:21.84
380	4:22.54	4:23.23	4:23.92	4:24.61	4:25.31	4:26.00	4:26.69	4:27.39	4:28.08	4:28.77
390	4:29.46	4:30.16	4:30.85	4:31.54	4:32.23	4:32.93	4:33.62	4:34.31	4:35.01	4:35.70
400	4:36.39	4:37.08	4:37.78	4:38.47	4:39.16	4:39.85	4:40.55	4:41.24	4:41.93	4:42.62
410	4:43.32	4:44.01	4:44.70	4:45.40	4:46.09	4:46.78	4:47.47	4:48.17	4:48.86	4:49.55
420	4:50.24	4:50.94	4:51.63	4:52.32	4:53.02	4:53.71	4:54.40	4:55.09	4:55.79	4:56.48
430	4:57.17	4:57.86	4:58.56	4:59.25	4:59.94	5:00.64	5:01.33	5:02.02	5:02.71	5:03.41
440	5:04.10	5:04.79	5:05.48	5:06.18	5:06.87	5:07.56	5:08.26	5:08.95	5:09.64	5:10.33
450	5:11.03	5:11.72	5:12.41	5:13.10	5:13.80	5:14.49	5:15.18	5:15.87	5:16.57	5:17.26
460	5:17.95	5:18.65	5:19.34	5:20.03	5:20.72	5:21.42	5:22.11	5:22.80	5:23.49	5:24.19
470	5:24.88	5:25.57	5:26.27	5:26.96	5:27.65	5:28.34	5:29.04	5:29.73	5:30.42	5:31.11
480	5:31.81	5:32.50	5:33.19	5:33.89	5:34.58	5:35.27	5:35.96	5:36.66	5:37.35	5:38.04
490	5:38.73	5:39.43	5:40.12	5:40.81	5:41.51	5:42.20	5:42.89	5:43.58	5:44.28	5:44.97
500	5:45.66	5:46.35	5:47.05	5:47.74	5:48.43	5:49.12	5:49.82	5:50.51	5:51.20	5:51.90
510	5:52.59	5:53.28	5:53.97	5:54.67	5:55.36	5:56.05	5:56.74	5:57.44	5:58.13	5:58.82
520	5:59.52	6:00.21	6:00.90	6:01.59	6:02.29	6:02.98	6:03.67	6:04.36	6:05.06	6:05.75
530	6:06.44	6:07.14	6:07.83	6:08.52	6:09.21	6:09.91	6:10.60	6:11.29	6:11.98	6:12.68
540	6:13.37	6:14.06	6:14.76	6:15.45	6:16.14	6:16.83	6:17.53	6:18.22	6:18.91	6:19.60
550	6:20.30	6:20.99	6:21.68	6:22.37	6:23.07	6:23.76	6:24.45	6:25.15	6:25.84	6:26.53
560	6:27.22	6:27.92	6:28.61	6:29.30	6:29.99	6:30.69	6:31.38	6:32.07	6:32.77	6:33.46
570	6:34.15	6:34.84	6:35.54	6:36.23	6:36.92	6:37.61	6:38.31	6:39.00	6:39.69	6:40.39
580	6:41.08	6:41.77	6:42.46	6:43.16	6:43.85	6:44.54	6:45.23	6:45.93	6:46.62	6:47.31
590	6:48.01	6:48.70	6:49.39	6:50.08	6:50.78	6:51.47	6:52.16	6:52.85	6:53.55	6:54.24

Dotted quarter note = 1.04; Quarter note = 0.69; Dotted eighth note = 0.52; Triplet (quarter, eighth rest) = 0.46; Eighth note = 0.35; Triplet (eighth, two eighth rests) = 0.23; Sixteenth note = 0.17 seconds

CLICK: 16 6/8 FRAMES; M.M.: 85.97

Click	0	1	2	3	4	5	6	7	8	9
000	0:00.00	0:00.00	0:00.70	0:01.40	0:02.09	0:02.79	0:03.49	0:04.19	0:04.89	0:05.58
010	0:06.28	0:06.98	0:07.68	0:08.38	0:09.07	0:09.77	0:10.47	0:11.17	0:11.86	0:12.56
020	0:13.26	0:13.96	0:14.66	0:15.35	0:16.05	0:16.75	0:17.45	0:18.15	0:18.84	0:19.54
030	0:20.24	0:20.94	0:21.64	0:22.33	0:23.03	0:23.73	0:24.43	0:25.13	0:25.82	0:26.52
040	0:27.22	0:27.92	0:28.61	0:29.31	0:30.01	0:30.71	0:31.41	0:32.10	0:32.80	0:33.50
050	0:34.20	0:34.90	0:35.59	0:36.29	0:36.99	0:37.69	0:38.39	0:39.08	0:39.78	0:40.48
060	0:41.18	0:41.88	0:42.57	0:43.27	0:43.97	0:44.67	0:45.36	0:46.06	0:46.76	0:47.46
070	0:48.16	0:48.85	0:49.55	0:50.25	0:50.95	0:51.65	0:52.34	0:53.04	0:53.74	0:54.44
080	0:55.14	0:55.83	0:56.53	0:57.23	0:57.93	0:58.63	0:59.32	1:00.02	1:00.72	1:01.42
090	1:02.11	1:02.81	1:03.51	1:04.21	1:04.91	1:05.60	1:06.30	1:07.00	1:07.70	1:08.40
100	1:09.09	1:09.79	1:10.49	1:11.19	1:11.89	1:12.58	1:13.28	1:13.98	1:14.68	1:15.38
110	1:16.07	1:16.77	1:17.47	1:18.17	1:18.86	1:19.56	1:20.26	1:20.96	1:21.66	1:22.35
120	1:23.05	1:23.75	1:24.45	1:25.15	1:25.84	1:26.54	1:27.24	1:27.94	1:28.64	1:29.33
130	1:30.03	1:30.73	1:31.43	1:32.13	1:32.82	1:33.52	1:34.22	1:34.92	1:35.61	1:36.31
140	1:37.01	1:37.71	1:38.41	1:39.10	1:39.80	1:40.50	1:41.20	1:41.90	1:42.59	1:43.29
150	1:43.99	1:44.69	1:45.39	1:46.08	1:46.78	1:47.48	1:48.18	1:48.88	1:49.57	1:50.27
160	1:50.97	1:51.67	1:52.36	1:53.06	1:53.76	1:54.46	1:55.16	1:55.85	1:56.55	1:57.25
170	1:57.95	1:58.65	1:59.34	2:00.04	2:00.74	2:01.44	2:02.14	2:02.83	2:03.53	2:04.23
180	2:04.93	2:05.63	2:06.32	2:07.02	2:07.72	2:08.42	2:09.11	2:09.81	2:10.51	2:11.21
190	2:11.91	2:12.60	2:13.30	2:14.00	2:14.70	2:15.40	2:16.09	2:16.79	2:17.49	2:18.19
200	2:18.89	2:19.58	2:20.28	2:20.98	2:21.68	2:22.38	2:23.07	2:23.77	2:24.47	2:25.17
210	2:25.86	2:26.56	2:27.26	2:27.96	2:28.66	2:29.35	2:30.05	2:30.75	2:31.45	2:32.15
220	2:32.84	2:33.54	2:34.24	2:34.94	2:35.64	2:36.33	2:37.03	2:37.73	2:38.43	2:39.13
230	2:39.82	2:40.52	2:41.22	2:41.92	2:42.61	2:43.31	2:44.01	2:44.71	2:45.41	2:46.10
240	2:46.80	2:47.50	2:48.20	2:48.90	2:49.59	2:50.29	2:50.99	2:51.69	2:52.39	2:53.08
250	2:53.78	2:54.48	2:55.18	2:55.88	2:56.57	2:57.27	2:57.97	2:58.67	2:59.36	3:00.06
260	3:00.76	3:01.46	3:02.16	3:02.85	3:03.55	3:04.25	3:04.95	3:05.65	3:06.34	3:07.04
270	3:07.74	3:08.44	3:09.14	3:09.83	3:10.53	3:11.23	3:11.93	3:12.63	3:13.32	3:14.02
280	3:14.72	3:15.42	3:16.11	3:16.81	3:17.51	3:18.21	3:18.91	3:19.60	3:20.30	3:21.00
290	3:21.70	3:22.40	3:23.09	3:23.79	3:24.49	3:25.19	3:25.89	3:26.58	3:27.28	3:27.98
300	3:28.68	3:29.38	3:30.07	3:30.77	3:31.47	3:32.17	3:32.86	3:33.56	3:34.26	3:34.96
310	3:35.66	3:36.35	3:37.05	3:37.75	3:38.45	3:39.15	3:39.84	3:40.54	3:41.24	3:41.94
320	3:42.64	3:43.33	3:44.03	3:44.73	3:45.43	3:46.13	3:46.82	3:47.52	3:48.22	3:48.92
330	3:49.61	3:50.31	3:51.01	3:51.71	3:52.41	3:53.10	3:53.80	3:54.50	3:55.20	3:55.90
340	3:56.59	3:57.29	3:57.99	3:58.69	3:59.39	4:00.08	4:00.78	4:01.48	4:02.18	4:02.88
350	4:03.57	4:04.27	4:04.97	4:05.67	4:06.36	4:07.06	4:07.76	4:08.46	4:09.16	4:09.85
360	4:10.55	4:11.25	4:11.95	4:12.65	4:13.34	4:14.04	4:14.74	4:15.44	4:16.14	4:16.83
370	4:17.53	4:18.23	4:18.93	4:19.63	4:20.32	4:21.02	4:21.72	4:22.42	4:23.11	4:23.81
380	4:24.51	4:25.21	4:25.91	4:26.60	4:27.30	4:28.00	4:28.70	4:29.40	4:30.09	4:30.79
390	4:31.49	4:32.19	4:32.89	4:33.58	4:34.28	4:34.98	4:35.68	4:36.38	4:37.07	4:37.77
400	4:38.47	4:39.17	4:39.86	4:40.56	4:41.26	4:41.96	4:42.66	4:43.35	4:44.05	4:44.75
410	4:45.45	4:46.15	4:46.84	4:47.54	4:48.24	4:48.94	4:49.64	4:50.33	4:51.03	4:51.73
420	4:52.43	4:53.13	4:53.82	4:54.52	4:55.22	4:55.92	4:56.61	4:57.31	4:58.01	4:58.71
430	4:59.41	5:00.10	5:00.80	5:01.50	5:02.20	5:02.90	5:03.59	5:04.29	5:04.99	5:05.69
440	5:06.39	5:07.08	5:07.78	5:08.48	5:09.18	5:09.88	5:10.57	5:11.27	5:11.97	5:12.67
450	5:13.36	5:14.06	5:14.76	5:15.46	5:16.16	5:16.85	5:17.55	5:18.25	5:18.95	5:19.65
460	5:20.34	5:21.04	5:21.74	5:22.44	5:23.14	5:23.83	5:24.53	5:25.23	5:25.93	5:26.63
470	5:27.32	5:28.02	5:28.72	5:29.42	5:30.11	5:30.81	5:31.51	5:32.21	5:32.91	5:33.60
480	5:34.30	5:35.00	5:35.70	5:36.40	5:37.09	5:37.79	5:38.49	5:39.19	5:39.89	5:40.58
490	5:41.28	5:41.98	5:42.68	5:43.38	5:44.07	5:44.77	5:45.47	5:46.17	5:46.86	5:47.56
500	5:48.26	5:48.96	5:49.66	5:50.35	5:51.05	5:51.75	5:52.45	5:53.15	5:53.84	5:54.54
510	5:55.24	5:55.94	5:56.64	5:57.33	5:58.03	5:58.73	5:59.43	6:00.13	6:00.82	6:01.52
520	6:02.22	6:02.92	6:03.61	6:04.31	6:05.01	6:05.71	6:06.41	6:07.10	6:07.80	6:08.50
530	6:09.20	6:09.90	6:10.59	6:11.29	6:11.99	6:12.69	6:13.39	6:14.08	6:14.78	6:15.48
540	6:16.18	6:16.88	6:17.57	6:18.27	6:18.97	6:19.67	6:20.36	6:21.06	6:21.76	6:22.46
550	6:23.16	6:23.85	6:24.55	6:25.25	6:25.95	6:26.65	6:27.34	6:28.04	6:28.74	6:29.44
560	6:30.14	6:30.83	6:31.53	6:32.23	6:32.93	6:33.63	6:34.32	6:35.02	6:35.72	6:36.42
570	6:37.11	6:37.81	6:38.51	6:39.21	6:39.91	6:40.60	6:41.30	6:42.00	6:42.70	6:43.40
580	6:44.09	6:44.79	6:45.49	6:46.19	6:46.89	6:47.58	6:48.28	6:48.98	6:49.68	6:50.38
590	6:51.07	6:51.77	6:52.47	6:53.17	6:53.86	6:54.56	6:55.26	6:55.96	6:56.66	6:57.35

♩. = 1.05; ♩ = 0.70; ♪. = 0.52; (triplet 3) ♩ 𝄾 = 0.47; ♪ = 0.35; (triplet 3) ♪𝄾𝄾 = 0.23; 𝅘𝅥𝅯 = 0.17 seconds

CLICK: 16⅞ FRAMES; M.M.: 85.33

Click	0	1	2	3	4	5	6	7	8	9
000	0:00.00	0:00.00	0:00.70	0:01.41	0:02.11	0:02.81	0:03.52	0:04.22	0:04.92	0:05.63
010	0:06.33	0:07.03	0:07.73	0:08.44	0:09.14	0:09.84	0:10.55	0:11.25	0:11.95	0:12.66
020	0:13.36	0:14.06	0:14.77	0:15.47	0:16.17	0:16.88	0:17.58	0:18.28	0:18.98	0:19.69
030	0:20.39	0:21.09	0:21.80	0:22.50	0:23.20	0:23.91	0:24.61	0:25.31	0:26.02	0:26.72
040	0:27.42	0:28.13	0:28.83	0:29.53	0:30.23	0:30.94	0:31.64	0:32.34	0:33.05	0:33.75
050	0:34.45	0:35.16	0:35.86	0:36.56	0:37.27	0:37.97	0:38.67	0:39.38	0:40.08	0:40.78
060	0:41.48	0:42.19	0:42.89	0:43.59	0:44.30	0:45.00	0:45.70	0:46.41	0:47.11	0:47.81
070	0:48.52	0:49.22	0:49.92	0:50.63	0:51.33	0:52.03	0:52.73	0:53.44	0:54.14	0:54.84
080	0:55.55	0:56.25	0:56.95	0:57.66	0:58.36	0:59.06	0:59.77	1:00.47	1:01.17	1:01.88
090	1:02.58	1:03.28	1:03.98	1:04.69	1:05.39	1:06.09	1:06.80	1:07.50	1:08.20	1:08.91
100	1:09.61	1:10.31	1:11.02	1:11.72	1:12.42	1:13.13	1:13.83	1:14.53	1:15.23	1:15.94
110	1:16.64	1:17.34	1:18.05	1:18.75	1:19.45	1:20.16	1:20.86	1:21.56	1:22.27	1:22.97
120	1:23.67	1:24.38	1:25.08	1:25.78	1:26.48	1:27.19	1:27.89	1:28.59	1:29.30	1:30.00
130	1:30.70	1:31.41	1:32.11	1:32.81	1:33.52	1:34.22	1:34.92	1:35.63	1:36.33	1:37.03
140	1:37.73	1:38.44	1:39.14	1:39.84	1:40.55	1:41.25	1:41.95	1:42.66	1:43.36	1:44.06
150	1:44.77	1:45.47	1:46.17	1:46.88	1:47.58	1:48.28	1:48.98	1:49.69	1:50.39	1:51.09
160	1:51.80	1:52.50	1:53.20	1:53.91	1:54.61	1:55.31	1:56.02	1:56.72	1:57.42	1:58.13
170	1:58.83	1:59.53	2:00.23	2:00.94	2:01.64	2:02.34	2:03.05	2:03.75	2:04.45	2:05.16
180	2:05.86	2:06.56	2:07.27	2:07.97	2:08.67	2:09.38	2:10.08	2:10.78	2:11.48	2:12.19
190	2:12.89	2:13.59	2:14.30	2:15.00	2:15.70	2:16.41	2:17.11	2:17.81	2:18.52	2:19.22
200	2:19.92	2:20.63	2:21.33	2:22.03	2:22.73	2:23.44	2:24.14	2:24.84	2:25.55	2:26.25
210	2:26.95	2:27.66	2:28.36	2:29.06	2:29.77	2:30.47	2:31.17	2:31.88	2:32.58	2:33.28
220	2:33.98	2:34.69	2:35.39	2:36.09	2:36.80	2:37.50	2:38.20	2:38.91	2:39.61	2:40.31
230	2:41.02	2:41.72	2:42.42	2:43.13	2:43.83	2:44.53	2:45.23	2:45.94	2:46.64	2:47.34
240	2:48.05	2:48.75	2:49.45	2:50.16	2:50.86	2:51.56	2:52.27	2:52.97	2:53.67	2:54.38
250	2:55.08	2:55.78	2:56.48	2:57.19	2:57.89	2:58.59	2:59.30	3:00.00	3:00.70	3:01.41
260	3:02.11	3:02.81	3:03.52	3:04.22	3:04.92	3:05.63	3:06.33	3:07.03	3:07.73	3:08.44
270	3:09.14	3:09.84	3:10.55	3:11.25	3:11.95	3:12.66	3:13.36	3:14.06	3:14.77	3:15.47
280	3:16.17	3:16.88	3:17.58	3:18.28	3:18.98	3:19.69	3:20.39	3:21.09	3:21.80	3:22.50
290	3:23.20	3:23.91	3:24.61	3:25.31	3:26.02	3:26.72	3:27.42	3:28.13	3:28.83	3:29.53
300	3:30.23	3:30.94	3:31.64	3:32.34	3:33.05	3:33.75	3:34.45	3:35.16	3:35.86	3:36.56
310	3:37.27	3:37.97	3:38.67	3:39.38	3:40.08	3:40.78	3:41.48	3:42.19	3:42.89	3:43.59
320	3:44.30	3:45.00	3:45.70	3:46.41	3:47.11	3:47.81	3:48.52	3:49.22	3:49.92	3:50.63
330	3:51.33	3:52.03	3:52.73	3:53.44	3:54.14	3:54.84	3:55.55	3:56.25	3:56.95	3:57.66
340	3:58.36	3:59.06	3:59.77	4:00.47	4:01.17	4:01.88	4:02.58	4:03.28	4:03.98	4:04.69
350	4:05.39	4:06.09	4:06.80	4:07.50	4:08.20	4:08.91	4:09.61	4:10.31	4:11.02	4:11.72
360	4:12.42	4:13.13	4:13.83	4:14.53	4:15.23	4:15.94	4:16.64	4:17.34	4:18.05	4:18.75
370	4:19.45	4:20.16	4:20.86	4:21.56	4:22.27	4:22.97	4:23.67	4:24.38	4:25.08	4:25.78
380	4:26.48	4:27.19	4:27.89	4:28.59	4:29.30	4:30.00	4:30.70	4:31.41	4:32.11	4:32.81
390	4:33.52	4:34.22	4:34.92	4:35.63	4:36.33	4:37.03	4:37.73	4:38.44	4:39.14	4:39.84
400	4:40.55	4:41.25	4:41.95	4:42.66	4:43.36	4:44.06	4:44.77	4:45.47	4:46.17	4:46.88
410	4:47.58	4:48.28	4:48.98	4:49.69	4:50.39	4:51.09	4:51.80	4:52.50	4:53.20	4:53.91
420	4:54.61	4:55.31	4:56.02	4:56.72	4:57.42	4:58.13	4:58.83	4:59.53	5:00.23	5:00.94
430	5:01.64	5:02.34	5:03.05	5:03.75	5:04.45	5:05.16	5:05.86	5:06.56	5:07.27	5:07.97
440	5:08.67	5:09.38	5:10.08	5:10.78	5:11.48	5:12.19	5:12.89	5:13.59	5:14.30	5:15.00
450	5:15.70	5:16.41	5:17.11	5:17.81	5:18.52	5:19.22	5:19.92	5:20.63	5:21.33	5:22.03
460	5:22.73	5:23.44	5:24.14	5:24.84	5:25.55	5:26.25	5:26.95	5:27.66	5:28.36	5:29.06
470	5:29.77	5:30.47	5:31.17	5:31.88	5:32.58	5:33.28	5:33.98	5:34.69	5:35.39	5:36.09
480	5:36.80	5:37.50	5:38.20	5:38.91	5:39.61	5:40.31	5:41.02	5:41.72	5:42.42	5:43.13
490	5:43.83	5:44.53	5:45.23	5:45.94	5:46.64	5:47.34	5:48.05	5:48.75	5:49.45	5:50.16
500	5:50.86	5:51.56	5:52.27	5:52.97	5:53.67	5:54.38	5:55.08	5:55.78	5:56.48	5:57.19
510	5:57.89	5:58.59	5:59.30	6:00.00	6:00.70	6:01.41	6:02.11	6:02.81	6:03.52	6:04.22
520	6:04.92	6:05.63	6:06.33	6:07.03	6:07.73	6:08.44	6:09.14	6:09.84	6:10.55	6:11.25
530	6:11.95	6:12.66	6:13.36	6:14.06	6:14.77	6:15.47	6:16.17	6:16.88	6:17.58	6:18.28
540	6:18.98	6:19.69	6:20.39	6:21.09	6:21.80	6:22.50	6:23.20	6:23.91	6:24.61	6:25.31
550	6:26.02	6:26.72	6:27.42	6:28.13	6:28.83	6:29.53	6:30.23	6:30.94	6:31.64	6:32.34
560	6:33.05	6:33.75	6:34.45	6:35.16	6:35.86	6:36.56	6:37.27	6:37.97	6:38.67	6:39.38
570	6:40.08	6:40.78	6:41.48	6:42.19	6:42.89	6:43.59	6:44.30	6:45.00	6:45.70	6:46.41
580	6:47.11	6:47.81	6:48.52	6:49.22	6:49.92	6:50.63	6:51.33	6:52.03	6:52.73	6:53.44
590	6:54.14	6:54.84	6:55.55	6:56.25	6:56.95	6:57.66	6:58.36	6:59.06	6:59.77	7:00.47

♩. = 1.05; ♩ = 0.70; ♪. = 0.53; (triplet) ♩ 𝄾 = 0.47; ♪ = 0.35; (triplet) ♪𝄾𝄾 = 0.23; 𝅘𝅥𝅯 = 0.18 seconds

CLICK: 17 0/8 FRAMES; M.M.: 84.71

Click	0	1	2	3	4	5	6	7	8	9
000	0:00.00	0:00.00	0:00.71	0:01.42	0:02.13	0:02.83	0:03.54	0:04.25	0:04.96	0:05.67
010	0:06.38	0:07.08	0:07.79	0:08.50	0:09.21	0:09.92	0:10.63	0:11.33	0:12.04	0:12.75
020	0:13.46	0:14.17	0:14.88	0:15.58	0:16.29	0:17.00	0:17.71	0:18.42	0:19.13	0:19.83
030	0:20.54	0:21.25	0:21.96	0:22.67	0:23.38	0:24.08	0:24.79	0:25.50	0:26.21	0:26.92
040	0:27.63	0:28.33	0:29.04	0:29.75	0:30.46	0:31.17	0:31.88	0:32.58	0:33.29	0:34.00
050	0:34.71	0:35.42	0:36.13	0:36.83	0:37.54	0:38.25	0:38.96	0:39.67	0:40.38	0:41.08
060	0:41.79	0:42.50	0:43.21	0:43.92	0:44.63	0:45.33	0:46.04	0:46.75	0:47.46	0:48.17
070	0:48.88	0:49.58	0:50.29	0:51.00	0:51.71	0:52.42	0:53.13	0:53.83	0:54.54	0:55.25
080	0:55.96	0:56.67	0:57.38	0:58.08	0:58.79	0:59.50	1:00.21	1:00.92	1:01.63	1:02.33
090	1:03.04	1:03.75	1:04.46	1:05.17	1:05.88	1:06.58	1:07.29	1:08.00	1:08.71	1:09.42
100	1:10.13	1:10.83	1:11.54	1:12.25	1:12.96	1:13.67	1:14.38	1:15.08	1:15.79	1:16.50
110	1:17.21	1:17.92	1:18.63	1:19.33	1:20.04	1:20.75	1:21.46	1:22.17	1:22.88	1:23.58
120	1:24.29	1:25.00	1:25.71	1:26.42	1:27.13	1:27.83	1:28.54	1:29.25	1:29.96	1:30.67
130	1:31.38	1:32.08	1:32.79	1:33.50	1:34.21	1:34.92	1:35.63	1:36.33	1:37.04	1:37.75
140	1:38.46	1:39.17	1:39.88	1:40.58	1:41.29	1:42.00	1:42.71	1:43.42	1:44.13	1:44.83
150	1:45.54	1:46.25	1:46.96	1:47.67	1:48.38	1:49.08	1:49.79	1:50.50	1:51.21	1:51.92
160	1:52.63	1:53.33	1:54.04	1:54.75	1:55.46	1:56.17	1:56.88	1:57.58	1:58.29	1:59.00
170	1:59.71	2:00.42	2:01.12	2:01.83	2:02.54	2:03.25	2:03.96	2:04.67	2:05.38	2:06.08
180	2:06.79	2:07.50	2:08.21	2:08.92	2:09.62	2:10.33	2:11.04	2:11.75	2:12.46	2:13.17
190	2:13.88	2:14.58	2:15.29	2:16.00	2:16.71	2:17.42	2:18.13	2:18.83	2:19.54	2:20.25
200	2:20.96	2:21.67	2:22.38	2:23.08	2:23.79	2:24.50	2:25.21	2:25.92	2:26.63	2:27.33
210	2:28.04	2:28.75	2:29.46	2:30.17	2:30.88	2:31.58	2:32.29	2:33.00	2:33.71	2:34.42
220	2:35.13	2:35.83	2:36.54	2:37.25	2:37.96	2:38.67	2:39.38	2:40.08	2:40.79	2:41.50
230	2:42.21	2:42.92	2:43.63	2:44.33	2:45.04	2:45.75	2:46.46	2:47.17	2:47.88	2:48.58
240	2:49.29	2:50.00	2:50.71	2:51.42	2:52.13	2:52.83	2:53.54	2:54.25	2:54.96	2:55.67
250	2:56.38	2:57.08	2:57.79	2:58.50	2:59.21	2:59.92	3:00.63	3:01.33	3:02.04	3:02.75
260	3:03.46	3:04.17	3:04.87	3:05.58	3:06.29	3:07.00	3:07.71	3:08.42	3:09.13	3:09.83
270	3:10.54	3:11.25	3:11.96	3:12.67	3:13.38	3:14.08	3:14.79	3:15.50	3:16.21	3:16.92
280	3:17.63	3:18.33	3:19.04	3:19.75	3:20.46	3:21.17	3:21.88	3:22.58	3:23.29	3:24.00
290	3:24.71	3:25.42	3:26.13	3:26.83	3:27.54	3:28.25	3:28.96	3:29.67	3:30.38	3:31.08
300	3:31.79	3:32.50	3:33.21	3:33.92	3:34.63	3:35.33	3:36.04	3:36.75	3:37.46	3:38.17
310	3:38.88	3:39.58	3:40.29	3:41.00	3:41.71	3:42.42	3:43.13	3:43.83	3:44.54	3:45.25
320	3:45.96	3:46.67	3:47.38	3:48.08	3:48.79	3:49.50	3:50.21	3:50.92	3:51.63	3:52.33
330	3:53.04	3:53.75	3:54.46	3:55.17	3:55.88	3:56.58	3:57.29	3:58.00	3:58.71	3:59.42
340	4:00.12	4:00.83	4:01.54	4:02.25	4:02.96	4:03.67	4:04.37	4:05.08	4:05.79	4:06.50
350	4:07.21	4:07.92	4:08.63	4:09.33	4:10.04	4:10.75	4:11.46	4:12.17	4:12.88	4:13.58
360	4:14.29	4:15.00	4:15.71	4:16.42	4:17.12	4:17.83	4:18.54	4:19.25	4:19.96	4:20.67
370	4:21.38	4:22.08	4:22.79	4:23.50	4:24.21	4:24.92	4:25.63	4:26.33	4:27.04	4:27.75
380	4:28.46	4:29.17	4:29.88	4:30.58	4:31.29	4:32.00	4:32.71	4:33.42	4:34.12	4:34.83
390	4:35.54	4:36.25	4:36.96	4:37.67	4:38.38	4:39.08	4:39.79	4:40.50	4:41.21	4:41.92
400	4:42.63	4:43.33	4:44.04	4:44.75	4:45.46	4:46.17	4:46.88	4:47.58	4:48.29	4:49.00
410	4:49.71	4:50.42	4:51.12	4:51.83	4:52.54	4:53.25	4:53.96	4:54.67	4:55.38	4:56.08
420	4:56.79	4:57.50	4:58.21	4:58.92	4:59.63	5:00.33	5:01.04	5:01.75	5:02.46	5:03.17
430	5:03.87	5:04.58	5:05.29	5:06.00	5:06.71	5:07.42	5:08.13	5:08.83	5:09.54	5:10.25
440	5:10.96	5:11.67	5:12.38	5:13.08	5:13.79	5:14.50	5:15.21	5:15.92	5:16.63	5:17.33
450	5:18.04	5:18.75	5:19.46	5:20.17	5:20.87	5:21.58	5:22.29	5:23.00	5:23.71	5:24.42
460	5:25.13	5:25.83	5:26.54	5:27.25	5:27.96	5:28.67	5:29.38	5:30.08	5:30.79	5:31.50
470	5:32.21	5:32.92	5:33.63	5:34.33	5:35.04	5:35.75	5:36.46	5:37.17	5:37.87	5:38.58
480	5:39.29	5:40.00	5:40.71	5:41.42	5:42.13	5:42.83	5:43.54	5:44.25	5:44.96	5:45.67
490	5:46.38	5:47.08	5:47.79	5:48.50	5:49.21	5:49.92	5:50.63	5:51.33	5:52.04	5:52.75
500	5:53.46	5:54.17	5:54.88	5:55.58	5:56.29	5:57.00	5:57.71	5:58.42	5:59.13	5:59.83
510	6:00.54	6:01.25	6:01.96	6:02.67	6:03.38	6:04.08	6:04.79	6:05.50	6:06.21	6:06.92
520	6:07.62	6:08.33	6:09.04	6:09.75	6:10.46	6:11.17	6:11.88	6:12.58	6:13.29	6:14.00
530	6:14.71	6:15.42	6:16.13	6:16.83	6:17.54	6:18.25	6:18.96	6:19.67	6:20.38	6:21.08
540	6:21.79	6:22.50	6:23.21	6:23.92	6:24.62	6:25.33	6:26.04	6:26.75	6:27.46	6:28.17
550	6:28.88	6:29.58	6:30.29	6:31.00	6:31.71	6:32.42	6:33.13	6:33.83	6:34.54	6:35.25
560	6:35.96	6:36.67	6:37.38	6:38.08	6:38.79	6:39.50	6:40.21	6:40.92	6:41.62	6:42.33
570	6:43.04	6:43.75	6:44.46	6:45.17	6:45.88	6:46.58	6:47.29	6:48.00	6:48.71	6:49.42
580	6:50.13	6:50.83	6:51.54	6:52.25	6:52.96	6:53.67	6:54.38	6:55.08	6:55.79	6:56.50
590	6:57.21	6:57.92	6:58.63	6:59.33	7:00.04	7:00.75	7:01.46	7:02.17	7:02.88	7:03.58

♩. = 1.06; ♩ = 0.71; ♪. = 0.53; (triplet) ♩ 𝄾 = 0.47; ♪ = 0.35; (triplet) ♪𝄾𝄾 = 0.24; 𝅘𝅥𝅯 = 0.18 seconds

CLICK: 17⅛ FRAMES; M.M.: 84.09

Click	0	1	2	3	4	5	6	7	8	9
000	0:00.00	0:00.00	0:00.71	0:01.43	0:02.14	0:02.85	0:03.57	0:04.28	0:04.99	0:05.71
010	0:06.42	0:07.14	0:07.85	0:08.56	0:09.28	0:09.99	0:10.70	0:11.42	0:12.13	0:12.84
020	0:13.56	0:14.27	0:14.98	0:15.70	0:16.41	0:17.13	0:17.84	0:18.55	0:19.27	0:19.98
030	0:20.69	0:21.41	0:22.12	0:22.83	0:23.55	0:24.26	0:24.97	0:25.69	0:26.40	0:27.11
040	0:27.83	0:28.54	0:29.26	0:29.97	0:30.68	0:31.40	0:32.11	0:32.82	0:33.54	0:34.25
050	0:34.96	0:35.68	0:36.39	0:37.10	0:37.82	0:38.53	0:39.24	0:39.96	0:40.67	0:41.39
060	0:42.10	0:42.81	0:43.53	0:44.24	0:44.95	0:45.67	0:46.38	0:47.09	0:47.81	0:48.52
070	0:49.23	0:49.95	0:50.66	0:51.38	0:52.09	0:52.80	0:53.52	0:54.23	0:54.94	0:55.66
080	0:56.37	0:57.08	0:57.80	0:58.51	0:59.22	0:59.94	1:00.65	1:01.36	1:02.08	1:02.79
090	1:03.51	1:04.22	1:04.93	1:05.65	1:06.36	1:07.07	1:07.79	1:08.50	1:09.21	1:09.93
100	1:10.64	1:11.35	1:12.07	1:12.78	1:13.49	1:14.21	1:14.92	1:15.64	1:16.35	1:17.06
110	1:17.78	1:18.49	1:19.20	1:19.92	1:20.63	1:21.34	1:22.06	1:22.77	1:23.48	1:24.20
120	1:24.91	1:25.62	1:26.34	1:27.05	1:27.77	1:28.48	1:29.19	1:29.91	1:30.62	1:31.33
130	1:32.05	1:32.76	1:33.47	1:34.19	1:34.90	1:35.61	1:36.33	1:37.04	1:37.76	1:38.47
140	1:39.18	1:39.90	1:40.61	1:41.32	1:42.04	1:42.75	1:43.46	1:44.18	1:44.89	1:45.60
150	1:46.32	1:47.03	1:47.74	1:48.46	1:49.17	1:49.89	1:50.60	1:51.31	1:52.03	1:52.74
160	1:53.45	1:54.17	1:54.88	1:55.59	1:56.31	1:57.02	1:57.73	1:58.45	1:59.16	1:59.87
170	2:00.59	2:01.30	2:02.02	2:02.73	2:03.44	2:04.16	2:04.87	2:05.58	2:06.30	2:07.01
180	2:07.72	2:08.44	2:09.15	2:09.86	2:10.58	2:11.29	2:12.01	2:12.72	2:13.43	2:14.15
190	2:14.86	2:15.57	2:16.29	2:17.00	2:17.71	2:18.43	2:19.14	2:19.85	2:20.57	2:21.28
200	2:21.99	2:22.71	2:23.42	2:24.14	2:24.85	2:25.56	2:26.28	2:26.99	2:27.70	2:28.42
210	2:29.13	2:29.84	2:30.56	2:31.27	2:31.98	2:32.70	2:33.41	2:34.12	2:34.84	2:35.55
220	2:36.27	2:36.98	2:37.69	2:38.41	2:39.12	2:39.83	2:40.55	2:41.26	2:41.97	2:42.69
230	2:43.40	2:44.11	2:44.83	2:45.54	2:46.26	2:46.97	2:47.68	2:48.40	2:49.11	2:49.82
240	2:50.54	2:51.25	2:51.96	2:52.68	2:53.39	2:54.10	2:54.82	2:55.53	2:56.24	2:56.96
250	2:57.67	2:58.39	2:59.10	2:59.81	3:00.53	3:01.24	3:01.95	3:02.67	3:03.38	3:04.09
260	3:04.81	3:05.52	3:06.23	3:06.95	3:07.66	3:08.37	3:09.09	3:09.80	3:10.52	3:11.23
270	3:11.94	3:12.66	3:13.37	3:14.08	3:14.80	3:15.51	3:16.22	3:16.94	3:17.65	3:18.36
280	3:19.08	3:19.79	3:20.51	3:21.22	3:21.93	3:22.65	3:23.36	3:24.07	3:24.79	3:25.50
290	3:26.21	3:26.93	3:27.64	3:28.35	3:29.07	3:29.78	3:30.49	3:31.21	3:31.92	3:32.64
300	3:33.35	3:34.06	3:34.78	3:35.49	3:36.20	3:36.92	3:37.63	3:38.34	3:39.06	3:39.77
310	3:40.48	3:41.20	3:41.91	3:42.62	3:43.34	3:44.05	3:44.77	3:45.48	3:46.19	3:46.91
320	3:47.62	3:48.33	3:49.05	3:49.76	3:50.47	3:51.19	3:51.90	3:52.61	3:53.33	3:54.04
330	3:54.76	3:55.47	3:56.18	3:56.90	3:57.61	3:58.32	3:59.04	3:59.75	4:00.46	4:01.18
340	4:01.89	4:02.60	4:03.32	4:04.03	4:04.74	4:05.46	4:06.17	4:06.89	4:07.60	4:08.31
350	4:09.03	4:09.74	4:10.45	4:11.17	4:11.88	4:12.59	4:13.31	4:14.02	4:14.73	4:15.45
360	4:16.16	4:16.88	4:17.59	4:18.30	4:19.02	4:19.73	4:20.44	4:21.16	4:21.87	4:22.58
370	4:23.30	4:24.01	4:24.72	4:25.44	4:26.15	4:26.86	4:27.58	4:28.29	4:29.01	4:29.72
380	4:30.43	4:31.15	4:31.86	4:32.57	4:33.29	4:34.00	4:34.71	4:35.43	4:36.14	4:36.85
390	4:37.57	4:38.28	4:38.99	4:39.71	4:40.42	4:41.14	4:41.85	4:42.56	4:43.28	4:43.99
400	4:44.70	4:45.42	4:46.13	4:46.84	4:47.56	4:48.27	4:48.98	4:49.70	4:50.41	4:51.12
410	4:51.84	4:52.55	4:53.27	4:53.98	4:54.69	4:55.41	4:56.12	4:56.83	4:57.55	4:58.26
420	4:58.97	4:59.69	5:00.40	5:01.11	5:01.83	5:02.54	5:03.26	5:03.97	5:04.68	5:05.40
430	5:06.11	5:06.82	5:07.54	5:08.25	5:08.96	5:09.68	5:10.39	5:11.10	5:11.82	5:12.53
440	5:13.24	5:13.96	5:14.67	5:15.39	5:16.10	5:16.81	5:17.53	5:18.24	5:18.95	5:19.67
450	5:20.38	5:21.09	5:21.81	5:22.52	5:23.23	5:23.95	5:24.66	5:25.37	5:26.09	5:26.80
460	5:27.52	5:28.23	5:28.94	5:29.66	5:30.37	5:31.08	5:31.80	5:32.51	5:33.22	5:33.94
470	5:34.65	5:35.36	5:36.08	5:36.79	5:37.51	5:38.22	5:38.93	5:39.65	5:40.36	5:41.07
480	5:41.79	5:42.50	5:43.21	5:43.93	5:44.64	5:45.35	5:46.07	5:46.78	5:47.49	5:48.21
490	5:48.92	5:49.64	5:50.35	5:51.06	5:51.78	5:52.49	5:53.20	5:53.92	5:54.63	5:55.34
500	5:56.06	5:56.77	5:57.48	5:58.20	5:58.91	5:59.62	6:00.34	6:01.05	6:01.77	6:02.48
510	6:03.19	6:03.91	6:04.62	6:05.33	6:06.05	6:06.76	6:07.47	6:08.19	6:08.90	6:09.61
520	6:10.33	6:11.04	6:11.76	6:12.47	6:13.18	6:13.90	6:14.61	6:15.32	6:16.04	6:16.75
530	6:17.46	6:18.18	6:18.89	6:19.60	6:20.32	6:21.03	6:21.74	6:22.46	6:23.17	6:23.89
540	6:24.60	6:25.31	6:26.03	6:26.74	6:27.45	6:28.17	6:28.88	6:29.59	6:30.31	6:31.02
550	6:31.73	6:32.45	6:33.16	6:33.88	6:34.59	6:35.30	6:36.02	6:36.73	6:37.44	6:38.16
560	6:38.87	6:39.58	6:40.30	6:41.01	6:41.72	6:42.44	6:43.15	6:43.86	6:44.58	6:45.29
570	6:46.01	6:46.72	6:47.43	6:48.15	6:48.86	6:49.57	6:50.29	6:51.00	6:51.71	6:52.43
580	6:53.14	6:53.85	6:54.57	6:55.28	6:55.99	6:56.71	6:57.42	6:58.14	6:58.85	6:59.56
590	7:00.28	7:00.99	7:01.70	7:02.42	7:03.13	7:03.84	7:04.56	7:05.27	7:05.98	7:06.70

♩. = 1.07; ♩ = 0.71; ♪. = 0.54; (triplet) ♩ 𝄾 = 0.48; ♪ = 0.36; (triplet) ♪ 𝄾 𝄾 = 0.24; 𝅘𝅥𝅯 = 0.18 seconds

CLICK: 17 2/8 FRAMES; M.M.: 83.48

Click	0	1	2	3	4	5	6	7	8	9
000	0:00.00	0:00.00	0:00.72	0:01.44	0:02.16	0:02.88	0:03.59	0:04.31	0:05.03	0:05.75
010	0:06.47	0:07.19	0:07.91	0:08.63	0:09.34	0:10.06	0:10.78	0:11.50	0:12.22	0:12.94
020	0:13.66	0:14.38	0:15.09	0:15.81	0:16.53	0:17.25	0:17.97	0:18.69	0:19.41	0:20.13
030	0:20.84	0:21.56	0:22.28	0:23.00	0:23.72	0:24.44	0:25.16	0:25.88	0:26.59	0:27.31
040	0:28.03	0:28.75	0:29.47	0:30.19	0:30.91	0:31.63	0:32.34	0:33.06	0:33.78	0:34.50
050	0:35.22	0:35.94	0:36.66	0:37.38	0:38.09	0:38.81	0:39.53	0:40.25	0:40.97	0:41.69
060	0:42.41	0:43.13	0:43.84	0:44.56	0:45.28	0:46.00	0:46.72	0:47.44	0:48.16	0:48.88
070	0:49.59	0:50.31	0:51.03	0:51.75	0:52.47	0:53.19	0:53.91	0:54.63	0:55.34	0:56.06
080	0:56.78	0:57.50	0:58.22	0:58.94	0:59.66	1:00.38	1:01.09	1:01.81	1:02.53	1:03.25
090	1:03.97	1:04.69	1:05.41	1:06.12	1:06.84	1:07.56	1:08.28	1:09.00	1:09.72	1:10.44
100	1:11.16	1:11.87	1:12.59	1:13.31	1:14.03	1:14.75	1:15.47	1:16.19	1:16.91	1:17.62
110	1:18.34	1:19.06	1:19.78	1:20.50	1:21.22	1:21.94	1:22.66	1:23.38	1:24.09	1:24.81
120	1:25.53	1:26.25	1:26.97	1:27.69	1:28.41	1:29.13	1:29.84	1:30.56	1:31.28	1:32.00
130	1:32.72	1:33.44	1:34.16	1:34.87	1:35.59	1:36.31	1:37.03	1:37.75	1:38.47	1:39.19
140	1:39.91	1:40.62	1:41.34	1:42.06	1:42.78	1:43.50	1:44.22	1:44.94	1:45.66	1:46.38
150	1:47.09	1:47.81	1:48.53	1:49.25	1:49.97	1:50.69	1:51.41	1:52.13	1:52.84	1:53.56
160	1:54.28	1:55.00	1:55.72	1:56.44	1:57.16	1:57.87	1:58.59	1:59.31	2:00.03	2:00.75
170	2:01.47	2:02.19	2:02.91	2:03.63	2:04.34	2:05.06	2:05.78	2:06.50	2:07.22	2:07.94
180	2:08.66	2:09.38	2:10.09	2:10.81	2:11.53	2:12.25	2:12.97	2:13.69	2:14.41	2:15.12
190	2:15.84	2:16.56	2:17.28	2:18.00	2:18.72	2:19.44	2:20.16	2:20.87	2:21.59	2:22.31
200	2:23.03	2:23.75	2:24.47	2:25.19	2:25.91	2:26.62	2:27.34	2:28.06	2:28.78	2:29.50
210	2:30.22	2:30.94	2:31.66	2:32.37	2:33.09	2:33.81	2:34.53	2:35.25	2:35.97	2:36.69
220	2:37.41	2:38.12	2:38.84	2:39.56	2:40.28	2:41.00	2:41.72	2:42.44	2:43.16	2:43.88
230	2:44.59	2:45.31	2:46.03	2:46.75	2:47.47	2:48.19	2:48.91	2:49.63	2:50.34	2:51.06
240	2:51.78	2:52.50	2:53.22	2:53.94	2:54.66	2:55.38	2:56.09	2:56.81	2:57.53	2:58.25
250	2:58.97	2:59.69	3:00.41	3:01.12	3:01.84	3:02.56	3:03.28	3:04.00	3:04.72	3:05.44
260	3:06.16	3:06.87	3:07.59	3:08.31	3:09.03	3:09.75	3:10.47	3:11.19	3:11.91	3:12.62
270	3:13.34	3:14.06	3:14.78	3:15.50	3:16.22	3:16.94	3:17.66	3:18.37	3:19.09	3:19.81
280	3:20.53	3:21.25	3:21.97	3:22.69	3:23.41	3:24.12	3:24.84	3:25.56	3:26.28	3:27.00
290	3:27.72	3:28.44	3:29.16	3:29.88	3:30.59	3:31.31	3:32.03	3:32.75	3:33.47	3:34.19
300	3:34.91	3:35.63	3:36.34	3:37.06	3:37.78	3:38.50	3:39.22	3:39.94	3:40.66	3:41.38
310	3:42.09	3:42.81	3:43.53	3:44.25	3:44.97	3:45.69	3:46.41	3:47.12	3:47.84	3:48.56
320	3:49.28	3:50.00	3:50.72	3:51.44	3:52.16	3:52.87	3:53.59	3:54.31	3:55.03	3:55.75
330	3:56.47	3:57.19	3:57.91	3:58.62	3:59.34	4:00.06	4:00.78	4:01.50	4:02.22	4:02.94
340	4:03.66	4:04.37	4:05.09	4:05.81	4:06.53	4:07.25	4:07.97	4:08.69	4:09.41	4:10.12
350	4:10.84	4:11.56	4:12.28	4:13.00	4:13.72	4:14.44	4:15.16	4:15.87	4:16.59	4:17.31
360	4:18.03	4:18.75	4:19.47	4:20.19	4:20.91	4:21.62	4:22.34	4:23.06	4:23.78	4:24.50
370	4:25.22	4:25.94	4:26.66	4:27.37	4:28.09	4:28.81	4:29.53	4:30.25	4:30.97	4:31.69
380	4:32.41	4:33.12	4:33.84	4:34.56	4:35.28	4:36.00	4:36.72	4:37.44	4:38.16	4:38.88
390	4:39.59	4:40.31	4:41.03	4:41.75	4:42.47	4:43.19	4:43.91	4:44.63	4:45.34	4:46.06
400	4:46.78	4:47.50	4:48.22	4:48.94	4:49.66	4:50.38	4:51.09	4:51.81	4:52.53	4:53.25
410	4:53.97	4:54.69	4:55.41	4:56.13	4:56.84	4:57.56	4:58.28	4:59.00	4:59.72	5:00.44
420	5:01.16	5:01.88	5:02.59	5:03.31	5:04.03	5:04.75	5:05.47	5:06.19	5:06.91	5:07.62
430	5:08.34	5:09.06	5:09.78	5:10.50	5:11.22	5:11.94	5:12.66	5:13.37	5:14.09	5:14.81
440	5:15.53	5:16.25	5:16.97	5:17.69	5:18.41	5:19.12	5:19.84	5:20.56	5:21.28	5:22.00
450	5:22.72	5:23.44	5:24.16	5:24.87	5:25.59	5:26.31	5:27.03	5:27.75	5:28.47	5:29.19
460	5:29.91	5:30.62	5:31.34	5:32.06	5:32.78	5:33.50	5:34.22	5:34.94	5:35.66	5:36.37
470	5:37.09	5:37.81	5:38.53	5:39.25	5:39.97	5:40.69	5:41.41	5:42.12	5:42.84	5:43.56
480	5:44.28	5:45.00	5:45.72	5:46.44	5:47.16	5:47.87	5:48.59	5:49.31	5:50.03	5:50.75
490	5:51.47	5:52.19	5:52.91	5:53.62	5:54.34	5:55.06	5:55.78	5:56.50	5:57.22	5:57.94
500	5:58.66	5:59.37	6:00.09	6:00.81	6:01.53	6:02.25	6:02.97	6:03.69	6:04.41	6:05.12
510	6:05.84	6:06.56	6:07.28	6:08.00	6:08.72	6:09.44	6:10.16	6:10.88	6:11.59	6:12.31
520	6:13.03	6:13.75	6:14.47	6:15.19	6:15.91	6:16.63	6:17.34	6:18.06	6:18.78	6:19.50
530	6:20.22	6:20.94	6:21.66	6:22.38	6:23.09	6:23.81	6:24.53	6:25.25	6:25.97	6:26.69
540	6:27.41	6:28.13	6:28.84	6:29.56	6:30.28	6:31.00	6:31.72	6:32.44	6:33.16	6:33.88
550	6:34.59	6:35.31	6:36.03	6:36.75	6:37.47	6:38.19	6:38.91	6:39.62	6:40.34	6:41.06
560	6:41.78	6:42.50	6:43.22	6:43.94	6:44.66	6:45.37	6:46.09	6:46.81	6:47.53	6:48.25
570	6:48.97	6:49.69	6:50.41	6:51.12	6:51.84	6:52.56	6:53.28	6:54.00	6:54.72	6:55.44
580	6:56.16	6:56.87	6:57.59	6:58.31	6:59.03	6:59.75	7:00.47	7:01.19	7:01.91	7:02.62
590	7:03.34	7:04.06	7:04.78	7:05.50	7:06.22	7:06.94	7:07.66	7:08.37	7:09.09	7:09.81

dotted half note = 1.08; quarter note = 0.72; dotted eighth note = 0.54; triplet (quarter note, eighth rest) = 0.48; eighth note = 0.36; triplet (eighth note, two eighth rests) = 0.24; sixteenth note = 0.18 seconds

CLICK: 17⅜ FRAMES; M.M.: 82.88

Click	0	1	2	3	4	5	6	7	8	9
000	0:00.00	0:00.00	0:00.72	0:01.45	0:02.17	0:02.90	0:03.62	0:04.34	0:05.07	0:05.79
010	0:06.52	0:07.24	0:07.96	0:08.69	0:09.41	0:10.14	0:10.86	0:11.58	0:12.31	0:13.03
020	0:13.76	0:14.48	0:15.20	0:15.93	0:16.65	0:17.38	0:18.10	0:18.82	0:19.55	0:20.27
030	0:20.99	0:21.72	0:22.44	0:23.17	0:23.89	0:24.61	0:25.34	0:26.06	0:26.79	0:27.51
040	0:28.23	0:28.96	0:29.68	0:30.41	0:31.13	0:31.85	0:32.58	0:33.30	0:34.03	0:34.75
050	0:35.47	0:36.20	0:36.92	0:37.65	0:38.37	0:39.09	0:39.82	0:40.54	0:41.27	0:41.99
060	0:42.71	0:43.44	0:44.16	0:44.89	0:45.61	0:46.33	0:47.06	0:47.78	0:48.51	0:49.23
070	0:49.95	0:50.68	0:51.40	0:52.13	0:52.85	0:53.57	0:54.30	0:55.02	0:55.74	0:56.47
080	0:57.19	0:57.92	0:58.64	0:59.36	1:00.09	1:00.81	1:01.54	1:02.26	1:02.98	1:03.71
090	1:04.43	1:05.16	1:05.88	1:06.60	1:07.33	1:08.05	1:08.78	1:09.50	1:10.22	1:10.95
100	1:11.67	1:12.40	1:13.12	1:13.84	1:14.57	1:15.29	1:16.02	1:16.74	1:17.46	1:18.19
110	1:18.91	1:19.64	1:20.36	1:21.08	1:21.81	1:22.53	1:23.26	1:23.98	1:24.70	1:25.43
120	1:26.15	1:26.87	1:27.60	1:28.32	1:29.05	1:29.77	1:30.49	1:31.22	1:31.94	1:32.67
130	1:33.39	1:34.11	1:34.84	1:35.56	1:36.29	1:37.01	1:37.73	1:38.46	1:39.18	1:39.91
140	1:40.63	1:41.35	1:42.08	1:42.80	1:43.53	1:44.25	1:44.97	1:45.70	1:46.42	1:47.15
150	1:47.87	1:48.59	1:49.32	1:50.04	1:50.77	1:51.49	1:52.21	1:52.94	1:53.66	1:54.39
160	1:55.11	1:55.83	1:56.56	1:57.28	1:58.01	1:58.73	1:59.45	2:00.18	2:00.90	2:01.63
170	2:02.35	2:03.07	2:03.80	2:04.52	2:05.24	2:05.97	2:06.69	2:07.42	2:08.14	2:08.86
180	2:09.59	2:10.31	2:11.04	2:11.76	2:12.48	2:13.21	2:13.93	2:14.66	2:15.38	2:16.10
190	2:16.83	2:17.55	2:18.28	2:19.00	2:19.72	2:20.45	2:21.17	2:21.90	2:22.62	2:23.34
200	2:24.07	2:24.79	2:25.52	2:26.24	2:26.96	2:27.69	2:28.41	2:29.14	2:29.86	2:30.58
210	2:31.31	2:32.03	2:32.76	2:33.48	2:34.20	2:34.93	2:35.65	2:36.38	2:37.10	2:37.82
220	2:38.55	2:39.27	2:39.99	2:40.72	2:41.44	2:42.17	2:42.89	2:43.61	2:44.34	2:45.06
230	2:45.79	2:46.51	2:47.23	2:47.96	2:48.68	2:49.41	2:50.13	2:50.85	2:51.58	2:52.30
240	2:53.03	2:53.75	2:54.47	2:55.20	2:55.92	2:56.65	2:57.37	2:58.09	2:58.82	2:59.54
250	3:00.27	3:00.99	3:01.71	3:02.44	3:03.16	3:03.89	3:04.61	3:05.33	3:06.06	3:06.78
260	3:07.51	3:08.23	3:08.95	3:09.68	3:10.40	3:11.13	3:11.85	3:12.57	3:13.30	3:14.02
270	3:14.74	3:15.47	3:16.19	3:16.92	3:17.64	3:18.36	3:19.09	3:19.81	3:20.54	3:21.26
280	3:21.98	3:22.71	3:23.43	3:24.16	3:24.88	3:25.60	3:26.33	3:27.05	3:27.78	3:28.50
290	3:29.22	3:29.95	3:30.67	3:31.40	3:32.12	3:32.84	3:33.57	3:34.29	3:35.02	3:35.74
300	3:36.46	3:37.19	3:37.91	3:38.64	3:39.36	3:40.08	3:40.81	3:41.53	3:42.26	3:42.98
310	3:43.70	3:44.43	3:45.15	3:45.88	3:46.60	3:47.32	3:48.05	3:48.77	3:49.49	3:50.22
320	3:50.94	3:51.67	3:52.39	3:53.11	3:53.84	3:54.56	3:55.29	3:56.01	3:56.73	3:57.46
330	3:58.18	3:58.91	3:59.63	4:00.35	4:01.08	4:01.80	4:02.53	4:03.25	4:03.97	4:04.70
340	4:05.42	4:06.15	4:06.87	4:07.59	4:08.32	4:09.04	4:09.77	4:10.49	4:11.21	4:11.94
350	4:12.66	4:13.39	4:14.11	4:14.83	4:15.56	4:16.28	4:17.01	4:17.73	4:18.45	4:19.18
360	4:19.90	4:20.63	4:21.35	4:22.07	4:22.80	4:23.52	4:24.24	4:24.97	4:25.69	4:26.42
370	4:27.14	4:27.86	4:28.59	4:29.31	4:30.04	4:30.76	4:31.48	4:32.21	4:32.93	4:33.66
380	4:34.38	4:35.10	4:35.83	4:36.55	4:37.28	4:38.00	4:38.72	4:39.45	4:40.17	4:40.90
390	4:41.62	4:42.34	4:43.07	4:43.79	4:44.52	4:45.24	4:45.96	4:46.69	4:47.41	4:48.14
400	4:48.86	4:49.58	4:50.31	4:51.03	4:51.76	4:52.48	4:53.20	4:53.93	4:54.65	4:55.38
410	4:56.10	4:56.82	4:57.55	4:58.27	4:58.99	4:59.72	5:00.44	5:01.17	5:01.89	5:02.61
420	5:03.34	5:04.06	5:04.79	5:05.51	5:06.23	5:06.96	5:07.68	5:08.41	5:09.13	5:09.85
430	5:10.58	5:11.30	5:12.03	5:12.75	5:13.47	5:14.20	5:14.92	5:15.65	5:16.37	5:17.09
440	5:17.82	5:18.54	5:19.27	5:19.99	5:20.71	5:21.44	5:22.16	5:22.89	5:23.61	5:24.33
450	5:25.06	5:25.78	5:26.51	5:27.23	5:27.95	5:28.68	5:29.40	5:30.12	5:30.85	5:31.57
460	5:32.30	5:33.02	5:33.74	5:34.47	5:35.19	5:35.92	5:36.64	5:37.36	5:38.09	5:38.81
470	5:39.54	5:40.26	5:40.98	5:41.71	5:42.43	5:43.16	5:43.88	5:44.60	5:45.33	5:46.05
480	5:46.78	5:47.50	5:48.22	5:48.95	5:49.67	5:50.40	5:51.12	5:51.84	5:52.57	5:53.29
490	5:54.02	5:54.74	5:55.46	5:56.19	5:56.91	5:57.64	5:58.36	5:59.08	5:59.81	6:00.53
500	6:01.26	6:01.98	6:02.70	6:03.43	6:04.15	6:04.88	6:05.60	6:06.32	6:07.05	6:07.77
510	6:08.49	6:09.22	6:09.94	6:10.67	6:11.39	6:12.11	6:12.84	6:13.56	6:14.29	6:15.01
520	6:15.73	6:16.46	6:17.18	6:17.91	6:18.63	6:19.35	6:20.08	6:20.80	6:21.53	6:22.25
530	6:22.97	6:23.70	6:24.42	6:25.15	6:25.87	6:26.59	6:27.32	6:28.04	6:28.77	6:29.49
540	6:30.21	6:30.94	6:31.66	6:32.39	6:33.11	6:33.83	6:34.56	6:35.28	6:36.01	6:36.73
550	6:37.45	6:38.18	6:38.90	6:39.62	6:40.35	6:41.07	6:41.80	6:42.52	6:43.24	6:43.97
560	6:44.69	6:45.42	6:46.14	6:46.86	6:47.59	6:48.31	6:49.04	6:49.76	6:50.48	6:51.21
570	6:51.93	6:52.66	6:53.38	6:54.10	6:54.83	6:55.55	6:56.28	6:57.00	6:57.72	6:58.45
580	6:59.17	6:59.90	7:00.62	7:01.34	7:02.07	7:02.79	7:03.52	7:04.24	7:04.96	7:05.69
590	7:06.41	7:07.14	7:07.86	7:08.58	7:09.31	7:10.03	7:10.76	7:11.48	7:12.20	7:12.93

♩. = 1.09; ♩ = 0.72; ♪. = 0.54; (triplet) ♩ 𝄾 = 0.48; ♪ = 0.36; (triplet) ♪ 𝄾 𝄾 = 0.24; 𝅘𝅥𝅯 = 0.18 seconds

CLICK: 17 4/8 FRAMES; M.M.: 82.29

Click	0	1	2	3	4	5	6	7	8	9
000	0:00.00	0:00.00	0:00.73	0:01.46	0:02.19	0:02.92	0:03.65	0:04.38	0:05.10	0:05.83
010	0:06.56	0:07.29	0:08.02	0:08.75	0:09.48	0:10.21	0:10.94	0:11.67	0:12.40	0:13.13
020	0:13.85	0:14.58	0:15.31	0:16.04	0:16.77	0:17.50	0:18.23	0:18.96	0:19.69	0:20.42
030	0:21.15	0:21.88	0:22.60	0:23.33	0:24.06	0:24.79	0:25.52	0:26.25	0:26.98	0:27.71
040	0:28.44	0:29.17	0:29.90	0:30.63	0:31.35	0:32.08	0:32.81	0:33.54	0:34.27	0:35.00
050	0:35.73	0:36.46	0:37.19	0:37.92	0:38.65	0:39.38	0:40.10	0:40.83	0:41.56	0:42.29
060	0:43.02	0:43.75	0:44.48	0:45.21	0:45.94	0:46.67	0:47.40	0:48.13	0:48.85	0:49.58
070	0:50.31	0:51.04	0:51.77	0:52.50	0:53.23	0:53.96	0:54.69	0:55.42	0:56.15	0:56.88
080	0:57.60	0:58.33	0:59.06	0:59.79	1:00.52	1:01.25	1:01.98	1:02.71	1:03.44	1:04.17
090	1:04.90	1:05.63	1:06.35	1:07.08	1:07.81	1:08.54	1:09.27	1:10.00	1:10.73	1:11.46
100	1:12.19	1:12.92	1:13.65	1:14.38	1:15.10	1:15.83	1:16.56	1:17.29	1:18.02	1:18.75
110	1:19.48	1:20.21	1:20.94	1:21.67	1:22.40	1:23.13	1:23.85	1:24.58	1:25.31	1:26.04
120	1:26.77	1:27.50	1:28.23	1:28.96	1:29.69	1:30.42	1:31.15	1:31.88	1:32.60	1:33.33
130	1:34.06	1:34.79	1:35.52	1:36.25	1:36.98	1:37.71	1:38.44	1:39.17	1:39.90	1:40.63
140	1:41.35	1:42.08	1:42.81	1:43.54	1:44.27	1:45.00	1:45.73	1:46.46	1:47.19	1:47.92
150	1:48.65	1:49.38	1:50.10	1:50.83	1:51.56	1:52.29	1:53.02	1:53.75	1:54.48	1:55.21
160	1:55.94	1:56.67	1:57.40	1:58.13	1:58.85	1:59.58	2:00.31	2:01.04	2:01.77	2:02.50
170	2:03.23	2:03.96	2:04.69	2:05.42	2:06.15	2:06.87	2:07.60	2:08.33	2:09.06	2:09.79
180	2:10.52	2:11.25	2:11.98	2:12.71	2:13.44	2:14.17	2:14.90	2:15.63	2:16.35	2:17.08
190	2:17.81	2:18.54	2:19.27	2:20.00	2:20.73	2:21.46	2:22.19	2:22.92	2:23.65	2:24.38
200	2:25.10	2:25.83	2:26.56	2:27.29	2:28.02	2:28.75	2:29.48	2:30.21	2:30.94	2:31.67
210	2:32.40	2:33.13	2:33.85	2:34.58	2:35.31	2:36.04	2:36.77	2:37.50	2:38.23	2:38.96
220	2:39.69	2:40.42	2:41.15	2:41.88	2:42.60	2:43.33	2:44.06	2:44.79	2:45.52	2:46.25
230	2:46.98	2:47.71	2:48.44	2:49.17	2:49.90	2:50.63	2:51.35	2:52.08	2:52.81	2:53.54
240	2:54.27	2:55.00	2:55.73	2:56.46	2:57.19	2:57.92	2:58.65	2:59.38	3:00.10	3:00.83
250	3:01.56	3:02.29	3:03.02	3:03.75	3:04.48	3:05.21	3:05.94	3:06.67	3:07.40	3:08.13
260	3:08.85	3:09.58	3:10.31	3:11.04	3:11.77	3:12.50	3:13.23	3:13.96	3:14.69	3:15.42
270	3:16.15	3:16.88	3:17.60	3:18.33	3:19.06	3:19.79	3:20.52	3:21.25	3:21.98	3:22.71
280	3:23.44	3:24.17	3:24.90	3:25.63	3:26.35	3:27.08	3:27.81	3:28.54	3:29.27	3:30.00
290	3:30.73	3:31.46	3:32.19	3:32.92	3:33.65	3:34.38	3:35.10	3:35.83	3:36.56	3:37.29
300	3:38.02	3:38.75	3:39.48	3:40.21	3:40.94	3:41.67	3:42.40	3:43.13	3:43.85	3:44.58
310	3:45.31	3:46.04	3:46.77	3:47.50	3:48.23	3:48.96	3:49.69	3:50.42	3:51.15	3:51.88
320	3:52.60	3:53.33	3:54.06	3:54.79	3:55.52	3:56.25	3:56.98	3:57.71	3:58.44	3:59.17
330	3:59.90	4:00.62	4:01.35	4:02.08	4:02.81	4:03.54	4:04.27	4:05.00	4:05.73	4:06.46
340	4:07.19	4:07.92	4:08.65	4:09.38	4:10.10	4:10.83	4:11.56	4:12.29	4:13.02	4:13.75
350	4:14.48	4:15.21	4:15.94	4:16.67	4:17.40	4:18.13	4:18.85	4:19.58	4:20.31	4:21.04
360	4:21.77	4:22.50	4:23.23	4:23.96	4:24.69	4:25.42	4:26.15	4:26.87	4:27.60	4:28.33
370	4:29.06	4:29.79	4:30.52	4:31.25	4:31.98	4:32.71	4:33.44	4:34.17	4:34.90	4:35.63
380	4:36.35	4:37.08	4:37.81	4:38.54	4:39.27	4:40.00	4:40.73	4:41.46	4:42.19	4:42.92
390	4:43.65	4:44.38	4:45.10	4:45.83	4:46.56	4:47.29	4:48.02	4:48.75	4:49.48	4:50.21
400	4:50.94	4:51.67	4:52.40	4:53.13	4:53.85	4:54.58	4:55.31	4:56.04	4:56.77	4:57.50
410	4:58.23	4:58.96	4:59.69	5:00.42	5:01.15	5:01.88	5:02.60	5:03.33	5:04.06	5:04.79
420	5:05.52	5:06.25	5:06.98	5:07.71	5:08.44	5:09.17	5:09.90	5:10.63	5:11.35	5:12.08
430	5:12.81	5:13.54	5:14.27	5:15.00	5:15.73	5:16.46	5:17.19	5:17.92	5:18.65	5:19.38
440	5:20.10	5:20.83	5:21.56	5:22.29	5:23.02	5:23.75	5:24.48	5:25.21	5:25.94	5:26.67
450	5:27.40	5:28.13	5:28.85	5:29.58	5:30.31	5:31.04	5:31.77	5:32.50	5:33.23	5:33.96
460	5:34.69	5:35.42	5:36.15	5:36.88	5:37.60	5:38.33	5:39.06	5:39.79	5:40.52	5:41.25
470	5:41.98	5:42.71	5:43.44	5:44.17	5:44.90	5:45.63	5:46.35	5:47.08	5:47.81	5:48.54
480	5:49.27	5:50.00	5:50.73	5:51.46	5:52.19	5:52.92	5:53.65	5:54.38	5:55.10	5:55.83
490	5:56.56	5:57.29	5:58.02	5:58.75	5:59.48	6:00.21	6:00.94	6:01.67	6:02.40	6:03.13
500	6:03.85	6:04.58	6:05.31	6:06.04	6:06.77	6:07.50	6:08.23	6:08.96	6:09.69	6:10.42
510	6:11.15	6:11.88	6:12.60	6:13.33	6:14.06	6:14.79	6:15.52	6:16.25	6:16.98	6:17.71
520	6:18.44	6:19.17	6:19.90	6:20.63	6:21.35	6:22.08	6:22.81	6:23.54	6:24.27	6:25.00
530	6:25.73	6:26.46	6:27.19	6:27.92	6:28.65	6:29.38	6:30.10	6:30.83	6:31.56	6:32.29
540	6:33.02	6:33.75	6:34.48	6:35.21	6:35.94	6:36.67	6:37.40	6:38.13	6:38.85	6:39.58
550	6:40.31	6:41.04	6:41.77	6:42.50	6:43.23	6:43.96	6:44.69	6:45.42	6:46.15	6:46.88
560	6:47.60	6:48.33	6:49.06	6:49.79	6:50.52	6:51.25	6:51.98	6:52.71	6:53.44	6:54.17
570	6:54.90	6:55.63	6:56.35	6:57.08	6:57.81	6:58.54	6:59.27	7:00.00	7:00.73	7:01.46
580	7:02.19	7:02.92	7:03.65	7:04.38	7:05.10	7:05.83	7:06.56	7:07.29	7:08.02	7:08.75
590	7:09.48	7:10.21	7:10.94	7:11.67	7:12.40	7:13.13	7:13.85	7:14.58	7:15.31	7:16.04

♩. = 1.09; ♩ = 0.73; ♪. = 0.55; (triplet) ♩ 𝄾 = 0.49; ♪ = 0.36; (triplet) ♪𝄾𝄾 = 0.24; 𝅘𝅥𝅯 = 0.18 seconds

CLICK: 17⅝ FRAMES; M.M.: 81.70

Click	0	1	2	3	4	5	6	7	8	9
000	0:00.00	0:00.00	0:00.73	0:01.47	0:02.20	0:02.94	0:03.67	0:04.41	0:05.14	0:05.88
010	0:06.61	0:07.34	0:08.08	0:08.81	0:09.55	0:10.28	0:11.02	0:11.75	0:12.48	0:13.22
020	0:13.95	0:14.69	0:15.42	0:16.16	0:16.89	0:17.63	0:18.36	0:19.09	0:19.83	0:20.56
030	0:21.30	0:22.03	0:22.77	0:23.50	0:24.23	0:24.97	0:25.70	0:26.44	0:27.17	0:27.91
040	0:28.64	0:29.38	0:30.11	0:30.84	0:31.58	0:32.31	0:33.05	0:33.78	0:34.52	0:35.25
050	0:35.98	0:36.72	0:37.45	0:38.19	0:38.92	0:39.66	0:40.39	0:41.13	0:41.86	0:42.59
060	0:43.33	0:44.06	0:44.80	0:45.53	0:46.27	0:47.00	0:47.73	0:48.47	0:49.20	0:49.94
070	0:50.67	0:51.41	0:52.14	0:52.88	0:53.61	0:54.34	0:55.08	0:55.81	0:56.55	0:57.28
080	0:58.02	0:58.75	0:59.48	1:00.22	1:00.95	1:01.69	1:02.42	1:03.16	1:03.89	1:04.63
090	1:05.36	1:06.09	1:06.83	1:07.56	1:08.30	1:09.03	1:09.77	1:10.50	1:11.23	1:11.97
100	1:12.70	1:13.44	1:14.17	1:14.91	1:15.64	1:16.38	1:17.11	1:17.84	1:18.58	1:19.31
110	1:20.05	1:20.78	1:21.52	1:22.25	1:22.98	1:23.72	1:24.45	1:25.19	1:25.92	1:26.66
120	1:27.39	1:28.13	1:28.86	1:29.59	1:30.33	1:31.06	1:31.80	1:32.53	1:33.27	1:34.00
130	1:34.73	1:35.47	1:36.20	1:36.94	1:37.67	1:38.41	1:39.14	1:39.88	1:40.61	1:41.34
140	1:42.08	1:42.81	1:43.55	1:44.28	1:45.02	1:45.75	1:46.48	1:47.22	1:47.95	1:48.69
150	1:49.42	1:50.16	1:50.89	1:51.63	1:52.36	1:53.09	1:53.83	1:54.56	1:55.30	1:56.03
160	1:56.77	1:57.50	1:58.23	1:58.97	1:59.70	2:00.44	2:01.17	2:01.91	2:02.64	2:03.38
170	2:04.11	2:04.84	2:05.58	2:06.31	2:07.05	2:07.78	2:08.52	2:09.25	2:09.98	2:10.72
180	2:11.45	2:12.19	2:12.92	2:13.66	2:14.39	2:15.12	2:15.86	2:16.59	2:17.33	2:18.06
190	2:18.80	2:19.53	2:20.27	2:21.00	2:21.73	2:22.47	2:23.20	2:23.94	2:24.67	2:25.41
200	2:26.14	2:26.88	2:27.61	2:28.34	2:29.08	2:29.81	2:30.55	2:31.28	2:32.02	2:32.75
210	2:33.48	2:34.22	2:34.95	2:35.69	2:36.42	2:37.16	2:37.89	2:38.63	2:39.36	2:40.09
220	2:40.83	2:41.56	2:42.30	2:43.03	2:43.77	2:44.50	2:45.23	2:45.97	2:46.70	2:47.44
230	2:48.17	2:48.91	2:49.64	2:50.38	2:51.11	2:51.84	2:52.58	2:53.31	2:54.05	2:54.78
240	2:55.52	2:56.25	2:56.98	2:57.72	2:58.45	2:59.19	2:59.92	3:00.66	3:01.39	3:02.13
250	3:02.86	3:03.59	3:04.33	3:05.06	3:05.80	3:06.53	3:07.27	3:08.00	3:08.73	3:09.47
260	3:10.20	3:10.94	3:11.67	3:12.41	3:13.14	3:13.88	3:14.61	3:15.34	3:16.08	3:16.81
270	3:17.55	3:18.28	3:19.02	3:19.75	3:20.48	3:21.22	3:21.95	3:22.69	3:23.42	3:24.16
280	3:24.89	3:25.63	3:26.36	3:27.09	3:27.83	3:28.56	3:29.30	3:30.03	3:30.77	3:31.50
290	3:32.23	3:32.97	3:33.70	3:34.44	3:35.17	3:35.91	3:36.64	3:37.38	3:38.11	3:38.84
300	3:39.58	3:40.31	3:41.05	3:41.78	3:42.52	3:43.25	3:43.98	3:44.72	3:45.45	3:46.19
310	3:46.92	3:47.66	3:48.39	3:49.13	3:49.86	3:50.59	3:51.33	3:52.06	3:52.80	3:53.53
320	3:54.27	3:55.00	3:55.73	3:56.47	3:57.20	3:57.94	3:58.67	3:59.41	4:00.14	4:00.88
330	4:01.61	4:02.34	4:03.08	4:03.81	4:04.55	4:05.28	4:06.02	4:06.75	4:07.48	4:08.22
340	4:08.95	4:09.69	4:10.42	4:11.16	4:11.89	4:12.63	4:13.36	4:14.09	4:14.83	4:15.56
350	4:16.30	4:17.03	4:17.77	4:18.50	4:19.23	4:19.97	4:20.70	4:21.44	4:22.17	4:22.91
360	4:23.64	4:24.38	4:25.11	4:25.84	4:26.58	4:27.31	4:28.05	4:28.78	4:29.52	4:30.25
370	4:30.98	4:31.72	4:32.45	4:33.19	4:33.92	4:34.66	4:35.39	4:36.13	4:36.86	4:37.59
380	4:38.33	4:39.06	4:39.80	4:40.53	4:41.27	4:42.00	4:42.73	4:43.47	4:44.20	4:44.94
390	4:45.67	4:46.41	4:47.14	4:47.88	4:48.61	4:49.34	4:50.08	4:50.81	4:51.55	4:52.28
400	4:53.02	4:53.75	4:54.48	4:55.22	4:55.95	4:56.69	4:57.42	4:58.16	4:58.89	4:59.63
410	5:00.36	5:01.09	5:01.83	5:02.56	5:03.30	5:04.03	5:04.77	5:05.50	5:06.23	5:06.97
420	5:07.70	5:08.44	5:09.17	5:09.91	5:10.64	5:11.37	5:12.11	5:12.84	5:13.58	5:14.31
430	5:15.05	5:15.78	5:16.52	5:17.25	5:17.98	5:18.72	5:19.45	5:20.19	5:20.92	5:21.66
440	5:22.39	5:23.13	5:23.86	5:24.59	5:25.33	5:26.06	5:26.80	5:27.53	5:28.27	5:29.00
450	5:29.73	5:30.47	5:31.20	5:31.94	5:32.67	5:33.41	5:34.14	5:34.88	5:35.61	5:36.34
460	5:37.08	5:37.81	5:38.55	5:39.28	5:40.02	5:40.75	5:41.48	5:42.22	5:42.95	5:43.69
470	5:44.42	5:45.16	5:45.89	5:46.63	5:47.36	5:48.09	5:48.83	5:49.56	5:50.30	5:51.03
480	5:51.77	5:52.50	5:53.23	5:53.97	5:54.70	5:55.44	5:56.17	5:56.91	5:57.64	5:58.38
490	5:59.11	5:59.84	6:00.58	6:01.31	6:02.05	6:02.78	6:03.52	6:04.25	6:04.98	6:05.72
500	6:06.45	6:07.19	6:07.92	6:08.66	6:09.39	6:10.13	6:10.86	6:11.59	6:12.33	6:13.06
510	6:13.80	6:14.53	6:15.27	6:16.00	6:16.73	6:17.47	6:18.20	6:18.94	6:19.67	6:20.41
520	6:21.14	6:21.88	6:22.61	6:23.34	6:24.08	6:24.81	6:25.55	6:26.28	6:27.02	6:27.75
530	6:28.48	6:29.22	6:29.95	6:30.69	6:31.42	6:32.16	6:32.89	6:33.63	6:34.36	6:35.09
540	6:35.83	6:36.56	6:37.30	6:38.03	6:38.77	6:39.50	6:40.23	6:40.97	6:41.70	6:42.44
550	6:43.17	6:43.91	6:44.64	6:45.38	6:46.11	6:46.84	6:47.58	6:48.31	6:49.05	6:49.78
560	6:50.52	6:51.25	6:51.98	6:52.72	6:53.45	6:54.19	6:54.92	6:55.66	6:56.39	6:57.13
570	6:57.86	6:58.59	6:59.33	7:00.06	7:00.80	7:01.53	7:02.27	7:03.00	7:03.73	7:04.47
580	7:05.20	7:05.94	7:06.67	7:07.41	7:08.14	7:08.88	7:09.61	7:10.34	7:11.08	7:11.81
590	7:12.55	7:13.28	7:14.02	7:14.75	7:15.48	7:16.22	7:16.95	7:17.69	7:18.42	7:19.16

♩. = 1.10; ♩ = 0.73; ♪. = 0.55; ♩ 𝄾 (triplet 3) = 0.49; ♪ = 0.37; ♪𝄾𝄾 (triplet 3) = 0.24; 𝅘𝅥𝅯 = 0.18 seconds

CLICK: 17 6/8 FRAMES; M.M.: 81.13

Click	0	1	2	3	4	5	6	7	8	9
000	0:00.00	0:00.00	0:00.74	0:01.48	0:02.22	0:02.96	0:03.70	0:04.44	0:05.18	0:05.92
010	0:06.66	0:07.40	0:08.14	0:08.88	0:09.61	0:10.35	0:11.09	0:11.83	0:12.57	0:13.31
020	0:14.05	0:14.79	0:15.53	0:16.27	0:17.01	0:17.75	0:18.49	0:19.23	0:19.97	0:20.71
030	0:21.45	0:22.19	0:22.93	0:23.67	0:24.41	0:25.15	0:25.89	0:26.63	0:27.36	0:28.10
040	0:28.84	0:29.58	0:30.32	0:31.06	0:31.80	0:32.54	0:33.28	0:34.02	0:34.76	0:35.50
050	0:36.24	0:36.98	0:37.72	0:38.46	0:39.20	0:39.94	0:40.68	0:41.42	0:42.16	0:42.90
060	0:43.64	0:44.38	0:45.11	0:45.85	0:46.59	0:47.33	0:48.07	0:48.81	0:49.55	0:50.29
070	0:51.03	0:51.77	0:52.51	0:53.25	0:53.99	0:54.73	0:55.47	0:56.21	0:56.95	0:57.69
080	0:58.43	0:59.17	0:59.91	1:00.65	1:01.39	1:02.12	1:02.86	1:03.60	1:04.34	1:05.08
090	1:05.82	1:06.56	1:07.30	1:08.04	1:08.78	1:09.52	1:10.26	1:11.00	1:11.74	1:12.48
100	1:13.22	1:13.96	1:14.70	1:15.44	1:16.18	1:16.92	1:17.66	1:18.40	1:19.14	1:19.87
110	1:20.61	1:21.35	1:22.09	1:22.83	1:23.57	1:24.31	1:25.05	1:25.79	1:26.53	1:27.27
120	1:28.01	1:28.75	1:29.49	1:30.23	1:30.97	1:31.71	1:32.45	1:33.19	1:33.93	1:34.67
130	1:35.41	1:36.15	1:36.89	1:37.63	1:38.36	1:39.10	1:39.84	1:40.58	1:41.32	1:42.06
140	1:42.80	1:43.54	1:44.28	1:45.02	1:45.76	1:46.50	1:47.24	1:47.98	1:48.72	1:49.46
150	1:50.20	1:50.94	1:51.68	1:52.42	1:53.16	1:53.90	1:54.64	1:55.38	1:56.11	1:56.85
160	1:57.59	1:58.33	1:59.07	1:59.81	2:00.55	2:01.29	2:02.03	2:02.77	2:03.51	2:04.25
170	2:04.99	2:05.73	2:06.47	2:07.21	2:07.95	2:08.69	2:09.43	2:10.17	2:10.91	2:11.65
180	2:12.39	2:13.13	2:13.86	2:14.60	2:15.34	2:16.08	2:16.82	2:17.56	2:18.30	2:19.04
190	2:19.78	2:20.52	2:21.26	2:22.00	2:22.74	2:23.48	2:24.22	2:24.96	2:25.70	2:26.44
200	2:27.18	2:27.92	2:28.66	2:29.40	2:30.14	2:30.88	2:31.61	2:32.35	2:33.09	2:33.83
210	2:34.57	2:35.31	2:36.05	2:36.79	2:37.53	2:38.27	2:39.01	2:39.75	2:40.49	2:41.23
220	2:41.97	2:42.71	2:43.45	2:44.19	2:44.93	2:45.67	2:46.41	2:47.15	2:47.89	2:48.63
230	2:49.36	2:50.10	2:50.84	2:51.58	2:52.32	2:53.06	2:53.80	2:54.54	2:55.28	2:56.02
240	2:56.76	2:57.50	2:58.24	2:58.98	2:59.72	3:00.46	3:01.20	3:01.94	3:02.68	3:03.42
250	3:04.16	3:04.90	3:05.64	3:06.38	3:07.11	3:07.85	3:08.59	3:09.33	3:10.07	3:10.81
260	3:11.55	3:12.29	3:13.03	3:13.77	3:14.51	3:15.25	3:15.99	3:16.73	3:17.47	3:18.21
270	3:18.95	3:19.69	3:20.43	3:21.17	3:21.91	3:22.65	3:23.39	3:24.12	3:24.86	3:25.60
280	3:26.34	3:27.08	3:27.82	3:28.56	3:29.30	3:30.04	3:30.78	3:31.52	3:32.26	3:33.00
290	3:33.74	3:34.48	3:35.22	3:35.96	3:36.70	3:37.44	3:38.18	3:38.92	3:39.66	3:40.40
300	3:41.14	3:41.87	3:42.61	3:43.35	3:44.09	3:44.83	3:45.57	3:46.31	3:47.05	3:47.79
310	3:48.53	3:49.27	3:50.01	3:50.75	3:51.49	3:52.23	3:52.97	3:53.71	3:54.45	3:55.19
320	3:55.93	3:56.67	3:57.41	3:58.15	3:58.89	3:59.62	4:00.36	4:01.10	4:01.84	4:02.58
330	4:03.32	4:04.06	4:04.80	4:05.54	4:06.28	4:07.02	4:07.76	4:08.50	4:09.24	4:09.98
340	4:10.72	4:11.46	4:12.20	4:12.94	4:13.68	4:14.42	4:15.16	4:15.90	4:16.64	4:17.37
350	4:18.11	4:18.85	4:19.59	4:20.33	4:21.07	4:21.81	4:22.55	4:23.29	4:24.03	4:24.77
360	4:25.51	4:26.25	4:26.99	4:27.73	4:28.47	4:29.21	4:29.95	4:30.69	4:31.43	4:32.17
370	4:32.91	4:33.65	4:34.39	4:35.13	4:35.86	4:36.60	4:37.34	4:38.08	4:38.82	4:39.56
380	4:40.30	4:41.04	4:41.78	4:42.52	4:43.26	4:44.00	4:44.74	4:45.48	4:46.22	4:46.96
390	4:47.70	4:48.44	4:49.18	4:49.92	4:50.66	4:51.40	4:52.14	4:52.87	4:53.61	4:54.35
400	4:55.09	4:55.83	4:56.57	4:57.31	4:58.05	4:58.79	4:59.53	5:00.27	5:01.01	5:01.75
410	5:02.49	5:03.23	5:03.97	5:04.71	5:05.45	5:06.19	5:06.93	5:07.67	5:08.41	5:09.15
420	5:09.89	5:10.62	5:11.36	5:12.10	5:12.84	5:13.58	5:14.32	5:15.06	5:15.80	5:16.54
430	5:17.28	5:18.02	5:18.76	5:19.50	5:20.24	5:20.98	5:21.72	5:22.46	5:23.20	5:23.94
440	5:24.68	5:25.42	5:26.16	5:26.90	5:27.64	5:28.37	5:29.11	5:29.85	5:30.59	5:31.33
450	5:32.07	5:32.81	5:33.55	5:34.29	5:35.03	5:35.77	5:36.51	5:37.25	5:37.99	5:38.73
460	5:39.47	5:40.21	5:40.95	5:41.69	5:42.43	5:43.17	5:43.91	5:44.65	5:45.39	5:46.12
470	5:46.86	5:47.60	5:48.34	5:49.08	5:49.82	5:50.56	5:51.30	5:52.04	5:52.78	5:53.52
480	5:54.26	5:55.00	5:55.74	5:56.48	5:57.22	5:57.96	5:58.70	5:59.44	6:00.18	6:00.92
490	6:01.66	6:02.40	6:03.14	6:03.87	6:04.61	6:05.35	6:06.09	6:06.83	6:07.57	6:08.31
500	6:09.05	6:09.79	6:10.53	6:11.27	6:12.01	6:12.75	6:13.49	6:14.23	6:14.97	6:15.71
510	6:16.45	6:17.19	6:17.93	6:18.67	6:19.41	6:20.15	6:20.89	6:21.62	6:22.36	6:23.10
520	6:23.84	6:24.58	6:25.32	6:26.06	6:26.80	6:27.54	6:28.28	6:29.02	6:29.76	6:30.50
530	6:31.24	6:31.98	6:32.72	6:33.46	6:34.20	6:34.94	6:35.68	6:36.42	6:37.16	6:37.90
540	6:38.64	6:39.38	6:40.11	6:40.85	6:41.59	6:42.33	6:43.07	6:43.81	6:44.55	6:45.29
550	6:46.03	6:46.77	6:47.51	6:48.25	6:48.99	6:49.73	6:50.47	6:51.21	6:51.95	6:52.69
560	6:53.43	6:54.17	6:54.91	6:55.65	6:56.39	6:57.12	6:57.86	6:58.60	6:59.34	7:00.08
570	7:00.82	7:01.56	7:02.30	7:03.04	7:03.78	7:04.52	7:05.26	7:06.00	7:06.74	7:07.48
580	7:08.22	7:08.96	7:09.70	7:10.44	7:11.18	7:11.92	7:12.66	7:13.40	7:14.14	7:14.88
590	7:15.61	7:16.35	7:17.09	7:17.83	7:18.57	7:19.31	7:20.05	7:20.79	7:21.53	7:22.27

♩. = 1.11; ♩ = 0.74; ♪. = 0.55; (triplet) ♩ 𝄾 = 0.49; ♪ = 0.37; (triplet) ♪ 𝄾 𝄾 = 0.25; 𝅘𝅥𝅯 = 0.18 seconds

CLICK: 17⅞ FRAMES; M.M.: 80.56

Click	0	1	2	3	4	5	6	7	8	9
000	0:00.00	0:00.00	0:00.74	0:01.49	0:02.23	0:02.98	0:03.72	0:04.47	0:05.21	0:05.96
010	0:06.70	0:07.45	0:08.19	0:08.94	0:09.68	0:10.43	0:11.17	0:11.92	0:12.66	0:13.41
020	0:14.15	0:14.90	0:15.64	0:16.39	0:17.13	0:17.88	0:18.62	0:19.36	0:20.11	0:20.85
030	0:21.60	0:22.34	0:23.09	0:23.83	0:24.58	0:25.32	0:26.07	0:26.81	0:27.56	0:28.30
040	0:29.05	0:29.79	0:30.54	0:31.28	0:32.03	0:32.77	0:33.52	0:34.26	0:35.01	0:35.75
050	0:36.49	0:37.24	0:37.98	0:38.73	0:39.47	0:40.22	0:40.96	0:41.71	0:42.45	0:43.20
060	0:43.94	0:44.69	0:45.43	0:46.18	0:46.92	0:47.67	0:48.41	0:49.16	0:49.90	0:50.65
070	0:51.39	0:52.14	0:52.88	0:53.63	0:54.37	0:55.11	0:55.86	0:56.60	0:57.35	0:58.09
080	0:58.84	0:59.58	1:00.33	1:01.07	1:01.82	1:02.56	1:03.31	1:04.05	1:04.80	1:05.54
090	1:06.29	1:07.03	1:07.78	1:08.52	1:09.27	1:10.01	1:10.76	1:11.50	1:12.24	1:12.99
100	1:13.73	1:14.48	1:15.22	1:15.97	1:16.71	1:17.46	1:18.20	1:18.95	1:19.69	1:20.44
110	1:21.18	1:21.93	1:22.67	1:23.42	1:24.16	1:24.91	1:25.65	1:26.40	1:27.14	1:27.89
120	1:28.63	1:29.38	1:30.12	1:30.86	1:31.61	1:32.35	1:33.10	1:33.84	1:34.59	1:35.33
130	1:36.08	1:36.82	1:37.57	1:38.31	1:39.06	1:39.80	1:40.55	1:41.29	1:42.04	1:42.78
140	1:43.53	1:44.27	1:45.02	1:45.76	1:46.51	1:47.25	1:47.99	1:48.74	1:49.48	1:50.23
150	1:50.97	1:51.72	1:52.46	1:53.21	1:53.95	1:54.70	1:55.44	1:56.19	1:56.93	1:57.68
160	1:58.42	1:59.17	1:59.91	2:00.66	2:01.40	2:02.15	2:02.89	2:03.64	2:04.38	2:05.12
170	2:05.87	2:06.61	2:07.36	2:08.10	2:08.85	2:09.59	2:10.34	2:11.08	2:11.83	2:12.57
180	2:13.32	2:14.06	2:14.81	2:15.55	2:16.30	2:17.04	2:17.79	2:18.53	2:19.28	2:20.02
190	2:20.77	2:21.51	2:22.26	2:23.00	2:23.74	2:24.49	2:25.23	2:25.98	2:26.72	2:27.47
200	2:28.21	2:28.96	2:29.70	2:30.45	2:31.19	2:31.94	2:32.68	2:33.43	2:34.17	2:34.92
210	2:35.66	2:36.41	2:37.15	2:37.90	2:38.64	2:39.39	2:40.13	2:40.88	2:41.62	2:42.36
220	2:43.11	2:43.85	2:44.60	2:45.34	2:46.09	2:46.83	2:47.58	2:48.32	2:49.07	2:49.81
230	2:50.56	2:51.30	2:52.05	2:52.79	2:53.54	2:54.28	2:55.03	2:55.77	2:56.52	2:57.26
240	2:58.01	2:58.75	2:59.49	3:00.24	3:00.98	3:01.73	3:02.47	3:03.22	3:03.96	3:04.71
250	3:05.45	3:06.20	3:06.94	3:07.69	3:08.43	3:09.18	3:09.92	3:10.67	3:11.41	3:12.16
260	3:12.90	3:13.65	3:14.39	3:15.14	3:15.88	3:16.63	3:17.37	3:18.11	3:18.86	3:19.60
270	3:20.35	3:21.09	3:21.84	3:22.58	3:23.33	3:24.07	3:24.82	3:25.56	3:26.31	3:27.05
280	3:27.80	3:28.54	3:29.29	3:30.03	3:30.78	3:31.52	3:32.27	3:33.01	3:33.76	3:34.50
290	3:35.24	3:35.99	3:36.73	3:37.48	3:38.22	3:38.97	3:39.71	3:40.46	3:41.20	3:41.95
300	3:42.69	3:43.44	3:44.18	3:44.93	3:45.67	3:46.42	3:47.16	3:47.91	3:48.65	3:49.40
310	3:50.14	3:50.89	3:51.63	3:52.38	3:53.12	3:53.86	3:54.61	3:55.35	3:56.10	3:56.84
320	3:57.59	3:58.33	3:59.08	3:59.82	4:00.57	4:01.31	4:02.06	4:02.80	4:03.55	4:04.29
330	4:05.04	4:05.78	4:06.53	4:07.27	4:08.02	4:08.76	4:09.51	4:10.25	4:10.99	4:11.74
340	4:12.48	4:13.23	4:13.97	4:14.72	4:15.46	4:16.21	4:16.95	4:17.70	4:18.44	4:19.19
350	4:19.93	4:20.68	4:21.42	4:22.17	4:22.91	4:23.66	4:24.40	4:25.15	4:25.89	4:26.64
360	4:27.38	4:28.13	4:28.87	4:29.61	4:30.36	4:31.10	4:31.85	4:32.59	4:33.34	4:34.08
370	4:34.83	4:35.57	4:36.32	4:37.06	4:37.81	4:38.55	4:39.30	4:40.04	4:40.79	4:41.53
380	4:42.28	4:43.02	4:43.77	4:44.51	4:45.26	4:46.00	4:46.74	4:47.49	4:48.23	4:48.98
390	4:49.72	4:50.47	4:51.21	4:51.96	4:52.70	4:53.45	4:54.19	4:54.94	4:55.68	4:56.43
400	4:57.17	4:57.92	4:58.66	4:59.41	5:00.15	5:00.90	5:01.64	5:02.39	5:03.13	5:03.87
410	5:04.62	5:05.36	5:06.11	5:06.85	5:07.60	5:08.34	5:09.09	5:09.83	5:10.58	5:11.32
420	5:12.07	5:12.81	5:13.56	5:14.30	5:15.05	5:15.79	5:16.54	5:17.28	5:18.03	5:18.77
430	5:19.52	5:20.26	5:21.01	5:21.75	5:22.49	5:23.24	5:23.98	5:24.73	5:25.47	5:26.22
440	5:26.96	5:27.71	5:28.45	5:29.20	5:29.94	5:30.69	5:31.43	5:32.18	5:32.92	5:33.67
450	5:34.41	5:35.16	5:35.90	5:36.65	5:37.39	5:38.14	5:38.88	5:39.62	5:40.37	5:41.11
460	5:41.86	5:42.60	5:43.35	5:44.09	5:44.84	5:45.58	5:46.33	5:47.07	5:47.82	5:48.56
470	5:49.31	5:50.05	5:50.80	5:51.54	5:52.29	5:53.03	5:53.78	5:54.52	5:55.27	5:56.01
480	5:56.76	5:57.50	5:58.24	5:58.99	5:59.73	6:00.48	6:01.22	6:01.97	6:02.71	6:03.46
490	6:04.20	6:04.95	6:05.69	6:06.44	6:07.18	6:07.93	6:08.67	6:09.42	6:10.16	6:10.91
500	6:11.65	6:12.40	6:13.14	6:13.89	6:14.63	6:15.37	6:16.12	6:16.86	6:17.61	6:18.35
510	6:19.10	6:19.84	6:20.59	6:21.33	6:22.08	6:22.82	6:23.57	6:24.31	6:25.06	6:25.80
520	6:26.55	6:27.29	6:28.04	6:28.78	6:29.53	6:30.27	6:31.02	6:31.76	6:32.51	6:33.25
530	6:33.99	6:34.74	6:35.48	6:36.23	6:36.97	6:37.72	6:38.46	6:39.21	6:39.95	6:40.70
540	6:41.44	6:42.19	6:42.93	6:43.68	6:44.42	6:45.17	6:45.91	6:46.66	6:47.40	6:48.15
550	6:48.89	6:49.64	6:50.38	6:51.12	6:51.87	6:52.61	6:53.36	6:54.10	6:54.85	6:55.59
560	6:56.34	6:57.08	6:57.83	6:58.57	6:59.32	7:00.06	7:00.81	7:01.55	7:02.30	7:03.04
570	7:03.79	7:04.53	7:05.28	7:06.02	7:06.77	7:07.51	7:08.26	7:09.00	7:09.74	7:10.49
580	7:11.23	7:11.98	7:12.72	7:13.47	7:14.21	7:14.96	7:15.70	7:16.45	7:17.19	7:17.94
590	7:18.68	7:19.43	7:20.17	7:20.92	7:21.66	7:22.41	7:23.15	7:23.90	7:24.64	7:25.39

♩. = 1.12; ♩ = 0.74; ♪. = 0.56; (triplet ♩ 𝄾) = 0.50; ♪ = 0.37; (triplet ♪ 𝄾 𝄾) = 0.25; 𝅘𝅥𝅯 = 0.19 seconds

CLICK: 18 0/8 FRAMES; M.M.: 80.00

Click	0	1	2	3	4	5	6	7	8	9
000	0:00.00	0:00.00	0:00.75	0:01.50	0:02.25	0:03.00	0:03.75	0:04.50	0:05.25	0:06.00
010	0:06.75	0:07.50	0:08.25	0:09.00	0:09.75	0:10.50	0:11.25	0:12.00	0:12.75	0:13.50
020	0:14.25	0:15.00	0:15.75	0:16.50	0:17.25	0:18.00	0:18.75	0:19.50	0:20.25	0:21.00
030	0:21.75	0:22.50	0:23.25	0:24.00	0:24.75	0:25.50	0:26.25	0:27.00	0:27.75	0:28.50
040	0:29.25	0:30.00	0:30.75	0:31.50	0:32.25	0:33.00	0:33.75	0:34.50	0:35.25	0:36.00
050	0:36.75	0:37.50	0:38.25	0:39.00	0:39.75	0:40.50	0:41.25	0:42.00	0:42.75	0:43.50
060	0:44.25	0:45.00	0:45.75	0:46.50	0:47.25	0:48.00	0:48.75	0:49.50	0:50.25	0:51.00
070	0:51.75	0:52.50	0:53.25	0:54.00	0:54.75	0:55.50	0:56.25	0:57.00	0:57.75	0:58.50
080	0:59.25	1:00.00	1:00.75	1:01.50	1:02.25	1:03.00	1:03.75	1:04.50	1:05.25	1:06.00
090	1:06.75	1:07.50	1:08.25	1:09.00	1:09.75	1:10.50	1:11.25	1:12.00	1:12.75	1:13.50
100	1:14.25	1:15.00	1:15.75	1:16.50	1:17.25	1:18.00	1:18.75	1:19.50	1:20.25	1:21.00
110	1:21.75	1:22.50	1:23.25	1:24.00	1:24.75	1:25.50	1:26.25	1:27.00	1:27.75	1:28.50
120	1:29.25	1:30.00	1:30.75	1:31.50	1:32.25	1:33.00	1:33.75	1:34.50	1:35.25	1:36.00
130	1:36.75	1:37.50	1:38.25	1:39.00	1:39.75	1:40.50	1:41.25	1:42.00	1:42.75	1:43.50
140	1:44.25	1:45.00	1:45.75	1:46.50	1:47.25	1:48.00	1:48.75	1:49.50	1:50.25	1:51.00
150	1:51.75	1:52.50	1:53.25	1:54.00	1:54.75	1:55.50	1:56.25	1:57.00	1:57.75	1:58.50
160	1:59.25	2:00.00	2:00.75	2:01.50	2:02.25	2:03.00	2:03.75	2:04.50	2:05.25	2:06.00
170	2:06.75	2:07.50	2:08.25	2:09.00	2:09.75	2:10.50	2:11.25	2:12.00	2:12.75	2:13.50
180	2:14.25	2:15.00	2:15.75	2:16.50	2:17.25	2:18.00	2:18.75	2:19.50	2:20.25	2:21.00
190	2:21.75	2:22.50	2:23.25	2:24.00	2:24.75	2:25.50	2:26.25	2:27.00	2:27.75	2:28.50
200	2:29.25	2:30.00	2:30.75	2:31.50	2:32.25	2:33.00	2:33.75	2:34.50	2:35.25	2:36.00
210	2:36.75	2:37.50	2:38.25	2:39.00	2:39.75	2:40.50	2:41.25	2:42.00	2:42.75	2:43.50
220	2:44.25	2:45.00	2:45.75	2:46.50	2:47.25	2:48.00	2:48.75	2:49.50	2:50.25	2:51.00
230	2:51.75	2:52.50	2:53.25	2:54.00	2:54.75	2:55.50	2:56.25	2:57.00	2:57.75	2:58.50
240	2:59.25	3:00.00	3:00.75	3:01.50	3:02.25	3:03.00	3:03.75	3:04.50	3:05.25	3:06.00
250	3:06.75	3:07.50	3:08.25	3:09.00	3:09.75	3:10.50	3:11.25	3:12.00	3:12.75	3:13.50
260	3:14.25	3:15.00	3:15.75	3:16.50	3:17.25	3:18.00	3:18.75	3:19.50	3:20.25	3:21.00
270	3:21.75	3:22.50	3:23.25	3:24.00	3:24.75	3:25.50	3:26.25	3:27.00	3:27.75	3:28.50
280	3:29.25	3:30.00	3:30.75	3:31.50	3:32.25	3:33.00	3:33.75	3:34.50	3:35.25	3:36.00
290	3:36.75	3:37.50	3:38.25	3:39.00	3:39.75	3:40.50	3:41.25	3:42.00	3:42.75	3:43.50
300	3:44.25	3:45.00	3:45.75	3:46.50	3:47.25	3:48.00	3:48.75	3:49.50	3:50.25	3:51.00
310	3:51.75	3:52.50	3:53.25	3:54.00	3:54.75	3:55.50	3:56.25	3:57.00	3:57.75	3:58.50
320	3:59.25	4:00.00	4:00.75	4:01.50	4:02.25	4:03.00	4:03.75	4:04.50	4:05.25	4:06.00
330	4:06.75	4:07.50	4:08.25	4:09.00	4:09.75	4:10.50	4:11.25	4:12.00	4:12.75	4:13.50
340	4:14.25	4:15.00	4:15.75	4:16.50	4:17.25	4:18.00	4:18.75	4:19.50	4:20.25	4:21.00
350	4:21.75	4:22.50	4:23.25	4:24.00	4:24.75	4:25.50	4:26.25	4:27.00	4:27.75	4:28.50
360	4:29.25	4:30.00	4:30.75	4:31.50	4:32.25	4:33.00	4:33.75	4:34.50	4:35.25	4:36.00
370	4:36.75	4:37.50	4:38.25	4:39.00	4:39.75	4:40.50	4:41.25	4:42.00	4:42.75	4:43.50
380	4:44.25	4:45.00	4:45.75	4:46.50	4:47.25	4:48.00	4:48.75	4:49.50	4:50.25	4:51.00
390	4:51.75	4:52.50	4:53.25	4:54.00	4:54.75	4:55.50	4:56.25	4:57.00	4:57.75	4:58.50
400	4:59.25	5:00.00	5:00.75	5:01.50	5:02.25	5:03.00	5:03.75	5:04.50	5:05.25	5:06.00
410	5:06.75	5:07.50	5:08.25	5:09.00	5:09.75	5:10.50	5:11.25	5:12.00	5:12.75	5:13.50
420	5:14.25	5:15.00	5:15.75	5:16.50	5:17.25	5:18.00	5:18.75	5:19.50	5:20.25	5:21.00
430	5:21.75	5:22.50	5:23.25	5:24.00	5:24.75	5:25.50	5:26.25	5:27.00	5:27.75	5:28.50
440	5:29.25	5:30.00	5:30.75	5:31.50	5:32.25	5:33.00	5:33.75	5:34.50	5:35.25	5:36.00
450	5:36.75	5:37.50	5:38.25	5:39.00	5:39.75	5:40.50	5:41.25	5:42.00	5:42.75	5:43.50
460	5:44.25	5:45.00	5:45.75	5:46.50	5:47.25	5:48.00	5:48.75	5:49.50	5:50.25	5:51.00
470	5:51.75	5:52.50	5:53.25	5:54.00	5:54.75	5:55.50	5:56.25	5:57.00	5:57.75	5:58.50
480	5:59.25	6:00.00	6:00.75	6:01.50	6:02.25	6:03.00	6:03.75	6:04.50	6:05.25	6:06.00
490	6:06.75	6:07.50	6:08.25	6:09.00	6:09.75	6:10.50	6:11.25	6:12.00	6:12.75	6:13.50
500	6:14.25	6:15.00	6:15.75	6:16.50	6:17.25	6:18.00	6:18.75	6:19.50	6:20.25	6:21.00
510	6:21.75	6:22.50	6:23.25	6:24.00	6:24.75	6:25.50	6:26.25	6:27.00	6:27.75	6:28.50
520	6:29.25	6:30.00	6:30.75	6:31.50	6:32.25	6:33.00	6:33.75	6:34.50	6:35.25	6:36.00
530	6:36.75	6:37.50	6:38.25	6:39.00	6:39.75	6:40.50	6:41.25	6:42.00	6:42.75	6:43.50
540	6:44.25	6:45.00	6:45.75	6:46.50	6:47.25	6:48.00	6:48.75	6:49.50	6:50.25	6:51.00
550	6:51.75	6:52.50	6:53.25	6:54.00	6:54.75	6:55.50	6:56.25	6:57.00	6:57.75	6:58.50
560	6:59.25	7:00.00	7:00.75	7:01.50	7:02.25	7:03.00	7:03.75	7:04.50	7:05.25	7:06.00
570	7:06.75	7:07.50	7:08.25	7:09.00	7:09.75	7:10.50	7:11.25	7:12.00	7:12.75	7:13.50
580	7:14.25	7:15.00	7:15.75	7:16.50	7:17.25	7:18.00	7:18.75	7:19.50	7:20.25	7:21.00
590	7:21.75	7:22.50	7:23.25	7:24.00	7:24.75	7:25.50	7:26.25	7:27.00	7:27.75	7:28.50

♩. = 1.13; ♩ = 0.75; ♪. = 0.56; (triplet ♩ 𝄾) = 0.50; ♪ = 0.38; (triplet ♪ 𝄾 𝄾) = 0.25; 𝅘𝅥𝅯 = 0.19 seconds

CLICK: 18⅛ FRAMES; M.M.: 79.45

Click	0	1	2	3	4	5	6	7	8	9
000	0:00.00	0:00.00	0:00.76	0:01.51	0:02.27	0:03.02	0:03.78	0:04.53	0:05.29	0:06.04
010	0:06.80	0:07.55	0:08.31	0:09.06	0:09.82	0:10.57	0:11.33	0:12.08	0:12.84	0:13.59
020	0:14.35	0:15.10	0:15.86	0:16.61	0:17.37	0:18.13	0:18.88	0:19.64	0:20.39	0:21.15
030	0:21.90	0:22.66	0:23.41	0:24.17	0:24.92	0:25.68	0:26.43	0:27.19	0:27.94	0:28.70
040	0:29.45	0:30.21	0:30.96	0:31.72	0:32.47	0:33.23	0:33.98	0:34.74	0:35.49	0:36.25
050	0:37.01	0:37.76	0:38.52	0:39.27	0:40.03	0:40.78	0:41.54	0:42.29	0:43.05	0:43.80
060	0:44.56	0:45.31	0:46.07	0:46.82	0:47.58	0:48.33	0:49.09	0:49.84	0:50.60	0:51.35
070	0:52.11	0:52.86	0:53.62	0:54.38	0:55.13	0:55.89	0:56.64	0:57.40	0:58.15	0:58.91
080	0:59.66	1:00.42	1:01.17	1:01.93	1:02.68	1:03.44	1:04.19	1:04.95	1:05.70	1:06.46
090	1:07.21	1:07.97	1:08.72	1:09.48	1:10.23	1:10.99	1:11.74	1:12.50	1:13.26	1:14.01
100	1:14.77	1:15.52	1:16.28	1:17.03	1:17.79	1:18.54	1:19.30	1:20.05	1:20.81	1:21.56
110	1:22.32	1:23.07	1:23.83	1:24.58	1:25.34	1:26.09	1:26.85	1:27.60	1:28.36	1:29.11
120	1:29.87	1:30.63	1:31.38	1:32.14	1:32.89	1:33.65	1:34.40	1:35.16	1:35.91	1:36.67
130	1:37.42	1:38.18	1:38.93	1:39.69	1:40.44	1:41.20	1:41.95	1:42.71	1:43.46	1:44.22
140	1:44.97	1:45.73	1:46.48	1:47.24	1:47.99	1:48.75	1:49.51	1:50.26	1:51.02	1:51.77
150	1:52.53	1:53.28	1:54.04	1:54.79	1:55.55	1:56.30	1:57.06	1:57.81	1:58.57	1:59.32
160	2:00.08	2:00.83	2:01.59	2:02.34	2:03.10	2:03.85	2:04.61	2:05.36	2:06.12	2:06.88
170	2:07.63	2:08.39	2:09.14	2:09.90	2:10.65	2:11.41	2:12.16	2:12.92	2:13.67	2:14.43
180	2:15.18	2:15.94	2:16.69	2:17.45	2:18.20	2:18.96	2:19.71	2:20.47	2:21.22	2:21.98
190	2:22.73	2:23.49	2:24.24	2:25.00	2:25.76	2:26.51	2:27.27	2:28.02	2:28.78	2:29.53
200	2:30.29	2:31.04	2:31.80	2:32.55	2:33.31	2:34.06	2:34.82	2:35.57	2:36.33	2:37.08
210	2:37.84	2:38.59	2:39.35	2:40.10	2:40.86	2:41.61	2:42.37	2:43.13	2:43.88	2:44.64
220	2:45.39	2:46.15	2:46.90	2:47.66	2:48.41	2:49.17	2:49.92	2:50.68	2:51.43	2:52.19
230	2:52.94	2:53.70	2:54.45	2:55.21	2:55.96	2:56.72	2:57.47	2:58.23	2:58.98	2:59.74
240	3:00.49	3:01.25	3:02.01	3:02.76	3:03.52	3:04.27	3:05.03	3:05.78	3:06.54	3:07.29
250	3:08.05	3:08.80	3:09.56	3:10.31	3:11.07	3:11.82	3:12.58	3:13.33	3:14.09	3:14.84
260	3:15.60	3:16.35	3:17.11	3:17.86	3:18.62	3:19.38	3:20.13	3:20.89	3:21.64	3:22.40
270	3:23.15	3:23.91	3:24.66	3:25.42	3:26.17	3:26.93	3:27.68	3:28.44	3:29.19	3:29.95
280	3:30.70	3:31.46	3:32.21	3:32.97	3:33.72	3:34.48	3:35.23	3:35.99	3:36.74	3:37.50
290	3:38.26	3:39.01	3:39.77	3:40.52	3:41.28	3:42.03	3:42.79	3:43.54	3:44.30	3:45.05
300	3:45.81	3:46.56	3:47.32	3:48.07	3:48.83	3:49.58	3:50.34	3:51.09	3:51.85	3:52.60
310	3:53.36	3:54.11	3:54.87	3:55.63	3:56.38	3:57.14	3:57.89	3:58.65	3:59.40	4:00.16
320	4:00.91	4:01.67	4:02.42	4:03.18	4:03.93	4:04.69	4:05.44	4:06.20	4:06.95	4:07.71
330	4:08.46	4:09.22	4:09.97	4:10.73	4:11.48	4:12.24	4:12.99	4:13.75	4:14.51	4:15.26
340	4:16.02	4:16.77	4:17.53	4:18.28	4:19.04	4:19.79	4:20.55	4:21.30	4:22.06	4:22.81
350	4:23.57	4:24.32	4:25.08	4:25.83	4:26.59	4:27.34	4:28.10	4:28.85	4:29.61	4:30.36
360	4:31.12	4:31.88	4:32.63	4:33.39	4:34.14	4:34.90	4:35.65	4:36.41	4:37.16	4:37.92
370	4:38.67	4:39.43	4:40.18	4:40.94	4:41.69	4:42.45	4:43.20	4:43.96	4:44.71	4:45.47
380	4:46.22	4:46.98	4:47.73	4:48.49	4:49.24	4:50.00	4:50.76	4:51.51	4:52.27	4:53.02
390	4:53.78	4:54.53	4:55.29	4:56.04	4:56.80	4:57.55	4:58.31	4:59.06	4:59.82	5:00.57
400	5:01.33	5:02.08	5:02.84	5:03.59	5:04.35	5:05.10	5:05.86	5:06.61	5:07.37	5:08.13
410	5:08.88	5:09.64	5:10.39	5:11.15	5:11.90	5:12.66	5:13.41	5:14.17	5:14.92	5:15.68
420	5:16.43	5:17.19	5:17.94	5:18.70	5:19.45	5:20.21	5:20.96	5:21.72	5:22.47	5:23.23
430	5:23.98	5:24.74	5:25.49	5:26.25	5:27.01	5:27.76	5:28.52	5:29.27	5:30.03	5:30.78
440	5:31.54	5:32.29	5:33.05	5:33.80	5:34.56	5:35.31	5:36.07	5:36.82	5:37.58	5:38.33
450	5:39.09	5:39.84	5:40.60	5:41.35	5:42.11	5:42.86	5:43.62	5:44.38	5:45.13	5:45.89
460	5:46.64	5:47.40	5:48.15	5:48.91	5:49.66	5:50.42	5:51.17	5:51.93	5:52.68	5:53.44
470	5:54.19	5:54.95	5:55.70	5:56.46	5:57.21	5:57.97	5:58.72	5:59.48	6:00.23	6:00.99
480	6:01.74	6:02.50	6:03.26	6:04.01	6:04.77	6:05.52	6:06.28	6:07.03	6:07.79	6:08.54
490	6:09.30	6:10.05	6:10.81	6:11.56	6:12.32	6:13.07	6:13.83	6:14.58	6:15.34	6:16.09
500	6:16.85	6:17.60	6:18.36	6:19.11	6:19.87	6:20.63	6:21.38	6:22.14	6:22.89	6:23.65
510	6:24.40	6:25.16	6:25.91	6:26.67	6:27.42	6:28.18	6:28.93	6:29.69	6:30.44	6:31.20
520	6:31.95	6:32.71	6:33.46	6:34.22	6:34.97	6:35.73	6:36.48	6:37.24	6:37.99	6:38.75
530	6:39.51	6:40.26	6:41.02	6:41.77	6:42.53	6:43.28	6:44.04	6:44.79	6:45.55	6:46.30
540	6:47.06	6:47.81	6:48.57	6:49.32	6:50.08	6:50.83	6:51.59	6:52.34	6:53.10	6:53.85
550	6:54.61	6:55.36	6:56.12	6:56.88	6:57.63	6:58.39	6:59.14	6:59.90	7:00.65	7:01.41
560	7:02.16	7:02.92	7:03.67	7:04.43	7:05.18	7:05.94	7:06.69	7:07.45	7:08.20	7:08.96
570	7:09.71	7:10.47	7:11.22	7:11.98	7:12.73	7:13.49	7:14.24	7:15.00	7:15.76	7:16.51
580	7:17.27	7:18.02	7:18.78	7:19.53	7:20.29	7:21.04	7:21.80	7:22.55	7:23.31	7:24.06
590	7:24.82	7:25.57	7:26.33	7:27.08	7:27.84	7:28.59	7:29.35	7:30.10	7:30.86	7:31.61

♩. = 1.13; ♩ = 0.76; ♪. = 0.57; (triplet ♩ 𝄾) = 0.50; ♪ = 0.38; (triplet ♪ 𝄾 𝄾) = 0.25; 𝅘𝅥𝅯 = 0.19 seconds

CLICK: 18 2/8 FRAMES; M.M.: 78.90

Click	0	1	2	3	4	5	6	7	8	9
000	0:00.00	0:00.00	0:00.76	0:01.52	0:02.28	0:03.04	0:03.80	0:04.56	0:05.32	0:06.08
010	0:06.84	0:07.60	0:08.36	0:09.13	0:09.89	0:10.65	0:11.41	0:12.17	0:12.93	0:13.69
020	0:14.45	0:15.21	0:15.97	0:16.73	0:17.49	0:18.25	0:19.01	0:19.77	0:20.53	0:21.29
030	0:22.05	0:22.81	0:23.57	0:24.33	0:25.09	0:25.85	0:26.61	0:27.38	0:28.14	0:28.90
040	0:29.66	0:30.42	0:31.18	0:31.94	0:32.70	0:33.46	0:34.22	0:34.98	0:35.74	0:36.50
050	0:37.26	0:38.02	0:38.78	0:39.54	0:40.30	0:41.06	0:41.82	0:42.58	0:43.34	0:44.10
060	0:44.86	0:45.63	0:46.39	0:47.15	0:47.91	0:48.67	0:49.43	0:50.19	0:50.95	0:51.71
070	0:52.47	0:53.23	0:53.99	0:54.75	0:55.51	0:56.27	0:57.03	0:57.79	0:58.55	0:59.31
080	1:00.07	1:00.83	1:01.59	1:02.35	1:03.11	1:03.88	1:04.64	1:05.40	1:06.16	1:06.92
090	1:07.68	1:08.44	1:09.20	1:09.96	1:10.72	1:11.48	1:12.24	1:13.00	1:13.76	1:14.52
100	1:15.28	1:16.04	1:16.80	1:17.56	1:18.32	1:19.08	1:19.84	1:20.60	1:21.36	1:22.13
110	1:22.89	1:23.65	1:24.41	1:25.17	1:25.93	1:26.69	1:27.45	1:28.21	1:28.97	1:29.73
120	1:30.49	1:31.25	1:32.01	1:32.77	1:33.53	1:34.29	1:35.05	1:35.81	1:36.57	1:37.33
130	1:38.09	1:38.85	1:39.61	1:40.38	1:41.14	1:41.90	1:42.66	1:43.42	1:44.18	1:44.94
140	1:45.70	1:46.46	1:47.22	1:47.98	1:48.74	1:49.50	1:50.26	1:51.02	1:51.78	1:52.54
150	1:53.30	1:54.06	1:54.82	1:55.58	1:56.34	1:57.10	1:57.86	1:58.63	1:59.39	2:00.15
160	2:00.91	2:01.67	2:02.43	2:03.19	2:03.95	2:04.71	2:05.47	2:06.23	2:06.99	2:07.75
170	2:08.51	2:09.27	2:10.03	2:10.79	2:11.55	2:12.31	2:13.07	2:13.83	2:14.59	2:15.35
180	2:16.11	2:16.88	2:17.64	2:18.40	2:19.16	2:19.92	2:20.68	2:21.44	2:22.20	2:22.96
190	2:23.72	2:24.48	2:25.24	2:26.00	2:26.76	2:27.52	2:28.28	2:29.04	2:29.80	2:30.56
200	2:31.32	2:32.08	2:32.84	2:33.60	2:34.36	2:35.13	2:35.89	2:36.65	2:37.41	2:38.17
210	2:38.93	2:39.69	2:40.45	2:41.21	2:41.97	2:42.73	2:43.49	2:44.25	2:45.01	2:45.77
220	2:46.53	2:47.29	2:48.05	2:48.81	2:49.57	2:50.33	2:51.09	2:51.85	2:52.61	2:53.38
230	2:54.14	2:54.90	2:55.66	2:56.42	2:57.18	2:57.94	2:58.70	2:59.46	3:00.22	3:00.98
240	3:01.74	3:02.50	3:03.26	3:04.02	3:04.78	3:05.54	3:06.30	3:07.06	3:07.82	3:08.58
250	3:09.34	3:10.10	3:10.86	3:11.63	3:12.39	3:13.15	3:13.91	3:14.67	3:15.43	3:16.19
260	3:16.95	3:17.71	3:18.47	3:19.23	3:19.99	3:20.75	3:21.51	3:22.27	3:23.03	3:23.79
270	3:24.55	3:25.31	3:26.07	3:26.83	3:27.59	3:28.35	3:29.11	3:29.88	3:30.64	3:31.40
280	3:32.16	3:32.92	3:33.68	3:34.44	3:35.20	3:35.96	3:36.72	3:37.48	3:38.24	3:39.00
290	3:39.76	3:40.52	3:41.28	3:42.04	3:42.80	3:43.56	3:44.32	3:45.08	3:45.84	3:46.60
300	3:47.36	3:48.13	3:48.89	3:49.65	3:50.41	3:51.17	3:51.93	3:52.69	3:53.45	3:54.21
310	3:54.97	3:55.73	3:56.49	3:57.25	3:58.01	3:58.77	3:59.53	4:00.29	4:01.05	4:01.81
320	4:02.57	4:03.33	4:04.09	4:04.85	4:05.61	4:06.38	4:07.14	4:07.90	4:08.66	4:09.42
330	4:10.18	4:10.94	4:11.70	4:12.46	4:13.22	4:13.98	4:14.74	4:15.50	4:16.26	4:17.02
340	4:17.78	4:18.54	4:19.30	4:20.06	4:20.82	4:21.58	4:22.34	4:23.10	4:23.86	4:24.63
350	4:25.39	4:26.15	4:26.91	4:27.67	4:28.43	4:29.19	4:29.95	4:30.71	4:31.47	4:32.23
360	4:32.99	4:33.75	4:34.51	4:35.27	4:36.03	4:36.79	4:37.55	4:38.31	4:39.07	4:39.83
370	4:40.59	4:41.35	4:42.11	4:42.88	4:43.64	4:44.40	4:45.16	4:45.92	4:46.68	4:47.44
380	4:48.20	4:48.96	4:49.72	4:50.48	4:51.24	4:52.00	4:52.76	4:53.52	4:54.28	4:55.04
390	4:55.80	4:56.56	4:57.32	4:58.08	4:58.84	4:59.60	5:00.36	5:01.13	5:01.89	5:02.65
400	5:03.41	5:04.17	5:04.93	5:05.69	5:06.45	5:07.21	5:07.97	5:08.73	5:09.49	5:10.25
410	5:11.01	5:11.77	5:12.53	5:13.29	5:14.05	5:14.81	5:15.57	5:16.33	5:17.09	5:17.85
420	5:18.61	5:19.38	5:20.14	5:20.90	5:21.66	5:22.42	5:23.18	5:23.94	5:24.70	5:25.46
430	5:26.22	5:26.98	5:27.74	5:28.50	5:29.26	5:30.02	5:30.78	5:31.54	5:32.30	5:33.06
440	5:33.82	5:34.58	5:35.34	5:36.10	5:36.86	5:37.63	5:38.39	5:39.15	5:39.91	5:40.67
450	5:41.43	5:42.19	5:42.95	5:43.71	5:44.47	5:45.23	5:45.99	5:46.75	5:47.51	5:48.27
460	5:49.03	5:49.79	5:50.55	5:51.31	5:52.07	5:52.83	5:53.59	5:54.35	5:55.11	5:55.88
470	5:56.64	5:57.40	5:58.16	5:58.92	5:59.68	6:00.44	6:01.20	6:01.96	6:02.72	6:03.48
480	6:04.24	6:05.00	6:05.76	6:06.52	6:07.28	6:08.04	6:08.80	6:09.56	6:10.32	6:11.08
490	6:11.84	6:12.60	6:13.36	6:14.13	6:14.89	6:15.65	6:16.41	6:17.17	6:17.93	6:18.69
500	6:19.45	6:20.21	6:20.97	6:21.73	6:22.49	6:23.25	6:24.01	6:24.77	6:25.53	6:26.29
510	6:27.05	6:27.81	6:28.57	6:29.33	6:30.09	6:30.85	6:31.61	6:32.38	6:33.14	6:33.90
520	6:34.66	6:35.42	6:36.18	6:36.94	6:37.70	6:38.46	6:39.22	6:39.98	6:40.74	6:41.50
530	6:42.26	6:43.02	6:43.78	6:44.54	6:45.30	6:46.06	6:46.82	6:47.58	6:48.34	6:49.10
540	6:49.86	6:50.63	6:51.39	6:52.15	6:52.91	6:53.67	6:54.43	6:55.19	6:55.95	6:56.71
550	6:57.47	6:58.23	6:58.99	6:59.75	7:00.51	7:01.27	7:02.03	7:02.79	7:03.55	7:04.31
560	7:05.07	7:05.83	7:06.59	7:07.35	7:08.11	7:08.88	7:09.64	7:10.40	7:11.16	7:11.92
570	7:12.68	7:13.44	7:14.20	7:14.96	7:15.72	7:16.48	7:17.24	7:18.00	7:18.76	7:19.52
580	7:20.28	7:21.04	7:21.80	7:22.56	7:23.32	7:24.08	7:24.84	7:25.60	7:26.36	7:27.13
590	7:27.89	7:28.65	7:29.41	7:30.17	7:30.93	7:31.69	7:32.45	7:33.21	7:33.97	7:34.73

𝅗𝅥. = 1.14; ♩ = 0.76; ♪. = 0.57; (triplet) ♩ 𝄾 = 0.51; ♪ = 0.38; (triplet) ♪𝄾𝄾 = 0.25; 𝅘𝅥𝅯 = 0.19 seconds

CLICK: 18⅜ FRAMES; M.M.: 78.37

Click	0	1	2	3	4	5	6	7	8	9
000	0:00.00	0:00.00	0:00.77	0:01.53	0:02.30	0:03.06	0:03.83	0:04.59	0:05.36	0:06.13
010	0:06.89	0:07.66	0:08.42	0:09.19	0:09.95	0:10.72	0:11.48	0:12.25	0:13.02	0:13.78
020	0:14.55	0:15.31	0:16.08	0:16.84	0:17.61	0:18.38	0:19.14	0:19.91	0:20.67	0:21.44
030	0:22.20	0:22.97	0:23.73	0:24.50	0:25.27	0:26.03	0:26.80	0:27.56	0:28.33	0:29.09
040	0:29.86	0:30.63	0:31.39	0:32.16	0:32.92	0:33.69	0:34.45	0:35.22	0:35.98	0:36.75
050	0:37.52	0:38.28	0:39.05	0:39.81	0:40.58	0:41.34	0:42.11	0:42.88	0:43.64	0:44.41
060	0:45.17	0:45.94	0:46.70	0:47.47	0:48.23	0:49.00	0:49.77	0:50.53	0:51.30	0:52.06
070	0:52.83	0:53.59	0:54.36	0:55.13	0:55.89	0:56.66	0:57.42	0:58.19	0:58.95	0:59.72
080	1:00.48	1:01.25	1:02.02	1:02.78	1:03.55	1:04.31	1:05.08	1:05.84	1:06.61	1:07.38
090	1:08.14	1:08.91	1:09.67	1:10.44	1:11.20	1:11.97	1:12.73	1:13.50	1:14.27	1:15.03
100	1:15.80	1:16.56	1:17.33	1:18.09	1:18.86	1:19.63	1:20.39	1:21.16	1:21.92	1:22.69
110	1:23.45	1:24.22	1:24.98	1:25.75	1:26.52	1:27.28	1:28.05	1:28.81	1:29.58	1:30.34
120	1:31.11	1:31.88	1:32.64	1:33.41	1:34.17	1:34.94	1:35.70	1:36.47	1:37.23	1:38.00
130	1:38.77	1:39.53	1:40.30	1:41.06	1:41.83	1:42.59	1:43.36	1:44.13	1:44.89	1:45.66
140	1:46.42	1:47.19	1:47.95	1:48.72	1:49.48	1:50.25	1:51.02	1:51.78	1:52.55	1:53.31
150	1:54.08	1:54.84	1:55.61	1:56.38	1:57.14	1:57.91	1:58.67	1:59.44	2:00.20	2:00.97
160	2:01.73	2:02.50	2:03.27	2:04.03	2:04.80	2:05.56	2:06.33	2:07.09	2:07.86	2:08.62
170	2:09.39	2:10.16	2:10.92	2:11.69	2:12.45	2:13.22	2:13.98	2:14.75	2:15.52	2:16.28
180	2:17.05	2:17.81	2:18.58	2:19.34	2:20.11	2:20.87	2:21.64	2:22.41	2:23.17	2:23.94
190	2:24.70	2:25.47	2:26.23	2:27.00	2:27.77	2:28.53	2:29.30	2:30.06	2:30.83	2:31.59
200	2:32.36	2:33.12	2:33.89	2:34.66	2:35.42	2:36.19	2:36.95	2:37.72	2:38.48	2:39.25
210	2:40.02	2:40.78	2:41.55	2:42.31	2:43.08	2:43.84	2:44.61	2:45.37	2:46.14	2:46.91
220	2:47.67	2:48.44	2:49.20	2:49.97	2:50.73	2:51.50	2:52.27	2:53.03	2:53.80	2:54.56
230	2:55.33	2:56.09	2:56.86	2:57.62	2:58.39	2:59.16	2:59.92	3:00.69	3:01.45	3:02.22
240	3:02.98	3:03.75	3:04.52	3:05.28	3:06.05	3:06.81	3:07.58	3:08.34	3:09.11	3:09.87
250	3:10.64	3:11.41	3:12.17	3:12.94	3:13.70	3:14.47	3:15.23	3:16.00	3:16.77	3:17.53
260	3:18.30	3:19.06	3:19.83	3:20.59	3:21.36	3:22.13	3:22.89	3:23.66	3:24.42	3:25.19
270	3:25.95	3:26.72	3:27.48	3:28.25	3:29.02	3:29.78	3:30.55	3:31.31	3:32.08	3:32.84
280	3:33.61	3:34.38	3:35.14	3:35.91	3:36.67	3:37.44	3:38.20	3:38.97	3:39.73	3:40.50
290	3:41.27	3:42.03	3:42.80	3:43.56	3:44.33	3:45.09	3:45.86	3:46.63	3:47.39	3:48.16
300	3:48.92	3:49.69	3:50.45	3:51.22	3:51.98	3:52.75	3:53.52	3:54.28	3:55.05	3:55.81
310	3:56.58	3:57.34	3:58.11	3:58.88	3:59.64	4:00.41	4:01.17	4:01.94	4:02.70	4:03.47
320	4:04.23	4:05.00	4:05.77	4:06.53	4:07.30	4:08.06	4:08.83	4:09.59	4:10.36	4:11.13
330	4:11.89	4:12.66	4:13.42	4:14.19	4:14.95	4:15.72	4:16.48	4:17.25	4:18.02	4:18.78
340	4:19.55	4:20.31	4:21.08	4:21.84	4:22.61	4:23.37	4:24.14	4:24.91	4:25.67	4:26.44
350	4:27.20	4:27.97	4:28.73	4:29.50	4:30.27	4:31.03	4:31.80	4:32.56	4:33.33	4:34.09
360	4:34.86	4:35.63	4:36.39	4:37.16	4:37.92	4:38.69	4:39.45	4:40.22	4:40.98	4:41.75
370	4:42.52	4:43.28	4:44.05	4:44.81	4:45.58	4:46.34	4:47.11	4:47.87	4:48.64	4:49.41
380	4:50.17	4:50.94	4:51.70	4:52.47	4:53.23	4:54.00	4:54.77	4:55.53	4:56.30	4:57.06
390	4:57.83	4:58.59	4:59.36	5:00.12	5:00.89	5:01.66	5:02.42	5:03.19	5:03.95	5:04.72
400	5:05.48	5:06.25	5:07.02	5:07.78	5:08.55	5:09.31	5:10.08	5:10.84	5:11.61	5:12.38
410	5:13.14	5:13.91	5:14.67	5:15.44	5:16.20	5:16.97	5:17.73	5:18.50	5:19.27	5:20.03
420	5:20.80	5:21.56	5:22.33	5:23.09	5:23.86	5:24.62	5:25.39	5:26.16	5:26.92	5:27.69
430	5:28.45	5:29.22	5:29.98	5:30.75	5:31.52	5:32.28	5:33.05	5:33.81	5:34.58	5:35.34
440	5:36.11	5:36.88	5:37.64	5:38.41	5:39.17	5:39.94	5:40.70	5:41.47	5:42.23	5:43.00
450	5:43.77	5:44.53	5:45.30	5:46.06	5:46.83	5:47.59	5:48.36	5:49.12	5:49.89	5:50.66
460	5:51.42	5:52.19	5:52.95	5:53.72	5:54.48	5:55.25	5:56.02	5:56.78	5:57.55	5:58.31
470	5:59.08	5:59.84	6:00.61	6:01.38	6:02.14	6:02.91	6:03.67	6:04.44	6:05.20	6:05.97
480	6:06.73	6:07.50	6:08.27	6:09.03	6:09.80	6:10.56	6:11.33	6:12.09	6:12.86	6:13.62
490	6:14.39	6:15.16	6:15.92	6:16.69	6:17.45	6:18.22	6:18.98	6:19.75	6:20.52	6:21.28
500	6:22.05	6:22.81	6:23.58	6:24.34	6:25.11	6:25.88	6:26.64	6:27.41	6:28.17	6:28.94
510	6:29.70	6:30.47	6:31.23	6:32.00	6:32.77	6:33.53	6:34.30	6:35.06	6:35.83	6:36.59
520	6:37.36	6:38.12	6:38.89	6:39.66	6:40.42	6:41.19	6:41.95	6:42.72	6:43.48	6:44.25
530	6:45.02	6:45.78	6:46.55	6:47.31	6:48.08	6:48.84	6:49.61	6:50.38	6:51.14	6:51.91
540	6:52.67	6:53.44	6:54.20	6:54.97	6:55.73	6:56.50	6:57.27	6:58.03	6:58.80	6:59.56
550	7:00.33	7:01.09	7:01.86	7:02.62	7:03.39	7:04.16	7:04.92	7:05.69	7:06.45	7:07.22
560	7:07.98	7:08.75	7:09.52	7:10.28	7:11.05	7:11.81	7:12.58	7:13.34	7:14.11	7:14.88
570	7:15.64	7:16.41	7:17.17	7:17.94	7:18.70	7:19.47	7:20.23	7:21.00	7:21.77	7:22.53
580	7:23.30	7:24.06	7:24.83	7:25.59	7:26.36	7:27.12	7:27.89	7:28.66	7:29.42	7:30.19
590	7:30.95	7:31.72	7:32.48	7:33.25	7:34.02	7:34.78	7:35.55	7:36.31	7:37.08	7:37.84

𝅗𝅥. = 1.15; ♩ = 0.77; ♪. = 0.57; (triplet ♩ 𝄾) = 0.51; ♪ = 0.38; (triplet ♪ 𝄾 𝄾) = 0.26; 𝅘𝅥𝅯 = 0.19 seconds

CLICK: 18 4/8 FRAMES; M.M.: 77.84

Click	0	1	2	3	4	5	6	7	8	9
000	0:00.00	0:00.00	0:00.77	0:01.54	0:02.31	0:03.08	0:03.85	0:04.63	0:05.40	0:06.17
010	0:06.94	0:07.71	0:08.48	0:09.25	0:10.02	0:10.79	0:11.56	0:12.33	0:13.10	0:13.88
020	0:14.65	0:15.42	0:16.19	0:16.96	0:17.73	0:18.50	0:19.27	0:20.04	0:20.81	0:21.58
030	0:22.35	0:23.13	0:23.90	0:24.67	0:25.44	0:26.21	0:26.98	0:27.75	0:28.52	0:29.29
040	0:30.06	0:30.83	0:31.60	0:32.38	0:33.15	0:33.92	0:34.69	0:35.46	0:36.23	0:37.00
050	0:37.77	0:38.54	0:39.31	0:40.08	0:40.85	0:41.63	0:42.40	0:43.17	0:43.94	0:44.71
060	0:45.48	0:46.25	0:47.02	0:47.79	0:48.56	0:49.33	0:50.10	0:50.88	0:51.65	0:52.42
070	0:53.19	0:53.96	0:54.73	0:55.50	0:56.27	0:57.04	0:57.81	0:58.58	0:59.35	1:00.12
080	1:00.90	1:01.67	1:02.44	1:03.21	1:03.98	1:04.75	1:05.52	1:06.29	1:07.06	1:07.83
090	1:08.60	1:09.38	1:10.15	1:10.92	1:11.69	1:12.46	1:13.23	1:14.00	1:14.77	1:15.54
100	1:16.31	1:17.08	1:17.85	1:18.63	1:19.40	1:20.17	1:20.94	1:21.71	1:22.48	1:23.25
110	1:24.02	1:24.79	1:25.56	1:26.33	1:27.10	1:27.88	1:28.65	1:29.42	1:30.19	1:30.96
120	1:31.73	1:32.50	1:33.27	1:34.04	1:34.81	1:35.58	1:36.35	1:37.13	1:37.90	1:38.67
130	1:39.44	1:40.21	1:40.98	1:41.75	1:42.52	1:43.29	1:44.06	1:44.83	1:45.60	1:46.38
140	1:47.15	1:47.92	1:48.69	1:49.46	1:50.23	1:51.00	1:51.77	1:52.54	1:53.31	1:54.08
150	1:54.85	1:55.63	1:56.40	1:57.17	1:57.94	1:58.71	1:59.48	2:00.25	2:01.02	2:01.79
160	2:02.56	2:03.33	2:04.10	2:04.87	2:05.65	2:06.42	2:07.19	2:07.96	2:08.73	2:09.50
170	2:10.27	2:11.04	2:11.81	2:12.58	2:13.35	2:14.12	2:14.90	2:15.67	2:16.44	2:17.21
180	2:17.98	2:18.75	2:19.52	2:20.29	2:21.06	2:21.83	2:22.60	2:23.38	2:24.15	2:24.92
190	2:25.69	2:26.46	2:27.23	2:28.00	2:28.77	2:29.54	2:30.31	2:31.08	2:31.85	2:32.63
200	2:33.40	2:34.17	2:34.94	2:35.71	2:36.48	2:37.25	2:38.02	2:38.79	2:39.56	2:40.33
210	2:41.10	2:41.88	2:42.65	2:43.42	2:44.19	2:44.96	2:45.73	2:46.50	2:47.27	2:48.04
220	2:48.81	2:49.58	2:50.35	2:51.13	2:51.90	2:52.67	2:53.44	2:54.21	2:54.98	2:55.75
230	2:56.52	2:57.29	2:58.06	2:58.83	2:59.60	3:00.38	3:01.15	3:01.92	3:02.69	3:03.46
240	3:04.23	3:05.00	3:05.77	3:06.54	3:07.31	3:08.08	3:08.85	3:09.62	3:10.40	3:11.17
250	3:11.94	3:12.71	3:13.48	3:14.25	3:15.02	3:15.79	3:16.56	3:17.33	3:18.10	3:18.87
260	3:19.65	3:20.42	3:21.19	3:21.96	3:22.73	3:23.50	3:24.27	3:25.04	3:25.81	3:26.58
270	3:27.35	3:28.13	3:28.90	3:29.67	3:30.44	3:31.21	3:31.98	3:32.75	3:33.52	3:34.29
280	3:35.06	3:35.83	3:36.60	3:37.38	3:38.15	3:38.92	3:39.69	3:40.46	3:41.23	3:42.00
290	3:42.77	3:43.54	3:44.31	3:45.08	3:45.85	3:46.63	3:47.40	3:48.17	3:48.94	3:49.71
300	3:50.48	3:51.25	3:52.02	3:52.79	3:53.56	3:54.33	3:55.10	3:55.88	3:56.65	3:57.42
310	3:58.19	3:58.96	3:59.73	4:00.50	4:01.27	4:02.04	4:02.81	4:03.58	4:04.35	4:05.13
320	4:05.90	4:06.67	4:07.44	4:08.21	4:08.98	4:09.75	4:10.52	4:11.29	4:12.06	4:12.83
330	4:13.60	4:14.38	4:15.15	4:15.92	4:16.69	4:17.46	4:18.23	4:19.00	4:19.77	4:20.54
340	4:21.31	4:22.08	4:22.85	4:23.63	4:24.40	4:25.17	4:25.94	4:26.71	4:27.48	4:28.25
350	4:29.02	4:29.79	4:30.56	4:31.33	4:32.10	4:32.88	4:33.65	4:34.42	4:35.19	4:35.96
360	4:36.73	4:37.50	4:38.27	4:39.04	4:39.81	4:40.58	4:41.35	4:42.13	4:42.90	4:43.67
370	4:44.44	4:45.21	4:45.98	4:46.75	4:47.52	4:48.29	4:49.06	4:49.83	4:50.60	4:51.38
380	4:52.15	4:52.92	4:53.69	4:54.46	4:55.23	4:56.00	4:56.77	4:57.54	4:58.31	4:59.08
390	4:59.85	5:00.62	5:01.40	5:02.17	5:02.94	5:03.71	5:04.48	5:05.25	5:06.02	5:06.79
400	5:07.56	5:08.33	5:09.10	5:09.87	5:10.65	5:11.42	5:12.19	5:12.96	5:13.73	5:14.50
410	5:15.27	5:16.04	5:16.81	5:17.58	5:18.35	5:19.12	5:19.90	5:20.67	5:21.44	5:22.21
420	5:22.98	5:23.75	5:24.52	5:25.29	5:26.06	5:26.83	5:27.60	5:28.37	5:29.15	5:29.92
430	5:30.69	5:31.46	5:32.23	5:33.00	5:33.77	5:34.54	5:35.31	5:36.08	5:36.85	5:37.63
440	5:38.40	5:39.17	5:39.94	5:40.71	5:41.48	5:42.25	5:43.02	5:43.79	5:44.56	5:45.33
450	5:46.10	5:46.88	5:47.65	5:48.42	5:49.19	5:49.96	5:50.73	5:51.50	5:52.27	5:53.04
460	5:53.81	5:54.58	5:55.35	5:56.13	5:56.90	5:57.67	5:58.44	5:59.21	5:59.98	6:00.75
470	6:01.52	6:02.29	6:03.06	6:03.83	6:04.60	6:05.38	6:06.15	6:06.92	6:07.69	6:08.46
480	6:09.23	6:10.00	6:10.77	6:11.54	6:12.31	6:13.08	6:13.85	6:14.63	6:15.40	6:16.17
490	6:16.94	6:17.71	6:18.48	6:19.25	6:20.02	6:20.79	6:21.56	6:22.33	6:23.10	6:23.88
500	6:24.65	6:25.42	6:26.19	6:26.96	6:27.73	6:28.50	6:29.27	6:30.04	6:30.81	6:31.58
510	6:32.35	6:33.13	6:33.90	6:34.67	6:35.44	6:36.21	6:36.98	6:37.75	6:38.52	6:39.29
520	6:40.06	6:40.83	6:41.60	6:42.38	6:43.15	6:43.92	6:44.69	6:45.46	6:46.23	6:47.00
530	6:47.77	6:48.54	6:49.31	6:50.08	6:50.85	6:51.63	6:52.40	6:53.17	6:53.94	6:54.71
540	6:55.48	6:56.25	6:57.02	6:57.79	6:58.56	6:59.33	7:00.10	7:00.88	7:01.65	7:02.42
550	7:03.19	7:03.96	7:04.73	7:05.50	7:06.27	7:07.04	7:07.81	7:08.58	7:09.35	7:10.13
560	7:10.90	7:11.67	7:12.44	7:13.21	7:13.98	7:14.75	7:15.52	7:16.29	7:17.06	7:17.83
570	7:18.60	7:19.38	7:20.15	7:20.92	7:21.69	7:22.46	7:23.23	7:24.00	7:24.77	7:25.54
580	7:26.31	7:27.08	7:27.85	7:28.62	7:29.40	7:30.17	7:30.94	7:31.71	7:32.48	7:33.25
590	7:34.02	7:34.79	7:35.56	7:36.33	7:37.10	7:37.87	7:38.65	7:39.42	7:40.19	7:40.96

♩. = 1.16; ♩ = 0.77; ♪. = 0.58; (triplet ♩ 𝄾) = 0.51; ♪ = 0.39; (triplet ♪ 𝄾 𝄾) = 0.26; 𝅘𝅥𝅯 = 0.19 seconds

CLICK: 18⅝ FRAMES; M.M.: 77.32

Click	0	1	2	3	4	5	6	7	8	9
000	0:00.00	0:00.00	0:00.78	0:01.55	0:02.33	0:03.10	0:03.88	0:04.66	0:05.43	0:06.21
010	0:06.98	0:07.76	0:08.54	0:09.31	0:10.09	0:10.86	0:11.64	0:12.42	0:13.19	0:13.97
020	0:14.74	0:15.52	0:16.30	0:17.07	0:17.85	0:18.63	0:19.40	0:20.18	0:20.95	0:21.73
030	0:22.51	0:23.28	0:24.06	0:24.83	0:25.61	0:26.39	0:27.16	0:27.94	0:28.71	0:29.49
040	0:30.27	0:31.04	0:31.82	0:32.59	0:33.37	0:34.15	0:34.92	0:35.70	0:36.47	0:37.25
050	0:38.03	0:38.80	0:39.58	0:40.35	0:41.13	0:41.91	0:42.68	0:43.46	0:44.23	0:45.01
060	0:45.79	0:46.56	0:47.34	0:48.11	0:48.89	0:49.67	0:50.44	0:51.22	0:51.99	0:52.77
070	0:53.55	0:54.32	0:55.10	0:55.88	0:56.65	0:57.43	0:58.20	0:58.98	0:59.76	1:00.53
080	1:01.31	1:02.08	1:02.86	1:03.64	1:04.41	1:05.19	1:05.96	1:06.74	1:07.52	1:08.29
090	1:09.07	1:09.84	1:10.62	1:11.40	1:12.17	1:12.95	1:13.72	1:14.50	1:15.28	1:16.05
100	1:16.83	1:17.60	1:18.38	1:19.16	1:19.93	1:20.71	1:21.48	1:22.26	1:23.04	1:23.81
110	1:24.59	1:25.36	1:26.14	1:26.92	1:27.69	1:28.47	1:29.24	1:30.02	1:30.80	1:31.57
120	1:32.35	1:33.12	1:33.90	1:34.68	1:35.45	1:36.23	1:37.01	1:37.78	1:38.56	1:39.33
130	1:40.11	1:40.89	1:41.66	1:42.44	1:43.21	1:43.99	1:44.77	1:45.54	1:46.32	1:47.09
140	1:47.87	1:48.65	1:49.42	1:50.20	1:50.97	1:51.75	1:52.53	1:53.30	1:54.08	1:54.85
150	1:55.63	1:56.41	1:57.18	1:57.96	1:58.73	1:59.51	2:00.29	2:01.06	2:01.84	2:02.61
160	2:03.39	2:04.17	2:04.94	2:05.72	2:06.49	2:07.27	2:08.05	2:08.82	2:09.60	2:10.37
170	2:11.15	2:11.93	2:12.70	2:13.48	2:14.26	2:15.03	2:15.81	2:16.58	2:17.36	2:18.14
180	2:18.91	2:19.69	2:20.46	2:21.24	2:22.02	2:22.79	2:23.57	2:24.34	2:25.12	2:25.90
190	2:26.67	2:27.45	2:28.22	2:29.00	2:29.78	2:30.55	2:31.33	2:32.10	2:32.88	2:33.66
200	2:34.43	2:35.21	2:35.98	2:36.76	2:37.54	2:38.31	2:39.09	2:39.86	2:40.64	2:41.42
210	2:42.19	2:42.97	2:43.74	2:44.52	2:45.30	2:46.07	2:46.85	2:47.62	2:48.40	2:49.18
220	2:49.95	2:50.73	2:51.51	2:52.28	2:53.06	2:53.83	2:54.61	2:55.39	2:56.16	2:56.94
230	2:57.71	2:58.49	2:59.27	3:00.04	3:00.82	3:01.59	3:02.37	3:03.15	3:03.92	3:04.70
240	3:05.47	3:06.25	3:07.03	3:07.80	3:08.58	3:09.35	3:10.13	3:10.91	3:11.68	3:12.46
250	3:13.23	3:14.01	3:14.79	3:15.56	3:16.34	3:17.11	3:17.89	3:18.67	3:19.44	3:20.22
260	3:20.99	3:21.77	3:22.55	3:23.32	3:24.10	3:24.87	3:25.65	3:26.43	3:27.20	3:27.98
270	3:28.76	3:29.53	3:30.31	3:31.08	3:31.86	3:32.64	3:33.41	3:34.19	3:34.96	3:35.74
280	3:36.52	3:37.29	3:38.07	3:38.84	3:39.62	3:40.40	3:41.17	3:41.95	3:42.72	3:43.50
290	3:44.28	3:45.05	3:45.83	3:46.60	3:47.38	3:48.16	3:48.93	3:49.71	3:50.48	3:51.26
300	3:52.04	3:52.81	3:53.59	3:54.36	3:55.14	3:55.92	3:56.69	3:57.47	3:58.24	3:59.02
310	3:59.80	4:00.57	4:01.35	4:02.12	4:02.90	4:03.68	4:04.45	4:05.23	4:06.01	4:06.78
320	4:07.56	4:08.33	4:09.11	4:09.89	4:10.66	4:11.44	4:12.21	4:12.99	4:13.77	4:14.54
330	4:15.32	4:16.09	4:16.87	4:17.65	4:18.42	4:19.20	4:19.97	4:20.75	4:21.53	4:22.30
340	4:23.08	4:23.85	4:24.63	4:25.41	4:26.18	4:26.96	4:27.73	4:28.51	4:29.29	4:30.06
350	4:30.84	4:31.61	4:32.39	4:33.17	4:33.94	4:34.72	4:35.49	4:36.27	4:37.05	4:37.82
360	4:38.60	4:39.38	4:40.15	4:40.93	4:41.70	4:42.48	4:43.26	4:44.03	4:44.81	4:45.58
370	4:46.36	4:47.14	4:47.91	4:48.69	4:49.46	4:50.24	4:51.02	4:51.79	4:52.57	4:53.34
380	4:54.12	4:54.90	4:55.67	4:56.45	4:57.22	4:58.00	4:58.78	4:59.55	5:00.33	5:01.10
390	5:01.88	5:02.66	5:03.43	5:04.21	5:04.98	5:05.76	5:06.54	5:07.31	5:08.09	5:08.86
400	5:09.64	5:10.42	5:11.19	5:11.97	5:12.74	5:13.52	5:14.30	5:15.07	5:15.85	5:16.62
410	5:17.40	5:18.18	5:18.95	5:19.73	5:20.51	5:21.28	5:22.06	5:22.83	5:23.61	5:24.39
420	5:25.16	5:25.94	5:26.71	5:27.49	5:28.27	5:29.04	5:29.82	5:30.59	5:31.37	5:32.15
430	5:32.92	5:33.70	5:34.47	5:35.25	5:36.03	5:36.80	5:37.58	5:38.35	5:39.13	5:39.91
440	5:40.68	5:41.46	5:42.23	5:43.01	5:43.79	5:44.56	5:45.34	5:46.11	5:46.89	5:47.67
450	5:48.44	5:49.22	5:49.99	5:50.77	5:51.55	5:52.32	5:53.10	5:53.87	5:54.65	5:55.43
460	5:56.20	5:56.98	5:57.76	5:58.53	5:59.31	6:00.08	6:00.86	6:01.64	6:02.41	6:03.19
470	6:03.96	6:04.74	6:05.52	6:06.29	6:07.07	6:07.84	6:08.62	6:09.40	6:10.17	6:10.95
480	6:11.72	6:12.50	6:13.28	6:14.05	6:14.83	6:15.60	6:16.38	6:17.16	6:17.93	6:18.71
490	6:19.48	6:20.26	6:21.04	6:21.81	6:22.59	6:23.36	6:24.14	6:24.92	6:25.69	6:26.47
500	6:27.24	6:28.02	6:28.80	6:29.57	6:30.35	6:31.12	6:31.90	6:32.68	6:33.45	6:34.23
510	6:35.01	6:35.78	6:36.56	6:37.33	6:38.11	6:38.89	6:39.66	6:40.44	6:41.21	6:41.99
520	6:42.77	6:43.54	6:44.32	6:45.09	6:45.87	6:46.65	6:47.42	6:48.20	6:48.97	6:49.75
530	6:50.53	6:51.30	6:52.08	6:52.85	6:53.63	6:54.41	6:55.18	6:55.96	6:56.73	6:57.51
540	6:58.29	6:59.06	6:59.84	7:00.61	7:01.39	7:02.17	7:02.94	7:03.72	7:04.49	7:05.27
550	7:06.05	7:06.82	7:07.60	7:08.37	7:09.15	7:09.93	7:10.70	7:11.48	7:12.26	7:13.03
560	7:13.81	7:14.58	7:15.36	7:16.14	7:16.91	7:17.69	7:18.46	7:19.24	7:20.02	7:20.79
570	7:21.57	7:22.34	7:23.12	7:23.90	7:24.67	7:25.45	7:26.22	7:27.00	7:27.78	7:28.55
580	7:29.33	7:30.10	7:30.88	7:31.66	7:32.43	7:33.21	7:33.98	7:34.76	7:35.54	7:36.31
590	7:37.09	7:37.86	7:38.64	7:39.42	7:40.19	7:40.97	7:41.74	7:42.52	7:43.30	7:44.07

♩. = 1.16; ♩ = 0.78; ♪. = 0.58; (triplet ♩ 𝄾) = 0.52; ♪ = 0.39; (triplet ♪ 𝄾 𝄾) = 0.26; 𝅘𝅥𝅯 = 0.19 seconds

CLICK: 18 6/8 FRAMES; M.M.: 76.80

Click	0	1	2	3	4	5	6	7	8	9
000	0:00.00	0:00.00	0:00.78	0:01.56	0:02.34	0:03.13	0:03.91	0:04.69	0:05.47	0:06.25
010	0:07.03	0:07.81	0:08.59	0:09.38	0:10.16	0:10.94	0:11.72	0:12.50	0:13.28	0:14.06
020	0:14.84	0:15.62	0:16.41	0:17.19	0:17.97	0:18.75	0:19.53	0:20.31	0:21.09	0:21.87
030	0:22.66	0:23.44	0:24.22	0:25.00	0:25.78	0:26.56	0:27.34	0:28.13	0:28.91	0:29.69
040	0:30.47	0:31.25	0:32.03	0:32.81	0:33.59	0:34.37	0:35.16	0:35.94	0:36.72	0:37.50
050	0:38.28	0:39.06	0:39.84	0:40.63	0:41.41	0:42.19	0:42.97	0:43.75	0:44.53	0:45.31
060	0:46.09	0:46.88	0:47.66	0:48.44	0:49.22	0:50.00	0:50.78	0:51.56	0:52.34	0:53.12
070	0:53.91	0:54.69	0:55.47	0:56.25	0:57.03	0:57.81	0:58.59	0:59.38	1:00.16	1:00.94
080	1:01.72	1:02.50	1:03.28	1:04.06	1:04.84	1:05.63	1:06.41	1:07.19	1:07.97	1:08.75
090	1:09.53	1:10.31	1:11.09	1:11.87	1:12.66	1:13.44	1:14.22	1:15.00	1:15.78	1:16.56
100	1:17.34	1:18.12	1:18.91	1:19.69	1:20.47	1:21.25	1:22.03	1:22.81	1:23.59	1:24.38
110	1:25.16	1:25.94	1:26.72	1:27.50	1:28.28	1:29.06	1:29.84	1:30.62	1:31.41	1:32.19
120	1:32.97	1:33.75	1:34.53	1:35.31	1:36.09	1:36.87	1:37.66	1:38.44	1:39.22	1:40.00
130	1:40.78	1:41.56	1:42.34	1:43.13	1:43.91	1:44.69	1:45.47	1:46.25	1:47.03	1:47.81
140	1:48.59	1:49.37	1:50.16	1:50.94	1:51.72	1:52.50	1:53.28	1:54.06	1:54.84	1:55.62
150	1:56.41	1:57.19	1:57.97	1:58.75	1:59.53	2:00.31	2:01.09	2:01.88	2:02.66	2:03.44
160	2:04.22	2:05.00	2:05.78	2:06.56	2:07.34	2:08.12	2:08.91	2:09.69	2:10.47	2:11.25
170	2:12.03	2:12.81	2:13.59	2:14.37	2:15.16	2:15.94	2:16.72	2:17.50	2:18.28	2:19.06
180	2:19.84	2:20.63	2:21.41	2:22.19	2:22.97	2:23.75	2:24.53	2:25.31	2:26.09	2:26.87
190	2:27.66	2:28.44	2:29.22	2:30.00	2:30.78	2:31.56	2:32.34	2:33.12	2:33.91	2:34.69
200	2:35.47	2:36.25	2:37.03	2:37.81	2:38.59	2:39.38	2:40.16	2:40.94	2:41.72	2:42.50
210	2:43.28	2:44.06	2:44.84	2:45.62	2:46.41	2:47.19	2:47.97	2:48.75	2:49.53	2:50.31
220	2:51.09	2:51.87	2:52.66	2:53.44	2:54.22	2:55.00	2:55.78	2:56.56	2:57.34	2:58.13
230	2:58.91	2:59.69	3:00.47	3:01.25	3:02.03	3:02.81	3:03.59	3:04.37	3:05.16	3:05.94
240	3:06.72	3:07.50	3:08.28	3:09.06	3:09.84	3:10.62	3:11.41	3:12.19	3:12.97	3:13.75
250	3:14.53	3:15.31	3:16.09	3:16.88	3:17.66	3:18.44	3:19.22	3:20.00	3:20.78	3:21.56
260	3:22.34	3:23.12	3:23.91	3:24.69	3:25.47	3:26.25	3:27.03	3:27.81	3:28.59	3:29.37
270	3:30.16	3:30.94	3:31.72	3:32.50	3:33.28	3:34.06	3:34.84	3:35.63	3:36.41	3:37.19
280	3:37.97	3:38.75	3:39.53	3:40.31	3:41.09	3:41.87	3:42.66	3:43.44	3:44.22	3:45.00
290	3:45.78	3:46.56	3:47.34	3:48.12	3:48.91	3:49.69	3:50.47	3:51.25	3:52.03	3:52.81
300	3:53.59	3:54.38	3:55.16	3:55.94	3:56.72	3:57.50	3:58.28	3:59.06	3:59.84	4:00.62
310	4:01.41	4:02.19	4:02.97	4:03.75	4:04.53	4:05.31	4:06.09	4:06.87	4:07.66	4:08.44
320	4:09.22	4:10.00	4:10.78	4:11.56	4:12.34	4:13.13	4:13.91	4:14.69	4:15.47	4:16.25
330	4:17.03	4:17.81	4:18.59	4:19.37	4:20.16	4:20.94	4:21.72	4:22.50	4:23.28	4:24.06
340	4:24.84	4:25.62	4:26.41	4:27.19	4:27.97	4:28.75	4:29.53	4:30.31	4:31.09	4:31.88
350	4:32.66	4:33.44	4:34.22	4:35.00	4:35.78	4:36.56	4:37.34	4:38.12	4:38.91	4:39.69
360	4:40.47	4:41.25	4:42.03	4:42.81	4:43.59	4:44.37	4:45.16	4:45.94	4:46.72	4:47.50
370	4:48.28	4:49.06	4:49.84	4:50.63	4:51.41	4:52.19	4:52.97	4:53.75	4:54.53	4:55.31
380	4:56.09	4:56.87	4:57.66	4:58.44	4:59.22	5:00.00	5:00.78	5:01.56	5:02.34	5:03.12
390	5:03.91	5:04.69	5:05.47	5:06.25	5:07.03	5:07.81	5:08.59	5:09.38	5:10.16	5:10.94
400	5:11.72	5:12.50	5:13.28	5:14.06	5:14.84	5:15.62	5:16.41	5:17.19	5:17.97	5:18.75
410	5:19.53	5:20.31	5:21.09	5:21.87	5:22.66	5:23.44	5:24.22	5:25.00	5:25.78	5:26.56
420	5:27.34	5:28.13	5:28.91	5:29.69	5:30.47	5:31.25	5:32.03	5:32.81	5:33.59	5:34.37
430	5:35.16	5:35.94	5:36.72	5:37.50	5:38.28	5:39.06	5:39.84	5:40.62	5:41.41	5:42.19
440	5:42.97	5:43.75	5:44.53	5:45.31	5:46.09	5:46.88	5:47.66	5:48.44	5:49.22	5:50.00
450	5:50.78	5:51.56	5:52.34	5:53.12	5:53.91	5:54.69	5:55.47	5:56.25	5:57.03	5:57.81
460	5:58.59	5:59.37	6:00.16	6:00.94	6:01.72	6:02.50	6:03.28	6:04.06	6:04.84	6:05.63
470	6:06.41	6:07.19	6:07.97	6:08.75	6:09.53	6:10.31	6:11.09	6:11.87	6:12.66	6:13.44
480	6:14.22	6:15.00	6:15.78	6:16.56	6:17.34	6:18.12	6:18.91	6:19.69	6:20.47	6:21.25
490	6:22.03	6:22.81	6:23.59	6:24.38	6:25.16	6:25.94	6:26.72	6:27.50	6:28.28	6:29.06
500	6:29.84	6:30.62	6:31.41	6:32.19	6:32.97	6:33.75	6:34.53	6:35.31	6:36.09	6:36.87
510	6:37.66	6:38.44	6:39.22	6:40.00	6:40.78	6:41.56	6:42.34	6:43.13	6:43.91	6:44.69
520	6:45.47	6:46.25	6:47.03	6:47.81	6:48.59	6:49.37	6:50.16	6:50.94	6:51.72	6:52.50
530	6:53.28	6:54.06	6:54.84	6:55.62	6:56.41	6:57.19	6:57.97	6:58.75	6:59.53	7:00.31
540	7:01.09	7:01.88	7:02.66	7:03.44	7:04.22	7:05.00	7:05.78	7:06.56	7:07.34	7:08.12
550	7:08.91	7:09.69	7:10.47	7:11.25	7:12.03	7:12.81	7:13.59	7:14.37	7:15.16	7:15.94
560	7:16.72	7:17.50	7:18.28	7:19.06	7:19.84	7:20.63	7:21.41	7:22.19	7:22.97	7:23.75
570	7:24.53	7:25.31	7:26.09	7:26.87	7:27.66	7:28.44	7:29.22	7:30.00	7:30.78	7:31.56
580	7:32.34	7:33.12	7:33.91	7:34.69	7:35.47	7:36.25	7:37.03	7:37.81	7:38.59	7:39.38
590	7:40.16	7:40.94	7:41.72	7:42.50	7:43.28	7:44.06	7:44.84	7:45.62	7:46.41	7:47.19

♩. = 1.17; ♩ = 0.78; ♪. = 0.59; (3: ♩ 𝄾) = 0.52; ♪ = 0.39; (3: ♪ 𝄾 𝄾) = 0.26; ♬ = 0.20 seconds

CLICK: 18⅞ FRAMES; M.M.: 76.29

Click	0	1	2	3	4	5	6	7	8	9
000	0:00.00	0:00.00	0:00.79	0:01.57	0:02.36	0:03.15	0:03.93	0:04.72	0:05.51	0:06.29
010	0:07.08	0:07.86	0:08.65	0:09.44	0:10.22	0:11.01	0:11.80	0:12.58	0:13.37	0:14.16
020	0:14.94	0:15.73	0:16.52	0:17.30	0:18.09	0:18.88	0:19.66	0:20.45	0:21.23	0:22.02
030	0:22.81	0:23.59	0:24.38	0:25.17	0:25.95	0:26.74	0:27.53	0:28.31	0:29.10	0:29.89
040	0:30.67	0:31.46	0:32.24	0:33.03	0:33.82	0:34.60	0:35.39	0:36.18	0:36.96	0:37.75
050	0:38.54	0:39.32	0:40.11	0:40.90	0:41.68	0:42.47	0:43.26	0:44.04	0:44.83	0:45.61
060	0:46.40	0:47.19	0:47.97	0:48.76	0:49.55	0:50.33	0:51.12	0:51.91	0:52.69	0:53.48
070	0:54.27	0:55.05	0:55.84	0:56.63	0:57.41	0:58.20	0:58.98	0:59.77	1:00.56	1:01.34
080	1:02.13	1:02.92	1:03.70	1:04.49	1:05.28	1:06.06	1:06.85	1:07.64	1:08.42	1:09.21
090	1:09.99	1:10.78	1:11.57	1:12.35	1:13.14	1:13.93	1:14.71	1:15.50	1:16.29	1:17.07
100	1:17.86	1:18.65	1:19.43	1:20.22	1:21.01	1:21.79	1:22.58	1:23.36	1:24.15	1:24.94
110	1:25.72	1:26.51	1:27.30	1:28.08	1:28.87	1:29.66	1:30.44	1:31.23	1:32.02	1:32.80
120	1:33.59	1:34.37	1:35.16	1:35.95	1:36.73	1:37.52	1:38.31	1:39.09	1:39.88	1:40.67
130	1:41.45	1:42.24	1:43.03	1:43.81	1:44.60	1:45.39	1:46.17	1:46.96	1:47.74	1:48.53
140	1:49.32	1:50.10	1:50.89	1:51.68	1:52.46	1:53.25	1:54.04	1:54.82	1:55.61	1:56.40
150	1:57.18	1:57.97	1:58.76	1:59.54	2:00.33	2:01.11	2:01.90	2:02.69	2:03.47	2:04.26
160	2:05.05	2:05.83	2:06.62	2:07.41	2:08.19	2:08.98	2:09.77	2:10.55	2:11.34	2:12.13
170	2:12.91	2:13.70	2:14.48	2:15.27	2:16.06	2:16.84	2:17.63	2:18.42	2:19.20	2:19.99
180	2:20.78	2:21.56	2:22.35	2:23.14	2:23.92	2:24.71	2:25.49	2:26.28	2:27.07	2:27.85
190	2:28.64	2:29.43	2:30.21	2:31.00	2:31.79	2:32.57	2:33.36	2:34.15	2:34.93	2:35.72
200	2:36.51	2:37.29	2:38.08	2:38.86	2:39.65	2:40.44	2:41.22	2:42.01	2:42.80	2:43.58
210	2:44.37	2:45.16	2:45.94	2:46.73	2:47.52	2:48.30	2:49.09	2:49.87	2:50.66	2:51.45
220	2:52.23	2:53.02	2:53.81	2:54.59	2:55.38	2:56.17	2:56.95	2:57.74	2:58.53	2:59.31
230	3:00.10	3:00.89	3:01.67	3:02.46	3:03.24	3:04.03	3:04.82	3:05.60	3:06.39	3:07.18
240	3:07.96	3:08.75	3:09.54	3:10.32	3:11.11	3:11.90	3:12.68	3:13.47	3:14.26	3:15.04
250	3:15.83	3:16.61	3:17.40	3:18.19	3:18.97	3:19.76	3:20.55	3:21.33	3:22.12	3:22.91
260	3:23.69	3:24.48	3:25.27	3:26.05	3:26.84	3:27.62	3:28.41	3:29.20	3:29.98	3:30.77
270	3:31.56	3:32.34	3:33.13	3:33.92	3:34.70	3:35.49	3:36.28	3:37.06	3:37.85	3:38.64
280	3:39.42	3:40.21	3:40.99	3:41.78	3:42.57	3:43.35	3:44.14	3:44.93	3:45.71	3:46.50
290	3:47.29	3:48.07	3:48.86	3:49.65	3:50.43	3:51.22	3:52.01	3:52.79	3:53.58	3:54.36
300	3:55.15	3:55.94	3:56.72	3:57.51	3:58.30	3:59.08	3:59.87	4:00.66	4:01.44	4:02.23
310	4:03.02	4:03.80	4:04.59	4:05.38	4:06.16	4:06.95	4:07.73	4:08.52	4:09.31	4:10.09
320	4:10.88	4:11.67	4:12.45	4:13.24	4:14.03	4:14.81	4:15.60	4:16.39	4:17.17	4:17.96
330	4:18.74	4:19.53	4:20.32	4:21.10	4:21.89	4:22.68	4:23.46	4:24.25	4:25.04	4:25.82
340	4:26.61	4:27.40	4:28.18	4:28.97	4:29.76	4:30.54	4:31.33	4:32.11	4:32.90	4:33.69
350	4:34.47	4:35.26	4:36.05	4:36.83	4:37.62	4:38.41	4:39.19	4:39.98	4:40.77	4:41.55
360	4:42.34	4:43.13	4:43.91	4:44.70	4:45.48	4:46.27	4:47.06	4:47.84	4:48.63	4:49.42
370	4:50.20	4:50.99	4:51.78	4:52.56	4:53.35	4:54.14	4:54.92	4:55.71	4:56.49	4:57.28
380	4:58.07	4:58.85	4:59.64	5:00.43	5:01.21	5:02.00	5:02.79	5:03.57	5:04.36	5:05.15
390	5:05.93	5:06.72	5:07.51	5:08.29	5:09.08	5:09.86	5:10.65	5:11.44	5:12.22	5:13.01
400	5:13.80	5:14.58	5:15.37	5:16.16	5:16.94	5:17.73	5:18.52	5:19.30	5:20.09	5:20.87
410	5:21.66	5:22.45	5:23.23	5:24.02	5:24.81	5:25.59	5:26.38	5:27.17	5:27.95	5:28.74
420	5:29.53	5:30.31	5:31.10	5:31.89	5:32.67	5:33.46	5:34.24	5:35.03	5:35.82	5:36.60
430	5:37.39	5:38.18	5:38.96	5:39.75	5:40.54	5:41.32	5:42.11	5:42.90	5:43.68	5:44.47
440	5:45.26	5:46.04	5:46.83	5:47.61	5:48.40	5:49.19	5:49.97	5:50.76	5:51.55	5:52.33
450	5:53.12	5:53.91	5:54.69	5:55.48	5:56.27	5:57.05	5:57.84	5:58.62	5:59.41	6:00.20
460	6:00.98	6:01.77	6:02.56	6:03.34	6:04.13	6:04.92	6:05.70	6:06.49	6:07.28	6:08.06
470	6:08.85	6:09.64	6:10.42	6:11.21	6:11.99	6:12.78	6:13.57	6:14.35	6:15.14	6:15.93
480	6:16.71	6:17.50	6:18.29	6:19.07	6:19.86	6:20.65	6:21.43	6:22.22	6:23.01	6:23.79
490	6:24.58	6:25.36	6:26.15	6:26.94	6:27.72	6:28.51	6:29.30	6:30.08	6:30.87	6:31.66
500	6:32.44	6:33.23	6:34.02	6:34.80	6:35.59	6:36.37	6:37.16	6:37.95	6:38.73	6:39.52
510	6:40.31	6:41.09	6:41.88	6:42.67	6:43.45	6:44.24	6:45.03	6:45.81	6:46.60	6:47.39
520	6:48.17	6:48.96	6:49.74	6:50.53	6:51.32	6:52.10	6:52.89	6:53.68	6:54.46	6:55.25
530	6:56.04	6:56.82	6:57.61	6:58.40	6:59.18	6:59.97	7:00.76	7:01.54	7:02.33	7:03.11
540	7:03.90	7:04.69	7:05.47	7:06.26	7:07.05	7:07.83	7:08.62	7:09.41	7:10.19	7:10.98
550	7:11.77	7:12.55	7:13.34	7:14.12	7:14.91	7:15.70	7:16.48	7:17.27	7:18.06	7:18.84
560	7:19.63	7:20.42	7:21.20	7:21.99	7:22.78	7:23.56	7:24.35	7:25.14	7:25.92	7:26.71
570	7:27.49	7:28.28	7:29.07	7:29.85	7:30.64	7:31.43	7:32.21	7:33.00	7:33.79	7:34.57
580	7:35.36	7:36.15	7:36.93	7:37.72	7:38.51	7:39.29	7:40.08	7:40.86	7:41.65	7:42.44
590	7:43.22	7:44.01	7:44.80	7:45.58	7:46.37	7:47.16	7:47.94	7:48.73	7:49.52	7:50.30

♩. = 1.18; ♩ = 0.79; ♪. = 0.59; (3) ♩ 𝄾 = 0.52; ♪ = 0.39; (3) ♪ 𝄾 𝄾 = 0.26; 𝅘𝅥𝅯 = 0.20 seconds

CLICK: 19 0/8 FRAMES; M.M.: 75.79

Click	0	1	2	3	4	5	6	7	8	9
000	0:00.00	0:00.00	0:00.79	0:01.58	0:02.38	0:03.17	0:03.96	0:04.75	0:05.54	0:06.33
010	0:07.13	0:07.92	0:08.71	0:09.50	0:10.29	0:11.08	0:11.88	0:12.67	0:13.46	0:14.25
020	0:15.04	0:15.83	0:16.63	0:17.42	0:18.21	0:19.00	0:19.79	0:20.58	0:21.38	0:22.17
030	0:22.96	0:23.75	0:24.54	0:25.33	0:26.13	0:26.92	0:27.71	0:28.50	0:29.29	0:30.08
040	0:30.88	0:31.67	0:32.46	0:33.25	0:34.04	0:34.83	0:35.63	0:36.42	0:37.21	0:38.00
050	0:38.79	0:39.58	0:40.38	0:41.17	0:41.96	0:42.75	0:43.54	0:44.33	0:45.13	0:45.92
060	0:46.71	0:47.50	0:48.29	0:49.08	0:49.88	0:50.67	0:51.46	0:52.25	0:53.04	0:53.83
070	0:54.63	0:55.42	0:56.21	0:57.00	0:57.79	0:58.58	0:59.38	1:00.17	1:00.96	1:01.75
080	1:02.54	1:03.33	1:04.13	1:04.92	1:05.71	1:06.50	1:07.29	1:08.08	1:08.88	1:09.67
090	1:10.46	1:11.25	1:12.04	1:12.83	1:13.63	1:14.42	1:15.21	1:16.00	1:16.79	1:17.58
100	1:18.37	1:19.17	1:19.96	1:20.75	1:21.54	1:22.33	1:23.12	1:23.92	1:24.71	1:25.50
110	1:26.29	1:27.08	1:27.88	1:28.67	1:29.46	1:30.25	1:31.04	1:31.83	1:32.63	1:33.42
120	1:34.21	1:35.00	1:35.79	1:36.58	1:37.38	1:38.17	1:38.96	1:39.75	1:40.54	1:41.33
130	1:42.13	1:42.92	1:43.71	1:44.50	1:45.29	1:46.08	1:46.88	1:47.67	1:48.46	1:49.25
140	1:50.04	1:50.83	1:51.63	1:52.42	1:53.21	1:54.00	1:54.79	1:55.58	1:56.38	1:57.17
150	1:57.96	1:58.75	1:59.54	2:00.33	2:01.12	2:01.92	2:02.71	2:03.50	2:04.29	2:05.08
160	2:05.87	2:06.67	2:07.46	2:08.25	2:09.04	2:09.83	2:10.62	2:11.42	2:12.21	2:13.00
170	2:13.79	2:14.58	2:15.38	2:16.17	2:16.96	2:17.75	2:18.54	2:19.33	2:20.13	2:20.92
180	2:21.71	2:22.50	2:23.29	2:24.08	2:24.88	2:25.67	2:26.46	2:27.25	2:28.04	2:28.83
190	2:29.63	2:30.42	2:31.21	2:32.00	2:32.79	2:33.58	2:34.38	2:35.17	2:35.96	2:36.75
200	2:37.54	2:38.33	2:39.13	2:39.92	2:40.71	2:41.50	2:42.29	2:43.08	2:43.88	2:44.67
210	2:45.46	2:46.25	2:47.04	2:47.83	2:48.63	2:49.42	2:50.21	2:51.00	2:51.79	2:52.58
220	2:53.38	2:54.17	2:54.96	2:55.75	2:56.54	2:57.33	2:58.13	2:58.92	2:59.71	3:00.50
230	3:01.29	3:02.08	3:02.87	3:03.67	3:04.46	3:05.25	3:06.04	3:06.83	3:07.62	3:08.42
240	3:09.21	3:10.00	3:10.79	3:11.58	3:12.37	3:13.17	3:13.96	3:14.75	3:15.54	3:16.33
250	3:17.12	3:17.92	3:18.71	3:19.50	3:20.29	3:21.08	3:21.87	3:22.67	3:23.46	3:24.25
260	3:25.04	3:25.83	3:26.63	3:27.42	3:28.21	3:29.00	3:29.79	3:30.58	3:31.38	3:32.17
270	3:32.96	3:33.75	3:34.54	3:35.33	3:36.13	3:36.92	3:37.71	3:38.50	3:39.29	3:40.08
280	3:40.88	3:41.67	3:42.46	3:43.25	3:44.04	3:44.83	3:45.63	3:46.42	3:47.21	3:48.00
290	3:48.79	3:49.58	3:50.38	3:51.17	3:51.96	3:52.75	3:53.54	3:54.33	3:55.13	3:55.92
300	3:56.71	3:57.50	3:58.29	3:59.08	3:59.88	4:00.67	4:01.46	4:02.25	4:03.04	4:03.83
310	4:04.63	4:05.42	4:06.21	4:07.00	4:07.79	4:08.58	4:09.38	4:10.17	4:10.96	4:11.75
320	4:12.54	4:13.33	4:14.13	4:14.92	4:15.71	4:16.50	4:17.29	4:18.08	4:18.87	4:19.67
330	4:20.46	4:21.25	4:22.04	4:22.83	4:23.63	4:24.42	4:25.21	4:26.00	4:26.79	4:27.58
340	4:28.37	4:29.17	4:29.96	4:30.75	4:31.54	4:32.33	4:33.13	4:33.92	4:34.71	4:35.50
350	4:36.29	4:37.08	4:37.87	4:38.67	4:39.46	4:40.25	4:41.04	4:41.83	4:42.63	4:43.42
360	4:44.21	4:45.00	4:45.79	4:46.58	4:47.37	4:48.17	4:48.96	4:49.75	4:50.54	4:51.33
370	4:52.13	4:52.92	4:53.71	4:54.50	4:55.29	4:56.08	4:56.87	4:57.67	4:58.46	4:59.25
380	5:00.04	5:00.83	5:01.63	5:02.42	5:03.21	5:04.00	5:04.79	5:05.58	5:06.38	5:07.17
390	5:07.96	5:08.75	5:09.54	5:10.33	5:11.13	5:11.92	5:12.71	5:13.50	5:14.29	5:15.08
400	5:15.88	5:16.67	5:17.46	5:18.25	5:19.04	5:19.83	5:20.63	5:21.42	5:22.21	5:23.00
410	5:23.79	5:24.58	5:25.38	5:26.17	5:26.96	5:27.75	5:28.54	5:29.33	5:30.12	5:30.92
420	5:31.71	5:32.50	5:33.29	5:34.08	5:34.88	5:35.67	5:36.46	5:37.25	5:38.04	5:38.83
430	5:39.62	5:40.42	5:41.21	5:42.00	5:42.79	5:43.58	5:44.38	5:45.17	5:45.96	5:46.75
440	5:47.54	5:48.33	5:49.12	5:49.92	5:50.71	5:51.50	5:52.29	5:53.08	5:53.88	5:54.67
450	5:55.46	5:56.25	5:57.04	5:57.83	5:58.62	5:59.42	6:00.21	6:01.00	6:01.79	6:02.58
460	6:03.38	6:04.17	6:04.96	6:05.75	6:06.54	6:07.33	6:08.12	6:08.92	6:09.71	6:10.50
470	6:11.29	6:12.08	6:12.88	6:13.67	6:14.46	6:15.25	6:16.04	6:16.83	6:17.63	6:18.42
480	6:19.21	6:20.00	6:20.79	6:21.58	6:22.38	6:23.17	6:23.96	6:24.75	6:25.54	6:26.33
490	6:27.13	6:27.92	6:28.71	6:29.50	6:30.29	6:31.08	6:31.88	6:32.67	6:33.46	6:34.25
500	6:35.04	6:35.83	6:36.63	6:37.42	6:38.21	6:39.00	6:39.79	6:40.58	6:41.38	6:42.17
510	6:42.96	6:43.75	6:44.54	6:45.33	6:46.13	6:46.92	6:47.71	6:48.50	6:49.29	6:50.08
520	6:50.87	6:51.67	6:52.46	6:53.25	6:54.04	6:54.83	6:55.63	6:56.42	6:57.21	6:58.00
530	6:58.79	6:59.58	7:00.37	7:01.17	7:01.96	7:02.75	7:03.54	7:04.33	7:05.13	7:05.92
540	7:06.71	7:07.50	7:08.29	7:09.08	7:09.87	7:10.67	7:11.46	7:12.25	7:13.04	7:13.83
550	7:14.63	7:15.42	7:16.21	7:17.00	7:17.79	7:18.58	7:19.38	7:20.17	7:20.96	7:21.75
560	7:22.54	7:23.33	7:24.13	7:24.92	7:25.71	7:26.50	7:27.29	7:28.08	7:28.88	7:29.67
570	7:30.46	7:31.25	7:32.04	7:32.83	7:33.63	7:34.42	7:35.21	7:36.00	7:36.79	7:37.58
580	7:38.38	7:39.17	7:39.96	7:40.75	7:41.54	7:42.33	7:43.13	7:43.92	7:44.71	7:45.50
590	7:46.29	7:47.08	7:47.88	7:48.67	7:49.46	7:50.25	7:51.04	7:51.83	7:52.63	7:53.42

♩. = 1.19; ♩ = 0.79; ♪. = 0.59; (triplet) ♩ 𝄾 = 0.53; ♪ = 0.40; (triplet) ♪ 𝄾 𝄾 = 0.26; 𝅘𝅥𝅯 = 0.20 seconds

CLICK: 19⅛ FRAMES; M.M.: 75.29

Click	0	1	2	3	4	5	6	7	8	9
000	0:00.00	0:00.00	0:00.80	0:01.59	0:02.39	0:03.19	0:03.98	0:04.78	0:05.58	0:06.37
010	0:07.17	0:07.97	0:08.77	0:09.56	0:10.36	0:11.16	0:11.95	0:12.75	0:13.55	0:14.34
020	0:15.14	0:15.94	0:16.73	0:17.53	0:18.33	0:19.13	0:19.92	0:20.72	0:21.52	0:22.31
030	0:23.11	0:23.91	0:24.70	0:25.50	0:26.30	0:27.09	0:27.89	0:28.69	0:29.48	0:30.28
040	0:31.08	0:31.88	0:32.67	0:33.47	0:34.27	0:35.06	0:35.86	0:36.66	0:37.45	0:38.25
050	0:39.05	0:39.84	0:40.64	0:41.44	0:42.23	0:43.03	0:43.83	0:44.63	0:45.42	0:46.22
060	0:47.02	0:47.81	0:48.61	0:49.41	0:50.20	0:51.00	0:51.80	0:52.59	0:53.39	0:54.19
070	0:54.98	0:55.78	0:56.58	0:57.37	0:58.17	0:58.97	0:59.77	1:00.56	1:01.36	1:02.16
080	1:02.95	1:03.75	1:04.55	1:05.34	1:06.14	1:06.94	1:07.73	1:08.53	1:09.33	1:10.12
090	1:10.92	1:11.72	1:12.52	1:13.31	1:14.11	1:14.91	1:15.70	1:16.50	1:17.30	1:18.09
100	1:18.89	1:19.69	1:20.48	1:21.28	1:22.08	1:22.87	1:23.67	1:24.47	1:25.27	1:26.06
110	1:26.86	1:27.66	1:28.45	1:29.25	1:30.05	1:30.84	1:31.64	1:32.44	1:33.23	1:34.03
120	1:34.83	1:35.62	1:36.42	1:37.22	1:38.02	1:38.81	1:39.61	1:40.41	1:41.20	1:42.00
130	1:42.80	1:43.59	1:44.39	1:45.19	1:45.98	1:46.78	1:47.58	1:48.38	1:49.17	1:49.97
140	1:50.77	1:51.56	1:52.36	1:53.16	1:53.95	1:54.75	1:55.55	1:56.34	1:57.14	1:57.94
150	1:58.73	1:59.53	2:00.33	2:01.12	2:01.92	2:02.72	2:03.52	2:04.31	2:05.11	2:05.91
160	2:06.70	2:07.50	2:08.30	2:09.09	2:09.89	2:10.69	2:11.48	2:12.28	2:13.08	2:13.87
170	2:14.67	2:15.47	2:16.27	2:17.06	2:17.86	2:18.66	2:19.45	2:20.25	2:21.05	2:21.84
180	2:22.64	2:23.44	2:24.23	2:25.03	2:25.83	2:26.62	2:27.42	2:28.22	2:29.02	2:29.81
190	2:30.61	2:31.41	2:32.20	2:33.00	2:33.80	2:34.59	2:35.39	2:36.19	2:36.98	2:37.78
200	2:38.58	2:39.38	2:40.17	2:40.97	2:41.77	2:42.56	2:43.36	2:44.16	2:44.95	2:45.75
210	2:46.55	2:47.34	2:48.14	2:48.94	2:49.73	2:50.53	2:51.33	2:52.12	2:52.92	2:53.72
220	2:54.52	2:55.31	2:56.11	2:56.91	2:57.70	2:58.50	2:59.30	3:00.09	3:00.89	3:01.69
230	3:02.48	3:03.28	3:04.08	3:04.87	3:05.67	3:06.47	3:07.27	3:08.06	3:08.86	3:09.66
240	3:10.45	3:11.25	3:12.05	3:12.84	3:13.64	3:14.44	3:15.23	3:16.03	3:16.83	3:17.62
250	3:18.42	3:19.22	3:20.02	3:20.81	3:21.61	3:22.41	3:23.20	3:24.00	3:24.80	3:25.59
260	3:26.39	3:27.19	3:27.98	3:28.78	3:29.58	3:30.37	3:31.17	3:31.97	3:32.77	3:33.56
270	3:34.36	3:35.16	3:35.95	3:36.75	3:37.55	3:38.34	3:39.14	3:39.94	3:40.73	3:41.53
280	3:42.33	3:43.12	3:43.92	3:44.72	3:45.52	3:46.31	3:47.11	3:47.91	3:48.70	3:49.50
290	3:50.30	3:51.09	3:51.89	3:52.69	3:53.48	3:54.28	3:55.08	3:55.87	3:56.67	3:57.47
300	3:58.27	3:59.06	3:59.86	4:00.66	4:01.45	4:02.25	4:03.05	4:03.84	4:04.64	4:05.44
310	4:06.23	4:07.03	4:07.83	4:08.62	4:09.42	4:10.22	4:11.02	4:11.81	4:12.61	4:13.41
320	4:14.20	4:15.00	4:15.80	4:16.59	4:17.39	4:18.19	4:18.98	4:19.78	4:20.58	4:21.37
330	4:22.17	4:22.97	4:23.77	4:24.56	4:25.36	4:26.16	4:26.95	4:27.75	4:28.55	4:29.34
340	4:30.14	4:30.94	4:31.73	4:32.53	4:33.33	4:34.12	4:34.92	4:35.72	4:36.52	4:37.31
350	4:38.11	4:38.91	4:39.70	4:40.50	4:41.30	4:42.09	4:42.89	4:43.69	4:44.48	4:45.28
360	4:46.08	4:46.88	4:47.67	4:48.47	4:49.27	4:50.06	4:50.86	4:51.66	4:52.45	4:53.25
370	4:54.05	4:54.84	4:55.64	4:56.44	4:57.23	4:58.03	4:58.83	4:59.62	5:00.42	5:01.22
380	5:02.02	5:02.81	5:03.61	5:04.41	5:05.20	5:06.00	5:06.80	5:07.59	5:08.39	5:09.19
390	5:09.98	5:10.78	5:11.58	5:12.37	5:13.17	5:13.97	5:14.77	5:15.56	5:16.36	5:17.16
400	5:17.95	5:18.75	5:19.55	5:20.34	5:21.14	5:21.94	5:22.73	5:23.53	5:24.33	5:25.12
410	5:25.92	5:26.72	5:27.52	5:28.31	5:29.11	5:29.91	5:30.70	5:31.50	5:32.30	5:33.09
420	5:33.89	5:34.69	5:35.48	5:36.28	5:37.08	5:37.87	5:38.67	5:39.47	5:40.27	5:41.06
430	5:41.86	5:42.66	5:43.45	5:44.25	5:45.05	5:45.84	5:46.64	5:47.44	5:48.23	5:49.03
440	5:49.83	5:50.62	5:51.42	5:52.22	5:53.02	5:53.81	5:54.61	5:55.41	5:56.20	5:57.00
450	5:57.80	5:58.59	5:59.39	6:00.19	6:00.98	6:01.78	6:02.58	6:03.37	6:04.17	6:04.97
460	6:05.77	6:06.56	6:07.36	6:08.16	6:08.95	6:09.75	6:10.55	6:11.34	6:12.14	6:12.94
470	6:13.73	6:14.53	6:15.33	6:16.12	6:16.92	6:17.72	6:18.52	6:19.31	6:20.11	6:20.91
480	6:21.70	6:22.50	6:23.30	6:24.09	6:24.89	6:25.69	6:26.48	6:27.28	6:28.08	6:28.87
490	6:29.67	6:30.47	6:31.27	6:32.06	6:32.86	6:33.66	6:34.45	6:35.25	6:36.05	6:36.84
500	6:37.64	6:38.44	6:39.23	6:40.03	6:40.83	6:41.62	6:42.42	6:43.22	6:44.02	6:44.81
510	6:45.61	6:46.41	6:47.20	6:48.00	6:48.80	6:49.59	6:50.39	6:51.19	6:51.98	6:52.78
520	6:53.58	6:54.37	6:55.17	6:55.97	6:56.77	6:57.56	6:58.36	6:59.16	6:59.95	7:00.75
530	7:01.55	7:02.34	7:03.14	7:03.94	7:04.73	7:05.53	7:06.33	7:07.12	7:07.92	7:08.72
540	7:09.52	7:10.31	7:11.11	7:11.91	7:12.70	7:13.50	7:14.30	7:15.09	7:15.89	7:16.69
550	7:17.48	7:18.28	7:19.08	7:19.87	7:20.67	7:21.47	7:22.27	7:23.06	7:23.86	7:24.66
560	7:25.45	7:26.25	7:27.05	7:27.84	7:28.64	7:29.44	7:30.23	7:31.03	7:31.83	7:32.62
570	7:33.42	7:34.22	7:35.02	7:35.81	7:36.61	7:37.41	7:38.20	7:39.00	7:39.80	7:40.59
580	7:41.39	7:42.19	7:42.98	7:43.78	7:44.58	7:45.37	7:46.17	7:46.97	7:47.77	7:48.56
590	7:49.36	7:50.16	7:50.95	7:51.75	7:52.55	7:53.34	7:54.14	7:54.94	7:55.73	7:56.53

♩. = 1.20; ♩ = 0.80; ♪. = 0.60; (triplet ♩ 𝄾) = 0.53; ♪ = 0.40; (triplet ♪ 𝄾 𝄾) = 0.27; 𝅘𝅥𝅯 = 0.20 seconds

CLICK: 19 2/8 FRAMES; M.M.: 74.81

Click	0	1	2	3	4	5	6	7	8	9
000	0:00.00	0:00.00	0:00.80	0:01.60	0:02.41	0:03.21	0:04.01	0:04.81	0:05.61	0:06.42
010	0:07.22	0:08.02	0:08.82	0:09.63	0:10.43	0:11.23	0:12.03	0:12.83	0:13.64	0:14.44
020	0:15.24	0:16.04	0:16.84	0:17.65	0:18.45	0:19.25	0:20.05	0:20.85	0:21.66	0:22.46
030	0:23.26	0:24.06	0:24.86	0:25.67	0:26.47	0:27.27	0:28.07	0:28.88	0:29.68	0:30.48
040	0:31.28	0:32.08	0:32.89	0:33.69	0:34.49	0:35.29	0:36.09	0:36.90	0:37.70	0:38.50
050	0:39.30	0:40.10	0:40.91	0:41.71	0:42.51	0:43.31	0:44.11	0:44.92	0:45.72	0:46.52
060	0:47.32	0:48.13	0:48.93	0:49.73	0:50.53	0:51.33	0:52.14	0:52.94	0:53.74	0:54.54
070	0:55.34	0:56.15	0:56.95	0:57.75	0:58.55	0:59.35	1:00.16	1:00.96	1:01.76	1:02.56
080	1:03.36	1:04.17	1:04.97	1:05.77	1:06.57	1:07.38	1:08.18	1:08.98	1:09.78	1:10.58
090	1:11.39	1:12.19	1:12.99	1:13.79	1:14.59	1:15.40	1:16.20	1:17.00	1:17.80	1:18.60
100	1:19.41	1:20.21	1:21.01	1:21.81	1:22.61	1:23.42	1:24.22	1:25.02	1:25.82	1:26.63
110	1:27.43	1:28.23	1:29.03	1:29.83	1:30.64	1:31.44	1:32.24	1:33.04	1:33.84	1:34.65
120	1:35.45	1:36.25	1:37.05	1:37.85	1:38.66	1:39.46	1:40.26	1:41.06	1:41.86	1:42.67
130	1:43.47	1:44.27	1:45.07	1:45.88	1:46.68	1:47.48	1:48.28	1:49.08	1:49.89	1:50.69
140	1:51.49	1:52.29	1:53.09	1:53.90	1:54.70	1:55.50	1:56.30	1:57.10	1:57.91	1:58.71
150	1:59.51	2:00.31	2:01.11	2:01.92	2:02.72	2:03.52	2:04.32	2:05.13	2:05.93	2:06.73
160	2:07.53	2:08.33	2:09.14	2:09.94	2:10.74	2:11.54	2:12.34	2:13.15	2:13.95	2:14.75
170	2:15.55	2:16.35	2:17.16	2:17.96	2:18.76	2:19.56	2:20.36	2:21.17	2:21.97	2:22.77
180	2:23.57	2:24.38	2:25.18	2:25.98	2:26.78	2:27.58	2:28.39	2:29.19	2:29.99	2:30.79
190	2:31.59	2:32.40	2:33.20	2:34.00	2:34.80	2:35.60	2:36.41	2:37.21	2:38.01	2:38.81
200	2:39.61	2:40.42	2:41.22	2:42.02	2:42.82	2:43.63	2:44.43	2:45.23	2:46.03	2:46.83
210	2:47.64	2:48.44	2:49.24	2:50.04	2:50.84	2:51.65	2:52.45	2:53.25	2:54.05	2:54.85
220	2:55.66	2:56.46	2:57.26	2:58.06	2:58.86	2:59.67	3:00.47	3:01.27	3:02.07	3:02.88
230	3:03.68	3:04.48	3:05.28	3:06.08	3:06.89	3:07.69	3:08.49	3:09.29	3:10.09	3:10.90
240	3:11.70	3:12.50	3:13.30	3:14.10	3:14.91	3:15.71	3:16.51	3:17.31	3:18.11	3:18.92
250	3:19.72	3:20.52	3:21.32	3:22.13	3:22.93	3:23.73	3:24.53	3:25.33	3:26.14	3:26.94
260	3:27.74	3:28.54	3:29.34	3:30.15	3:30.95	3:31.75	3:32.55	3:33.35	3:34.16	3:34.96
270	3:35.76	3:36.56	3:37.36	3:38.17	3:38.97	3:39.77	3:40.57	3:41.38	3:42.18	3:42.98
280	3:43.78	3:44.58	3:45.39	3:46.19	3:46.99	3:47.79	3:48.59	3:49.40	3:50.20	3:51.00
290	3:51.80	3:52.60	3:53.41	3:54.21	3:55.01	3:55.81	3:56.61	3:57.42	3:58.22	3:59.02
300	3:59.82	4:00.63	4:01.43	4:02.23	4:03.03	4:03.83	4:04.64	4:05.44	4:06.24	4:07.04
310	4:07.84	4:08.65	4:09.45	4:10.25	4:11.05	4:11.85	4:12.66	4:13.46	4:14.26	4:15.06
320	4:15.86	4:16.67	4:17.47	4:18.27	4:19.07	4:19.88	4:20.68	4:21.48	4:22.28	4:23.08
330	4:23.89	4:24.69	4:25.49	4:26.29	4:27.09	4:27.90	4:28.70	4:29.50	4:30.30	4:31.10
340	4:31.91	4:32.71	4:33.51	4:34.31	4:35.11	4:35.92	4:36.72	4:37.52	4:38.32	4:39.13
350	4:39.93	4:40.73	4:41.53	4:42.33	4:43.14	4:43.94	4:44.74	4:45.54	4:46.34	4:47.15
360	4:47.95	4:48.75	4:49.55	4:50.35	4:51.16	4:51.96	4:52.76	4:53.56	4:54.36	4:55.17
370	4:55.97	4:56.77	4:57.57	4:58.38	4:59.18	4:59.98	5:00.78	5:01.58	5:02.39	5:03.19
380	5:03.99	5:04.79	5:05.59	5:06.40	5:07.20	5:08.00	5:08.80	5:09.60	5:10.41	5:11.21
390	5:12.01	5:12.81	5:13.61	5:14.42	5:15.22	5:16.02	5:16.82	5:17.63	5:18.43	5:19.23
400	5:20.03	5:20.83	5:21.64	5:22.44	5:23.24	5:24.04	5:24.84	5:25.65	5:26.45	5:27.25
410	5:28.05	5:28.85	5:29.66	5:30.46	5:31.26	5:32.06	5:32.86	5:33.67	5:34.47	5:35.27
420	5:36.07	5:36.88	5:37.68	5:38.48	5:39.28	5:40.08	5:40.89	5:41.69	5:42.49	5:43.29
430	5:44.09	5:44.90	5:45.70	5:46.50	5:47.30	5:48.10	5:48.91	5:49.71	5:50.51	5:51.31
440	5:52.11	5:52.92	5:53.72	5:54.52	5:55.32	5:56.13	5:56.93	5:57.73	5:58.53	5:59.33
450	6:00.14	6:00.94	6:01.74	6:02.54	6:03.34	6:04.15	6:04.95	6:05.75	6:06.55	6:07.35
460	6:08.16	6:08.96	6:09.76	6:10.56	6:11.36	6:12.17	6:12.97	6:13.77	6:14.57	6:15.38
470	6:16.18	6:16.98	6:17.78	6:18.58	6:19.39	6:20.19	6:20.99	6:21.79	6:22.59	6:23.40
480	6:24.20	6:25.00	6:25.80	6:26.60	6:27.41	6:28.21	6:29.01	6:29.81	6:30.61	6:31.42
490	6:32.22	6:33.02	6:33.82	6:34.63	6:35.43	6:36.23	6:37.03	6:37.83	6:38.64	6:39.44
500	6:40.24	6:41.04	6:41.84	6:42.65	6:43.45	6:44.25	6:45.05	6:45.85	6:46.66	6:47.46
510	6:48.26	6:49.06	6:49.86	6:50.67	6:51.47	6:52.27	6:53.07	6:53.88	6:54.68	6:55.48
520	6:56.28	6:57.08	6:57.89	6:58.69	6:59.49	7:00.29	7:01.09	7:01.90	7:02.70	7:03.50
530	7:04.30	7:05.10	7:05.91	7:06.71	7:07.51	7:08.31	7:09.11	7:09.92	7:10.72	7:11.52
540	7:12.32	7:13.13	7:13.93	7:14.73	7:15.53	7:16.33	7:17.14	7:17.94	7:18.74	7:19.54
550	7:20.34	7:21.15	7:21.95	7:22.75	7:23.55	7:24.35	7:25.16	7:25.96	7:26.76	7:27.56
560	7:28.36	7:29.17	7:29.97	7:30.77	7:31.57	7:32.38	7:33.18	7:33.98	7:34.78	7:35.58
570	7:36.39	7:37.19	7:37.99	7:38.79	7:39.59	7:40.40	7:41.20	7:42.00	7:42.80	7:43.60
580	7:44.41	7:45.21	7:46.01	7:46.81	7:47.61	7:48.42	7:49.22	7:50.02	7:50.82	7:51.63
590	7:52.43	7:53.23	7:54.03	7:54.83	7:55.64	7:56.44	7:57.24	7:58.04	7:58.84	7:59.65

♩. = 1.20; ♩ = 0.80; ♪. = 0.60; (triplet ♩ 𝄾) = 0.53; ♪ = 0.40; (triplet ♪ 𝄾 𝄾) = 0.27; 𝅘𝅥𝅯 = 0.20 seconds

CLICK: 19⅜ FRAMES; M.M.: 74.32

Click	0	1	2	3	4	5	6	7	8	9
000	0:00.00	0:00.00	0:00.81	0:01.61	0:02.42	0:03.23	0:04.04	0:04.84	0:05.65	0:06.46
010	0:07.27	0:08.07	0:08.88	0:09.69	0:10.49	0:11.30	0:12.11	0:12.92	0:13.72	0:14.53
020	0:15.34	0:16.15	0:16.95	0:17.76	0:18.57	0:19.38	0:20.18	0:20.99	0:21.80	0:22.60
030	0:23.41	0:24.22	0:25.03	0:25.83	0:26.64	0:27.45	0:28.26	0:29.06	0:29.87	0:30.68
040	0:31.48	0:32.29	0:33.10	0:33.91	0:34.71	0:35.52	0:36.33	0:37.14	0:37.94	0:38.75
050	0:39.56	0:40.36	0:41.17	0:41.98	0:42.79	0:43.59	0:44.40	0:45.21	0:46.02	0:46.82
060	0:47.63	0:48.44	0:49.24	0:50.05	0:50.86	0:51.67	0:52.47	0:53.28	0:54.09	0:54.90
070	0:55.70	0:56.51	0:57.32	0:58.13	0:58.93	0:59.74	1:00.55	1:01.35	1:02.16	1:02.97
080	1:03.78	1:04.58	1:05.39	1:06.20	1:07.01	1:07.81	1:08.62	1:09.43	1:10.23	1:11.04
090	1:11.85	1:12.66	1:13.46	1:14.27	1:15.08	1:15.89	1:16.69	1:17.50	1:18.31	1:19.11
100	1:19.92	1:20.73	1:21.54	1:22.34	1:23.15	1:23.96	1:24.77	1:25.57	1:26.38	1:27.19
110	1:27.99	1:28.80	1:29.61	1:30.42	1:31.22	1:32.03	1:32.84	1:33.65	1:34.45	1:35.26
120	1:36.07	1:36.88	1:37.68	1:38.49	1:39.30	1:40.10	1:40.91	1:41.72	1:42.53	1:43.33
130	1:44.14	1:44.95	1:45.76	1:46.56	1:47.37	1:48.18	1:48.98	1:49.79	1:50.60	1:51.41
140	1:52.21	1:53.02	1:53.83	1:54.64	1:55.44	1:56.25	1:57.06	1:57.86	1:58.67	1:59.48
150	2:00.29	2:01.09	2:01.90	2:02.71	2:03.52	2:04.32	2:05.13	2:05.94	2:06.74	2:07.55
160	2:08.36	2:09.17	2:09.97	2:10.78	2:11.59	2:12.40	2:13.20	2:14.01	2:14.82	2:15.63
170	2:16.43	2:17.24	2:18.05	2:18.85	2:19.66	2:20.47	2:21.28	2:22.08	2:22.89	2:23.70
180	2:24.51	2:25.31	2:26.12	2:26.93	2:27.73	2:28.54	2:29.35	2:30.16	2:30.96	2:31.77
190	2:32.58	2:33.39	2:34.19	2:35.00	2:35.81	2:36.61	2:37.42	2:38.23	2:39.04	2:39.84
200	2:40.65	2:41.46	2:42.27	2:43.07	2:43.88	2:44.69	2:45.49	2:46.30	2:47.11	2:47.92
210	2:48.72	2:49.53	2:50.34	2:51.15	2:51.95	2:52.76	2:53.57	2:54.38	2:55.18	2:55.99
220	2:56.80	2:57.60	2:58.41	2:59.22	3:00.03	3:00.83	3:01.64	3:02.45	3:03.26	3:04.06
230	3:04.87	3:05.68	3:06.48	3:07.29	3:08.10	3:08.91	3:09.71	3:10.52	3:11.33	3:12.14
240	3:12.94	3:13.75	3:14.56	3:15.36	3:16.17	3:16.98	3:17.79	3:18.59	3:19.40	3:20.21
250	3:21.02	3:21.82	3:22.63	3:23.44	3:24.24	3:25.05	3:25.86	3:26.67	3:27.47	3:28.28
260	3:29.09	3:29.90	3:30.70	3:31.51	3:32.32	3:33.13	3:33.93	3:34.74	3:35.55	3:36.35
270	3:37.16	3:37.97	3:38.78	3:39.58	3:40.39	3:41.20	3:42.01	3:42.81	3:43.62	3:44.43
280	3:45.23	3:46.04	3:46.85	3:47.66	3:48.46	3:49.27	3:50.08	3:50.89	3:51.69	3:52.50
290	3:53.31	3:54.11	3:54.92	3:55.73	3:56.54	3:57.34	3:58.15	3:58.96	3:59.77	4:00.57
300	4:01.38	4:02.19	4:02.99	4:03.80	4:04.61	4:05.42	4:06.22	4:07.03	4:07.84	4:08.65
310	4:09.45	4:10.26	4:11.07	4:11.88	4:12.68	4:13.49	4:14.30	4:15.10	4:15.91	4:16.72
320	4:17.53	4:18.33	4:19.14	4:19.95	4:20.76	4:21.56	4:22.37	4:23.18	4:23.98	4:24.79
330	4:25.60	4:26.41	4:27.21	4:28.02	4:28.83	4:29.64	4:30.44	4:31.25	4:32.06	4:32.86
340	4:33.67	4:34.48	4:35.29	4:36.09	4:36.90	4:37.71	4:38.52	4:39.32	4:40.13	4:40.94
350	4:41.74	4:42.55	4:43.36	4:44.17	4:44.97	4:45.78	4:46.59	4:47.40	4:48.20	4:49.01
360	4:49.82	4:50.63	4:51.43	4:52.24	4:53.05	4:53.85	4:54.66	4:55.47	4:56.28	4:57.08
370	4:57.89	4:58.70	4:59.51	5:00.31	5:01.12	5:01.93	5:02.73	5:03.54	5:04.35	5:05.16
380	5:05.96	5:06.77	5:07.58	5:08.39	5:09.19	5:10.00	5:10.81	5:11.61	5:12.42	5:13.23
390	5:14.04	5:14.84	5:15.65	5:16.46	5:17.27	5:18.07	5:18.88	5:19.69	5:20.49	5:21.30
400	5:22.11	5:22.92	5:23.72	5:24.53	5:25.34	5:26.15	5:26.95	5:27.76	5:28.57	5:29.38
410	5:30.18	5:30.99	5:31.80	5:32.60	5:33.41	5:34.22	5:35.03	5:35.83	5:36.64	5:37.45
420	5:38.26	5:39.06	5:39.87	5:40.68	5:41.48	5:42.29	5:43.10	5:43.91	5:44.71	5:45.52
430	5:46.33	5:47.14	5:47.94	5:48.75	5:49.56	5:50.36	5:51.17	5:51.98	5:52.79	5:53.59
440	5:54.40	5:55.21	5:56.02	5:56.82	5:57.63	5:58.44	5:59.24	6:00.05	6:00.86	6:01.67
450	6:02.47	6:03.28	6:04.09	6:04.90	6:05.70	6:06.51	6:07.32	6:08.13	6:08.93	6:09.74
460	6:10.55	6:11.35	6:12.16	6:12.97	6:13.78	6:14.58	6:15.39	6:16.20	6:17.01	6:17.81
470	6:18.62	6:19.43	6:20.23	6:21.04	6:21.85	6:22.66	6:23.46	6:24.27	6:25.08	6:25.89
480	6:26.69	6:27.50	6:28.31	6:29.11	6:29.92	6:30.73	6:31.54	6:32.34	6:33.15	6:33.96
490	6:34.77	6:35.57	6:36.38	6:37.19	6:37.99	6:38.80	6:39.61	6:40.42	6:41.22	6:42.03
500	6:42.84	6:43.65	6:44.45	6:45.26	6:46.07	6:46.88	6:47.68	6:48.49	6:49.30	6:50.10
510	6:50.91	6:51.72	6:52.53	6:53.33	6:54.14	6:54.95	6:55.76	6:56.56	6:57.37	6:58.18
520	6:58.98	6:59.79	7:00.60	7:01.41	7:02.21	7:03.02	7:03.83	7:04.64	7:05.44	7:06.25
530	7:07.06	7:07.86	7:08.67	7:09.48	7:10.29	7:11.09	7:11.90	7:12.71	7:13.52	7:14.32
540	7:15.13	7:15.94	7:16.74	7:17.55	7:18.36	7:19.17	7:19.97	7:20.78	7:21.59	7:22.40
550	7:23.20	7:24.01	7:24.82	7:25.63	7:26.43	7:27.24	7:28.05	7:28.85	7:29.66	7:30.47
560	7:31.28	7:32.08	7:32.89	7:33.70	7:34.51	7:35.31	7:36.12	7:36.93	7:37.73	7:38.54
570	7:39.35	7:40.16	7:40.96	7:41.77	7:42.58	7:43.39	7:44.19	7:45.00	7:45.81	7:46.61
580	7:47.42	7:48.23	7:49.04	7:49.84	7:50.65	7:51.46	7:52.27	7:53.07	7:53.88	7:54.69
590	7:55.49	7:56.30	7:57.11	7:57.92	7:58.72	7:59.53	8:00.34	8:01.15	8:01.95	8:02.76

♩. = 1.21; ♩ = 0.81; ♪. = 0.61; (triplet: ♩ 𝄾) = 0.54; ♪ = 0.40; (triplet: ♪ 𝄾 𝄾) = 0.27; 𝅘𝅥𝅯 = 0.20 seconds

CLICK: 19 4/8 FRAMES; M.M.: 73.85

Click	0	1	2	3	4	5	6	7	8	9
000	0:00.00	0:00.00	0:00.81	0:01.63	0:02.44	0:03.25	0:04.06	0:04.88	0:05.69	0:06.50
010	0:07.31	0:08.13	0:08.94	0:09.75	0:10.56	0:11.38	0:12.19	0:13.00	0:13.81	0:14.63
020	0:15.44	0:16.25	0:17.06	0:17.88	0:18.69	0:19.50	0:20.31	0:21.13	0:21.94	0:22.75
030	0:23.56	0:24.38	0:25.19	0:26.00	0:26.81	0:27.63	0:28.44	0:29.25	0:30.06	0:30.88
040	0:31.69	0:32.50	0:33.31	0:34.13	0:34.94	0:35.75	0:36.56	0:37.38	0:38.19	0:39.00
050	0:39.81	0:40.63	0:41.44	0:42.25	0:43.06	0:43.88	0:44.69	0:45.50	0:46.31	0:47.13
060	0:47.94	0:48.75	0:49.56	0:50.38	0:51.19	0:52.00	0:52.81	0:53.63	0:54.44	0:55.25
070	0:56.06	0:56.88	0:57.69	0:58.50	0:59.31	1:00.12	1:00.94	1:01.75	1:02.56	1:03.37
080	1:04.19	1:05.00	1:05.81	1:06.62	1:07.44	1:08.25	1:09.06	1:09.88	1:10.69	1:11.50
090	1:12.31	1:13.13	1:13.94	1:14.75	1:15.56	1:16.38	1:17.19	1:18.00	1:18.81	1:19.63
100	1:20.44	1:21.25	1:22.06	1:22.88	1:23.69	1:24.50	1:25.31	1:26.13	1:26.94	1:27.75
110	1:28.56	1:29.38	1:30.19	1:31.00	1:31.81	1:32.63	1:33.44	1:34.25	1:35.06	1:35.88
120	1:36.69	1:37.50	1:38.31	1:39.13	1:39.94	1:40.75	1:41.56	1:42.38	1:43.19	1:44.00
130	1:44.81	1:45.62	1:46.44	1:47.25	1:48.06	1:48.88	1:49.69	1:50.50	1:51.31	1:52.13
140	1:52.94	1:53.75	1:54.56	1:55.38	1:56.19	1:57.00	1:57.81	1:58.63	1:59.44	2:00.25
150	2:01.06	2:01.88	2:02.69	2:03.50	2:04.31	2:05.13	2:05.94	2:06.75	2:07.56	2:08.38
160	2:09.19	2:10.00	2:10.81	2:11.62	2:12.44	2:13.25	2:14.06	2:14.88	2:15.69	2:16.50
170	2:17.31	2:18.12	2:18.94	2:19.75	2:20.56	2:21.38	2:22.19	2:23.00	2:23.81	2:24.62
180	2:25.44	2:26.25	2:27.06	2:27.88	2:28.69	2:29.50	2:30.31	2:31.12	2:31.94	2:32.75
190	2:33.56	2:34.38	2:35.19	2:36.00	2:36.81	2:37.63	2:38.44	2:39.25	2:40.06	2:40.88
200	2:41.69	2:42.50	2:43.31	2:44.13	2:44.94	2:45.75	2:46.56	2:47.38	2:48.19	2:49.00
210	2:49.81	2:50.63	2:51.44	2:52.25	2:53.06	2:53.88	2:54.69	2:55.50	2:56.31	2:57.13
220	2:57.94	2:58.75	2:59.56	3:00.38	3:01.19	3:02.00	3:02.81	3:03.63	3:04.44	3:05.25
230	3:06.06	3:06.87	3:07.69	3:08.50	3:09.31	3:10.13	3:10.94	3:11.75	3:12.56	3:13.37
240	3:14.19	3:15.00	3:15.81	3:16.63	3:17.44	3:18.25	3:19.06	3:19.87	3:20.69	3:21.50
250	3:22.31	3:23.13	3:23.94	3:24.75	3:25.56	3:26.37	3:27.19	3:28.00	3:28.81	3:29.63
260	3:30.44	3:31.25	3:32.06	3:32.88	3:33.69	3:34.50	3:35.31	3:36.13	3:36.94	3:37.75
270	3:38.56	3:39.38	3:40.19	3:41.00	3:41.81	3:42.63	3:43.44	3:44.25	3:45.06	3:45.88
280	3:46.69	3:47.50	3:48.31	3:49.13	3:49.94	3:50.75	3:51.56	3:52.38	3:53.19	3:54.00
290	3:54.81	3:55.62	3:56.44	3:57.25	3:58.06	3:58.88	3:59.69	4:00.50	4:01.31	4:02.12
300	4:02.94	4:03.75	4:04.56	4:05.38	4:06.19	4:07.00	4:07.81	4:08.63	4:09.44	4:10.25
310	4:11.06	4:11.87	4:12.69	4:13.50	4:14.31	4:15.12	4:15.94	4:16.75	4:17.56	4:18.38
320	4:19.19	4:20.00	4:20.81	4:21.63	4:22.44	4:23.25	4:24.06	4:24.87	4:25.69	4:26.50
330	4:27.31	4:28.13	4:28.94	4:29.75	4:30.56	4:31.38	4:32.19	4:33.00	4:33.81	4:34.63
340	4:35.44	4:36.25	4:37.06	4:37.87	4:38.69	4:39.50	4:40.31	4:41.13	4:41.94	4:42.75
350	4:43.56	4:44.38	4:45.19	4:46.00	4:46.81	4:47.62	4:48.44	4:49.25	4:50.06	4:50.87
360	4:51.69	4:52.50	4:53.31	4:54.13	4:54.94	4:55.75	4:56.56	4:57.38	4:58.19	4:59.00
370	4:59.81	5:00.62	5:01.44	5:02.25	5:03.06	5:03.87	5:04.69	5:05.50	5:06.31	5:07.13
380	5:07.94	5:08.75	5:09.56	5:10.38	5:11.19	5:12.00	5:12.81	5:13.62	5:14.44	5:15.25
390	5:16.06	5:16.88	5:17.69	5:18.50	5:19.31	5:20.13	5:20.94	5:21.75	5:22.56	5:23.38
400	5:24.19	5:25.00	5:25.81	5:26.62	5:27.44	5:28.25	5:29.06	5:29.88	5:30.69	5:31.50
410	5:32.31	5:33.13	5:33.94	5:34.75	5:35.56	5:36.38	5:37.19	5:38.00	5:38.81	5:39.62
420	5:40.44	5:41.25	5:42.06	5:42.88	5:43.69	5:44.50	5:45.31	5:46.13	5:46.94	5:47.75
430	5:48.56	5:49.37	5:50.19	5:51.00	5:51.81	5:52.63	5:53.44	5:54.25	5:55.06	5:55.88
440	5:56.69	5:57.50	5:58.31	5:59.13	5:59.94	6:00.75	6:01.56	6:02.37	6:03.19	6:04.00
450	6:04.81	6:05.63	6:06.44	6:07.25	6:08.06	6:08.88	6:09.69	6:10.50	6:11.31	6:12.13
460	6:12.94	6:13.75	6:14.56	6:15.37	6:16.19	6:17.00	6:17.81	6:18.63	6:19.44	6:20.25
470	6:21.06	6:21.88	6:22.69	6:23.50	6:24.31	6:25.13	6:25.94	6:26.75	6:27.56	6:28.37
480	6:29.19	6:30.00	6:30.81	6:31.63	6:32.44	6:33.25	6:34.06	6:34.88	6:35.69	6:36.50
490	6:37.31	6:38.12	6:38.94	6:39.75	6:40.56	6:41.38	6:42.19	6:43.00	6:43.81	6:44.63
500	6:45.44	6:46.25	6:47.06	6:47.88	6:48.69	6:49.50	6:50.31	6:51.12	6:51.94	6:52.75
510	6:53.56	6:54.38	6:55.19	6:56.00	6:56.81	6:57.63	6:58.44	6:59.25	7:00.06	7:00.88
520	7:01.69	7:02.50	7:03.31	7:04.12	7:04.94	7:05.75	7:06.56	7:07.38	7:08.19	7:09.00
530	7:09.81	7:10.63	7:11.44	7:12.25	7:13.06	7:13.88	7:14.69	7:15.50	7:16.31	7:17.12
540	7:17.94	7:18.75	7:19.56	7:20.38	7:21.19	7:22.00	7:22.81	7:23.63	7:24.44	7:25.25
550	7:26.06	7:26.87	7:27.69	7:28.50	7:29.31	7:30.12	7:30.94	7:31.75	7:32.56	7:33.38
560	7:34.19	7:35.00	7:35.81	7:36.63	7:37.44	7:38.25	7:39.06	7:39.87	7:40.69	7:41.50
570	7:42.31	7:43.13	7:43.94	7:44.75	7:45.56	7:46.38	7:47.19	7:48.00	7:48.81	7:49.63
580	7:50.44	7:51.25	7:52.06	7:52.87	7:53.69	7:54.50	7:55.31	7:56.13	7:56.94	7:57.75
590	7:58.56	7:59.38	8:00.19	8:01.00	8:01.81	8:02.62	8:03.44	8:04.25	8:05.06	8:05.87

♩. = 1.22; ♩ = 0.81; ♪. = 0.61; (triplet 3) ♩ 𝄾 = 0.54; ♪ = 0.41; (triplet 3) ♪𝄾𝄾 = 0.27; 𝅘𝅥𝅯 = 0.20 seconds

CLICK: 19⅝ FRAMES; M.M.: 73.38

Click	0	1	2	3	4	5	6	7	8	9
000	0:00.00	0:00.00	0:00.82	0:01.64	0:02.45	0:03.27	0:04.09	0:04.91	0:05.72	0:06.54
010	0:07.36	0:08.18	0:08.99	0:09.81	0:10.63	0:11.45	0:12.27	0:13.08	0:13.90	0:14.72
020	0:15.54	0:16.35	0:17.17	0:17.99	0:18.81	0:19.63	0:20.44	0:21.26	0:22.08	0:22.90
030	0:23.71	0:24.53	0:25.35	0:26.17	0:26.98	0:27.80	0:28.62	0:29.44	0:30.26	0:31.07
040	0:31.89	0:32.71	0:33.53	0:34.34	0:35.16	0:35.98	0:36.80	0:37.61	0:38.43	0:39.25
050	0:40.07	0:40.89	0:41.70	0:42.52	0:43.34	0:44.16	0:44.97	0:45.79	0:46.61	0:47.43
060	0:48.24	0:49.06	0:49.88	0:50.70	0:51.52	0:52.33	0:53.15	0:53.97	0:54.79	0:55.60
070	0:56.42	0:57.24	0:58.06	0:58.88	0:59.69	1:00.51	1:01.33	1:02.15	1:02.96	1:03.78
080	1:04.60	1:05.42	1:06.23	1:07.05	1:07.87	1:08.69	1:09.51	1:10.32	1:11.14	1:11.96
090	1:12.78	1:13.59	1:14.41	1:15.23	1:16.05	1:16.86	1:17.68	1:18.50	1:19.32	1:20.14
100	1:20.95	1:21.77	1:22.59	1:23.41	1:24.22	1:25.04	1:25.86	1:26.68	1:27.49	1:28.31
110	1:29.13	1:29.95	1:30.77	1:31.58	1:32.40	1:33.22	1:34.04	1:34.85	1:35.67	1:36.49
120	1:37.31	1:38.12	1:38.94	1:39.76	1:40.58	1:41.40	1:42.21	1:43.03	1:43.85	1:44.67
130	1:45.48	1:46.30	1:47.12	1:47.94	1:48.76	1:49.57	1:50.39	1:51.21	1:52.03	1:52.84
140	1:53.66	1:54.48	1:55.30	1:56.11	1:56.93	1:57.75	1:58.57	1:59.39	2:00.20	2:01.02
150	2:01.84	2:02.66	2:03.47	2:04.29	2:05.11	2:05.93	2:06.74	2:07.56	2:08.38	2:09.20
160	2:10.02	2:10.83	2:11.65	2:12.47	2:13.29	2:14.10	2:14.92	2:15.74	2:16.56	2:17.37
170	2:18.19	2:19.01	2:19.83	2:20.65	2:21.46	2:22.28	2:23.10	2:23.92	2:24.73	2:25.55
180	2:26.37	2:27.19	2:28.01	2:28.82	2:29.64	2:30.46	2:31.28	2:32.09	2:32.91	2:33.73
190	2:34.55	2:35.36	2:36.18	2:37.00	2:37.82	2:38.64	2:39.45	2:40.27	2:41.09	2:41.91
200	2:42.72	2:43.54	2:44.36	2:45.18	2:45.99	2:46.81	2:47.63	2:48.45	2:49.27	2:50.08
210	2:50.90	2:51.72	2:52.54	2:53.35	2:54.17	2:54.99	2:55.81	2:56.62	2:57.44	2:58.26
220	2:59.08	2:59.90	3:00.71	3:01.53	3:02.35	3:03.17	3:03.98	3:04.80	3:05.62	3:06.44
230	3:07.26	3:08.07	3:08.89	3:09.71	3:10.53	3:11.34	3:12.16	3:12.98	3:13.80	3:14.61
240	3:15.43	3:16.25	3:17.07	3:17.89	3:18.70	3:19.52	3:20.34	3:21.16	3:21.97	3:22.79
250	3:23.61	3:24.43	3:25.24	3:26.06	3:26.88	3:27.70	3:28.52	3:29.33	3:30.15	3:30.97
260	3:31.79	3:32.60	3:33.42	3:34.24	3:35.06	3:35.87	3:36.69	3:37.51	3:38.33	3:39.15
270	3:39.96	3:40.78	3:41.60	3:42.42	3:43.23	3:44.05	3:44.87	3:45.69	3:46.51	3:47.32
280	3:48.14	3:48.96	3:49.78	3:50.59	3:51.41	3:52.23	3:53.05	3:53.86	3:54.68	3:55.50
290	3:56.32	3:57.14	3:57.95	3:58.77	3:59.59	4:00.41	4:01.22	4:02.04	4:02.86	4:03.68
300	4:04.49	4:05.31	4:06.13	4:06.95	4:07.77	4:08.58	4:09.40	4:10.22	4:11.04	4:11.85
310	4:12.67	4:13.49	4:14.31	4:15.12	4:15.94	4:16.76	4:17.58	4:18.40	4:19.21	4:20.03
320	4:20.85	4:21.67	4:22.48	4:23.30	4:24.12	4:24.94	4:25.76	4:26.57	4:27.39	4:28.21
330	4:29.03	4:29.84	4:30.66	4:31.48	4:32.30	4:33.11	4:33.93	4:34.75	4:35.57	4:36.39
340	4:37.20	4:38.02	4:38.84	4:39.66	4:40.47	4:41.29	4:42.11	4:42.93	4:43.74	4:44.56
350	4:45.38	4:46.20	4:47.02	4:47.83	4:48.65	4:49.47	4:50.29	4:51.10	4:51.92	4:52.74
360	4:53.56	4:54.38	4:55.19	4:56.01	4:56.83	4:57.65	4:58.46	4:59.28	5:00.10	5:00.92
370	5:01.73	5:02.55	5:03.37	5:04.19	5:05.01	5:05.82	5:06.64	5:07.46	5:08.28	5:09.09
380	5:09.91	5:10.73	5:11.55	5:12.36	5:13.18	5:14.00	5:14.82	5:15.64	5:16.45	5:17.27
390	5:18.09	5:18.91	5:19.72	5:20.54	5:21.36	5:22.18	5:22.99	5:23.81	5:24.63	5:25.45
400	5:26.27	5:27.08	5:27.90	5:28.72	5:29.54	5:30.35	5:31.17	5:31.99	5:32.81	5:33.62
410	5:34.44	5:35.26	5:36.08	5:36.90	5:37.71	5:38.53	5:39.35	5:40.17	5:40.98	5:41.80
420	5:42.62	5:43.44	5:44.26	5:45.07	5:45.89	5:46.71	5:47.53	5:48.34	5:49.16	5:49.98
430	5:50.80	5:51.61	5:52.43	5:53.25	5:54.07	5:54.89	5:55.70	5:56.52	5:57.34	5:58.16
440	5:58.97	5:59.79	6:00.61	6:01.43	6:02.24	6:03.06	6:03.88	6:04.70	6:05.52	6:06.33
450	6:07.15	6:07.97	6:08.79	6:09.60	6:10.42	6:11.24	6:12.06	6:12.87	6:13.69	6:14.51
460	6:15.33	6:16.15	6:16.96	6:17.78	6:18.60	6:19.42	6:20.23	6:21.05	6:21.87	6:22.69
470	6:23.51	6:24.32	6:25.14	6:25.96	6:26.78	6:27.59	6:28.41	6:29.23	6:30.05	6:30.86
480	6:31.68	6:32.50	6:33.32	6:34.14	6:34.95	6:35.77	6:36.59	6:37.41	6:38.22	6:39.04
490	6:39.86	6:40.68	6:41.49	6:42.31	6:43.13	6:43.95	6:44.77	6:45.58	6:46.40	6:47.22
500	6:48.04	6:48.85	6:49.67	6:50.49	6:51.31	6:52.12	6:52.94	6:53.76	6:54.58	6:55.40
510	6:56.21	6:57.03	6:57.85	6:58.67	6:59.48	7:00.30	7:01.12	7:01.94	7:02.76	7:03.57
520	7:04.39	7:05.21	7:06.03	7:06.84	7:07.66	7:08.48	7:09.30	7:10.11	7:10.93	7:11.75
530	7:12.57	7:13.39	7:14.20	7:15.02	7:15.84	7:16.66	7:17.47	7:18.29	7:19.11	7:19.93
540	7:20.74	7:21.56	7:22.38	7:23.20	7:24.02	7:24.83	7:25.65	7:26.47	7:27.29	7:28.10
550	7:28.92	7:29.74	7:30.56	7:31.37	7:32.19	7:33.01	7:33.83	7:34.65	7:35.46	7:36.28
560	7:37.10	7:37.92	7:38.73	7:39.55	7:40.37	7:41.19	7:42.01	7:42.82	7:43.64	7:44.46
570	7:45.28	7:46.09	7:46.91	7:47.73	7:48.55	7:49.36	7:50.18	7:51.00	7:51.82	7:52.64
580	7:53.45	7:54.27	7:55.09	7:55.91	7:56.72	7:57.54	7:58.36	7:59.18	7:59.99	8:00.81
590	8:01.63	8:02.45	8:03.27	8:04.08	8:04.90	8:05.72	8:06.54	8:07.35	8:08.17	8:08.99

♩. = 1.23; ♩ = 0.82; ♪. = 0.61; (3) ♩ 𝄾 = 0.55; ♪ = 0.41; (3) ♪𝄾𝄾 = 0.27; 𝅘𝅥𝅯 = 0.20 seconds

CLICK: 19 6/8 FRAMES; M.M.: 72.91

Click	0	1	2	3	4	5	6	7	8	9
000	0:00.00	0:00.00	0:00.82	0:01.65	0:02.47	0:03.29	0:04.11	0:04.94	0:05.76	0:06.58
010	0:07.41	0:08.23	0:09.05	0:09.88	0:10.70	0:11.52	0:12.34	0:13.17	0:13.99	0:14.81
020	0:15.64	0:16.46	0:17.28	0:18.10	0:18.93	0:19.75	0:20.57	0:21.40	0:22.22	0:23.04
030	0:23.86	0:24.69	0:25.51	0:26.33	0:27.16	0:27.98	0:28.80	0:29.62	0:30.45	0:31.27
040	0:32.09	0:32.92	0:33.74	0:34.56	0:35.39	0:36.21	0:37.03	0:37.85	0:38.68	0:39.50
050	0:40.32	0:41.15	0:41.97	0:42.79	0:43.61	0:44.44	0:45.26	0:46.08	0:46.91	0:47.73
060	0:48.55	0:49.37	0:50.20	0:51.02	0:51.84	0:52.67	0:53.49	0:54.31	0:55.14	0:55.96
070	0:56.78	0:57.60	0:58.43	0:59.25	1:00.07	1:00.90	1:01.72	1:02.54	1:03.36	1:04.19
080	1:05.01	1:05.83	1:06.66	1:07.48	1:08.30	1:09.12	1:09.95	1:10.77	1:11.59	1:12.42
090	1:13.24	1:14.06	1:14.89	1:15.71	1:16.53	1:17.35	1:18.18	1:19.00	1:19.82	1:20.65
100	1:21.47	1:22.29	1:23.11	1:23.94	1:24.76	1:25.58	1:26.41	1:27.23	1:28.05	1:28.87
110	1:29.70	1:30.52	1:31.34	1:32.17	1:32.99	1:33.81	1:34.64	1:35.46	1:36.28	1:37.10
120	1:37.93	1:38.75	1:39.57	1:40.40	1:41.22	1:42.04	1:42.86	1:43.69	1:44.51	1:45.33
130	1:46.16	1:46.98	1:47.80	1:48.62	1:49.45	1:50.27	1:51.09	1:51.92	1:52.74	1:53.56
140	1:54.39	1:55.21	1:56.03	1:56.85	1:57.68	1:58.50	1:59.32	2:00.15	2:00.97	2:01.79
150	2:02.61	2:03.44	2:04.26	2:05.08	2:05.91	2:06.73	2:07.55	2:08.38	2:09.20	2:10.02
160	2:10.84	2:11.67	2:12.49	2:13.31	2:14.14	2:14.96	2:15.78	2:16.60	2:17.43	2:18.25
170	2:19.07	2:19.90	2:20.72	2:21.54	2:22.36	2:23.19	2:24.01	2:24.83	2:25.66	2:26.48
180	2:27.30	2:28.13	2:28.95	2:29.77	2:30.59	2:31.42	2:32.24	2:33.06	2:33.89	2:34.71
190	2:35.53	2:36.35	2:37.18	2:38.00	2:38.82	2:39.65	2:40.47	2:41.29	2:42.11	2:42.94
200	2:43.76	2:44.58	2:45.41	2:46.23	2:47.05	2:47.88	2:48.70	2:49.52	2:50.34	2:51.17
210	2:51.99	2:52.81	2:53.64	2:54.46	2:55.28	2:56.10	2:56.93	2:57.75	2:58.57	2:59.40
220	3:00.22	3:01.04	3:01.86	3:02.69	3:03.51	3:04.33	3:05.16	3:05.98	3:06.80	3:07.62
230	3:08.45	3:09.27	3:10.09	3:10.92	3:11.74	3:12.56	3:13.39	3:14.21	3:15.03	3:15.85
240	3:16.68	3:17.50	3:18.32	3:19.15	3:19.97	3:20.79	3:21.61	3:22.44	3:23.26	3:24.08
250	3:24.91	3:25.73	3:26.55	3:27.37	3:28.20	3:29.02	3:29.84	3:30.67	3:31.49	3:32.31
260	3:33.14	3:33.96	3:34.78	3:35.60	3:36.43	3:37.25	3:38.07	3:38.90	3:39.72	3:40.54
270	3:41.36	3:42.19	3:43.01	3:43.83	3:44.66	3:45.48	3:46.30	3:47.12	3:47.95	3:48.77
280	3:49.59	3:50.42	3:51.24	3:52.06	3:52.89	3:53.71	3:54.53	3:55.35	3:56.18	3:57.00
290	3:57.82	3:58.65	3:59.47	4:00.29	4:01.11	4:01.94	4:02.76	4:03.58	4:04.41	4:05.23
300	4:06.05	4:06.87	4:07.70	4:08.52	4:09.34	4:10.17	4:10.99	4:11.81	4:12.64	4:13.46
310	4:14.28	4:15.10	4:15.93	4:16.75	4:17.57	4:18.40	4:19.22	4:20.04	4:20.86	4:21.69
320	4:22.51	4:23.33	4:24.16	4:24.98	4:25.80	4:26.62	4:27.45	4:28.27	4:29.09	4:29.92
330	4:30.74	4:31.56	4:32.39	4:33.21	4:34.03	4:34.85	4:35.68	4:36.50	4:37.32	4:38.15
340	4:38.97	4:39.79	4:40.61	4:41.44	4:42.26	4:43.08	4:43.91	4:44.73	4:45.55	4:46.37
350	4:47.20	4:48.02	4:48.84	4:49.67	4:50.49	4:51.31	4:52.14	4:52.96	4:53.78	4:54.60
360	4:55.43	4:56.25	4:57.07	4:57.90	4:58.72	4:59.54	5:00.36	5:01.19	5:02.01	5:02.83
370	5:03.66	5:04.48	5:05.30	5:06.12	5:06.95	5:07.77	5:08.59	5:09.42	5:10.24	5:11.06
380	5:11.89	5:12.71	5:13.53	5:14.35	5:15.18	5:16.00	5:16.82	5:17.65	5:18.47	5:19.29
390	5:20.11	5:20.94	5:21.76	5:22.58	5:23.41	5:24.23	5:25.05	5:25.88	5:26.70	5:27.52
400	5:28.34	5:29.17	5:29.99	5:30.81	5:31.64	5:32.46	5:33.28	5:34.10	5:34.93	5:35.75
410	5:36.57	5:37.40	5:38.22	5:39.04	5:39.86	5:40.69	5:41.51	5:42.33	5:43.16	5:43.98
420	5:44.80	5:45.62	5:46.45	5:47.27	5:48.09	5:48.92	5:49.74	5:50.56	5:51.39	5:52.21
430	5:53.03	5:53.85	5:54.68	5:55.50	5:56.32	5:57.15	5:57.97	5:58.79	5:59.61	6:00.44
440	6:01.26	6:02.08	6:02.91	6:03.73	6:04.55	6:05.38	6:06.20	6:07.02	6:07.84	6:08.67
450	6:09.49	6:10.31	6:11.14	6:11.96	6:12.78	6:13.60	6:14.43	6:15.25	6:16.07	6:16.90
460	6:17.72	6:18.54	6:19.36	6:20.19	6:21.01	6:21.83	6:22.66	6:23.48	6:24.30	6:25.12
470	6:25.95	6:26.77	6:27.59	6:28.42	6:29.24	6:30.06	6:30.89	6:31.71	6:32.53	6:33.35
480	6:34.18	6:35.00	6:35.82	6:36.65	6:37.47	6:38.29	6:39.11	6:39.94	6:40.76	6:41.58
490	6:42.41	6:43.23	6:44.05	6:44.88	6:45.70	6:46.52	6:47.34	6:48.17	6:48.99	6:49.81
500	6:50.64	6:51.46	6:52.28	6:53.10	6:53.93	6:54.75	6:55.57	6:56.40	6:57.22	6:58.04
510	6:58.86	6:59.69	7:00.51	7:01.33	7:02.16	7:02.98	7:03.80	7:04.62	7:05.45	7:06.27
520	7:07.09	7:07.92	7:08.74	7:09.56	7:10.39	7:11.21	7:12.03	7:12.85	7:13.68	7:14.50
530	7:15.32	7:16.15	7:16.97	7:17.79	7:18.61	7:19.44	7:20.26	7:21.08	7:21.91	7:22.73
540	7:23.55	7:24.38	7:25.20	7:26.02	7:26.84	7:27.67	7:28.49	7:29.31	7:30.14	7:30.96
550	7:31.78	7:32.60	7:33.43	7:34.25	7:35.07	7:35.90	7:36.72	7:37.54	7:38.36	7:39.19
560	7:40.01	7:40.83	7:41.66	7:42.48	7:43.30	7:44.12	7:44.95	7:45.77	7:46.59	7:47.42
570	7:48.24	7:49.06	7:49.89	7:50.71	7:51.53	7:52.35	7:53.18	7:54.00	7:54.82	7:55.65
580	7:56.47	7:57.29	7:58.11	7:58.94	7:59.76	8:00.58	8:01.41	8:02.23	8:03.05	8:03.87
590	8:04.70	8:05.52	8:06.34	8:07.17	8:07.99	8:08.81	8:09.64	8:10.46	8:11.28	8:12.10

♩. = 1.23; ♩ = 0.82; ♪. = 0.62; (triplet ♩ 𝄾) = 0.55; ♪ = 0.41; (triplet ♪ 𝄾 𝄾) = 0.27; 𝅘𝅥𝅯 = 0.21 seconds

CLICK: 19⅞ FRAMES; M.M.: 72.45

Click	0	1	2	3	4	5	6	7	8	9
000	0:00.00	0:00.00	0:00.83	0:01.66	0:02.48	0:03.31	0:04.14	0:04.97	0:05.80	0:06.63
010	0:07.45	0:08.28	0:09.11	0:09.94	0:10.77	0:11.59	0:12.42	0:13.25	0:14.08	0:14.91
020	0:15.73	0:16.56	0:17.39	0:18.22	0:19.05	0:19.88	0:20.70	0:21.53	0:22.36	0:23.19
030	0:24.02	0:24.84	0:25.67	0:26.50	0:27.33	0:28.16	0:28.98	0:29.81	0:30.64	0:31.47
040	0:32.30	0:33.13	0:33.95	0:34.78	0:35.61	0:36.44	0:37.27	0:38.09	0:38.92	0:39.75
050	0:40.58	0:41.41	0:42.23	0:43.06	0:43.89	0:44.72	0:45.55	0:46.38	0:47.20	0:48.03
060	0:48.86	0:49.69	0:50.52	0:51.34	0:52.17	0:53.00	0:53.83	0:54.66	0:55.48	0:56.31
070	0:57.14	0:57.97	0:58.80	0:59.63	1:00.45	1:01.28	1:02.11	1:02.94	1:03.77	1:04.59
080	1:05.42	1:06.25	1:07.08	1:07.91	1:08.73	1:09.56	1:10.39	1:11.22	1:12.05	1:12.88
090	1:13.70	1:14.53	1:15.36	1:16.19	1:17.02	1:17.84	1:18.67	1:19.50	1:20.33	1:21.16
100	1:21.98	1:22.81	1:23.64	1:24.47	1:25.30	1:26.13	1:26.95	1:27.78	1:28.61	1:29.44
110	1:30.27	1:31.09	1:31.92	1:32.75	1:33.58	1:34.41	1:35.23	1:36.06	1:36.89	1:37.72
120	1:38.55	1:39.38	1:40.20	1:41.03	1:41.86	1:42.69	1:43.52	1:44.34	1:45.17	1:46.00
130	1:46.83	1:47.66	1:48.48	1:49.31	1:50.14	1:50.97	1:51.80	1:52.63	1:53.45	1:54.28
140	1:55.11	1:55.94	1:56.77	1:57.59	1:58.42	1:59.25	2:00.08	2:00.91	2:01.73	2:02.56
150	2:03.39	2:04.22	2:05.05	2:05.88	2:06.70	2:07.53	2:08.36	2:09.19	2:10.02	2:10.84
160	2:11.67	2:12.50	2:13.33	2:14.16	2:14.98	2:15.81	2:16.64	2:17.47	2:18.30	2:19.13
170	2:19.95	2:20.78	2:21.61	2:22.44	2:23.27	2:24.09	2:24.92	2:25.75	2:26.58	2:27.41
180	2:28.23	2:29.06	2:29.89	2:30.72	2:31.55	2:32.38	2:33.20	2:34.03	2:34.86	2:35.69
190	2:36.52	2:37.34	2:38.17	2:39.00	2:39.83	2:40.66	2:41.48	2:42.31	2:43.14	2:43.97
200	2:44.80	2:45.63	2:46.45	2:47.28	2:48.11	2:48.94	2:49.77	2:50.59	2:51.42	2:52.25
210	2:53.08	2:53.91	2:54.73	2:55.56	2:56.39	2:57.22	2:58.05	2:58.88	2:59.70	3:00.53
220	3:01.36	3:02.19	3:03.02	3:03.84	3:04.67	3:05.50	3:06.33	3:07.16	3:07.98	3:08.81
230	3:09.64	3:10.47	3:11.30	3:12.13	3:12.95	3:13.78	3:14.61	3:15.44	3:16.27	3:17.09
240	3:17.92	3:18.75	3:19.58	3:20.41	3:21.23	3:22.06	3:22.89	3:23.72	3:24.55	3:25.38
250	3:26.20	3:27.03	3:27.86	3:28.69	3:29.52	3:30.34	3:31.17	3:32.00	3:32.83	3:33.66
260	3:34.48	3:35.31	3:36.14	3:36.97	3:37.80	3:38.63	3:39.45	3:40.28	3:41.11	3:41.94
270	3:42.77	3:43.59	3:44.42	3:45.25	3:46.08	3:46.91	3:47.73	3:48.56	3:49.39	3:50.22
280	3:51.05	3:51.88	3:52.70	3:53.53	3:54.36	3:55.19	3:56.02	3:56.84	3:57.67	3:58.50
290	3:59.33	4:00.16	4:00.98	4:01.81	4:02.64	4:03.47	4:04.30	4:05.13	4:05.95	4:06.78
300	4:07.61	4:08.44	4:09.27	4:10.09	4:10.92	4:11.75	4:12.58	4:13.41	4:14.23	4:15.06
310	4:15.89	4:16.72	4:17.55	4:18.38	4:19.20	4:20.03	4:20.86	4:21.69	4:22.52	4:23.34
320	4:24.17	4:25.00	4:25.83	4:26.66	4:27.48	4:28.31	4:29.14	4:29.97	4:30.80	4:31.63
330	4:32.45	4:33.28	4:34.11	4:34.94	4:35.77	4:36.59	4:37.42	4:38.25	4:39.08	4:39.91
340	4:40.73	4:41.56	4:42.39	4:43.22	4:44.05	4:44.88	4:45.70	4:46.53	4:47.36	4:48.19
350	4:49.02	4:49.84	4:50.67	4:51.50	4:52.33	4:53.16	4:53.98	4:54.81	4:55.64	4:56.47
360	4:57.30	4:58.13	4:58.95	4:59.78	5:00.61	5:01.44	5:02.27	5:03.09	5:03.92	5:04.75
370	5:05.58	5:06.41	5:07.23	5:08.06	5:08.89	5:09.72	5:10.55	5:11.38	5:12.20	5:13.03
380	5:13.86	5:14.69	5:15.52	5:16.34	5:17.17	5:18.00	5:18.83	5:19.66	5:20.48	5:21.31
390	5:22.14	5:22.97	5:23.80	5:24.63	5:25.45	5:26.28	5:27.11	5:27.94	5:28.77	5:29.59
400	5:30.42	5:31.25	5:32.08	5:32.91	5:33.73	5:34.56	5:35.39	5:36.22	5:37.05	5:37.88
410	5:38.70	5:39.53	5:40.36	5:41.19	5:42.02	5:42.84	5:43.67	5:44.50	5:45.33	5:46.16
420	5:46.98	5:47.81	5:48.64	5:49.47	5:50.30	5:51.13	5:51.95	5:52.78	5:53.61	5:54.44
430	5:55.27	5:56.09	5:56.92	5:57.75	5:58.58	5:59.41	6:00.23	6:01.06	6:01.89	6:02.72
440	6:03.55	6:04.38	6:05.20	6:06.03	6:06.86	6:07.69	6:08.52	6:09.34	6:10.17	6:11.00
450	6:11.83	6:12.66	6:13.48	6:14.31	6:15.14	6:15.97	6:16.80	6:17.63	6:18.45	6:19.28
460	6:20.11	6:20.94	6:21.77	6:22.59	6:23.42	6:24.25	6:25.08	6:25.91	6:26.73	6:27.56
470	6:28.39	6:29.22	6:30.05	6:30.88	6:31.70	6:32.53	6:33.36	6:34.19	6:35.02	6:35.84
480	6:36.67	6:37.50	6:38.33	6:39.16	6:39.98	6:40.81	6:41.64	6:42.47	6:43.30	6:44.13
490	6:44.95	6:45.78	6:46.61	6:47.44	6:48.27	6:49.09	6:49.92	6:50.75	6:51.58	6:52.41
500	6:53.23	6:54.06	6:54.89	6:55.72	6:56.55	6:57.38	6:58.20	6:59.03	6:59.86	7:00.69
510	7:01.52	7:02.34	7:03.17	7:04.00	7:04.83	7:05.66	7:06.48	7:07.31	7:08.14	7:08.97
520	7:09.80	7:10.63	7:11.45	7:12.28	7:13.11	7:13.94	7:14.77	7:15.59	7:16.42	7:17.25
530	7:18.08	7:18.91	7:19.73	7:20.56	7:21.39	7:22.22	7:23.05	7:23.88	7:24.70	7:25.53
540	7:26.36	7:27.19	7:28.02	7:28.84	7:29.67	7:30.50	7:31.33	7:32.16	7:32.98	7:33.81
550	7:34.64	7:35.47	7:36.30	7:37.13	7:37.95	7:38.78	7:39.61	7:40.44	7:41.27	7:42.09
560	7:42.92	7:43.75	7:44.58	7:45.41	7:46.23	7:47.06	7:47.89	7:48.72	7:49.55	7:50.38
570	7:51.20	7:52.03	7:52.86	7:53.69	7:54.52	7:55.34	7:56.17	7:57.00	7:57.83	7:58.66
580	7:59.48	8:00.31	8:01.14	8:01.97	8:02.80	8:03.63	8:04.45	8:05.28	8:06.11	8:06.94
590	8:07.77	8:08.59	8:09.42	8:10.25	8:11.08	8:11.91	8:12.73	8:13.56	8:14.39	8:15.22

♩. = 1.24; ♩ = 0.83; ♪. = 0.62; (3: ♩ 𝄾) = 0.55; ♪ = 0.41; (3: ♪ 𝄾 𝄾) = 0.28; 𝅘𝅥𝅯 = 0.21 seconds

CLICK: 20 0/8 FRAMES; M.M.: 72.00

Click	0	1	2	3	4	5	6	7	8	9
000	0:00.00	0:00.00	0:00.83	0:01.67	0:02.50	0:03.33	0:04.17	0:05.00	0:05.83	0:06.67
010	0:07.50	0:08.33	0:09.17	0:10.00	0:10.83	0:11.67	0:12.50	0:13.33	0:14.17	0:15.00
020	0:15.83	0:16.67	0:17.50	0:18.33	0:19.17	0:20.00	0:20.83	0:21.67	0:22.50	0:23.33
030	0:24.17	0:25.00	0:25.83	0:26.67	0:27.50	0:28.33	0:29.17	0:30.00	0:30.83	0:31.67
040	0:32.50	0:33.33	0:34.17	0:35.00	0:35.83	0:36.67	0:37.50	0:38.33	0:39.17	0:40.00
050	0:40.83	0:41.67	0:42.50	0:43.33	0:44.17	0:45.00	0:45.83	0:46.67	0:47.50	0:48.33
060	0:49.17	0:50.00	0:50.83	0:51.67	0:52.50	0:53.33	0:54.17	0:55.00	0:55.83	0:56.67
070	0:57.50	0:58.33	0:59.17	1:00.00	1:00.83	1:01.67	1:02.50	1:03.33	1:04.17	1:05.00
080	1:05.83	1:06.67	1:07.50	1:08.33	1:09.17	1:10.00	1:10.83	1:11.67	1:12.50	1:13.33
090	1:14.17	1:15.00	1:15.83	1:16.67	1:17.50	1:18.33	1:19.17	1:20.00	1:20.83	1:21.67
100	1:22.50	1:23.33	1:24.17	1:25.00	1:25.83	1:26.67	1:27.50	1:28.33	1:29.17	1:30.00
110	1:30.83	1:31.67	1:32.50	1:33.33	1:34.17	1:35.00	1:35.83	1:36.67	1:37.50	1:38.33
120	1:39.17	1:40.00	1:40.83	1:41.67	1:42.50	1:43.33	1:44.17	1:45.00	1:45.83	1:46.67
130	1:47.50	1:48.33	1:49.17	1:50.00	1:50.83	1:51.67	1:52.50	1:53.33	1:54.17	1:55.00
140	1:55.83	1:56.67	1:57.50	1:58.33	1:59.17	2:00.00	2:00.83	2:01.67	2:02.50	2:03.33
150	2:04.17	2:05.00	2:05.83	2:06.67	2:07.50	2:08.33	2:09.17	2:10.00	2:10.83	2:11.67
160	2:12.50	2:13.33	2:14.17	2:15.00	2:15.83	2:16.67	2:17.50	2:18.33	2:19.17	2:20.00
170	2:20.83	2:21.67	2:22.50	2:23.33	2:24.17	2:25.00	2:25.83	2:26.67	2:27.50	2:28.33
180	2:29.17	2:30.00	2:30.83	2:31.67	2:32.50	2:33.33	2:34.17	2:35.00	2:35.83	2:36.67
190	2:37.50	2:38.33	2:39.17	2:40.00	2:40.83	2:41.67	2:42.50	2:43.33	2:44.17	2:45.00
200	2:45.83	2:46.67	2:47.50	2:48.33	2:49.17	2:50.00	2:50.83	2:51.67	2:52.50	2:53.33
210	2:54.17	2:55.00	2:55.83	2:56.67	2:57.50	2:58.33	2:59.17	3:00.00	3:00.83	3:01.67
220	3:02.50	3:03.33	3:04.17	3:05.00	3:05.83	3:06.67	3:07.50	3:08.33	3:09.17	3:10.00
230	3:10.83	3:11.67	3:12.50	3:13.33	3:14.17	3:15.00	3:15.83	3:16.67	3:17.50	3:18.33
240	3:19.17	3:20.00	3:20.83	3:21.67	3:22.50	3:23.33	3:24.17	3:25.00	3:25.83	3:26.67
250	3:27.50	3:28.33	3:29.17	3:30.00	3:30.83	3:31.67	3:32.50	3:33.33	3:34.17	3:35.00
260	3:35.83	3:36.67	3:37.50	3:38.33	3:39.17	3:40.00	3:40.83	3:41.67	3:42.50	3:43.33
270	3:44.17	3:45.00	3:45.83	3:46.67	3:47.50	3:48.33	3:49.17	3:50.00	3:50.83	3:51.67
280	3:52.50	3:53.33	3:54.17	3:55.00	3:55.83	3:56.67	3:57.50	3:58.33	3:59.17	4:00.00
290	4:00.83	4:01.67	4:02.50	4:03.33	4:04.17	4:05.00	4:05.83	4:06.67	4:07.50	4:08.33
300	4:09.17	4:10.00	4:10.83	4:11.67	4:12.50	4:13.33	4:14.17	4:15.00	4:15.83	4:16.67
310	4:17.50	4:18.33	4:19.17	4:20.00	4:20.83	4:21.67	4:22.50	4:23.33	4:24.17	4:25.00
320	4:25.83	4:26.67	4:27.50	4:28.33	4:29.17	4:30.00	4:30.83	4:31.67	4:32.50	4:33.33
330	4:34.17	4:35.00	4:35.83	4:36.67	4:37.50	4:38.33	4:39.17	4:40.00	4:40.83	4:41.67
340	4:42.50	4:43.33	4:44.17	4:45.00	4:45.83	4:46.67	4:47.50	4:48.33	4:49.17	4:50.00
350	4:50.83	4:51.67	4:52.50	4:53.33	4:54.17	4:55.00	4:55.83	4:56.67	4:57.50	4:58.33
360	4:59.17	5:00.00	5:00.83	5:01.67	5:02.50	5:03.33	5:04.17	5:05.00	5:05.83	5:06.67
370	5:07.50	5:08.33	5:09.17	5:10.00	5:10.83	5:11.67	5:12.50	5:13.33	5:14.17	5:15.00
380	5:15.83	5:16.67	5:17.50	5:18.33	5:19.17	5:20.00	5:20.83	5:21.67	5:22.50	5:23.33
390	5:24.17	5:25.00	5:25.83	5:26.67	5:27.50	5:28.33	5:29.17	5:30.00	5:30.83	5:31.67
400	5:32.50	5:33.33	5:34.17	5:35.00	5:35.83	5:36.67	5:37.50	5:38.33	5:39.17	5:40.00
410	5:40.83	5:41.67	5:42.50	5:43.33	5:44.17	5:45.00	5:45.83	5:46.67	5:47.50	5:48.33
420	5:49.17	5:50.00	5:50.83	5:51.67	5:52.50	5:53.33	5:54.17	5:55.00	5:55.83	5:56.67
430	5:57.50	5:58.33	5:59.17	6:00.00	6:00.83	6:01.67	6:02.50	6:03.33	6:04.17	6:05.00
440	6:05.83	6:06.67	6:07.50	6:08.33	6:09.17	6:10.00	6:10.83	6:11.67	6:12.50	6:13.33
450	6:14.17	6:15.00	6:15.83	6:16.67	6:17.50	6:18.33	6:19.17	6:20.00	6:20.83	6:21.67
460	6:22.50	6:23.33	6:24.17	6:25.00	6:25.83	6:26.67	6:27.50	6:28.33	6:29.17	6:30.00
470	6:30.83	6:31.67	6:32.50	6:33.33	6:34.17	6:35.00	6:35.83	6:36.67	6:37.50	6:38.33
480	6:39.17	6:40.00	6:40.83	6:41.67	6:42.50	6:43.33	6:44.17	6:45.00	6:45.83	6:46.67
490	6:47.50	6:48.33	6:49.17	6:50.00	6:50.83	6:51.67	6:52.50	6:53.33	6:54.17	6:55.00
500	6:55.83	6:56.67	6:57.50	6:58.33	6:59.17	7:00.00	7:00.83	7:01.67	7:02.50	7:03.33
510	7:04.17	7:05.00	7:05.83	7:06.67	7:07.50	7:08.33	7:09.17	7:10.00	7:10.83	7:11.67
520	7:12.50	7:13.33	7:14.17	7:15.00	7:15.83	7:16.67	7:17.50	7:18.33	7:19.17	7:20.00
530	7:20.83	7:21.67	7:22.50	7:23.33	7:24.17	7:25.00	7:25.83	7:26.67	7:27.50	7:28.33
540	7:29.17	7:30.00	7:30.83	7:31.67	7:32.50	7:33.33	7:34.17	7:35.00	7:35.83	7:36.67
550	7:37.50	7:38.33	7:39.17	7:40.00	7:40.83	7:41.67	7:42.50	7:43.33	7:44.17	7:45.00
560	7:45.83	7:46.67	7:47.50	7:48.33	7:49.17	7:50.00	7:50.83	7:51.67	7:52.50	7:53.33
570	7:54.17	7:55.00	7:55.83	7:56.67	7:57.50	7:58.33	7:59.17	8:00.00	8:00.83	8:01.67
580	8:02.50	8:03.33	8:04.17	8:05.00	8:05.83	8:06.67	8:07.50	8:08.33	8:09.17	8:10.00
590	8:10.83	8:11.67	8:12.50	8:13.33	8:14.17	8:15.00	8:15.83	8:16.67	8:17.50	8:18.33

𝅗𝅥. = 1.25; ♩ = 0.83; ♪. = 0.63; ♩ 𝄾 (triplet) = 0.56; ♪ = 0.42; ♪ 𝄾 𝄾 (triplet) = 0.28; 𝅘𝅥𝅯 = 0.21 seconds

CLICK: 20⅛ FRAMES; M.M.: 71.55

Click	0	1	2	3	4	5	6	7	8	9
000	0:00.00	0:00.00	0:00.84	0:01.68	0:02.52	0:03.35	0:04.19	0:05.03	0:05.87	0:06.71
010	0:07.55	0:08.39	0:09.22	0:10.06	0:10.90	0:11.74	0:12.58	0:13.42	0:14.26	0:15.09
020	0:15.93	0:16.77	0:17.61	0:18.45	0:19.29	0:20.13	0:20.96	0:21.80	0:22.64	0:23.48
030	0:24.32	0:25.16	0:25.99	0:26.83	0:27.67	0:28.51	0:29.35	0:30.19	0:31.03	0:31.86
040	0:32.70	0:33.54	0:34.38	0:35.22	0:36.06	0:36.90	0:37.73	0:38.57	0:39.41	0:40.25
050	0:41.09	0:41.93	0:42.77	0:43.60	0:44.44	0:45.28	0:46.12	0:46.96	0:47.80	0:48.64
060	0:49.47	0:50.31	0:51.15	0:51.99	0:52.83	0:53.67	0:54.51	0:55.34	0:56.18	0:57.02
070	0:57.86	0:58.70	0:59.54	1:00.38	1:01.21	1:02.05	1:02.89	1:03.73	1:04.57	1:05.41
080	1:06.24	1:07.08	1:07.92	1:08.76	1:09.60	1:10.44	1:11.28	1:12.11	1:12.95	1:13.79
090	1:14.63	1:15.47	1:16.31	1:17.15	1:17.98	1:18.82	1:19.66	1:20.50	1:21.34	1:22.18
100	1:23.02	1:23.85	1:24.69	1:25.53	1:26.37	1:27.21	1:28.05	1:28.89	1:29.72	1:30.56
110	1:31.40	1:32.24	1:33.08	1:33.92	1:34.76	1:35.59	1:36.43	1:37.27	1:38.11	1:38.95
120	1:39.79	1:40.63	1:41.46	1:42.30	1:43.14	1:43.98	1:44.82	1:45.66	1:46.49	1:47.33
130	1:48.17	1:49.01	1:49.85	1:50.69	1:51.53	1:52.36	1:53.20	1:54.04	1:54.88	1:55.72
140	1:56.56	1:57.40	1:58.23	1:59.07	1:59.91	2:00.75	2:01.59	2:02.43	2:03.27	2:04.10
150	2:04.94	2:05.78	2:06.62	2:07.46	2:08.30	2:09.14	2:09.97	2:10.81	2:11.65	2:12.49
160	2:13.33	2:14.17	2:15.01	2:15.84	2:16.68	2:17.52	2:18.36	2:19.20	2:20.04	2:20.88
170	2:21.71	2:22.55	2:23.39	2:24.23	2:25.07	2:25.91	2:26.74	2:27.58	2:28.42	2:29.26
180	2:30.10	2:30.94	2:31.78	2:32.61	2:33.45	2:34.29	2:35.13	2:35.97	2:36.81	2:37.65
190	2:38.48	2:39.32	2:40.16	2:41.00	2:41.84	2:42.68	2:43.52	2:44.35	2:45.19	2:46.03
200	2:46.87	2:47.71	2:48.55	2:49.39	2:50.22	2:51.06	2:51.90	2:52.74	2:53.58	2:54.42
210	2:55.26	2:56.09	2:56.93	2:57.77	2:58.61	2:59.45	3:00.29	3:01.13	3:01.96	3:02.80
220	3:03.64	3:04.48	3:05.32	3:06.16	3:06.99	3:07.83	3:08.67	3:09.51	3:10.35	3:11.19
230	3:12.03	3:12.86	3:13.70	3:14.54	3:15.38	3:16.22	3:17.06	3:17.90	3:18.73	3:19.57
240	3:20.41	3:21.25	3:22.09	3:22.93	3:23.77	3:24.60	3:25.44	3:26.28	3:27.12	3:27.96
250	3:28.80	3:29.64	3:30.47	3:31.31	3:32.15	3:32.99	3:33.83	3:34.67	3:35.51	3:36.34
260	3:37.18	3:38.02	3:38.86	3:39.70	3:40.54	3:41.38	3:42.21	3:43.05	3:43.89	3:44.73
270	3:45.57	3:46.41	3:47.24	3:48.08	3:48.92	3:49.76	3:50.60	3:51.44	3:52.28	3:53.11
280	3:53.95	3:54.79	3:55.63	3:56.47	3:57.31	3:58.15	3:58.98	3:59.82	4:00.66	4:01.50
290	4:02.34	4:03.18	4:04.02	4:04.85	4:05.69	4:06.53	4:07.37	4:08.21	4:09.05	4:09.89
300	4:10.72	4:11.56	4:12.40	4:13.24	4:14.08	4:14.92	4:15.76	4:16.59	4:17.43	4:18.27
310	4:19.11	4:19.95	4:20.79	4:21.63	4:22.46	4:23.30	4:24.14	4:24.98	4:25.82	4:26.66
320	4:27.49	4:28.33	4:29.17	4:30.01	4:30.85	4:31.69	4:32.53	4:33.36	4:34.20	4:35.04
330	4:35.88	4:36.72	4:37.56	4:38.40	4:39.23	4:40.07	4:40.91	4:41.75	4:42.59	4:43.43
340	4:44.27	4:45.10	4:45.94	4:46.78	4:47.62	4:48.46	4:49.30	4:50.14	4:50.97	4:51.81
350	4:52.65	4:53.49	4:54.33	4:55.17	4:56.01	4:56.84	4:57.68	4:58.52	4:59.36	5:00.20
360	5:01.04	5:01.88	5:02.71	5:03.55	5:04.39	5:05.23	5:06.07	5:06.91	5:07.74	5:08.58
370	5:09.42	5:10.26	5:11.10	5:11.94	5:12.78	5:13.61	5:14.45	5:15.29	5:16.13	5:16.97
380	5:17.81	5:18.65	5:19.48	5:20.32	5:21.16	5:22.00	5:22.84	5:23.68	5:24.52	5:25.35
390	5:26.19	5:27.03	5:27.87	5:28.71	5:29.55	5:30.39	5:31.22	5:32.06	5:32.90	5:33.74
400	5:34.58	5:35.42	5:36.26	5:37.09	5:37.93	5:38.77	5:39.61	5:40.45	5:41.29	5:42.13
410	5:42.96	5:43.80	5:44.64	5:45.48	5:46.32	5:47.16	5:47.99	5:48.83	5:49.67	5:50.51
420	5:51.35	5:52.19	5:53.03	5:53.86	5:54.70	5:55.54	5:56.38	5:57.22	5:58.06	5:58.90
430	5:59.73	6:00.57	6:01.41	6:02.25	6:03.09	6:03.93	6:04.77	6:05.60	6:06.44	6:07.28
440	6:08.12	6:08.96	6:09.80	6:10.64	6:11.47	6:12.31	6:13.15	6:13.99	6:14.83	6:15.67
450	6:16.51	6:17.34	6:18.18	6:19.02	6:19.86	6:20.70	6:21.54	6:22.38	6:23.21	6:24.05
460	6:24.89	6:25.73	6:26.57	6:27.41	6:28.24	6:29.08	6:29.92	6:30.76	6:31.60	6:32.44
470	6:33.28	6:34.11	6:34.95	6:35.79	6:36.63	6:37.47	6:38.31	6:39.15	6:39.98	6:40.82
480	6:41.66	6:42.50	6:43.34	6:44.18	6:45.02	6:45.85	6:46.69	6:47.53	6:48.37	6:49.21
490	6:50.05	6:50.89	6:51.72	6:52.56	6:53.40	6:54.24	6:55.08	6:55.92	6:56.76	6:57.59
500	6:58.43	6:59.27	7:00.11	7:00.95	7:01.79	7:02.63	7:03.46	7:04.30	7:05.14	7:05.98
510	7:06.82	7:07.66	7:08.49	7:09.33	7:10.17	7:11.01	7:11.85	7:12.69	7:13.53	7:14.36
520	7:15.20	7:16.04	7:16.88	7:17.72	7:18.56	7:19.40	7:20.23	7:21.07	7:21.91	7:22.75
530	7:23.59	7:24.43	7:25.27	7:26.10	7:26.94	7:27.78	7:28.62	7:29.46	7:30.30	7:31.14
540	7:31.97	7:32.81	7:33.65	7:34.49	7:35.33	7:36.17	7:37.01	7:37.84	7:38.68	7:39.52
550	7:40.36	7:41.20	7:42.04	7:42.88	7:43.71	7:44.55	7:45.39	7:46.23	7:47.07	7:47.91
560	7:48.74	7:49.58	7:50.42	7:51.26	7:52.10	7:52.94	7:53.78	7:54.61	7:55.45	7:56.29
570	7:57.13	7:57.97	7:58.81	7:59.65	8:00.48	8:01.32	8:02.16	8:03.00	8:03.84	8:04.68
580	8:05.52	8:06.35	8:07.19	8:08.03	8:08.87	8:09.71	8:10.55	8:11.39	8:12.22	8:13.06
590	8:13.90	8:14.74	8:15.58	8:16.42	8:17.26	8:18.09	8:18.93	8:19.77	8:20.61	8:21.45

♩. = 1.26; ♩ = 0.84; ♪. = 0.63; (3) ♩ 𝄾 = 0.56; ♪ = 0.42; (3) ♪ 𝄾 𝄾 = 0.28; 𝅘𝅥𝅯 = 0.21 seconds

CLICK: 20 2/8 FRAMES; M.M.: 71.11

Click	0	1	2	3	4	5	6	7	8	9
000	0:00.00	0:00.00	0:00.84	0:01.69	0:02.53	0:03.38	0:04.22	0:05.06	0:05.91	0:06.75
010	0:07.59	0:08.44	0:09.28	0:10.13	0:10.97	0:11.81	0:12.66	0:13.50	0:14.34	0:15.19
020	0:16.03	0:16.88	0:17.72	0:18.56	0:19.41	0:20.25	0:21.09	0:21.94	0:22.78	0:23.62
030	0:24.47	0:25.31	0:26.16	0:27.00	0:27.84	0:28.69	0:29.53	0:30.37	0:31.22	0:32.06
040	0:32.91	0:33.75	0:34.59	0:35.44	0:36.28	0:37.13	0:37.97	0:38.81	0:39.66	0:40.50
050	0:41.34	0:42.19	0:43.03	0:43.88	0:44.72	0:45.56	0:46.41	0:47.25	0:48.09	0:48.94
060	0:49.78	0:50.63	0:51.47	0:52.31	0:53.16	0:54.00	0:54.84	0:55.69	0:56.53	0:57.37
070	0:58.22	0:59.06	0:59.91	1:00.75	1:01.59	1:02.44	1:03.28	1:04.13	1:04.97	1:05.81
080	1:06.66	1:07.50	1:08.34	1:09.19	1:10.03	1:10.87	1:11.72	1:12.56	1:13.41	1:14.25
090	1:15.09	1:15.94	1:16.78	1:17.62	1:18.47	1:19.31	1:20.16	1:21.00	1:21.84	1:22.69
100	1:23.53	1:24.38	1:25.22	1:26.06	1:26.91	1:27.75	1:28.59	1:29.44	1:30.28	1:31.12
110	1:31.97	1:32.81	1:33.66	1:34.50	1:35.34	1:36.19	1:37.03	1:37.87	1:38.72	1:39.56
120	1:40.41	1:41.25	1:42.09	1:42.94	1:43.78	1:44.63	1:45.47	1:46.31	1:47.16	1:48.00
130	1:48.84	1:49.69	1:50.53	1:51.37	1:52.22	1:53.06	1:53.91	1:54.75	1:55.59	1:56.44
140	1:57.28	1:58.13	1:58.97	1:59.81	2:00.66	2:01.50	2:02.34	2:03.19	2:04.03	2:04.87
150	2:05.72	2:06.56	2:07.41	2:08.25	2:09.09	2:09.94	2:10.78	2:11.62	2:12.47	2:13.31
160	2:14.16	2:15.00	2:15.84	2:16.69	2:17.53	2:18.37	2:19.22	2:20.06	2:20.91	2:21.75
170	2:22.59	2:23.44	2:24.28	2:25.13	2:25.97	2:26.81	2:27.66	2:28.50	2:29.34	2:30.19
180	2:31.03	2:31.88	2:32.72	2:33.56	2:34.41	2:35.25	2:36.09	2:36.94	2:37.78	2:38.62
190	2:39.47	2:40.31	2:41.16	2:42.00	2:42.84	2:43.69	2:44.53	2:45.37	2:46.22	2:47.06
200	2:47.91	2:48.75	2:49.59	2:50.44	2:51.28	2:52.12	2:52.97	2:53.81	2:54.66	2:55.50
210	2:56.34	2:57.19	2:58.03	2:58.87	2:59.72	3:00.56	3:01.41	3:02.25	3:03.09	3:03.94
220	3:04.78	3:05.63	3:06.47	3:07.31	3:08.16	3:09.00	3:09.84	3:10.69	3:11.53	3:12.37
230	3:13.22	3:14.06	3:14.91	3:15.75	3:16.59	3:17.44	3:18.28	3:19.12	3:19.97	3:20.81
240	3:21.66	3:22.50	3:23.34	3:24.19	3:25.03	3:25.87	3:26.72	3:27.56	3:28.41	3:29.25
250	3:30.09	3:30.94	3:31.78	3:32.62	3:33.47	3:34.31	3:35.16	3:36.00	3:36.84	3:37.69
260	3:38.53	3:39.38	3:40.22	3:41.06	3:41.91	3:42.75	3:43.59	3:44.44	3:45.28	3:46.12
270	3:46.97	3:47.81	3:48.66	3:49.50	3:50.34	3:51.19	3:52.03	3:52.87	3:53.72	3:54.56
280	3:55.41	3:56.25	3:57.09	3:57.94	3:58.78	3:59.62	4:00.47	4:01.31	4:02.16	4:03.00
290	4:03.84	4:04.69	4:05.53	4:06.37	4:07.22	4:08.06	4:08.91	4:09.75	4:10.59	4:11.44
300	4:12.28	4:13.13	4:13.97	4:14.81	4:15.66	4:16.50	4:17.34	4:18.19	4:19.03	4:19.87
310	4:20.72	4:21.56	4:22.41	4:23.25	4:24.09	4:24.94	4:25.78	4:26.62	4:27.47	4:28.31
320	4:29.16	4:30.00	4:30.84	4:31.69	4:32.53	4:33.38	4:34.22	4:35.06	4:35.91	4:36.75
330	4:37.59	4:38.44	4:39.28	4:40.12	4:40.97	4:41.81	4:42.66	4:43.50	4:44.34	4:45.19
340	4:46.03	4:46.88	4:47.72	4:48.56	4:49.41	4:50.25	4:51.09	4:51.94	4:52.78	4:53.62
350	4:54.47	4:55.31	4:56.16	4:57.00	4:57.84	4:58.69	4:59.53	5:00.37	5:01.22	5:02.06
360	5:02.91	5:03.75	5:04.59	5:05.44	5:06.28	5:07.13	5:07.97	5:08.81	5:09.66	5:10.50
370	5:11.34	5:12.19	5:13.03	5:13.87	5:14.72	5:15.56	5:16.41	5:17.25	5:18.09	5:18.94
380	5:19.78	5:20.63	5:21.47	5:22.31	5:23.16	5:24.00	5:24.84	5:25.69	5:26.53	5:27.37
390	5:28.22	5:29.06	5:29.91	5:30.75	5:31.59	5:32.44	5:33.28	5:34.12	5:34.97	5:35.81
400	5:36.66	5:37.50	5:38.34	5:39.19	5:40.03	5:40.87	5:41.72	5:42.56	5:43.41	5:44.25
410	5:45.09	5:45.94	5:46.78	5:47.62	5:48.47	5:49.31	5:50.16	5:51.00	5:51.84	5:52.69
420	5:53.53	5:54.38	5:55.22	5:56.06	5:56.91	5:57.75	5:58.59	5:59.44	6:00.28	6:01.12
430	6:01.97	6:02.81	6:03.66	6:04.50	6:05.34	6:06.19	6:07.03	6:07.87	6:08.72	6:09.56
440	6:10.41	6:11.25	6:12.09	6:12.94	6:13.78	6:14.62	6:15.47	6:16.31	6:17.16	6:18.00
450	6:18.84	6:19.69	6:20.53	6:21.37	6:22.22	6:23.06	6:23.91	6:24.75	6:25.59	6:26.44
460	6:27.28	6:28.13	6:28.97	6:29.81	6:30.66	6:31.50	6:32.34	6:33.19	6:34.03	6:34.87
470	6:35.72	6:36.56	6:37.41	6:38.25	6:39.09	6:39.94	6:40.78	6:41.62	6:42.47	6:43.31
480	6:44.16	6:45.00	6:45.84	6:46.69	6:47.53	6:48.37	6:49.22	6:50.06	6:50.91	6:51.75
490	6:52.59	6:53.44	6:54.28	6:55.12	6:55.97	6:56.81	6:57.66	6:58.50	6:59.34	7:00.19
500	7:01.03	7:01.88	7:02.72	7:03.56	7:04.41	7:05.25	7:06.09	7:06.94	7:07.78	7:08.62
510	7:09.47	7:10.31	7:11.16	7:12.00	7:12.84	7:13.69	7:14.53	7:15.37	7:16.22	7:17.06
520	7:17.91	7:18.75	7:19.59	7:20.44	7:21.28	7:22.12	7:22.97	7:23.81	7:24.66	7:25.50
530	7:26.34	7:27.19	7:28.03	7:28.87	7:29.72	7:30.56	7:31.41	7:32.25	7:33.09	7:33.94
540	7:34.78	7:35.63	7:36.47	7:37.31	7:38.16	7:39.00	7:39.84	7:40.69	7:41.53	7:42.37
550	7:43.22	7:44.06	7:44.91	7:45.75	7:46.59	7:47.44	7:48.28	7:49.12	7:49.97	7:50.81
560	7:51.66	7:52.50	7:53.34	7:54.19	7:55.03	7:55.87	7:56.72	7:57.56	7:58.41	7:59.25
570	8:00.09	8:00.94	8:01.78	8:02.62	8:03.47	8:04.31	8:05.16	8:06.00	8:06.84	8:07.69
580	8:08.53	8:09.38	8:10.22	8:11.06	8:11.91	8:12.75	8:13.59	8:14.44	8:15.28	8:16.13
590	8:16.97	8:17.81	8:18.66	8:19.50	8:20.34	8:21.19	8:22.03	8:22.87	8:23.72	8:24.56

♩. = 1.27; ♩ = 0.84; ♪. = 0.63; (triplet ♩ 𝄾) = 0.56; ♪ = 0.42; (triplet ♪ 𝄾 𝄾) = 0.28; 𝅘𝅥𝅯 = 0.21 seconds

CLICK: 20⅜ FRAMES; M.M.: 70.67

Click	0	1	2	3	4	5	6	7	8	9
000	0:00.00	0:00.00	0:00.85	0:01.70	0:02.55	0:03.40	0:04.24	0:05.09	0:05.94	0:06.79
010	0:07.64	0:08.49	0:09.34	0:10.19	0:11.04	0:11.89	0:12.73	0:13.58	0:14.43	0:15.28
020	0:16.13	0:16.98	0:17.83	0:18.68	0:19.53	0:20.38	0:21.22	0:22.07	0:22.92	0:23.77
030	0:24.62	0:25.47	0:26.32	0:27.17	0:28.02	0:28.86	0:29.71	0:30.56	0:31.41	0:32.26
040	0:33.11	0:33.96	0:34.81	0:35.66	0:36.51	0:37.35	0:38.20	0:39.05	0:39.90	0:40.75
050	0:41.60	0:42.45	0:43.30	0:44.15	0:44.99	0:45.84	0:46.69	0:47.54	0:48.39	0:49.24
060	0:50.09	0:50.94	0:51.79	0:52.64	0:53.48	0:54.33	0:55.18	0:56.03	0:56.88	0:57.73
070	0:58.58	0:59.43	1:00.28	1:01.13	1:01.97	1:02.82	1:03.67	1:04.52	1:05.37	1:06.22
080	1:07.07	1:07.92	1:08.77	1:09.61	1:10.46	1:11.31	1:12.16	1:13.01	1:13.86	1:14.71
090	1:15.56	1:16.41	1:17.26	1:18.10	1:18.95	1:19.80	1:20.65	1:21.50	1:22.35	1:23.20
100	1:24.05	1:24.90	1:25.74	1:26.59	1:27.44	1:28.29	1:29.14	1:29.99	1:30.84	1:31.69
110	1:32.54	1:33.39	1:34.23	1:35.08	1:35.93	1:36.78	1:37.63	1:38.48	1:39.33	1:40.18
120	1:41.03	1:41.88	1:42.72	1:43.57	1:44.42	1:45.27	1:46.12	1:46.97	1:47.82	1:48.67
130	1:49.52	1:50.36	1:51.21	1:52.06	1:52.91	1:53.76	1:54.61	1:55.46	1:56.31	1:57.16
140	1:58.01	1:58.85	1:59.70	2:00.55	2:01.40	2:02.25	2:03.10	2:03.95	2:04.80	2:05.65
150	2:06.49	2:07.34	2:08.19	2:09.04	2:09.89	2:10.74	2:11.59	2:12.44	2:13.29	2:14.14
160	2:14.98	2:15.83	2:16.68	2:17.53	2:18.38	2:19.23	2:20.08	2:20.93	2:21.78	2:22.63
170	2:23.47	2:24.32	2:25.17	2:26.02	2:26.87	2:27.72	2:28.57	2:29.42	2:30.27	2:31.11
180	2:31.96	2:32.81	2:33.66	2:34.51	2:35.36	2:36.21	2:37.06	2:37.91	2:38.76	2:39.60
190	2:40.45	2:41.30	2:42.15	2:43.00	2:43.85	2:44.70	2:45.55	2:46.40	2:47.24	2:48.09
200	2:48.94	2:49.79	2:50.64	2:51.49	2:52.34	2:53.19	2:54.04	2:54.89	2:55.73	2:56.58
210	2:57.43	2:58.28	2:59.13	2:59.98	3:00.83	3:01.68	3:02.53	3:03.38	3:04.22	3:05.07
220	3:05.92	3:06.77	3:07.62	3:08.47	3:09.32	3:10.17	3:11.02	3:11.86	3:12.71	3:13.56
230	3:14.41	3:15.26	3:16.11	3:16.96	3:17.81	3:18.66	3:19.51	3:20.35	3:21.20	3:22.05
240	3:22.90	3:23.75	3:24.60	3:25.45	3:26.30	3:27.15	3:27.99	3:28.84	3:29.69	3:30.54
250	3:31.39	3:32.24	3:33.09	3:33.94	3:34.79	3:35.64	3:36.48	3:37.33	3:38.18	3:39.03
260	3:39.88	3:40.73	3:41.58	3:42.43	3:43.28	3:44.13	3:44.97	3:45.82	3:46.67	3:47.52
270	3:48.37	3:49.22	3:50.07	3:50.92	3:51.77	3:52.61	3:53.46	3:54.31	3:55.16	3:56.01
280	3:56.86	3:57.71	3:58.56	3:59.41	4:00.26	4:01.10	4:01.95	4:02.80	4:03.65	4:04.50
290	4:05.35	4:06.20	4:07.05	4:07.90	4:08.74	4:09.59	4:10.44	4:11.29	4:12.14	4:12.99
300	4:13.84	4:14.69	4:15.54	4:16.39	4:17.23	4:18.08	4:18.93	4:19.78	4:20.63	4:21.48
310	4:22.33	4:23.18	4:24.03	4:24.88	4:25.72	4:26.57	4:27.42	4:28.27	4:29.12	4:29.97
320	4:30.82	4:31.67	4:32.52	4:33.36	4:34.21	4:35.06	4:35.91	4:36.76	4:37.61	4:38.46
330	4:39.31	4:40.16	4:41.01	4:41.85	4:42.70	4:43.55	4:44.40	4:45.25	4:46.10	4:46.95
340	4:47.80	4:48.65	4:49.49	4:50.34	4:51.19	4:52.04	4:52.89	4:53.74	4:54.59	4:55.44
350	4:56.29	4:57.14	4:57.98	4:58.83	4:59.68	5:00.53	5:01.38	5:02.23	5:03.08	5:03.93
360	5:04.78	5:05.63	5:06.47	5:07.32	5:08.17	5:09.02	5:09.87	5:10.72	5:11.57	5:12.42
370	5:13.27	5:14.11	5:14.96	5:15.81	5:16.66	5:17.51	5:18.36	5:19.21	5:20.06	5:20.91
380	5:21.76	5:22.60	5:23.45	5:24.30	5:25.15	5:26.00	5:26.85	5:27.70	5:28.55	5:29.40
390	5:30.24	5:31.09	5:31.94	5:32.79	5:33.64	5:34.49	5:35.34	5:36.19	5:37.04	5:37.89
400	5:38.73	5:39.58	5:40.43	5:41.28	5:42.13	5:42.98	5:43.83	5:44.68	5:45.53	5:46.38
410	5:47.22	5:48.07	5:48.92	5:49.77	5:50.62	5:51.47	5:52.32	5:53.17	5:54.02	5:54.86
420	5:55.71	5:56.56	5:57.41	5:58.26	5:59.11	5:59.96	6:00.81	6:01.66	6:02.51	6:03.35
430	6:04.20	6:05.05	6:05.90	6:06.75	6:07.60	6:08.45	6:09.30	6:10.15	6:10.99	6:11.84
440	6:12.69	6:13.54	6:14.39	6:15.24	6:16.09	6:16.94	6:17.79	6:18.64	6:19.48	6:20.33
450	6:21.18	6:22.03	6:22.88	6:23.73	6:24.58	6:25.43	6:26.28	6:27.13	6:27.97	6:28.82
460	6:29.67	6:30.52	6:31.37	6:32.22	6:33.07	6:33.92	6:34.77	6:35.61	6:36.46	6:37.31
470	6:38.16	6:39.01	6:39.86	6:40.71	6:41.56	6:42.41	6:43.26	6:44.10	6:44.95	6:45.80
480	6:46.65	6:47.50	6:48.35	6:49.20	6:50.05	6:50.90	6:51.74	6:52.59	6:53.44	6:54.29
490	6:55.14	6:55.99	6:56.84	6:57.69	6:58.54	6:59.39	7:00.23	7:01.08	7:01.93	7:02.78
500	7:03.63	7:04.48	7:05.33	7:06.18	7:07.03	7:07.88	7:08.72	7:09.57	7:10.42	7:11.27
510	7:12.12	7:12.97	7:13.82	7:14.67	7:15.52	7:16.36	7:17.21	7:18.06	7:18.91	7:19.76
520	7:20.61	7:21.46	7:22.31	7:23.16	7:24.01	7:24.85	7:25.70	7:26.55	7:27.40	7:28.25
530	7:29.10	7:29.95	7:30.80	7:31.65	7:32.49	7:33.34	7:34.19	7:35.04	7:35.89	7:36.74
540	7:37.59	7:38.44	7:39.29	7:40.14	7:40.98	7:41.83	7:42.68	7:43.53	7:44.38	7:45.23
550	7:46.08	7:46.93	7:47.78	7:48.63	7:49.47	7:50.32	7:51.17	7:52.02	7:52.87	7:53.72
560	7:54.57	7:55.42	7:56.27	7:57.11	7:57.96	7:58.81	7:59.66	8:00.51	8:01.36	8:02.21
570	8:03.06	8:03.91	8:04.76	8:05.60	8:06.45	8:07.30	8:08.15	8:09.00	8:09.85	8:10.70
580	8:11.55	8:12.40	8:13.24	8:14.09	8:14.94	8:15.79	8:16.64	8:17.49	8:18.34	8:19.19
590	8:20.04	8:20.89	8:21.73	8:22.58	8:23.43	8:24.28	8:25.13	8:25.98	8:26.83	8:27.68

♩. = 1.27; ♩ = 0.85; ♪. = 0.64; (3: ♩ 𝄾) = 0.57; ♪ = 0.42; (3: ♪ 𝄾 𝄾) = 0.28; 𝅘𝅥𝅯 = 0.21 seconds

CLICK: 20 4/8 FRAMES; M.M.: 70.24

Click	0	1	2	3	4	5	6	7	8	9
000	0:00.00	0:00.00	0:00.85	0:01.71	0:02.56	0:03.42	0:04.27	0:05.13	0:05.98	0:06.83
010	0:07.69	0:08.54	0:09.40	0:10.25	0:11.10	0:11.96	0:12.81	0:13.67	0:14.52	0:15.38
020	0:16.23	0:17.08	0:17.94	0:18.79	0:19.65	0:20.50	0:21.35	0:22.21	0:23.06	0:23.92
030	0:24.77	0:25.63	0:26.48	0:27.33	0:28.19	0:29.04	0:29.90	0:30.75	0:31.60	0:32.46
040	0:33.31	0:34.17	0:35.02	0:35.88	0:36.73	0:37.58	0:38.44	0:39.29	0:40.15	0:41.00
050	0:41.85	0:42.71	0:43.56	0:44.42	0:45.27	0:46.13	0:46.98	0:47.83	0:48.69	0:49.54
060	0:50.40	0:51.25	0:52.10	0:52.96	0:53.81	0:54.67	0:55.52	0:56.38	0:57.23	0:58.08
070	0:58.94	0:59.79	1:00.65	1:01.50	1:02.35	1:03.21	1:04.06	1:04.92	1:05.77	1:06.63
080	1:07.48	1:08.33	1:09.19	1:10.04	1:10.90	1:11.75	1:12.60	1:13.46	1:14.31	1:15.17
090	1:16.02	1:16.88	1:17.73	1:18.58	1:19.44	1:20.29	1:21.15	1:22.00	1:22.85	1:23.71
100	1:24.56	1:25.42	1:26.27	1:27.13	1:27.98	1:28.83	1:29.69	1:30.54	1:31.40	1:32.25
110	1:33.10	1:33.96	1:34.81	1:35.67	1:36.52	1:37.38	1:38.23	1:39.08	1:39.94	1:40.79
120	1:41.65	1:42.50	1:43.35	1:44.21	1:45.06	1:45.92	1:46.77	1:47.63	1:48.48	1:49.33
130	1:50.19	1:51.04	1:51.90	1:52.75	1:53.60	1:54.46	1:55.31	1:56.17	1:57.02	1:57.88
140	1:58.73	1:59.58	2:00.44	2:01.29	2:02.15	2:03.00	2:03.85	2:04.71	2:05.56	2:06.42
150	2:07.27	2:08.13	2:08.98	2:09.83	2:10.69	2:11.54	2:12.40	2:13.25	2:14.10	2:14.96
160	2:15.81	2:16.67	2:17.52	2:18.38	2:19.23	2:20.08	2:20.94	2:21.79	2:22.65	2:23.50
170	2:24.35	2:25.21	2:26.06	2:26.92	2:27.77	2:28.63	2:29.48	2:30.33	2:31.19	2:32.04
180	2:32.90	2:33.75	2:34.60	2:35.46	2:36.31	2:37.17	2:38.02	2:38.88	2:39.73	2:40.58
190	2:41.44	2:42.29	2:43.15	2:44.00	2:44.85	2:45.71	2:46.56	2:47.42	2:48.27	2:49.13
200	2:49.98	2:50.83	2:51.69	2:52.54	2:53.40	2:54.25	2:55.10	2:55.96	2:56.81	2:57.67
210	2:58.52	2:59.38	3:00.23	3:01.08	3:01.94	3:02.79	3:03.65	3:04.50	3:05.35	3:06.21
220	3:07.06	3:07.92	3:08.77	3:09.63	3:10.48	3:11.33	3:12.19	3:13.04	3:13.90	3:14.75
230	3:15.60	3:16.46	3:17.31	3:18.17	3:19.02	3:19.88	3:20.73	3:21.58	3:22.44	3:23.29
240	3:24.15	3:25.00	3:25.85	3:26.71	3:27.56	3:28.42	3:29.27	3:30.13	3:30.98	3:31.83
250	3:32.69	3:33.54	3:34.40	3:35.25	3:36.10	3:36.96	3:37.81	3:38.67	3:39.52	3:40.38
260	3:41.23	3:42.08	3:42.94	3:43.79	3:44.65	3:45.50	3:46.35	3:47.21	3:48.06	3:48.92
270	3:49.77	3:50.63	3:51.48	3:52.33	3:53.19	3:54.04	3:54.90	3:55.75	3:56.60	3:57.46
280	3:58.31	3:59.17	4:00.02	4:00.88	4:01.73	4:02.58	4:03.44	4:04.29	4:05.15	4:06.00
290	4:06.85	4:07.71	4:08.56	4:09.42	4:10.27	4:11.13	4:11.98	4:12.83	4:13.69	4:14.54
300	4:15.40	4:16.25	4:17.10	4:17.96	4:18.81	4:19.67	4:20.52	4:21.38	4:22.23	4:23.08
310	4:23.94	4:24.79	4:25.65	4:26.50	4:27.35	4:28.21	4:29.06	4:29.92	4:30.77	4:31.63
320	4:32.48	4:33.33	4:34.19	4:35.04	4:35.90	4:36.75	4:37.60	4:38.46	4:39.31	4:40.17
330	4:41.02	4:41.88	4:42.73	4:43.58	4:44.44	4:45.29	4:46.15	4:47.00	4:47.85	4:48.71
340	4:49.56	4:50.42	4:51.27	4:52.13	4:52.98	4:53.83	4:54.69	4:55.54	4:56.40	4:57.25
350	4:58.10	4:58.96	4:59.81	5:00.67	5:01.52	5:02.38	5:03.23	5:04.08	5:04.94	5:05.79
360	5:06.65	5:07.50	5:08.35	5:09.21	5:10.06	5:10.92	5:11.77	5:12.63	5:13.48	5:14.33
370	5:15.19	5:16.04	5:16.90	5:17.75	5:18.60	5:19.46	5:20.31	5:21.17	5:22.02	5:22.88
380	5:23.73	5:24.58	5:25.44	5:26.29	5:27.15	5:28.00	5:28.85	5:29.71	5:30.56	5:31.42
390	5:32.27	5:33.13	5:33.98	5:34.83	5:35.69	5:36.54	5:37.40	5:38.25	5:39.10	5:39.96
400	5:40.81	5:41.67	5:42.52	5:43.38	5:44.23	5:45.08	5:45.94	5:46.79	5:47.65	5:48.50
410	5:49.35	5:50.21	5:51.06	5:51.92	5:52.77	5:53.63	5:54.48	5:55.33	5:56.19	5:57.04
420	5:57.90	5:58.75	5:59.60	6:00.46	6:01.31	6:02.17	6:03.02	6:03.88	6:04.73	6:05.58
430	6:06.44	6:07.29	6:08.15	6:09.00	6:09.85	6:10.71	6:11.56	6:12.42	6:13.27	6:14.13
440	6:14.98	6:15.83	6:16.69	6:17.54	6:18.40	6:19.25	6:20.10	6:20.96	6:21.81	6:22.67
450	6:23.52	6:24.38	6:25.23	6:26.08	6:26.94	6:27.79	6:28.65	6:29.50	6:30.35	6:31.21
460	6:32.06	6:32.92	6:33.77	6:34.63	6:35.48	6:36.33	6:37.19	6:38.04	6:38.90	6:39.75
470	6:40.60	6:41.46	6:42.31	6:43.17	6:44.02	6:44.88	6:45.73	6:46.58	6:47.44	6:48.29
480	6:49.15	6:50.00	6:50.85	6:51.71	6:52.56	6:53.42	6:54.27	6:55.13	6:55.98	6:56.83
490	6:57.69	6:58.54	6:59.40	7:00.25	7:01.10	7:01.96	7:02.81	7:03.67	7:04.52	7:05.38
500	7:06.23	7:07.08	7:07.94	7:08.79	7:09.65	7:10.50	7:11.35	7:12.21	7:13.06	7:13.92
510	7:14.77	7:15.63	7:16.48	7:17.33	7:18.19	7:19.04	7:19.90	7:20.75	7:21.60	7:22.46
520	7:23.31	7:24.17	7:25.02	7:25.88	7:26.73	7:27.58	7:28.44	7:29.29	7:30.15	7:31.00
530	7:31.85	7:32.71	7:33.56	7:34.42	7:35.27	7:36.13	7:36.98	7:37.83	7:38.69	7:39.54
540	7:40.40	7:41.25	7:42.10	7:42.96	7:43.81	7:44.67	7:45.52	7:46.38	7:47.23	7:48.08
550	7:48.94	7:49.79	7:50.65	7:51.50	7:52.35	7:53.21	7:54.06	7:54.92	7:55.77	7:56.63
560	7:57.48	7:58.33	7:59.19	8:00.04	8:00.90	8:01.75	8:02.60	8:03.46	8:04.31	8:05.17
570	8:06.02	8:06.88	8:07.73	8:08.58	8:09.44	8:10.29	8:11.15	8:12.00	8:12.85	8:13.71
580	8:14.56	8:15.42	8:16.27	8:17.13	8:17.98	8:18.83	8:19.69	8:20.54	8:21.40	8:22.25
590	8:23.10	8:23.96	8:24.81	8:25.67	8:26.52	8:27.38	8:28.23	8:29.08	8:29.94	8:30.79

♩. = 1.28; ♩ = 0.85; ♪. = 0.64; (triplet ♩ 𝄾) = 0.57; ♪ = 0.43; (triplet ♪ 𝄾 𝄾) = 0.28; 𝅘𝅥𝅯 = 0.21 seconds

CLICK: 20⅝ FRAMES; M.M.: 69.82

Click	0	1	2	3	4	5	6	7	8	9
000	0:00.00	0:00.00	0:00.86	0:01.72	0:02.58	0:03.44	0:04.30	0:05.16	0:06.02	0:06.88
010	0:07.73	0:08.59	0:09.45	0:10.31	0:11.17	0:12.03	0:12.89	0:13.75	0:14.61	0:15.47
020	0:16.33	0:17.19	0:18.05	0:18.91	0:19.77	0:20.63	0:21.48	0:22.34	0:23.20	0:24.06
030	0:24.92	0:25.78	0:26.64	0:27.50	0:28.36	0:29.22	0:30.08	0:30.94	0:31.80	0:32.66
040	0:33.52	0:34.38	0:35.23	0:36.09	0:36.95	0:37.81	0:38.67	0:39.53	0:40.39	0:41.25
050	0:42.11	0:42.97	0:43.83	0:44.69	0:45.55	0:46.41	0:47.27	0:48.13	0:48.98	0:49.84
060	0:50.70	0:51.56	0:52.42	0:53.28	0:54.14	0:55.00	0:55.86	0:56.72	0:57.58	0:58.44
070	0:59.30	1:00.16	1:01.02	1:01.88	1:02.73	1:03.59	1:04.45	1:05.31	1:06.17	1:07.03
080	1:07.89	1:08.75	1:09.61	1:10.47	1:11.33	1:12.19	1:13.05	1:13.91	1:14.77	1:15.63
090	1:16.48	1:17.34	1:18.20	1:19.06	1:19.92	1:20.78	1:21.64	1:22.50	1:23.36	1:24.22
100	1:25.08	1:25.94	1:26.80	1:27.66	1:28.52	1:29.38	1:30.23	1:31.09	1:31.95	1:32.81
110	1:33.67	1:34.53	1:35.39	1:36.25	1:37.11	1:37.97	1:38.83	1:39.69	1:40.55	1:41.41
120	1:42.27	1:43.13	1:43.98	1:44.84	1:45.70	1:46.56	1:47.42	1:48.28	1:49.14	1:50.00
130	1:50.86	1:51.72	1:52.58	1:53.44	1:54.30	1:55.16	1:56.02	1:56.88	1:57.73	1:58.59
140	1:59.45	2:00.31	2:01.17	2:02.03	2:02.89	2:03.75	2:04.61	2:05.47	2:06.33	2:07.19
150	2:08.05	2:08.91	2:09.77	2:10.63	2:11.48	2:12.34	2:13.20	2:14.06	2:14.92	2:15.78
160	2:16.64	2:17.50	2:18.36	2:19.22	2:20.08	2:20.94	2:21.80	2:22.66	2:23.52	2:24.38
170	2:25.23	2:26.09	2:26.95	2:27.81	2:28.67	2:29.53	2:30.39	2:31.25	2:32.11	2:32.97
180	2:33.83	2:34.69	2:35.55	2:36.41	2:37.27	2:38.13	2:38.98	2:39.84	2:40.70	2:41.56
190	2:42.42	2:43.28	2:44.14	2:45.00	2:45.86	2:46.72	2:47.58	2:48.44	2:49.30	2:50.16
200	2:51.02	2:51.88	2:52.73	2:53.59	2:54.45	2:55.31	2:56.17	2:57.03	2:57.89	2:58.75
210	2:59.61	3:00.47	3:01.33	3:02.19	3:03.05	3:03.91	3:04.77	3:05.63	3:06.48	3:07.34
220	3:08.20	3:09.06	3:09.92	3:10.78	3:11.64	3:12.50	3:13.36	3:14.22	3:15.08	3:15.94
230	3:16.80	3:17.66	3:18.52	3:19.38	3:20.23	3:21.09	3:21.95	3:22.81	3:23.67	3:24.53
240	3:25.39	3:26.25	3:27.11	3:27.97	3:28.83	3:29.69	3:30.55	3:31.41	3:32.27	3:33.13
250	3:33.98	3:34.84	3:35.70	3:36.56	3:37.42	3:38.28	3:39.14	3:40.00	3:40.86	3:41.72
260	3:42.58	3:43.44	3:44.30	3:45.16	3:46.02	3:46.88	3:47.73	3:48.59	3:49.45	3:50.31
270	3:51.17	3:52.03	3:52.89	3:53.75	3:54.61	3:55.47	3:56.33	3:57.19	3:58.05	3:58.91
280	3:59.77	4:00.63	4:01.48	4:02.34	4:03.20	4:04.06	4:04.92	4:05.78	4:06.64	4:07.50
290	4:08.36	4:09.22	4:10.08	4:10.94	4:11.80	4:12.66	4:13.52	4:14.38	4:15.23	4:16.09
300	4:16.95	4:17.81	4:18.67	4:19.53	4:20.39	4:21.25	4:22.11	4:22.97	4:23.83	4:24.69
310	4:25.55	4:26.41	4:27.27	4:28.13	4:28.98	4:29.84	4:30.70	4:31.56	4:32.42	4:33.28
320	4:34.14	4:35.00	4:35.86	4:36.72	4:37.58	4:38.44	4:39.30	4:40.16	4:41.02	4:41.88
330	4:42.73	4:43.59	4:44.45	4:45.31	4:46.17	4:47.03	4:47.89	4:48.75	4:49.61	4:50.47
340	4:51.33	4:52.19	4:53.05	4:53.91	4:54.77	4:55.63	4:56.48	4:57.34	4:58.20	4:59.06
350	4:59.92	5:00.78	5:01.64	5:02.50	5:03.36	5:04.22	5:05.08	5:05.94	5:06.80	5:07.66
360	5:08.52	5:09.38	5:10.23	5:11.09	5:11.95	5:12.81	5:13.67	5:14.53	5:15.39	5:16.25
370	5:17.11	5:17.97	5:18.83	5:19.69	5:20.55	5:21.41	5:22.27	5:23.13	5:23.98	5:24.84
380	5:25.70	5:26.56	5:27.42	5:28.28	5:29.14	5:30.00	5:30.86	5:31.72	5:32.58	5:33.44
390	5:34.30	5:35.16	5:36.02	5:36.88	5:37.73	5:38.59	5:39.45	5:40.31	5:41.17	5:42.03
400	5:42.89	5:43.75	5:44.61	5:45.47	5:46.33	5:47.19	5:48.05	5:48.91	5:49.77	5:50.63
410	5:51.48	5:52.34	5:53.20	5:54.06	5:54.92	5:55.78	5:56.64	5:57.50	5:58.36	5:59.22
420	6:00.08	6:00.94	6:01.80	6:02.66	6:03.52	6:04.38	6:05.23	6:06.09	6:06.95	6:07.81
430	6:08.67	6:09.53	6:10.39	6:11.25	6:12.11	6:12.97	6:13.83	6:14.69	6:15.55	6:16.41
440	6:17.27	6:18.13	6:18.98	6:19.84	6:20.70	6:21.56	6:22.42	6:23.28	6:24.14	6:25.00
450	6:25.86	6:26.72	6:27.58	6:28.44	6:29.30	6:30.16	6:31.02	6:31.88	6:32.73	6:33.59
460	6:34.45	6:35.31	6:36.17	6:37.03	6:37.89	6:38.75	6:39.61	6:40.47	6:41.33	6:42.19
470	6:43.05	6:43.91	6:44.77	6:45.63	6:46.48	6:47.34	6:48.20	6:49.06	6:49.92	6:50.78
480	6:51.64	6:52.50	6:53.36	6:54.22	6:55.08	6:55.94	6:56.80	6:57.66	6:58.52	6:59.38
490	7:00.23	7:01.09	7:01.95	7:02.81	7:03.67	7:04.53	7:05.39	7:06.25	7:07.11	7:07.97
500	7:08.83	7:09.69	7:10.55	7:11.41	7:12.27	7:13.13	7:13.98	7:14.84	7:15.70	7:16.56
510	7:17.42	7:18.28	7:19.14	7:20.00	7:20.86	7:21.72	7:22.58	7:23.44	7:24.30	7:25.16
520	7:26.02	7:26.88	7:27.73	7:28.59	7:29.45	7:30.31	7:31.17	7:32.03	7:32.89	7:33.75
530	7:34.61	7:35.47	7:36.33	7:37.19	7:38.05	7:38.91	7:39.77	7:40.63	7:41.48	7:42.34
540	7:43.20	7:44.06	7:44.92	7:45.78	7:46.64	7:47.50	7:48.36	7:49.22	7:50.08	7:50.94
550	7:51.80	7:52.66	7:53.52	7:54.38	7:55.23	7:56.09	7:56.95	7:57.81	7:58.67	7:59.53
560	8:00.39	8:01.25	8:02.11	8:02.97	8:03.83	8:04.69	8:05.55	8:06.41	8:07.27	8:08.13
570	8:08.98	8:09.84	8:10.70	8:11.56	8:12.42	8:13.28	8:14.14	8:15.00	8:15.86	8:16.72
580	8:17.58	8:18.44	8:19.30	8:20.16	8:21.02	8:21.88	8:22.73	8:23.59	8:24.45	8:25.31
590	8:26.17	8:27.03	8:27.89	8:28.75	8:29.61	8:30.47	8:31.33	8:32.19	8:33.05	8:33.91

♩. = 1.29; ♩ = 0.86; ♪. = 0.64; (triplet) ♩ 𝄾 = 0.57; ♪ = 0.43; (triplet) ♪ 𝄾 𝄾 = 0.29; 𝅘𝅥𝅯 = 0.21 seconds

CLICK: 20 6/8 FRAMES; M.M.: 69.40

Click	0	1	2	3	4	5	6	7	8	9
000	0:00.00	0:00.00	0:00.86	0:01.73	0:02.59	0:03.46	0:04.32	0:05.19	0:06.05	0:06.92
010	0:07.78	0:08.65	0:09.51	0:10.38	0:11.24	0:12.10	0:12.97	0:13.83	0:14.70	0:15.56
020	0:16.43	0:17.29	0:18.16	0:19.02	0:19.89	0:20.75	0:21.61	0:22.48	0:23.34	0:24.21
030	0:25.07	0:25.94	0:26.80	0:27.67	0:28.53	0:29.40	0:30.26	0:31.13	0:31.99	0:32.85
040	0:33.72	0:34.58	0:35.45	0:36.31	0:37.18	0:38.04	0:38.91	0:39.77	0:40.64	0:41.50
050	0:42.36	0:43.23	0:44.09	0:44.96	0:45.82	0:46.69	0:47.55	0:48.42	0:49.28	0:50.15
060	0:51.01	0:51.88	0:52.74	0:53.60	0:54.47	0:55.33	0:56.20	0:57.06	0:57.93	0:58.79
070	0:59.66	1:00.52	1:01.39	1:02.25	1:03.11	1:03.98	1:04.84	1:05.71	1:06.57	1:07.44
080	1:08.30	1:09.17	1:10.03	1:10.90	1:11.76	1:12.63	1:13.49	1:14.35	1:15.22	1:16.08
090	1:16.95	1:17.81	1:18.68	1:19.54	1:20.41	1:21.27	1:22.14	1:23.00	1:23.86	1:24.73
100	1:25.59	1:26.46	1:27.32	1:28.19	1:29.05	1:29.92	1:30.78	1:31.65	1:32.51	1:33.38
110	1:34.24	1:35.10	1:35.97	1:36.83	1:37.70	1:38.56	1:39.43	1:40.29	1:41.16	1:42.02
120	1:42.89	1:43.75	1:44.61	1:45.48	1:46.34	1:47.21	1:48.07	1:48.94	1:49.80	1:50.67
130	1:51.53	1:52.40	1:53.26	1:54.12	1:54.99	1:55.85	1:56.72	1:57.58	1:58.45	1:59.31
140	2:00.18	2:01.04	2:01.91	2:02.77	2:03.64	2:04.50	2:05.36	2:06.23	2:07.09	2:07.96
150	2:08.82	2:09.69	2:10.55	2:11.42	2:12.28	2:13.15	2:14.01	2:14.88	2:15.74	2:16.60
160	2:17.47	2:18.33	2:19.20	2:20.06	2:20.93	2:21.79	2:22.66	2:23.52	2:24.39	2:25.25
170	2:26.11	2:26.98	2:27.84	2:28.71	2:29.57	2:30.44	2:31.30	2:32.17	2:33.03	2:33.90
180	2:34.76	2:35.63	2:36.49	2:37.35	2:38.22	2:39.08	2:39.95	2:40.81	2:41.68	2:42.54
190	2:43.41	2:44.27	2:45.14	2:46.00	2:46.86	2:47.73	2:48.59	2:49.46	2:50.32	2:51.19
200	2:52.05	2:52.92	2:53.78	2:54.65	2:55.51	2:56.38	2:57.24	2:58.10	2:58.97	2:59.83
210	3:00.70	3:01.56	3:02.43	3:03.29	3:04.16	3:05.02	3:05.89	3:06.75	3:07.61	3:08.48
220	3:09.34	3:10.21	3:11.07	3:11.94	3:12.80	3:13.67	3:14.53	3:15.40	3:16.26	3:17.12
230	3:17.99	3:18.85	3:19.72	3:20.58	3:21.45	3:22.31	3:23.18	3:24.04	3:24.91	3:25.77
240	3:26.64	3:27.50	3:28.36	3:29.23	3:30.09	3:30.96	3:31.82	3:32.69	3:33.55	3:34.42
250	3:35.28	3:36.15	3:37.01	3:37.87	3:38.74	3:39.60	3:40.47	3:41.33	3:42.20	3:43.06
260	3:43.93	3:44.79	3:45.66	3:46.52	3:47.39	3:48.25	3:49.11	3:49.98	3:50.84	3:51.71
270	3:52.57	3:53.44	3:54.30	3:55.17	3:56.03	3:56.90	3:57.76	3:58.62	3:59.49	4:00.35
280	4:01.22	4:02.08	4:02.95	4:03.81	4:04.68	4:05.54	4:06.41	4:07.27	4:08.14	4:09.00
290	4:09.86	4:10.73	4:11.59	4:12.46	4:13.32	4:14.19	4:15.05	4:15.92	4:16.78	4:17.65
300	4:18.51	4:19.37	4:20.24	4:21.10	4:21.97	4:22.83	4:23.70	4:24.56	4:25.43	4:26.29
310	4:27.16	4:28.02	4:28.89	4:29.75	4:30.61	4:31.48	4:32.34	4:33.21	4:34.07	4:34.94
320	4:35.80	4:36.67	4:37.53	4:38.40	4:39.26	4:40.12	4:40.99	4:41.85	4:42.72	4:43.58
330	4:44.45	4:45.31	4:46.18	4:47.04	4:47.91	4:48.77	4:49.64	4:50.50	4:51.36	4:52.23
340	4:53.09	4:53.96	4:54.82	4:55.69	4:56.55	4:57.42	4:58.28	4:59.15	5:00.01	5:00.87
350	5:01.74	5:02.60	5:03.47	5:04.33	5:05.20	5:06.06	5:06.93	5:07.79	5:08.66	5:09.52
360	5:10.39	5:11.25	5:12.11	5:12.98	5:13.84	5:14.71	5:15.57	5:16.44	5:17.30	5:18.17
370	5:19.03	5:19.90	5:20.76	5:21.62	5:22.49	5:23.35	5:24.22	5:25.08	5:25.95	5:26.81
380	5:27.68	5:28.54	5:29.41	5:30.27	5:31.14	5:32.00	5:32.86	5:33.73	5:34.59	5:35.46
390	5:36.32	5:37.19	5:38.05	5:38.92	5:39.78	5:40.65	5:41.51	5:42.37	5:43.24	5:44.10
400	5:44.97	5:45.83	5:46.70	5:47.56	5:48.43	5:49.29	5:50.16	5:51.02	5:51.89	5:52.75
410	5:53.61	5:54.48	5:55.34	5:56.21	5:57.07	5:57.94	5:58.80	5:59.67	6:00.53	6:01.40
420	6:02.26	6:03.12	6:03.99	6:04.85	6:05.72	6:06.58	6:07.45	6:08.31	6:09.18	6:10.04
430	6:10.91	6:11.77	6:12.64	6:13.50	6:14.36	6:15.23	6:16.09	6:16.96	6:17.82	6:18.69
440	6:19.55	6:20.42	6:21.28	6:22.15	6:23.01	6:23.87	6:24.74	6:25.60	6:26.47	6:27.33
450	6:28.20	6:29.06	6:29.93	6:30.79	6:31.66	6:32.52	6:33.39	6:34.25	6:35.11	6:35.98
460	6:36.84	6:37.71	6:38.57	6:39.44	6:40.30	6:41.17	6:42.03	6:42.90	6:43.76	6:44.62
470	6:45.49	6:46.35	6:47.22	6:48.08	6:48.95	6:49.81	6:50.68	6:51.54	6:52.41	6:53.27
480	6:54.14	6:55.00	6:55.86	6:56.73	6:57.59	6:58.46	6:59.32	7:00.19	7:01.05	7:01.92
490	7:02.78	7:03.65	7:04.51	7:05.37	7:06.24	7:07.10	7:07.97	7:08.83	7:09.70	7:10.56
500	7:11.43	7:12.29	7:13.16	7:14.02	7:14.89	7:15.75	7:16.61	7:17.48	7:18.34	7:19.21
510	7:20.07	7:20.94	7:21.80	7:22.67	7:23.53	7:24.40	7:25.26	7:26.13	7:26.99	7:27.85
520	7:28.72	7:29.58	7:30.45	7:31.31	7:32.18	7:33.04	7:33.91	7:34.77	7:35.64	7:36.50
530	7:37.36	7:38.23	7:39.09	7:39.96	7:40.82	7:41.69	7:42.55	7:43.42	7:44.28	7:45.15
540	7:46.01	7:46.88	7:47.74	7:48.60	7:49.47	7:50.33	7:51.20	7:52.06	7:52.93	7:53.79
550	7:54.66	7:55.52	7:56.39	7:57.25	7:58.11	7:58.98	7:59.84	8:00.71	8:01.57	8:02.44
560	8:03.30	8:04.17	8:05.03	8:05.90	8:06.76	8:07.62	8:08.49	8:09.35	8:10.22	8:11.08
570	8:11.95	8:12.81	8:13.68	8:14.54	8:15.41	8:16.27	8:17.14	8:18.00	8:18.86	8:19.73
580	8:20.59	8:21.46	8:22.32	8:23.19	8:24.05	8:24.92	8:25.78	8:26.65	8:27.51	8:28.37
590	8:29.24	8:30.10	8:30.97	8:31.83	8:32.70	8:33.56	8:34.43	8:35.29	8:36.16	8:37.02

♩. = 1.30; ♩ = 0.86; ♪. = 0.65; (3: ♩ 𝄾) = 0.58; ♪ = 0.43; (3: ♪ 𝄾 𝄾) = 0.29; 𝅘𝅥𝅯 = 0.22 seconds

CLICK: 20⅞ FRAMES; M.M.: 68.98

Click	0	1	2	3	4	5	6	7	8	9
000	0:00.00	0:00.00	0:00.87	0:01.74	0:02.61	0:03.48	0:04.35	0:05.22	0:06.09	0:06.96
010	0:07.83	0:08.70	0:09.57	0:10.44	0:11.31	0:12.18	0:13.05	0:13.92	0:14.79	0:15.66
020	0:16.53	0:17.40	0:18.27	0:19.14	0:20.01	0:20.87	0:21.74	0:22.61	0:23.48	0:24.35
030	0:25.22	0:26.09	0:26.96	0:27.83	0:28.70	0:29.57	0:30.44	0:31.31	0:32.18	0:33.05
040	0:33.92	0:34.79	0:35.66	0:36.53	0:37.40	0:38.27	0:39.14	0:40.01	0:40.88	0:41.75
050	0:42.62	0:43.49	0:44.36	0:45.23	0:46.10	0:46.97	0:47.84	0:48.71	0:49.58	0:50.45
060	0:51.32	0:52.19	0:53.06	0:53.93	0:54.80	0:55.67	0:56.54	0:57.41	0:58.28	0:59.15
070	1:00.02	1:00.89	1:01.76	1:02.62	1:03.49	1:04.36	1:05.23	1:06.10	1:06.97	1:07.84
080	1:08.71	1:09.58	1:10.45	1:11.32	1:12.19	1:13.06	1:13.93	1:14.80	1:15.67	1:16.54
090	1:17.41	1:18.28	1:19.15	1:20.02	1:20.89	1:21.76	1:22.63	1:23.50	1:24.37	1:25.24
100	1:26.11	1:26.98	1:27.85	1:28.72	1:29.59	1:30.46	1:31.33	1:32.20	1:33.07	1:33.94
110	1:34.81	1:35.68	1:36.55	1:37.42	1:38.29	1:39.16	1:40.03	1:40.90	1:41.77	1:42.64
120	1:43.51	1:44.37	1:45.24	1:46.11	1:46.98	1:47.85	1:48.72	1:49.59	1:50.46	1:51.33
130	1:52.20	1:53.07	1:53.94	1:54.81	1:55.68	1:56.55	1:57.42	1:58.29	1:59.16	2:00.03
140	2:00.90	2:01.77	2:02.64	2:03.51	2:04.38	2:05.25	2:06.12	2:06.99	2:07.86	2:08.73
150	2:09.60	2:10.47	2:11.34	2:12.21	2:13.08	2:13.95	2:14.82	2:15.69	2:16.56	2:17.43
160	2:18.30	2:19.17	2:20.04	2:20.91	2:21.78	2:22.65	2:23.52	2:24.39	2:25.26	2:26.12
170	2:26.99	2:27.86	2:28.73	2:29.60	2:30.47	2:31.34	2:32.21	2:33.08	2:33.95	2:34.82
180	2:35.69	2:36.56	2:37.43	2:38.30	2:39.17	2:40.04	2:40.91	2:41.78	2:42.65	2:43.52
190	2:44.39	2:45.26	2:46.13	2:47.00	2:47.87	2:48.74	2:49.61	2:50.48	2:51.35	2:52.22
200	2:53.09	2:53.96	2:54.83	2:55.70	2:56.57	2:57.44	2:58.31	2:59.18	3:00.05	3:00.92
210	3:01.79	3:02.66	3:03.53	3:04.40	3:05.27	3:06.14	3:07.01	3:07.87	3:08.74	3:09.61
220	3:10.48	3:11.35	3:12.22	3:13.09	3:13.96	3:14.83	3:15.70	3:16.57	3:17.44	3:18.31
230	3:19.18	3:20.05	3:20.92	3:21.79	3:22.66	3:23.53	3:24.40	3:25.27	3:26.14	3:27.01
240	3:27.88	3:28.75	3:29.62	3:30.49	3:31.36	3:32.23	3:33.10	3:33.97	3:34.84	3:35.71
250	3:36.58	3:37.45	3:38.32	3:39.19	3:40.06	3:40.93	3:41.80	3:42.67	3:43.54	3:44.41
260	3:45.28	3:46.15	3:47.02	3:47.89	3:48.76	3:49.62	3:50.49	3:51.36	3:52.23	3:53.10
270	3:53.97	3:54.84	3:55.71	3:56.58	3:57.45	3:58.32	3:59.19	4:00.06	4:00.93	4:01.80
280	4:02.67	4:03.54	4:04.41	4:05.28	4:06.15	4:07.02	4:07.89	4:08.76	4:09.63	4:10.50
290	4:11.37	4:12.24	4:13.11	4:13.98	4:14.85	4:15.72	4:16.59	4:17.46	4:18.33	4:19.20
300	4:20.07	4:20.94	4:21.81	4:22.68	4:23.55	4:24.42	4:25.29	4:26.16	4:27.03	4:27.90
310	4:28.77	4:29.64	4:30.51	4:31.37	4:32.24	4:33.11	4:33.98	4:34.85	4:35.72	4:36.59
320	4:37.46	4:38.33	4:39.20	4:40.07	4:40.94	4:41.81	4:42.68	4:43.55	4:44.42	4:45.29
330	4:46.16	4:47.03	4:47.90	4:48.77	4:49.64	4:50.51	4:51.38	4:52.25	4:53.12	4:53.99
340	4:54.86	4:55.73	4:56.60	4:57.47	4:58.34	4:59.21	5:00.08	5:00.95	5:01.82	5:02.69
350	5:03.56	5:04.43	5:05.30	5:06.17	5:07.04	5:07.91	5:08.78	5:09.65	5:10.52	5:11.39
360	5:12.26	5:13.12	5:13.99	5:14.86	5:15.73	5:16.60	5:17.47	5:18.34	5:19.21	5:20.08
370	5:20.95	5:21.82	5:22.69	5:23.56	5:24.43	5:25.30	5:26.17	5:27.04	5:27.91	5:28.78
380	5:29.65	5:30.52	5:31.39	5:32.26	5:33.13	5:34.00	5:34.87	5:35.74	5:36.61	5:37.48
390	5:38.35	5:39.22	5:40.09	5:40.96	5:41.83	5:42.70	5:43.57	5:44.44	5:45.31	5:46.18
400	5:47.05	5:47.92	5:48.79	5:49.66	5:50.53	5:51.40	5:52.27	5:53.14	5:54.01	5:54.87
410	5:55.74	5:56.61	5:57.48	5:58.35	5:59.22	6:00.09	6:00.96	6:01.83	6:02.70	6:03.57
420	6:04.44	6:05.31	6:06.18	6:07.05	6:07.92	6:08.79	6:09.66	6:10.53	6:11.40	6:12.27
430	6:13.14	6:14.01	6:14.88	6:15.75	6:16.62	6:17.49	6:18.36	6:19.23	6:20.10	6:20.97
440	6:21.84	6:22.71	6:23.58	6:24.45	6:25.32	6:26.19	6:27.06	6:27.93	6:28.80	6:29.67
450	6:30.54	6:31.41	6:32.28	6:33.15	6:34.02	6:34.89	6:35.76	6:36.62	6:37.49	6:38.36
460	6:39.23	6:40.10	6:40.97	6:41.84	6:42.71	6:43.58	6:44.45	6:45.32	6:46.19	6:47.06
470	6:47.93	6:48.80	6:49.67	6:50.54	6:51.41	6:52.28	6:53.15	6:54.02	6:54.89	6:55.76
480	6:56.63	6:57.50	6:58.37	6:59.24	7:00.11	7:00.98	7:01.85	7:02.72	7:03.59	7:04.46
490	7:05.33	7:06.20	7:07.07	7:07.94	7:08.81	7:09.68	7:10.55	7:11.42	7:12.29	7:13.16
500	7:14.03	7:14.90	7:15.77	7:16.64	7:17.51	7:18.37	7:19.24	7:20.11	7:20.98	7:21.85
510	7:22.72	7:23.59	7:24.46	7:25.33	7:26.20	7:27.07	7:27.94	7:28.81	7:29.68	7:30.55
520	7:31.42	7:32.29	7:33.16	7:34.03	7:34.90	7:35.77	7:36.64	7:37.51	7:38.38	7:39.25
530	7:40.12	7:40.99	7:41.86	7:42.73	7:43.60	7:44.47	7:45.34	7:46.21	7:47.08	7:47.95
540	7:48.82	7:49.69	7:50.56	7:51.43	7:52.30	7:53.17	7:54.04	7:54.91	7:55.78	7:56.65
550	7:57.52	7:58.39	7:59.26	8:00.12	8:00.99	8:01.86	8:02.73	8:03.60	8:04.47	8:05.34
560	8:06.21	8:07.08	8:07.95	8:08.82	8:09.69	8:10.56	8:11.43	8:12.30	8:13.17	8:14.04
570	8:14.91	8:15.78	8:16.65	8:17.52	8:18.39	8:19.26	8:20.13	8:21.00	8:21.87	8:22.74
580	8:23.61	8:24.48	8:25.35	8:26.22	8:27.09	8:27.96	8:28.83	8:29.70	8:30.57	8:31.44
590	8:32.31	8:33.18	8:34.05	8:34.92	8:35.79	8:36.66	8:37.53	8:38.40	8:39.27	8:40.14

♩. = 1.30; ♩ = 0.87; ♪. = 0.65; (triplet ♩ 𝄾) = 0.58; ♪ = 0.43; (triplet ♪ 𝄾 𝄾) = 0.29; 𝅘𝅥𝅯 = 0.22 seconds

CLICK: 21 0/8 FRAMES; M.M.: 68.57

Click	0	1	2	3	4	5	6	7	8	9
000	0:00.00	0:00.00	0:00.88	0:01.75	0:02.63	0:03.50	0:04.38	0:05.25	0:06.13	0:07.00
010	0:07.87	0:08.75	0:09.63	0:10.50	0:11.38	0:12.25	0:13.13	0:14.00	0:14.88	0:15.75
020	0:16.63	0:17.50	0:18.38	0:19.25	0:20.13	0:21.00	0:21.88	0:22.75	0:23.63	0:24.50
030	0:25.38	0:26.25	0:27.13	0:28.00	0:28.88	0:29.75	0:30.63	0:31.50	0:32.38	0:33.25
040	0:34.13	0:35.00	0:35.88	0:36.75	0:37.63	0:38.50	0:39.38	0:40.25	0:41.13	0:42.00
050	0:42.88	0:43.75	0:44.63	0:45.50	0:46.38	0:47.25	0:48.13	0:49.00	0:49.88	0:50.75
060	0:51.63	0:52.50	0:53.38	0:54.25	0:55.13	0:56.00	0:56.88	0:57.75	0:58.63	0:59.50
070	1:00.38	1:01.25	1:02.13	1:03.00	1:03.87	1:04.75	1:05.63	1:06.50	1:07.38	1:08.25
080	1:09.13	1:10.00	1:10.87	1:11.75	1:12.63	1:13.50	1:14.38	1:15.25	1:16.12	1:17.00
090	1:17.88	1:18.75	1:19.63	1:20.50	1:21.38	1:22.25	1:23.12	1:24.00	1:24.88	1:25.75
100	1:26.63	1:27.50	1:28.38	1:29.25	1:30.12	1:31.00	1:31.88	1:32.75	1:33.63	1:34.50
110	1:35.38	1:36.25	1:37.13	1:38.00	1:38.88	1:39.75	1:40.63	1:41.50	1:42.37	1:43.25
120	1:44.13	1:45.00	1:45.88	1:46.75	1:47.63	1:48.50	1:49.37	1:50.25	1:51.13	1:52.00
130	1:52.88	1:53.75	1:54.63	1:55.50	1:56.38	1:57.25	1:58.13	1:59.00	1:59.88	2:00.75
140	2:01.63	2:02.50	2:03.38	2:04.25	2:05.13	2:06.00	2:06.87	2:07.75	2:08.62	2:09.50
150	2:10.37	2:11.25	2:12.13	2:13.00	2:13.88	2:14.75	2:15.63	2:16.50	2:17.38	2:18.25
160	2:19.12	2:20.00	2:20.87	2:21.75	2:22.62	2:23.50	2:24.38	2:25.25	2:26.13	2:27.00
170	2:27.88	2:28.75	2:29.63	2:30.50	2:31.38	2:32.25	2:33.12	2:34.00	2:34.87	2:35.75
180	2:36.63	2:37.50	2:38.38	2:39.25	2:40.13	2:41.00	2:41.88	2:42.75	2:43.63	2:44.50
190	2:45.37	2:46.25	2:47.12	2:48.00	2:48.88	2:49.75	2:50.63	2:51.50	2:52.38	2:53.25
200	2:54.13	2:55.00	2:55.88	2:56.75	2:57.63	2:58.50	2:59.37	3:00.25	3:01.12	3:02.00
210	3:02.87	3:03.75	3:04.63	3:05.50	3:06.38	3:07.25	3:08.13	3:09.00	3:09.88	3:10.75
220	3:11.62	3:12.50	3:13.37	3:14.25	3:15.12	3:16.00	3:16.88	3:17.75	3:18.63	3:19.50
230	3:20.38	3:21.25	3:22.13	3:23.00	3:23.88	3:24.75	3:25.62	3:26.50	3:27.37	3:28.25
240	3:29.13	3:30.00	3:30.88	3:31.75	3:32.63	3:33.50	3:34.38	3:35.25	3:36.13	3:37.00
250	3:37.87	3:38.75	3:39.62	3:40.50	3:41.38	3:42.25	3:43.13	3:44.00	3:44.88	3:45.75
260	3:46.63	3:47.50	3:48.38	3:49.25	3:50.13	3:51.00	3:51.87	3:52.75	3:53.62	3:54.50
270	3:55.38	3:56.25	3:57.13	3:58.00	3:58.88	3:59.75	4:00.62	4:01.50	4:02.37	4:03.25
280	4:04.12	4:05.00	4:05.87	4:06.75	4:07.62	4:08.50	4:09.38	4:10.25	4:11.13	4:12.00
290	4:12.88	4:13.75	4:14.63	4:15.50	4:16.38	4:17.25	4:18.13	4:19.00	4:19.88	4:20.75
300	4:21.63	4:22.50	4:23.38	4:24.25	4:25.12	4:26.00	4:26.87	4:27.75	4:28.62	4:29.50
310	4:30.37	4:31.25	4:32.12	4:33.00	4:33.88	4:34.75	4:35.63	4:36.50	4:37.38	4:38.25
320	4:39.13	4:40.00	4:40.88	4:41.75	4:42.63	4:43.50	4:44.38	4:45.25	4:46.13	4:47.00
330	4:47.88	4:48.75	4:49.63	4:50.50	4:51.37	4:52.25	4:53.12	4:54.00	4:54.87	4:55.75
340	4:56.62	4:57.50	4:58.37	4:59.25	5:00.12	5:01.00	5:01.88	5:02.75	5:03.63	5:04.50
350	5:05.38	5:06.25	5:07.13	5:08.00	5:08.88	5:09.75	5:10.63	5:11.50	5:12.38	5:13.25
360	5:14.13	5:15.00	5:15.88	5:16.75	5:17.62	5:18.50	5:19.37	5:20.25	5:21.12	5:22.00
370	5:22.87	5:23.75	5:24.62	5:25.50	5:26.37	5:27.25	5:28.13	5:29.00	5:29.88	5:30.75
380	5:31.63	5:32.50	5:33.38	5:34.25	5:35.13	5:36.00	5:36.88	5:37.75	5:38.63	5:39.50
390	5:40.38	5:41.25	5:42.13	5:43.00	5:43.87	5:44.75	5:45.62	5:46.50	5:47.37	5:48.25
400	5:49.12	5:50.00	5:50.87	5:51.75	5:52.63	5:53.50	5:54.38	5:55.25	5:56.13	5:57.00
410	5:57.88	5:58.75	5:59.63	6:00.50	6:01.38	6:02.25	6:03.13	6:04.00	6:04.88	6:05.75
420	6:06.63	6:07.50	6:08.38	6:09.25	6:10.12	6:11.00	6:11.87	6:12.75	6:13.62	6:14.50
430	6:15.37	6:16.25	6:17.12	6:18.00	6:18.87	6:19.75	6:20.63	6:21.50	6:22.38	6:23.25
440	6:24.13	6:25.00	6:25.88	6:26.75	6:27.63	6:28.50	6:29.38	6:30.25	6:31.13	6:32.00
450	6:32.88	6:33.75	6:34.63	6:35.50	6:36.37	6:37.25	6:38.12	6:39.00	6:39.87	6:40.75
460	6:41.62	6:42.50	6:43.37	6:44.25	6:45.13	6:46.00	6:46.88	6:47.75	6:48.63	6:49.50
470	6:50.38	6:51.25	6:52.13	6:53.00	6:53.88	6:54.75	6:55.63	6:56.50	6:57.38	6:58.25
480	6:59.13	7:00.00	7:00.88	7:01.75	7:02.62	7:03.50	7:04.37	7:05.25	7:06.12	7:07.00
490	7:07.87	7:08.75	7:09.62	7:10.50	7:11.37	7:12.25	7:13.13	7:14.00	7:14.88	7:15.75
500	7:16.63	7:17.50	7:18.38	7:19.25	7:20.13	7:21.00	7:21.88	7:22.75	7:23.63	7:24.50
510	7:25.38	7:26.25	7:27.13	7:28.00	7:28.87	7:29.75	7:30.62	7:31.50	7:32.37	7:33.25
520	7:34.12	7:35.00	7:35.87	7:36.75	7:37.63	7:38.50	7:39.38	7:40.25	7:41.13	7:42.00
530	7:42.88	7:43.75	7:44.63	7:45.50	7:46.38	7:47.25	7:48.13	7:49.00	7:49.88	7:50.75
540	7:51.63	7:52.50	7:53.38	7:54.25	7:55.12	7:56.00	7:56.87	7:57.75	7:58.62	7:59.50
550	8:00.38	8:01.25	8:02.12	8:03.00	8:03.88	8:04.75	8:05.63	8:06.50	8:07.38	8:08.25
560	8:09.13	8:10.00	8:10.87	8:11.75	8:12.63	8:13.50	8:14.37	8:15.25	8:16.13	8:17.00
570	8:17.87	8:18.75	8:19.63	8:20.50	8:21.37	8:22.25	8:23.13	8:24.00	8:24.87	8:25.75
580	8:26.63	8:27.50	8:28.37	8:29.25	8:30.13	8:31.00	8:31.88	8:32.75	8:33.63	8:34.50
590	8:35.38	8:36.25	8:37.12	8:38.00	8:38.88	8:39.75	8:40.62	8:41.50	8:42.38	8:43.25

♩. = 1.31; ♩ = 0.88; ♪. = 0.66; (triplet ♩ 𝄾) = 0.58; ♪ = 0.44; (triplet ♪ 𝄾 𝄾) = 0.29; 𝅘𝅥𝅯 = 0.22 seconds

CLICK: 21⅛ FRAMES; M.M.: 68.17

Click	0	1	2	3	4	5	6	7	8	9
000	0:00.00	0:00.00	0:00.88	0:01.76	0:02.64	0:03.52	0:04.40	0:05.28	0:06.16	0:07.04
010	0:07.92	0:08.80	0:09.68	0:10.56	0:11.44	0:12.32	0:13.20	0:14.08	0:14.96	0:15.84
020	0:16.72	0:17.60	0:18.48	0:19.36	0:20.24	0:21.13	0:22.01	0:22.89	0:23.77	0:24.65
030	0:25.53	0:26.41	0:27.29	0:28.17	0:29.05	0:29.93	0:30.81	0:31.69	0:32.57	0:33.45
040	0:34.33	0:35.21	0:36.09	0:36.97	0:37.85	0:38.73	0:39.61	0:40.49	0:41.37	0:42.25
050	0:43.13	0:44.01	0:44.89	0:45.77	0:46.65	0:47.53	0:48.41	0:49.29	0:50.17	0:51.05
060	0:51.93	0:52.81	0:53.69	0:54.57	0:55.45	0:56.33	0:57.21	0:58.09	0:58.97	0:59.85
070	1:00.73	1:01.61	1:02.49	1:03.37	1:04.26	1:05.14	1:06.02	1:06.90	1:07.78	1:08.66
080	1:09.54	1:10.42	1:11.30	1:12.18	1:13.06	1:13.94	1:14.82	1:15.70	1:16.58	1:17.46
090	1:18.34	1:19.22	1:20.10	1:20.98	1:21.86	1:22.74	1:23.62	1:24.50	1:25.38	1:26.26
100	1:27.14	1:28.02	1:28.90	1:29.78	1:30.66	1:31.54	1:32.42	1:33.30	1:34.18	1:35.06
110	1:35.94	1:36.82	1:37.70	1:38.58	1:39.46	1:40.34	1:41.22	1:42.10	1:42.98	1:43.86
120	1:44.74	1:45.63	1:46.51	1:47.39	1:48.27	1:49.15	1:50.03	1:50.91	1:51.79	1:52.67
130	1:53.55	1:54.43	1:55.31	1:56.19	1:57.07	1:57.95	1:58.83	1:59.71	2:00.59	2:01.47
140	2:02.35	2:03.23	2:04.11	2:04.99	2:05.87	2:06.75	2:07.63	2:08.51	2:09.39	2:10.27
150	2:11.15	2:12.03	2:12.91	2:13.79	2:14.67	2:15.55	2:16.43	2:17.31	2:18.19	2:19.07
160	2:19.95	2:20.83	2:21.71	2:22.59	2:23.47	2:24.35	2:25.23	2:26.11	2:26.99	2:27.88
170	2:28.76	2:29.64	2:30.52	2:31.40	2:32.28	2:33.16	2:34.04	2:34.92	2:35.80	2:36.68
180	2:37.56	2:38.44	2:39.32	2:40.20	2:41.08	2:41.96	2:42.84	2:43.72	2:44.60	2:45.48
190	2:46.36	2:47.24	2:48.12	2:49.00	2:49.88	2:50.76	2:51.64	2:52.52	2:53.40	2:54.28
200	2:55.16	2:56.04	2:56.92	2:57.80	2:58.68	2:59.56	3:00.44	3:01.32	3:02.20	3:03.08
210	3:03.96	3:04.84	3:05.72	3:06.60	3:07.48	3:08.36	3:09.24	3:10.13	3:11.01	3:11.89
220	3:12.77	3:13.65	3:14.53	3:15.41	3:16.29	3:17.17	3:18.05	3:18.93	3:19.81	3:20.69
230	3:21.57	3:22.45	3:23.33	3:24.21	3:25.09	3:25.97	3:26.85	3:27.73	3:28.61	3:29.49
240	3:30.37	3:31.25	3:32.13	3:33.01	3:33.89	3:34.77	3:35.65	3:36.53	3:37.41	3:38.29
250	3:39.17	3:40.05	3:40.93	3:41.81	3:42.69	3:43.57	3:44.45	3:45.33	3:46.21	3:47.09
260	3:47.97	3:48.85	3:49.73	3:50.61	3:51.49	3:52.38	3:53.26	3:54.14	3:55.02	3:55.90
270	3:56.78	3:57.66	3:58.54	3:59.42	4:00.30	4:01.18	4:02.06	4:02.94	4:03.82	4:04.70
280	4:05.58	4:06.46	4:07.34	4:08.22	4:09.10	4:09.98	4:10.86	4:11.74	4:12.62	4:13.50
290	4:14.38	4:15.26	4:16.14	4:17.02	4:17.90	4:18.78	4:19.66	4:20.54	4:21.42	4:22.30
300	4:23.18	4:24.06	4:24.94	4:25.82	4:26.70	4:27.58	4:28.46	4:29.34	4:30.22	4:31.10
310	4:31.98	4:32.86	4:33.74	4:34.63	4:35.51	4:36.39	4:37.27	4:38.15	4:39.03	4:39.91
320	4:40.79	4:41.67	4:42.55	4:43.43	4:44.31	4:45.19	4:46.07	4:46.95	4:47.83	4:48.71
330	4:49.59	4:50.47	4:51.35	4:52.23	4:53.11	4:53.99	4:54.87	4:55.75	4:56.63	4:57.51
340	4:58.39	4:59.27	5:00.15	5:01.03	5:01.91	5:02.79	5:03.67	5:04.55	5:05.43	5:06.31
350	5:07.19	5:08.07	5:08.95	5:09.83	5:10.71	5:11.59	5:12.47	5:13.35	5:14.23	5:15.11
360	5:15.99	5:16.88	5:17.76	5:18.64	5:19.52	5:20.40	5:21.28	5:22.16	5:23.04	5:23.92
370	5:24.80	5:25.68	5:26.56	5:27.44	5:28.32	5:29.20	5:30.08	5:30.96	5:31.84	5:32.72
380	5:33.60	5:34.48	5:35.36	5:36.24	5:37.12	5:38.00	5:38.88	5:39.76	5:40.64	5:41.52
390	5:42.40	5:43.28	5:44.16	5:45.04	5:45.92	5:46.80	5:47.68	5:48.56	5:49.44	5:50.32
400	5:51.20	5:52.08	5:52.96	5:53.84	5:54.72	5:55.60	5:56.48	5:57.36	5:58.24	5:59.13
410	6:00.01	6:00.89	6:01.77	6:02.65	6:03.53	6:04.41	6:05.29	6:06.17	6:07.05	6:07.93
420	6:08.81	6:09.69	6:10.57	6:11.45	6:12.33	6:13.21	6:14.09	6:14.97	6:15.85	6:16.73
430	6:17.61	6:18.49	6:19.37	6:20.25	6:21.13	6:22.01	6:22.89	6:23.77	6:24.65	6:25.53
440	6:26.41	6:27.29	6:28.17	6:29.05	6:29.93	6:30.81	6:31.69	6:32.57	6:33.45	6:34.33
450	6:35.21	6:36.09	6:36.97	6:37.85	6:38.73	6:39.61	6:40.49	6:41.38	6:42.26	6:43.14
460	6:44.02	6:44.90	6:45.78	6:46.66	6:47.54	6:48.42	6:49.30	6:50.18	6:51.06	6:51.94
470	6:52.82	6:53.70	6:54.58	6:55.46	6:56.34	6:57.22	6:58.10	6:58.98	6:59.86	7:00.74
480	7:01.62	7:02.50	7:03.38	7:04.26	7:05.14	7:06.02	7:06.90	7:07.78	7:08.66	7:09.54
490	7:10.42	7:11.30	7:12.18	7:13.06	7:13.94	7:14.82	7:15.70	7:16.58	7:17.46	7:18.34
500	7:19.22	7:20.10	7:20.98	7:21.86	7:22.74	7:23.63	7:24.51	7:25.39	7:26.27	7:27.15
510	7:28.03	7:28.91	7:29.79	7:30.67	7:31.55	7:32.43	7:33.31	7:34.19	7:35.07	7:35.95
520	7:36.83	7:37.71	7:38.59	7:39.47	7:40.35	7:41.23	7:42.11	7:42.99	7:43.87	7:44.75
530	7:45.63	7:46.51	7:47.39	7:48.27	7:49.15	7:50.03	7:50.91	7:51.79	7:52.67	7:53.55
540	7:54.43	7:55.31	7:56.19	7:57.07	7:57.95	7:58.83	7:59.71	8:00.59	8:01.47	8:02.35
550	8:03.23	8:04.11	8:04.99	8:05.87	8:06.76	8:07.64	8:08.52	8:09.40	8:10.28	8:11.16
560	8:12.04	8:12.92	8:13.80	8:14.68	8:15.56	8:16.44	8:17.32	8:18.20	8:19.08	8:19.96
570	8:20.84	8:21.72	8:22.60	8:23.48	8:24.36	8:25.24	8:26.12	8:27.00	8:27.88	8:28.76
580	8:29.64	8:30.52	8:31.40	8:32.28	8:33.16	8:34.04	8:34.92	8:35.80	8:36.68	8:37.56
590	8:38.44	8:39.32	8:40.20	8:41.08	8:41.96	8:42.84	8:43.72	8:44.60	8:45.48	8:46.36

♩. = 1.32; ♩ = 0.88; ♪. = 0.66; 3 ♩ 𝄾 = 0.59; ♪ = 0.44; 3 ♪ 𝄾 𝄾 = 0.29; 𝅘𝅥𝅯 = 0.22 seconds

CLICK: $21\frac{2}{8}$ FRAMES; M.M.: 67.76

Click	0	1	2	3	4	5	6	7	8	9
000	0:00.00	0:00.00	0:00.89	0:01.77	0:02.66	0:03.54	0:04.43	0:05.31	0:06.20	0:07.08
010	0:07.97	0:08.85	0:09.74	0:10.63	0:11.51	0:12.40	0:13.28	0:14.17	0:15.05	0:15.94
020	0:16.82	0:17.71	0:18.59	0:19.48	0:20.36	0:21.25	0:22.14	0:23.02	0:23.91	0:24.79
030	0:25.68	0:26.56	0:27.45	0:28.33	0:29.22	0:30.10	0:30.99	0:31.88	0:32.76	0:33.65
040	0:34.53	0:35.42	0:36.30	0:37.19	0:38.07	0:38.96	0:39.84	0:40.73	0:41.61	0:42.50
050	0:43.39	0:44.27	0:45.16	0:46.04	0:46.93	0:47.81	0:48.70	0:49.58	0:50.47	0:51.35
060	0:52.24	0:53.12	0:54.01	0:54.90	0:55.78	0:56.67	0:57.55	0:58.44	0:59.32	1:00.21
070	1:01.09	1:01.98	1:02.86	1:03.75	1:04.64	1:05.52	1:06.41	1:07.29	1:08.18	1:09.06
080	1:09.95	1:10.83	1:11.72	1:12.60	1:13.49	1:14.37	1:15.26	1:16.15	1:17.03	1:17.92
090	1:18.80	1:19.69	1:20.57	1:21.46	1:22.34	1:23.23	1:24.11	1:25.00	1:25.89	1:26.77
100	1:27.66	1:28.54	1:29.43	1:30.31	1:31.20	1:32.08	1:32.97	1:33.85	1:34.74	1:35.63
110	1:36.51	1:37.40	1:38.28	1:39.17	1:40.05	1:40.94	1:41.82	1:42.71	1:43.59	1:44.48
120	1:45.36	1:46.25	1:47.14	1:48.02	1:48.91	1:49.79	1:50.68	1:51.56	1:52.45	1:53.33
130	1:54.22	1:55.10	1:55.99	1:56.87	1:57.76	1:58.65	1:59.53	2:00.42	2:01.30	2:02.19
140	2:03.07	2:03.96	2:04.84	2:05.73	2:06.61	2:07.50	2:08.39	2:09.27	2:10.16	2:11.04
150	2:11.93	2:12.81	2:13.70	2:14.58	2:15.47	2:16.35	2:17.24	2:18.12	2:19.01	2:19.90
160	2:20.78	2:21.67	2:22.55	2:23.44	2:24.32	2:25.21	2:26.09	2:26.98	2:27.86	2:28.75
170	2:29.64	2:30.52	2:31.41	2:32.29	2:33.18	2:34.06	2:34.95	2:35.83	2:36.72	2:37.60
180	2:38.49	2:39.38	2:40.26	2:41.15	2:42.03	2:42.92	2:43.80	2:44.69	2:45.57	2:46.46
190	2:47.34	2:48.23	2:49.11	2:50.00	2:50.89	2:51.77	2:52.66	2:53.54	2:54.43	2:55.31
200	2:56.20	2:57.08	2:57.97	2:58.85	2:59.74	3:00.62	3:01.51	3:02.40	3:03.28	3:04.17
210	3:05.05	3:05.94	3:06.82	3:07.71	3:08.59	3:09.48	3:10.36	3:11.25	3:12.14	3:13.02
220	3:13.91	3:14.79	3:15.68	3:16.56	3:17.45	3:18.33	3:19.22	3:20.10	3:20.99	3:21.87
230	3:22.76	3:23.65	3:24.53	3:25.42	3:26.30	3:27.19	3:28.07	3:28.96	3:29.84	3:30.73
240	3:31.61	3:32.50	3:33.39	3:34.27	3:35.16	3:36.04	3:36.93	3:37.81	3:38.70	3:39.58
250	3:40.47	3:41.35	3:42.24	3:43.13	3:44.01	3:44.90	3:45.78	3:46.67	3:47.55	3:48.44
260	3:49.32	3:50.21	3:51.09	3:51.98	3:52.86	3:53.75	3:54.64	3:55.52	3:56.41	3:57.29
270	3:58.18	3:59.06	3:59.95	4:00.83	4:01.72	4:02.60	4:03.49	4:04.37	4:05.26	4:06.15
280	4:07.03	4:07.92	4:08.80	4:09.69	4:10.57	4:11.46	4:12.34	4:13.23	4:14.11	4:15.00
290	4:15.89	4:16.77	4:17.66	4:18.54	4:19.43	4:20.31	4:21.20	4:22.08	4:22.97	4:23.85
300	4:24.74	4:25.62	4:26.51	4:27.40	4:28.28	4:29.17	4:30.05	4:30.94	4:31.82	4:32.71
310	4:33.59	4:34.48	4:35.36	4:36.25	4:37.14	4:38.02	4:38.91	4:39.79	4:40.68	4:41.56
320	4:42.45	4:43.33	4:44.22	4:45.10	4:45.99	4:46.88	4:47.76	4:48.65	4:49.53	4:50.42
330	4:51.30	4:52.19	4:53.07	4:53.96	4:54.84	4:55.73	4:56.61	4:57.50	4:58.39	4:59.27
340	5:00.16	5:01.04	5:01.93	5:02.81	5:03.70	5:04.58	5:05.47	5:06.35	5:07.24	5:08.12
350	5:09.01	5:09.90	5:10.78	5:11.67	5:12.55	5:13.44	5:14.32	5:15.21	5:16.09	5:16.98
360	5:17.86	5:18.75	5:19.64	5:20.52	5:21.41	5:22.29	5:23.18	5:24.06	5:24.95	5:25.83
370	5:26.72	5:27.60	5:28.49	5:29.37	5:30.26	5:31.15	5:32.03	5:32.92	5:33.80	5:34.69
380	5:35.57	5:36.46	5:37.34	5:38.23	5:39.11	5:40.00	5:40.89	5:41.77	5:42.66	5:43.54
390	5:44.43	5:45.31	5:46.20	5:47.08	5:47.97	5:48.85	5:49.74	5:50.63	5:51.51	5:52.40
400	5:53.28	5:54.17	5:55.05	5:55.94	5:56.82	5:57.71	5:58.59	5:59.48	6:00.36	6:01.25
410	6:02.14	6:03.02	6:03.91	6:04.79	6:05.68	6:06.56	6:07.45	6:08.33	6:09.22	6:10.10
420	6:10.99	6:11.87	6:12.76	6:13.65	6:14.53	6:15.42	6:16.30	6:17.19	6:18.07	6:18.96
430	6:19.84	6:20.73	6:21.61	6:22.50	6:23.39	6:24.27	6:25.16	6:26.04	6:26.93	6:27.81
440	6:28.70	6:29.58	6:30.47	6:31.35	6:32.24	6:33.12	6:34.01	6:34.90	6:35.78	6:36.67
450	6:37.55	6:38.44	6:39.32	6:40.21	6:41.09	6:41.98	6:42.86	6:43.75	6:44.64	6:45.52
460	6:46.41	6:47.29	6:48.18	6:49.06	6:49.95	6:50.83	6:51.72	6:52.60	6:53.49	6:54.38
470	6:55.26	6:56.15	6:57.03	6:57.92	6:58.80	6:59.69	7:00.57	7:01.46	7:02.34	7:03.23
480	7:04.11	7:05.00	7:05.89	7:06.77	7:07.66	7:08.54	7:09.43	7:10.31	7:11.20	7:12.08
490	7:12.97	7:13.85	7:14.74	7:15.62	7:16.51	7:17.40	7:18.28	7:19.17	7:20.05	7:20.94
500	7:21.82	7:22.71	7:23.59	7:24.48	7:25.36	7:26.25	7:27.14	7:28.02	7:28.91	7:29.79
510	7:30.68	7:31.56	7:32.45	7:33.33	7:34.22	7:35.10	7:35.99	7:36.87	7:37.76	7:38.65
520	7:39.53	7:40.42	7:41.30	7:42.19	7:43.07	7:43.96	7:44.84	7:45.73	7:46.61	7:47.50
530	7:48.39	7:49.27	7:50.16	7:51.04	7:51.93	7:52.81	7:53.70	7:54.58	7:55.47	7:56.35
540	7:57.24	7:58.13	7:59.01	7:59.90	8:00.78	8:01.67	8:02.55	8:03.44	8:04.32	8:05.21
550	8:06.09	8:06.98	8:07.86	8:08.75	8:09.64	8:10.52	8:11.41	8:12.29	8:13.18	8:14.06
560	8:14.95	8:15.83	8:16.72	8:17.60	8:18.49	8:19.37	8:20.26	8:21.15	8:22.03	8:22.92
570	8:23.80	8:24.69	8:25.57	8:26.46	8:27.34	8:28.23	8:29.11	8:30.00	8:30.89	8:31.77
580	8:32.66	8:33.54	8:34.43	8:35.31	8:36.20	8:37.08	8:37.97	8:38.85	8:39.74	8:40.62
590	8:41.51	8:42.40	8:43.28	8:44.17	8:45.05	8:45.94	8:46.82	8:47.71	8:48.59	8:49.48

♩. = 1.33; ♩ = 0.89; ♪. = 0.66; (triplet ♩ 𝄾) = 0.59; ♪ = 0.44; (triplet ♪ 𝄾 𝄾) = 0.30; 𝅘𝅥𝅯 = 0.22 seconds

CLICK: 21⅜ FRAMES; M.M.: 67.37

Click	0	1	2	3	4	5	6	7	8	9
000	0:00.00	0:00.00	0:00.89	0:01.78	0:02.67	0:03.56	0:04.45	0:05.34	0:06.23	0:07.13
010	0:08.02	0:08.91	0:09.80	0:10.69	0:11.58	0:12.47	0:13.36	0:14.25	0:15.14	0:16.03
020	0:16.92	0:17.81	0:18.70	0:19.59	0:20.48	0:21.38	0:22.27	0:23.16	0:24.05	0:24.94
030	0:25.83	0:26.72	0:27.61	0:28.50	0:29.39	0:30.28	0:31.17	0:32.06	0:32.95	0:33.84
040	0:34.73	0:35.63	0:36.52	0:37.41	0:38.30	0:39.19	0:40.08	0:40.97	0:41.86	0:42.75
050	0:43.64	0:44.53	0:45.42	0:46.31	0:47.20	0:48.09	0:48.98	0:49.88	0:50.77	0:51.66
060	0:52.55	0:53.44	0:54.33	0:55.22	0:56.11	0:57.00	0:57.89	0:58.78	0:59.67	1:00.56
070	1:01.45	1:02.34	1:03.23	1:04.13	1:05.02	1:05.91	1:06.80	1:07.69	1:08.58	1:09.47
080	1:10.36	1:11.25	1:12.14	1:13.03	1:13.92	1:14.81	1:15.70	1:16.59	1:17.48	1:18.37
090	1:19.27	1:20.16	1:21.05	1:21.94	1:22.83	1:23.72	1:24.61	1:25.50	1:26.39	1:27.28
100	1:28.17	1:29.06	1:29.95	1:30.84	1:31.73	1:32.62	1:33.52	1:34.41	1:35.30	1:36.19
110	1:37.08	1:37.97	1:38.86	1:39.75	1:40.64	1:41.53	1:42.42	1:43.31	1:44.20	1:45.09
120	1:45.98	1:46.88	1:47.77	1:48.66	1:49.55	1:50.44	1:51.33	1:52.22	1:53.11	1:54.00
130	1:54.89	1:55.78	1:56.67	1:57.56	1:58.45	1:59.34	2:00.23	2:01.12	2:02.02	2:02.91
140	2:03.80	2:04.69	2:05.58	2:06.47	2:07.36	2:08.25	2:09.14	2:10.03	2:10.92	2:11.81
150	2:12.70	2:13.59	2:14.48	2:15.37	2:16.27	2:17.16	2:18.05	2:18.94	2:19.83	2:20.72
160	2:21.61	2:22.50	2:23.39	2:24.28	2:25.17	2:26.06	2:26.95	2:27.84	2:28.73	2:29.62
170	2:30.52	2:31.41	2:32.30	2:33.19	2:34.08	2:34.97	2:35.86	2:36.75	2:37.64	2:38.53
180	2:39.42	2:40.31	2:41.20	2:42.09	2:42.98	2:43.88	2:44.77	2:45.66	2:46.55	2:47.44
190	2:48.33	2:49.22	2:50.11	2:51.00	2:51.89	2:52.78	2:53.67	2:54.56	2:55.45	2:56.34
200	2:57.23	2:58.13	2:59.02	2:59.91	3:00.80	3:01.69	3:02.58	3:03.47	3:04.36	3:05.25
210	3:06.14	3:07.03	3:07.92	3:08.81	3:09.70	3:10.59	3:11.48	3:12.37	3:13.27	3:14.16
220	3:15.05	3:15.94	3:16.83	3:17.72	3:18.61	3:19.50	3:20.39	3:21.28	3:22.17	3:23.06
230	3:23.95	3:24.84	3:25.73	3:26.62	3:27.52	3:28.41	3:29.30	3:30.19	3:31.08	3:31.97
240	3:32.86	3:33.75	3:34.64	3:35.53	3:36.42	3:37.31	3:38.20	3:39.09	3:39.98	3:40.87
250	3:41.77	3:42.66	3:43.55	3:44.44	3:45.33	3:46.22	3:47.11	3:48.00	3:48.89	3:49.78
260	3:50.67	3:51.56	3:52.45	3:53.34	3:54.23	3:55.13	3:56.02	3:56.91	3:57.80	3:58.69
270	3:59.58	4:00.47	4:01.36	4:02.25	4:03.14	4:04.03	4:04.92	4:05.81	4:06.70	4:07.59
280	4:08.48	4:09.38	4:10.27	4:11.16	4:12.05	4:12.94	4:13.83	4:14.72	4:15.61	4:16.50
290	4:17.39	4:18.28	4:19.17	4:20.06	4:20.95	4:21.84	4:22.73	4:23.62	4:24.52	4:25.41
300	4:26.30	4:27.19	4:28.08	4:28.97	4:29.86	4:30.75	4:31.64	4:32.53	4:33.42	4:34.31
310	4:35.20	4:36.09	4:36.98	4:37.87	4:38.77	4:39.66	4:40.55	4:41.44	4:42.33	4:43.22
320	4:44.11	4:45.00	4:45.89	4:46.78	4:47.67	4:48.56	4:49.45	4:50.34	4:51.23	4:52.13
330	4:53.02	4:53.91	4:54.80	4:55.69	4:56.58	4:57.47	4:58.36	4:59.25	5:00.14	5:01.03
340	5:01.92	5:02.81	5:03.70	5:04.59	5:05.48	5:06.37	5:07.27	5:08.16	5:09.05	5:09.94
350	5:10.83	5:11.72	5:12.61	5:13.50	5:14.39	5:15.28	5:16.17	5:17.06	5:17.95	5:18.84
360	5:19.73	5:20.63	5:21.52	5:22.41	5:23.30	5:24.19	5:25.08	5:25.97	5:26.86	5:27.75
370	5:28.64	5:29.53	5:30.42	5:31.31	5:32.20	5:33.09	5:33.98	5:34.87	5:35.77	5:36.66
380	5:37.55	5:38.44	5:39.33	5:40.22	5:41.11	5:42.00	5:42.89	5:43.78	5:44.67	5:45.56
390	5:46.45	5:47.34	5:48.23	5:49.12	5:50.02	5:50.91	5:51.80	5:52.69	5:53.58	5:54.47
400	5:55.36	5:56.25	5:57.14	5:58.03	5:58.92	5:59.81	6:00.70	6:01.59	6:02.48	6:03.38
410	6:04.27	6:05.16	6:06.05	6:06.94	6:07.83	6:08.72	6:09.61	6:10.50	6:11.39	6:12.28
420	6:13.17	6:14.06	6:14.95	6:15.84	6:16.73	6:17.62	6:18.52	6:19.41	6:20.30	6:21.19
430	6:22.08	6:22.97	6:23.86	6:24.75	6:25.64	6:26.53	6:27.42	6:28.31	6:29.20	6:30.09
440	6:30.98	6:31.88	6:32.77	6:33.66	6:34.55	6:35.44	6:36.33	6:37.22	6:38.11	6:39.00
450	6:39.89	6:40.78	6:41.67	6:42.56	6:43.45	6:44.34	6:45.23	6:46.12	6:47.02	6:47.91
460	6:48.80	6:49.69	6:50.58	6:51.47	6:52.36	6:53.25	6:54.14	6:55.03	6:55.92	6:56.81
470	6:57.70	6:58.59	6:59.48	7:00.37	7:01.27	7:02.16	7:03.05	7:03.94	7:04.83	7:05.72
480	7:06.61	7:07.50	7:08.39	7:09.28	7:10.17	7:11.06	7:11.95	7:12.84	7:13.73	7:14.63
490	7:15.52	7:16.41	7:17.30	7:18.19	7:19.08	7:19.97	7:20.86	7:21.75	7:22.64	7:23.53
500	7:24.42	7:25.31	7:26.20	7:27.09	7:27.98	7:28.87	7:29.77	7:30.66	7:31.55	7:32.44
510	7:33.33	7:34.22	7:35.11	7:36.00	7:36.89	7:37.78	7:38.67	7:39.56	7:40.45	7:41.34
520	7:42.23	7:43.13	7:44.02	7:44.91	7:45.80	7:46.69	7:47.58	7:48.47	7:49.36	7:50.25
530	7:51.14	7:52.03	7:52.92	7:53.81	7:54.70	7:55.59	7:56.48	7:57.37	7:58.27	7:59.16
540	8:00.05	8:00.94	8:01.83	8:02.72	8:03.61	8:04.50	8:05.39	8:06.28	8:07.17	8:08.06
550	8:08.95	8:09.84	8:10.73	8:11.62	8:12.52	8:13.41	8:14.30	8:15.19	8:16.08	8:16.97
560	8:17.86	8:18.75	8:19.64	8:20.53	8:21.42	8:22.31	8:23.20	8:24.09	8:24.98	8:25.87
570	8:26.77	8:27.66	8:28.55	8:29.44	8:30.33	8:31.22	8:32.11	8:33.00	8:33.89	8:34.78
580	8:35.67	8:36.56	8:37.45	8:38.34	8:39.23	8:40.12	8:41.02	8:41.91	8:42.80	8:43.69
590	8:44.58	8:45.47	8:46.36	8:47.25	8:48.14	8:49.03	8:49.92	8:50.81	8:51.70	8:52.59

♩. = 1.34; ♩ = 0.89; ♪. = 0.67; (3) ♩ 𝄾 = 0.59; ♪ = 0.45; (3) ♪ 𝄾 𝄾 = 0.30; 𝅘𝅥𝅯 = 0.22 seconds

CLICK: 21 4/8 FRAMES; M.M.: 66.98

Click	0	1	2	3	4	5	6	7	8	9
000	0:00.00	0:00.00	0:00.90	0:01.79	0:02.69	0:03.58	0:04.48	0:05.38	0:06.27	0:07.17
010	0:08.06	0:08.96	0:09.85	0:10.75	0:11.65	0:12.54	0:13.44	0:14.33	0:15.23	0:16.13
020	0:17.02	0:17.92	0:18.81	0:19.71	0:20.60	0:21.50	0:22.40	0:23.29	0:24.19	0:25.08
030	0:25.98	0:26.88	0:27.77	0:28.67	0:29.56	0:30.46	0:31.35	0:32.25	0:33.15	0:34.04
040	0:34.94	0:35.83	0:36.73	0:37.63	0:38.52	0:39.42	0:40.31	0:41.21	0:42.10	0:43.00
050	0:43.90	0:44.79	0:45.69	0:46.58	0:47.48	0:48.38	0:49.27	0:50.17	0:51.06	0:51.96
060	0:52.85	0:53.75	0:54.65	0:55.54	0:56.44	0:57.33	0:58.23	0:59.13	1:00.02	1:00.92
070	1:01.81	1:02.71	1:03.60	1:04.50	1:05.40	1:06.29	1:07.19	1:08.08	1:08.98	1:09.88
080	1:10.77	1:11.67	1:12.56	1:13.46	1:14.35	1:15.25	1:16.15	1:17.04	1:17.94	1:18.83
090	1:19.73	1:20.63	1:21.52	1:22.42	1:23.31	1:24.21	1:25.10	1:26.00	1:26.90	1:27.79
100	1:28.69	1:29.58	1:30.48	1:31.38	1:32.27	1:33.17	1:34.06	1:34.96	1:35.85	1:36.75
110	1:37.65	1:38.54	1:39.44	1:40.33	1:41.23	1:42.13	1:43.02	1:43.92	1:44.81	1:45.71
120	1:46.60	1:47.50	1:48.40	1:49.29	1:50.19	1:51.08	1:51.98	1:52.88	1:53.77	1:54.67
130	1:55.56	1:56.46	1:57.35	1:58.25	1:59.15	2:00.04	2:00.94	2:01.83	2:02.73	2:03.63
140	2:04.52	2:05.42	2:06.31	2:07.21	2:08.10	2:09.00	2:09.90	2:10.79	2:11.69	2:12.58
150	2:13.48	2:14.37	2:15.27	2:16.17	2:17.06	2:17.96	2:18.85	2:19.75	2:20.65	2:21.54
160	2:22.44	2:23.33	2:24.23	2:25.13	2:26.02	2:26.92	2:27.81	2:28.71	2:29.60	2:30.50
170	2:31.40	2:32.29	2:33.19	2:34.08	2:34.98	2:35.87	2:36.77	2:37.67	2:38.56	2:39.46
180	2:40.35	2:41.25	2:42.15	2:43.04	2:43.94	2:44.83	2:45.73	2:46.63	2:47.52	2:48.42
190	2:49.31	2:50.21	2:51.10	2:52.00	2:52.90	2:53.79	2:54.69	2:55.58	2:56.48	2:57.37
200	2:58.27	2:59.17	3:00.06	3:00.96	3:01.85	3:02.75	3:03.65	3:04.54	3:05.44	3:06.33
210	3:07.23	3:08.13	3:09.02	3:09.92	3:10.81	3:11.71	3:12.60	3:13.50	3:14.40	3:15.29
220	3:16.19	3:17.08	3:17.98	3:18.87	3:19.77	3:20.67	3:21.56	3:22.46	3:23.35	3:24.25
230	3:25.15	3:26.04	3:26.94	3:27.83	3:28.73	3:29.63	3:30.52	3:31.42	3:32.31	3:33.21
240	3:34.10	3:35.00	3:35.90	3:36.79	3:37.69	3:38.58	3:39.48	3:40.38	3:41.27	3:42.17
250	3:43.06	3:43.96	3:44.85	3:45.75	3:46.65	3:47.54	3:48.44	3:49.33	3:50.23	3:51.13
260	3:52.02	3:52.92	3:53.81	3:54.71	3:55.60	3:56.50	3:57.40	3:58.29	3:59.19	4:00.08
270	4:00.98	4:01.88	4:02.77	4:03.67	4:04.56	4:05.46	4:06.35	4:07.25	4:08.15	4:09.04
280	4:09.94	4:10.83	4:11.73	4:12.63	4:13.52	4:14.42	4:15.31	4:16.21	4:17.10	4:18.00
290	4:18.90	4:19.79	4:20.69	4:21.58	4:22.48	4:23.37	4:24.27	4:25.17	4:26.06	4:26.96
300	4:27.85	4:28.75	4:29.65	4:30.54	4:31.44	4:32.33	4:33.23	4:34.12	4:35.02	4:35.92
310	4:36.81	4:37.71	4:38.60	4:39.50	4:40.40	4:41.29	4:42.19	4:43.08	4:43.98	4:44.88
320	4:45.77	4:46.67	4:47.56	4:48.46	4:49.35	4:50.25	4:51.15	4:52.04	4:52.94	4:53.83
330	4:54.73	4:55.63	4:56.52	4:57.42	4:58.31	4:59.21	5:00.10	5:01.00	5:01.90	5:02.79
340	5:03.69	5:04.58	5:05.48	5:06.37	5:07.27	5:08.17	5:09.06	5:09.96	5:10.85	5:11.75
350	5:12.65	5:13.54	5:14.44	5:15.33	5:16.23	5:17.12	5:18.02	5:18.92	5:19.81	5:20.71
360	5:21.60	5:22.50	5:23.40	5:24.29	5:25.19	5:26.08	5:26.98	5:27.88	5:28.77	5:29.67
370	5:30.56	5:31.46	5:32.35	5:33.25	5:34.15	5:35.04	5:35.94	5:36.83	5:37.73	5:38.63
380	5:39.52	5:40.42	5:41.31	5:42.21	5:43.10	5:44.00	5:44.90	5:45.79	5:46.69	5:47.58
390	5:48.48	5:49.37	5:50.27	5:51.17	5:52.06	5:52.96	5:53.85	5:54.75	5:55.65	5:56.54
400	5:57.44	5:58.33	5:59.23	6:00.12	6:01.02	6:01.92	6:02.81	6:03.71	6:04.60	6:05.50
410	6:06.40	6:07.29	6:08.19	6:09.08	6:09.98	6:10.88	6:11.77	6:12.67	6:13.56	6:14.46
420	6:15.35	6:16.25	6:17.15	6:18.04	6:18.94	6:19.83	6:20.73	6:21.63	6:22.52	6:23.42
430	6:24.31	6:25.21	6:26.10	6:27.00	6:27.90	6:28.79	6:29.69	6:30.58	6:31.48	6:32.37
440	6:33.27	6:34.17	6:35.06	6:35.96	6:36.85	6:37.75	6:38.65	6:39.54	6:40.44	6:41.33
450	6:42.23	6:43.13	6:44.02	6:44.92	6:45.81	6:46.71	6:47.60	6:48.50	6:49.40	6:50.29
460	6:51.19	6:52.08	6:52.98	6:53.88	6:54.77	6:55.67	6:56.56	6:57.46	6:58.35	6:59.25
470	7:00.15	7:01.04	7:01.94	7:02.83	7:03.73	7:04.63	7:05.52	7:06.42	7:07.31	7:08.21
480	7:09.10	7:10.00	7:10.90	7:11.79	7:12.69	7:13.58	7:14.48	7:15.37	7:16.27	7:17.17
490	7:18.06	7:18.96	7:19.85	7:20.75	7:21.65	7:22.54	7:23.44	7:24.33	7:25.23	7:26.13
500	7:27.02	7:27.92	7:28.81	7:29.71	7:30.60	7:31.50	7:32.40	7:33.29	7:34.19	7:35.08
510	7:35.98	7:36.88	7:37.77	7:38.67	7:39.56	7:40.46	7:41.35	7:42.25	7:43.15	7:44.04
520	7:44.94	7:45.83	7:46.73	7:47.62	7:48.52	7:49.42	7:50.31	7:51.21	7:52.10	7:53.00
530	7:53.90	7:54.79	7:55.69	7:56.58	7:57.48	7:58.37	7:59.27	8:00.17	8:01.06	8:01.96
540	8:02.85	8:03.75	8:04.65	8:05.54	8:06.44	8:07.33	8:08.23	8:09.13	8:10.02	8:10.92
550	8:11.81	8:12.71	8:13.60	8:14.50	8:15.40	8:16.29	8:17.19	8:18.08	8:18.98	8:19.88
560	8:20.77	8:21.67	8:22.56	8:23.46	8:24.35	8:25.25	8:26.15	8:27.04	8:27.94	8:28.83
570	8:29.73	8:30.63	8:31.52	8:32.42	8:33.31	8:34.21	8:35.10	8:36.00	8:36.90	8:37.79
580	8:38.69	8:39.58	8:40.48	8:41.38	8:42.27	8:43.17	8:44.06	8:44.96	8:45.85	8:46.75
590	8:47.65	8:48.54	8:49.44	8:50.33	8:51.23	8:52.12	8:53.02	8:53.92	8:54.81	8:55.71

♩. = 1.34; ♩ = 0.90; ♪. = 0.67; (triplet) ♩ 𝄾 = 0.60; ♪ = 0.45; (triplet) ♪ 𝄾 𝄾 = 0.30; 𝅘𝅥𝅯 = 0.22 seconds

CLICK: 21⅝ FRAMES; M.M.: 66.59

Click	0	1	2	3	4	5	6	7	8	9
000	0:00.00	0:00.00	0:00.90	0:01.80	0:02.70	0:03.60	0:04.51	0:05.41	0:06.31	0:07.21
010	0:08.11	0:09.01	0:09.91	0:10.81	0:11.71	0:12.61	0:13.52	0:14.42	0:15.32	0:16.22
020	0:17.12	0:18.02	0:18.92	0:19.82	0:20.72	0:21.63	0:22.53	0:23.43	0:24.33	0:25.23
030	0:26.13	0:27.03	0:27.93	0:28.83	0:29.73	0:30.64	0:31.54	0:32.44	0:33.34	0:34.24
040	0:35.14	0:36.04	0:36.94	0:37.84	0:38.74	0:39.65	0:40.55	0:41.45	0:42.35	0:43.25
050	0:44.15	0:45.05	0:45.95	0:46.85	0:47.76	0:48.66	0:49.56	0:50.46	0:51.36	0:52.26
060	0:53.16	0:54.06	0:54.96	0:55.86	0:56.77	0:57.67	0:58.57	0:59.47	1:00.37	1:01.27
070	1:02.17	1:03.07	1:03.97	1:04.88	1:05.78	1:06.68	1:07.58	1:08.48	1:09.38	1:10.28
080	1:11.18	1:12.08	1:12.98	1:13.89	1:14.79	1:15.69	1:16.59	1:17.49	1:18.39	1:19.29
090	1:20.19	1:21.09	1:21.99	1:22.90	1:23.80	1:24.70	1:25.60	1:26.50	1:27.40	1:28.30
100	1:29.20	1:30.10	1:31.01	1:31.91	1:32.81	1:33.71	1:34.61	1:35.51	1:36.41	1:37.31
110	1:38.21	1:39.11	1:40.02	1:40.92	1:41.82	1:42.72	1:43.62	1:44.52	1:45.42	1:46.32
120	1:47.22	1:48.13	1:49.03	1:49.93	1:50.83	1:51.73	1:52.63	1:53.53	1:54.43	1:55.33
130	1:56.23	1:57.14	1:58.04	1:58.94	1:59.84	2:00.74	2:01.64	2:02.54	2:03.44	2:04.34
140	2:05.24	2:06.15	2:07.05	2:07.95	2:08.85	2:09.75	2:10.65	2:11.55	2:12.45	2:13.35
150	2:14.26	2:15.16	2:16.06	2:16.96	2:17.86	2:18.76	2:19.66	2:20.56	2:21.46	2:22.36
160	2:23.27	2:24.17	2:25.07	2:25.97	2:26.87	2:27.77	2:28.67	2:29.57	2:30.47	2:31.38
170	2:32.28	2:33.18	2:34.08	2:34.98	2:35.88	2:36.78	2:37.68	2:38.58	2:39.48	2:40.39
180	2:41.29	2:42.19	2:43.09	2:43.99	2:44.89	2:45.79	2:46.69	2:47.59	2:48.49	2:49.40
190	2:50.30	2:51.20	2:52.10	2:53.00	2:53.90	2:54.80	2:55.70	2:56.60	2:57.51	2:58.41
200	2:59.31	3:00.21	3:01.11	3:02.01	3:02.91	3:03.81	3:04.71	3:05.61	3:06.52	3:07.42
210	3:08.32	3:09.22	3:10.12	3:11.02	3:11.92	3:12.82	3:13.72	3:14.63	3:15.53	3:16.43
220	3:17.33	3:18.23	3:19.13	3:20.03	3:20.93	3:21.83	3:22.73	3:23.64	3:24.54	3:25.44
230	3:26.34	3:27.24	3:28.14	3:29.04	3:29.94	3:30.84	3:31.74	3:32.65	3:33.55	3:34.45
240	3:35.35	3:36.25	3:37.15	3:38.05	3:38.95	3:39.85	3:40.76	3:41.66	3:42.56	3:43.46
250	3:44.36	3:45.26	3:46.16	3:47.06	3:47.96	3:48.86	3:49.77	3:50.67	3:51.57	3:52.47
260	3:53.37	3:54.27	3:55.17	3:56.07	3:56.97	3:57.88	3:58.78	3:59.68	4:00.58	4:01.48
270	4:02.38	4:03.28	4:04.18	4:05.08	4:05.98	4:06.89	4:07.79	4:08.69	4:09.59	4:10.49
280	4:11.39	4:12.29	4:13.19	4:14.09	4:14.99	4:15.90	4:16.80	4:17.70	4:18.60	4:19.50
290	4:20.40	4:21.30	4:22.20	4:23.10	4:24.01	4:24.91	4:25.81	4:26.71	4:27.61	4:28.51
300	4:29.41	4:30.31	4:31.21	4:32.11	4:33.02	4:33.92	4:34.82	4:35.72	4:36.62	4:37.52
310	4:38.42	4:39.32	4:40.22	4:41.13	4:42.03	4:42.93	4:43.83	4:44.73	4:45.63	4:46.53
320	4:47.43	4:48.33	4:49.23	4:50.14	4:51.04	4:51.94	4:52.84	4:53.74	4:54.64	4:55.54
330	4:56.44	4:57.34	4:58.24	4:59.15	5:00.05	5:00.95	5:01.85	5:02.75	5:03.65	5:04.55
340	5:05.45	5:06.35	5:07.26	5:08.16	5:09.06	5:09.96	5:10.86	5:11.76	5:12.66	5:13.56
350	5:14.46	5:15.36	5:16.27	5:17.17	5:18.07	5:18.97	5:19.87	5:20.77	5:21.67	5:22.57
360	5:23.47	5:24.38	5:25.28	5:26.18	5:27.08	5:27.98	5:28.88	5:29.78	5:30.68	5:31.58
370	5:32.48	5:33.39	5:34.29	5:35.19	5:36.09	5:36.99	5:37.89	5:38.79	5:39.69	5:40.59
380	5:41.49	5:42.40	5:43.30	5:44.20	5:45.10	5:46.00	5:46.90	5:47.80	5:48.70	5:49.60
390	5:50.51	5:51.41	5:52.31	5:53.21	5:54.11	5:55.01	5:55.91	5:56.81	5:57.71	5:58.61
400	5:59.52	6:00.42	6:01.32	6:02.22	6:03.12	6:04.02	6:04.92	6:05.82	6:06.72	6:07.63
410	6:08.53	6:09.43	6:10.33	6:11.23	6:12.13	6:13.03	6:13.93	6:14.83	6:15.73	6:16.64
420	6:17.54	6:18.44	6:19.34	6:20.24	6:21.14	6:22.04	6:22.94	6:23.84	6:24.74	6:25.65
430	6:26.55	6:27.45	6:28.35	6:29.25	6:30.15	6:31.05	6:31.95	6:32.85	6:33.76	6:34.66
440	6:35.56	6:36.46	6:37.36	6:38.26	6:39.16	6:40.06	6:40.96	6:41.86	6:42.77	6:43.67
450	6:44.57	6:45.47	6:46.37	6:47.27	6:48.17	6:49.07	6:49.97	6:50.88	6:51.78	6:52.68
460	6:53.58	6:54.48	6:55.38	6:56.28	6:57.18	6:58.08	6:58.98	6:59.89	7:00.79	7:01.69
470	7:02.59	7:03.49	7:04.39	7:05.29	7:06.19	7:07.09	7:07.99	7:08.90	7:09.80	7:10.70
480	7:11.60	7:12.50	7:13.40	7:14.30	7:15.20	7:16.10	7:17.01	7:17.91	7:18.81	7:19.71
490	7:20.61	7:21.51	7:22.41	7:23.31	7:24.21	7:25.11	7:26.02	7:26.92	7:27.82	7:28.72
500	7:29.62	7:30.52	7:31.42	7:32.32	7:33.22	7:34.13	7:35.03	7:35.93	7:36.83	7:37.73
510	7:38.63	7:39.53	7:40.43	7:41.33	7:42.23	7:43.14	7:44.04	7:44.94	7:45.84	7:46.74
520	7:47.64	7:48.54	7:49.44	7:50.34	7:51.24	7:52.15	7:53.05	7:53.95	7:54.85	7:55.75
530	7:56.65	7:57.55	7:58.45	7:59.35	8:00.26	8:01.16	8:02.06	8:02.96	8:03.86	8:04.76
540	8:05.66	8:06.56	8:07.46	8:08.36	8:09.27	8:10.17	8:11.07	8:11.97	8:12.87	8:13.77
550	8:14.67	8:15.57	8:16.47	8:17.38	8:18.28	8:19.18	8:20.08	8:20.98	8:21.88	8:22.78
560	8:23.68	8:24.58	8:25.48	8:26.39	8:27.29	8:28.19	8:29.09	8:29.99	8:30.89	8:31.79
570	8:32.69	8:33.59	8:34.49	8:35.40	8:36.30	8:37.20	8:38.10	8:39.00	8:39.90	8:40.80
580	8:41.70	8:42.60	8:43.51	8:44.41	8:45.31	8:46.21	8:47.11	8:48.01	8:48.91	8:49.81
590	8:50.71	8:51.61	8:52.52	8:53.42	8:54.32	8:55.22	8:56.12	8:57.02	8:57.92	8:58.82

♩. = 1.35; ♩ = 0.90; ♪. = 0.68; (triplet) ♩ 𝄾 = 0.60; ♪ = 0.45; (triplet) ♪𝄾𝄾 = 0.30; 𝅘𝅥𝅯 = 0.23 seconds

CLICK: 21 6/8 FRAMES; M.M.: 66.21

Click	0	1	2	3	4	5	6	7	8	9
000	0:00.00	0:00.00	0:00.91	0:01.81	0:02.72	0:03.63	0:04.53	0:05.44	0:06.34	0:07.25
010	0:08.16	0:09.06	0:09.97	0:10.88	0:11.78	0:12.69	0:13.59	0:14.50	0:15.41	0:16.31
020	0:17.22	0:18.13	0:19.03	0:19.94	0:20.84	0:21.75	0:22.66	0:23.56	0:24.47	0:25.38
030	0:26.28	0:27.19	0:28.09	0:29.00	0:29.91	0:30.81	0:31.72	0:32.63	0:33.53	0:34.44
040	0:35.34	0:36.25	0:37.16	0:38.06	0:38.97	0:39.88	0:40.78	0:41.69	0:42.59	0:43.50
050	0:44.41	0:45.31	0:46.22	0:47.13	0:48.03	0:48.94	0:49.84	0:50.75	0:51.66	0:52.56
060	0:53.47	0:54.38	0:55.28	0:56.19	0:57.09	0:58.00	0:58.91	0:59.81	1:00.72	1:01.63
070	1:02.53	1:03.44	1:04.34	1:05.25	1:06.16	1:07.06	1:07.97	1:08.88	1:09.78	1:10.69
080	1:11.59	1:12.50	1:13.41	1:14.31	1:15.22	1:16.13	1:17.03	1:17.94	1:18.84	1:19.75
090	1:20.66	1:21.56	1:22.47	1:23.38	1:24.28	1:25.19	1:26.09	1:27.00	1:27.91	1:28.81
100	1:29.72	1:30.63	1:31.53	1:32.44	1:33.34	1:34.25	1:35.16	1:36.06	1:36.97	1:37.88
110	1:38.78	1:39.69	1:40.59	1:41.50	1:42.41	1:43.31	1:44.22	1:45.13	1:46.03	1:46.94
120	1:47.84	1:48.75	1:49.66	1:50.56	1:51.47	1:52.38	1:53.28	1:54.19	1:55.09	1:56.00
130	1:56.91	1:57.81	1:58.72	1:59.63	2:00.53	2:01.44	2:02.34	2:03.25	2:04.16	2:05.06
140	2:05.97	2:06.88	2:07.78	2:08.69	2:09.59	2:10.50	2:11.41	2:12.31	2:13.22	2:14.12
150	2:15.03	2:15.94	2:16.84	2:17.75	2:18.66	2:19.56	2:20.47	2:21.38	2:22.28	2:23.19
160	2:24.09	2:25.00	2:25.91	2:26.81	2:27.72	2:28.63	2:29.53	2:30.44	2:31.34	2:32.25
170	2:33.16	2:34.06	2:34.97	2:35.88	2:36.78	2:37.69	2:38.59	2:39.50	2:40.41	2:41.31
180	2:42.22	2:43.13	2:44.03	2:44.94	2:45.84	2:46.75	2:47.66	2:48.56	2:49.47	2:50.38
190	2:51.28	2:52.19	2:53.09	2:54.00	2:54.91	2:55.81	2:56.72	2:57.63	2:58.53	2:59.44
200	3:00.34	3:01.25	3:02.16	3:03.06	3:03.97	3:04.88	3:05.78	3:06.69	3:07.59	3:08.50
210	3:09.41	3:10.31	3:11.22	3:12.13	3:13.03	3:13.94	3:14.84	3:15.75	3:16.66	3:17.56
220	3:18.47	3:19.38	3:20.28	3:21.19	3:22.09	3:23.00	3:23.91	3:24.81	3:25.72	3:26.63
230	3:27.53	3:28.44	3:29.34	3:30.25	3:31.16	3:32.06	3:32.97	3:33.88	3:34.78	3:35.69
240	3:36.59	3:37.50	3:38.41	3:39.31	3:40.22	3:41.13	3:42.03	3:42.94	3:43.84	3:44.75
250	3:45.66	3:46.56	3:47.47	3:48.38	3:49.28	3:50.19	3:51.09	3:52.00	3:52.91	3:53.81
260	3:54.72	3:55.63	3:56.53	3:57.44	3:58.34	3:59.25	4:00.16	4:01.06	4:01.97	4:02.88
270	4:03.78	4:04.69	4:05.59	4:06.50	4:07.41	4:08.31	4:09.22	4:10.13	4:11.03	4:11.94
280	4:12.84	4:13.75	4:14.66	4:15.56	4:16.47	4:17.38	4:18.28	4:19.19	4:20.09	4:21.00
290	4:21.91	4:22.81	4:23.72	4:24.62	4:25.53	4:26.44	4:27.34	4:28.25	4:29.16	4:30.06
300	4:30.97	4:31.88	4:32.78	4:33.69	4:34.59	4:35.50	4:36.41	4:37.31	4:38.22	4:39.13
310	4:40.03	4:40.94	4:41.84	4:42.75	4:43.66	4:44.56	4:45.47	4:46.38	4:47.28	4:48.19
320	4:49.09	4:50.00	4:50.91	4:51.81	4:52.72	4:53.63	4:54.53	4:55.44	4:56.34	4:57.25
330	4:58.16	4:59.06	4:59.97	5:00.88	5:01.78	5:02.69	5:03.59	5:04.50	5:05.41	5:06.31
340	5:07.22	5:08.13	5:09.03	5:09.94	5:10.84	5:11.75	5:12.66	5:13.56	5:14.47	5:15.38
350	5:16.28	5:17.19	5:18.09	5:19.00	5:19.91	5:20.81	5:21.72	5:22.62	5:23.53	5:24.44
360	5:25.34	5:26.25	5:27.16	5:28.06	5:28.97	5:29.88	5:30.78	5:31.69	5:32.59	5:33.50
370	5:34.41	5:35.31	5:36.22	5:37.13	5:38.03	5:38.94	5:39.84	5:40.75	5:41.66	5:42.56
380	5:43.47	5:44.38	5:45.28	5:46.19	5:47.09	5:48.00	5:48.91	5:49.81	5:50.72	5:51.63
390	5:52.53	5:53.44	5:54.34	5:55.25	5:56.16	5:57.06	5:57.97	5:58.88	5:59.78	6:00.69
400	6:01.59	6:02.50	6:03.41	6:04.31	6:05.22	6:06.13	6:07.03	6:07.94	6:08.84	6:09.75
410	6:10.66	6:11.56	6:12.47	6:13.38	6:14.28	6:15.19	6:16.09	6:17.00	6:17.91	6:18.81
420	6:19.72	6:20.63	6:21.53	6:22.44	6:23.34	6:24.25	6:25.16	6:26.06	6:26.97	6:27.88
430	6:28.78	6:29.69	6:30.59	6:31.50	6:32.41	6:33.31	6:34.22	6:35.13	6:36.03	6:36.94
440	6:37.84	6:38.75	6:39.66	6:40.56	6:41.47	6:42.38	6:43.28	6:44.19	6:45.09	6:46.00
450	6:46.91	6:47.81	6:48.72	6:49.63	6:50.53	6:51.44	6:52.34	6:53.25	6:54.16	6:55.06
460	6:55.97	6:56.88	6:57.78	6:58.69	6:59.59	7:00.50	7:01.41	7:02.31	7:03.22	7:04.13
470	7:05.03	7:05.94	7:06.84	7:07.75	7:08.66	7:09.56	7:10.47	7:11.38	7:12.28	7:13.19
480	7:14.09	7:15.00	7:15.91	7:16.81	7:17.72	7:18.63	7:19.53	7:20.44	7:21.34	7:22.25
490	7:23.16	7:24.06	7:24.97	7:25.88	7:26.78	7:27.69	7:28.59	7:29.50	7:30.41	7:31.31
500	7:32.22	7:33.13	7:34.03	7:34.94	7:35.84	7:36.75	7:37.66	7:38.56	7:39.47	7:40.38
510	7:41.28	7:42.19	7:43.09	7:44.00	7:44.91	7:45.81	7:46.72	7:47.63	7:48.53	7:49.44
520	7:50.34	7:51.25	7:52.16	7:53.06	7:53.97	7:54.88	7:55.78	7:56.69	7:57.59	7:58.50
530	7:59.41	8:00.31	8:01.22	8:02.12	8:03.03	8:03.94	8:04.84	8:05.75	8:06.66	8:07.56
540	8:08.47	8:09.38	8:10.28	8:11.19	8:12.09	8:13.00	8:13.91	8:14.81	8:15.72	8:16.63
550	8:17.53	8:18.44	8:19.34	8:20.25	8:21.16	8:22.06	8:22.97	8:23.88	8:24.78	8:25.69
560	8:26.59	8:27.50	8:28.41	8:29.31	8:30.22	8:31.13	8:32.03	8:32.94	8:33.84	8:34.75
570	8:35.66	8:36.56	8:37.47	8:38.38	8:39.28	8:40.19	8:41.09	8:42.00	8:42.91	8:43.81
580	8:44.72	8:45.63	8:46.53	8:47.44	8:48.34	8:49.25	8:50.16	8:51.06	8:51.97	8:52.88
590	8:53.78	8:54.69	8:55.59	8:56.50	8:57.41	8:58.31	8:59.22	9:00.13	9:01.03	9:01.94

𝅗𝅥. = 1.36; ♩ = 0.91; ♪. = 0.68; (triplet) ♩ 𝄾 = 0.60; ♪ = 0.45; (triplet) ♪ 𝄾 𝄾 = 0.30; 𝅘𝅥𝅯 = 0.23 seconds

CLICK: 21⅞ FRAMES; M.M.: 65.83

Click	0	1	2	3	4	5	6	7	8	9
000	0:00.00	0:00.00	0:00.91	0:01.82	0:02.73	0:03.65	0:04.56	0:05.47	0:06.38	0:07.29
010	0:08.20	0:09.11	0:10.03	0:10.94	0:11.85	0:12.76	0:13.67	0:14.58	0:15.49	0:16.41
020	0:17.32	0:18.23	0:19.14	0:20.05	0:20.96	0:21.88	0:22.79	0:23.70	0:24.61	0:25.52
030	0:26.43	0:27.34	0:28.26	0:29.17	0:30.08	0:30.99	0:31.90	0:32.81	0:33.72	0:34.64
040	0:35.55	0:36.46	0:37.37	0:38.28	0:39.19	0:40.10	0:41.02	0:41.93	0:42.84	0:43.75
050	0:44.66	0:45.57	0:46.48	0:47.40	0:48.31	0:49.22	0:50.13	0:51.04	0:51.95	0:52.86
060	0:53.78	0:54.69	0:55.60	0:56.51	0:57.42	0:58.33	0:59.24	1:00.16	1:01.07	1:01.98
070	1:02.89	1:03.80	1:04.71	1:05.63	1:06.54	1:07.45	1:08.36	1:09.27	1:10.18	1:11.09
080	1:12.01	1:12.92	1:13.83	1:14.74	1:15.65	1:16.56	1:17.47	1:18.39	1:19.30	1:20.21
090	1:21.12	1:22.03	1:22.94	1:23.85	1:24.77	1:25.68	1:26.59	1:27.50	1:28.41	1:29.32
100	1:30.23	1:31.15	1:32.06	1:32.97	1:33.88	1:34.79	1:35.70	1:36.61	1:37.53	1:38.44
110	1:39.35	1:40.26	1:41.17	1:42.08	1:42.99	1:43.91	1:44.82	1:45.73	1:46.64	1:47.55
120	1:48.46	1:49.38	1:50.29	1:51.20	1:52.11	1:53.02	1:53.93	1:54.84	1:55.76	1:56.67
130	1:57.58	1:58.49	1:59.40	2:00.31	2:01.22	2:02.14	2:03.05	2:03.96	2:04.87	2:05.78
140	2:06.69	2:07.60	2:08.52	2:09.43	2:10.34	2:11.25	2:12.16	2:13.07	2:13.98	2:14.90
150	2:15.81	2:16.72	2:17.63	2:18.54	2:19.45	2:20.36	2:21.28	2:22.19	2:23.10	2:24.01
160	2:24.92	2:25.83	2:26.74	2:27.66	2:28.57	2:29.48	2:30.39	2:31.30	2:32.21	2:33.13
170	2:34.04	2:34.95	2:35.86	2:36.77	2:37.68	2:38.59	2:39.51	2:40.42	2:41.33	2:42.24
180	2:43.15	2:44.06	2:44.97	2:45.89	2:46.80	2:47.71	2:48.62	2:49.53	2:50.44	2:51.35
190	2:52.27	2:53.18	2:54.09	2:55.00	2:55.91	2:56.82	2:57.73	2:58.65	2:59.56	3:00.47
200	3:01.38	3:02.29	3:03.20	3:04.11	3:05.03	3:05.94	3:06.85	3:07.76	3:08.67	3:09.58
210	3:10.49	3:11.41	3:12.32	3:13.23	3:14.14	3:15.05	3:15.96	3:16.88	3:17.79	3:18.70
220	3:19.61	3:20.52	3:21.43	3:22.34	3:23.26	3:24.17	3:25.08	3:25.99	3:26.90	3:27.81
230	3:28.72	3:29.64	3:30.55	3:31.46	3:32.37	3:33.28	3:34.19	3:35.10	3:36.02	3:36.93
240	3:37.84	3:38.75	3:39.66	3:40.57	3:41.48	3:42.40	3:43.31	3:44.22	3:45.13	3:46.04
250	3:46.95	3:47.86	3:48.78	3:49.69	3:50.60	3:51.51	3:52.42	3:53.33	3:54.24	3:55.16
260	3:56.07	3:56.98	3:57.89	3:58.80	3:59.71	4:00.63	4:01.54	4:02.45	4:03.36	4:04.27
270	4:05.18	4:06.09	4:07.01	4:07.92	4:08.83	4:09.74	4:10.65	4:11.56	4:12.47	4:13.39
280	4:14.30	4:15.21	4:16.12	4:17.03	4:17.94	4:18.85	4:19.77	4:20.68	4:21.59	4:22.50
290	4:23.41	4:24.32	4:25.23	4:26.15	4:27.06	4:27.97	4:28.88	4:29.79	4:30.70	4:31.61
300	4:32.53	4:33.44	4:34.35	4:35.26	4:36.17	4:37.08	4:37.99	4:38.91	4:39.82	4:40.73
310	4:41.64	4:42.55	4:43.46	4:44.38	4:45.29	4:46.20	4:47.11	4:48.02	4:48.93	4:49.84
320	4:50.76	4:51.67	4:52.58	4:53.49	4:54.40	4:55.31	4:56.22	4:57.14	4:58.05	4:58.96
330	4:59.87	5:00.78	5:01.69	5:02.60	5:03.52	5:04.43	5:05.34	5:06.25	5:07.16	5:08.07
340	5:08.98	5:09.90	5:10.81	5:11.72	5:12.63	5:13.54	5:14.45	5:15.36	5:16.28	5:17.19
350	5:18.10	5:19.01	5:19.92	5:20.83	5:21.74	5:22.66	5:23.57	5:24.48	5:25.39	5:26.30
360	5:27.21	5:28.13	5:29.04	5:29.95	5:30.86	5:31.77	5:32.68	5:33.59	5:34.51	5:35.42
370	5:36.33	5:37.24	5:38.15	5:39.06	5:39.97	5:40.89	5:41.80	5:42.71	5:43.62	5:44.53
380	5:45.44	5:46.35	5:47.27	5:48.18	5:49.09	5:50.00	5:50.91	5:51.82	5:52.73	5:53.65
390	5:54.56	5:55.47	5:56.38	5:57.29	5:58.20	5:59.11	6:00.03	6:00.94	6:01.85	6:02.76
400	6:03.67	6:04.58	6:05.49	6:06.41	6:07.32	6:08.23	6:09.14	6:10.05	6:10.96	6:11.88
410	6:12.79	6:13.70	6:14.61	6:15.52	6:16.43	6:17.34	6:18.26	6:19.17	6:20.08	6:20.99
420	6:21.90	6:22.81	6:23.72	6:24.64	6:25.55	6:26.46	6:27.37	6:28.28	6:29.19	6:30.10
430	6:31.02	6:31.93	6:32.84	6:33.75	6:34.66	6:35.57	6:36.48	6:37.40	6:38.31	6:39.22
440	6:40.13	6:41.04	6:41.95	6:42.86	6:43.78	6:44.69	6:45.60	6:46.51	6:47.42	6:48.33
450	6:49.24	6:50.16	6:51.07	6:51.98	6:52.89	6:53.80	6:54.71	6:55.63	6:56.54	6:57.45
460	6:58.36	6:59.27	7:00.18	7:01.09	7:02.01	7:02.92	7:03.83	7:04.74	7:05.65	7:06.56
470	7:07.47	7:08.39	7:09.30	7:10.21	7:11.12	7:12.03	7:12.94	7:13.85	7:14.77	7:15.68
480	7:16.59	7:17.50	7:18.41	7:19.32	7:20.23	7:21.15	7:22.06	7:22.97	7:23.88	7:24.79
490	7:25.70	7:26.61	7:27.53	7:28.44	7:29.35	7:30.26	7:31.17	7:32.08	7:32.99	7:33.91
500	7:34.82	7:35.73	7:36.64	7:37.55	7:38.46	7:39.38	7:40.29	7:41.20	7:42.11	7:43.02
510	7:43.93	7:44.84	7:45.76	7:46.67	7:47.58	7:48.49	7:49.40	7:50.31	7:51.22	7:52.14
520	7:53.05	7:53.96	7:54.87	7:55.78	7:56.69	7:57.60	7:58.52	7:59.43	8:00.34	8:01.25
530	8:02.16	8:03.07	8:03.98	8:04.90	8:05.81	8:06.72	8:07.63	8:08.54	8:09.45	8:10.36
540	8:11.28	8:12.19	8:13.10	8:14.01	8:14.92	8:15.83	8:16.74	8:17.66	8:18.57	8:19.48
550	8:20.39	8:21.30	8:22.21	8:23.13	8:24.04	8:24.95	8:25.86	8:26.77	8:27.68	8:28.59
560	8:29.51	8:30.42	8:31.33	8:32.24	8:33.15	8:34.06	8:34.97	8:35.89	8:36.80	8:37.71
570	8:38.62	8:39.53	8:40.44	8:41.35	8:42.27	8:43.18	8:44.09	8:45.00	8:45.91	8:46.82
580	8:47.73	8:48.65	8:49.56	8:50.47	8:51.38	8:52.29	8:53.20	8:54.11	8:55.03	8:55.94
590	8:56.85	8:57.76	8:58.67	8:59.58	9:00.49	9:01.41	9:02.32	9:03.23	9:04.14	9:05.05

♩. = 1.37; ♩ = 0.91; ♪. = 0.68; ⌐3¬ ♩ 𝄾 = 0.61; ♪ = 0.46; ⌐3¬ ♪𝄾𝄾 = 0.30; 𝅘𝅥𝅯 = 0.23 seconds

CLICK: 22 0/8 FRAMES; M.M.: 65.45

Click	0	1	2	3	4	5	6	7	8	9
000	0:00.00	0:00.00	0:00.92	0:01.83	0:02.75	0:03.67	0:04.58	0:05.50	0:06.42	0:07.33
010	0:08.25	0:09.17	0:10.08	0:11.00	0:11.92	0:12.83	0:13.75	0:14.67	0:15.58	0:16.50
020	0:17.42	0:18.33	0:19.25	0:20.17	0:21.08	0:22.00	0:22.92	0:23.83	0:24.75	0:25.67
030	0:26.58	0:27.50	0:28.42	0:29.33	0:30.25	0:31.17	0:32.08	0:33.00	0:33.92	0:34.83
040	0:35.75	0:36.67	0:37.58	0:38.50	0:39.42	0:40.33	0:41.25	0:42.17	0:43.08	0:44.00
050	0:44.92	0:45.83	0:46.75	0:47.67	0:48.58	0:49.50	0:50.42	0:51.33	0:52.25	0:53.17
060	0:54.08	0:55.00	0:55.92	0:56.83	0:57.75	0:58.67	0:59.58	1:00.50	1:01.42	1:02.33
070	1:03.25	1:04.17	1:05.08	1:06.00	1:06.92	1:07.83	1:08.75	1:09.67	1:10.58	1:11.50
080	1:12.42	1:13.33	1:14.25	1:15.17	1:16.08	1:17.00	1:17.92	1:18.83	1:19.75	1:20.67
090	1:21.58	1:22.50	1:23.42	1:24.33	1:25.25	1:26.17	1:27.08	1:28.00	1:28.92	1:29.83
100	1:30.75	1:31.67	1:32.58	1:33.50	1:34.42	1:35.33	1:36.25	1:37.17	1:38.08	1:39.00
110	1:39.92	1:40.83	1:41.75	1:42.67	1:43.58	1:44.50	1:45.42	1:46.33	1:47.25	1:48.17
120	1:49.08	1:50.00	1:50.92	1:51.83	1:52.75	1:53.67	1:54.58	1:55.50	1:56.42	1:57.33
130	1:58.25	1:59.17	2:00.08	2:01.00	2:01.92	2:02.83	2:03.75	2:04.67	2:05.58	2:06.50
140	2:07.42	2:08.33	2:09.25	2:10.17	2:11.08	2:12.00	2:12.92	2:13.83	2:14.75	2:15.67
150	2:16.58	2:17.50	2:18.42	2:19.33	2:20.25	2:21.17	2:22.08	2:23.00	2:23.92	2:24.83
160	2:25.75	2:26.67	2:27.58	2:28.50	2:29.42	2:30.33	2:31.25	2:32.17	2:33.08	2:34.00
170	2:34.92	2:35.83	2:36.75	2:37.67	2:38.58	2:39.50	2:40.42	2:41.33	2:42.25	2:43.17
180	2:44.08	2:45.00	2:45.92	2:46.83	2:47.75	2:48.67	2:49.58	2:50.50	2:51.42	2:52.33
190	2:53.25	2:54.17	2:55.08	2:56.00	2:56.92	2:57.83	2:58.75	2:59.67	3:00.58	3:01.50
200	3:02.42	3:03.33	3:04.25	3:05.17	3:06.08	3:07.00	3:07.92	3:08.83	3:09.75	3:10.67
210	3:11.58	3:12.50	3:13.42	3:14.33	3:15.25	3:16.17	3:17.08	3:18.00	3:18.92	3:19.83
220	3:20.75	3:21.67	3:22.58	3:23.50	3:24.42	3:25.33	3:26.25	3:27.17	3:28.08	3:29.00
230	3:29.92	3:30.83	3:31.75	3:32.67	3:33.58	3:34.50	3:35.42	3:36.33	3:37.25	3:38.17
240	3:39.08	3:40.00	3:40.92	3:41.83	3:42.75	3:43.67	3:44.58	3:45.50	3:46.42	3:47.33
250	3:48.25	3:49.17	3:50.08	3:51.00	3:51.92	3:52.83	3:53.75	3:54.67	3:55.58	3:56.50
260	3:57.42	3:58.33	3:59.25	4:00.17	4:01.08	4:02.00	4:02.92	4:03.83	4:04.75	4:05.67
270	4:06.58	4:07.50	4:08.42	4:09.33	4:10.25	4:11.17	4:12.08	4:13.00	4:13.92	4:14.83
280	4:15.75	4:16.67	4:17.58	4:18.50	4:19.42	4:20.33	4:21.25	4:22.17	4:23.08	4:24.00
290	4:24.92	4:25.83	4:26.75	4:27.67	4:28.58	4:29.50	4:30.42	4:31.33	4:32.25	4:33.17
300	4:34.08	4:35.00	4:35.92	4:36.83	4:37.75	4:38.67	4:39.58	4:40.50	4:41.42	4:42.33
310	4:43.25	4:44.17	4:45.08	4:46.00	4:46.92	4:47.83	4:48.75	4:49.67	4:50.58	4:51.50
320	4:52.42	4:53.33	4:54.25	4:55.17	4:56.08	4:57.00	4:57.92	4:58.83	4:59.75	5:00.67
330	5:01.58	5:02.50	5:03.42	5:04.33	5:05.25	5:06.17	5:07.08	5:08.00	5:08.92	5:09.83
340	5:10.75	5:11.67	5:12.58	5:13.50	5:14.42	5:15.33	5:16.25	5:17.17	5:18.08	5:19.00
350	5:19.92	5:20.83	5:21.75	5:22.67	5:23.58	5:24.50	5:25.42	5:26.33	5:27.25	5:28.17
360	5:29.08	5:30.00	5:30.92	5:31.83	5:32.75	5:33.67	5:34.58	5:35.50	5:36.42	5:37.33
370	5:38.25	5:39.17	5:40.08	5:41.00	5:41.92	5:42.83	5:43.75	5:44.67	5:45.58	5:46.50
380	5:47.42	5:48.33	5:49.25	5:50.17	5:51.08	5:52.00	5:52.92	5:53.83	5:54.75	5:55.67
390	5:56.58	5:57.50	5:58.42	5:59.33	6:00.25	6:01.17	6:02.08	6:03.00	6:03.92	6:04.83
400	6:05.75	6:06.67	6:07.58	6:08.50	6:09.42	6:10.33	6:11.25	6:12.17	6:13.08	6:14.00
410	6:14.92	6:15.83	6:16.75	6:17.67	6:18.58	6:19.50	6:20.42	6:21.33	6:22.25	6:23.17
420	6:24.08	6:25.00	6:25.92	6:26.83	6:27.75	6:28.67	6:29.58	6:30.50	6:31.42	6:32.33
430	6:33.25	6:34.17	6:35.08	6:36.00	6:36.92	6:37.83	6:38.75	6:39.67	6:40.58	6:41.50
440	6:42.42	6:43.33	6:44.25	6:45.17	6:46.08	6:47.00	6:47.92	6:48.83	6:49.75	6:50.67
450	6:51.58	6:52.50	6:53.42	6:54.33	6:55.25	6:56.17	6:57.08	6:58.00	6:58.92	6:59.83
460	7:00.75	7:01.67	7:02.58	7:03.50	7:04.42	7:05.33	7:06.25	7:07.17	7:08.08	7:09.00
470	7:09.92	7:10.83	7:11.75	7:12.67	7:13.58	7:14.50	7:15.42	7:16.33	7:17.25	7:18.17
480	7:19.08	7:20.00	7:20.92	7:21.83	7:22.75	7:23.67	7:24.58	7:25.50	7:26.42	7:27.33
490	7:28.25	7:29.17	7:30.08	7:31.00	7:31.92	7:32.83	7:33.75	7:34.67	7:35.58	7:36.50
500	7:37.42	7:38.33	7:39.25	7:40.17	7:41.08	7:42.00	7:42.92	7:43.83	7:44.75	7:45.67
510	7:46.58	7:47.50	7:48.42	7:49.33	7:50.25	7:51.17	7:52.08	7:53.00	7:53.92	7:54.83
520	7:55.75	7:56.67	7:57.58	7:58.50	7:59.42	8:00.33	8:01.25	8:02.17	8:03.08	8:04.00
530	8:04.92	8:05.83	8:06.75	8:07.67	8:08.58	8:09.50	8:10.42	8:11.33	8:12.25	8:13.17
540	8:14.08	8:15.00	8:15.92	8:16.83	8:17.75	8:18.67	8:19.58	8:20.50	8:21.42	8:22.33
550	8:23.25	8:24.17	8:25.08	8:26.00	8:26.92	8:27.83	8:28.75	8:29.67	8:30.58	8:31.50
560	8:32.42	8:33.33	8:34.25	8:35.17	8:36.08	8:37.00	8:37.92	8:38.83	8:39.75	8:40.67
570	8:41.58	8:42.50	8:43.42	8:44.33	8:45.25	8:46.17	8:47.08	8:48.00	8:48.92	8:49.83
580	8:50.75	8:51.67	8:52.58	8:53.50	8:54.42	8:55.33	8:56.25	8:57.17	8:58.08	8:59.00
590	8:59.92	9:00.83	9:01.75	9:02.67	9:03.58	9:04.50	9:05.42	9:06.33	9:07.25	9:08.17

♩. = 1.38; ♩ = 0.92; ♪. = 0.69; (triplet ♩ 𝄾) = 0.61; ♪ = 0.46; (triplet ♪ 𝄾 𝄾) = 0.31; 𝅘𝅥𝅯 = 0.23 seconds

CLICK: 22⅛ FRAMES; M.M.: 65.08

Click	0	1	2	3	4	5	6	7	8	9
000	0:00.00	0:00.00	0:00.92	0:01.84	0:02.77	0:03.69	0:04.61	0:05.53	0:06.45	0:07.37
010	0:08.30	0:09.22	0:10.14	0:11.06	0:11.98	0:12.91	0:13.83	0:14.75	0:15.67	0:16.59
020	0:17.52	0:18.44	0:19.36	0:20.28	0:21.20	0:22.12	0:23.05	0:23.97	0:24.89	0:25.81
030	0:26.73	0:27.66	0:28.58	0:29.50	0:30.42	0:31.34	0:32.27	0:33.19	0:34.11	0:35.03
040	0:35.95	0:36.88	0:37.80	0:38.72	0:39.64	0:40.56	0:41.48	0:42.41	0:43.33	0:44.25
050	0:45.17	0:46.09	0:47.02	0:47.94	0:48.86	0:49.78	0:50.70	0:51.63	0:52.55	0:53.47
060	0:54.39	0:55.31	0:56.23	0:57.16	0:58.08	0:59.00	0:59.92	1:00.84	1:01.77	1:02.69
070	1:03.61	1:04.53	1:05.45	1:06.37	1:07.30	1:08.22	1:09.14	1:10.06	1:10.98	1:11.91
080	1:12.83	1:13.75	1:14.67	1:15.59	1:16.52	1:17.44	1:18.36	1:19.28	1:20.20	1:21.13
090	1:22.05	1:22.97	1:23.89	1:24.81	1:25.73	1:26.66	1:27.58	1:28.50	1:29.42	1:30.34
100	1:31.27	1:32.19	1:33.11	1:34.03	1:34.95	1:35.87	1:36.80	1:37.72	1:38.64	1:39.56
110	1:40.48	1:41.41	1:42.33	1:43.25	1:44.17	1:45.09	1:46.02	1:46.94	1:47.86	1:48.78
120	1:49.70	1:50.62	1:51.55	1:52.47	1:53.39	1:54.31	1:55.23	1:56.16	1:57.08	1:58.00
130	1:58.92	1:59.84	2:00.77	2:01.69	2:02.61	2:03.53	2:04.45	2:05.37	2:06.30	2:07.22
140	2:08.14	2:09.06	2:09.98	2:10.91	2:11.83	2:12.75	2:13.67	2:14.59	2:15.52	2:16.44
150	2:17.36	2:18.28	2:19.20	2:20.12	2:21.05	2:21.97	2:22.89	2:23.81	2:24.73	2:25.66
160	2:26.58	2:27.50	2:28.42	2:29.34	2:30.27	2:31.19	2:32.11	2:33.03	2:33.95	2:34.87
170	2:35.80	2:36.72	2:37.64	2:38.56	2:39.48	2:40.41	2:41.33	2:42.25	2:43.17	2:44.09
180	2:45.02	2:45.94	2:46.86	2:47.78	2:48.70	2:49.62	2:50.55	2:51.47	2:52.39	2:53.31
190	2:54.23	2:55.16	2:56.08	2:57.00	2:57.92	2:58.84	2:59.77	3:00.69	3:01.61	3:02.53
200	3:03.45	3:04.37	3:05.30	3:06.22	3:07.14	3:08.06	3:08.98	3:09.91	3:10.83	3:11.75
210	3:12.67	3:13.59	3:14.52	3:15.44	3:16.36	3:17.28	3:18.20	3:19.12	3:20.05	3:20.97
220	3:21.89	3:22.81	3:23.73	3:24.66	3:25.58	3:26.50	3:27.42	3:28.34	3:29.27	3:30.19
230	3:31.11	3:32.03	3:32.95	3:33.87	3:34.80	3:35.72	3:36.64	3:37.56	3:38.48	3:39.41
240	3:40.33	3:41.25	3:42.17	3:43.09	3:44.02	3:44.94	3:45.86	3:46.78	3:47.70	3:48.62
250	3:49.55	3:50.47	3:51.39	3:52.31	3:53.23	3:54.16	3:55.08	3:56.00	3:56.92	3:57.84
260	3:58.77	3:59.69	4:00.61	4:01.53	4:02.45	4:03.37	4:04.30	4:05.22	4:06.14	4:07.06
270	4:07.98	4:08.91	4:09.83	4:10.75	4:11.67	4:12.59	4:13.52	4:14.44	4:15.36	4:16.28
280	4:17.20	4:18.12	4:19.05	4:19.97	4:20.89	4:21.81	4:22.73	4:23.66	4:24.58	4:25.50
290	4:26.42	4:27.34	4:28.27	4:29.19	4:30.11	4:31.03	4:31.95	4:32.87	4:33.80	4:34.72
300	4:35.64	4:36.56	4:37.48	4:38.41	4:39.33	4:40.25	4:41.17	4:42.09	4:43.02	4:43.94
310	4:44.86	4:45.78	4:46.70	4:47.62	4:48.55	4:49.47	4:50.39	4:51.31	4:52.23	4:53.16
320	4:54.08	4:55.00	4:55.92	4:56.84	4:57.77	4:58.69	4:59.61	5:00.53	5:01.45	5:02.37
330	5:03.30	5:04.22	5:05.14	5:06.06	5:06.98	5:07.91	5:08.83	5:09.75	5:10.67	5:11.59
340	5:12.52	5:13.44	5:14.36	5:15.28	5:16.20	5:17.12	5:18.05	5:18.97	5:19.89	5:20.81
350	5:21.73	5:22.66	5:23.58	5:24.50	5:25.42	5:26.34	5:27.27	5:28.19	5:29.11	5:30.03
360	5:30.95	5:31.87	5:32.80	5:33.72	5:34.64	5:35.56	5:36.48	5:37.41	5:38.33	5:39.25
370	5:40.17	5:41.09	5:42.02	5:42.94	5:43.86	5:44.78	5:45.70	5:46.62	5:47.55	5:48.47
380	5:49.39	5:50.31	5:51.23	5:52.16	5:53.08	5:54.00	5:54.92	5:55.84	5:56.77	5:57.69
390	5:58.61	5:59.53	6:00.45	6:01.37	6:02.30	6:03.22	6:04.14	6:05.06	6:05.98	6:06.91
400	6:07.83	6:08.75	6:09.67	6:10.59	6:11.52	6:12.44	6:13.36	6:14.28	6:15.20	6:16.12
410	6:17.05	6:17.97	6:18.89	6:19.81	6:20.73	6:21.66	6:22.58	6:23.50	6:24.42	6:25.34
420	6:26.27	6:27.19	6:28.11	6:29.03	6:29.95	6:30.87	6:31.80	6:32.72	6:33.64	6:34.56
430	6:35.48	6:36.41	6:37.33	6:38.25	6:39.17	6:40.09	6:41.02	6:41.94	6:42.86	6:43.78
440	6:44.70	6:45.62	6:46.55	6:47.47	6:48.39	6:49.31	6:50.23	6:51.16	6:52.08	6:53.00
450	6:53.92	6:54.84	6:55.77	6:56.69	6:57.61	6:58.53	6:59.45	7:00.37	7:01.30	7:02.22
460	7:03.14	7:04.06	7:04.98	7:05.91	7:06.83	7:07.75	7:08.67	7:09.59	7:10.52	7:11.44
470	7:12.36	7:13.28	7:14.20	7:15.12	7:16.05	7:16.97	7:17.89	7:18.81	7:19.73	7:20.66
480	7:21.58	7:22.50	7:23.42	7:24.34	7:25.27	7:26.19	7:27.11	7:28.03	7:28.95	7:29.87
490	7:30.80	7:31.72	7:32.64	7:33.56	7:34.48	7:35.41	7:36.33	7:37.25	7:38.17	7:39.09
500	7:40.02	7:40.94	7:41.86	7:42.78	7:43.70	7:44.62	7:45.55	7:46.47	7:47.39	7:48.31
510	7:49.23	7:50.16	7:51.08	7:52.00	7:52.92	7:53.84	7:54.77	7:55.69	7:56.61	7:57.53
520	7:58.45	7:59.37	8:00.30	8:01.22	8:02.14	8:03.06	8:03.98	8:04.91	8:05.83	8:06.75
530	8:07.67	8:08.59	8:09.52	8:10.44	8:11.36	8:12.28	8:13.20	8:14.12	8:15.05	8:15.97
540	8:16.89	8:17.81	8:18.73	8:19.66	8:20.58	8:21.50	8:22.42	8:23.34	8:24.27	8:25.19
550	8:26.11	8:27.03	8:27.95	8:28.87	8:29.80	8:30.72	8:31.64	8:32.56	8:33.48	8:34.41
560	8:35.33	8:36.25	8:37.17	8:38.09	8:39.02	8:39.94	8:40.86	8:41.78	8:42.70	8:43.62
570	8:44.55	8:45.47	8:46.39	8:47.31	8:48.23	8:49.16	8:50.08	8:51.00	8:51.92	8:52.84
580	8:53.77	8:54.69	8:55.61	8:56.53	8:57.45	8:58.37	8:59.30	9:00.22	9:01.14	9:02.06
590	9:02.98	9:03.91	9:04.83	9:05.75	9:06.67	9:07.59	9:08.52	9:09.44	9:10.36	9:11.28

dotted quarter = 1.38; quarter = 0.92; dotted eighth = 0.69; triplet (quarter, eighth rest) = 0.61; eighth = 0.46; triplet (eighth, eighth rest, eighth rest) = 0.31; sixteenth = 0.23 seconds

CLICK: 22 2/8 FRAMES; M.M.: 64.72

Click	0	1	2	3	4	5	6	7	8	9
000	0:00.00	0:00.00	0:00.93	0:01.85	0:02.78	0:03.71	0:04.64	0:05.56	0:06.49	0:07.42
010	0:08.34	0:09.27	0:10.20	0:11.13	0:12.05	0:12.98	0:13.91	0:14.83	0:15.76	0:16.69
020	0:17.61	0:18.54	0:19.47	0:20.40	0:21.32	0:22.25	0:23.18	0:24.10	0:25.03	0:25.96
030	0:26.89	0:27.81	0:28.74	0:29.67	0:30.59	0:31.52	0:32.45	0:33.38	0:34.30	0:35.23
040	0:36.16	0:37.08	0:38.01	0:38.94	0:39.86	0:40.79	0:41.72	0:42.65	0:43.57	0:44.50
050	0:45.43	0:46.35	0:47.28	0:48.21	0:49.14	0:50.06	0:50.99	0:51.92	0:52.84	0:53.77
060	0:54.70	0:55.63	0:56.55	0:57.48	0:58.41	0:59.33	1:00.26	1:01.19	1:02.11	1:03.04
070	1:03.97	1:04.90	1:05.82	1:06.75	1:07.68	1:08.60	1:09.53	1:10.46	1:11.39	1:12.31
080	1:13.24	1:14.17	1:15.09	1:16.02	1:16.95	1:17.88	1:18.80	1:19.73	1:20.66	1:21.58
090	1:22.51	1:23.44	1:24.36	1:25.29	1:26.22	1:27.15	1:28.07	1:29.00	1:29.93	1:30.85
100	1:31.78	1:32.71	1:33.64	1:34.56	1:35.49	1:36.42	1:37.34	1:38.27	1:39.20	1:40.13
110	1:41.05	1:41.98	1:42.91	1:43.83	1:44.76	1:45.69	1:46.61	1:47.54	1:48.47	1:49.40
120	1:50.32	1:51.25	1:52.18	1:53.10	1:54.03	1:54.96	1:55.89	1:56.81	1:57.74	1:58.67
130	1:59.59	2:00.52	2:01.45	2:02.38	2:03.30	2:04.23	2:05.16	2:06.08	2:07.01	2:07.94
140	2:08.86	2:09.79	2:10.72	2:11.65	2:12.57	2:13.50	2:14.43	2:15.35	2:16.28	2:17.21
150	2:18.14	2:19.06	2:19.99	2:20.92	2:21.84	2:22.77	2:23.70	2:24.63	2:25.55	2:26.48
160	2:27.41	2:28.33	2:29.26	2:30.19	2:31.11	2:32.04	2:32.97	2:33.90	2:34.82	2:35.75
170	2:36.68	2:37.60	2:38.53	2:39.46	2:40.39	2:41.31	2:42.24	2:43.17	2:44.09	2:45.02
180	2:45.95	2:46.88	2:47.80	2:48.73	2:49.66	2:50.58	2:51.51	2:52.44	2:53.36	2:54.29
190	2:55.22	2:56.15	2:57.07	2:58.00	2:58.93	2:59.85	3:00.78	3:01.71	3:02.64	3:03.56
200	3:04.49	3:05.42	3:06.34	3:07.27	3:08.20	3:09.13	3:10.05	3:10.98	3:11.91	3:12.83
210	3:13.76	3:14.69	3:15.61	3:16.54	3:17.47	3:18.40	3:19.32	3:20.25	3:21.18	3:22.10
220	3:23.03	3:23.96	3:24.89	3:25.81	3:26.74	3:27.67	3:28.59	3:29.52	3:30.45	3:31.38
230	3:32.30	3:33.23	3:34.16	3:35.08	3:36.01	3:36.94	3:37.86	3:38.79	3:39.72	3:40.65
240	3:41.57	3:42.50	3:43.43	3:44.35	3:45.28	3:46.21	3:47.14	3:48.06	3:48.99	3:49.92
250	3:50.84	3:51.77	3:52.70	3:53.63	3:54.55	3:55.48	3:56.41	3:57.33	3:58.26	3:59.19
260	4:00.11	4:01.04	4:01.97	4:02.90	4:03.82	4:04.75	4:05.68	4:06.60	4:07.53	4:08.46
270	4:09.39	4:10.31	4:11.24	4:12.17	4:13.09	4:14.02	4:14.95	4:15.88	4:16.80	4:17.73
280	4:18.66	4:19.58	4:20.51	4:21.44	4:22.36	4:23.29	4:24.22	4:25.15	4:26.07	4:27.00
290	4:27.93	4:28.85	4:29.78	4:30.71	4:31.64	4:32.56	4:33.49	4:34.42	4:35.34	4:36.27
300	4:37.20	4:38.13	4:39.05	4:39.98	4:40.91	4:41.83	4:42.76	4:43.69	4:44.61	4:45.54
310	4:46.47	4:47.40	4:48.32	4:49.25	4:50.18	4:51.10	4:52.03	4:52.96	4:53.89	4:54.81
320	4:55.74	4:56.67	4:57.59	4:58.52	4:59.45	5:00.38	5:01.30	5:02.23	5:03.16	5:04.08
330	5:05.01	5:05.94	5:06.86	5:07.79	5:08.72	5:09.65	5:10.57	5:11.50	5:12.43	5:13.35
340	5:14.28	5:15.21	5:16.14	5:17.06	5:17.99	5:18.92	5:19.84	5:20.77	5:21.70	5:22.62
350	5:23.55	5:24.48	5:25.41	5:26.33	5:27.26	5:28.19	5:29.11	5:30.04	5:30.97	5:31.90
360	5:32.82	5:33.75	5:34.68	5:35.60	5:36.53	5:37.46	5:38.39	5:39.31	5:40.24	5:41.17
370	5:42.09	5:43.02	5:43.95	5:44.88	5:45.80	5:46.73	5:47.66	5:48.58	5:49.51	5:50.44
380	5:51.36	5:52.29	5:53.22	5:54.15	5:55.07	5:56.00	5:56.93	5:57.85	5:58.78	5:59.71
390	6:00.64	6:01.56	6:02.49	6:03.42	6:04.34	6:05.27	6:06.20	6:07.13	6:08.05	6:08.98
400	6:09.91	6:10.83	6:11.76	6:12.69	6:13.61	6:14.54	6:15.47	6:16.40	6:17.32	6:18.25
410	6:19.18	6:20.10	6:21.03	6:21.96	6:22.89	6:23.81	6:24.74	6:25.67	6:26.59	6:27.52
420	6:28.45	6:29.38	6:30.30	6:31.23	6:32.16	6:33.08	6:34.01	6:34.94	6:35.86	6:36.79
430	6:37.72	6:38.65	6:39.57	6:40.50	6:41.43	6:42.35	6:43.28	6:44.21	6:45.14	6:46.06
440	6:46.99	6:47.92	6:48.84	6:49.77	6:50.70	6:51.63	6:52.55	6:53.48	6:54.41	6:55.33
450	6:56.26	6:57.19	6:58.11	6:59.04	6:59.97	7:00.90	7:01.82	7:02.75	7:03.68	7:04.60
460	7:05.53	7:06.46	7:07.39	7:08.31	7:09.24	7:10.17	7:11.09	7:12.02	7:12.95	7:13.88
470	7:14.80	7:15.73	7:16.66	7:17.58	7:18.51	7:19.44	7:20.36	7:21.29	7:22.22	7:23.15
480	7:24.07	7:25.00	7:25.93	7:26.85	7:27.78	7:28.71	7:29.64	7:30.56	7:31.49	7:32.42
490	7:33.34	7:34.27	7:35.20	7:36.13	7:37.05	7:37.98	7:38.91	7:39.83	7:40.76	7:41.69
500	7:42.61	7:43.54	7:44.47	7:45.40	7:46.32	7:47.25	7:48.18	7:49.10	7:50.03	7:50.96
510	7:51.89	7:52.81	7:53.74	7:54.67	7:55.59	7:56.52	7:57.45	7:58.38	7:59.30	8:00.23
520	8:01.16	8:02.08	8:03.01	8:03.94	8:04.86	8:05.79	8:06.72	8:07.65	8:08.57	8:09.50
530	8:10.43	8:11.35	8:12.28	8:13.21	8:14.14	8:15.06	8:15.99	8:16.92	8:17.84	8:18.77
540	8:19.70	8:20.63	8:21.55	8:22.48	8:23.41	8:24.33	8:25.26	8:26.19	8:27.11	8:28.04
550	8:28.97	8:29.90	8:30.82	8:31.75	8:32.68	8:33.60	8:34.53	8:35.46	8:36.39	8:37.31
560	8:38.24	8:39.17	8:40.09	8:41.02	8:41.95	8:42.88	8:43.80	8:44.73	8:45.66	8:46.58
570	8:47.51	8:48.44	8:49.36	8:50.29	8:51.22	8:52.15	8:53.07	8:54.00	8:54.93	8:55.85
580	8:56.78	8:57.71	8:58.64	8:59.56	9:00.49	9:01.42	9:02.34	9:03.27	9:04.20	9:05.13
590	9:06.05	9:06.98	9:07.91	9:08.83	9:09.76	9:10.69	9:11.61	9:12.54	9:13.47	9:14.40

♩. = 1.39; ♩ = 0.93; ♪. = 0.70; (triplet ♩ 𝄾) = 0.62; ♪ = 0.46; (triplet ♪𝄾𝄾) = 0.31; 𝅘𝅥𝅯 = 0.23 seconds

CLICK: 22⅜ FRAMES; M.M.: 64.36

Click	0	1	2	3	4	5	6	7	8	9
000	0:00.00	0:00.00	0:00.93	0:01.86	0:02.80	0:03.73	0:04.66	0:05.59	0:06.53	0:07.46
010	0:08.39	0:09.32	0:10.26	0:11.19	0:12.12	0:13.05	0:13.98	0:14.92	0:15.85	0:16.78
020	0:17.71	0:18.65	0:19.58	0:20.51	0:21.44	0:22.38	0:23.31	0:24.24	0:25.17	0:26.10
030	0:27.04	0:27.97	0:28.90	0:29.83	0:30.77	0:31.70	0:32.63	0:33.56	0:34.49	0:35.43
040	0:36.36	0:37.29	0:38.22	0:39.16	0:40.09	0:41.02	0:41.95	0:42.89	0:43.82	0:44.75
050	0:45.68	0:46.61	0:47.55	0:48.48	0:49.41	0:50.34	0:51.28	0:52.21	0:53.14	0:54.07
060	0:55.01	0:55.94	0:56.87	0:57.80	0:58.73	0:59.67	1:00.60	1:01.53	1:02.46	1:03.40
070	1:04.33	1:05.26	1:06.19	1:07.13	1:08.06	1:08.99	1:09.92	1:10.85	1:11.79	1:12.72
080	1:13.65	1:14.58	1:15.52	1:16.45	1:17.38	1:18.31	1:19.24	1:20.18	1:21.11	1:22.04
090	1:22.97	1:23.91	1:24.84	1:25.77	1:26.70	1:27.64	1:28.57	1:29.50	1:30.43	1:31.36
100	1:32.30	1:33.23	1:34.16	1:35.09	1:36.03	1:36.96	1:37.89	1:38.82	1:39.76	1:40.69
110	1:41.62	1:42.55	1:43.48	1:44.42	1:45.35	1:46.28	1:47.21	1:48.15	1:49.08	1:50.01
120	1:50.94	1:51.88	1:52.81	1:53.74	1:54.67	1:55.60	1:56.54	1:57.47	1:58.40	1:59.33
130	2:00.27	2:01.20	2:02.13	2:03.06	2:03.99	2:04.93	2:05.86	2:06.79	2:07.72	2:08.66
140	2:09.59	2:10.52	2:11.45	2:12.39	2:13.32	2:14.25	2:15.18	2:16.11	2:17.05	2:17.98
150	2:18.91	2:19.84	2:20.78	2:21.71	2:22.64	2:23.57	2:24.51	2:25.44	2:26.37	2:27.30
160	2:28.23	2:29.17	2:30.10	2:31.03	2:31.96	2:32.90	2:33.83	2:34.76	2:35.69	2:36.63
170	2:37.56	2:38.49	2:39.42	2:40.35	2:41.29	2:42.22	2:43.15	2:44.08	2:45.02	2:45.95
180	2:46.88	2:47.81	2:48.74	2:49.68	2:50.61	2:51.54	2:52.47	2:53.41	2:54.34	2:55.27
190	2:56.20	2:57.14	2:58.07	2:59.00	2:59.93	3:00.86	3:01.80	3:02.73	3:03.66	3:04.59
200	3:05.53	3:06.46	3:07.39	3:08.32	3:09.26	3:10.19	3:11.12	3:12.05	3:12.98	3:13.92
210	3:14.85	3:15.78	3:16.71	3:17.65	3:18.58	3:19.51	3:20.44	3:21.38	3:22.31	3:23.24
220	3:24.17	3:25.10	3:26.04	3:26.97	3:27.90	3:28.83	3:29.77	3:30.70	3:31.63	3:32.56
230	3:33.49	3:34.43	3:35.36	3:36.29	3:37.22	3:38.16	3:39.09	3:40.02	3:40.95	3:41.89
240	3:42.82	3:43.75	3:44.68	3:45.61	3:46.55	3:47.48	3:48.41	3:49.34	3:50.28	3:51.21
250	3:52.14	3:53.07	3:54.01	3:54.94	3:55.87	3:56.80	3:57.73	3:58.67	3:59.60	4:00.53
260	4:01.46	4:02.40	4:03.33	4:04.26	4:05.19	4:06.13	4:07.06	4:07.99	4:08.92	4:09.85
270	4:10.79	4:11.72	4:12.65	4:13.58	4:14.52	4:15.45	4:16.38	4:17.31	4:18.24	4:19.18
280	4:20.11	4:21.04	4:21.97	4:22.91	4:23.84	4:24.77	4:25.70	4:26.64	4:27.57	4:28.50
290	4:29.43	4:30.36	4:31.30	4:32.23	4:33.16	4:34.09	4:35.03	4:35.96	4:36.89	4:37.82
300	4:38.76	4:39.69	4:40.62	4:41.55	4:42.48	4:43.42	4:44.35	4:45.28	4:46.21	4:47.15
310	4:48.08	4:49.01	4:49.94	4:50.88	4:51.81	4:52.74	4:53.67	4:54.60	4:55.54	4:56.47
320	4:57.40	4:58.33	4:59.27	5:00.20	5:01.13	5:02.06	5:02.99	5:03.93	5:04.86	5:05.79
330	5:06.72	5:07.66	5:08.59	5:09.52	5:10.45	5:11.39	5:12.32	5:13.25	5:14.18	5:15.11
340	5:16.05	5:16.98	5:17.91	5:18.84	5:19.78	5:20.71	5:21.64	5:22.57	5:23.51	5:24.44
350	5:25.37	5:26.30	5:27.23	5:28.17	5:29.10	5:30.03	5:30.96	5:31.90	5:32.83	5:33.76
360	5:34.69	5:35.63	5:36.56	5:37.49	5:38.42	5:39.35	5:40.29	5:41.22	5:42.15	5:43.08
370	5:44.02	5:44.95	5:45.88	5:46.81	5:47.74	5:48.68	5:49.61	5:50.54	5:51.47	5:52.41
380	5:53.34	5:54.27	5:55.20	5:56.14	5:57.07	5:58.00	5:58.93	5:59.86	6:00.80	6:01.73
390	6:02.66	6:03.59	6:04.53	6:05.46	6:06.39	6:07.32	6:08.26	6:09.19	6:10.12	6:11.05
400	6:11.98	6:12.92	6:13.85	6:14.78	6:15.71	6:16.65	6:17.58	6:18.51	6:19.44	6:20.38
410	6:21.31	6:22.24	6:23.17	6:24.10	6:25.04	6:25.97	6:26.90	6:27.83	6:28.77	6:29.70
420	6:30.63	6:31.56	6:32.49	6:33.43	6:34.36	6:35.29	6:36.22	6:37.16	6:38.09	6:39.02
430	6:39.95	6:40.89	6:41.82	6:42.75	6:43.68	6:44.61	6:45.55	6:46.48	6:47.41	6:48.34
440	6:49.28	6:50.21	6:51.14	6:52.07	6:53.01	6:53.94	6:54.87	6:55.80	6:56.73	6:57.67
450	6:58.60	6:59.53	7:00.46	7:01.40	7:02.33	7:03.26	7:04.19	7:05.13	7:06.06	7:06.99
460	7:07.92	7:08.85	7:09.79	7:10.72	7:11.65	7:12.58	7:13.52	7:14.45	7:15.38	7:16.31
470	7:17.24	7:18.18	7:19.11	7:20.04	7:20.97	7:21.91	7:22.84	7:23.77	7:24.70	7:25.64
480	7:26.57	7:27.50	7:28.43	7:29.36	7:30.30	7:31.23	7:32.16	7:33.09	7:34.03	7:34.96
490	7:35.89	7:36.82	7:37.76	7:38.69	7:39.62	7:40.55	7:41.48	7:42.42	7:43.35	7:44.28
500	7:45.21	7:46.15	7:47.08	7:48.01	7:48.94	7:49.88	7:50.81	7:51.74	7:52.67	7:53.60
510	7:54.54	7:55.47	7:56.40	7:57.33	7:58.27	7:59.20	8:00.13	8:01.06	8:01.99	8:02.93
520	8:03.86	8:04.79	8:05.72	8:06.66	8:07.59	8:08.52	8:09.45	8:10.39	8:11.32	8:12.25
530	8:13.18	8:14.11	8:15.05	8:15.98	8:16.91	8:17.84	8:18.78	8:19.71	8:20.64	8:21.57
540	8:22.51	8:23.44	8:24.37	8:25.30	8:26.23	8:27.17	8:28.10	8:29.03	8:29.96	8:30.90
550	8:31.83	8:32.76	8:33.69	8:34.63	8:35.56	8:36.49	8:37.42	8:38.35	8:39.29	8:40.22
560	8:41.15	8:42.08	8:43.02	8:43.95	8:44.88	8:45.81	8:46.74	8:47.68	8:48.61	8:49.54
570	8:50.47	8:51.41	8:52.34	8:53.27	8:54.20	8:55.14	8:56.07	8:57.00	8:57.93	8:58.86
580	8:59.80	9:00.73	9:01.66	9:02.59	9:03.53	9:04.46	9:05.39	9:06.32	9:07.26	9:08.19
590	9:09.12	9:10.05	9:10.98	9:11.92	9:12.85	9:13.78	9:14.71	9:15.65	9:16.58	9:17.51

♩. = 1.40; ♩ = 0.93; ♪. = 0.70; (triplet ♩ 𝄾) = 0.62; ♪ = 0.47; (triplet ♪ 𝄾 𝄾) = 0.31; 𝅘𝅥𝅯 = 0.23 seconds

CLICK: 22 4/8 FRAMES; M.M.: 64.00

Click	0	1	2	3	4	5	6	7	8	9
000	0:00.00	0:00.00	0:00.94	0:01.88	0:02.81	0:03.75	0:04.69	0:05.63	0:06.56	0:07.50
010	0:08.44	0:09.38	0:10.31	0:11.25	0:12.19	0:13.13	0:14.06	0:15.00	0:15.94	0:16.88
020	0:17.81	0:18.75	0:19.69	0:20.63	0:21.56	0:22.50	0:23.44	0:24.38	0:25.31	0:26.25
030	0:27.19	0:28.13	0:29.06	0:30.00	0:30.94	0:31.88	0:32.81	0:33.75	0:34.69	0:35.63
040	0:36.56	0:37.50	0:38.44	0:39.38	0:40.31	0:41.25	0:42.19	0:43.13	0:44.06	0:45.00
050	0:45.94	0:46.88	0:47.81	0:48.75	0:49.69	0:50.63	0:51.56	0:52.50	0:53.44	0:54.38
060	0:55.31	0:56.25	0:57.19	0:58.13	0:59.06	1:00.00	1:00.94	1:01.88	1:02.81	1:03.75
070	1:04.69	1:05.63	1:06.56	1:07.50	1:08.44	1:09.38	1:10.31	1:11.25	1:12.19	1:13.13
080	1:14.06	1:15.00	1:15.94	1:16.88	1:17.81	1:18.75	1:19.69	1:20.63	1:21.56	1:22.50
090	1:23.44	1:24.38	1:25.31	1:26.25	1:27.19	1:28.13	1:29.06	1:30.00	1:30.94	1:31.88
100	1:32.81	1:33.75	1:34.69	1:35.63	1:36.56	1:37.50	1:38.44	1:39.38	1:40.31	1:41.25
110	1:42.19	1:43.13	1:44.06	1:45.00	1:45.94	1:46.88	1:47.81	1:48.75	1:49.69	1:50.63
120	1:51.56	1:52.50	1:53.44	1:54.38	1:55.31	1:56.25	1:57.19	1:58.13	1:59.06	2:00.00
130	2:00.94	2:01.88	2:02.81	2:03.75	2:04.69	2:05.63	2:06.56	2:07.50	2:08.44	2:09.38
140	2:10.31	2:11.25	2:12.19	2:13.13	2:14.06	2:15.00	2:15.94	2:16.88	2:17.81	2:18.75
150	2:19.69	2:20.63	2:21.56	2:22.50	2:23.44	2:24.38	2:25.31	2:26.25	2:27.19	2:28.13
160	2:29.06	2:30.00	2:30.94	2:31.88	2:32.81	2:33.75	2:34.69	2:35.63	2:36.56	2:37.50
170	2:38.44	2:39.38	2:40.31	2:41.25	2:42.19	2:43.13	2:44.06	2:45.00	2:45.94	2:46.88
180	2:47.81	2:48.75	2:49.69	2:50.63	2:51.56	2:52.50	2:53.44	2:54.38	2:55.31	2:56.25
190	2:57.19	2:58.13	2:59.06	3:00.00	3:00.94	3:01.88	3:02.81	3:03.75	3:04.69	3:05.63
200	3:06.56	3:07.50	3:08.44	3:09.38	3:10.31	3:11.25	3:12.19	3:13.13	3:14.06	3:15.00
210	3:15.94	3:16.88	3:17.81	3:18.75	3:19.69	3:20.63	3:21.56	3:22.50	3:23.44	3:24.38
220	3:25.31	3:26.25	3:27.19	3:28.13	3:29.06	3:30.00	3:30.94	3:31.88	3:32.81	3:33.75
230	3:34.69	3:35.63	3:36.56	3:37.50	3:38.44	3:39.38	3:40.31	3:41.25	3:42.19	3:43.13
240	3:44.06	3:45.00	3:45.94	3:46.88	3:47.81	3:48.75	3:49.69	3:50.63	3:51.56	3:52.50
250	3:53.44	3:54.38	3:55.31	3:56.25	3:57.19	3:58.13	3:59.06	4:00.00	4:00.94	4:01.88
260	4:02.81	4:03.75	4:04.69	4:05.63	4:06.56	4:07.50	4:08.44	4:09.38	4:10.31	4:11.25
270	4:12.19	4:13.13	4:14.06	4:15.00	4:15.94	4:16.88	4:17.81	4:18.75	4:19.69	4:20.63
280	4:21.56	4:22.50	4:23.44	4:24.38	4:25.31	4:26.25	4:27.19	4:28.13	4:29.06	4:30.00
290	4:30.94	4:31.88	4:32.81	4:33.75	4:34.69	4:35.63	4:36.56	4:37.50	4:38.44	4:39.38
300	4:40.31	4:41.25	4:42.19	4:43.13	4:44.06	4:45.00	4:45.94	4:46.88	4:47.81	4:48.75
310	4:49.69	4:50.63	4:51.56	4:52.50	4:53.44	4:54.38	4:55.31	4:56.25	4:57.19	4:58.13
320	4:59.06	5:00.00	5:00.94	5:01.88	5:02.81	5:03.75	5:04.69	5:05.63	5:06.56	5:07.50
330	5:08.44	5:09.38	5:10.31	5:11.25	5:12.19	5:13.13	5:14.06	5:15.00	5:15.94	5:16.88
340	5:17.81	5:18.75	5:19.69	5:20.63	5:21.56	5:22.50	5:23.44	5:24.38	5:25.31	5:26.25
350	5:27.19	5:28.13	5:29.06	5:30.00	5:30.94	5:31.88	5:32.81	5:33.75	5:34.69	5:35.63
360	5:36.56	5:37.50	5:38.44	5:39.38	5:40.31	5:41.25	5:42.19	5:43.13	5:44.06	5:45.00
370	5:45.94	5:46.88	5:47.81	5:48.75	5:49.69	5:50.63	5:51.56	5:52.50	5:53.44	5:54.38
380	5:55.31	5:56.25	5:57.19	5:58.13	5:59.06	6:00.00	6:00.94	6:01.88	6:02.81	6:03.75
390	6:04.69	6:05.63	6:06.56	6:07.50	6:08.44	6:09.38	6:10.31	6:11.25	6:12.19	6:13.13
400	6:14.06	6:15.00	6:15.94	6:16.88	6:17.81	6:18.75	6:19.69	6:20.63	6:21.56	6:22.50
410	6:23.44	6:24.38	6:25.31	6:26.25	6:27.19	6:28.13	6:29.06	6:30.00	6:30.94	6:31.88
420	6:32.81	6:33.75	6:34.69	6:35.63	6:36.56	6:37.50	6:38.44	6:39.38	6:40.31	6:41.25
430	6:42.19	6:43.13	6:44.06	6:45.00	6:45.94	6:46.88	6:47.81	6:48.75	6:49.69	6:50.63
440	6:51.56	6:52.50	6:53.44	6:54.38	6:55.31	6:56.25	6:57.19	6:58.13	6:59.06	7:00.00
450	7:00.94	7:01.88	7:02.81	7:03.75	7:04.69	7:05.63	7:06.56	7:07.50	7:08.44	7:09.38
460	7:10.31	7:11.25	7:12.19	7:13.13	7:14.06	7:15.00	7:15.94	7:16.88	7:17.81	7:18.75
470	7:19.69	7:20.63	7:21.56	7:22.50	7:23.44	7:24.38	7:25.31	7:26.25	7:27.19	7:28.13
480	7:29.06	7:30.00	7:30.94	7:31.88	7:32.81	7:33.75	7:34.69	7:35.63	7:36.56	7:37.50
490	7:38.44	7:39.38	7:40.31	7:41.25	7:42.19	7:43.13	7:44.06	7:45.00	7:45.94	7:46.88
500	7:47.81	7:48.75	7:49.69	7:50.63	7:51.56	7:52.50	7:53.44	7:54.38	7:55.31	7:56.25
510	7:57.19	7:58.13	7:59.06	8:00.00	8:00.94	8:01.88	8:02.81	8:03.75	8:04.69	8:05.63
520	8:06.56	8:07.50	8:08.44	8:09.38	8:10.31	8:11.25	8:12.19	8:13.13	8:14.06	8:15.00
530	8:15.94	8:16.88	8:17.81	8:18.75	8:19.69	8:20.63	8:21.56	8:22.50	8:23.44	8:24.38
540	8:25.31	8:26.25	8:27.19	8:28.13	8:29.06	8:30.00	8:30.94	8:31.88	8:32.81	8:33.75
550	8:34.69	8:35.63	8:36.56	8:37.50	8:38.44	8:39.38	8:40.31	8:41.25	8:42.19	8:43.13
560	8:44.06	8:45.00	8:45.94	8:46.88	8:47.81	8:48.75	8:49.69	8:50.63	8:51.56	8:52.50
570	8:53.44	8:54.38	8:55.31	8:56.25	8:57.19	8:58.13	8:59.06	9:00.00	9:00.94	9:01.88
580	9:02.81	9:03.75	9:04.69	9:05.63	9:06.56	9:07.50	9:08.44	9:09.38	9:10.31	9:11.25
590	9:12.19	9:13.13	9:14.06	9:15.00	9:15.94	9:16.88	9:17.81	9:18.75	9:19.69	9:20.63

♩. = 1.41; ♩ = 0.94; ♪. = 0.70; (triplet ♩ 𝄾) = 0.63; ♪ = 0.47; (triplet ♪𝄾𝄾) = 0.31; 𝅘𝅥𝅯 = 0.23 seconds

CLICK: 22⅝ FRAMES; M.M.: 63.65

Click	0	1	2	3	4	5	6	7	8	9
000	0:00.00	0:00.00	0:00.94	0:01.89	0:02.83	0:03.77	0:04.71	0:05.66	0:06.60	0:07.54
010	0:08.48	0:09.43	0:10.37	0:11.31	0:12.26	0:13.20	0:14.14	0:15.08	0:16.03	0:16.97
020	0:17.91	0:18.85	0:19.80	0:20.74	0:21.68	0:22.63	0:23.57	0:24.51	0:25.45	0:26.40
030	0:27.34	0:28.28	0:29.22	0:30.17	0:31.11	0:32.05	0:32.99	0:33.94	0:34.88	0:35.82
040	0:36.77	0:37.71	0:38.65	0:39.59	0:40.54	0:41.48	0:42.42	0:43.36	0:44.31	0:45.25
050	0:46.19	0:47.14	0:48.08	0:49.02	0:49.96	0:50.91	0:51.85	0:52.79	0:53.73	0:54.68
060	0:55.62	0:56.56	0:57.51	0:58.45	0:59.39	1:00.33	1:01.28	1:02.22	1:03.16	1:04.10
070	1:05.05	1:05.99	1:06.93	1:07.87	1:08.82	1:09.76	1:10.70	1:11.65	1:12.59	1:13.53
080	1:14.47	1:15.42	1:16.36	1:17.30	1:18.24	1:19.19	1:20.13	1:21.07	1:22.02	1:22.96
090	1:23.90	1:24.84	1:25.79	1:26.73	1:27.67	1:28.61	1:29.56	1:30.50	1:31.44	1:32.39
100	1:33.33	1:34.27	1:35.21	1:36.16	1:37.10	1:38.04	1:38.98	1:39.93	1:40.87	1:41.81
110	1:42.76	1:43.70	1:44.64	1:45.58	1:46.53	1:47.47	1:48.41	1:49.35	1:50.30	1:51.24
120	1:52.18	1:53.12	1:54.07	1:55.01	1:55.95	1:56.90	1:57.84	1:58.78	1:59.72	2:00.67
130	2:01.61	2:02.55	2:03.49	2:04.44	2:05.38	2:06.32	2:07.27	2:08.21	2:09.15	2:10.09
140	2:11.04	2:11.98	2:12.92	2:13.86	2:14.81	2:15.75	2:16.69	2:17.64	2:18.58	2:19.52
150	2:20.46	2:21.41	2:22.35	2:23.29	2:24.23	2:25.18	2:26.12	2:27.06	2:28.01	2:28.95
160	2:29.89	2:30.83	2:31.78	2:32.72	2:33.66	2:34.60	2:35.55	2:36.49	2:37.43	2:38.37
170	2:39.32	2:40.26	2:41.20	2:42.15	2:43.09	2:44.03	2:44.97	2:45.92	2:46.86	2:47.80
180	2:48.74	2:49.69	2:50.63	2:51.57	2:52.52	2:53.46	2:54.40	2:55.34	2:56.29	2:57.23
190	2:58.17	2:59.11	3:00.06	3:01.00	3:01.94	3:02.89	3:03.83	3:04.77	3:05.71	3:06.66
200	3:07.60	3:08.54	3:09.48	3:10.43	3:11.37	3:12.31	3:13.26	3:14.20	3:15.14	3:16.08
210	3:17.03	3:17.97	3:18.91	3:19.85	3:20.80	3:21.74	3:22.68	3:23.62	3:24.57	3:25.51
220	3:26.45	3:27.40	3:28.34	3:29.28	3:30.22	3:31.17	3:32.11	3:33.05	3:33.99	3:34.94
230	3:35.88	3:36.82	3:37.77	3:38.71	3:39.65	3:40.59	3:41.54	3:42.48	3:43.42	3:44.36
240	3:45.31	3:46.25	3:47.19	3:48.14	3:49.08	3:50.02	3:50.96	3:51.91	3:52.85	3:53.79
250	3:54.73	3:55.68	3:56.62	3:57.56	3:58.51	3:59.45	4:00.39	4:01.33	4:02.28	4:03.22
260	4:04.16	4:05.10	4:06.05	4:06.99	4:07.93	4:08.87	4:09.82	4:10.76	4:11.70	4:12.65
270	4:13.59	4:14.53	4:15.47	4:16.42	4:17.36	4:18.30	4:19.24	4:20.19	4:21.13	4:22.07
280	4:23.02	4:23.96	4:24.90	4:25.84	4:26.79	4:27.73	4:28.67	4:29.61	4:30.56	4:31.50
290	4:32.44	4:33.39	4:34.33	4:35.27	4:36.21	4:37.16	4:38.10	4:39.04	4:39.98	4:40.93
300	4:41.87	4:42.81	4:43.76	4:44.70	4:45.64	4:46.58	4:47.53	4:48.47	4:49.41	4:50.35
310	4:51.30	4:52.24	4:53.18	4:54.12	4:55.07	4:56.01	4:56.95	4:57.90	4:58.84	4:59.78
320	5:00.72	5:01.67	5:02.61	5:03.55	5:04.49	5:05.44	5:06.38	5:07.32	5:08.27	5:09.21
330	5:10.15	5:11.09	5:12.04	5:12.98	5:13.92	5:14.86	5:15.81	5:16.75	5:17.69	5:18.64
340	5:19.58	5:20.52	5:21.46	5:22.41	5:23.35	5:24.29	5:25.23	5:26.18	5:27.12	5:28.06
350	5:29.01	5:29.95	5:30.89	5:31.83	5:32.78	5:33.72	5:34.66	5:35.60	5:36.55	5:37.49
360	5:38.43	5:39.37	5:40.32	5:41.26	5:42.20	5:43.15	5:44.09	5:45.03	5:45.97	5:46.92
370	5:47.86	5:48.80	5:49.74	5:50.69	5:51.63	5:52.57	5:53.52	5:54.46	5:55.40	5:56.34
380	5:57.29	5:58.23	5:59.17	6:00.11	6:01.06	6:02.00	6:02.94	6:03.89	6:04.83	6:05.77
390	6:06.71	6:07.66	6:08.60	6:09.54	6:10.48	6:11.43	6:12.37	6:13.31	6:14.26	6:15.20
400	6:16.14	6:17.08	6:18.03	6:18.97	6:19.91	6:20.85	6:21.80	6:22.74	6:23.68	6:24.62
410	6:25.57	6:26.51	6:27.45	6:28.40	6:29.34	6:30.28	6:31.22	6:32.17	6:33.11	6:34.05
420	6:34.99	6:35.94	6:36.88	6:37.82	6:38.77	6:39.71	6:40.65	6:41.59	6:42.54	6:43.48
430	6:44.42	6:45.36	6:46.31	6:47.25	6:48.19	6:49.14	6:50.08	6:51.02	6:51.96	6:52.91
440	6:53.85	6:54.79	6:55.73	6:56.68	6:57.62	6:58.56	6:59.51	7:00.45	7:01.39	7:02.33
450	7:03.28	7:04.22	7:05.16	7:06.10	7:07.05	7:07.99	7:08.93	7:09.87	7:10.82	7:11.76
460	7:12.70	7:13.65	7:14.59	7:15.53	7:16.47	7:17.42	7:18.36	7:19.30	7:20.24	7:21.19
470	7:22.13	7:23.07	7:24.02	7:24.96	7:25.90	7:26.84	7:27.79	7:28.73	7:29.67	7:30.61
480	7:31.56	7:32.50	7:33.44	7:34.39	7:35.33	7:36.27	7:37.21	7:38.16	7:39.10	7:40.04
490	7:40.98	7:41.93	7:42.87	7:43.81	7:44.76	7:45.70	7:46.64	7:47.58	7:48.53	7:49.47
500	7:50.41	7:51.35	7:52.30	7:53.24	7:54.18	7:55.12	7:56.07	7:57.01	7:57.95	7:58.90
510	7:59.84	8:00.78	8:01.72	8:02.67	8:03.61	8:04.55	8:05.49	8:06.44	8:07.38	8:08.32
520	8:09.27	8:10.21	8:11.15	8:12.09	8:13.04	8:13.98	8:14.92	8:15.86	8:16.81	8:17.75
530	8:18.69	8:19.64	8:20.58	8:21.52	8:22.46	8:23.41	8:24.35	8:25.29	8:26.23	8:27.18
540	8:28.12	8:29.06	8:30.01	8:30.95	8:31.89	8:32.83	8:33.78	8:34.72	8:35.66	8:36.60
550	8:37.55	8:38.49	8:39.43	8:40.37	8:41.32	8:42.26	8:43.20	8:44.15	8:45.09	8:46.03
560	8:46.97	8:47.92	8:48.86	8:49.80	8:50.74	8:51.69	8:52.63	8:53.57	8:54.52	8:55.46
570	8:56.40	8:57.34	8:58.29	8:59.23	9:00.17	9:01.11	9:02.06	9:03.00	9:03.94	9:04.89
580	9:05.83	9:06.77	9:07.71	9:08.66	9:09.60	9:10.54	9:11.48	9:12.43	9:13.37	9:14.31
590	9:15.26	9:16.20	9:17.14	9:18.08	9:19.03	9:19.97	9:20.91	9:21.85	9:22.80	9:23.74

♩. = 1.41; ♩ = 0.94; ♪. = 0.71; (3) ♩ 𝄾 = 0.63; ♪ = 0.47; (3) ♪ 𝄾 𝄾 = 0.31; 𝅘𝅥𝅯 = 0.24 seconds

CLICK: 22 6/8 FRAMES; M.M.: 63.30

Click	0	1	2	3	4	5	6	7	8	9
000	0:00.00	0:00.00	0:00.95	0:01.90	0:02.84	0:03.79	0:04.74	0:05.69	0:06.64	0:07.58
010	0:08.53	0:09.48	0:10.43	0:11.38	0:12.32	0:13.27	0:14.22	0:15.17	0:16.11	0:17.06
020	0:18.01	0:18.96	0:19.91	0:20.85	0:21.80	0:22.75	0:23.70	0:24.65	0:25.59	0:26.54
030	0:27.49	0:28.44	0:29.39	0:30.33	0:31.28	0:32.23	0:33.18	0:34.13	0:35.07	0:36.02
040	0:36.97	0:37.92	0:38.86	0:39.81	0:40.76	0:41.71	0:42.66	0:43.60	0:44.55	0:45.50
050	0:46.45	0:47.40	0:48.34	0:49.29	0:50.24	0:51.19	0:52.14	0:53.08	0:54.03	0:54.98
060	0:55.93	0:56.88	0:57.82	0:58.77	0:59.72	1:00.67	1:01.61	1:02.56	1:03.51	1:04.46
070	1:05.41	1:06.35	1:07.30	1:08.25	1:09.20	1:10.15	1:11.09	1:12.04	1:12.99	1:13.94
080	1:14.89	1:15.83	1:16.78	1:17.73	1:18.68	1:19.63	1:20.57	1:21.52	1:22.47	1:23.42
090	1:24.36	1:25.31	1:26.26	1:27.21	1:28.16	1:29.10	1:30.05	1:31.00	1:31.95	1:32.90
100	1:33.84	1:34.79	1:35.74	1:36.69	1:37.64	1:38.58	1:39.53	1:40.48	1:41.43	1:42.38
110	1:43.32	1:44.27	1:45.22	1:46.17	1:47.11	1:48.06	1:49.01	1:49.96	1:50.91	1:51.85
120	1:52.80	1:53.75	1:54.70	1:55.65	1:56.59	1:57.54	1:58.49	1:59.44	2:00.39	2:01.33
130	2:02.28	2:03.23	2:04.18	2:05.13	2:06.07	2:07.02	2:07.97	2:08.92	2:09.86	2:10.81
140	2:11.76	2:12.71	2:13.66	2:14.60	2:15.55	2:16.50	2:17.45	2:18.40	2:19.34	2:20.29
150	2:21.24	2:22.19	2:23.14	2:24.08	2:25.03	2:25.98	2:26.93	2:27.88	2:28.82	2:29.77
160	2:30.72	2:31.67	2:32.61	2:33.56	2:34.51	2:35.46	2:36.41	2:37.35	2:38.30	2:39.25
170	2:40.20	2:41.15	2:42.09	2:43.04	2:43.99	2:44.94	2:45.89	2:46.83	2:47.78	2:48.73
180	2:49.68	2:50.63	2:51.57	2:52.52	2:53.47	2:54.42	2:55.36	2:56.31	2:57.26	2:58.21
190	2:59.16	3:00.10	3:01.05	3:02.00	3:02.95	3:03.90	3:04.84	3:05.79	3:06.74	3:07.69
200	3:08.64	3:09.58	3:10.53	3:11.48	3:12.43	3:13.38	3:14.32	3:15.27	3:16.22	3:17.17
210	3:18.11	3:19.06	3:20.01	3:20.96	3:21.91	3:22.85	3:23.80	3:24.75	3:25.70	3:26.65
220	3:27.59	3:28.54	3:29.49	3:30.44	3:31.39	3:32.33	3:33.28	3:34.23	3:35.18	3:36.13
230	3:37.07	3:38.02	3:38.97	3:39.92	3:40.86	3:41.81	3:42.76	3:43.71	3:44.66	3:45.60
240	3:46.55	3:47.50	3:48.45	3:49.40	3:50.34	3:51.29	3:52.24	3:53.19	3:54.14	3:55.08
250	3:56.03	3:56.98	3:57.93	3:58.88	3:59.82	4:00.77	4:01.72	4:02.67	4:03.61	4:04.56
260	4:05.51	4:06.46	4:07.41	4:08.35	4:09.30	4:10.25	4:11.20	4:12.15	4:13.09	4:14.04
270	4:14.99	4:15.94	4:16.89	4:17.83	4:18.78	4:19.73	4:20.68	4:21.63	4:22.57	4:23.52
280	4:24.47	4:25.42	4:26.36	4:27.31	4:28.26	4:29.21	4:30.16	4:31.10	4:32.05	4:33.00
290	4:33.95	4:34.90	4:35.84	4:36.79	4:37.74	4:38.69	4:39.64	4:40.58	4:41.53	4:42.48
300	4:43.43	4:44.38	4:45.32	4:46.27	4:47.22	4:48.17	4:49.11	4:50.06	4:51.01	4:51.96
310	4:52.91	4:53.85	4:54.80	4:55.75	4:56.70	4:57.65	4:58.59	4:59.54	5:00.49	5:01.44
320	5:02.39	5:03.33	5:04.28	5:05.23	5:06.18	5:07.13	5:08.07	5:09.02	5:09.97	5:10.92
330	5:11.86	5:12.81	5:13.76	5:14.71	5:15.66	5:16.60	5:17.55	5:18.50	5:19.45	5:20.40
340	5:21.34	5:22.29	5:23.24	5:24.19	5:25.14	5:26.08	5:27.03	5:27.98	5:28.93	5:29.88
350	5:30.82	5:31.77	5:32.72	5:33.67	5:34.61	5:35.56	5:36.51	5:37.46	5:38.41	5:39.35
360	5:40.30	5:41.25	5:42.20	5:43.15	5:44.09	5:45.04	5:45.99	5:46.94	5:47.89	5:48.83
370	5:49.78	5:50.73	5:51.68	5:52.63	5:53.57	5:54.52	5:55.47	5:56.42	5:57.36	5:58.31
380	5:59.26	6:00.21	6:01.16	6:02.10	6:03.05	6:04.00	6:04.95	6:05.90	6:06.84	6:07.79
390	6:08.74	6:09.69	6:10.64	6:11.58	6:12.53	6:13.48	6:14.43	6:15.38	6:16.32	6:17.27
400	6:18.22	6:19.17	6:20.11	6:21.06	6:22.01	6:22.96	6:23.91	6:24.85	6:25.80	6:26.75
410	6:27.70	6:28.65	6:29.59	6:30.54	6:31.49	6:32.44	6:33.39	6:34.33	6:35.28	6:36.23
420	6:37.18	6:38.13	6:39.07	6:40.02	6:40.97	6:41.92	6:42.86	6:43.81	6:44.76	6:45.71
430	6:46.66	6:47.60	6:48.55	6:49.50	6:50.45	6:51.40	6:52.34	6:53.29	6:54.24	6:55.19
440	6:56.14	6:57.08	6:58.03	6:58.98	6:59.93	7:00.88	7:01.82	7:02.77	7:03.72	7:04.67
450	7:05.61	7:06.56	7:07.51	7:08.46	7:09.41	7:10.35	7:11.30	7:12.25	7:13.20	7:14.15
460	7:15.09	7:16.04	7:16.99	7:17.94	7:18.89	7:19.83	7:20.78	7:21.73	7:22.68	7:23.63
470	7:24.57	7:25.52	7:26.47	7:27.42	7:28.36	7:29.31	7:30.26	7:31.21	7:32.16	7:33.10
480	7:34.05	7:35.00	7:35.95	7:36.90	7:37.84	7:38.79	7:39.74	7:40.69	7:41.64	7:42.58
490	7:43.53	7:44.48	7:45.43	7:46.38	7:47.32	7:48.27	7:49.22	7:50.17	7:51.11	7:52.06
500	7:53.01	7:53.96	7:54.91	7:55.85	7:56.80	7:57.75	7:58.70	7:59.65	8:00.59	8:01.54
510	8:02.49	8:03.44	8:04.39	8:05.33	8:06.28	8:07.23	8:08.18	8:09.13	8:10.07	8:11.02
520	8:11.97	8:12.92	8:13.86	8:14.81	8:15.76	8:16.71	8:17.66	8:18.60	8:19.55	8:20.50
530	8:21.45	8:22.40	8:23.34	8:24.29	8:25.24	8:26.19	8:27.14	8:28.08	8:29.03	8:29.98
540	8:30.93	8:31.88	8:32.82	8:33.77	8:34.72	8:35.67	8:36.61	8:37.56	8:38.51	8:39.46
550	8:40.41	8:41.35	8:42.30	8:43.25	8:44.20	8:45.15	8:46.09	8:47.04	8:47.99	8:48.94
560	8:49.89	8:50.83	8:51.78	8:52.73	8:53.68	8:54.62	8:55.57	8:56.52	8:57.47	8:58.42
570	8:59.36	9:00.31	9:01.26	9:02.21	9:03.16	9:04.10	9:05.05	9:06.00	9:06.95	9:07.90
580	9:08.84	9:09.79	9:10.74	9:11.69	9:12.64	9:13.58	9:14.53	9:15.48	9:16.43	9:17.37
590	9:18.32	9:19.27	9:20.22	9:21.17	9:22.11	9:23.06	9:24.01	9:24.96	9:25.91	9:26.85

♩. = 1.42; ♩ = 0.95; ♪. = 0.71; (3: ♩ 𝄾) = 0.63; ♪ = 0.47; (3: ♪ 𝄾 𝄾) = 0.32; 𝅘𝅥𝅯 = 0.24 seconds

CLICK: 22⅞ FRAMES; M.M.: 62.95

Click	0	1	2	3	4	5	6	7	8	9
000	0:00.00	0:00.00	0:00.95	0:01.91	0:02.86	0:03.81	0:04.77	0:05.72	0:06.67	0:07.63
010	0:08.58	0:09.53	0:10.48	0:11.44	0:12.39	0:13.34	0:14.30	0:15.25	0:16.20	0:17.16
020	0:18.11	0:19.06	0:20.02	0:20.97	0:21.92	0:22.88	0:23.83	0:24.78	0:25.73	0:26.69
030	0:27.64	0:28.59	0:29.55	0:30.50	0:31.45	0:32.41	0:33.36	0:34.31	0:35.27	0:36.22
040	0:37.17	0:38.13	0:39.08	0:40.03	0:40.98	0:41.94	0:42.89	0:43.84	0:44.80	0:45.75
050	0:46.70	0:47.66	0:48.61	0:49.56	0:50.52	0:51.47	0:52.42	0:53.38	0:54.33	0:55.28
060	0:56.23	0:57.19	0:58.14	0:59.09	1:00.05	1:01.00	1:01.95	1:02.91	1:03.86	1:04.81
070	1:05.77	1:06.72	1:07.67	1:08.62	1:09.58	1:10.53	1:11.48	1:12.44	1:13.39	1:14.34
080	1:15.30	1:16.25	1:17.20	1:18.16	1:19.11	1:20.06	1:21.02	1:21.97	1:22.92	1:23.88
090	1:24.83	1:25.78	1:26.73	1:27.69	1:28.64	1:29.59	1:30.55	1:31.50	1:32.45	1:33.41
100	1:34.36	1:35.31	1:36.27	1:37.22	1:38.17	1:39.12	1:40.08	1:41.03	1:41.98	1:42.94
110	1:43.89	1:44.84	1:45.80	1:46.75	1:47.70	1:48.66	1:49.61	1:50.56	1:51.52	1:52.47
120	1:53.42	1:54.38	1:55.33	1:56.28	1:57.23	1:58.19	1:59.14	2:00.09	2:01.05	2:02.00
130	2:02.95	2:03.91	2:04.86	2:05.81	2:06.77	2:07.72	2:08.67	2:09.62	2:10.58	2:11.53
140	2:12.48	2:13.44	2:14.39	2:15.34	2:16.30	2:17.25	2:18.20	2:19.16	2:20.11	2:21.06
150	2:22.02	2:22.97	2:23.92	2:24.87	2:25.83	2:26.78	2:27.73	2:28.69	2:29.64	2:30.59
160	2:31.55	2:32.50	2:33.45	2:34.41	2:35.36	2:36.31	2:37.27	2:38.22	2:39.17	2:40.13
170	2:41.08	2:42.03	2:42.98	2:43.94	2:44.89	2:45.84	2:46.80	2:47.75	2:48.70	2:49.66
180	2:50.61	2:51.56	2:52.52	2:53.47	2:54.42	2:55.38	2:56.33	2:57.28	2:58.23	2:59.19
190	3:00.14	3:01.09	3:02.05	3:03.00	3:03.95	3:04.91	3:05.86	3:06.81	3:07.77	3:08.72
200	3:09.67	3:10.62	3:11.58	3:12.53	3:13.48	3:14.44	3:15.39	3:16.34	3:17.30	3:18.25
210	3:19.20	3:20.16	3:21.11	3:22.06	3:23.02	3:23.97	3:24.92	3:25.87	3:26.83	3:27.78
220	3:28.73	3:29.69	3:30.64	3:31.59	3:32.55	3:33.50	3:34.45	3:35.41	3:36.36	3:37.31
230	3:38.27	3:39.22	3:40.17	3:41.13	3:42.08	3:43.03	3:43.98	3:44.94	3:45.89	3:46.84
240	3:47.80	3:48.75	3:49.70	3:50.66	3:51.61	3:52.56	3:53.52	3:54.47	3:55.42	3:56.38
250	3:57.33	3:58.28	3:59.23	4:00.19	4:01.14	4:02.09	4:03.05	4:04.00	4:04.95	4:05.91
260	4:06.86	4:07.81	4:08.77	4:09.72	4:10.67	4:11.62	4:12.58	4:13.53	4:14.48	4:15.44
270	4:16.39	4:17.34	4:18.30	4:19.25	4:20.20	4:21.16	4:22.11	4:23.06	4:24.02	4:24.97
280	4:25.92	4:26.87	4:27.83	4:28.78	4:29.73	4:30.69	4:31.64	4:32.59	4:33.55	4:34.50
290	4:35.45	4:36.41	4:37.36	4:38.31	4:39.27	4:40.22	4:41.17	4:42.12	4:43.08	4:44.03
300	4:44.98	4:45.94	4:46.89	4:47.84	4:48.80	4:49.75	4:50.70	4:51.66	4:52.61	4:53.56
310	4:54.52	4:55.47	4:56.42	4:57.37	4:58.33	4:59.28	5:00.23	5:01.19	5:02.14	5:03.09
320	5:04.05	5:05.00	5:05.95	5:06.91	5:07.86	5:08.81	5:09.77	5:10.72	5:11.67	5:12.63
330	5:13.58	5:14.53	5:15.48	5:16.44	5:17.39	5:18.34	5:19.30	5:20.25	5:21.20	5:22.16
340	5:23.11	5:24.06	5:25.02	5:25.97	5:26.92	5:27.88	5:28.83	5:29.78	5:30.73	5:31.69
350	5:32.64	5:33.59	5:34.55	5:35.50	5:36.45	5:37.41	5:38.36	5:39.31	5:40.27	5:41.22
360	5:42.17	5:43.13	5:44.08	5:45.03	5:45.98	5:46.94	5:47.89	5:48.84	5:49.80	5:50.75
370	5:51.70	5:52.66	5:53.61	5:54.56	5:55.52	5:56.47	5:57.42	5:58.37	5:59.33	6:00.28
380	6:01.23	6:02.19	6:03.14	6:04.09	6:05.05	6:06.00	6:06.95	6:07.91	6:08.86	6:09.81
390	6:10.77	6:11.72	6:12.67	6:13.62	6:14.58	6:15.53	6:16.48	6:17.44	6:18.39	6:19.34
400	6:20.30	6:21.25	6:22.20	6:23.16	6:24.11	6:25.06	6:26.02	6:26.97	6:27.92	6:28.87
410	6:29.83	6:30.78	6:31.73	6:32.69	6:33.64	6:34.59	6:35.55	6:36.50	6:37.45	6:38.41
420	6:39.36	6:40.31	6:41.27	6:42.22	6:43.17	6:44.12	6:45.08	6:46.03	6:46.98	6:47.94
430	6:48.89	6:49.84	6:50.80	6:51.75	6:52.70	6:53.66	6:54.61	6:55.56	6:56.52	6:57.47
440	6:58.42	6:59.37	7:00.33	7:01.28	7:02.23	7:03.19	7:04.14	7:05.09	7:06.05	7:07.00
450	7:07.95	7:08.91	7:09.86	7:10.81	7:11.77	7:12.72	7:13.67	7:14.63	7:15.58	7:16.53
460	7:17.48	7:18.44	7:19.39	7:20.34	7:21.30	7:22.25	7:23.20	7:24.16	7:25.11	7:26.06
470	7:27.02	7:27.97	7:28.92	7:29.88	7:30.83	7:31.78	7:32.73	7:33.69	7:34.64	7:35.59
480	7:36.55	7:37.50	7:38.45	7:39.41	7:40.36	7:41.31	7:42.27	7:43.22	7:44.17	7:45.13
490	7:46.08	7:47.03	7:47.98	7:48.94	7:49.89	7:50.84	7:51.80	7:52.75	7:53.70	7:54.66
500	7:55.61	7:56.56	7:57.52	7:58.47	7:59.42	8:00.37	8:01.33	8:02.28	8:03.23	8:04.19
510	8:05.14	8:06.09	8:07.05	8:08.00	8:08.95	8:09.91	8:10.86	8:11.81	8:12.77	8:13.72
520	8:14.67	8:15.63	8:16.58	8:17.53	8:18.48	8:19.44	8:20.39	8:21.34	8:22.30	8:23.25
530	8:24.20	8:25.16	8:26.11	8:27.06	8:28.02	8:28.97	8:29.92	8:30.88	8:31.83	8:32.78
540	8:33.73	8:34.69	8:35.64	8:36.59	8:37.55	8:38.50	8:39.45	8:40.41	8:41.36	8:42.31
550	8:43.27	8:44.22	8:45.17	8:46.13	8:47.08	8:48.03	8:48.98	8:49.94	8:50.89	8:51.84
560	8:52.80	8:53.75	8:54.70	8:55.66	8:56.61	8:57.56	8:58.52	8:59.47	9:00.42	9:01.38
570	9:02.33	9:03.28	9:04.23	9:05.19	9:06.14	9:07.09	9:08.05	9:09.00	9:09.95	9:10.91
580	9:11.86	9:12.81	9:13.77	9:14.72	9:15.67	9:16.63	9:17.58	9:18.53	9:19.48	9:20.44
590	9:21.39	9:22.34	9:23.30	9:24.25	9:25.20	9:26.16	9:27.11	9:28.06	9:29.02	9:29.97

♩. = 1.43; ♩ = 0.95; ♪. = 0.71; (triplet 3: ♩ 𝄾) = 0.64; ♪ = 0.48; (triplet 3: ♪ 𝄾 𝄾) = 0.32; 𝅘𝅥𝅯 = 0.24 seconds

CLICK: 23 0/8 FRAMES; M.M.: 62.61

Click	0	1	2	3	4	5	6	7	8	9
000	0:00.00	0:00.00	0:00.96	0:01.92	0:02.88	0:03.83	0:04.79	0:05.75	0:06.71	0:07.67
010	0:08.63	0:09.58	0:10.54	0:11.50	0:12.46	0:13.42	0:14.37	0:15.33	0:16.29	0:17.25
020	0:18.21	0:19.17	0:20.12	0:21.08	0:22.04	0:23.00	0:23.96	0:24.92	0:25.87	0:26.83
030	0:27.79	0:28.75	0:29.71	0:30.67	0:31.62	0:32.58	0:33.54	0:34.50	0:35.46	0:36.42
040	0:37.38	0:38.33	0:39.29	0:40.25	0:41.21	0:42.17	0:43.12	0:44.08	0:45.04	0:46.00
050	0:46.96	0:47.92	0:48.88	0:49.83	0:50.79	0:51.75	0:52.71	0:53.67	0:54.62	0:55.58
060	0:56.54	0:57.50	0:58.46	0:59.42	1:00.37	1:01.33	1:02.29	1:03.25	1:04.21	1:05.17
070	1:06.12	1:07.08	1:08.04	1:09.00	1:09.96	1:10.92	1:11.87	1:12.83	1:13.79	1:14.75
080	1:15.71	1:16.67	1:17.62	1:18.58	1:19.54	1:20.50	1:21.46	1:22.42	1:23.37	1:24.33
090	1:25.29	1:26.25	1:27.21	1:28.17	1:29.12	1:30.08	1:31.04	1:32.00	1:32.96	1:33.92
100	1:34.87	1:35.83	1:36.79	1:37.75	1:38.71	1:39.67	1:40.62	1:41.58	1:42.54	1:43.50
110	1:44.46	1:45.42	1:46.37	1:47.33	1:48.29	1:49.25	1:50.21	1:51.17	1:52.12	1:53.08
120	1:54.04	1:55.00	1:55.96	1:56.92	1:57.87	1:58.83	1:59.79	2:00.75	2:01.71	2:02.67
130	2:03.62	2:04.58	2:05.54	2:06.50	2:07.46	2:08.42	2:09.37	2:10.33	2:11.29	2:12.25
140	2:13.21	2:14.17	2:15.12	2:16.08	2:17.04	2:18.00	2:18.96	2:19.92	2:20.87	2:21.83
150	2:22.79	2:23.75	2:24.71	2:25.67	2:26.62	2:27.58	2:28.54	2:29.50	2:30.46	2:31.42
160	2:32.37	2:33.33	2:34.29	2:35.25	2:36.21	2:37.17	2:38.12	2:39.08	2:40.04	2:41.00
170	2:41.96	2:42.92	2:43.87	2:44.83	2:45.79	2:46.75	2:47.71	2:48.67	2:49.62	2:50.58
180	2:51.54	2:52.50	2:53.46	2:54.42	2:55.37	2:56.33	2:57.29	2:58.25	2:59.21	3:00.17
190	3:01.12	3:02.08	3:03.04	3:04.00	3:04.96	3:05.92	3:06.87	3:07.83	3:08.79	3:09.75
200	3:10.71	3:11.67	3:12.62	3:13.58	3:14.54	3:15.50	3:16.46	3:17.42	3:18.37	3:19.33
210	3:20.29	3:21.25	3:22.21	3:23.17	3:24.12	3:25.08	3:26.04	3:27.00	3:27.96	3:28.92
220	3:29.87	3:30.83	3:31.79	3:32.75	3:33.71	3:34.67	3:35.62	3:36.58	3:37.54	3:38.50
230	3:39.46	3:40.42	3:41.37	3:42.33	3:43.29	3:44.25	3:45.21	3:46.17	3:47.12	3:48.08
240	3:49.04	3:50.00	3:50.96	3:51.92	3:52.87	3:53.83	3:54.79	3:55.75	3:56.71	3:57.67
250	3:58.62	3:59.58	4:00.54	4:01.50	4:02.46	4:03.42	4:04.37	4:05.33	4:06.29	4:07.25
260	4:08.21	4:09.17	4:10.12	4:11.08	4:12.04	4:13.00	4:13.96	4:14.92	4:15.87	4:16.83
270	4:17.79	4:18.75	4:19.71	4:20.67	4:21.62	4:22.58	4:23.54	4:24.50	4:25.46	4:26.42
280	4:27.37	4:28.33	4:29.29	4:30.25	4:31.21	4:32.17	4:33.12	4:34.08	4:35.04	4:36.00
290	4:36.96	4:37.92	4:38.87	4:39.83	4:40.79	4:41.75	4:42.71	4:43.67	4:44.62	4:45.58
300	4:46.54	4:47.50	4:48.46	4:49.42	4:50.37	4:51.33	4:52.29	4:53.25	4:54.21	4:55.17
310	4:56.12	4:57.08	4:58.04	4:59.00	4:59.96	5:00.92	5:01.87	5:02.83	5:03.79	5:04.75
320	5:05.71	5:06.67	5:07.62	5:08.58	5:09.54	5:10.50	5:11.46	5:12.42	5:13.37	5:14.33
330	5:15.29	5:16.25	5:17.21	5:18.17	5:19.12	5:20.08	5:21.04	5:22.00	5:22.96	5:23.92
340	5:24.87	5:25.83	5:26.79	5:27.75	5:28.71	5:29.67	5:30.62	5:31.58	5:32.54	5:33.50
350	5:34.46	5:35.42	5:36.37	5:37.33	5:38.29	5:39.25	5:40.21	5:41.17	5:42.12	5:43.08
360	5:44.04	5:45.00	5:45.96	5:46.92	5:47.87	5:48.83	5:49.79	5:50.75	5:51.71	5:52.67
370	5:53.62	5:54.58	5:55.54	5:56.50	5:57.46	5:58.42	5:59.37	6:00.33	6:01.29	6:02.25
380	6:03.21	6:04.17	6:05.12	6:06.08	6:07.04	6:08.00	6:08.96	6:09.92	6:10.87	6:11.83
390	6:12.79	6:13.75	6:14.71	6:15.67	6:16.62	6:17.58	6:18.54	6:19.50	6:20.46	6:21.42
400	6:22.37	6:23.33	6:24.29	6:25.25	6:26.21	6:27.17	6:28.12	6:29.08	6:30.04	6:31.00
410	6:31.96	6:32.92	6:33.87	6:34.83	6:35.79	6:36.75	6:37.71	6:38.67	6:39.62	6:40.58
420	6:41.54	6:42.50	6:43.46	6:44.42	6:45.37	6:46.33	6:47.29	6:48.25	6:49.21	6:50.17
430	6:51.12	6:52.08	6:53.04	6:54.00	6:54.96	6:55.92	6:56.87	6:57.83	6:58.79	6:59.75
440	7:00.71	7:01.67	7:02.62	7:03.58	7:04.54	7:05.50	7:06.46	7:07.42	7:08.37	7:09.33
450	7:10.29	7:11.25	7:12.21	7:13.17	7:14.12	7:15.08	7:16.04	7:17.00	7:17.96	7:18.92
460	7:19.87	7:20.83	7:21.79	7:22.75	7:23.71	7:24.67	7:25.62	7:26.58	7:27.54	7:28.50
470	7:29.46	7:30.42	7:31.37	7:32.33	7:33.29	7:34.25	7:35.21	7:36.17	7:37.12	7:38.08
480	7:39.04	7:40.00	7:40.96	7:41.92	7:42.87	7:43.83	7:44.79	7:45.75	7:46.71	7:47.67
490	7:48.62	7:49.58	7:50.54	7:51.50	7:52.46	7:53.42	7:54.37	7:55.33	7:56.29	7:57.25
500	7:58.21	7:59.17	8:00.12	8:01.08	8:02.04	8:03.00	8:03.96	8:04.92	8:05.87	8:06.83
510	8:07.79	8:08.75	8:09.71	8:10.67	8:11.62	8:12.58	8:13.54	8:14.50	8:15.46	8:16.42
520	8:17.37	8:18.33	8:19.29	8:20.25	8:21.21	8:22.17	8:23.12	8:24.08	8:25.04	8:26.00
530	8:26.96	8:27.92	8:28.87	8:29.83	8:30.79	8:31.75	8:32.71	8:33.67	8:34.62	8:35.58
540	8:36.54	8:37.50	8:38.46	8:39.42	8:40.37	8:41.33	8:42.29	8:43.25	8:44.21	8:45.17
550	8:46.12	8:47.08	8:48.04	8:49.00	8:49.96	8:50.92	8:51.87	8:52.83	8:53.79	8:54.75
560	8:55.71	8:56.67	8:57.62	8:58.58	8:59.54	9:00.50	9:01.46	9:02.42	9:03.37	9:04.33
570	9:05.29	9:06.25	9:07.21	9:08.17	9:09.12	9:10.08	9:11.04	9:12.00	9:12.96	9:13.92
580	9:14.87	9:15.83	9:16.79	9:17.75	9:18.71	9:19.67	9:20.62	9:21.58	9:22.54	9:23.50
590	9:24.46	9:25.42	9:26.37	9:27.33	9:28.29	9:29.25	9:30.21	9:31.17	9:32.12	9:33.08

♩. = 1.44; ♩ = 0.96; ♪. = 0.72; (triplet) ♩ 𝄾 = 0.64; ♪ = 0.48; (triplet) ♪𝄾𝄾 = 0.32; ♬ = 0.24 seconds

CLICK: 23⅛ FRAMES; M.M.: 62.27

Click	0	1	2	3	4	5	6	7	8	9
000	0:00.00	0:00.00	0:00.96	0:01.93	0:02.89	0:03.85	0:04.82	0:05.78	0:06.74	0:07.71
010	0:08.67	0:09.64	0:10.60	0:11.56	0:12.53	0:13.49	0:14.45	0:15.42	0:16.38	0:17.34
020	0:18.31	0:19.27	0:20.23	0:21.20	0:22.16	0:23.13	0:24.09	0:25.05	0:26.02	0:26.98
030	0:27.94	0:28.91	0:29.87	0:30.83	0:31.80	0:32.76	0:33.72	0:34.69	0:35.65	0:36.61
040	0:37.58	0:38.54	0:39.51	0:40.47	0:41.43	0:42.40	0:43.36	0:44.32	0:45.29	0:46.25
050	0:47.21	0:48.18	0:49.14	0:50.10	0:51.07	0:52.03	0:52.99	0:53.96	0:54.92	0:55.89
060	0:56.85	0:57.81	0:58.78	0:59.74	1:00.70	1:01.67	1:02.63	1:03.59	1:04.56	1:05.52
070	1:06.48	1:07.45	1:08.41	1:09.38	1:10.34	1:11.30	1:12.27	1:13.23	1:14.19	1:15.16
080	1:16.12	1:17.08	1:18.05	1:19.01	1:19.97	1:20.94	1:21.90	1:22.86	1:23.83	1:24.79
090	1:25.76	1:26.72	1:27.68	1:28.65	1:29.61	1:30.57	1:31.54	1:32.50	1:33.46	1:34.43
100	1:35.39	1:36.35	1:37.32	1:38.28	1:39.24	1:40.21	1:41.17	1:42.14	1:43.10	1:44.06
110	1:45.03	1:45.99	1:46.95	1:47.92	1:48.88	1:49.84	1:50.81	1:51.77	1:52.73	1:53.70
120	1:54.66	1:55.63	1:56.59	1:57.55	1:58.52	1:59.48	2:00.44	2:01.41	2:02.37	2:03.33
130	2:04.30	2:05.26	2:06.22	2:07.19	2:08.15	2:09.11	2:10.08	2:11.04	2:12.01	2:12.97
140	2:13.93	2:14.90	2:15.86	2:16.82	2:17.79	2:18.75	2:19.71	2:20.68	2:21.64	2:22.60
150	2:23.57	2:24.53	2:25.49	2:26.46	2:27.42	2:28.39	2:29.35	2:30.31	2:31.28	2:32.24
160	2:33.20	2:34.17	2:35.13	2:36.09	2:37.06	2:38.02	2:38.98	2:39.95	2:40.91	2:41.88
170	2:42.84	2:43.80	2:44.77	2:45.73	2:46.69	2:47.66	2:48.62	2:49.58	2:50.55	2:51.51
180	2:52.47	2:53.44	2:54.40	2:55.36	2:56.33	2:57.29	2:58.26	2:59.22	3:00.18	3:01.15
190	3:02.11	3:03.07	3:04.04	3:05.00	3:05.96	3:06.93	3:07.89	3:08.85	3:09.82	3:10.78
200	3:11.74	3:12.71	3:13.67	3:14.64	3:15.60	3:16.56	3:17.53	3:18.49	3:19.45	3:20.42
210	3:21.38	3:22.34	3:23.31	3:24.27	3:25.23	3:26.20	3:27.16	3:28.13	3:29.09	3:30.05
220	3:31.02	3:31.98	3:32.94	3:33.91	3:34.87	3:35.83	3:36.80	3:37.76	3:38.72	3:39.69
230	3:40.65	3:41.61	3:42.58	3:43.54	3:44.51	3:45.47	3:46.43	3:47.40	3:48.36	3:49.32
240	3:50.29	3:51.25	3:52.21	3:53.18	3:54.14	3:55.10	3:56.07	3:57.03	3:57.99	3:58.96
250	3:59.92	4:00.89	4:01.85	4:02.81	4:03.78	4:04.74	4:05.70	4:06.67	4:07.63	4:08.59
260	4:09.56	4:10.52	4:11.48	4:12.45	4:13.41	4:14.38	4:15.34	4:16.30	4:17.27	4:18.23
270	4:19.19	4:20.16	4:21.12	4:22.08	4:23.05	4:24.01	4:24.97	4:25.94	4:26.90	4:27.86
280	4:28.83	4:29.79	4:30.76	4:31.72	4:32.68	4:33.65	4:34.61	4:35.57	4:36.54	4:37.50
290	4:38.46	4:39.43	4:40.39	4:41.35	4:42.32	4:43.28	4:44.24	4:45.21	4:46.17	4:47.14
300	4:48.10	4:49.06	4:50.03	4:50.99	4:51.95	4:52.92	4:53.88	4:54.84	4:55.81	4:56.77
310	4:57.73	4:58.70	4:59.66	5:00.62	5:01.59	5:02.55	5:03.52	5:04.48	5:05.44	5:06.41
320	5:07.37	5:08.33	5:09.30	5:10.26	5:11.22	5:12.19	5:13.15	5:14.11	5:15.08	5:16.04
330	5:17.01	5:17.97	5:18.93	5:19.90	5:20.86	5:21.82	5:22.79	5:23.75	5:24.71	5:25.68
340	5:26.64	5:27.60	5:28.57	5:29.53	5:30.49	5:31.46	5:32.42	5:33.39	5:34.35	5:35.31
350	5:36.28	5:37.24	5:38.20	5:39.17	5:40.13	5:41.09	5:42.06	5:43.02	5:43.98	5:44.95
360	5:45.91	5:46.88	5:47.84	5:48.80	5:49.77	5:50.73	5:51.69	5:52.66	5:53.62	5:54.58
370	5:55.55	5:56.51	5:57.47	5:58.44	5:59.40	6:00.36	6:01.33	6:02.29	6:03.26	6:04.22
380	6:05.18	6:06.15	6:07.11	6:08.07	6:09.04	6:10.00	6:10.96	6:11.93	6:12.89	6:13.85
390	6:14.82	6:15.78	6:16.74	6:17.71	6:18.67	6:19.64	6:20.60	6:21.56	6:22.53	6:23.49
400	6:24.45	6:25.42	6:26.38	6:27.34	6:28.31	6:29.27	6:30.23	6:31.20	6:32.16	6:33.13
410	6:34.09	6:35.05	6:36.02	6:36.98	6:37.94	6:38.91	6:39.87	6:40.83	6:41.80	6:42.76
420	6:43.72	6:44.69	6:45.65	6:46.61	6:47.58	6:48.54	6:49.51	6:50.47	6:51.43	6:52.40
430	6:53.36	6:54.32	6:55.29	6:56.25	6:57.21	6:58.18	6:59.14	7:00.10	7:01.07	7:02.03
440	7:02.99	7:03.96	7:04.92	7:05.89	7:06.85	7:07.81	7:08.78	7:09.74	7:10.70	7:11.67
450	7:12.63	7:13.59	7:14.56	7:15.52	7:16.48	7:17.45	7:18.41	7:19.38	7:20.34	7:21.30
460	7:22.27	7:23.23	7:24.19	7:25.16	7:26.12	7:27.08	7:28.05	7:29.01	7:29.97	7:30.94
470	7:31.90	7:32.86	7:33.83	7:34.79	7:35.76	7:36.72	7:37.68	7:38.65	7:39.61	7:40.57
480	7:41.54	7:42.50	7:43.46	7:44.43	7:45.39	7:46.35	7:47.32	7:48.28	7:49.24	7:50.21
490	7:51.17	7:52.14	7:53.10	7:54.06	7:55.03	7:55.99	7:56.95	7:57.92	7:58.88	7:59.84
500	8:00.81	8:01.77	8:02.73	8:03.70	8:04.66	8:05.63	8:06.59	8:07.55	8:08.52	8:09.48
510	8:10.44	8:11.41	8:12.37	8:13.33	8:14.30	8:15.26	8:16.22	8:17.19	8:18.15	8:19.11
520	8:20.08	8:21.04	8:22.01	8:22.97	8:23.93	8:24.90	8:25.86	8:26.82	8:27.79	8:28.75
530	8:29.71	8:30.68	8:31.64	8:32.60	8:33.57	8:34.53	8:35.49	8:36.46	8:37.42	8:38.39
540	8:39.35	8:40.31	8:41.28	8:42.24	8:43.20	8:44.17	8:45.13	8:46.09	8:47.06	8:48.02
550	8:48.98	8:49.95	8:50.91	8:51.87	8:52.84	8:53.80	8:54.77	8:55.73	8:56.69	8:57.66
560	8:58.62	8:59.58	9:00.55	9:01.51	9:02.47	9:03.44	9:04.40	9:05.36	9:06.33	9:07.29
570	9:08.26	9:09.22	9:10.18	9:11.15	9:12.11	9:13.07	9:14.04	9:15.00	9:15.96	9:16.93
580	9:17.89	9:18.85	9:19.82	9:20.78	9:21.74	9:22.71	9:23.67	9:24.64	9:25.60	9:26.56
590	9:27.53	9:28.49	9:29.45	9:30.42	9:31.38	9:32.34	9:33.31	9:34.27	9:35.23	9:36.20

♩. = 1.45; ♩ = 0.96; ♪. = 0.72; (triplet) ♩ 𝄾 = 0.64; ♪ = 0.48; (triplet) ♪ 𝄾 𝄾 = 0.32; 𝅘𝅥𝅯 = 0.24 seconds

CLICK: $23\frac{2}{8}$ FRAMES; M.M.: 61.94

Click	0	1	2	3	4	5	6	7	8	9
000	0:00.00	0:00.00	0:00.97	0:01.94	0:02.91	0:03.88	0:04.84	0:05.81	0:06.78	0:07.75
010	0:08.72	0:09.69	0:10.66	0:11.63	0:12.59	0:13.56	0:14.53	0:15.50	0:16.47	0:17.44
020	0:18.41	0:19.38	0:20.34	0:21.31	0:22.28	0:23.25	0:24.22	0:25.19	0:26.16	0:27.13
030	0:28.09	0:29.06	0:30.03	0:31.00	0:31.97	0:32.94	0:33.91	0:34.88	0:35.84	0:36.81
040	0:37.78	0:38.75	0:39.72	0:40.69	0:41.66	0:42.63	0:43.59	0:44.56	0:45.53	0:46.50
050	0:47.47	0:48.44	0:49.41	0:50.38	0:51.34	0:52.31	0:53.28	0:54.25	0:55.22	0:56.19
060	0:57.16	0:58.13	0:59.09	1:00.06	1:01.03	1:02.00	1:02.97	1:03.94	1:04.91	1:05.88
070	1:06.84	1:07.81	1:08.78	1:09.75	1:10.72	1:11.69	1:12.66	1:13.63	1:14.59	1:15.56
080	1:16.53	1:17.50	1:18.47	1:19.44	1:20.41	1:21.38	1:22.34	1:23.31	1:24.28	1:25.25
090	1:26.22	1:27.19	1:28.16	1:29.13	1:30.09	1:31.06	1:32.03	1:33.00	1:33.97	1:34.94
100	1:35.91	1:36.88	1:37.84	1:38.81	1:39.78	1:40.75	1:41.72	1:42.69	1:43.66	1:44.63
110	1:45.59	1:46.56	1:47.53	1:48.50	1:49.47	1:50.44	1:51.41	1:52.38	1:53.34	1:54.31
120	1:55.28	1:56.25	1:57.22	1:58.19	1:59.16	2:00.13	2:01.09	2:02.06	2:03.03	2:04.00
130	2:04.97	2:05.94	2:06.91	2:07.88	2:08.84	2:09.81	2:10.78	2:11.75	2:12.72	2:13.69
140	2:14.66	2:15.63	2:16.59	2:17.56	2:18.53	2:19.50	2:20.47	2:21.44	2:22.41	2:23.38
150	2:24.34	2:25.31	2:26.28	2:27.25	2:28.22	2:29.19	2:30.16	2:31.13	2:32.09	2:33.06
160	2:34.03	2:35.00	2:35.97	2:36.94	2:37.91	2:38.88	2:39.84	2:40.81	2:41.78	2:42.75
170	2:43.72	2:44.69	2:45.66	2:46.63	2:47.59	2:48.56	2:49.53	2:50.50	2:51.47	2:52.44
180	2:53.41	2:54.38	2:55.34	2:56.31	2:57.28	2:58.25	2:59.22	3:00.19	3:01.16	3:02.13
190	3:03.09	3:04.06	3:05.03	3:06.00	3:06.97	3:07.94	3:08.91	3:09.88	3:10.84	3:11.81
200	3:12.78	3:13.75	3:14.72	3:15.69	3:16.66	3:17.63	3:18.59	3:19.56	3:20.53	3:21.50
210	3:22.47	3:23.44	3:24.41	3:25.38	3:26.34	3:27.31	3:28.28	3:29.25	3:30.22	3:31.19
220	3:32.16	3:33.13	3:34.09	3:35.06	3:36.03	3:37.00	3:37.97	3:38.94	3:39.91	3:40.88
230	3:41.84	3:42.81	3:43.78	3:44.75	3:45.72	3:46.69	3:47.66	3:48.63	3:49.59	3:50.56
240	3:51.53	3:52.50	3:53.47	3:54.44	3:55.41	3:56.38	3:57.34	3:58.31	3:59.28	4:00.25
250	4:01.22	4:02.19	4:03.16	4:04.13	4:05.09	4:06.06	4:07.03	4:08.00	4:08.97	4:09.94
260	4:10.91	4:11.88	4:12.84	4:13.81	4:14.78	4:15.75	4:16.72	4:17.69	4:18.66	4:19.63
270	4:20.59	4:21.56	4:22.53	4:23.50	4:24.47	4:25.44	4:26.41	4:27.38	4:28.34	4:29.31
280	4:30.28	4:31.25	4:32.22	4:33.19	4:34.16	4:35.13	4:36.09	4:37.06	4:38.03	4:39.00
290	4:39.97	4:40.94	4:41.91	4:42.88	4:43.84	4:44.81	4:45.78	4:46.75	4:47.72	4:48.69
300	4:49.66	4:50.63	4:51.59	4:52.56	4:53.53	4:54.50	4:55.47	4:56.44	4:57.41	4:58.38
310	4:59.34	5:00.31	5:01.28	5:02.25	5:03.22	5:04.19	5:05.16	5:06.13	5:07.09	5:08.06
320	5:09.03	5:10.00	5:10.97	5:11.94	5:12.91	5:13.88	5:14.84	5:15.81	5:16.78	5:17.75
330	5:18.72	5:19.69	5:20.66	5:21.63	5:22.59	5:23.56	5:24.53	5:25.50	5:26.47	5:27.44
340	5:28.41	5:29.38	5:30.34	5:31.31	5:32.28	5:33.25	5:34.22	5:35.19	5:36.16	5:37.13
350	5:38.09	5:39.06	5:40.03	5:41.00	5:41.97	5:42.94	5:43.91	5:44.88	5:45.84	5:46.81
360	5:47.78	5:48.75	5:49.72	5:50.69	5:51.66	5:52.63	5:53.59	5:54.56	5:55.53	5:56.50
370	5:57.47	5:58.44	5:59.41	6:00.38	6:01.34	6:02.31	6:03.28	6:04.25	6:05.22	6:06.19
380	6:07.16	6:08.13	6:09.09	6:10.06	6:11.03	6:12.00	6:12.97	6:13.94	6:14.91	6:15.88
390	6:16.84	6:17.81	6:18.78	6:19.75	6:20.72	6:21.69	6:22.66	6:23.63	6:24.59	6:25.56
400	6:26.53	6:27.50	6:28.47	6:29.44	6:30.41	6:31.38	6:32.34	6:33.31	6:34.28	6:35.25
410	6:36.22	6:37.19	6:38.16	6:39.13	6:40.09	6:41.06	6:42.03	6:43.00	6:43.97	6:44.94
420	6:45.91	6:46.88	6:47.84	6:48.81	6:49.78	6:50.75	6:51.72	6:52.69	6:53.66	6:54.63
430	6:55.59	6:56.56	6:57.53	6:58.50	6:59.47	7:00.44	7:01.41	7:02.38	7:03.34	7:04.31
440	7:05.28	7:06.25	7:07.22	7:08.19	7:09.16	7:10.13	7:11.09	7:12.06	7:13.03	7:14.00
450	7:14.97	7:15.94	7:16.91	7:17.88	7:18.84	7:19.81	7:20.78	7:21.75	7:22.72	7:23.69
460	7:24.66	7:25.63	7:26.59	7:27.56	7:28.53	7:29.50	7:30.47	7:31.44	7:32.41	7:33.38
470	7:34.34	7:35.31	7:36.28	7:37.25	7:38.22	7:39.19	7:40.16	7:41.13	7:42.09	7:43.06
480	7:44.03	7:45.00	7:45.97	7:46.94	7:47.91	7:48.88	7:49.84	7:50.81	7:51.78	7:52.75
490	7:53.72	7:54.69	7:55.66	7:56.63	7:57.59	7:58.56	7:59.53	8:00.50	8:01.47	8:02.44
500	8:03.41	8:04.38	8:05.34	8:06.31	8:07.28	8:08.25	8:09.22	8:10.19	8:11.16	8:12.13
510	8:13.09	8:14.06	8:15.03	8:16.00	8:16.97	8:17.94	8:18.91	8:19.88	8:20.84	8:21.81
520	8:22.78	8:23.75	8:24.72	8:25.69	8:26.66	8:27.63	8:28.59	8:29.56	8:30.53	8:31.50
530	8:32.47	8:33.44	8:34.41	8:35.38	8:36.34	8:37.31	8:38.28	8:39.25	8:40.22	8:41.19
540	8:42.16	8:43.13	8:44.09	8:45.06	8:46.03	8:47.00	8:47.97	8:48.94	8:49.91	8:50.88
550	8:51.84	8:52.81	8:53.78	8:54.75	8:55.72	8:56.69	8:57.66	8:58.63	8:59.59	9:00.56
560	9:01.53	9:02.50	9:03.47	9:04.44	9:05.41	9:06.38	9:07.34	9:08.31	9:09.28	9:10.25
570	9:11.22	9:12.19	9:13.16	9:14.13	9:15.09	9:16.06	9:17.03	9:18.00	9:18.97	9:19.94
580	9:20.91	9:21.88	9:22.84	9:23.81	9:24.78	9:25.75	9:26.72	9:27.69	9:28.66	9:29.63
590	9:30.59	9:31.56	9:32.53	9:33.50	9:34.47	9:35.44	9:36.41	9:37.38	9:38.34	9:39.31

♩. = 1.45; ♩ = 0.97; ♪. = 0.73; (3) ♩ 𝄾 = 0.65; ♪ = 0.48; (3) 𝅘𝅥𝅯 𝄾 𝄾 = 0.32; 𝅘𝅥𝅯 = 0.24 seconds

CLICK: 23⅜ FRAMES; M.M.: 61.60

Click	0	1	2	3	4	5	6	7	8	9
000	0:00.00	0:00.00	0:00.97	0:01.95	0:02.92	0:03.90	0:04.87	0:05.84	0:06.82	0:07.79
010	0:08.77	0:09.74	0:10.71	0:11.69	0:12.66	0:13.64	0:14.61	0:15.58	0:16.56	0:17.53
020	0:18.51	0:19.48	0:20.45	0:21.43	0:22.40	0:23.38	0:24.35	0:25.32	0:26.30	0:27.27
030	0:28.24	0:29.22	0:30.19	0:31.17	0:32.14	0:33.11	0:34.09	0:35.06	0:36.04	0:37.01
040	0:37.98	0:38.96	0:39.93	0:40.91	0:41.88	0:42.85	0:43.83	0:44.80	0:45.78	0:46.75
050	0:47.72	0:48.70	0:49.67	0:50.65	0:51.62	0:52.59	0:53.57	0:54.54	0:55.52	0:56.49
060	0:57.46	0:58.44	0:59.41	1:00.39	1:01.36	1:02.33	1:03.31	1:04.28	1:05.26	1:06.23
070	1:07.20	1:08.18	1:09.15	1:10.13	1:11.10	1:12.07	1:13.05	1:14.02	1:14.99	1:15.97
080	1:16.94	1:17.92	1:18.89	1:19.86	1:20.84	1:21.81	1:22.79	1:23.76	1:24.73	1:25.71
090	1:26.68	1:27.66	1:28.63	1:29.60	1:30.58	1:31.55	1:32.53	1:33.50	1:34.47	1:35.45
100	1:36.42	1:37.40	1:38.37	1:39.34	1:40.32	1:41.29	1:42.27	1:43.24	1:44.21	1:45.19
110	1:46.16	1:47.14	1:48.11	1:49.08	1:50.06	1:51.03	1:52.01	1:52.98	1:53.95	1:54.93
120	1:55.90	1:56.88	1:57.85	1:58.82	1:59.80	2:00.77	2:01.74	2:02.72	2:03.69	2:04.67
130	2:05.64	2:06.61	2:07.59	2:08.56	2:09.54	2:10.51	2:11.48	2:12.46	2:13.43	2:14.41
140	2:15.38	2:16.35	2:17.33	2:18.30	2:19.28	2:20.25	2:21.22	2:22.20	2:23.17	2:24.15
150	2:25.12	2:26.09	2:27.07	2:28.04	2:29.02	2:29.99	2:30.96	2:31.94	2:32.91	2:33.89
160	2:34.86	2:35.83	2:36.81	2:37.78	2:38.76	2:39.73	2:40.70	2:41.68	2:42.65	2:43.63
170	2:44.60	2:45.57	2:46.55	2:47.52	2:48.49	2:49.47	2:50.44	2:51.42	2:52.39	2:53.36
180	2:54.34	2:55.31	2:56.29	2:57.26	2:58.23	2:59.21	3:00.18	3:01.16	3:02.13	3:03.10
190	3:04.08	3:05.05	3:06.03	3:07.00	3:07.97	3:08.95	3:09.92	3:10.90	3:11.87	3:12.84
200	3:13.82	3:14.79	3:15.77	3:16.74	3:17.71	3:18.69	3:19.66	3:20.64	3:21.61	3:22.58
210	3:23.56	3:24.53	3:25.51	3:26.48	3:27.45	3:28.43	3:29.40	3:30.38	3:31.35	3:32.32
220	3:33.30	3:34.27	3:35.24	3:36.22	3:37.19	3:38.17	3:39.14	3:40.11	3:41.09	3:42.06
230	3:43.04	3:44.01	3:44.98	3:45.96	3:46.93	3:47.91	3:48.88	3:49.85	3:50.83	3:51.80
240	3:52.78	3:53.75	3:54.72	3:55.70	3:56.67	3:57.65	3:58.62	3:59.59	4:00.57	4:01.54
250	4:02.52	4:03.49	4:04.46	4:05.44	4:06.41	4:07.39	4:08.36	4:09.33	4:10.31	4:11.28
260	4:12.26	4:13.23	4:14.20	4:15.18	4:16.15	4:17.13	4:18.10	4:19.07	4:20.05	4:21.02
270	4:21.99	4:22.97	4:23.94	4:24.92	4:25.89	4:26.86	4:27.84	4:28.81	4:29.79	4:30.76
280	4:31.73	4:32.71	4:33.68	4:34.66	4:35.63	4:36.60	4:37.58	4:38.55	4:39.53	4:40.50
290	4:41.47	4:42.45	4:43.42	4:44.40	4:45.37	4:46.34	4:47.32	4:48.29	4:49.27	4:50.24
300	4:51.21	4:52.19	4:53.16	4:54.14	4:55.11	4:56.08	4:57.06	4:58.03	4:59.01	4:59.98
310	5:00.95	5:01.93	5:02.90	5:03.88	5:04.85	5:05.82	5:06.80	5:07.77	5:08.74	5:09.72
320	5:10.69	5:11.67	5:12.64	5:13.61	5:14.59	5:15.56	5:16.54	5:17.51	5:18.48	5:19.46
330	5:20.43	5:21.41	5:22.38	5:23.35	5:24.33	5:25.30	5:26.28	5:27.25	5:28.22	5:29.20
340	5:30.17	5:31.15	5:32.12	5:33.09	5:34.07	5:35.04	5:36.02	5:36.99	5:37.96	5:38.94
350	5:39.91	5:40.89	5:41.86	5:42.83	5:43.81	5:44.78	5:45.76	5:46.73	5:47.70	5:48.68
360	5:49.65	5:50.63	5:51.60	5:52.57	5:53.55	5:54.52	5:55.49	5:56.47	5:57.44	5:58.42
370	5:59.39	6:00.36	6:01.34	6:02.31	6:03.29	6:04.26	6:05.23	6:06.21	6:07.18	6:08.16
380	6:09.13	6:10.10	6:11.08	6:12.05	6:13.03	6:14.00	6:14.97	6:15.95	6:16.92	6:17.90
390	6:18.87	6:19.84	6:20.82	6:21.79	6:22.77	6:23.74	6:24.71	6:25.69	6:26.66	6:27.64
400	6:28.61	6:29.58	6:30.56	6:31.53	6:32.51	6:33.48	6:34.45	6:35.43	6:36.40	6:37.38
410	6:38.35	6:39.32	6:40.30	6:41.27	6:42.24	6:43.22	6:44.19	6:45.17	6:46.14	6:47.11
420	6:48.09	6:49.06	6:50.04	6:51.01	6:51.98	6:52.96	6:53.93	6:54.91	6:55.88	6:56.85
430	6:57.83	6:58.80	6:59.78	7:00.75	7:01.72	7:02.70	7:03.67	7:04.65	7:05.62	7:06.59
440	7:07.57	7:08.54	7:09.52	7:10.49	7:11.46	7:12.44	7:13.41	7:14.39	7:15.36	7:16.33
450	7:17.31	7:18.28	7:19.26	7:20.23	7:21.20	7:22.18	7:23.15	7:24.13	7:25.10	7:26.07
460	7:27.05	7:28.02	7:28.99	7:29.97	7:30.94	7:31.92	7:32.89	7:33.86	7:34.84	7:35.81
470	7:36.79	7:37.76	7:38.73	7:39.71	7:40.68	7:41.66	7:42.63	7:43.60	7:44.58	7:45.55
480	7:46.53	7:47.50	7:48.47	7:49.45	7:50.42	7:51.40	7:52.37	7:53.34	7:54.32	7:55.29
490	7:56.27	7:57.24	7:58.21	7:59.19	8:00.16	8:01.14	8:02.11	8:03.08	8:04.06	8:05.03
500	8:06.01	8:06.98	8:07.95	8:08.93	8:09.90	8:10.88	8:11.85	8:12.82	8:13.80	8:14.77
510	8:15.74	8:16.72	8:17.69	8:18.67	8:19.64	8:20.61	8:21.59	8:22.56	8:23.54	8:24.51
520	8:25.48	8:26.46	8:27.43	8:28.41	8:29.38	8:30.35	8:31.33	8:32.30	8:33.28	8:34.25
530	8:35.22	8:36.20	8:37.17	8:38.15	8:39.12	8:40.09	8:41.07	8:42.04	8:43.02	8:43.99
540	8:44.96	8:45.94	8:46.91	8:47.89	8:48.86	8:49.83	8:50.81	8:51.78	8:52.76	8:53.73
550	8:54.70	8:55.68	8:56.65	8:57.63	8:58.60	8:59.57	9:00.55	9:01.52	9:02.49	9:03.47
560	9:04.44	9:05.42	9:06.39	9:07.36	9:08.34	9:09.31	9:10.29	9:11.26	9:12.23	9:13.21
570	9:14.18	9:15.16	9:16.13	9:17.10	9:18.08	9:19.05	9:20.03	9:21.00	9:21.97	9:22.95
580	9:23.92	9:24.90	9:25.87	9:26.84	9:27.82	9:28.79	9:29.77	9:30.74	9:31.71	9:32.69
590	9:33.66	9:34.64	9:35.61	9:36.58	9:37.56	9:38.53	9:39.51	9:40.48	9:41.45	9:42.43

♩. = 1.46; ♩ = 0.97; ♪. = 0.73; (triplet ♩ 𝄾) = 0.65; ♪ = 0.49; (triplet ♪ 𝄾 𝄾) = 0.32; 𝅘𝅥𝅯 = 0.24 seconds

CLICK: 23 4/8 FRAMES; M.M.: 61.28

Click	0	1	2	3	4	5	6	7	8	9
000	0:00.00	0:00.00	0:00.98	0:01.96	0:02.94	0:03.92	0:04.90	0:05.88	0:06.85	0:07.83
010	0:08.81	0:09.79	0:10.77	0:11.75	0:12.73	0:13.71	0:14.69	0:15.67	0:16.65	0:17.63
020	0:18.60	0:19.58	0:20.56	0:21.54	0:22.52	0:23.50	0:24.48	0:25.46	0:26.44	0:27.42
030	0:28.40	0:29.38	0:30.35	0:31.33	0:32.31	0:33.29	0:34.27	0:35.25	0:36.23	0:37.21
040	0:38.19	0:39.17	0:40.15	0:41.13	0:42.10	0:43.08	0:44.06	0:45.04	0:46.02	0:47.00
050	0:47.98	0:48.96	0:49.94	0:50.92	0:51.90	0:52.88	0:53.85	0:54.83	0:55.81	0:56.79
060	0:57.77	0:58.75	0:59.73	1:00.71	1:01.69	1:02.67	1:03.65	1:04.63	1:05.60	1:06.58
070	1:07.56	1:08.54	1:09.52	1:10.50	1:11.48	1:12.46	1:13.44	1:14.42	1:15.40	1:16.38
080	1:17.35	1:18.33	1:19.31	1:20.29	1:21.27	1:22.25	1:23.23	1:24.21	1:25.19	1:26.17
090	1:27.15	1:28.13	1:29.10	1:30.08	1:31.06	1:32.04	1:33.02	1:34.00	1:34.98	1:35.96
100	1:36.94	1:37.92	1:38.90	1:39.88	1:40.85	1:41.83	1:42.81	1:43.79	1:44.77	1:45.75
110	1:46.73	1:47.71	1:48.69	1:49.67	1:50.65	1:51.63	1:52.60	1:53.58	1:54.56	1:55.54
120	1:56.52	1:57.50	1:58.48	1:59.46	2:00.44	2:01.42	2:02.40	2:03.38	2:04.35	2:05.33
130	2:06.31	2:07.29	2:08.27	2:09.25	2:10.23	2:11.21	2:12.19	2:13.17	2:14.15	2:15.13
140	2:16.10	2:17.08	2:18.06	2:19.04	2:20.02	2:21.00	2:21.98	2:22.96	2:23.94	2:24.92
150	2:25.90	2:26.88	2:27.85	2:28.83	2:29.81	2:30.79	2:31.77	2:32.75	2:33.73	2:34.71
160	2:35.69	2:36.67	2:37.65	2:38.63	2:39.60	2:40.58	2:41.56	2:42.54	2:43.52	2:44.50
170	2:45.48	2:46.46	2:47.44	2:48.42	2:49.40	2:50.38	2:51.35	2:52.33	2:53.31	2:54.29
180	2:55.27	2:56.25	2:57.23	2:58.21	2:59.19	3:00.17	3:01.15	3:02.13	3:03.10	3:04.08
190	3:05.06	3:06.04	3:07.02	3:08.00	3:08.98	3:09.96	3:10.94	3:11.92	3:12.90	3:13.88
200	3:14.85	3:15.83	3:16.81	3:17.79	3:18.77	3:19.75	3:20.73	3:21.71	3:22.69	3:23.67
210	3:24.65	3:25.63	3:26.60	3:27.58	3:28.56	3:29.54	3:30.52	3:31.50	3:32.48	3:33.46
220	3:34.44	3:35.42	3:36.40	3:37.38	3:38.35	3:39.33	3:40.31	3:41.29	3:42.27	3:43.25
230	3:44.23	3:45.21	3:46.19	3:47.17	3:48.15	3:49.13	3:50.10	3:51.08	3:52.06	3:53.04
240	3:54.02	3:55.00	3:55.98	3:56.96	3:57.94	3:58.92	3:59.90	4:00.88	4:01.85	4:02.83
250	4:03.81	4:04.79	4:05.77	4:06.75	4:07.73	4:08.71	4:09.69	4:10.67	4:11.65	4:12.63
260	4:13.60	4:14.58	4:15.56	4:16.54	4:17.52	4:18.50	4:19.48	4:20.46	4:21.44	4:22.42
270	4:23.40	4:24.38	4:25.35	4:26.33	4:27.31	4:28.29	4:29.27	4:30.25	4:31.23	4:32.21
280	4:33.19	4:34.17	4:35.15	4:36.13	4:37.10	4:38.08	4:39.06	4:40.04	4:41.02	4:42.00
290	4:42.98	4:43.96	4:44.94	4:45.92	4:46.90	4:47.88	4:48.85	4:49.83	4:50.81	4:51.79
300	4:52.77	4:53.75	4:54.73	4:55.71	4:56.69	4:57.67	4:58.65	4:59.63	5:00.60	5:01.58
310	5:02.56	5:03.54	5:04.52	5:05.50	5:06.48	5:07.46	5:08.44	5:09.42	5:10.40	5:11.38
320	5:12.35	5:13.33	5:14.31	5:15.29	5:16.27	5:17.25	5:18.23	5:19.21	5:20.19	5:21.17
330	5:22.15	5:23.13	5:24.10	5:25.08	5:26.06	5:27.04	5:28.02	5:29.00	5:29.98	5:30.96
340	5:31.94	5:32.92	5:33.90	5:34.88	5:35.85	5:36.83	5:37.81	5:38.79	5:39.77	5:40.75
350	5:41.73	5:42.71	5:43.69	5:44.67	5:45.65	5:46.63	5:47.60	5:48.58	5:49.56	5:50.54
360	5:51.52	5:52.50	5:53.48	5:54.46	5:55.44	5:56.42	5:57.40	5:58.38	5:59.35	6:00.33
370	6:01.31	6:02.29	6:03.27	6:04.25	6:05.23	6:06.21	6:07.19	6:08.17	6:09.15	6:10.13
380	6:11.10	6:12.08	6:13.06	6:14.04	6:15.02	6:16.00	6:16.98	6:17.96	6:18.94	6:19.92
390	6:20.90	6:21.88	6:22.85	6:23.83	6:24.81	6:25.79	6:26.77	6:27.75	6:28.73	6:29.71
400	6:30.69	6:31.67	6:32.65	6:33.63	6:34.60	6:35.58	6:36.56	6:37.54	6:38.52	6:39.50
410	6:40.48	6:41.46	6:42.44	6:43.42	6:44.40	6:45.38	6:46.35	6:47.33	6:48.31	6:49.29
420	6:50.27	6:51.25	6:52.23	6:53.21	6:54.19	6:55.17	6:56.15	6:57.13	6:58.10	6:59.08
430	7:00.06	7:01.04	7:02.02	7:03.00	7:03.98	7:04.96	7:05.94	7:06.92	7:07.90	7:08.88
440	7:09.85	7:10.83	7:11.81	7:12.79	7:13.77	7:14.75	7:15.73	7:16.71	7:17.69	7:18.67
450	7:19.65	7:20.63	7:21.60	7:22.58	7:23.56	7:24.54	7:25.52	7:26.50	7:27.48	7:28.46
460	7:29.44	7:30.42	7:31.40	7:32.38	7:33.35	7:34.33	7:35.31	7:36.29	7:37.27	7:38.25
470	7:39.23	7:40.21	7:41.19	7:42.17	7:43.15	7:44.13	7:45.10	7:46.08	7:47.06	7:48.04
480	7:49.02	7:50.00	7:50.98	7:51.96	7:52.94	7:53.92	7:54.90	7:55.88	7:56.85	7:57.83
490	7:58.81	7:59.79	8:00.77	8:01.75	8:02.73	8:03.71	8:04.69	8:05.67	8:06.65	8:07.63
500	8:08.60	8:09.58	8:10.56	8:11.54	8:12.52	8:13.50	8:14.48	8:15.46	8:16.44	8:17.42
510	8:18.40	8:19.38	8:20.35	8:21.33	8:22.31	8:23.29	8:24.27	8:25.25	8:26.23	8:27.21
520	8:28.19	8:29.17	8:30.15	8:31.13	8:32.10	8:33.08	8:34.06	8:35.04	8:36.02	8:37.00
530	8:37.98	8:38.96	8:39.94	8:40.92	8:41.90	8:42.88	8:43.85	8:44.83	8:45.81	8:46.79
540	8:47.77	8:48.75	8:49.73	8:50.71	8:51.69	8:52.67	8:53.65	8:54.63	8:55.60	8:56.58
550	8:57.56	8:58.54	8:59.52	9:00.50	9:01.48	9:02.46	9:03.44	9:04.42	9:05.40	9:06.38
560	9:07.35	9:08.33	9:09.31	9:10.29	9:11.27	9:12.25	9:13.23	9:14.21	9:15.19	9:16.17
570	9:17.15	9:18.13	9:19.10	9:20.08	9:21.06	9:22.04	9:23.02	9:24.00	9:24.98	9:25.96
580	9:26.94	9:27.92	9:28.90	9:29.88	9:30.85	9:31.83	9:32.81	9:33.79	9:34.77	9:35.75
590	9:36.73	9:37.71	9:38.69	9:39.67	9:40.65	9:41.63	9:42.60	9:43.58	9:44.56	9:45.54

♩. = 1.47; ♩ = 0.98; ♪. = 0.73; (triplet ♩ 𝄾) = 0.65; ♪ = 0.49; (triplet ♪ 𝄾 𝄾) = 0.33; 𝅘𝅥𝅯 = 0.24 seconds

CLICK: 23⅝ FRAMES; M.M.: 60.95

Click	0	1	2	3	4	5	6	7	8	9
000	0:00.00	0:00.00	0:00.98	0:01.97	0:02.95	0:03.94	0:04.92	0:05.91	0:06.89	0:07.88
010	0:08.86	0:09.84	0:10.83	0:11.81	0:12.80	0:13.78	0:14.77	0:15.75	0:16.73	0:17.72
020	0:18.70	0:19.69	0:20.67	0:21.66	0:22.64	0:23.63	0:24.61	0:25.59	0:26.58	0:27.56
030	0:28.55	0:29.53	0:30.52	0:31.50	0:32.48	0:33.47	0:34.45	0:35.44	0:36.42	0:37.41
040	0:38.39	0:39.38	0:40.36	0:41.34	0:42.33	0:43.31	0:44.30	0:45.28	0:46.27	0:47.25
050	0:48.23	0:49.22	0:50.20	0:51.19	0:52.17	0:53.16	0:54.14	0:55.13	0:56.11	0:57.09
060	0:58.08	0:59.06	1:00.05	1:01.03	1:02.02	1:03.00	1:03.98	1:04.97	1:05.95	1:06.94
070	1:07.92	1:08.91	1:09.89	1:10.88	1:11.86	1:12.84	1:13.83	1:14.81	1:15.80	1:16.78
080	1:17.77	1:18.75	1:19.73	1:20.72	1:21.70	1:22.69	1:23.67	1:24.66	1:25.64	1:26.63
090	1:27.61	1:28.59	1:29.58	1:30.56	1:31.55	1:32.53	1:33.52	1:34.50	1:35.48	1:36.47
100	1:37.45	1:38.44	1:39.42	1:40.41	1:41.39	1:42.38	1:43.36	1:44.34	1:45.33	1:46.31
110	1:47.30	1:48.28	1:49.27	1:50.25	1:51.23	1:52.22	1:53.20	1:54.19	1:55.17	1:56.16
120	1:57.14	1:58.13	1:59.11	2:00.09	2:01.08	2:02.06	2:03.05	2:04.03	2:05.02	2:06.00
130	2:06.98	2:07.97	2:08.95	2:09.94	2:10.92	2:11.91	2:12.89	2:13.88	2:14.86	2:15.84
140	2:16.83	2:17.81	2:18.80	2:19.78	2:20.77	2:21.75	2:22.73	2:23.72	2:24.70	2:25.69
150	2:26.67	2:27.66	2:28.64	2:29.63	2:30.61	2:31.59	2:32.58	2:33.56	2:34.55	2:35.53
160	2:36.52	2:37.50	2:38.48	2:39.47	2:40.45	2:41.44	2:42.42	2:43.41	2:44.39	2:45.38
170	2:46.36	2:47.34	2:48.33	2:49.31	2:50.30	2:51.28	2:52.27	2:53.25	2:54.23	2:55.22
180	2:56.20	2:57.19	2:58.17	2:59.16	3:00.14	3:01.13	3:02.11	3:03.09	3:04.08	3:05.06
190	3:06.05	3:07.03	3:08.02	3:09.00	3:09.98	3:10.97	3:11.95	3:12.94	3:13.92	3:14.91
200	3:15.89	3:16.88	3:17.86	3:18.84	3:19.83	3:20.81	3:21.80	3:22.78	3:23.77	3:24.75
210	3:25.73	3:26.72	3:27.70	3:28.69	3:29.67	3:30.66	3:31.64	3:32.63	3:33.61	3:34.59
220	3:35.58	3:36.56	3:37.55	3:38.53	3:39.52	3:40.50	3:41.48	3:42.47	3:43.45	3:44.44
230	3:45.42	3:46.41	3:47.39	3:48.38	3:49.36	3:50.34	3:51.33	3:52.31	3:53.30	3:54.28
240	3:55.27	3:56.25	3:57.23	3:58.22	3:59.20	4:00.19	4:01.17	4:02.16	4:03.14	4:04.13
250	4:05.11	4:06.09	4:07.08	4:08.06	4:09.05	4:10.03	4:11.02	4:12.00	4:12.98	4:13.97
260	4:14.95	4:15.94	4:16.92	4:17.91	4:18.89	4:19.88	4:20.86	4:21.84	4:22.83	4:23.81
270	4:24.80	4:25.78	4:26.77	4:27.75	4:28.73	4:29.72	4:30.70	4:31.69	4:32.67	4:33.66
280	4:34.64	4:35.63	4:36.61	4:37.59	4:38.58	4:39.56	4:40.55	4:41.53	4:42.52	4:43.50
290	4:44.48	4:45.47	4:46.45	4:47.44	4:48.42	4:49.41	4:50.39	4:51.38	4:52.36	4:53.34
300	4:54.33	4:55.31	4:56.30	4:57.28	4:58.27	4:59.25	5:00.23	5:01.22	5:02.20	5:03.19
310	5:04.17	5:05.16	5:06.14	5:07.13	5:08.11	5:09.09	5:10.08	5:11.06	5:12.05	5:13.03
320	5:14.02	5:15.00	5:15.98	5:16.97	5:17.95	5:18.94	5:19.92	5:20.91	5:21.89	5:22.88
330	5:23.86	5:24.84	5:25.83	5:26.81	5:27.80	5:28.78	5:29.77	5:30.75	5:31.73	5:32.72
340	5:33.70	5:34.69	5:35.67	5:36.66	5:37.64	5:38.63	5:39.61	5:40.59	5:41.58	5:42.56
350	5:43.55	5:44.53	5:45.52	5:46.50	5:47.48	5:48.47	5:49.45	5:50.44	5:51.42	5:52.41
360	5:53.39	5:54.38	5:55.36	5:56.34	5:57.33	5:58.31	5:59.30	6:00.28	6:01.27	6:02.25
370	6:03.23	6:04.22	6:05.20	6:06.19	6:07.17	6:08.16	6:09.14	6:10.13	6:11.11	6:12.09
380	6:13.08	6:14.06	6:15.05	6:16.03	6:17.02	6:18.00	6:18.98	6:19.97	6:20.95	6:21.94
390	6:22.92	6:23.91	6:24.89	6:25.88	6:26.86	6:27.84	6:28.83	6:29.81	6:30.80	6:31.78
400	6:32.77	6:33.75	6:34.73	6:35.72	6:36.70	6:37.69	6:38.67	6:39.66	6:40.64	6:41.63
410	6:42.61	6:43.59	6:44.58	6:45.56	6:46.55	6:47.53	6:48.52	6:49.50	6:50.48	6:51.47
420	6:52.45	6:53.44	6:54.42	6:55.41	6:56.39	6:57.38	6:58.36	6:59.34	7:00.33	7:01.31
430	7:02.30	7:03.28	7:04.27	7:05.25	7:06.23	7:07.22	7:08.20	7:09.19	7:10.17	7:11.16
440	7:12.14	7:13.13	7:14.11	7:15.09	7:16.08	7:17.06	7:18.05	7:19.03	7:20.02	7:21.00
450	7:21.98	7:22.97	7:23.95	7:24.94	7:25.92	7:26.91	7:27.89	7:28.88	7:29.86	7:30.84
460	7:31.83	7:32.81	7:33.80	7:34.78	7:35.77	7:36.75	7:37.73	7:38.72	7:39.70	7:40.69
470	7:41.67	7:42.66	7:43.64	7:44.63	7:45.61	7:46.59	7:47.58	7:48.56	7:49.55	7:50.53
480	7:51.52	7:52.50	7:53.48	7:54.47	7:55.45	7:56.44	7:57.42	7:58.41	7:59.39	8:00.38
490	8:01.36	8:02.34	8:03.33	8:04.31	8:05.30	8:06.28	8:07.27	8:08.25	8:09.23	8:10.22
500	8:11.20	8:12.19	8:13.17	8:14.16	8:15.14	8:16.13	8:17.11	8:18.09	8:19.08	8:20.06
510	8:21.05	8:22.03	8:23.02	8:24.00	8:24.98	8:25.97	8:26.95	8:27.94	8:28.92	8:29.91
520	8:30.89	8:31.88	8:32.86	8:33.84	8:34.83	8:35.81	8:36.80	8:37.78	8:38.77	8:39.75
530	8:40.73	8:41.72	8:42.70	8:43.69	8:44.67	8:45.66	8:46.64	8:47.63	8:48.61	8:49.59
540	8:50.58	8:51.56	8:52.55	8:53.53	8:54.52	8:55.50	8:56.48	8:57.47	8:58.45	8:59.44
550	9:00.42	9:01.41	9:02.39	9:03.38	9:04.36	9:05.34	9:06.33	9:07.31	9:08.30	9:09.28
560	9:10.27	9:11.25	9:12.23	9:13.22	9:14.20	9:15.19	9:16.17	9:17.16	9:18.14	9:19.13
570	9:20.11	9:21.09	9:22.08	9:23.06	9:24.05	9:25.03	9:26.02	9:27.00	9:27.98	9:28.97
580	9:29.95	9:30.94	9:31.92	9:32.91	9:33.89	9:34.88	9:35.86	9:36.84	9:37.83	9:38.81
590	9:39.80	9:40.78	9:41.77	9:42.75	9:43.73	9:44.72	9:45.70	9:46.69	9:47.67	9:48.66

♩. = 1.48; ♩ = 0.98; ♪. = 0.74; (triplet ♩ 𝄾) = 0.66; ♪ = 0.49; (triplet ♪ 𝄾 𝄾) = 0.33; 𝅘𝅥𝅯 = 0.25 seconds

CLICK: 23 6/8 FRAMES; M.M.: 60.63

Click	0	1	2	3	4	5	6	7	8	9
000	0:00.00	0:00.00	0:00.99	0:01.98	0:02.97	0:03.96	0:04.95	0:05.94	0:06.93	0:07.92
010	0:08.91	0:09.90	0:10.89	0:11.88	0:12.86	0:13.85	0:14.84	0:15.83	0:16.82	0:17.81
020	0:18.80	0:19.79	0:20.78	0:21.77	0:22.76	0:23.75	0:24.74	0:25.73	0:26.72	0:27.71
030	0:28.70	0:29.69	0:30.68	0:31.67	0:32.66	0:33.65	0:34.64	0:35.63	0:36.61	0:37.60
040	0:38.59	0:39.58	0:40.57	0:41.56	0:42.55	0:43.54	0:44.53	0:45.52	0:46.51	0:47.50
050	0:48.49	0:49.48	0:50.47	0:51.46	0:52.45	0:53.44	0:54.43	0:55.42	0:56.41	0:57.40
060	0:58.39	0:59.38	1:00.36	1:01.35	1:02.34	1:03.33	1:04.32	1:05.31	1:06.30	1:07.29
070	1:08.28	1:09.27	1:10.26	1:11.25	1:12.24	1:13.23	1:14.22	1:15.21	1:16.20	1:17.19
080	1:18.18	1:19.17	1:20.16	1:21.15	1:22.14	1:23.13	1:24.11	1:25.10	1:26.09	1:27.08
090	1:28.07	1:29.06	1:30.05	1:31.04	1:32.03	1:33.02	1:34.01	1:35.00	1:35.99	1:36.98
100	1:37.97	1:38.96	1:39.95	1:40.94	1:41.93	1:42.92	1:43.91	1:44.90	1:45.89	1:46.88
110	1:47.86	1:48.85	1:49.84	1:50.83	1:51.82	1:52.81	1:53.80	1:54.79	1:55.78	1:56.77
120	1:57.76	1:58.75	1:59.74	2:00.73	2:01.72	2:02.71	2:03.70	2:04.69	2:05.68	2:06.67
130	2:07.66	2:08.65	2:09.64	2:10.63	2:11.61	2:12.60	2:13.59	2:14.58	2:15.57	2:16.56
140	2:17.55	2:18.54	2:19.53	2:20.52	2:21.51	2:22.50	2:23.49	2:24.48	2:25.47	2:26.46
150	2:27.45	2:28.44	2:29.43	2:30.42	2:31.41	2:32.40	2:33.39	2:34.38	2:35.36	2:36.35
160	2:37.34	2:38.33	2:39.32	2:40.31	2:41.30	2:42.29	2:43.28	2:44.27	2:45.26	2:46.25
170	2:47.24	2:48.23	2:49.22	2:50.21	2:51.20	2:52.19	2:53.18	2:54.17	2:55.16	2:56.15
180	2:57.14	2:58.13	2:59.11	3:00.10	3:01.09	3:02.08	3:03.07	3:04.06	3:05.05	3:06.04
190	3:07.03	3:08.02	3:09.01	3:10.00	3:10.99	3:11.98	3:12.97	3:13.96	3:14.95	3:15.94
200	3:16.93	3:17.92	3:18.91	3:19.90	3:20.89	3:21.88	3:22.86	3:23.85	3:24.84	3:25.83
210	3:26.82	3:27.81	3:28.80	3:29.79	3:30.78	3:31.77	3:32.76	3:33.75	3:34.74	3:35.73
220	3:36.72	3:37.71	3:38.70	3:39.69	3:40.68	3:41.67	3:42.66	3:43.65	3:44.64	3:45.63
230	3:46.61	3:47.60	3:48.59	3:49.58	3:50.57	3:51.56	3:52.55	3:53.54	3:54.53	3:55.52
240	3:56.51	3:57.50	3:58.49	3:59.48	4:00.47	4:01.46	4:02.45	4:03.44	4:04.43	4:05.42
250	4:06.41	4:07.40	4:08.39	4:09.38	4:10.36	4:11.35	4:12.34	4:13.33	4:14.32	4:15.31
260	4:16.30	4:17.29	4:18.28	4:19.27	4:20.26	4:21.25	4:22.24	4:23.23	4:24.22	4:25.21
270	4:26.20	4:27.19	4:28.18	4:29.17	4:30.16	4:31.15	4:32.14	4:33.13	4:34.11	4:35.10
280	4:36.09	4:37.08	4:38.07	4:39.06	4:40.05	4:41.04	4:42.03	4:43.02	4:44.01	4:45.00
290	4:45.99	4:46.98	4:47.97	4:48.96	4:49.95	4:50.94	4:51.93	4:52.92	4:53.91	4:54.90
300	4:55.89	4:56.88	4:57.86	4:58.85	4:59.84	5:00.83	5:01.82	5:02.81	5:03.80	5:04.79
310	5:05.78	5:06.77	5:07.76	5:08.75	5:09.74	5:10.73	5:11.72	5:12.71	5:13.70	5:14.69
320	5:15.68	5:16.67	5:17.66	5:18.65	5:19.64	5:20.63	5:21.61	5:22.60	5:23.59	5:24.58
330	5:25.57	5:26.56	5:27.55	5:28.54	5:29.53	5:30.52	5:31.51	5:32.50	5:33.49	5:34.48
340	5:35.47	5:36.46	5:37.45	5:38.44	5:39.43	5:40.42	5:41.41	5:42.40	5:43.39	5:44.38
350	5:45.36	5:46.35	5:47.34	5:48.33	5:49.32	5:50.31	5:51.30	5:52.29	5:53.28	5:54.27
360	5:55.26	5:56.25	5:57.24	5:58.23	5:59.22	6:00.21	6:01.20	6:02.19	6:03.18	6:04.17
370	6:05.16	6:06.15	6:07.14	6:08.13	6:09.11	6:10.10	6:11.09	6:12.08	6:13.07	6:14.06
380	6:15.05	6:16.04	6:17.03	6:18.02	6:19.01	6:20.00	6:20.99	6:21.98	6:22.97	6:23.96
390	6:24.95	6:25.94	6:26.93	6:27.92	6:28.91	6:29.90	6:30.89	6:31.88	6:32.86	6:33.85
400	6:34.84	6:35.83	6:36.82	6:37.81	6:38.80	6:39.79	6:40.78	6:41.77	6:42.76	6:43.75
410	6:44.74	6:45.73	6:46.72	6:47.71	6:48.70	6:49.69	6:50.68	6:51.67	6:52.66	6:53.65
420	6:54.64	6:55.63	6:56.61	6:57.60	6:58.59	6:59.58	7:00.57	7:01.56	7:02.55	7:03.54
430	7:04.53	7:05.52	7:06.51	7:07.50	7:08.49	7:09.48	7:10.47	7:11.46	7:12.45	7:13.44
440	7:14.43	7:15.42	7:16.41	7:17.40	7:18.39	7:19.38	7:20.36	7:21.35	7:22.34	7:23.33
450	7:24.32	7:25.31	7:26.30	7:27.29	7:28.28	7:29.27	7:30.26	7:31.25	7:32.24	7:33.23
460	7:34.22	7:35.21	7:36.20	7:37.19	7:38.18	7:39.17	7:40.16	7:41.15	7:42.14	7:43.13
470	7:44.11	7:45.10	7:46.09	7:47.08	7:48.07	7:49.06	7:50.05	7:51.04	7:52.03	7:53.02
480	7:54.01	7:55.00	7:55.99	7:56.98	7:57.97	7:58.96	7:59.95	8:00.94	8:01.93	8:02.92
490	8:03.91	8:04.90	8:05.89	8:06.88	8:07.86	8:08.85	8:09.84	8:10.83	8:11.82	8:12.81
500	8:13.80	8:14.79	8:15.78	8:16.77	8:17.76	8:18.75	8:19.74	8:20.73	8:21.72	8:22.71
510	8:23.70	8:24.69	8:25.68	8:26.67	8:27.66	8:28.65	8:29.64	8:30.63	8:31.61	8:32.60
520	8:33.59	8:34.58	8:35.57	8:36.56	8:37.55	8:38.54	8:39.53	8:40.52	8:41.51	8:42.50
530	8:43.49	8:44.48	8:45.47	8:46.46	8:47.45	8:48.44	8:49.43	8:50.42	8:51.41	8:52.40
540	8:53.39	8:54.38	8:55.36	8:56.35	8:57.34	8:58.33	8:59.32	9:00.31	9:01.30	9:02.29
550	9:03.28	9:04.27	9:05.26	9:06.25	9:07.24	9:08.23	9:09.22	9:10.21	9:11.20	9:12.19
560	9:13.18	9:14.17	9:15.16	9:16.15	9:17.14	9:18.13	9:19.11	9:20.10	9:21.09	9:22.08
570	9:23.07	9:24.06	9:25.05	9:26.04	9:27.03	9:28.02	9:29.01	9:30.00	9:30.99	9:31.98
580	9:32.97	9:33.96	9:34.95	9:35.94	9:36.93	9:37.92	9:38.91	9:39.90	9:40.89	9:41.88
590	9:42.86	9:43.85	9:44.84	9:45.83	9:46.82	9:47.81	9:48.80	9:49.79	9:50.78	9:51.77

𝅘𝅥. = 1.48; 𝅘𝅥 = 0.99; 𝅘𝅥𝅮. = 0.74; (triplet) 𝅘𝅥 𝄾 = 0.66; 𝅘𝅥𝅮 = 0.49; (triplet) 𝅘𝅥𝅮 𝄾 𝄾 = 0.33; 𝅘𝅥𝅯 = 0.25 seconds

CLICK: 23⅞ FRAMES; M.M.: 60.31

Click	0	1	2	3	4	5	6	7	8	9
000	0:00.00	0:00.00	0:00.99	0:01.99	0:02.98	0:03.98	0:04.97	0:05.97	0:06.96	0:07.96
010	0:08.95	0:09.95	0:10.94	0:11.94	0:12.93	0:13.93	0:14.92	0:15.92	0:16.91	0:17.91
020	0:18.90	0:19.90	0:20.89	0:21.89	0:22.88	0:23.88	0:24.87	0:25.86	0:26.86	0:27.85
030	0:28.85	0:29.84	0:30.84	0:31.83	0:32.83	0:33.82	0:34.82	0:35.81	0:36.81	0:37.80
040	0:38.80	0:39.79	0:40.79	0:41.78	0:42.78	0:43.77	0:44.77	0:45.76	0:46.76	0:47.75
050	0:48.74	0:49.74	0:50.73	0:51.73	0:52.72	0:53.72	0:54.71	0:55.71	0:56.70	0:57.70
060	0:58.69	0:59.69	1:00.68	1:01.68	1:02.67	1:03.67	1:04.66	1:05.66	1:06.65	1:07.65
070	1:08.64	1:09.64	1:10.63	1:11.63	1:12.62	1:13.61	1:14.61	1:15.60	1:16.60	1:17.59
080	1:18.59	1:19.58	1:20.58	1:21.57	1:22.57	1:23.56	1:24.56	1:25.55	1:26.55	1:27.54
090	1:28.54	1:29.53	1:30.53	1:31.52	1:32.52	1:33.51	1:34.51	1:35.50	1:36.49	1:37.49
100	1:38.48	1:39.48	1:40.47	1:41.47	1:42.46	1:43.46	1:44.45	1:45.45	1:46.44	1:47.44
110	1:48.43	1:49.43	1:50.42	1:51.42	1:52.41	1:53.41	1:54.40	1:55.40	1:56.39	1:57.39
120	1:58.38	1:59.37	2:00.37	2:01.36	2:02.36	2:03.35	2:04.35	2:05.34	2:06.34	2:07.33
130	2:08.33	2:09.32	2:10.32	2:11.31	2:12.31	2:13.30	2:14.30	2:15.29	2:16.29	2:17.28
140	2:18.28	2:19.27	2:20.27	2:21.26	2:22.26	2:23.25	2:24.24	2:25.24	2:26.23	2:27.23
150	2:28.22	2:29.22	2:30.21	2:31.21	2:32.20	2:33.20	2:34.19	2:35.19	2:36.18	2:37.18
160	2:38.17	2:39.17	2:40.16	2:41.16	2:42.15	2:43.15	2:44.14	2:45.14	2:46.13	2:47.12
170	2:48.12	2:49.11	2:50.11	2:51.10	2:52.10	2:53.09	2:54.09	2:55.08	2:56.08	2:57.07
180	2:58.07	2:59.06	3:00.06	3:01.05	3:02.05	3:03.04	3:04.04	3:05.03	3:06.03	3:07.02
190	3:08.02	3:09.01	3:10.01	3:11.00	3:11.99	3:12.99	3:13.98	3:14.98	3:15.97	3:16.97
200	3:17.96	3:18.96	3:19.95	3:20.95	3:21.94	3:22.94	3:23.93	3:24.93	3:25.92	3:26.92
210	3:27.91	3:28.91	3:29.90	3:30.90	3:31.89	3:32.89	3:33.88	3:34.87	3:35.87	3:36.86
220	3:37.86	3:38.85	3:39.85	3:40.84	3:41.84	3:42.83	3:43.83	3:44.82	3:45.82	3:46.81
230	3:47.81	3:48.80	3:49.80	3:50.79	3:51.79	3:52.78	3:53.78	3:54.77	3:55.77	3:56.76
240	3:57.76	3:58.75	3:59.74	4:00.74	4:01.73	4:02.73	4:03.72	4:04.72	4:05.71	4:06.71
250	4:07.70	4:08.70	4:09.69	4:10.69	4:11.68	4:12.68	4:13.67	4:14.67	4:15.66	4:16.66
260	4:17.65	4:18.65	4:19.64	4:20.64	4:21.63	4:22.62	4:23.62	4:24.61	4:25.61	4:26.60
270	4:27.60	4:28.59	4:29.59	4:30.58	4:31.58	4:32.57	4:33.57	4:34.56	4:35.56	4:36.55
280	4:37.55	4:38.54	4:39.54	4:40.53	4:41.53	4:42.52	4:43.52	4:44.51	4:45.51	4:46.50
290	4:47.49	4:48.49	4:49.48	4:50.48	4:51.47	4:52.47	4:53.46	4:54.46	4:55.45	4:56.45
300	4:57.44	4:58.44	4:59.43	5:00.43	5:01.42	5:02.42	5:03.41	5:04.41	5:05.40	5:06.40
310	5:07.39	5:08.39	5:09.38	5:10.37	5:11.37	5:12.36	5:13.36	5:14.35	5:15.35	5:16.34
320	5:17.34	5:18.33	5:19.33	5:20.32	5:21.32	5:22.31	5:23.31	5:24.30	5:25.30	5:26.29
330	5:27.29	5:28.28	5:29.28	5:30.27	5:31.27	5:32.26	5:33.26	5:34.25	5:35.24	5:36.24
340	5:37.23	5:38.23	5:39.22	5:40.22	5:41.21	5:42.21	5:43.20	5:44.20	5:45.19	5:46.19
350	5:47.18	5:48.18	5:49.17	5:50.17	5:51.16	5:52.16	5:53.15	5:54.15	5:55.14	5:56.14
360	5:57.13	5:58.13	5:59.12	6:00.11	6:01.11	6:02.10	6:03.10	6:04.09	6:05.09	6:06.08
370	6:07.08	6:08.07	6:09.07	6:10.06	6:11.06	6:12.05	6:13.05	6:14.04	6:15.04	6:16.03
380	6:17.03	6:18.02	6:19.02	6:20.01	6:21.01	6:22.00	6:22.99	6:23.99	6:24.98	6:25.98
390	6:26.97	6:27.97	6:28.96	6:29.96	6:30.95	6:31.95	6:32.94	6:33.94	6:34.93	6:35.93
400	6:36.92	6:37.92	6:38.91	6:39.91	6:40.90	6:41.90	6:42.89	6:43.89	6:44.88	6:45.87
410	6:46.87	6:47.86	6:48.86	6:49.85	6:50.85	6:51.84	6:52.84	6:53.83	6:54.83	6:55.82
420	6:56.82	6:57.81	6:58.81	6:59.80	7:00.80	7:01.79	7:02.79	7:03.78	7:04.78	7:05.77
430	7:06.77	7:07.76	7:08.76	7:09.75	7:10.74	7:11.74	7:12.73	7:13.73	7:14.72	7:15.72
440	7:16.71	7:17.71	7:18.70	7:19.70	7:20.69	7:21.69	7:22.68	7:23.68	7:24.67	7:25.67
450	7:26.66	7:27.66	7:28.65	7:29.65	7:30.64	7:31.64	7:32.63	7:33.63	7:34.62	7:35.61
460	7:36.61	7:37.60	7:38.60	7:39.59	7:40.59	7:41.58	7:42.58	7:43.57	7:44.57	7:45.56
470	7:46.56	7:47.55	7:48.55	7:49.54	7:50.54	7:51.53	7:52.53	7:53.52	7:54.52	7:55.51
480	7:56.51	7:57.50	7:58.49	7:59.49	8:00.48	8:01.48	8:02.47	8:03.47	8:04.46	8:05.46
490	8:06.45	8:07.45	8:08.44	8:09.44	8:10.43	8:11.43	8:12.42	8:13.42	8:14.41	8:15.41
500	8:16.40	8:17.40	8:18.39	8:19.39	8:20.38	8:21.37	8:22.37	8:23.36	8:24.36	8:25.35
510	8:26.35	8:27.34	8:28.34	8:29.33	8:30.33	8:31.32	8:32.32	8:33.31	8:34.31	8:35.30
520	8:36.30	8:37.29	8:38.29	8:39.28	8:40.28	8:41.27	8:42.27	8:43.26	8:44.26	8:45.25
530	8:46.24	8:47.24	8:48.23	8:49.23	8:50.22	8:51.22	8:52.21	8:53.21	8:54.20	8:55.20
540	8:56.19	8:57.19	8:58.18	8:59.18	9:00.17	9:01.17	9:02.16	9:03.16	9:04.15	9:05.15
550	9:06.14	9:07.14	9:08.13	9:09.13	9:10.12	9:11.11	9:12.11	9:13.10	9:14.10	9:15.09
560	9:16.09	9:17.08	9:18.08	9:19.07	9:20.07	9:21.06	9:22.06	9:23.05	9:24.05	9:25.04
570	9:26.04	9:27.03	9:28.03	9:29.02	9:30.02	9:31.01	9:32.01	9:33.00	9:33.99	9:34.99
580	9:35.98	9:36.98	9:37.97	9:38.97	9:39.96	9:40.96	9:41.95	9:42.95	9:43.94	9:44.94
590	9:45.93	9:46.93	9:47.92	9:48.92	9:49.91	9:50.91	9:51.90	9:52.90	9:53.89	9:54.89

♩. = 1.49; ♩ = 0.99; ♪. = 0.75; (3) ♩ 𝄾 = 0.66; ♪ = 0.50; (3) ♪𝄾𝄾 = 0.33; 𝅘𝅥𝅯 = 0.25 seconds

CLICK: 24 0/8 FRAMES; M.M.: 60.00

Click	0	1	2	3	4	5	6	7	8	9
000	0:00.00	0:00.00	0:01.00	0:02.00	0:03.00	0:04.00	0:05.00	0:06.00	0:07.00	0:08.00
010	0:09.00	0:10.00	0:11.00	0:12.00	0:13.00	0:14.00	0:15.00	0:16.00	0:17.00	0:18.00
020	0:19.00	0:20.00	0:21.00	0:22.00	0:23.00	0:24.00	0:25.00	0:26.00	0:27.00	0:28.00
030	0:29.00	0:30.00	0:31.00	0:32.00	0:33.00	0:34.00	0:35.00	0:36.00	0:37.00	0:38.00
040	0:39.00	0:40.00	0:41.00	0:42.00	0:43.00	0:44.00	0:45.00	0:46.00	0:47.00	0:48.00
050	0:49.00	0:50.00	0:51.00	0:52.00	0:53.00	0:54.00	0:55.00	0:56.00	0:57.00	0:58.00
060	0:59.00	1:00.00	1:01.00	1:02.00	1:03.00	1:04.00	1:05.00	1:06.00	1:07.00	1:08.00
070	1:09.00	1:10.00	1:11.00	1:12.00	1:13.00	1:14.00	1:15.00	1:16.00	1:17.00	1:18.00
080	1:19.00	1:20.00	1:21.00	1:22.00	1:23.00	1:24.00	1:25.00	1:26.00	1:27.00	1:28.00
090	1:29.00	1:30.00	1:31.00	1:32.00	1:33.00	1:34.00	1:35.00	1:36.00	1:37.00	1:38.00
100	1:39.00	1:40.00	1:41.00	1:42.00	1:43.00	1:44.00	1:45.00	1:46.00	1:47.00	1:48.00
110	1:49.00	1:50.00	1:51.00	1:52.00	1:53.00	1:54.00	1:55.00	1:56.00	1:57.00	1:58.00
120	1:59.00	2:00.00	2:01.00	2:02.00	2:03.00	2:04.00	2:05.00	2:06.00	2:07.00	2:08.00
130	2:09.00	2:10.00	2:11.00	2:12.00	2:13.00	2:14.00	2:15.00	2:16.00	2:17.00	2:18.00
140	2:19.00	2:20.00	2:21.00	2:22.00	2:23.00	2:24.00	2:25.00	2:26.00	2:27.00	2:28.00
150	2:29.00	2:30.00	2:31.00	2:32.00	2:33.00	2:34.00	2:35.00	2:36.00	2:37.00	2:38.00
160	2:39.00	2:40.00	2:41.00	2:42.00	2:43.00	2:44.00	2:45.00	2:46.00	2:47.00	2:48.00
170	2:49.00	2:50.00	2:51.00	2:52.00	2:53.00	2:54.00	2:55.00	2:56.00	2:57.00	2:58.00
180	2:59.00	3:00.00	3:01.00	3:02.00	3:03.00	3:04.00	3:05.00	3:06.00	3:07.00	3:08.00
190	3:09.00	3:10.00	3:11.00	3:12.00	3:13.00	3:14.00	3:15.00	3:16.00	3:17.00	3:18.00
200	3:19.00	3:20.00	3:21.00	3:22.00	3:23.00	3:24.00	3:25.00	3:26.00	3:27.00	3:28.00
210	3:29.00	3:30.00	3:31.00	3:32.00	3:33.00	3:34.00	3:35.00	3:36.00	3:37.00	3:38.00
220	3:39.00	3:40.00	3:41.00	3:42.00	3:43.00	3:44.00	3:45.00	3:46.00	3:47.00	3:48.00
230	3:49.00	3:50.00	3:51.00	3:52.00	3:53.00	3:54.00	3:55.00	3:56.00	3:57.00	3:58.00
240	3:59.00	4:00.00	4:01.00	4:02.00	4:03.00	4:04.00	4:05.00	4:06.00	4:07.00	4:08.00
250	4:09.00	4:10.00	4:11.00	4:12.00	4:13.00	4:14.00	4:15.00	4:16.00	4:17.00	4:18.00
260	4:19.00	4:20.00	4:21.00	4:22.00	4:23.00	4:24.00	4:25.00	4:26.00	4:27.00	4:28.00
270	4:29.00	4:30.00	4:31.00	4:32.00	4:33.00	4:34.00	4:35.00	4:36.00	4:37.00	4:38.00
280	4:39.00	4:40.00	4:41.00	4:42.00	4:43.00	4:44.00	4:45.00	4:46.00	4:47.00	4:48.00
290	4:49.00	4:50.00	4:51.00	4:52.00	4:53.00	4:54.00	4:55.00	4:56.00	4:57.00	4:58.00
300	4:59.00	5:00.00	5:01.00	5:02.00	5:03.00	5:04.00	5:05.00	5:06.00	5:07.00	5:08.00
310	5:09.00	5:10.00	5:11.00	5:12.00	5:13.00	5:14.00	5:15.00	5:16.00	5:17.00	5:18.00
320	5:19.00	5:20.00	5:21.00	5:22.00	5:23.00	5:24.00	5:25.00	5:26.00	5:27.00	5:28.00
330	5:29.00	5:30.00	5:31.00	5:32.00	5:33.00	5:34.00	5:35.00	5:36.00	5:37.00	5:38.00
340	5:39.00	5:40.00	5:41.00	5:42.00	5:43.00	5:44.00	5:45.00	5:46.00	5:47.00	5:48.00
350	5:49.00	5:50.00	5:51.00	5:52.00	5:53.00	5:54.00	5:55.00	5:56.00	5:57.00	5:58.00
360	5:59.00	6:00.00	6:01.00	6:02.00	6:03.00	6:04.00	6:05.00	6:06.00	6:07.00	6:08.00
370	6:09.00	6:10.00	6:11.00	6:12.00	6:13.00	6:14.00	6:15.00	6:16.00	6:17.00	6:18.00
380	6:19.00	6:20.00	6:21.00	6:22.00	6:23.00	6:24.00	6:25.00	6:26.00	6:27.00	6:28.00
390	6:29.00	6:30.00	6:31.00	6:32.00	6:33.00	6:34.00	6:35.00	6:36.00	6:37.00	6:38.00
400	6:39.00	6:40.00	6:41.00	6:42.00	6:43.00	6:44.00	6:45.00	6:46.00	6:47.00	6:48.00
410	6:49.00	6:50.00	6:51.00	6:52.00	6:53.00	6:54.00	6:55.00	6:56.00	6:57.00	6:58.00
420	6:59.00	7:00.00	7:01.00	7:02.00	7:03.00	7:04.00	7:05.00	7:06.00	7:07.00	7:08.00
430	7:09.00	7:10.00	7:11.00	7:12.00	7:13.00	7:14.00	7:15.00	7:16.00	7:17.00	7:18.00
440	7:19.00	7:20.00	7:21.00	7:22.00	7:23.00	7:24.00	7:25.00	7:26.00	7:27.00	7:28.00
450	7:29.00	7:30.00	7:31.00	7:32.00	7:33.00	7:34.00	7:35.00	7:36.00	7:37.00	7:38.00
460	7:39.00	7:40.00	7:41.00	7:42.00	7:43.00	7:44.00	7:45.00	7:46.00	7:47.00	7:48.00
470	7:49.00	7:50.00	7:51.00	7:52.00	7:53.00	7:54.00	7:55.00	7:56.00	7:57.00	7:58.00
480	7:59.00	8:00.00	8:01.00	8:02.00	8:03.00	8:04.00	8:05.00	8:06.00	8:07.00	8:08.00
490	8:09.00	8:10.00	8:11.00	8:12.00	8:13.00	8:14.00	8:15.00	8:16.00	8:17.00	8:18.00
500	8:19.00	8:20.00	8:21.00	8:22.00	8:23.00	8:24.00	8:25.00	8:26.00	8:27.00	8:28.00
510	8:29.00	8:30.00	8:31.00	8:32.00	8:33.00	8:34.00	8:35.00	8:36.00	8:37.00	8:38.00
520	8:39.00	8:40.00	8:41.00	8:42.00	8:43.00	8:44.00	8:45.00	8:46.00	8:47.00	8:48.00
530	8:49.00	8:50.00	8:51.00	8:52.00	8:53.00	8:54.00	8:55.00	8:56.00	8:57.00	8:58.00
540	8:59.00	9:00.00	9:01.00	9:02.00	9:03.00	9:04.00	9:05.00	9:06.00	9:07.00	9:08.00
550	9:09.00	9:10.00	9:11.00	9:12.00	9:13.00	9:14.00	9:15.00	9:16.00	9:17.00	9:18.00
560	9:19.00	9:20.00	9:21.00	9:22.00	9:23.00	9:24.00	9:25.00	9:26.00	9:27.00	9:28.00
570	9:29.00	9:30.00	9:31.00	9:32.00	9:33.00	9:34.00	9:35.00	9:36.00	9:37.00	9:38.00
580	9:39.00	9:40.00	9:41.00	9:42.00	9:43.00	9:44.00	9:45.00	9:46.00	9:47.00	9:48.00
590	9:49.00	9:50.00	9:51.00	9:52.00	9:53.00	9:54.00	9:55.00	9:56.00	9:57.00	9:58.00

♩. = 1.50; ♩ = 1.00; ♪. = 0.75; (3) ♩ 𝄾 = 0.67; ♪ = 0.50; (3) ♪ 𝄾 𝄾 = 0.33; 𝅘𝅥𝅯 = 0.25 seconds

CLICK: 24⅛ FRAMES; M.M.: 59.69

Click	0	1	2	3	4	5	6	7	8	9
000	0:00.00	0:00.00	0:01.01	0:02.01	0:03.02	0:04.02	0:05.03	0:06.03	0:07.04	0:08.04
010	0:09.05	0:10.05	0:11.06	0:12.06	0:13.07	0:14.07	0:15.08	0:16.08	0:17.09	0:18.09
020	0:19.10	0:20.10	0:21.11	0:22.11	0:23.12	0:24.13	0:25.13	0:26.14	0:27.14	0:28.15
030	0:29.15	0:30.16	0:31.16	0:32.17	0:33.17	0:34.18	0:35.18	0:36.19	0:37.19	0:38.20
040	0:39.20	0:40.21	0:41.21	0:42.22	0:43.22	0:44.23	0:45.23	0:46.24	0:47.24	0:48.25
050	0:49.26	0:50.26	0:51.27	0:52.27	0:53.28	0:54.28	0:55.29	0:56.29	0:57.30	0:58.30
060	0:59.31	1:00.31	1:01.32	1:02.32	1:03.33	1:04.33	1:05.34	1:06.34	1:07.35	1:08.35
070	1:09.36	1:10.36	1:11.37	1:12.38	1:13.38	1:14.39	1:15.39	1:16.40	1:17.40	1:18.41
080	1:19.41	1:20.42	1:21.42	1:22.43	1:23.43	1:24.44	1:25.44	1:26.45	1:27.45	1:28.46
090	1:29.46	1:30.47	1:31.47	1:32.48	1:33.48	1:34.49	1:35.49	1:36.50	1:37.51	1:38.51
100	1:39.52	1:40.52	1:41.53	1:42.53	1:43.54	1:44.54	1:45.55	1:46.55	1:47.56	1:48.56
110	1:49.57	1:50.57	1:51.58	1:52.58	1:53.59	1:54.59	1:55.60	1:56.60	1:57.61	1:58.61
120	1:59.62	2:00.63	2:01.63	2:02.64	2:03.64	2:04.65	2:05.65	2:06.66	2:07.66	2:08.67
130	2:09.67	2:10.68	2:11.68	2:12.69	2:13.69	2:14.70	2:15.70	2:16.71	2:17.71	2:18.72
140	2:19.72	2:20.73	2:21.73	2:22.74	2:23.74	2:24.75	2:25.76	2:26.76	2:27.77	2:28.77
150	2:29.78	2:30.78	2:31.79	2:32.79	2:33.80	2:34.80	2:35.81	2:36.81	2:37.82	2:38.82
160	2:39.83	2:40.83	2:41.84	2:42.84	2:43.85	2:44.85	2:45.86	2:46.86	2:47.87	2:48.88
170	2:49.88	2:50.89	2:51.89	2:52.90	2:53.90	2:54.91	2:55.91	2:56.92	2:57.92	2:58.93
180	2:59.93	3:00.94	3:01.94	3:02.95	3:03.95	3:04.96	3:05.96	3:06.97	3:07.97	3:08.98
190	3:09.98	3:10.99	3:11.99	3:13.00	3:14.01	3:15.01	3:16.02	3:17.02	3:18.03	3:19.03
200	3:20.04	3:21.04	3:22.05	3:23.05	3:24.06	3:25.06	3:26.07	3:27.07	3:28.08	3:29.08
210	3:30.09	3:31.09	3:32.10	3:33.10	3:34.11	3:35.11	3:36.12	3:37.13	3:38.13	3:39.14
220	3:40.14	3:41.15	3:42.15	3:43.16	3:44.16	3:45.17	3:46.17	3:47.18	3:48.18	3:49.19
230	3:50.19	3:51.20	3:52.20	3:53.21	3:54.21	3:55.22	3:56.22	3:57.23	3:58.23	3:59.24
240	4:00.24	4:01.25	4:02.26	4:03.26	4:04.27	4:05.27	4:06.28	4:07.28	4:08.29	4:09.29
250	4:10.30	4:11.30	4:12.31	4:13.31	4:14.32	4:15.32	4:16.33	4:17.33	4:18.34	4:19.34
260	4:20.35	4:21.35	4:22.36	4:23.36	4:24.37	4:25.38	4:26.38	4:27.39	4:28.39	4:29.40
270	4:30.40	4:31.41	4:32.41	4:33.42	4:34.42	4:35.43	4:36.43	4:37.44	4:38.44	4:39.45
280	4:40.45	4:41.46	4:42.46	4:43.47	4:44.47	4:45.48	4:46.48	4:47.49	4:48.49	4:49.50
290	4:50.51	4:51.51	4:52.52	4:53.52	4:54.53	4:55.53	4:56.54	4:57.54	4:58.55	4:59.55
300	5:00.56	5:01.56	5:02.57	5:03.57	5:04.58	5:05.58	5:06.59	5:07.59	5:08.60	5:09.60
310	5:10.61	5:11.61	5:12.62	5:13.62	5:14.63	5:15.64	5:16.64	5:17.65	5:18.65	5:19.66
320	5:20.66	5:21.67	5:22.67	5:23.68	5:24.68	5:25.69	5:26.69	5:27.70	5:28.70	5:29.71
330	5:30.71	5:31.72	5:32.72	5:33.73	5:34.73	5:35.74	5:36.74	5:37.75	5:38.76	5:39.76
340	5:40.77	5:41.77	5:42.78	5:43.78	5:44.79	5:45.79	5:46.80	5:47.80	5:48.81	5:49.81
350	5:50.82	5:51.82	5:52.83	5:53.83	5:54.84	5:55.84	5:56.85	5:57.85	5:58.86	5:59.86
360	6:00.87	6:01.88	6:02.88	6:03.89	6:04.89	6:05.90	6:06.90	6:07.91	6:08.91	6:09.92
370	6:10.92	6:11.93	6:12.93	6:13.94	6:14.94	6:15.95	6:16.95	6:17.96	6:18.96	6:19.97
380	6:20.97	6:21.98	6:22.98	6:23.99	6:24.99	6:26.00	6:27.01	6:28.01	6:29.02	6:30.02
390	6:31.03	6:32.03	6:33.04	6:34.04	6:35.05	6:36.05	6:37.06	6:38.06	6:39.07	6:40.07
400	6:41.08	6:42.08	6:43.09	6:44.09	6:45.10	6:46.10	6:47.11	6:48.11	6:49.12	6:50.13
410	6:51.13	6:52.14	6:53.14	6:54.15	6:55.15	6:56.16	6:57.16	6:58.17	6:59.17	7:00.18
420	7:01.18	7:02.19	7:03.19	7:04.20	7:05.20	7:06.21	7:07.21	7:08.22	7:09.22	7:10.23
430	7:11.23	7:12.24	7:13.24	7:14.25	7:15.26	7:16.26	7:17.27	7:18.27	7:19.28	7:20.28
440	7:21.29	7:22.29	7:23.30	7:24.30	7:25.31	7:26.31	7:27.32	7:28.32	7:29.33	7:30.33
450	7:31.34	7:32.34	7:33.35	7:34.35	7:35.36	7:36.36	7:37.37	7:38.38	7:39.38	7:40.39
460	7:41.39	7:42.40	7:43.40	7:44.41	7:45.41	7:46.42	7:47.42	7:48.43	7:49.43	7:50.44
470	7:51.44	7:52.45	7:53.45	7:54.46	7:55.46	7:56.47	7:57.47	7:58.48	7:59.48	8:00.49
480	8:01.49	8:02.50	8:03.51	8:04.51	8:05.52	8:06.52	8:07.53	8:08.53	8:09.54	8:10.54
490	8:11.55	8:12.55	8:13.56	8:14.56	8:15.57	8:16.57	8:17.58	8:18.58	8:19.59	8:20.59
500	8:21.60	8:22.60	8:23.61	8:24.61	8:25.62	8:26.63	8:27.63	8:28.64	8:29.64	8:30.65
510	8:31.65	8:32.66	8:33.66	8:34.67	8:35.67	8:36.68	8:37.68	8:38.69	8:39.69	8:40.70
520	8:41.70	8:42.71	8:43.71	8:44.72	8:45.72	8:46.73	8:47.73	8:48.74	8:49.74	8:50.75
530	8:51.76	8:52.76	8:53.77	8:54.77	8:55.78	8:56.78	8:57.79	8:58.79	8:59.80	9:00.80
540	9:01.81	9:02.81	9:03.82	9:04.82	9:05.83	9:06.83	9:07.84	9:08.84	9:09.85	9:10.85
550	9:11.86	9:12.86	9:13.87	9:14.88	9:15.88	9:16.89	9:17.89	9:18.90	9:19.90	9:20.91
560	9:21.91	9:22.92	9:23.92	9:24.93	9:25.93	9:26.94	9:27.94	9:28.95	9:29.95	9:30.96
570	9:31.96	9:32.97	9:33.97	9:34.98	9:35.98	9:36.99	9:37.99	9:39.00	9:40.01	9:41.01
580	9:42.02	9:43.02	9:44.03	9:45.03	9:46.04	9:47.04	9:48.05	9:49.05	9:50.06	9:51.06
590	9:52.07	9:53.07	9:54.08	9:55.08	9:56.09	9:57.09	9:58.10	9:59.10	10:00.11	10:01.11

♩. = 1.51; ♩ = 1.01; ♪. = 0.75; (triplet ♩ 𝄾) = 0.67; ♪ = 0.50; (triplet ♪ 𝄾 𝄾) = 0.34; 𝅘𝅥𝅯 = 0.25 seconds

CLICK: 24 2/8 FRAMES; M.M.: 59.38

Click	0	1	2	3	4	5	6	7	8	9
000	0:00.00	0:00.00	0:01.01	0:02.02	0:03.03	0:04.04	0:05.05	0:06.06	0:07.07	0:08.08
010	0:09.09	0:10.10	0:11.11	0:12.13	0:13.14	0:14.15	0:15.16	0:16.17	0:17.18	0:18.19
020	0:19.20	0:20.21	0:21.22	0:22.23	0:23.24	0:24.25	0:25.26	0:26.27	0:27.28	0:28.29
030	0:29.30	0:30.31	0:31.32	0:32.33	0:33.34	0:34.35	0:35.36	0:36.38	0:37.39	0:38.40
040	0:39.41	0:40.42	0:41.43	0:42.44	0:43.45	0:44.46	0:45.47	0:46.48	0:47.49	0:48.50
050	0:49.51	0:50.52	0:51.53	0:52.54	0:53.55	0:54.56	0:55.57	0:56.58	0:57.59	0:58.60
060	0:59.61	1:00.62	1:01.64	1:02.65	1:03.66	1:04.67	1:05.68	1:06.69	1:07.70	1:08.71
070	1:09.72	1:10.73	1:11.74	1:12.75	1:13.76	1:14.77	1:15.78	1:16.79	1:17.80	1:18.81
080	1:19.82	1:20.83	1:21.84	1:22.85	1:23.86	1:24.88	1:25.89	1:26.90	1:27.91	1:28.92
090	1:29.93	1:30.94	1:31.95	1:32.96	1:33.97	1:34.98	1:35.99	1:37.00	1:38.01	1:39.02
100	1:40.03	1:41.04	1:42.05	1:43.06	1:44.07	1:45.08	1:46.09	1:47.10	1:48.11	1:49.12
110	1:50.14	1:51.15	1:52.16	1:53.17	1:54.18	1:55.19	1:56.20	1:57.21	1:58.22	1:59.23
120	2:00.24	2:01.25	2:02.26	2:03.27	2:04.28	2:05.29	2:06.30	2:07.31	2:08.32	2:09.33
130	2:10.34	2:11.35	2:12.36	2:13.37	2:14.39	2:15.40	2:16.41	2:17.42	2:18.43	2:19.44
140	2:20.45	2:21.46	2:22.47	2:23.48	2:24.49	2:25.50	2:26.51	2:27.52	2:28.53	2:29.54
150	2:30.55	2:31.56	2:32.57	2:33.58	2:34.59	2:35.60	2:36.61	2:37.63	2:38.64	2:39.65
160	2:40.66	2:41.67	2:42.68	2:43.69	2:44.70	2:45.71	2:46.72	2:47.73	2:48.74	2:49.75
170	2:50.76	2:51.77	2:52.78	2:53.79	2:54.80	2:55.81	2:56.82	2:57.83	2:58.84	2:59.85
180	3:00.86	3:01.88	3:02.89	3:03.90	3:04.91	3:05.92	3:06.93	3:07.94	3:08.95	3:09.96
190	3:10.97	3:11.98	3:12.99	3:14.00	3:15.01	3:16.02	3:17.03	3:18.04	3:19.05	3:20.06
200	3:21.07	3:22.08	3:23.09	3:24.10	3:25.11	3:26.12	3:27.14	3:28.15	3:29.16	3:30.17
210	3:31.18	3:32.19	3:33.20	3:34.21	3:35.22	3:36.23	3:37.24	3:38.25	3:39.26	3:40.27
220	3:41.28	3:42.29	3:43.30	3:44.31	3:45.32	3:46.33	3:47.34	3:48.35	3:49.36	3:50.37
230	3:51.39	3:52.40	3:53.41	3:54.42	3:55.43	3:56.44	3:57.45	3:58.46	3:59.47	4:00.48
240	4:01.49	4:02.50	4:03.51	4:04.52	4:05.53	4:06.54	4:07.55	4:08.56	4:09.57	4:10.58
250	4:11.59	4:12.60	4:13.61	4:14.63	4:15.64	4:16.65	4:17.66	4:18.67	4:19.68	4:20.69
260	4:21.70	4:22.71	4:23.72	4:24.73	4:25.74	4:26.75	4:27.76	4:28.77	4:29.78	4:30.79
270	4:31.80	4:32.81	4:33.82	4:34.83	4:35.84	4:36.85	4:37.86	4:38.87	4:39.89	4:40.90
280	4:41.91	4:42.92	4:43.93	4:44.94	4:45.95	4:46.96	4:47.97	4:48.98	4:49.99	4:51.00
290	4:52.01	4:53.02	4:54.03	4:55.04	4:56.05	4:57.06	4:58.07	4:59.08	5:00.09	5:01.10
300	5:02.11	5:03.12	5:04.14	5:05.15	5:06.16	5:07.17	5:08.18	5:09.19	5:10.20	5:11.21
310	5:12.22	5:13.23	5:14.24	5:15.25	5:16.26	5:17.27	5:18.28	5:19.29	5:20.30	5:21.31
320	5:22.32	5:23.33	5:24.34	5:25.35	5:26.36	5:27.37	5:28.39	5:29.40	5:30.41	5:31.42
330	5:32.43	5:33.44	5:34.45	5:35.46	5:36.47	5:37.48	5:38.49	5:39.50	5:40.51	5:41.52
340	5:42.53	5:43.54	5:44.55	5:45.56	5:46.57	5:47.58	5:48.59	5:49.60	5:50.61	5:51.62
350	5:52.64	5:53.65	5:54.66	5:55.67	5:56.68	5:57.69	5:58.70	5:59.71	6:00.72	6:01.73
360	6:02.74	6:03.75	6:04.76	6:05.77	6:06.78	6:07.79	6:08.80	6:09.81	6:10.82	6:11.83
370	6:12.84	6:13.85	6:14.86	6:15.87	6:16.89	6:17.90	6:18.91	6:19.92	6:20.93	6:21.94
380	6:22.95	6:23.96	6:24.97	6:25.98	6:26.99	6:28.00	6:29.01	6:30.02	6:31.03	6:32.04
390	6:33.05	6:34.06	6:35.07	6:36.08	6:37.09	6:38.10	6:39.11	6:40.12	6:41.14	6:42.15
400	6:43.16	6:44.17	6:45.18	6:46.19	6:47.20	6:48.21	6:49.22	6:50.23	6:51.24	6:52.25
410	6:53.26	6:54.27	6:55.28	6:56.29	6:57.30	6:58.31	6:59.32	7:00.33	7:01.34	7:02.35
420	7:03.36	7:04.37	7:05.39	7:06.40	7:07.41	7:08.42	7:09.43	7:10.44	7:11.45	7:12.46
430	7:13.47	7:14.48	7:15.49	7:16.50	7:17.51	7:18.52	7:19.53	7:20.54	7:21.55	7:22.56
440	7:23.57	7:24.58	7:25.59	7:26.60	7:27.61	7:28.62	7:29.64	7:30.65	7:31.66	7:32.67
450	7:33.68	7:34.69	7:35.70	7:36.71	7:37.72	7:38.73	7:39.74	7:40.75	7:41.76	7:42.77
460	7:43.78	7:44.79	7:45.80	7:46.81	7:47.82	7:48.83	7:49.84	7:50.85	7:51.86	7:52.87
470	7:53.89	7:54.90	7:55.91	7:56.92	7:57.93	7:58.94	7:59.95	8:00.96	8:01.97	8:02.98
480	8:03.99	8:05.00	8:06.01	8:07.02	8:08.03	8:09.04	8:10.05	8:11.06	8:12.07	8:13.08
490	8:14.09	8:15.10	8:16.11	8:17.12	8:18.14	8:19.15	8:20.16	8:21.17	8:22.18	8:23.19
500	8:24.20	8:25.21	8:26.22	8:27.23	8:28.24	8:29.25	8:30.26	8:31.27	8:32.28	8:33.29
510	8:34.30	8:35.31	8:36.32	8:37.33	8:38.34	8:39.35	8:40.36	8:41.37	8:42.39	8:43.40
520	8:44.41	8:45.42	8:46.43	8:47.44	8:48.45	8:49.46	8:50.47	8:51.48	8:52.49	8:53.50
530	8:54.51	8:55.52	8:56.53	8:57.54	8:58.55	8:59.56	9:00.57	9:01.58	9:02.59	9:03.60
540	9:04.61	9:05.63	9:06.64	9:07.65	9:08.66	9:09.67	9:10.68	9:11.69	9:12.70	9:13.71
550	9:14.72	9:15.73	9:16.74	9:17.75	9:18.76	9:19.77	9:20.78	9:21.79	9:22.80	9:23.81
560	9:24.82	9:25.83	9:26.84	9:27.85	9:28.86	9:29.87	9:30.89	9:31.90	9:32.91	9:33.92
570	9:34.93	9:35.94	9:36.95	9:37.96	9:38.97	9:39.98	9:40.99	9:42.00	9:43.01	9:44.02
580	9:45.03	9:46.04	9:47.05	9:48.06	9:49.07	9:50.08	9:51.09	9:52.10	9:53.11	9:54.13
590	9:55.14	9:56.15	9:57.16	9:58.17	9:59.18	10:00.19	10:01.20	10:02.21	10:03.22	10:04.23

♩. = 1.52; ♩ = 1.01; ♪. = 0.76; (triplet) ♩ 𝄾 = 0.67; ♪ = 0.51; (triplet) ♪ 𝄾 𝄾 = 0.34; 𝅘𝅥𝅯 = 0.25 seconds

CLICK: 24⅜ FRAMES; M.M.: 59.08

Click	0	1	2	3	4	5	6	7	8	9
000	0:00.00	0:00.00	0:01.02	0:02.03	0:03.05	0:04.06	0:05.08	0:06.09	0:07.11	0:08.13
010	0:09.14	0:10.16	0:11.17	0:12.19	0:13.20	0:14.22	0:15.23	0:16.25	0:17.27	0:18.28
020	0:19.30	0:20.31	0:21.33	0:22.34	0:23.36	0:24.38	0:25.39	0:26.41	0:27.42	0:28.44
030	0:29.45	0:30.47	0:31.48	0:32.50	0:33.52	0:34.53	0:35.55	0:36.56	0:37.58	0:38.59
040	0:39.61	0:40.63	0:41.64	0:42.66	0:43.67	0:44.69	0:45.70	0:46.72	0:47.73	0:48.75
050	0:49.77	0:50.78	0:51.80	0:52.81	0:53.83	0:54.84	0:55.86	0:56.88	0:57.89	0:58.91
060	0:59.92	1:00.94	1:01.95	1:02.97	1:03.98	1:05.00	1:06.02	1:07.03	1:08.05	1:09.06
070	1:10.08	1:11.09	1:12.11	1:13.13	1:14.14	1:15.16	1:16.17	1:17.19	1:18.20	1:19.22
080	1:20.23	1:21.25	1:22.27	1:23.28	1:24.30	1:25.31	1:26.33	1:27.34	1:28.36	1:29.38
090	1:30.39	1:31.41	1:32.42	1:33.44	1:34.45	1:35.47	1:36.48	1:37.50	1:38.52	1:39.53
100	1:40.55	1:41.56	1:42.58	1:43.59	1:44.61	1:45.63	1:46.64	1:47.66	1:48.67	1:49.69
110	1:50.70	1:51.72	1:52.73	1:53.75	1:54.77	1:55.78	1:56.80	1:57.81	1:58.83	1:59.84
120	2:00.86	2:01.88	2:02.89	2:03.91	2:04.92	2:05.94	2:06.95	2:07.97	2:08.98	2:10.00
130	2:11.02	2:12.03	2:13.05	2:14.06	2:15.08	2:16.09	2:17.11	2:18.13	2:19.14	2:20.16
140	2:21.17	2:22.19	2:23.20	2:24.22	2:25.23	2:26.25	2:27.27	2:28.28	2:29.30	2:30.31
150	2:31.33	2:32.34	2:33.36	2:34.38	2:35.39	2:36.41	2:37.42	2:38.44	2:39.45	2:40.47
160	2:41.48	2:42.50	2:43.52	2:44.53	2:45.55	2:46.56	2:47.58	2:48.59	2:49.61	2:50.63
170	2:51.64	2:52.66	2:53.67	2:54.69	2:55.70	2:56.72	2:57.73	2:58.75	2:59.77	3:00.78
180	3:01.80	3:02.81	3:03.83	3:04.84	3:05.86	3:06.88	3:07.89	3:08.91	3:09.92	3:10.94
190	3:11.95	3:12.97	3:13.98	3:15.00	3:16.02	3:17.03	3:18.05	3:19.06	3:20.08	3:21.09
200	3:22.11	3:23.13	3:24.14	3:25.16	3:26.17	3:27.19	3:28.20	3:29.22	3:30.23	3:31.25
210	3:32.27	3:33.28	3:34.30	3:35.31	3:36.33	3:37.34	3:38.36	3:39.38	3:40.39	3:41.41
220	3:42.42	3:43.44	3:44.45	3:45.47	3:46.48	3:47.50	3:48.52	3:49.53	3:50.55	3:51.56
230	3:52.58	3:53.59	3:54.61	3:55.63	3:56.64	3:57.66	3:58.67	3:59.69	4:00.70	4:01.72
240	4:02.73	4:03.75	4:04.77	4:05.78	4:06.80	4:07.81	4:08.83	4:09.84	4:10.86	4:11.88
250	4:12.89	4:13.91	4:14.92	4:15.94	4:16.95	4:17.97	4:18.98	4:20.00	4:21.02	4:22.03
260	4:23.05	4:24.06	4:25.08	4:26.09	4:27.11	4:28.13	4:29.14	4:30.16	4:31.17	4:32.19
270	4:33.20	4:34.22	4:35.23	4:36.25	4:37.27	4:38.28	4:39.30	4:40.31	4:41.33	4:42.34
280	4:43.36	4:44.38	4:45.39	4:46.41	4:47.42	4:48.44	4:49.45	4:50.47	4:51.48	4:52.50
290	4:53.52	4:54.53	4:55.55	4:56.56	4:57.58	4:58.59	4:59.61	5:00.63	5:01.64	5:02.66
300	5:03.67	5:04.69	5:05.70	5:06.72	5:07.73	5:08.75	5:09.77	5:10.78	5:11.80	5:12.81
310	5:13.83	5:14.84	5:15.86	5:16.88	5:17.89	5:18.91	5:19.92	5:20.94	5:21.95	5:22.97
320	5:23.98	5:25.00	5:26.02	5:27.03	5:28.05	5:29.06	5:30.08	5:31.09	5:32.11	5:33.13
330	5:34.14	5:35.16	5:36.17	5:37.19	5:38.20	5:39.22	5:40.23	5:41.25	5:42.27	5:43.28
340	5:44.30	5:45.31	5:46.33	5:47.34	5:48.36	5:49.38	5:50.39	5:51.41	5:52.42	5:53.44
350	5:54.45	5:55.47	5:56.48	5:57.50	5:58.52	5:59.53	6:00.55	6:01.56	6:02.58	6:03.59
360	6:04.61	6:05.63	6:06.64	6:07.66	6:08.67	6:09.69	6:10.70	6:11.72	6:12.73	6:13.75
370	6:14.77	6:15.78	6:16.80	6:17.81	6:18.83	6:19.84	6:20.86	6:21.88	6:22.89	6:23.91
380	6:24.92	6:25.94	6:26.95	6:27.97	6:28.98	6:30.00	6:31.02	6:32.03	6:33.05	6:34.06
390	6:35.08	6:36.09	6:37.11	6:38.13	6:39.14	6:40.16	6:41.17	6:42.19	6:43.20	6:44.22
400	6:45.23	6:46.25	6:47.27	6:48.28	6:49.30	6:50.31	6:51.33	6:52.34	6:53.36	6:54.38
410	6:55.39	6:56.41	6:57.42	6:58.44	6:59.45	7:00.47	7:01.48	7:02.50	7:03.52	7:04.53
420	7:05.55	7:06.56	7:07.58	7:08.59	7:09.61	7:10.63	7:11.64	7:12.66	7:13.67	7:14.69
430	7:15.70	7:16.72	7:17.73	7:18.75	7:19.77	7:20.78	7:21.80	7:22.81	7:23.83	7:24.84
440	7:25.86	7:26.88	7:27.89	7:28.91	7:29.92	7:30.94	7:31.95	7:32.97	7:33.98	7:35.00
450	7:36.02	7:37.03	7:38.05	7:39.06	7:40.08	7:41.09	7:42.11	7:43.13	7:44.14	7:45.16
460	7:46.17	7:47.19	7:48.20	7:49.22	7:50.23	7:51.25	7:52.27	7:53.28	7:54.30	7:55.31
470	7:56.33	7:57.34	7:58.36	7:59.38	8:00.39	8:01.41	8:02.42	8:03.44	8:04.45	8:05.47
480	8:06.48	8:07.50	8:08.52	8:09.53	8:10.55	8:11.56	8:12.58	8:13.59	8:14.61	8:15.63
490	8:16.64	8:17.66	8:18.67	8:19.69	8:20.70	8:21.72	8:22.73	8:23.75	8:24.77	8:25.78
500	8:26.80	8:27.81	8:28.83	8:29.84	8:30.86	8:31.88	8:32.89	8:33.91	8:34.92	8:35.94
510	8:36.95	8:37.97	8:38.98	8:40.00	8:41.02	8:42.03	8:43.05	8:44.06	8:45.08	8:46.09
520	8:47.11	8:48.13	8:49.14	8:50.16	8:51.17	8:52.19	8:53.20	8:54.22	8:55.23	8:56.25
530	8:57.27	8:58.28	8:59.30	9:00.31	9:01.33	9:02.34	9:03.36	9:04.38	9:05.39	9:06.41
540	9:07.42	9:08.44	9:09.45	9:10.47	9:11.48	9:12.50	9:13.52	9:14.53	9:15.55	9:16.56
550	9:17.58	9:18.59	9:19.61	9:20.63	9:21.64	9:22.66	9:23.67	9:24.69	9:25.70	9:26.72
560	9:27.73	9:28.75	9:29.77	9:30.78	9:31.80	9:32.81	9:33.83	9:34.84	9:35.86	9:36.88
570	9:37.89	9:38.91	9:39.92	9:40.94	9:41.95	9:42.97	9:43.98	9:45.00	9:46.02	9:47.03
580	9:48.05	9:49.06	9:50.08	9:51.09	9:52.11	9:53.13	9:54.14	9:55.16	9:56.17	9:57.19
590	9:58.20	9:59.22	10:00.23	10:01.25	10:02.27	10:03.28	10:04.30	10:05.31	10:06.33	10:07.34

♩. = 1.52; ♩ = 1.02; ♪. = 0.76; (3: ♩ 𝄾) = 0.68; ♪ = 0.51; (3: ♪ 𝄾 𝄾) = 0.34; 𝅘𝅥𝅯 = 0.25 seconds

CLICK: 24 4/8 FRAMES; M.M.: 58.78

Click	0	1	2	3	4	5	6	7	8	9
000	0:00.00	0:00.00	0:01.02	0:02.04	0:03.06	0:04.08	0:05.10	0:06.13	0:07.15	0:08.17
010	0:09.19	0:10.21	0:11.23	0:12.25	0:13.27	0:14.29	0:15.31	0:16.33	0:17.35	0:18.38
020	0:19.40	0:20.42	0:21.44	0:22.46	0:23.48	0:24.50	0:25.52	0:26.54	0:27.56	0:28.58
030	0:29.60	0:30.63	0:31.65	0:32.67	0:33.69	0:34.71	0:35.73	0:36.75	0:37.77	0:38.79
040	0:39.81	0:40.83	0:41.85	0:42.88	0:43.90	0:44.92	0:45.94	0:46.96	0:47.98	0:49.00
050	0:50.02	0:51.04	0:52.06	0:53.08	0:54.10	0:55.13	0:56.15	0:57.17	0:58.19	0:59.21
060	1:00.23	1:01.25	1:02.27	1:03.29	1:04.31	1:05.33	1:06.35	1:07.38	1:08.40	1:09.42
070	1:10.44	1:11.46	1:12.48	1:13.50	1:14.52	1:15.54	1:16.56	1:17.58	1:18.60	1:19.63
080	1:20.65	1:21.67	1:22.69	1:23.71	1:24.73	1:25.75	1:26.77	1:27.79	1:28.81	1:29.83
090	1:30.85	1:31.88	1:32.90	1:33.92	1:34.94	1:35.96	1:36.98	1:38.00	1:39.02	1:40.04
100	1:41.06	1:42.08	1:43.10	1:44.13	1:45.15	1:46.17	1:47.19	1:48.21	1:49.23	1:50.25
110	1:51.27	1:52.29	1:53.31	1:54.33	1:55.35	1:56.38	1:57.40	1:58.42	1:59.44	2:00.46
120	2:01.48	2:02.50	2:03.52	2:04.54	2:05.56	2:06.58	2:07.60	2:08.62	2:09.65	2:10.67
130	2:11.69	2:12.71	2:13.73	2:14.75	2:15.77	2:16.79	2:17.81	2:18.83	2:19.85	2:20.87
140	2:21.90	2:22.92	2:23.94	2:24.96	2:25.98	2:27.00	2:28.02	2:29.04	2:30.06	2:31.08
150	2:32.10	2:33.12	2:34.15	2:35.17	2:36.19	2:37.21	2:38.23	2:39.25	2:40.27	2:41.29
160	2:42.31	2:43.33	2:44.35	2:45.37	2:46.40	2:47.42	2:48.44	2:49.46	2:50.48	2:51.50
170	2:52.52	2:53.54	2:54.56	2:55.58	2:56.60	2:57.62	2:58.65	2:59.67	3:00.69	3:01.71
180	3:02.73	3:03.75	3:04.77	3:05.79	3:06.81	3:07.83	3:08.85	3:09.87	3:10.90	3:11.92
190	3:12.94	3:13.96	3:14.98	3:16.00	3:17.02	3:18.04	3:19.06	3:20.08	3:21.10	3:22.13
200	3:23.15	3:24.17	3:25.19	3:26.21	3:27.23	3:28.25	3:29.27	3:30.29	3:31.31	3:32.33
210	3:33.35	3:34.38	3:35.40	3:36.42	3:37.44	3:38.46	3:39.48	3:40.50	3:41.52	3:42.54
220	3:43.56	3:44.58	3:45.60	3:46.63	3:47.65	3:48.67	3:49.69	3:50.71	3:51.73	3:52.75
230	3:53.77	3:54.79	3:55.81	3:56.83	3:57.85	3:58.88	3:59.90	4:00.92	4:01.94	4:02.96
240	4:03.98	4:05.00	4:06.02	4:07.04	4:08.06	4:09.08	4:10.10	4:11.13	4:12.15	4:13.17
250	4:14.19	4:15.21	4:16.23	4:17.25	4:18.27	4:19.29	4:20.31	4:21.33	4:22.35	4:23.37
260	4:24.40	4:25.42	4:26.44	4:27.46	4:28.48	4:29.50	4:30.52	4:31.54	4:32.56	4:33.58
270	4:34.60	4:35.63	4:36.65	4:37.67	4:38.69	4:39.71	4:40.73	4:41.75	4:42.77	4:43.79
280	4:44.81	4:45.83	4:46.85	4:47.87	4:48.90	4:49.92	4:50.94	4:51.96	4:52.98	4:54.00
290	4:55.02	4:56.04	4:57.06	4:58.08	4:59.10	5:00.12	5:01.15	5:02.17	5:03.19	5:04.21
300	5:05.23	5:06.25	5:07.27	5:08.29	5:09.31	5:10.33	5:11.35	5:12.38	5:13.40	5:14.42
310	5:15.44	5:16.46	5:17.48	5:18.50	5:19.52	5:20.54	5:21.56	5:22.58	5:23.60	5:24.62
320	5:25.65	5:26.67	5:27.69	5:28.71	5:29.73	5:30.75	5:31.77	5:32.79	5:33.81	5:34.83
330	5:35.85	5:36.88	5:37.90	5:38.92	5:39.94	5:40.96	5:41.98	5:43.00	5:44.02	5:45.04
340	5:46.06	5:47.08	5:48.10	5:49.12	5:50.15	5:51.17	5:52.19	5:53.21	5:54.23	5:55.25
350	5:56.27	5:57.29	5:58.31	5:59.33	6:00.35	6:01.38	6:02.40	6:03.42	6:04.44	6:05.46
360	6:06.48	6:07.50	6:08.52	6:09.54	6:10.56	6:11.58	6:12.60	6:13.62	6:14.65	6:15.67
370	6:16.69	6:17.71	6:18.73	6:19.75	6:20.77	6:21.79	6:22.81	6:23.83	6:24.85	6:25.88
380	6:26.90	6:27.92	6:28.94	6:29.96	6:30.98	6:32.00	6:33.02	6:34.04	6:35.06	6:36.08
390	6:37.10	6:38.12	6:39.15	6:40.17	6:41.19	6:42.21	6:43.23	6:44.25	6:45.27	6:46.29
400	6:47.31	6:48.33	6:49.35	6:50.38	6:51.40	6:52.42	6:53.44	6:54.46	6:55.48	6:56.50
410	6:57.52	6:58.54	6:59.56	7:00.58	7:01.60	7:02.62	7:03.65	7:04.67	7:05.69	7:06.71
420	7:07.73	7:08.75	7:09.77	7:10.79	7:11.81	7:12.83	7:13.85	7:14.88	7:15.90	7:16.92
430	7:17.94	7:18.96	7:19.98	7:21.00	7:22.02	7:23.04	7:24.06	7:25.08	7:26.10	7:27.12
440	7:28.15	7:29.17	7:30.19	7:31.21	7:32.23	7:33.25	7:34.27	7:35.29	7:36.31	7:37.33
450	7:38.35	7:39.38	7:40.40	7:41.42	7:42.44	7:43.46	7:44.48	7:45.50	7:46.52	7:47.54
460	7:48.56	7:49.58	7:50.60	7:51.62	7:52.65	7:53.67	7:54.69	7:55.71	7:56.73	7:57.75
470	7:58.77	7:59.79	8:00.81	8:01.83	8:02.85	8:03.87	8:04.90	8:05.92	8:06.94	8:07.96
480	8:08.98	8:10.00	8:11.02	8:12.04	8:13.06	8:14.08	8:15.10	8:16.13	8:17.15	8:18.17
490	8:19.19	8:20.21	8:21.23	8:22.25	8:23.27	8:24.29	8:25.31	8:26.33	8:27.35	8:28.37
500	8:29.40	8:30.42	8:31.44	8:32.46	8:33.48	8:34.50	8:35.52	8:36.54	8:37.56	8:38.58
510	8:39.60	8:40.62	8:41.65	8:42.67	8:43.69	8:44.71	8:45.73	8:46.75	8:47.77	8:48.79
520	8:49.81	8:50.83	8:51.85	8:52.88	8:53.90	8:54.92	8:55.94	8:56.96	8:57.98	8:59.00
530	9:00.02	9:01.04	9:02.06	9:03.08	9:04.10	9:05.13	9:06.15	9:07.17	9:08.19	9:09.21
540	9:10.23	9:11.25	9:12.27	9:13.29	9:14.31	9:15.33	9:16.35	9:17.37	9:18.40	9:19.42
550	9:20.44	9:21.46	9:22.48	9:23.50	9:24.52	9:25.54	9:26.56	9:27.58	9:28.60	9:29.62
560	9:30.65	9:31.67	9:32.69	9:33.71	9:34.73	9:35.75	9:36.77	9:37.79	9:38.81	9:39.83
570	9:40.85	9:41.88	9:42.90	9:43.92	9:44.94	9:45.96	9:46.98	9:48.00	9:49.02	9:50.04
580	9:51.06	9:52.08	9:53.10	9:54.13	9:55.15	9:56.17	9:57.19	9:58.21	9:59.23	10:00.25
590	10:01.27	10:02.29	10:03.31	10:04.33	10:05.35	10:06.37	10:07.40	10:08.42	10:09.44	10:10.46

♩. = 1.53; ♩ = 1.02; ♪. = 0.77; (3: ♩ 𝄾) = 0.68; ♪ = 0.51; (3: ♪ 𝄾 𝄾) = 0.34; 𝅘𝅥𝅯 = 0.26 seconds

CLICK: 24⅝ FRAMES; M.M.: 58.48

Click	0	1	2	3	4	5	6	7	8	9
000	0:00.00	0:00.00	0:01.03	0:02.05	0:03.08	0:04.10	0:05.13	0:06.16	0:07.18	0:08.21
010	0:09.23	0:10.26	0:11.29	0:12.31	0:13.34	0:14.36	0:15.39	0:16.42	0:17.44	0:18.47
020	0:19.49	0:20.52	0:21.55	0:22.57	0:23.60	0:24.63	0:25.65	0:26.68	0:27.70	0:28.73
030	0:29.76	0:30.78	0:31.81	0:32.83	0:33.86	0:34.89	0:35.91	0:36.94	0:37.96	0:38.99
040	0:40.02	0:41.04	0:42.07	0:43.09	0:44.12	0:45.15	0:46.17	0:47.20	0:48.22	0:49.25
050	0:50.28	0:51.30	0:52.33	0:53.35	0:54.38	0:55.41	0:56.43	0:57.46	0:58.48	0:59.51
060	1:00.54	1:01.56	1:02.59	1:03.61	1:04.64	1:05.67	1:06.69	1:07.72	1:08.74	1:09.77
070	1:10.80	1:11.82	1:12.85	1:13.87	1:14.90	1:15.93	1:16.95	1:17.98	1:19.01	1:20.03
080	1:21.06	1:22.08	1:23.11	1:24.14	1:25.16	1:26.19	1:27.21	1:28.24	1:29.27	1:30.29
090	1:31.32	1:32.34	1:33.37	1:34.40	1:35.42	1:36.45	1:37.47	1:38.50	1:39.53	1:40.55
100	1:41.58	1:42.60	1:43.63	1:44.66	1:45.68	1:46.71	1:47.73	1:48.76	1:49.79	1:50.81
110	1:51.84	1:52.86	1:53.89	1:54.92	1:55.94	1:56.97	1:57.99	1:59.02	2:00.05	2:01.07
120	2:02.10	2:03.12	2:04.15	2:05.18	2:06.20	2:07.23	2:08.26	2:09.28	2:10.31	2:11.33
130	2:12.36	2:13.39	2:14.41	2:15.44	2:16.46	2:17.49	2:18.52	2:19.54	2:20.57	2:21.59
140	2:22.62	2:23.65	2:24.67	2:25.70	2:26.72	2:27.75	2:28.78	2:29.80	2:30.83	2:31.85
150	2:32.88	2:33.91	2:34.93	2:35.96	2:36.98	2:38.01	2:39.04	2:40.06	2:41.09	2:42.11
160	2:43.14	2:44.17	2:45.19	2:46.22	2:47.24	2:48.27	2:49.30	2:50.32	2:51.35	2:52.37
170	2:53.40	2:54.43	2:55.45	2:56.48	2:57.51	2:58.53	2:59.56	3:00.58	3:01.61	3:02.64
180	3:03.66	3:04.69	3:05.71	3:06.74	3:07.77	3:08.79	3:09.82	3:10.84	3:11.87	3:12.90
190	3:13.92	3:14.95	3:15.97	3:17.00	3:18.03	3:19.05	3:20.08	3:21.10	3:22.13	3:23.16
200	3:24.18	3:25.21	3:26.23	3:27.26	3:28.29	3:29.31	3:30.34	3:31.36	3:32.39	3:33.42
210	3:34.44	3:35.47	3:36.49	3:37.52	3:38.55	3:39.57	3:40.60	3:41.62	3:42.65	3:43.68
220	3:44.70	3:45.73	3:46.76	3:47.78	3:48.81	3:49.83	3:50.86	3:51.89	3:52.91	3:53.94
230	3:54.96	3:55.99	3:57.02	3:58.04	3:59.07	4:00.09	4:01.12	4:02.15	4:03.17	4:04.20
240	4:05.22	4:06.25	4:07.28	4:08.30	4:09.33	4:10.35	4:11.38	4:12.41	4:13.43	4:14.46
250	4:15.48	4:16.51	4:17.54	4:18.56	4:19.59	4:20.61	4:21.64	4:22.67	4:23.69	4:24.72
260	4:25.74	4:26.77	4:27.80	4:28.82	4:29.85	4:30.87	4:31.90	4:32.93	4:33.95	4:34.98
270	4:36.01	4:37.03	4:38.06	4:39.08	4:40.11	4:41.14	4:42.16	4:43.19	4:44.21	4:45.24
280	4:46.27	4:47.29	4:48.32	4:49.34	4:50.37	4:51.40	4:52.42	4:53.45	4:54.47	4:55.50
290	4:56.53	4:57.55	4:58.58	4:59.60	5:00.63	5:01.66	5:02.68	5:03.71	5:04.73	5:05.76
300	5:06.79	5:07.81	5:08.84	5:09.86	5:10.89	5:11.92	5:12.94	5:13.97	5:14.99	5:16.02
310	5:17.05	5:18.07	5:19.10	5:20.12	5:21.15	5:22.18	5:23.20	5:24.23	5:25.26	5:26.28
320	5:27.31	5:28.33	5:29.36	5:30.39	5:31.41	5:32.44	5:33.46	5:34.49	5:35.52	5:36.54
330	5:37.57	5:38.59	5:39.62	5:40.65	5:41.67	5:42.70	5:43.72	5:44.75	5:45.78	5:46.80
340	5:47.83	5:48.85	5:49.88	5:50.91	5:51.93	5:52.96	5:53.98	5:55.01	5:56.04	5:57.06
350	5:58.09	5:59.11	6:00.14	6:01.17	6:02.19	6:03.22	6:04.24	6:05.27	6:06.30	6:07.32
360	6:08.35	6:09.37	6:10.40	6:11.43	6:12.45	6:13.48	6:14.51	6:15.53	6:16.56	6:17.58
370	6:18.61	6:19.64	6:20.66	6:21.69	6:22.71	6:23.74	6:24.77	6:25.79	6:26.82	6:27.84
380	6:28.87	6:29.90	6:30.92	6:31.95	6:32.97	6:34.00	6:35.03	6:36.05	6:37.08	6:38.10
390	6:39.13	6:40.16	6:41.18	6:42.21	6:43.23	6:44.26	6:45.29	6:46.31	6:47.34	6:48.36
400	6:49.39	6:50.42	6:51.44	6:52.47	6:53.49	6:54.52	6:55.55	6:56.57	6:57.60	6:58.62
410	6:59.65	7:00.68	7:01.70	7:02.73	7:03.76	7:04.78	7:05.81	7:06.83	7:07.86	7:08.89
420	7:09.91	7:10.94	7:11.96	7:12.99	7:14.02	7:15.04	7:16.07	7:17.09	7:18.12	7:19.15
430	7:20.17	7:21.20	7:22.22	7:23.25	7:24.28	7:25.30	7:26.33	7:27.35	7:28.38	7:29.41
440	7:30.43	7:31.46	7:32.48	7:33.51	7:34.54	7:35.56	7:36.59	7:37.61	7:38.64	7:39.67
450	7:40.69	7:41.72	7:42.74	7:43.77	7:44.80	7:45.82	7:46.85	7:47.87	7:48.90	7:49.93
460	7:50.95	7:51.98	7:53.01	7:54.03	7:55.06	7:56.08	7:57.11	7:58.14	7:59.16	8:00.19
470	8:01.21	8:02.24	8:03.27	8:04.29	8:05.32	8:06.34	8:07.37	8:08.40	8:09.42	8:10.45
480	8:11.47	8:12.50	8:13.53	8:14.55	8:15.58	8:16.60	8:17.63	8:18.66	8:19.68	8:20.71
490	8:21.73	8:22.76	8:23.79	8:24.81	8:25.84	8:26.86	8:27.89	8:28.92	8:29.94	8:30.97
500	8:31.99	8:33.02	8:34.05	8:35.07	8:36.10	8:37.12	8:38.15	8:39.18	8:40.20	8:41.23
510	8:42.26	8:43.28	8:44.31	8:45.33	8:46.36	8:47.39	8:48.41	8:49.44	8:50.46	8:51.49
520	8:52.52	8:53.54	8:54.57	8:55.59	8:56.62	8:57.65	8:58.67	8:59.70	9:00.72	9:01.75
530	9:02.78	9:03.80	9:04.83	9:05.85	9:06.88	9:07.91	9:08.93	9:09.96	9:10.98	9:12.01
540	9:13.04	9:14.06	9:15.09	9:16.11	9:17.14	9:18.17	9:19.19	9:20.22	9:21.24	9:22.27
550	9:23.30	9:24.32	9:25.35	9:26.37	9:27.40	9:28.43	9:29.45	9:30.48	9:31.51	9:32.53
560	9:33.56	9:34.58	9:35.61	9:36.64	9:37.66	9:38.69	9:39.71	9:40.74	9:41.77	9:42.79
570	9:43.82	9:44.84	9:45.87	9:46.90	9:47.92	9:48.95	9:49.97	9:51.00	9:52.03	9:53.05
580	9:54.08	9:55.10	9:56.13	9:57.16	9:58.18	9:59.21	10:00.23	10:01.26	10:02.29	10:03.31
590	10:04.34	10:05.36	10:06.39	10:07.42	10:08.44	10:09.47	10:10.49	10:11.52	10:12.55	10:13.57

♩. = 1.54; ♩ = 1.03; ♪. = 0.77; (triplet ♩ 𝄾) = 0.68; ♪ = 0.51; (triplet ♪ 𝄾 𝄾) = 0.34; 𝅘𝅥𝅯 = 0.26 seconds

CLICK: 24 6/8 FRAMES; M.M.: 58.18

Click	0	1	2	3	4	5	6	7	8	9
000	0:00.00	0:00.00	0:01.03	0:02.06	0:03.09	0:04.13	0:05.16	0:06.19	0:07.22	0:08.25
010	0:09.28	0:10.31	0:11.34	0:12.38	0:13.41	0:14.44	0:15.47	0:16.50	0:17.53	0:18.56
020	0:19.59	0:20.63	0:21.66	0:22.69	0:23.72	0:24.75	0:25.78	0:26.81	0:27.84	0:28.88
030	0:29.91	0:30.94	0:31.97	0:33.00	0:34.03	0:35.06	0:36.09	0:37.13	0:38.16	0:39.19
040	0:40.22	0:41.25	0:42.28	0:43.31	0:44.34	0:45.38	0:46.41	0:47.44	0:48.47	0:49.50
050	0:50.53	0:51.56	0:52.59	0:53.63	0:54.66	0:55.69	0:56.72	0:57.75	0:58.78	0:59.81
060	1:00.84	1:01.88	1:02.91	1:03.94	1:04.97	1:06.00	1:07.03	1:08.06	1:09.09	1:10.13
070	1:11.16	1:12.19	1:13.22	1:14.25	1:15.28	1:16.31	1:17.34	1:18.37	1:19.41	1:20.44
080	1:21.47	1:22.50	1:23.53	1:24.56	1:25.59	1:26.63	1:27.66	1:28.69	1:29.72	1:30.75
090	1:31.78	1:32.81	1:33.84	1:34.88	1:35.91	1:36.94	1:37.97	1:39.00	1:40.03	1:41.06
100	1:42.09	1:43.13	1:44.16	1:45.19	1:46.22	1:47.25	1:48.28	1:49.31	1:50.34	1:51.38
110	1:52.41	1:53.44	1:54.47	1:55.50	1:56.53	1:57.56	1:58.59	1:59.63	2:00.66	2:01.69
120	2:02.72	2:03.75	2:04.78	2:05.81	2:06.84	2:07.88	2:08.91	2:09.94	2:10.97	2:12.00
130	2:13.03	2:14.06	2:15.09	2:16.12	2:17.16	2:18.19	2:19.22	2:20.25	2:21.28	2:22.31
140	2:23.34	2:24.38	2:25.41	2:26.44	2:27.47	2:28.50	2:29.53	2:30.56	2:31.59	2:32.63
150	2:33.66	2:34.69	2:35.72	2:36.75	2:37.78	2:38.81	2:39.84	2:40.88	2:41.91	2:42.94
160	2:43.97	2:45.00	2:46.03	2:47.06	2:48.09	2:49.13	2:50.16	2:51.19	2:52.22	2:53.25
170	2:54.28	2:55.31	2:56.34	2:57.37	2:58.41	2:59.44	3:00.47	3:01.50	3:02.53	3:03.56
180	3:04.59	3:05.63	3:06.66	3:07.69	3:08.72	3:09.75	3:10.78	3:11.81	3:12.84	3:13.88
190	3:14.91	3:15.94	3:16.97	3:18.00	3:19.03	3:20.06	3:21.09	3:22.13	3:23.16	3:24.19
200	3:25.22	3:26.25	3:27.28	3:28.31	3:29.34	3:30.38	3:31.41	3:32.44	3:33.47	3:34.50
210	3:35.53	3:36.56	3:37.59	3:38.63	3:39.66	3:40.69	3:41.72	3:42.75	3:43.78	3:44.81
220	3:45.84	3:46.88	3:47.91	3:48.94	3:49.97	3:51.00	3:52.03	3:53.06	3:54.09	3:55.13
230	3:56.16	3:57.19	3:58.22	3:59.25	4:00.28	4:01.31	4:02.34	4:03.38	4:04.41	4:05.44
240	4:06.47	4:07.50	4:08.53	4:09.56	4:10.59	4:11.62	4:12.66	4:13.69	4:14.72	4:15.75
250	4:16.78	4:17.81	4:18.84	4:19.88	4:20.91	4:21.94	4:22.97	4:24.00	4:25.03	4:26.06
260	4:27.09	4:28.13	4:29.16	4:30.19	4:31.22	4:32.25	4:33.28	4:34.31	4:35.34	4:36.38
270	4:37.41	4:38.44	4:39.47	4:40.50	4:41.53	4:42.56	4:43.59	4:44.63	4:45.66	4:46.69
280	4:47.72	4:48.75	4:49.78	4:50.81	4:51.84	4:52.87	4:53.91	4:54.94	4:55.97	4:57.00
290	4:58.03	4:59.06	5:00.09	5:01.13	5:02.16	5:03.19	5:04.22	5:05.25	5:06.28	5:07.31
300	5:08.34	5:09.38	5:10.41	5:11.44	5:12.47	5:13.50	5:14.53	5:15.56	5:16.59	5:17.63
310	5:18.66	5:19.69	5:20.72	5:21.75	5:22.78	5:23.81	5:24.84	5:25.88	5:26.91	5:27.94
320	5:28.97	5:30.00	5:31.03	5:32.06	5:33.09	5:34.12	5:35.16	5:36.19	5:37.22	5:38.25
330	5:39.28	5:40.31	5:41.34	5:42.38	5:43.41	5:44.44	5:45.47	5:46.50	5:47.53	5:48.56
340	5:49.59	5:50.63	5:51.66	5:52.69	5:53.72	5:54.75	5:55.78	5:56.81	5:57.84	5:58.88
350	5:59.91	6:00.94	6:01.97	6:03.00	6:04.03	6:05.06	6:06.09	6:07.13	6:08.16	6:09.19
360	6:10.22	6:11.25	6:12.28	6:13.31	6:14.34	6:15.37	6:16.41	6:17.44	6:18.47	6:19.50
370	6:20.53	6:21.56	6:22.59	6:23.63	6:24.66	6:25.69	6:26.72	6:27.75	6:28.78	6:29.81
380	6:30.84	6:31.88	6:32.91	6:33.94	6:34.97	6:36.00	6:37.03	6:38.06	6:39.09	6:40.13
390	6:41.16	6:42.19	6:43.22	6:44.25	6:45.28	6:46.31	6:47.34	6:48.38	6:49.41	6:50.44
400	6:51.47	6:52.50	6:53.53	6:54.56	6:55.59	6:56.63	6:57.66	6:58.69	6:59.72	7:00.75
410	7:01.78	7:02.81	7:03.84	7:04.88	7:05.91	7:06.94	7:07.97	7:09.00	7:10.03	7:11.06
420	7:12.09	7:13.13	7:14.16	7:15.19	7:16.22	7:17.25	7:18.28	7:19.31	7:20.34	7:21.38
430	7:22.41	7:23.44	7:24.47	7:25.50	7:26.53	7:27.56	7:28.59	7:29.63	7:30.66	7:31.69
440	7:32.72	7:33.75	7:34.78	7:35.81	7:36.84	7:37.88	7:38.91	7:39.94	7:40.97	7:42.00
450	7:43.03	7:44.06	7:45.09	7:46.13	7:47.16	7:48.19	7:49.22	7:50.25	7:51.28	7:52.31
460	7:53.34	7:54.38	7:55.41	7:56.44	7:57.47	7:58.50	7:59.53	8:00.56	8:01.59	8:02.62
470	8:03.66	8:04.69	8:05.72	8:06.75	8:07.78	8:08.81	8:09.84	8:10.88	8:11.91	8:12.94
480	8:13.97	8:15.00	8:16.03	8:17.06	8:18.09	8:19.13	8:20.16	8:21.19	8:22.22	8:23.25
490	8:24.28	8:25.31	8:26.34	8:27.38	8:28.41	8:29.44	8:30.47	8:31.50	8:32.53	8:33.56
500	8:34.59	8:35.63	8:36.66	8:37.69	8:38.72	8:39.75	8:40.78	8:41.81	8:42.84	8:43.87
510	8:44.91	8:45.94	8:46.97	8:48.00	8:49.03	8:50.06	8:51.09	8:52.13	8:53.16	8:54.19
520	8:55.22	8:56.25	8:57.28	8:58.31	8:59.34	9:00.38	9:01.41	9:02.44	9:03.47	9:04.50
530	9:05.53	9:06.56	9:07.59	9:08.63	9:09.66	9:10.69	9:11.72	9:12.75	9:13.78	9:14.81
540	9:15.84	9:16.88	9:17.91	9:18.94	9:19.97	9:21.00	9:22.03	9:23.06	9:24.09	9:25.12
550	9:26.16	9:27.19	9:28.22	9:29.25	9:30.28	9:31.31	9:32.34	9:33.38	9:34.41	9:35.44
560	9:36.47	9:37.50	9:38.53	9:39.56	9:40.59	9:41.63	9:42.66	9:43.69	9:44.72	9:45.75
570	9:46.78	9:47.81	9:48.84	9:49.88	9:50.91	9:51.94	9:52.97	9:54.00	9:55.03	9:56.06
580	9:57.09	9:58.13	9:59.16	10:00.19	10:01.22	10:02.25	10:03.28	10:04.31	10:05.34	10:06.37
590	10:07.41	10:08.44	10:09.47	10:10.50	10:11.53	10:12.56	10:13.59	10:14.63	10:15.66	10:16.69

𝅗𝅥. = 1.55; ♩ = 1.03; ♪. = 0.77; (triplet ♩ 𝄾) = 0.69; ♪ = 0.52; (triplet ♪ 𝄾 𝄾) = 0.34; 𝅘𝅥𝅯 = 0.26 seconds

CLICK: 24⅞ FRAMES; M.M.: 57.89

Click	0	1	2	3	4	5	6	7	8	9
000	0:00.00	0:00.00	0:01.04	0:02.07	0:03.11	0:04.15	0:05.18	0:06.22	0:07.26	0:08.29
010	0:09.33	0:10.36	0:11.40	0:12.44	0:13.47	0:14.51	0:15.55	0:16.58	0:17.62	0:18.66
020	0:19.69	0:20.73	0:21.77	0:22.80	0:23.84	0:24.88	0:25.91	0:26.95	0:27.98	0:29.02
030	0:30.06	0:31.09	0:32.13	0:33.17	0:34.20	0:35.24	0:36.28	0:37.31	0:38.35	0:39.39
040	0:40.42	0:41.46	0:42.49	0:43.53	0:44.57	0:45.60	0:46.64	0:47.68	0:48.71	0:49.75
050	0:50.79	0:51.82	0:52.86	0:53.90	0:54.93	0:55.97	0:57.01	0:58.04	0:59.08	1:00.11
060	1:01.15	1:02.19	1:03.22	1:04.26	1:05.30	1:06.33	1:07.37	1:08.41	1:09.44	1:10.48
070	1:11.52	1:12.55	1:13.59	1:14.62	1:15.66	1:16.70	1:17.73	1:18.77	1:19.81	1:20.84
080	1:21.88	1:22.92	1:23.95	1:24.99	1:26.03	1:27.06	1:28.10	1:29.14	1:30.17	1:31.21
090	1:32.24	1:33.28	1:34.32	1:35.35	1:36.39	1:37.43	1:38.46	1:39.50	1:40.54	1:41.57
100	1:42.61	1:43.65	1:44.68	1:45.72	1:46.76	1:47.79	1:48.83	1:49.86	1:50.90	1:51.94
110	1:52.97	1:54.01	1:55.05	1:56.08	1:57.12	1:58.16	1:59.19	2:00.23	2:01.27	2:02.30
120	2:03.34	2:04.38	2:05.41	2:06.45	2:07.48	2:08.52	2:09.56	2:10.59	2:11.63	2:12.67
130	2:13.70	2:14.74	2:15.78	2:16.81	2:17.85	2:18.89	2:19.92	2:20.96	2:21.99	2:23.03
140	2:24.07	2:25.10	2:26.14	2:27.18	2:28.21	2:29.25	2:30.29	2:31.32	2:32.36	2:33.40
150	2:34.43	2:35.47	2:36.51	2:37.54	2:38.58	2:39.61	2:40.65	2:41.69	2:42.72	2:43.76
160	2:44.80	2:45.83	2:46.87	2:47.91	2:48.94	2:49.98	2:51.02	2:52.05	2:53.09	2:54.13
170	2:55.16	2:56.20	2:57.23	2:58.27	2:59.31	3:00.34	3:01.38	3:02.42	3:03.45	3:04.49
180	3:05.53	3:06.56	3:07.60	3:08.64	3:09.67	3:10.71	3:11.74	3:12.78	3:13.82	3:14.85
190	3:15.89	3:16.93	3:17.96	3:19.00	3:20.04	3:21.07	3:22.11	3:23.15	3:24.18	3:25.22
200	3:26.26	3:27.29	3:28.33	3:29.36	3:30.40	3:31.44	3:32.47	3:33.51	3:34.55	3:35.58
210	3:36.62	3:37.66	3:38.69	3:39.73	3:40.77	3:41.80	3:42.84	3:43.88	3:44.91	3:45.95
220	3:46.98	3:48.02	3:49.06	3:50.09	3:51.13	3:52.17	3:53.20	3:54.24	3:55.28	3:56.31
230	3:57.35	3:58.39	3:59.42	4:00.46	4:01.49	4:02.53	4:03.57	4:04.60	4:05.64	4:06.68
240	4:07.71	4:08.75	4:09.79	4:10.82	4:11.86	4:12.90	4:13.93	4:14.97	4:16.01	4:17.04
250	4:18.08	4:19.11	4:20.15	4:21.19	4:22.22	4:23.26	4:24.30	4:25.33	4:26.37	4:27.41
260	4:28.44	4:29.48	4:30.52	4:31.55	4:32.59	4:33.63	4:34.66	4:35.70	4:36.73	4:37.77
270	4:38.81	4:39.84	4:40.88	4:41.92	4:42.95	4:43.99	4:45.03	4:46.06	4:47.10	4:48.14
280	4:49.17	4:50.21	4:51.24	4:52.28	4:53.32	4:54.35	4:55.39	4:56.43	4:57.46	4:58.50
290	4:59.54	5:00.57	5:01.61	5:02.65	5:03.68	5:04.72	5:05.76	5:06.79	5:07.83	5:08.86
300	5:09.90	5:10.94	5:11.97	5:13.01	5:14.05	5:15.08	5:16.12	5:17.16	5:18.19	5:19.23
310	5:20.27	5:21.30	5:22.34	5:23.37	5:24.41	5:25.45	5:26.48	5:27.52	5:28.56	5:29.59
320	5:30.63	5:31.67	5:32.70	5:33.74	5:34.78	5:35.81	5:36.85	5:37.89	5:38.92	5:39.96
330	5:40.99	5:42.03	5:43.07	5:44.10	5:45.14	5:46.18	5:47.21	5:48.25	5:49.29	5:50.32
340	5:51.36	5:52.40	5:53.43	5:54.47	5:55.51	5:56.54	5:57.58	5:58.61	5:59.65	6:00.69
350	6:01.72	6:02.76	6:03.80	6:04.83	6:05.87	6:06.91	6:07.94	6:08.98	6:10.02	6:11.05
360	6:12.09	6:13.13	6:14.16	6:15.20	6:16.23	6:17.27	6:18.31	6:19.34	6:20.38	6:21.42
370	6:22.45	6:23.49	6:24.53	6:25.56	6:26.60	6:27.64	6:28.67	6:29.71	6:30.74	6:31.78
380	6:32.82	6:33.85	6:34.89	6:35.93	6:36.96	6:38.00	6:39.04	6:40.07	6:41.11	6:42.15
390	6:43.18	6:44.22	6:45.26	6:46.29	6:47.33	6:48.36	6:49.40	6:50.44	6:51.47	6:52.51
400	6:53.55	6:54.58	6:55.62	6:56.66	6:57.69	6:58.73	6:59.77	7:00.80	7:01.84	7:02.87
410	7:03.91	7:04.95	7:05.98	7:07.02	7:08.06	7:09.09	7:10.13	7:11.17	7:12.20	7:13.24
420	7:14.28	7:15.31	7:16.35	7:17.39	7:18.42	7:19.46	7:20.49	7:21.53	7:22.57	7:23.60
430	7:24.64	7:25.68	7:26.71	7:27.75	7:28.79	7:29.82	7:30.86	7:31.90	7:32.93	7:33.97
440	7:35.01	7:36.04	7:37.08	7:38.11	7:39.15	7:40.19	7:41.22	7:42.26	7:43.30	7:44.33
450	7:45.37	7:46.41	7:47.44	7:48.48	7:49.52	7:50.55	7:51.59	7:52.63	7:53.66	7:54.70
460	7:55.73	7:56.77	7:57.81	7:58.84	7:59.88	8:00.92	8:01.95	8:02.99	8:04.03	8:05.06
470	8:06.10	8:07.14	8:08.17	8:09.21	8:10.24	8:11.28	8:12.32	8:13.35	8:14.39	8:15.43
480	8:16.46	8:17.50	8:18.54	8:19.57	8:20.61	8:21.65	8:22.68	8:23.72	8:24.76	8:25.79
490	8:26.83	8:27.86	8:28.90	8:29.94	8:30.97	8:32.01	8:33.05	8:34.08	8:35.12	8:36.16
500	8:37.19	8:38.23	8:39.27	8:40.30	8:41.34	8:42.38	8:43.41	8:44.45	8:45.48	8:46.52
510	8:47.56	8:48.59	8:49.63	8:50.67	8:51.70	8:52.74	8:53.78	8:54.81	8:55.85	8:56.89
520	8:57.92	8:58.96	8:59.99	9:01.03	9:02.07	9:03.10	9:04.14	9:05.18	9:06.21	9:07.25
530	9:08.29	9:09.32	9:10.36	9:11.40	9:12.43	9:13.47	9:14.51	9:15.54	9:16.58	9:17.61
540	9:18.65	9:19.69	9:20.72	9:21.76	9:22.80	9:23.83	9:24.87	9:25.91	9:26.94	9:27.98
550	9:29.02	9:30.05	9:31.09	9:32.12	9:33.16	9:34.20	9:35.23	9:36.27	9:37.31	9:38.34
560	9:39.38	9:40.42	9:41.45	9:42.49	9:43.53	9:44.56	9:45.60	9:46.64	9:47.67	9:48.71
570	9:49.74	9:50.78	9:51.82	9:52.85	9:53.89	9:54.93	9:55.96	9:57.00	9:58.04	9:59.07
580	10:00.11	10:01.15	10:02.18	10:03.22	10:04.26	10:05.29	10:06.33	10:07.36	10:08.40	10:09.44
590	10:10.47	10:11.51	10:12.55	10:13.58	10:14.62	10:15.66	10:16.69	10:17.73	10:18.77	10:19.80

♩. = 1.55; ♩ = 1.04; ♪. = 0.78; (triplet ♩ 𝄾) = 0.69; ♪ = 0.52; (triplet ♪ 𝄾 𝄾) = 0.35; 𝅘𝅥𝅯 = 0.26 seconds

CLICK: 25 0/8 FRAMES; M.M.: 57.60

Click	0	1	2	3	4	5	6	7	8	9
000	0:00.00	0:00.00	0:01.04	0:02.08	0:03.13	0:04.17	0:05.21	0:06.25	0:07.29	0:08.33
010	0:09.38	0:10.42	0:11.46	0:12.50	0:13.54	0:14.58	0:15.63	0:16.67	0:17.71	0:18.75
020	0:19.79	0:20.83	0:21.88	0:22.92	0:23.96	0:25.00	0:26.04	0:27.08	0:28.13	0:29.17
030	0:30.21	0:31.25	0:32.29	0:33.33	0:34.38	0:35.42	0:36.46	0:37.50	0:38.54	0:39.58
040	0:40.63	0:41.67	0:42.71	0:43.75	0:44.79	0:45.83	0:46.88	0:47.92	0:48.96	0:50.00
050	0:51.04	0:52.08	0:53.13	0:54.17	0:55.21	0:56.25	0:57.29	0:58.33	0:59.38	1:00.42
060	1:01.46	1:02.50	1:03.54	1:04.58	1:05.63	1:06.67	1:07.71	1:08.75	1:09.79	1:10.83
070	1:11.88	1:12.92	1:13.96	1:15.00	1:16.04	1:17.08	1:18.13	1:19.17	1:20.21	1:21.25
080	1:22.29	1:23.33	1:24.38	1:25.42	1:26.46	1:27.50	1:28.54	1:29.58	1:30.63	1:31.67
090	1:32.71	1:33.75	1:34.79	1:35.83	1:36.88	1:37.92	1:38.96	1:40.00	1:41.04	1:42.08
100	1:43.13	1:44.17	1:45.21	1:46.25	1:47.29	1:48.33	1:49.38	1:50.42	1:51.46	1:52.50
110	1:53.54	1:54.58	1:55.63	1:56.67	1:57.71	1:58.75	1:59.79	2:00.83	2:01.88	2:02.92
120	2:03.96	2:05.00	2:06.04	2:07.08	2:08.13	2:09.17	2:10.21	2:11.25	2:12.29	2:13.33
130	2:14.38	2:15.42	2:16.46	2:17.50	2:18.54	2:19.58	2:20.63	2:21.67	2:22.71	2:23.75
140	2:24.79	2:25.83	2:26.88	2:27.92	2:28.96	2:30.00	2:31.04	2:32.08	2:33.13	2:34.17
150	2:35.21	2:36.25	2:37.29	2:38.33	2:39.38	2:40.42	2:41.46	2:42.50	2:43.54	2:44.58
160	2:45.63	2:46.67	2:47.71	2:48.75	2:49.79	2:50.83	2:51.88	2:52.92	2:53.96	2:55.00
170	2:56.04	2:57.08	2:58.13	2:59.17	3:00.21	3:01.25	3:02.29	3:03.33	3:04.38	3:05.42
180	3:06.46	3:07.50	3:08.54	3:09.58	3:10.63	3:11.67	3:12.71	3:13.75	3:14.79	3:15.83
190	3:16.88	3:17.92	3:18.96	3:20.00	3:21.04	3:22.08	3:23.13	3:24.17	3:25.21	3:26.25
200	3:27.29	3:28.33	3:29.38	3:30.42	3:31.46	3:32.50	3:33.54	3:34.58	3:35.63	3:36.67
210	3:37.71	3:38.75	3:39.79	3:40.83	3:41.88	3:42.92	3:43.96	3:45.00	3:46.04	3:47.08
220	3:48.13	3:49.17	3:50.21	3:51.25	3:52.29	3:53.33	3:54.38	3:55.42	3:56.46	3:57.50
230	3:58.54	3:59.58	4:00.63	4:01.67	4:02.71	4:03.75	4:04.79	4:05.83	4:06.88	4:07.92
240	4:08.96	4:10.00	4:11.04	4:12.08	4:13.13	4:14.17	4:15.21	4:16.25	4:17.29	4:18.33
250	4:19.38	4:20.42	4:21.46	4:22.50	4:23.54	4:24.58	4:25.63	4:26.67	4:27.71	4:28.75
260	4:29.79	4:30.83	4:31.88	4:32.92	4:33.96	4:35.00	4:36.04	4:37.08	4:38.13	4:39.17
270	4:40.21	4:41.25	4:42.29	4:43.33	4:44.38	4:45.42	4:46.46	4:47.50	4:48.54	4:49.58
280	4:50.63	4:51.67	4:52.71	4:53.75	4:54.79	4:55.83	4:56.88	4:57.92	4:58.96	5:00.00
290	5:01.04	5:02.08	5:03.13	5:04.17	5:05.21	5:06.25	5:07.29	5:08.33	5:09.38	5:10.42
300	5:11.46	5:12.50	5:13.54	5:14.58	5:15.63	5:16.67	5:17.71	5:18.75	5:19.79	5:20.83
310	5:21.88	5:22.92	5:23.96	5:25.00	5:26.04	5:27.08	5:28.13	5:29.17	5:30.21	5:31.25
320	5:32.29	5:33.33	5:34.38	5:35.42	5:36.46	5:37.50	5:38.54	5:39.58	5:40.63	5:41.67
330	5:42.71	5:43.75	5:44.79	5:45.83	5:46.88	5:47.92	5:48.96	5:50.00	5:51.04	5:52.08
340	5:53.13	5:54.17	5:55.21	5:56.25	5:57.29	5:58.33	5:59.38	6:00.42	6:01.46	6:02.50
350	6:03.54	6:04.58	6:05.63	6:06.67	6:07.71	6:08.75	6:09.79	6:10.83	6:11.88	6:12.92
360	6:13.96	6:15.00	6:16.04	6:17.08	6:18.13	6:19.17	6:20.21	6:21.25	6:22.29	6:23.33
370	6:24.38	6:25.42	6:26.46	6:27.50	6:28.54	6:29.58	6:30.63	6:31.67	6:32.71	6:33.75
380	6:34.79	6:35.83	6:36.88	6:37.92	6:38.96	6:40.00	6:41.04	6:42.08	6:43.13	6:44.17
390	6:45.21	6:46.25	6:47.29	6:48.33	6:49.38	6:50.42	6:51.46	6:52.50	6:53.54	6:54.58
400	6:55.63	6:56.67	6:57.71	6:58.75	6:59.79	7:00.83	7:01.88	7:02.92	7:03.96	7:05.00
410	7:06.04	7:07.08	7:08.13	7:09.17	7:10.21	7:11.25	7:12.29	7:13.33	7:14.38	7:15.42
420	7:16.46	7:17.50	7:18.54	7:19.58	7:20.63	7:21.67	7:22.71	7:23.75	7:24.79	7:25.83
430	7:26.88	7:27.92	7:28.96	7:30.00	7:31.04	7:32.08	7:33.13	7:34.17	7:35.21	7:36.25
440	7:37.29	7:38.33	7:39.38	7:40.42	7:41.46	7:42.50	7:43.54	7:44.58	7:45.63	7:46.67
450	7:47.71	7:48.75	7:49.79	7:50.83	7:51.88	7:52.92	7:53.96	7:55.00	7:56.04	7:57.08
460	7:58.13	7:59.17	8:00.21	8:01.25	8:02.29	8:03.33	8:04.38	8:05.42	8:06.46	8:07.50
470	8:08.54	8:09.58	8:10.63	8:11.67	8:12.71	8:13.75	8:14.79	8:15.83	8:16.88	8:17.92
480	8:18.96	8:20.00	8:21.04	8:22.08	8:23.13	8:24.17	8:25.21	8:26.25	8:27.29	8:28.33
490	8:29.38	8:30.42	8:31.46	8:32.50	8:33.54	8:34.58	8:35.63	8:36.67	8:37.71	8:38.75
500	8:39.79	8:40.83	8:41.88	8:42.92	8:43.96	8:45.00	8:46.04	8:47.08	8:48.13	8:49.17
510	8:50.21	8:51.25	8:52.29	8:53.33	8:54.38	8:55.42	8:56.46	8:57.50	8:58.54	8:59.58
520	9:00.63	9:01.67	9:02.71	9:03.75	9:04.79	9:05.83	9:06.88	9:07.92	9:08.96	9:10.00
530	9:11.04	9:12.08	9:13.13	9:14.17	9:15.21	9:16.25	9:17.29	9:18.33	9:19.38	9:20.42
540	9:21.46	9:22.50	9:23.54	9:24.58	9:25.63	9:26.67	9:27.71	9:28.75	9:29.79	9:30.83
550	9:31.88	9:32.92	9:33.96	9:35.00	9:36.04	9:37.08	9:38.13	9:39.17	9:40.21	9:41.25
560	9:42.29	9:43.33	9:44.38	9:45.42	9:46.46	9:47.50	9:48.54	9:49.58	9:50.63	9:51.67
570	9:52.71	9:53.75	9:54.79	9:55.83	9:56.88	9:57.92	9:58.96	10:00.00	10:01.04	10:02.08
580	10:03.13	10:04.17	10:05.21	10:06.25	10:07.29	10:08.33	10:09.38	10:10.42	10:11.46	10:12.50
590	10:13.54	10:14.58	10:15.63	10:16.67	10:17.71	10:18.75	10:19.79	10:20.83	10:21.88	10:22.92

♩. = 1.56; ♩ = 1.04; ♪. = 0.78; ♩ 𝄾 (triplet) = 0.69; ♪ = 0.52; ♪ 𝄾 𝄾 (triplet) = 0.35; 𝅘𝅥𝅯 = 0.26 seconds

CLICK: 25⅛ FRAMES; M.M.: 57.31

Click	0	1	2	3	4	5	6	7	8	9
000	0:00.00	0:00.00	0:01.05	0:02.09	0:03.14	0:04.19	0:05.23	0:06.28	0:07.33	0:08.38
010	0:09.42	0:10.47	0:11.52	0:12.56	0:13.61	0:14.66	0:15.70	0:16.75	0:17.80	0:18.84
020	0:19.89	0:20.94	0:21.98	0:23.03	0:24.08	0:25.13	0:26.17	0:27.22	0:28.27	0:29.31
030	0:30.36	0:31.41	0:32.45	0:33.50	0:34.55	0:35.59	0:36.64	0:37.69	0:38.73	0:39.78
040	0:40.83	0:41.88	0:42.92	0:43.97	0:45.02	0:46.06	0:47.11	0:48.16	0:49.20	0:50.25
050	0:51.30	0:52.34	0:53.39	0:54.44	0:55.48	0:56.53	0:57.58	0:58.63	0:59.67	1:00.72
060	1:01.77	1:02.81	1:03.86	1:04.91	1:05.95	1:07.00	1:08.05	1:09.09	1:10.14	1:11.19
070	1:12.23	1:13.28	1:14.33	1:15.38	1:16.42	1:17.47	1:18.52	1:19.56	1:20.61	1:21.66
080	1:22.70	1:23.75	1:24.80	1:25.84	1:26.89	1:27.94	1:28.98	1:30.03	1:31.08	1:32.13
090	1:33.17	1:34.22	1:35.27	1:36.31	1:37.36	1:38.41	1:39.45	1:40.50	1:41.55	1:42.59
100	1:43.64	1:44.69	1:45.73	1:46.78	1:47.83	1:48.88	1:49.92	1:50.97	1:52.02	1:53.06
110	1:54.11	1:55.16	1:56.20	1:57.25	1:58.30	1:59.34	2:00.39	2:01.44	2:02.48	2:03.53
120	2:04.58	2:05.63	2:06.67	2:07.72	2:08.77	2:09.81	2:10.86	2:11.91	2:12.95	2:14.00
130	2:15.05	2:16.09	2:17.14	2:18.19	2:19.23	2:20.28	2:21.33	2:22.38	2:23.42	2:24.47
140	2:25.52	2:26.56	2:27.61	2:28.66	2:29.70	2:30.75	2:31.80	2:32.84	2:33.89	2:34.94
150	2:35.98	2:37.03	2:38.08	2:39.13	2:40.17	2:41.22	2:42.27	2:43.31	2:44.36	2:45.41
160	2:46.45	2:47.50	2:48.55	2:49.59	2:50.64	2:51.69	2:52.73	2:53.78	2:54.83	2:55.88
170	2:56.92	2:57.97	2:59.02	3:00.06	3:01.11	3:02.16	3:03.20	3:04.25	3:05.30	3:06.34
180	3:07.39	3:08.44	3:09.48	3:10.53	3:11.58	3:12.63	3:13.67	3:14.72	3:15.77	3:16.81
190	3:17.86	3:18.91	3:19.95	3:21.00	3:22.05	3:23.09	3:24.14	3:25.19	3:26.23	3:27.28
200	3:28.33	3:29.37	3:30.42	3:31.47	3:32.52	3:33.56	3:34.61	3:35.66	3:36.70	3:37.75
210	3:38.80	3:39.84	3:40.89	3:41.94	3:42.98	3:44.03	3:45.08	3:46.12	3:47.17	3:48.22
220	3:49.27	3:50.31	3:51.36	3:52.41	3:53.45	3:54.50	3:55.55	3:56.59	3:57.64	3:58.69
230	3:59.73	4:00.78	4:01.83	4:02.88	4:03.92	4:04.97	4:06.02	4:07.06	4:08.11	4:09.16
240	4:10.20	4:11.25	4:12.30	4:13.34	4:14.39	4:15.44	4:16.48	4:17.53	4:18.58	4:19.63
250	4:20.67	4:21.72	4:22.77	4:23.81	4:24.86	4:25.91	4:26.95	4:28.00	4:29.05	4:30.09
260	4:31.14	4:32.19	4:33.23	4:34.28	4:35.33	4:36.37	4:37.42	4:38.47	4:39.52	4:40.56
270	4:41.61	4:42.66	4:43.70	4:44.75	4:45.80	4:46.84	4:47.89	4:48.94	4:49.98	4:51.03
280	4:52.08	4:53.12	4:54.17	4:55.22	4:56.27	4:57.31	4:58.36	4:59.41	5:00.45	5:01.50
290	5:02.55	5:03.59	5:04.64	5:05.69	5:06.73	5:07.78	5:08.83	5:09.87	5:10.92	5:11.97
300	5:13.02	5:14.06	5:15.11	5:16.16	5:17.20	5:18.25	5:19.30	5:20.34	5:21.39	5:22.44
310	5:23.48	5:24.53	5:25.58	5:26.62	5:27.67	5:28.72	5:29.77	5:30.81	5:31.86	5:32.91
320	5:33.95	5:35.00	5:36.05	5:37.09	5:38.14	5:39.19	5:40.23	5:41.28	5:42.33	5:43.37
330	5:44.42	5:45.47	5:46.52	5:47.56	5:48.61	5:49.66	5:50.70	5:51.75	5:52.80	5:53.84
340	5:54.89	5:55.94	5:56.98	5:58.03	5:59.08	6:00.12	6:01.17	6:02.22	6:03.27	6:04.31
350	6:05.36	6:06.41	6:07.45	6:08.50	6:09.55	6:10.59	6:11.64	6:12.69	6:13.73	6:14.78
360	6:15.83	6:16.88	6:17.92	6:18.97	6:20.02	6:21.06	6:22.11	6:23.16	6:24.20	6:25.25
370	6:26.30	6:27.34	6:28.39	6:29.44	6:30.48	6:31.53	6:32.58	6:33.63	6:34.67	6:35.72
380	6:36.77	6:37.81	6:38.86	6:39.91	6:40.95	6:42.00	6:43.05	6:44.09	6:45.14	6:46.19
390	6:47.23	6:48.28	6:49.33	6:50.38	6:51.42	6:52.47	6:53.52	6:54.56	6:55.61	6:56.66
400	6:57.70	6:58.75	6:59.80	7:00.84	7:01.89	7:02.94	7:03.98	7:05.03	7:06.08	7:07.13
410	7:08.17	7:09.22	7:10.27	7:11.31	7:12.36	7:13.41	7:14.45	7:15.50	7:16.55	7:17.59
420	7:18.64	7:19.69	7:20.73	7:21.78	7:22.83	7:23.88	7:24.92	7:25.97	7:27.02	7:28.06
430	7:29.11	7:30.16	7:31.20	7:32.25	7:33.30	7:34.34	7:35.39	7:36.44	7:37.48	7:38.53
440	7:39.58	7:40.63	7:41.67	7:42.72	7:43.77	7:44.81	7:45.86	7:46.91	7:47.95	7:49.00
450	7:50.05	7:51.09	7:52.14	7:53.19	7:54.23	7:55.28	7:56.33	7:57.38	7:58.42	7:59.47
460	8:00.52	8:01.56	8:02.61	8:03.66	8:04.70	8:05.75	8:06.80	8:07.84	8:08.89	8:09.94
470	8:10.98	8:12.03	8:13.08	8:14.12	8:15.17	8:16.22	8:17.27	8:18.31	8:19.36	8:20.41
480	8:21.45	8:22.50	8:23.55	8:24.59	8:25.64	8:26.69	8:27.73	8:28.78	8:29.83	8:30.88
490	8:31.92	8:32.97	8:34.02	8:35.06	8:36.11	8:37.16	8:38.20	8:39.25	8:40.30	8:41.34
500	8:42.39	8:43.44	8:44.48	8:45.53	8:46.58	8:47.62	8:48.67	8:49.72	8:50.77	8:51.81
510	8:52.86	8:53.91	8:54.95	8:56.00	8:57.05	8:58.09	8:59.14	9:00.19	9:01.23	9:02.28
520	9:03.33	9:04.38	9:05.42	9:06.47	9:07.52	9:08.56	9:09.61	9:10.66	9:11.70	9:12.75
530	9:13.80	9:14.84	9:15.89	9:16.94	9:17.98	9:19.03	9:20.08	9:21.12	9:22.17	9:23.22
540	9:24.27	9:25.31	9:26.36	9:27.41	9:28.45	9:29.50	9:30.55	9:31.59	9:32.64	9:33.69
550	9:34.73	9:35.78	9:36.83	9:37.88	9:38.92	9:39.97	9:41.02	9:42.06	9:43.11	9:44.16
560	9:45.20	9:46.25	9:47.30	9:48.34	9:49.39	9:50.44	9:51.48	9:52.53	9:53.58	9:54.62
570	9:55.67	9:56.72	9:57.77	9:58.81	9:59.86	10:00.91	10:01.95	10:03.00	10:04.05	10:05.09
580	10:06.14	10:07.19	10:08.23	10:09.28	10:10.33	10:11.38	10:12.42	10:13.47	10:14.52	10:15.56
590	10:16.61	10:17.66	10:18.70	10:19.75	10:20.80	10:21.84	10:22.89	10:23.94	10:24.98	10:26.03

♩. = 1.57; ♩ = 1.05; ♪. = 0.79; (3: ♩ 𝄾) = 0.70; ♪ = 0.52; (3: ♪ 𝄾 𝄾) = 0.35; 𝅘𝅥𝅯 = 0.26 seconds

CLICK: 25 2/8 FRAMES; M.M.: 57.03

Click	0	1	2	3	4	5	6	7	8	9
000	0:00.00	0:00.00	0:01.05	0:02.10	0:03.16	0:04.21	0:05.26	0:06.31	0:07.36	0:08.42
010	0:09.47	0:10.52	0:11.57	0:12.63	0:13.68	0:14.73	0:15.78	0:16.83	0:17.89	0:18.94
020	0:19.99	0:21.04	0:22.09	0:23.15	0:24.20	0:25.25	0:26.30	0:27.35	0:28.41	0:29.46
030	0:30.51	0:31.56	0:32.61	0:33.67	0:34.72	0:35.77	0:36.82	0:37.88	0:38.93	0:39.98
040	0:41.03	0:42.08	0:43.14	0:44.19	0:45.24	0:46.29	0:47.34	0:48.40	0:49.45	0:50.50
050	0:51.55	0:52.60	0:53.66	0:54.71	0:55.76	0:56.81	0:57.86	0:58.92	0:59.97	1:01.02
060	1:02.07	1:03.13	1:04.18	1:05.23	1:06.28	1:07.33	1:08.39	1:09.44	1:10.49	1:11.54
070	1:12.59	1:13.65	1:14.70	1:15.75	1:16.80	1:17.85	1:18.91	1:19.96	1:21.01	1:22.06
080	1:23.11	1:24.17	1:25.22	1:26.27	1:27.32	1:28.38	1:29.43	1:30.48	1:31.53	1:32.58
090	1:33.64	1:34.69	1:35.74	1:36.79	1:37.84	1:38.90	1:39.95	1:41.00	1:42.05	1:43.10
100	1:44.16	1:45.21	1:46.26	1:47.31	1:48.36	1:49.42	1:50.47	1:51.52	1:52.57	1:53.63
110	1:54.68	1:55.73	1:56.78	1:57.83	1:58.89	1:59.94	2:00.99	2:02.04	2:03.09	2:04.15
120	2:05.20	2:06.25	2:07.30	2:08.35	2:09.41	2:10.46	2:11.51	2:12.56	2:13.61	2:14.67
130	2:15.72	2:16.77	2:17.82	2:18.88	2:19.93	2:20.98	2:22.03	2:23.08	2:24.14	2:25.19
140	2:26.24	2:27.29	2:28.34	2:29.40	2:30.45	2:31.50	2:32.55	2:33.60	2:34.66	2:35.71
150	2:36.76	2:37.81	2:38.86	2:39.92	2:40.97	2:42.02	2:43.07	2:44.13	2:45.18	2:46.23
160	2:47.28	2:48.33	2:49.39	2:50.44	2:51.49	2:52.54	2:53.59	2:54.65	2:55.70	2:56.75
170	2:57.80	2:58.85	2:59.91	3:00.96	3:02.01	3:03.06	3:04.11	3:05.17	3:06.22	3:07.27
180	3:08.32	3:09.38	3:10.43	3:11.48	3:12.53	3:13.58	3:14.64	3:15.69	3:16.74	3:17.79
190	3:18.84	3:19.90	3:20.95	3:22.00	3:23.05	3:24.10	3:25.16	3:26.21	3:27.26	3:28.31
200	3:29.36	3:30.42	3:31.47	3:32.52	3:33.57	3:34.63	3:35.68	3:36.73	3:37.78	3:38.83
210	3:39.89	3:40.94	3:41.99	3:43.04	3:44.09	3:45.15	3:46.20	3:47.25	3:48.30	3:49.35
220	3:50.41	3:51.46	3:52.51	3:53.56	3:54.61	3:55.67	3:56.72	3:57.77	3:58.82	3:59.88
230	4:00.93	4:01.98	4:03.03	4:04.08	4:05.14	4:06.19	4:07.24	4:08.29	4:09.34	4:10.40
240	4:11.45	4:12.50	4:13.55	4:14.60	4:15.66	4:16.71	4:17.76	4:18.81	4:19.86	4:20.92
250	4:21.97	4:23.02	4:24.07	4:25.13	4:26.18	4:27.23	4:28.28	4:29.33	4:30.39	4:31.44
260	4:32.49	4:33.54	4:34.59	4:35.65	4:36.70	4:37.75	4:38.80	4:39.85	4:40.91	4:41.96
270	4:43.01	4:44.06	4:45.11	4:46.17	4:47.22	4:48.27	4:49.32	4:50.38	4:51.43	4:52.48
280	4:53.53	4:54.58	4:55.64	4:56.69	4:57.74	4:58.79	4:59.84	5:00.90	5:01.95	5:03.00
290	5:04.05	5:05.10	5:06.16	5:07.21	5:08.26	5:09.31	5:10.36	5:11.42	5:12.47	5:13.52
300	5:14.57	5:15.63	5:16.68	5:17.73	5:18.78	5:19.83	5:20.89	5:21.94	5:22.99	5:24.04
310	5:25.09	5:26.15	5:27.20	5:28.25	5:29.30	5:30.35	5:31.41	5:32.46	5:33.51	5:34.56
320	5:35.61	5:36.67	5:37.72	5:38.77	5:39.82	5:40.88	5:41.93	5:42.98	5:44.03	5:45.08
330	5:46.14	5:47.19	5:48.24	5:49.29	5:50.34	5:51.40	5:52.45	5:53.50	5:54.55	5:55.60
340	5:56.66	5:57.71	5:58.76	5:59.81	6:00.86	6:01.92	6:02.97	6:04.02	6:05.07	6:06.13
350	6:07.18	6:08.23	6:09.28	6:10.33	6:11.39	6:12.44	6:13.49	6:14.54	6:15.59	6:16.65
360	6:17.70	6:18.75	6:19.80	6:20.85	6:21.91	6:22.96	6:24.01	6:25.06	6:26.11	6:27.17
370	6:28.22	6:29.27	6:30.32	6:31.38	6:32.43	6:33.48	6:34.53	6:35.58	6:36.64	6:37.69
380	6:38.74	6:39.79	6:40.84	6:41.90	6:42.95	6:44.00	6:45.05	6:46.10	6:47.16	6:48.21
390	6:49.26	6:50.31	6:51.36	6:52.42	6:53.47	6:54.52	6:55.57	6:56.63	6:57.68	6:58.73
400	6:59.78	7:00.83	7:01.89	7:02.94	7:03.99	7:05.04	7:06.09	7:07.15	7:08.20	7:09.25
410	7:10.30	7:11.35	7:12.41	7:13.46	7:14.51	7:15.56	7:16.61	7:17.67	7:18.72	7:19.77
420	7:20.82	7:21.88	7:22.93	7:23.98	7:25.03	7:26.08	7:27.14	7:28.19	7:29.24	7:30.29
430	7:31.34	7:32.40	7:33.45	7:34.50	7:35.55	7:36.60	7:37.66	7:38.71	7:39.76	7:40.81
440	7:41.86	7:42.92	7:43.97	7:45.02	7:46.07	7:47.13	7:48.18	7:49.23	7:50.28	7:51.33
450	7:52.39	7:53.44	7:54.49	7:55.54	7:56.59	7:57.65	7:58.70	7:59.75	8:00.80	8:01.85
460	8:02.91	8:03.96	8:05.01	8:06.06	8:07.11	8:08.17	8:09.22	8:10.27	8:11.32	8:12.38
470	8:13.43	8:14.48	8:15.53	8:16.58	8:17.64	8:18.69	8:19.74	8:20.79	8:21.84	8:22.90
480	8:23.95	8:25.00	8:26.05	8:27.10	8:28.16	8:29.21	8:30.26	8:31.31	8:32.36	8:33.42
490	8:34.47	8:35.52	8:36.57	8:37.63	8:38.68	8:39.73	8:40.78	8:41.83	8:42.89	8:43.94
500	8:44.99	8:46.04	8:47.09	8:48.15	8:49.20	8:50.25	8:51.30	8:52.35	8:53.41	8:54.46
510	8:55.51	8:56.56	8:57.61	8:58.67	8:59.72	9:00.77	9:01.82	9:02.88	9:03.93	9:04.98
520	9:06.03	9:07.08	9:08.14	9:09.19	9:10.24	9:11.29	9:12.34	9:13.40	9:14.45	9:15.50
530	9:16.55	9:17.60	9:18.66	9:19.71	9:20.76	9:21.81	9:22.86	9:23.92	9:24.97	9:26.02
540	9:27.07	9:28.13	9:29.18	9:30.23	9:31.28	9:32.33	9:33.39	9:34.44	9:35.49	9:36.54
550	9:37.59	9:38.65	9:39.70	9:40.75	9:41.80	9:42.85	9:43.91	9:44.96	9:46.01	9:47.06
560	9:48.11	9:49.17	9:50.22	9:51.27	9:52.32	9:53.38	9:54.43	9:55.48	9:56.53	9:57.58
570	9:58.64	9:59.69	10:00.74	10:01.79	10:02.84	10:03.90	10:04.95	10:06.00	10:07.05	10:08.10
580	10:09.16	10:10.21	10:11.26	10:12.31	10:13.36	10:14.42	10:15.47	10:16.52	10:17.57	10:18.63
590	10:19.68	10:20.73	10:21.78	10:22.83	10:23.89	10:24.94	10:25.99	10:27.04	10:28.09	10:29.15

♩. = 1.58; ♩ = 1.05; ♪. = 0.79; (3) ♩ 𝄾 = 0.70; ♪ = 0.53; (3) ♪𝄾𝄾 = 0.35; 𝅘𝅥𝅯 = 0.26 seconds

CLICK: 25⅜ FRAMES; M.M.: 56.75

Click	0	1	2	3	4	5	6	7	8	9
000	0:00.00	0:00.00	0:01.06	0:02.11	0:03.17	0:04.23	0:05.29	0:06.34	0:07.40	0:08.46
010	0:09.52	0:10.57	0:11.63	0:12.69	0:13.74	0:14.80	0:15.86	0:16.92	0:17.97	0:19.03
020	0:20.09	0:21.15	0:22.20	0:23.26	0:24.32	0:25.38	0:26.43	0:27.49	0:28.55	0:29.60
030	0:30.66	0:31.72	0:32.78	0:33.83	0:34.89	0:35.95	0:37.01	0:38.06	0:39.12	0:40.18
040	0:41.23	0:42.29	0:43.35	0:44.41	0:45.46	0:46.52	0:47.58	0:48.64	0:49.69	0:50.75
050	0:51.81	0:52.86	0:53.92	0:54.98	0:56.04	0:57.09	0:58.15	0:59.21	1:00.27	1:01.32
060	1:02.38	1:03.44	1:04.49	1:05.55	1:06.61	1:07.67	1:08.72	1:09.78	1:10.84	1:11.90
070	1:12.95	1:14.01	1:15.07	1:16.13	1:17.18	1:18.24	1:19.30	1:20.35	1:21.41	1:22.47
080	1:23.53	1:24.58	1:25.64	1:26.70	1:27.76	1:28.81	1:29.87	1:30.93	1:31.98	1:33.04
090	1:34.10	1:35.16	1:36.21	1:37.27	1:38.33	1:39.39	1:40.44	1:41.50	1:42.56	1:43.61
100	1:44.67	1:45.73	1:46.79	1:47.84	1:48.90	1:49.96	1:51.02	1:52.07	1:53.13	1:54.19
110	1:55.24	1:56.30	1:57.36	1:58.42	1:59.47	2:00.53	2:01.59	2:02.65	2:03.70	2:04.76
120	2:05.82	2:06.88	2:07.93	2:08.99	2:10.05	2:11.10	2:12.16	2:13.22	2:14.28	2:15.33
130	2:16.39	2:17.45	2:18.51	2:19.56	2:20.62	2:21.68	2:22.73	2:23.79	2:24.85	2:25.91
140	2:26.96	2:28.02	2:29.08	2:30.14	2:31.19	2:32.25	2:33.31	2:34.36	2:35.42	2:36.48
150	2:37.54	2:38.59	2:39.65	2:40.71	2:41.77	2:42.82	2:43.88	2:44.94	2:45.99	2:47.05
160	2:48.11	2:49.17	2:50.22	2:51.28	2:52.34	2:53.40	2:54.45	2:55.51	2:56.57	2:57.63
170	2:58.68	2:59.74	3:00.80	3:01.85	3:02.91	3:03.97	3:05.03	3:06.08	3:07.14	3:08.20
180	3:09.26	3:10.31	3:11.37	3:12.43	3:13.48	3:14.54	3:15.60	3:16.66	3:17.71	3:18.77
190	3:19.83	3:20.89	3:21.94	3:23.00	3:24.06	3:25.11	3:26.17	3:27.23	3:28.29	3:29.34
200	3:30.40	3:31.46	3:32.52	3:33.57	3:34.63	3:35.69	3:36.74	3:37.80	3:38.86	3:39.92
210	3:40.97	3:42.03	3:43.09	3:44.15	3:45.20	3:46.26	3:47.32	3:48.38	3:49.43	3:50.49
220	3:51.55	3:52.60	3:53.66	3:54.72	3:55.78	3:56.83	3:57.89	3:58.95	4:00.01	4:01.06
230	4:02.12	4:03.18	4:04.23	4:05.29	4:06.35	4:07.41	4:08.46	4:09.52	4:10.58	4:11.64
240	4:12.69	4:13.75	4:14.81	4:15.86	4:16.92	4:17.98	4:19.04	4:20.09	4:21.15	4:22.21
250	4:23.27	4:24.32	4:25.38	4:26.44	4:27.49	4:28.55	4:29.61	4:30.67	4:31.72	4:32.78
260	4:33.84	4:34.90	4:35.95	4:37.01	4:38.07	4:39.13	4:40.18	4:41.24	4:42.30	4:43.35
270	4:44.41	4:45.47	4:46.53	4:47.58	4:48.64	4:49.70	4:50.76	4:51.81	4:52.87	4:53.93
280	4:54.98	4:56.04	4:57.10	4:58.16	4:59.21	5:00.27	5:01.33	5:02.39	5:03.44	5:04.50
290	5:05.56	5:06.61	5:07.67	5:08.73	5:09.79	5:10.84	5:11.90	5:12.96	5:14.02	5:15.07
300	5:16.13	5:17.19	5:18.24	5:19.30	5:20.36	5:21.42	5:22.47	5:23.53	5:24.59	5:25.65
310	5:26.70	5:27.76	5:28.82	5:29.88	5:30.93	5:31.99	5:33.05	5:34.10	5:35.16	5:36.22
320	5:37.28	5:38.33	5:39.39	5:40.45	5:41.51	5:42.56	5:43.62	5:44.68	5:45.73	5:46.79
330	5:47.85	5:48.91	5:49.96	5:51.02	5:52.08	5:53.14	5:54.19	5:55.25	5:56.31	5:57.36
340	5:58.42	5:59.48	6:00.54	6:01.59	6:02.65	6:03.71	6:04.77	6:05.82	6:06.88	6:07.94
350	6:08.99	6:10.05	6:11.11	6:12.17	6:13.22	6:14.28	6:15.34	6:16.40	6:17.45	6:18.51
360	6:19.57	6:20.63	6:21.68	6:22.74	6:23.80	6:24.85	6:25.91	6:26.97	6:28.03	6:29.08
370	6:30.14	6:31.20	6:32.26	6:33.31	6:34.37	6:35.43	6:36.48	6:37.54	6:38.60	6:39.66
380	6:40.71	6:41.77	6:42.83	6:43.89	6:44.94	6:46.00	6:47.06	6:48.11	6:49.17	6:50.23
390	6:51.29	6:52.34	6:53.40	6:54.46	6:55.52	6:56.57	6:57.63	6:58.69	6:59.74	7:00.80
400	7:01.86	7:02.92	7:03.97	7:05.03	7:06.09	7:07.15	7:08.20	7:09.26	7:10.32	7:11.38
410	7:12.43	7:13.49	7:14.55	7:15.60	7:16.66	7:17.72	7:18.78	7:19.83	7:20.89	7:21.95
420	7:23.01	7:24.06	7:25.12	7:26.18	7:27.23	7:28.29	7:29.35	7:30.41	7:31.46	7:32.52
430	7:33.58	7:34.64	7:35.69	7:36.75	7:37.81	7:38.86	7:39.92	7:40.98	7:42.04	7:43.09
440	7:44.15	7:45.21	7:46.27	7:47.32	7:48.38	7:49.44	7:50.49	7:51.55	7:52.61	7:53.67
450	7:54.72	7:55.78	7:56.84	7:57.90	7:58.95	8:00.01	8:01.07	8:02.12	8:03.18	8:04.24
460	8:05.30	8:06.35	8:07.41	8:08.47	8:09.53	8:10.58	8:11.64	8:12.70	8:13.76	8:14.81
470	8:15.87	8:16.93	8:17.98	8:19.04	8:20.10	8:21.16	8:22.21	8:23.27	8:24.33	8:25.39
480	8:26.44	8:27.50	8:28.56	8:29.61	8:30.67	8:31.73	8:32.79	8:33.84	8:34.90	8:35.96
490	8:37.02	8:38.07	8:39.13	8:40.19	8:41.24	8:42.30	8:43.36	8:44.42	8:45.47	8:46.53
500	8:47.59	8:48.65	8:49.70	8:50.76	8:51.82	8:52.88	8:53.93	8:54.99	8:56.05	8:57.10
510	8:58.16	8:59.22	9:00.28	9:01.33	9:02.39	9:03.45	9:04.51	9:05.56	9:06.62	9:07.68
520	9:08.73	9:09.79	9:10.85	9:11.91	9:12.96	9:14.02	9:15.08	9:16.14	9:17.19	9:18.25
530	9:19.31	9:20.36	9:21.42	9:22.48	9:23.54	9:24.59	9:25.65	9:26.71	9:27.77	9:28.82
540	9:29.88	9:30.94	9:31.99	9:33.05	9:34.11	9:35.17	9:36.22	9:37.28	9:38.34	9:39.40
550	9:40.45	9:41.51	9:42.57	9:43.62	9:44.68	9:45.74	9:46.80	9:47.85	9:48.91	9:49.97
560	9:51.03	9:52.08	9:53.14	9:54.20	9:55.26	9:56.31	9:57.37	9:58.43	9:59.48	10:00.54
570	10:01.60	10:02.66	10:03.71	10:04.77	10:05.83	10:06.89	10:07.94	10:09.00	10:10.06	10:11.11
580	10:12.17	10:13.23	10:14.29	10:15.34	10:16.40	10:17.46	10:18.52	10:19.57	10:20.63	10:21.69
590	10:22.74	10:23.80	10:24.86	10:25.92	10:26.97	10:28.03	10:29.09	10:30.15	10:31.20	10:32.26

♩. = 1.59; ♩ = 1.06; ♪. = 0.79; (triplet ♩ 𝄾) = 0.70; ♪ = 0.53; (triplet ♪ 𝄾 𝄾) = 0.35; 𝅘𝅥𝅯 = 0.26 seconds

CLICK: 25 4/8 FRAMES; M.M.: 56.47

Click	0	1	2	3	4	5	6	7	8	9
000	0:00.00	0:00.00	0:01.06	0:02.13	0:03.19	0:04.25	0:05.31	0:06.38	0:07.44	0:08.50
010	0:09.56	0:10.63	0:11.69	0:12.75	0:13.81	0:14.88	0:15.94	0:17.00	0:18.06	0:19.13
020	0:20.19	0:21.25	0:22.31	0:23.38	0:24.44	0:25.50	0:26.56	0:27.63	0:28.69	0:29.75
030	0:30.81	0:31.88	0:32.94	0:34.00	0:35.06	0:36.13	0:37.19	0:38.25	0:39.31	0:40.38
040	0:41.44	0:42.50	0:43.56	0:44.63	0:45.69	0:46.75	0:47.81	0:48.88	0:49.94	0:51.00
050	0:52.06	0:53.13	0:54.19	0:55.25	0:56.31	0:57.38	0:58.44	0:59.50	1:00.56	1:01.62
060	1:02.69	1:03.75	1:04.81	1:05.87	1:06.94	1:08.00	1:09.06	1:10.13	1:11.19	1:12.25
070	1:13.31	1:14.38	1:15.44	1:16.50	1:17.56	1:18.63	1:19.69	1:20.75	1:21.81	1:22.88
080	1:23.94	1:25.00	1:26.06	1:27.13	1:28.19	1:29.25	1:30.31	1:31.38	1:32.44	1:33.50
090	1:34.56	1:35.63	1:36.69	1:37.75	1:38.81	1:39.88	1:40.94	1:42.00	1:43.06	1:44.13
100	1:45.19	1:46.25	1:47.31	1:48.38	1:49.44	1:50.50	1:51.56	1:52.63	1:53.69	1:54.75
110	1:55.81	1:56.87	1:57.94	1:59.00	2:00.06	2:01.12	2:02.19	2:03.25	2:04.31	2:05.38
120	2:06.44	2:07.50	2:08.56	2:09.62	2:10.69	2:11.75	2:12.81	2:13.88	2:14.94	2:16.00
130	2:17.06	2:18.12	2:19.19	2:20.25	2:21.31	2:22.38	2:23.44	2:24.50	2:25.56	2:26.62
140	2:27.69	2:28.75	2:29.81	2:30.88	2:31.94	2:33.00	2:34.06	2:35.12	2:36.19	2:37.25
150	2:38.31	2:39.38	2:40.44	2:41.50	2:42.56	2:43.62	2:44.69	2:45.75	2:46.81	2:47.88
160	2:48.94	2:50.00	2:51.06	2:52.13	2:53.19	2:54.25	2:55.31	2:56.38	2:57.44	2:58.50
170	2:59.56	3:00.63	3:01.69	3:02.75	3:03.81	3:04.87	3:05.94	3:07.00	3:08.06	3:09.13
180	3:10.19	3:11.25	3:12.31	3:13.37	3:14.44	3:15.50	3:16.56	3:17.63	3:18.69	3:19.75
190	3:20.81	3:21.87	3:22.94	3:24.00	3:25.06	3:26.13	3:27.19	3:28.25	3:29.31	3:30.37
200	3:31.44	3:32.50	3:33.56	3:34.63	3:35.69	3:36.75	3:37.81	3:38.87	3:39.94	3:41.00
210	3:42.06	3:43.13	3:44.19	3:45.25	3:46.31	3:47.37	3:48.44	3:49.50	3:50.56	3:51.63
220	3:52.69	3:53.75	3:54.81	3:55.87	3:56.94	3:58.00	3:59.06	4:00.12	4:01.19	4:02.25
230	4:03.31	4:04.37	4:05.44	4:06.50	4:07.56	4:08.63	4:09.69	4:10.75	4:11.81	4:12.88
240	4:13.94	4:15.00	4:16.06	4:17.12	4:18.19	4:19.25	4:20.31	4:21.37	4:22.44	4:23.50
250	4:24.56	4:25.63	4:26.69	4:27.75	4:28.81	4:29.88	4:30.94	4:32.00	4:33.06	4:34.12
260	4:35.19	4:36.25	4:37.31	4:38.37	4:39.44	4:40.50	4:41.56	4:42.63	4:43.69	4:44.75
270	4:45.81	4:46.88	4:47.94	4:49.00	4:50.06	4:51.12	4:52.19	4:53.25	4:54.31	4:55.37
280	4:56.44	4:57.50	4:58.56	4:59.63	5:00.69	5:01.75	5:02.81	5:03.87	5:04.94	5:06.00
290	5:07.06	5:08.12	5:09.19	5:10.25	5:11.31	5:12.38	5:13.44	5:14.50	5:15.56	5:16.63
300	5:17.69	5:18.75	5:19.81	5:20.87	5:21.94	5:23.00	5:24.06	5:25.12	5:26.19	5:27.25
310	5:28.31	5:29.38	5:30.44	5:31.50	5:32.56	5:33.63	5:34.69	5:35.75	5:36.81	5:37.87
320	5:38.94	5:40.00	5:41.06	5:42.12	5:43.19	5:44.25	5:45.31	5:46.38	5:47.44	5:48.50
330	5:49.56	5:50.63	5:51.69	5:52.75	5:53.81	5:54.87	5:55.94	5:57.00	5:58.06	5:59.12
340	6:00.19	6:01.25	6:02.31	6:03.38	6:04.44	6:05.50	6:06.56	6:07.62	6:08.69	6:09.75
350	6:10.81	6:11.87	6:12.94	6:14.00	6:15.06	6:16.13	6:17.19	6:18.25	6:19.31	6:20.38
360	6:21.44	6:22.50	6:23.56	6:24.62	6:25.69	6:26.75	6:27.81	6:28.87	6:29.94	6:31.00
370	6:32.06	6:33.13	6:34.19	6:35.25	6:36.31	6:37.38	6:38.44	6:39.50	6:40.56	6:41.62
380	6:42.69	6:43.75	6:44.81	6:45.87	6:46.94	6:48.00	6:49.06	6:50.13	6:51.19	6:52.25
390	6:53.31	6:54.38	6:55.44	6:56.50	6:57.56	6:58.62	6:59.69	7:00.75	7:01.81	7:02.87
400	7:03.94	7:05.00	7:06.06	7:07.13	7:08.19	7:09.25	7:10.31	7:11.37	7:12.44	7:13.50
410	7:14.56	7:15.62	7:16.69	7:17.75	7:18.81	7:19.87	7:20.94	7:22.00	7:23.06	7:24.13
420	7:25.19	7:26.25	7:27.31	7:28.37	7:29.44	7:30.50	7:31.56	7:32.62	7:33.69	7:34.75
430	7:35.81	7:36.88	7:37.94	7:39.00	7:40.06	7:41.13	7:42.19	7:43.25	7:44.31	7:45.37
440	7:46.44	7:47.50	7:48.56	7:49.62	7:50.69	7:51.75	7:52.81	7:53.88	7:54.94	7:56.00
450	7:57.06	7:58.13	7:59.19	8:00.25	8:01.31	8:02.37	8:03.44	8:04.50	8:05.56	8:06.62
460	8:07.69	8:08.75	8:09.81	8:10.87	8:11.94	8:13.00	8:14.06	8:15.12	8:16.19	8:17.25
470	8:18.31	8:19.38	8:20.44	8:21.50	8:22.56	8:23.63	8:24.69	8:25.75	8:26.81	8:27.88
480	8:28.94	8:30.00	8:31.06	8:32.12	8:33.19	8:34.25	8:35.31	8:36.37	8:37.44	8:38.50
490	8:39.56	8:40.62	8:41.69	8:42.75	8:43.81	8:44.87	8:45.94	8:47.00	8:48.06	8:49.13
500	8:50.19	8:51.25	8:52.31	8:53.38	8:54.44	8:55.50	8:56.56	8:57.63	8:58.69	8:59.75
510	9:00.81	9:01.88	9:02.94	9:04.00	9:05.06	9:06.12	9:07.19	9:08.25	9:09.31	9:10.37
520	9:11.44	9:12.50	9:13.56	9:14.62	9:15.69	9:16.75	9:17.81	9:18.87	9:19.94	9:21.00
530	9:22.06	9:23.13	9:24.19	9:25.25	9:26.31	9:27.38	9:28.44	9:29.50	9:30.56	9:31.63
540	9:32.69	9:33.75	9:34.81	9:35.87	9:36.94	9:38.00	9:39.06	9:40.12	9:41.19	9:42.25
550	9:43.31	9:44.37	9:45.44	9:46.50	9:47.56	9:48.62	9:49.69	9:50.75	9:51.81	9:52.88
560	9:53.94	9:55.00	9:56.06	9:57.13	9:58.19	9:59.25	10:00.31	10:01.38	10:02.44	10:03.50
570	10:04.56	10:05.63	10:06.69	10:07.75	10:08.81	10:09.87	10:10.94	10:12.00	10:13.06	10:14.12
580	10:15.19	10:16.25	10:17.31	10:18.37	10:19.44	10:20.50	10:21.56	10:22.62	10:23.69	10:24.75
590	10:25.81	10:26.88	10:27.94	10:29.00	10:30.06	10:31.13	10:32.19	10:33.25	10:34.31	10:35.38

(dotted quarter) = 1.59; (quarter) = 1.06; (dotted eighth) = 0.80; (quarter-note triplet figure) = 0.71; (eighth) = 0.53; (eighth-note triplet figure) = 0.35; (sixteenth) = 0.27 seconds

CLICK: 25⅝ FRAMES; M.M.: 56.20

Click	0	1	2	3	4	5	6	7	8	9
000	0:00.00	0:00.00	0:01.07	0:02.14	0:03.20	0:04.27	0:05.34	0:06.41	0:07.47	0:08.54
010	0:09.61	0:10.68	0:11.74	0:12.81	0:13.88	0:14.95	0:16.02	0:17.08	0:18.15	0:19.22
020	0:20.29	0:21.35	0:22.42	0:23.49	0:24.56	0:25.62	0:26.69	0:27.76	0:28.83	0:29.90
030	0:30.96	0:32.03	0:33.10	0:34.17	0:35.23	0:36.30	0:37.37	0:38.44	0:39.51	0:40.57
040	0:41.64	0:42.71	0:43.78	0:44.84	0:45.91	0:46.98	0:48.05	0:49.11	0:50.18	0:51.25
050	0:52.32	0:53.39	0:54.45	0:55.52	0:56.59	0:57.66	0:58.72	0:59.79	1:00.86	1:01.93
060	1:02.99	1:04.06	1:05.13	1:06.20	1:07.27	1:08.33	1:09.40	1:10.47	1:11.54	1:12.60
070	1:13.67	1:14.74	1:15.81	1:16.88	1:17.94	1:19.01	1:20.08	1:21.15	1:22.21	1:23.28
080	1:24.35	1:25.42	1:26.48	1:27.55	1:28.62	1:29.69	1:30.76	1:31.82	1:32.89	1:33.96
090	1:35.03	1:36.09	1:37.16	1:38.23	1:39.30	1:40.36	1:41.43	1:42.50	1:43.57	1:44.64
100	1:45.70	1:46.77	1:47.84	1:48.91	1:49.97	1:51.04	1:52.11	1:53.18	1:54.24	1:55.31
110	1:56.38	1:57.45	1:58.52	1:59.58	2:00.65	2:01.72	2:02.79	2:03.85	2:04.92	2:05.99
120	2:07.06	2:08.12	2:09.19	2:10.26	2:11.33	2:12.40	2:13.46	2:14.53	2:15.60	2:16.67
130	2:17.73	2:18.80	2:19.87	2:20.94	2:22.01	2:23.07	2:24.14	2:25.21	2:26.28	2:27.34
140	2:28.41	2:29.48	2:30.55	2:31.61	2:32.68	2:33.75	2:34.82	2:35.89	2:36.95	2:38.02
150	2:39.09	2:40.16	2:41.22	2:42.29	2:43.36	2:44.43	2:45.49	2:46.56	2:47.63	2:48.70
160	2:49.77	2:50.83	2:51.90	2:52.97	2:54.04	2:55.10	2:56.17	2:57.24	2:58.31	2:59.37
170	3:00.44	3:01.51	3:02.58	3:03.65	3:04.71	3:05.78	3:06.85	3:07.92	3:08.98	3:10.05
180	3:11.12	3:12.19	3:13.26	3:14.32	3:15.39	3:16.46	3:17.53	3:18.59	3:19.66	3:20.73
190	3:21.80	3:22.86	3:23.93	3:25.00	3:26.07	3:27.14	3:28.20	3:29.27	3:30.34	3:31.41
200	3:32.47	3:33.54	3:34.61	3:35.68	3:36.74	3:37.81	3:38.88	3:39.95	3:41.02	3:42.08
210	3:43.15	3:44.22	3:45.29	3:46.35	3:47.42	3:48.49	3:49.56	3:50.62	3:51.69	3:52.76
220	3:53.83	3:54.90	3:55.96	3:57.03	3:58.10	3:59.17	4:00.23	4:01.30	4:02.37	4:03.44
230	4:04.51	4:05.57	4:06.64	4:07.71	4:08.78	4:09.84	4:10.91	4:11.98	4:13.05	4:14.11
240	4:15.18	4:16.25	4:17.32	4:18.39	4:19.45	4:20.52	4:21.59	4:22.66	4:23.72	4:24.79
250	4:25.86	4:26.93	4:27.99	4:29.06	4:30.13	4:31.20	4:32.27	4:33.33	4:34.40	4:35.47
260	4:36.54	4:37.60	4:38.67	4:39.74	4:40.81	4:41.87	4:42.94	4:44.01	4:45.08	4:46.15
270	4:47.21	4:48.28	4:49.35	4:50.42	4:51.48	4:52.55	4:53.62	4:54.69	4:55.76	4:56.82
280	4:57.89	4:58.96	5:00.03	5:01.09	5:02.16	5:03.23	5:04.30	5:05.36	5:06.43	5:07.50
290	5:08.57	5:09.64	5:10.70	5:11.77	5:12.84	5:13.91	5:14.97	5:16.04	5:17.11	5:18.18
300	5:19.24	5:20.31	5:21.38	5:22.45	5:23.52	5:24.58	5:25.65	5:26.72	5:27.79	5:28.85
310	5:29.92	5:30.99	5:32.06	5:33.12	5:34.19	5:35.26	5:36.33	5:37.40	5:38.46	5:39.53
320	5:40.60	5:41.67	5:42.73	5:43.80	5:44.87	5:45.94	5:47.01	5:48.07	5:49.14	5:50.21
330	5:51.28	5:52.34	5:53.41	5:54.48	5:55.55	5:56.61	5:57.68	5:58.75	5:59.82	6:00.89
340	6:01.95	6:03.02	6:04.09	6:05.16	6:06.22	6:07.29	6:08.36	6:09.43	6:10.49	6:11.56
350	6:12.63	6:13.70	6:14.77	6:15.83	6:16.90	6:17.97	6:19.04	6:20.10	6:21.17	6:22.24
360	6:23.31	6:24.37	6:25.44	6:26.51	6:27.58	6:28.65	6:29.71	6:30.78	6:31.85	6:32.92
370	6:33.98	6:35.05	6:36.12	6:37.19	6:38.26	6:39.32	6:40.39	6:41.46	6:42.53	6:43.59
380	6:44.66	6:45.73	6:46.80	6:47.86	6:48.93	6:50.00	6:51.07	6:52.14	6:53.20	6:54.27
390	6:55.34	6:56.41	6:57.47	6:58.54	6:59.61	7:00.68	7:01.74	7:02.81	7:03.88	7:04.95
400	7:06.02	7:07.08	7:08.15	7:09.22	7:10.29	7:11.35	7:12.42	7:13.49	7:14.56	7:15.62
410	7:16.69	7:17.76	7:18.83	7:19.90	7:20.96	7:22.03	7:23.10	7:24.17	7:25.23	7:26.30
420	7:27.37	7:28.44	7:29.51	7:30.57	7:31.64	7:32.71	7:33.78	7:34.84	7:35.91	7:36.98
430	7:38.05	7:39.11	7:40.18	7:41.25	7:42.32	7:43.39	7:44.45	7:45.52	7:46.59	7:47.66
440	7:48.72	7:49.79	7:50.86	7:51.93	7:52.99	7:54.06	7:55.13	7:56.20	7:57.27	7:58.33
450	7:59.40	8:00.47	8:01.54	8:02.60	8:03.67	8:04.74	8:05.81	8:06.87	8:07.94	8:09.01
460	8:10.08	8:11.15	8:12.21	8:13.28	8:14.35	8:15.42	8:16.48	8:17.55	8:18.62	8:19.69
470	8:20.76	8:21.82	8:22.89	8:23.96	8:25.03	8:26.09	8:27.16	8:28.23	8:29.30	8:30.36
480	8:31.43	8:32.50	8:33.57	8:34.64	8:35.70	8:36.77	8:37.84	8:38.91	8:39.97	8:41.04
490	8:42.11	8:43.18	8:44.24	8:45.31	8:46.38	8:47.45	8:48.52	8:49.58	8:50.65	8:51.72
500	8:52.79	8:53.85	8:54.92	8:55.99	8:57.06	8:58.13	8:59.19	9:00.26	9:01.33	9:02.40
510	9:03.46	9:04.53	9:05.60	9:06.67	9:07.73	9:08.80	9:09.87	9:10.94	9:12.01	9:13.07
520	9:14.14	9:15.21	9:16.28	9:17.34	9:18.41	9:19.48	9:20.55	9:21.61	9:22.68	9:23.75
530	9:24.82	9:25.89	9:26.95	9:28.02	9:29.09	9:30.16	9:31.22	9:32.29	9:33.36	9:34.43
540	9:35.49	9:36.56	9:37.63	9:38.70	9:39.77	9:40.83	9:41.90	9:42.97	9:44.04	9:45.10
550	9:46.17	9:47.24	9:48.31	9:49.37	9:50.44	9:51.51	9:52.58	9:53.65	9:54.71	9:55.78
560	9:56.85	9:57.92	9:58.98	10:00.05	10:01.12	10:02.19	10:03.26	10:04.32	10:05.39	10:06.46
570	10:07.53	10:08.59	10:09.66	10:10.73	10:11.80	10:12.86	10:13.93	10:15.00	10:16.07	10:17.14
580	10:18.20	10:19.27	10:20.34	10:21.41	10:22.47	10:23.54	10:24.61	10:25.68	10:26.74	10:27.81
590	10:28.88	10:29.95	10:31.02	10:32.08	10:33.15	10:34.22	10:35.29	10:36.35	10:37.42	10:38.49

♩. = 1.60; ♩ = 1.07; ♪. = 0.80; (triplet ♩ 𝄾) = 0.71; ♪ = 0.53; (triplet ♪ 𝄾 𝄾) = 0.36; 𝅘𝅥𝅯 = 0.27 seconds

CLICK: 25⅝ FRAMES; M.M.: 55.92

Click	0	1	2	3	4	5	6	7	8	9
000	0:00.00	0:00.00	0:01.07	0:02.15	0:03.22	0:04.29	0:05.36	0:06.44	0:07.51	0:08.58
010	0:09.66	0:10.73	0:11.80	0:12.88	0:13.95	0:15.02	0:16.09	0:17.17	0:18.24	0:19.31
020	0:20.39	0:21.46	0:22.53	0:23.60	0:24.68	0:25.75	0:26.82	0:27.90	0:28.97	0:30.04
030	0:31.11	0:32.19	0:33.26	0:34.33	0:35.41	0:36.48	0:37.55	0:38.63	0:39.70	0:40.77
040	0:41.84	0:42.92	0:43.99	0:45.06	0:46.14	0:47.21	0:48.28	0:49.35	0:50.43	0:51.50
050	0:52.57	0:53.65	0:54.72	0:55.79	0:56.86	0:57.94	0:59.01	1:00.08	1:01.16	1:02.23
060	1:03.30	1:04.38	1:05.45	1:06.52	1:07.59	1:08.67	1:09.74	1:10.81	1:11.89	1:12.96
070	1:14.03	1:15.10	1:16.18	1:17.25	1:18.32	1:19.40	1:20.47	1:21.54	1:22.61	1:23.69
080	1:24.76	1:25.83	1:26.91	1:27.98	1:29.05	1:30.13	1:31.20	1:32.27	1:33.34	1:34.42
090	1:35.49	1:36.56	1:37.64	1:38.71	1:39.78	1:40.85	1:41.93	1:43.00	1:44.07	1:45.15
100	1:46.22	1:47.29	1:48.36	1:49.44	1:50.51	1:51.58	1:52.66	1:53.73	1:54.80	1:55.88
110	1:56.95	1:58.02	1:59.09	2:00.17	2:01.24	2:02.31	2:03.39	2:04.46	2:05.53	2:06.60
120	2:07.68	2:08.75	2:09.82	2:10.90	2:11.97	2:13.04	2:14.11	2:15.19	2:16.26	2:17.33
130	2:18.41	2:19.48	2:20.55	2:21.63	2:22.70	2:23.77	2:24.84	2:25.92	2:26.99	2:28.06
140	2:29.14	2:30.21	2:31.28	2:32.35	2:33.43	2:34.50	2:35.57	2:36.65	2:37.72	2:38.79
150	2:39.86	2:40.94	2:42.01	2:43.08	2:44.16	2:45.23	2:46.30	2:47.38	2:48.45	2:49.52
160	2:50.59	2:51.67	2:52.74	2:53.81	2:54.89	2:55.96	2:57.03	2:58.10	2:59.18	3:00.25
170	3:01.32	3:02.40	3:03.47	3:04.54	3:05.61	3:06.69	3:07.76	3:08.83	3:09.91	3:10.98
180	3:12.05	3:13.13	3:14.20	3:15.27	3:16.34	3:17.42	3:18.49	3:19.56	3:20.64	3:21.71
190	3:22.78	3:23.85	3:24.93	3:26.00	3:27.07	3:28.15	3:29.22	3:30.29	3:31.36	3:32.44
200	3:33.51	3:34.58	3:35.66	3:36.73	3:37.80	3:38.88	3:39.95	3:41.02	3:42.09	3:43.17
210	3:44.24	3:45.31	3:46.39	3:47.46	3:48.53	3:49.60	3:50.68	3:51.75	3:52.82	3:53.90
220	3:54.97	3:56.04	3:57.11	3:58.19	3:59.26	4:00.33	4:01.41	4:02.48	4:03.55	4:04.63
230	4:05.70	4:06.77	4:07.84	4:08.92	4:09.99	4:11.06	4:12.14	4:13.21	4:14.28	4:15.35
240	4:16.43	4:17.50	4:18.57	4:19.65	4:20.72	4:21.79	4:22.86	4:23.94	4:25.01	4:26.08
250	4:27.16	4:28.23	4:29.30	4:30.37	4:31.45	4:32.52	4:33.59	4:34.67	4:35.74	4:36.81
260	4:37.89	4:38.96	4:40.03	4:41.10	4:42.18	4:43.25	4:44.32	4:45.40	4:46.47	4:47.54
270	4:48.61	4:49.69	4:50.76	4:51.83	4:52.91	4:53.98	4:55.05	4:56.13	4:57.20	4:58.27
280	4:59.34	5:00.42	5:01.49	5:02.56	5:03.64	5:04.71	5:05.78	5:06.85	5:07.93	5:09.00
290	5:10.07	5:11.15	5:12.22	5:13.29	5:14.36	5:15.44	5:16.51	5:17.58	5:18.66	5:19.73
300	5:20.80	5:21.88	5:22.95	5:24.02	5:25.09	5:26.17	5:27.24	5:28.31	5:29.39	5:30.46
310	5:31.53	5:32.60	5:33.68	5:34.75	5:35.82	5:36.90	5:37.97	5:39.04	5:40.11	5:41.19
320	5:42.26	5:43.33	5:44.41	5:45.48	5:46.55	5:47.63	5:48.70	5:49.77	5:50.84	5:51.92
330	5:52.99	5:54.06	5:55.14	5:56.21	5:57.28	5:58.35	5:59.43	6:00.50	6:01.57	6:02.65
340	6:03.72	6:04.79	6:05.86	6:06.94	6:08.01	6:09.08	6:10.16	6:11.23	6:12.30	6:13.37
350	6:14.45	6:15.52	6:16.59	6:17.67	6:18.74	6:19.81	6:20.89	6:21.96	6:23.03	6:24.10
360	6:25.18	6:26.25	6:27.32	6:28.40	6:29.47	6:30.54	6:31.61	6:32.69	6:33.76	6:34.83
370	6:35.91	6:36.98	6:38.05	6:39.13	6:40.20	6:41.27	6:42.34	6:43.42	6:44.49	6:45.56
380	6:46.64	6:47.71	6:48.78	6:49.85	6:50.93	6:52.00	6:53.07	6:54.15	6:55.22	6:56.29
390	6:57.36	6:58.44	6:59.51	7:00.58	7:01.66	7:02.73	7:03.80	7:04.88	7:05.95	7:07.02
400	7:08.09	7:09.17	7:10.24	7:11.31	7:12.39	7:13.46	7:14.53	7:15.60	7:16.68	7:17.75
410	7:18.82	7:19.90	7:20.97	7:22.04	7:23.11	7:24.19	7:25.26	7:26.33	7:27.41	7:28.48
420	7:29.55	7:30.63	7:31.70	7:32.77	7:33.84	7:34.92	7:35.99	7:37.06	7:38.14	7:39.21
430	7:40.28	7:41.35	7:42.43	7:43.50	7:44.57	7:45.65	7:46.72	7:47.79	7:48.86	7:49.94
440	7:51.01	7:52.08	7:53.16	7:54.23	7:55.30	7:56.38	7:57.45	7:58.52	7:59.59	8:00.67
450	8:01.74	8:02.81	8:03.89	8:04.96	8:06.03	8:07.10	8:08.18	8:09.25	8:10.32	8:11.40
460	8:12.47	8:13.54	8:14.61	8:15.69	8:16.76	8:17.83	8:18.91	8:19.98	8:21.05	8:22.13
470	8:23.20	8:24.27	8:25.34	8:26.42	8:27.49	8:28.56	8:29.64	8:30.71	8:31.78	8:32.85
480	8:33.93	8:35.00	8:36.07	8:37.15	8:38.22	8:39.29	8:40.36	8:41.44	8:42.51	8:43.58
490	8:44.66	8:45.73	8:46.80	8:47.87	8:48.95	8:50.02	8:51.09	8:52.17	8:53.24	8:54.31
500	8:55.39	8:56.46	8:57.53	8:58.60	8:59.68	9:00.75	9:01.82	9:02.90	9:03.97	9:05.04
510	9:06.11	9:07.19	9:08.26	9:09.33	9:10.41	9:11.48	9:12.55	9:13.62	9:14.70	9:15.77
520	9:16.84	9:17.92	9:18.99	9:20.06	9:21.14	9:22.21	9:23.28	9:24.35	9:25.43	9:26.50
530	9:27.57	9:28.65	9:29.72	9:30.79	9:31.86	9:32.94	9:34.01	9:35.08	9:36.16	9:37.23
540	9:38.30	9:39.38	9:40.45	9:41.52	9:42.59	9:43.67	9:44.74	9:45.81	9:46.89	9:47.96
550	9:49.03	9:50.10	9:51.18	9:52.25	9:53.32	9:54.40	9:55.47	9:56.54	9:57.61	9:58.69
560	9:59.76	10:00.83	10:01.91	10:02.98	10:04.05	10:05.13	10:06.20	10:07.27	10:08.34	10:09.42
570	10:10.49	10:11.56	10:12.64	10:13.71	10:14.78	10:15.85	10:16.93	10:18.00	10:19.07	10:20.15
580	10:21.22	10:22.29	10:23.36	10:24.44	10:25.51	10:26.58	10:27.66	10:28.73	10:29.80	10:30.88
590	10:31.95	10:33.02	10:34.09	10:35.17	10:36.24	10:37.31	10:38.39	10:39.46	10:40.53	10:41.60

𝅗𝅥. = 1.61; ♩ = 1.07; ♪. = 0.80; (triplet ♩ 𝄾) = 0.72; ♪ = 0.54; (triplet ♪ 𝄾 𝄾) = 0.36; 𝅘𝅥𝅯 = 0.27 seconds

CLICK: 25⅞ FRAMES; M.M.: 55.65

Click	0	1	2	3	4	5	6	7	8	9
000	0:00.00	0:00.00	0:01.08	0:02.16	0:03.23	0:04.31	0:05.39	0:06.47	0:07.55	0:08.63
010	0:09.70	0:10.78	0:11.86	0:12.94	0:14.02	0:15.09	0:16.17	0:17.25	0:18.33	0:19.41
020	0:20.48	0:21.56	0:22.64	0:23.72	0:24.80	0:25.88	0:26.95	0:28.03	0:29.11	0:30.19
030	0:31.27	0:32.34	0:33.42	0:34.50	0:35.58	0:36.66	0:37.73	0:38.81	0:39.89	0:40.97
040	0:42.05	0:43.13	0:44.20	0:45.28	0:46.36	0:47.44	0:48.52	0:49.59	0:50.67	0:51.75
050	0:52.83	0:53.91	0:54.98	0:56.06	0:57.14	0:58.22	0:59.30	1:00.38	1:01.45	1:02.53
060	1:03.61	1:04.69	1:05.77	1:06.84	1:07.92	1:09.00	1:10.08	1:11.16	1:12.23	1:13.31
070	1:14.39	1:15.47	1:16.55	1:17.63	1:18.70	1:19.78	1:20.86	1:21.94	1:23.02	1:24.09
080	1:25.17	1:26.25	1:27.33	1:28.41	1:29.48	1:30.56	1:31.64	1:32.72	1:33.80	1:34.88
090	1:35.95	1:37.03	1:38.11	1:39.19	1:40.27	1:41.34	1:42.42	1:43.50	1:44.58	1:45.66
100	1:46.73	1:47.81	1:48.89	1:49.97	1:51.05	1:52.13	1:53.20	1:54.28	1:55.36	1:56.44
110	1:57.52	1:58.59	1:59.67	2:00.75	2:01.83	2:02.91	2:03.98	2:05.06	2:06.14	2:07.22
120	2:08.30	2:09.38	2:10.45	2:11.53	2:12.61	2:13.69	2:14.77	2:15.84	2:16.92	2:18.00
130	2:19.08	2:20.16	2:21.23	2:22.31	2:23.39	2:24.47	2:25.55	2:26.63	2:27.70	2:28.78
140	2:29.86	2:30.94	2:32.02	2:33.09	2:34.17	2:35.25	2:36.33	2:37.41	2:38.48	2:39.56
150	2:40.64	2:41.72	2:42.80	2:43.88	2:44.95	2:46.03	2:47.11	2:48.19	2:49.27	2:50.34
160	2:51.42	2:52.50	2:53.58	2:54.66	2:55.73	2:56.81	2:57.89	2:58.97	3:00.05	3:01.13
170	3:02.20	3:03.28	3:04.36	3:05.44	3:06.52	3:07.59	3:08.67	3:09.75	3:10.83	3:11.91
180	3:12.98	3:14.06	3:15.14	3:16.22	3:17.30	3:18.38	3:19.45	3:20.53	3:21.61	3:22.69
190	3:23.77	3:24.84	3:25.92	3:27.00	3:28.08	3:29.16	3:30.23	3:31.31	3:32.39	3:33.47
200	3:34.55	3:35.63	3:36.70	3:37.78	3:38.86	3:39.94	3:41.02	3:42.09	3:43.17	3:44.25
210	3:45.33	3:46.41	3:47.48	3:48.56	3:49.64	3:50.72	3:51.80	3:52.88	3:53.95	3:55.03
220	3:56.11	3:57.19	3:58.27	3:59.34	4:00.42	4:01.50	4:02.58	4:03.66	4:04.73	4:05.81
230	4:06.89	4:07.97	4:09.05	4:10.13	4:11.20	4:12.28	4:13.36	4:14.44	4:15.52	4:16.59
240	4:17.67	4:18.75	4:19.83	4:20.91	4:21.98	4:23.06	4:24.14	4:25.22	4:26.30	4:27.38
250	4:28.45	4:29.53	4:30.61	4:31.69	4:32.77	4:33.84	4:34.92	4:36.00	4:37.08	4:38.16
260	4:39.23	4:40.31	4:41.39	4:42.47	4:43.55	4:44.63	4:45.70	4:46.78	4:47.86	4:48.94
270	4:50.02	4:51.09	4:52.17	4:53.25	4:54.33	4:55.41	4:56.48	4:57.56	4:58.64	4:59.72
280	5:00.80	5:01.88	5:02.95	5:04.03	5:05.11	5:06.19	5:07.27	5:08.34	5:09.42	5:10.50
290	5:11.58	5:12.66	5:13.73	5:14.81	5:15.89	5:16.97	5:18.05	5:19.13	5:20.20	5:21.28
300	5:22.36	5:23.44	5:24.52	5:25.59	5:26.67	5:27.75	5:28.83	5:29.91	5:30.98	5:32.06
310	5:33.14	5:34.22	5:35.30	5:36.38	5:37.45	5:38.53	5:39.61	5:40.69	5:41.77	5:42.84
320	5:43.92	5:45.00	5:46.08	5:47.16	5:48.23	5:49.31	5:50.39	5:51.47	5:52.55	5:53.63
330	5:54.70	5:55.78	5:56.86	5:57.94	5:59.02	6:00.09	6:01.17	6:02.25	6:03.33	6:04.41
340	6:05.48	6:06.56	6:07.64	6:08.72	6:09.80	6:10.88	6:11.95	6:13.03	6:14.11	6:15.19
350	6:16.27	6:17.34	6:18.42	6:19.50	6:20.58	6:21.66	6:22.73	6:23.81	6:24.89	6:25.97
360	6:27.05	6:28.13	6:29.20	6:30.28	6:31.36	6:32.44	6:33.52	6:34.59	6:35.67	6:36.75
370	6:37.83	6:38.91	6:39.98	6:41.06	6:42.14	6:43.22	6:44.30	6:45.38	6:46.45	6:47.53
380	6:48.61	6:49.69	6:50.77	6:51.84	6:52.92	6:54.00	6:55.08	6:56.16	6:57.23	6:58.31
390	6:59.39	7:00.47	7:01.55	7:02.63	7:03.70	7:04.78	7:05.86	7:06.94	7:08.02	7:09.09
400	7:10.17	7:11.25	7:12.33	7:13.41	7:14.48	7:15.56	7:16.64	7:17.72	7:18.80	7:19.88
410	7:20.95	7:22.03	7:23.11	7:24.19	7:25.27	7:26.34	7:27.42	7:28.50	7:29.58	7:30.66
420	7:31.73	7:32.81	7:33.89	7:34.97	7:36.05	7:37.13	7:38.20	7:39.28	7:40.36	7:41.44
430	7:42.52	7:43.59	7:44.67	7:45.75	7:46.83	7:47.91	7:48.98	7:50.06	7:51.14	7:52.22
440	7:53.30	7:54.38	7:55.45	7:56.53	7:57.61	7:58.69	7:59.77	8:00.84	8:01.92	8:03.00
450	8:04.08	8:05.16	8:06.23	8:07.31	8:08.39	8:09.47	8:10.55	8:11.63	8:12.70	8:13.78
460	8:14.86	8:15.94	8:17.02	8:18.09	8:19.17	8:20.25	8:21.33	8:22.41	8:23.48	8:24.56
470	8:25.64	8:26.72	8:27.80	8:28.88	8:29.95	8:31.03	8:32.11	8:33.19	8:34.27	8:35.34
480	8:36.42	8:37.50	8:38.58	8:39.66	8:40.73	8:41.81	8:42.89	8:43.97	8:45.05	8:46.13
490	8:47.20	8:48.28	8:49.36	8:50.44	8:51.52	8:52.59	8:53.67	8:54.75	8:55.83	8:56.91
500	8:57.98	8:59.06	9:00.14	9:01.22	9:02.30	9:03.38	9:04.45	9:05.53	9:06.61	9:07.69
510	9:08.77	9:09.84	9:10.92	9:12.00	9:13.08	9:14.16	9:15.23	9:16.31	9:17.39	9:18.47
520	9:19.55	9:20.63	9:21.70	9:22.78	9:23.86	9:24.94	9:26.02	9:27.09	9:28.17	9:29.25
530	9:30.33	9:31.41	9:32.48	9:33.56	9:34.64	9:35.72	9:36.80	9:37.88	9:38.95	9:40.03
540	9:41.11	9:42.19	9:43.27	9:44.34	9:45.42	9:46.50	9:47.58	9:48.66	9:49.73	9:50.81
550	9:51.89	9:52.97	9:54.05	9:55.13	9:56.20	9:57.28	9:58.36	9:59.44	10:00.52	10:01.59
560	10:02.67	10:03.75	10:04.83	10:05.91	10:06.98	10:08.06	10:09.14	10:10.22	10:11.30	10:12.38
570	10:13.45	10:14.53	10:15.61	10:16.69	10:17.77	10:18.84	10:19.92	10:21.00	10:22.08	10:23.16
580	10:24.23	10:25.31	10:26.39	10:27.47	10:28.55	10:29.63	10:30.70	10:31.78	10:32.86	10:33.94
590	10:35.02	10:36.09	10:37.17	10:38.25	10:39.33	10:40.41	10:41.48	10:42.56	10:43.64	10:44.72

♩. = 1.62; ♩ = 1.08; ♪. = 0.81; (3: ♩ 𝄾) = 0.72; ♪ = 0.54; (3: ♪ 𝄾 𝄾) = 0.36; 𝅘𝅥𝅯 = 0.27 seconds

CLICK: 26 0/8 FRAMES; M.M.: 55.38

Click	0	1	2	3	4	5	6	7	8	9
000	0:00.00	0:00.00	0:01.08	0:02.17	0:03.25	0:04.33	0:05.42	0:06.50	0:07.58	0:08.67
010	0:09.75	0:10.83	0:11.92	0:13.00	0:14.08	0:15.17	0:16.25	0:17.33	0:18.42	0:19.50
020	0:20.58	0:21.67	0:22.75	0:23.83	0:24.92	0:26.00	0:27.08	0:28.17	0:29.25	0:30.33
030	0:31.42	0:32.50	0:33.58	0:34.67	0:35.75	0:36.83	0:37.92	0:39.00	0:40.08	0:41.17
040	0:42.25	0:43.33	0:44.42	0:45.50	0:46.58	0:47.67	0:48.75	0:49.83	0:50.92	0:52.00
050	0:53.08	0:54.17	0:55.25	0:56.33	0:57.42	0:58.50	0:59.58	1:00.67	1:01.75	1:02.83
060	1:03.92	1:05.00	1:06.08	1:07.17	1:08.25	1:09.33	1:10.42	1:11.50	1:12.58	1:13.67
070	1:14.75	1:15.83	1:16.92	1:18.00	1:19.08	1:20.17	1:21.25	1:22.33	1:23.42	1:24.50
080	1:25.58	1:26.67	1:27.75	1:28.83	1:29.92	1:31.00	1:32.08	1:33.17	1:34.25	1:35.33
090	1:36.42	1:37.50	1:38.58	1:39.67	1:40.75	1:41.83	1:42.92	1:44.00	1:45.08	1:46.17
100	1:47.25	1:48.33	1:49.42	1:50.50	1:51.58	1:52.67	1:53.75	1:54.83	1:55.92	1:57.00
110	1:58.08	1:59.17	2:00.25	2:01.33	2:02.42	2:03.50	2:04.58	2:05.67	2:06.75	2:07.83
120	2:08.92	2:10.00	2:11.08	2:12.17	2:13.25	2:14.33	2:15.42	2:16.50	2:17.58	2:18.67
130	2:19.75	2:20.83	2:21.92	2:23.00	2:24.08	2:25.17	2:26.25	2:27.33	2:28.42	2:29.50
140	2:30.58	2:31.67	2:32.75	2:33.83	2:34.92	2:36.00	2:37.08	2:38.17	2:39.25	2:40.33
150	2:41.42	2:42.50	2:43.58	2:44.67	2:45.75	2:46.83	2:47.92	2:49.00	2:50.08	2:51.17
160	2:52.25	2:53.33	2:54.42	2:55.50	2:56.58	2:57.67	2:58.75	2:59.83	3:00.92	3:02.00
170	3:03.08	3:04.17	3:05.25	3:06.33	3:07.42	3:08.50	3:09.58	3:10.67	3:11.75	3:12.83
180	3:13.92	3:15.00	3:16.08	3:17.17	3:18.25	3:19.33	3:20.42	3:21.50	3:22.58	3:23.67
190	3:24.75	3:25.83	3:26.92	3:28.00	3:29.08	3:30.17	3:31.25	3:32.33	3:33.42	3:34.50
200	3:35.58	3:36.67	3:37.75	3:38.83	3:39.92	3:41.00	3:42.08	3:43.17	3:44.25	3:45.33
210	3:46.42	3:47.50	3:48.58	3:49.67	3:50.75	3:51.83	3:52.92	3:54.00	3:55.08	3:56.17
220	3:57.25	3:58.33	3:59.42	4:00.50	4:01.58	4:02.67	4:03.75	4:04.83	4:05.92	4:07.00
230	4:08.08	4:09.17	4:10.25	4:11.33	4:12.42	4:13.50	4:14.58	4:15.67	4:16.75	4:17.83
240	4:18.92	4:20.00	4:21.08	4:22.17	4:23.25	4:24.33	4:25.42	4:26.50	4:27.58	4:28.67
250	4:29.75	4:30.83	4:31.92	4:33.00	4:34.08	4:35.17	4:36.25	4:37.33	4:38.42	4:39.50
260	4:40.58	4:41.67	4:42.75	4:43.83	4:44.92	4:46.00	4:47.08	4:48.17	4:49.25	4:50.33
270	4:51.42	4:52.50	4:53.58	4:54.67	4:55.75	4:56.83	4:57.92	4:59.00	5:00.08	5:01.17
280	5:02.25	5:03.33	5:04.42	5:05.50	5:06.58	5:07.67	5:08.75	5:09.83	5:10.92	5:12.00
290	5:13.08	5:14.17	5:15.25	5:16.33	5:17.42	5:18.50	5:19.58	5:20.67	5:21.75	5:22.83
300	5:23.92	5:25.00	5:26.08	5:27.17	5:28.25	5:29.33	5:30.42	5:31.50	5:32.58	5:33.67
310	5:34.75	5:35.83	5:36.92	5:38.00	5:39.08	5:40.17	5:41.25	5:42.33	5:43.42	5:44.50
320	5:45.58	5:46.67	5:47.75	5:48.83	5:49.92	5:51.00	5:52.08	5:53.17	5:54.25	5:55.33
330	5:56.42	5:57.50	5:58.58	5:59.67	6:00.75	6:01.83	6:02.92	6:04.00	6:05.08	6:06.17
340	6:07.25	6:08.33	6:09.42	6:10.50	6:11.58	6:12.67	6:13.75	6:14.83	6:15.92	6:17.00
350	6:18.08	6:19.17	6:20.25	6:21.33	6:22.42	6:23.50	6:24.58	6:25.67	6:26.75	6:27.83
360	6:28.92	6:30.00	6:31.08	6:32.17	6:33.25	6:34.33	6:35.42	6:36.50	6:37.58	6:38.67
370	6:39.75	6:40.83	6:41.92	6:43.00	6:44.08	6:45.17	6:46.25	6:47.33	6:48.42	6:49.50
380	6:50.58	6:51.67	6:52.75	6:53.83	6:54.92	6:56.00	6:57.08	6:58.17	6:59.25	7:00.33
390	7:01.42	7:02.50	7:03.58	7:04.67	7:05.75	7:06.83	7:07.92	7:09.00	7:10.08	7:11.17
400	7:12.25	7:13.33	7:14.42	7:15.50	7:16.58	7:17.67	7:18.75	7:19.83	7:20.92	7:22.00
410	7:23.08	7:24.17	7:25.25	7:26.33	7:27.42	7:28.50	7:29.58	7:30.67	7:31.75	7:32.83
420	7:33.92	7:35.00	7:36.08	7:37.17	7:38.25	7:39.33	7:40.42	7:41.50	7:42.58	7:43.67
430	7:44.75	7:45.83	7:46.92	7:48.00	7:49.08	7:50.17	7:51.25	7:52.33	7:53.42	7:54.50
440	7:55.58	7:56.67	7:57.75	7:58.83	7:59.92	8:01.00	8:02.08	8:03.17	8:04.25	8:05.33
450	8:06.42	8:07.50	8:08.58	8:09.67	8:10.75	8:11.83	8:12.92	8:14.00	8:15.08	8:16.17
460	8:17.25	8:18.33	8:19.42	8:20.50	8:21.58	8:22.67	8:23.75	8:24.83	8:25.92	8:27.00
470	8:28.08	8:29.17	8:30.25	8:31.33	8:32.42	8:33.50	8:34.58	8:35.67	8:36.75	8:37.83
480	8:38.92	8:40.00	8:41.08	8:42.17	8:43.25	8:44.33	8:45.42	8:46.50	8:47.58	8:48.67
490	8:49.75	8:50.83	8:51.92	8:53.00	8:54.08	8:55.17	8:56.25	8:57.33	8:58.42	8:59.50
500	9:00.58	9:01.67	9:02.75	9:03.83	9:04.92	9:06.00	9:07.08	9:08.17	9:09.25	9:10.33
510	9:11.42	9:12.50	9:13.58	9:14.67	9:15.75	9:16.83	9:17.92	9:19.00	9:20.08	9:21.17
520	9:22.25	9:23.33	9:24.42	9:25.50	9:26.58	9:27.67	9:28.75	9:29.83	9:30.92	9:32.00
530	9:33.08	9:34.17	9:35.25	9:36.33	9:37.42	9:38.50	9:39.58	9:40.67	9:41.75	9:42.83
540	9:43.92	9:45.00	9:46.08	9:47.17	9:48.25	9:49.33	9:50.42	9:51.50	9:52.58	9:53.67
550	9:54.75	9:55.83	9:56.92	9:58.00	9:59.08	10:00.17	10:01.25	10:02.33	10:03.42	10:04.50
560	10:05.58	10:06.67	10:07.75	10:08.83	10:09.92	10:11.00	10:12.08	10:13.17	10:14.25	10:15.33
570	10:16.42	10:17.50	10:18.58	10:19.67	10:20.75	10:21.83	10:22.92	10:24.00	10:25.08	10:26.17
580	10:27.25	10:28.33	10:29.42	10:30.50	10:31.58	10:32.67	10:33.75	10:34.83	10:35.92	10:37.00
590	10:38.08	10:39.17	10:40.25	10:41.33	10:42.42	10:43.50	10:44.58	10:45.67	10:46.75	10:47.83

♩. = 1.62; ♩ = 1.08; ♪. = 0.81; [triplet: ♩ 𝄾] = 0.72; ♪ = 0.54; [triplet: ♪ 𝄾 𝄾] = 0.36; 𝅘𝅥𝅯 = 0.27 seconds

CLICK: 26⅛ FRAMES; M.M.: 55.12

Click	0	1	2	3	4	5	6	7	8	9
000	0:00.00	0:00.00	0:01.09	0:02.18	0:03.27	0:04.35	0:05.44	0:06.53	0:07.62	0:08.71
010	0:09.80	0:10.89	0:11.97	0:13.06	0:14.15	0:15.24	0:16.33	0:17.42	0:18.51	0:19.59
020	0:20.68	0:21.77	0:22.86	0:23.95	0:25.04	0:26.13	0:27.21	0:28.30	0:29.39	0:30.48
030	0:31.57	0:32.66	0:33.74	0:34.83	0:35.92	0:37.01	0:38.10	0:39.19	0:40.28	0:41.36
040	0:42.45	0:43.54	0:44.63	0:45.72	0:46.81	0:47.90	0:48.98	0:50.07	0:51.16	0:52.25
050	0:53.34	0:54.43	0:55.52	0:56.60	0:57.69	0:58.78	0:59.87	1:00.96	1:02.05	1:03.14
060	1:04.22	1:05.31	1:06.40	1:07.49	1:08.58	1:09.67	1:10.76	1:11.84	1:12.93	1:14.02
070	1:15.11	1:16.20	1:17.29	1:18.38	1:19.46	1:20.55	1:21.64	1:22.73	1:23.82	1:24.91
080	1:25.99	1:27.08	1:28.17	1:29.26	1:30.35	1:31.44	1:32.53	1:33.61	1:34.70	1:35.79
090	1:36.88	1:37.97	1:39.06	1:40.15	1:41.23	1:42.32	1:43.41	1:44.50	1:45.59	1:46.68
100	1:47.77	1:48.85	1:49.94	1:51.03	1:52.12	1:53.21	1:54.30	1:55.39	1:56.47	1:57.56
110	1:58.65	1:59.74	2:00.83	2:01.92	2:03.01	2:04.09	2:05.18	2:06.27	2:07.36	2:08.45
120	2:09.54	2:10.63	2:11.71	2:12.80	2:13.89	2:14.98	2:16.07	2:17.16	2:18.24	2:19.33
130	2:20.42	2:21.51	2:22.60	2:23.69	2:24.78	2:25.86	2:26.95	2:28.04	2:29.13	2:30.22
140	2:31.31	2:32.40	2:33.48	2:34.57	2:35.66	2:36.75	2:37.84	2:38.93	2:40.02	2:41.10
150	2:42.19	2:43.28	2:44.37	2:45.46	2:46.55	2:47.64	2:48.72	2:49.81	2:50.90	2:51.99
160	2:53.08	2:54.17	2:55.26	2:56.34	2:57.43	2:58.52	2:59.61	3:00.70	3:01.79	3:02.88
170	3:03.96	3:05.05	3:06.14	3:07.23	3:08.32	3:09.41	3:10.49	3:11.58	3:12.67	3:13.76
180	3:14.85	3:15.94	3:17.03	3:18.11	3:19.20	3:20.29	3:21.38	3:22.47	3:23.56	3:24.65
190	3:25.73	3:26.82	3:27.91	3:29.00	3:30.09	3:31.18	3:32.27	3:33.35	3:34.44	3:35.53
200	3:36.62	3:37.71	3:38.80	3:39.89	3:40.97	3:42.06	3:43.15	3:44.24	3:45.33	3:46.42
210	3:47.51	3:48.59	3:49.68	3:50.77	3:51.86	3:52.95	3:54.04	3:55.13	3:56.21	3:57.30
220	3:58.39	3:59.48	4:00.57	4:01.66	4:02.74	4:03.83	4:04.92	4:06.01	4:07.10	4:08.19
230	4:09.28	4:10.36	4:11.45	4:12.54	4:13.63	4:14.72	4:15.81	4:16.90	4:17.98	4:19.07
240	4:20.16	4:21.25	4:22.34	4:23.43	4:24.52	4:25.60	4:26.69	4:27.78	4:28.87	4:29.96
250	4:31.05	4:32.14	4:33.22	4:34.31	4:35.40	4:36.49	4:37.58	4:38.67	4:39.76	4:40.84
260	4:41.93	4:43.02	4:44.11	4:45.20	4:46.29	4:47.38	4:48.46	4:49.55	4:50.64	4:51.73
270	4:52.82	4:53.91	4:54.99	4:56.08	4:57.17	4:58.26	4:59.35	5:00.44	5:01.53	5:02.61
280	5:03.70	5:04.79	5:05.88	5:06.97	5:08.06	5:09.15	5:10.23	5:11.32	5:12.41	5:13.50
290	5:14.59	5:15.68	5:16.77	5:17.85	5:18.94	5:20.03	5:21.12	5:22.21	5:23.30	5:24.39
300	5:25.47	5:26.56	5:27.65	5:28.74	5:29.83	5:30.92	5:32.01	5:33.09	5:34.18	5:35.27
310	5:36.36	5:37.45	5:38.54	5:39.63	5:40.71	5:41.80	5:42.89	5:43.98	5:45.07	5:46.16
320	5:47.24	5:48.33	5:49.42	5:50.51	5:51.60	5:52.69	5:53.78	5:54.86	5:55.95	5:57.04
330	5:58.13	5:59.22	6:00.31	6:01.40	6:02.48	6:03.57	6:04.66	6:05.75	6:06.84	6:07.93
340	6:09.02	6:10.10	6:11.19	6:12.28	6:13.37	6:14.46	6:15.55	6:16.64	6:17.72	6:18.81
350	6:19.90	6:20.99	6:22.08	6:23.17	6:24.26	6:25.34	6:26.43	6:27.52	6:28.61	6:29.70
360	6:30.79	6:31.88	6:32.96	6:34.05	6:35.14	6:36.23	6:37.32	6:38.41	6:39.49	6:40.58
370	6:41.67	6:42.76	6:43.85	6:44.94	6:46.03	6:47.11	6:48.20	6:49.29	6:50.38	6:51.47
380	6:52.56	6:53.65	6:54.73	6:55.82	6:56.91	6:58.00	6:59.09	7:00.18	7:01.27	7:02.35
390	7:03.44	7:04.53	7:05.62	7:06.71	7:07.80	7:08.89	7:09.97	7:11.06	7:12.15	7:13.24
400	7:14.33	7:15.42	7:16.51	7:17.59	7:18.68	7:19.77	7:20.86	7:21.95	7:23.04	7:24.13
410	7:25.21	7:26.30	7:27.39	7:28.48	7:29.57	7:30.66	7:31.74	7:32.83	7:33.92	7:35.01
420	7:36.10	7:37.19	7:38.28	7:39.36	7:40.45	7:41.54	7:42.63	7:43.72	7:44.81	7:45.90
430	7:46.98	7:48.07	7:49.16	7:50.25	7:51.34	7:52.43	7:53.52	7:54.60	7:55.69	7:56.78
440	7:57.87	7:58.96	8:00.05	8:01.14	8:02.22	8:03.31	8:04.40	8:05.49	8:06.58	8:07.67
450	8:08.76	8:09.84	8:10.93	8:12.02	8:13.11	8:14.20	8:15.29	8:16.38	8:17.46	8:18.55
460	8:19.64	8:20.73	8:21.82	8:22.91	8:23.99	8:25.08	8:26.17	8:27.26	8:28.35	8:29.44
470	8:30.53	8:31.61	8:32.70	8:33.79	8:34.88	8:35.97	8:37.06	8:38.15	8:39.23	8:40.32
480	8:41.41	8:42.50	8:43.59	8:44.68	8:45.77	8:46.85	8:47.94	8:49.03	8:50.12	8:51.21
490	8:52.30	8:53.39	8:54.47	8:55.56	8:56.65	8:57.74	8:58.83	8:59.92	9:01.01	9:02.09
500	9:03.18	9:04.27	9:05.36	9:06.45	9:07.54	9:08.63	9:09.71	9:10.80	9:11.89	9:12.98
510	9:14.07	9:15.16	9:16.24	9:17.33	9:18.42	9:19.51	9:20.60	9:21.69	9:22.78	9:23.86
520	9:24.95	9:26.04	9:27.13	9:28.22	9:29.31	9:30.40	9:31.48	9:32.57	9:33.66	9:34.75
530	9:35.84	9:36.93	9:38.02	9:39.10	9:40.19	9:41.28	9:42.37	9:43.46	9:44.55	9:45.64
540	9:46.72	9:47.81	9:48.90	9:49.99	9:51.08	9:52.17	9:53.26	9:54.34	9:55.43	9:56.52
550	9:57.61	9:58.70	9:59.79	10:00.88	10:01.96	10:03.05	10:04.14	10:05.23	10:06.32	10:07.41
560	10:08.49	10:09.58	10:10.67	10:11.76	10:12.85	10:13.94	10:15.03	10:16.11	10:17.20	10:18.29
570	10:19.38	10:20.47	10:21.56	10:22.65	10:23.73	10:24.82	10:25.91	10:27.00	10:28.09	10:29.18
580	10:30.27	10:31.35	10:32.44	10:33.53	10:34.62	10:35.71	10:36.80	10:37.89	10:38.97	10:40.06
590	10:41.15	10:42.24	10:43.33	10:44.42	10:45.51	10:46.59	10:47.68	10:48.77	10:49.86	10:50.95

♩. = 1.63; ♩ = 1.09; ♪. = 0.82; (3: ♩ 𝄾) = 0.73; ♪ = 0.54; (3: ♪ 𝄾 𝄾) = 0.36; 𝅘𝅥𝅯 = 0.27 seconds

CLICK: 26 2/8 FRAMES; M.M.: 54.86

Click	0	1	2	3	4	5	6	7	8	9
000	0:00.00	0:00.00	0:01.09	0:02.19	0:03.28	0:04.38	0:05.47	0:06.56	0:07.66	0:08.75
010	0:09.84	0:10.94	0:12.03	0:13.13	0:14.22	0:15.31	0:16.41	0:17.50	0:18.59	0:19.69
020	0:20.78	0:21.87	0:22.97	0:24.06	0:25.16	0:26.25	0:27.34	0:28.44	0:29.53	0:30.62
030	0:31.72	0:32.81	0:33.91	0:35.00	0:36.09	0:37.19	0:38.28	0:39.38	0:40.47	0:41.56
040	0:42.66	0:43.75	0:44.84	0:45.94	0:47.03	0:48.13	0:49.22	0:50.31	0:51.41	0:52.50
050	0:53.59	0:54.69	0:55.78	0:56.87	0:57.97	0:59.06	1:00.16	1:01.25	1:02.34	1:03.44
060	1:04.53	1:05.63	1:06.72	1:07.81	1:08.91	1:10.00	1:11.09	1:12.19	1:13.28	1:14.37
070	1:15.47	1:16.56	1:17.66	1:18.75	1:19.84	1:20.94	1:22.03	1:23.12	1:24.22	1:25.31
080	1:26.41	1:27.50	1:28.59	1:29.69	1:30.78	1:31.88	1:32.97	1:34.06	1:35.16	1:36.25
090	1:37.34	1:38.44	1:39.53	1:40.62	1:41.72	1:42.81	1:43.91	1:45.00	1:46.09	1:47.19
100	1:48.28	1:49.37	1:50.47	1:51.56	1:52.66	1:53.75	1:54.84	1:55.94	1:57.03	1:58.12
110	1:59.22	2:00.31	2:01.41	2:02.50	2:03.59	2:04.69	2:05.78	2:06.87	2:07.97	2:09.06
120	2:10.16	2:11.25	2:12.34	2:13.44	2:14.53	2:15.62	2:16.72	2:17.81	2:18.91	2:20.00
130	2:21.09	2:22.19	2:23.28	2:24.38	2:25.47	2:26.56	2:27.66	2:28.75	2:29.84	2:30.94
140	2:32.03	2:33.12	2:34.22	2:35.31	2:36.41	2:37.50	2:38.59	2:39.69	2:40.78	2:41.87
150	2:42.97	2:44.06	2:45.16	2:46.25	2:47.34	2:48.44	2:49.53	2:50.63	2:51.72	2:52.81
160	2:53.91	2:55.00	2:56.09	2:57.19	2:58.28	2:59.37	3:00.47	3:01.56	3:02.66	3:03.75
170	3:04.84	3:05.94	3:07.03	3:08.12	3:09.22	3:10.31	3:11.41	3:12.50	3:13.59	3:14.69
180	3:15.78	3:16.88	3:17.97	3:19.06	3:20.16	3:21.25	3:22.34	3:23.44	3:24.53	3:25.62
190	3:26.72	3:27.81	3:28.91	3:30.00	3:31.09	3:32.19	3:33.28	3:34.37	3:35.47	3:36.56
200	3:37.66	3:38.75	3:39.84	3:40.94	3:42.03	3:43.12	3:44.22	3:45.31	3:46.41	3:47.50
210	3:48.59	3:49.69	3:50.78	3:51.87	3:52.97	3:54.06	3:55.16	3:56.25	3:57.34	3:58.44
220	3:59.53	4:00.62	4:01.72	4:02.81	4:03.91	4:05.00	4:06.09	4:07.19	4:08.28	4:09.38
230	4:10.47	4:11.56	4:12.66	4:13.75	4:14.84	4:15.94	4:17.03	4:18.12	4:19.22	4:20.31
240	4:21.41	4:22.50	4:23.59	4:24.69	4:25.78	4:26.87	4:27.97	4:29.06	4:30.16	4:31.25
250	4:32.34	4:33.44	4:34.53	4:35.63	4:36.72	4:37.81	4:38.91	4:40.00	4:41.09	4:42.19
260	4:43.28	4:44.37	4:45.47	4:46.56	4:47.66	4:48.75	4:49.84	4:50.94	4:52.03	4:53.12
270	4:54.22	4:55.31	4:56.41	4:57.50	4:58.59	4:59.69	5:00.78	5:01.88	5:02.97	5:04.06
280	5:05.16	5:06.25	5:07.34	5:08.44	5:09.53	5:10.62	5:11.72	5:12.81	5:13.91	5:15.00
290	5:16.09	5:17.19	5:18.28	5:19.37	5:20.47	5:21.56	5:22.66	5:23.75	5:24.84	5:25.94
300	5:27.03	5:28.13	5:29.22	5:30.31	5:31.41	5:32.50	5:33.59	5:34.69	5:35.78	5:36.87
310	5:37.97	5:39.06	5:40.16	5:41.25	5:42.34	5:43.44	5:44.53	5:45.62	5:46.72	5:47.81
320	5:48.91	5:50.00	5:51.09	5:52.19	5:53.28	5:54.38	5:55.47	5:56.56	5:57.66	5:58.75
330	5:59.84	6:00.94	6:02.03	6:03.12	6:04.22	6:05.31	6:06.41	6:07.50	6:08.59	6:09.69
340	6:10.78	6:11.87	6:12.97	6:14.06	6:15.16	6:16.25	6:17.34	6:18.44	6:19.53	6:20.63
350	6:21.72	6:22.81	6:23.91	6:25.00	6:26.09	6:27.19	6:28.28	6:29.37	6:30.47	6:31.56
360	6:32.66	6:33.75	6:34.84	6:35.94	6:37.03	6:38.12	6:39.22	6:40.31	6:41.41	6:42.50
370	6:43.59	6:44.69	6:45.78	6:46.88	6:47.97	6:49.06	6:50.16	6:51.25	6:52.34	6:53.44
380	6:54.53	6:55.62	6:56.72	6:57.81	6:58.91	7:00.00	7:01.09	7:02.19	7:03.28	7:04.37
390	7:05.47	7:06.56	7:07.66	7:08.75	7:09.84	7:10.94	7:12.03	7:13.12	7:14.22	7:15.31
400	7:16.41	7:17.50	7:18.59	7:19.69	7:20.78	7:21.87	7:22.97	7:24.06	7:25.16	7:26.25
410	7:27.34	7:28.44	7:29.53	7:30.62	7:31.72	7:32.81	7:33.91	7:35.00	7:36.09	7:37.19
420	7:38.28	7:39.37	7:40.47	7:41.56	7:42.66	7:43.75	7:44.84	7:45.94	7:47.03	7:48.12
430	7:49.22	7:50.31	7:51.41	7:52.50	7:53.59	7:54.69	7:55.78	7:56.87	7:57.97	7:59.06
440	8:00.16	8:01.25	8:02.34	8:03.44	8:04.53	8:05.63	8:06.72	8:07.81	8:08.91	8:10.00
450	8:11.09	8:12.19	8:13.28	8:14.37	8:15.47	8:16.56	8:17.66	8:18.75	8:19.84	8:20.94
460	8:22.03	8:23.12	8:24.22	8:25.31	8:26.41	8:27.50	8:28.59	8:29.69	8:30.78	8:31.88
470	8:32.97	8:34.06	8:35.16	8:36.25	8:37.34	8:38.44	8:39.53	8:40.62	8:41.72	8:42.81
480	8:43.91	8:45.00	8:46.09	8:47.19	8:48.28	8:49.37	8:50.47	8:51.56	8:52.66	8:53.75
490	8:54.84	8:55.94	8:57.03	8:58.13	8:59.22	9:00.31	9:01.41	9:02.50	9:03.59	9:04.69
500	9:05.78	9:06.87	9:07.97	9:09.06	9:10.16	9:11.25	9:12.34	9:13.44	9:14.53	9:15.62
510	9:16.72	9:17.81	9:18.91	9:20.00	9:21.09	9:22.19	9:23.28	9:24.38	9:25.47	9:26.56
520	9:27.66	9:28.75	9:29.84	9:30.94	9:32.03	9:33.12	9:34.22	9:35.31	9:36.41	9:37.50
530	9:38.59	9:39.69	9:40.78	9:41.87	9:42.97	9:44.06	9:45.16	9:46.25	9:47.34	9:48.44
540	9:49.53	9:50.63	9:51.72	9:52.81	9:53.91	9:55.00	9:56.09	9:57.19	9:58.28	9:59.37
550	10:00.47	10:01.56	10:02.66	10:03.75	10:04.84	10:05.94	10:07.03	10:08.12	10:09.22	10:10.31
560	10:11.41	10:12.50	10:13.59	10:14.69	10:15.78	10:16.88	10:17.97	10:19.06	10:20.16	10:21.25
570	10:22.34	10:23.44	10:24.53	10:25.62	10:26.72	10:27.81	10:28.91	10:30.00	10:31.09	10:32.19
580	10:33.28	10:34.37	10:35.47	10:36.56	10:37.66	10:38.75	10:39.84	10:40.94	10:42.03	10:43.13
590	10:44.22	10:45.31	10:46.41	10:47.50	10:48.59	10:49.69	10:50.78	10:51.87	10:52.97	10:54.06

♩. = 1.64; ♩ = 1.09; ♪. = 0.82; (3: ♩ 𝄾) = 0.73; ♪ = 0.55; (3: ♪ 𝄾 𝄾) = 0.36; 𝅘𝅥𝅯 = 0.27 seconds

CLICK: 26⅜ FRAMES; M.M.: 54.60

Click	0	1	2	3	4	5	6	7	8	9
000	0:00.00	0:00.00	0:01.10	0:02.20	0:03.30	0:04.40	0:05.49	0:06.59	0:07.69	0:08.79
010	0:09.89	0:10.99	0:12.09	0:13.19	0:14.29	0:15.39	0:16.48	0:17.58	0:18.68	0:19.78
020	0:20.88	0:21.98	0:23.08	0:24.18	0:25.28	0:26.37	0:27.47	0:28.57	0:29.67	0:30.77
030	0:31.87	0:32.97	0:34.07	0:35.17	0:36.27	0:37.36	0:38.46	0:39.56	0:40.66	0:41.76
040	0:42.86	0:43.96	0:45.06	0:46.16	0:47.26	0:48.35	0:49.45	0:50.55	0:51.65	0:52.75
050	0:53.85	0:54.95	0:56.05	0:57.15	0:58.24	0:59.34	1:00.44	1:01.54	1:02.64	1:03.74
060	1:04.84	1:05.94	1:07.04	1:08.14	1:09.23	1:10.33	1:11.43	1:12.53	1:13.63	1:14.73
070	1:15.83	1:16.93	1:18.03	1:19.12	1:20.22	1:21.32	1:22.42	1:23.52	1:24.62	1:25.72
080	1:26.82	1:27.92	1:29.02	1:30.11	1:31.21	1:32.31	1:33.41	1:34.51	1:35.61	1:36.71
090	1:37.81	1:38.91	1:40.01	1:41.10	1:42.20	1:43.30	1:44.40	1:45.50	1:46.60	1:47.70
100	1:48.80	1:49.90	1:50.99	1:52.09	1:53.19	1:54.29	1:55.39	1:56.49	1:57.59	1:58.69
110	1:59.79	2:00.89	2:01.98	2:03.08	2:04.18	2:05.28	2:06.38	2:07.48	2:08.58	2:09.68
120	2:10.78	2:11.87	2:12.97	2:14.07	2:15.17	2:16.27	2:17.37	2:18.47	2:19.57	2:20.67
130	2:21.77	2:22.86	2:23.96	2:25.06	2:26.16	2:27.26	2:28.36	2:29.46	2:30.56	2:31.66
140	2:32.76	2:33.85	2:34.95	2:36.05	2:37.15	2:38.25	2:39.35	2:40.45	2:41.55	2:42.65
150	2:43.74	2:44.84	2:45.94	2:47.04	2:48.14	2:49.24	2:50.34	2:51.44	2:52.54	2:53.64
160	2:54.73	2:55.83	2:56.93	2:58.03	2:59.13	3:00.23	3:01.33	3:02.43	3:03.53	3:04.62
170	3:05.72	3:06.82	3:07.92	3:09.02	3:10.12	3:11.22	3:12.32	3:13.42	3:14.52	3:15.61
180	3:16.71	3:17.81	3:18.91	3:20.01	3:21.11	3:22.21	3:23.31	3:24.41	3:25.51	3:26.60
190	3:27.70	3:28.80	3:29.90	3:31.00	3:32.10	3:33.20	3:34.30	3:35.40	3:36.49	3:37.59
200	3:38.69	3:39.79	3:40.89	3:41.99	3:43.09	3:44.19	3:45.29	3:46.39	3:47.48	3:48.58
210	3:49.68	3:50.78	3:51.88	3:52.98	3:54.08	3:55.18	3:56.28	3:57.37	3:58.47	3:59.57
220	4:00.67	4:01.77	4:02.87	4:03.97	4:05.07	4:06.17	4:07.27	4:08.36	4:09.46	4:10.56
230	4:11.66	4:12.76	4:13.86	4:14.96	4:16.06	4:17.16	4:18.26	4:19.35	4:20.45	4:21.55
240	4:22.65	4:23.75	4:24.85	4:25.95	4:27.05	4:28.15	4:29.24	4:30.34	4:31.44	4:32.54
250	4:33.64	4:34.74	4:35.84	4:36.94	4:38.04	4:39.14	4:40.23	4:41.33	4:42.43	4:43.53
260	4:44.63	4:45.73	4:46.83	4:47.93	4:49.03	4:50.12	4:51.22	4:52.32	4:53.42	4:54.52
270	4:55.62	4:56.72	4:57.82	4:58.92	5:00.02	5:01.11	5:02.21	5:03.31	5:04.41	5:05.51
280	5:06.61	5:07.71	5:08.81	5:09.91	5:11.01	5:12.10	5:13.20	5:14.30	5:15.40	5:16.50
290	5:17.60	5:18.70	5:19.80	5:20.90	5:21.99	5:23.09	5:24.19	5:25.29	5:26.39	5:27.49
300	5:28.59	5:29.69	5:30.79	5:31.89	5:32.98	5:34.08	5:35.18	5:36.28	5:37.38	5:38.48
310	5:39.58	5:40.68	5:41.78	5:42.87	5:43.97	5:45.07	5:46.17	5:47.27	5:48.37	5:49.47
320	5:50.57	5:51.67	5:52.77	5:53.86	5:54.96	5:56.06	5:57.16	5:58.26	5:59.36	6:00.46
330	6:01.56	6:02.66	6:03.76	6:04.85	6:05.95	6:07.05	6:08.15	6:09.25	6:10.35	6:11.45
340	6:12.55	6:13.65	6:14.74	6:15.84	6:16.94	6:18.04	6:19.14	6:20.24	6:21.34	6:22.44
350	6:23.54	6:24.64	6:25.73	6:26.83	6:27.93	6:29.03	6:30.13	6:31.23	6:32.33	6:33.43
360	6:34.53	6:35.62	6:36.72	6:37.82	6:38.92	6:40.02	6:41.12	6:42.22	6:43.32	6:44.42
370	6:45.52	6:46.61	6:47.71	6:48.81	6:49.91	6:51.01	6:52.11	6:53.21	6:54.31	6:55.41
380	6:56.51	6:57.60	6:58.70	6:59.80	7:00.90	7:02.00	7:03.10	7:04.20	7:05.30	7:06.40
390	7:07.49	7:08.59	7:09.69	7:10.79	7:11.89	7:12.99	7:14.09	7:15.19	7:16.29	7:17.39
400	7:18.48	7:19.58	7:20.68	7:21.78	7:22.88	7:23.98	7:25.08	7:26.18	7:27.28	7:28.37
410	7:29.47	7:30.57	7:31.67	7:32.77	7:33.87	7:34.97	7:36.07	7:37.17	7:38.27	7:39.36
420	7:40.46	7:41.56	7:42.66	7:43.76	7:44.86	7:45.96	7:47.06	7:48.16	7:49.26	7:50.35
430	7:51.45	7:52.55	7:53.65	7:54.75	7:55.85	7:56.95	7:58.05	7:59.15	8:00.24	8:01.34
440	8:02.44	8:03.54	8:04.64	8:05.74	8:06.84	8:07.94	8:09.04	8:10.14	8:11.23	8:12.33
450	8:13.43	8:14.53	8:15.63	8:16.73	8:17.83	8:18.93	8:20.03	8:21.12	8:22.22	8:23.32
460	8:24.42	8:25.52	8:26.62	8:27.72	8:28.82	8:29.92	8:31.02	8:32.11	8:33.21	8:34.31
470	8:35.41	8:36.51	8:37.61	8:38.71	8:39.81	8:40.91	8:42.01	8:43.10	8:44.20	8:45.30
480	8:46.40	8:47.50	8:48.60	8:49.70	8:50.80	8:51.90	8:52.99	8:54.09	8:55.19	8:56.29
490	8:57.39	8:58.49	8:59.59	9:00.69	9:01.79	9:02.89	9:03.98	9:05.08	9:06.18	9:07.28
500	9:08.38	9:09.48	9:10.58	9:11.68	9:12.78	9:13.87	9:14.97	9:16.07	9:17.17	9:18.27
510	9:19.37	9:20.47	9:21.57	9:22.67	9:23.77	9:24.86	9:25.96	9:27.06	9:28.16	9:29.26
520	9:30.36	9:31.46	9:32.56	9:33.66	9:34.76	9:35.85	9:36.95	9:38.05	9:39.15	9:40.25
530	9:41.35	9:42.45	9:43.55	9:44.65	9:45.74	9:46.84	9:47.94	9:49.04	9:50.14	9:51.24
540	9:52.34	9:53.44	9:54.54	9:55.64	9:56.73	9:57.83	9:58.93	10:00.03	10:01.13	10:02.23
550	10:03.33	10:04.43	10:05.53	10:06.62	10:07.72	10:08.82	10:09.92	10:11.02	10:12.12	10:13.22
560	10:14.32	10:15.42	10:16.52	10:17.61	10:18.71	10:19.81	10:20.91	10:22.01	10:23.11	10:24.21
570	10:25.31	10:26.41	10:27.51	10:28.60	10:29.70	10:30.80	10:31.90	10:33.00	10:34.10	10:35.20
580	10:36.30	10:37.40	10:38.49	10:39.59	10:40.69	10:41.79	10:42.89	10:43.99	10:45.09	10:46.19
590	10:47.29	10:48.39	10:49.48	10:50.58	10:51.68	10:52.78	10:53.88	10:54.98	10:56.08	10:57.18

♩. = 1.65; ♩ = 1.10; ♪. = 0.82; (3) ♩ 𝄾 = 0.73; ♪ = 0.55; (3) ♪ 𝄾 𝄾 = 0.37; 𝅘𝅥𝅯 = 0.27 seconds

CLICK: 26 4/8 FRAMES; M.M.: 54.34

Click	0	1	2	3	4	5	6	7	8	9
000	0:00.00	0:00.00	0:01.10	0:02.21	0:03.31	0:04.42	0:05.52	0:06.63	0:07.73	0:08.83
010	0:09.94	0:11.04	0:12.15	0:13.25	0:14.35	0:15.46	0:16.56	0:17.67	0:18.77	0:19.88
020	0:20.98	0:22.08	0:23.19	0:24.29	0:25.40	0:26.50	0:27.60	0:28.71	0:29.81	0:30.92
030	0:32.02	0:33.13	0:34.23	0:35.33	0:36.44	0:37.54	0:38.65	0:39.75	0:40.85	0:41.96
040	0:43.06	0:44.17	0:45.27	0:46.38	0:47.48	0:48.58	0:49.69	0:50.79	0:51.90	0:53.00
050	0:54.10	0:55.21	0:56.31	0:57.42	0:58.52	0:59.63	1:00.73	1:01.83	1:02.94	1:04.04
060	1:05.15	1:06.25	1:07.35	1:08.46	1:09.56	1:10.67	1:11.77	1:12.87	1:13.98	1:15.08
070	1:16.19	1:17.29	1:18.40	1:19.50	1:20.60	1:21.71	1:22.81	1:23.92	1:25.02	1:26.13
080	1:27.23	1:28.33	1:29.44	1:30.54	1:31.65	1:32.75	1:33.85	1:34.96	1:36.06	1:37.17
090	1:38.27	1:39.38	1:40.48	1:41.58	1:42.69	1:43.79	1:44.90	1:46.00	1:47.10	1:48.21
100	1:49.31	1:50.42	1:51.52	1:52.63	1:53.73	1:54.83	1:55.94	1:57.04	1:58.15	1:59.25
110	2:00.35	2:01.46	2:02.56	2:03.67	2:04.77	2:05.87	2:06.98	2:08.08	2:09.19	2:10.29
120	2:11.40	2:12.50	2:13.60	2:14.71	2:15.81	2:16.92	2:18.02	2:19.12	2:20.23	2:21.33
130	2:22.44	2:23.54	2:24.65	2:25.75	2:26.85	2:27.96	2:29.06	2:30.17	2:31.27	2:32.37
140	2:33.48	2:34.58	2:35.69	2:36.79	2:37.90	2:39.00	2:40.10	2:41.21	2:42.31	2:43.42
150	2:44.52	2:45.63	2:46.73	2:47.83	2:48.94	2:50.04	2:51.15	2:52.25	2:53.35	2:54.46
160	2:55.56	2:56.67	2:57.77	2:58.88	2:59.98	3:01.08	3:02.19	3:03.29	3:04.40	3:05.50
170	3:06.60	3:07.71	3:08.81	3:09.92	3:11.02	3:12.13	3:13.23	3:14.33	3:15.44	3:16.54
180	3:17.65	3:18.75	3:19.85	3:20.96	3:22.06	3:23.17	3:24.27	3:25.38	3:26.48	3:27.58
190	3:28.69	3:29.79	3:30.90	3:32.00	3:33.10	3:34.21	3:35.31	3:36.42	3:37.52	3:38.62
200	3:39.73	3:40.83	3:41.94	3:43.04	3:44.15	3:45.25	3:46.35	3:47.46	3:48.56	3:49.67
210	3:50.77	3:51.87	3:52.98	3:54.08	3:55.19	3:56.29	3:57.40	3:58.50	3:59.60	4:00.71
220	4:01.81	4:02.92	4:04.02	4:05.13	4:06.23	4:07.33	4:08.44	4:09.54	4:10.65	4:11.75
230	4:12.85	4:13.96	4:15.06	4:16.17	4:17.27	4:18.38	4:19.48	4:20.58	4:21.69	4:22.79
240	4:23.90	4:25.00	4:26.10	4:27.21	4:28.31	4:29.42	4:30.52	4:31.63	4:32.73	4:33.83
250	4:34.94	4:36.04	4:37.15	4:38.25	4:39.35	4:40.46	4:41.56	4:42.67	4:43.77	4:44.88
260	4:45.98	4:47.08	4:48.19	4:49.29	4:50.40	4:51.50	4:52.60	4:53.71	4:54.81	4:55.92
270	4:57.02	4:58.13	4:59.23	5:00.33	5:01.44	5:02.54	5:03.65	5:04.75	5:05.85	5:06.96
280	5:08.06	5:09.17	5:10.27	5:11.37	5:12.48	5:13.58	5:14.69	5:15.79	5:16.90	5:18.00
290	5:19.10	5:20.21	5:21.31	5:22.42	5:23.52	5:24.62	5:25.73	5:26.83	5:27.94	5:29.04
300	5:30.15	5:31.25	5:32.35	5:33.46	5:34.56	5:35.67	5:36.77	5:37.87	5:38.98	5:40.08
310	5:41.19	5:42.29	5:43.40	5:44.50	5:45.60	5:46.71	5:47.81	5:48.92	5:50.02	5:51.12
320	5:52.23	5:53.33	5:54.44	5:55.54	5:56.65	5:57.75	5:58.85	5:59.96	6:01.06	6:02.17
330	6:03.27	6:04.37	6:05.48	6:06.58	6:07.69	6:08.79	6:09.90	6:11.00	6:12.10	6:13.21
340	6:14.31	6:15.42	6:16.52	6:17.62	6:18.73	6:19.83	6:20.94	6:22.04	6:23.15	6:24.25
350	6:25.35	6:26.46	6:27.56	6:28.67	6:29.77	6:30.87	6:31.98	6:33.08	6:34.19	6:35.29
360	6:36.40	6:37.50	6:38.60	6:39.71	6:40.81	6:41.92	6:43.02	6:44.12	6:45.23	6:46.33
370	6:47.44	6:48.54	6:49.65	6:50.75	6:51.85	6:52.96	6:54.06	6:55.17	6:56.27	6:57.37
380	6:58.48	6:59.58	7:00.69	7:01.79	7:02.90	7:04.00	7:05.10	7:06.21	7:07.31	7:08.42
390	7:09.52	7:10.63	7:11.73	7:12.83	7:13.94	7:15.04	7:16.15	7:17.25	7:18.35	7:19.46
400	7:20.56	7:21.67	7:22.77	7:23.88	7:24.98	7:26.08	7:27.19	7:28.29	7:29.40	7:30.50
410	7:31.60	7:32.71	7:33.81	7:34.92	7:36.02	7:37.13	7:38.23	7:39.33	7:40.44	7:41.54
420	7:42.65	7:43.75	7:44.85	7:45.96	7:47.06	7:48.17	7:49.27	7:50.38	7:51.48	7:52.58
430	7:53.69	7:54.79	7:55.90	7:57.00	7:58.10	7:59.21	8:00.31	8:01.42	8:02.52	8:03.62
440	8:04.73	8:05.83	8:06.94	8:08.04	8:09.15	8:10.25	8:11.35	8:12.46	8:13.56	8:14.67
450	8:15.77	8:16.88	8:17.98	8:19.08	8:20.19	8:21.29	8:22.40	8:23.50	8:24.60	8:25.71
460	8:26.81	8:27.92	8:29.02	8:30.12	8:31.23	8:32.33	8:33.44	8:34.54	8:35.65	8:36.75
470	8:37.85	8:38.96	8:40.06	8:41.17	8:42.27	8:43.37	8:44.48	8:45.58	8:46.69	8:47.79
480	8:48.90	8:50.00	8:51.10	8:52.21	8:53.31	8:54.42	8:55.52	8:56.63	8:57.73	8:58.83
490	8:59.94	9:01.04	9:02.15	9:03.25	9:04.35	9:05.46	9:06.56	9:07.67	9:08.77	9:09.87
500	9:10.98	9:12.08	9:13.19	9:14.29	9:15.40	9:16.50	9:17.60	9:18.71	9:19.81	9:20.92
510	9:22.02	9:23.13	9:24.23	9:25.33	9:26.44	9:27.54	9:28.65	9:29.75	9:30.85	9:31.96
520	9:33.06	9:34.17	9:35.27	9:36.37	9:37.48	9:38.58	9:39.69	9:40.79	9:41.90	9:43.00
530	9:44.10	9:45.21	9:46.31	9:47.42	9:48.52	9:49.63	9:50.73	9:51.83	9:52.94	9:54.04
540	9:55.15	9:56.25	9:57.35	9:58.46	9:59.56	10:00.67	10:01.77	10:02.87	10:03.98	10:05.08
550	10:06.19	10:07.29	10:08.40	10:09.50	10:10.60	10:11.71	10:12.81	10:13.92	10:15.02	10:16.13
560	10:17.23	10:18.33	10:19.44	10:20.54	10:21.65	10:22.75	10:23.85	10:24.96	10:26.06	10:27.17
570	10:28.27	10:29.37	10:30.48	10:31.58	10:32.69	10:33.79	10:34.90	10:36.00	10:37.10	10:38.21
580	10:39.31	10:40.42	10:41.52	10:42.63	10:43.73	10:44.83	10:45.94	10:47.04	10:48.15	10:49.25
590	10:50.35	10:51.46	10:52.56	10:53.67	10:54.77	10:55.87	10:56.98	10:58.08	10:59.19	11:00.29

♩. = 1.66; ♩ = 1.10; ♪. = 0.83; (triplet 3: ♩ 𝄾) = 0.74; ♪ = 0.55; (triplet 3: ♪ 𝄾 𝄾) = 0.37; 𝅘𝅥𝅯 = 0.28 seconds

CLICK: $26\frac{5}{8}$ FRAMES; M.M.: 54.08

Click	0	1	2	3	4	5	6	7	8	9
000	0:00.00	0:00.00	0:01.11	0:02.22	0:03.33	0:04.44	0:05.55	0:06.66	0:07.77	0:08.88
010	0:09.98	0:11.09	0:12.20	0:13.31	0:14.42	0:15.53	0:16.64	0:17.75	0:18.86	0:19.97
020	0:21.08	0:22.19	0:23.30	0:24.41	0:25.52	0:26.63	0:27.73	0:28.84	0:29.95	0:31.06
030	0:32.17	0:33.28	0:34.39	0:35.50	0:36.61	0:37.72	0:38.83	0:39.94	0:41.05	0:42.16
040	0:43.27	0:44.38	0:45.48	0:46.59	0:47.70	0:48.81	0:49.92	0:51.03	0:52.14	0:53.25
050	0:54.36	0:55.47	0:56.58	0:57.69	0:58.80	0:59.91	1:01.02	1:02.12	1:03.23	1:04.34
060	1:05.45	1:06.56	1:07.67	1:08.78	1:09.89	1:11.00	1:12.11	1:13.22	1:14.33	1:15.44
070	1:16.55	1:17.66	1:18.77	1:19.87	1:20.98	1:22.09	1:23.20	1:24.31	1:25.42	1:26.53
080	1:27.64	1:28.75	1:29.86	1:30.97	1:32.08	1:33.19	1:34.30	1:35.41	1:36.52	1:37.63
090	1:38.73	1:39.84	1:40.95	1:42.06	1:43.17	1:44.28	1:45.39	1:46.50	1:47.61	1:48.72
100	1:49.83	1:50.94	1:52.05	1:53.16	1:54.27	1:55.37	1:56.48	1:57.59	1:58.70	1:59.81
110	2:00.92	2:02.03	2:03.14	2:04.25	2:05.36	2:06.47	2:07.58	2:08.69	2:09.80	2:10.91
120	2:12.02	2:13.13	2:14.23	2:15.34	2:16.45	2:17.56	2:18.67	2:19.78	2:20.89	2:22.00
130	2:23.11	2:24.22	2:25.33	2:26.44	2:27.55	2:28.66	2:29.77	2:30.87	2:31.98	2:33.09
140	2:34.20	2:35.31	2:36.42	2:37.53	2:38.64	2:39.75	2:40.86	2:41.97	2:43.08	2:44.19
150	2:45.30	2:46.41	2:47.52	2:48.62	2:49.73	2:50.84	2:51.95	2:53.06	2:54.17	2:55.28
160	2:56.39	2:57.50	2:58.61	2:59.72	3:00.83	3:01.94	3:03.05	3:04.16	3:05.27	3:06.37
170	3:07.48	3:08.59	3:09.70	3:10.81	3:11.92	3:13.03	3:14.14	3:15.25	3:16.36	3:17.47
180	3:18.58	3:19.69	3:20.80	3:21.91	3:23.02	3:24.12	3:25.23	3:26.34	3:27.45	3:28.56
190	3:29.67	3:30.78	3:31.89	3:33.00	3:34.11	3:35.22	3:36.33	3:37.44	3:38.55	3:39.66
200	3:40.77	3:41.87	3:42.98	3:44.09	3:45.20	3:46.31	3:47.42	3:48.53	3:49.64	3:50.75
210	3:51.86	3:52.97	3:54.08	3:55.19	3:56.30	3:57.41	3:58.52	3:59.62	4:00.73	4:01.84
220	4:02.95	4:04.06	4:05.17	4:06.28	4:07.39	4:08.50	4:09.61	4:10.72	4:11.83	4:12.94
230	4:14.05	4:15.16	4:16.27	4:17.37	4:18.48	4:19.59	4:20.70	4:21.81	4:22.92	4:24.03
240	4:25.14	4:26.25	4:27.36	4:28.47	4:29.58	4:30.69	4:31.80	4:32.91	4:34.02	4:35.12
250	4:36.23	4:37.34	4:38.45	4:39.56	4:40.67	4:41.78	4:42.89	4:44.00	4:45.11	4:46.22
260	4:47.33	4:48.44	4:49.55	4:50.66	4:51.77	4:52.87	4:53.98	4:55.09	4:56.20	4:57.31
270	4:58.42	4:59.53	5:00.64	5:01.75	5:02.86	5:03.97	5:05.08	5:06.19	5:07.30	5:08.41
280	5:09.52	5:10.62	5:11.73	5:12.84	5:13.95	5:15.06	5:16.17	5:17.28	5:18.39	5:19.50
290	5:20.61	5:21.72	5:22.83	5:23.94	5:25.05	5:26.16	5:27.27	5:28.37	5:29.48	5:30.59
300	5:31.70	5:32.81	5:33.92	5:35.03	5:36.14	5:37.25	5:38.36	5:39.47	5:40.58	5:41.69
310	5:42.80	5:43.91	5:45.02	5:46.12	5:47.23	5:48.34	5:49.45	5:50.56	5:51.67	5:52.78
320	5:53.89	5:55.00	5:56.11	5:57.22	5:58.33	5:59.44	6:00.55	6:01.66	6:02.77	6:03.87
330	6:04.98	6:06.09	6:07.20	6:08.31	6:09.42	6:10.53	6:11.64	6:12.75	6:13.86	6:14.97
340	6:16.08	6:17.19	6:18.30	6:19.41	6:20.52	6:21.62	6:22.73	6:23.84	6:24.95	6:26.06
350	6:27.17	6:28.28	6:29.39	6:30.50	6:31.61	6:32.72	6:33.83	6:34.94	6:36.05	6:37.16
360	6:38.27	6:39.37	6:40.48	6:41.59	6:42.70	6:43.81	6:44.92	6:46.03	6:47.14	6:48.25
370	6:49.36	6:50.47	6:51.58	6:52.69	6:53.80	6:54.91	6:56.02	6:57.12	6:58.23	6:59.34
380	7:00.45	7:01.56	7:02.67	7:03.78	7:04.89	7:06.00	7:07.11	7:08.22	7:09.33	7:10.44
390	7:11.55	7:12.66	7:13.77	7:14.87	7:15.98	7:17.09	7:18.20	7:19.31	7:20.42	7:21.53
400	7:22.64	7:23.75	7:24.86	7:25.97	7:27.08	7:28.19	7:29.30	7:30.41	7:31.52	7:32.62
410	7:33.73	7:34.84	7:35.95	7:37.06	7:38.17	7:39.28	7:40.39	7:41.50	7:42.61	7:43.72
420	7:44.83	7:45.94	7:47.05	7:48.16	7:49.27	7:50.37	7:51.48	7:52.59	7:53.70	7:54.81
430	7:55.92	7:57.03	7:58.14	7:59.25	8:00.36	8:01.47	8:02.58	8:03.69	8:04.80	8:05.91
440	8:07.02	8:08.12	8:09.23	8:10.34	8:11.45	8:12.56	8:13.67	8:14.78	8:15.89	8:17.00
450	8:18.11	8:19.22	8:20.33	8:21.44	8:22.55	8:23.66	8:24.77	8:25.87	8:26.98	8:28.09
460	8:29.20	8:30.31	8:31.42	8:32.53	8:33.64	8:34.75	8:35.86	8:36.97	8:38.08	8:39.19
470	8:40.30	8:41.41	8:42.52	8:43.62	8:44.73	8:45.84	8:46.95	8:48.06	8:49.17	8:50.28
480	8:51.39	8:52.50	8:53.61	8:54.72	8:55.83	8:56.94	8:58.05	8:59.16	9:00.27	9:01.37
490	9:02.48	9:03.59	9:04.70	9:05.81	9:06.92	9:08.03	9:09.14	9:10.25	9:11.36	9:12.47
500	9:13.58	9:14.69	9:15.80	9:16.91	9:18.02	9:19.12	9:20.23	9:21.34	9:22.45	9:23.56
510	9:24.67	9:25.78	9:26.89	9:28.00	9:29.11	9:30.22	9:31.33	9:32.44	9:33.55	9:34.66
520	9:35.77	9:36.87	9:37.98	9:39.09	9:40.20	9:41.31	9:42.42	9:43.53	9:44.64	9:45.75
530	9:46.86	9:47.97	9:49.08	9:50.19	9:51.30	9:52.41	9:53.52	9:54.62	9:55.73	9:56.84
540	9:57.95	9:59.06	10:00.17	10:01.28	10:02.39	10:03.50	10:04.61	10:05.72	10:06.83	10:07.94
550	10:09.05	10:10.16	10:11.27	10:12.37	10:13.48	10:14.59	10:15.70	10:16.81	10:17.92	10:19.03
560	10:20.14	10:21.25	10:22.36	10:23.47	10:24.58	10:25.69	10:26.80	10:27.91	10:29.02	10:30.12
570	10:31.23	10:32.34	10:33.45	10:34.56	10:35.67	10:36.78	10:37.89	10:39.00	10:40.11	10:41.22
580	10:42.33	10:43.44	10:44.55	10:45.66	10:46.77	10:47.87	10:48.98	10:50.09	10:51.20	10:52.31
590	10:53.42	10:54.53	10:55.64	10:56.75	10:57.86	10:58.97	11:00.08	11:01.19	11:02.30	11:03.41

♩. = 1.66; ♩ = 1.11; ♪. = 0.83; (triplet ♩ 𝄾) = 0.74; ♪ = 0.55; (triplet ♪ 𝄾 𝄾) = 0.37; 𝅘𝅥𝅯 = 0.28 seconds

CLICK: 26 6/8 FRAMES; M.M.: 53.83

Click	0	1	2	3	4	5	6	7	8	9
000	0:00.00	0:00.00	0:01.11	0:02.23	0:03.34	0:04.46	0:05.57	0:06.69	0:07.80	0:08.92
010	0:10.03	0:11.15	0:12.26	0:13.38	0:14.49	0:15.60	0:16.72	0:17.83	0:18.95	0:20.06
020	0:21.18	0:22.29	0:23.41	0:24.52	0:25.64	0:26.75	0:27.86	0:28.98	0:30.09	0:31.21
030	0:32.32	0:33.44	0:34.55	0:35.67	0:36.78	0:37.90	0:39.01	0:40.13	0:41.24	0:42.35
040	0:43.47	0:44.58	0:45.70	0:46.81	0:47.93	0:49.04	0:50.16	0:51.27	0:52.39	0:53.50
050	0:54.61	0:55.73	0:56.84	0:57.96	0:59.07	1:00.19	1:01.30	1:02.42	1:03.53	1:04.65
060	1:05.76	1:06.88	1:07.99	1:09.10	1:10.22	1:11.33	1:12.45	1:13.56	1:14.68	1:15.79
070	1:16.91	1:18.02	1:19.14	1:20.25	1:21.36	1:22.48	1:23.59	1:24.71	1:25.82	1:26.94
080	1:28.05	1:29.17	1:30.28	1:31.40	1:32.51	1:33.63	1:34.74	1:35.85	1:36.97	1:38.08
090	1:39.20	1:40.31	1:41.43	1:42.54	1:43.66	1:44.77	1:45.89	1:47.00	1:48.11	1:49.23
100	1:50.34	1:51.46	1:52.57	1:53.69	1:54.80	1:55.92	1:57.03	1:58.15	1:59.26	2:00.38
110	2:01.49	2:02.60	2:03.72	2:04.83	2:05.95	2:07.06	2:08.18	2:09.29	2:10.41	2:11.52
120	2:12.64	2:13.75	2:14.86	2:15.98	2:17.09	2:18.21	2:19.32	2:20.44	2:21.55	2:22.67
130	2:23.78	2:24.90	2:26.01	2:27.13	2:28.24	2:29.35	2:30.47	2:31.58	2:32.70	2:33.81
140	2:34.93	2:36.04	2:37.16	2:38.27	2:39.39	2:40.50	2:41.61	2:42.73	2:43.84	2:44.96
150	2:46.07	2:47.19	2:48.30	2:49.42	2:50.53	2:51.65	2:52.76	2:53.88	2:54.99	2:56.10
160	2:57.22	2:58.33	2:59.45	3:00.56	3:01.68	3:02.79	3:03.91	3:05.02	3:06.14	3:07.25
170	3:08.36	3:09.48	3:10.59	3:11.71	3:12.82	3:13.94	3:15.05	3:16.17	3:17.28	3:18.40
180	3:19.51	3:20.63	3:21.74	3:22.85	3:23.97	3:25.08	3:26.20	3:27.31	3:28.43	3:29.54
190	3:30.66	3:31.77	3:32.89	3:34.00	3:35.11	3:36.23	3:37.34	3:38.46	3:39.57	3:40.69
200	3:41.80	3:42.92	3:44.03	3:45.15	3:46.26	3:47.38	3:48.49	3:49.60	3:50.72	3:51.83
210	3:52.95	3:54.06	3:55.18	3:56.29	3:57.41	3:58.52	3:59.64	4:00.75	4:01.86	4:02.98
220	4:04.09	4:05.21	4:06.32	4:07.44	4:08.55	4:09.67	4:10.78	4:11.90	4:13.01	4:14.13
230	4:15.24	4:16.35	4:17.47	4:18.58	4:19.70	4:20.81	4:21.93	4:23.04	4:24.16	4:25.27
240	4:26.39	4:27.50	4:28.61	4:29.73	4:30.84	4:31.96	4:33.07	4:34.19	4:35.30	4:36.42
250	4:37.53	4:38.65	4:39.76	4:40.88	4:41.99	4:43.10	4:44.22	4:45.33	4:46.45	4:47.56
260	4:48.68	4:49.79	4:50.91	4:52.02	4:53.14	4:54.25	4:55.36	4:56.48	4:57.59	4:58.71
270	4:59.82	5:00.94	5:02.05	5:03.17	5:04.28	5:05.40	5:06.51	5:07.62	5:08.74	5:09.85
280	5:10.97	5:12.08	5:13.20	5:14.31	5:15.43	5:16.54	5:17.66	5:18.77	5:19.89	5:21.00
290	5:22.11	5:23.23	5:24.34	5:25.46	5:26.57	5:27.69	5:28.80	5:29.92	5:31.03	5:32.15
300	5:33.26	5:34.38	5:35.49	5:36.60	5:37.72	5:38.83	5:39.95	5:41.06	5:42.18	5:43.29
310	5:44.41	5:45.52	5:46.64	5:47.75	5:48.86	5:49.98	5:51.09	5:52.21	5:53.32	5:54.44
320	5:55.55	5:56.67	5:57.78	5:58.90	6:00.01	6:01.13	6:02.24	6:03.35	6:04.47	6:05.58
330	6:06.70	6:07.81	6:08.93	6:10.04	6:11.16	6:12.27	6:13.39	6:14.50	6:15.61	6:16.73
340	6:17.84	6:18.96	6:20.07	6:21.19	6:22.30	6:23.42	6:24.53	6:25.65	6:26.76	6:27.88
350	6:28.99	6:30.10	6:31.22	6:32.33	6:33.45	6:34.56	6:35.68	6:36.79	6:37.91	6:39.02
360	6:40.14	6:41.25	6:42.36	6:43.48	6:44.59	6:45.71	6:46.82	6:47.94	6:49.05	6:50.17
370	6:51.28	6:52.40	6:53.51	6:54.62	6:55.74	6:56.85	6:57.97	6:59.08	7:00.20	7:01.31
380	7:02.43	7:03.54	7:04.66	7:05.77	7:06.89	7:08.00	7:09.11	7:10.23	7:11.34	7:12.46
390	7:13.57	7:14.69	7:15.80	7:16.92	7:18.03	7:19.15	7:20.26	7:21.38	7:22.49	7:23.60
400	7:24.72	7:25.83	7:26.95	7:28.06	7:29.18	7:30.29	7:31.41	7:32.52	7:33.64	7:34.75
410	7:35.86	7:36.98	7:38.09	7:39.21	7:40.32	7:41.44	7:42.55	7:43.67	7:44.78	7:45.90
420	7:47.01	7:48.13	7:49.24	7:50.35	7:51.47	7:52.58	7:53.70	7:54.81	7:55.93	7:57.04
430	7:58.16	7:59.27	8:00.39	8:01.50	8:02.61	8:03.73	8:04.84	8:05.96	8:07.07	8:08.19
440	8:09.30	8:10.42	8:11.53	8:12.65	8:13.76	8:14.88	8:15.99	8:17.10	8:18.22	8:19.33
450	8:20.45	8:21.56	8:22.68	8:23.79	8:24.91	8:26.02	8:27.14	8:28.25	8:29.36	8:30.48
460	8:31.59	8:32.71	8:33.82	8:34.94	8:36.05	8:37.17	8:38.28	8:39.40	8:40.51	8:41.63
470	8:42.74	8:43.85	8:44.97	8:46.08	8:47.20	8:48.31	8:49.43	8:50.54	8:51.66	8:52.77
480	8:53.89	8:55.00	8:56.11	8:57.23	8:58.34	8:59.46	9:00.57	9:01.69	9:02.80	9:03.92
490	9:05.03	9:06.15	9:07.26	9:08.38	9:09.49	9:10.60	9:11.72	9:12.83	9:13.95	9:15.06
500	9:16.18	9:17.29	9:18.41	9:19.52	9:20.64	9:21.75	9:22.86	9:23.98	9:25.09	9:26.21
510	9:27.32	9:28.44	9:29.55	9:30.67	9:31.78	9:32.90	9:34.01	9:35.13	9:36.24	9:37.35
520	9:38.47	9:39.58	9:40.70	9:41.81	9:42.93	9:44.04	9:45.16	9:46.27	9:47.39	9:48.50
530	9:49.61	9:50.73	9:51.84	9:52.96	9:54.07	9:55.19	9:56.30	9:57.42	9:58.53	9:59.65
540	10:00.76	10:01.88	10:02.99	10:04.10	10:05.22	10:06.33	10:07.45	10:08.56	10:09.68	10:10.79
550	10:11.91	10:13.02	10:14.14	10:15.25	10:16.36	10:17.48	10:18.59	10:19.71	10:20.82	10:21.94
560	10:23.05	10:24.17	10:25.28	10:26.40	10:27.51	10:28.62	10:29.74	10:30.85	10:31.97	10:33.08
570	10:34.20	10:35.31	10:36.43	10:37.54	10:38.66	10:39.77	10:40.89	10:42.00	10:43.11	10:44.23
580	10:45.34	10:46.46	10:47.57	10:48.69	10:49.80	10:50.92	10:52.03	10:53.15	10:54.26	10:55.37
590	10:56.49	10:57.60	10:58.72	10:59.83	11:00.95	11:02.06	11:03.18	11:04.29	11:05.41	11:06.52

♩. = 1.67; ♩ = 1.11; ♪. = 0.84; (triplet ♩ 𝄾) = 0.74; ♪ = 0.56; (triplet ♪ 𝄾 𝄾) = 0.37; 𝅘𝅥𝅯 = 0.28 seconds

CLICK: 26⅞ FRAMES; M.M.: 53.58

Click	0	1	2	3	4	5	6	7	8	9
000	0:00.00	0:00.00	0:01.12	0:02.24	0:03.36	0:04.48	0:05.60	0:06.72	0:07.84	0:08.96
010	0:10.08	0:11.20	0:12.32	0:13.44	0:14.56	0:15.68	0:16.80	0:17.92	0:19.04	0:20.16
020	0:21.28	0:22.40	0:23.52	0:24.64	0:25.76	0:26.88	0:27.99	0:29.11	0:30.23	0:31.35
030	0:32.47	0:33.59	0:34.71	0:35.83	0:36.95	0:38.07	0:39.19	0:40.31	0:41.43	0:42.55
040	0:43.67	0:44.79	0:45.91	0:47.03	0:48.15	0:49.27	0:50.39	0:51.51	0:52.63	0:53.75
050	0:54.87	0:55.99	0:57.11	0:58.23	0:59.35	1:00.47	1:01.59	1:02.71	1:03.83	1:04.95
060	1:06.07	1:07.19	1:08.31	1:09.43	1:10.55	1:11.67	1:12.79	1:13.91	1:15.03	1:16.15
070	1:17.27	1:18.39	1:19.51	1:20.63	1:21.74	1:22.86	1:23.98	1:25.10	1:26.22	1:27.34
080	1:28.46	1:29.58	1:30.70	1:31.82	1:32.94	1:34.06	1:35.18	1:36.30	1:37.42	1:38.54
090	1:39.66	1:40.78	1:41.90	1:43.02	1:44.14	1:45.26	1:46.38	1:47.50	1:48.62	1:49.74
100	1:50.86	1:51.98	1:53.10	1:54.22	1:55.34	1:56.46	1:57.58	1:58.70	1:59.82	2:00.94
110	2:02.06	2:03.18	2:04.30	2:05.42	2:06.54	2:07.66	2:08.78	2:09.90	2:11.02	2:12.14
120	2:13.26	2:14.37	2:15.49	2:16.61	2:17.73	2:18.85	2:19.97	2:21.09	2:22.21	2:23.33
130	2:24.45	2:25.57	2:26.69	2:27.81	2:28.93	2:30.05	2:31.17	2:32.29	2:33.41	2:34.53
140	2:35.65	2:36.77	2:37.89	2:39.01	2:40.13	2:41.25	2:42.37	2:43.49	2:44.61	2:45.73
150	2:46.85	2:47.97	2:49.09	2:50.21	2:51.33	2:52.45	2:53.57	2:54.69	2:55.81	2:56.93
160	2:58.05	2:59.17	3:00.29	3:01.41	3:02.53	3:03.65	3:04.77	3:05.89	3:07.01	3:08.12
170	3:09.24	3:10.36	3:11.48	3:12.60	3:13.72	3:14.84	3:15.96	3:17.08	3:18.20	3:19.32
180	3:20.44	3:21.56	3:22.68	3:23.80	3:24.92	3:26.04	3:27.16	3:28.28	3:29.40	3:30.52
190	3:31.64	3:32.76	3:33.88	3:35.00	3:36.12	3:37.24	3:38.36	3:39.48	3:40.60	3:41.72
200	3:42.84	3:43.96	3:45.08	3:46.20	3:47.32	3:48.44	3:49.56	3:50.68	3:51.80	3:52.92
210	3:54.04	3:55.16	3:56.28	3:57.40	3:58.52	3:59.64	4:00.76	4:01.88	4:02.99	4:04.11
220	4:05.23	4:06.35	4:07.47	4:08.59	4:09.71	4:10.83	4:11.95	4:13.07	4:14.19	4:15.31
230	4:16.43	4:17.55	4:18.67	4:19.79	4:20.91	4:22.03	4:23.15	4:24.27	4:25.39	4:26.51
240	4:27.63	4:28.75	4:29.87	4:30.99	4:32.11	4:33.23	4:34.35	4:35.47	4:36.59	4:37.71
250	4:38.83	4:39.95	4:41.07	4:42.19	4:43.31	4:44.43	4:45.55	4:46.67	4:47.79	4:48.91
260	4:50.03	4:51.15	4:52.27	4:53.39	4:54.51	4:55.62	4:56.74	4:57.86	4:58.98	5:00.10
270	5:01.22	5:02.34	5:03.46	5:04.58	5:05.70	5:06.82	5:07.94	5:09.06	5:10.18	5:11.30
280	5:12.42	5:13.54	5:14.66	5:15.78	5:16.90	5:18.02	5:19.14	5:20.26	5:21.38	5:22.50
290	5:23.62	5:24.74	5:25.86	5:26.98	5:28.10	5:29.22	5:30.34	5:31.46	5:32.58	5:33.70
300	5:34.82	5:35.94	5:37.06	5:38.18	5:39.30	5:40.42	5:41.54	5:42.66	5:43.78	5:44.90
310	5:46.02	5:47.14	5:48.26	5:49.37	5:50.49	5:51.61	5:52.73	5:53.85	5:54.97	5:56.09
320	5:57.21	5:58.33	5:59.45	6:00.57	6:01.69	6:02.81	6:03.93	6:05.05	6:06.17	6:07.29
330	6:08.41	6:09.53	6:10.65	6:11.77	6:12.89	6:14.01	6:15.13	6:16.25	6:17.37	6:18.49
340	6:19.61	6:20.73	6:21.85	6:22.97	6:24.09	6:25.21	6:26.33	6:27.45	6:28.57	6:29.69
350	6:30.81	6:31.93	6:33.05	6:34.17	6:35.29	6:36.41	6:37.53	6:38.65	6:39.77	6:40.89
360	6:42.01	6:43.13	6:44.24	6:45.36	6:46.48	6:47.60	6:48.72	6:49.84	6:50.96	6:52.08
370	6:53.20	6:54.32	6:55.44	6:56.56	6:57.68	6:58.80	6:59.92	7:01.04	7:02.16	7:03.28
380	7:04.40	7:05.52	7:06.64	7:07.76	7:08.88	7:10.00	7:11.12	7:12.24	7:13.36	7:14.48
390	7:15.60	7:16.72	7:17.84	7:18.96	7:20.08	7:21.20	7:22.32	7:23.44	7:24.56	7:25.68
400	7:26.80	7:27.92	7:29.04	7:30.16	7:31.28	7:32.40	7:33.52	7:34.64	7:35.76	7:36.87
410	7:37.99	7:39.11	7:40.23	7:41.35	7:42.47	7:43.59	7:44.71	7:45.83	7:46.95	7:48.07
420	7:49.19	7:50.31	7:51.43	7:52.55	7:53.67	7:54.79	7:55.91	7:57.03	7:58.15	7:59.27
430	8:00.39	8:01.51	8:02.63	8:03.75	8:04.87	8:05.99	8:07.11	8:08.23	8:09.35	8:10.47
440	8:11.59	8:12.71	8:13.83	8:14.95	8:16.07	8:17.19	8:18.31	8:19.43	8:20.55	8:21.67
450	8:22.79	8:23.91	8:25.03	8:26.15	8:27.27	8:28.39	8:29.51	8:30.62	8:31.74	8:32.86
460	8:33.98	8:35.10	8:36.22	8:37.34	8:38.46	8:39.58	8:40.70	8:41.82	8:42.94	8:44.06
470	8:45.18	8:46.30	8:47.42	8:48.54	8:49.66	8:50.78	8:51.90	8:53.02	8:54.14	8:55.26
480	8:56.38	8:57.50	8:58.62	8:59.74	9:00.86	9:01.98	9:03.10	9:04.22	9:05.34	9:06.46
490	9:07.58	9:08.70	9:09.82	9:10.94	9:12.06	9:13.18	9:14.30	9:15.42	9:16.54	9:17.66
500	9:18.78	9:19.90	9:21.02	9:22.14	9:23.26	9:24.38	9:25.49	9:26.61	9:27.73	9:28.85
510	9:29.97	9:31.09	9:32.21	9:33.33	9:34.45	9:35.57	9:36.69	9:37.81	9:38.93	9:40.05
520	9:41.17	9:42.29	9:43.41	9:44.53	9:45.65	9:46.77	9:47.89	9:49.01	9:50.13	9:51.25
530	9:52.37	9:53.49	9:54.61	9:55.73	9:56.85	9:57.97	9:59.09	10:00.21	10:01.33	10:02.45
540	10:03.57	10:04.69	10:05.81	10:06.93	10:08.05	10:09.17	10:10.29	10:11.41	10:12.53	10:13.65
550	10:14.77	10:15.89	10:17.01	10:18.12	10:19.24	10:20.36	10:21.48	10:22.60	10:23.72	10:24.84
560	10:25.96	10:27.08	10:28.20	10:29.32	10:30.44	10:31.56	10:32.68	10:33.80	10:34.92	10:36.04
570	10:37.16	10:38.28	10:39.40	10:40.52	10:41.64	10:42.76	10:43.88	10:45.00	10:46.12	10:47.24
580	10:48.36	10:49.48	10:50.60	10:51.72	10:52.84	10:53.96	10:55.08	10:56.20	10:57.32	10:58.44
590	10:59.56	11:00.68	11:01.80	11:02.92	11:04.04	11:05.16	11:06.28	11:07.40	11:08.52	11:09.64

♩. = 1.68; ♩ = 1.12; ♪. = 0.84; (triplet ♩ 𝄾) = 0.75; ♪ = 0.56; (triplet ♪ 𝄾 𝄾) = 0.37; 𝅘𝅥𝅯 = 0.28 seconds

CLICK: 27 0/8 FRAMES; M.M.: 53.33

Click	0	1	2	3	4	5	6	7	8	9
000	0:00.00	0:00.00	0:01.13	0:02.25	0:03.38	0:04.50	0:05.63	0:06.75	0:07.88	0:09.00
010	0:10.13	0:11.25	0:12.38	0:13.50	0:14.63	0:15.75	0:16.88	0:18.00	0:19.13	0:20.25
020	0:21.38	0:22.50	0:23.63	0:24.75	0:25.88	0:27.00	0:28.13	0:29.25	0:30.38	0:31.50
030	0:32.63	0:33.75	0:34.88	0:36.00	0:37.13	0:38.25	0:39.38	0:40.50	0:41.63	0:42.75
040	0:43.88	0:45.00	0:46.13	0:47.25	0:48.38	0:49.50	0:50.63	0:51.75	0:52.88	0:54.00
050	0:55.13	0:56.25	0:57.38	0:58.50	0:59.63	1:00.75	1:01.88	1:03.00	1:04.13	1:05.25
060	1:06.38	1:07.50	1:08.63	1:09.75	1:10.88	1:12.00	1:13.13	1:14.25	1:15.38	1:16.50
070	1:17.63	1:18.75	1:19.88	1:21.00	1:22.13	1:23.25	1:24.38	1:25.50	1:26.63	1:27.75
080	1:28.88	1:30.00	1:31.13	1:32.25	1:33.38	1:34.50	1:35.63	1:36.75	1:37.88	1:39.00
090	1:40.13	1:41.25	1:42.38	1:43.50	1:44.63	1:45.75	1:46.88	1:48.00	1:49.13	1:50.25
100	1:51.38	1:52.50	1:53.63	1:54.75	1:55.88	1:57.00	1:58.13	1:59.25	2:00.38	2:01.50
110	2:02.63	2:03.75	2:04.88	2:06.00	2:07.13	2:08.25	2:09.38	2:10.50	2:11.63	2:12.75
120	2:13.88	2:15.00	2:16.13	2:17.25	2:18.38	2:19.50	2:20.63	2:21.75	2:22.88	2:24.00
130	2:25.13	2:26.25	2:27.38	2:28.50	2:29.63	2:30.75	2:31.88	2:33.00	2:34.13	2:35.25
140	2:36.38	2:37.50	2:38.63	2:39.75	2:40.88	2:42.00	2:43.13	2:44.25	2:45.38	2:46.50
150	2:47.63	2:48.75	2:49.88	2:51.00	2:52.13	2:53.25	2:54.38	2:55.50	2:56.63	2:57.75
160	2:58.88	3:00.00	3:01.13	3:02.25	3:03.38	3:04.50	3:05.63	3:06.75	3:07.88	3:09.00
170	3:10.13	3:11.25	3:12.38	3:13.50	3:14.63	3:15.75	3:16.88	3:18.00	3:19.13	3:20.25
180	3:21.38	3:22.50	3:23.63	3:24.75	3:25.88	3:27.00	3:28.13	3:29.25	3:30.38	3:31.50
190	3:32.63	3:33.75	3:34.88	3:36.00	3:37.13	3:38.25	3:39.38	3:40.50	3:41.63	3:42.75
200	3:43.88	3:45.00	3:46.13	3:47.25	3:48.38	3:49.50	3:50.63	3:51.75	3:52.88	3:54.00
210	3:55.13	3:56.25	3:57.38	3:58.50	3:59.63	4:00.75	4:01.88	4:03.00	4:04.13	4:05.25
220	4:06.38	4:07.50	4:08.63	4:09.75	4:10.88	4:12.00	4:13.13	4:14.25	4:15.38	4:16.50
230	4:17.63	4:18.75	4:19.88	4:21.00	4:22.13	4:23.25	4:24.38	4:25.50	4:26.63	4:27.75
240	4:28.88	4:30.00	4:31.13	4:32.25	4:33.38	4:34.50	4:35.63	4:36.75	4:37.88	4:39.00
250	4:40.13	4:41.25	4:42.38	4:43.50	4:44.63	4:45.75	4:46.88	4:48.00	4:49.13	4:50.25
260	4:51.38	4:52.50	4:53.63	4:54.75	4:55.88	4:57.00	4:58.13	4:59.25	5:00.38	5:01.50
270	5:02.63	5:03.75	5:04.88	5:06.00	5:07.13	5:08.25	5:09.38	5:10.50	5:11.63	5:12.75
280	5:13.88	5:15.00	5:16.13	5:17.25	5:18.38	5:19.50	5:20.63	5:21.75	5:22.88	5:24.00
290	5:25.13	5:26.25	5:27.38	5:28.50	5:29.63	5:30.75	5:31.88	5:33.00	5:34.13	5:35.25
300	5:36.38	5:37.50	5:38.63	5:39.75	5:40.88	5:42.00	5:43.13	5:44.25	5:45.38	5:46.50
310	5:47.63	5:48.75	5:49.88	5:51.00	5:52.13	5:53.25	5:54.38	5:55.50	5:56.63	5:57.75
320	5:58.88	6:00.00	6:01.13	6:02.25	6:03.38	6:04.50	6:05.63	6:06.75	6:07.88	6:09.00
330	6:10.13	6:11.25	6:12.38	6:13.50	6:14.63	6:15.75	6:16.88	6:18.00	6:19.13	6:20.25
340	6:21.38	6:22.50	6:23.63	6:24.75	6:25.88	6:27.00	6:28.13	6:29.25	6:30.38	6:31.50
350	6:32.63	6:33.75	6:34.88	6:36.00	6:37.13	6:38.25	6:39.38	6:40.50	6:41.63	6:42.75
360	6:43.88	6:45.00	6:46.13	6:47.25	6:48.38	6:49.50	6:50.63	6:51.75	6:52.88	6:54.00
370	6:55.13	6:56.25	6:57.38	6:58.50	6:59.63	7:00.75	7:01.88	7:03.00	7:04.13	7:05.25
380	7:06.38	7:07.50	7:08.63	7:09.75	7:10.88	7:12.00	7:13.13	7:14.25	7:15.38	7:16.50
390	7:17.63	7:18.75	7:19.88	7:21.00	7:22.13	7:23.25	7:24.38	7:25.50	7:26.63	7:27.75
400	7:28.88	7:30.00	7:31.13	7:32.25	7:33.38	7:34.50	7:35.63	7:36.75	7:37.88	7:39.00
410	7:40.13	7:41.25	7:42.38	7:43.50	7:44.63	7:45.75	7:46.88	7:48.00	7:49.13	7:50.25
420	7:51.38	7:52.50	7:53.63	7:54.75	7:55.88	7:57.00	7:58.13	7:59.25	8:00.38	8:01.50
430	8:02.63	8:03.75	8:04.88	8:06.00	8:07.13	8:08.25	8:09.38	8:10.50	8:11.63	8:12.75
440	8:13.88	8:15.00	8:16.13	8:17.25	8:18.38	8:19.50	8:20.63	8:21.75	8:22.88	8:24.00
450	8:25.13	8:26.25	8:27.38	8:28.50	8:29.63	8:30.75	8:31.88	8:33.00	8:34.13	8:35.25
460	8:36.38	8:37.50	8:38.63	8:39.75	8:40.88	8:42.00	8:43.13	8:44.25	8:45.38	8:46.50
470	8:47.63	8:48.75	8:49.88	8:51.00	8:52.13	8:53.25	8:54.38	8:55.50	8:56.63	8:57.75
480	8:58.88	9:00.00	9:01.13	9:02.25	9:03.38	9:04.50	9:05.63	9:06.75	9:07.88	9:09.00
490	9:10.13	9:11.25	9:12.38	9:13.50	9:14.63	9:15.75	9:16.88	9:18.00	9:19.13	9:20.25
500	9:21.38	9:22.50	9:23.63	9:24.75	9:25.88	9:27.00	9:28.13	9:29.25	9:30.38	9:31.50
510	9:32.63	9:33.75	9:34.88	9:36.00	9:37.13	9:38.25	9:39.38	9:40.50	9:41.63	9:42.75
520	9:43.88	9:45.00	9:46.13	9:47.25	9:48.38	9:49.50	9:50.63	9:51.75	9:52.88	9:54.00
530	9:55.13	9:56.25	9:57.38	9:58.50	9:59.63	10:00.75	10:01.88	10:03.00	10:04.13	10:05.25
540	10:06.38	10:07.50	10:08.63	10:09.75	10:10.88	10:12.00	10:13.13	10:14.25	10:15.38	10:16.50
550	10:17.63	10:18.75	10:19.88	10:21.00	10:22.13	10:23.25	10:24.38	10:25.50	10:26.63	10:27.75
560	10:28.88	10:30.00	10:31.13	10:32.25	10:33.38	10:34.50	10:35.63	10:36.75	10:37.88	10:39.00
570	10:40.13	10:41.25	10:42.38	10:43.50	10:44.63	10:45.75	10:46.88	10:48.00	10:49.13	10:50.25
580	10:51.38	10:52.50	10:53.63	10:54.75	10:55.88	10:57.00	10:58.13	10:59.25	11:00.38	11:01.50
590	11:02.63	11:03.75	11:04.88	11:06.00	11:07.13	11:08.25	11:09.38	11:10.50	11:11.63	11:12.75

♩. = 1.69; ♩ = 1.13; ♪. = 0.84; (triplet: ♩ 𝄾) = 0.75; ♪ = 0.56; (triplet: ♪ 𝄾 𝄾) = 0.38; 𝅘𝅥𝅯 = 0.28 seconds

CLICK: 27⅛ FRAMES; M.M.: 53.09

Click	0	1	2	3	4	5	6	7	8	9
000	0:00.00	0:00.00	0:01.13	0:02.26	0:03.39	0:04.52	0:05.65	0:06.78	0:07.91	0:09.04
010	0:10.17	0:11.30	0:12.43	0:13.56	0:14.69	0:15.82	0:16.95	0:18.08	0:19.21	0:20.34
020	0:21.47	0:22.60	0:23.73	0:24.86	0:25.99	0:27.13	0:28.26	0:29.39	0:30.52	0:31.65
030	0:32.78	0:33.91	0:35.04	0:36.17	0:37.30	0:38.43	0:39.56	0:40.69	0:41.82	0:42.95
040	0:44.08	0:45.21	0:46.34	0:47.47	0:48.60	0:49.73	0:50.86	0:51.99	0:53.12	0:54.25
050	0:55.38	0:56.51	0:57.64	0:58.77	0:59.90	1:01.03	1:02.16	1:03.29	1:04.42	1:05.55
060	1:06.68	1:07.81	1:08.94	1:10.07	1:11.20	1:12.33	1:13.46	1:14.59	1:15.72	1:16.85
070	1:17.98	1:19.11	1:20.24	1:21.38	1:22.51	1:23.64	1:24.77	1:25.90	1:27.03	1:28.16
080	1:29.29	1:30.42	1:31.55	1:32.68	1:33.81	1:34.94	1:36.07	1:37.20	1:38.33	1:39.46
090	1:40.59	1:41.72	1:42.85	1:43.98	1:45.11	1:46.24	1:47.37	1:48.50	1:49.63	1:50.76
100	1:51.89	1:53.02	1:54.15	1:55.28	1:56.41	1:57.54	1:58.67	1:59.80	2:00.93	2:02.06
110	2:03.19	2:04.32	2:05.45	2:06.58	2:07.71	2:08.84	2:09.97	2:11.10	2:12.23	2:13.36
120	2:14.49	2:15.63	2:16.76	2:17.89	2:19.02	2:20.15	2:21.28	2:22.41	2:23.54	2:24.67
130	2:25.80	2:26.93	2:28.06	2:29.19	2:30.32	2:31.45	2:32.58	2:33.71	2:34.84	2:35.97
140	2:37.10	2:38.23	2:39.36	2:40.49	2:41.62	2:42.75	2:43.88	2:45.01	2:46.14	2:47.27
150	2:48.40	2:49.53	2:50.66	2:51.79	2:52.92	2:54.05	2:55.18	2:56.31	2:57.44	2:58.57
160	2:59.70	3:00.83	3:01.96	3:03.09	3:04.22	3:05.35	3:06.48	3:07.61	3:08.74	3:09.88
170	3:11.01	3:12.14	3:13.27	3:14.40	3:15.53	3:16.66	3:17.79	3:18.92	3:20.05	3:21.18
180	3:22.31	3:23.44	3:24.57	3:25.70	3:26.83	3:27.96	3:29.09	3:30.22	3:31.35	3:32.48
190	3:33.61	3:34.74	3:35.87	3:37.00	3:38.13	3:39.26	3:40.39	3:41.52	3:42.65	3:43.78
200	3:44.91	3:46.04	3:47.17	3:48.30	3:49.43	3:50.56	3:51.69	3:52.82	3:53.95	3:55.08
210	3:56.21	3:57.34	3:58.47	3:59.60	4:00.73	4:01.86	4:02.99	4:04.12	4:05.26	4:06.39
220	4:07.52	4:08.65	4:09.78	4:10.91	4:12.04	4:13.17	4:14.30	4:15.43	4:16.56	4:17.69
230	4:18.82	4:19.95	4:21.08	4:22.21	4:23.34	4:24.47	4:25.60	4:26.73	4:27.86	4:28.99
240	4:30.12	4:31.25	4:32.38	4:33.51	4:34.64	4:35.77	4:36.90	4:38.03	4:39.16	4:40.29
250	4:41.42	4:42.55	4:43.68	4:44.81	4:45.94	4:47.07	4:48.20	4:49.33	4:50.46	4:51.59
260	4:52.72	4:53.85	4:54.98	4:56.11	4:57.24	4:58.37	4:59.51	5:00.64	5:01.77	5:02.90
270	5:04.03	5:05.16	5:06.29	5:07.42	5:08.55	5:09.68	5:10.81	5:11.94	5:13.07	5:14.20
280	5:15.33	5:16.46	5:17.59	5:18.72	5:19.85	5:20.98	5:22.11	5:23.24	5:24.37	5:25.50
290	5:26.63	5:27.76	5:28.89	5:30.02	5:31.15	5:32.28	5:33.41	5:34.54	5:35.67	5:36.80
300	5:37.93	5:39.06	5:40.19	5:41.32	5:42.45	5:43.58	5:44.71	5:45.84	5:46.97	5:48.10
310	5:49.23	5:50.36	5:51.49	5:52.63	5:53.76	5:54.89	5:56.02	5:57.15	5:58.28	5:59.41
320	6:00.54	6:01.67	6:02.80	6:03.93	6:05.06	6:06.19	6:07.32	6:08.45	6:09.58	6:10.71
330	6:11.84	6:12.97	6:14.10	6:15.23	6:16.36	6:17.49	6:18.62	6:19.75	6:20.88	6:22.01
340	6:23.14	6:24.27	6:25.40	6:26.53	6:27.66	6:28.79	6:29.92	6:31.05	6:32.18	6:33.31
350	6:34.44	6:35.57	6:36.70	6:37.83	6:38.96	6:40.09	6:41.22	6:42.35	6:43.48	6:44.61
360	6:45.74	6:46.88	6:48.01	6:49.14	6:50.27	6:51.40	6:52.53	6:53.66	6:54.79	6:55.92
370	6:57.05	6:58.18	6:59.31	7:00.44	7:01.57	7:02.70	7:03.83	7:04.96	7:06.09	7:07.22
380	7:08.35	7:09.48	7:10.61	7:11.74	7:12.87	7:14.00	7:15.13	7:16.26	7:17.39	7:18.52
390	7:19.65	7:20.78	7:21.91	7:23.04	7:24.17	7:25.30	7:26.43	7:27.56	7:28.69	7:29.82
400	7:30.95	7:32.08	7:33.21	7:34.34	7:35.47	7:36.60	7:37.73	7:38.86	7:39.99	7:41.13
410	7:42.26	7:43.39	7:44.52	7:45.65	7:46.78	7:47.91	7:49.04	7:50.17	7:51.30	7:52.43
420	7:53.56	7:54.69	7:55.82	7:56.95	7:58.08	7:59.21	8:00.34	8:01.47	8:02.60	8:03.73
430	8:04.86	8:05.99	8:07.12	8:08.25	8:09.38	8:10.51	8:11.64	8:12.77	8:13.90	8:15.03
440	8:16.16	8:17.29	8:18.42	8:19.55	8:20.68	8:21.81	8:22.94	8:24.07	8:25.20	8:26.33
450	8:27.46	8:28.59	8:29.72	8:30.85	8:31.98	8:33.11	8:34.24	8:35.38	8:36.51	8:37.64
460	8:38.77	8:39.90	8:41.03	8:42.16	8:43.29	8:44.42	8:45.55	8:46.68	8:47.81	8:48.94
470	8:50.07	8:51.20	8:52.33	8:53.46	8:54.59	8:55.72	8:56.85	8:57.98	8:59.11	9:00.24
480	9:01.37	9:02.50	9:03.63	9:04.76	9:05.89	9:07.02	9:08.15	9:09.28	9:10.41	9:11.54
490	9:12.67	9:13.80	9:14.93	9:16.06	9:17.19	9:18.32	9:19.45	9:20.58	9:21.71	9:22.84
500	9:23.97	9:25.10	9:26.23	9:27.36	9:28.49	9:29.62	9:30.76	9:31.89	9:33.02	9:34.15
510	9:35.28	9:36.41	9:37.54	9:38.67	9:39.80	9:40.93	9:42.06	9:43.19	9:44.32	9:45.45
520	9:46.58	9:47.71	9:48.84	9:49.97	9:51.10	9:52.23	9:53.36	9:54.49	9:55.62	9:56.75
530	9:57.88	9:59.01	10:00.14	10:01.27	10:02.40	10:03.53	10:04.66	10:05.79	10:06.92	10:08.05
540	10:09.18	10:10.31	10:11.44	10:12.57	10:13.70	10:14.83	10:15.96	10:17.09	10:18.22	10:19.35
550	10:20.48	10:21.61	10:22.74	10:23.88	10:25.01	10:26.14	10:27.27	10:28.40	10:29.53	10:30.66
560	10:31.79	10:32.92	10:34.05	10:35.18	10:36.31	10:37.44	10:38.57	10:39.70	10:40.83	10:41.96
570	10:43.09	10:44.22	10:45.35	10:46.48	10:47.61	10:48.74	10:49.87	10:51.00	10:52.13	10:53.26
580	10:54.39	10:55.52	10:56.65	10:57.78	10:58.91	11:00.04	11:01.17	11:02.30	11:03.43	11:04.56
590	11:05.69	11:06.82	11:07.95	11:09.08	11:10.21	11:11.34	11:12.47	11:13.60	11:14.73	11:15.86

♩. = 1.70; ♩ = 1.13; ♪. = 0.85; (triplet ♩ 𝄾) = 0.75; ♪ = 0.57; (triplet ♪ 𝄾 𝄾) = 0.38; 𝅘𝅥𝅯 = 0.28 seconds

CLICK: 27⅞ FRAMES; M.M.: 52.84

Click	0	1	2	3	4	5	6	7	8	9
000	0:00.00	0:00.00	0:01.14	0:02.27	0:03.41	0:04.54	0:05.68	0:06.81	0:07.95	0:09.08
010	0:10.22	0:11.35	0:12.49	0:13.63	0:14.76	0:15.90	0:17.03	0:18.17	0:19.30	0:20.44
020	0:21.57	0:22.71	0:23.84	0:24.98	0:26.11	0:27.25	0:28.39	0:29.52	0:30.66	0:31.79
030	0:32.93	0:34.06	0:35.20	0:36.33	0:37.47	0:38.60	0:39.74	0:40.88	0:42.01	0:43.15
040	0:44.28	0:45.42	0:46.55	0:47.69	0:48.82	0:49.96	0:51.09	0:52.23	0:53.36	0:54.50
050	0:55.64	0:56.77	0:57.91	0:59.04	1:00.18	1:01.31	1:02.45	1:03.58	1:04.72	1:05.85
060	1:06.99	1:08.12	1:09.26	1:10.40	1:11.53	1:12.67	1:13.80	1:14.94	1:16.07	1:17.21
070	1:18.34	1:19.48	1:20.61	1:21.75	1:22.89	1:24.02	1:25.16	1:26.29	1:27.43	1:28.56
080	1:29.70	1:30.83	1:31.97	1:33.10	1:34.24	1:35.37	1:36.51	1:37.65	1:38.78	1:39.92
090	1:41.05	1:42.19	1:43.32	1:44.46	1:45.59	1:46.73	1:47.86	1:49.00	1:50.14	1:51.27
100	1:52.41	1:53.54	1:54.68	1:55.81	1:56.95	1:58.08	1:59.22	2:00.35	2:01.49	2:02.63
110	2:03.76	2:04.90	2:06.03	2:07.17	2:08.30	2:09.44	2:10.57	2:11.71	2:12.84	2:13.98
120	2:15.11	2:16.25	2:17.39	2:18.52	2:19.66	2:20.79	2:21.93	2:23.06	2:24.20	2:25.33
130	2:26.47	2:27.60	2:28.74	2:29.88	2:31.01	2:32.15	2:33.28	2:34.42	2:35.55	2:36.69
140	2:37.82	2:38.96	2:40.09	2:41.23	2:42.36	2:43.50	2:44.64	2:45.77	2:46.91	2:48.04
150	2:49.18	2:50.31	2:51.45	2:52.58	2:53.72	2:54.85	2:55.99	2:57.13	2:58.26	2:59.40
160	3:00.53	3:01.67	3:02.80	3:03.94	3:05.07	3:06.21	3:07.34	3:08.48	3:09.61	3:10.75
170	3:11.89	3:13.02	3:14.16	3:15.29	3:16.43	3:17.56	3:18.70	3:19.83	3:20.97	3:22.10
180	3:23.24	3:24.38	3:25.51	3:26.65	3:27.78	3:28.92	3:30.05	3:31.19	3:32.32	3:33.46
190	3:34.59	3:35.73	3:36.86	3:38.00	3:39.14	3:40.27	3:41.41	3:42.54	3:43.68	3:44.81
200	3:45.95	3:47.08	3:48.22	3:49.35	3:50.49	3:51.63	3:52.76	3:53.90	3:55.03	3:56.17
210	3:57.30	3:58.44	3:59.57	4:00.71	4:01.84	4:02.98	4:04.11	4:05.25	4:06.39	4:07.52
220	4:08.66	4:09.79	4:10.93	4:12.06	4:13.20	4:14.33	4:15.47	4:16.60	4:17.74	4:18.87
230	4:20.01	4:21.15	4:22.28	4:23.42	4:24.55	4:25.69	4:26.82	4:27.96	4:29.09	4:30.23
240	4:31.36	4:32.50	4:33.64	4:34.77	4:35.91	4:37.04	4:38.18	4:39.31	4:40.45	4:41.58
250	4:42.72	4:43.85	4:44.99	4:46.12	4:47.26	4:48.40	4:49.53	4:50.67	4:51.80	4:52.94
260	4:54.07	4:55.21	4:56.34	4:57.48	4:58.61	4:59.75	5:00.89	5:02.02	5:03.16	5:04.29
270	5:05.43	5:06.56	5:07.70	5:08.83	5:09.97	5:11.10	5:12.24	5:13.37	5:14.51	5:15.65
280	5:16.78	5:17.92	5:19.05	5:20.19	5:21.32	5:22.46	5:23.59	5:24.73	5:25.86	5:27.00
290	5:28.14	5:29.27	5:30.41	5:31.54	5:32.68	5:33.81	5:34.95	5:36.08	5:37.22	5:38.35
300	5:39.49	5:40.62	5:41.76	5:42.90	5:44.03	5:45.17	5:46.30	5:47.44	5:48.57	5:49.71
310	5:50.84	5:51.98	5:53.11	5:54.25	5:55.39	5:56.52	5:57.66	5:58.79	5:59.93	6:01.06
320	6:02.20	6:03.33	6:04.47	6:05.60	6:06.74	6:07.87	6:09.01	6:10.15	6:11.28	6:12.42
330	6:13.55	6:14.69	6:15.82	6:16.96	6:18.09	6:19.23	6:20.36	6:21.50	6:22.64	6:23.77
340	6:24.91	6:26.04	6:27.18	6:28.31	6:29.45	6:30.58	6:31.72	6:32.85	6:33.99	6:35.12
350	6:36.26	6:37.40	6:38.53	6:39.67	6:40.80	6:41.94	6:43.07	6:44.21	6:45.34	6:46.48
360	6:47.61	6:48.75	6:49.89	6:51.02	6:52.16	6:53.29	6:54.43	6:55.56	6:56.70	6:57.83
370	6:58.97	7:00.10	7:01.24	7:02.37	7:03.51	7:04.65	7:05.78	7:06.92	7:08.05	7:09.19
380	7:10.32	7:11.46	7:12.59	7:13.73	7:14.86	7:16.00	7:17.14	7:18.27	7:19.41	7:20.54
390	7:21.68	7:22.81	7:23.95	7:25.08	7:26.22	7:27.35	7:28.49	7:29.62	7:30.76	7:31.90
400	7:33.03	7:34.17	7:35.30	7:36.44	7:37.57	7:38.71	7:39.84	7:40.98	7:42.11	7:43.25
410	7:44.39	7:45.52	7:46.66	7:47.79	7:48.93	7:50.06	7:51.20	7:52.33	7:53.47	7:54.60
420	7:55.74	7:56.87	7:58.01	7:59.15	8:00.28	8:01.42	8:02.55	8:03.69	8:04.82	8:05.96
430	8:07.09	8:08.23	8:09.36	8:10.50	8:11.64	8:12.77	8:13.91	8:15.04	8:16.18	8:17.31
440	8:18.45	8:19.58	8:20.72	8:21.85	8:22.99	8:24.13	8:25.26	8:26.40	8:27.53	8:28.67
450	8:29.80	8:30.94	8:32.07	8:33.21	8:34.34	8:35.48	8:36.61	8:37.75	8:38.89	8:40.02
460	8:41.16	8:42.29	8:43.43	8:44.56	8:45.70	8:46.83	8:47.97	8:49.10	8:50.24	8:51.37
470	8:52.51	8:53.65	8:54.78	8:55.92	8:57.05	8:58.19	8:59.32	9:00.46	9:01.59	9:02.73
480	9:03.86	9:05.00	9:06.14	9:07.27	9:08.41	9:09.54	9:10.68	9:11.81	9:12.95	9:14.08
490	9:15.22	9:16.35	9:17.49	9:18.62	9:19.76	9:20.90	9:22.03	9:23.17	9:24.30	9:25.44
500	9:26.57	9:27.71	9:28.84	9:29.98	9:31.11	9:32.25	9:33.39	9:34.52	9:35.66	9:36.79
510	9:37.93	9:39.06	9:40.20	9:41.33	9:42.47	9:43.60	9:44.74	9:45.87	9:47.01	9:48.15
520	9:49.28	9:50.42	9:51.55	9:52.69	9:53.82	9:54.96	9:56.09	9:57.23	9:58.36	9:59.50
530	10:00.64	10:01.77	10:02.91	10:04.04	10:05.18	10:06.31	10:07.45	10:08.58	10:09.72	10:10.85
540	10:11.99	10:13.13	10:14.26	10:15.40	10:16.53	10:17.67	10:18.80	10:19.94	10:21.07	10:22.21
550	10:23.34	10:24.48	10:25.61	10:26.75	10:27.89	10:29.02	10:30.16	10:31.29	10:32.43	10:33.56
560	10:34.70	10:35.83	10:36.97	10:38.10	10:39.24	10:40.37	10:41.51	10:42.65	10:43.78	10:44.92
570	10:46.05	10:47.19	10:48.32	10:49.46	10:50.59	10:51.73	10:52.86	10:54.00	10:55.14	10:56.27
580	10:57.41	10:58.54	10:59.68	11:00.81	11:01.95	11:03.08	11:04.22	11:05.35	11:06.49	11:07.62
590	11:08.76	11:09.90	11:11.03	11:12.17	11:13.30	11:14.44	11:15.57	11:16.71	11:17.84	11:18.98

♩. = 1.70; ♩ = 1.14; ♪. = 0.85; (triplet) ♩ 𝄾 = 0.76; ♪ = 0.57; (triplet) ♪𝄾𝄾 = 0.38; 𝅘𝅥𝅯 = 0.28 seconds

CLICK: 27⅜ FRAMES; M.M.: 52.60

Click	0	1	2	3	4	5	6	7	8	9
000	0:00.00	0:00.00	0:01.14	0:02.28	0:03.42	0:04.56	0:05.70	0:06.84	0:07.98	0:09.13
010	0:10.27	0:11.41	0:12.55	0:13.69	0:14.83	0:15.97	0:17.11	0:18.25	0:19.39	0:20.53
020	0:21.67	0:22.81	0:23.95	0:25.09	0:26.23	0:27.38	0:28.52	0:29.66	0:30.80	0:31.94
030	0:33.08	0:34.22	0:35.36	0:36.50	0:37.64	0:38.78	0:39.92	0:41.06	0:42.20	0:43.34
040	0:44.48	0:45.63	0:46.77	0:47.91	0:49.05	0:50.19	0:51.33	0:52.47	0:53.61	0:54.75
050	0:55.89	0:57.03	0:58.17	0:59.31	1:00.45	1:01.59	1:02.73	1:03.88	1:05.02	1:06.16
060	1:07.30	1:08.44	1:09.58	1:10.72	1:11.86	1:13.00	1:14.14	1:15.28	1:16.42	1:17.56
070	1:18.70	1:19.84	1:20.98	1:22.13	1:23.27	1:24.41	1:25.55	1:26.69	1:27.83	1:28.97
080	1:30.11	1:31.25	1:32.39	1:33.53	1:34.67	1:35.81	1:36.95	1:38.09	1:39.23	1:40.38
090	1:41.52	1:42.66	1:43.80	1:44.94	1:46.08	1:47.22	1:48.36	1:49.50	1:50.64	1:51.78
100	1:52.92	1:54.06	1:55.20	1:56.34	1:57.48	1:58.63	1:59.77	2:00.91	2:02.05	2:03.19
110	2:04.33	2:05.47	2:06.61	2:07.75	2:08.89	2:10.03	2:11.17	2:12.31	2:13.45	2:14.59
120	2:15.73	2:16.88	2:18.02	2:19.16	2:20.30	2:21.44	2:22.58	2:23.72	2:24.86	2:26.00
130	2:27.14	2:28.28	2:29.42	2:30.56	2:31.70	2:32.84	2:33.98	2:35.13	2:36.27	2:37.41
140	2:38.55	2:39.69	2:40.83	2:41.97	2:43.11	2:44.25	2:45.39	2:46.53	2:47.67	2:48.81
150	2:49.95	2:51.09	2:52.23	2:53.38	2:54.52	2:55.66	2:56.80	2:57.94	2:59.08	3:00.22
160	3:01.36	3:02.50	3:03.64	3:04.78	3:05.92	3:07.06	3:08.20	3:09.34	3:10.48	3:11.63
170	3:12.77	3:13.91	3:15.05	3:16.19	3:17.33	3:18.47	3:19.61	3:20.75	3:21.89	3:23.03
180	3:24.17	3:25.31	3:26.45	3:27.59	3:28.73	3:29.88	3:31.02	3:32.16	3:33.30	3:34.44
190	3:35.58	3:36.72	3:37.86	3:39.00	3:40.14	3:41.28	3:42.42	3:43.56	3:44.70	3:45.84
200	3:46.98	3:48.13	3:49.27	3:50.41	3:51.55	3:52.69	3:53.83	3:54.97	3:56.11	3:57.25
210	3:58.39	3:59.53	4:00.67	4:01.81	4:02.95	4:04.09	4:05.23	4:06.38	4:07.52	4:08.66
220	4:09.80	4:10.94	4:12.08	4:13.22	4:14.36	4:15.50	4:16.64	4:17.78	4:18.92	4:20.06
230	4:21.20	4:22.34	4:23.48	4:24.62	4:25.77	4:26.91	4:28.05	4:29.19	4:30.33	4:31.47
240	4:32.61	4:33.75	4:34.89	4:36.03	4:37.17	4:38.31	4:39.45	4:40.59	4:41.73	4:42.88
250	4:44.02	4:45.16	4:46.30	4:47.44	4:48.58	4:49.72	4:50.86	4:52.00	4:53.14	4:54.28
260	4:55.42	4:56.56	4:57.70	4:58.84	4:59.98	5:01.13	5:02.27	5:03.41	5:04.55	5:05.69
270	5:06.83	5:07.97	5:09.11	5:10.25	5:11.39	5:12.53	5:13.67	5:14.81	5:15.95	5:17.09
280	5:18.23	5:19.38	5:20.52	5:21.66	5:22.80	5:23.94	5:25.08	5:26.22	5:27.36	5:28.50
290	5:29.64	5:30.78	5:31.92	5:33.06	5:34.20	5:35.34	5:36.48	5:37.63	5:38.77	5:39.91
300	5:41.05	5:42.19	5:43.33	5:44.47	5:45.61	5:46.75	5:47.89	5:49.03	5:50.17	5:51.31
310	5:52.45	5:53.59	5:54.73	5:55.88	5:57.02	5:58.16	5:59.30	6:00.44	6:01.58	6:02.72
320	6:03.86	6:05.00	6:06.14	6:07.28	6:08.42	6:09.56	6:10.70	6:11.84	6:12.98	6:14.13
330	6:15.27	6:16.41	6:17.55	6:18.69	6:19.83	6:20.97	6:22.11	6:23.25	6:24.39	6:25.53
340	6:26.67	6:27.81	6:28.95	6:30.09	6:31.23	6:32.38	6:33.52	6:34.66	6:35.80	6:36.94
350	6:38.08	6:39.22	6:40.36	6:41.50	6:42.64	6:43.78	6:44.92	6:46.06	6:47.20	6:48.34
360	6:49.48	6:50.63	6:51.77	6:52.91	6:54.05	6:55.19	6:56.33	6:57.47	6:58.61	6:59.75
370	7:00.89	7:02.03	7:03.17	7:04.31	7:05.45	7:06.59	7:07.73	7:08.88	7:10.02	7:11.16
380	7:12.30	7:13.44	7:14.58	7:15.72	7:16.86	7:18.00	7:19.14	7:20.28	7:21.42	7:22.56
390	7:23.70	7:24.84	7:25.98	7:27.13	7:28.27	7:29.41	7:30.55	7:31.69	7:32.83	7:33.97
400	7:35.11	7:36.25	7:37.39	7:38.53	7:39.67	7:40.81	7:41.95	7:43.09	7:44.23	7:45.38
410	7:46.52	7:47.66	7:48.80	7:49.94	7:51.08	7:52.22	7:53.36	7:54.50	7:55.64	7:56.78
420	7:57.92	7:59.06	8:00.20	8:01.34	8:02.48	8:03.63	8:04.77	8:05.91	8:07.05	8:08.19
430	8:09.33	8:10.47	8:11.61	8:12.75	8:13.89	8:15.03	8:16.17	8:17.31	8:18.45	8:19.59
440	8:20.73	8:21.88	8:23.02	8:24.16	8:25.30	8:26.44	8:27.58	8:28.72	8:29.86	8:31.00
450	8:32.14	8:33.28	8:34.42	8:35.56	8:36.70	8:37.84	8:38.98	8:40.12	8:41.27	8:42.41
460	8:43.55	8:44.69	8:45.83	8:46.97	8:48.11	8:49.25	8:50.39	8:51.53	8:52.67	8:53.81
470	8:54.95	8:56.09	8:57.23	8:58.37	8:59.52	9:00.66	9:01.80	9:02.94	9:04.08	9:05.22
480	9:06.36	9:07.50	9:08.64	9:09.78	9:10.92	9:12.06	9:13.20	9:14.34	9:15.48	9:16.63
490	9:17.77	9:18.91	9:20.05	9:21.19	9:22.33	9:23.47	9:24.61	9:25.75	9:26.89	9:28.03
500	9:29.17	9:30.31	9:31.45	9:32.59	9:33.73	9:34.88	9:36.02	9:37.16	9:38.30	9:39.44
510	9:40.58	9:41.72	9:42.86	9:44.00	9:45.14	9:46.28	9:47.42	9:48.56	9:49.70	9:50.84
520	9:51.98	9:53.13	9:54.27	9:55.41	9:56.55	9:57.69	9:58.83	9:59.97	10:01.11	10:02.25
530	10:03.39	10:04.53	10:05.67	10:06.81	10:07.95	10:09.09	10:10.23	10:11.38	10:12.52	10:13.66
540	10:14.80	10:15.94	10:17.08	10:18.22	10:19.36	10:20.50	10:21.64	10:22.78	10:23.92	10:25.06
550	10:26.20	10:27.34	10:28.48	10:29.63	10:30.77	10:31.91	10:33.05	10:34.19	10:35.33	10:36.47
560	10:37.61	10:38.75	10:39.89	10:41.03	10:42.17	10:43.31	10:44.45	10:45.59	10:46.73	10:47.88
570	10:49.02	10:50.16	10:51.30	10:52.44	10:53.58	10:54.72	10:55.86	10:57.00	10:58.14	10:59.28
580	11:00.42	11:01.56	11:02.70	11:03.84	11:04.98	11:06.12	11:07.27	11:08.41	11:09.55	11:10.69
590	11:11.83	11:12.97	11:14.11	11:15.25	11:16.39	11:17.53	11:18.67	11:19.81	11:20.95	11:22.09

♩. = 1.71; ♩ = 1.14; ♪. = 0.86; (triplet ♩ 𝄾) = 0.76; ♪ = 0.57; (triplet ♪ 𝄾 𝄾) = 0.38; 𝅘𝅥𝅯 = 0.29 seconds

CLICK: 27⅝ FRAMES; M.M.: 52.36

Click	0	1	2	3	4	5	6	7	8	9
000	0:00.00	0:00.00	0:01.15	0:02.29	0:03.44	0:04.58	0:05.73	0:06.88	0:08.02	0:09.17
010	0:10.31	0:11.46	0:12.60	0:13.75	0:14.90	0:16.04	0:17.19	0:18.33	0:19.48	0:20.63
020	0:21.77	0:22.92	0:24.06	0:25.21	0:26.35	0:27.50	0:28.65	0:29.79	0:30.94	0:32.08
030	0:33.23	0:34.38	0:35.52	0:36.67	0:37.81	0:38.96	0:40.10	0:41.25	0:42.40	0:43.54
040	0:44.69	0:45.83	0:46.98	0:48.13	0:49.27	0:50.42	0:51.56	0:52.71	0:53.85	0:55.00
050	0:56.15	0:57.29	0:58.44	0:59.58	1:00.73	1:01.88	1:03.02	1:04.17	1:05.31	1:06.46
060	1:07.60	1:08.75	1:09.90	1:11.04	1:12.19	1:13.33	1:14.48	1:15.62	1:16.77	1:17.92
070	1:19.06	1:20.21	1:21.35	1:22.50	1:23.65	1:24.79	1:25.94	1:27.08	1:28.23	1:29.38
080	1:30.52	1:31.67	1:32.81	1:33.96	1:35.10	1:36.25	1:37.40	1:38.54	1:39.69	1:40.83
090	1:41.98	1:43.13	1:44.27	1:45.42	1:46.56	1:47.71	1:48.85	1:50.00	1:51.15	1:52.29
100	1:53.44	1:54.58	1:55.73	1:56.87	1:58.02	1:59.17	2:00.31	2:01.46	2:02.60	2:03.75
110	2:04.90	2:06.04	2:07.19	2:08.33	2:09.48	2:10.62	2:11.77	2:12.92	2:14.06	2:15.21
120	2:16.35	2:17.50	2:18.65	2:19.79	2:20.94	2:22.08	2:23.23	2:24.38	2:25.52	2:26.67
130	2:27.81	2:28.96	2:30.10	2:31.25	2:32.40	2:33.54	2:34.69	2:35.83	2:36.98	2:38.13
140	2:39.27	2:40.42	2:41.56	2:42.71	2:43.85	2:45.00	2:46.15	2:47.29	2:48.44	2:49.58
150	2:50.73	2:51.87	2:53.02	2:54.17	2:55.31	2:56.46	2:57.60	2:58.75	2:59.90	3:01.04
160	3:02.19	3:03.33	3:04.48	3:05.63	3:06.77	3:07.92	3:09.06	3:10.21	3:11.35	3:12.50
170	3:13.65	3:14.79	3:15.94	3:17.08	3:18.23	3:19.38	3:20.52	3:21.67	3:22.81	3:23.96
180	3:25.10	3:26.25	3:27.40	3:28.54	3:29.69	3:30.83	3:31.98	3:33.12	3:34.27	3:35.42
190	3:36.56	3:37.71	3:38.85	3:40.00	3:41.15	3:42.29	3:43.44	3:44.58	3:45.73	3:46.88
200	3:48.02	3:49.17	3:50.31	3:51.46	3:52.60	3:53.75	3:54.90	3:56.04	3:57.19	3:58.33
210	3:59.48	4:00.62	4:01.77	4:02.92	4:04.06	4:05.21	4:06.35	4:07.50	4:08.65	4:09.79
220	4:10.94	4:12.08	4:13.23	4:14.38	4:15.52	4:16.67	4:17.81	4:18.96	4:20.10	4:21.25
230	4:22.40	4:23.54	4:24.69	4:25.83	4:26.98	4:28.13	4:29.27	4:30.42	4:31.56	4:32.71
240	4:33.85	4:35.00	4:36.15	4:37.29	4:38.44	4:39.58	4:40.73	4:41.87	4:43.02	4:44.17
250	4:45.31	4:46.46	4:47.60	4:48.75	4:49.90	4:51.04	4:52.19	4:53.33	4:54.48	4:55.63
260	4:56.77	4:57.92	4:59.06	5:00.21	5:01.35	5:02.50	5:03.65	5:04.79	5:05.94	5:07.08
270	5:08.23	5:09.38	5:10.52	5:11.67	5:12.81	5:13.96	5:15.10	5:16.25	5:17.40	5:18.54
280	5:19.69	5:20.83	5:21.98	5:23.12	5:24.27	5:25.42	5:26.56	5:27.71	5:28.85	5:30.00
290	5:31.15	5:32.29	5:33.44	5:34.58	5:35.73	5:36.88	5:38.02	5:39.17	5:40.31	5:41.46
300	5:42.60	5:43.75	5:44.90	5:46.04	5:47.19	5:48.33	5:49.48	5:50.63	5:51.77	5:52.92
310	5:54.06	5:55.21	5:56.35	5:57.50	5:58.65	5:59.79	6:00.94	6:02.08	6:03.23	6:04.37
320	6:05.52	6:06.67	6:07.81	6:08.96	6:10.10	6:11.25	6:12.40	6:13.54	6:14.69	6:15.83
330	6:16.98	6:18.13	6:19.27	6:20.42	6:21.56	6:22.71	6:23.85	6:25.00	6:26.15	6:27.29
340	6:28.44	6:29.58	6:30.73	6:31.88	6:33.02	6:34.17	6:35.31	6:36.46	6:37.60	6:38.75
350	6:39.90	6:41.04	6:42.19	6:43.33	6:44.48	6:45.62	6:46.77	6:47.92	6:49.06	6:50.21
360	6:51.35	6:52.50	6:53.65	6:54.79	6:55.94	6:57.08	6:58.23	6:59.38	7:00.52	7:01.67
370	7:02.81	7:03.96	7:05.10	7:06.25	7:07.40	7:08.54	7:09.69	7:10.83	7:11.98	7:13.13
380	7:14.27	7:15.42	7:16.56	7:17.71	7:18.85	7:20.00	7:21.15	7:22.29	7:23.44	7:24.58
390	7:25.73	7:26.87	7:28.02	7:29.17	7:30.31	7:31.46	7:32.60	7:33.75	7:34.90	7:36.04
400	7:37.19	7:38.33	7:39.48	7:40.62	7:41.77	7:42.92	7:44.06	7:45.21	7:46.35	7:47.50
410	7:48.65	7:49.79	7:50.94	7:52.08	7:53.23	7:54.38	7:55.52	7:56.67	7:57.81	7:58.96
420	8:00.10	8:01.25	8:02.40	8:03.54	8:04.69	8:05.83	8:06.98	8:08.13	8:09.27	8:10.42
430	8:11.56	8:12.71	8:13.85	8:15.00	8:16.15	8:17.29	8:18.44	8:19.58	8:20.73	8:21.87
440	8:23.02	8:24.17	8:25.31	8:26.46	8:27.60	8:28.75	8:29.90	8:31.04	8:32.19	8:33.33
450	8:34.48	8:35.63	8:36.77	8:37.92	8:39.06	8:40.21	8:41.35	8:42.50	8:43.65	8:44.79
460	8:45.94	8:47.08	8:48.23	8:49.38	8:50.52	8:51.67	8:52.81	8:53.96	8:55.10	8:56.25
470	8:57.40	8:58.54	8:59.69	9:00.83	9:01.98	9:03.12	9:04.27	9:05.42	9:06.56	9:07.71
480	9:08.85	9:10.00	9:11.15	9:12.29	9:13.44	9:14.58	9:15.73	9:16.88	9:18.02	9:19.17
490	9:20.31	9:21.46	9:22.60	9:23.75	9:24.90	9:26.04	9:27.19	9:28.33	9:29.48	9:30.63
500	9:31.77	9:32.92	9:34.06	9:35.21	9:36.35	9:37.50	9:38.65	9:39.79	9:40.94	9:42.08
510	9:43.23	9:44.37	9:45.52	9:46.67	9:47.81	9:48.96	9:50.10	9:51.25	9:52.40	9:53.54
520	9:54.69	9:55.83	9:56.98	9:58.13	9:59.27	10:00.42	10:01.56	10:02.71	10:03.85	10:05.00
530	10:06.15	10:07.29	10:08.44	10:09.58	10:10.73	10:11.88	10:13.02	10:14.17	10:15.31	10:16.46
540	10:17.60	10:18.75	10:19.90	10:21.04	10:22.19	10:23.33	10:24.48	10:25.62	10:26.77	10:27.92
550	10:29.06	10:30.21	10:31.35	10:32.50	10:33.65	10:34.79	10:35.94	10:37.08	10:38.23	10:39.38
560	10:40.52	10:41.67	10:42.81	10:43.96	10:45.10	10:46.25	10:47.40	10:48.54	10:49.69	10:50.83
570	10:51.98	10:53.13	10:54.27	10:55.42	10:56.56	10:57.71	10:58.85	11:00.00	11:01.15	11:02.29
580	11:03.44	11:04.58	11:05.73	11:06.87	11:08.02	11:09.17	11:10.31	11:11.46	11:12.60	11:13.75
590	11:14.90	11:16.04	11:17.19	11:18.33	11:19.48	11:20.63	11:21.77	11:22.92	11:24.06	11:25.21

♩. = 1.72; ♩ = 1.15; ♪. = 0.86; (triplet) ♩ 𝄾 = 0.76; ♪ = 0.57; (triplet) ♪ 𝄾 𝄾 = 0.38; 𝅘𝅥𝅯 = 0.29 seconds

CLICK: 27⅝ FRAMES; M.M.: 52.13

Click	0	1	2	3	4	5	6	7	8	9
000	0:00.00	0:00.00	0:01.15	0:02.30	0:03.45	0:04.60	0:05.76	0:06.91	0:08.06	0:09.21
010	0:10.36	0:11.51	0:12.66	0:13.81	0:14.96	0:16.11	0:17.27	0:18.42	0:19.57	0:20.72
020	0:21.87	0:23.02	0:24.17	0:25.32	0:26.47	0:27.62	0:28.78	0:29.93	0:31.08	0:32.23
030	0:33.38	0:34.53	0:35.68	0:36.83	0:37.98	0:39.14	0:40.29	0:41.44	0:42.59	0:43.74
040	0:44.89	0:46.04	0:47.19	0:48.34	0:49.49	0:50.65	0:51.80	0:52.95	0:54.10	0:55.25
050	0:56.40	0:57.55	0:58.70	0:59.85	1:01.01	1:02.16	1:03.31	1:04.46	1:05.61	1:06.76
060	1:07.91	1:09.06	1:10.21	1:11.36	1:12.52	1:13.67	1:14.82	1:15.97	1:17.12	1:18.27
070	1:19.42	1:20.57	1:21.72	1:22.87	1:24.03	1:25.18	1:26.33	1:27.48	1:28.63	1:29.78
080	1:30.93	1:32.08	1:33.23	1:34.39	1:35.54	1:36.69	1:37.84	1:38.99	1:40.14	1:41.29
090	1:42.44	1:43.59	1:44.74	1:45.90	1:47.05	1:48.20	1:49.35	1:50.50	1:51.65	1:52.80
100	1:53.95	1:55.10	1:56.26	1:57.41	1:58.56	1:59.71	2:00.86	2:02.01	2:03.16	2:04.31
110	2:05.46	2:06.61	2:07.77	2:08.92	2:10.07	2:11.22	2:12.37	2:13.52	2:14.67	2:15.82
120	2:16.97	2:18.12	2:19.28	2:20.43	2:21.58	2:22.73	2:23.88	2:25.03	2:26.18	2:27.33
130	2:28.48	2:29.64	2:30.79	2:31.94	2:33.09	2:34.24	2:35.39	2:36.54	2:37.69	2:38.84
140	2:39.99	2:41.15	2:42.30	2:43.45	2:44.60	2:45.75	2:46.90	2:48.05	2:49.20	2:50.35
150	2:51.51	2:52.66	2:53.81	2:54.96	2:56.11	2:57.26	2:58.41	2:59.56	3:00.71	3:01.86
160	3:03.02	3:04.17	3:05.32	3:06.47	3:07.62	3:08.77	3:09.92	3:11.07	3:12.22	3:13.37
170	3:14.53	3:15.68	3:16.83	3:17.98	3:19.13	3:20.28	3:21.43	3:22.58	3:23.73	3:24.89
180	3:26.04	3:27.19	3:28.34	3:29.49	3:30.64	3:31.79	3:32.94	3:34.09	3:35.24	3:36.40
190	3:37.55	3:38.70	3:39.85	3:41.00	3:42.15	3:43.30	3:44.45	3:45.60	3:46.76	3:47.91
200	3:49.06	3:50.21	3:51.36	3:52.51	3:53.66	3:54.81	3:55.96	3:57.11	3:58.27	3:59.42
210	4:00.57	4:01.72	4:02.87	4:04.02	4:05.17	4:06.32	4:07.47	4:08.62	4:09.78	4:10.93
220	4:12.08	4:13.23	4:14.38	4:15.53	4:16.68	4:17.83	4:18.98	4:20.14	4:21.29	4:22.44
230	4:23.59	4:24.74	4:25.89	4:27.04	4:28.19	4:29.34	4:30.49	4:31.65	4:32.80	4:33.95
240	4:35.10	4:36.25	4:37.40	4:38.55	4:39.70	4:40.85	4:42.01	4:43.16	4:44.31	4:45.46
250	4:46.61	4:47.76	4:48.91	4:50.06	4:51.21	4:52.36	4:53.52	4:54.67	4:55.82	4:56.97
260	4:58.12	4:59.27	5:00.42	5:01.57	5:02.72	5:03.87	5:05.03	5:06.18	5:07.33	5:08.48
270	5:09.63	5:10.78	5:11.93	5:13.08	5:14.23	5:15.39	5:16.54	5:17.69	5:18.84	5:19.99
280	5:21.14	5:22.29	5:23.44	5:24.59	5:25.74	5:26.90	5:28.05	5:29.20	5:30.35	5:31.50
290	5:32.65	5:33.80	5:34.95	5:36.10	5:37.26	5:38.41	5:39.56	5:40.71	5:41.86	5:43.01
300	5:44.16	5:45.31	5:46.46	5:47.61	5:48.77	5:49.92	5:51.07	5:52.22	5:53.37	5:54.52
310	5:55.67	5:56.82	5:57.97	5:59.12	6:00.28	6:01.43	6:02.58	6:03.73	6:04.88	6:06.03
320	6:07.18	6:08.33	6:09.48	6:10.64	6:11.79	6:12.94	6:14.09	6:15.24	6:16.39	6:17.54
330	6:18.69	6:19.84	6:20.99	6:22.15	6:23.30	6:24.45	6:25.60	6:26.75	6:27.90	6:29.05
340	6:30.20	6:31.35	6:32.51	6:33.66	6:34.81	6:35.96	6:37.11	6:38.26	6:39.41	6:40.56
350	6:41.71	6:42.86	6:44.02	6:45.17	6:46.32	6:47.47	6:48.62	6:49.77	6:50.92	6:52.07
360	6:53.22	6:54.37	6:55.53	6:56.68	6:57.83	6:58.98	7:00.13	7:01.28	7:02.43	7:03.58
370	7:04.73	7:05.89	7:07.04	7:08.19	7:09.34	7:10.49	7:11.64	7:12.79	7:13.94	7:15.09
380	7:16.24	7:17.40	7:18.55	7:19.70	7:20.85	7:22.00	7:23.15	7:24.30	7:25.45	7:26.60
390	7:27.76	7:28.91	7:30.06	7:31.21	7:32.36	7:33.51	7:34.66	7:35.81	7:36.96	7:38.11
400	7:39.27	7:40.42	7:41.57	7:42.72	7:43.87	7:45.02	7:46.17	7:47.32	7:48.47	7:49.62
410	7:50.78	7:51.93	7:53.08	7:54.23	7:55.38	7:56.53	7:57.68	7:58.83	7:59.98	8:01.14
420	8:02.29	8:03.44	8:04.59	8:05.74	8:06.89	8:08.04	8:09.19	8:10.34	8:11.49	8:12.65
430	8:13.80	8:14.95	8:16.10	8:17.25	8:18.40	8:19.55	8:20.70	8:21.85	8:23.01	8:24.16
440	8:25.31	8:26.46	8:27.61	8:28.76	8:29.91	8:31.06	8:32.21	8:33.36	8:34.52	8:35.67
450	8:36.82	8:37.97	8:39.12	8:40.27	8:41.42	8:42.57	8:43.72	8:44.87	8:46.03	8:47.18
460	8:48.33	8:49.48	8:50.63	8:51.78	8:52.93	8:54.08	8:55.23	8:56.39	8:57.54	8:58.69
470	8:59.84	9:00.99	9:02.14	9:03.29	9:04.44	9:05.59	9:06.74	9:07.90	9:09.05	9:10.20
480	9:11.35	9:12.50	9:13.65	9:14.80	9:15.95	9:17.10	9:18.26	9:19.41	9:20.56	9:21.71
490	9:22.86	9:24.01	9:25.16	9:26.31	9:27.46	9:28.61	9:29.77	9:30.92	9:32.07	9:33.22
500	9:34.37	9:35.52	9:36.67	9:37.82	9:38.97	9:40.12	9:41.28	9:42.43	9:43.58	9:44.73
510	9:45.88	9:47.03	9:48.18	9:49.33	9:50.48	9:51.64	9:52.79	9:53.94	9:55.09	9:56.24
520	9:57.39	9:58.54	9:59.69	10:00.84	10:01.99	10:03.15	10:04.30	10:05.45	10:06.60	10:07.75
530	10:08.90	10:10.05	10:11.20	10:12.35	10:13.51	10:14.66	10:15.81	10:16.96	10:18.11	10:19.26
540	10:20.41	10:21.56	10:22.71	10:23.86	10:25.02	10:26.17	10:27.32	10:28.47	10:29.62	10:30.77
550	10:31.92	10:33.07	10:34.22	10:35.37	10:36.53	10:37.68	10:38.83	10:39.98	10:41.13	10:42.28
560	10:43.43	10:44.58	10:45.73	10:46.89	10:48.04	10:49.19	10:50.34	10:51.49	10:52.64	10:53.79
570	10:54.94	10:56.09	10:57.24	10:58.40	10:59.55	11:00.70	11:01.85	11:03.00	11:04.15	11:05.30
580	11:06.45	11:07.60	11:08.76	11:09.91	11:11.06	11:12.21	11:13.36	11:14.51	11:15.66	11:16.81
590	11:17.96	11:19.11	11:20.27	11:21.42	11:22.57	11:23.72	11:24.87	11:26.02	11:27.17	11:28.32

♩. = 1.73; ♩ = 1.15; ♪. = 0.86; (triplet ♩ 𝄾) = 0.77; ♪ = 0.58; (triplet ♪ 𝄾 𝄾) = 0.38; 𝅘𝅥𝅯 = 0.29 seconds

CLICK: 27⅝ FRAMES; M.M.: 51.89

Click	0	1	2	3	4	5	6	7	8	9
000	0:00.00	0:00.00	0:01.16	0:02.31	0:03.47	0:04.63	0:05.78	0:06.94	0:08.09	0:09.25
010	0:10.41	0:11.56	0:12.72	0:13.88	0:15.03	0:16.19	0:17.34	0:18.50	0:19.66	0:20.81
020	0:21.97	0:23.13	0:24.28	0:25.44	0:26.59	0:27.75	0:28.91	0:30.06	0:31.22	0:32.38
030	0:33.53	0:34.69	0:35.84	0:37.00	0:38.16	0:39.31	0:40.47	0:41.63	0:42.78	0:43.94
040	0:45.09	0:46.25	0:47.41	0:48.56	0:49.72	0:50.88	0:52.03	0:53.19	0:54.34	0:55.50
050	0:56.66	0:57.81	0:58.97	1:00.12	1:01.28	1:02.44	1:03.59	1:04.75	1:05.91	1:07.06
060	1:08.22	1:09.38	1:10.53	1:11.69	1:12.84	1:14.00	1:15.16	1:16.31	1:17.47	1:18.63
070	1:19.78	1:20.94	1:22.09	1:23.25	1:24.41	1:25.56	1:26.72	1:27.88	1:29.03	1:30.19
080	1:31.34	1:32.50	1:33.66	1:34.81	1:35.97	1:37.13	1:38.28	1:39.44	1:40.59	1:41.75
090	1:42.91	1:44.06	1:45.22	1:46.38	1:47.53	1:48.69	1:49.84	1:51.00	1:52.16	1:53.31
100	1:54.47	1:55.63	1:56.78	1:57.94	1:59.09	2:00.25	2:01.41	2:02.56	2:03.72	2:04.87
110	2:06.03	2:07.19	2:08.34	2:09.50	2:10.66	2:11.81	2:12.97	2:14.12	2:15.28	2:16.44
120	2:17.59	2:18.75	2:19.91	2:21.06	2:22.22	2:23.38	2:24.53	2:25.69	2:26.84	2:28.00
130	2:29.16	2:30.31	2:31.47	2:32.63	2:33.78	2:34.94	2:36.09	2:37.25	2:38.41	2:39.56
140	2:40.72	2:41.88	2:43.03	2:44.19	2:45.34	2:46.50	2:47.66	2:48.81	2:49.97	2:51.13
150	2:52.28	2:53.44	2:54.59	2:55.75	2:56.91	2:58.06	2:59.22	3:00.38	3:01.53	3:02.69
160	3:03.84	3:05.00	3:06.16	3:07.31	3:08.47	3:09.62	3:10.78	3:11.94	3:13.09	3:14.25
170	3:15.41	3:16.56	3:17.72	3:18.87	3:20.03	3:21.19	3:22.34	3:23.50	3:24.66	3:25.81
180	3:26.97	3:28.13	3:29.28	3:30.44	3:31.59	3:32.75	3:33.91	3:35.06	3:36.22	3:37.38
190	3:38.53	3:39.69	3:40.84	3:42.00	3:43.16	3:44.31	3:45.47	3:46.63	3:47.78	3:48.94
200	3:50.09	3:51.25	3:52.41	3:53.56	3:54.72	3:55.88	3:57.03	3:58.19	3:59.34	4:00.50
210	4:01.66	4:02.81	4:03.97	4:05.13	4:06.28	4:07.44	4:08.59	4:09.75	4:10.91	4:12.06
220	4:13.22	4:14.38	4:15.53	4:16.69	4:17.84	4:19.00	4:20.16	4:21.31	4:22.47	4:23.63
230	4:24.78	4:25.94	4:27.09	4:28.25	4:29.41	4:30.56	4:31.72	4:32.88	4:34.03	4:35.19
240	4:36.34	4:37.50	4:38.66	4:39.81	4:40.97	4:42.13	4:43.28	4:44.44	4:45.59	4:46.75
250	4:47.91	4:49.06	4:50.22	4:51.38	4:52.53	4:53.69	4:54.84	4:56.00	4:57.16	4:58.31
260	4:59.47	5:00.62	5:01.78	5:02.94	5:04.09	5:05.25	5:06.41	5:07.56	5:08.72	5:09.87
270	5:11.03	5:12.19	5:13.34	5:14.50	5:15.66	5:16.81	5:17.97	5:19.12	5:20.28	5:21.44
280	5:22.59	5:23.75	5:24.91	5:26.06	5:27.22	5:28.37	5.29.53	5:30.69	5:31.84	5:33.00
290	5:34.16	5:35.31	5:36.47	5:37.63	5:38.78	5:39.94	5:41.09	5:42.25	5:43.41	5:44.56
300	5:45.72	5:46.88	5:48.03	5:49.19	5:50.34	5:51.50	5:52.66	5:53.81	5:54.97	5:56.13
310	5:57.28	5:58.44	5:59.59	6:00.75	6:01.91	6:03.06	6:04.22	6:05.38	6:06.53	6:07.69
320	6:08.84	6:10.00	6:11.16	6:12.31	6:13.47	6:14.63	6:15.78	6:16.94	6:18.09	6:19.25
330	6:20.41	6:21.56	6:22.72	6:23.88	6:25.03	6:26.19	6:27.34	6:28.50	6:29.66	6:30.81
340	6:31.97	6:33.13	6:34.28	6:35.44	6:36.59	6:37.75	6:38.91	6:40.06	6:41.22	6:42.38
350	6:43.53	6:44.69	6:45.84	6:47.00	6:48.16	6:49.31	6:50.47	6:51.63	6:52.78	6:53.94
360	6:55.09	6:56.25	6:57.41	6:58.56	6:59.72	7:00.88	7:02.03	7:03.19	7:04.34	7:05.50
370	7:06.66	7:07.81	7:08.97	7:10.13	7:11.28	7:12.44	7:13.59	7:14.75	7:15.91	7:17.06
380	7:18.22	7:19.38	7:20.53	7:21.69	7:22.84	7:24.00	7:25.16	7:26.31	7:27.47	7:28.62
390	7:29.78	7:30.94	7:32.09	7:33.25	7:34.41	7:35.56	7:36.72	7:37.87	7:39.03	7:40.19
400	7:41.34	7:42.50	7:43.66	7:44.81	7:45.97	7:47.12	7:48.28	7:49.44	7:50.59	7:51.75
410	7:52.91	7:54.06	7:55.22	7:56.38	7:57.53	7:58.69	7:59.84	8:01.00	8:02.16	8:03.31
420	8:04.47	8:05.63	8:06.78	8:07.94	8:09.09	8:10.25	8:11.41	8:12.56	8:13.72	8:14.88
430	8:16.03	8:17.19	8:18.34	8:19.50	8:20.66	8:21.81	8:22.97	8:24.13	8:25.28	8:26.44
440	8:27.59	8:28.75	8:29.91	8:31.06	8:32.22	8:33.38	8:34.53	8:35.69	8:36.84	8:38.00
450	8:39.16	8:40.31	8:41.47	8:42.63	8:43.78	8:44.94	8:46.09	8:47.25	8:48.41	8:49.56
460	8:50.72	8:51.87	8:53.03	8:54.19	8:55.34	8:56.50	8:57.66	8:58.81	8:59.97	9:01.13
470	9:02.28	9:03.44	9:04.59	9:05.75	9:06.91	9:08.06	9:09.22	9:10.37	9:11.53	9:12.69
480	9:13.84	9:15.00	9:16.16	9:17.31	9:18.47	9:19.63	9:20.78	9:21.94	9:23.09	9:24.25
490	9:25.41	9:26.56	9:27.72	9:28.87	9:30.03	9:31.19	9:32.34	9:33.50	9:34.66	9:35.81
500	9:36.97	9:38.13	9:39.28	9:40.44	9:41.59	9:42.75	9:43.91	9:45.06	9:46.22	9:47.37
510	9:48.53	9:49.69	9:50.84	9:52.00	9:53.16	9:54.31	9:55.47	9:56.63	9:57.78	9:58.94
520	10:00.09	10:01.25	10:02.41	10:03.56	10:04.72	10:05.87	10:07.03	10:08.19	10:09.34	10:10.50
530	10:11.66	10:12.81	10:13.97	10:15.13	10:16.28	10:17.44	10:18.59	10:19.75	10:20.91	10:22.06
540	10:23.22	10:24.38	10:25.53	10:26.69	10:27.84	10:29.00	10:30.16	10:31.31	10:32.47	10:33.63
550	10:34.78	10:35.94	10:37.09	10:38.25	10:39.41	10:40.56	10:41.72	10:42.88	10:44.03	10:45.19
560	10:46.34	10:47.50	10:48.66	10:49.81	10:50.97	10:52.13	10:53.28	10:54.44	10:55.59	10:56.75
570	10:57.91	10:59.06	11:00.22	11:01.38	11:02.53	11:03.69	11:04.84	11:06.00	11:07.16	11:08.31
580	11:09.47	11:10.62	11:11.78	11:12.94	11:14.09	11:15.25	11:16.41	11:17.56	11:18.72	11:19.88
590	11:21.03	11:22.19	11:23.34	11:24.50	11:25.66	11:26.81	11:27.97	11:29.12	11:30.28	11:31.44

♩. = 1.73; ♩ = 1.16; ♪. = 0.87; (triplet) ♩ 𝄾 = 0.77; ♪ = 0.58; (triplet) ♪𝄾𝄾 = 0.39; 𝅘𝅥𝅯 = 0.29 seconds

CLICK: 27⅞ FRAMES; M.M.: 51.66

Click	0	1	2	3	4	5	6	7	8	9
000	0:00.00	0:00.00	0:01.16	0:02.32	0:03.48	0:04.65	0:05.81	0:06.97	0:08.13	0:09.29
010	0:10.45	0:11.61	0:12.78	0:13.94	0:15.10	0:16.26	0:17.42	0:18.58	0:19.74	0:20.91
020	0:22.07	0:23.23	0:24.39	0:25.55	0:26.71	0:27.88	0:29.04	0:30.20	0:31.36	0:32.52
030	0:33.68	0:34.84	0:36.01	0:37.17	0:38.33	0:39.49	0:40.65	0:41.81	0:42.97	0:44.14
040	0:45.30	0:46.46	0:47.62	0:48.78	0:49.94	0:51.10	0:52.27	0:53.43	0:54.59	0:55.75
050	0:56.91	0:58.07	0:59.23	1:00.40	1:01.56	1:02.72	1:03.88	1:05.04	1:06.20	1:07.36
060	1:08.53	1:09.69	1:10.85	1:12.01	1:13.17	1:14.33	1:15.49	1:16.66	1:17.82	1:18.98
070	1:20.14	1:21.30	1:22.46	1:23.62	1:24.79	1:25.95	1:27.11	1:28.27	1:29.43	1:30.59
080	1:31.76	1:32.92	1:34.08	1:35.24	1:36.40	1:37.56	1:38.72	1:39.89	1:41.05	1:42.21
090	1:43.37	1:44.53	1:45.69	1:46.85	1:48.02	1:49.18	1:50.34	1:51.50	1:52.66	1:53.82
100	1:54.98	1:56.15	1:57.31	1:58.47	1:59.63	2:00.79	2:01.95	2:03.11	2:04.28	2:05.44
110	2:06.60	2:07.76	2:08.92	2:10.08	2:11.24	2:12.41	2:13.57	2:14.73	2:15.89	2:17.05
120	2:18.21	2:19.37	2:20.54	2:21.70	2:22.86	2:24.02	2:25.18	2:26.34	2:27.51	2:28.67
130	2:29.83	2:30.99	2:32.15	2:33.31	2:34.47	2:35.64	2:36.80	2:37.96	2:39.12	2:40.28
140	2:41.44	2:42.60	2:43.77	2:44.93	2:46.09	2:47.25	2:48.41	2:49.57	2:50.73	2:51.90
150	2:53.06	2:54.22	2:55.38	2:56.54	2:57.70	2:58.86	3:00.03	3:01.19	3:02.35	3:03.51
160	3:04.67	3:05.83	3:06.99	3:08.16	3:09.32	3:10.48	3:11.64	3:12.80	3:13.96	3:15.12
170	3:16.29	3:17.45	3:18.61	3:19.77	3:20.93	3:22.09	3:23.26	3:24.42	3:25.58	3:26.74
180	3:27.90	3:29.06	3:30.22	3:31.39	3:32.55	3:33.71	3:34.87	3:36.03	3:37.19	3:38.35
190	3:39.52	3:40.68	3:41.84	3:43.00	3:44.16	3:45.32	3:46.48	3:47.65	3:48.81	3:49.97
200	3:51.13	3:52.29	3:53.45	3:54.61	3:55.78	3:56.94	3:58.10	3:59.26	4:00.42	4:01.58
210	4:02.74	4:03.91	4:05.07	4:06.23	4:07.39	4:08.55	4:09.71	4:10.88	4:12.04	4:13.20
220	4:14.36	4:15.52	4:16.68	4:17.84	4:19.01	4:20.17	4:21.33	4:22.49	4:23.65	4:24.81
230	4:25.97	4:27.14	4:28.30	4:29.46	4:30.62	4:31.78	4:32.94	4:34.10	4:35.27	4:36.43
240	4:37.59	4:38.75	4:39.91	4:41.07	4:42.23	4:43.40	4:44.56	4:45.72	4:46.88	4:48.04
250	4:49.20	4:50.36	4:51.53	4:52.69	4:53.85	4:55.01	4:56.17	4:57.33	4:58.49	4:59.66
260	5:00.82	5:01.98	5:03.14	5:04.30	5:05.46	5:06.62	5:07.79	5:08.95	5:10.11	5:11.27
270	5:12.43	5:13.59	5:14.76	5:15.92	5:17.08	5:18.24	5:19.40	5:20.56	5:21.72	5:22.89
280	5:24.05	5:25.21	5:26.37	5:27.53	5:28.69	5:29.85	5:31.02	5:32.18	5:33.34	5:34.50
290	5:35.66	5:36.82	5:37.98	5:39.15	5:40.31	5:41.47	5:42.63	5:43.79	5:44.95	5:46.11
300	5:47.28	5:48.44	5:49.60	5:50.76	5:51.92	5:53.08	5:54.24	5:55.41	5:56.57	5:57.73
310	5:58.89	6:00.05	6:01.21	6:02.37	6:03.54	6:04.70	6:05.86	6:07.02	6:08.18	6:09.34
320	6:10.51	6:11.67	6:12.83	6:13.99	6:15.15	6:16.31	6:17.47	6:18.64	6:19.80	6:20.96
330	6:22.12	6:23.28	6:24.44	6:25.60	6:26.77	6:27.93	6:29.09	6:30.25	6:31.41	6:32.57
340	6:33.73	6:34.90	6:36.06	6:37.22	6:38.38	6:39.54	6:40.70	6:41.86	6:43.03	6:44.19
350	6:45.35	6:46.51	6:47.67	6:48.83	6:49.99	6:51.16	6:52.32	6:53.48	6:54.64	6:55.80
360	6:56.96	6:58.13	6:59.29	7:00.45	7:01.61	7:02.77	7:03.93	7:05.09	7:06.26	7:07.42
370	7:08.58	7:09.74	7:10.90	7:12.06	7:13.22	7:14.39	7:15.55	7:16.71	7:17.87	7:19.03
380	7:20.19	7:21.35	7:22.52	7:23.68	7:24.84	7:26.00	7:27.16	7:28.32	7:29.48	7:30.65
390	7:31.81	7:32.97	7:34.13	7:35.29	7:36.45	7:37.61	7:38.78	7:39.94	7:41.10	7:42.26
400	7:43.42	7:44.58	7:45.74	7:46.91	7:48.07	7:49.23	7:50.39	7:51.55	7:52.71	7:53.87
410	7:55.04	7:56.20	7:57.36	7:58.52	7:59.68	8:00.84	8:02.01	8:03.17	8:04.33	8:05.49
420	8:06.65	8:07.81	8:08.97	8:10.14	8:11.30	8:12.46	8:13.62	8:14.78	8:15.94	8:17.10
430	8:18.27	8:19.43	8:20.59	8:21.75	8:22.91	8:24.07	8:25.23	8:26.40	8:27.56	8:28.72
440	8:29.88	8:31.04	8:32.20	8:33.36	8:34.53	8:35.69	8:36.85	8:38.01	8:39.17	8:40.33
450	8:41.49	8:42.66	8:43.82	8:44.98	8:46.14	8:47.30	8:48.46	8:49.63	8:50.79	8:51.95
460	8:53.11	8:54.27	8:55.43	8:56.59	8:57.76	8:58.92	9:00.08	9:01.24	9:02.40	9:03.56
470	9:04.72	9:05.89	9:07.05	9:08.21	9:09.37	9:10.53	9:11.69	9:12.85	9:14.02	9:15.18
480	9:16.34	9:17.50	9:18.66	9:19.82	9:20.98	9:22.15	9:23.31	9:24.47	9:25.63	9:26.79
490	9:27.95	9:29.11	9:30.28	9:31.44	9:32.60	9:33.76	9:34.92	9:36.08	9:37.24	9:38.41
500	9:39.57	9:40.73	9:41.89	9:43.05	9:44.21	9:45.37	9:46.54	9:47.70	9:48.86	9:50.02
510	9:51.18	9:52.34	9:53.51	9:54.67	9:55.83	9:56.99	9:58.15	9:59.31	10:00.47	10:01.64
520	10:02.80	10:03.96	10:05.12	10:06.28	10:07.44	10:08.60	10:09.77	10:10.93	10:12.09	10:13.25
530	10:14.41	10:15.57	10:16.73	10:17.90	10:19.06	10:20.22	10:21.38	10:22.54	10:23.70	10:24.86
540	10:26.03	10:27.19	10:28.35	10:29.51	10:30.67	10:31.83	10:32.99	10:34.16	10:35.32	10:36.48
550	10:37.64	10:38.80	10:39.96	10:41.12	10:42.29	10:43.45	10:44.61	10:45.77	10:46.93	10:48.09
560	10:49.26	10:50.42	10:51.58	10:52.74	10:53.90	10:55.06	10:56.22	10:57.39	10:58.55	10:59.71
570	11:00.87	11:02.03	11:03.19	11:04.35	11:05.52	11:06.68	11:07.84	11:09.00	11:10.16	11:11.32
580	11:12.48	11:13.65	11:14.81	11:15.97	11:17.13	11:18.29	11:19.45	11:20.61	11:21.78	11:22.94
590	11:24.10	11:25.26	11:26.42	11:27.58	11:28.74	11:29.91	11:31.07	11:32.23	11:33.39	11:34.55

♩. = 1.74; ♩ = 1.16; ♪. = 0.87; ⌐3¬ ♩ 𝄾 = 0.77; ♪ = 0.58; ⌐3¬ ♪𝄾𝄾 = 0.39; 𝅘𝅥𝅯 = 0.29 seconds

CLICK: 28 0/8 FRAMES; M.M.: 51.43

Click	0	1	2	3	4	5	6	7	8	9
000	0:00.00	0:00.00	0:01.17	0:02.33	0:03.50	0:04.67	0:05.83	0:07.00	0:08.17	0:09.33
010	0:10.50	0:11.67	0:12.83	0:14.00	0:15.17	0:16.33	0:17.50	0:18.67	0:19.83	0:21.00
020	0:22.17	0:23.33	0:24.50	0:25.67	0:26.83	0:28.00	0:29.17	0:30.33	0:31.50	0:32.67
030	0:33.83	0:35.00	0:36.17	0:37.33	0:38.50	0:39.67	0:40.83	0:42.00	0:43.17	0:44.33
040	0:45.50	0:46.67	0:47.83	0:49.00	0:50.17	0:51.33	0:52.50	0:53.67	0:54.83	0:56.00
050	0:57.17	0:58.33	0:59.50	1:00.67	1:01.83	1:03.00	1:04.17	1:05.33	1:06.50	1:07.67
060	1:08.83	1:10.00	1:11.17	1:12.33	1:13.50	1:14.67	1:15.83	1:17.00	1:18.17	1:19.33
070	1:20.50	1:21.67	1:22.83	1:24.00	1:25.17	1:26.33	1:27.50	1:28.67	1:29.83	1:31.00
080	1:32.17	1:33.33	1:34.50	1:35.67	1:36.83	1:38.00	1:39.17	1:40.33	1:41.50	1:42.67
090	1:43.83	1:45.00	1:46.17	1:47.33	1:48.50	1:49.67	1:50.83	1:52.00	1:53.17	1:54.33
100	1:55.50	1:56.67	1:57.83	1:59.00	2:00.17	2:01.33	2:02.50	2:03.67	2:04.83	2:06.00
110	2:07.17	2:08.33	2:09.50	2:10.67	2:11.83	2:13.00	2:14.17	2:15.33	2:16.50	2:17.67
120	2:18.83	2:20.00	2:21.17	2:22.33	2:23.50	2:24.67	2:25.83	2:27.00	2:28.17	2:29.33
130	2:30.50	2:31.67	2:32.83	2:34.00	2:35.17	2:36.33	2:37.50	2:38.67	2:39.83	2:41.00
140	2:42.17	2:43.33	2:44.50	2:45.67	2:46.83	2:48.00	2:49.17	2:50.33	2:51.50	2:52.67
150	2:53.83	2:55.00	2:56.17	2:57.33	2:58.50	2:59.67	3:00.83	3:02.00	3:03.17	3:04.33
160	3:05.50	3:06.67	3:07.83	3:09.00	3:10.17	3:11.33	3:12.50	3:13.67	3:14.83	3:16.00
170	3:17.17	3:18.33	3:19.50	3:20.67	3:21.83	3:23.00	3:24.17	3:25.33	3:26.50	3:27.67
180	3:28.83	3:30.00	3:31.17	3:32.33	3:33.50	3:34.67	3:35.83	3:37.00	3:38.17	3:39.33
190	3:40.50	3:41.67	3:42.83	3:44.00	3:45.17	3:46.33	3:47.50	3:48.67	3:49.83	3:51.00
200	3:52.17	3:53.33	3:54.50	3:55.67	3:56.83	3:58.00	3:59.17	4:00.33	4:01.50	4:02.67
210	4:03.83	4:05.00	4:06.17	4:07.33	4:08.50	4:09.67	4:10.83	4:12.00	4:13.17	4:14.33
220	4:15.50	4:16.67	4:17.83	4:19.00	4:20.17	4:21.33	4:22.50	4:23.67	4:24.83	4:26.00
230	4:27.17	4:28.33	4:29.50	4:30.67	4:31.83	4:33.00	4:34.17	4:35.33	4:36.50	4:37.67
240	4:38.83	4:40.00	4:41.17	4:42.33	4:43.50	4:44.67	4:45.83	4:47.00	4:48.17	4:49.33
250	4:50.50	4:51.67	4:52.83	4:54.00	4:55.17	4:56.33	4:57.50	4:58.67	4:59.83	5:01.00
260	5:02.17	5:03.33	5:04.50	5:05.67	5:06.83	5:08.00	5:09.17	5:10.33	5:11.50	5:12.67
270	5:13.83	5:15.00	5:16.17	5:17.33	5:18.50	5:19.67	5:20.83	5:22.00	5:23.17	5:24.33
280	5:25.50	5:26.67	5:27.83	5:29.00	5:30.17	5:31.33	5:32.50	5:33.67	5:34.83	5:36.00
290	5:37.17	5:38.33	5:39.50	5:40.67	5:41.83	5:43.00	5:44.17	5:45.33	5:46.50	5:47.67
300	5:48.83	5:50.00	5:51.17	5:52.33	5:53.50	5:54.67	5:55.83	5:57.00	5:58.17	5:59.33
310	6:00.50	6:01.67	6:02.83	6:04.00	6:05.17	6:06.33	6:07.50	6:08.67	6:09.83	6:11.00
320	6:12.17	6:13.33	6:14.50	6:15.67	6:16.83	6:18.00	6:19.17	6:20.33	6:21.50	6:22.67
330	6:23.83	6:25.00	6:26.17	6:27.33	6:28.50	6:29.67	6:30.83	6:32.00	6:33.17	6:34.33
340	6:35.50	6:36.67	6:37.83	6:39.00	6:40.17	6:41.33	6:42.50	6:43.67	6:44.83	6:46.00
350	6:47.17	6:48.33	6:49.50	6:50.67	6:51.83	6:53.00	6:54.17	6:55.33	6:56.50	6:57.67
360	6:58.83	6:60.00	7:01.17	7:02.33	7:03.50	7:04.67	7:05.83	7:07.00	7:08.17	7:09.33
370	7:10.50	7:11.67	7:12.83	7:14.00	7:15.17	7:16.33	7:17.50	7:18.67	7:19.83	7:21.00
380	7:22.17	7:23.33	7:24.50	7:25.67	7:26.83	7:28.00	7:29.17	7:30.33	7:31.50	7:32.67
390	7:33.83	7:35.00	7:36.17	7:37.33	7:38.50	7:39.67	7:40.83	7:42.00	7:43.17	7:44.33
400	7:45.50	7:46.67	7:47.83	7:49.00	7:50.17	7:51.33	7:52.50	7:53.67	7:54.83	7:56.00
410	7:57.17	7:58.33	7:59.50	8:00.67	8:01.83	8:03.00	8:04.17	8:05.33	8:06.50	8:07.67
420	8:08.83	8:10.00	8:11.17	8:12.33	8:13.50	8:14.67	8:15.83	8:17.00	8:18.17	8:19.33
430	8:20.50	8:21.67	8:22.83	8:24.00	8:25.17	8:26.33	8:27.50	8:28.67	8:29.83	8:31.00
440	8:32.17	8:33.33	8:34.50	8:35.67	8:36.83	8:38.00	8:39.17	8:40.33	8:41.50	8:42.67
450	8:43.83	8:45.00	8:46.17	8:47.33	8:48.50	8:49.67	8:50.83	8:52.00	8:53.17	8:54.33
460	8:55.50	8:56.67	8:57.83	8:59.00	9:00.17	9:01.33	9:02.50	9:03.67	9:04.83	9:06.00
470	9:07.17	9:08.33	9:09.50	9:10.67	9:11.83	9:13.00	9:14.17	9:15.33	9:16.50	9:17.67
480	9:18.83	9:20.00	9:21.17	9:22.33	9:23.50	9:24.67	9:25.83	9:27.00	9:28.17	9:29.33
490	9:30.50	9:31.67	9:32.83	9:34.00	9:35.17	9:36.33	9:37.50	9:38.67	9:39.83	9:41.00
500	9:42.17	9:43.33	9:44.50	9:45.67	9:46.83	9:48.00	9:49.17	9:50.33	9:51.50	9:52.67
510	9:53.83	9:55.00	9:56.17	9:57.33	9:58.50	9:59.67	10:00.83	10:02.00	10:03.17	10:04.33
520	10:05.50	10:06.67	10:07.83	10:09.00	10:10.17	10:11.33	10:12.50	10:13.67	10:14.83	10:16.00
530	10:17.17	10:18.33	10:19.50	10:20.67	10:21.83	10:23.00	10:24.17	10:25.33	10:26.50	10:27.67
540	10:28.83	10:30.00	10:31.17	10:32.33	10:33.50	10:34.67	10:35.83	10:37.00	10:38.17	10:39.33
550	10:40.50	10:41.67	10:42.83	10:44.00	10:45.17	10:46.33	10:47.50	10:48.67	10:49.83	10:51.00
560	10:52.17	10:53.33	10:54.50	10:55.67	10:56.83	10:58.00	10:59.17	11:00.33	11:01.50	11:02.67
570	11:03.83	11:05.00	11:06.17	11:07.33	11:08.50	11:09.67	11:10.83	11:12.00	11:13.17	11:14.33
580	11:15.50	11:16.67	11:17.83	11:19.00	11:20.17	11:21.33	11:22.50	11:23.67	11:24.83	11:26.00
590	11:27.17	11:28.33	11:29.50	11:30.67	11:31.83	11:33.00	11:34.17	11:35.33	11:36.50	11:37.67

♩. = 1.75; ♩ = 1.17; ♪. = 0.88; (triplet ♩ 𝄾) = 0.78; ♪ = 0.58; (triplet ♪ 𝄾 𝄾) = 0.39; 𝅘𝅥𝅯 = 0.29 seconds

INDEX

References to films are indexed in the Filmography.

C

D

P

R

S